Abraham Lincoln
THE WAR YEARS
IN FOUR VOLUMES
Volume 3

Abraham Lincoln, Washington, D. C., February 9, 1864
Photograph by Brady, estimated by Robert T. Lincoln "the best portrait" of his father
Original in the Barrett collection

ABRAHAM LINCOLN

The War Years

BY CARL SANDBURG

WITH 426 HALF-TONES OF PHOTOGRAPHS, AND
244 CUTS OF CARTOONS, LETTERS, DOCUMENTS

Volume Three

HARCOURT, BRACE & COMPANY
NEW YORK

W

Typography by Robert Josephy

PRINTED IN THE UNITED STATES OF AMERICA

CONTENTS

LIST OF ILLUSTRATIONS

Abraham Lincoln
THE WAR YEARS

ABRAHAM LINCOLN: The War Years

CHAPTER 50

SPRING OF '64—BLOOD AND ANGER

BETWEEN the Missouri River and California Lincoln wanted a line of Free States. Congress in April of '64 gave Nebraska authority to form a State and come into the Union. The 28,000 people of that Territory by entering the Union as a State could have one Congressman, two Senators, and political power. But they voted against it. They were mostly poor farmers acquainted with good land, variable crops, drouth, hot winds, grasshoppers, hostile Indians. Out of the Union, their expense of being governed was paid from Washington. They voted for that. Lincoln would have been glad to see them come in. So would Ben Wade. But they could not afford it.

Nevada was different. Out in that Territory of gray desert, cactus, and the coyote, ore of silver hid in the stark mountains. Her pay streaks would rival those of California, claimed several observers. The few shacks of Virginia City had in four years grown into the second city in size west of the Rocky Mountains, with churches, schools, stores, theatres, saloons. And Nevada's population of miners, prospectors, gamblers, gold- and silver-hunters, with 26,000 voters, wanted to have a State and be in the Union. She could afford her own government and liked the idea of her little desert population sending a Congressman and two Senators to Washington. Two out of three voters were Republican. Before authority came from Congress in 1863 they elected delegates to a convention and wrote a State constitution. The voters had rejected this constitution, but since then a new and fresh population had swarmed in by wagon, on horseback, in stagecoaches, and sentiment was overwhelming that Nevada must be a State. In Congress were those who agreed. Ben Wade of the Senate Territorial Committee reported out a bill which among other provisions decreed that Nevada must forever be free of slavery. Lincoln joined his efforts with Wade in the Senate and Stevens in the House to pass the bill.

The President called on Assistant Secretary of War Charles A. Dana. He told Dana the Administration had decided that the Constitution of the United States should be amended to prohibit slavery; this was not only a change in national policy but also a most important military measure in its effect on the judgment, feelings, anticipations, of those in rebellion. Such a Constitutional Amendment would be equivalent to new armies in the field.

worth at least a million men, tending to paralyze the enemy and break the continuity of his ideas. To pass such an Amendment to the Constitution would require approval by three-fourths of the States. Nevada might be of critical importance as a State.

Thus ran Lincoln's argument, according to Dana, who quoted him, "It is easier to admit Nevada than to raise another million soldiers."

The Senate bill of February 24, 1864, authorized a Nevada convention to meet on the first Monday in July, to declare on behalf of the people that they adopt the Constitution of the United States and to frame a State government. In the House through weeks of March this bill was held up. Not by long, earnest speeches nor by parliamentary tactics of delay and confusion, but by lack of votes. Stevens, the floor leader, simply couldn't line up a majority for it.

Lincoln knew the anxiety and need of Stevens as to the bill. He walked from the White House and late one afternoon came into Dana's third-floor office in the War Department building. Other times too Lincoln had walked over to Dana's office because he liked a walk and it took him away from the White House crowds. This visit, however, Dana remembered particularly. Lincoln came in, shut the door.

"Dana, I am very anxious about this vote. It has got to be taken next week. The time is very short. It is going to be a great deal closer than I wish it was."

"There are plenty of Democrats who will vote for it. There is James E. English of Connecticut. I think he is sure, isn't he?"

"Oh, yes; he is sure on the merits of the question."

"Then there's Sunset Cox of Ohio. How is he?"

"He is sure and fearless. But there are some others that I am not clear about. There are three that you can deal with better than anybody else, perhaps, as you know them all. I wish you would send for them."

Lincoln told Dana who they were. Dana considered it unnecessary to tell their names to anyone not immediately concerned. One of the Congressmen was from New Jersey and two from New York.

"What will they be likely to want?" asked Dana.

"I don't know," said the President. "I don't know. It makes no difference, though, what they want. Here is the alternative: that we carry this vote, or be compelled to raise another million, and I don't know how many more, men, and fight no one knows how long. It is a question of three votes or new armies."

"Well, sir, what shall I say to these gentlemen?"

"I don't know, but whatever promise you make to them I will perform."

So Dana sent for the men and saw them one by one. Dana found they were afraid of their party. They said that some fellows in the party would be down on them. Two of them wanted each an internal-revenue collector's appointment. "You shall have it," said Dana. Another wanted an important customhouse appointment in New York. Dana knew well the man whom the Congressman wanted to have appointed; he was a Republican, though the Congressman was a Democrat. Dana had served with him in the Republican county committee of New York. The office was worth about $20,000 a year. When the Congressman had stated his case, Dana asked, "Do you want that?"

"Yes."

"Well, you shall have it."

"I understand, of course, that you are not saying this on your own authority?"

"No. I am saying it on the authority of the President."

So the extra votes needed to pass the Nevada bill through the House were gotten.

And the Yeas and Nays on the vote in Senate and House were not indexed nor recorded in the *Congressional Globe*, whether through clerical inattention or by official arrangement.

Dana believed that he and Lincoln knew precisely the fine, thin lines of right, wrong, and expediency that wove through this piece of politics. Lincoln had chosen for an intermediary in an intricate operation a man of delicate methods, who was a terror to fraudulent contractors and get-rich-quick cotton-traders, and whose faith in Lincoln had depths.

"Lincoln was a supreme politician," wrote Dana. "He understood politics because he understood human nature. . . . There was no flabby philanthropy about Abraham Lincoln. He was all solid, hard, keen intelligence combined with goodness. . . . The expression of his face and of his bearing which impressed one most, after his benevolence and benignity, was his intelligent understanding. You felt that here was a man who saw through things, who understood, and you respected him accordingly."

Far more difficult than the Nevada affair was the joint adventure of Hay and Lincoln in reconstruction politics in Florida. Before it was over the two heard a harsh outcry against them. Lincoln was used to it, but to Hay it would have a bitter taste he had not hitherto met. In his diary of December 28, 1863, Hay wrote of receiving letters from Paige and Stickney, two Unionist friends down in Florida, "asking me to come down . . . and be their Representative in Congress." In May of the year before Hay had been down there and written a brother that the soil of Florida was almost as rich as Illinois prairie, while to Nicolay he poetized on South Carolina: "The sun goes down over the pines through a sky like ashes-of-roses and hangs for an instant on the horizon like a bubble of blood." A majority of the people there Hay found "bitter rebels" and yet "a good many sound Union people."

Hay talked with the President late in December about reconstruction in Florida, the possibility of getting one-tenth of the voters in the State to swear Union allegiance and be recorded as United States citizens in an oath book. Possibly Hay or Lincoln mentioned John Hay, the humorist, quipster, and literary artist, becoming a Congressman from the land of bananas, tarantulas, and flaring sunsets, as between two half-serious jokers. The President "will appoint me a Commissioner to go to Florida and engineer the business there," wrote Hay. . . . "There seems a prospect of getting the State under way early next spring. I will go down there & form my plans after I get there, as to my own course."

To General Q. A. Gillmore, in whose department Florida lay, the President wrote on January 13 that he had commissioned Hay a major in the army and that Hay with blankbooks and oath blanks would arrive and explain to General Gillmore the President's general views on the subject of reconstructing a loyal State government in Florida. "It is desirable for all to coöperate, but if irreconcilable differences of opinion shall arise, you are master. I wish the thing done in the most speedy way possible, so that when done, it lie within the range of the late proclamation on the subject. The detail labor, of course, will have to be done by others; but I shall be greatly obliged if you will give it such general supervision as you can find consistent with your more strictly military duties."

On this same day young Hay came into the President's room and said he was starting for Florida. "Great good luck and God's blessing go with you, John." And John wrote in his diary, "How long will you stay? One month or six months?"

Hay sailed to Gillmore's headquarters on the South Carolina coast, handed the General the President's letter, noticed that the General probably thought he was expected to undertake some immediate military operation, and assured the General it was not the President's intention to do anything to embarrass his military operations, "that all I wished from him was an order directing me to go to Florida & open my books of record for the oathes [sic], as preliminary to future proceedings."

At Jacksonville, Florida, Hay read the President's proclamation of amnesty to a line-up of guardhouse prisoners, explained that if they signed the oath book, certificates to that effect would be issued to them and they would be allowed to go home. Otherwise they would be sent North as prisoners of war for exchange. "There is to be neither force nor persuasion used in the matter. You decide for y^{r}selves." They signed, nearly half making their mark. They were tired of the war. Some of the more intelligent cursed their politicians and especially South Carolina. In the city of Jacksonville Hay felt encouraged at enrolling sixty names, "some of them men of substance and influence." The future of Florida looked somewhat assuring to Hay, enough so that he made a $500 investment in land.

Then came shocking news. General Truman Seymour, a regular-army officer in charge of some 5,500 men, sought out a Confederate force of about the same size at Olustee River under General Joseph Finegan in a picked position, welcoming battle. The Union loss was 1,800, the Confederate half that. Seymour's orders from Gillmore had been to wait. But he had plunged and his army was routed. From Sanderson to Barber's Station, wrote one of the routed, "ten miles we wended or crawled along, the wounded filling the night air with lamentations, the crippled horses neighing in pain, and a full moon kissing the cold, clammy lips of the dying." Wrote another, "This moment of grief is too sacred for anger."

With Union bayonets in disgrace for the moment, Hay had a harder time enrolling loyal Unionists. He went to Fernandina, got a few more names, noted: "Some refused to sign, on the ground that they were not repentant rebels." On March 3 he wrote, "I am sure that we cannot now get the President's 10th." His hopes vanished that the required 10 per cent of voters to form a State government could be enrolled. He sailed to Key West on a sea that held "a miracle of color, ripples of pale green water, whitened by coral." In Key West proper he wrote of finding, outside of a decent darkey and a horse doctor, only "a race of thieves and a degeneration of vipers."

Sailing back to Washington, Hay could read in newspapers, the *New York Herald* or *World*, that President Lincoln would not hesitate at murder to win political ends, that Hay had joined with the President in a reckless conspiracy to overawe Florida with military power, to elect himself as a Congressman, to deliver a set of Florida delegates for the President at the nominating convention in June; that the President's eager and precipitant haste to push the scheme through had resulted in the useless slaughter of General Seymour's army. Beyond such allegations the newspaper stories did not go.

"Price of Three Votes for the Presidency! One Thousand Lives!" trumpeted the *New York Herald*, while the *World* day after day rehearsed the allegations in new phrases. The *Chicago Times* gloated. "Butchery to bring into Congress Hay, Lincoln's hireling and *private* servant," wrote radical Gurowski in his diary. "The greatest efforts are made to hush up the infamy. Mr. Lincoln has in hand a full report from his agent, Hay, a report reeking with blood, but, of course, Mr. Lincoln does not show it. Everybody is exasperated."

The hue and cry threw fear and foreboding into men easily shaken, like Senator James W. Grimes of Iowa. Grimes told his colleagues this needless slaughter of troops required congressional inquiry. Greeley, like Grimes, had during the war spent sleepless nights over needless slaughter and might have been expected in this matter to join with Grimes and call for stern investigation and punishment. Greeley, however, saw the *World* playing politics and Bennett's *Herald* again sharpshooting at Lincoln in the style of the man who asked a Yes-or-No answer to the question "Have you stopped beating your wife?" Greeley printed a long editorial taking the blame off the Administration. Still later and more deliberately Greeley wrote, "President Lincoln, who had never dreamed of such a folly, was assailed and held up to execration as having fooled away 2,000 men in a sordid attempt to manufacture for himself three additional votes in the approaching Presidential election."

The written instructions of Lincoln to Hay and to Gillmore, along with Gillmore's explicit orders to General Seymour, were made public, and it was seen that a brave general down in Florida had taken a chance, risked a battle, and lost. This amid the hullabaloo of passing weeks came to be regarded as the central fact. Senator Grimes cooled off. The *Washington*

Chronicle, the *New York Times*, *Harper's Weekly*, explained that war is murder of a sort and the killings in Florida were only the same kind of manslaughter as other battles, and there is no telling when a gallant, impetuous general will win or lose. This too was the gist of the evidence and findings of the Committee on the Conduct of the War. Fanatic Gurowski wrote on March 21 that the Administration press "still tenderly attempts to whitewash Lincoln from the Florida massacre, but it will not do, it will not do." Like the *New York World*, Gurowski hoped the affair could be made into a tempestuous campaign issue that would end Lincoln politically. The repeated cry of murder in politics became feebler, however, as an unconvinced public wearied of what hostile journals fed it about Lincoln and Hay slaughtering Federal troops for the sake of Lincoln presidential delegates.

"I had an unusually long and interesting sitting from the President," wrote Carpenter of March 2, when the Florida news had brought the murder cry against the President. . . . "Mr. Lincoln was deeply wounded by these charges. He referred to them during the sitting; and gave a simple . . . statement of the affair. . . . A few days afterward, an editorial appeared in the New York 'Tribune' . . . entirely exonerating him from all blame. I took the article to him in his study and he expressed much gratification at its candor." To Carpenter it seemed that Lincoln had in mind the savage newspaper attacks of the hour as he told about a backwoods traveler lost in a terrific thunderstorm. The rider floundered along till his horse gave out and he stood alone where lightning streaked and the shocks of thunder came in bolts. The wrath of God seemed let loose from the overhead sky. One bolt seemed to crash the earth underfoot. It brought him to his knees. He was not a praying man but he made a petition short and to the point: "O Lord, if it is all the same to you, give us a little more light and a little less noise!"

Hay arrived from Florida March 24, went upstairs in the White House, and talked at seven in the morning with Nicolay in bed. "After breakfast I talked with the President. There was no special necessity of my presenting my papers as I found he thoroughly understood the state of affairs in Florida and did not seem in the least annoyed by the newspaper falsehoods about the matter." Many miles had Hay come since he had seen a Southern evening sky like ashes of roses and sundown on the horizon like a bubble of blood.

In many forms ran accusations that the President had an eye on Southern delegates to help renominate him. The accusers hoped he would wait until after the November elections before taking a hand in reconstruction, out of fear that anything he did might look as though he were hunting delegates. Sardonic and miserable contradictions were beginning to whirl around the very word "reconstruction." Out of so much death, ashes, and devastation, what could in the end be reconstructed? Who could take the ruins and erect them into something worth looking at? What would the finished structure be? In its beginning it was to rest on a 10 per cent of oath-bound voters regarded as betrayers and outcasts by those whose bayonets and taxes were still keeping the Confederacy alive. The oath itself had lost sanctity in the story of the soldiers who caught a rattlesnake, took it to camp, administered the oath, and let it go.

That wholesale and regimented oath-taking business might easily become ridiculous was in Lincoln's mind when he issued the Amnesty Proclamation in December; he had warned that it was only a method, a mode, for re-establishing national authority. He heard in January of '64 from General Banks, commanding the Department of the Gulf, that there were loyal Union people in Louisiana who wished to avoid taking the oath prescribed. The President replied quoting from his proclamation and message of December to show that the oath itself, as well as the reconstruction method in general, was not final and could be revised. That the Federal authority in Louisiana must not be absolute about the oath of Union allegiance was made clear in his letter to Banks January 31: "These things were put into these documents on purpose that some conformity to circumstances should be admissible; and when I have, more than once, said to you in my letters that available labor already done should not be thrown away, I had in my mind the very class of cases you now mention. So you see it is not even a modification of anything I have heretofore said, when I tell you that you are at liberty to adopt any rule which shall admit to vote any unquestionably loyal free-State men and none others. And yet I do wish they would all take the oath."

Far down in that crisscross of population, that changing patchwork of military and civil governments, in Louisiana, Lincoln tried to guide General Nathaniel Prentiss Banks, a Massachusetts Democrat, three times Governor of Massachusetts. Several times amid clashing authorities Lincoln wrote him assurance. "I deeply regret to have said or done anything which could give you pain or uneasiness. I have all the while intended you to be master . . . hence my letters on reconstruction have nearly, if not quite, all been addressed to you." Though Banks had come far short of touching glory as a military commander, neither money-chasing nor fool political ambitions had muddled his motives in Louisiana. While fortunes large and small were being harvested in a thousand shady Gulf Coast traffickings, Banks kept an instinct for what Nicolay and Hay named "honorable poverty" rather than such cash winnings as Ben Butler and his brother took out of the Crescent City.

Through the many mentions of making him President, Banks kept his head, even though the *Beadle Dime Library* had spread his name and career. "As a boy he was the best swimmer, the best ball-player, and the fleetest runner of his age in Waltham, Massachusetts, and, withal, was a manly, brave, truthful boy who abhorred a mean action." Another biography, *The Bobbin Boy*, told of Banks as a textile worker at a spinning machine twelve hours a day for $2 a week. He became a skilled machinist, read Shakespeare, lectured on temperance, went in for stump speaking, and under President Polk took a place in the Boston Customs House. In Congress, elected Speaker of the House in 1854, one Southern member said of Banks, "He stood so straight that he almost leaned to the other side." After three terms as Governor of Massachusetts Banks sat at a desk as President of the Illinois Central Railroad for a few months and, like McClellan, gave up railroading for war, stars of a major general on his shoulder straps. His troops in '63 had taken Port Hudson and its garrison of 6,000 on the Mississippi below Vicksburg, Lincoln writing Banks that this final stroke in opening the Mississippi "never should, and I think never will, be forgotten."

By private letter and publicly announced policies Lincoln tried to steer Banks in the governing of some seventeen of the forty-eight parishes of Louisiana controlled by Union armies, an area holding a fourth of the slaves of Louisiana. "While I very well know what I would be glad for Louisiana to do," wrote Lincoln to Banks, "it is quite a different thing for me to assume direction of the matter." He would like to see the State recognize the Emancipation Proclamation. "And while she is at it, I think it would not be objectionable for her to adopt some practical system by which the two races could gradually live themselves out of the old relation to each other, and both come out better prepared for the new. Education for young blacks should be included in the plan." Lincoln hoped that even proslavery men could see that they had strong reason to place themselves again under the shield of the Union and "thus perpetually hedge against the recurrence of the scenes through which we are now passing." He stressed the plight of "the landless and homeless freed people" and made clear: "My word is out to be for and not against them on the question of their permanent freedom."

Thus with bayonets of military control in one hand, advices from Washington in the other, besides what he had learned of the Negro and the Southern planter and the Creole in Massachusetts, Banks was "master" in the procedure of erecting a new Louisiana government to carry on as one of the States of the Union. No other military or civil magistrate in the country had a more picaresque lot of human odds and ends to govern than Banks. "Wonders are becoming common," said *Leslie's* of February 27. "There is an Abraham Lincoln Club in New Orleans, and the chairman is a large slave owner." Into the United States Senate came a Louisiana petition from 1,000 colored persons (white blood preponderant) representing $15,000,000 of property, praying they might be allowed to vote as United States citizens.

Two Creoles, Mr. J. B. Rodanez and Captain Arnold Bertonneau, came to the White House bearing a petition signed by 1,000 ancient freedmen of New Orleans, nearly all of French descent, natives of Louisiana, owners of real and personal property, having among their signers twenty-eight veterans of the War of 1812 who had served under General Andrew Jackson, not to mention one ancient freedman who was a lieutenant in the French army under Napoleon before Louisiana was sold to the United States. They prayed now to have under the newly announced free government some of the rights they had under the old French government. "The President in replying to the petition," wrote the *Chicago Tribune* correspondent, "said it was his business to finish the job he had on hand, and that if he were convinced it was necessary in order to the restoration of Louisiana that they should be allowed to vote, he would do it, but this petition rests its claims on racial grounds, and with those he had and would have nothing to do; he must therefore refer them to the Constitutional Convention soon to be held in Louisiana. The creoles mean to lay their petition before Congress."

Out over his checkered domain Banks on January 11 proclaimed an election to be held on February 22 of State officers to govern under the constitution and laws of Louisiana except as to laws related to slavery. Banks announced too that in the coming April delegates would be chosen to make a constitution and arrange for election of members of Congress; meanwhile martial law was fundamental, though the military government was prepared to surrender gradually its power as events moved toward full restoration of the State to the Union. Free white male voters who had taken the oath of allegiance cast over 11,000 ballots on February 22, of which the Banks candidate Michael Hahn received 6,183, J. Q. A. Fellows, a proslavery conservative, 2,996, and B. F. Flanders 2,232. Flanders was a horse of hope put into the field by a Free State committee. Before the election the committee charged that Banks with the President's sanction was mismanaging reconstruction and emancipation. After the election the Free State committee charged that the election was not valid and Congress ought to declare it null and void. Before and after the election Flanders, a New Hampshire-born New Orleans lawyer, held office and drew pay as a supervising special agent of the Treasury Department for Louisiana, Mississippi, and Texas, appointed by Secretary Chase.

In his Louisiana domain Governor Michael Hahn counted a mass of people, three-fourths of the State, whose allegiance mainly lay with the Confederate Governor and the legislature in session at the capitol in Shreveport. Hahn was only thirty-four years old, born in Bavaria, as a baby carried by his parents to a ship for New York. He moved with them to New Orleans, where he graduated from high school and the law department of the University of Louisiana, became president of the school board in New Orleans, clung fast to Douglas in politics, though an outspoken antislavery man. When the Confederacy was established and all officials were called to swear allegiance to it, Hahn in renewing his oath as a notary public managed to neglect being sworn in. With the Union capture of New Orleans Hahn swore allegiance to the United States, was elected to Congress from the Second Louisiana District in 1862, took his seat as a Republican in Washington on February 17, 1863, and served through March 3, returning to advise that no more congressional elections be held till the State was more thoroughly reconstructed. His newspaper, the *True Delta*, was a journal of emancipation in support of Lincoln policies and Lincoln's renomination in June.

Of Hahn's inaugural day, wrote one reporter, "The dawn was ushered in by the clangor of the iron-tongued bells, and the roar of artillery, waking the slumberous echoes from their lairs, and proclaiming to a disenthralled people the glad tidings of the reëstablishment of civil liberty." In Lafayette Square, where, in replica of the Clark Mills statue across from the White House at Washington, Andrew Jackson rode a prancing horse symbolic of the Union forever, crowds gathered, including 6,000 schoolchildren "from the lisping five year old to the radiant maiden of sixteen." In the center of the amphitheater a large banner pictured a prolific pelican feeding a brood of fledglings from her torn and bleeding breast (meaning the war); a phoenix bird above symbolized the Union that would rise out of the ashes. Banners and bunting had inscriptions to Farragut, Banks, and Hahn as heroes of freedom and men of duty. An orchestra of three hundred pieces, and forty anvils for beating out the "Anvil Chorus," performed next to a tall flagstaff and a platform with "Michael Hahn, Our Governor" wrought in evergreen. Hahn swore in the presence of Almighty God that he would henceforward faithfully support, protect, and defend the Constitution of the United States, and in like manner abide by the acts of Congress and in like manner abide by all proclamations of the President having reference to slaves, so long and so far as not modified or declared void by the Supreme Court.

To Hahn, Lincoln wrote a letter marked "Private" at the top and saying at the bottom it was "only a suggestion, not to the public, but to you alone." It held Lincoln's first important committal on Negro suffrage and read: "I congratulate you on having fixed your name in history as the first free-State governor of Louisiana. Now you are about to have a convention, which, among other things, will probably define the elective franchise. I barely suggest for your private consideration, whether some of the colored people may not be let in—as, for instance, the very intelligent, and especially those who have fought gallantly in our ranks. They would probably help, in some trying time to come, to keep the jewel of liberty within the family of freedom."

To this the President added a one-sentence letter, perhaps equally important, notifying Hahn that until further orders he would be Military Governor of Lousiana. Thus if his civil authority given him by election was questioned, he could call out the troops and riot squads.

Governor Hahn's new Secretary of State, S. Wrotnowski, issued a proclamation on March 16 notifying electors, sheriffs, and election commissioners to prepare for electing delegates to the Constitutional Convention to be held in April. Before that convention met and while it held sessions, General Banks was to ride in one of the most heartsickening adventures that ever befell a man on horseback leading men afoot into weariness, despair, and death.

Banks headed in March the Red River expedition of some 40,000 men, hundreds of wagons, a fleet of 20 gunboats, as many more transports, tenders, and supply ships. They started across western Louisiana aiming to stop interference from that direction with Mississippi River navigation, to put down whatever Confederate armies joined up against them, and to take

Shreveport and have Governor Hahn and a Union legislature sit there and rule Louisiana. This would make a starting-point from which to overrun Texas and set up the United States flag as a warning to the French imperial army across the Mexican border, where the Austrian Archduke Maximilian had been put on a throne by Napoleon III. Seward wanted this last objective very much. Lincoln wrote Banks that recent events in Mexico rendered early action in Texas "more important than ever." Halleck with Banks had worked out the campaign plan. Grant opposed it, though Grant in his first days as lieutenant general would not go so far as to countermand the Red River expedition.

His army at Natchitoches was over halfway to Shreveport on April 2 when General Banks wrote to John Hay that the enemy seemed to be fortifying far away on the Sabine River and he was only anxious lest he should not have a battle with the foe. Hay showed the Banks letter to Lincoln and Hay thought it set going in Lincoln an instinct like a sixth sense for bad news to come. "I am sorry," said Lincoln, "to see this tone of confidence; the next news we shall hear from there will be of a defeat."

Amid pine barrens in a broken hill country, with wagon roads few and cleared spaces for open battle rare, the Banks forces moved against inferior-numbered Confederate forces who knew the land and how to live on it and maneuver rapidly across it. And the Banks forces were mishandled and beaten and sent reeling so that Banks was glad to get his army safe in Alexandria, eighty miles back eastward from the town where twenty days earlier he had written John Hay he was anxious lest the enemy might not give him battle. A bullet had torn through Banks's coat in one major action where General William B. Franklin had two horses killed under him and where Franklin said of the wild runaway of a scared army, "Bull Run was not a circumstance in comparison." The *Philadelphia Press* correspondent, who had also been at Bull Run, saw it as the same kind of a rout, except that fewer men were engaged and before their flight they fought with a valor not seen at the first panic of the war. It started like a thunderbolt, how or why the correspondent could not see. "We found ourselves swallowed up in a hissing, seething, bubbling whirlpool of agitated men . . . and if we hoped to live we must ride with the rest of them. Our line of battle had given way."

At Pleasant Hill General A. J. Smith, who had trained under Grant and Sherman in the Vicksburg campaign, commanded troops who threw back the enemy with heavy punishment. An Ohio soldier wrote home that General Banks remarked, "General Smith, you have saved my army," and General Smith busted out, "By God! I know it, sir." When told that Banks would soon have reinforcements, General Smith flashed, "The fellow has more men now than he knows how to use." No other Western military operation brought such disgust over the commander as did the Red River expedition. "There is great dissatisfaction expressed on all sides at the generalship displayed by General Banks," wrote the *Missouri Republican* correspondent. "He has lost the confidence of the entire army. The privates are ridiculing him. Officers are not loudly but deeply cursing him and civilians are unanimous in condemnation."

Far up the river was the navy, Admiral Porter's fleet of boats he figured worth $2,000,000, stranded in rapids and shallow water, unable to move down-river. The officers prepared in their minds to hand over the fleet to Confederate armies due to arrive soon. Then a young Wisconsin engineer, Lieutenant Colonel Joseph Bailey, worked out a scheme of dams, cribs, and chutes, built in record time by thousands of soldiers cutting down trees and toiling to their armpits in running water. The job began on April 30 and was finished May 8. They raised the river-water level seven feet. The fleet moved down-river and was saved. Young Bailey, at first laughed at as crackbrained, was a hero.

Banks called his generals for a council of war. The council voted to retreat. At Alexandria General David Hunter arrived with dispatches ordering Banks to end the expedition. These orders were countermanded in fresh dispatches from Halleck. Grant sent peremptory orders that 10,000 troops loaned by Sherman be sent back May 1. A crop of quarrels sprang up among the generals. Cotton-traders and speculators trailing the expedition made themselves heard through their political fronts at Washington, spreading word that Banks was feathering his own nest. Uncalled-for newspaper insinuations had it that Banks was running for President.

Lincoln, Seward, Halleck, Grant, Sherman, newspaper correspondents, and the cotton-traders had, each and all, affirmatively or negatively, shared in getting the expedition started and in direction of it after it got going. Banks was pleased to get back with it to the Mississippi and disperse it into various commands. In all engagements except one, wrote Banks in his official report, his army had been successful, had marched by land four hundred miles and fought with a total loss of 3,980 men. "The failure to accomplish the main object was due to other considerations than the actual superiority of the enemy in the field."

Charges arose that, after all, the collapsed and inglorious Red River expedition was not so much to win Texas and threaten the French imperialists in Mexico, nor to widen the area of reconstruction across Louisiana, nor incidentally to clear the Southwest of armed Confederate forces. The main objective, these charges implied, was capture of immense supplies of cotton to be sold by the Union Government to relieve the textile-mill famine and to put millions of dollars into the United States Treasury. General Banks the year before had urged a plan for cotton seizures which he believed would bring in from $50,000,000 to $100,000,000 cash profits to the Government, besides replenishing the world markets and perhaps giving work to the unemployed of Liverpool and Manchester. A congressional committee, investigating the many vague charges and rumors, found no evidence to go against Banks's word that every dollar's worth of property taken by his army was properly accounted for.

"Reflections more or less severe were cast upon the President," wrote Nicolay and Hay, "because two men appeared at Alexandria [on the Red

River] bearing passes in his handwriting authorizing them to trade in cotton." The secretaries pointed to a pressure "almost incredible" on the President to grant such permits, "and he sometimes, though very seldom, gave way." The letter of the President to Congressman William Kellogg of Illinois, audibly groaning his refusal to give a trading permit, was quoted. "I think you do not know how embarrassing your request is," he wrote. Few things were so troublesome to the Government as the fierceness with which the profits in cotton-trading were sought. "The temptation is so great that nearly everybody wishes to be in it; and, when in, the question of profit controls all, regardless of whether the cotton-seller is loyal or rebel, or whether he is paid in corn-meal or gunpowder," the President informed Kellogg. "The officers of the army, in numerous instances, are believed to connive and share the profits, and thus the army itself is diverted from fighting the rebels to speculating in cotton, and steamboats and wagons in the pay of the government are set to gathering and carrying cotton, and the soldiers to loading cotton-trains and guarding them." The Treasury and War departments had brought the matter up again and again for Cabinet discussions. "What can and what cannot be done has for the time been settled, and it seems to me I cannot safely break over it. I know it is thought that one case is not much, but how can I favor one and deny another?"

Kellogg had urged or implied that the President could let him have one or two trading permits and the public need know nothing of it. That had been done. The President noted: "One case cannot be kept a secret. The authority given would be utterly ineffectual until it is shown, and when shown, everybody knows of it." Having previously seen Kellogg flare up in anger at being refused an official favor, Lincoln wrote in much the same tone as on that previous occasion. "The administration would do for you as much as for any other man; and I personally would do some more than for most others; but really I cannot involve myself and the government as this would do."

Two men turned up at Alexandria on the Red River with cotton-trading permits in the President's personal handwriting. They were William Butler and Thomas L. Casey of Springfield, Illinois, old personal friends of Lincoln. Butler had taken Lincoln in as a boarder when Lincoln first came to Springfield with little cash and heavy debts. Butler and Lincoln had been two of the members of the Illinois Legislature who had brought about the removal of the State capital from Vandalia to Springfield. Lincoln had boarded with Butler from the time he came to Springfield until he married and set up housekeeping. Butler's plea for a trading permit Lincoln could not resist, as he did that of Congressman Kellogg.

What little cotton Butler and Casey collected at Alexandria was taken away from them by the army and put to military use, some bales of it going into the dam that saved the gunboat fleet. But their appearance at the Red River camp with presidential permits made a hullabaloo and set many tongues going. "Much odium was excited by the circumstance," wrote Greeley.

The navy managed to gather in some cotton which the Government sold at St. Louis, but the available bulk of it went out of sight when the Confederate General Kirby Smith first became sure that the army and navy were coming up Red River. He then ordered bonfires south of Alexandria and east of the Ouachita River that sent up in smoke 150,000 bales valued at $60,000,000.

Admiral Porter sent a clerk named Heap from Alexandria on the Red River to Washington with confidential dispatches, to which Heap verbally added details, telling President Lincoln and Secretary Welles that failure of the expedition should be laid to imbecility. Heap and his Admiral accused Banks of equivocating, of electioneering, of speculating in cotton, of general malfeasance and mismanagement, wrote Welles, and: "I took Heap with me to the President and had him tell his own story. It was less full and denunciatory than to me, but it seemed to convince the President, who I have thought was over-partial to Banks, and I have thought that Seward contributed to that feeling. The President, after hearing Heap, said he had rather cousined up to Banks, but for some time past had begun to think he was erring in so doing. He repeated two verses from Moore, commencing

> "Oh, ever thus, from childhood's hour,
> I've seen my fondest hopes decay."

"In the midst of all the painful controversies that grew out of the Red River mischance," said Nicolay and Hay, it was gratifying to know "that no officer of rank in army or navy was shown to be guilty of any act of dishonesty." Particularly they felt that the "honorable poverty" which followed General Banks in afterdays was the best answer to his loose-tongued enemies.

In May, Banks was relieved of his command and resigned his army commission. West Pointers hated him and called him a "political general." His Red River campaign had been "one damned blunder from beginning to end," said Sherman. At two points in the Red River campaign Banks had spent time with the natives electioneering for the coming Louisiana Constitutional Convention and working on Louisiana reconstruction. The job handed to Banks mixed the political and the military more intricately perhaps than any assignment Lincoln had given during the war. He faced meshes of the race question in immediate administration. "The President gave me too much to do—more than any other major-general in the army," he wrote, as fact and not complaint. Sherman had written Lincoln and Halleck he deemed it "very unwise at this time or for years to come, to revive the State governments of Louisiana, etc., or to institute in this quarter any civil government in which the local people have much to say." This, however, was precisely what Banks under Lincoln's guidance was trying to do with one hand while with the other he was to slay Confederate armies.

Lincoln sought to implant the seeds of a new society, freed of Negro slavery, into an organism that had deep strength of both active and passive resistance. Banks was an instrument of political and social science attempting this cultural experiment in many-complexioned Louisiana. The political phase of it interested Banks more than the military, as Sherman saw when on March 3 Banks invited him to stay the next day and see the Hahn inauguration, with cannon salvos by electrical signal to synchronize with three hundred band instruments and forty anvils. Sherman declined with thanks, went away feeling that Banks was a politician rather than a soldier, that Banks should have been looking to his Red River campaign, which turned out in Sherman's view to be "one damned blunder from beginning to end."

Lincoln and Banks agreed that, if only for its effect on politics and war morale in the North, the ballot should be given to at least a part of the free Negro population. Governor Hahn hoped to work out Lincoln's suggestion that Negroes who had fought for the Union, and possibly those who could read and write, should be the first Negro voters. Banks had a plan for the first Negro voters to come from the social ranks of those who had more white than Negro blood in their veins. A United States court decree should be obtained "fixing the standard of citizenship as to color, and declaring that a man, with a major part of white blood, should possess all the rights of a white man." On such a decision Banks would have had 30,000 Negro voters to begin with, and from that starting-point extended the franchise gradually to other Negroes.

He had made his arrangements with Judge Durell of the United States Court, wrote Banks, but a few men, radicals who opposed step-by-step tactics, managed to defeat him. To these radicals and their friends in the North, Banks pointed out that if he had met their wishes and given the ballot to all Negroes, he would have given political domination to an exclusively Negro constituency. "You might not object to this; but I know perfectly well that, while a Government formed, as heretofore, by white men, may clothe negroes with the right of suffrage, a Government, organized by negro voters, that should give the elective franchise to white men, would not be acceptable to the Administration, to Congress, nor to the country, nor any part of it. Such would have been the result in Louisiana under a general order conferring suffrage upon negroes."

When Banks had tried to keep for his own department the 10,000 troops loaned to him from Sherman's army, Grant telegraphed Halleck ordering their return and added gently, "I do think it is a waste of strength to trust General Banks with a large command or an important expedition." When Grant telegraphed Halleck about replacing Banks with another commander, Halleck replied that the President had been reading all of Grant's telegrams but so far had not said anything about replacing Banks. "General Banks is a personal friend of the President," wrote Halleck, "and has strong political supporters in and out of Congress. There will undoubtedly be a very strong opposition to his being removed or superseded, and I think the President will hesitate to act unless he has a definite request from you to do so, as a military necessity, you designating his superior in command. On receiving such a formal request (not a mere suggestion) I believe he would act immediately. I have no authority for saying this, but give it simply as my own opinion, formed from the last two years' experience, and the reason, I think, is obvious. To do an act which will give offense to a large number of his political friends the President will require some evidence in a positive form to show the military necessity of that act. In other words, he must have something in a definite shape to fall back upon as his justification. You will perceive that the press in New Orleans and in the Eastern States are already beginning to open in General Banks' favor. The administration would be immediately attacked for his removal. Do not understand me as advocating his retention in command. On the contrary I expressed to the President months ago my own opinion of General Banks' want of capacity."

Grant suggested General E. R. S. Canby to supersede Banks and it was so ordered. But Lincoln and Banks remained friends and Banks was staying on in New Orleans advising with the Louisiana Constitutional Convention and reporting to Lincoln.

The State of Arkansas, lying north of Louisiana and west of the Mississippi River, had fewer slaveholders and less pride of breeding and wealth, made lesser claim to chivalry, than its neighbor Slave States to the east. After General Frederick Steele's column of 13,000 Union troops had marched into Little Rock, the capital of Arkansas, on September 13 of 1863, a large part of the State came under Union control. Eight regiments of Arkansas citizens had been enlisted for service under the Union flag. And early in January President Lincoln sent oath books and blank certificates to General Steele, for use in reorganizing a State government. As the plan of Lincoln and Banks for Louisiana unfolded, Lincoln gave General Steele the details of it, and General Steele was proceeding with it when word came to Lincoln of a series of Union meetings with speeches and resolutions and election of delegates to a convention of 44 members who claimed to represent twenty-two of the fifty-four counties of the State of Arkansas.

This convention on January 22 of '64 declared secession null and void, slavery abolished immediately and unconditionally, and the Confederate debt repudiated. An address to the voters of Arkansas adopted on January 23 frankly acknowledged "that while we could not properly claim to be the people of Arkansas in convention assembled," yet as representatives of a considerable portion of the State, and understanding the sentiment of citizens desiring a government under United States authority, they had determined to present a State constitution for the voters to ballot on. They arranged a provisional State government, provided for an election on March 14 with state, county, and legislative tickets, and candidates for Congress. Also they appointed and inaugurated for Provisional Governor one Isaac Murphy, sixty-two years old, born near Pittsburgh, Pennsylvania, schoolteacher, lawyer, California gold-hunter, civil engineer and public-land surveyor. As a member in May of '61 of the State convention which decided

William ("Deacon") Bross

Ward Hill Lamon

Richard James Oglesby

Isaac Newton Arnold

FOUR ILLINOIS MEN

From the author's collection

Francis Preston Blair, Sr.

Francis Preston Blair, Jr.

William Dennison

Reuben Eaton Fenton

From the author's collection

that Arkansas would secede, Murphy was the one lone delegate voting against secession. He went back home to Huntsville, but soon found it safer to travel north to Missouri, where he became a staff officer of General Steele; his son Frank was a major in the 1st Arkansas United States Infantry.

As word of this movement headed by Isaac Murphy came to Lincoln, along with telegrams asking him to change a date set by Steele for an election to the same date as their convention had set, Lincoln wrote on February 17 to one of the delegates, William M. Fishback, at Little Rock: "When I fixed a plan for an election in Arkansas I did it in ignorance that your convention was doing the same work. Since I learned the latter fact I have been constantly trying to yield my plan to them. I have sent two letters to General Steele, and three or four despatches to you and others, saying that he, General Steele, must be master, but that it will probably be best for him to merely help the convention on its own plan. Some single mind must be master, else there will be no agreement in anything, and General Steele, commanding the military and being on the ground, is the best man to be that master. Even now citizens are telegraphing me to postpone the election to a later day than either that fixed by the convention or by me. This discord must be silenced."

General Steele proclaimed the election for March 14 as scheduled by the convention, the polls to be kept open three days. The returns gave 12,179 votes for the new constitution and 226 against it, and for Murphy, with no opposition candidate for governor, 12,430 ballots cast by oath-of-allegiance voters in forty counties. With brass bands, flags, and formalities the new State government was sworn in and took office on April 11. On May 12, when Steele's army had vanished south to help Banks, the new State government trembled as if it hung by an eyelash and Governor Murphy telegraphed the Big Father in Washington: "Banks and Steele have been defeated. Little Rock is threatened. . . . We need protection now, or will be lost." The protection came. And the State government held on—even though its two United States Senators-elect and its three Congressmen-elect went to Washington, presented their credentials, heard the wrangling and the squabbling in Senate and House over how the occupied Southern States should be reconstructed, and came back home to tell their people that not yet, though maybe after a while, they might be admitted to seats. Decision was postponed.

The President wrote to General Steele a short letter that he could have made much longer, though in the case there really did not seem to be much more to say: "I understand that Congress declines to admit to seats the persons sent as senators and representatives from Arkansas. These persons apprehend that, in consequence, you may not support the new State government there as you otherwise would. My wish is that you give that government and the people there the same support and protection that you would if the members had been admitted, because in no event, nor in any view of the case, can this do any harm, while it will be the best you can do toward suppressing the rebellion."

Along the Red River area in Louisiana and in many counties in Arkansas murder, barn-burning, and horse-stealing became applied arts. When for reasons of war the Union forces vanished from a neighborhood, those families where a man had taken the Union oath took their punishment unless they fled. The town of Alexandria was wiped out by fire because so many of its citizens had sworn loyalty to the Louisiana government. Neighborhoods in Arkansas that had cast a heavy vote for the new Murphy government, and for Senators and Congressmen to go to Washington, whenever their military protection moved away witnessed murder, mayhem, fire, and the wild night cry of vengeance and reprisal from mobs, gangs, guerrillas, and squads of roving desperadoes.

In southern Missouri the Union men had, as the war progressed more in their favor, developed illegal violence to the point where it seemed to Lincoln they were going too far, and he wrote April 4 to his military head, General Rosecrans: "It is said, I know not whether truly, that in some parts of Missouri assassinations are systematically committed upon returned rebels who wish to ground arms and behave themselves. This should not be. Of course I have not heard that you give countenance to or wink at such assassinations." The President hoped too that there would be less disorder in the enrolling of Negro troops in Missouri. The sight of black men in the national military uniform handling guns and bayonets was still annoying to some white men who could not get accustomed to the new regime. In the many combustible and hair-trigger situations where Rosecrans had to make decisions Lincoln believed Old Rosy had done not so bad. "So far you have got along in the Department of the Missouri rather better than I dared to hope, and I congratulate you and myself upon it." The President gave Rosecrans "suggestions rather than orders" regarding a Rosecrans ruling that church organizations such as conventions, synods, councils, should before transacting business take the Union oath of allegiance. "I have found that men who have not even been suspected of disloyalty are very averse to taking an oath of any sort as a condition to exercising an ordinary right of citizenship."

Bushwhackers had sprung up around Little Rock in such force that it was not safe to go a mile out of the capital. Brigadier General C. C. Andrews wrote to Lincoln: "A large majority of planters have taken the oath, pretend to acquiesce in the proclamation setting their slaves free, and still cling to their slaves and to the hope that they will sometime again hold them as slaves." From Chariton County, Missouri, a legislative member wrote to Rosecrans that the country was overrun with thieves armed with oaths and certificates of citizenship, the question being, "How are we to get rid of them?" He hoped these oaths would not go into use "as a cloak to cover crimes." To Lincoln as well as to Rosecrans came Missouri reports now from one town or county and then from another telling of vagabonds, thieves, marauders, bushwhackers, guerrillas, incendiaries, by tens, twenties, hundreds, often wearing the Federal uniform. The mail for Kansas City was abstracted at Pleasant Hill, the telegraph wires from Lexington to Independence cut in two places. The bulletins pictured confusion and personal distress. J. P. Sanderson, Provost Marshal General of the State, reported he believed it was a settled policy of the Confederacy to give furloughs to soldiers who would return home to Missouri, talk like they were disgusted deserters, take the Union oath of allegiance, then go in for bushwhacking. Nearly every bushwhacker arrested or killed with his hands in murder or robbery had in his pockets the oath of allegiance to the United States sworn in the presence of Almighty God, said Sanderson. Lincoln believed only part of this, deeming Sanderson flighty.

Rosecrans telegraphed the President that he had "detailed information of high national importance, of a plot to overthrow the Government," which could not be entrusted to the mails. Lincoln telegraphed to send it by express—"no danger of its miscarriage." The nature of the information was too grave for transmissal through by express, Rosecrans telegraphed; "a sense of duty obliges me to refrain from so transmitting it." Lincoln telegraphed that express was safer than a staff officer. "If you send a verbal message, the messenger is one additional person let into the secret." Then came a telegram from Governor Yates of Illinois. Yates too had received information from Rosecrans of vital importance to the Government which could not be conveyed in full import by mail or express, and Rosecrans or his Provost Marshal should be summoned to Washington immediately.

Lincoln came into Hay's room in the White House just before bedtime that night and explained that Governor Yates of Illinois was joining in Rosecrans' request that John P. Sanderson, Provost Marshal General of Missouri, be called to Washington by the President to lay bare a vast conspiracy. "If it is a matter of such overwhelming importance," said Lincoln, "I don't think Sanderson is the proper person to whom to entrust it. I am inclined to think that the object of the General is to force me into a conflict with the Secretary of War and to make me overrule him in this matter. This at present I am not inclined to do. I have concluded to send you out there to talk it over with Rosecrans and to ascertain just what he has."

Hay started for St. Louis next morning with a letter from the President to Rosecrans. He lay over and changed trains at Cincinnati, rode to St. Louis writing rhymes in a compartment with a pair of whisky-smugglers. He found Rosecrans agreeable and chatty. "Hay, where were you born? How long have you been with the President?" They partook of a savorless hotel dinner, went to Rosecrans' private room. The commander of the Department of Missouri lit a cigar, offered Hay one, and said, "No? Long-necked fellows like you don't need them." Between puffs then Rosecrans began talking about the conspiracy, first in a loud voice, then in lowered tones as he cast a glance over his shoulder and moved his chair closer to Hay. He outlined a secret organization, the Order of American Knights, the O.A.K., having high priests and oaths, contacts with returned rebel soldiers and guerrillas, with plans for plunder, murder, and persecution of Union men. His secret-service men had found many recent massacres directly chargeable to this secret society. The intensely active and widespread O.A.K. had in Missouri 13,000 sworn members, in Illinois 140,000, in Ohio and Indiana almost as large a membership.

Hay the next day went to the office of Sanderson, who read from heavy reports and showed a few documents. Hay spent one more evening with Rosecrans, said he would go back to Washington and lay the matter before the President as it had been presented to him. He did not ask for any of Sanderson's reports or any papers in the case. He noticed that both Rosecrans and Sanderson inclined to insist on Sanderson's going to Washington in person to discuss the matter with the President without Stanton's touching it. The young bland, innocent-looking messenger from the President figured the lay of the land and what was in the wind: "Rosecrans is bitterly hostile to Stanton: he is full of the idea that Stanton has wronged him & is continually seeking opportunities to thwart and humiliate him. Then Sand^{n} himself is rather proud of his work in ferreting out this business and is not unwilling to come to Wash^{n} & impress the Pres^{t} with the same sense: then they wish a program for future opportunities determined, & finally they want money for the Secret Service fund."

These impressions Hay talked of to Lincoln at Washington, noting that the President seemed not overwell pleased that Rosecrans had not sent all the necessary papers by Hay, speaking again his want of confidence in Sanderson, declining to be made a party to a quarrel between Stanton and Rosecrans, and in reply to Rosecrans' suggestion that the greatest of secrecy was important saying that a secret already confided to the four State Governors Yates, Morton, Brough, Bramlette, and their circles of officers could scarcely be worth the keeping now. As to the O.A.K. and its conspiracy in the North, it was politics again, with an organization of about the same sort of malice and childishness as the Knights of the Golden Circle.

Neither Rosecrans nor Sanderson was permitted to go to Washington in the matter, and Rosecrans by messenger sent on a Sanderson report, "covering 1,000 pages of foolscap," elaborating no essential points beyond what Rosecrans had told Hay between cigar puffs in his hotel room in St. Louis.

A dramatic history-making figure rising out of Missouri affairs, ready to embroil Lincoln in a fiery episode, was Francis Preston Blair, Jr. Early in the game he had joined hands with General Lyon to clinch possession of St. Louis and northern Missouri for the Union and run the "neutral" Governor Jackson out of the State capital as a fugitive. Early Blair had raised seven regiments in Missouri, and he and his brother Montgomery had given Lincoln the name of Frémont, their St. Louis friend, as the man to head military operations in Missouri. And as a Border State man, moderate on the slavery question, having acquaintance with slaveholders, he came into collision with Frémont, Chase, Henry Winter Davis, and the extremists. For the slave as a human being Blair pleaded freedom and opportunity, yet he held that with the Negro population of the South so often equal to, or outnumbering, that of the whites the enforcement of race equality by laws would require bayonets and martial rule for a long time. The cost and pain of political equality would run high, believed Blair, and passionately so. He fought the Frémont and Chase cohorts with resentment, contempt, intolerance; he hated them and said he thrived on it. The tradition of Jackson was on him and the Blair tribe—out of natural disposition and his father's long confidential service with Jackson.

Forty-three years old, born in Lexington, Kentucky, a Princeton graduate who studied law in Washington, Frank Blair, Jr., was admitted to the bar in Kentucky, practiced in St. Louis, trapped bear and wolf in the Rocky Mountains, fought in the Mexican War, again practiced law in St. Louis, edited the *Missouri Democrat,* went to the legislature, helped found the Republican party in 1856. One of the first Republicans in Congress, in 1857 he advocated compensated emancipation and colonization of the Negroes five years before Lincoln brought those issues to Congress. When Congress opened on July 4 of '61, Vallandigham challenged Blair's right to a seat on the ground that he was holding a military commission from the United States Government. Blair informed Vallandigham and the House that he had not been sworn in to the United States Army service and therefore would take his seat. In the balloting for Speaker of the House Blair received 50 votes and retired in favor of Galusha Grow, whom he had voted for. He won adoption of a resolution to expel Congressman John B. Clark of Missouri as having taken up arms for the Confederate Government. He defended President Lincoln from the charge of having forced General Scott to order the battle of Bull Run against that General's better judgment.

Then Blair had been commissioned general of a brigade he raised himself, and ordered to join Grant at Milliken's Bend down in Mississippi. "I dreaded his coming," said Grant, who had known Blair at St. Louis and voted against him for Congress in 1858. To Grant, Blair seemed one more political general, one more politician with unearned stars on the shoulder straps. "I knew him as a frank, positive and generous man," said Grant, "true to his friends even to a fault, but always a leader. I knew from experience that it was more difficult to command two generals desiring to be leaders than it was to command one army officered intelligently and with subordination."

Then at Chickasaw bluffs, Arkansas Post, at Hard Times Landing and Champion's Hill, on the Big Black and the Yazoo, Blair had fought in muddy bayous and across cornfields, sending lines of skirmishers or storming columns against the enemy trying to keep Grant from getting a death clutch on Vicksburg. Grant said he was disappointed, agreeably so, in Frank Blair, "no man braver than he, nor . . . any who obeyed all orders . . . with more unquestioning alacrity." Therefore Grant deduced that Blair was "one man as a soldier, another as a politician." The Senate approved President Lincoln's commissioning him major general. He had handled his 15th Corps under Sherman's eye, and that redheaded apostle of conquest had only enthusiasm for the way Blair marched and fought his men at Jackson, Tuscumbia, Missionary Ridge, and the relief of Knoxville.

Then Stanton out of suspicion and dislike of the Blair tribe issued an order relieving General Blair of command, having, the Blairs and their friends said, "the effrontery to declare that he did so by order of the President." Sherman still wanted Blair in the saddle with the 15th Corps. So did Grant. And Lincoln called on Stanton to revoke the order relieving Blair.

By this time Blair himself began to have doubts whether he ought to stay with the army. Perhaps he would do better to take his seat in Congress. So he asked his brother Montgomery in the Cabinet to find out the wishes of President Lincoln. He would be guided by those wishes. Lincoln saw that if Blair could come on to Washington and win place as Speaker of the House that would help. Lincoln wrote a letter dated November 2, 1863, which if made public would let people know how things stood between him and the Blair brothers, the kind and degree of understanding they had. This fatherly epistle, strangely affectionate and wistful, addressed to the Honorable Montgomery Blair, read:

> Some days ago I understood you to say that your brother, General Frank Blair, desires to be guided by my wishes as to whether he will occupy his seat in Congress or remain in the field. My wish, then, is compounded of what I believe will be best for the country and best for him, and it is that he will come here, put his military commission in my hands, take his seat, go into caucus with our friends, abide the nominations, help elect the nominees, and thus aid to organize a House of Representatives which will really support the government in the war. If the result shall be the election of himself as Speaker, let him serve in that position; if not, let him retake his commission and return to the army. For the country this will heal a dangerous schism; for him it will relieve from a dangerous position. By a misunderstanding, as I think, he is in danger of being permanently separated from those with whom only he can ever have a real sympathy—the sincere opponents of slavery. It will be a mistake if he shall allow the provocations offered him by insincere time-servers to drive him out of the house of his own building. He is young yet. He has abundant talent—quite enough to occupy all his time without devoting any to temper. He is rising in military skill and usefulness. His recent appointment to the command of a corps by one so competent to judge as General Sherman proves this. In that line he can serve both the country and himself more profitably than he could as a member of Congress on the floor. The foregoing is what I would say if Frank Blair were my brother instead of yours.

On the day Lincoln wrote this letter he let one main point of it—that he was friendly with the Blairs but independent of their control—along with other bits of information, get to his radical opposition. These points were eagerly picked up by Whitelaw Reid and sent on to Greeley, with no delay—in fact on the very day that Lincoln wrote his remarkable letter to Monty Blair. Reid, twenty-seven years old, Washington correspondent of the *Cincinnati Gazette*, a personal friend of Chase and foremost of young journalists in the movement to nominate Chase for President in '64, was also librarian of the House of Representatives, with admittance to the floor of the House and access to "inside" news and views. Reid wrote to Greeley as though he had on this November 2 interviewed the President, or received his information from someone who had personally spoken with the President—possibly John Hay, for there was a growing friendship between the President's secretary and Reid. It was one of those unusual interviews in which the President was heard to use the word "durned." Addressing "My Dear Mr. Greeley" Reid wrote:

> I snatch a moment to say that the Frank Blair danger has just been handsomely averted. He [Frank Blair] sent Montgomery to the President to ask him whether he should remain in the army or come to Congress. Mr. Lincoln took the question as intimating that Blair gave him absolute authority to decide the matter. So he took time to consider;—then told Montgomery to tell Frank that if he would come on, go into the Administration Caucus and help organize the House, he would then give him back his Major Generalship and let him at once return to the army. That would, he told him, harmonize all these difficulties, and do a world of good. "I don't know," said Mr. Lincoln this morning, "whether Frank will do this or not, but it will show durned quick," (I quote literally,) "whether he's honest or not."

Frank Blair was as yet in rain and sleet among Union fighters in Tennessee while Congress organized and elected Colfax Speaker of the House, Montgomery Blair telling Welles that he did his best, at Lincoln's suggestion, to get Washburne for Speaker. On January 12 of '64, however, Frank Blair took his seat in Congress. Those who had hated the sight of him the last time they saw him now hated him all the more. Stanton's relieving him from command was considered personal animus. They were uneasy. Blair outclassed them in the point that he could sit a horse and keep a cool head while handling a corps of 30,000 troops in a style up to the requirements of the terrible Sherman. "Tall, well-formed with a sandy complexion, light-gray eyes, heavy moustache," wrote the war correspondent Wilkie, "a fine forehead covered with a mass of reddish hair, distingué in style and bearing, handsome and commanding, slow and deliberate in speech, doing everything well from leading a charge to uncorking a bottle."

Blair defended the President's Amnesty Proclamation as wise statesmanship, a procedure without violence toward reconstruction of the seceded States. He argued extensively that those States were not, as Stevens and Winter Davis contended, a foreign nation at war with the United States. He challenged a provision for the lands, estates, and properties of the South to be seized and partitioned among freed slaves and Union soldiers. Congressman James F. Wilson of Iowa had urged confiscation, saying that honeyed words, soothing syrup, mercy, would have to wait, saying that no marvelously kindhearted gentlemen could "stay the fury of a tornado by singing a lullaby to it." Blair countered that with the end of the rebellion not far off there was need of moderation and forbearance. He would recall Senator Benton's aphorism, "Our troubles come from the uneasy politicians and our safety from the tranquil masses." A vindictive and acrimonious spirit would defeat permanent results. Blair cited English tragedies dealing with treason, persecution of Jews and Moors in Spain; wholesale confiscation of land and property in the South would bring misery to the women and children of the present and the succeeding generations. He quoted his colleague Spalding, "Even the innocence of women and children does not screen them from the fate of their nation," and countered of Stevens: "I must do the gentleman the justice to declare that I cannot believe he means what he has said. He has a shrewd tongue, but it does not find its severity in his heart. His speech is that of a party advocate, seeking to . . . cut the States of the South from their constitutional moorings and make a hotch-potch . . . a revolutionary caldron."

With praise for the President, Blair mingled his plea for slaveholders loyal to the Union to be paid for their slaves made free. "The President, in my judgment, expressed more clearly the sense of the entire nation in his proclamations than was supposed by either those who most applauded or those who denounced the act. The pledge which he gave to use all his efforts to compensate the loyal owners of slaves, which was ignored by one class and distrusted by the other, was, in my opinion, the pledge of the nation, and will be redeemed. It was an act too grand and noble to be stained by any leaven of injustice or dishonesty."

In this speech of February 5, 1864, Blair put himself on record with the few Lincoln men in Congress. In doing so he set himself up as an interpreter of the President's mind and took on the tone of a spokesman and a defender, so that those who heard or read his speech might believe that the Blair family and the President were in perfect accord. It was a habit and a method that both Montgomery and Frank Blair had. And Lincoln knew its political folly when he wrote to Montgomery that Frank was "in danger of being permanently separated from those with whom only he can ever have a real sympathy—the sincere opponents of slavery." Only in case Frank could be elected Speaker of the House would Lincoln have cared to have him back in Congress, for he had advised "if not [elected Speaker], let him . . . return to the army." By going back to the army Frank Blair would "heal a dangerous schism."

Grant and Sherman had yet to open their big drives aimed to crush the Southern armies, and the pleas of Blair in Congress for moderation and mercy were so framed that they sounded, as Wilson said, like singing a lullaby to stop a tornado. Blair talked as a dogged fighter facing his enemies with blunt weapons, yet in his speech of February 5, 1864, he cut deeper the dangerous schism that Lincoln said needed healing. Very personal and tantalizing was Blair in this speech flavored as follows:

> Allow me to say to the gentleman from Pennsylvania [Stevens] that the President's policy of amnesty, reconstruction of the States, and the segregation of the white and black races, bears not the slightest resemblance to the doctrine of the spoliation of an entire people, the annihilation of the States, and the disfranchisement of the people of our own race, thus putting them upon equality with the blacks.
>
> So far from being the truth that the President and the gentleman from Pennsylvania stand upon "common ground," I am apprehensive that the gentleman is anxious to

saddle the President with the odium of doctrines which are known to be those of rival aspirants for the Presidency, and which have proved fatal to their aspirations.

It is because the President has soared above these unconstitutional and inhuman dogmas, and has shown in his whole Administration, and more especially in his recent proclamations, that he was for amnesty and the restoration of the Union as soon as the inhabitants of the revolted States would resume their allegiance and provide against the recurrence of revolt by removing its cause, that the great body of the loyal people of the country have responded to his words of wisdom and patriotism, and have demanded his renomination by an almost universal acclaim, thus dissipating the hopes of those rival aspirants. . . .

I am not without the apprehension that the gentleman from Pennsylvania wishes also to destroy the President by attributing to him sentiments so justly obnoxious to a great and magnanimous people.

The plain-speaking tone, with its baffling personal and political motives underlying, only deepened the resolves of powerful party men who heard it that they would somehow, even at high cost, wreck the power of the Blairs in the counsels of the President. They said eventually they would have a scalp or know why. Lincoln saw Blair tearing wider the split between radicals and moderates in Congress, and therefore was making arrangements with Grant and Sherman for Blair to take again his corps command.

Blair struck at Chase in a resolution calling for a committee of five from Congress to investigate acts of the Treasury Department, "to report whether any frauds have been practiced on the Government," whether any favoritism had been shown, and whether the enemy had been helped. The Chase men struck back.

Blair had bought brandy to the amount of 225 gallons and a scandalously large amount of whisky, claret, Catawba wine, besides 25 half-barrels of ale and 225 boxes of canned fruit, while he was at Vicksburg in June of '63, according to photographic copies of an order signed by Major General Blair and eight staff officers. This order was published in newspapers and photographic copies of it were circulated among members of Congress. The permit of the customs collector at St. Louis invoiced the purchase at $8,651. The inference of the Chase men and the Missouri radicals seeking Blair's scalp was that Blair and his staff men on duty at Vicksburg could not possibly drink 225 gallons of brandy apiece and a larger amount of whisky, claret, Catawba, and ale during the war, and the goods had been ordered for speculation, sale, and profits.

On March 23 the Missouri radical J. W. McClurg rose in his seat to say that he was sorry his colleague Mr. Blair was not in his seat and he hoped Mr. Blair's friends would send for him. McClurg then made a speech saying that Blair had been a poor witness for himself, had given one false explanation of the liquor order, and "false in one false in all." Blair had told the House that the liquor order was a forgery and B. R. Bonner, Assistant Special Treasury Agent at St. Louis, would substantiate the fact. McClurg was replying with a long letter from Mr. Bonner at St. Louis in which Mr. Bonner denied that he had ever made an admission to Mr. Blair that the liquor order was a forgery. Mr. Bonner's letter, as read by McClurg and as it went into the *Congressional Globe*, ended: "It will thus be seen that General Blair, without the slightest excuse, has coolly and impudently, in the House of Representatives of the United States, uttered a willful, malicious, and deliberate falsehood; and now stands branded and must forever stand branded as a reckless and unscrupulous slanderer, utterly regardless of truth."

Speaker Colfax interrupted to say that the gentleman's speech was clearly out of order as violating the House rule forbidding personalities. Mr. McClurg explained that Mr. Bonner had held only kindness of feeling toward Mr. Blair when this matter arose, that Mr. Blair had induced Mr. Bonner "to commit the indiscretion of saying there appeared to be some disagreement in the chirography of the [liquor] order, in one or two parts," that Mr. Blair had returned Mr. Bonner's kindness with abuse. They had loved each other, these two St. Louis citizens, Blair and Bonner, and now Blair "attempts to place a dagger in the heart of an old friend." No one would deny that the signature "Frank P. Blair, jr." on the liquor order was genuine, said McClurg, with further remarks implying that Blair was a hard drinker as well as a soiled speculator, and closing: "*Justice must be done*, though tears of anguish be drawn from the past and present friends of the condemned criminal."

Blair had come in and had heard his enemy's speech. For such language, in Missouri and Kentucky where he had lived, men drew their guns and shot it out. He took the floor and requested the House to appoint a committee of three to investigate the entire matter and report. As to his colleague McClurg, "I pronounce his allegation from beginning to end a base and miserable falsehood. He has taken the place of the forger and falsifier, and I pronounce him an infamous liar and scoundrel. [Great sensation.]"

Speaker Colfax said he would have to enforce the rule of the House forbidding such language. Blair said there was no other fit language to use, that if he was guilty of the crime charged he was not a fit person to sit in the House. A coast-to-coast committee of William Higby of California, Brutus J. Clay of Kentucky, and John V. S. L. Pruyn of New York was appointed and reported a month later, on April 23, that they had given full opportunity to both parties to produce witnesses and had taken all testimony offered on the subject. It appeared satisfactorily in evidence before them that "one Michael Powers, representing himself to be an agent of the Treasury Department . . . had offered his services" to procure a moderate amount of liquor, tobacco, and cigars for General Blair and his staff, to cost not more than $175. Since Blair and his officers had signed the order, it had been altered. "The original order was for five gallons [of brandy]; by inserting the figure 2 before the figure 5, and adding the word 'each,' it became an order (as nine persons had signed it) for two hundred twenty-five gallons."

Thus an order for goods to cost less than $175 had been item by item changed to cost $8,651. "Judging from all the circumstances, they [the changes] were probably made for the purpose of realizing a profitable speculation under cover of the original order. That they were made by Powers, there cannot from the testimony be any reasonable doubt. At the time the order was delivered to Powers, there was no law or military regulation in any way prohibiting it." The committee were agreed that the evidence sustained Blair in his denial of being engaged in liquor speculation and his charges that the figures in the liquor order had been raised. As to the issues between Blair and McClurg in the House, the chairman from California had doubts, the gentleman from Kentucky could not concur with the chairman, the member from New York said it was outside the scope of the committee.

Blair arose to give notice that he was not to stay in the House much longer and he would best deliver now his remarks on the extraordinary, malicious, and unjust attacks made on him. Others demurred, but Winter Davis said it was due to the gentleman from Missouri that he should be indulged in remarks. "I am . . . loth . . . to consume the time," began Blair in a speech that ran ten columns in the *Congressional Globe.* When the atrocious slander against him had first been published he was commanding the 15th Army Corps on its march from Memphis to Chattanooga to drive Bragg from Lookout Mountain and Missionary Ridge. Following publication of the slander, he had been superseded in command. Not satisfied with having thus humiliated him, the originators of the calumny had reiterated it on his return to the House. He spoke regrets at having employed the language ("liar, falsifier, scoundrel") which he did in the House, though making it clear he was still using that same language outside of the House. The accusation that he had prostituted his office for speculation and profits was made (by McClurg) in an insulting manner, purposely provocative. "I found it impossible to restrain myself, and used language for which I am willing to apologize to the House, but for which I shall never apologize to him." He would not go extensively into the matter of the "forgery perpetrated by a person in the employ of the Treasury Department, uttered and put into circulation by a special agent of the Treasury Department, and printed in a newspaper pensioned by the Secretary of the Treasury." These guilty men he would not follow longer. "These dogs have been set on me by their master, and since I have whipped them back into their kennel I mean to hold their master responsible for this outrage and not the curs who have been set upon me." The liquor order had been made public by a Treasury agent who knew that it was a forgery, after the goods it called for had been seized as contraband, after he, Blair, had been assailed in newspapers as a whisky speculator, and "because I had attacked Mr. Chase in a speech in St. Louis and assailed his trade regulations."

Everything true or false that Blair could think of that might possibly blacken or smear Chase was hurled out before a gaping, amazed audience of Congressmen and press gallery. The same Chase who had opposed the President on the reinforcement of Fort Sumter and would have abandoned the war at the start now favored a war to annihilate the loyal State governments of the South. The congressional committee which was trying to destroy the President's reconstruction plan was composed of the Pomeroy committee with its "private circular" intended to destroy the President. The bill to disfranchise Southern whites and to enfranchise the Negroes was "to prevent any of the States coming back in time to vote for Mr. Lincoln for President, and to promote the ambition of the Secretary of the Treasury." He, Blair, had been refused the opportunity he requested when he had said he could prove frauds and corruptions in trade between the insurrectionary States. He read long letters from businessmen in Vicksburg, Memphis, New Orleans, New York, Philadelphia, outlining possible frauds in cotton- and flour-trading, in percussion caps, in seized plantations leased by the Government. One letter from the head of a large financial institution in New York City mentioned rumors afloat there: the Secretary of the Treasury had "given to his son-in-law, Governor Sprague, a permit to buy cotton at the South, by which he will probably make . . . $2,000,000." When a congressional committee should make the inquiry that he, Blair, had called for, they would find plenty. "And Mr. Chase cannot escape. . . . However deeply the committee may lay the whitewash on, it cannot conceal the dark background."

Among the Chase understrappers who had tried to drag him down, continued Blair, was Jay Cooke & Company, whose *Philadelphia Inquirer* had led in abuse of him as a liquor speculator. The $11,000,000 of five-twenty bonds sold by Jay Cooke & Company above the prescribed $500,000,000 in January "were twelve per cent. above par at the time of their issue, the profits on them must have exceeded a million and a quarter of dollars." This added to the $450,000 profit reported by Secretary Chase, Blair figured as total Cooke earnings of $1,375,000 in nine months, which "would aid in the establishment of a good many newspapers in the interest of Mr. Chase." And though Mr. Chase had written a letter saying he had retired from the canvass for the presidential nomination, that letter was written because the "strictly private" Pomeroy Circular, being made public, had cut the ground from under him. "He wanted to get down under the ground and work there in the dark as he is now doing, running the Pomeroy machine on the public money as vigorously as ever." The open Frémont candidacy was a cat's-paw and a stalking horse yet to be used for Chase, and its tactics embraced intrigue, corruption, and fraud.

When Blair had finished, he had only come short of openly saying that he believed Chase to be a respectable masquerading scoundrel, a whited sepulcher, coward, liar, hypocrite, thief, and snake in the grass.

The friends of Blair were as correct in saying the speech was "acrimonious" as the friends of Chase were in saying it was "scurrilous." The leader of one factional clan in politics had been hit below the belt and had hit back—below the belt. It was a double foul, and not easy for Lincoln to referee. "In defending himself on the floor of Congress," said Nicolay and Hay from their White House post, "the natural pugnacity of his

[Blair's] disposition led him to what soldiers call an offensive return." Out of knowing Blair a long time the secretaries judged, "Anyone who knew Blair, however slightly, should have known that personal dishonesty could never have offered him the least temptation." Also the secretaries found personal "integrity beyond question" in Chase. That is, neither Blair nor Chase had ever taken a dirty dollar, so to speak, but when the two of them got snarled in a factional fight in politics each hoped to leave the other with the odor forever on him of a polecat. The rule of the factional leaders was from the French: "Throw mud, throw mud; some of it is sure to stick."

Having spoken his farewell to Congress, having given them something to remember him by, Frank Blair the same night left Washington with a commission as major general assigned by Sherman to command the 17th Corps in the coming campaign against Atlanta. When Lincoln had first heard of the roughshod speech that day, he said he knew "another beehive was kicked over." The House two days later asked the President to tell them whether Blair was a Congressman or a general, and if so how. The President three days later sent the House "in obedience to the resolution of your honorable body" an explanation:

Prior to and at the meeting of the present Congress, Robert C. Schenck, of Ohio, and Frank P. Blair, Jr., of Missouri, members elect thereto, by and with the consent of the Senate held commissions from the executive as major-generals in the volunteer army. General Schenck tendered the resignation of his said commission, and took his seat in the House of Representatives, at the assembling thereof, upon the distinct verbal understanding with the Secretary of War and the executive that he might, at any time during the session, at his own pleasure, withdraw said resignation and return to the field.

General Blair was, by temporary assignment of General Sherman, in command of a corps through the battles in front of Chattanooga, and in the march to the relief of Knoxville, which occurred in the latter days of November and early days of December last, and of course was not present at the assembling of Congress. When he subsequently arrived here, he sought, and was allowed by the Secretary of War and the executive, the same conditions and promise as allowed and made to General Schenck.

General Schenck has not applied to withdraw his resignation; but when General Grant was made lieutenant-general, producing some change of commanders, General Blair sought to be assigned to the command of a corps. This was made known to Generals Grant and Sherman, and assented to by them, and the particular corps for him designated. This was all arranged and understood, as now remembered, so much as a month ago; but the formal withdrawal of General Blair's resignation, and making the order assigning him to the command of the corps, were not consummated at the War Department until last week, perhaps on the 23d of April instant.

As a summary of the whole, it may be stated that General Blair holds no military commission or appointment other than as herein stated, and that it is believed he is now acting as major-general upon the assumed validity of the commission herein stated, in connection with the facts herein stated, and not otherwise.

There are some letters, notes, telegrams, orders, entries, and perhaps other documents, in connection with this subject, which it is believed would throw no additional light upon it, but which will be cheerfully furnished if desired.

The House next day by a vote of 84 to 28 requested the President to send over copies of all notes, letters, telegrams, orders, entries, and other documents concerned in the matter. He did so, and Senate and House threshed over the question of whether the President had authority thus to hold resignations. Again the President was overstepping the Constitution and taking powers that belonged to Congress, said several earnest, worthy statesmen, besides several windy blatherskites. The matter finally was referred to a committee, where it lingered and was not brought up.

Also another committee was ordered in the House, this one to investigate the Treasury Department, the Speaker to name the members. "It is made up," wrote Welles, "as only Colfax could do it. Some able friends of Chase are on it." Not much more came from this committee than from the one to report on the President's authority to cancel the resignation of Blair while Blair was a Congressman. The two committees may have had an understanding. The radical *St. Louis Democrat* and other newspapers cried the evidence was now complete that the President was "Blair-ridden" and under the control of "advisers morally and politically of the lowest description." The *Chicago Tribune*, which had persistently joined with the Missouri radicals in trying to pry loose the President from the Blairs, said it was not a pleasant sight to see the President illegally appoint to high command a man who had poured a flood of billingsgate on a trustworthy Cabinet member. Yet it was also plain to see that the President had managed to pack off from Congress and rid Washington of a good soldier, a commander Sherman and Grant were calling for. To construe the President's act as an endorsement of the attack on Chase was an "utter mistake," said the *Chicago Tribune*. Lincoln would have done the same thing if Blair's attack had been upon Lincoln. "It is his habit to disregard personal considerations. The President is not one of the thin-skinned; he goes for things, and not words. But by what 'good story' he will get out of the legal predicament he is in, does not yet appear." However, to a pair of Congressmen, friends of Chase, Lincoln soon did tell a long story, taking a half-hour in the telling.

Late in the day of Blair's speech burning up Chase, Albert Gallatin Riddle, an Ohio friend of Chase, was shown into the railroad car on which Chase was soon starting for Baltimore. "He [Chase] was alone, and in a frightful rage, and controlled himself with difficulty while he explained the cause," noted Riddle. "The recital in a hoarse, constrained voice, seemed to rekindle his anger and aggravate its intensity. The spacious car fairly trembled under his feet." The news had come to Mr. Chase, since arriving at the railroad station, that Blair, after his abusive speech, had held a brief interview with the President, received his old commission as a corps commander, and had left for the front. "The circumstances left no shade of doubt in Mr. Chase's mind but that all this, including Blair's speech, had been done with the cordial approval of the President, a view fully shared by some of his [Chase's] immediate friends. Mr. Chase thought of remaining in the city, and at once tendering his resignation to the President."

The train was pulling out of the station as Riddle implored Mr. Chase not to resign. "I was much relieved to find the train in motion," wrote Riddle, "and mentally made up my course of action." He rode to Baltimore with Mr. Chase arguing and pleading with Mr. Chase not to resign, "that to permit himself to be driven from a post more important than the command of armies in the field, by a speech on the floor of the House, would fill the world with amazement." Furthermore, said Riddle, he, Riddle, would return from Baltimore to Washington, interview the President, and secure personal assurance that the Blair speech had the President's condemnation.

Jay Cooke wrote to Chase that he did not wonder "somebody was a little wrathy." Chase answered Cooke: "I hope my wrathiness was not excessive. Indeed, it was vexatious to think that all my labors to serve our country had found recompense, so far as Mr. Lincoln's special friends were concerned, and with his apparent (but, as I hope and believe, merely apparent) endorsement, only in outrageous calumny." Chase had suppressed his inclinations to resign his office and to denounce the Blairs, he wrote Cooke. He had returned from Baltimore, conferred with Governor Brough of Ohio and other friends who advised against resignation. "I yielded to their judgment, which, indeed, coincided with my own, though exceedingly contrary to my impulses." An Ohio delegation, he had learned, had visited the President, "who disavowed in the most explicit terms all connection with, or responsibility for, Blair's assault, and expressed his decided disapproval of it." This disavowal being merely verbal, however, the delegation, as Chase understood it, "determined to call on the President in a body, and make and present a distinct statement in writing—on their part, of their advice and my action, and their conviction of what was due from the President to me, to Ohio, and to the country; and on his part, such reply as he should see fit to give."

This to Chase seemed only simple justice against "the unworthy men who have set on foot and propagated these vile calumnies." To his daughter Nettie Chase he wrote the same day, "I wish I were out of official harness. . . . It is painful to find my labors made the occasion of calumny and reviling." To Edward Haight also the same day: "I am not in the least concerned about misrepresentations." To Colonel R. C. Parsons he wrote that the President's disavowal must be public; it was due to Ohio and would probably be cheerfully conceded by Mr. Lincoln. "This done I shall have no personal ground of complaint; though nothing can change the character of the Blair-Lincoln transaction so far as the public is concerned."

Former Congressman Riddle, whose final words in the House the year before were high praise of Lincoln, had taken the next train back to Washington on leaving Chase at Baltimore, and had called on the President with another Ohio Congressman, Rufus Paine Spalding, who was, said Riddle, "the personal and confidential friend nearest the Secretary [Chase]." These two constituted "the Ohio delegation" to which Chase referred in his letters. "Mr. Lincoln received us politely but with no pretence of cordiality," noted Riddle. "After brief salutations he passed around to the other side of the long wide table, and sat down by a bundle of papers, grimly awaiting my assault." The first remark of Riddle could not have been better aimed. "Mr. President," he said, "I am one of the personal and political friends of Mr. Chase, who believes that the safety of the Union cause requires that you should be unanimously nominated at the June Convention, and should receive in November the eagerly cast ballot of every man devoted to our country." Riddle referred to Blair's getting his military commission on the same day that he made an acrimonious speech, how these events "seemed planned for dramatic effect, as parts of a conspiracy" against the Secretary of the Treasury. "The . . . jealous and exacting . . . abolitionists," said the standing Riddle to the seated Lincoln, "forgetting how impossible it is that you can be guilty of an attack upon your Secretary . . . believe that Blair must have had at least your countenance in this wretched business, and they demand the instant resignation of Mr. Chase. It is only by the strenuous exertions of one or two persons that this has been delayed." For Chase to resign would be equal to a severe setback for Grant's army in its effect on the public morale. For the Chase men to leave the Administration party would mean its defeat in November, which might result in a lost cause. The abolitionists urging Chase to resign were the oldest antislavery men, who with later allies "made your accession to power possible." Though overhasty, they were sincere and loyal.

"Mr. President, I am not the emissary of these men," pointedly said Riddle. "I am not the agent of Mr. Chase." Then he gave the few simple words he would like to take back to them from Lincoln. "I have said to them that I would return to them your word that you were in no way a party to or responsible for a word uttered by Mr. Blair. He was an independent representative of his constituency and spoke for them and himself, and could no more be dictated to by the President than you could think of dictating to him; and, having spoken, he was not responsible to you for his utterances.'

The standing Congressman Spalding, sixty-six years old, a former Ohio supreme-court judge, added a few words; his views agreed with those spoken by Mr. Riddle. The President rose from his chair, came around the table, took the two men by the hand, and made it clear that they had happily surprised him by their sentiments. The President then went to the table, took up some papers, and, standing, addressed the two Congressmen for half an hour. "He spoke in his best manner, as if before a very select audience," thought Riddle. Out of their frankness and cordiality his statement to them would be easier than he had expected. He asked them if they had read his letter of February 29 to Mr. Chase concerning his candidacy. Spalding had read it, Riddle had not. The President gave it aloud with quiet emphasis on his writing the Secretary, "I assure you, as you have assured me, that no assault has been made upon you by my instigation, or with my countenance." They talked about the Blairs.

LINCOLN. The Blairs are, as you know, strong, tenacious men, having some peculiarities, among them the energy with which their feuds are carried on.

RIDDLE. Yes, Montgomery says that when the Blairs go in for a fight they go in for a funeral.

LINCOLN. Exactly. As you know, they labored for ten years to build up an anti-slavery party in Missouri, and in an action of ejectment to recover that party in the State, they could prove title in any common law court. Frank has in some way permitted himself to be put in a false position. He is in danger of being kicked out of the house built by himself, and by a set of men rather new to it. You know that they contributed more than any twenty men to bring forward Fremont in 1855. I know that they mainly induced me to make him a Major-General and send him to Missouri.

The President gave them his explanations as later sent to the House, told of his arrangements with Frank Blair for future service, and read the letter of guidance for Frank as written to Montgomery Blair. Grant wanted Blair in the army. The President had made the arrangement for Blair to go back to the army, without reference to any possible question of law. If he had no power to make it, Frank Blair was in fact no major general. Early in the year, when Frank had said he wanted to make a speech on Mississippi trade regulations, he had warned Frank not to make it the occasion of pursuing a personal warfare. Then the speech had come and he was annoyed and mortified by it.

Long before the speech, he had sent, on Frank's request, an order to the War Department to have him restored as a major general. He heard no more of it till about noon of the day of Frank's last speech, when Frank had called and said the all-important order had not been made. The President then sent a messenger to the Adjutant General, who replied that Mr. Blair was not known in the department as an officer, whereupon the President ordered his resignation to be canceled, which was done. "Within three hours," said Lincoln as Riddle noted it, "I heard that this speech had been made, when I knew *that another beehive was kicked over*. My first thought was to have cancelled the orders restoring him to the army and assigning him to command. Perhaps this would have been best. On such reflection as I was able to give to the matter, however, I concluded to let them stand. If I was wrong in this, the injury to the service can be set right. And thus you see how far I am responsible for Frank Blair's assaults on Mr. Chase."

When Lincoln several times appealed to proofs of his statements and reasserted their accuracy, Mr. Spalding said, "Mr. President, spare us all other evidence. We only ask your word." And Mr. Riddle said, "Your word, Mr. President, is the highest human evidence." The conversation ranged into Maryland politics, Lincoln saying he had balanced between Montgomery Blair and Henry Winter Davis for Postmaster General and finally chose Blair. He had tried to meet the wishes of Winter Davis in the Maryland patronage, had later regarded him as holding ground not favorable to the best interests of the country; a speech from the gentleman one day in the House had wholly disabused his mind and he was greatly rejoiced to find his first opinion of Winter Davis to have been correct. He had rendered Davis as a candidate for Congress all the help he consistently could, though he understood that Mr. Chase favored Davis's Union-party opponent. Since that election Mr. Davis in the Maryland constitutional election had asked help that Lincoln could not afford to give, and Mr. Winter Davis had become "very cool" toward him.

The visit of Riddle and Spalding with the President lasted two hours, and they were pleased to go away with their message for Mr. Chase and the abolitionists. As matters stood, Mr. Chase did not insist on the President's making the public disavowal which at first he had said must be conceded.

It was the third time Riddle had called on Lincoln. The second time was the afternoon of the Blair speech, just before Riddle went to the train and saw Chase. Riddle was a little shocked at the change in the President's looks and manner since five months before. "He looked like a man worn and harassed with political faultfinding and criticism, until he had turned at bay, like an old stag pursued and hunted by a cowardly rabble of men and dogs. He received me as if he hardly knew whether he had not to ward off a baiting." While Riddle waited in the anteroom of the President's office that day he heard "rude roasting" of the President by some of those waiting to enter. A friend named Worcester whom he considered amiable and excellent had to speak ironically of Lincoln as "that great and good man." Senator Henry Wilson of Massachusetts, an antislavery extremist, a factory boy who had worked his way up, was the one most loud and bitter in the anteroom. The assaults of Wilson amazed Riddle. He asked Wilson why he did not open on the President in the Senate instead of the streets and in the lobbies and offices of the Executive Mansion. Wilson conceded Riddle's point that the North was solid for the President and would renominate him, and "bad as that would be, the best must be made of it." "Yes," said Riddle, "and this is the way you are doing your share of that best work."

Meanwhile in this month of April, 1864, came news of an affair alongside which the Blair-Chase imbroglio was a merry and comic incident. The central figure of this affair was Major General Nathan Bedford Forrest, born for war. Fifteen horses had been killed under him in various actions. In the battles at Murfreesboro, Shiloh, Chickamauga, he was in the vortex. "War means fighting and fighting means killing," was a saying from him, and no other commanding officer North or South, it was believed, had sat his horse and personally sabered to death so many of the enemy. A log-cabin boy from middle Tennessee, Forrest had never seen West Point nor read a book on military tactics. In Memphis as a real-estate dealer and slave-trader he had made a fortune, bought cotton plantations, and when the war started had an income of $30,000 a year. He had raised several regiments, sometimes outfitting them with horses, equipment, and rations by raids on Union supply centers. His record for swift movement and fast fighting was compared to that of Stonewall Jackson. His answer to a woman who asked him the secret of his success was, "Ma'am, I got thar fust with the most men." One of his written orders read, "Tell Bell to move up and fetch all he's got." In battles his usually sober face flooded with a scarlet rage, the blood vessels bulged, and his eyes reddened. He took whisky only when wounded, spoke prayers in his tent every night, and before wading into the enemy, if there were time, he had a chaplain ask God's blessing on ranks of men with hats off. He had sent pistol balls into more than one runaway trooper, had learned that by trying to cleave the head of another rider he would merely knock him off the horse alive and jumping. "I then tried the p'int on one and when he fell he lay thar."

Having fired the opening and closing guns at Chickamauga, Forrest sought Bragg and said to Bragg: "You have played the part of a damned scoundrel, and are a coward, and if you were any part of a man I would slap your jaws and force you to resent it. You have threatened to arrest me for not obeying your orders promptly. I dare you to do it, and I say to you that if you ever again try to interfere with me or cross my path it will be at the peril of your life." The powerful two hands of Forrest had more than once knocked the head of a soldier against a tree. Whether it was a superior officer or a private in the ranks, he invoked physical force, a beating of some kind, the mode and procedure used in what he sometimes referred to as "my nigger-yard in Memphis." As a slave-trader he had the faint enigmatic odor of something or other that traditionally excluded slave-traders from exclusive social circles of the South. When it was urged that the war was for Southern independence and not slavery, Forrest replied, "If we aint fightin' fer slavery then I'd like to know what we are fightin' fer." Slowly and by degrees he had built so solid a record as a military leader, as a brilliant and incessant destroyer of the enemy, that it became ridiculous for the West Pointers at Richmond to hold off appointing him a major general. A born killer made for war, he was tireless, sudden, merciless, with a gorgeous abandon, a high scorn of any death to come.

With some 4,000 men Forrest moved up from Mississippi into Tennessee, jolted 7,000 Union troops under General William Sooy Smith aiming to join Sherman farther South at Meridian, sent Smith reeling back to Memphis. Forrest carried his columns up north across Kentucky to the Ohio River, held Paducah for hours while he mounted a command of new Kentucky recruits who insisted on horses. He struck at Sherman's supply connections, enlarged and strengthened his army, and took several Union garrisons. One of these was at Fort Pillow, on the Mississippi forty miles north of Memphis.

What happened there at Fort Pillow on April 12 of '64 became a livid national issue. Forrest with 6,000 troops drove the 600 defenders from outworks into the fort. While his white flags of truce were in the air he served notice that he would storm the fort. The Union commanders claimed that while thus negotiating under flags of truce Forrest moved his troops into better positions, violating the laws of civilized warfare. Forrest's regiments rushed the fort, took it, and put to death over half the garrison, Forrest claiming that the fort flag had not been hauled down in token of surrender and in accord with civilized military law. Of the 262 Negro soldiers in the garrison nearly all were killed, wounded in escape, or buried alive.

The news shocked the North. Press, pulpit, and politicians of antislavery trend cried the affair as a fiendish atrocity demanding retaliation. Ben Wade for the Senate and Daniel W. Gooch of Massachusetts for the House were appointed a committee to go find the facts and report. In western Kentucky and Tennessee they interviewed the Union survivors and eyewitnesses and reported "at least 300 were murdered in cold blood after the post was in possession of the rebels and our men had thrown down their arms and ceased to offer resistance." The tomahawk and scalping knife of the Indians had never matched this "devilish work," said the report, alleging: "Men, women, even children, were shot down, beaten, hacked with sabres; children not more than ten years old were forced to stand up and face their murderers while being shot; sick and wounded were butchered without mercy, the rebels even entering the hospital-building and dragging them out to be shot. . . . Some were shot in the river; others on the bank were shot and their bodies kicked into the water, many of them still living but . . . drowning . . . cries of 'No quarter!' 'Kill the damned niggers; shoot them down!' . . . Huts and tents of the wounded were set on fire . . . those seeking to escape the flames . . . shot down, or . . . their brains beaten out. One man was fastened to the floor of a tent, face upward, nails driven through his clothing and into the boards under him, and then the tent set on fire; another was nailed to the side of a building outside of the fort, and then the building set on fire and burned . . . charred remains of five bodies were afterward found, so disfigured they could not be identified."

This Wade-Gooch report was a propaganda document intended to emphasize every fact that would infuriate the North for war and to minimize points the South might plead in justification. Whether one side tricked the other under a flag of truce was left in doubt; perhaps neither side could have cleared up the point. But a historian would have to record that a certain moment arrived when Forrest's men were no longer fighting a battle in a war between civilized nations. They were from that moment on sharing in a race riot, a mass lynching, and the event became an orgy of unleashed primitive human animals riding a storm of anger and vengeance directed at their sworn enemy, whom they considered less than human and beyond all laws of civilized war: the Negro. "Kill the God damned nigger!" ran the recurring line of the published testimony. "Kill all the niggers!" shouted one Confederate officer. "There's another dead nigger," called a captain as his pistol cracked and sent toppling a private, 6th United States Colored Artillery. In the head, in the shoulder, in the right wrist, in the head again, the Negro Private Arthur Edwards, 6th United States Colored Artillery, received bullets from four marksmen, the fourth crying, "God damn you, you are fighting against your master." General Forrest, riding among the scattered wounded Negroes, called out that he knew some of them.

"They've been in my nigger-yard in Memphis." A white private of the 13th Tennessee Cavalry, Woodford Cooksey, testified he lay on the ground with a musket ball and three buckshot in his shoulder, and the man who shot him said, "Hand me up your money, you damned son of a bitch." Cooksey handed up four bits, "two bits in silver and two in paper," and the man who took it "said he had damned nigh a notion to hit me in the head on account of staying there and fighting with the niggers." Cooksey's testimony vignetted a moment of race war:

> I saw one of them shoot a black fellow in the head with three buckshot and a musket-ball. The man held up his head, and then the fellow took his pistol and fired that at his head. The black man still moved, and then the fellow took his sabre and stuck it in the hole in the Negro's head and rammed it way down, and said: "Now, God damn you, die!" The Negro did not say anything, but he moved, and the fellow took his carbine and beat his head soft with it. That was the next morning after the fight.

Another white private, D. W. Harrison of the 13th Tennessee Cavalry, testified he threw up his hands and said, "I surrender," received a bullet in the shoulder, and lay on the ground, where later he begged a drink of water from one of Forrest's men who refused it with "Damn you, I have nothing for you fellows; you Tennesseeans pretend to be men, and you fight side by side with niggers," and then took $90 in greenbacks and a gold watch from Harrison's pockets. Another of Forrest's men, "who was a man, came along and brought me some water," said Harrison.

Another white cavalryman from Tennessee, Nathan Fulks, had thrown away his gun, begged they wouldn't shoot him, went down with a bullet in the thigh and heard the words, "God damn you, you fight with the niggers, and we will kill the last one of you!" One aimed a rifle to shoot him again when another said, "Don't shoot the white fellows any more."

From Detroit, Michigan, John Penwell, white, had wandered south, joined the Tennessee cavalry. His gun thrown away and his hands in the air, he fell with a bullet from one of Forrest's men, crying, "Die, you damned Yankee son of a bitch!" While they stripped him of $50 in greenbacks and hat, boots, coat, he moaned, "Kill me, out and out." Three voices came to his ears, one saying, "He ain't dead yet," another, "Hit him a crack on the head," another: "Let the poor fellow be, and get well if he can. He has nothing more left now." Then Penwell of Detroit fainted and heard no more till rescuers came.

"I saw four white men and at least twenty-five negroes shot while begging for mercy," testified William J. Mays, white, of the 13th Tennessee Cavalry. "I saw one negro dragged from a hollow log within ten feet of where I lay, and as one rebel held him by the foot another shot him. These were all soldiers. Two negro women and three little children stood within twenty-five steps from me, when a rebel stepped up to them and said, 'Yes, God damn you, you thought you were free, did you?' and shot them all. They all fell but one child, when he knocked it in the head with the breech of his gun."

Perhaps half or more than half of Forrest's men were horrified at what was happening. What they saw was not war but mass murder out of race hatred. They tried to stop it. But it was a cyclone. According to a private of the 6th United States Colored Artillery one Confederate officer shouted to his men, "Boys, I will have you arrested if you don't stop killing them boys," another Confederate officer yelling the answer, "Damn it, let them go on; it isn't our law to take any negro prisoners; kill every one of them." Repeatedly the witnesses told of Southern officers ordering men not to shoot, or of Confederate men in the ranks pleading for mercy to enemy Negroes and whites. But discipline was gone. What began as a battle ended as a mob scene with wholesale lynching.

As testimony from scores of witnesses filled the newspaper columns of the North during early April there were horror and rage. While it was plain that Wade and Gooch had heard the witnesses of only one side, it was also clear from a telegram of Forrest received at Richmond that a terrible event and far out of the ordinary had taken place. Forrest reported driving the enemy into Fort Pillow and demanding surrender, "which was declined." Then: "I stormed the fort, and after a contest of thirty minutes captured the entire garrison, killing 500 and taking 100 prisoners, and a large amount of quartermaster stores. The officers in the fort were killed, including Major Booth [commanding]. I sustained a loss of 20 killed and 60 wounded."

Forrest at Paducah and at Columbus in weeks immediately preceding had indicated that if he must storm the works "no quarter" would be shown the Negro troops. His view was made clearer a few weeks later when he wrote to a Union general, "I regard captured negroes as I do other captured property, and not as captured soldiers."

Of course, Forrest in what he let happen at Fort Pillow, whatever it was, did not know that he was playing into the hands of the abolitionists, whose fury and thirst for vengeance were beginning to match his own lust for the kill. Whatever happened at Fort Pillow could be made by the pro-Negro, antislavery press, pulpit, and politicians of the North to look like Negroes fighting for freedom given mass murder by cruel masters who would rather kill them than see them have freedom. It seemed a flaring sequel and corollary to the lurid pages of *Uncle Tom's Cabin.* The accomplished propagandists of the antislavery cause leaped at the chance and proclaimed that never before did it seem so necessary to kill off the whole ruling class of the South.

Lincoln gazed on the event of Fort Pillow and its results and knew that Providence had been with him, that he would have had to face the same tumult of accusation from the South if it had happened after his Emancipation Proclamation that so much as one group of Negroes somewhere in the South had arisen with gun, knife, and torch and slain their masters by scores. Such a slave insurrection would have justified Forrest in what seemed to have happened at Fort Pillow. That the Negro had thus far made war only according to the rules of war established by the civilized nations of the earth was in favor of the President.

Six days after the Fort Pillow massacre, as it was most often called, Lincoln sat in a railroad car going to Baltimore to speak at a Sanitary Fair. Over the country was deep expectation that he would say something about Fort Pillow, great hope among radicals that he would call for a war to exterminate the ruling class of the South, take their lands and property, and make their names a byword and a hissing among nations.

The President reminded his Baltimore audience that in looking out on so many people assembled to serve the Union soldiers, the fact was that three years ago the same soldiers could not so much as pass through Baltimore. He would call blessings on the "brave men" who had wrought the change and "the fair women" who strove to reward them for it. He then repeated from the Hodges letter his point that neither party to the war had expected it to go so long. "But here we are; the war has not ended, and slavery has been much affected–how much needs not now to be recounted. So true is it that man proposes and God disposes."

He swung then to the point that the world had never had a good definition of liberty, and the American people, just then, were much in want of one. "We all declare for liberty; but in using the same word we do not all mean the same thing. With some the word liberty may mean for each man to do as he pleases with himself, and the product of his labor; while with others the same word may mean for some men to do as they please with other men, and the product of other men's labor. Here are two, not only different, but incompatible things, called by the same name, liberty. And it follows that each of the things is, by the respective parties, called by two different and incompatible names–liberty and tyranny."

Then as if he had fished a long time in deep waters of contemplation and at last found words for an inkling of what the war was about, he told his Sanitary Fair hearers: "The shepherd drives the wolf from the sheep's throat, for which the sheep thanks the shepherd as his liberator, while the wolf denounces him for the same act, as the destroyer of liberty, especially as the sheep was a black one. Plainly, the sheep and the wolf are not agreed upon a definition of the word liberty; and precisely the same difference prevails to-day among us human creatures, even in the North, and all professing to love liberty. Hence we behold the process by which thousands are daily passing from under the yoke of bondage hailed by some as the advance of liberty, and bewailed by others as the destruction of all liberty. Recently, as it seems, the people of Maryland have been doing something to define liberty, and thanks to them that, in what they have done, the wolf's dictionary has been repudiated."

His address had now gone about the usual distance for a Sanitary Fair and he half apologized, "It is not very becoming for one in my position to make speeches at great length." But there was another subject on which he felt he ought to say a word. "A painful rumor–true, I fear–has reached us of the massacre by the rebel forces at Fort Pillow, in the west end of Tennessee, on the Mississippi River, of some three hundred colored soldiers and white officers. . . . There seems to be some anxiety in the public mind whether the government is doing its duty to the colored soldier, and to the service, at this point."

Then he told a vast and waiting audience that would eagerly read it precisely where the Government, as he represented it, stood on the issue of the hour: "At the beginning of the war, and for some time, the use of colored troops was not contemplated; and how the change of purpose was wrought I will not now take time to explain. Upon a clear conviction of duty I resolved to turn that element of strength to account; and I am responsible for it to the American people, to the Christian world, to history, and in my final account to God. Having determined to use the negro as a soldier, there is no way but to give him all the protection given to any other soldier. The difficulty is not in stating the principle, but in practically applying it. It is a mistake to suppose the government is indifferent to this matter, or is not doing the best it can in regard to it. We do not to-day know that a colored soldier, or white officer commanding colored soldiers, has been massacred by the rebels when made a prisoner. We fear it,—believe it, I may say,—but we do not know it. To take the life of one of their prisoners on the assumption that they murder ours, when it is short of certainty that they do murder ours, might be too serious, too cruel, a mistake. We are having the Fort Pillow affair thoroughly investigated; and such investigation will probably show conclusively how the truth is. If after all that has been said it shall turn out that there has been no massacre at Fort Pillow, it will be almost safe to say there has been none, and will be none, elsewhere. If there has been the massacre of three hundred there, or even the tenth part of three hundred, it will be conclusively proved; and being so proved, the retribution shall as surely come. It will be matter of grave consideration in what exact course to apply the retribution; but in the supposed case it must come."

Two weeks later the President asked his Cabinet members to give him in writing their opinions as to what course the Government should take as to Fort Pillow. Seward was for great caution in any proceeding looking toward retaliation and advised for the present only the setting apart and rigorous confinement of an equal number of Confederate prisoners as hostages until the Confederate Government could be called on to explain or disavow the cruelties and give pledges they should not be repeated. Chase advised the same except that the hostages should be from Confederate prisoners of the highest rank. Stanton's view was much the same as Chase's, with the additional point that Forrest and all Confederate officers and soldiers at Fort Pillow be excluded from the benefits of the President's Amnesty Proclamation and from the privilege of exchange. Also Stanton would have the President demand from the Richmond Government that they hand over Forrest and his associates for punishment, and that, the Richmond Government failing so to do, the President should take such measures against the hostages as existing circumstances made necessary. Welles practically agreed with Stanton. Blair said he was against retaliation, man for man; it would not be civilized warfare. "The inclination of my mind is, to pursue the actual offenders alone . . . to order the most energetic measures for their capture, and the most summary punishment when captured. . . . A proclamation of order that the guilty individuals are to be hunted down will have far greater terrors, and be far more effectual to prevent the repetition of the crime, than the punishment of parties not concerned in that crime." Bates of Missouri agreed with Blair of Missouri. "I would have no cartel of blood and murder; no stipulation to the effect that if you murder one of my men I will murder one of yours. Retaliation is not mere justice. It is avowedly revenge." Usher of Indiana agreed chiefly with Blair and Bates, urging that great battles were at hand and until the results were known it would be inexpedient to take extreme action in the premises.

In the storm of guns and blood and death soon to be let loose by Grant and Sherman against Lee and Johnston, in the reddening streams and the shouting and the crying with black silence after, and then the renewal of crimson explosions and the gray monotonous weariness—in this terrific grapple of guns and living wills and dying testaments the Fort Pillow affair was to sink to a lesser significance.

CHAPTER 51

GRANT'S OFFENSIVE '64—FREE PRESS —LINCOLN VISITS THE ARMY

A MEMBER of Congress asked what Grant was doing. Lincoln gave what he had: "I can't tell much about it. You see, Grant has gone to the Wilderness, crawled in, drawn up the ladder, and pulled in the hole after him, and I guess we'll have to wait till he comes out before we know just what he's up to."

Wrote Welles in his diary that same day, May 6 of '64: "We get no tidings from the front. There is an impression that we are on the eve of a great battle and that it may already have commenced." The next day "fragmentary intelligence" arrived of a two days' fight. "The President came into my room about 1 P.M., and told me he had slept none last night. He lay down for a short time on the sofa in my room and detailed all the news he had gathered."

Across the Rapidan River and into the Wilderness of Spotsylvania, Grant with some 120,000 men had vanished at midnight of May 4. On a piece of ground ranging ten to twelve miles across in any direction Grant was to meet Lee's army. Grant had two men to Lee's one. Lee, as Grant came on, could choose where he wanted to fight Grant. For Grant's men, crossing a river, seeking their opponent and going to him, it would be at times a groping in the dark. Around swampland and swale, in red clay and sandy land, in thickets of jack pine intermixed with scrub oak, cedar, ash, walnut, and a tanglefoot underbrush, the men of Grant and Lee were to grapple and to lie by thousands in rows and piles and sudden disorderly huddles, some of them pillowed in peace on a smooth green wilderness moss that had seldom seen the great white sun.

On part of this very ground these same armies, then under Hooker and Lee, had fought just a year ago, and their campfires and rusty canteens, their rotting artillery axes, their skeletons of men and horses, met the eyes of living fighting men. On one spot ten rods square could be counted fifty skulls of men, their eye sockets staring at the path of war. From a half-open grave would stand out a rotted trouser leg and a knee bone or a mildewed sleeve and the clean frame of a man's hand.

Amid scrawny and tenacious timbers the wild rose came because it was spring. Out of a reddish bitter clay stood honeysuckle and huckleberry in bloom. The dogwood and the shad-blow floated their accustomed annual blossoms.

Here where Hooker had failed and Jackson had died and Lee had earned new stars of military merit, Grant was to hammer and recoil to a standstill and then return to hammer again.

Along the gravel path to the War Office Lincoln had gone, had sat scanning flimsies in the telegraph room, and during Thursday, May 5, and past midnight of Friday, May 6, had no news of Grant. Friday morning came a dribble from some newspaper reporter who had left the army at four o'clock and on foot had reached Union Mills, Virginia, and told a telegrapher, "Everything pushing along favorably." Later in the morning Lincoln entered the telegraph office to find Stanton telegraphing this newspaperman that he would be arrested as a spy unless he uncovered the news he had from the army. Then a telegram went to the correspondent asking if he would tell the President where Grant was. His reply offered to tell everything if he would be permitted to send a hundred-word dispatch to his paper, the *New York Tribune*. His offer accepted, with the proviso that the dispatch could run over one hundred words, Lincoln arranged with the *New York Tribune* to give the Associated Press a summary for all the newspapers.

A locomotive ordered by Lincoln brought the correspondent, a cub reporter named Henry E. Wing, from thirty miles away to Washington, for a two-o'clock-in-the-morning interview with Lincoln. And as Wing told it, his information to Lincoln was that Grant had given orders for a daybreak offensive against the enemy, and that Grant had said to him on leaving, "If you do see the President, see him alone and tell him that General Grant says there will be no turning back." Until four o'clock that Saturday morning the man and the youth talked, Lincoln squeezing from Wing every last point as to what he had seen and heard.

The same night a messenger summoned the Assistant Secretary of War Charles A. Dana from a pleasant evening party. At the War Office he found the President "talking very soberly" with Stanton. The Administration was "in the dark" about what was happening, the President said to Dana. "We are very much troubled, and have concluded to send you down there. How soon can you start?" Dana said in a half-hour, went away, arranged for a locomotive to wait with steam up at Alexandria, got into his camp clothes, borrowed a pistol, and with no more baggage than a toothbrush was on his horse ready to go. An orderly galloped up with word that the President wished to see him. He rode to the War Office, found Lincoln in the same chair.

"Well, Dana," said he, looking up, "since you went away I've been thinking about it. I don't like to send you down there."

"But why not, Mr. President?"

"You can't tell," continued the President, "just where Lee is or what he is doing, and Jeb Stuart is rampaging around pretty lively in between the Rappahannock and the Rapidan. It's a considerable risk, and I don't like to expose you to it."

"Mr. President," Dana said, "I have a cavalry guard ready and a good horse myself. If we are attacked, we probably will be strong enough to fight. If we are not strong enough to fight, and it comes to the worst, we are equipped to run. It's getting late, and I want to get down to the Rappahannock by daylight. I think I'll start."

"Well, now, Dana," said the President, with a little twinkle in his eyes, "if you feel that way, I rather wish you would. Good night, and God bless you."

While Dana rode southward and Lincoln tried to sleep after midnight, Grant sat by a campfire, his hat slouched low, the collar of his blue overcoat hiding most of his worn, haggard face. He smoked a cigar, he slowly chewed the cigar, he sat motionless except for an occasional shift of one leg over the other. Grant had lost 14,000 men, killed, wounded, or missing, in forty-eight hours of fighting. The ambulances streaming north choked the roadways. Lee had lost more than he could spare as Grant hour on hour ordered up assaulting columns. After such desperate fighting it was customary to rest an army. Grant could decide to hold back—or go on. His decision must consider his promise to Sherman that he would keep Lee fighting so hard and fast that Lee would send no troops to Georgia to oppose Sherman's campaign against Johnston and Atlanta. Also Ben Butler was landing an army near Richmond and by moving into another battle with Lee, Grant would stop Lee from action against Butler.

Sitting at a campfire as hours passed after midnight, slouched and grizzled, outwardly calm as bronze and steel but underneath shaken in turmoil, Grant did his thinking and made his decision. He would move on. His reasoning included his proposition "Accident often decides the fate of battle." He could name the simple accidents that had operated against him and against Lee that day. He reasoned too that there would be an advantage in doing what the other fellow did not want him to do. He would move on, toward Richmond, by the left, toward Spotsylvania Court House. He determined "to use the greatest number of troops practicable" and to hammer the enemy, "until, by mere attrition, if in no other way, there should be nothing left to him."

By a keen guess or by accident Lee was at Spotsylvania, again in Grant's path. Back and forth in smoke and fog and rain sagged the battle lines. At the parapet of one salient men were pulled over the bloody slippery logs and made prisoner. Bayoneted muskets were hurled like spears. Over ditches filled with dead, in mud and blood, the living waded and clambered at Bloody Angle. One tree of twenty-two inches diameter and another of two inches less were gnawed and cut down clean by bullet fire. Till the dawn of May 13 the combat went on at Spotsylvania. For ten days the Army of the Potomac had marched and fought continuously, losing 26,815 killed and wounded, 4,183 missing. The Confederates gave out no records of losses, though on the basis of prisoners taken by Grant, it was plain that Lee's army was being mercilessly slashed of irreplaceable man power.

"I have been very anxious for some days in regard to our armies in the field," wrote Lincoln May 9 to Mrs. Sarah B. Meconkey, West Chester, Pennsylvania, "but am considerably cheered, just now, by favorable news from them." She and other "good mothers, wives, sisters, and daughters" would do all they could, he was sure, to relieve and comfort the gallant soldiers. He issued the same day to the "Friends of Union and Liberty" a recommendation of Thanksgiving. "Enough is known of army operations, within the last five days to claim an especial gratitude to God."

In the evening to serenaders Lincoln spoke of "Our commanders following up their victories resolutely and successfully." In a tone as though giving the public a frank opinion to which it was entitled, he said: "I think, without knowing the particulars of the plans of General Grant, that what has been accomplished is of more importance than at first appears. I believe, I know—and am especially grateful to know—that General Grant has not been jostled in his purposes, that he has made all his points, and to-day he is on his line as he purposed before he moved his armies. I will volunteer to say that I am very glad at what has happened, but there is a great deal still to be done." Loyal men and patriots would follow the example of "the modest general at the head of our armies," and in the work ahead, sink all personal considerations for the sake of the country. "I commend you to keep yourselves in the same tranquil mood that is characteristic of that brave and loyal man." He closed with telling the crowd on the White House lawn that he had said more than he had expected to when he came before them. What he said to the evening crowd, however, had the same color as his private remarks, Hay writing in his diary:

"May 9, 1864. Received today the first despatches from Grant. The President thinks very highly of what Grant has done. He was talking about it today with me, and said: 'How near we have been to this thing before and failed. I believe if any other general had been at the head of that army it would have now been on this side of the Rapidan. It is the dogged pertinacity of Grant that wins.' "

Hay seemed to enjoy with the President a rumor of Meade's observing to Grant that the enemy seemed inclined to make a Kilkenny cat fight of the affair, Grant answering "Our cat has the longest tail."

Newspapers chronicled: "A remark is reported of the President's on this campaign, which may or may not be authentic, but which conveys much truth. 'Any other commander that the Army of the Potomac has had,' he is rumored to have said, 'would have at once withdrawn his army over the Rapidan, after that first day's reception!' " This was the *New York World's* cue to observe editorially, "The most fortuitous circumstance in connection with the battles on the Rapidan is the fact that President Lincoln had nothing to do with them."

During this week the painter Carpenter, resident at the White House, studied every line and shade of expression in the exterior Lincoln. "Absorbed in his papers, he would become unconscious of my presence. . . . In repose, it was the saddest face I ever knew. There were days when I could scarcely look into it without crying. The first week of the battles of the Wilderness he scarcely slept at all. . . . One of these days, I met him, clad in a long morning wrapper, pacing back and forth a narrow passage leading to one of the windows, his hands behind him, great black rings under his eyes, his head bent forward upon his breast." Of this same day John W. Forney wrote that he heard Lincoln cry "My God! my God!" over 20,000 men killed and wounded in a few days' fighting, and "I cannot bear it! I cannot bear it!" This heavy solemnity re-echoed in his speech to the serenaders of May 9: "I am indeed very grateful to the brave men who have been struggling with the enemy in the field, to their noble commanders who have directed them, and especially to our Maker. . . . We should, above all, be very grateful to Almighty God, who gives us victory." Forney on an evening visit that week found him "ghastly pale, dark rings under his caverned eyes, hair brushed back from his temples," hunched in a chair, reading Shakespeare, and greeting Forney, "Let me read you this from Macbeth. I cannot read it like Forrest, but it comes to me tonight like a consolation:

> " 'To-morrow, and to-morrow, and to-morrow,
> Creeps in this petty pace from day to day,
> To the last syllable of recorded time;
> And all our yesterdays have lighted fools
> The way to dusty death. Out, out, brief candle!
> Life's but a walking shadow; a poor player
> That struts and frets his hour upon the stage,
> And then is heard no more; it is a tale
> Told by an idiot, full of sound and fury,
> Signifying nothing.' "

Never before had such lines of ambulances rumbled along the streets of Washington, carrying shell-torn and bullet-racked boys in blue. Evening haze had settled over the Potomac sky, and in twilight the President in his carriage slowly driving to the Soldiers' Home stopped for a talk with Congressman Isaac N. Arnold. Pointing his hand toward a line of wounded men near by, Lincoln said to his Chicago friend: "Look yonder at those poor fellows. I cannot bear it. This suffering, this loss of life, is dreadful." Arnold recalled to him a consoling letter he had written once with the words "And this too shall pass away. Never fear. Victory will come." Lincoln: "Yes, victory will come, but it comes slowly."

Good news from the battle front had to be shared. Lincoln could not lie abed with it. "The President came in last night in his shirt & told us of the retirement of the enemy from his works at Spottsylvania & our pursuit," wrote Hay on May 14. Considering the wear and tear of events, Hay estimated that Lincoln was holding his weight well. "I complimented him on the amount of underpinning he still has left & he said he weighed 180 pounds. Important if true." On this day too Hay saw Lincoln deeply moved by the death in the Wilderness battle of General James S. Wadsworth of New York, an original Republican-party man with a remarkable civic and military record. No loss of a personal friend had so touched Lincoln since the death of Ned Baker. "No man has given himself up to the war with such self-sacrificing patriotism as General Wadsworth," he said to Hay. "He went into the service, not wishing or expecting great success or distinction in his military career, and profoundly indifferent to popular applause, actuated only by a sense of duty which he neither evaded nor sought to evade."

Month by month as the war had gone on the personal ambitions and petty devices of Benjamin Butler had been less easy to look at. Heading an army that landed from transports near Richmond, he had failed to get the results Grant asked for, was quarreling with good generals given him, and in his communications was still more of an adroit politician and resourceful criminal lawyer than a military commander. Hay noted in his diary: "I said to the President today that I thought Butler was the only man in the army to whom power would be dangerous. McClellan was too timid & vacillating to usurp. Grant was too sound and cool headed & too unselfish; Banks also. Frémont would be dangerous if he had more ability & energy." This brought Lincoln's offhand estimate of Butler as "like Jim Jett's brother . . . the damndest scoundrel that ever lived, but in the infinite mercy of Providence . . . also the damndest fool."

In public and private utterance Lincoln was upholding Grant as he had no previous commander. At the vortex now was a man terribly alive, creating history. Lincoln gave his impression in a story which passed on to the newspapers. Lincoln had once used it with reference to himself in the White House heading the Government, the incident of the celebrated chess-player who could not beat an automaton at the game and ended with crying to the machine, "There's a man in it!" In this case Lincoln meant Grant, and added his point: "This, sir, is just the secret of our present success." *Leslie's Weekly* recorded a gentleman as remarking to Lincoln that nothing could cheat him of election as President again except Grant's capture of Richmond followed by the Democrats nominating Grant for President. "Well," said the President, "I feel very much like the man who said he didn't want to die particularly, but if he had got to die that was precisely the disease he would like to die of." Isaac Arnold one evening at the White House alluded to pending attempts to make Grant a candidate for the Presidency, saying the Union *people* were for Lincoln, but not many politicians. Lincoln: "If General Grant could be more useful as President in putting down the rebellion, I would be content. He is fully pledged to our policy of emancipation and the employment of negro soldiers; and if this policy is carried out, it won't make much difference who is President." Worrying friends suggested more than once that he should beware of General Grant. His usual reply, according to his secretaries: "If he takes Richmond, let him have it."

"What word have you to send?" asked Grant's home-town Congressman Washburne as he started to leave Grant's headquarters for Washington on May 11 after the hardest fighting was over at Spotsylvania Court House.

GRANT. None I think, except that we are fighting away here.

WASHBURNE. Hadn't you better send Stanton just a scratch of the pen?

GRANT. Perhaps so.

In his tent, with no pauses, and without reading it after it was written, Grant scribbled a note which Stanton gave to the country: "We have now ended the 6th day of very hard fighting. The result to this time is much in our favor. But our losses have been heavy as well as those of the enemy. I think the loss of the enemy must be greater; we have taken over four thousand prisoners in battle, whilst he has taken from us but few except . . . stragglers. I purpose to fight it out on this line if it takes all summer."

Now emerged Phil Sheridan. His cavalry swept round the flank of Lee's army, tore up ten miles of railway, released 400 Union prisoners, struck the reserve stores of Lee's supplies, destroyed 504,000 rations of bread and 904,000 of meat, and in combat six miles from Richmond killed the dauntless and priceless J. E. B. Stuart, thirty-one years old, Lee's most irreplaceable general officer, "the eyes of the army."

Grant's pride and joy among major generals, the dauntless and priceless John Sedgwick, took a sharpshooter's bullet in his brain one May day as he smiled in jest to his soldiers his last words, "Don't duck; they couldn't hit an elephant at that distance." Once Lincoln offered him command of the Army of the Potomac and in modesty Sedgwick declined it. He was afraid of nothing except immeasurable personal responsibility.

"The importance of this campaign to the administration of Mr. Lincoln and to General Grant leaves no doubt that every effort and every sacrifice will be made to secure its success," wrote Lee to Davis on May 18. The hope at Richmond was that they might be able in defensive tactics to drag out the contest and make the Northern people war-weary and ready to negotiate.

By the left again Grant moved, to Cold Harbor, almost in sight of the steeples of Richmond. There he ordered a frontal assault that in twenty-two minutes lost 3,000 men. The night of June 3 saw 7,000 Union soldiers dead or ready for hospitals, as against Confederate losses of 1,200 to 1,500. "I have always regretted that the last assault at Cold Harbor was ever made," wrote Grant later. It was thirty days since he had crossed the Rapidan and forced Lee into a succession of battles. Never before had the Army of Northern Virginia been pressed from point to point and day to day of fighting by an Army of the Potomac that never rested nor quit. A new mental and psychic factor was entering the war.

Who and what was this hammer Grant that came and came and never gave way? Was he some merciless incarnation of a prophecy that the North was stronger than the South and it was written in a Book of Fate that the Union of States in blood and iron should be welded together for all time? What was this new triple combination of Grant in Virginia, Sherman in Georgia, and Lincoln at Washington? Would Lincoln, the recruiting agent and supply man at Washington, and Grant and Sherman with men and bayonets, carry on till they established the authority of the Federal Government at Washington over all the States that had each a star in the Union flag? Was this as a grim portent and a melancholy idea beginning to seep through the mass of the Southern people?

Soaked in mud and blood, soaked in a psychic bewilderment of issues and methods, yet managed by Grant as a force that persisted in going on, the Army of the Potomac in its vital centers was beginning to suspect itself a tool of destiny, an Instrument of History.

No longer could Lee go out in the open and send assaulting columns at the Army of the Potomac. The Richmond Government was near its last line of conscripts. Against McClellan, Burnside, Hooker, Pope, Meade, on Virginia soil Lee could afford to spend men and win delay. Other commanders when punished and beaten retreated or stood still and waited. Grant came on for more. It was not a duel or a sporting affair between gentlemen. It was war and the Four Horsemen of the Apocalypse.

Grant "puzzles me as much as he appears to the rebels," wrote in a letter Charles Francis Adams, Jr., a cavalry officer at Grant's headquarters. "He fights when we expect him to march, waits when we look for motion, and moves when we expect him to fight."

"I now find, after over thirty days of trial, the enemy deems it of first importance to run no risks with the armies they now have," Grant wrote to Halleck after the Cold Harbor slaughter.

Thirty days' fighting had changed morale in both armies. Among Lee's men the question was: Will this battle never end? Why kill and kill only to see that army come further south? Among Grant's men the question was: Why should we over and again lose two and three to one fighting an entrenched enemy who forces us to come to him?

Union trenches, shelters, and bombproofs at the siege of Petersburg

Grant

Grant's staff during the battle of Cold Harbor, the General at the left stooping over the back of a bench

From stereographs in the Barrett collection

Harper's Weekly presents

Benjamin Franklin Butler

Horatio Seymour

Wilbur Fisk Storey

A LIAR, A POLITICAL GENERAL, AND TWO COPPERHEADS

From the author's collection

Suddenly Grant made a complete shift in his style of fighting. While Lee waited for direct combat and bloody frontal assaults, Grant moved—by night—in so shrouded a secrecy that only a few high officers knew where the army was going. Lee's skirmishers the next day brought him word that the long trenches in front of Cold Harbor were empty. Grant was gone. A long march, and the wide James River crossed, brought Grant's army to the Petersburg defenses of Richmond. In four days of assaults 10,000 Union troops were lost as against half that number of the enemy. On June 19 Grant sent word to Washington that he would order no more assaults. For a time he would rest his army. From the Wilderness through Cold Harbor he had lost 54,000 men, nearly as many as the entire force under Lee, but reinforcements had brought his army to about the same number he had when he crossed the Rapidan in early May.

While the bloody assaults at Petersburg were under way Grant had a telegram from Lincoln dated June 15, 1864, 7 A.M., a greeting over the adroit transfer of the Army of the Potomac to Petersburg. "I have just received your despatch of 1 P.M. yesterday. I begin to see it: you will succeed. God bless you all." This implied complete approval and measured admiration not merely for what Grant had done in battering Lee's army and relentlessly moving south. It meant salutations on the grand strategy conducted. For Grant was directing several armies. Sigel in the Shenandoah had failed him. Butler on the James River had dallied and lost big chances. But Sheridan had come through and performed, while Sherman in a series of flanking movements and battles was steadily approaching Atlanta. Long toils were ahead. Could Sherman and Grant press through and join their armies? If so, the war would be over. "I begin to see it," Lincoln wired Grant.

A world-wide argument, to last long, began. Was Grant or Lee the greatest general of the war? In the Confederate War Office in Richmond an official of peculiar discrimination, John Tyler, wrote on June 7 to General Sterling Price in Arkansas an estimate: "From first to last Grant has shown great skill and prudence, combined with remorseless persistency and brutality. He is a scientific Goth, resembling Alaric, destroying the country as he goes and delivering the people over to starvation. Nor does he bury his dead, but leaves them to rot on the battlefield." Of Lee by contrast Tyler wrote: "He is almost unapproachable, and yet no man is more simple, or less ostentatious, hating all pretension. It would be impossible for an officer to be more reverenced, admired, and respected. He eats the rations of the soldier and quarters alone in his tent. Without parade, haughtiness or assumption, he is elevated in his thought and feeling, and is worthy of the cause he represents and the army he commands." And of the game between the two Tyler wrote it was grand and surpassing, both sides having consummate mastery of the art of war. "It is admitted that Lee has at last met with a foeman who matches his steel, although he may not be worthy of it. Each guards himself perfectly and gives his blow with a precise eye and cool and sanguinary nerve."

Lincoln continued service as Grant's head recruiting officer. "War at the best is terrible, and this of ours in its magnitude and duration is one of the most terrible the world has ever known," said the President at a Sanitary Fair in Philadelphia. Business was deranged, the load of debt and taxes heavier. The war had ruined homes, destroyed life and property, caused mourning until almost the heavens hung with black. "Yet it continues." The labors and voluntary contributions of the Sanitary and Christian commissions in relief of soldiers were proof of national resources not at all exhausted. The women had done "much, very much" for the soldier, continually reminding him of care and thought for him at home. "The knowledge that he is not forgotten is grateful to his heart."

And when was this war to end? "I do not wish to name the day when it will end, lest the end should not come at the given time. We accepted this war, and did not begin it. We accepted it for an object, and when that object is accomplished the war will end, and I hope to God that it will never end until that object is accomplished. We are going through with our task, so far as I am concerned, if it takes us three years longer.

"I have not been in the habit of making predictions, but I am almost tempted now to hazard one. I will. It is, that Grant is this evening in a position, with Meade and Hancock, of Pennsylvania, whence he can never be dislodged by the enemy until Richmond is taken.

"If I shall discover that General Grant may be greatly facilitated in the capture of Richmond by rapidly pouring to him a large number of armed men at the briefest notice, will you go? Will you march on with him? [Cries of "Yes, yes."] Then I shall call upon you when it is necessary." Thus spoke Grant's foremost recruiting agent.

No other man, unless the late Henry Clay, could have gone through the same amount of handshaking in one day with such untiring good humor as did President Lincoln, said the *Philadelphia News*. "Mr. Lincoln is certainly not what would be called a 'handsome man' but he has a face stamped with the impress which nature ever bestows upon an honest man." From the time he arrived until a late hour the streets were alive with joyous and excited crowds who were delighted with the President and his ways, said the *News*. The *New York World* man, however, wrote that the President's carriage from the Broad Street depot was flanked by plenty of policemen as a precaution against the rag, tag, and bobtail. In a barouche with four horses and a military escort he arrived at the Eighteenth Street entrance of the fair and the police squeezed a path through a shoving crowd.

"Mr. Lincoln," wrote the *World* man, "with great difficulty reached the reception room of the executive committee. Here he gave wings to one of those terse, clear-cut and original expressions which so mark the man. 'I'd like,' said he, 'I'd like a little cold water.' Rumor has it, also, that he electrified his loyal hearers shortly afterward by suddenly saying, with solemnity, 'It's warm.' Whether he referred to the water just mentioned, or to the weather, or whether he said it at all, I am not certain—I simply repeat what I have heard; for in these times, when we are making a page of history a day, the expressions of our great men must not be forgotten or pass unnoticed. . . . The President spent about an hour in making the tour of the Fair. Your reporter was not near enough to catch the President's first words upon entering the banquet-hall, but is informed that he whispered to a companion 'This is a right smart set-out.' "

The President's gestures when speaking revealed the rail-splitter rather than the orator of true grace, wrote the *World* man, while his handshaking was neither pump-handle, twist, nor reach, but a sudden thrust and a corkscrew burrow. "You carefully count your fingers to see that none of them are missing, and wonder why Mr. Lincoln does not put that 'hand' on the throat of the rebellion, instead of employing it in writing proclamations." In dwelling on the general aspect of the President, the *World* man was not pleased. In connection with the President's necktie he suggested that the President might yet be hanged by the neck till he was dead. "His neck-tie is an outrage and the manner in which he wears it a still greater atrocity. Why should he allow an unseemly knot to show itself under his left ear? It gives rise to unpleasant thoughts in the minds of the faithful and wicked comparisons among his numerous enemies."

Whether the occasion was too solemn or the President was bilious, the *World* man could not say, but " 'The Second Washington' did not, that I can learn, crack many jokes—smutty or otherwise." He heard that as the President began filling himself at the table, he exclaimed, "I'll fight it out on this line, if it takes all summer." Toward the end of his story the *World* man recorded that the Loyal Leaguers and others who heard the President "roared themselves hoarse" in approval of what he said.

The cleverly barbed malice streaking through the *World* man's report of Lincoln at Philadelphia had its motive partly in events of four weeks back. The President then had suppressed the *New York World* and the *New York Journal of Commerce*, arrested their editors, and for two days stopped them from printing and selling their papers. Seward and Stanton originated these arbitrary actions and Lincoln let them have their way. At the bottom of the affair was a hoodoo creature once before giving trouble to Lincoln, the same Joseph Howard who had invented "the Scotch cap and long military cloak" in which Lincoln had secretly passed through Baltimore and arrived in Washington, the same Joseph Howard who at Lincoln's inauguration had written that Douglas nodded approval and said "That's good" and "No doubt about that," expressions that none of the others, closer than Howard to Douglas, had heard.

On May 18 at 4 A.M. and the press deadline near, Howard sent to all the newspapers of New York a forged proclamation in which the President fixed May 26 as a day of fasting, humiliation, and prayer for the nation, called for 400,000 men to be conscripted, and took on a tone of mourning as though the war was lost. Dated at the Executive Mansion, Washington, it opened: "In all exigencies it becomes a Nation to carefully scrutinize its line of conduct, humbly to approach the Throne of Grace and meekly to implore forgiveness, wisdom and guidance. For reasons known only to Him, it has been decreed that this country should be the scene of unparalleled outrage, and this Nation the monumental sufferer of the nineteenth century. With a heavy heart but an undiminished confidence in our cause, I approach the performance of duty, rendered imperative by sense of weakness before the Almighty, and of justice to the people."

The *Herald*, *Tribune*, and *Times* editors had received in their offices the same Associated Press manifold sheets as the *World* and the *Journal of Commerce*. But the late hour of arrival for such a document from the President, the fishy tone of its opening: "Fellow-Citizens of the United States"—a phrase of address not employed by the President in his proclamations—made it suspect. The *Herald* printed it, but did not send out the early edition containing it. The two newspapers foremost in violent opposition to the President, however, could not resist the temptation to print and circulate it. As news it was what they wanted as a follow-up on their repeated items about the President's shattered physical health, on their exaggerations of Grant's colossal battle losses in the Wilderness and their picture of Grant coldly sending boys by thousands into unprecedented slaughter "at the behest of a President who demanded victories with an eye on reëlection in November."

Stanton the next morning, according to Nicolay and Hay, wrote a dispatch, followed by Lincoln's signature, to Major General John A. Dix, commanding in New York: "Whereas there has been wickedlly and traitorously printed and published this morning in the New York 'World' and New York 'Journal of Commerce' . . . a false and spurious proclamation, purporting to be signed by the President, and to be countersigned by the Secretary of State, which publication is of a treasonable nature designed to give aid and comfort to the enemies of the United States and to the rebels now at war against the government . . . you are therefore hereby commanded forthwith to arrest and imprison . . . the editors, proprietors, and publishers of the aforesaid newspapers." To Governor Yates at Springfield, Illinois, Lincoln wired that day, "If any such proclamation has appeared, it is a forgery." Seward issued a statement to the public: "The paper is an absolute forgery." Stanton sent orders for the seizure of the offices, arrest of managers, superintendents, and operators of the Independent Telegraph Company, and later in the day had telegrams from New York, Harrisburg, Baltimore, Pittsburgh, that those offices had been closed and the arrests made. Dix at New York arrested the editors of the *World* and the *Journal of Commerce*, under later orders let them go, but for two days would not let them print and sell their papers.

Dix telegraphed Stanton on May 20 he had arrested and was sending to Fort Lafayette one Joseph Howard, found to be the author of the forged proclamation. "He is a newspaper man and is known as Howard of the 'Times.' He has been very frank in his confession, says it was a stockjobbing operation and that no person connected with the press had any agency in the transaction, except another reporter, who distributed the copies to the newspapers." This telegram, Stanton shortly wired Dix, had been submitted to the President, who directed that, while the editors had no right to shield themselves behind a plea of ignorance or want of criminal intent, he was not disposed "to visit them with vindictive punishment," hoped they would exercise more caution in the future, and authorized Dix to restore to them their establishments. So once more they could print and sell papers. The editor of the *World*, Manton Marble, put his signature to column on column of editorials addressed to President Lincoln, calling the Chief Magistrate tyrant, usurper, and despot who had destroyed "freedom of the press." By his methods Marble invited and defied the President to again close down the *World*, which didn't happen.

In his diary of May 19 Welles wrote: "The bogus proclamation has been the principal topic to-day. The knowledge that it is a forgery has not quieted the public mind."

The offhand way in which a Government having enough guns and troops could proceed to suppress a newspaper was touched briefly in Welles's diary of May 18: "Seward . . . asked if the *World* and *Journal of Commerce* had been shut up. Stanton said he knew of their course only a minute before. Seward said the papers had been published a minute too long; and Stanton said if he [Seward] and the President directed, they should be suspended. Seward thought there should be no delay."

Stanton, "the fiery Secretary," had then rushed the matter without asking the President about it, according to Nicolay and Hay, had written the telegraphic order to General Dix which closed: "You will also take possession, by military force, of the printing establishments of the New York 'World' and 'Journal of Commerce,' and hold the same until further orders, and prevent any further publication therefrom," and signed it: "A. Lincoln, President of the United States" and "By the President: William H. Seward, Secretary of State." The President's secretaries implied that it was a case similar to that of General Burnside's summary actions in the arrest of Vallandigham and the suppression of the *Chicago Times*, in both of which the President indicated afterward that he would have preferred another course of action. "The momentary suppression of the two New York newspapers," wrote Nicolay and Hay . . . "arose from an error which was, after all, sufficiently natural on the part of the Secretary of War." Seward, it was evident from Welles's diary, had no hesitations and wanted the two newspapers "shut up"; they had been "published a minute too long."

Meantime Joe Howard, as the newspapermen called him, meditated behind the bars of a cell at Fort Lafayette on what his lively imagination had brought him to, on the easy money he had expected from the rise of gold resulting from his hoax, on the brokers in cahoots with him who had also lost out, on his former days as secretary to the Reverend Henry Ward Beecher, on newspapers over the country saying with the *New York Tribune*, "Howard was with President Lincoln at the time of his tour from Springfield to Washington and wrote the hoax story in relation to Mr. Lincoln's escape 'in a Scotch cap and long military cloak,' which had not a shadow of truth in it."

Weeks passed with Howard in his cell considering whether his field was not in romance and fiction rather than news fact and current history. Then Lincoln to Stanton: "I very much wish to oblige Henry Ward Beecher by releasing Howard; but I wish you to be satisfied when it is done. What say you?" And Stanton in reply: "I have no objection if you think it is right—and this is a proper time," leaving the inference that Stanton would just as soon let Howard languish in jail a while yet. But Lincoln next day wrote, "Let Howard, imprisoned in regard to the bogus proclamation, be discharged." Thus Lincoln was kind to Beecher and kind to the hoodoo hoaxer who in '61 invented "the Scotch cap and long military cloak" and in '64 gave his notorious, flagrant, criminal imitation of Lincoln writing a proclamation.

"I am no Howard," wrote the *World* man at the Sanitary Fair in Philadelphia, "and should a fluctuation of gold take place because of this report, I shall feel perfectly blameless." Undoubtedly too he felt blameless over his sentences suggesting that Lincoln's necktie formed "an unseemly knot . . . under his left ear," giving rise to "wicked comparisons among his numerous enemies."

Governor Seymour of New York publicly called on District Attorney A. Oakey Hall of New York City to punish those who in the suppression of newspapers had offended the law. General John A. Dix and four other army officers were arrested, though not jailed; the proceedings were polite and legal. In court the attorney for the defense said the President of the United States had issued another order to Dix, directing that while the war lasted "he must not relieve himself from his command or be deprived of his liberty for obeying any order of a military nature which the President of the United States directs him to execute." The orders of the President to Dix were inadmissible as evidence, contended Hall, in defense of the charges against Dix of: (1) inciting to riot; (2) forcible entry and detainer; (3) false imprisonment. Hall's argument pointed to the Roman emperor Caligula writing his own laws, hanging them up so high they could not be read, and then punishing citizens who did not know the law. Thus Congress "allows the President to frame the law within his own breast." Had not the President in an address to Chicago clergymen in 1862 pleaded, "As commander-in-chief of the army and navy, in time of war I suppose I have a right to take any measure which may best subdue the enemy"?

Hall read from Section 4 of the act of Congress of March 3, 1863, which decreed "that any order of the President, or under his authority, made at any time during the existence of the present rebellion, shall be a defence in all courts . . . for any seizure, arrest, or imprisonment, made, done, or committed, or acts omitted to be done under and by virtue of such order." This, said Hall, might be entitled "An act to authorize the commission of wrongs." Hall became specific. Suppose the President should by telegraph order a United States Marshal to arrest Governor Seymour, and if Seymour resisted, to shoot him. Suppose the Governor did resist, and the Marshal killed the Governor, and was tried in Albany for murder, would that order of the President set him free?

Ex-Judge Pierrepont for the defense asked whether or not, in view of the mourning for thousands of New York boys who had fallen in battle, New York was at war. And in whom did the war power exist if not in the President of the United States? The question to be determined by the court was whether General Dix, in obeying the orders of the Chief Executive like a soldier and a patriot, had kidnapped his fellow man (the editors of the *World* and the *Journal of Commerce*) and incited a riot.

The court, Judge A. D. Russel, gave a decision that he would hold for the grand jury General Dix and the four other defendants who had carried out the orders of the President. If the powers given by Congress were constitutional, they clothed the President of the United States with the authority of an absolute monarch, "incapable of doing any wrong," said the court. "This is a very novel and startling doctrine to advance under a republican form of government." One grand jury refused to agree with this view of wartime powers of the President. And the matter never reached a second grand jury. Governor Seymour in these actions, as in the Vallandigham affair and the draft riots, could not guess Lincoln's next move. In the Vallandigham affair Seymour had drawn from Lincoln the devastating propaganda letter "To Erastus Corning and Others"; in the draft riots he had been forced finally to see peace brought to New York City by Lincoln's troops from the Army of the Potomac; and now he was baffled by Lincoln's order to Major General Dix that Dix until further orders must stay in command in New York and, in effect, use the United States Army and Navy before he let the likes of Seymour and the *New York World* put him in jail.

And while it seemed that Lincoln did not initiate the suppression of the two New York newspapers, it did appear that he originated and pressed the issue of whether Governor Seymour of New York could during wartime remove Federal military commanders from service by the classical due process of throwing them into jail. Some Cabinet members were "squeamish" in discussion of the matter when the President called for opinions, according to Welles, who wrote: "The President very frankly avowed the act to be his, and he thought the government should protect Dix. Seward was positive and bold on that. I expressed no opinion, nor did Blair or Bates." And in his diary Welles wrote what he held back from saying at Cabinet meeting: "While I regret that the papers should have been suppressed or meddled with [Welles during twenty-eight years was editor and part owner of the *Hartford Times*], I would not, I think, permit a general officer to be arrested and tried by a State judge for obeying an order of the President."

Elsewhere over the land mobs of Union men had gone much farther than Dix in New York under Lincoln's orders, in the suppression of newspapers. In the three preceding months the *Constitution and Union* at Fairfield, Iowa, was destroyed, likewise the *Northumberland Democrat* and the *Sunbury Democrat* in Pennsylvania, also the Youngstown *Mahoning Sen-*

tinel and the *Dayton Empire* and the *Greenville Democrat* and the *Lancaster Eagle* and the *Wauseon Democrat* in Ohio, likewise the *Laporte Democrat* in Indiana, also the *Chester Picket Guard* and the *Gallatin County Democrat* in Illinois, the *Belleville Volksblatt* and the *Louisiana Union* in Missouri. In these cases the mobs wrecked and demolished office and plant so it could not get out a paper. In Columbus, Ohio, the editor of the *Crisis* was seized and imprisoned; the editor of the *Mahoning Sentinel* narrowly escaped death. Editors at several points were "seized" and sometimes roughly handled. In his two-day suppression of two New York newspapers Lincoln was in accord with a mass trend of the first half of that year and could have gone farther had he chosen.

For weeks in the spring of that year the public heard from the newspapers about the Arguelles case. It sprang up and died down. A grand jury in New York indicted United States Marshal Robert Murray on the charge of kidnapping Arguelles. The Marshal pleaded that what he had done was under orders from the President and therefore his case should be transferred to the United States court. In the end the case never came to trial, the facts favoring the Marshal. Arguelles, a colonel in the Spanish army and serving as lieutenant governor of the district of Colon in Cuba, had captured a cargo of African slaves and thereby acquired a reputation as an efficient public officer, besides $15,000 of the usual prize money awarded. Soon afterward Arguelles quit Cuba and was in New York, buying a Spanish newspaper, settling down to life as an American and spending money in amounts beyond expectation. The Cuban Government laid before Seward, according to Nicolay and Hay and Raymond of the *Times*, the evidence that Arguelles in cahoots with another Cuban had sold one hundred fifty of the slaves from the captured African cargo, had kept the money for himself and officially reported the slaves as dying of smallpox.

The return of Arguelles to Cuba was wanted mainly for the sake of liberating the slaves Arguelles had sold. But no extradition treaty then existed between Spain and the United States. Lincoln and Seward could not in strict international law return Arguelles to Cuba. But the facts laid before them were such that they issued orders in line with "the laws of common humanity and international courtesy." Arguelles was arrested in New York by the United States Marshal, put in charge of a Spanish officer waiting to take him, and carried to Havana. Had there been an extradition treaty with Spain what Lincoln and Seward did would have been extradition instead of kidnapping.

Anti-Lincoln newspapers made the Arguelles case first-page news joined to editorial shrieks, but it was one of those affairs where few got excited except the editorial writers, and their excitement did not last beyond the office of the paper. Little was said about the case in the President's Cabinet meetings, Welles writing that he knew nothing of it "except what I see in the papers." Seward had acted on his own again without seeing the President about it, Welles suspected. "I am persuaded he [the President] has nothing to do in this affair beyond acquiescing without knowledge in what has been done." As a news event the Arguelles case was sunk in the public prints when two New York editors arose to cry that they had been kidnapped and their establishments stolen by a power-drunk despotism at Washington.

On the morning the bogus proclamation was published, the price of gold made fast upswings and the New York Stock Exchange was feverish. To those gold speculators who took it as genuine the proclamation meant that Grant was losing and gold would go higher. The antics and greed of these gamblers had recently been attacked by Congress in a bill empowering the Secretary of the Treasury to sell surplus gold. The painter Carpenter in the White House heard Governor Curtin remark to Lincoln one day, "I see by the quotations that Chase's movement has already knocked gold down several per cent."

Lincoln's face knotted. "Curtin, what do you think of those fellows in Wall Street, who are gambling in gold at such a time as this?"

"They are a set of sharks."

"For my part," bringing a clenched fist down on a table, "I wish every one of them had his *devilish* head shot off."

In his own mind the President believed the war would last a longer time than he dared to tell the public, according to Noah Brooks, who wrote that on June 14 the President was impatient with the people who expected that Grant would close the war and enter Richmond before the autumn leaves began to fall. "The solemn manner of the President, and the weightiness of his utterance, so impressed me that I drew toward me a sheet of paper and wrote down his words then and there," noted Brooks. "Then I read to him what I had written, in order that I might be sure that he was correctly reported. He suggested a verbal change, and I carried the paper away with me." This sheet of paper recorded Lincoln's private anxiety of which he could not be entirely frank with the divided country:

"I wish, when you write or speak to people, you would do all you can to correct the impression that the war in Virginia will end right off and victoriously. To me the most trying thing of all this war is that the people are too sanguine; they expect too much at once. I declare to you, sir, that we are to-day farther ahead than I thought, one year and a half ago, that we should be; and yet there are plenty of people who believe that the war is about to be substantially closed. As God is my judge, I shall be satisfied if we are over with the fight in Virginia within a year. I hope we shall be 'happily disappointed,' as the saying is; but I am afraid not—I am afraid not."

"I approve . . . whatever may tend to strengthen and sustain General Grant and the noble armies under his direction," wrote Lincoln in a letter to a New York mass meeting held to express gratitude to Grant for signal services, and to project Grant as a presidential candidate. "My previous high estimate of Grant has been maintained and heightened by what has occurred in the remarkable campaign he is now conducting, while the magnitude and difficulty of the task before him do not prove less than I expected. He and his brave soldiers are now in the midst of their great trial, and I trust that at your meeting you will so shape your good words that they may turn to men and guns, moving to his and their support."

This public tone of Lincoln with relation to Grant was kept in his private contacts. His word to immediate associates was the same as what he gave the country. He could not withhold grief over the slaughter. They saw him moan and mourn over the killed and wounded. But Grant the hammer, Grant the relentless, he would stand by. If the work needed could be done, Grant was the man.

Down the Potomac and around to the James River Lincoln and Tad rode on a white river steamer and on June 21 Lincoln stepped from upper deck to gangway, wrung the hand of his General in Chief, spoke appreciation. Grant with Colonel Horace Porter and others went with Lincoln to the after cabin, Grant saying, "I hope you are very well, Mr. President."

"Yes, I am in very good health, but I don't feel very comfortable after my trip last night on the bay. It was rough, and I was considerably shaken up. My stomach has not yet entirely recovered from the effects."

A wiseacre interposed: "Try a glass of champagne, Mr. President. That is always a certain cure for seasickness."

Lincoln with lighted face eyed him a moment. "No, my friend. I have seen too many fellows seasick ashore from drinking that very stuff."

This, as Horace Porter noted it, was "a knockdown for the officer," and in the laugh at his expense Lincoln and Grant joined.

Grant. I know it would be a great satisfaction for the troops to have an opportunity of seeing you, Mr. President; and I am sure your presence among them would have a very gratifying effect. I can furnish you a good horse, and will be most happy to escort you to points of interest along the line.

Lincoln. Why, yes; I had fully intended to go out and take a look at the brave fellows who have fought their way down to Petersburg in this wonderful campaign, and I am ready to start at any time.

The staff officers were presented for greetings and cordial words. Lincoln stepped ashore, chatted at Grant's headquarters, then mounted the large bay horse Cincinnati, while Grant sat Jeff Davis. With three staff men they rode to the Butler and Meade commands. Astride of a horse Lincoln wore a tall black silk hat, black trousers, and frock coat. He sat his horse well enough. "But," wrote Horace Porter, "it must be acknowledged that in appearance he [Lincoln] was not a very dashing rider. On this occasion, by the time he had reached the troops he was completely covered with dust, and the black color of his clothes had changed to Confederate gray. As he had no straps, his trousers gradually worked up above his ankles, and gave him the appearance of a country farmer riding into town wearing his Sunday clothes. However, the troops were so lost in admiration of the man that the humorous aspect did not seem to strike them. The soldiers rapidly passed the word along the line that 'Uncle Abe' had joined them, and cheers broke forth from all the commands, and enthusiastic shouts and even words of familiar greeting met him on all sides."

After a while of this Grant suggested they should ride on and see the colored troops who the week before had behaved handsomely in General Baldy Smith's attack on the Petersburg defenses.

LINCOLN. Oh, yes. I want to take a look at those boys. I read with the greatest delight the account in Mr. Dana's despatch of how gallantly they behaved. He said they took six out of the sixteen guns captured that day. I was opposed on nearly every side when I first favored the raising of colored regiments; but they have proved their efficiency, and I am glad they have kept pace with the white troops in the recent assaults. When we wanted every able-bodied man who could be spared to go to the front, and my opposers kept objecting to the negroes, I used to tell them that at such times it was just as well to be a little color-blind. I think, General, we can say of the black boys what a country fellow who was an old-time abolitionist in Illinois said when he went to a theater in Chicago and saw Forrest playing Othello. He was not very well up in Shakespeare, and didn't know that the tragedian was a white man who had blacked up for the purpose. After the play was over the folks who had invited him to go to the show wanted to know what he thought of the actors, and he said, "Waal, layin' aside all sectional prejudices and any partiality I may have for the race, derned ef I don't think the nigger held his own with any on 'em."

Riding into the camp of the colored troops of the 18th Corps, Lincoln met a torrent of black men who circled roundabout a strange figure on a horse who was to them the Liberator, the Chain-Breaker, the Giver of Freedom. Tears ran down some faces. Cheers, laughter, songs, mixed and rang in the air. "God bress Massa Linkum!" "De Lawd save Fader Abraham!" "De day ob jubilee am come, shuah." They waved their hands, brandished their arms, kissed the hands of their mystic hero, crowded around fondling his horse, bridle, and saddle. "The President," noted Porter, "rode with bared head; the tears had started to his eyes and his voice was broken."

That evening Grant and his staff had Lincoln as headquarters guest. "His anecdotes possessed the true geometric requisite of excellence: they were neither too broad nor too long," wrote Porter. "He seemed to recollect every incident in his experience and to weave it into material for his stories." A sentinel posted near enough to gather the President's talk was heard to say, "That man's got a powerful memory and a mighty poor forgettery."

The low camp chair lacked the rungs on which Lincoln customarily put his feet when at ease in storytelling, with the result that this evening he "wound his legs around each other as if in an effort to get them out of the way." The gyrations of his arms and hands ran an accompaniment to his verbal text. One officer said he would prize a photograph of one of Mr. Lincoln's jokes. At one point he drifted into talk about improved firearms and a new powder used in 15-inch guns which he had not seen but he understood differed much from any other powder ever used. Colonel Porter spoke of having a specimen of this identical powder in his tent. He brought to Lincoln a grain of the powder about the size of a walnut. Lincoln handled it, scrutinized it carefully, and rambled into an anecdote of associated interest:

"Well, it's rather larger than the powder we used to buy in my shooting days. It reminds me of what occurred once in a country meeting-house in Sangamon County. You see, there were very few newspapers then, and the country storekeepers had to resort to some other means of advertising their wares. If, for instance, the preacher happened to be late in coming to a prayer-meeting of an evening, the shopkeepers would often put in the time while the people were waiting by notifying them of any new arrival of an attractive line of goods. One evening a man rose up and said: 'Brethren, let me take occasion to say, while we're a-waitin', that I have jest received a new inv'ice of sportin' powder. The grains are so small you kin sca'cely see 'em with the naked eye, and polished up so fine you kin stand up and comb yer ha'r in front of one o' them grains jest like it was a lookin'-glass. Hope you'll come down to my store at the cross-roads and examine that powder for yourselves.' When he had got about this far a rival powder-merchant in the meeting, who had been boiling over with indignation at the amount of advertising the opposition powder was getting, jumped up and cried out: 'Brethren, I hope you'll not believe a single word Brother Jones has been sayin' about that powder. I've been down thar and seen it for myself, and I pledge you my word that the grains is bigger than the lumps in a coal-pile; and any one of you, brethren, ef you was in your future state, could put a bar'l o' that powder on your shoulder and march squar' through the sulphurious flames surroundin' you without the least danger of an explosion.' "

The pleasant party drew to a close. Porter, carrying the walnut-sized grain of powder, walked to his tent, put it away safely, and turned to find Lincoln looking into his tent. Porter asked him in. The President stepped inside a moment, and his eye fell on a specimen artillery trace, a patented article which some inventor wished the army to adopt.

"Why, what's that?"

"That is a trace."

"Oh, that recalls what the poet wrote: 'Sorrow had fled, but left her traces there.' What became of the rest of the harness he didn't mention."

After a night's sleep on the river steamer, Lincoln the next morning cruised up-river, amid the gunboats, met Admiral Lee and General Benjamin Butler, saw breastworks and parapets and heard army men explain them. Some particularly strong positions recently seized and fortified were pointed out and brought Lincoln's remark to Butler, "When Grant once gets possession of a place, he holds on to it as if he had inherited it."

The limb of a tree meeting Lincoln's hat as he rode that day, the hat fell to the ground. Dana was interested to see forty-five-year-old Admiral Lee off his horse and handing the President a hat while officers twenty years younger sat their horses.

Someone referring that day to the presidential campaign and the number of men who composed the Electoral College, Lincoln said, "Among all our colleges, the Electoral College is the only one where they choose their own masters."

Light moments of humor and byplay came and went but the prevailing mood was anxiety. The short shafts of laughter punctuated a gravity lost and resumed. His mind seemed completely absorbed in the operations of the army, wrote Porter. Several times, when contemplated battles were spoken of, he said, "I cannot pretend to advise, but I do sincerely hope that all may be accomplished with as little bloodshed as possible."

He sailed back to Washington with new-made friends in the army, not the least of them the General in Chief. Their bonds were drawing closer and would need yet to be stronger.

Aboard the steamer returning to Washington was Dana, who may have given more than inklings to Lincoln of the views he would soon report in writing: that Meade was showing violent temper toward subordinates, that generals were losing confidence in him, that Grant was disposed to place much of the blame for inconclusive results on Meade, that Meade's queer orders for the last series of assaults on Petersburg, losing 10,000 men to little advantage, were to the effect that he had found it impracticable to secure the co-operation of corps commanders and therefore each was to attack on his own account and do the best he could by himself.

Perhaps it was the wear and tear of the war telling on Meade. His letters to his wife lacked the ease and generosity they had the year before. He was obeying orders and coming clean as a soldier and officer, but his mind could not approve and accept the strategy and methods of Grant. This blunted in Meade the edge of his desire for action and immediate results, having its effect on staff and line. Grant had given him promotions but they came slowly, Meade felt, and in this feeling his wife aggressively supported him. Meade did not understand that Grant at Cold Harbor, as at Donelson and Vicksburg, was playing with imponderables, gambling that Lee's line was so thin and his reserves so ragged that any one of the desperate assaulting columns breaking through might have ended the war. Grant was born tough for war. Meade had a finer temperament than Grant. Grant brought a new vocabulary to the Army of the Potomac. Sherman and Sheridan knew his answers. Meade never would.

But Meade was no double-dealer mixing a political game with the military as McClellan did. His flaws were otherwise. "A battle always put him in a fury," wrote Grant later. "He raged from beginning to end. His own staff officers would dread to bring him a report of anything wrong. Meade's anger would overflow on the heads of his nearest and best friends." General Schaff, a friend of Meade, wrote, "I have seen him so cross and ugly that no man dared to speak to him—in fact, at such times his staff and everybody kept as clear of him as possible." A medical officer complained to Meade that soldiers were jeering "Old Pills" at him and he wanted it stopped. Meade clapped on his big eyeglasses, glared furiously, and snarled: "Well, what of it? How can I prevent it? Why, I hear that when I rode out the other day some of the men called me a 'damned old goggle-eyed snapping turtle!'"

On the very day that Lincoln steamed away for Washington Meade wrote to his wife a letter reflecting no true, hard, and indurated soldier. He unbosomed himself to his wife of secret thoughts that if spoken aloud would have been regarded as defeatist in tone, for he told her: "I conversed with some prisoners yesterday, who said they were completely exhausted, having had no rest or sleep for days, and being compelled to be all the time marching. I said to one of them, 'Well, we will treat you well,' and he replied, 'Oh, sir, you cannot treat us worse than we are treated on the other side.' In flags of truce, and on all occasions that we meet the rebel officers, they always begin conversation by asking when the war is going to be over, and expressing themselves as most heartily tired and anxious for peace. I believe these two armies would fraternize and make peace in an hour, if the matter rested with them; not on terms to suit politicians on either side, but such as the world at large would acknowledge as honorable, and which would be satisfactory to the mass of people on both sides." On the picket lines flung out at night after the day's fighting were laughter and goodwill across enemy fronts, Meade's staff man Lyman writing: "These men are incomprehensible—now standing from daylight to dark killing and wounding each other by thousands and now making jokes and exchanging newspapers, despite orders to the contrary. You see them lying side by side in the hospitals, talking together in that prosaic way that characterizes Americans. The great staples of conversation are the size and quality of rations, the marches they have made, and the regiments they have fought against. All sense of personal spite is sunk in the immensity of the contest."

One letter to Mrs. Meade from her husband's headquarters informed her, "Mr. Lincoln honored the army with his presence this afternoon, and was so gracious as to say he had seen you in Philadelphia, etc., etc."

Dana and Lincoln on the river steamer may have talked about Ben Butler, of whom General Baldy Smith wrote to Grant, "I want simply . . . to ask you how you can place a man in command of two army corps who is as helpless as a child on the field of battle and as visionary as an opium-eater in council?"

Not yet could they put Butler on the shelf. Over the country he had a strange popularity, resting on little real achievement but rather on his sense of drama and utterance. He was a Democratic-party man of power, often mentioned for the Presidency, and Grant and Lincoln were handling him as with gentle tongs. The lawyer and the politician stood uppermost in Major General Butler. He recorded how he responded to a message from his two corps commanders suggesting a change in plans. "To that letter I at once replied that, while regretting the infirmity of purpose which did not permit them to state to me while personally present the suggestion contained in their note, but allowed me to go to my headquarters under the impression that a far different purpose was advised by them, I should not yield to their written suggestions which implied a change of plan within thirty minutes after I left them." Butler liked disputes and came away with the last word. Also in some responsible military matters he would rather give a verbal order than put it in writing. His relations with Grant and Lincoln ran into many twilight zones where Butler and other witnesses mixed fact, falsehood, and prejudice. As days heavy with fate wore on, the accumulated circumstances indicated that Butler was, as Lincoln had casually told Hay by anecdote, both scoundrel and fool.

From New Orleans, where current reports credited Butler's brother with having gleaned there a fortune of from $1,000,000 to $2,000,000, and where Butler himself admitted his brother's holdings ran to $200,000, he had come to Virginia, was blaming his failures on others, and according to Dana, was exercising a peculiarly sinister influence over Grant. To General Lew Wallace, General Robert Schenck said: "Ben Butler is the only man Stanton fears. Butler can do the most atrocious things—steal or murder—and be let alone. I always think of Ben as a cross-eyed cuttle-fish swimming about in waters of his own muddying." A 660-page book, *General Butler in New Orleans* by James Parton, was published and went to a large audience of readers. "One who can rule and dare not lie," was the judgment of the book. Butler was a fertile genius of brains, valor, patriotism, honesty, ran the recurring theme. "You have told me what I was *not* recalled for," the book related his saying to Stanton. "I now ask you to tell me what I *was* recalled for." And Stanton had laughed. "You and I are both lawyers, and it is of no use your filing a bill of discovery upon *me*, for I shan't tell you." In all the departments Butler met cordiality and consideration. "He asked the President the reason of his recall, and the President referred him to the Secretary of State and the Secretary of War, who, the President said, had recommended the measure [for his recall]."

Of his claim that he was the senior major general, entitled to outrank all others, and the almanac would prove his case, the President, according to Butler, said he knew nothing about the dates of the several commissions, and added, "I know only that I gave you your commission the first of anybody." A board of officers to whom the question was referred decided that the President was not bound by the almanac and could make a junior senior if he pleased, and that Generals McClellan, Frémont, Dix, and Banks took rank before Butler. This, Parton's book alleged, was "merely one instance more of the systematic snubbing" given Butler.

Parton saw they were handling his hero with tongs but seemed innocent of any knowledge of Butler's devious and ramified financial, cotton, and supply operations while Military Governor of New Orleans. Enough light on those operations had come to Lincoln, Stanton, and Seward to satisfy them Butler should be recalled. "He was recalled for the purpose of conciliating the French government," was Parton's conclusion joined to that of Butler. Those who recalled him, however. had more evidence than they cared to bring out bearing on what Admiral Farragut at New Orleans wrote to his family of the war running a course like a violent disease with strange contaminations resulting from "vice and extravagance" preceding the war.

"I scarcely know what to hope. I do not see any improvement in the moral condition of the country. Those who can, seem to be doing all they can to swindle the Government."

In January of '64 Stanton wrote with his own hand—as he seldom did and in this case possibly because he would rather that no subordinate should know of the delicate matter involved—a letter to Butler commanding at Fortress Monroe. From the Unionist Governor of Virginia, Pierpont, Stanton had word, he informed Butler, "that you have ordered all the Municipal officers of Norfolk and Portsmouth to report to you in detail the amounts of all money received by them, &c., and also that you have constituted a Commission to investigate the conditions of the Savings Funds and Banking institutions there, and he, as Governor, feels aggrieved by these measures." And Stanton in this case had talked the matter over with Lincoln and gave Butler the order: "The President directs me to request you to suspend these measures, until you can state to him, in writing or otherwise, your views of the necessity or propriety of them."

The most recent muddying of the waters by Butler went into an entry of Welles's diary of June 23, 1864. Papers from Admiral Lee informed Welles of Butler's addressing a letter to the President with a proposal to send plows, harrows, and farming utensils to loyal farmers in North Carolina in exchange for cotton and other products. To Welles this seemed "a little, dirty, speculating intrigue" having the usual "plausible and taking rascality" of Butler. A man named Lane and his steamer the *Philadelphia* had started for the Chowan River in North Carolina carrying a permit from Butler. "The President indorsed that he approved the project. On this General Butler granted a permit. Captain Smith, senior officer in the Sounds, declined to recognize it, detained the boat and sent the papers to Admiral Lee. The latter failed—called the paper many names, said the President's permit must be respected." Welles showed the papers to Seward and Blair, mentioning that he was disposed to telegraph and detain the vessel. Blair was inclined, with hesitations, to favor Welles's view. Admiral Lee had married a sister of Blair and out of their associations Blair understood Lee's inclinations. Seward advised waiting the arrival of the President. But Seward and Blair "both condemned the proceedings as wholly improper," wrote Welles. Of Lincoln's major generals Butler was the only one of whom there were continuous reports that he was lining his own pockets out of the war. Some said he was blemished, others that he was rotten. All agreed he was smooth and adroit, by habit, as Welles put it, "plausible and taking."

On arriving in Washington after three days' and four nights' absence, Lincoln telegraphed Mrs. Lincoln in Boston: "All well and very warm. Tad and I have been to General Grant's army. Returned yesterday safe and sound." He talked with Sumner, who wrote to the Duchess of Argyll the latest inside news, an item that would have leaped to the front pages had the press received it:

"The President, on his return from General Grant's headquarters, told me that the general, who is a man of very few words, said to him: 'I am as far from Richmond now as I ever shall be. I shall take the place; but as the rebel papers say, it may require a long summer's day.' The President describes Grant as full of confidence, and as wanting nothing."

Welles noted the President at Cabinet meeting as "in very good spirits," the journey having "done him good physically, and strengthened him mentally and inspired confidence in the General and army." Seward still bothered Welles by discussing matters alone with the President, and "Stanton is but little better. If he comes, it is to whisper to the President, or take the dispatches or the papers from his pocket and go into a corner with the President."

The President returned, wrote Bates in his diary, "perceptably [sic] disappointed at the small measures of our success, in that region; but encouraged by Grant's persistent confidence." On this same day Bates had from United States District Attorney Chandler of West Virginia an account of "how he was abused by Brigr. Genl. Wilde [sic], at Norfolk." Wild had earned a queer name for himself by giving former slaves whips with which they lashed the bare back of their former owner. "Wilde," wrote Bates, "is the same ruffian that caused a gentleman to be stripped and whipped by his own slaves, and called it *poetic justice!* (I heard the President quote his words.) The wretch ought to be punished in emphatic *prose.*"

The *Chicago Times* quoted a Missouri Frémonter as saying Lincoln's head was "too light for the weight of his foot," and the war was conducted in the manner of the man found climbing trees to catch woodpeckers. On being told he could never catch woodpeckers in that way, he hollered back, "Well, if I don't catch any I'll worry them like hell."

The *Rochester Democrat* countered the *Chicago Times* allegation that Grant was really retreating and Lee pursuing. An Iowa editor, it was recalled, took a beating in his office and wrote of it in his paper: "There was a blow. Somebody fell. We got up. Turning upon our antagonist, we then succeeded in winding his arms around our waist, and by a quick manoeuvre threw him on the top of us, bringing our back at the same time in contact with the bed of the printing press. Then inserting our nose between his teeth, and his hands in our hair, we had him."

Partly as propaganda and partly as fact having point, Unionist newspapers dwelt on Libby Prison in Richmond limiting letters to six lines and one prisoner writing: "My dear Wife—Yours received—no hope of exchange—send corn starch—want socks—no money—rheumatism in left shoulder—pickles very good—send sausages—God bless you—kiss the baby—Hail Columbia! Your devoted Husband."

For an album that held the autographs of all the Presidents of the United States Lincoln wrote his signature. The actress Fanny Kemble donated it to the New York Sanitary Fair. The publisher Robert Bonner gave the fair the celebrated trotting mare Lady Woodruff, who had done a mile in two minutes and twenty-seven seconds. She went at auction for the ridiculously low price of $1,800. "Among contributions," said *Leslie's*, "is that of a Spanish lady, who, having renounced the world and become a nun in the Convent of the Sacred Heart, sends all her earthly treasures, consisting of jewelry and gems valued at $2,500, to the Fair." Old John Burns, who at seventy years of age had volunteered and taken wounds at Gettysburg, was on view for crowds in the Trophy Room. "Another living history in the same room, is a soldier named William Mudge, whose sightless eyes are made the subject of especial appeal by a beautiful lady who recites his services and condition to those who have hearts and pockets. A ball has stricken away the soldier's sight, affected his palate, and taken from him a large share of enjoyment for life. Such sights bring home to us the realities of our great struggle, and make us see the earnestness of purpose and necessity that underlies all the dazzle, beauty, fashion, flirtation and poetry of the great Sanitary Fair."

Over the land stood houses where the war losses came close home. "My oldest boy, not yet twenty," wrote the poet Longfellow to a friend, "in the last battle on the Rapidan shot through both shoulders with a rifle-ball, is now at home. He comes down into my study every day, and is propped up in a great chair. How brave these boys are! Not a single murmur or complaint, though he has a wound through him a foot long. He pretends it does not hurt him."

Homeward went a musician from the Virginia fighting. When he had arrived in hospital, according to the *New York Tribune*, the surgeon said he must be lashed down while a leg was amputated. "No," said the soldier. "Never! Is there a violin in camp?" They brought one. He put it under his chin, tuned it, laughed. "Now, doctor, begin." And he went on playing the violin "without missing a note or moving a muscle" during some forty minutes while they sawed his leg off.

Patriotism before the war had been fireworks, salutes, serenades for holidays and summer evenings, though the reality was "cotton thread and complaisance," wrote Emerson in his diary. "Now the deaths of thousands and the determination of millions of men and women show it real."

The *Buffalo Express* hung up a slogan: "God–Grant–Victory."

From Cold Harbor on June 7 Grant's kindly shadow, Rawlins, wrote to his wife that he had taken dinner in the house of Edmund Ruffin, who at Sumter had fired the first gun of the war. "His fine plantation is abandoned, and I understand that he is dead. I enclose a lily picked in the yard." Ruffin, in fact, was not dead—but his house and lands were lost and the lily that dropped out of the letter Mrs. Rawlins had from her husband might be a foretokening.

CHAPTER 52

THE LINCOLN-JOHNSON TICKET

IN the family of Vice-President Hannibal Hamlin in his Maine home they had laughed over his telling them early in '64 while snow was still on the ground that Mr. Lincoln, looking toward the presidential campaign of the coming summer and fall, had sent for Mr. Hamlin and suggested, "Hamlin, I want you to pick out some bright, likely man to look after delegates in Maine, and keep a weather eye for squalls in New England."

And Hamlin had mentioned the young Congressman James G. Blaine, chairman of the Republican State Committee, as a brilliant organizer. Whereat Mr. Lincoln seemed pleased and dismissed the matter. "You and Cameron fix it up between you."

And the snows melted in New England and on the Western prairies and Lincoln had not done bad in picking up delegates. Yet he was careless in his ways and could be doing better, older heads urged.

David Davis, Associate Justice of the Supreme Court of the United States, was in '64 as sharply interested in practical politics as in '60 when he was the leading manager of the Lincoln campaign organization. Late in March of '64 Davis wrote to Thurlow Weed as between two practical party managers who were not doing very much managing just then. "I showed your letter to the President. It pains him when you are not satisfied with what he does. He stated to me that he has the highest esteem for you, knows that you are patriotic, and that it hurts him when he cannot do what you think advisable." Both Weed and Davis wanted more action from the President. They tried to get him to take steps toward clinching the nomination. They were exchanging letters about an "important matter" where they sought the President's immediate Yes. But the President said he would wait. "I think he ought to act, and act promptly," wrote Davis to Weed, "but his mind is constituted differently from yours and mine. We will have to wait for his decision in the important matter."

Davis's judgment was that Chase's letter following the Pomeroy Secret Circular scandal, in which Chase declined to run for the Presidency, had weasel words in it, and Chase might yet be a formidable contender against Lincoln. "Mr. Chase's declination is a mere sham," wrote Davis to Weed as he indicated what would be attempted. "The plan is to get up a great opposition to Lincoln, use Frémont and others, and represent, when the convention meets, the necessity of united effort, that anybody can unite except Lincoln, etc., etc., and then to present Chase. There was a meeting of Chase's friends in the city last night [May 20]. They resolved not to support Lincoln, etc., etc.; the greater part present were Treasury office-holders. How long can these things last?"

Weed seemed to lose interest as a fixer and became an onlooker. In mid-April he wrote to an Englishman, Joseph Parkes, that all eyes and hopes centered on Grant. "If he wins in Virginia, it will brighten the horizon and make him President." The English friend wrote back that he might in a few years visit the United States and sojourn with Weed, Mrs. Weed, and their daughter Harriet. "My dear old friend," he told Weed, "I should really like to go to the United States, if only to see your Lincoln. But will he soon be in Fort Lafayette, or here [in England] in exile?"

One of the powers with the German vote, Carl Schurz, offered to come on and get results. But Lincoln had to write Schurz it would be dangerous for him to get temporarily out of military service. "A major-general once out, it is next to impossible for even the President to get him in again. . . . Of course I would be very glad to have your service for the country in the approaching political canvass; but I fear we cannot properly have it without separating you from the military."

To General Orme, Justice Davis confided in letters: "Mr. Lincoln seems disposed to let the thing run itself and if the people elect him he will be thankful, but won't use means to secure the thing. Mr. Lincoln annoys me more than I can express, by his persistence in letting things take their course —without effort or organization."

The impression of Davis and Swett that Lincoln was letting the thing run itself, letting things take their course, was in the main correct. Eight weeks after Davis had written to Orme that he was annoyed and anxious about Lincoln doing nothing, Swett wrote to Orme, "Lincoln out of 150 delegates elected previous to May 25, figures them all up for him." The National Union convention was ten days away. And so far no delegates had been picked for anyone but Lincoln. In one State, Missouri, were two sets of delegates, and Lincoln could have the say as to which of the two would be seated in the convention.

As matters stood ten days before the convention, Lincoln seemed to have everything he needed for a nomination by acclamation.

The *Chicago Times* alleged "wire-pullers and bottle-washers" had so arranged matters that the President could lay his hand upon each individual delegate and say, "This man is the creature of my will." The *New York Times* and *Harper's Weekly* held, on the other hand, that the prairies and mountains were afire with pro-Lincoln sentiment, that against the wishes of many powerful politicians, the people, the masses, were going to name the President for a second term.

The two Lincoln friends, Davis and Swett, who in '60 had played important roles in practical organization, were in '64 asked to do little or nothing toward a nomination. And the influential and practical Weed had asked to help and was hurt by the President's advice to do nothing. Yet on May 27 of '64 Swett heard Lincoln figuring that of the total of 150 delegates thus far elected to the Baltimore convention all were for Lincoln. Without incurring any political debts to Davis, Swett, and Weed, and "letting the thing run itself," Lincoln's progress toward nomination was almost incredibly smooth and perfect. He was reducing trades, deals, pledges, and manipulations to a minimum.

Into the scene then stepped John Charles Frémont, John Cochrane, Wendell Phillips, Emil Preetorius, Worthington G. Smythers, Elizabeth Cady Stanton, Caspar Butz, B. Gratz Brown, Pantaleon Candidus, General Gustave Paul Cluseret, and others, including the Reverend George Barrell Cheever of the Church of the Puritans of New York City. In Cosmopolitan Hall in Cleveland, Ohio, May 31 of '64, they organized a political party having a single main objective declared by its leaders—the defeat of the Lincoln Administration. They met eight days before the National Union convention at Baltimore in order to notify that convention that it must not nominate Abraham Lincoln for President. Their platform: the constitutional prohibition of slavery, free speech and a free press, a one-term Presidency, reconstruction of States to be left entirely with Congress. For President their candidate was Major General John C. Frémont of New York, and for Vice-President Brigadier General John Cochrane of New York.

Cochrane in accepting as a candidate was moderate in tone and seemed too amiable really to belong, Nicolay and Hay noting that he was an adroit and experienced politician and "had, in fact, thrown an anchor to windward by visiting Mr. Lincoln before the Convention met and assuring him of his continued friendship." New York and St. Louis, the draft-riots metropolis and the war-torn Border State of Missouri, were the main centers of the movement, with an added contingent from the antislavery societies who could not travel with William Lloyd Garrison in his support of President Lincoln. The rules had not been very strict as to who could be a delegate, and the proceedings at moments had comedy. The convention laughed at a shrill speaker from Illinois saying, "These are solemn times." His treble tones and his hesitations brought further amusement and when he shouted his rebuke, "I believe there is a God who holds the universe in his hand as you would hold an egg," the hall rocked with jeers and roars, and the delegate took his hat and marched out in contempt of unbelievers. Among former military associates of General Frémont present was Cluseret, a Frenchman born to adventure, who had won the Legion of Honor ribbon suppressing street insurrections in Paris in 1848, served in Algeria and the Crimea for France and under Garibaldi for Italy, taking wounds at Capua. After gallant service under Frémont and a brevet of brigadier general, Cluseret resigned in March of '63, and in '64 began editing the *New Nation* in New York.

"We are annoyed and irritated at hearing the words of Abraham Lincoln and honesty always coupled together," said General Cluseret's weekly paper, "but we propose before ostracizing honest Abe from the White House to consider his right to the name of 'Honest.' To call one man honest out of a population of thirty millions, is not so much of a compliment to him as a sarcasm upon the rest. . . . Mr. Lincoln's honesty is of a strange description. It consists in nearly ruining his country and in disregarding its interests in order to make sure of power for four years longer. . . . Even if President Lincoln were the honest man that his paid organs represent him to be, how dangerous would his reëlection prove to the liberties of the people, under existing circumstances, surrounded as he is with the military influences that he has at his back!"

On the reading of a letter from Wendell Phillips the delegates hung with eager interest. They knew him as a bugler and fugleman of their ranks. They had read Phillips's speech earlier that month in which he reviewed Lincoln's Baltimore remarks on the Fort Pillow massacre: "At last we wrenched from the evasive lips of the President the announcement, 'If I could only find a case.' When had the government made a step of a single inch toward trying to find one? I arraign that speech of the President's as the foulest insult to the black race ever uttered on this continent." Now they heard from Phillips: "For three years the Administration has poured out the public treasure and blood of the country. Meanwhile slavery was too sacred to be used; that was saved, lest the feelings of rebels should be hurt. . . . Men say, if we elect Mr. Lincoln, we may change his views. Possibly. But three years has been a long time for a man's education in such hours as these. The nation cannot afford any more. At any rate, the Constitution gives us, this summer, an opportunity to make President a man fully educated. . . . I shall support the Convention's action, if it puts the name of Frémont or Butler on its flag. Frémont is my first choice. . . . Mr. Lincoln may wish the end—peace and freedom—but he is wholly unwilling to use the means which can secure that end. If Mr. Lincoln is reelected I do not expect to see the Union reconstructed in my day, unless on terms more disastrous to liberty than even disunion would be. If I turn to General Frémont, I see a man whose first act was to use the freedom of the negro as his weapon. . . . If the Baltimore Convention shall nominate Mr. Lincoln then I hope we shall fling our candidate's name—the long-honored one of John C. Frémont—to the breeze and appeal to the patriotism and common sense of the people to save us from another such three years as we have seen."

New York delegates styling themselves War Democrats tried to swing a nomination of General Grant. A letter from an Albany Democrat was read pledging a majority of 100,000 for Grant in November. An Albany delegate rising to name Grant was denounced as a Lincoln hireling. Amid roars from Missouri, a uniformed general of the Missouri militia moved Frémont's nomination by acclamation, and it was done.

A committee brought in a name for the new party: Radical Democracy. Another committee, with Worthington G. Smythers of Maryland as chairman, was appointed to notify Frémont of his nomination. Frémont replied to Mr. Smythers' notification. General Frémont accepted, and so doing, announced that he had resigned his commission as major general in the United States Army. He approved of the Cleveland platform, except the plank which called for seizure of conquered slave soil and its division among soldiers and sailors of the United States. "Had Mr. Lincoln remained faith-

LINCOLN—" *Well, Master Fremont, that's rather a long reach, ain't it? You might fetch it with your sword, perhaps, in the proper time, but it isn't ripe yet.*"

Harper's Weekly opposes the new third party

ful to the principles he was elected to defend, no schism could have been created and no contest would have been possible," declared the man who had been the Republican-party candidate for President in 1856. If the Baltimore convention should nominate a man of fidelity "to our cardinal principles," there need be no division among really patriotic men. "My own decided preference is to aid in this way and not to be myself a candidate. But if Mr. Lincoln should be nominated, as I believe it would be fatal to

HARPER'S WEEKLY: JUNE 18, 1864.

JUST SO!

FREMONT. "Well, Sir! I am nominated, you see!"
COCHRANE. "Yes, Sir; WE are nominated."
LINCOLN. "Well, Gentlemen; and what then?"
FREMONT and COCHRANE. "Oh! nothing, Sir; nothing—that's all!"

the country, cost us the lives of thousands of men and needlessly put the country on the road to bankruptcy, there will remain no other alternative but to organize against him every element of conscientious opposition with a view to prevent the misfortune of his election. In this contingency I accept the nomination."

The news from Cleveland put wrath into some of Lincoln's friends. The President himself saw comedy elements. On the morning after the convention, according to Nicolay and Hay, a friend gave him an account of it, and said that instead of the many thousands expected there were present at no time more than 400 people. The President, struck by the number mentioned, reached for the Bible on his desk, searched a moment, then read the words: "And everyone that was in distress, and everyone that was in debt, and everyone that was discontented, gathered themselves unto him;

and he became a captain over them; and there were with him about four hundred men."

To illustrate the positions of the extremist Garrison trailing with Lincoln and the other extremist Phillips flying the Frémont kite, there was rehearsal of old lines, of Horace Mann sniffing to Samuel J. May, "I hate your doctrine that we should think only of the right and not at all of the expedient," and Samuel J. May sniffing in return, "And I hate your doctrine that we should think of the expedient, and not only of the right."

In the week of the Cleveland convention the *New York Herald* gave its readers another of the hymns of hate to which the ears of Lincoln had now become accustomed. The *Chicago Times* and other newspapers reprinted the editorial as something to read. The subject was a National Union mass meeting in Cooper Union, New York, "a gathering of ghouls, vultures, hyenas and other feeders upon carrion" authorized by "the great ghoul at Washington," ran the poisoned pen. "In the midst of the terrible conflicts of the past three weeks, while thousands of lives were being sacrificed for the national cause, and while every patriotic man was watching with intense and anxious interest the painful progress of events, these ghouls thought only of Lincoln's renomination, the control of the Baltimore convention and their own chances for petty offices. At the sound of the cannon which was to decide the fate of the country, these ghouls hurried down from the mountains, these vultures flocked from the plains, these hyenas sneaked out of their holes to feast upon the bodies of the slain. There was Clay Smith, the Kentucky ghoul, and Oglesby, the military ghoul, and Arnold, the Congressional ghoul, and Spencer, the legal ghoul. These were the orators of the meeting, and they all devoted themselves to praising Lincoln, the great Presidential ghoul, and advocating his renomination and reëlection. Their logic was that because Lincoln had killed so many men he ought to be allowed another term to kill as many more. The head ghoul at Washington had not sense enough to forbid the meeting."

Toward its end the motive for the editorial became more evident. Lincoln's re-election was impossible, said the same *New York Herald* which four and five months before had declared nothing could stop him. Now it again saw hopes of Grant. The shadowy and powerful interests to which the *Herald* was responsive had chosen Grant as the best man to run if they could somehow put Grant at the head of a ticket. The editorial was a final shriek of horror meant to have its effect on the Baltimore convention twenty days off. "The people long ago decided that Grant is to be our next President," shouted the *Herald* editorial near its close.

The melodramatic ghoul editorial was one stage effect of a tremendous effort to project Grant into a spot where his name would cut down Lincoln. On June 4, three days before the Baltimore convention was to meet, a mass meeting of 20,000 people in Union Square heard ex-Mayor George Opdyke, Senator Pomeroy, Magnus Gross, Hiram Walbridge, James T. Brady, General T. F. Meagher, and other orators pay tributes to General Grant. The announced and express purpose of the meeting was "to honor General Grant." The inference was that Grant should be nominated at Baltimore instead of Lincoln. Grant's name in the air as the man of the hour, the doer of straightway deeds, might suddenly be plucked for service by the emotional delegates of the Baltimore convention. Had not Seward in 1860 just before the hour of fate looked nearly as formidable as Lincoln in 1864? Therefore keep Grant's name and deeds where the delegates could never for a moment forget him in case any of them should suddenly be asking who could do better than Lincoln. This was the motive of the New York glory-to-Grant mass meetings and the Lincoln-is-a-ghoul editorials.

In Chase's reply to an invitation to be present at the New York glory-to-Grant mass meeting was a little sentence he hoped would be devastating: "It will be the marvel of future historians that men of this day were willing to risk the success of the rebellion, rather than entrust to black loyalists bullets and ballots."

Senator Morgan of New York, executive committee chairman of the Baltimore convention, came to his brother-in-law Welles on May 9 with worries. Such criticism had been piled on him for calling the National Union convention at so early a date that he had sent out a circular defending himself. Morgan knew Welles would stand by him. The answers to his circular were all one way, except for an Ohio man who favored postponement. Welles saw this as Chase influence. The next day came more worries. "Tonight," wrote Welles, "Governor Morgan informs me that the hall in which the convention is to meet has been hired by the malcontents, through the treachery and connivance of H. Winter Davis, in whom he confided." Morgan and Welles talked about whether to rent a theatre, build a wigwam, or move the convention to Philadelphia. After more worrying Morgan rented the Front Street Theatre in Baltimore, had stage scenery shifted away, floored the parquet, and finally had a place for the convention to sit and deliberate.

As the convention date drew near it was evident that many a radical politician had seen that it would be easier sledding in his home territory if he was for Lincoln. Senator Jim Lane of Kansas, who had once led in taking a committee of Missouri-Kansas radicals to the White House for protest of the President's policy, was now on the band wagon, and bringing to Baltimore a set of delegates who he said were "all vindictive friends of the President." Congressman William D. Kelley of Pennsylvania was publicly hailing the President as "the wisest radical of us all." In his paper, the *Philadelphia Press,* John W. Forney, clerk of the Senate and a political informant and adviser of the President, wrote and published an article the day before the convention saying the delegates could not originate but would simply republish a policy already absolutely established by the acts of the President and accepted and ratified by Congress and the people. "Yet for this reason it is transcendently the more imposing in its expression of the national will." The convention had no candidate for President to *choose.* "Choice is forbidden it by the previous action of the people. It is a body which almost beyond parallel is directly responsible to the people, and little more than an instrument of their will. Mr. Lincoln is already renominated, and the Convention will but formally announce the decision of the people. If this absence lessens the mere political interest of the Convention in one respect, the fact that it will thoroughly and unquestionably obey national instructions gives it higher importance."

Of the many who took the road to Washington to win perhaps an inkling of what the President might wish or to let him know their names and faces and that they were for him, Lincoln's secretaries noted: "They were all welcomed with genial and cordial courtesy, but received not the slightest intimation of what would be agreeable to him. The most powerful politicians from New York and Pennsylvania were listened to with no more confidential consideration than the shy and awkward representatives of the rebellious States, who had elected themselves in sutlers' tents and in the shadow of department headquarters."

Baltimore was only two hours by rail from Washington. Delegates, party leaders, and aspirants visited the White House on their way to the convention. Hay wrote in his diary on June 5 that for a day or two the Executive Mansion was "full of patriots on their way to Baltimore who wish to pay their respects & engrave on the expectant mind of the Tycoon, their images in view of future contingencies." Delegations genuine, bogus, and irregular saw the President. C. Bullitt "with Louisiana in his trousers' pocket," somewhat stampeded by political rumors in New York, was feeling "uneasy in his seat." "Florida was sending two delegations," Hay noted. "Neither will get in. Each attacks the other as unprincipled tricksters." Then came an odd paragraph in Hay's diary:

"The South Carolina delegation came in yesterday. The Pres^{t} says, 'Let them in.' 'They are a swindle,' I said. 'They won't swindle me,' quoth the Tycoon. They filed in: a few sutlers, cotton-dealers. and negroes, presented a petition & retired."

The irony of reconstruction, thus far, stood forth in that delegation. The camp-following sutler, the profit-itched cotton-trader, the politically minded Negro who in the crisis preferred civic life to the army—these were to begin the reconstruction of South Carolina?

The effort to manipulate opinion in advance of the Baltimore convention was tremendous. Lincoln's health was worse than ever and he had become a worn skeleton, shattered in nerves and afraid of his own shadow, according to hostile newspapers. The Chase faction was preparing to abandon Lincoln and support the Frémont ticket, said the bogeyman. That Congress had struck directly at the President in taking away from the President's friend and intimate, Marshal Ward Hill Lamon, the profitable management of the District of Columbia jail was an indication that the Republicans were a broken party and could not afford to nominate Lincoln; thus another report.

June 7 the convention met. June 7 Grant was still burying his dead four days after the bloody repulse at Cold Harbor. June 7 the gold-speculators in New York were crazy and wild-eyed over the betting that gold, now higher than ever, would go higher yet. June 7 and potatoes quoted at $160 a bushel in Richmond, cabbageheads $10 apiece.

Yes, on June 7 the convention met. The croaker Gurowski was there and saw "everywhere shoddy, contractors, schemers, pap-journalists," although present were Parson Brownlow of Tennessee and Robert J. Breckinridge of Kentucky and Jim Lane of Kansas and others whose lives in the drive of civil war had often been as candle flame in a wind. Of course the schemers, soiled adventurers who sought what they could lay their hands on, creatures hunting pelf and loot, were there, some of them in high places. Yet there was also a long roll call of the men who had stood fast when the Union was crumbling and had at personal cost and with toil helped buttress the Union.

To what extent Lincoln had indicated his wishes to the executive chairman, the temporary chairman, the permanent chairman, the platform-committee chairman, who swayed the proceedings, was not known to such intimates of the President as Nicolay and Hay, Brooks. It was assumed that the color of doctrine and idea that dominated the convention had come directly or indirectly from the President.

The executive committee chairman, Senator Morgan, called the convention to order at noon of June 7 in sweltering hot weather, after music from the military band of Fort McHenry, while a brigade of boys passed along the aisles with ice water. Morgan's speech was short and warned that the convention would fail of its great mission unless it should declare "for such an amendment of the Constitution as would positively prohibit African slavery in the United States." Morgan then turned the convention over to the Reverend Dr. Robert J. Breckinridge of Kentucky, chosen by the National Committee for temporary chairman, though it became a tradition of the Breckinridge family that President Lincoln had asked the National Committee to choose Breckinridge. The white-haired, bearded, and grizzled preacher took the platform while the roof rang with cheers for the "Old War Horse of Kentucky."

At that very moment the Confederate cavalry raider John Morgan was loose in Kentucky, that week seizing $60,000 from the Farmer's Bank of Mount Sterling, and at Lexington taking all the hats, shoes, saddles, horses, in the town, including the famous stallion Skedaddle, valued at $8,000. Delegates knew they were gazing on an old man who had a nephew and two sons serving as officers in the Confederate Army. He spoke with "a weak voice and an irresolute manner," according to one reporter, while another heard low melodious tones with "every word dropping from his lips like a coin of gold—clear-cut, bright and beautiful."

A whirlwind of applause shook rafters and beams at a sentence near Breckinridge's: "Does any man doubt . . . that Abraham Lincoln shall be the nominee?" But other solemn duties lay ahead. They would have to tell the country why they were fighting the war. They would have to beware of party politics and sink all for the Union. "As a Union party, I will follow you to the ends of the earth, and to the gates of death. [Applause.] But as an Abolition party—as a Republican party—as a Whig party—as a Democratic party—as an American party, I will not follow you one foot."

The tall, slender Kentuckian, with eyes peering from heavy, overhanging brows, with words issuing amidst a long, pointed, patriarchal beard, was telling the convention something from the depths of personal tragedy. They hung on his words. They wondered what would come next. He spoke terrible words. "The only enduring, the only imperishable cement of all free institutions has been the blood of traitors. . . . It is a fearful truth, but we had as well avow it at once; and every blow you strike, and every rebel you kill, every battle you win, dreadful as it is to do it, you are adding, it may be, a year . . . it may be a century—it may be ten centuries to the life of the Government and the freedom of your children." Breckinridge made reference to the bones of two generations of his ancestors in his home State that he loved, of his children there, buried where his own bones would soon lie, and of how some would hate him for what he was saying. Lifting his long arms over his head, he rang the slow words "We have put our faces toward the way in which we intend to go, and we will go in it to the end."

The outcry that the Constitution had been violated Breckinridge would answer with saying the present living generation and the present Union party were more thoroughly devoted to that Constitution than any generation that ever lived under it. He would contend also that sacred as was the Constitution, the nation was not its slave. "We ought to have it distinctly understood by friends and enemies that while we love that instrument we will maintain it, and will, with undoubted certainty, put to death friend or foe who undertakes to trample it under foot; yet, beyond a doubt, we will reserve the right to alter it to suit ourselves from time to time and from generation to generation. [Applause.]"

As to slavery the venerable Kentuckian was equally crystalline. "I join myself with those who say, away with it forever; and I fervently pray God that the day may come when throughout the whole land every man may be as free as you are, and as capable of enjoying regulated liberty."

After a prayer was offered, Thad Stevens took the floor and objected to the admission of delegates from States "in secession." He had no doubt "excellent men . . . from such States" were present, but protested against any "recognition of the right of States which now belong to the Southern Confederacy to be represented here, and, of course, to be represented in the Electoral College."

Then arose Horace Maynard of Tennessee, tall and spare, his long black hair, high brow, and strong straight nose having brought him the nickname of "The Narragansett Indian." Maynard's high-pitched voice measured out sentences, punctuated by gestures with a forearm and a quivering index finger; he carried to every seat in the theatre. His eyes grew wet with tears and many in the audience sobbed aloud as he pictured the conditions of his people and faltered at voicing their desolation. "For you that drink in the cool breezes of the Northern air, it is easy to rally to the flag. . . . But we represent those who have stood in the very furnace of the rebellion, those who have met treason eye to eye, and face to face, and fought from the beginning for the support of the flag and the honor of our country. [Great applause.]" Outnumbered and often outlawed, they had seen their sons conscripted in the Confederate Army, their property confiscated, homes burned, brutal guerrilla raids, imprisonment and execution of leaders, and all the woe of a land where contending armies sweep back and forth. A storm of applause swept the main floor and galleries when Maynard finished. He had said to begin with that he was speaking not so much for the political rights of his delegation as of the heroic suffering, loyalty, and patriotism of the hundreds of thousands of Unionists in the South.

At the evening session the speech of the permanent chairman of the convention, ex-Governor William Dennison of Ohio, was "drab and meaningless," according to one reporter, and if you believed others it was "brief and eloquent." He too alluded to the forthcoming unanimous nomination for the Presidency of the United States. The nomination would go to "the wise and good man whose unselfish devotion to the country, in the administration of the Government has secured to him not only the admiration, but the warmest affection of every friend of constitutional liberty. [Applause.]"

The lean and stubborn Parson Brownlow of Tennessee, just out of a sickbed, was given the floor near adjournment, after the appointment of organizational committees. So "rash an act" as excluding the Tennessee delegation would be a recognition of secession, he warned, with thrusts that won him the crowd. "We don't recognize it in Tennessee. [Applause.] We deny that we are out. [Applause.] We deny that we have been out. [Applause.] We maintain that a minority first voted us out, and then a majority whipped the minority out of the State with bayonets." And while he rattled along in a stump speech the words tumbled from Brownlow that "as an inducement not to exclude our delegation . . . we may take it into our heads, before the thing is over, to present a candidate from that State in rebellion for the second office in the gift of the people." This first reference to Governor Andrew Johnson of Tennessee as a possible vice-presidential candidate brought applause from the galleries. "We have a man down there," continued Brownlow, "whom it has been my good luck and bad fortune to fight untiringly and perseveringly for the last twenty-five years—Andrew Johnson. [Applause.] For the first time, in the Providence of God, three years ago we got together on the same platform, and we are fighting the devil, Tom Walker and Jeff Davis side by side. [Applause.]"

The next morning, besides the naming of a candidate for President the convention program had three items: (1) a decision as to which contested delegations should have seats and on what conditions; (2) the framing of a platform; (3) the naming of a candidate for the Vice-Presidency.

The booming bass voice of Chairman Preston King of the Credentials Committee reported its majority recommendation that the "Radical Union" delegation from Missouri be seated. Having thus reported, King joined with Jim Lane in fighting the acceptance of the report. King and Lane would amend the report so as to seat both the "Radical Union" delegates and a set of Blair delegates from Missouri. Dr. Breckinridge of Kentucky rose to protest that the favored delegates came from a Missouri party supporting Lincoln only "on the condition that the President of the United States will agree to be brow-beaten by them." The convention then voted 440 to 4 in favor of seating the Missouri radicals. The vote meant that a convention overwhelmingly committed to Lincoln was giving seats to a set of delegates who had obstructed and harassed Lincoln the year before to the point where he said he was "tormented" by them. They were the fellows of whom he had remarked to Hay they were "the unhandiest devils in the world to deal with" though after all "their faces are set Zionwards." They were welcomed into the convention almost unanimously, while the Blair delegates from Missouri were frozen out.

What of the delegations from Virginia, Tennessee, Louisiana, Florida, Arkansas? The majority report of the Credentials Committee said they should have seats in the convention without the right to vote. What would the convention do about the report? The convention might indicate where it stood on the issue between Lincoln on the one hand and Sumner and Stevens on the other, Lincoln holding that no State could secede and therefore none had seceded, while Sumner and Stevens held that in seceding each State had committed suicide and would again have to be admitted to the Union in order to be a State. Of course the issue was not clear-cut, because of the fact that some of the delegations came from States where a process of reconstruction had begun and the Union Government had started to re-establish its authority. For the delegates from these States an argument could be made.

By a series of roll calls the convention sifted what it wanted. Only the delegates from South Carolina were thrown out entirely, "a swindle," as Hay in his diary had predicted when they had called on the President. The Virginia and Florida delegations were admitted to seats with no right to vote. Arkansas and Louisiana were given seats and the right to vote. By 310 to 151 the convention gave Tennessee delegates seats with the right to vote, this being welcome to the boomers of Andrew Johnson for Vice-President.

The report of the Platform Committee was offered by its chairman, Henry J. Raymond, a confidant of Lincoln, editor of the *New York Times*, the one Manhattan newspaper then unfailing in co-operation with Lincoln. The platform resolved in favor of the war, the Union, the Constitution; pledged itself to everything possible to quell the then raging rebellion; no compromise with rebels; a deathblow at the gigantic evil of slavery through a constitutional prohibition of it; thanks and everlasting gratitude to the soldiers and sailors of the Union cause and promise of "ample and permanent provision for those of their survivors who have received disabling and honorable wounds in the service of the country"; approval and applause of "the practical wisdom, the unselfish patriotism and unswerving fidelity to the Constitution and the principles of American liberty, with which Abraham Lincoln has discharged, under circumstances of unparalleled difficulty, the great duties and responsibilities of the Presidential office," and full confidence in his future determinations; justice and protection to all men employed in the Union armies "without regard to distinction of color"; liberal and just encouragement of foreign immigration to "this nation, the asylum of the oppressed of all nations"; speedy construction of the railroad to the Pacific Coast; inviolate redemption of the public debt, economy and responsibility in public expenditures, vigorous and just taxation.

Two planks of the platform had hidden meanings. One of them approved "the position taken by the Government that the people of the United States can never regard with indifference the attempt of any European Power to overthrow by force or to supplant by fraud the institutions of any Republican Government on the Western continent." This was a compromise with radicals who wished to censure the President's policy in Mexico. What the radicals accepted was a statement that the Government favored the Monroe Doctrine.

Another plank was a thrust at Blair in the Cabinet—and might even be taken as a reflection on whichever Cabinet member anyone believed he had a case against. It was a plank to be called on in the future: "We deem it essential to the general welfare that harmony should prevail in the National Councils, and we regard as worthy of public confidence and official trust those only who cordially endorse the principles proclaimed in these resolutions, and which should characterize the administration of the government."

The radical mood was seen in a pledge of the first plank for "bringing to the punishment due to their crimes the Rebels and traitors arrayed against" the Government. Lincoln had often let it be known that he favored the killing of rebels until the rebellion was put down. Beyond that he was completely reserved. The platform indicated criminal trials and hanging of Confederate leaders if the North won the war. This part of the platform Lincoln would have revised or deleted. As it stood it could not belong among his platform views.

The platform adopted and out of the way, nominations were in order for President of the United States. A clamor arose. "Sundry well-meaning persons were almost ready to fly at one another's throats in their anxiety to have the honor of nominating Abraham Lincoln for the presidency," wrote Noah Brooks, who was there partly as an unofficial observer for Lincoln. "As one sat on the platform, looking over the tempest-tossed assemblage, watching . . . the frantic efforts of a score of men to climb over one another's heads, as it were . . . one could not help thinking of the frequently repeated assertion of certain small politicians that Lincoln could not possibly be nominated by that convention."

Foremost in claiming the floor were Cameron of Pennsylvania, Governor William Stone of Iowa, Burton C. Cook of Illinois, and a California dele-

John Cochrane

Benjamin Gratz Brown (*above*)
George Washington Julian (*below*)

Jessie Benton Frémont

John Charles Frémont

NORTHERN RADICAL OPPONENTS OF LINCOLN

From the Meserve collection

Henry Jarvis Raymond
(The *New York Times*)

James Gordon Bennett
(The *New York Herald*)

From the Meserve collection

John Albion Andrew
(The Commonwealth of Massachusetts)

Harriet Beecher Stowe
(*Uncle Tom's Cabin*)

From the author's collection

gate, Thompson Campbell, who in days long gone had known Lincoln in Springfield, Illinois, and was now afire to name him for President. Campbell had been told from high up that this privilege would be accorded him, but before he could get the floor Cameron had sent to the clerk's desk a written resolution with a demand it be read. It was. The convention heard a call for the unanimous renomination of Abraham Lincoln of Illinois and Hannibal Hamlin of Maine.

"No sooner had the clerk finished reading the resolution than a frightful clamor shook the hall," wrote Brooks. "Almost every delegate was on his feet objecting or hurrahing. . . . For a few minutes pandemonium reigned, and in the midst of it Cameron stood with his arms folded, grimly smiling, regarding with composure the storm that he had raised. After the turmoil had spent itself . . . Raymond of New York, in an incisive, clear-cut speech, advocated nomination by a call of States. He urged that as entire unanimity in the choice of the presidential candidate was expected, the moral effect would be better if no noisy acclamation were made, which would give slanderers an opportunity to say that the nomination was rushed through."

Raymond's resolution passed. The applause over it was just fading away when Burton C. Cook of Illinois mounted a settee and shouted with a glad hosanna: "Illinois again presents to the loyal people of this nation, for President of the United States, Abraham Lincoln. God bless him." Another roar of applause swept the theatre, and Governor Stone of Iowa seconded Cook's nomination. But Thompson Campbell of California, the delegate who had known Lincoln in Springfield in the days long gone, refused to be thrust aside by parliamentary tricks, leaped on a settee and addressed the chair amid unceasing interruptions of "Meeouw! meeouw!" and cries of "No speeches!" "Get down!" "Dry up!" "Call the roll!" Campbell would neither get down nor dry up. He seemed oath-bound to nominate Lincoln that day. "In the midst of the confusion," noted Brooks, "Campbell, who was a tall, spare man with a saturnine visage and tremendous lung power, kept on speaking in dumb show, wildly gesticulating, not a word of his speech being audible. Campbell was evidently beside himself with rage and disappointment; but those nearest him finally succeeded in coaxing him off his perch, and he sat down sullen with anger."

The roll call began. Maine announced 16 votes for Lincoln. New Hampshire, coming next, tried a little speechmaking but was choked off with cries of "No speeches!" From then on each State announced its vote without oratory. One by one the undivided delegations threw in their ballots for Lincoln. Only one snag broke the smooth and orderly unanimity. The Missouri delegation, its chairman John F. Hume announced, was under positive instructions to cast its 22 votes for Ulysses S. Grant; he and his associates would support any nominee of the convention, but they must obey orders from home. "This caused a sensation," wrote Brooks, "and growls of disapproval arose from all parts of the convention." Before the result of the balloting was announced Hume of Missouri moved that the nomination of Lincoln be declared unanimous. This under the rules could not be done until the secretary read the results: 484 votes for Lincoln, 22 for Grant.

Missouri then changed its vote, and the secretary gave the grand total of 506 for Lincoln.

A storm of cheers was let loose, lasting many minutes, dying down and then flaring up again. "Men hurrahed, embraced one another," noted Brooks, "threw up their hats, danced in the aisles or on the platform, jumped on the benches, waved flags, yelled, and committed every possible extravagance. . . . One of the most comical sights I beheld was that of Horace Maynard and Henry J. Raymond alternately hugging each other and shaking hands. . . . And when the big brass band burst forth with 'Hail, Columbia!' the racket was so intolerable that I involuntarily looked up to see if the roof . . . were not lifted. . . . When quiet was restored . . . the band struck up 'Yankee Doodle' . . . and another torrent of enthusiasm broke forth."

The chairman now read a telegram from the Secretary of War that victory had perched on the banners of Hunter's army in the Shenandoah, routing the Confederates beyond Staunton. Again the convention went into a season of cheers. The Reverend T. H. Pearne of Oregon read a telegram from his State that the Union party had swept everything in a general election the day before. Another roar belched from the vocal guns of the convention.

The hilarity over, they settled down to nominating a candidate for Vice-President. Cameron presented, under instructions of his State, he said, the name of Hannibal Hamlin. A New York delegate "in behalf of a portion" of his delegation proposed Daniel S. Dickinson of New York. Indiana, under instructions of its State convention, offered the name of Governor Andrew Johnson of Tennessee. Horace Maynard seconded this, saying Johnson "in the furnace of treason" would stand by the convention's declarations "as long as his reason remains unimpaired, and as long as breath is given him by his God."

On roll call Maine was solid for Hamlin. The number of votes that Johnson had picked up in other New England States was surprising. Connecticut plopped solid its 12 for Johnson. Massachusetts split with 17 for Dickinson, 3 for Hamlin, 2 for Butler. What would New York do? The chairman was solemn, the convention too, as the tally was read: Johnson 32, Dickinson 28, Hamlin 6. Had Seward, Weed, Raymond, been at work, and with whom were they in league and how far had this thing been worked out? Delegates pondered. Louisiana split evenly between Dickinson and Johnson. Arkansas threw its 10 votes to Johnson. Tennessee's 15 went likewise. The Missouri radicals gladly pinned a rose on Ben Butler with 20 votes, though 2 put in for Johnson. The final total was shocking and almost unbelievable to the Hamlin men: Johnson 200, Dickinson 108, Hamlin 150.

Kentucky now announced that its complimentary vote of 21 for its

General Rousseau and 1 for Tod would be thrown to Johnson. Oregon and Kansas followed for Johnson. A wave of applause came with Cameron handing Pennsylvania's 52 to Johnson. As New Jersey swung into line Senator Morrill of Maine, Hamlin's manager, who the night before had been publicly and privately confident of Hamlin's chances, changed the vote of Maine in favor of the Tennessee tailor described that day as "the noblest Roman in the country." The convention secretary announced the result of the first and only ballot: Johnson 494, Dickinson 27, Hamlin 9.

What had happened? Practically all the political forecasters, friendly and hostile, had taken it as a matter of course that Hamlin would be renominated, that the 1860 ticket would be named again. Who had brought this change with results that looked as though a spontaneous upheaval had dictated Johnson as Lincoln's running mate? The croaker and inveterate gossip Gurowski wished that he knew and of this matter and others wrote that week: "Find out how many bargains were made in advance, how many promissory notes were delivered and similar facts, and the true character of that convention would be understood, and the people would see how it was cheated out of its trust."

To what extent had Lincoln's hand moved to pick Johnson for a running mate? Nicolay would answer that. He would point first to Leonard Swett, Lincoln's old associate and confidant who had helped manage the 1860 campaign. From Swett had come a telegram to Delegate B. C. Cook of Illinois urging the Illinois delegation to go for Joseph Holt of Kentucky. And Cook had buttonholed Nicolay and asked confidentially whether Swett was all right and whether in urging Holt, Swett was reflecting the wishes of the President. Cook was "suspicious that Swett may be untrue to Lincoln." This information Nicolay relayed to Lincoln through Hay, saying Cook wanted to know "whether the President has any preference, either personally or on the score of policy; or whether he wishes not even to interfere by a confidential intimation." Nicolay in this letter urged Hay, "Please get this information for me, if possible."

Hay took the letter to the President, who endorsed it in writing: "Swett is unquestionably all right. Mr. Holt is good man, but I had not heard or thought of him for V.P. . . . Can not interfere about platform. Convention must judge for itself."

Nicolay took this instruction and communicated it, he said, "to the President's most intimate friends in the Convention," not naming the friends. Nicolay believed that "therefore with minds absolutely untrammeled by even any knowledge of the President's wishes the Convention went about its work of selecting his associate on the ticket." Johnson's nomination Nicolay would chiefly ascribe to "the general impression, in and out of the Convention, that it would be advisable to select as a candidate for the Vice-Presidency a war Democrat."

Noah Brooks had his impression. The night before the convention he held a long conversation with the President, who, he wrote, "requested me to come to him when I should return from Baltimore, and bring him the odd bits of political gossip that I might pick up . . . and which, as he said, would not get into the newspapers." Brooks hoped to see Hamlin renominated, and of this he wrote: "I . . . had anxiously given Mr. Lincoln many opportunities to say whether he preferred the renomination of the Vice-President; but he was craftily and rigidly non-committal, knowing, as he did, what was in my mind concerning Mr. Hamlin. He would refer to the matter only in the vaguest phrase, as, 'Mr. Hamlin is a very good man,' or, 'You, being a New Englander, would naturally like to see Mr. Hamlin renominated; and you are quite right,' and so on. . . . He could not be induced to express any opinion on the subject of the selection of a candidate for vice-president. He did go so far as to say that he hoped that the convention would declare in favor of the constitutional amendment abolishing slavery. . . . But beyond that, nothing."

And was the President under the surface really for the renomination of Hamlin? Brooks would answer Yes. He went to the White House after the convention, entertained the President with a recital of "doings of which he had not previously heard," and he quoted the President as then saying, "Some of our folks [referring, as I believed, to Republican leaders] had expressed the opinion that it would be wise to take a War Democrat as candidate for vice-president, and that, if possible, a border-State man should be the nominee." To Brooks, Lincoln seemed satisfied with the final result; he said, "Andy Johnson, I think, is a good man." This to Brooks was the President's cheerful acceptance of an inevitable result, Brooks writing: "Nevertheless, I have always been confident that Lincoln, left to himself, would have chosen . . . the old ticket of 1860—Lincoln and Hamlin. . . . It is reasonable to suppose that he had resolved to leave the convention entirely free in its choice of a candidate for the second place on the ticket."

In writing his impressions of Lincoln and the Baltimore convention Brooks for some reason known to himself omitted the circumstances underlying what he wrote from Washington on March 11 of '64, published in the *Sacramento Union* April 11 of '64. Then Brooks set forth that the coon up a tree cried, "Don't shoot, I'll come down," and descended gracefully before a shot was fired. This coon, wrote Brooks in this news letter, "has successors nowadays and one is Vice-President Hamlin, who has been using his influence against Lincoln wherever practicable, but who has just authorized a Portland paper to say that he is in favor of Lincoln's renomination."

Burton C. Cook of Illinois, on seeing Lincoln's noncommittal endorsement of Nicolay's letter, had suspected the President might have some wish in the matter that could not be committed to writing. Cook took a train for Washington and interviewed the President. What he learned through oral statement from the President was merely the same as what the President had written to Nicolay. Lincoln told Cook he was "particularly anxious" not to make known his preference. Cook's conclusion, however, was that Hamlin was Lincoln's "favorite" for the nomination. Governor Austin Blair of Michigan also took a train for Washington to satisfy himself regarding a hotel-lobby rumor of Lincoln picking Johnson for Vice-

President. The Michigan Governor before returning to the convention at Baltimore had extracted nothing more definite than Cook or Noah Brooks had got from the President. Nicolay learned of Indiana, Illinois, and California delegates also calling on the President about his choice for Vice-President. To each he was cordial—and gave them nothing specific to guide them.

If other actors in the scene should have their words taken at anywhere near face value, however, Lincoln had in the spring of '64, for reasons that seemed to him vital and formidable, decided on someone else than Hamlin for a running mate and for the awful work that would fall to whoever would step into Lincoln's place in the event of his death. Fate was in the air, and immense hazards lurked in the question of who should supersede the amiable and solid Yankee Hamlin.

Lincoln's first choice was the most dramatic rogue in the American political scene, if Simon Cameron and the rogue himself should be credited. In the spring of '64, according to Cameron: "It was the desire of Lincoln, and also of Stanton . . . that Butler should run as the candidate for Vice-President. I was called into consultation and heartily endorsed the scheme. Accordingly Lincoln sent me on a mission to Fort Monroe to see General Butler, and to say to him that it was his [Lincoln's] request that he [Butler] should allow himself to run as second on the ticket. I, accompanied by William H. Armstrong, afterward a member of Congress, did visit General Butler and made the tender according to instructions. To our astonishment, Butler refused to agree to the proposition. He said there was nothing in the Vice-Presidency."

According to Butler himself, he had only three weeks before turned down an offer from Chase emissaries to run on a ticket of Chase for President and Butler for Vice-President. Butler wrote that his own words in reply to Cameron were: "Please say to Mr. Lincoln that while I appreciate with the fullest sensibilities his act of friendship and the high compliment he pays me, yet I must decline. Tell him that I said laughingly that with the prospects of a campaign before me I would not quit the field to be Vice-President even with himself as President. Ask him what he thinks I have done to deserve to be punished at forty-six years of age by being made to sit as presiding officer of the Senate and listen to debates more or less stupid in which I could take no part or say a word." Cameron took Butler's reply back to Lincoln, who, said Cameron, "seemed to regret General Butler's decision." In Cameron's judgment "Mr. Hamlin never had a serious chance to become the Vice-Presidential candidate after Mr. Lincoln's renomination was assured."

Lamon, when asked whether Lincoln had left the choice of Vice-President entirely with the Baltimore convention, was to answer that the President preferred a Southern man, seeing Johnson as the most expedient choice. Lamon was to say that the President sent for Swett before the convention met, and he was present when the President surprised Swett by saying another man than Hamlin should be nominated for the Vice-

Presidency, a proposition to which Swett replied: "Lincoln, if it were known in New England that you are in favor of leaving Hamlin off the ticket it would raise the devil among the Yankees [Swett was a Maine-born Yankee], and it would raise a bumble-bee's nest about your ears that would appall the country. . . . Your tardiness in issuing your Emancipation Proclamation and your liberal reconstruction policy . . . these people think two great blunders of your administration." Lincoln produced arguments. Swett went to the convention and joined Cameron and others in working for Johnson. Nor was this all. Lamon was to further say that Swett asked Mr. Lincoln, as he was leaving the White House, whether he was authorized to use Mr. Lincoln's name in his efforts at the convention. Mr. Lincoln's reply was: "No; I will address a letter to Lamon here embodying my views, which you, McClure, and other friends may use if it be found absolutely necessary. Otherwise, it may be better that I should not appear actively on this stage of the theater."

Furthermore, Lamon was to say: "The letter was written, and I took it to the Convention with me. It was not used, as there was no occasion for its use, and it was afterward returned to Mr. Lincoln at his request. Mr. Lincoln was beset before the Convention by the friends of the Hamlin interest for his opinion and preference for Vice-President. To such he invariably dodged the question, sometimes saying, 'It perhaps would not become me to interfere with the will of the people,' always evading a direct answer." Lamon had his views as to whether the President was in this lacking in candor. "The success of the party and the safety of the Union were the paramount objects that moved him. He did not, by suppressing the truth to those whom he thought had no right to cross-question him, purpose conveying a false impression. If this is to be construed as duplicity, be it so; he was still 'Honest Old Abe,' and he thought the end justified the means."

Whether Lincoln favored Hamlin or Johnson in the days immediately preceding the convention was indicated in John Hay's diary entry for June 5 of '64. On that day Hay went to see Lamon, who had the day before hurt himself badly in a fall from his carriage to the pavement. "I . . . found him bruised but plucky," wrote Hay. "Says he intends to go to Baltimore tomorrow. Says he feels inclined to go for Cameron for Vice-Pres[t] on personal grounds. Says he thinks Lincoln rather prefers Johnson or some War Democrat as calculated to give more strength to the ticket." This could hardly mean anything else than that Lincoln for reasons of his own had decided that Hamlin was not the man, that he was willing Lamon should be for Cameron at that particular hour, and that in so far as he was naming anyone, it was Johnson. Lamon was the man Lincoln had sent to notify the Governor of South Carolina that the Federal Government intended to provision the garrison of Fort Sumter in April of '61 and Lamon was the man Lincoln chose to introduce him for the Gettysburg speech in November of '63 and Lamon was in June of '64 not likely to be the man to whom Lincoln would give a mistaken impression about who should run for the Vice-Presidency.

S. Newton Pettis, a Pennsylvania delegate from Meadville, was to enter the discussion later and say of the day the Baltimore convention was organizing: "I called upon Mr. Lincoln in his study and stated that I called especially to ask him whom he desired put on the ticket with him as Vice-President. He leaned forward and in a low but distinct tone of voice said, 'Governor Johnson of Tennessee.'" That was all. In two brief sentences Mr. Pettis told of his extracting from Lincoln what no other unsent-for caller had been told. Why Mr. Pettis should be singled out for such a confidence he did not bother to explain. The President in speaking "leaned forward," said Mr. Pettis, as though he would on the other hand have noted it had the President leaned backward. Also the President supplied the information "in a low but distinct tone of voice." That is, Mr. Pettis could testify that for sure the President hadn't hollered "Governor Johnson of Tennessee!" at him. At a later time Mr. Pettis thrust on Hamlin the information that Lincoln was for Johnson and that Lincoln had so told Pettis before the Baltimore convention. Hamlin hadn't asked Pettis about it or led up to it in any way. But Pettis felt called on to blab what it seemed nobody else had cared to pour into Hamlin's ear. Hamlin wearily sighed. "Judge Pettis, I am sorry you told me that." Pettis was to make public a letter quoting Hamlin as saying, "Mr. L.[incoln] evidently became alarmed about his reëlection and changed his position. That is all I care to say." But a son of Hamlin said that he heard from his father's lips a repudiation of Pettis and what had been written to Pettis. And though Pettis was to hold office as Congressman, judge, foreign Minister, what he had to say about Lincoln leaning forward and in a low but distinct voice saying "Governor Johnson of Tennessee" had a fishy savor. It was too easy, short, offhand, said Nicolay.

More circumstantial and more credible was the story of Alexander K. McClure, editor of the *Chambersburg Repository*, superintendent of the draft in Pennsylvania, member of the State senate, chairman of its committee on military affairs, and party lieutenant of Governor Curtin, who headed one faction of the Republicans of Pennsylvania, and Cameron the other. These factions about equally divided the Republican strength of their State and usually spoke to each other in a language of tomahawks and scalps. Only the tact and sagacity of Lincoln had held the party together in an unbroken front in Pennsylvania during the war, many commentators said. Lincoln refereed their disputes and shared patronage carefully between them. McClure as an editor to whom politics was the breath of his nostrils on occasion had been called in by Lincoln who sought information or might have an errand for McClure.

One May day of '64 McClure had a telegram from Lincoln to come to Washington. As McClure rode the cars toward the national capital the inexorable process of drafting fresh levies of troops to replace losses in the field was proceeding ruthlessly over the country, the war costing almost

$2.000,000 a day and the end not in sight, Grant bloodily pounding Lee in Virginia, and the opposition to Lincoln holding great mass meetings to express thanks to Grant for victories. In their interview Lincoln remarked, according to McClure, "I don't quite forget that I was nominated for President in a convention that was two-thirds for the other fellow." What Lincoln asked specifically was that McClure, already chosen a delegate to the Baltimore convention from his home district, should arrange to have the Republican State Convention name him, McClure, one of the four delegates at large to the Baltimore convention. Cameron had written to the President that he would be a delegate at large, the President informed McClure, adding that while he had no question of Cameron's fidelity, he thought it most desirable that if Cameron was a delegate at large McClure should be one with him. "He was most importunate on the subject and finally said, 'I think you can accomplish it, and I want you to try.' "

McClure stopped off at Harrisburg, talked with a Cameron organization man, George Bergner, and learned that "the old man," meaning Cameron, wanted to be a delegate at large to Baltimore but didn't like the idea of sitting so near Curtin when they were not on speaking terms. McClure and Bergner agreed that "we were now all for Lincoln," and on McClure's suggestion Bergner stepped over to Cameron's house and came back in a few minutes saying it was fixed and that every Cameron man in the State convention would heartily support McClure for delegate at large. McClure then saw Governor Curtin and explained what was happening, and Curtin "insisted that the plan should be carried out."

McClure was mystified as to what special purpose Lincoln had in view. The solution came when three days before the Baltimore convention, the President again telegraphed him to come to Washington. In this second interview, wrote McClure: "The President startled me by stating that he desired me to support Andrew Johnson for Vice-President. . . . I did not then know that Cameron had been taken into the confidence of Lincoln several months before, that Cameron was present when it was finally decided to make Johnson the candidate for Vice-President. . . . Lincoln doubtless knew that I would readily accede to his request to vote for Johnson, and as the movement required the severest discretion, he permitted no one of those to whom he confided his purpose to know of others whom he had consulted. He knew that Cameron was for Johnson at the time he insisted upon me becoming a delegate-at-large, and knowing that I would readily accept his advice, he logically argued that with Cameron and myself delegates-at-large representing the two great factions of the State, enlisted in the support of Johnson, the entire delegation would be certain to follow, and it did follow precisely as Lincoln had planned it.

"So cautious was Lincoln in the movement," wrote McClure, "that Cameron did not know of my position on the Vice-Presidency, nor did I know what Cameron's was. Soon after I reached Baltimore to attend the convention Cameron came to my room, pulled the bell, ordered a bottle of wine for the room, and informed me that he had come to discuss the question of the Vice-Presidency. His first proposition was that the Pennsylvania delegation should unite and give a complimentary vote to himself, which he knew I would object to. I told him that we had a very important duty to perform and that we would settle down at once, without playing marbles, to decide what the delegation should do. Cameron said that he was very friendly to Hamlin, but was entirely satisfied that Hamlin could not be renominated, in which I concurred. He next stated that he was inclined to favor Johnson of Tennessee, in which I also concurred. He next proposed that, as he was somewhat embarrassed by his relations with Hamlin in the Senate, we should line up both sides of the delegation, cast a unanimous vote for Hamlin when the State was called, and at the end of the roll-call before the vote was computed, change the vote of the State to a unanimous vote for Johnson, to which I readily concurred. Then for the first time, Cameron knew that I was to support Johnson, and I, for the first time, knew that Cameron was to do the same."

When the plan was put up to the Pennsylvania delegation they lined up for it to a man except Thad Stevens, who turned a cold gray eye on McClure and scowled. "Can't you get a candidate for Vice-President without going down into a damned rebel province for one?" And later as Stevens saw he stood alone he permitted the vote of the State to be cast according to program.

McClure's judgment ran with Lamon's that Lincoln rejected Hamlin not because he hated him and accepted Johnson not because he loved him. "Lincoln was guided in what he did, or what he did not, in planning the great campaign of his life that involved the destiny of the country itself, by the single purpose of making success as nearly certain as possible." McClure saw "not a trace of prejudice or even unfriendliness toward Hamlin" in all that Lincoln said in their second interview. "He was careful to say that he did not desire the nomination of Johnson to gratify any personal preference of his own. He naturally preferred a new man, as Hamlin was not in sympathy with Lincoln personally or with the general policy of his administration."

Two reasons Lincoln gave McClure for Johnson's candidacy. First, he was the ablest of all War Democrats and in a position to draw that element toward the Government. Johnson was then dramatically before the people in his work of restoring his State to the Union. The second reason was with Lincoln stronger and more imperative, according to McClure. "The great peril of the Union was the recognition of the Confederacy by England and France, and every month's delay of the overthrow of the rebellious armies increased the danger. Extraordinary efforts had been made by Lincoln to stimulate the Union sentiment, especially in England, but with only moderate success, and there was no safety from one day to another against a war with England and France that would have been fatal to the success of the Union cause. The only possible way to hinder recognition was to show successful results of the war in restoring the dissevered States to their old allegiance, and Lincoln was firmly convinced that by no other method could the Union sentiment abroad be so greatly inspired and strengthened as by the nomination and election of a representative Southern man to the Vice-Presidency from one of the rebellious States in the very heart of the Confederacy."

Nicolay was to say that McClure misstated the facts, that Lincoln had kept his hand out of the nomination of Johnson, that McClure imputed double-dealing to an honest Chief Magistrate. McClure was to reply that he did not at all accuse Lincoln of deceit or insincerity. "It was quite as much a necessity for Lincoln to conceal his movements for the nomination of Johnson as it was, in his judgment, a necessity for him to nominate a Southern man and a War Democrat. He simply acted with rare sagacity and discretion in his movements, and with fidelity to the country."

Aside from and beyond any personal hand of Lincoln in the matter were the seething hatreds of two peculiar political feuds. Sumner detested Senator Fessenden of Maine for several reasons, though chiefly because Fessenden had a way of plucking Sumner's forensic feathers in Senate debate, sometimes leaving Sumner without a leg of logic to stand on. And the record was plain that when Sumner went to Baltimore it was his dominance over the Massachusetts delegation that split it several ways so word spread that Hamlin's renomination was impossible because even Massachusetts was against him. And Sumner's motive was known definitely. He wanted Hamlin out as Vice-President because then, as he planned, Hamlin would replace Fessenden as Senator from Maine. These slender facts stood evident from many testimonies. The second feud was the old one of the Seward crowd against the field in New York. The theory of Seward's opposition was that if they could nominate Daniel S. Dickinson of New York and elect him as Vice-President, that would make two high places in possession of New York, and two was too many and Seward eventually would have to walk the plank as Secretary of State. This too stood forth from many accounts.

Senator Lot Morrill of Maine, who managed Hamlin's canvass at Baltimore, wrote to Hamlin the day after the convention a terse recital of Machiavellian strategies. "Tuesday morning [the second day of the convention] early I learned from Mr. Weed that gentlemen from the Massachusetts delegation had late the night before called upon their delegation [New York], had said to them that the Massachusetts delegates were opposed to you, and would take the lead for Dickinson. They threw the New York delegation into confusion. Those who had voted for you were willing to go for Dickinson, and upon the representation that New England would not support you, but could not hold their men for Dickinson except upon a new man, and therefore went for Johnson. The Massachusetts delegation had made some revelation to Maryland, New Jersey, Ohio, and other delegations, and the result was that those States changed their support to others. The division of New England was made great use of with Western delegations. . . . I do not doubt but for the movement of Massachusetts you would have gone through. Connecticut was against you, but that would not have damaged us much, as she is generally with New York. Massachusetts intrigued for Dickinson with New York. That broke up the order of things for you. We then were committed to chance. To keep Seward in the Cabinet his friends would take [the] Vice-President out of New York, and went for Johnson, not supposing he would be nominated on [the] first ballot. The Massachusetts delegates are not pleased with the result."

Lot Morrill thus set forth the moving human diagrams that spun in swift confusions to end spelling a ticket: Lincoln and Johnson. Amid those confusions the slightest signals from Lincoln could have brought the result that came. Did Lincoln give those signals and if so, to whom? Could he possibly have been unaware of Sumner's manipulations of the Massachusetts delegation against Hamlin and of the New York fight on Seward with Dickinson as the spearhead? Had he estimated that the longer those operations lasted, the more they would grind down Hamlin's chances, and if he gave the word the detached fractions would join up for Johnson? What would the meager and indirect disclosures of Cameron have lighted had they been enlarged with what he knew further? Was the procedure as simple as McClure related, or did Cameron have an understanding with Lincoln that if the balloting toward the end showed a majority for Hamlin, then Hamlin should have the nomination and Cameron would not reverse the Pennsylvania vote and throw it to Johnson?

To Senator Fessenden one week after the event Cameron wrote, "I strove hard to renominate Hamlin, as well for his own sake as for yours, but failed only because New England, especially Massachusetts, did not adhere to him." Cameron was elusive. So was Swett. Did Swett on his own initiative send to Cook the telegram advising the Illinois delegation to go for Holt? Would Swett at the national capital near Lincoln have sent a telegram breaking Hamlin's chances on his own authority and without a guiding intimation from Lincoln? He had guiding intimations or explicit instructions—what were they? And why in the family of Hamlin was Sumner held most responsible for what happened to Hamlin at Baltimore on June 8 of '64?

One of the Hamlin family wrote that at this time "Mr. Sumner was Mr. Hamlin's personal friend, strange as it may seem" and that "Mr. Hamlin's preference for a seat in the Senate" was known to Mr. Sumner, Mr. Hamlin saying, "I am only the fifth wheel of a coach and can do little for my friends." As a son and a grandson of Hamlin saw it, Sumner took Mr. Hamlin at his word and conceived the plan of retiring Mr. Hamlin from the Vice-Presidency in the expectation that the people of Maine would return Mr. Hamlin to the Senate in '65 in Fessenden's place—Fessenden with whom Sumner's feud was open. "Thus Mr. Sumner figured that he would hit two birds with one stone, as it were. By nominating Dickinson for Vice-President he would drive Seward into private life, and by sending Mr. Hamlin back to the Senate he would get rid of Fessenden." The Hamlin kin quoted a Boston paper: "Sumner was an unsafe man, doing far more harm than good." Taking it by and large, it was an hour when Sumner could have quoted himself, "I am in morals, not politics," and lived to it. But he didn't. He was in morals and politics both.

And while Sumner laid his undercover mine by which he hoped to hoist Seward out of the Cabinet, what was Seward doing? Could anyone who knew Seward picture him unaware and uninformed of the foot tracks of Sumner over the landscape and what the game was that Sumner stalked?

"Largely without their knowledge, Sumner's influence was strong upon his friends both from his own state and elsewhere to persuade them to the choice of Johnson," wrote Anna Laurens Dawes, daughter of Congressman Henry Laurens Dawes. She saw Sumner's hostility and distrust of Fessenden and Fessenden's friend, Hamlin, operating, "while, on the other hand, he [Sumner] greatly admired Johnson, who was just then in so radical a mood as to seize every opportunity to antagonize the President." Miss Dawes believed Sumner well pleased with the nomination of Johnson. She credited one Massachusetts delegate justifying himself to a Hamlin friend: "Do you know what Sumner says? He says he wishes the ticket were turned round, and it was Johnson and Lincoln." Also Miss Dawes wrote of knowing a colleague to whom Sumner "in still less guarded phrase complained that the American people were so deluded as to renominate Lincoln, for the weakest man in the Massachusetts delegation was better qualified to be President." This last was perhaps a distortion of something Sumner had said. His Massachusetts colleague, Henry Wilson, who in feeling traveled close to Frémonters who outrightly hated Lincoln, would in the hour not have hesitated to color with his own temperament something Sumner had said, changing a regret into a disgust.

Did Seward and Lincoln, the two leading masters of political art in the Republican party, talk it over and garnish with anecdotes the entry of Sumner into the deals, dickers, and combinations of candidate-making? They talked it over probably; it was fantastic; but the hour was too dark for any merriment about such realities. They had some sort of an understanding about running Andy Johnson for the Vice-Presidency, probably, and there were several indications that delegates asked Seward who was the man and heard Seward say Johnson was the man and without asking Seward if he spoke for the President, delegates assumed that he did. Seward was joined as with steel to Lincoln on the policy of gentling the South back into the Union through reconstructed States theoretically in law never out of the Union. Johnson incarnated that idea as did no other candidate proposed.

The open influence of the New York and Massachusetts delegations, joined to the quiet though powerful efforts of the President, brought about Johnson's nomination, according to Anna Laurens Dawes. Among Republican leaders, she wrote in a study of Sumner's life, it was "hardly a secret" that "confidential embassies" had sounded different prominent Democrats, among them General Butler and Governor Johnson, "the first refusing curtly, the second eagerly welcoming the suggestion." Lincoln had been among the foremost of those believing that the party should, as it did, call itself National Union instead of Republican, that its ticket should include a Democrat as a sign of loyalty to War Democrats and to draw as many as possible of the wavering Democrats into Union support. "This feeling," wrote Miss Dawes, "he [Lincoln] refused to make public even under the greatest pressure, but it was discussed freely in private conferences, and well known in trusted quarters. . . . This desire of Lincoln was in no sense personal, but a firm conviction that the welfare of the country absolutely required such a course." To what extent Miss Dawes had her information from her able father, who kept himself rather free from extremists of all camps and yet was no outsider in party councils, she did not reveal. Impressions and facts from her father, however, definitely shaped her statements.

The ancient factor of effective oratory had swayed the convention toward Johnson, several observers noted. The most memorable voices were those of the Border State men, Breckinridge, Brownlow, and Maynard. In two speeches Maynard with fierce and moving phrases named Johnson as someone to think about. There was design wrought from some quarter in the staging of these scarred orators for their early roles at the convention. Details were scant in Johnson's secretary, Benjamin C. Truman, writing: "Brownlow and Maynard went to Baltimore at the request of Lincoln and Johnson to promote the nomination [of Johnson]. Forney wrote to Johnson saying that General Sickles would be in Tennessee to canvass Johnson's availability, and that Lincoln, on the whole, preferred Johnson [of Tennessee] first and Holt [of Kentucky] next." Sickles denied that he was sent on any other mission than to survey Johnson's administration as Governor of Tennessee and then report to Lincoln and Seward. Forney as an old Douglas Democrat might have sounded Johnson as to whether he would run if nominated. Johnson's secretary was confused as to just what Forney did write to Johnson. Forney could distill subtle expressions as a letter-writer, and the purport of what he did write Johnson, and whether he assumed to speak for Lincoln, did not become known. That Johnson had a record for courage and personal integrity out of the ordinary was evident: no scandal or shadow trailed with his name at Baltimore. He had walked as a living target so many days in paths where life was cheap that to many he was a little unreal. In the poverty and obscurity of his early days he was compared to Lincoln. In the choice of him by the Baltimore convention was a touch of the unreal, of a guess in twilight and prayers such as fishermen say when violence of wind and water lash a boat and the steersman can only hope.

"Of Andrew Johnson it is enough to say that there is no man in the country, unless it be Mr. Lincoln himself, whom the rebels more cordially hate," said *Harper's Weekly* in June. "He fought them in the Senate, when they counted upon his aid, and he has fought them steadily ever since." Greeley in the *Tribune* saw as "happy" the nomination of Johnson, who had "never wavered or faltered" in the Union cause, a man who would be hanged at noon on the day the Confederates captured him. From various points now was voiced one thought or instinct that had lain behind the framing of the Lincoln-Johnson ticket: it would nationalize the Republican party; no longer would Lincoln stand as the head of a sectional party.

Before Lincoln's policy of reconstruction had become defined Johnson had written to Monty Blair, "I hope the President will not be led to make territories out of the rebellious states." The plan so odious and stench-laden to the radicals, known as "Lincoln's ten-per-cent plan," had only to be announced for Johnson to leap to embrace it. In a speech six months before his nomination for Vice-President Johnson said: "Abraham Lincoln is a honest man and is going to put down this infernal rebellion. He is for a free government and I stand by him. . . . Why this feeling on the part of the leaders of rebellion against Abraham Lincoln? It is because Lincoln is a Democrat in principle; he is for the people and for free government and he rose from the masses." And to his Slave State audience Johnson laid down the propositions: "As for the negro I am for setting him free but at the same time I assert that this is a white man's government. . . . If whites and blacks can't get along together arrangements must be made to colonize the blacks."

At a mass meeting with brass bands and a big crowd jubilating before him on the capitol grounds at Nashville just after his nomination, Johnson said, "Slavery is dead and you must pardon me if I do not mourn over its dead body . . . in the emancipation of the slaves we break down an odious and dangerous aristocracy. I think we are freeing more whites than blacks in Tennessee." From his beginnings in politics Johnson had voiced the poor whites as against the exclusive and propertied aristocracy which for thirty years had ruled the South and controlled at Washington. "This aristocracy," he now said in '64, "hated Mr. Lincoln because he was of humble origin, a railsplitter in early life. . . . If this aristocracy is so violently opposed to being governed by Mr. Lincoln, what in the name of conscience will it do with Lincoln and Johnson, a railsplitter and a tailor?"

Of medium height, a little swarthy of skin, well formed with fine shoulders and a deep chest, Johnson carried a massive head of which Charles Dickens was to write to a son that it was splendidly shaped and that no judge of human nature could look upon Johnson and doubt that he was an extraordinary man. His deep-set and darkly piercing eyes looked at men without fear. The strangest thing about him was just that. He seemed to be afraid of nothing. Weapons and threats had no effect on him. And if an idea, a method of action, or an impulse of depth moved him, he acted on it and stood by it. Physically he trusted the revolver in his right hip pocket and spiritually he had an ego that could rest on a bulwark he called his conscience. He wore clean linen, was almost dainty about his collar and his shirt front, had small hands and feet; but the blandishments of the social set couldn't sway him. His square chin and large mobile mouth had a way. The strut and bluster of Ben Butler was not here, nor the itching palm.

Such a man could hardly escape the faults to go with such excesses of merit. Sometimes he was brave unto stubborn folly. He could wear his hate of the aristocrats and his passion for democracy till it was a pose and an overdone attitude. Johnson could be so overly zealous to stand square and clear on a human issue that important half-lights of it were lost to him. Perhaps only such a man could have been the outstanding, effective, spectacular Unionist of the South. Perhaps only such a man could have been the first to so manage a seceded State that it could give some color of promise to "Lincoln's ten-per-cent plan."

Of the many messages of congratulation that rolled in to Lincoln on his renomination there was none from Johnson. Of the many telegrams and letters that came to Johnson there was none from Lincoln. Each said publicly that the ticket was a good one. But neither sent word to the other that it was pleasant they were running mates. Much was happening. They were in toils. Each had probably asked himself whether he should send such a customary message. And each had given himself answer, and nobody else.

An officious suggestion to Mr. Lincoln that it might be good politics to have Andy Johnson write a radical letter of acceptance, according to the *Chicago Journal* drew from the President the response that it was unnecessary, that Johnson was known to be sufficiently radical. Another anxious inquirer quoted the President: "Don't be concerned, sir; when Andy Johnson was last here he said if it was necessary to carry on the war for thirty years he was for carrying it on."

"Everybody comes back from the Convention tired but sober," wrote Hay in his diary. "Nicolay says it was a very quiet Convention. Little drinking—little quarreling—an earnest intention. . . . They were intolerant of speeches—remorselessly coughed down the crack orators of the party."

A newsman, Horace White, from a wire in the convention hall had sent Lincoln the first message of congratulation on renomination. This and a telegram from Nicolay with the news arrived at the War Department telegraph office. No one bothered to rush them over to Lincoln at the White House. It was assumed that he was keeping in touch with Baltimore. When the President after a time strolled into the telegraph office Major Eckert congratulated him. His face lighted elusively. "What! Am I renominated?" Operator Tinker showed him Nicolay's telegram. "Send it right over to the Madam. She will be more interested than I am."

When the news of the nomination of Johnson for Vice-President came through, according to Operator Tinker, Lincoln looked at the telegram and in a soliloquizing way said slowly, "Well, I thought possibly he might be the man; perhaps he is the best man, but—" And rising from his chair, he walked from the room. Operator Tinker was afterwards sure that he caught the exact words and that his memory served him correctly. Tinker's derivation was that the President would have preferred Hamlin. The enigmatic "but," however, could be construed forty ways.

A committee called the next day. Dennison of Ohio spoke notifying Lincoln of his nomination, and predicted "triumphant election" to follow.

The President answered: "I will neither conceal my gratification nor restrain the expression of my gratitude. . . . I know no reason to doubt that I shall accept the nomination tendered; and yet perhaps I should not declare definitely before reading and considering what is called the platform." He would emphatically approve of a constitutional prohibition of slavery. Unconditional Union men, North and South, perceived its importance. "Let us labor to give it legal form and practical effect."

To serenading Ohio delegates in the evening Lincoln said he was much obliged even though "the hardest of all speeches I have to answer is a serenade," for "I never know what to say on these occasions." They were doing him "this kindness," he supposed, in connection with the action of the Baltimore convention, with which of course he was satisfied. "What we want, still more than Baltimore conventions or presidential elections, is success under General Grant." And he proposed three rousing cheers for Grant and his men.

The National Grand Council of the Union League had met in Baltimore during the convention and adopted a platform similar to that of the convention, with an added plank. Considering the wealth and respectability of the Union League clubs over the country, this added plank was significant, declaring as it did, in key with the Cleveland Radical Democracy, for confiscation of the property of the "rebels." The propertied class of the North, it would seem, in part favored expropriation and obliteration of the propertied class of the South. The National Grand Council endorsed the Lincoln and Johnson ticket, and to a Union League committee the President said he could not take the nomination as a personal compliment. "I have not permitted myself, gentlemen, to conclude that I am the best man in the country; but I am reminded in this connection of a story of an old Dutch farmer who remarked to a companion once that 'it was not best to swap horses when crossing a stream.' "

In handshaking with the Union League committee Lincoln was particularly interested in Henry G. Blasdel of Nevada, candidate for governor out there. Blasdel stood six feet five inches in height.

The convention's formal letter of notification, written by George William Curtis of the Harper publications in New York, was lavish as to the President and his people. "Amid the bitter taunts of eager friends and the fierce denunciation of enemies, now moving too fast for some, now too slowly for others, they have seen you throughout this tremendous contest patient, sagacious, just; leaning upon the heart of the great mass of the people, and satisfied to be moved by its mighty pulsations." The President replied briefly that he gratefully accepted the nomination, that he approved the platform, that he was especially gratified the soldier and the seaman were not forgotten by the convention, and would subscribe himself "Your obedient servant."

The convention platform and the President's public addresses had projected above all other immediate issues the need of a Constitutional Amendment to prohibit slavery. But one week after the convention adjourned, when the House of Representatives took up a joint resolution to that effect, 64 members voted Nay, and it failed for lack of a two-thirds majority. The Nay votes were all Democratic and forecast a campaign issue.

Normain Doane got his furlough from a Washington hospital on an

THE HARDEST SHELL YET.
Jeff Davis's breakfast spoilt by a shot from Baltimore.

Harper's Weekly sees Jeff Davis shaken by the Baltimore nomination

application reading: "Dear Sir: The Union is saved. Hurrah! Make room in Abraham's bosom. My wife has twins. Both boys! Do please grant me a furlough for twenty or thirty days to go to Fort Wayne, Indiana, to christen 'em Abe and Andy; and besides, I would like to see if they look like me."

Rumor credited a German trooper in the Army of the Potomac with saying: "I goes for Fader Abraham. Fader Abraham, he likes the soldier-boy. Ven he serves tree years he gives him four hundred tollar, and reënlists him von veteran. Now Fader Abraham, he serve four years. We reënlist him four years more, and make *von veteran of him.*"

In Middletown, Connecticut, a clergyman lighted his front door with a transparency quoting from Genesis 22:15: "The angel of the Lord called unto Abraham out of heaven a second time."

The *Troy Times* was naïve. "If Mr. Lincoln has fallen into errors and made mistakes—if he has done some things that he ought not to have done, and left undone some things that he ought to have done, who that was ever called upon to do so much has erred so little?"

Hannibal Hamlin at a ratification meeting in Bangor, Maine, three days after the Baltimore convention repeated his belief that the President was "a man of eminent abilities" who would "lead the nation out of its present difficulty and plant it on the eternal principle of liberty." Hamlin spoke of Lincoln as one "whom the people loved."

The *New York World* spoke for August Belmont and many wealthy and respectable Democrats on June 9. "The age of statesmen is gone; the age of rail-splitters and tailors, of buffoons, boors and fanatics, has succeeded. . . . In a crisis of the most appalling magnitude, requiring statesmanship of the highest order, the country is asked to consider the claims of two ignorant, boorish, third-rate backwoods lawyers, for the highest stations in the government. Such nominations, in such a conjuncture, are an insult to the common-sense of the people. God save the Republic!" Later in the month the *World* mentioned an "eminent divine," without naming him, as having departed abruptly from a call on Lincoln, sickened with "low and obscene stories," exclaiming, "We have a buffoon and a gawk for President." To those who wished to know the character of the Chief Magistrate the *World* counseled: "Ask the gentlemen who fêted Mr. Lincoln in New York and escorted him to the clubs on his visit here [en route to inauguration in '61]. Ask the Republican who left the room where the President was recounting experiences of his early life rather than that his ears should be defiled with the echoes of such filthiness. Ask the staff officers who galloped behind the President when he visited the battlefield of Antietam and who increased their distance from him rather than listen longer to the low nigger song of 'Picayune Butler' which Mr. Lincoln called on Marshal Lamon to sing as he rode." And there was more of this. The tone of the campaign was being set.

"I, A. Lincoln, hereby nominate myself as a candidate for reëlection," said the *Chicago Times* of June 11, later in the month reprinting a *Richmond Examiner* article which said, "If either Grant or Butler had taken Richmond before the Baltimore Convention, then Grant or Butler would have been nominated," and further related: "The *New York Times*, Lincoln's organ, took care to publish at length a dismal account of the bloody defeat inflicted on the Federals June 3 [Cold Harbor], and to express the opinion that it was a most disastrous affair. This was true; but the *Times* did not state it because it was true. The *Times* stated it notwithstanding that it was true, in order to lower Grant's stock in the convention, just in the nick of time. Lincoln and his gang have been lucky." The high enthusiasm of the *New York Times* over the Lincoln renomination needed correction, in the view of the *Detroit Free Press*, which emitted several sentences of this tone: "The *New York Times* gets into a lather of delight on Old Abe's renomination, and makes a perfect diarrhoea over its pages to show that rail-splitters and flatboatmen are the true benefactors of the race, and that a triumph of thieves and public plunderers and shoddyites will continue the millennium, a sample of which has been given us during the past three years' sway of fraud, corruption and other Lincolnisms." Various anti-Lincoln journals, including the *Chicago Times*, reprinted a long editorial from the *Richmond Dispatch*. "We say of Old Abe it would be impossible to find such another ass in the United States; and therefore, we say let him stay."

Hostile country weekly newspapers cheeped with the *Bureau County Patriot* in Illinois, "The 4th of next March Old Abe will be obliged to pack up his duds and retire to the shades of Springfield, where he can spend the rest of his life relating anecdotes he learned at Washington."

A one-column letter of Wendell Phillips in the *Independent* was reprinted in the *New York Tribune*, the *New York World*, and across the country. "The Baltimore Convention was largely a mob of speculators and contractors willing to leave to their friend, Mr. Lincoln, his usurped power of reconstruction," wrote Phillips. Its "meaningless and hypocritical platform" was "a mixture of claptrap compliments and brave demands forced by the Cleveland movement." Phillips trusted that the Cleveland movement might still be "made effectual to prevent the disaster of Mr. Lincoln's reelection." He still held that Lincoln heading the Government spelled disaster. "We shall never have peace until slavery is destroyed. As long as you keep the present turtle at the head of the Government you make a pit with one hand and fill it with the other."

Of the gyrations of Phillips *Harper's* remarked that to his cry of "Hypocrites!" they could retort that he himself was a hypocrite. Why catfight? They wouldn't. "For we confide in his [Phillips's] honesty, and if he does not confide in the honesty of the men who met at Baltimore, it is simply because he knows nothing about them, and is much too swift to assume the dishonesty of all who do not agree with him. . . . There are men [Baltimore delegates] who oppose Mr. Lincoln, there are others who support him reluctantly. . . . Mr. Phillips has no right whatever to call them hypocrites. . . . To his chosen and well-filled part of moral agitator they forgive his caustic and contemptuous criticism of all expedients by which great moral principles are to be reduced to practice. But his vast vituperation and bitter assaults upon the characters and motives of men who love liberty and their country not less than he, however they may differ from him as to the means of serving them, these are things which make many an admiring friend sad and sorry for him, and will they not one day make him profoundly sorry for himself?"

From an open letter of Thurlow Weed *Harper's Weekly* took one of his sentences for discussion. Weed's latest letter had these words: "Though always treated courteously by Mr. Lincoln, my views and suggestions have not concurred with his convictions of duty; and from my first interview with the President, at Springfield [in 1860] to my last in January [of '64], I have been of no account." Whether these facts implied a misfortune for the country or an incompetency in the President, the people must determine, said *Harper's*. "Whether the war would have been more clearly comprehended and more wisely prosecuted if Mr. Weed or Mr. Parker Pillsbury had been President than it has been by Mr. Lincoln, are questions that the election will determine. If we might express an opinion, we should say that Mr. Lincoln has probably more faith in the people than Mr. Weed, and more practical sagacity than Mr. Pillsbury. We certainly do not impugn the patriotism or the good faith of either of these gentlemen when we say that Mr. Lincoln seems to us to have apprehended more correctly than either of them both the significance of the contest and the conditions of ultimate success."

Party lines were shaken and old political bonds sundered in the sight of two men, one Republican and the other Democratic, heading a national ticket. The great American game of politics was in chaos. In Maine and California, in Ohio and Connecticut, the State governors were War Democrats. In the patronage portioned out by the President, the War Democrats got more than a fair share, said organization Republicans. "Of the more earnest and thorough-going Republicans in both Houses of Congress," wrote Congressman George Julian, "probably not one in ten really favored it [Lincoln's nomination]. It was not only very distasteful to a large majority of Congress but to many of the most prominent men of the [Republican] party throughout the country. During the month of June ['64] the feeling against Mr. Lincoln became more and more bitter and intense, but its expression never found its way to the people." These dissatisfied Republican-party men had expression from editors such as Greeley and Bryant, *Harper's Weekly* saying that journals "truly and not technically 'democratic' . . . regret to see that Mr. Lincoln has been renominated, confess that he is beyond any question the man and the choice of the people. . . . Fortunately for the good cause, the people differ from these journals." Bryant's version in the *New York Evening Post* was that "many of the thieving and corrupt scoundrels" of the political stables had capitalized the President's popularity with the common man.

The renomination of Lincoln would deepen his idea of becoming king, said the *New York World*. "His adherents do not blush in comparing him to God, a custom received from the annals of the Roman Caesar." The *World* fetched up a loyalist named Breckinridge at the Republican State Convention at Springfield, Illinois, "who does not hesitate in using the following profane language: 'That great man Old Abe Lincoln is a special gift from God Almighty, and if we reject him from this convention, we reject God Almighty.'"

Greeley in the *New York Tribune* saw the renomination as "unquestionably in accord with public sentiment and all its manifestations," yet he believed another man for President would minimize the "venom" in the national situation. As an outsider Lincoln would have had "no more to expect or hope, could be impelled by no conceivable motive but a desire to serve and save his country, and thus win for himself an enviable and enduring fame." The renomination, said the *New York Evening Post,* was "so universally expected that it takes nobody by surprise . . . it is not to be denied that Mr. Lincoln enjoys the favor and confidence of the people." So convinced were the people of "Mr. Lincoln's complete integrity, of his homely good sense and honesty of purpose," that they overlooked his defects. "They pardon his mistakes, they are prone to forgive even his occasional lapses into serious and dangerous abuse of power." The people were unaware of other distinguished men "capable of a more comprehensive, consistent and dignified statesmanship" and of the estimates that "Mr. Lincoln is slow and suffers the best opportunities to pass; without knowledge of men he gets about him unworthy persons like Cameron. . . . He listens too patiently to mere schemers or men of management and intrigue, and he either drifts into the right course or assumes it with an embarrassed air, as if he took shelter in it as a final expedient. There is nothing high, generous, heroic in the tone of his administration." In this as in similar editorial expressions the *New York Evening Post* was saying what the radical faction wanted said.

"Let partisans rave as they will," wrote Forney in a *Washington Chronicle* article, "the nomination of President Lincoln is the work of the people. With what reluctance after his inaugural he undertook his sworn duty against warring malcontents, and how tenderly and how forbearingly he has dealt with armed traitors, history will attest; for the history of Abraham Lincoln for the last three years is the history of the nation. By one party he has been denounced as a tyrant, but the past will be searched in vain for a parallel of one clothed with such vast authority who so little abused it. . . . Noisy adherents of almost every shade of opinion have censured and commended him by turns. Through all the vicissitudes of a social upheaval such as never before perhaps convulsed a nation, he has kept one purpose steadily in view, that of preserving the integrity of the national life. Throughout he has grown in the confidence and kindly regards of the people. Fashionable exquisites sneer at his manners. Dilettanti scholars criticise his speech. Radical politicians denounce his want of pluck. Conservative ultraists grow fierce over his unconstitutional aggressions. Shallow brains carp at his inferior intellect. But his homely manners win the popular heart. His clear, terse utterances sink into the public mind. His timidity is felt to be the caution of a statesman oppressed with the magnitude of the interests in his hands, and who believes in the maxim 'make haste slowly.' " The President's arbitrary exercise of authority, what was it but the reluctant concession to the truth that revolutionary times occasionally demand extreme measures? The masses of people had been won by "the magnanimity which forgives mistakes and refuses to worry over trifles, the honesty which scorns corruption and frankly confesses mental processes that a weaker nature is eager to conceal, and the earnest patriotism which, though indulging in an occasional humorous flash, is ever up to the mark of its most serious and solemn responsibilities." The man now at the center of clamors, jars, intrigues, would yet "preside over a reunited and regenerated republic."

The supreme American botanist, president of the American Academy of Arts and Sciences, Asa Gray, saw Lincoln at this time as having deep roots in good loam. "The people," he wrote to an American friend, "are determined to support and reëlect their excellent President Lincoln, whether Frémont and the like make a coalition with copperheads or not. . . . Lincoln will walk the course. God bless him!" To his English friend Charles Darwin, Asa Gray wrote, "Homely, honest, ungainly Lincoln is the representative man of the country."

The Irish-born New York attorney E. L. Godkin, who had turned journalist as correspondent for the London *Daily News*, wrote for his paper a review of Lincoln's public career, seeing the renomination as "long foreseen by all intelligent observers of the drift of public sentiment," brought about by "general confidence in his honesty and general approval of his policy" and by fear of changing administrations while war raged. Godkin had noticed in America a change of viewpoint as to "Mr. Lincoln's defects" both of manner and of looks. "When the war broke out and Mr. Lincoln became the cynosure of all eyes, the horror felt by the 'nobility, gentry, and clergy' in England at the cut of his clothes, the length of his legs, his way of wearing his beard, and his manner of receiving company, called forth a corresponding amount of sympathy here. People were rather disposed to be ashamed of their President when they found he was likely to excite so much attention. Lamentations were heard on every side over his want of education. Many persons were greatly distressed when they found that Southerners in England were contrasting his deportment with that of Jefferson Davis. They wished they had not elected him, and declared they never would have voted for him if they had known he was to represent the nation through such a crisis as was then impending." During his first year as President he grew in popularity, and "The dissatisfaction of the genteel people with his exterior was drowned in the general devotion to him as the emblem of national unity. There was probably never before at the North such devotion to the Presidency, and reverence for it."

Then, ran Godkin's survey, came the McClellan campaigns, some of Mr. Lincoln's dealings with McClellan having "an unpleasant look of undue interference," and in the maze of troubles Lincoln in the autumn of 1862 reached the lowest point in the estimation of all classes. Yet amid gloom the President held to faith in the national destiny. "The more furiously the factions raged, the more completely he emancipated himself from their control . . . he has been gaining ground steadily with all the moderates, though losing it with the radicals. . . . The suspension of the *Habeas Corpus* was generally acknowledged to be necessary, but it was grossly abused by Mr. Stanton and many of his subordinates, and the tenacity with which Mr.

Lincoln retained Stanton in office in the teeth of such hostility, and I think well-merited hostility, irritated and disgusted a good many men of all parties." Through it all however, in Godkin's view, the President had retained "a high character for justice, sagacity, firmness, and above all for honesty," which explained the renomination at Baltimore.

Twice in the week of the Baltimore convention William Lloyd Garrison had interviews with Lincoln, and the news went far and wide and the opposition expanded and expounded on the report of Mr. Garrison, who had once railed at the Constitution as "a league with death and a covenant with hell," saying that what he heard from the President was "satisfactory." At one interview Theodore Tilton of the *Independent* accompanied Garrison, and it seemed that Tilton would swing in for the Lincoln and Johnson ticket.

Garrison and Tilton had taken a walk around Baltimore and tried to find the old jail in which abolitionist Garrison had done time many years back for voicing subversive doctrines. They told Lincoln they couldn't find the jail and Lincoln laughed. "Well, Mr. Garrison, when you first went to Baltimore you couldn't get *out;* but the second time you couldn't get *in!*"

Tilton wrote for the *Independent:* "The President's . . . reception of Mr. Garrison was an equal honor to host and guest. . . . When one of us mentioned the great enthusiasm at the convention, after Senator Morgan's proposition to amend the Constitution, abolishing slavery, Mr. Lincoln instantly said,—'It was I who suggested to Mr. Morgan that he should put that idea into his opening speech.' "

One White House visitor grinned at Lincoln with a prediction that the people would sure re-elect him. Lincoln said he had lately heard this often. When it was first mentioned to him he was reminded of a farmer in Illinois who tried his hand as a beginner at blasting. This farmer was good at boring and was no slouch at filling in with powder, but somehow he couldn't make the powder go off. So he began talking with another man standing by and looking on, about why the powder would not go off though it seemed to be the real thing. And in the midst of talking with the other fellow about what was wrong the farmer suddenly had an idea, "I know what's the matter. That powder won't go off because it's been shot before!"

A story got around that the President one day dropped in at the corner where Carpenter was painting "The Happy Family," Lincoln and his Cabinet. Lincoln guessed it looked sort of nice and the artist believed before long it would be done, and then, "I intend to travel through the country and exhibit it."

"What! exhibit that all over the country! It will ruin my chances for re-election. Everybody expects me to change my Cabinet."

The chairman of a Philadelphia Union League delegation introduced a colleague, giving name and district. "He has . . . been good enough to paint, and present to our League rooms, a most beautiful portrait of yourself." Lincoln took the man's hand and while shaking it said, "I presume, sir, in painting your beautiful portrait, you took your idea of me from my principles, and not from my person." This, noted Carpenter, "created considerable amusement."

From a photograph by Gardner of Lincoln seated, with Nicolay and Hay standing, *Harper's Weekly* made a drawing which it presented to its readers in a full-page illustration the week after the Baltimore convention. "In this earnest care-worn face," it commented, "saddened by a solemn sense of the great responsibility which in God's providence has devolved upon him, we see the man who said to his neighbors, as he left his home three years ago, that he was called to a graver task than any chief magistrate since Washington. Through an infinite perplexity of events the faith of the President has never faltered. . . . Look thoughtfully at this rugged face. In its candor, its sagacity, its calmness, its steadiness and strength, there is especially conspicuous the distinctive American. Turn then to the portrait of General Grant in our paper of three weeks ago, and there you see another purely American face, the same homely honesty, capacity and tenacity. Children of the people both of them, sprung from the poorest and plainest ancestry, as unpretending and unselfish in their high places today as in the time when they were both unknown, these two men illustrate at once the character of American civilization. There is but one prayer in the great multitude of American hearts today, God bless President Lincoln and General Grant!"

For the eyes of his family, in a letter strictly private, Richard Henry Dana, author of *Two Years before the Mast,* sketched his impression of Lincoln at this time. Dana was a United States district attorney of Massachusetts in charge of prize-court cases, and had spent a half-hour with the President officially and socially, writing of it: "I cannot describe the President; it is impossible. He was sobered in his talk, told no extreme stories, said some good things and some helplessly natural and naïve things. You cannot help feeling an interest in him, a sympathy and a kind of pity; feeling, too, that he has some qualities of great value, yet fearing that his weak points may wreck him or wreck something. His life seems a series of wise sound conclusions, slowly reached, oddly worked out, on great questions, with constant failures in administration of details and dealings with individuals. When I return I will tell you of a high compliment he paid me, in a sincere, awkward manner."

A Supreme Court decision had been analyzed by Dana and Lincoln told Dana that he had read this analysis, "that it cleared up his mind on the subject entirely; that it reasoned out and put into scientific statement what he had all along felt in his bones must be the truth of the matter, and was not able to find anywhere in the books, or to reason out satisfactorily to himself." Having had interviews with the President, Seward, Blair, Stanton, Welles, Chase, Dana wrote of this same visit to Washington: "The cabinet is at sixes and sevens, or 'Isaac and Josh,' as my witness said. They say dreadful things of one another. (Not Seward; I have never heard him speak *harshly* of one of them.)"

In a thin mist of evening air with willows near by trembling to a low breeze, amid a cool dew flung out by old oaks above them, Lincoln on the Soldiers' Home grounds stood with others silent over a thoughtful twilight. By and by, as a California woman remembered it and soon wrote home to San Francisco, Lincoln said softly:

> "'How sleep the brave, who sink to rest
> By all their country's wishes blest–'"

She was too "easily melted," wrote the California woman. "It made us cry." And she heard him further in the purpling shadows:

> "'And women o'er the graves shall weep,
> Where nameless heroes calmly sleep.'"

CHAPTER 53

WASHINGTON BELEAGUERED AND TUMULTUOUS

ON the night of June 14, 1864, a man in his room in the Hiron's House in Windsor, Canada, stands before a mirror and in an amateur way arranges himself a disguise. On his unshaven upper lip he smooths down a large mustache, over the close-trimmed beard of his chin and jaws a long luxuriant flowing set of whiskers. He blackens his reddish eyebrows. Under trousers and vest he buttons a bed pillow.

Nobody bothers him as he rides the ferry from Her Majesty's dominion to Detroit and the U.S.A. A customs officer punches him lightly in the stomach asking what he's got there, and lets it go at that. A policeman in Detroit is suspicious, takes him to a street gaslight, looks him over and lets him go. On a train out of Detroit a passenger bends down to whisper in his ear, "I know your voice but you are safe from me." Snuggled in the berth of a sleeping-car he rides safely overnight to Hamilton, Ohio.

This is the return on June 15, 1864, of the Honorable Clement L. Vallandigham from alien lands to the soil of his native country and the domain of the Buckeye. "Men of Ohio: To-day I am again in your midst," he said to the Congressional District Convention at Hamilton that day. . . . "I return of my own act. . . . I was abducted from my home and forced into banishment. The assertion or insinuation of the President, that I was arrested because laboring with some effect to prevent the raising of troops . . . is absolutely false. . . . To-day my only 'crime' is that, in the way which they call treason, worship I the Constitution of my fathers. . . . Indorsed by nearly two hundred thousand freemen of the Democratic party of my native State at the late election, and still with the sympathy and support of millions more, I do not mean any longer to be the only man of that party who is to be the victim of arbitrary power. If Abraham Lincoln seeks my life, let him so declare; but he shall not again restrain me of my personal liberty, except upon 'due process of law.' "

And now what? Now Vallandigham would join what he termed "a conspiracy known as the Democratic party" and next November through the ballot box elect "a President true to his oath, to liberty, and the Constitution." He admonished all persons against armed resistance to the Federal and State authorities. He denied connection with the secret Order of Knights of the Golden Circle. He was covering himself. He was speaking for the record. What Vallandigham did not say was that while in Canada he had taken a hand in organizing the secret order of the Sons of Liberty and had been sworn in as Grand Commander. Nor could he tell the Buckeyes before him there at Dayton that he had become disgusted with the way things were run in the Sons of Liberty, that the secret peace societies over the country were getting in each other's way, that he had refused to join the Order of American Knights because it was so plainly a Confederate organization committed to Southern independence.

Nor could Vallandigham tell them that he was disgusted with the ritual and mummery of his own order in which he was Grand Commander. In that ritual three raps at the wicket in a dark cellar would bring the triple query "Who cometh? Who cometh? Who cometh?" and after three raps more the response: "A citizen we found in the hands of the sons of despotism, bound and well-nigh crushed to death beneath their oppression. We have brought him hither, and would now restore him to the blessings of liberty and law." Thousands initiated in the dark-lantern Sons of Liberty had stood in the "vestibule of the temple," the right hand under the left arm, the left arm under the right, the forefingers over and the thumb hidden under the right arm; and again with "hands crossed on his bowels, representing the belt of Orion." Something about the passwords, the grips, and the secrecy did not sit well with Vallandigham. He was too parliamentary and argumentative to enjoy undercover work—or violence. He had heard of some of the lodges buying hardware and getting ready to shoot their way to liberty. And he didn't like that. Worse yet were indications that outright Confederates had wormed their way into membership and were trying to arm it against the Union.

When Vallandigham slipped across the border at Detroit for his electrifying public reappearance in Ohio he sent no word to the brothers of the order of which he was Grand Commander. Now he would try to fix his fences. But he would have to be careful. And he believed it would not hurt anybody to give it out that the Sons of Liberty numbered 300,000, though he may have known it was nearer to one-tenth of that figure. Of course he could not agree with a Hoosier editor who said the membership was drawn from "the assorted lot of ninny-hammers and zanies, to be found in all communities, whose heads are emptier than an idiot's skull, and should be bored for simples."

The Democratic press in general saw eye to eye with the *Philadelphia Age:* "If Mr. Lincoln allows Mr. Vallandigham to remain in Ohio unmolested, he virtually acknowledges that the arrest and punishment by military commission was an outrage. If, on the contrary, Mr. Lincoln sends his minions to again arrest Mr. Vallandigham, he will provoke a new contest. Already the fanatics are beginning to urge a second arrest of Mr. Vallandigham. We think Mr. Lincoln will quail before the firm front of the West. The joker and his party will be too cowardly to try a new outrage."

Some days later Noah Brooks dropped into Lincoln's office and referred to Vallandigham speaking in Ohio. The President, with a quizzical look: "What! has Vallandigham got back?" Brooks had to say everybody knew it and noted the President with a fussy and pretended solemnity: "Dear me! I supposed he was in a foreign land. Anyhow, I hope I do not know that he is in the United States; and I shall not, unless he says or does something to draw attention to him." Going to a table, he drew out his notes of an interview with Fernando Wood, who had said to him, "We Peace Democrats are the only Democrats; all others are bastards and impostors; there is no such thing as a War Democrat, for that is a contradiction in terms." They didn't expect to elect a President in the fall, Wood went on, but would hold their party together for the time when peace came. "Now, Mr. President, you cannot find fault with that; it is not going to hurt you any." And Lincoln had told Wood he was disposed to be generous and then asked if Vallandigham's return was any part of a program, Wood replying: "You may not believe me, but I assure you that I never knew or expected that he would return, though I acknowledge that I have had a letter from him since he got back. He has already had more notoriety than he deserves, and I warn you that the true policy is that he be severely let alone."

Lincoln then, according to his notes of what he said to Wood: "I don't believe that Vallandigham has returned; I never can believe it until he forces himself offensively upon the public attention and upon my attention. Then we shall have to deal with him. So long as he behaves himself decently, he is as effectually in disguise as the man who went to a masquerade party with a clean face."

In this latter June of '64 when Vallandigham made an entry into the country Salmon P. Chase made an exit from the Cabinet by handing the President another one of his resignations. Chase had lost standing and dignity when his boom for the Presidency collapsed, and in a letter he had blamed mainly Monty Blair and Blair's politically busy postmasters. The Baltimore convention, Chase had written, would be simply a Blair-Lincoln affair; many held that "some popular movement for Grant" would offer a better hope of saving the country. In the same key as three years before Chase wrote in a May letter, "The Executive does not, I fear, sufficiently realize the importance of an energetic and comprehensive policy in all departments." Something might yet happen that would put him at the head of a winning ticket that year; this was the obvious hope of his earnest bosom. The *New York Herald* had wronged him in saying he had intentionally put the President's face on the two-dollar bill and his own manly features on the one-dollar bill. Had he not held matters even by seeing to it that Lincoln's face adorned the paper half-dollar?

An issue had arisen between President and Finance Minister over who should fill the place of John J. Cisco, Assistant Treasurer at New York, resigned in May. Chase at first agreed with Lincoln that the new appointment should not be objectionable to Senator Morgan of New York, who had the confidence of the leading banks and commercial interests of New York City. Chase consulted and conferred with Senator Morgan. They agreed on one New York man of high standing, who said No. They agreed on a second, who also said No, politely, but No. Then Chase brought out his personal choice, Maunsell B. Field, Third Assistant Secretary of the Treasury, a smooth-tongued, ready-witted writer and social mixer who had served as a manner of press agent and political scout in confidential errands for Chase. From several quarters came protest that Field was impossible. Senator Morgan was just short of furious and could see wreck of the Union party in New York. He begged first Lincoln and then Chase to make a choice from three eminent citizens of New York whose names he presented.

Chase had his mind made up. Without further consultation with the President he sent him June 27 the nomination of Field. The President next day wrote Chase a letter: "I cannot, without much embarrassment, make this appointment, principally because of Senator Morgan's very firm opposition to it," and naming three men whom Morgan had mentioned to Chase. "It will really oblige me if you will make choice among these three, or any other man that Senators Morgan and Harris will be satisfied with."

Chase sent a note to the President asking an interview, wired Cisco begging him to withdraw his resignation, went to the House and to the Senate to see how they were getting along, read his mail, considered better ink and paper for the dollar bills, wrote in his diary that no answer had come from his request to the President for an interview, and meditations: "This morning I read part of Paul to the Ephesians, and, as usual, endeavored to seek God in prayer. Oh, for more faith and clearer sight! How stable is the City of God! How disordered is the City of Man!" Welles in his diary the same June 28 was writing: "The President, like myself, slightly indisposed. . . . Gold has gone up to 240. Paper . . . is settling down out of sight. . . . Chase learns no wisdom. We are hurrying onward into a financial abyss." Three days before Welles had written, "Chase, though a man of mark, has not the sagacity, knowledge, taste, or ability of a financier. Has expedients, and will break down the government. There is no one to check him. The President has surrendered the finances to his management entirely. Other members of the Cabinet are not consulted. . . . I believe I am the only one who has expressed opinions that questioned his policy, and that expression was mild and kindly uttered. . . . Congress surrenders to his capricious and superficial qualities as pliantly as the President and the Cabinet."

What Welles did not enter in his diary was the peculiar fact that Chase spent so much of his time in party and factional politics that what Chase did as a Finance Minister in colossal money affairs gave no indication of what Chase could do in that field if it had all of his time and talents. In his diary of June 28 Chase wrote of trade regulations, speculations, and "I wish we could have good commissioners to manage these things, and also loans. But the President would almost certainly put in men from political considerations, and, after all, the responsibility would still be on me."

The President meanwhile this June 28 was writing Chase a compressed and careful statement: "When I received your note this forenoon suggesting a verbal conversation in relation to the appointment of a successor to Mr. Cisco, I hesitated, because the difficulty does not, in the main part, lie within the range of a conversation between you and me. As the proverb goes, no man knows so well where the shoe pinches as he who wears it. I do not think Mr. Field a very proper man for the place, but I would trust your judgment and forego this were the greater difficulty out of the way. Much as I personally like Mr. Barney [port collector at New York], it has been a great burden to me to retain him in his place when nearly all our friends in New York were directly or indirectly urging his removal. Then the appointment of Judge Hogeboom to be general appraiser brought me to, and has ever since kept me at, the verge of open revolt. Now the appointment of Mr. Field would precipitate me in it unless Senator Morgan and those feeling as he does, could be brought to concur in it. Strained as I already am at this point, I do not think I can make this appointment in the direction of still greater strain."

The tone of this was a little new to Chase. What could there be not "within the range of a conversation between you and me"? And whose was the foot being pinched? And who should be "at the verge of open revolt"? Chase would see about this.

Meanwhile a telegram had come from Mr. Cisco. He would yield to the pressure and stay on for a time, say, three months. So the situation had cleared. The weather was fair again. So it might have seemed. But not for Chase. The more he studied the President's letter, the more he felt called on to take steps. He wrote to the President: "I have received your note and I have read it with great attention. I was not aware of the extent of the embarrassment to which you refer." He mentioned Cisco's telegram as relieving the present difficulty; "but I cannot help feeling that my position here is not altogether agreeable to you; and it is certainly too full of embarrassment and difficulty and painful responsibility, to allow in me the least desire to retain it. I think it my duty, therefore, to inclose to you my resignation. I shall regard it as a real relief if you think proper to accept it." With this letter he enclosed a formal notice of resignation.

Once more Mr. Chase had resigned. This made four times. His letter of resignation arrived on Lincoln's desk along with other papers, including the telegram from Cisco saying he would stay on. Lincoln read the Cisco telegram, and somehow missed seeing Chase's resignation. The next morning,

June 30, he was going to write Chase on how nicely the matter had sort of settled itself when his eyes came across the words that Chase was quitting again.

This time he wrote to Chase: "Your resignation of the office of Secretary of the Treasury sent me yesterday is accepted. Of all I have said in commendation of your ability and fidelity I have nothing to unsay; and yet you and I have reached a point of mutual embarrassment in our official relations which it seems cannot be overcome or longer sustained consistently with the public service."

In his diary Chase wrote: "So my official life closes. I have laid broad foundations. . . . I am too earnest, too anti-slavery, and, say, too radical, to make the President willing to have me connected with the Administration, just as my opinion is that he is not earnest enough, not anti-slavery enough, not radical enough." A letter came from Jay Cooke, whose early access to official financial information might not hereafter be so easy. "For our dear country's sake, I am deeply pained to hear of your resignation. How was it possible for you to leave the helm of finance in the midst of this great storm? The reasons must be mighty and all-powerful. . . . God keep us."

Besides heavy routine duty the summer had brought stench of scandal. The *New York World* and other hostile newspapers day on day aired the matter of women from the Printing Bureau of the Treasury Department dressing in the attire of men and attending at the Canterbury Inn in Washington lewd performances to which men only were supposed to have admission. Two newspaper columns of affidavits recited details giving the impression that the Treasury Department offices held a fast and loose set of public servants. This to one so spotless as Chase in relation to women was not to be laughed off. The *New York Tribune* presented Chase's view that the affair was a conspiracy on the part of conniving Colonel La Fayette C. Baker, that Baker utilized a disreputable actress and women of the streets as informers and operatives to discredit women employees of the Printing Bureau and thereby cast a shadow over the Treasury Department. It was not an agreeable matter to read about in the morning newspaper over the breakfast table.

Hay read mixed motives in Chase's quitting as he did. Personal pride and ambition were there. Yet the resignation came when gold reached a new high point, when despair over government finance was deepest. Hay noted Congressman Hooper of Massachusetts, on whom Chase and Lincoln had leaned for guiding financial measures through the House, saying, as between friends, "A point has been reached where he [Chase] does not clearly see what comes next; and at this point the President allows him to step from under the load." A touch of desperation was in the Chase diary on the day his resignation was accepted: "I did not see how I could carry on the department without more means than Congress was likely to supply." To William G. Hosea he wrote that he had "felt able with God's favor to carry the load" if only he could have had "the cordial support of Mr. Lincoln." The political motive, however, overweighed all others in the

Chase communications, the definite yearnings of his remark to the editor of the *Indianapolis Independent*, "After all, I believe that I would rather that the people should wonder why I wasn't President than why I was."

Governor Brough of Ohio walking to the War Department met the President, who insisted on Brough's going to the Executive Mansion. "What is it, another Treasury imbroglio?" asked Brough.

"Right."

"Well, Mr. President, before going further, I have a question to ask: Is it beyond mediation?"

"Well—perhaps and perhaps not. What do you propose?"

"First tell me the nature of the difficulty."

"It's about the Cisco business."

"I don't wish to intrude, but for the interest of the country, and it being nothing more serious than that, if you will delay action until tomorrow morning when I can get the Ohio men together, I think it can be arranged."

"But this is the third time he has thrown it at me, and I don't think I am called on to continue to beg him to take it back, especially when the country would not go to destruction in consequence."

"This is not simply a personal matter. The people will not understand it. . . . If you will give me time, I think Ohio can close the breach and the world be none the wiser."

"You doctored the business up once, but on the whole, Brough, I reckon you had better let it alone this time."

Thus Brough reported the conversation to his secretary of state, William Henry Smith, who made an immediate diary entry of it.

The *New York Herald* was pleased at Chase's leaving. Greeley in the *Tribune* bemoaned the loss of "one of the few great men left" from the days of Webster, Clay, Calhoun. The *New York World* said this Cabinet explosion came from disputes and corruption and would be followed by other surprises.

Sumner gave his view in writing to Richard Cobden in England: "The President made a great mistake in compelling him [Chase] to resign. It was very much as when Louis XVI. threw overboard Necker,—and, by the way, I have often observed that Mr. Lincoln resembles Louis XVI. more than any other ruler in history. I once said to Chase that I should not be astonished if, like Necker, he was recalled; to which he replied, 'That might be if Mr. Lincoln were king and not politician.' "

No sooner had Lincoln notified Chase that they could no longer travel together officially than he sent to the Senate a message. It amazed that body, for he named former Governor David Tod of Ohio, an old Douglas Democrat, to be Secretary of the Treasury. Then the President telegraphed to Tod this news entirely unexpected by Tod. By his action the President was showing first that he could offer a high Cabinet place to a good War Democrat, and second that he was not sore at Ohio just because he had thrown out the Ohioan Chase.

The Senate Finance Committee went into executive session. They agreed

Tod had just about everything wanted except national reputation and financial ability. They called in a body on Lincoln to protest that Tod was not the man for the place. Lincoln said he had met many men "since our troubles began," and comparing him with others, all in all, he thought

HARPER'S WEEKLY. ULY 16, 1864.

Mr. Lincoln. "Mike, remove the Salmon and bring me a Tod."
Mike. "The Tod's out; but can't I fitch something else, Sir?"

Puns on political fish

"Dave Tod was considerable of a man." He went into a history of his relations with "Governor Chase," how he designed his Cabinet to represent regional interests and political views, so that abolitionists, conservatives, and the Blair family found their way to his council table. He took from pigeonholes letters between him and Chase, read them to the Senators, recounted the times Chase had resigned, and in particular how the latest eruption had come, and why he could not permit Chase to name his personal choice for Third Assistant Secretary of the Treasury. "Now, gentlemen," continued

Wall Street, New York, looking east from Nassau Street; the United States Subtreasury at the left, 23 Wall Street at the right, the United States Customs House in the distance at the right

From an engraving in the Barrett collection

John Wien Forney

Leonard Swett

Whitelaw Reid

Henry Wager Halleck

Henry Wilson

William Kellogg

THEY HELPED LINCOLN—AND HINDERED HIM

the President, as Conness of California noted it, "I could not appoint him He [Chase's nominee] had only recently at a social gathering, in the presence of ladies and gentlemen, while intoxicated, kicked his hat up against the ceiling, bringing discredit upon us all, and proving his unfitness." The President had no objection to Governor Chase's candidacy for the Presidency—Chase had a right to be a candidate; but there had grown such a state of feeling that it was unpleasant for them to meet each other. So he had taken Chase at his word and accepted the resignation. Furthermore: "I will not longer continue the association. I am ready and willing to resign the office of President, and let you have Mr. Hamlin for your President, but I will no longer endure the state I have been in." These, according to Conness, were nearly his words, spoken with deep seriousness.

Hay's diary gave Lincoln's account of the meeting with the Senate Finance Committee. "Fessenden was frightened, Conness was mad, Sherman thought we could not have gotten on together much longer anyhow," Cowan and Van Winkle were indifferent. The Senators had not only objected to any change, but protested against Tod as too little known and too inexperienced. The President replied he had little personal acquaintance with Tod, that he had nominated him on account of the high opinion he had formed of him as Governor of Ohio; but that the Senate had the duty and responsibility of passing upon the question of fitness, in which it must be entirely untrammeled; he could not, in justice to himself or Tod, withdraw the nomination.

Meanwhile excitement kept up over Tod. He was known to be "a hard-money man." Why couldn't the President have picked a man friendly to greenbacks? And why had the President consulted no one about this choice?

In the evening of this day came a telegram from Tod to the President saying his health would not permit him to be Secretary of the Treasury. The President sent a secretary to the Capitol with this information for the Senate. The President's appointment of Tod was thus out of the way. The Senators could now dismiss that from their minds. But what next?

Early the next morning the President wrote out a nomination for William Pitt Fessenden, Senator from Maine, to be Secretary of the Treasury. As he gave Hay this paper of nomination, to be carried to the Senate, Hay said Fessenden was waiting outside in the anteroom to see him. "Send him in and go at once to the Senate," said Lincoln.

Fessenden's business with Lincoln was to suggest Hugh McCulloch for the vacant place. The President listened, smiled a brief moment, and then told Fessenden that the President had already sent the nomination of Fessenden to the Senate.

Fessenden leaped to his feet. "You must withdraw it—I can't accept."

"If you decline, you must do it in open day, for I shall not recall the nomination."

They talked about it. Fessenden pleaded ill-health. He went away less decided in his refusal. He reached the Senate to find that the Senate had taken about one minute to confirm unanimously the President's nomination. He went to his room and commenced writing a letter to the President declining the appointment. While he tried to write he was interrupted by telegrams of congratulation from chambers of commerce and from individual friends, by delegations from the House and by nearly every member of the Senate calling to say he must accept. He finished a letter of mixed thanks and regrets saying he was thoroughly exhausted and medical opinion joined his own that he must recover from his fatigue or wreck himself beyond restoration.

Fessenden took this letter to the Executive Mansion near ten o'clock that night. The President had gone to bed. He left word for the President that he would call again in the morning. "I accordingly did so," Fessenden wrote to ex-Chief Justice Tenney of Maine, "and told the President that I had a letter for him which I deemed it most respectful to present in person. He said that if it was a letter declining to accept the Treasury, he would not receive it. Much conversation followed . . . personal appeals to my sense of duty, and expressions of belief that there was no other man with whom the country would be satisfied. He said the crisis was such as demanded any sacrifice, even life itself; that Providence had never deserted him or the country, and that his choice of me was a special proof that Providence would not desert him. All this and more. Failing, however, to convince me, he requested, as a favor, that I would let the matter stand until after Congress adjourned, in order that, as it would then be a vacancy occurring in the recess, he might have a chance to fill it more deliberately. To this I, of course, assented."

As chairman of the Senate Finance Committee Fessenden knew the money market was feverish, public confidence wavering, and there was basis for his friends saying a financial crash would follow his refusal. "I did not dare to hesitate longer, whatever might be the consequences," he wrote in the letter to Tenney. "Foreseeing nothing but entire prostration of my physical powers, and feeling that to take the Treasury in its exhausted condition would probably result in destroying what little reputation I had, it was still my duty to hazard both life and reputation if by so doing I could avert a crisis so imminent. I consented, therefore, to make the sacrifice, having, however, a clear understanding with the President that I might retire when I could do so without public injury."

Three of Fessenden's four sons had gone into the army; one had been killed in battle at Centerville in '62; the others had won advancement by valor and ability to brigadier general and colonel. The Fessendens had a good war record. Stanton attacked the Senator's hesitations: "You can no more refuse than your son could have refused to attack Monet's Bluff, and you cannot look him in the face if you do."

"It will kill me."

"Very well, you cannot die better."

"The President's course is a riddle," said Welles's diary. "Tod is a hard-money man; Fessenden has pressed through Congress the paper system of

Chase. One day Tod is selected; on his refusal, Fessenden is brought forward. This can in no other way be reconciled than in the President's want of knowledge of the subject. His attention never has been given to the finances. He seems not aware that within twenty-four hours he has swung to opposite extremes. Seward can hardly have been consulted, for Fessenden has been his sharp and avowed opponent of late, and unless he has changed, or shall change, will prove a troublesome man for him in the Cabinet."

Chase in his diary wrote: "He [Fessenden] has the confidence of the country, and many who have become inimical to me will give him their support. Perhaps they will do more than they otherwise would to sustain him, in order to show how much better a Secretary he is than I was."

Telegrams and letters of approval beyond precedent had poured in on Fessenden. The New York and Boston clearinghouses, bankers and merchants in all quarters, it seemed, urged his acceptance of the President's nomination when it was reported he would refuse. At the first report that Fessenden was to be Secretary of the Treasury, Government bonds advanced, pork declined $10 a barrel, and all provisions went to lower prices. Gold opened at 250, being 30 per cent lower than the highest figure of the day before, and fell to 220. A rumor that Fessenden had refused the office sent gold up twenty-five points. "Men went about with smiling faces at the news of his appointment," said one newspaper.

On July 5 of '64 Fessenden was sworn in and took over the portfolio abandoned by Salmon P. Chase. The press held forth in compliments such as never before, except in the case of Grant, over a major Lincoln appointment. "Mr. Lincoln was in fine spirits," wrote the *Springfield Republican* correspondent, quoting the President as exclaiming to Seward, "The Lord has never yet deserted me, and I did not believe he would this time!"

New York World readers on July 1 gathered the editorial opinion that "the backwoods lawyer at the head of the government has not sufficient mental enlargement to go outside of the walks of politics for a Secretary of the Treasury. . . . Mr. Lincoln wanted a facile man with the instincts of a politician; a mere nose-of-wax with little knowledge of finance, a supple tool. The treasury is to be run as an electioneering engine for the benefit of Mr. Lincoln. The hand of that arch-contriver, Secretary Seward, is discernible in this flinging of Mr. Chase's corpse to the sharks." On July 4, however, *World* readers gathered again: "The Hon. W. P. Fessenden, who has been appointed to fill the office of Secretary of the Treasury, is a gentleman of unimpeachable integrity. . . . It is reasonable to assume that we shall have a continuance of Mr. Chase's paper money system, but without the rascality and gold-gambling and stock-jobbing trickery which accompanied Mr. Chase's 'financial strategy.' "

Lincoln was surprised and pleased at one of his appointments being taken in this way. Into Hay's diary went an entry of the President saying: "It is very singular, considering that this appointment of F.'s is so popular when made, that no one ever mentioned his name to me for that place. Thinking over the matter two or three points occurred to me. *First,* he knows the ropes thoroughly: as Chairman of the Senate Committee on Finance he knows as much of this special subject as Mr. Chase. 2nd, he is a man possessing a national reputation and the confidence of the country. 3[d], he is a radical—without the petulant and vicious fretfulness of many radicals. On the other hand I considered the objections: the Vice President & Sec. Treasury coming from the same small state—though I thought little of that; then that Fessenden from the state of his health is of rather a quick & irritable temper: but in this respect he should be pleased with this incident; for, while for some time he has been running in rather a pocket of bad luck—such as the failure to renominate Mr. Hamlin which makes possible a contest between him & the V.P., the most popular man in Maine for the election which is now imminent, & the fact of his recent spat in the Senate where Trumbull told him his ill-temper had left him no friends—this thing has developed a sudden and very gratifying manifestation of good feeling in his appointment, his instant confirmation, the earnest entreaties of everybody that he may accept & all that. It cannot but be very grateful to his feelings."

On the day Fessenden was nominated Noah Brooks had a message to call on the President at the White House and found the President in the library, lying on his back on a sofa, hands clasped over his chest, "looking weary beyond description. But he was in a comfortable frame of mind." He rehearsed the day's incidents, and "When I finally struck the name of Fessenden as Governor Chase's successor, I felt as if the Lord hadn't forsaken me yet."

The defensive tactics of Lincoln in this affair came in an odd version to A. K. McClure. "Secretary Chase is today a national necessity," one adviser urged. Lincoln in quiet tone: "I used to have similar notions. No! If we should all be turned out tomorrow and could come back here in a week, we should find our places filled by a lot of fellows doing just as well as we did, and in many instances better. The Irishman said, 'In this country one man is as good as another, and for the matter of that, very often a good deal better.' No; this Government does not depend upon the life of any man."

In an affectionate letter plainly having no other intention than frank and honest counsel Senator Grimes of Iowa, before starting for home, wrote to Fessenden, with the incidental parting advice: "Get rid of Mr. Chase's agents as soon as possible. I believe many of them are corrupt, but whether they be so or not they are thought to be, and that is sufficient reason for supplanting them with new men." But Fessenden proceeded in no such line of theory or action as Grimes advised. Fessenden called on Chase July 4 to say that, as to appointments, he and the President were agreed. Wrote Chase, "The President only requiring that, should he himself [the President] desire any particular appointments made, his wishes in that regard should be fully considered. He [Lincoln] said, too, that he hoped Mr. Fessenden would not, without a real necessity, remove any friends of Governor Chase." It was evident from Chase's diary that he was trying to make himself believe that Lincoln had adopted a different tone with Fessenden, and that had Lincoln used this tone with Chase then Chase would not have resigned. "Had the President, in reply to my note tendering resignation, expressed himself as he did now to Mr. Fessenden, I should cheerfully have withdrawn it." Which was merely another case of Chase not really being aware of what was going on past and present. The understanding about offices and appointments between Lincoln and Fessenden went into a memorandum which Lincoln wrote and gave to Fessenden. It was an explicit and delicate document:

Executive Mansion, Washington, July 4, 1864

I have today said to Hon. W. P. Fessenden, on his assuming the office of Secretary of the Treasury, that I will keep no person in office in his department, against his express will, so long as I choose to continue him; and he has said to me, that in filling vacancies he will strive to give his willing consent to my wishes in cases when I may let him know that I have such wishes. It is, and will be, my sincere desire, not only to advance the public interest, by giving him complete control of the department, but also to make his position agreeable to him.

In Cabinet my view is that in questions affecting the whole country there should be full and frequent consultations, and that nothing should be done particularly affecting any department without consultation with the head of that department.

A man not lacking an eye for the comic had replaced in the Cabinet a dignitary low in humor. In one letter home in 1859 the widower Fessenden had written from Washington: "This is a great place for widows in the fashionable season. We have some half dozen of them now staying at the hotels and creating a sensation." A friend told one widow he could think of but two unmarried men in the Senate, Clingman and Fessenden. "She said that one was 'dried up' and the other 'too old.' As I have never seen her, it is impossible to estimate my loss." Though usually voting with the radicals on antislavery bills, Fessenden had held back from some of the harsh and peremptory steps of the extremists. He was his own man. He opposed naming Grant in the bill creating the office of lieutenant general, saying they could trust the President for that. He opposed naming a congressional committee to investigate the Fort Pillow killings, on the ground that the Secretary of War could make the inquiry just as well and that more immediately practical work demanded the time of Congress. He had a habit of insisting that when measures of war and finance had been set for Senate discussion they should not give way to the latest antislavery proposals of Sumner, Wade, and Trumbull. For this he was represented as a milk-and-water emancipation man, though the Yeas and Nays showed otherwise.

Fessenden had served in the Senate as a foil for the overrighteousness of the radicals. His cameo-carved face had incisive lines, would suggest the ascetic and the relentless if not for a second thought that the face looked ready for a smile when chance offered. Behind his relentless face he could be pleasantly relenting, as when he attacked the administration of the $300 clause of the draft law. He would credit the Government with the best intentions and would sustain it thoroughly, but he was opposed to "the system of high bounties which made people forget that their first duty was to the country." He wrote to his family that if they would read the *Congressional Globe* he had sent them, they would see "that I have been pitching into the government a little." The Secretary of War was "a good deal cut up about it . . . seemed to be more hurt than angry, and I shall set him right by and by, when occasion offers, as he is really much the best of the lot. I have not been to see the President yet, which I must do soon, as he has done me the honor to notice the fact."

Maunsell B. Field, the Chase press agent and wirepuller, still held his desk as Third Assistant Secretary of the Treasury, and wrote of one day: "Immediately after a Cabinet meeting, Mr. Fessenden, entering his room in the Department where I was awaiting his return, advanced toward me with a glowing countenance, and said, 'I tell you, Mr. Field, Mr. Lincoln is more of a politician than all his Cabinet put together!' Before he had opportunity to explain what had so excited his enthusiasm, somebody came in upon business and the matter was dropped." This may have been one of the times Field was telling precisely what happened.

As a Cabinet member Fessenden came to see from the inside that what he had once interpreted as "Lincoln's weakness and obstinacy" was something else. In his many family letters Fessenden had weighed the President with kindliness, usually in the light of his writing December 20 of '62: "We are in a crisis, and such a curious compound is our good Abraham that no one knows how it will eventuate. His attachment to individuals and his tenderness of heart are fatal to his efficiency in times like these. In the hands of some men who had integrity, sternness, and will, he would do well enough, but he must depend upon his surroundings."

Seven months before entry as Secretary of the Treasury, Fessenden had written of Lincoln's proposed amnesty oath: "I think Abe's proclamation, take it altogether, was a silly performance, but he is lucky, and I hope it may work well. Think of telling the rebels they may fight as long as they can, and take a pardon when they have had enough of it. He *is funny*—speaking of his smallpox, he said he had one thing that nobody wanted." Where Chase's sensitivity chiefly concerned Chase, Fessenden would writhe over the selfish and quarreling generals, the officeholder urging a salary raise. "Many of our poor soldiers have not had a dime in months," he wrote in January of '63. "Hard, isn't it? I would be content to borrow and mortgage my house, if that would help them. Nobody can blame them for deserting. I am heartsick when I think of the miserable mismanagement of our army. In the 'Convalescent Camps' thousands are almost without shelter, and miserably provided with food—all through the stupidity of our officers, for there have been ample means provided. If I was secretary of war, wouldn't heads fall? The simple truth is, there never was such a shambling, half and half set of incapables collected in one government before since the world began. I saw a letter this morning written in good English by the King of Siam to Admiral Foote, which had more good sense in it, and a better comprehensiveness of our troubles, I do verily believe, than *Abe* has had from the beginning. But it's of no use to scold."

Fessenden in the Senate had punctured Sumner's pompous heroics with the most casual and unexpected points bearing on what was immediately practical. He had favored a moderate rather than extreme policy in the use of Negro troops, and once wrote to his family: "I see Phillips, Douglass, the *Tribune*, and the whole tribe of such dogs, have been barking at me. . . . Well, they are wrong and I am right. So they may bark or howl as suits them best, and I shall stick to my text as usual." On a resolution to expel, with an amendment to censure "Garrulous" Garrett Davis, the Senator from Kentucky, Fessenden stood against both proposals, held that the Senate was a sort of Liberty Hall where each gentleman had his say, and the fool would be known by his folly. Considering there in the year of '64 that of his three boys who had gone into the army Sam was dead, Frank was on the Red River in Arkansas, Jim with one leg gone was on Hooker's staff with Sherman trying to take Atlanta, Fessenden could have joined the Vindictives.

Measuring the amount of devoted toil that had nearly wrecked his health in the raging fury and the grinding monotony of a war between States, Fessenden was of rather extraordinary human stuff. On first look he might be pointed to as the typical "hatchet-faced Yankee," but on closer scrutiny he evaded classification as a type. Starting as a young lawyer in Portland, Maine, he had become a Whig Congressman, later a Senator, was one of the founders of the Republican party, watched the tariff, fisheries, and shipping interests of his State, clashed with Welles over Maine's share of favors and patronage, and was now to head a great department and undergo the trials of an executive. The national debt was $1,700,000,000. The Treasury was almost empty and the war was costing $2,000,000 a day.

Jay Cooke still had his impressive new office building across the street from the Treasury Department. But neither Jay nor his brother Henry crossed the street for a talk with the new Secretary. Henry in a letter to Jay mentioned talk of Chase returning to the Treasury: "It is not impossible in the event of Lincoln's re-election. Governor C. is not averse to the idea but feels in regard to Mr. Lincoln a good deal as you do towards Mr. Fessenden—that the overtures should come from Mr. Lincoln." Brother Jay wrote his feeling, "I cannot . . . with self-respect push myself upon Mr. Fessenden's notice."

Fessenden sent for Cooke. And Cooke crossed the street from his office to the Treasury Department and talked with Fessenden, and went away, as he said, "hurt" by a "cruel" thing Fessenden told him.

Cooke had one national bank in Philadelphia and another in Washington. The cashier of the Washington bank, William S. Huntington, went to see Lincoln on Cooke business. Huntington reported to his chief that the President made inquiries as though he regarded a close connection between the Treasury and the Cooke houses as indispensable, asking several times that Cooke should visit him. Days passed with Cooke saying nothing. Again the cashier Huntington wrote Jay Cooke: "I have heard nothing from you in reply to the President's invitation to you to see him. What do you think of it? I saw him again yesterday and he again assured me he would be very glad to see you." Cooke's explanation was simple and was given in a letter to Chase. "The President has several times, as Huntington and Fahny [H. C. Fahnestock, a Cooke partner] will tell you, requested that I should go over and see him. This was during Mr. Fessenden's absence [on a personal business trip to Maine] and I did not go because I felt, if I did, I should be interfering with Mr. Fessenden, and until I saw whether he intended to adopt the views I had expressed to him I thought it indelicate to urge them on the President."

To Chase, Jay Cooke confided what Fessenden told him at their first interview, being probably the same as what Fessenden told Lincoln about the Cookes. "He has the fullest confidence in me and in our firms. Yet he expressed to me a sentiment that has hurt me ever since: that he thought it right to say to me that he could not think of engaging in any business negotiations with our firms. As such matters had in the past been animadverted upon so constantly by the press and various parties disadvantageously to the Treasury (as I interpreted it) he thought it best to steer clear of anything that could be found fault with. I thought it cruel after all my hard night and day services, which as far as I know my heart were as disinterested and patriotic and pure as earth ever saw, to be thus insulted by Mr. F. I promptly assured him that I never, and did not then seek any favors of the government."

For several weeks it would seem Fessenden held off from making arrangements with Cooke, saying to Cooke in effect that only one reason stood in the way, that newspapers and politicians had made out too strong a case against Cooke's garnering a large comfortable fortune for himself in the selling of government bonds. Too many people believed Cooke was taking more than was right during a war in which patriots put personal sacrifice first and money rewards second. This was the "sentiment" which Fessenden presented to Cooke as having existence to such an extent that he, Fessenden, the new Secretary of the Treasury, "could not think of engaging in any business negotiations" with Jay Cooke & Company. Cooke's reply was as natural to him as the horns of a Texas longhorn. He would say his services were "as disinterested and patriotic and pure as earth ever saw." He could go into details. His commissions on sales were a fraction of 1 per cent, and the more money he raised, the more difficult was it for him to get that fractional percentage increased. Around him centered the question whether men or money were more needed for the war. Could a war be run without money? Had it ever been done? Were there not hoary and respected proverbs of money as the sinews of war, the lifeblood of commerce, the basis of transport and supply?

Fessenden knew this. He was kindly and courteous with Jay Cooke. "We parted good friends," wrote Cooke. "I know just what ought to be done and could in one week put the machinery in motion, and save our finances from utter ruin." Chase believed this too, letting Cooke know, "I have both written and spoken to him [Fessenden] very decidedly." And incidentally neither Chase nor Cooke saw Fessenden as any genius of finance, Chase writing Cooke, "I do not think, perhaps I may be overvain, that Mr. Fessenden quite draws my bow," and "However much cause I may think I have to dislike certain acts of Mr. Lincoln I cannot but feel that my duty to sustain the government remains unaffected," and so on.

Out of interviews with Fessenden and Lincoln it followed that Jay Cooke & Company were once more harnessed into government service. Nowhere in sight prepared and ready to go was anything to compare with the Cooke machinery and methods for coaxing bankers, investors, and the masses of people into putting their money into government bonds as a good investment. Once when Fessenden returned from New York with a $10,000,000 lot of bonds and no takers at acceptable prices, Cooke said to Fessenden: "I will take them myself. I will take three millions at once, and you can give me an option on the rest of the ten millions, which I will close after a visit to New York."

Fessenden smiled and made a remark often thereafter quoted in the Cooke firm's banks and offices: "I have heretofore thought you a protégé of Mr. Chase, but now I see that he was your protégé."

Seventeen days before Chase had resigned Congress passed the Gold Bill and the President signed it. To buy or sell gold for delivery later than the day of signing the contract was made a crime. To contract to buy or sell gold not in the hands of the seller when selling was made a crime. The purpose was to stop speculation and gambling in gold. In six months gold had steadily climbed from 150 to 250. The Gold Bill made the course of gold crazier than before. It cavorted and somersaulted so fast in such a price range that it was the gambler's perfect delight. And actual gold was sent into deeper hiding and became more scarce for its functions of paying interest on government bonds and foreign exchange.

After the seventeen days of gold-price acrobatics Congress repealed the Gold Bill and the President signed the repeal. From then on the gold gamblers were accepted by the Government as an evil beyond control.

Whether Copperhead or Confederate manipulation was present could not be proved, though Unionists continued to denounce "unpatriotic criminal efforts of speculators and probably of secret enemies to raise the price of gold regardless of the injury inflicted on the country." Gold gamblers as a class were "disloyal men in sympathy with the South," said one Senator. The distinction between a legitimate gold speculator on the one hand, and a gambler indifferent to the Union cause on the other, could not be strictly drawn.

The young banker J. Pierpont Morgan in his public statement that the Gold Bill was "only one more instance of the utter lawlessness of Congress to interfere with the ordinary business transactions of a commercial city" voiced the legitimate protest of the bankers' meeting of which he was secretary. And in joining secretly with Morris Ketchum, Secretary Chase's loan representative in New York City, to buy $5,000,000 of gold, ship half of it abroad, resell the other half at home, and otherwise juggle the gold back and forth in sales and purchases where it was not known that Ketchum was Morgan's associate—in this too J. Pierpont Morgan was strictly within the law and could not be accused of the "utter lawlessness" he charged upon Congress in its Gold Bill. The joint profit of Morgan and Ketchum in this one deal was $160,000. The *New York Times* exposed the transaction and identified the "respectably connected young" Morgan as operating it. The respectability of Morgan was not affected by the *New York Times* ascribing "the enormous and unprincipled speculation in gold" to "a knot of unscrupulous gamblers who care nothing for the credit of the country." Lincoln in May of '64 could only clutch at empty air as he cried in the hearing of Carpenter that every one of the gold gamblers "ought to have his *devilish* head shot off."

Nothing came of a Union League meeting in June of '64 urging that "Congress at once order the erection of scaffolds for hanging" the speculators, nor of Jay Cooke saying they were "evil geniuses," nor of the New York Stock Exchange frowning on gold-buyers. Those who wanted money from tricks in gold first had met in the Coal Hole, a basement, and then moved to larger quarters, the Gold Room. Into this room flowed various information services from the battlefields. Bets on the gold price range hung on how many boys lay mangled in the Wilderness, at Spotsylvania, or on Kenesaw Mountain. Union defeats sent gold up, and the Gold Room seemed to attract gamblers who could be glad over Confederate victories. "Men stand in groups upon the floor," said the *New York Evening Post*, "and openly manifest their sympathy with the rebels." They added to the confusion that worked against the Union cause. They further muddled economic conditions that had made money cheaper. Rising prices of the goods of life had made the private soldier's $13 a month look so ridiculous that Congress on May 1 of '64 raised it to $16.

In the deep-gloom months of July and August, 1864, the barometric indicator, gold, was to say that Lincoln and the Union Government were failing. Against the peak price of gold during three years of war could be cited figures and facts favoring Lincoln. What gold commanded in exchange, however, represented an imponderable human factor. It registered in those two summer months. Thirty-nine dollars of gold would buy $100 of greenbacks. This was the bottom gold price of the Union Government's paper promises to pay. One interpretation was that the holders of gold in those months had less hope than ever of the Union Government's winning its war. Daniel Drew, who won millions in jugglery of Erie Railroad securities, said gold speculation was hardly in his line, but "it's good fishing in troubled waters," and so he was in the Gold Room with others, such as the swift and furtive little Jay Gould with a curly black beard, and the bovine and blond-mustached Jim Fisk, who in playing cards preferred a marked deck. Of the international bankers Peabody & Morgan, sturdy Samuel Bowles said in the *Springfield Republican* that their agencies in New York and London had induced during the war a flight of capital from America. "They gave us no faith and no help in our struggle for national existence.

. . . No individuals contributed so much to flooding the money markets with evidences of our debts to Europe, and breaking down their prices and weakening financial confidence in our nationality, and none made more money by the operation."

On July 4 of this gloomy summer Congress adjourned. Among the bills piled on the President's desk for signature was one that would slash the slender supports on which the "Lincoln ten-per-cent plan" rested. Since December of '63, when the President had launched his plan, much had happened to it. Then Hay wrote in his diary that all factions in Congress seemed to agree, and on the reading of the President's message, "Men acted as if the millennium had come. Chandler was delighted, Sumner was beaming." Border State men said they were satisfied; Senator Wilson of Massachusetts gave Hay a message for the President, "Tell him for me, 'God bless him.' " Kellogg of Michigan shouted in a lobby, "The President is the only man . . . none like him in the world. He sees more widely and more clearly than anybody"; the St. Louis radical Henry T. Blow was wrought up to say: "God bless Our Abe. I am one of the Radicals who have always believed in the President."

Then slowly and week by week had come a change, deepening suspicions of the President's motives, more open claims that the States in secession had committed suicide and that the President was impossible in his plan for a loyal 10 per cent to be authorized to reorganize the governments of those States. Representative Henry Winter Davis of Maryland led this opposition in the House, and Ben Wade in the Senate. Henry Winter Davis was a cousin of Judge David Davis, one radical and the other conservative. Davis was tall, slender, with wavy hair and a curly mustache, a musical voice, mental caliber, oratorical style, and nerve. Born in a Maryland slaveholding family, he had come to hate slavery as fiercely as any New Englander. In politics first a Whig, then an American or Know-Nothing, he became a Republican and in 1860 refused offers of second place on the ticket with Lincoln.

When the suggestion was made to Henry Winter Davis that he should be Attorney General in Lincoln's Cabinet he urged that John A. Gilmer of North Carolina have the place. That Monty Blair of Maryland should be named Postmaster General was a stench in his nostrils. He was leading a Maryland faction that hated Blair. Of the many haters of Blair perhaps none equaled Henry Winter Davis. In Maryland appointive offices Davis had received a fair share, even though Blair men and others advised the President otherwise. "The President was a man so persistently and incorrigibly just, that, even in the face of provocation, he never lost his high opinion of Mr. Davis' ability nor his confidence in his inherent good intentions," wrote Nicolay and Hay. Why Davis should from the start be on the warpath against Lincoln was a puzzle to Nicolay and Hay, for in their judgment, "Mr. Davis was a man of too much integrity and elevation of character to allow the imputation that his action on public matters was dictated entirely by personal feeling or prejudice."

In short, Davis seemed to be clean, honest, flaming, impetuous, and temperamental, like Wendell Phillips, the difficult key to him found perhaps in his saying that he who compromised a moral principle was a scoundrel, but that he who would not compromise a political measure was a fool. He had talked with the President in the spring of '63 about his campaign for Congress and the President next day had written him a letter with a postscript advising Davis that the letter was not for publication "but to prevent misunderstanding of what I verbally said to you yesterday." This, as Lincoln wrote it, was what he had said verbally:

"There will be in the new House of Representatives, as there were in the old, some members openly opposing the war, some supporting it unconditionally, and some supporting it with 'buts,' and 'ifs,' and 'ands.' They will divide on the organization of the House—on the election of a Speaker. As you ask my opinion, I give it, that the supporters of the war should send no man to Congress who will not pledge himself to go into caucus with the unconditional supporters of the war, and to abide the action of such caucus and vote for the person therein nominated for Speaker. Let the friends of the Government first save the Government, and then administer it to their own liking."

Davis replied this "favor" was "all that could be desired," won his election, began his service in the Congress. Immediately on the House receiving the President's message Davis called for a select committee to "guarantee" its reconstruction proposals. In the course of a few months Davis denounced Seward as a truckler to foreign Powers and hardly less than a traitor, shamed the Administration's policy in Mexico, demanded "explanations" of the President's relations to Napoleon III, and flung into the arena a bill intended to block the restoration efforts already started by the President in Louisiana and Tennessee and to stop the spread of the President's policy in other Southern States.

This open antagonism to the President was doing harm politically in Maryland. A delegation of Administration supporters interviewed Lincoln to say so and to add that the President might lose the electoral vote of the State. The President, according to Nicolay and Hay, replied: "I understand that Mr. Davis is doing all in his power to secure the success of the emancipation ticket in Maryland. If he does this, I care nothing about the electoral vote." As between the Blair influence in Maryland and that of Henry Winter Davis, it seemed that Lincoln at this hour would prefer that Davis should prevail in idea and spirit. In the House Davis was the one radical most often reminded by Thaddeus Stevens that he was going too far and ought to take what he could get now. The one speaker who could draw in more members from the cloakrooms than any other was Davis. Many had risen to tell what their minds read across the mist of years and what the future held for the Negro race whose slave chains were being pounded loose by far-flung armies with cannon and flame. None had spoken their guess and vision with stranger cadences than Henry Winter Davis:

"The folly of our ancestors and the wisdom of the Almighty, in its inscrutable purpose, having allowed them to come here and planted them here, they have a right to remain here to the latest syllable of recorded time. And whether they become our equals or our superiors, whether they blend or remain a distinct race, your posterity will know, for their eyes will behold them as ours do now. These are things which we cannot control. Laws do not make, laws cannot unmake them. If God has made them our equals, then they will work out the problem which He has sent them to work out; and if God has stamped upon them an ineradicable inferiority, you cannot make one hair white or black or add a cubit to their stature."

His intimates knew that Henry Winter Davis favored giving all Negroes the ballot, just as Governor Hahn in Louisiana knew by a private letter from Lincoln that Lincoln favored giving the ballot to "the very intelligent, and especially those who have fought gallantly in our ranks." That Lincoln had so written to Governor Hahn may have come to Davis, who through letters kept close touch with abolitionist staff officers of General Banks at New Orleans. That William Lloyd Garrison explicitly stood with Lincoln on this issue had no weight with Winter Davis, who ranged himself in spirit and in specific demands with the Wendell Phillips faction of the divided American Anti-Slavery Society. In his cries for death to slaveholders and confiscation of their property, for immediate Negro emancipation and universal Negro political equality, Davis was a manner of twin to Wendell Phillips. In his flush and flowing sentiment that the march of universal human freedom "is destined to continue until nations shall roll up like a scroll, and all created things shall be wrapped in the bosom of the Creator," he had the Phillips drumbeat. And though he was an abolitionist in everything except formal membership, Davis could and did go to Cooper Union in October of '63 and in the course of a speech declare, "I never sympathized with the radical abolitionists, for I thought them one hair's breadth this side of craziness."

Such in degree was the quixotic political artist who with his ally Ben Wade saw a wide chasm between them and the President. They could not trust him. They nursed suspicions into what they believed were facts. The President was too slow, too hesitant, too loose with expedient, they believed, and Congress would be more firm. And beyond this personal matter lay an idea and a theory of republican government; the reconstruction of the seceded Slave States, if and when conquered, was so momentous a project that it should be directed by the legislative body and not by the Executive. The Constitution vested Congress with "a plenary, supreme, unlimited political jurisdiction," and new State governments could be referred "to no authority except the judgment and will of the majority of Congress," said Davis in behalf of a bill he introduced February 15 of '64.

Under the bill the President with Senate consent would appoint for each State in rebellion a provisional governor to serve until Congress recognized a regular civil government as existing therein. As soon as military resistance to Federal authority had been suppressed, "and the people had sufficiently returned to their obedience to the Constitution and the laws," it was made the duty of the governor "to enroll all white male citizens of the United States," and wherever a majority of them took the oath of allegiance, the loyal people of the State were entitled to elect delegates to re-establish a State government. Confederate soldiers and officers were barred as delegates and from voting for delegates, as were also all civil officers of the Confederate Government. Whatever constitution a State convention should adopt must require: (1) that no Confederate colonel or officer of higher rank than colonel could be governor or have a seat in the legislature; (2) that slavery be abolished and "involuntary servitude forever prohibited"; (3) that no Confederate or State debts should be recognized.

"Until therefore," said Davis, "Congress recognize a State government, organized under its auspices, there is no government in the rebel States except the authority of Congress." Looking southward, he could see in "the darkness of that bottomless pit" no hope of co-operation with a Union Government, no willingness to accept terms that even the Democrats were offering. His language and viewpoint were strikingly parallel to that of General Tecumseh Sherman, also saying that no beginning of legal and orderly government could be made until military opposition was absolutely annihilated, "trampled in the dust."

Davis rejected the President's Amnesty Proclamation and its "ten-per-cent plan" as lacking guarantees. "If . . . under the dictation of any military authority, or under the prescriptions of a provost marshal, something in the form of a government shall be presented, the President will recognize that." Under the President's plan, surmised Davis, the newly organized government of a State might combine all the population, or one-tenth only, "or ten governments may come competing for recognition at the door of the Executive Mansion."

The debate ran long, a festival of constitutional lawyers. How and when does a State become a State, and under what conditions can it lose its face as a State and again later have its face put back? This question, and what many eminent legal minds had spoken and written about it, was argued up, down, and across.

The amnesty oath devised by the President, said Ignatius Donnelly of Minnesota, could be viewed in the light of the Confederate General Jeff Thompson, now a prisoner at St. Louis, saying he had been in regions where men consulted their memorandum books to see what oath they had taken last. Thousands of Confederate dead had been found on battlefields, Donnelly asserted, with oaths of allegiance to the Federal Government, sworn and subscribed to, in their pockets. The propping up of an old fabric, "a patching together of the broken shreds and fragments" giving the *appearance* of what had been, did not meet with favor from Donnelly, and he was for the Davis bill.

Donnelly said he was aware however of "great claims" which Mr. Lincoln had on the People. "I recognize that popularity which accompanies him, and which, considering the ordeal through which he has passed, is little less than miraculous. I recognize that unquestioning faith in his honesty and ability which pervades all classes, and that sincere affection with which almost the entire population regard him. We must not underrate him even in our praises. He is a great man. Great not after the old models of the world, but with a homely and original greatness. He will stand out to future ages in the history of these crowded and confused times with wonderful distinctness. He has carried a vast and discordant population safely and peacefully through the greatest of political revolutions with such consummate sagacity and skill that while he led he appeared to follow; while he innovated beyond all precedent he has been denounced as tardy; while he struck the shackles from the limbs of three million slaves he has been hailed as a conservative! If to adapt, persistently and continuously, just and righteous principles to all the perplexed windings and changes of human events, and to secure in the end the complete triumph of those principles, be statesmanship, then Abraham Lincoln is the first of statesmen." This was Donnelly's notice to the radicals that he would not join those who questioned the motives and ability of the President. It was a charming panegyric to come from a man preparing to write a thick book in support of the proposition that Lord Bacon wrote the plays of William Shakespeare and nobody else could have.

The unconstitutional and despotic acts of the President would be legalized and perpetuated by the proposed bill, declared Representative Charles Denison of Pennsylvania. Perry of New Jersey was positive that the Machiavellian hand of the President was behind the bill. "Mr. Speaker, I denominate the whole plan a political trick worthy of the most adroit and unscrupulous wire-puller of our ward primary meetings." Fernando Wood held it to be "the worst kind of tyranny" to pretend to give the reorganized Southern States a republican form of government while dictating to them they must abolish slavery. Another Peace Democrat, George Pendleton of Ohio, said that all pretense was now thrust aside and the avowal was evident that an old Constitution was treasonably being ingrafted with new principles and a revolution instituted. "Admit you are in revolution; admit you are revolutionists; admit that you do not desire to restore the old order. Avow that you are not bound by the Constitution, but by your own sense of right. Avow that resistance to your schemes is not treason, but war. Dissolve the spell which you have woven around the hearts of our people by the cunning use of the words conservatism, patriotism, Union. And . . . we will hush all reproaches . . . fight you with your weapons."

Again as so often before the sense of word values between Peace Democrats on the one hand, and War Democrats and Republicans on the other, was blunted. S. S. Cox of Ohio, whose later nickname of "Sunset" arose from his use of burning adjectives to describe an Ohio sunset, saw the

Republic writing in the final sweats and ravings that precede Death, the skeleton, and Time, the shadow. In Cox's view, "He [the President] only draws over the mailed hand a silken though transparent glove. His plan is the will of the commander, while pretending to be the wisdom of the civilian." Cox saw the same fatal defect in the plans of both Lincoln and Davis: they would both abolish slavery without constitutional authority. Cox wandered far afield in historical parallels from Rome, Greece, Mesopotamia, England, and Ireland, and closed with saying he would have the Government animated by a voice soft as an angel's lute or a seraph's song, promising redress for wrong,

> " 'Speaking of peace, speaking of love,
> Speaking as angels speak above.' "

No sooner had Cox finished speaking of conciliation and love than the Massachusetts Republican George Boutwell arose to say the Davis bill should in justice provide that South Carolina, Georgia, Florida, could never come back into the Union except as strictly Negro States. "Let these three States be set apart as the home of the negro. Invite him there by giving to him local political power. Give them local self-government, and let them defend themselves as a portion of this Republic." Boutwell said that it ill became any believers in liberty to arraign the President or his own lifelong personal friend General Banks for mistakes in Louisiana. "She is becoming free through the fact that her people are being identified day by day and week by week with the institutions and principles of freedom." Boutwell would nevertheless vote for the Davis bill. His trust was in Congress rather than the President, of whom he gave the shaded estimate: "Whatever may be our opinion of the President on certain points, and I do not stand here or anywhere as his defender, I think I am justified in saying that they are manifest only in the lack of executive control over those intrusted with the performance of administrative duties."

Nor was Thaddeus Stevens satisfied with the Davis bill. "It does not, in my judgment, meet the evil." Its acknowledgment that the "rebel States have rights under the Constitution" he would deny. "I do not inquire what rights we have under it, but they have none. The bill takes for granted that the President may partially interfere in their civil administration, not as conqueror, but as President of the United States. It adopts in some measure the idea that less than a majority may regulate to some extent the affairs of a republic." Stevens's chief objection was that the bill removed the opportunity of confiscating the property of the disloyal.

Davis consented to a preamble by Stevens which declared "the so-called confederate States are a public enemy, waging an unjust war, whose injustice is so glaring that they have no right to claim the mitigation of the extreme rights of war which are accorded by modern usage to an enemy who has a right to consider the war a just one," from which it should follow that "none of the States which, by a regularly recorded majority of its citizens, have joined the so-called southern confederacy can be considered and treated as entitled to be represented in Congress, or to take any part in the political government of the Union."

A number of Republicans and War Democrats joined with Peace Democrats and by a vote of 76 to 57 rejected this preamble of Stevens. In the Yeas and Nays immediately thereafter on the Davis bill, however, these votes returned to the Republicans. By 73 to 59 the Davis bill passed the House May 4, 1864. In the Senate its course had been guided by Wade, who said: "The Executive ought not to be permitted to handle this great question to his own liking. It does not belong, under the Constitution, to the President to prescribe the rule, and it is a base abandonment of our own powers and our own duties to cast this great principle upon the decision of the executive branch of the Government . . . I know very well that the President from the best motives undertook to fix a rule upon which he would admit these States back into the Union." Nevertheless, that a State should have self-government originated by one-tenth of the population seemed to Wade absurd, antirepublican, anomalous, and entirely subversive.

In what the President had thus far done he was "equally a usurper with Caesar, Cromwell and Bonaparte," said Garrett Davis of Kentucky. In exploiting the Peace Democrat viewpoint Garrett Davis spread over the pages of the *Congressional Globe* a diatribe of several thousand words on Lincoln's ambition, desire for re-election, love of power and money. "He is no statesman, but a mere political charlatan. He has inordinate vanity and conceit. He is a consummate dissembler, and an adroit and sagacious demagogue. He has the illusion of making a great historical name for himself in connection with the total abolition of slavery in the United States. He is not fierce or revengeful, or even boldly audacious and radical; and though not marked by any sense of benevolence, humanity, or justice, he does not possess positively the opposite qualities, and, though a radical, is not reckless or rash. He is, and always has been, as uncompromisingly opposed to slavery as the most ultra radical, but preferred to overthrow it with some show of legal and constitutional authority; and that it should be effected gradually, and not by sudden and violent change. Being rather of flexible but still obstinate nature, the pressure of the bold and more energetic radicals has pushed him pretty well nigh to their extreme position." The tentative and hazardous State governments set up by the President in Louisiana, Tennessee, and Arkansas were denounced by Garrett Davis as "lawless and daring political enterprises" intended to garner electoral votes in the coming November.

Carlile of Virginia offered arguments that the Constitution made it "the duty of the Government of the United States, not of Congress" to do what the Wade bill proposed, and to questions of Wade replied with quotations from the forty-third number of the *Federalist* by James Madison, author of the Constitution, on what the Government could "guaranty" a State. "He is too good a lawyer not to know the meaning of the word 'guaranty,'" said Carlile of Wade. And Carlile pushed Wade on constitutional points to where Wade gave no reply. Carlile mixed his strictly legal argument with no personal accusations and insinuations. As a member of the convention by which Virginia had seceded from the Union, and in which he fought to the last against secession, Carlile had studied the Constitution closely. And again in the movement by which western Virginia was carved out and set up as the part of Virginia still in the Union, he had become expert on what the Constitution said as to the making of States. Wade for once seemed to be stumped, and offered no dispute of Carlile's proposition that Congress was taking to itself powers which the Constitution gave to the whole Government.

B. Gratz Brown of Missouri, now hovering in mid-air as between the Republican party and the Frémont Radical Democracy, put in an amendment which would bar inhabitants of the insurrectionary States from voting for presidential Electors or members of Congress until the President by act of Congress had declared the rebellion abandoned. By a vote of 17 to 16 the Senate adopted this amendment. Sumner too had an amendment. He would enact the Emancipation Proclamation into a law. The Senate rejected this by 21 to 11.

On the main bill of Wade, which had been on the Senators' desks for five months, the Senate voted July 2, 1864, and passed it by 26 Yeas to 3 Nays, with no less than 20 Senators absent. The bill went into conference. The House refused to accept the Gratz Brown amendment. Wade moved that the Senate recede from its amendment and agree to the House (Davis) bill. The Senate agreed by 18 Yeas and 14 Nays, no less than 17 Senators being absent.

On July 4 Congress was to adjourn. The President in his room at the Capitol was signing bills as they were brought to him from Senate and House. The Wade-Davis bill was placed before him, and he laid it aside. Members of Congress entered. Hay saw Sumner in "a state of intense anxiety" over the bill. Boutwell was somewhat nervous but said little. Zachariah Chandler, "unabashed in any mortal presence, roundly asked the President if he intended to sign the bill."

Lincoln. This bill was placed before me a few moments before Congress adjourns. It is a matter of too much importance to be swallowed in that way.

Chandler. If it is vetoed it will damage us fearfully in the Northwest. The important point is that one prohibiting slavery in the reconstructed States.

Lincoln. That is the point on which I doubt the authority of Congress to act.

Chandler. It is no more than you have done yourself.

Lincoln. I conceive that I may in an emergency do things on military grounds which cannot be done constitutionally by Congress.

Chandler went out. The President turned to Cabinet members at the table: "I do not see how any of us can now deny and contradict what we have always said, that Congress has no constitutional power over slavery in the States." Fessenden agreed entirely, saying, "I even had my doubts as to the constitutional efficacy of your own decree of emancipation, in such cases where it has not been carried into effect by the actual advance of the Army."

The President said: "This bill and the position of these gentlemen seems to me to make the fatal admission (in asserting that the insurrectionary States are no longer in the Union) that States whenever they please may of their own motion dissolve their connection with the Union. Now we cannot survive that admission, I am convinced. If that be true, I am not President, these gentlemen are not Congress. I have laboriously endeavored to avoid that question ever since it first began to be mooted & thus to avoid confusion and disturbance in our own counsels. It was to obviate this question that I earnestly favored the movement for an amendment to the Constitution abolishing slavery, which passed the Senate and failed in the House. I thought it much better, if it were possible, to restore the Union without the necessity of a violent quarrel among its friends, as to whether certain States have been in or out of the Union during the war: a merely metaphysical question, and one unnecessary to be forced into discussion."

Every Cabinet member present agreed with this view, Hay noted, and when the President a few minutes later stepped into his carriage to go to the White House, he was already aware of the step he would take and of possible disaster ahead. Someone said to him that the threats of the extreme radicals had no foundation and the people would not bolt their ticket on a question of metaphysics, and he answered: "If they choose to make a point upon this, I do not doubt that they can do harm. They have never been friendly to me. . . . At all events, I must keep some consciousness of being somewhere near right: I must keep some standard of principle fixed within myself."

For five months the bill had been before Congress. "The President declined to exercise any influence on the debate," said his secretaries, meaning that no Senators or Representatives were privately called in by the President for discussion of the bill with executive request that they should do the best they could against it. While the House during five months had the bill, the President in public addresses repeatedly emphasized the immediate necessity for moving toward abolition of slavery by Constitutional Amendment. He stressed this so plainly that Congress and the country could hardly get any other impression than that he believed Congress did not have the authority to prohibit slavery and the only way was the slow process of having three-fourths of the State legislatures thus instruct Congress and the President. The projection of this idea was perhaps the extent of the President's influence on debate in Congress. Indications were, however, that he did take a hand in the parliamentary procedure, that it was his wish the Senate should put off its debate and its vote on the bill till the end of the session.

The inside history of the peculiar voting record of the Senate on July 1 and July 2 might or might not have revealed the President in an effort to kill the bill. Those two days showed a surprising change in shift in

Yeas and Nays. On July 1 the Wade bill with the B. Gratz Brown amendment passed by 26 to 3, with 20 Senators absent. The next day the Wade bill, divested by House conference of the Brown amendment, passed by 18 to 14, with 17 Senators absent. Four more Nay votes would have tied the vote and killed the bill. The names of Senators Doolittle of Wisconsin, Henderson of Missouri, Ten Eyck of New York, and Trumbull of Illinois shifted from the Yea column of July 1 to the Nays of July 2. Of these Henderson, as a moderate opposed in Missouri to Gratz Brown, voted logically on the second day, and Trumbull was an independent whose present and later record showed he was not always to be counted with the radicals.

Into this confusion and perplexity four days after Congress adjourned the President stepped with an amazing document. He issued a proclamation reciting that whereas Congress had passed a bill to guarantee republican form of government to certain States, and whereas "the said bill was presented to the President of the United States for his approval less than one hour before the *sine die* adjournment of said session, and was not signed by him," that the plan expressing the sense of Congress on restoration of the proper, practical relation of States in rebellion, was now before the people for their consideration:

"Now, therefore, I, Abraham Lincoln, President of the United States, do proclaim, declare, and make known that while I am—as I was in December last, when by proclamation I propounded a plan of restoration—unprepared by a formal approval of this bill to be inflexibly committed to any single plan of restoration, and while I am also unprepared to declare that the free State constitutions and governments, already adopted and installed in Arkansas and Louisiana, shall be set aside and held for naught, thereby repelling and discouraging the loyal citizens who have set up the same as to further effort, or to declare a constitutional competency in Congress to abolish slavery in States, but am at the same time sincerely hoping and expecting that a constitutional amendment abolishing slavery throughout the nation may be adopted, nevertheless, I am fully satisfied with the system for restoration contained in the bill as one very proper plan for the loyal people of any State choosing to adopt it; and that I am, and at all times shall be, prepared to give the executive aid and assistance to any such people, so soon as military resistance to the United States shall have been suppressed in any such State, and the people thereof shall have sufficiently returned to their obedience to the Constitution and the laws of the United States, in which cases military governors will be appointed, with directions to proceed according to the bill."

Nothing quite like this had happened before in the history of the Republic. Never before had an Executive assumed to reject those provisions in a legislative measure which he disliked and to adopt those acceptable to him. This was precisely what Lincoln did. And in the very hour of doing it he went straight to the people proclaiming it. He had neither signed the bill nor vetoed it. "He put it in his pocket." The method became known as the pocket veto. He was "fully satisfied" with part of the bill but as to other parts he was "unprepared." The key of the matter was in his saying he could not be "inflexibly committed to any single plan of restoration." Over the heads of Congress and its embittered and warring factions, he put his case to the country and the people.

Ben Wade and Henry Winter Davis were good haters and liked a fight. They raged privately. And publicly they stormed. In the *New York Tribune* of August 5 they published their joint answer to Lincoln, picked up and reprinted over the country, "The Wade-Davis Manifesto." The language was fierce and polite at once. They hoped to blast the pinions from under the President and blister his name and give him a lesson. Addressing themselves "To the Supporters of the Government," they said they had "read without surprise, but not without indignation" the President's proclamation of July 8. They would maintain it was a right and a duty "to check the encroachments of the Executive on the authority of Congress, and to require it to confine itself to its proper sphere." The President did not sign the bill in question. "The bill did not therefore become a law; and it is therefore nothing. The proclamation is neither an approval nor a veto of the bill; it is therefore a document unknown to the laws and Constitution of the United States. . . . The committee sent to ascertain if the President had any further communication for the House of Representatives reported that he had none; and the friends of the bill, who had anxiously waited on him to ascertain its fate, had already been informed that the President had resolved not to sign it. The time of presentation, therefore, had nothing to do with his failure to approve it."

Wade and Davis pointed to the length of time the bill had been discussed and considered and how there was no reason to believe "that this method of preventing the bill from becoming a law without the constitutional responsibility of a vote had been resolved on long before the bill passed the Senate." They set forth information "by a gentleman entitled to entire confidence" that before June 22 in New Orleans, it was stated by a member of General Banks's staff, in the presence of other gentlemen in official position, that Senator Doolittle in a letter to the department had written that the House Reconstruction bill "would be stayed off in the Senate to a period too late in the session to require the President to veto it in order to defeat it, and that Mr. Lincoln would retain the bill, if necessary, and thereby defeat it."

The reasons of the President for his action Wade and Davis found full of ominous significance. "The President persists in recognizing those shadows of governments in Arkansas and Louisiana, which Congress formally declared should not be recognized—whose representatives and senators were repelled by formal votes of both Houses of Congress. . . . They are the mere creatures of his will." Wade and Davis dwelt on the slender supports of those State governments, alleged the elections were a farce, and declared the President held "the electoral votes of the rebel states at the dictation of his personal ambition." They presented constitutional arguments which had become familiar in the debates in Congress, questioned the sincerity of the President in giving his "blessing" to emancipation, quoted from his latest proclamation and commented, "A more studied outrage on the legislative authority of the people has never been perpetrated."

Wade and Davis urged at length that where their bill would bring organization and order in republican form, there was now only chaos and delusion in Louisiana and Arkansas resulting from "this rash and fatal act of the President." The President had "greatly presumed" and they would give warning. "He must understand that our support is of a cause and not of a man; that the authority of Congress is paramount and must be respected; that the whole body of the Union men of Congress will not submit to be impeached by him of rash and unconstitutional legislation; and if he wishes our support he must confine himself to his executive duties—to obey and to execute, not make the laws—to suppress by arms armed rebellion, and leave political reorganization to Congress. If the supporters of the Government fail to insist on this they become responsible for the usurpations which they fail to rebuke. . . . Let them consider the remedy for these usurpations, and, having found it, fearlessly execute it."

On hearing the rasp and snarl of this family quarrel in the Republican party the opposition rejoiced. It was campaign year and their best verbal sharpshooters on the stump could not pick off the high stovepipe hat of Abe Lincoln, metaphorically, with the skill of Wade and Davis. Republican organization men who wanted to win in November said the party's best orators should not "wash dirty linen in public." One who was hot under the collar came to Lincoln about it. And according to Carpenter, the painter resident at the White House, the President philosophized: "It is not worth fretting about; it reminds me of an old acquaintance, who, having a son of a scientific turn, bought him a microscope. The boy went around experimenting with his glass on everything that came in his way. One day, at the dinner-table, his father took up a piece of cheese. 'Don't eat that, father,' said the boy; 'it is full of *wrigglers.*' 'My son,' replied the old gentleman, taking, at the same time, a huge bite, 'let 'em *wriggle;* I can stand it if they can.' "

Welles, so constantly eager to read ambition and personal advancement as a controlling motive, believed that Wade and Winter Davis each wanted to be President. "I remarked [to the President]," he wrote August 6, "that I had seen the Wade and Winter Davis protest. He said, Well, let them wriggle, but it was strange that Greeley, whom they made their organ in publishing the protest, approved his [the President's] course and therein differed from the protestants." Two days later Welles wrote: "The President, in a conversation with Blair and myself on the Wade and Davis protest, remarked that he had not, and probably should not read it. From what was said of it he had no desire to, could himself take no part in such a controversy as they seemed to wish to provoke. Perhaps he is right, provided he has some judicious friend to state to him what there is really substantial . . . without the vituperative asperity." From this point Welles strayed into dejection over the President's having advised only with Seward on his pocket-veto proclamation, having called no Cabinet meeting on it.

To Carpenter, Welles, and probably others, the President said, "Let them wriggle," but humor over what Wade and Davis were doing did not come easy. The main landscape of the country was too somber for people to care that Wade and Davis had lost their heads or that Winter Davis by his false stride was to fail of nomination and lose his seat in Congress to a Unionist colonel who had come near death from wounds in the Wilderness. One viewpoint was given by *Harper's Weekly*. "We have read with pain the manifesto of Messrs. Wade and Winter Davis," ran its editorial, "not because of its envenomed hostility to the President, but because of its ill-tempered spirit, which proves conclusively the unfitness of either of the gentlemen for grave counselors in a time of national peril. . . . It was the President's constitutional right to let the bill drop and say nothing more about it. But he chose to say that while he could not approve, and consequently obey it as a law, yet that he would follow it within the unquestioned domain of his own action so far as it seemed to him wise. In other words, he accepted parts of the bill as suggestions to guide him in all his executive conduct. Messrs. Wade and Davis complain that he did not accept the bill altogether or reject it entirely. As a law he did reject it; but, like a wise man, he embraced the sound principles he found in it, and will act upon them. . . . To charge him with extraordinary and dangerous assumptions of power, is childish. . . . It is simply impossible to make the American people believe that the President is a wily despot or a political gambler."

An underlying animus with Wade, Winter Davis, and their allies arose from fear and suspicion that Lincoln used the executive power to thwart the intentions of Congress as expressed in legislation. When after much heaving and hauling they passed a law, what use was it when the President didn't care about enforcing it? So they inquired, pointing to the Confiscation Act of '62. Lincoln had signed it and sent with his signature his explanation of why he seriously considered vetoing it. He was willing to confiscate slave property but not real estate in perpetuity. And his radical opposition knew that the President had let this law become a dead letter except as to slave property.

Where Wade and Davis had hoped for many million-dollar seizures of property the Treasury Department reported total proceeds of the confiscation had brought in $129,680. The Attorney General, a moderate particularly in agreement with the President on this law, had charge of its enforcement, though in practice it was performed by army officers. An instance was General Lew Wallace at Baltimore issuing two orders that declared his intention to confiscate the property of certain persons who were either serving in the Confederate Army or giving aid to the Confederate cause. Attorney General Bates on seeing these orders published in newspapers at once reminded Wallace that execution of the Confiscation Act was in the hands of the Attorney General and that Wallace had no legal warrant to seize private property. A dispute arose between Bates and Wallace. "Thereupon," wrote Horace White, "Bates took the orders and the correspondence to the President and declared his intention to resign his office if his functions were usurped by military men in the field, or by the War Department. Lincoln took the papers, and directed Secretary Stanton to require Wallace to withdraw the two orders and to desist from confiscation altogether. This was done by Stanton, but the orders were never publicly withdrawn although action under them was discontinued."

In the three days immediately preceding his proclamation concerning the Wade-Davis bill the President issued, with detailed reasons, a proclamation suspending the writ of habeas corpus in Kentucky, and another proclamation, by direction of Congress, appointing the first Thursday of August as a day of national humiliation and prayer. The President set forth the concordant resolution of Congress which urged that on this day all servants of the Government should convene at their usual places of worship "to confess and to repent of their manifold sins; to implore the compassion and forgiveness of the Almighty, that, if consistent with his will, the existing rebellion may be speedily suppressed . . . to implore him, as the supreme ruler of the world, not to destroy us as a people, nor suffer us to be destroyed by the hostility or the connivance of other nations, or by obstinate adhesion to our own counsels which may be in conflict with his eternal purposes."

To the 43 Democrats in Congress this proclamation was a propaganda of hypocrites. They one and all signed an address to the people of the United States, pointing to what they regarded as the shortcomings and evil-doings of Lincoln in his "bogus" State governments, in the swindle of paper money, in the cruelty of a mismanaged war. They concluded: "There are but two classes of men in this country who may rejoice in existing conditions: First, those who make money out of the war; and second, those who desire to achieve emancipation by it." The capital causes of danger were "corruption and fanaticism" and the Peace Democrats offered themselves and their party as a means of light and leadership to overcome these evils.

In almost the same calendar week that Ben Wade and Winter Davis shot their political venom at Lincoln, it happened that Confederate sharpshooters aimed their rifles at the President and sent cold lead bullets whining and snarling around their target. This was in the first battle fought on District of Columbia soil with the Capitol dome and its Goddess of Liberty looking on.

Once more General Robert E. Lee played a bold defensive game and struck fear into the heart of the Union cause. He gave Jubal A. Early and John C. Breckinridge an army of 20,000 men. Sheltered by the Blue Ridge Mountains, they marched up the Shenandoah Valley, slipped through a pass, headed for Washington, and only by a nod of fate as whimsical as a throw of dice John C. Breckinridge failed to pay that visit he had in the spring of '61 promised his kinswoman in the White House.

Early's men had legs and grit, could march thirty miles a day, and in their stride toward Washington their commander collected $20,000 cash at Hagerstown and from Frederick City, Maryland, which he threatened to lay in ashes, came $200,000 more. The foot soldiers tore up twenty-four miles of Baltimore & Ohio Railroad tracks, wrecked and burned mills, workshops, factories, while Early's horsemen got as far as the environs of Baltimore and burned the home of Governor Bradford of Maryland. Turning their horses toward Washington, they reached Silver Spring and in sight of the Capitol dome seized private papers, valuables, whisky, in the homes of Postmaster General Blair and Old Man Blair, and then set the houses afire.

"Baltimore is in great peril," telegraphed a mayor's committee to President Lincoln, asking for troops. From Philadelphia arrived a telegram that some "assuring announcement" must come from Washington to quiet the public mind. A Confederate army of 75,000 to 100,000 under Lee himself was again footloose and aiming for a stranglehold on Washington, ran another telegram that tumbled into Washington. Gustavus Vasa Fox, without the President's knowing it, had a steamer docked and ready for him in case the city was taken. In the Gold Room in New York the wild-eyed gamblers saw gold on June 11 go to its peak price of 285. "The panic here is heavy and increasing," telegraphed Lew Wallace, department commander at Baltimore. "Do not think there is just cause for it." To the Baltimore mayor's committee Lincoln wired: "I have not a single soldier but whom is being disposed by the military for the best protection of all. By latest accounts the enemy is moving on Washington. They cannot fly to either place. Let us be vigilant, but keep cool. I hope neither Baltimore nor Washington will be sacked."

Wallace had marched troops out to Monocacy, fought a battle, and, heavily outnumbered, was routed. His defeat delayed Early's army one day. That one day, it was generally admitted, saved Washington from the disgrace of capture. At Point Lookout near by were 17,000 Confederate prisoners whom Lee hoped Early would free and arm. But Early didn't find time. Every hour counted. His objective, as he later told of it, was practically the same as reported by a Union prisoner, Artificer N. A. Fitts, who escaped from Early's men and informed the War Department, "They claimed the object of their raid was to get horses and provisions, that they did not expect to take Washington and hold it, but thought they could raid through the city and capture the President, if there, and draw Grant's forces from Petersburg."

Raw troops and soldiers just out of hospital made up the 20,000 men scraped together for manning the forts around Washington against Early, who had cut all wires north and July 11 marched his men on the Seventh Street Road that would lead him straight to the offices, the arsenals, the gold and silver, of the United States Government. Early halted his men just a little over two miles from the Soldiers' Home, where Lincoln the night before had gone to bed when a squad from the War Department arrived with word from Stanton that he must get back into the city in a hurry. The President put on his clothes and rode to the Executive Mansion.

The next day would decide whether a Confederate flag was for once to be run up over the Capitol dome. The next day the President looked from the south windows of the White House and saw through a glass transport steamers at Alexandria coming to unload two magnificent divisions of veteran troops fresh from Grant at City Point. The President met them at the wharf, touched his hat to them, and they cheered and he waved his hand and smiled and they sent up more and more cheers.

Out on the Seventh Street Road the same day Jubal Early sat his horse and looked at Fort Stevens (later Stephens), which blocked his path. The fort was "feebly manned," as he saw it. And he was correct. But while he was still gazing, and while the attack he had ordered was getting under way, his eye caught a column of men in blue filing into the works. The fort guns began speaking. A line of skirmishers strung out in front. On one of the parapets Lincoln was a watcher and saw the first shots traded. He was too tall a target, said officers who insisted till he put himself below the danger line.

Early stopped his attack, sent his cavalry to hunt another door into the city. That night while Early held a council of war just north of Washington, more newly arrived troops at the south stepped off transports and tramped through the streets with a certainty that the Capitol dome the next day would be saved from a Confederate flag over it. The sun was throwing long slants of gold over that dome the next morning as Jubal Early looked at it and wondered what this day of July 12 would bring.

No mail, no telegrams, arrived from the outer world that day of July 12 in Washington. At a noon Cabinet meeting the President was signing a batch of commissions. "The President," wrote Welles, "said he and Seward had visited several of the fortifications. I asked where the Rebels were in force. He said he did not know with certainty, but he thought the main body at Silver Spring. I expressed a doubt whether there was any large force at any one point, but that they were in squads of from 500 to perhaps 1500 scattered along . . . the Potomac. . . . The President did not respond farther than to again remark he thought there must be a pretty large force in the neighborhood of Silver Spring."

From where Lincoln stood on a Fort Stevens rampart that afternoon he could see the swaying skirmish lines and later the marching brigade of General Daniel Davidson Bidwell, a police justice from Buffalo, New York, who had enlisted in '61 as a private, was a colonel through the Seven Days and Malvern Hill, and with his men had heard the bullets sing from Antietam through Gettysburg and the Wilderness. Out across parched fields, dust, and a haze of summer heat marched Bidwell's men in perfect order, to drive the enemy from a house and orchard near the Silver Spring Road. Up a rise of ground in the face of a withering fire they moved and

SCENES NEAR WASHINGTON, DURING THE REBEL RAID—NIGHT ATTACK, JULY 11, ON FORT STEVENS WHILE THE PRESIDENT WAS THERE.

took their point and pushed the enemy pickets back for a mile. The cost was 280 men killed and wounded.

For the first time in his life Abraham Lincoln saw men in battle action go to their knees and sprawl on the earth with cold lead in their vitals, with holes plowed by metal through their heads. Before this day he had seen them marching away cheering and laughing, and he had seen them return in ambulances, and had met them on crutches and in slings and casts, and in hospitals he had held their hands and talked with them. Now for the first time he saw them as the rain of enemy rifle shots picked them off.

While he stood watching this bloody drama a bullet whizzed five feet from him, was deflected, and struck Surgeon Crawford of the 102d Pennsylvania in the ankle. While he yet stood there, within three feet of the President an officer fell with a death wound. Those who were there that afternoon said he was cool and thoughtful, seemed unconscious of danger, and looked like a Commander in Chief.

In officially reporting the afternoon's losses at 300, Halleck wrote that "a few men in the trenches were picked off by rebel sharpshooters." The fire of those who came near picking off Lincoln was at long range, it would seem from the report of a chief of staff who suggested to Major General Augur, in command, the driving away of "a thin line of the enemy (not more than 500), who occupy a crest and house near our line and 1,100 yards only from Fort Stevens," the special object being "to put them out of a large house occupied by sharpshooters." So it was probable the men 1,100 yards away were shooting that day at a man, any man on a rampart or in a trench who made a good target, though they would concede that a man six feet four in height was a shade the easier to draw a bead on. Twice they nearly got the tall man. "Amid the whizzing bullets," wrote Nicolay and Hay, the President held to his place "with . . . grave and passive countenance," till finally "General Wright peremptorily represented to him the needless risk he was running."

Another onlooker that day, facing Lincoln from a mile away, was the man whom the South in 1860 voted for overwhelmingly as its choice for President of the United States, the Kentuckian who hoped to pay a promised call at the Executive Mansion, General John C. Breckinridge.

In his diary Welles wrote of riding out in the afternoon to Fort Stevens, of Senator Wade coming up beside him, the two of them entering the fort, "where we found the President, who was sitting in the shade, his back against the parapet towards the enemy." The impression of Welles, and probably of Wade, was that the President might at least have been standing up during the battle, and perhaps should have had curiosity enough to have faced toward the enemy. Their visit was short, all hands were busy, and Welles went away unaware of the music the President had faced before sitting in the shade, his back against the parapet towards the enemy. "As we came out of the fort," wrote Welles, "four or five of the wounded men were carried by on stretchers. It was nearly dark as we left. Driving . . . out, we passed fields as well as roads full of soldiers, horses, teams, mules. Camp-fires lighted up the woods . . . stragglers by the wayside were many. Some were doubtless sick, some were drunk, some weary and exhausted. Then men on horseback, on mules, in wagons as well as on foot, batteries of artillery, caissons, an innumerable throng. It was exciting and wild. Much of life and much of sadness. Strange that in this age and country there is this strife and struggle, under one of the most beneficent governments which ever blessed mankind and all in sight of the Capitol."

Official records of the only battle of the war where Lincoln was an eyewitness and a target gave the Union losses at 380 killed and 319 wounded.

The next morning Early's army was gone. Again on July 14 Washington had mail and telegrams. Somewhere toward the Shenandoah Valley marched Early's army with its plunder-laden wagons, audacity on its banners, money in its strongboxes, shoes on feet that had started north barefoot.

Early got away for the same reason that he arrived. "Nobody stopped him."

And why? The answer would require a diagram of the overlapping authorities and departments; of many physical and psychic factors, of slackness, fears, jealousies, rivalries; of Dana, the Assistant Secretary of War, telegraphing Grant on the night of July 12 when Early was leaving Washington by a night march: "General Halleck will not give orders except as he receives them; the President will give none, and until you direct positively and explicitly what is to be done, everything will go on in the deplorable and fatal way in which it has gone on for the past week." Nicolay and Hay recorded: "Everybody was eager for the pursuit [of Early] to begin; but Grant was too far away to give the necessary orders; the President, true to the position he had taken when Grant was made general-in-chief, would not interfere, though he observed with anguish the undisturbed retreat of Early." Halleck assumed that he was in fact, as he ranked, a chief of staff and not a commander from whom strategy was required.

As late as July 15, however, there was no good reason for Halleck's sending Grant the information that Early had 30,000 to 40,000 men when those figures should have been cut in half. Halleck continued to follow routine, scratch his elbows, and hold the role of a muddler who wrote lucid textbooks on the art of war. "Put Halleck in command of 20,000 men," said Ben Wade, "and he would not scare three sitting geese from their nests." Halleck concocted a telegram to Hunter, commanding an army at Harper's Ferry, that was either pathetically stupid or intentionally malicious, for it conveyed the impression that the President was taking Hunter's army away from him and giving it to another commander because Hunter was slow and dumb. Hunter at once wrote the President asking to be relieved and the President had to write another of his conciliatory letters to one of his few abolitionist major generals. It was Grant and not the President who originated the order that General Horatio G. Wright should be put in supreme command of all available troops, including Hunter's, for the pursuit of Early.

Hay wrote of July 14, "The Chief is evidently disgusted," and noted the President saying in the evening just before he started to the Soldiers' Home: "Wright telegraphs that he thinks the enemy are all across the Potomac but that he has halted & sent out an infantry reconnoissance, for fear he might come across the rebels & catch some of them."

"Today," wrote Bates in his diary, "I spoke my mind very plainly, to the Prest. (in presence of Seward, Welles and Usher) about the ignorant imbecility of the late military operations, and my contempt for Genl. Halleck." Possibly the Attorney General paused over whether he should use the phrase "imbecile ignorance" in preference to "ignorant imbecility."

Others, including Mrs. Lincoln, blamed Stanton with Halleck. As Carpenter told it, the War Secretary at the Soldiers' Home one evening spoke playfully: "Mrs. Lincoln, I intend to have a full-length portrait of you painted, standing on the ramparts at Fort Stevens overlooking the fight!" "That is very well," she flashed; "and I can assure you of one thing, Mr. Secretary, if I had had a few *ladies* with me the Rebels would not have been permitted to get away as they did!"

Twelve days after Early quit the outskirts of Washington Dana sent word to Grant's chief of staff Rawlins: "The pursuit of Early, on the whole, has proved an egregious blunder. Early has got off with the whole of his plunder." Grant ordered Wright and his 6th Corps to return to City Point with the main Army of the Potomac; sent Rawlins to Washington to see Lincoln and Stanton; exchanged several telegrams with Lincoln about when they could meet for a talk at Washington; decided it would not do at all to leave the Army of the Potomac and go to Washington, as the move would be nationally misinterpreted; suggested that Hunter should keep a defensive army between Washington and any possible invader from the South; and gave his theory that the enemy could capture no important point "whilst the main Union army is within thirty hours of the capital."

On July 25 Grant sent a dynamic constructive proposal in a letter to President Lincoln on "the necessity of having the four departments of the Susquehanna, the Middle, West Virginia, and Washington, under one head." He had made this proposal before and the War Department had rejected it. Now he was urging it again. And again he was naming General William B. Franklin, clearly one of the cleaner and abler major generals of distinguished field service, "as a suitable person to command the whole."

Two days after Lincoln received this proposal from Grant, the Secretary of War notified not General Franklin, but Halleck, that "the President directs me to instruct you that all the military operations" of the four departments and all the forces in those departments, "are placed under your general command."

Why the President did this and whether he did it as peremptorily as Stanton's order indicated, the record did not show. It seemed to be the first time that Grant had asked for something definitely important that rested on Lincoln's Yes and Lincoln said No.

In telegraphing his policy to Halleck, Grant had added, "If the President thinks it advisable that I should go to Washington in person, I can start in an hour after receiving notice, leaving everything here on the defensive." Lincoln telegraphed Grant that his dispatch "referring to what I may think in the present emergency" had been read. "What I think is, that you should provide to retain your hold where you are, certainly, and bring the rest with you personally, and make a vigorous effort to destroy the enemy's forces in this vicinity. I think there is really a fair chance to do this, if the movement is prompt. This is what I think upon your suggestion, and is not an order."

When this dispatch from Lincoln came into Grant's hands July 11, he was about ready to start for Washington. What Rawlins said and did at that moment was described by Rawlins in a letter to his wife: "I differed with any and all such propositions and told the General that his place was here—that he had started out to defeat Lee and capture Richmond—that his appearance in Washington would be heralded all over the country as an abandonment of his campaign, a faltering at least in his purpose; that he had under orders to Washington full thirty thousand men, with able and efficient officers, besides the troops of Hunter and those already at Washington and Baltimore, and if they could not defeat, rout and capture Early, whose force never could exceed twenty-five thousand, I did not think his presence would help the thing enough to justify his going from here. Falling in with my view, he telegraphed the President in accordance therewith." The telegram began: "I think, on reflection, it would have a bad effect for me to leave here" and closed: "I have great faith that the enemy will never be able to get back with much of his force." To staff men in conversation Grant said that his going to Washington would probably be "just what Lee wants me to do," and that in staying near Petersburg he would be protecting Sherman against Lee's detaching any forces to be used against Sherman, who was now "a long distance from his base of supplies."

It seemed that Grant wanted Franklin, or some other proven field general, at the head of the defense of Washington, while Stanton wanted the desk strategist, Halleck, elevated from staff chief to commander. And as between Stanton and Grant the President was saying Yes to Stanton and No to Grant. On the face of the matter Lincoln was going back on Grant and taking a stand with the established political bureaucrats who muddled instead of performing. Stanton's order accommodating Grant by joining four departments into one, and then giving Grant the last man Grant would have picked to head the new four-in-one department, was dated July 27.

And on that day Grant took to drink. Had Rawlins been there, Rawlins would have cursed him and put up arguments and returned to cursing and Grant would have stayed sober. As it was, Rawlins on July 28 got back from Washington to write his wife in the morning the news: "I find the General in my absence digressed from his true path. The God of Heaven only knows how long I am to serve my country as the guardian of the habits of him whom it has honored. It shall not be always thus. Owing to this faltering of his, I shall not be able to leave here." And Rawlins wrote his wife in the afternoon: "Active operations have commenced, which with the fact of the General's forgetting himself, in that one danger of which I wrote you this morning, renders my being here of an importance that you can appreciate as fully as any person living, although it deprives you of an immediate visit from me, a visit which my health demands."

Whether the death of McPherson could have had anything to do with Grant's drinking on July 27, Rawlins did not write his wife. Five days before Major General James B. McPherson, bronzed, tall, tireless, in boots and gauntlets on a beautiful black horse, had ridden away from a talk with Sherman to examine the cause of a new roaring note in the firing on the left of their army near Atlanta. McPherson was only thirty-five years old, with a future of hope ahead of him and a sweetheart dated to marry him when Atlanta should be taken. And McPherson's black horse had come racing back with saddle empty and later they had found McPherson with a bullet near his heart—a soldier so rare that Grant had him in mind to take Sherman's place if anything happened to Sherman, a friend and comrade so rare that Sherman at the news paced back and forth in a headquarters room barking orders, barking his grief, tears running down his cheeks into the red beard and off on the floor. Grant too at the news had wet eyes, and his voice broke in saying, "The country has lost one of its best soldiers, and I have lost my best friend."

On the heels of this tragic personal loss came the first refusal Grant had received from Lincoln. What could have been the guiding animus back of that refusal? The man Grant asked for, General Franklin, had been on McClellan's staff from the beginning and taken a hand in the major actions of the Army of the Potomac. In the feuds and quarrels of that staff among themselves and with the War Department and Stanton and Halleck, had Franklin been overly loyal to McClellan, or was something more specific held against him? Or was Stanton, so distinctly of autocratic disposition, showing the same spirit now that he did when he tried to dictate that Grant could not take certain troops away from Washington and Lincoln as umpire had decided for Grant? What was the balancing circumstance that made Lincoln say Yes when Stanton brought him the suggestion that Halleck and not Franklin must head the new four-in-one department? Could Stanton have boldly said to Lincoln that he must have this point or he would resign? Would that have been past Stanton? And could Lincoln at this hour have taken on himself the burden of finding a new Secretary of War to replace Stanton? If so, who would make a better one than Stanton? Would either Stanton or Lincoln have taken a different course had they known their refusal would bring the coincidence that the General in Chief of the armies of the United States would take to the bottle?

Was Lincoln's retention of Halleck in response to some political instinct that told him not to accommodate Horace Greeley, who months before had referred to the New York upstate cabbage-raising section from which Halleck came, with the suggestion Halleck should return to his "ancestral

"Never abashed," said Nicolay and Hay of the Michigan Senator and Detroit merchant (*below*)

"A brilliant, fascinating orator," so rated the Maryland Congressman (*left*). Keen, unafraid, sarcastic, was the Ohio Senator (*below*)

Zachariah Chandler

Henry Winter Davis (*above*)
Lincoln in '64 (*below*)

Benjamin Franklin Wade

THREE RADICALS AND THE EXECUTIVE WHOSE POWER THEY FEARED AND CHALLENGED

Lincoln. Photograph by Brady, probably '64

Joseph Holt

James Rood Doolittle

Samuel Shellabarger

Hiram Barney

From the Meserve collection

krout gardens on the Mohawk"? The ridicule of Halleck in some quarters had become a habit, the *New York Tribune* saying: "The country inquires why it is that Halleck with that cabbage head of his, retains his place. . . . We, who do not care for all the epauletted dignity that the President can confer on mediocrity, press the demand now. Cabbage for Halleck, and war for those who have the genius to comprehend it."

What did Halleck have that the grizzly realist Sherman should be constantly writing him with respect and affection? In '61, sunk in a "slough of despond," he would have run away "and hid from dangers and complications" but for Halleck, Sherman wrote Halleck in early September of '64. "I owe you all I now enjoy of fame." And when Sherman read news of Democrats booming him for President, suggesting him for the head of the ticket, he wrote Halleck: "Some fool seems to have used my name. If forced to choose between the penitentiary and the White House for four years . . . I would say the penitentiary, thank you." Of various newspaper stories that he favored McClellan, that he was pledging his soldiers to vote Democratic, Sherman wrote Halleck that he was not a voter and would support neither candidate in the campaign. This letter, saying he hated to express a political opinion because its test was not reason nor general principles but "some dirty political platform," closed: "Show this to the President, except this conclusion; Damn the mischievous newspapers."

The Washington miasma of politics, intrigue, and crossed authorities of which Sherman warned him had come home to Grant. From Dana July 12 Grant had a dispatch with one item: "The Secretary of War directs me to tell you, in his judgment Hunter ought instantly to be relieved, having proven himself far more incapable than even Sigel. He also directs me to say that advice or suggestions from you will not be sufficient." This was crisp and had the curl of Stanton's upper lip. And when Grant did specifically name Franklin for his co-operating military head at Washington, what he got was Halleck. Again and again Grant had directed Halleck to give orders on his own responsibility, Halleck being the senior officer near the field of operations, but again and again Halleck declined. And on the point whether Hunter should be removed, though Stanton cried for it, both Grant and Lincoln defended Hunter.

Lincoln's own share in handling the Early raid had in it the sensitivity of the political leader who must consider that in his own country and abroad the national capital was a symbol. Lincoln did not have Grant's confidence that the farther Early was detached from Lee, the worse was Early's danger, that when Early got far enough north the 6th Corps from the Army of the Potomac could join with Hunter, get south of Early, and never let him get home. At Donelson and at Vicksburg, however, Grant had performed this very operation of bagging an army that got isolated.

Owing to breaks in wire and cable, dispatches took from twelve to twenty-four hours between Grant and the national capital. Grant cited this to Lincoln as one circumstance rendering it "difficult for me to give orders or directions" in any rapidly shifting situation in northern Virginia, Maryland, and Pennsylvania. In telegrams they exchanged July 28 and 29 it was evident that Grant and Lincoln each understood very well that there were delicate and involved matters of administration and personnel they could neither write nor telegraph, and a personal meeting at Fortress Monroe would clear somewhat hazy points. Arrangements were made to meet on July 30, changed to July 31, and then dropped. Both men were working at a furious pace in the fevered air of decisive events. On July 19 Grant had telegraphed the President a suggestion to call for another draft of 300,000 men and Lincoln replied: "I suppose you had not seen the call for 500,000, made the day before, and which, I suppose, covers the case. Always glad to have your suggestions."

Not yet had sudden circumstance or disaster arisen to spoil the bond of understanding between Lincoln and Grant. Each had his own fools and malcontents to deal with. It had happened that when Early's men came to Silver Spring they saved the home of Old Man Blair on the word of General Breckinridge, but the house of Monty Blair they ransacked, looted, and burned. In grief over losing his library and many valuable papers Monty Blair said nothing better could be expected while "poltroons and cowards" manned the War Department. This was carried by ready tongues to Halleck. At once Halleck had to write about it to Stanton. "I desire to know whether such wholesale denouncement and accusation by a member of the Cabinet receives the sanction and support of the President of the United States." Stanton chose to pass the letter without comment to the President, who remarked, "Men will speak their minds freely in this country," and wrote his reply of July 14 to the Secretary of War:

"Your note of to-day inclosing General Halleck's letter of yesterday relative to offensive remarks supposed to have been made by the Postmaster-General concerning the military officers on duty about Washington is received. The general's letter in substance demands of me that if I approve the remarks I shall strike the names of those officers from the rolls; and that if I do not approve them the Postmaster-General shall be dismissed from the Cabinet.

"Whether the remarks were really made I do not know, nor do I suppose such knowledge is necessary to a correct response. If they were made, I do not approve them; and yet, under the circumstances, I would not dismiss a member of the Cabinet therefor. I do not consider what may have been hastily said in a moment of vexation at so severe a loss is sufficient ground for so grave a step. Besides this, truth is generally the best vindication against slander. I propose continuing to be myself the judge as to when a member of the Cabinet shall be dismissed."

Stanton could not have spoken likewise to Halleck, because Stanton was among those who wanted Blair thrown out of the Cabinet. Others, including Welles, still wanted Seward thrown out. And the President followed his letter to Stanton with a memorandum for Cabinet members:

"I must myself be the judge how long to retain in and when to remove any of you from his position. It would greatly pain me to discover any of you endeavoring to procure another's removal, or in any way to prejudice him before the public. Such endeavor would be a wrong to me, and, much worse, a wrong to the country. My wish is that on this subject no remark be made nor question asked by any of you, here or elsewhere, now or hereafter."

This had slight effect on Welles or Blair, Welles writing a few days later: "Blair is sore and vexed because the President frequently makes a confidant and adviser of Seward, without consulting the rest of the Cabinet. I told him this had been the course from the beginning." Three years had passed and Welles was in '64 writing in his diary of the same jealousies and rivalries as in '61, '62, '63. The entries were monotonously alike and the oddity of it never dawned on him. "Stanton dislikes to meet Blair in council, knowing that B. dislikes and distrusts him," wrote Welles. "Seward and Stanton move together in all matters [which was not the fact], yet Seward fears a quarrel with Blair, and he tries to keep in with him and at the same time preserve his intimacy with Stanton. Both mouse about the President, who, in his intense interest and inquisitiveness, spends much of his time at the War Department, watching the telegraph. Of course, opportunities like these are not lost by Stanton, and, General Halleck being placed here indorsed by General Scott as the military adviser to the President, he has equal or greater advantages to play the sycophant, and does so. . . . Seward and Stanton make themselves the special confidants of the President, and they also consult with Halleck, so that the country is in a great degree in the hands of this triumvirate, who, while they have little confidence in each other, can yet combine to control or influence the President, who is honest."

Welles assumed that he could thus easily and briefly dispose of a wonderfully tangled mesh of relationships. He was in the main correct in what he said, though the way he said it had earned him the nickname of "The Old Lady of the Navy Department" and given rise to a circulated and published fable that when a delirious soldier in a hospital had cried to the visiting President that he must see his old mother or he would die, Lincoln had thereupon tried to induce Welles to put on petticoats, tuck the beard in the folds of a large-bosomed gown, and bring comfort to a patriotic trooper. But Noah, as some called the navy head, refused.

An incidental adventure of the Early raid was the ride of McCausland's gray cavalry up into Chambersburg, Pennsylvania, where a demand was presented for payment of $100,000 in gold or $500,000 in greenbacks. The citizens said they couldn't scrape together any such amount of money. An officer drew from his pocket a paper and read to the citizens a written order from General Early that on refusal of payment of the money demanded the Confederate troops should burn the town "in retaliation for the depredations committed by General Hunter." The courthouse, town hall, banks and stores were first set blazing. Then a turpentine supply in a drugstore was used to soak cotton balls which riders lighted and threw into shops and houses. Women and children took to the woods and fields, to near-by farms, where they watched nearly two-thirds of Chambersburg go up in smoke.

Three hours later Union cavalry reached the town and began pursuit of McCausland, somewhat crippling his force in skirmishes. "The affair," commented Early later, "had a very damaging effect upon my cavalry for the rest of the campaign." The regrets of Alexander K. McClure were that several letters he had received in the handwriting of Abraham Lincoln were burned when his house and home in Chambersburg was licked up in the general blaze.

Ten miles east of Chambersburg, the Confederates did their best to give Thad Stevens something to remember them by. They rode straight to an ironworks property of Stevens and laid in ashes a large charcoal furnace, forge, rolling mill, coal house, shops, valued at $50,000. "General Early rode up to the works accompanied by his staff," said the *Chambersburg Repository*, "and avowed his intentions to destroy them. Reminded that he would inflict a much more serious injury upon some hundred poor laborers who worked there, General Early replied that Mr. Stevens was an 'enemy of the South, in favor of confiscating their property and arming their negroes, and the property must be destroyed.'" Stevens's manager at the ironworks dropped a remark to General Early, according to the *Baltimore American*, that he guessed Stevens if captured would be sent to Libby Prison. Early: "No, sir, I would hang him on the spot and divide his bones and send them to the several States as curiosities."

The burning of the Blair homes at Silver Spring, declared Early's men, was a specific act of retaliation for Hunter at Lexington putting the torch to the Virginia Military Institute and the home of Governor Letcher. The news of the Blair houses afire reaching General Butler, he sent gunboats and troops to Fredericksburg and laid in ashes the fine country mansion of James Seddon, once Confederate War Secretary. He had been sparing that house for several days, wrote Butler, but now considered it good policy to let it incinerate. Word of this coming to Monty Blair, he begged Butler not again to so retaliate. "I have a great horror of lawlessness, and it does not improve my repugnance to it that it is practiced upon the lawless."

In the cross play of hates, guesses were made as to whether some of the Federal Government servants hated each other any less than they hated the enemy they were at war with. A peculiar mental attitude or a hoodoo spell pervaded much of Washington. Lincoln and Grant were aware of it. Grant on August 1 acted to evade it. Lincoln approved the action. Grant notified Halleck that he was sending Sheridan to "expel the enemy from the border." Sheridan's record and status, his complete aloofness from the desk strategists of Washington, were such that there was nothing they could do about it. They could officially harass him and they could look on skeptically at what he was attempting and they would change their minds about him if and when he did what was expected. Lincoln lighted up and August 3 sent to Grant a telegram momentous in its confession of a spirit that held powerful sway, reading:

"I have seen your despatch in which you say, 'I want Sheridan put in command of all the troops in the field, with instructions to put himself south of the enemy, and follow him to the death. Wherever the enemy goes, let our troops go also.' This, I think, is exactly right as to how our forces should move; but please look over the despatches you may have received from here, ever since you made that order, and discover, if you can, that there is any idea in the head of anyone here of 'putting our army south of the enemy,' or of following him to the 'death,' in any direction. I repeat to you, it will neither be done nor attempted, unless you watch it every day and hour, and force it."

Sheridan arrived in Washington the day after Lincoln sent Grant this dispatch and the next day was ordered to report to General Grant at Monocacy Junction. So important did Grant consider the work of clearing the Shenandoah Valley that he had left the Army of the Potomac south of Richmond and journeyed to the north of Washington without paying a call at the War Department or the White House in Washington. Grant had found General Hunter's army at Monocacy. "I asked the general where the enemy was," wrote Grant later. "He replied that he did not know. He said the fact was, that he was so embarrassed with orders from Washington moving him first to the right and then to the left that he had lost all trace of the enemy." When Grant suggested that Hunter could have his headquarters at Baltimore or Cumberland while Sheridan took charge of the troops in the field, General Hunter said he thought he had better be relieved entirely. "He said," Grant noted, "that General Halleck seemed so much to distrust his fitness for the position he was in that he thought somebody else ought to be there. He did not want, in any way, to embarrass the cause; thus showing a patriotism none too common in the army. . . . Not many major-generals . . . would voluntarily have asked to have the command of a department taken from them on the supposition that for some particular reason, or for any reason, the service would be better performed. I told him, 'very well then,' and telegraphed at once for Sheridan."

Lincoln was aware of this condition. He so implied directly in his dispatch of August 3 to Grant. He could have enlarged vastly on Grant's point: "It seemed to be the policy of General Halleck and Secretary Stanton to keep any force sent there [the Shenandoah Valley], in pursuit of the invading army, moving right and left so as to keep between the enemy and our capital; and, generally speaking, they pursued this policy until all knowledge of the whereabouts of the enemy was lost." Grant personally journeyed from south of Richmond to north of Washington, to Monocacy August 6, 1864, for personal communication with Sheridan; his telegrams through the War Department were too often translated into something else. Or as he put it when a short time later he again made a personal trip to confer with Sheridan: "I knew it was impossible for me to get orders through Washington to Sheridan to make a move, because they would be stopped there and such orders as Halleck's caution (and that of the Secretary of War) would suggest would be given instead, and would, no doubt, be contradictory to mine." The four times' use of "would" had to be read more than once—and then there was no mistaking what Grant meant to say.

This was the atmosphere when Sheridan before leaving Washington called on the President in company with Stanton. The President admitted that the Secretary of War had objected to the assignment of Sheridan to General Hunter's command for field duty in the Shenandoah, the Secretary thinking Sheridan was too young for such a responsibility. The President made it plain he was inclined to agree with this, but he ended by saying that, since Grant had plowed around the difficulties of the situation by picking Sheridan to command the boys in the field, he hoped for the best. Stanton stood by tight-lipped and cold with nothing to say, and it seemed to be one of the moments when the President was again siding with Grant and overruling Stanton's judgment. Out of the White House, as they walked away Stanton talked freely with Sheridan. He tried to impress the young cavalry leader with the importance, from every standpoint, of winning the campaign into which Sheridan would soon plunge. Sheridan gathered that Stanton might be pleased to hear of battles won over in the Shenandoah, of the enemy routed and destroyed.

On Sherman's hearing of Sheridan's new assignment he wrote to Grant, "I am glad you have given General Sheridan the command of the forces to defend Washington. He will worry Early to death."

Weeks were to pass with Sheridan on trial, with Sherman on trial, one in the Shenandoah, the other in Georgia, two commanders not yet proved as Grant had been proved, both of them held by Grant as unbeatable. And the delays and failure of immediate victory were blamed, by those in black moods for blaming that summer, chiefly on President Lincoln, who upheld all three and never let up on his efforts to meet their requirements.

It was at a later time in a political matter that Sherman refused to correct a policy of Grant when so requested. Then Sherman said, "Grant stood by me when I was crazy, and I stood by him when he was drunk, and now we stand by each other." Sherman was now writing, "War is cruelty and you can't refine it." How much longer the Union armies would have to kill, burn, mangle, and destroy in the South before the war ended Sherman wouldn't guess. His roving mind seemed never to rest. He asked a soldier for a cigar light one day, the soldier handing him a freshly lighted cigar; Sherman put it in his mouth, threw away his short butt, thanked the soldier, and walked on. The puzzled soldier laughed in an undertone, "That's cool, isn't it." Of what was the absent-minded general thinking? Perhaps of what he wrote home in the field from Big Shanty, from the Chattahoochee, from Peach Tree Creek, from Marietta, of fat country stripped of cattle, horses, hogs, and grain, of his food and munitions depending on a 500-mile line of railroad through hostile or semihostile territory, of starving thousands imploring him for food, "crowds of idlers, sanitary agents, Christian commissions, and all sort of curiosity hunters" with whom he had dealt using a stern hand. "People may starve, and go without, but an army cannot and do its work. A howl was raised, but the President and Secretary of War backed me, and now all recognize the wisdom and humanity of the thing."

At the start of his campaign toward Atlanta Halleck had written to Sherman that the President wished to give him appointment as a major general in the regular army. "I wish you to say to the President," wrote Sherman in reply, "that I would prefer he should not nominate me or anyone." He had all the rank necessary to command, believed those with him so conceded, "yet accidents may happen and I don't care about increasing the distance of my fall." Sherman knew his own weak points. "I will try and hold my tongue and pen and give my undivided thoughts and attention to the military duties devolving on me."

With the Armies of the Cumberland, Tennessee, and Ohio joined into a force of 99,000 Sherman began his campaign from Chattanooga aimed at the capture of Atlanta. Between him and Atlanta was the Confederate army of 41,000, soon reinforced to 62,000, commanded by the master strategist General Joseph E. Johnston. Carrying scars of wounds from Florida Indian wars, from wounds at Cerro Gordo and Chapultepec in the Mexican War, from wounds at Seven Pines in the Peninsular campaign near Richmond, now fifty-seven years of age, a West Pointer, a Virginian who had never owned slaves, a clean sportsman of a fighter, a silent, cautious Fabian—little Joe Johnston, familiar with the red hills of Georgia, seemed the one marshal in gray best able to stop or delay Sherman. He led Sherman on. He fought and faded and waited. At Dalton, past Buzzard's Roost, through Snake Creek Gap, back to Resaca and Cassville, across the Etowah, through Allatoona Pass, and after clashes at New Hope Church, not until Kenesaw Mountain did Johnston in his slowly maneuvered retreat lure Sherman into a frontal attack.

The two armies were twenty-five miles from Atlanta and Sherman piled in his men on the fortified lines of Johnston hoping to break through and win victory and Atlanta. Sherman lost 3,000 as against the Confederate's 800. "One or two more such assaults would use up this army," said Old Pap Thomas.

Johnston persisted in waiting, fading, waiting. He had several hopes. One was that Sherman would be led so far south that his food and munitions line running hundreds of miles toward the north would in its requirements draw off more and more men from Sherman's army, bringing it down to a size where Johnston would have better hope in combat with it. Johnston hoped also for some misplay on the part of the younger and perhaps rasher Sherman. Not least of Johnston's hopes was the one that he could hold off any Sherman victory until the November elections in the North. He would like to make Sherman's efforts look useless so as to persuade Northern citizens that the Lincoln Administration was useless. With his admirable management, his care and saving of resources, in two months of skirmishes and minor brushes without a decisive battle the Union losses were 16,800 as against the Confederate 14,500.

Davis and Bragg at Richmond wanted more decisive action. Johnston on July 17 was replaced by General John B. Hood, who, they knew, would not wait and fade and hope. In eleven days Hood fought and lost three battles at a cost of 10,841 men to Sherman's 9,719. Sherman had at last reached the Atlanta area. But would he take Atlanta? This was the question over the North and the South during the hot weeks of August. The North hoped. And the North despaired. Why did it take so long? Why had the whole war gone on so long?

One of the hopers, the *Chicago Journal*, as early as June 21 published an item of a captured Johnston trooper being asked what he thought of the Union fighters and General Sherman; he answered, "Sherman gits on a hill, flops his wings and crows; then yells out, 'Attention! creation! By kingdoms right wheel! march!' And then we git!" In the same week Sherman wrote home: "I am now 105 miles from Chattanooga, and all our provisions have come over that single road, which is almost daily broken somewhere, but thus far our supplies have been ample. We have devoured the land and our animals eat up the wheat and corn field close. All the people retire before us and desolation is behind. To realize what war is one should follow our tracks. . . . Though not conscious of danger at this moment, I know the country swarms with thousands who would shoot me, and thank their God they had slain a monster; and yet I have been more kindly disposed to the people of the South than any general officer of the whole army."

Not often does a director of havoc pause to write his contemplations over it as did Sherman in the field at Marietta: "It is enough to make the whole world start at the awful amount of death and destruction that now stalks abroad. Daily for the past two months has the work progressed and I see no signs of a remission till one or both and all the armies are destroyed, when I suppose the balance of the people will tear each other up, as Grant says, re-enacting the story of the Kilkenny cats. I begin to regard the death and mangling of a couple thousand men as a small affair, a kind of morning dash—and it may be well that we become so hardened."

From Lincoln in this last week of July Sherman had a long telegram which closed: "My profoundest thanks to you and your whole army for the present campaign so far." In the preceding part of the message Lincoln was replying to Sherman's telegram of the previous day to the War Department protesting the appointment of two new major generals, Alvin P. Hovey and Peter J. Osterhaus. Hovey had quit Sherman at Kenesaw Mountain after disputes over the mixing of infantry with his cavalry brigade. Osterhaus was on sick leave. "It is an act of injustice," wired Sherman, "to officers who stand by their posts in the day of danger to neglect them and advance such as Hovey and Osterhaus, who left us in the midst of bullets to go to the rear in search of personal advancement. If the rear be the post of honor, then we had all better change front on Washington." As though he fully realized the sources of Sherman's wrath and scorn, Lincoln stated his case fully: "The point you make is unquestionably a good one, and yet, please hear a word from us. My recollection is that both General Grant and yourself recommended both Hovey and Osterhaus for promotion, and these, with other strong recommendations, drew committals from us which we could neither honorably nor safely disregard. We blamed Hovey for coming away in the manner in which he did, but we knew he had apparent reason to feel disappointed and mortified, and we felt it was not best to crush one who had certainly been a good soldier. As to Osterhaus, we did not know of his leaving, at the time we made the appointment, and do not now know the terms on which he left. Not to have appointed him, as the case appeared to us at the time, would have been almost, if not quite, a violation of our word. The word was given on what we thought was high merit, and somewhat on his nationality. I beg you to believe we do not act in a spirit of disregarding merit; we expect to await your program for further changes and promotions in your army."

In an immediate reply to the President Sherman apologized and begged that he be not regarded as faultfinding. Sherman explained that if his own recommendation for the promotions of Hovey and Osterhaus had been acted on when made, just after the Vicksburg campaign, all would have been well, but coming at the present time, it led his officers to believe that advancement "results from importunity and not from actual service." Lincoln could know that this was a delicate way of saying that Sherman's officers would resent favors given to generals playing politics instead of fighting. Lincoln might too be pleased at Sherman's telegraphing his surprise that the President should take on himself the wrath that Sherman had meant for the War Department alone. "I assert that I have been well sustained in every respect during my entire service. I did not suppose my dispatches would go outside the War Department. I did not suppose you were troubled with such things."

Sherman would no more take Atlanta than Grant would take Richmond, the incessant critics said. Even Grant came under a shadow early in August as the reports came through of the battle in the Crater. An enormous dynamite mine was sprung at Petersburg, hoisting some two hundred Confederate troops into the air and burying some of them alive, demolishing Confederate trenches, and leaving a huge crater into which Union troops marched. The Confederates in a quick recovery soon had artillery at the crater's edge playing on a disordered, helpless mass of Union troops. "The effort was a stupendous failure," was Grant's later comment. "It cost us about four thousand men, mostly, however, captured; and all due to inefficiency on the part of the corps commander and the incompetency of the division commander who was sent to lead the assault." General Meade preferred charges of disobedience against General Burnside and ordered a court-martial for his trial. Grant disapproved of this, and at Burnside's request, a court of inquiry was ordered which eventually found Burnside "answerable for the want of success." In a letter home Meade wrote, "I feel sorry for Burnside, because I really believe the man half the time don't know what he is about, and is hardly responsible for his acts." Two weeks after the Crater blunder Meade wrote home: "I have insisted on Burnside's being relieved. Grant has let him go on a leave, but he will never return whilst I am here."

Thus Grant had deflected Meade from the more bitter procedure of a court-martial for Burnside, Lincoln had appointed a court of inquiry, and Burnside was out of active service—the Burnside who had admitted publicly that he was unfit to command a large army, the Burnside who months before had requested Lincoln to let him resign because of physical disability incurred by reason of chronic dysentery.

In Meade's letters home it was evident he rankled under promotions withheld from him and given to Sherman, Hancock, and Sheridan, under Grant's nomination and Lincoln's signature of them. Others than Meade's aide, Colonel Theodore Lyman, thrust in sarcasm as did Lyman in a letter of August 1, "I presume our father Abraham looks on his election prospects as waning, and wants to know of Ulysses, the warrior, if some *man* or some *plan* can't be got to do some *thing*. In one word he wants to know—WHY THE ARMY OF THE POTOMAC DON'T MOVE."

That citizens loyal and disloyal over the country should be talking as Colonel Lyman in Meade's headquarters was writing need not have been strange. Many were tired of the war, its cost, its betrayals and corruptions. Peace movements gained headway from this feeling in the North and the South. Fernando Wood of New York in seeking to have Congress empower the President to appoint commissioners to discuss peace terms with Southern representatives was playing with this sentiment. So was Long of Ohio; he moved that the President be requested to appoint the two ex-Presidents Pierce and Fillmore, with Thomas Ewing, to meet like commissioners from the South and discuss peace. To President Davis in Richmond and to others Governor Zebulon B. Vance of North Carolina wrote of "discontent" in his State. "I have concluded it will be impossible to remove it except by some effort at negotiation with the enemy." Davis gave Vance three instances wherein he had made "distinct efforts" to communicate with Lincoln, never once connecting, and to send peace proposals was "to invite insult and contumely, and to subject ourselves to indignity without the slightest chance of being listened to." Before hostilities began Confederate proposals were rejected, noted Davis for Vance, and "A second time I sent a military officer with a communication addressed by myself to President Lincoln. The letter was received by General Scott, who did not permit the officer to see Mr. Lincoln. . . . No answer has ever been received." (What Davis did not pause to explain for Vance was that in this instance he was notifying Lincoln that for every seaman captured on a Confederate privateer whom Lincoln hanged for piracy Davis would hang one Union prisoner in reprisal.) He had "cheerfully yielded," wrote Davis, to Vice-President Stephens's tender of his services as a lone peace negotiator and had seen Stephens stopped before he reached Washington. That peace sentiment spotted the South was revealed in Davis's writing to Vance: "I fear much, from the tenor of the news I receive from North Carolina, that an attempt will be made by some bad men to inaugurate movements which must be considered as equivalent to aid and comfort to the enemy, and which all patriots should combine to put down at any cost."

The *New York World* and its country newspaper following would not let their readers forget that Lincoln's inaugural address carried the portentous words: "Suppose you go to war, you cannot fight always; and when, after much loss on both sides, and no gain on either, you cease fighting, the identical old questions as to terms of intercourse are again upon you."

The quavering and uncertain Horace Greeley had resisted peace proposals through the first six months of '64, writing in the *Tribune* of peace discussions in the Confederate Congress, "There can be no peace the terms of which are not dictated and enforced by the Congress of the United States," writing in May of '64, when Congressman Dawson asked the North to "tender the olive branch of peace," that nobody would care if Dawson on his own should drive into General Lee's camp "with a whole cart-load of olive branches," and furthermore, "Some good may come of it. Mr. Dawson may be treated as a spy."

In July of '64, however, Greeley made one of his peculiar shifts. A letter came to him from a fellow signing himself "William Cornell Jewett of Colorado," as though he might possibly be mistaken for other Jewetts. This Jewett wrote many letters. He was *pro bono publico*. He wrote letters ornamented with his elaborate signature to Lincoln, to Jeff Davis, to the *New York Herald*. Jewett needed listeners. Now he picked on Greeley, writing, "I am authorized to state to you, for your use only, not the public, that two ambassadors of Davis & Co. are now in Canada, with full and complete powers for a peace." If President Lincoln would accord protection for these "ambassadors" they would meet in Niagara Falls whomsoever Lincoln might choose to send them for a private interview. Jewett quoted one George N. Sanders of Kentucky, also now resident in Canada, as saying, "The whole matter [of peace terms] can be consummated by you, them, and President Lincoln."

To Greeley this letter seemed to be an eye-opener. Just around the corner he could see peace. Again he wrote to Lincoln one of his long letters, both pleading and cudgeling. "Our bleeding, bankrupt, almost dying country longs for peace." The Baltimore platform cried war too fiercely. Lincoln had been false to his trust in not receiving Stephens and his peace proposals. "Mr. President, I fear you do not realize how intently the people desire any peace consistent with the national integrity and honor, and how joyously they would hail its achievements and bless its authors." And in his six peace conditions Greeley would put as the first two the restoration of the Union, and slavery "utterly and forever abolished."

Lincoln discounted Jewett's story and "doubted whether the embassy had any existence, except in the imagination of Sanders and Jewett," according to Nicolay and Hay. But within two days Lincoln wrote to Greeley:

"If you can find any person, anywhere, professing to have any proposition of Jefferson Davis in writing, for peace, embracing the restoration of the Union and abandonment of slavery, whatever else it embraces, say to him he may come to me with you; and that if he really brings such proposition, he shall at the least have safe conduct with the paper (and without publicity, if he chooses) to the point where you shall have met him. The same if there be two or more persons."

Greeley's immediate reply gave his belief the negotiators would not "open their budget" to him, again reproached Lincoln for his "rude repulse" of Stephens, put in various admonitions, and closed with saying he would try to get a look into the hand of the men at Niagara though he had "little heart for it." On July 13 Greeley again wrote Lincoln, saying now he had confidential information that the two Confederate ambassadors waiting and ready to cross over from Canada and talk peace terms at Niagara Falls were the Honorable Clement C. Clay of Alabama and the Honorable Jacob Thompson of Mississippi, each an ex-United States Senator from his State. As to their terms he knew nothing, had proposed nothing, though it seemed to him high time for efforts to terminate the wholesale slaughter of the war, and he hoped the President would act in the premises. Lincoln telegraphed two days later: "I was not expecting you to send me a letter, but to bring me a man, or men. Mr. Hay goes to you with my answer."

Hay in a New York hotel room was washing his face when Greeley's card was brought in. He dried his face, went down to the parlor, and handed Greeley Lincoln's letter. Greeley read that Lincoln was disappointed over Greeley's not having yet produced authorized Confederate peace commissioners in Washington. "I am disappointed that you have not already reached here with those commissioners, if they would consent to come on being shown my letter to you of the 9th instant. Show that and this to them, and if they will come on the terms stated in the former, bring them. I not only intend a sincere effort for peace, but I intend that you shall be a personal witness that it is made."

Greeley didn't like the letter, noted Hay, said he was the worst man the President could have picked for such a mission, that the newspapers would be full of it and he would be abused and blackguarded. Greeley had Hay telegraph to Washington and get Lincoln's authority to issue safe-conducts for four persons, saying for himself: "I want no safe-conduct. If they will catch me and put me in Fort La Fayette, it will suit me first-rate." The confusions of Greeley's mind in his *New York Tribune* office were noted in Hay's diary: "He was all along opposed to the President proposing terms. He was in favor of some palaver anyhow; wanted them to propose terms which we could not accept, if no better, for us to go to the country on; wanted the government to appear anxious for peace, and yet was strenuous in demanding as our ultimatum proper terms. As I left his office, Mr. Chase entered."

Lincoln, it was evident to Hay, was pressing the matter. He wrote Hay, "If there is or is not anything in the affair, I wish to know it without unnecessary delay." Whatever reality or illusion might be hovering on the Canadian border, he was going to smoke it out.

At the town of Niagara Falls Greeley met Jewett and sent by him a letter to Clay, Thompson, and a University of Virginia professor, James P. Holcombe, saying to them that he was informed they were accredited from Richmond as bearing propositions looking toward peace, that they desired to visit Washington in their mission with Mr. George N. Sanders accompanying them. "If my information be thus far substantially correct, I am

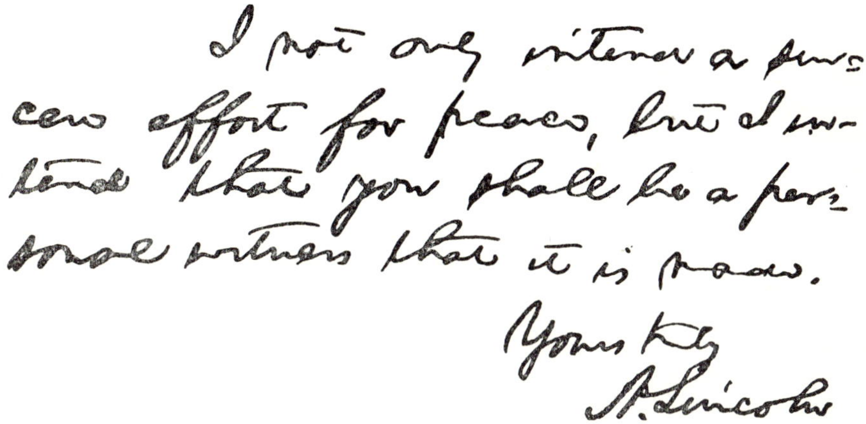
I not only intend a sincere effort for peace, but I intend that you shall be a personal witness that it is made.

Yours truly
A. Lincoln

Last lines of Lincoln's letter to Greeley on the Niagara peace effort. From the original in the Barrett collection.

authorized by the President of the United States to tender you his safe conduct on the journey proposed."

Greeley heard in reply from the supposed Confederate commissioners that Jacob Thompson was not one of them, that none of them had any authority to act for the Richmond Government, that they were acquainted nevertheless with the views of their Government and could easily get credentials, or other agents could be accredited in their place, if they could be sent to Richmond armed with "the circumstances disclosed in this correspondence."

Greeley acknowledged their letter, promised them he would report to Washington and solicit fresh instructions, and then telegraphed Lincoln the substance of what the supposed and unauthorized Confederate commissioners had written to him. Lincoln consulted with Seward and gave Hay a paper in his own handwriting to take to Niagara. There on July 20 Hay saw Sanders as "a seedy-looking rebel, with grizzled whiskers, and a flavor of old clo'," while Professor James P. Holcombe he saw as "a tall, solemn, spare, false-looking man, with false teeth, false eyes, and false hair." There Hay saw Greeley nettled and perplexed at reading the paper in the President's handwriting with affixed signature:

Executive Mansion, Washington, July 18, 1864

To whom it may concern: Any proposition which embraces the restoration of peace, the integrity of the whole Union, and the abandonment of slavery, and which comes by and with an authority that can control the armies now at war against the United States, will be received and considered by the executive government of the United States, and will be met by liberal terms on other substantial and collateral points, and the bearer or bearers thereof shall have safe conduct both ways.

Abraham Lincoln

Greeley proposed bringing Jewett into conference. Hay declined. Greeley then refused to cross the suspension bridge over into Canada unless Hay would go with him and deliver the Lincoln paper into Confederate hands. The two then crossed the bridge, met Holcombe in a hotel room in Clifton, Canada, and handed him the President's letter addressed "To whom it may concern." Greeley took a train for New York, but before doing so had an interview with Jewett, unknown to Hay. Hay stayed on a day and then wrote Holcombe asking when he might be favored with a reply to the communication addressed "To whom it may concern." "Mr. Holcombe greatly regrets," was the reply, "if his [Hay's] return to Washington has been delayed by any expectation of an answer." Jewett then wrote the Confederate emissaries that Greeley was gone and he regretted "the sad termination of the initiatory steps taken for peace," placing the blame on "the change made by the President in his instructions"; they could communicate to Greeley through him, Jewett.

The Confederates replied with compliments and a long letter to Greeley, holding the President responsible for the collapse of peace hopes. Without notifying Hay, Jewett gave this letter to the press, letting Hay know afterward that this was a mild form of revenge. The letter made interesting reading for a gloom-struck nation. There was drama bordering on farce in the Confederate diplomats, at the end of the suspension bridge connecting the United States and Canada, accusing Lincoln of high crimes. They assumed people would believe the President's duty was to invite unauthorized Confederate diplomats to Washington to receive peace terms from the President which they were to carry to Richmond.

"Instead of the safe conduct which we solicited . . . a document had been presented which provoked as much indignation as surprise," proceeded the chaste English of the letter signed by C. C. Clay, Jr., and James P. Holcombe. "It bears no feature of resemblance to that which was originally offered and is unlike any paper which ever before emanated from the constitutional executive of a free people. Addressed 'To whom it may concern,' it precludes negotiation." The explanation of "this sudden and entire change in the views of the President," of this "rude withdrawal of a courteous overture for negotiations," they would leave "for the speculation of those who have the means or inclination to penetrate the mysteries of his Cabinet, or fathom the caprice of his [Lincoln's] imperial will." As though they were sincere participants in a sober puppet play of pious motives they declared: "We have no use whatever for the paper which has been placed in our hands. We could not transmit it to the President of the Confederate States without offering him an indignity, dishonoring ourselves, and incurring the well-merited scorn of our countrymen." They valued themselves as lords of language and cast forth gleaming sentiments in their letter to Greeley, made public by Jewett. "If there be any patriots . . . in your land who shrink appalled from the illimitable vista of private misery and public calamity which stretches before them, we pray that in their bosoms a resolution may be quickened to recall the abused authority and vindicate the outraged civilization of their country."

They had hoped to use Bennett of the *New York Herald* for their game, Sanders remarking to Hay once, "I wanted old Bennett to come up, but he was afraid to come." They had used Jewett to lure Greeley, Jewett having followed his first letter to Greeley with a telegram: "Will you come here? Parties have full power." Greeley to begin with believed the parties had full power, which Lincoln didn't. Greeley's course in the end brought ridicule on him; Lincoln at a climactic point turned the incident into a dramatic presentation of his Government's viewpoint as to peace proposals. "Dealing with nameless men exposed him to the risk of a repudiation which would make him very nearly ridiculous," said the London *Spectator*, seeing "a touch of not undignified pride in the old workman who rules the North." Lincoln's reply to Greeley's final telegram, this editor noted, "when analyzed, will be found a model of diplomatic adroitness." The *Spectator* reprinted it with italicized explanations in brackets:

Executive Mansion, Washington, 18th.

"To whom it may concern—[*Envoys or unaccredited persons, whichever you are*],—Any proposition which embraces the restoration of peace [*which I also, you see, desire*], the integrity of the whole Union [*which is the Democrat point*], and the abandonment of slavery [*which is the Republican point and mine*], and which could be proposed by and with an authority that can control the armies now at war against the United States [*not the rebels, or the nation, but only the armies*], will be received and considered [*leaves the matter open to the people still*] by the Executive Government of the United States, and will be met by liberal terms on substantial and collateral points [*dismisses talk about debts; the question not being one of chandlery!*] and the bearer or bearers thereof shall have safe conduct both ways. [*I, you perceive, settle the bases, being your legal ruler.*] (Signed) Abraham Lincoln,

"President of the United States."

As Greeley writhed and fumed in his latest muddle he wrote to Lincoln declining the President's "Please come over and see me." The President was surrounded by Greeley's "bitterest personal enemies" and his going to Washington would only result in further mischief, as at Niagara. "I will gladly go whenever I feel a hope that their influence has waned." This was mainly Greeley's old feud with Seward. "Knowing who are nearest you," he told Lincoln, for the time being he wouldn't visit the White House. With a fine brief gesture Greeley wrote, "Let the past go," and then had to add in juvenile air the caution to the President, "Do not let this month pass without an earnest effort for peace." To a conciliatory telegram from the President, Greeley replied by refusing to telegraph: "Since I learned by sad experience at Niagara that my dispatches go to the War Department before reaching you." If he did go to Washington as the President wished, what could he do? "Your trusted advisers nearly all think I ought to go to Fort La Fayette for what I have done already." And he proceeded with gloom, with easy expedients, with predictions of nothing but disaster ahead.

Lincoln had consented to Greeley's publishing their correspondence: "With the suppression of a few passages in your letters in regard to which I think you and I would not disagree." And Greeley was adding final letters excoriating the Government and the Executive, which brought Lincoln to write: "The parts of your letters which I wish suppressed are only those which, as I think, give too gloomy an aspect to our cause, and those which present the carrying of elections as a motive of action. I have, as you see, drawn a red pencil over the parts I wish suppressed."

Greeley then insisted his letters must be published entire, if at all, which, noted Nicolay and Hay, "was accepted by Mr. Lincoln as a veto upon their publication." The country had enough gloom and exasperation without adding the Greeley mood of indigo. "I firmly believe," ran one specimen sentence in a Greeley letter, "that, were the election to take place tomorrow, the Democratic majority in this State and Pennsylvania would amount to 100,000, and that we should lose Connecticut also." This and similar expressions from the most important organ of opinion in the North Lincoln held it would be better to keep out of the public prints.

"As to the Alexander H. Stephens matter, so much pressed by you," wrote Lincoln in his final letter to Greeley, "I can only say that he sought to come to Washington in the name of the 'Confederate States,' in a vessel of 'the Confederate States navy,' and with no pretense even that he would bear any proposal for peace; but with language showing that his mission would be military, and not civil or diplomatic. Nor has he at any time since pretended that he had terms of peace, so far as I know or believe. On the contrary, Jefferson Davis has, in the most formal manner, declared that Stephens had no terms of peace."

Perhaps one minor motive of Lincoln in the affair was to reveal to the country that Greeley's habitual self-assurance might not be of service to the Government. Charles A. Dana wrote of "a funny twinkle" in the President's eye and his remark: "I sent Brother Greeley a commission. I guess I am about even with him now." Of reports of Republicans condemning his procedure, Lincoln was quoted in a retort: "It is hardly fair for them to say the letter amounts to nothing. It will shut up Greeley, and satisfy the people who are clamoring for peace. That's something, anyhow!"

At the Cabinet meeting August 19 Blair inquired about the Niagara peace correspondence. "The President," wrote Welles in his diary, "went over the particulars" of his sending "the whole correspondence to Greeley for publication, excepting one or two passages . . . which spoke of a bankrupted country and awful calamities." Of Greeley's reply that he would consent to no suppression of any part of his letters "the President remarked that, though G. had put him (the President) in a false attitude, he thought it better he should bear it, than that the country should be distressed by such a howl, from such a person, on such an occasion."

Then came this graphic notation in Welles's diary: "Concerning Greeley, to whom the President has clung too long and confidingly, he said to-day that Greeley is an old shoe—good for nothing now, whatever he has been. 'In early life, and with few mechanics and but little means in the West, we used,' said he, 'to make our shoes last a great while with much mending, and sometimes, when far gone, we found the leather so rotten the stitches would not hold. Greeley is so rotten that nothing can be done with him. He is not truthful; the stitches all tear out.' "

Over the country the Greeley Niagara conference resulted in fresh attacks on Lincoln in the role of abolitionist. The Northern people were not interested in freeing the slaves, urged the *New York Herald.* "What they want is the Union. The people have never before been officially told that the abolition of slavery will be insisted on as a *ne plus ultra* in the terms of peace, and are by no means pleased with the idea." On the other hand, the many who represented the growing trend of belief that slavery lay at the root of the war, and the war would never end till slavery was ended, took the President as on record saying that the "abandonment of slavery" was necessary to peace. Those who saw the President as "indecisive" had a new item to contemplate. Others saw the President as more astute, if not wiser, than they had expected. A contrivance for the benefit of the peace faction interested in the coming Chicago Democratic convention had failed, said *Leslie's Weekly.* "President Lincoln saw through the game and effectually blocked it." Professor Charles Eliot Norton wrote in a letter: "Lincoln showed as usual his straightforward good sense. What a contrast between him and the politicians who fancy themselves his superiors in insight and shrewdness." *Harper's Weekly* queried, "Every time George N. Sanders or Colorado Jewett chooses to announce that a couple of rebels wish to talk about peace, is the President to say that they have only to get authorized and he will hear them?" By a little memorandum addressed to nobody or anybody they had been thwarted. "The President's honesty, as usual, utterly outwitted diplomacy."

Another secret peace mission, later made public, carried on in 1863. It originated with the Reverend Colonel James Frazier Jaquess, a Methodist clergyman from Illinois, commissioned to raise and lead the 73d Illinois Volunteers. To General Garfield, Colonel Jaquess wrote in '63 that from conversations with ministers and members of the Methodist Episcopal Church South he had learned that peace sentiment was so prevalent in the South that "on the first offer coming from a reliable source" there would be an immediate return of the Southern people "to allegiance to church and state." A fanatic tint ran through parts of the letter. "*I will go into the Southern Confederacy and return within* NINETY DAYS *with terms of peace that the Government will accept.*"

General Rosecrans forwarded this letter, with approval of a furlough for Jaquess, to President Lincoln, who agreed, with reservations. "Such a mission as he proposes I think promises good, if it were free from difficulties, which I fear it cannot be. First. He cannot go with any government authority whatever. This is absolute and imperative. Secondly. If he goes without authority he takes a great deal of personal risk—he may be condemned and executed as a spy." Jaquess went to Baltimore and soon General Schenck was telegraphing Lincoln that Jaquess wanted a permit taking him South, Lincoln replying, "Mr. Jaquess is a very worthy gentleman, but I can have nothing to do, directly, or indirectly, with the matter he has in view." Jaquess went to Fortress Monroe, under permission, and returned to Baltimore, writing to Lincoln that he had unofficial information from "men of character and great influence in the South" concerning peace proposals. For two weeks Jaquess stayed at Barnum's Hotel in Baltimore awaiting reply from Lincoln. No reply came. Jaquess in Baltimore heard that his regiment would soon go into action down near Chattanooga. He hurried down there and after the action wrote to James R. Gilmore: "I lost over two hundred of my men, nineteen commissioned officers in killed and wounded, and I had two horses shot under me. I was not touched. I cannot perceive why President L. should decline any communication with me. I can give him some *most valuable* information." Gilmore connected with General Garfield, who, as he wrote to Gilmore, "after two ineffectual attempts" interviewed Lincoln when other persons were present, Lincoln saying: "Tell Gilmore to bring Jaquess here, and I will see him. Of course it should be done very quietly."

After joint interviews with Jaquess and Gilmore the President insisted that the two of them should go to Richmond if either went. Under flags of truce they were conducted from one of General Butler's outposts on the James River, and between the army lines met a Confederate commissioner for the exchange of prisoners, who lodged them under guard in the Spotswood Hotel in Richmond overnight. Their note addressed to Secretary Judah P. Benjamin brought on Sunday, July 17, 1864, an interview in which they were cross-examined down to fine points on whether Abraham Lincoln had in any way authorized them to come. In an evening interview with Jefferson Davis, the Confederate President, as Gilmore saw him in a suit of grayish brown clothes, was spare, even emaciated, having "a clear gray eye, full of life and vigor." Davis was agreeable, with "a peculiar charm" in his voice as he shook hands. "I am glad to see you, gentlemen. You are very welcome to Richmond." Then came conversation. Could any means be tried leading to peace? The ballot would not do it, Davis made clear, when it was suggested that North and South might abide by a majority vote. "Neither current events nor history show that the majority rules, or ever did rule," said Davis, according to Gilmore. "The contrary, I think, is true." The Southern people would hang the man who should go before them "with any proposition which implied that the North was to have a voice in determining the domestic relations of the South." Furthermore, "If one

Southern State objected to emancipation it would nullify the whole thing, for you are aware the people of Virginia cannot vote slavery out of South Carolina, or the people of South Carolina vote it out of Virginia."

With a touch of anger Davis said they could not accept the pardon implied in any amnesty act. "Amnesty, sir, applies to criminals. We have committed no crime." The key declaration of the Confederate Executive was in saying: "I worked night and day for twelve years to prevent it [war], but I could not. The North was mad and blind, would not let us govern ourselves, and so the war came; now it must go on until the last man of this generation falls in his tracks and his children seize his musket and fight our battles, *unless you acknowledge our right to self-government.* We are not fighting for slavery. We are fighting for independence, and that, or extermination, we *will* have."

Grant had lost more men than Lee had when Grant started, being now "no nearer taking Richmond than at first," urged Davis. Confederate paper money was not yet worthless, while the North owed money to all the world. "We do not lack arms and ammunition, and we have a wide territory from which to draw supplies."

Arriving in Washington with this interview written out, Gilmore found the President in a conference with Senator Sumner, and read it to them. Lincoln asked what he proposed doing with his notes of the interview at Richmond.

"Put a beginning and an end to it, sir, on my way home, and hand it to the *Tribune*."

"Can't you get it into the *Atlantic Monthly?* It would have less of a partisan look there."

"No doubt, but there would be some delay about it."

"And it is important that Davis's position should be known at once. It will show the country that I didn't fight shy of Greeley's Niagara business without a reason. Let it go into the *Tribune*."

"Permit me to suggest," interposed Sumner as a publicity expert himself, "that Mr. Gilmore put at once a short card, with the separation declaration of Davis, into one of the Boston papers, and then, as soon as he can, the fuller report into the *Atlantic*."

Lincoln approved. "Put Davis's 'We are not fighting for slavery; we are fighting for independence' into the card—that is enough; and send me the proof of what goes into the *Atlantic*. Don't let it appear till I return the proof. Some day all this will come out, but just now we must use discretion."

The "card" ran in the *Boston Evening Transcript* July 22 and proofs of the *Atlantic* article went to Lincoln in a few days. He kept them a week and deleted a page and a half, chiefly "the terms he was willing to grant, and all reference which I had made to compensation for the slaves," noted Gilmore, who added, "Mr. Lincoln told me . . . that while he was at first tempted to let the article stand as I had written it, fuller reflection convinced him that the publication of his terms would sow dissension in the South, and he was unwilling that his words should have any such effect."

The *Atlantic* article, widely reprinted, went to millions of readers, Oliver Wendell Holmes writing to Gilmore that it had a larger number of readers than any magazine article ever written. All the leading American newspapers, besides the London *Times*, *News* and *Telegraph*, copied it entire. As a document the Gilmore article projected the interlocked antagonists, Davis and Lincoln, with a degree of drama, following the Niagara Greeley affair. At Niagara Lincoln had given the world his peace terms; at Richmond Davis made himself clear.

And privately Lincoln held more than suspicions that Davis had a hand in what was doing at Niagara, that Davis might be having an eye on the Democratic convention soon to meet in Chicago. A spare and sober letter it was that Lincoln wrote to Postmaster Abram Wakeman at New York. "The men of the South recently (and perhaps still) at Niagara Falls tell us distinctly that they *are* in the confidential employment of the rebellion; and they tell us as distinctly that they are *not* empowered to offer terms of peace. Does any one doubt that what they *are* empowered to do is to assist in selecting and arranging a candidate and a platform for the Chicago convention? Who could have given them this confidential employment but he who, only a week since, declared, to Jaquess and Gilmore, that he had no terms of peace but the independence of the South—the dissolution of the Union? Thus, the present presidential contest will almost certainly be no other than a contest between a union and a disunion candidate, disunion certainly following the success of the latter. The issue is a mighty one, for all people, and all times; and whoever aids the right will be appreciated and remembered." He began the letter and went nearly to the end of it in quiet musings as between two friends, shifting in the last two sentences into the tone and flow of his public addresses.

Lincoln's knowledge of Jefferson Davis having Clement C. Clay, Jacob Thompson, and others in "confidential employment" in Canada was direct, according to Assistant Secretary of War Dana. A young man rated as having "good character," wrote Dana, wished to exchange his place as a War Department clerk for service as a spy. He was given a horse, money, an order passing him safely through the Federal lines. And that was the last seen of him—until he later showed up in Washington as a dispatch-carrier with letters sealed and signed by Jefferson Davis, addressed to Clement C. Clay at St. Catharine's, Canada, near Niagara Falls. He also carried a letter in the handwriting of the Confederate chief recommending him to Clay and Thompson as worthy of confidence and loyal to the Confederate cause. The young man was a perfect actor, a genius of pretense, "one of the cleverest creatures I ever saw," wrote Dana. "His style of patriotic lying was sublime." During the first eight months of '64 the letters which he brought to the War Department at Washington had the seals broken, the envelopes destroyed, the text of the letters copied, and the letter forwarded in what should appear to be original wrappers.

"Coming from Canada [with dispatches for Davis at Richmond], the paper employed was English and there was a good deal of trouble in procuring paper of the same appearance," wrote Dana. . . . "One important dispatch, which was sealed with Mr. Clay's seal, had to be delayed somewhat while we had an imitation seal engraved. These delays were easily accounted for at Richmond by the pretense that they had been caused by accidents upon the road and by the necessity of avoiding Federal pickets." Not until the service of this spy had gone on for some eight months did he gather information of prime importance. Meantime he established proof to Lincoln that Davis's associates of "confidential employment" in Canada were "empowered to assist in selecting and arranging a candidate and platform for the Chicago convention."

The Greeley and Jaquess-Gilmore peace missions had been affairs of risk. Any slight circumstance could have put Lincoln in a false light. Had Lincoln asked Gilmore to undertake another similar errand, Gilmore would have told Lincoln of the Quaker girl who married a military man. As the wife of a husband devoted to war she was called before elders who told her that she had violated the society's rule but she would be forgiven if she would say that she was sorry. She answered, "I can't truly say that I am sorry—but I will say that I will not do it again."

Only a certain procedure of guns, men, blood and iron, could bring peace, it seemed. "Peace," said *Leslie's Weekly* August 6 of '64, "must come through the powerful negotiations of Gens. Grant and Sherman."

"War is the remedy our enemies have chosen," wrote Sherman in this August of '64. . . . "And I say let us give them all they want . . . not a sign of let-up, no cave in till we are whipped or they are. . . . The only principle in this war is, which party can whip. It is as simple as a schoolboy's fight and when one or the other party gives in, we will be the better friends."

CHAPTER 54

"THE DARKEST MONTH OF THE WAR —AUGUST '64

IN rain or shine, amid good or evil reports, in Lafayette Park across the avenue from the White House the bronze Andrew Jackson sat his bronze horse of the poised and upreared forepaws. Here in this city square given to grass and trees Lincoln walked forgetful and indifferent or again with a curious eye for whoever else might have been drawn to a little haven saying welcome.

"Mister, can you spare a dime?" came one morning from a disheveled but sturdy-looking stick of a man who said he was in need of something to eat.

"You look like an able-bodied man—why don't you join the army?"

"They won't let me. I'd be glad enough to die for my country, sir, if they would give me a chance."

"Well, maybe I can be of service." And Lincoln took pencil and paper from his pocket, wrote a note, sealed it in an envelope, and addressed it to an office near by at 714 Fifteenth Street. "Give it to the officer there. If he can't do anything for you, come back here to me. I'm just walking around."

And the able-bodied stranger was not seen again on Lafayette Square nor did he report at the Fifteenth Street recruiting office with Lincoln's note, which, according to the anecdote in circulation, read: "Col. Fielding—The bearer is anxious to go to the front and die for his country. Can't you give him a chance?"

The draft laws of '64 were peculiar and brought to light many human peculiarities.

While considering further draft legislation the House of Representatives in February of '64 requested of the President a statement showing the number of re-enlisted veteran volunteers from each State. The President's reply was transmittal of a letter from the Secretary of War, who believed "it would prove prejudicial to the public service" for the House to receive the information requested. Month by month fewer volunteers came forward, a lesser proportion of veterans re-enlisted. A statement of the exact numbers would have been welcomed by Administration critics.

Speaking in this February of '64 for a group of Senators never quite able to muster a majority of votes for what they wanted in a conscription act, Senator Henry S. Lane of Indiana said the operation of the $300 clause had not been in favor of the poor man. "The poor man had to go at all events; he could not raise the $300; but it has operated, perhaps, beneficially upon the middle classes, and has exempted the rich entirely, for they could all pay the $300 exemption." Lane had regrets that throughout the whole country the $300 exemption feature had been denounced "as class legislation in favor of the rich and against the poor." He had come to the definite opinion: "We cannot fill our armies under any conscription law which retains the $300 clause."

In Lane's own Hoosier State it operated to this effect: "Those who are indisposed to go into the Army, as long as they can shield themselves under the $300 exemption clause, will not volunteer. If you repeal that clause there is an additional inducement held out to them to go into the service of the country." What did it matter that $12,000,000 had been paid into the government Treasury for draft exemptions? The measure was not intended to raise revenue. "We need men more than money. If we could print soldiers as fast as we print greenbacks, there would be something in this argument; but it cannot be done."

Since August of '63 Lincoln had carried farther the points he then wrote on the $300 clause. He had then found his written argument for it not worth giving to the people. As a method it was more than doubtful. The natural and expected difficulties of draft enforcement carried an added load:

one feature of it gave color to the cry of New York City rioters that the war took "the rich man's money and the poor man's blood."

Lincoln's young friend Brooks, under the heading "The Draft a Failure," wrote for the *Sacramento Union* an article "not pleasant to write," he confessed. "So far as results are concerned, the Conscription Law has failed to produce men enough to swell the armies of the Union to anything like their maximum standard." This he would ascribe first to "the too liberal margin for exemption from service on account of physical disability," and secondly to "the incompetence and weakness, to say the least, of enrolling officers and examining officers." Brooks saw personal advantages, personal favors, or actual money payments resulting in men well able to go to the army fronts staying at home. "Discouraging and sickening" were details that arrived to Brooks from New England. "Men perfectly able-bodied and hale have been exempted on the grounds of physical disability; and it is notorious that such exemption was the result of favoritism, political chicanery, or downright bribery." And throughout the country "a system of corruption, imbecility, and mismanagement has characterized the machinery of the draft, which has tended to bring the measure into disrepute and has filled the hearts of all loyal and patriotic men with sorrow and mortification. The traitorous doings of these wretches which have come to my own personal knowledge would fill pages."

Now the matter of conscription was one wherein Congress had kept to itself certain very strict powers. The President could be a dictator in enforcement of the draft law, but as to what that law provided—whether the commutation should be $300, $500, $1,000, or whether no man could buy exemption with money—Congress held the powers and the President was no dictator at all. He was limited to *advising* Congress what the draft law should say. And so, Executive Document No. 97 went to Congress.

The first item in this document had the signature of Abraham Lincoln, the date of June 8, 1864, the address "To the Senate and House of Representatives," and the text: "I have the honor to submit for the consideration of Congress a letter and inclosure from the Secretary of War, with my concurrence in the recommendation therein made." The letter enclosed, signed by Stanton and addressed "To the President," recommended "a repeal of the clause in the enrollment act commonly known as the $300 clause." By a maintenance of military strength, giving it such increase as extended operations required, an early termination of the war might be attained, suggested the War Minister. "But to accomplish this it is absolutely necessary that efficient means be taken, with vigor and promptness, to keep the Army up to its strength and supply deficiencies occasioned by the losses . . . in the field. To that end resort must be had to a draft; but ample experience has now shown that the pecuniary exemption from service frustrates the object of the enrollment law by furnishing money instead of men." Attached to Stanton's recommendation was a report signed by James B. Fry, Provost Marshal General, on the operation of the enrollment act as amended by Congress February 24, 1864.

No one would have said, on scrutiny of Fry's report, that he was trying to laugh in the face of Congress over the results of its draft legislation. The matter was in a realm beyond laughter. It was a commentary some might laugh at and others study somberly. It charted the patriotic response to the President's needs in the spring of '64. General Fry, Secretary Stanton, and the President himself endorsed the figures showing "the results of this draft, so far as shown by reports to this date . . . from sub-districts in eight different States, for their respective deficiencies on quotas of troops."

Number of drafted men examined		14,741
Number exempted for physical disability	4,374	
Number exempted for all other causes	2,642	
Total exempted	7,016	7,016
Number paid commutation money	5,050	
Number who have furnished substitutes	1,416	
Number held for personal service	1,259	
(This last includes some who may yet pay commutation money.)		
Total not exempted	7,725	7,725

"I invite your attention," noted General Fry, "to the small proportion of soldiers being obtained under the existing law. I see no reason to believe that the Army can be materially strengthened by draft so long as the $300 clause is in force, nor do I think it safe to assume that the commutation paid by a drafted man will enable the Government to procure a volunteer or substitute in his place. I do not think that bounties by the United States should be again resorted to for raising troops. I recommend that the $300 clause, as it is known, be repealed."

And this recommendation, said the President's letter of transmittal, was submitted to Congress "with my concurrence." Many months of involved administration of a draft law discriminating in favor of those having $300, as against those who hadn't, indicated positively to the President that another conscription act, beyond the reproach of class discrimination, would bring more troops and a war record less spotted.

Congressman Schenck brought before the House a bill to repeal previous draft laws. It declared "hereafter no payment of money shall be accepted or received by the Government to release any enrolled or drafted man from obligation to perform military duty." One exception was made. Any man could send a substitute for himself if it be his father, brother, or son. Schenck's opening speech was in a tone as though he might have come from a conference with Lincoln on the bill, mentioning the President of the United States as seeing "the necessity for having men and not money only to carry on this war against the rebels, and finding the present existing enrolling act does not produce men by a draft, because of . . . circumstances, such as commutation and substitution, and other things which intervene to prevent the procuring of men."

Peculiar features of the draft stood out from Schenck's speech. He pointed to the $300 clause by which any man wishing to escape the army would pay the Government that amount of money with which to hire some man not in the draft. Also he pointed to another clause by which any drafted man could hire an able-bodied substitute, at a price arranged between himself and the substitute, a current market figure in the substitute market which had become wide and flourishing. Both the $300 bounty clause and the substitute clause would be struck out by the Schenck bill. To repeal the $300 clause and let the substitute clause stand would run the price of substitutes up beyond the reach of drafted men of limited means. "The truth is," said Schenck, "that so far as the $300 clause operates it operates to the protection of men of limited means, and therefore I say that if you repeal it and go no further you leave them a right to complain that you run up substitutes in the market so as to make it impossible for them to obtain substitutes and compel them to go. Seeing the difficulty, the committee go one step further, and in the second section propose to repeal the provision allowing substitutes to be taken."

Schenck was speaking for the Military Affairs Committee in laying down the principle that the draft act should make no exceptions at all, as in any case where a substitute could be hired "a man of means will have the advantage over the others." Schenck raised a class issue in his argument, saying the committee proposed such limits in conscription that "no man, whether a man of means or not, whether rich or poor, shall in any case get rid of furnishing a substitute unless he be one of his own blood."

James G. Blaine of Maine moved to strike out the first section of the bill, saying it was made to appear "that the *people* need to be goaded and driven," saying a "*compulsory* draft" would require troops to shoot down rioters and demonstrators, saying the people were "patriotically willing" and there was no necessity for a conscription "absolutely merciless and sweeping," saying the draft as it was being enforced would bring "a very large amount of money with which to pay bounties to volunteers." His own State was raising its quota, said Blaine; other parts of the Union might be disorderly, but not Maine.

Representative John W. Chanler of New York said that though the bill masked itself as "a poor man's friend" it was nevertheless drawn from "the horrid example of the European system of government," which, requiring universal selective military service, "outrages all the affections of family and ties of blood." The section of the bill which would give the President authority to call a draft at his discretion would develop the hideous monster of war under the plea of military necessity, a power unheard of before this Administration. "The President is given unlimited control over the lives of every family in the land."

The debate was brief, its record taking only four pages of the *Congressional Globe*. If Blaine's motion to strike out the first section of the bill should pass, it would kill the bill and defeat Lincoln, Stanton, Schenck, and the Military Affairs Committee in their attempt to get universal selective military service, making money payments unlawful. "Do not, I pray you," cried Blaine, "by any action here proclaim to the world that you have no faith in the loyal people of the United States." The Yeas and Nays were called for. And the President, the War Department, and Schenck were beaten by a vote of Yeas 100, Nays 50, not voting 32, as follows:

YEAS—Messrs. James C. Allen, William J. Allen, Alley, Ames, Ancona, Baily, Augustus C. Baldwin, John D. Baldwin, Blaine, Bliss, Boutwell, Brooks, Broomall, James S. Brown, William G. Brown, Chanler, Freeman Clarke, Coffroth, Cravens, Thomas T. Davis, Dawes, Dawson, Deming, Denison, Eden, Edgerton, Eldridge, Eliot, English, Fenton, Finck, Frank, Ganson, Gooch, Grider, Griswold, Hale, Harding, Harrington, Benjamin G. Harris, Herrick, Holman, Hooper, Hotchkiss, Hutchins, Philip Johnson, William Johnson, Kalbfleisch, Knapp, Law, Lazear, Le Blond, Mallory, Marcy, McDowell, McKinney, Middleton, Samuel F. Miller, William H. Miller, Daniel Morris, James R. Morris, Morrison, Amos Myers, Leonard Myers, Nelson, Noble, Odell, John O'Neill, Patterson, Pendleton, Perham, Perry, Pruyn, Radford, Samuel J. Randall, Alexander H. Rice, Robinson, Rogers, Edward H. Rollins, Scofield, Scott, John B. Steele, William G. Steele, Stevens, Stiles, Strouse, Stuart, Sweat, Thomas, Upson, Wadsworth, Ward, William B. Washburn, Webster, Whaley, Wheeler, Chilton A. White, Joseph W. White, Williams, and Winfield—100.

NAYS—Messrs. Arnold, Ashley, Baxter, Beaman, Blair, Blow, Boyd, Ambrose W. Clark, Cobb, Cole, Dixon, Donnelly, Driggs, Eckley, Farnsworth, Garfield, Higby, Asahel W. Hubbard, John H. Hubbard, Hulburd, Ingersoll, Julian, Kelley, Francis W. Kellogg, Knox, Loan, Longyear, Marvin, McClurg, Moorhead, Morrill, Norton, Charles O'Neill, Orth, Pike, Pomeroy, Price, John H. Rice, Ross, Schenck, Shannon, Sloan, Smithers, Thayer, Tracy, Van Valkenburgh, Elihu B. Washburne, Wilder, Wilson, and Windom—50.

NOT VOTING—Messrs. Allison, Anderson, Brandegee, Clay, Cox, Creswell, Henry Winter Davis, Dumont, Grinnell, Hall, Charles M. Harris, Jenckes, Kasson, Orlando Kellogg, Kernan, King, Littlejohn, Long, McAllister, McBride, McIndoe, William H. Randall, James S. Rollins, Smith, Spalding, Starr, Stebbins, Voorhees, Benjamin Wood, Fernando Wood, Woodbridge, and Yeaman—32.

The 50 Congressmen who with Lincoln gambled their political futures (by risking the ill will of all potential drafted men having $300 with which they wished to buy exemption) were Republicans. The 100 who voted to keep the $300 exemption clause were Republicans joined by a minority of Democrats, including George H. Pendleton of Ohio, close political ally of Vallandigham. The 100 who thus voted counter to Lincoln's plan to put the draft on a new basis, eliminating class discrimination, included scores of politicians who had publicly and privately spoken in derision of Lincoln as lacking initiative and decision. Likewise among the 32 not voting were Republicans and Democrats who had repeatedly deprecated Lincoln's vacillation. It was to have been expected that the Wood brothers of New York, Ben and Fernando, would say neither Yea nor Nay, though their mouths and their newspaper had clamored that one of the main causes of the New York draft riots was the $300 clause favoring the rich against the poor; the banners of the Manhattan mobs that waded into slaughter and arson had proclaimed nothing else so mightily as a slogan than that the $300 exemption law was a crime against the poor.

Off and on then for days the House took up amendments—and amendments to amendments—of the draft law. Thaddeus Stevens proposed a $600 exemption clause, modified it, and inserted in lieu thereof $500, which was not adopted. Frank P. Blair of Missouri in a slightly modified form brought up the original proposition that no payment of money should release a drafted man from service—and it was beaten by about the same vote as at first. Nathaniel B. Smithers of Delaware brought up an intricate substitute bill which tinkered a little with the several features of drafting, and the House voted Yeas 75, Nays 77, not voting 30. The next day this action was reconsidered by a vote of Yeas 83, Nays 71, not voting 28. And the House adopted the Smithers bill by about the same vote. Frederick A. Pike of Maine moved to have the draft extend to persons between forty-five and fifty years the same as between the ages of twenty and forty-five, which was defeated by Yeas 47, Nays 102, not voting 33, the latter including the Wood brothers again. Stevens in behalf of Pennsylvania Quakers moved that the Smithers law should not apply to "those conscientiously opposed to bearing arms," Mallory of Kentucky asking whether this could apply to Peace Democrats. This Stevens amendment was passed by Yeas 79, Nays 64, not voting 39, again including the Wood brothers, Benjamin and Fernando.

Among minor matters arranged by the House for the bounty-paid soldier was a decree that when dying he might be permitted to make a last will and testament giving the bounty due him from the Government to a relative, but not to someone other than a relative. "We have no reason," said Stevens, "as long as the relatives of the soldier do not receive it, to give to a stranger the bounty . . . designed personally for the soldier." The vote was decisive against drafting Indians; they would be permitted to volunteer. Also there were fears expressed that Negroes would be put into depleted white regiments, thus bringing mutiny.

Congressmen plainly were afraid that the drastic action proposed by Stanton, concurred in by Lincoln, and advocated by Schenck, Frank P. Blair, and others on the floor, would offend men of influence and property in their home districts, resulting possibly in upheavals and violence. Mostly these fears were kept under, were left plainly implied. More often the Congressmen spoke strongly a confidence that the war could be won by using the traditional approved American plan of volunteers modified by drafting, bounty payments, and substitutes for whoever wished to pay. Stevens summed it up June 27:

> I do not think the time has come when it is absolutely necessary, arbitrarily, without recourse, to sweep our whole population into the Army as is done in the South. I believe that by voluntary action, if we are sufficiently liberal and wise, we can obtain sufficient money to raise an army and to supply all the deficiencies that may arise between this and a year hence. . . . I oppose, and shall continue to oppose, the repeal of the commutation clause; but I desire that a bill shall be passed that shall be so effective, so seductive if you please, as that within the shortest possible time a large army of five hundred thousand men can be raised.

In the Senate political instinct ran the same as in the House. The Senators were decisively for bounties and substitutes. Also they were as hazy and groping as House members on the ways and means of getting soldiers. The ballots ran close, as in the House, and about a proportional number stayed away and didn't get into the record. The first Senate ballot on one section of the House conference bill ran Yeas 16, Nays 18, absent 15, while final adoption was by a vote of Yeas 18, Nays 17, absent 14. These ballots revealed a touch of bewilderment in the Senate as to what methods to use for raising troops. There was no bewilderment, however, on the question of substitutes and the rights of those who could raise the money to pay others for performing their military service.

McDougall of California moved to insert a proviso in the Senate bill. It was the Stanton-Lincoln item and declared that "substitutes shall not be allowed in place of persons subject to draft." Wilson of Massachusetts spoke against this proviso. "I do not agree to these ideas that have been put forth that the Government ought to cast a drag-net over the nation and say to every man, 'Come out; serve the country; you shall have no bounty; you shall pay no commutation; you shall get no substitute.' The country is not in any such distressed condition as to require it. We have got the business interests of the country to take care of as well as the military interests. We must get the money to carry on the war. . . . We have got to watch and nurse and take care of the agricultural, manufacturing, mechanical, and commercial interests of the country." McDougall urged that for three years they had been talking of triumph, victory, and peace but they were not yet in sight; he didn't want the war to go for ten years. The Senators however killed McDougall's proviso (the Stanton-Lincoln item) by Yeas 6, Nays 35, absent 8; as follows:

YEAS—Messrs. Chandler, Doolittle, Grimes, McDougall, Ramsey, and Wilkinson—6.

NAYS—Messrs. Brown, Buckalew, Carlile, Clark, Collamer, Conness, Cowan, Davis, Dixon, Foot, Foster, Harlan, Harris, Hendricks, Howard, Howe, Johnson, Lane of Indiana, Lane of Kansas, Morgan, Morrill, Nesmith, Pomeroy, Powell, Richardson, Riddle, Sherman, Sprague, Sumner, Ten Eyck, Trumbull, Van Winkle, Wade, Willey, and Wilson—35.

ABSENT—Messrs. Anthony, Fessenden, Hale, Harding, Henderson, Hicks, Saulsbury, and Wright—8.

Wade, Wilson, Reverdy Johnson, and other Senators spoke fears of giving the President power to draft men for three years. The result might be a country ruled by a military despotism working through a horde of professional soldiers. A proposal of Chandler that the President be given authority to draft men for not less nor more than three years was beaten by 23 to 16. Senator Morgan of New York brought up an amendment requiring that in draft calls thereafter the terms of service for the drafted men should be as the President directed but "not exceeding one year." This passed by 25 to 14. The conflict of feeling as to whether Lincoln should be made a complete dictator over conscription was brought out in the speeches of

Sprague of Rhode Island and Wade of Ohio. Said Wade, "I do not know what the executive authorities would do if we gave them the whole power over it [conscription]. . . . I am not willing to invest them with this discretion." Said Sprague: "Until the Senate of the United States can resolve themselves into a Council of Ten, and be themselves the Secretary of War, the Secretary of the Treasury, and the President of the United States, they must delegate the execution of their decrees and of their laws to somebody, and that somebody must have their confidence, and if that officer has not their confidence it certainly is due from them to the people of this country that they should indicate that idea."

Schenck in the House and Sprague in the Senate had pointed out how clear it was that the President, the Cabinet, and the War Department wanted the $300 commutation clause absolutely repealed. This was done, in a way, by such a device that in the campaign of that year it could be said in speech and pamphlet and editorial that the commutation clause was absolutely repealed. And in place of the $300 clause which was absolutely repealed, a House and Senate conference bill, the act of July 4, 1864, provided that the President had authority to call for volunteers for one, two, or three years, the one-year men to be paid $100 bounty, the two-year men $200, the three-year men $300, each receiving the final one-third installment of his bounty on completion of service. Recruiting agents for volunteers were authorized to be sent into any State in rebellion except Tennessee, Arkansas, and Louisiana. If any State did not within fifty days furnish its quota as called for by the President, the draft must be held to fill the quota with men to serve for one year, and such draft must be repeated until deficits of men were made up.

Thus on a clear-cut issue between Lincoln and Congress he was refused by overwhelming votes what he asked for in an essential point for carrying on the war. The refusal of Congress extended to Grant and Sherman, who favored a policy of no money payments and no substitutes entangling and retarding the draft. Grant and Sherman stressed the point that money payments brought a poorer brand of soldiers. Both Schenck in the House and Sprague in the Senate urged that a better quality of fighting men and more efficient armies would be called into service with no cash payments and no drafted man buying another to take his place. Those who had directly operated the draft, Lincoln, Stanton, and Provost Marshal General Fry, had found the machinery of it slowed down and bungled because the Government endorsed the principle of money payments releasing men from service. Out of this experience Lincoln was speaking both as an executive in office and as a political candidate with his re-election at stake in four months. He was willing to take his chances on whatever disorder might result from the new principle in the draft. From the speeches on conscription spread across many pages of the *Congressional Globe* it was evident that more political fear was unspoken than found tongue regarding Lincoln's simple and decisive concurrence with the War Department in its request that it should no longer be an agency and recording office for bounty collections and substitutes.

Thus Senators and Representatives acting in protection of the safety and convenience of constituents in their home districts refused Lincoln the essential points he wanted in a draft law. And in face of political unrest and a vast gloom savage with suspicion and recrimination, Lincoln two weeks after the draft act was passed by Congress on July 4, 1864, proclaimed a call for a half-million volunteers. Again came the language now grown familiar. "Now, therefore, I, Abraham Lincoln, President of the United States, do issue this my call for 500,000 volunteers for the military service." And with the unrelenting exactitude of legal forms the proclamation made it clear that inside of fifty days, or the fifth day of September, 1864, "in every town, township, ward of a city, precinct or election district" where they had failed of their quota of troops, "a draft . . . shall be had." The call was for "volunteers." And "volunteers" not forthcoming, the new enrollment ordered by act of Congress would operate to recruit the strength of armies "required for the purpose of suppressing the rebellion and restoring the authority of the United States Government."

From Grant's headquarters Rawlins wrote to his wife that the President's call for 500,000 men was better late than never. "Had Congress given him the power to conscript, with the commuting clause left out, at the beginning of the last session, instead of at its close, and he had exercised it, the end of the war, so much hoped for, would have been reached in the campaign begun last May, but such was not the action of the Government and hence the unfinished work yet to be done."

With the $300 clause done away with, any man drafted must either go into the army himself or pay someone else to go for him. Such a substitute had to be either an alien, a veteran of two years' service, or a boy under twenty. Hustlers in the business of finding substitutes and selling them to those who wished to buy—hustlers came forward. "Wanted. Irishmen, Englishmen, Scotchmen, Germans, Frenchmen, to enlist as volunteers." Thus one amid columns of similar ads, paid for at regular rates, in the *New York Herald*. "Who wants a one-year substitute for eight hundred dollars?" Thus another also paid for at regular rates. "Forty-one were furnished by us on Monday," ran another. "Thirty-four more are wanted at the same price, nine hundred and fifty dollars each." Only four days after the President's proclamation one *New York Herald* ad made the appeal: "It is clearly to the interest of every man liable to military duty to procure an alien substitute at once and save dollars, cents and worry. The price of substitutes will soon reach $1,200, because of the great bounties that will be offered by cities, towns and States."

Prices for substitutes were boosted so high that a Supervisors' Committee in New York City publicly took steps to help those who desired at a low and reasonable rate to make their purchases. By entering their names in a book and paying $335 the committee would serve them, the $300 being for the substitute, the $35 for the person bringing the substitute. In Philadelphia, the Citizens' Volunteer Substitute Committee opened an exchange, received applications from those seeking substitutes, urged aliens and veterans to enlist as substitutes, offered $650 over and above the government bounty and charged no commission nor brokerage.

"Six hundred dollars cash paid for substitutes," ran one of many ads in newspapers of Cincinnati, where on August 20 prices went to $1,200 and $1,500 for substitutes, for men to replace the fallen or the vanished in the ranks of Grant and Sherman. "A nice farm of eighty acres worth $600" was offered by one lacking cash and seeking a substitute. Another would give a 200-acre Illinois farm, which two years before had sold for $3,000, to any two substitutes who might offer themselves. From another advertiser a substitute could choose a 40-acre farm partly under cultivation plus $300 cash or on the other hand no cash but a 42-acre farm all under cultivation plus a four-room frame house and a stable.

The Governor of Ohio issued a public warning that armed bodies of men resisting the draft law would be guilty of treason, and the penalty for treason was death; heavy fines and long prison terms awaited those who took a hand in insurrection. The Governor of Ohio was serving notice on secret organizations not to draw their weapons. In Indiana the Governor saw such signs of strength in the southern section of the State among secret organizations in opposition to the draft that he appealed to the War Department for military aid. For somewhat like reasons the Governor of Illinois suggested to the War Department that his State be made a military district with an officer in command.

Under way in northern New York State was a stampede of men seeking draft evasion, wrote the Provost Marshal of Albany requesting authority to stop the men at the Canadian border. In New York City draft enforcement would result in the sacking of every Provost Marshal's office, according to "reliable information" which General Sanford reported, without detailing it, to Stanton, who replied that "if those in command have not nerve, the Government will try to find some who have." Thousands of "miserable, cowardly Copperhead scoundrels" were fleeing across Minnesota for the Canadian border, ran a report from Milwaukee. An Ohio writer put the case with more care, observing for *Appleton's Annual Cyclopaedia:* "The voluntary absenteeism from the State of persons liable to military service, on the approach or during the pendency of the draft, was estimated to exceed twenty thousand. A large number left during the ten days allowed by law between draft and notification. To meet all these deficiencies supplementary drafts became necessary, and then the same process went on until, in some cases, there were not men enough left in the townships to fill the quota. Many men drafted in one section of the State went into other sections; many went into other States and the territories, and not a few fled to Canada." In some States army officers issued orders similar to one of Major General Hovey in Indiana requiring Provost Marshals to register "all persons known as refugees in their respective jurisdictions, stating where and from what place they arrived, their intention as to their future residence."

Three days before the draft was to begin Seward in a speech at Auburn, New York, told his home-town folks in his occasional slack way of talking, "We shall have no draft because the army is being recruited at the rate of from five to ten thousand a day by veterans." To Grant far down on the battle fronts this seemed a backdown from the draft. The moment he read Seward's words he telegraphed Stanton not to postpone the draft to allow time to fill the ranks with recruits. The men Grant had been getting that way nearly all deserted. Out of five reported North as having enlisted Grant said he did not get more than one. Stanton replied that he did not intend to delay the draft a single day, and asked of Grant a telegram for publication urging the immediate filling up of the army by draft. In some localities would be difficulties, not one regiment of volunteers having been organized in Indiana, not a regiment nor even a company of volunteers being on the way from Illinois, Stanton informed Grant. The General in Chief didn't hesitate about sending a telegram endorsing the draft and urging the need of more recruits.

On the date set by the President in his proclamation the draft began. Amid chaos, gloom, forebodings over the country, amid howlings that they were inhuman monsters and God would bring them retribution, Lincoln and Stanton carried through, with every employable resource at their hands, the procurement of troops to maintain the strength of Grant's and Sherman's armies, to impress the Southern people anew with the man power of the North. "All who will not help should be put in petticoats and deprived of the right to vote in the affairs of the nation," Sherman wrote home. "This army is much reduced in strength by deaths, sickness, and expiration of service. It looks hard to see regiments march away when their time is up." Sherman fretted over what the draft might bring him. "I suppose it will consist mostly of niggers and bought recruits that must be kept well to the rear. I sometimes think our people do not deserve to succeed in war; they are so apathetic."

In a dispute with a Massachusetts agent, John Spooner, seeking Negro recruits, Sherman wrote that he doubted the wisdom of Congress in authorizing civilian agents to come South and buy Negro substitutes to take the places of comfortable white men in the North. "The duty of citizens to fight for their country is too sacred a one to be peddled off by buying the refuse of other States . . . it is unjust to the soldiers and volunteers who are fighting, to place them on a par with the class of recruits you are after." Sherman startled the Massachusetts agent with his further points: "The negro is in a transition state and is not the equal of the white man . . . he is liberated by act of war, and the armies in the field are entitled to all his assistance in labor and fighting in addition to the proper quota of the states." Was Sherman nevertheless a friend of the Negro? He would claim that he had escorted into the Union lines more Negroes than had

Henry Wadsworth Longfellow

George Bancroft

Julia Ward Howe

Oliver Wendell Holmes

Photographs presented to the author in 1928 by A. W. Hannah of Chicago

William Lewis Dayton

John Lothrop Motley

From the Meserve collection

Cassius Marcellus Clay

Carl Schurz

FOREIGN ENVOYS NAMED BY LINCOLN, THE LOWER TWO LATER RECEIVING MAJOR GENERAL'S COMMISSIONS

From the author's collection

any other general, and that his policy was to detail Negroes, whenever practicable, for labor and garrison duty.

When Sherman's letter to Spooner found its way, through the kindness of Spooner, into the newspapers North and South, Sherman suddenly was a target for abolitionist criticism and Confederate approval. And the race issue did not become less intricate. The antislavery forces, and Lincoln with them, had hoped for Negro enlistments in such numbers and with such a military record as would lend new light to the question "Can you refuse freedom or citizenship to men who have fought in the Union ranks under the United States flag?" But the matter was becoming confused through the fact that each Negro recruited in the South for the Union Army was accredited to whatever Northern State the recruiting agent came from and was thereby taking the place of some white man who was staying at home.

From the field John C. Gray, Jr., wrote home to his mother in Massachusetts of "contempt and sneers" for Massachusetts because of its recruiting system. "This traffic of New England towns in the bodies of wretched negroes, bidding against each other for these miserable beings who are deluded, and if some affidavits that I have in my office are true, tortured into military service, forms too good a justification against the Yankees." It had become notorious, though not many details were published about it, that the lobby at Washington which had influenced Congress in the passage of the act included New England textile, arms, and munitions manufacturers anxious to have their white mill hands exempt from draft in a period when profits were running higher than at any time during the war. Such matters with others had led Noah Brooks to write for his California readers, "The traitorous doings of these wretches which have come to my personal knowledge would fill pages." It was carrying too far the intention voiced by Senator Henry Wilson of Massachusetts in his speech favoring substitute soldiers for those who could pay, saying, "We have got the business interests of the country to take care of as well as the military interests."

Lincoln in his War Department telegraph office corner saw dispatches of Sherman protesting against these recruiting agents, these "civilian nuisances" that hampered the running of his army. Lincoln telegraphed Sherman that Congress had given the appointment of these agents to the various States, and not to the executive government. "It is not for the War Department or myself to restrain or modify the law in its execution further than actual necessity may require. To be candid, I was for the passage of the law, not apprehending at the time that it would produce such inconvenience to the armies in the field, as you now cause me to fear. Many of the States were very anxious for it, and I hoped that, with their State bounties, and active exertions, they would get out substantial additions to our colored forces, which, unlike white recruits, help us where they came from, as well as where they go to. I still hope advantage from the law; and, being a law, it must be treated as such by all of us. We here will do what we consistently can to save you from difficulties arising out of it. May I ask therefore that you will give your hearty coöperation?"

The tone of this from Lincoln didn't worry Sherman. He went on by various devices harassing the recruiting agents sent by Northern governors into his military area. War Department investigators later reported that 237 agents had enlisted only 400 Negroes, one-fourth of them physically unfit. To Halleck, Sherman wrote that he did not wish to be "construed as unfriendly to Mr. Lincoln" but "it is not fair to our men to count negroes as equals. Cannot we at this day drop our theories and be reasonable men?" Of Negroes taken to Nashville by recruiting agents Sherman would say, "so far as my experience goes, they disappear." The best young white men of the land, having the pride of freemen, were wanted to fight for their country, continued Sherman to Halleck. "If Mr. Lincoln or Stanton could walk through the camps and hear the soldiers talk they would hear new ideas. I have had the question put to me often: 'Is not a negro as good as a white man to stop a bullet?' Yes; and a sand-bag is better; but can a negro do our skirmishing and picket duty? . . . Can they improvise roads, bridges, sorties, flank movements, etc., like the white man? I say no."

On the other hand one controlling factor in Massachusetts was the purpose of Governor Andrew and his antislavery associates to put into the field as large a force of Negro troops as possible; to them every added black trooper in Union blue was one more clincher for emancipation. Also Andrew believed, and with some justification, that the Massachusetts contribution of war supplies from her mills and factories was imperative, and if by any steps that might serve the antislavery cause he could also hold unimpeded the flow of needed articles and commodities to the war fronts, he would take those steps. Andrew's disappointment would have been less had the schemes for Negro recruitment worked to satisfaction, and his embarrassment would have been easier had the manufacturers and capitalists of the Bay State not reaped fortunes from profits deemed extortionate in time of war, profits that represented none of the "consecration" embodied in the dead of whom Lincoln spoke at Gettysburg.

In February of '64 Andrew had clashed with Lincoln, when a Massachusetts agent tried to carry a handful of Negroes into Maryland "to chop wood," half of them being stopped and sent back to Virginia. Andrew inquired of the President "by what color of pretended authority people not charged with crime, and not being engaged in the military service, and being in peace of the law, are thus subject to hardship and wrong?" A similar stoppage of Germans or Irishmen seeking to leave New England for Illinois would bring "a universal outcry in which every man would unite who had an acre of land to sell," wrote Andrew. With an utter gravity Andrew reminded Lincoln of the industrial contribution of Massachusetts to the war, the need of more workmen in her shops and fields. "Yet in the capital of the Nation federal officers forbid Southern refugees to come to Massachusetts, where there are work and wages for all." This appeal was carried to the White House by a Massachusetts recruiting agent, who informed Lincoln that in Virginia were hundreds of Negroes anxious to go to Massachusetts to enlist. “President Lincoln,” so the agent wrote of it, “only asked that Governor Pierrepont of Virginia, who then had the headquarters of his peripatetic Government at Alexandria, should write him a letter, stating that there were numbers of refugees in his bailiwick who

A befuddled British cartoonist in *Punch* titles this “The Black Draft,” neither Lincoln, Davis, nor the Negro enacting like roles in the American scene

desired to go North, and he would give his consent. The letter was obtained, Mr. Lincoln perused it, carefully folded it, as for filing, and wrote upon the back: ‘I understand from the within that there are a hundred colored men in Alexandria who desire to go to Massachusetts and enlist in the United States service. *Let them go!* A. Lincoln.’ The President never detailed anybody to count them.” This action of the President, Andrew termed the “letting down of the bars,” and from then on his recruiting agents picked up Negro enlistments wherever they could.

And again Lincoln had written one of those letters which he didn’t send. Once more he gave release to himself by a statement of what went on in his mind with relation to a given situation, not forwarding the statement because the one receiving it already believed him too much of a funny-man under grave circumstances. What he did write and didn't send Governor Andrew read as follows: "Yours of the 12th was received yesterday. If I were to judge from the letter, without any external knowledge, I should suppose that all the colored people south of Washington were struggling to get to Massachusetts; that Massachusetts was anxious to receive and retain the whole of them as permanent citizens, and that the United States Government here was interposing and preventing this. But I suppose these are neither really the facts nor meant to be asserted as true by you. Coming down to what I suppose to be the real facts, you are engaged in trying to raise colored troops for the United States, and wish to take recruits from Virginia through Washington to Massachusetts for that object, and the loyal governor of Virginia, also trying to raise troops for us, objects to your taking his material away, while we, having to care for all and being responsible alike to all, have to do as much for him as we would have to do for you if he was by our authority taking men from Massachusetts to fill up Virginia regiments. No more than this has been intended by me, nor, as I think, by the Secretary of War. There may have been some abuses of this, as a rule, which, if known, should be prevented in future. If, however, it be really true that Massachusetts wishes to afford a permanent home within her borders for all or even a large number of colored persons who will come to her, I shall be only too glad to know it. It would give relief in a very difficult point, and I would not for a moment hinder from going any person who is free by the terms of the proclamation or any of the acts of Congress."

The next matter on which Governor Andrew pointedly pressed Lincoln was that of colored soldiers receiving pay equal to the whites. Under an order of the War Department, based on a decision of the department's solicitor, William Whiting, "persons of African descent" were "entitled to ten dollars per month" or $6 less than white troops. The colonel of one Massachusetts Negro regiment having written to Andrew that the men "should be mustered out of the service, or receive the full pay which was promised them," Andrew went to Washington, talked with Lincoln, Stanton, Chase, Seward, suggested that Lincoln require an opinion from the Attorney General and that Stanton ask legislation from Congress righting the matter. Then Andrew went back to Boston and got legislative action for payment by the State of Massachusetts of $6 extra per month to its Negro troops, Andrew being shocked at the later news from his black regiments that they had stacked arms, were refusing the extra pay, were verging on mutiny, and held that they would not accept a $6 pay raise till it came from the Federal Government.

Andrew watched the failure of a bill in Congress "for equalizing the pay of soldiers," considered Stanton now useless for his purpose, and then wrote an appeal to the President, which he forwarded to Senator Sumner, charging Sumner to carry it to the White House and himself read it to Lincoln, so that if it failed its failure should be not by miscarriage but "by the positive order of refusal of the President." Andrew as a test was demanding of the President that he should approve the claim for $100 per month of Samuel Harrison, chaplain of the 54th Massachusetts regiment of Negro troops.

"For good and sufficient reasons," later wrote a secretary of Andrew, "Lincoln was determined not to put himself on record. Since the whole matter of the pay of colored troops was before Congress, he did not choose by independent action to point the way for legislation to follow; it was not a case in which he cared to overrule Stanton's decision; and, finally, with the presidential campaign at hand, he was unwilling either to offend the conservative element in his own party or to put a new weapon of attack into the hands of the opposition." Lincoln did go so far as to request an opinion from Attorney General Bates in the case on which Andrew based his appeal. The Attorney General supported Andrew, held that Congress had in view "persons who were slaves" and who by enlistment gained freedom and $10 a month pay, that other persons were entitled to a higher rate of pay. The Attorney General instructed the President that constitutional obligation "makes it your duty to direct the Secretary of War to inform the officers of the Pay Department of the Army that such is your view of the law." But Lincoln took no action.

Andrew made a second appeal, reciting the sullen mood of Negro troops "trembling on the verge of military demoralization." This in a letter Andrew sent to Sumner, with a request that he read it to the President and "telegraph result." Sumner went to the White House. He wired Andrew that the President would "act promptly." But nothing was done. Andrew now was writing to Thaddeus Stevens: "I will never give up my demand . . . I will neither forget nor forgive, nor intermit my effort, though I should stand unsupported and alone. And if I should leave this world with this work undone, and there should be any hearing for such as I elsewhere in the Universe, I will carry the appeal before the tribunal of Infinite Justice." Andrew's letter to Lincoln on May 13, 1864, closed, "in behalf of the rights of brave men in arms for their country" and in behalf of "the honor of the Nation," with the appeal, "I pray your Excellency to interpose the rightful power of the Chief Executive Magistrate of the United States, who is bound by his oath 'to take care that the laws be faithfully executed'; and by its immediate exercise right these wrongs."

The reading of this by Sumner to Lincoln was taken as part of the day's routine, as was also a letter from Andrew quoting an opinion of a United States Attorney General in 1823, bearing on the case. "Though Andrew had lost all hope of stirring Lincoln to action," wrote Andrew's secretary, "he was resolved, partly because he wished to put the blame where it belonged, partly because his fighting blood was up, to give him [Lincoln] no peace."

George S. Hale of Boston was going to Washington and Andrew pressed him into service for another appeal to Lincoln. Hale from Washington reported that the Republican convention meeting the next week in Baltimore gave every executive matter a political color, that Sumner positively refused to go to the White House with Hale on this mission, that Lincoln, expecting action soon from Congress, would be more firm than ever in refusal of immediate action. Andrew told Hale nevertheless to see Lincoln, which Hale did, writing of it to Andrew: "He intimated that he had been pressed with much urgency by your Excellency upon the subject, but before the interview closed, spoke in high and laudatory terms of you. He said his wishes and feelings were in favor of paying the Colored troops, but that he did not act, as had sometimes been charged against him, upon grounds of moral right without regard to his Constitutional powers. . . . He spoke at much length, and with some warmth, and I have not attempted to give all that he said or that passed between us, but mainly to state his position. I perceived that he was decided and that there was no probability of varying his action at present. I suggested that the proposed Legislation might fail and asked what he would then do. He replied he should then have to take it up anew."

What Congress did, after many conferences between Senate and House, was to provide that pay equal to that of the white soldiers should be given to all regularly enlisted "persons of color who were free" on April 19, 1861. This resulted in an ingenious oath being used in many of the Negro regiments. Drawn up by Colonel E. N. Hallowell of the Massachusetts 54th, it required men to swear that they "owed no man unrequited labor on or before the 19th day of April, 1861." Thus they might be swearing to the truth and the fact, though they would be evading the category in which the United States Constitution still held them as chattels and property. Here and there, said Massachusetts colonels, were black men whose pride would not let them take the oath that would bring them higher pay. They had been fugitive slaves, hunted by bloodhounds, starved in swamps, and considered they had earned a freedom that put them above a trick oath for evading a Constitution which still held them chattels and property.

Zeal for the Negro undoubtedly predominated in Andrew's scheme for recruiting agents from Massachusetts to enlist black men in the South, which enlistments would be credited to the Massachusetts quota, and his declaration, of his State: "Every man she might thus induce to join her ranks would be one civilian saved to the national industry, one soldier added to the army of the Union, one the less possible victim of rebel conscription, one Union man of the South enjoying, in the form of a Massachusetts bounty, some compensation for the waste and want with which the rebellion had visited him."

The agents went forth to garner in a strange harvest. And what were the eventual findings? First, the number of Negroes available, it was found, had been exaggerated. Second, in Virginia and along the coast, the blacks willing to volunteer had already enlisted. Third, a surprisingly large number were not sufficiently able-bodied to pass the physical tests, one observer far South holding there were but two kinds of Negroes, "the *bust* and the *robust*," and "None but the *bust* remain." Fourth, in Georgia and Alabama, the best field, Sherman chased them away. Fifth, noted Andrew's secretary, the recruiting agents were the chief obstacle. "The sum total of honesty among them was probably as small as in any set of men to be found outside prison, and the conditions under which they worked were such that no state could properly protect itself against their corrupt practices."

The report of a United States Provost Marshal General, after four months of operation of the system, was cited. "There were 1,045 men employed in this business, the actual sum of whose labors was 2,831 recruits in camp." From A. G. Browne, Sr., a treasury agent at Beaufort, South Carolina, and father of Governor Andrew's military secretary, Governor Andrew had a "hurried note" reporting that most of the white "negro brokers" were in the business from "mercenary motives" and it was a disgrace to all concerned. "The poor negroes are hunted like wild beasts, and besides, there are few sound, able-bodied men among them. There is a perfect panic throughout all these islands. Old men and invalids have taken to the bush through fear of the conscription; one poor fellow jumped overboard at St. Helena last week and was drowned."

"If Governor Andrew has really only imported a few thousand negroes and Dutchmen, it merely shows that he has disgraced himself for nothing," wrote John C. Gray, Jr., from the field to his mother at home in Massachusetts. "I really feel too indignant to write or talk about the subject." This was the tone of much condemnation, extreme and unfair, in its interpretation of Andrew. Gray's reference to "Dutchmen" meant an experiment begun early in '64 by bounty speculators who brought over more than 200 "voluntary immigrants" from Prussia and Switzerland, of whom 160 were passed and sent to the front. Later the same speculators imported three shiploads of men, hardly a word of English among them, which ran the enlisted men from two importations into a total of 907, to be credited to the Massachusetts quota. "Whether the gain were large or small," wrote Henry Greenleaf Pearson, a friend of Andrew, "the arrival of these shiploads of foreign mercenaries—for such in effect they were—was of enough importance to attract attention outside the State. The enemies of Massachusetts showed the fact in its ugliest light; the ministers of the countries from which the men had come beset Seward with complaints; Stanton's quick tongue was active at the Governor's expense; the men themselves, who, on their way to the front, were somewhat roughly handled and preyed upon by runners, had a grievance; those of them who, failing to pass the surgical examination, had to betake themselves to civil employments, complained of broken contracts; colonels of regiments were unanimous in declaring that their ignorance of English was a fatal weakness." Governor Andrew did his best to have them fitted in with German-American units. "The fortunes of war, however, from which this regiment suffered probably more than any other in the whole volunteer army, had left little of the German element in it, and these new recruits, from failing to understand the orders given to them, were massacred like sheep in one of the early days of the Wilderness."

Governor Andrew's only part in the importation of these aliens had been to accept the recommendation of a committee that the experiment was worth trying. And, continued Pearson, "When once the men [the aliens] were Massachusetts soldiers, however, the whole responsibility for having procured them, as well as for their behavior as soldiers, was of course charged upon him. In self-defense he had the partners in the enterprise make reports to himself and the State Department at Washington, demonstrating their scrupulous dealings; he listened to and endeavored to remedy the complaints of the men; to the public he tried to minimize the importance of the whole thing. Though technically he won his case, the State had undoubtedly suffered a loss of prestige for which the small number of men obtained was no compensation."

Andrew, like Lincoln and Stanton, was learning. All three were slowly being taught, for instance, to listen more closely to Grant and Sherman on the conduct of the war. They had seen regiments of "three months' men," organized contrary to the wish of Grant and Sherman, turn out to be hardly worth the effort and money. They had in one draft organized regiments so that officers could be appointed by State governors or elected by the rank and file. This resulted in such newly enlisted men losing the advantage of getting from tried veterans the knack of camp life, marching, quick trench-digging. "New regiments," wrote Sherman to Grant in the hope it would be emphasized for Lincoln, "for want of this knowledge [of the details of camp life], have measles, mumps, diarrhea and the whole catalogue of infantile diseases whereas the same number of men, distributed among the older regiments would learn from the sergeants and corporals and privates the art of taking care of themselves which would actually save their lives and preserve their health against the host of diseases which invariably attack new regiments. Also recruits, distributed among the older companies catch up, from close and intimate contact, a knowledge of drill, the care and use of arms and all the instructions which otherwise would take months to impart."

When in a draft of the year before Sherman had read that the President intended to consolidate veteran regiments whose membership had fallen below 300, such regiments to fight and march alongside greenhorn units, he begged Grant to try to get Lincoln to let go this idea and to use all recruits as replacements. To his wife Sherman wrote that the worst enemy of the United States could not devise a better plan to break down the army. "It may be that the whole war will be turned over to the negroes, and I begin to believe that they will do as well as Lincoln and his advisers."

Now that bridge had been crossed. Grant and Sherman in that particular were getting what they wanted, though they knew it would be a long time before Negro recruits would be used as replacements in white regiments.

Some of the old regiments of service at Shiloh and Corinth had lost 70 per cent of their men in battle, Sherman wrote Halleck, in telling of his eager interest in what the draft might do. Some of the veterans were feeling discouraged, "whereas if we could have a steady influx of recruits, the living would soon forget the dead."

A press item went the rounds. A White House visitor, George W. Dole, Commissioner of Indian Affairs, had suggested to the President that his call for 500,000 more troops would mean a draft and would spoil his re-election chances. The President: "It matters not. We must have the men. If I go down I intend to go like the *Cumberland* with my colors flying." Wrote the *New York Times* correspondent: "Mr. Lincoln in private conversation previous to the issue of the new call for 500,000 men, recognized all the elements of dissatisfaction which that measure was likely to bring with it, and to breed; but he stated most emphatically that the men were needed, and that should he fail in consequence, he would have at least the satisfaction of going down with flying colors."

The picture Lincoln would call up was a wooden frigate, the *Cumberland*. Shattered and splintered, her hull gashed and torn by the big guns of the Confederate ironclad *Merrimac*, she floated her flag so long as she could be seen. Slowly she went under, sinking with men and guns, the last of her to vanish from daylight being the Union Jack.

A political leader holding authority of Commander in Chief of the armies, Lincoln had made his call. No matter how many were shrinking, his own doggedness might be communicated to others. The theory of political and military leadership tightly involved was set forth in a volume by Clausewitz over in the Library of Congress: "The spark in the breast of the commander must rekindle hope in the hearts of his men, and so long as he is equal to his task he remains their commander. When his influence ceases and his own spirit is no longer strong enough to revive the spirits of others, the masses, drawing him with them, sink into the lower region of animal nature which recoils from danger and knows not shame."

The necessity of men killing men, since there was a war on, stood forth in Lincoln's writing to Vice-President Hamlin that on the issuance of the Emancipation Proclamation troops came forward more slowly than ever: "The North responds to the proclamation sufficiently in breath; but breath alone kills no rebels." Killings were wanted. Enough killings would end the war. "I have seen your despatch," he wired Grant one hot August day of '64, "expressing your unwillingness to break your hold where you are. Neither am I willing. Hold on with bulldog grip, and chew and choke as much as possible."

A committee of three came from Chicago. A mass meeting had appointed them to go to Washington and ask the Secretary of War for a new enrollment figure. Their quota had been put too high, they believed. Stanton refused to give them any concession. So they went to Lincoln. He said, "I will go with you to Stanton and hear both sides." Heading the committee was Joseph Medill, editor of the *Chicago Tribune*, who argued before Lincoln, Stanton, and Fry that the Chicago quota should be lowered. Chicago had already sent 22,000 men and was drained. Lincoln heard the argument sitting quietly, and in time lifted his head and spoke as though what he had to say was unanswerable.

"Gentlemen," he said, as Medill's memory served, "after Boston, Chicago has been the chief instrument in bringing this war on the country. The Northwest has opposed the South as the Northeast has opposed the South. You called for war until we had it. You called for emancipation and I have given it to you. Whatever you have asked for you have had. Now you come here begging to be let off from the call for men which I have made to carry out the war which you have demanded. You ought to be ashamed of yourselves. I have a right to expect better things of you. Go home and raise your 6,000 extra men. And you, Medill, are acting like a coward. You and your *Tribune* have had more influence than any paper in the Northwest in making this war. You can influence great masses, and yet you cry to be spared at a moment when your cause is suffering. Go home and send us those men."

Some sort of writhing, intense speech like that came from Lincoln, and as Medill confessed: "I couldn't say anything. It was the first time I ever was whipped, and I didn't have an answer. We all got up and went out, and when the door closed, one of my colleagues said, 'Well, gentlemen, the old man is right. We ought to be ashamed of ourselves. Let us never say anything about this, but go home and raise the men.' And we did, 6,000 men, making 28,000 in the war from a city of 156,000."

Few were the days that brought to Lincoln and Stanton no reports or rumors of bribery and corruption in draft administration. In some localities the morale ran high. In others it was low. Governor Brough of Ohio estimated "more or less corruption in at least one-half of the subordinate provost-marshalships" of his State, and wrote, "I know the fact that some men of heretofore moderate means have retired from these positions with handsome competencies while some remaining in them are manifesting outward tokens of worldly means not derived from salaries." In many newspapers and in sidewalk talk it was assumed that plenty of surgeons in government service were willing to find defects of hearing, eyesight, heart action, or other disabilities if their palms were crossed with a fat fee. In a letter to Senator Wilson, Provost Marshal General Fry admitted there was "bribery and corruption among the surgeons." Many failures and incompetents of the medical profession had drifted into government service, yet Fry was also aware that many of them had received their appointments unsought on account of reputations in their communities for ability and honesty, and they gave their Government "high professional service in a patriotic spirit beyond reproach." Both Lincoln and Stanton seemed to have kept a close association with General Fry and to have believed that he directed a widespread, complicated machinery with rare skill and decency.

"I hev lost, sence Stanton's order to draft, the use of wun eye entirely, and hev kronic inflammashen in the other," wrote Petroleum V. Nasby, gloom-chaser for the President. "My teeth is all unsound, my palit ain't eggsactly rite, and I hev hed bronkeetis 31 yeres last Joon. At present I hev a koff, the paroxisms uv wich is friteful 2 behold. I am afflictid with kronic diarrear and kostivness. I am rupcherd in 9 places, and am entirely enveloped with trusses. I hev korns and bunions on both feet, wich wood prevent me from marchin." And Nasby "in company with 5 other invalids" rowed a boat across Lake Erie landing "safe under the protectin tail of the British Lion," where he explained, "I hev twict as menny diseases ez wood hev eggsemptid me, but I wuz afeerd the Eggsaminer woodent see em, ez he aint much of a physician anyhow; besides, he votes the Union tickit, and hez, uv coarse, prejudisis."

Still later Nasby strays back to Ohio, is drafted, goes to the front, deserts to the Louisiana Pelicans and there becomes familiar with a Confederate conscript who confesses: "I hed 18 niggers, and they kept me as poor as a skim-milk cheese. The hogs eat the corn, the niggers eat the hogs, and I lived on what they left. To defend my property in these niggers, we seceshed and startid a new guvment. The new guvment took the corn, the hogs, the niggers, and finally took me."

Vast, cruel, comic, heroic, paradoxical, were events in the wake of the human dragnet thrown out by the Lincoln Government for men, more men, to uphold that Government. "Even in the hospitals," wrote Walt Whitman from Washington to his mother, the feeling was "savage & hot" against draft-evaders. "I do not feel it in my heart to abuse the poor people, or call for a rope or bullets for them, but that is all the talk here, even in the hospitals." The author of "Blow, Bugles, Blow!" who had welcomed war, like many others who brooded over the balances of justice in it now felt himself blown to and fro in its windy passions. "The deeper they go in with the draft, the more trouble it is likely to make. I have changed my opinions and feelings on the subject. We are in the midst of strange and terrible times. One is pulled a dozen different ways in his mind, & hardly knows what to think or do."

Men in hospital had told Whitman vividly of lying amid "four or five acres" of dead. "Mother, one's heart grows sick of war . . . a great slaughter-house and the men mutually butchering each other—then I feel how impossible it appears, again, to retire from this contest, until we have carried our points—it is cruel to be so tossed from pillar to post in one's judgment." The matronly bronze figure of Liberty atop the Capitol dome fascinated Whitman. "It looks wonderful toward sundown, I love to go down & look at it, the sun when it is nearly down shines on the headpiece & it dazzles & glitters like a big star." Writing again to "dearest mother" of the President and General Burnside reviewing the 9th Corps parade up Pennsylvania Avenue, "many more than half the army passed without noticing Mr. Lincoln & the others, for there was a great crowd all through the streets, & the place where the President stood was not conspicuous. Five regiments of new black troops looked and marched very well. It looked funny to see the President standing with his hat off to them just the same as the rest as they passed by."

Thus ran blurs of mind and feeling, images of foul slaughter and shining heroism seen through the changing smokes and confusions of the hour. And doubtless the President went on asking himself the question which he had put to General Couch when they sat their horses at the Chancellorsville grand review: "What is going to become of all these men when the war is over?"

When a man enlisted as a substitute, pocketed the cash bounty, jumped elsewhere to enlist again and pocket another cash bounty, he was known as a "bounty-jumper." Newspapers carried a stream of items about fugitive and captured bounty-jumpers. One sentenced to four years in the Albany penitentiary confessed to having jumped the bounty thirty-two times. According to records of the Provost Marshal General, "out of a detachment of 625 recruits sent to reinforce a New Hampshire regiment in the Army of the Potomac, 137 deserted on the passage, 82 to the enemy's picket line and 36 to the rear, leaving but 370 men."

One verse of "He's Gone to the Arms of Abraham" ended: "For what's the use of dying, just for Jeff or Abraham?" Another song, "How Are You, Conscript?" told him to take his medicine cheerfully along with the many others who didn't have "three hundred greenbacks to pony up," who gave their girls a lock of hair and marched away. "And when you do come home again, you'll see it same as I, For you're only going to Dixie to fight and 'mind your eye.'" Yes, you were your "mother's joy" and now you're a "goner," but don't you fret and cry, "For you're only going to Dixie to fight and 'mind your eye.'"

Those who took flight to evade the draft, known as "skedaddlers," changed their names and sought localities where voters and officials were hostile to the Lincoln Administration. They moved to lonely mining camps or settlements unfriendly to Provost Marshals and reached by hard travel. They fixed their abodes beyond the authority of the United States, *Leslie's Weekly* reporting: "On the western margin of the grand lake abreast of the town of Weston, Maine, and on the New Brunswick [Canadian] side of the line, a settlement has lately sprung up, which goes by the name of 'Skedaddler's Ridge,' as the dwellers there have fled from their country because of a mortal dread of the draft."

A Vermont woman, according to *Leslie's*, having an errand in Canada, was shocked at meeting her husband in Montreal. Had she not received official word from the Government that her husband had died on the field of battle as a hero? Had she not mourned and put on widow's garb, and later married another man? She had. Now she learned from him that he had nursed no wish to fall with honor on the field of glory, and therefore had stuffed her letters to him, her photographs, her locks of shining bronze hair, into the pockets and bosom of a dead soldier, removing from the corpse any evidence contradicting the letters, the pictures, the hair. Then he had deserted and made his way to Canada. He promised her, "I'll never trouble you again," and she warned him not to.

The distinguished patriotic poet Thomas Bailey Aldrich, having been drafted, hired as a substitute another poet, by name Fitz-James O'Brien, by breed a fighting Irishman. In front-line action O'Brien was shot; taken to hospital, he died of his wounds, at a later time a literary commentator alluding to "Thomas Bailey Aldrich, who was shot through Fitz-James O'Brien's shoulder."

In the war chronicle of the summer of '64, with its plodding in blood and muck, were two bright spots for the Union cause. On a Sunday morning in June, outside the international line off the coast of France at Cherbourg, two ships met and battled, in view of thousands of spectators on the French shore five miles away and other gazers on boats that had come out to be near the fight. In length, beam, guns, and men, the equipment of the fighting ships was about equal, though the one flying the Union flag had 400 horse power against 300 of its opponent. The one flying the Confederate flag had cruised thousands of miles in the South Atlantic and Indian oceans since August of '63, had captured 62 merchantmen, and burned most of them at sea. She was the hated and feared *Alabama*, her commander, Raphael Semmes. She was British-built, her seamen and gunners mainly British.

The *Kearsarge* had long trailed the *Alabama* and at last penned her in Cherbourg Harbor. Now the *Alabama* must fight for her freedom of the seas. Ninety minutes the two ships circled, shifted, blazed at each other. Three hundred and seventy shells from the *Alabama* left the *Kearsarge* practically undamaged, with only the loss of a smokestack, while nearly every one of the 173 projectiles from the *Kearsarge* found its target and tore the sides of the *Alabama* open till she began sinking. Forty were killed on the *Alabama* under the Confederate flag; on the *Kearsarge* the losses were three men wounded, of whom one died.

As the immemorial waters of the ancient sea took to their bosom the vanished *Alabama*, the only formidable dread that had haunted United States merchantmen on the seven seas was gone. It would not matter that the *Alabama* commander was picked up by a British vessel, the *Deerhound*, and taken to London, where he was dined by officers of the British Army and Navy and presented with a sword to replace the one he had thrown into the sea from the deck of his sinking ship. The army and navy cliques of London would have been pleased to lend swords and ships to the Confederate States of America. They were overbalanced by the mass sentiment of the workingmen of Britain about slavery and the Union cause in America. Spokesmen for powerful peace movements had presented petitions and requested Lord Palmerston to use his friendly relations with the United States Government to end hostilities. The Prime Minister quoted an old couplet—

They who in quarrels interpose
Will often wipe a bloody nose

—and gave assurances that if, at any time in the future, reasonable grounds could be shown for supposing friendly suggestions would be heard, Her Majesty's Government would be happy to use their efforts. "All of which means," said the foiled London *Times*, "that the Premier will support such an effort at a more opportune moment, that is to say when Grant and Sherman are defeated and the Confederacy stands in no need of recognition."

With its last important sea raider gone in June, the Confederacy lost in August its most essential port on the Gulf of Mexico. Lashed to a flagship mast and leading his fleet into Mobile Bay, Admiral Farragut saw one of his ships wavering, shouted through his trumpet, "What is the trouble?"

"Torpedoes."

"Damn the torpedoes! Captain Drayton, go ahead! Jouett, full speed!"

One of the monitors sank with crew and commander. Ahead were torpedoes. Behind was retreat. "O God," prayed Farragut, "who created man and gave him reason, direct me what to do. Shall I go on?"

His order, "Damn the torpedoes! Full speed ahead!" became a Unionist slogan. His fleet captured the ram *Tennessee*, rated one of the most power-

Farragut's fleet passing the forts of Mobile Bay

ful vessels of war afloat on any waters, and with land forces reduced the three forts guarding Mobile. Lincoln termed it a "brilliant achievement."

Lincoln with Grant believed a stranglehold was being put on the South. But a large number of people, some of them highly vocal in this August of '64, did not so believe or were not particularly interested in believing in anything connected with continuance of the war.

Near the town of Mount Vernon, Ohio, lived a farmer and his wife who believed that Vallandigham was telling the truth about the war, that Lincoln was a deceiver, a monster and a fiend perpetuating a needless war, the woman saying to her children, "Lincoln! how I loathe that name between my lips!" Sometimes of nights she could not sleep for her visions of men killing each other and the load of death, cripples, taxes, misery, hunger, put on the people. To her Vallandigham was a hero and brave truthteller. Nothing Lincoln said reached her. Whatever he might say she took as the word of a high hypocrite clothed with power he misused. She and her husband worked their farm without help, kept a sober and orderly household, read their Bible and went to a Congregational church on the Sabbath, had no traffic with ill-gotten gains of the war. They were for peace. They saw Lincoln as against peace. And her children, not yet of an age to be drafted, heard her say with immemorial woe and hate in her voice, "Lincoln! how I loathe that name between my lips!" She may have been in the crowd that heard Congressman Samuel S. Cox speak from the courthouse steps on the night of July 23, as reported in the *Crisis* of August 3. She was too quiet a woman to cheer, but she approved the surging murmurs and the "immense applause" indicated by the reporter who took down the speech and its interruptions:

MR. COX: So far as Mr. Lincoln is concerned, he made peace impossible by his own conduct. . . . Will not history, nay, will not the living present, curse the execrable tool of fanaticism, who thus, even in the agony and article of our national demise, flings away the hopes and interests of this nation?

A VOICE: God damn him. [Laughter and cheers.]

MR. COX: I cannot join in the earnest imprecation of my gentle friend. [Laughter.] While I do invoke that Providence may deal mercifully with the President, I pray that the people in November will damn him to an immortality of infamy. [Immense applause.] Think of it, in the very midst of the strife, while calling aloud to some seventeen States of the old Union to send him a half million more men to be added to the two millions who are wasted and wasting—when about to consume $300,000,000 more of the results of labor, to be added to the two thousand millions already spent; in the midst of a war of bereavement, destruction, desolation and death unequalled, this executive trifler; this retailer of smutty stories; this vulgar tyrant over men's thoughts, opinions, presses, letters, persons and lives, rejects the blessed opportunity which the Angel of Peace tenders to our afflicted land. [Cheers.]

The Democratic press over and again reprinted from Lincoln's 1848 Mexican War speech: "Any people anywhere being inclined and having the power have a right to rise up and shake off the existing government, and form a new one that suits them better. This is a most valuable, a most sacred right." To the *New York World* this was evidence that "Mr. Lincoln looks downward to the uneducated, unenlightened, and vicious for inspiration or guidance, and not upward to the intelligence and virtue of the republic. He follows the lowest strata of public opinion. . . . Let us return to the Constitution and banish into outer darkness the superficial demagogue whose jesting, jibing tongue, amid our awful sorrows, betokens the presence of a buffoon and something worse."

The *Richmond Examiner*, of course, spoke for the most extreme opposition to Lincoln in a sentence which *Harper's Weekly* reprinted in August—"The obscene ape of Illinois is about to be deposed from the Washington purple"—with the comment, "There is a great deal more in this strain, which is peculiar to a baby-selling chivalry—a strain in which Jefferson Davis showed himself an accomplished adept when he called his fellow-citizens against whom he has drawn the sword 'hyenas.'"

In doggerel not lacking in pertinency to the hour the *Boston Courier* published verses relating how

> Lank Abraham lolled in his library chair,
> Consulting "Joe Miller" and "Vanity Fair,"
> When in swept Columbia careworn and pale,
> But dauntless and haughty 'mid Fortune's assail—
> "Come, steward," she said, "now explain if you can
> Why shan't I discharge you and try a new man?"
>
> Then Abraham the wily replied with a grin,
> "A Dutchman once said in the county of Quinn,
> (The story is old but in point as I deem)
> Tain't safe to swap hosses when crossing a stream."
>
> "Cease, sirrah, your jesting! remember," she said,
> "My fields with the blood of my yeomanry red!
> The wail of the widow, the orphan's sad eye
> Rebuke the rude trifling of lowly or high.
> My children are warring along my green slopes—
> I come for your counsels, your plans and your hopes."

Across nine more verses Lincoln was posed as arguing with Columbia, who replied that a fool counseled by thieves and clowns held sway in the White House, the final rhyme going:

> Columbia, disgusted, would listen no more,
> But cried in a rage, as she stormed through the door—
> "I have kept an old donkey for nearly four years,
> Who brings me but scorn and disaster and tears!
> I vow I will drive a respectable team,
> Though forced to swap horses when crossing a stream!"

A Syracuse, New York, mass meeting and rally at which Vallandigham and others spoke in August carried mottoes on banners: "No more victims for the slaughter pens—not a man nor a dollar." "Let the tyrant tremble when the people speak." "Crush the Tyrant Lincoln before he crushes you." Someone in July signed a letter to the *New York World* "A Workingman" and began the letter: "I give a few of the crimes with which a workingman charges the present administration" and listed the crimes: (1) a fearful lowering of the standard of morality; (2) destruction of the national honor; (3) overturning of the Constitution and the established laws of the land; (4) putting military above civil authority; (5) causing the loss of tens of thousands of valuable lives; (6) making the workingman labor half the year to pay the interest of the debt with which they have saddled the nation; (7) putting the price of the necessaries of life all but out of the laborer's reach; (8) unsettling life with drafts, imprisonment; (9) incompetency; (10) obstinate determination to pursue a former suicidal policy. The anonymous writer who signed himself "A Workingman" had no less hate of Lincoln than the *New York World* editorial writer two days later: "Some of the shoddy papers profess to believe that because Lincoln and Hamlin have no middle names and were elected, Lincoln and Johnson, for a similar reason, will be successful. They call this a good omen. Some other noted individuals had no middle names; for instance, Judas Iscariot and Benedict Arnold."

At the Church of the Puritans in Union Square, New York, it was evident that Lincoln had earned the disapproval of the Reverend Dr. George Barrell Cheever, who for eighteen years had presided over the pulpit of that house of worship. Where Dr. Cheever saw what he believed evil he attacked it. *The Guilt of Slavery and Crime of Slave-holding* was one of his later books. *Defence of Capital Punishment* and *Punishment by Death, Its Authority and Expediency* were his two books attacking those who would abolish the death penalty. *The Right of the Bible in Our Public Schools* leveled a spear at those who would ban the Christian Scriptures from public schools. In detestation of those who would operate railroads or open saloons on Sunday Dr. Cheever had not written books, though he had lifted his voice unmistakably. Some of his gentler volumes were titled *The Winding of the River of the Water of Life* and *Thoughts for the Afflicted.* In Salem, Massachusetts, in younger days Dr. Cheever had issued a fable on the liquor traffic, "Inquire at Deacon Giles' Distillery," and the deacon's friends had put him on trial for libel and then enforced a thirty-day jail sentence on him. He had his milder moods, but Dr. Cheever rejoiced most in the thick of an onslaught on evil. The prime evil he now saw was the man Lincoln.

On a Monday evening in July Dr. Cheever's church was hung with mottoes: "This is the time to swap horses." "Lincoln weighed in the balance and found wanting." "Frémont the pathfinder of freedom." President Lincoln's public letters and state papers, said Dr. Cheever, according to press reports, "reveal his moral and political policy, and it is not safe for the nation to run upon it any longer." The President lacked guide and compass. "Events control him, not conscience, nor justice, nor God. Necessity is the whole of his creed. Indispensable necessity! The instrument of the tyrant to measure how much torture can be endured by his victim, how much blood taken, without swooning or dying. The calculating machine, whose weights and pulleys are the skeletons of armies, and the heads of your first born! How long shall this man be a snare to us? Know ye not that the people are destroyed? . . . Yet it comes to this—President Lincoln steadily opposed the gathering of colored troops, when he might have had hundreds of thousands from the heart of rebeldom . . . having given to the rebels meanwhile the advantage of three millions of laborers."

The view of the *New York Evening Post,* in an editorial immediately after the President's draft proclamation, was different. "This proclamation, cold, lifeless, rigid, bound round with red tape, clothed in the formal language of the bureau, sounds as though its author thought the people could bear to be chilled and disheartened. . . . It is the tone of a European sovereign telling his subjects what he requires of them." The *Post* would prefer that the President speak to the people, to his fellow citizens, simply, truly, with unreserved trust and confidence. "Is it the truth that we must now enlist for three years? Is it true that military affairs are in that condition? Then let us know it at once; let the people hear it from Mr. Lincoln in words which shall leave no doubt. Why should the whole people be in doubt, and in such distressing doubt, at this time, in regard to our military prospects?" *Harper's Weekly* held there was neither "chill" nor "red tape" in the President's proclamation, but a grave and properly confident tone. "It is surely much more dignified that a summons of the President should be calm, brief, and direct. Nothing is gained by what is called rhetoric in State papers; no statement the President might make of the situation could deepen the general feeling in regard to it; and no impassioned appeal could be more persuasive than the simple call."

Repeatedly in pretended news items and in editorial squibs opposition organs, the *New York World*, the *Detroit Free Press*, the *Chicago Times*, alleged that Lincoln was selfishly drawing his own salary in gold while paying the soldiers, if at all, in greenbacks. This had gone on for a year and longer before a statement of fact coming from L. E. Chittenden of Vermont, Register of the Treasury, in charge of payments, appeared in Administration newspapers. "Mr. Lincoln, and all his Cabinet, receive the ordinary greenbacks, just like ordinary men in ordinary business, and the regular income tax is regularly deducted from Mr. Lincoln's salary, just as it is from every other salary. The only officers paid in gold are our ministers abroad, in places where our currency is not recognized."

Three columns of allegations, rumors, charges, and suspicions in the *New York World* of July 21, 1864, persuaded those who read, and who believed without proof, that the Post Office Department was opening, before delivery, the mail of the *World*, of Generals McClellan and Frémont, of Mrs. Frémont, and that letters containing money were not delivered at all.

One peculiar fabrication originated in sick imagination and was later instructed by malice, barbed with evil intent. It seemed the same handicraft of the same reporter who invented the Scotch cap and long military cloak in which Lincoln rode at night through Baltimore to Washington, the same roguish muddler whose forged proclamation in May had brought newspaper suppressions by the Government. A New York Harbor commissioner, George W. Blunt, wrote to Assistant Secretary of the Navy Fox about it, Fox replying, "The slip of paper from the Sunday Times, about Pres. Lincoln calling for a song, whilst riding over the field with Gen'l McClellan is too absurd to contradict. No one here ever heard of it." This was December 30, 1862, and since then the story had been magnified with repeated telling, reappearing with many details in the *New York World*, the *Chicago Times*, the *Essex Statesman*, and scores of other newspapers.

"It would have been indecorous to name Mr. Lincoln the buffoon that he is, if he had been merely the Chief Magistrate," said the *New York World* of June 20, 1864. "But the truth must be told when he is a *Chief Magistrate seeking re-election.* . . . The American people are in no mood to re-elect a man to the highest office whose daily language is indecent, and who, riding over the field of Antietam, when thirty thousand of his fellow citizens were yet warm in their freshly-made graves, could slap Marshal Lamon on the knee, and call for the Negro song of 'Picayune Butler.' The war is a serious business to men whose sons have bitten the dust, whose brothers are under the Virginia hill-sides; it is a very serious business to women whose children have come home to them maimed for life, or whose husbands pine in the hospitals or have perished in the swamps of Virginia. They cannot be reminded of a smutty song; they cannot tread on fresh graves and grin and roar over a ribald nigger song. Nor do we believe the American people want to re-elect to the Presidency the man who can. The abolition abettors of traitors who fan the flames of treason, are shocked, nice souls! when he is called a fiddler who fiddles in the midst of this conflagration, when he is called a buffoon who tramples the holy dust of our gallant dead to the tune of 'Picayune Butler.' "

With no testimony from anyone directly concerned, without even so much as an anonymous comment from someone close enough to the persons of the incident to be regarded as halfway responsible, the *New York World* on the next day, June 21, 1864, reprinted from an upstate country newspaper, the *Essex Statesman*, an article headed LINCOLN UPON THE BATTLE-FIELD, and duly copied in anti-Administration newspapers:

We see that the papers are referring to the fact that Lincoln ordered a comic song to be sung upon a battle-field. We have known the facts about the transaction for some time, but have refrained from speaking them. As the newspapers are now stating some of the facts we will give the whole. Soon after one of the most desperate and sanguinary battles, Mr. Lincoln visited the commanding general and the army. While on his visit the commanding general, with his staff, took him over the field in a carriage and explained to him the plan of the battle, and the particular places where the fight was most fierce. At one point the commanding general said, "Here on this side of the road, five hundred of our brave fellows were killed, and just on the other side of the road four hundred more were slain, and right on the other side of the wall five hundred rebels were destroyed. We have buried them where they fell."

"I declare," said the President, "this is getting gloomy. Let us drive away." After driving a few rods, the President said, "This makes a fellow feel gloomy." "Jack" (speaking to a companion), "can't you give us something to cheer us up? Give us a song, and give us a lively one." Thereupon Jack struck up, as loud as he could bawl, a comic negro song, which he continued to sing while they were riding off from the battle-ground, and till they approached a regiment drawn up, when the commanding-general said, "Mr. President, wouldn't it be well for your friend to cease his song till we have passed this regiment? The poor fellows have lost more than half their numbers. They are feeling very badly, and I should be afraid of the effect that it may have on them."

The President then asked his companion to stop his singing till they got by that regiment. We know that this story is incredible, that it is impossible that a man who could be elected President of the United States, could so conduct himself over the fresh-made graves of the heroic dead. When this story was told us we said that it was *incredible, impossible,* but the story is told on such authority that we *know* it is true. We tell the story that the people may have some idea of this four years more of such rule. If any Republican holds up his hands in horror, and says this story *Can't* be true, we say we sympathize with him from the bottom of our soul; the story can't be true of any man fit for any office of trust, or even for decent society; but the story is every whit true of Abraham Lincoln, *incredible* and *impossible* as it may seem.

A few days afterward on the seriocomic collapse of the Greeley-Jewett peace negotiations at Niagara, the *New York World* deplored Lincoln's having learned "neither solemnity of feeling nor dignity of thought, nor so much as decency of demeanor from the dread circumstances which surround him." Lacking respect for himself, his office, and his country, he seemed incapable of understanding that "vulgar buffoonery and a coarse contempt for the commonest proprieties of life" were not required of him. "But it is wholly in the order of nature that a President who could divert himself with negro minstrelsy among the fresh graves of dead soldiers of the republic at Antietam, should see nothing odious or unbecoming in making sport of the public diplomacy."

Then passed gloomy weeks of August. Lamon repeated his suggestion that the Antietam slander should be refuted, that a word from the President would silence his defamers. Lincoln replied, as Lamon noted it: "No, Hill; there has already been too much said about this falsehood. Let the thing alone. If I have not established character enough to give the lie to this charge, I can only say that I am mistaken in my own estimate of myself. In politics, every man must skin his own skunk. These fellows are welcome to the hide of this one. Its body has already given forth its unsavory odor." Early in September Lamon brought to the President's attention one of many letters he had received. This began with an extract from the *New York World* of September 9, 1864. Under the heading "One of Mr. Lincoln's Jokes" it read:

The second verse of our campaign song published on this page was probably suggested by an incident which occurred on the battle-field of Antietam a few days after the fight. While the President was driving over the field in an ambulance, accompanied by Marshal Lamon, General McClellan, and another officer, heavy details of men were engaged in the task of burying the dead. The ambulance had just reached the neighborhood of the old stone bridge, where the dead were piled highest, when Mr. Lincoln, suddenly slapping Marshal Lamon on the knee, exclaimed: 'Come, Lamon, give us that song about Picayune Butler; McClellan has never heard it.' 'Not now, if you please,' said General McClellan, with a shudder; 'I would prefer to hear it some other place and time.'"

The letter-writer, A. J. Perkins, was worried over the story's having been "repeated in the *New York World* almost daily for the past three months," and saw it as a damaging story, if believed. That some believed it or pretended so was evident from mailbag doggerel with which the *World* accompanied the story:

Abe may crack his jolly jokes
O'er bloody fields of stricken battle,
While yet the ebbing life-tide smokes
From men that die like butchered cattle;
He, ere yet the guns grow cold,
To pimps and pets may crack his stories, etc.

Mr. Perkins closed his letter with direct inquiries as to what took place. Lamon wrote a reply with "a large infusion of 'vinegar and gall.' " Lincoln read both letters, shook his head. "No, Lamon, I would not publish this reply; it is too belligerent in tone for so grave a matter. There is a heap of 'cussedness' mixed up with your usual amiability, and you are at times too fond of a fight. If I were you, I would simply state the facts as they were. I would give the statement as you have here, without the pepper and salt. Let me try my hand at it." And taking a pen Lincoln wrote:

"The President has known me intimately for nearly twenty years, and has often heard me sing little ditties. The battle of Antietam was fought on the 17th day of September, 1862. On the first day of October, just two weeks after the battle, the President, with some others including myself, started from Washington to visit the Army, reaching Harper's Ferry at noon of that day. In a short while Gen. McClellan came from his Head Quarters near the battle ground, joined the President, and with him, reviewed the troops at Bolivar Heights that afternoon, and, at night, returned to his Head Quarters, leaving the President at Harper's Ferry. On the morning of the second the President, with Gen. Sumner, reviewed the troops respectively at Loudon Heights and Maryland Heights, and at about noon, started to Gen. McClellan's Head Quarters, reaching there only in time to see very little before night. On the morning of the third all started on a review of the third corps, and the cavalry, in the vicinity of the Antietam battle ground. After getting through with Gen. Burnside's Corps, at the suggestion of Gen. McClellan he and the President left their horses to be led, and went into an ambulance or ambulances to go to Gen. Fitz John Porter's Corps, which was two or three miles distant. I am not sure whether the President and Gen. McC. were in the same ambulance, or in different ones; but myself and some others were in the same with the President. On the way, and on no part of the battle ground, and on what suggestions I do not remember, the President asked me to sing the little sad song that follows, which he had often heard me sing, and had always seemed to like very much. I sang it. After it was over, some one of the party (I do not think it was the President) asked me to sing something else; and I sang two or three little comic things, of which 'Picayune Butler' was one.

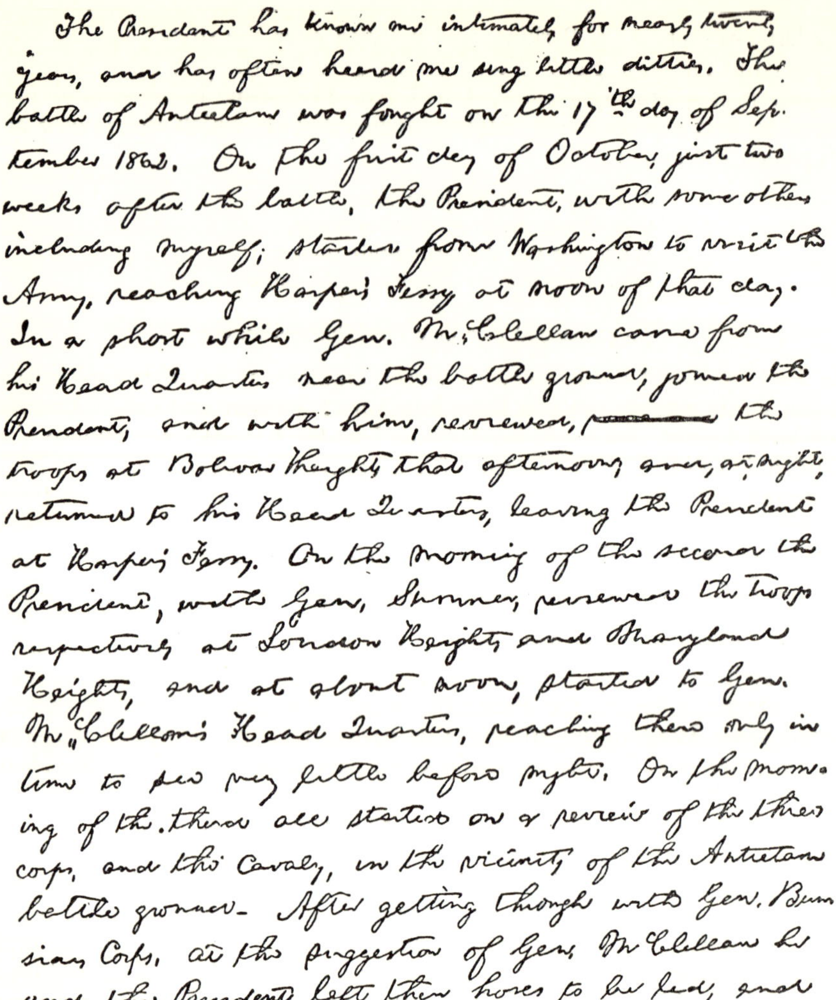

The President has known me intimately for nearly twenty years, and has often heard me sing little ditties. The battle of Antietam was fought on the 17th day of September 1862. On the first day of October, just two weeks after the battle, the President, with some others including myself, started from Washington to visit the Army, reaching Harper's Ferry at noon of that day. In a short while Gen. McClellan came from his Head Quarters near the battle ground, joined the President, and with him, reviewed the troops at Bolivar Heights that afternoon; and, at night, returned to his Head Quarters, leaving the President at Harper's Ferry. On the morning of the second the President, with Gen. Sumner, reviewed the troops respectively at Loudon Heights and Maryland Heights, and at about noon, started to Gen. McClellan's Head Quarters, reaching there only in time to see very little before night. On the morning of the third all started on a review of the three corps, and the Cavalry, in the vicinity of the Antietam battle ground. After getting through with Gen. Burnside's Corps, at the suggestion of Gen. McClellan he and the President left their horses to be led, and went into an ambulance or ambulances to go to Gen. Fitz John Porter's Corps, which was two or three miles distant. I am not sure whether the President and Gen. McC. were in the same ambulance, or in different ones; but myself and some others were in the same with the President. On the way, and on no part of the

Lincoln writes—for Lamon to sign—a statement on a "little ditty" at Antietam. Original in the possession of Dorothy Lamon Teillard.

Porter's corps was reached and reviewed; then the battle ground was passed over, and the most noted parts examined; then, in succession, the cavalry and Franklin's corps were reviewed, and the President and party returned to Gen. McClellan's headquarters at the end of a very hard, hot, and dusty day's work. Next day, the 4th, the President and Gen. McClellan visited such of the wounded as still remained in the vicinity, including the now lamented Gen. Richardson; then proceeded to and examined the South-Mountain battle-ground, at which point they parted,—Gen. McClellan returning to his camp, and the President returning to Washington, seeing, on the way, Gen. Hartsoff [sic], who lay wounded at Frederick Town.

"This is the whole story of the singing and its surroundings. Neither Gen. McClellan nor anyone else made any objections to the singing; the place was not on the battle-field; the time was sixteen days after the battle; no dead body was seen during the whole time the President was absent from Washington, nor even a grave that had not been rained on since it was made."

In rehearsing the facts and going over in his mind his relation to them, Lincoln shifted to a determination to say nothing and to see what would result from his keeping silence. "You know, Hill," he said to Lamon, "that this is the truth and the whole truth about that affair; but I dislike to appear as an apologist for an act of my own which I know was right. Keep this paper and we will see about it."

Wherefore in the tumult of that year of '64 neither Mr. Perkins nor the press nor the American electorate received any denial from Abraham Lincoln regarding the most malicious fabrication brought against him in that campaign year. Had the statement been given out, Lamon would have added the verses of "the little sad song" called "Twenty Years Ago," which was Lincoln's favorite in Lamon's repertoire, three verses that, according to Lamon, always had a special interest and appealing sentiment for Lincoln.

While the official journal of the Frémont Radical Democracy shouted a slogan—"Down with Lincoln! Such be our battlecry! Let there be but two parties; let all be for or against Lincoln"—the *Atlanta* (Georgia) *Register* agreed: "If they will use the ballot-box against Mr. Lincoln while we use the cartridge-box, each side will be a helper to the other, and both coöperate in accomplishing the greatest work which this country and the continent have witnessed." *Harper's Weekly* quoted a New York Copperhead paper, "It is the duty of the country to rally at the next election and put down Lincoln as well as his confederate, Jeff Davis."

Would former President Millard Fillmore be so patriotic as to accept a presidential nomination for President, if his friends would manage it? A friend asked him, for Fillmore was known to have little faith in Lincoln. Fillmore wrote in response, "I can assure you in all sincerity that I have no desire ever to occupy that exalted station again, and more especially at a time like this."

Here and there despair over the war became despair over the President and his seeming failures. "The war and its constant expectations and anxieties oppress me," wrote James Russell Lowell. "I cannot think. I hear bad things about Mr. Lincoln and try not to believe them." William Cullen Bryant wrote to John M. Forbes of "the Seward and Weed faction filling all the offices with its creatures," saying further, "I am so disgusted with Lincoln's behavior that I cannot muster respectful terms in which to write

This little card printed with green ink broadcast by the Lincoln opposition lets the reader guess who is the Baboon pictured. From the Barrett collection.

him." From Bloomington on August 4 David Davis wrote to a brother that while in Chicago he had talked with many people from different parts of the country and found growing uneasiness and distrust. "People are getting tired of the war. Some of them can't see a ray of light. I am speaking of good men. Two years ago I succeeded in raising 1,300 men in this county. It took about ten days. There is no note now of any volunteering. . . . There is faith in the administration, and yet you will hear *whispering* inquiries as to whether the plan they are pursuing is the best. . . . Keep these views to yourself, and burn this letter." Gurowski, who had so often and unwillingly confessed to his diary that Lincoln held the favor of the plain people in spite of the politicians, wrote August 1 of '64: "From almost all points very bad news in relation to Mr. Lincoln's chances of re-election. The people at large seems not at all so enthusiastic for him now."

Across weeks of August, 1864, a movement, necessarily secret, among Republican-party leaders operated with the aim of replacing Lincoln with another nominee for President. The Jonah of the Ship of State was Lincoln. He should be flung overboard. Among Republican conferences in New York City was one at the home of David Dudley Field August 14, with Greeley, Mayor George Opdyke, Parke Godwin of the *Evening Post*, William Curtis Noyes, Henry Winter Davis, Theodore Tilton, Franz Lieber, and twenty or more others. It was agreed that a committee should request Lincoln to withdraw as a presidential candidate. The name of Grant was most favored to replace that of Lincoln. A call was prepared for a convention to be held in Cincinnati September 28, signatures to the call to be requested in a circular letter signed only by John Austin Stevens, Secretary of the National War Committee, an active Republican since the formation of the party. "The present distraction and apathy which depress the friends of the Union threaten to throw the Government into the hands of its enemies," the call set forth, urging "that a convention of the people should be assembled to consider the state of the nation and to concentrate the Union strength on some one candidate, who commands the confidence of the country, *even by a new nomination if necessary*."

"Mr. Lincoln is already beaten," wrote Greeley to Mayor Opdyke, one of the organizers of the movement. "We must have another ticket to save us from utter overthrow. If we had such a ticket as could be had by naming Grant, Butler, or Sherman for President, and Farragut as Vice, we could make a fight yet." Chase wrote to Opdyke as though he were half-willing to go along, though, "my views are, by no means, as clear as I could wish." That Chase was no longer even mentioned for the head of the ticket may have had to do with his hesitancy. Chase was certain that the country was "never more in need of wise counsel and fearless action by and among patriotic men." Congressman Roscoe Conkling wrote to John Austin Stevens, who handled the bulk of the correspondence relating to the convention call, "I do not approve of the call or of the movement." Senator Collamer wrote to Stevens that he could not approve a change of front in the face of the enemy. Daniel S. Dickinson of New York wrote that "necessities of shoddy contractors and longing officeholders" had unwisely dictated the June convention which nominated Lincoln too previously, and, "I cannot believe that Mr. Lincoln, if fully advised of the state of the public mind, would desire to enter upon a canvass."

J. W. Shaffer wrote from Butler's army headquarters that General Butler was journeying north to visit his home in Lowell, Massachusetts, and would stop two days at the Fifth Avenue Hotel in New York, where he could be seen on political matters. Shaffer seemed a little worried over information that "Lincoln had copies of despatches to Chase, Ashley, and Sprague" but ended on the note that "it makes little difference what Mr. Lincoln knows." Also Shaffer covered himself and Butler against future contingencies with the line "I with you think the call might have been made without the back-handed lick at the President." Butler himself later wrote from Lowell naming two friends who knew his views and indicating his own availability for the emergency. "I agree with you that a most momentous crisis in our history approaches, nay, now is. The true friends of the Union, laying aside all else, must work to meet it."

The antislavery wheel horse, John Jay, believed a letter might be prepared which would "compel Mr. Lincoln's acquiescence" to another nominating convention, in which event "if Lincoln won't withdraw, the only effect of the new convention may be to elect a Copperhead, which would be much worse." J. S. Prettyman of Milford, Delaware, wrote that, his views being solicited, he would give them. "Thousands fear to trust the country in Mr. Lincoln's hands another term. They would desire a man of more force of character. Under these circumstances if the Cincinnati movement is to be strong and influential enough to scare Lincoln from the track, it will not do good, but evil." N. McBride of Morris, Illinois, wrote: "After conversing with different parties here, I am convinced that a large portion of loyal men in this country would hail the Cincinnati Convention movement with joy. We want decision, nerve and energy, and can trust Butler." Emil Preetorius voiced the German radicals of St. Louis in seeking "untrammelled expression of the popular voice" and indicated his preference that a Cincinnati convention reject Lincoln and nominate Frémont.

Senator Charles Sumner indicated his wish that Lincoln should withdraw, but in case Lincoln should refuse it would not be so good. "It may be," wrote Sumner, "that Mr. Lincoln will see that we shall all be stronger and more united under another candidate. But if he does not see it so, our duty is none the less clear to unite in the opposition to the common enemy." To Governor Andrew, Sumner wrote much the same view. "I see no way of meeting the difficulties from the candidacy of Mr. Lincoln unless he withdraws patriotically and kindly, so as to leave no breach in the party. Will he do this? I can imagine a patriotism looking singly to the good of the country at this trying moment."

An article by Whitelaw Reid in the *Cincinnati Gazette* suggested the advisability of Lincoln's withdrawal as a candidate, and Reid wrote to the committee's secretary Stevens at New York: "That which I could do in the direction you indicate has been done in inducing the *Gazette* to come out for Mr. Lincoln's withdrawal. The article has been telegraphed east, and I hope has done some good." The *Cincinnati Gazette* publisher, Richard Smith, wrote to Stevens: "The people regard Mr. Lincoln's candidacy as a misfortune. His apparent strength when nominated was fictitious, and now the fiction has disappeared, and instead of confidence there is distrust. I do not know a Lincoln man, and in all our correspondence, which is large and varied, I have seen few letters from Lincoln men." To keep Lincoln at the head of the ticket would make uphill work and be a dangerous experiment, in Smith's view. Smith could see there would be "general delight" over the nomination of "a man that would inspire confidence and infuse life into our ranks," though he was mentioning no name of any such bannerman. "Whatever is done should be cautiously managed, as the patient requires delicate treatment." In one direction might lie ill fate. "If the move should be made, and then Mr. Lincoln refuse to withdraw, our condition would be a great deal worse than it is now. Consequently a Convention to force Lincoln from the track would not be popular, but would be disastrous."

While John Austin Stevens was receiving these letters several Republican newspapers, besides opposition journals, printed items in tone with that of the *Buffalo Courier:* "It is rumored in New York, and the report is believed by many who are in a position to be well-informed, that, at an early date, Abraham Lincoln will withdraw his name as a candidate for re-election, and urge the assembling of another nomination convention." This was in key with the Whitelaw Reid article "telegraphed east" from Cincinnati, which spread a rumor, "a report believed by many," that Lincoln was actually going to do what those who regarded him as a Jonah wanted him to do.

Rugged John Andrew spoke for himself and others of unquestionably clean motives when he wrote to Greeley his gravely considered judgment of the President: "Mr. Lincoln *ought* to lead the country. But he is essentially lacking in the quality of leadership, which is a gift of God and not a device of man. Without this, his other qualities, as an able and devoted magistrate and most estimable citizen, leave it necessary for us to make a certain allowance for a measure of success which, under the more magnetic influence of a positive man, of clear purpose and more prophetic insight, would surely be ours." Andrew would support Lincoln so long as Lincoln was the candidate. So early a nomination of a candidate had been a political blunder. "Will the attempt to change front be a probable success? If any other man did now attract the spontaneous and united support of loyal and patriotic men, my answer might be, to yield to a suggestion which would then seem providential. As it is, I cannot venture, myself, without knowing what I do not know of opinion elsewhere, to advise the experiment."

How far would the Jonah movement go? How would it affect the party morale? A few weeks would give the answer. And what was Lincoln's own view of the proposal that he should withdraw? Carl Schurz was to say that one hot afternoon he rode with Lincoln in a carriage from the White House to the Soldiers' Home and the two of them that evening sat on a parlor lounge in conversation. And Schurz had afterward, while the language was still fresh in his mind, written a letter to a friend, giving his impression of how Lincoln felt about the movement to unseat him. Lincoln said to Schurz he would not complain of the burden of care put on his shoulders. Nobody knew that weight but himself. But was it necessary, generous, right, to impeach his motives? "They urge me with almost violent language to withdraw from the contest, although I have been unanimously nominated, in order to make room for a better man. I wish I could. Perhaps some other man might do this business better than I. That is possible. I do not deny it. But I am here, and that better man is not here. And if I should step aside to make room for him, it is not at all sure—perhaps not even probable—that he would get here. It is much more likely that the factions opposed to me would fall to fighting among themselves, and that those who want me to make room for a better man would get a man whom most of them would not want in at all. My withdrawal, therefore, might, and probably would, bring on a confusion worse confounded. God knows, I have at least tried very hard to do my duty, to do right to everybody and wrong to nobody. And now to have it said by men who have been my friends and who ought to know me better, that I have been seduced by what they call the lust of power, and that I have been doing this and that unscrupulous thing hurtful to the common cause, only to keep myself in office! Have they thought of that common cause when trying to break me down? I hope they have."

So he went on, as if speaking to himself, noted Schurz, sometimes as if Schurz were not there at all, now pausing for a second, then uttering a sentence or two with "vehement emphasis." Evening deepened, dusk came, and when the room had lamplight Schurz thought he saw Lincoln's eyes moist and his face working under strong emotion. "At last he stopped, as if waiting for me to say something." And Schurz could only offer his confident assurance that "the people" were not hearing the bickerings of the critics, believed in him and would faithfully stand by him. As the talk turned on things to be done and Lincoln explained various acts which in the coming campaign might be questioned, he was more at ease, bantered playfully, and calmly shook hands in parting with Schurz. "Well, things might look better, and they might look worse. Go in, and let us all do the best we can."

Up and down the length of his White House office walked Lincoln another hot afternoon, with Thaddeus Stevens and Simon Cameron present, and politics in Pennsylvania under consideration. Said Stevens, as Nicolay had it from one who was there, "In order that we may be able in our State to go to work with a good will I want you to make us one promise, that you will reorganize your cabinet and leave Montgomery Blair out of it." The discussion ran more than two hours, Lincoln rising from his chair and pacing the room as he told Stevens he was sorry to be compelled to deny the request, that even if he inclined to do it he had no right to do so. "Has it come to this, that the voters of this country are asked to elect a man to be President—to be Executive—to administer the Government, and yet that man is to have no will or discretion of his own? Am I to be the mere puppet of power? To have my constitutional advisers selected beforehand, to be told I must do this, or leave that undone? It would be degrading to my manhood to consent to any such bargain—I was about to say it is equally degrading to your manhood to ask it." Yes, he desired re-election, having pride enough to wish that his four years of administration should be endorsed, and believing he could serve better than any new man in putting down the rebellion and restoring peace and prosperity to the country. "But I would have the courage to refuse the office rather than to accept on such disgraceful terms as really not to be President after I am elected."

From Chicago and Philadelphia this summer Lincoln heard complaints requiring his interference. He wrote to Postmaster John L. Scripps in Chicago that he was "well satisfied" with Isaac N. Arnold as a member of Congress, did not know that the man who might supplant him would be as satisfactory. "But the correct principle, I think, is that all our friends should have absolute freedom of choice among our friends. My wish, therefore, is that you will do just as you think fit with your own suffrage in the case, and not constrain any of your subordinates to [do] other than [as] he thinks fit with his." Had Lincoln been nearer to Chicago, he might have brought co-operation from Scripps and others. What happened was that Isaac Arnold, the one most unquenchable pro-Lincoln Congressman, lost the nomination through generous withdrawal in favor of a candidate favored by John L. Scripps, writer of the first and most able campaign biography of Lincoln in the 1860 campaign.

In the case of the Philadelphia postmaster Lincoln sent for him and read to him from a written paper which the postmaster could carry away and read over to be sure what he had heard and there could be no dispute about precisely what was said. Lincoln read: "Complaint is made to me that you are using your official power to defeat Judge Kelley's renomination to Congress. I am well satisfied with Judge Kelley as a member of Congress, and I do not know that the man who might supplant him would be as satisfactory." Then followed the rule he had lain down for Scripps in Chicago, adding that this was "the rule I inculcated and adhered to on my part" in the case of another recent renomination. Back to Philadelphia went the postmaster. Also from Philadelphia came word later that not one of the two hundred and more post-office workers there was openly for Kelley. To a Republican of influence there Lincoln wrote, "This, if true, is not accidental." Left to free choice, maybe half or more would be for Kelley. "Please tell the postmaster he must find a way to relieve me from the suspicion that he is not keeping his promise to me in good faith." This brought a change. Soon plenty of post-office workers were coming out for Kelley. In fact, what with the post-office workers and others, Kelley rode into a handsome renomination.

Congressman George Julian brought Lincoln his complaint that Commissioner of Patents David P. Holloway, editor and owner of the *Richmond* (Indiana) *Palladium*, refused to recognize Julian as the proper party candidate, and was keeping the name of Julian's defeated rival standing in his newspaper. "This threatens discord and mischief" was Julian's way of putting it. And he demanded that the President remove Holloway from office.

"If I remove Mr. Holloway," said the President, "I shall have a quarrel with Senator Lane on my hands." Julian was sure Senator Lane would not quarrel over removal of a man fighting his own party and Administration friends. "Your nomination," then said the President, as Julian noted it, "is as binding on Republicans as mine, and you can rest assured that Mr. Holloway shall support you, openly and unconditionally, or lose his head." This satisfied Julian. He went away. A week passed. Again came Hoosier Julian to Lincoln on the case of Mr. Holloway, who he said had not changed his ways and was still snubbing Julian, Lincoln, and the Administration by keeping Julian's name out of the paper and flaunting that of the defeated rival. "I saw in an instant," noted Julian, "that the President meant business. He dispatched a messenger at once, asking Mr. Holloway to report to him forthwith, in person, and in a few days my name was announced in his paper as the Republican candidate, and that of my competitor withdrawn."

A considerable Republican faction in Congressman Roscoe Conkling's district in New York was threatening to unseat that young orator and actor. His friends sent word to Lincoln that Seward clansmen were the disturbers. Lincoln wrote to their spokesman that he had submitted their case to Seward and as for himself, "I am for the regular nominee in all cases . . . no one could be more satisfactory to me . . . than Mr. Conkling." Others in the district might be as good as Conkling "but I think I know him to be at least good enough." And Conkling was nominated and during August Conkling was emphatic in written refusals to join the Jonah movement.

With some of the unnecessary quiet of an eel swimming in oil, Ben Butler through July had lent his consent, though not on paper, to the radicals who favored a withdrawal of both Frémont and Lincoln in behalf of Butler for President. Written word came to Butler of Wade telling one of his friends that Butler could be "triumphantly elected President" if nominated. The Ohio Congressman Ashley wrote Butler that he had seen and talked confidentially with Thurlow Weed, Thomas Corwin, John W. Forney, and others, and that all wished a national convention of War Democrats to nominate Butler. Ashley seems to have been the only one who convinced himself that Weed, Corwin, and Forney, if and when they should leave the Lincoln ship, would go over into the Butler craft. Wendell Phillips, however, was for Butler. Phillips agreed with the New Yorker who suggested to Butler the ticket Benjamin F. Butler and Benjamin F. Wade, "two earnest men for country, humanity, God's truth and eternal justice."

At a Cabinet meeting July 19 Lincoln brought up the matter of a dispute between Butler and Governor Francis H. Pierpont, who had been elected by Unionist delegates from forty Virginia counties as governor of the State. Butler's military authorities at Norfolk had announced they would submit a vote to the citizens on whether they would be governed by martial law, Welles writing of it in his diary: "Of course the friends of civil administration, who denied the validity of the whole proceeding, would not vote, and the military had it all as they pleased. . . . While Butler has talents and capacity, he is not to be trusted. The more I see of him, the greater is my distrust of his integrity." Out of the Cabinet discussion came no decision of the President to act in favor of a governor holding capably to the President's reconstruction policy. One of the rare occasions this was when Attorney General Bates wrote with visible emotion in his diary: "Alas! that I should live to see such abject fear—such stolid indifference to duty. . . . My heart is sick, when I see the President shrinking from the correction of gross and heinous wrong because he is afraid 'Genl Butler will raise a hubbub about it'! . . . The Prest knows what is right, as well as any man, and will be glad to *see it done*, but, unhappily, lacks the nerve to do it."

And it also may have been that Lincoln knew better than Bates what would be the political ravages resulting from a dramatic attempt openly to discipline and correct the diabolically cunning lawyer-politician-general from Massachusetts. That Lincoln and Grant were meekly biding their time, waiting the occasion when they could without risk to the Union cause quietly drop Butler overboard—this Bates did not even faintly surmise.

Not entirely an invention was one *Cincinnati Commercial* item in June from its Washington correspondent, reprinted in various newspapers as follows: "Some gentlemen in conversation with the President a few days ago, expressed their doubts as to Butler's capacity as an officer in the field. 'Well,' said Mr. Lincoln, 'if he does not succeed it will not be my fault. I have set three of my best Generals to watch him—Baldy Smith, Gillmore, and Weitzel. Now, if they can't keep him from doing harm, I am sure I ought not to be held accountable for what he does.' " The fact was, of course, that Grant and not Lincoln named those stationed where they could "watch" Butler. Also the fact was that Grant was doing precisely what the newspaper item credited Lincoln with doing. Both Lincoln and Grant hoped that Butler's low performance as a military commander would be overcome by the better grade of generals assigned to Butler's staff.

The London *Spectator* in an extended consideration of Thurlow Weed as a Republican spokesman, "a chafferer," and "a wire-puller," quoted from his published words: "If Mr. Lincoln's opponent be, in the unpatriotic sense of the term, of 'Copperhead' proclivities, I shall heartily support Mr. Lincoln. But if I can see a reasonable probability of electing a President who would prosecute the war for objects declared to the world in the resolution offered by Mr. Crittenden and adopted by Congress, I should give my voice and vote for such a candidate." The *Spectator* then quoted the *New York Times* as quietly remarking, "We believe this to be substantially the position of the great body of the Union men throughout the country," the *Spectator* saying it wished to reply to the *New York Times:* "If it is so, which we do *not* believe, the great body of Union men throughout the country seem to be destitute of both good sense and good faith. . . . It would be a flagrant breach of contract on the strength of which 150,000 negroes are already fighting the battles *not* of the Northern States, but, as they suppose, as we believe, of freedom."

"Ten days since, I told Mr. Lincoln that his re-election was an impossibility," wrote Thurlow Weed to Seward August 22. "I also told him that the information would soon come to him through other channels. . . . Mr. Raymond, who has just left me, says that unless some prompt and bold step be now taken all is lost. The people are wild for peace. They are told that the President will only listen to terms of peace on condition slavery be abandoned." Therefore Weed was urging that the President should offer the Richmond Government the conditions of the Crittenden Compromise of the winter of '60-'61, with the Union to be restored and the South writing its own constitutional sanction of slave property. David Dudley Field thereupon let it be known he considered Weed no Republican-party man at all,

Weed then publishing a letter wherein he commented: "Field reads me out of his party. This is as it should be, for in attempting to fraternize, the Scripture, which forbids the yoking of an ox and an ass together, would be violated." The *Independent* suggested, "If we were Mr. Field we would have no more dealings with a man who called us an ox."

The smooth and easy-spoken Weed wandered into the Democratic camp this summer to the extent of talking with some of them till they believed he was going to travel with them. One of McClellan's close friends, a Wall Street gold speculator, S. L. M. Barlow, later wrote in a letter as to Weed: "He was with us and against the Republicans for about a month. Then we lost him."

Weed could only shake his head glumly over Lincoln's having suggested in his Niagara letter that peace through "the abandonment of slavery would be considered." General Meade wrote to his wife that in this the President was going too far with the radicals. A War Democrat editor in Wisconsin, Charles D. Robinson, wrote to Lincoln: "This puts the whole war question on a new basis, and takes us war Democrats clear off our feet, leaving us no ground to stand upon. I venture to write you . . . in the hope that you may suggest some interpretation of it." Lincoln wrote, left unfinished, and probably never sent to Robinson, a reply which began: "To me it seems plain that saying reunion and abandonment of slavery would be considered, if offered, is not saying that nothing else or less would be considered, if offered. But I will not stand upon the mere construction of language." He took up Robinson's quotation from the letter to Greeley in '62, wherein the President had said: "If I could save the Union without freeing any slave I would do it; and if I could save it by freeing all the slaves I would do it; and if I could save it by freeing some and leaving others alone I would also do that." He reminded Robinson that he had continued in that same letter, "What I do about slavery and the colored race, I do because I believe it helps to save the Union; and what I forbear, I forbear because I do not believe it would help to save the Union. I shall do less whenever I shall believe what I am doing hurts the cause; and I shall do more whenever I shall believe doing more will help the cause."

And of this written in '62 what would he say in '64? "I am as true to the whole of it now, as when I first said it." Emancipation and the employment of Negro soldiers were measures to help the cause not "by magic or miracles, but by inducing the colored people to come bodily over from the rebel side to ours." He quoted from his Conkling letter of September, '63, on the promise of freedom to Negro soldiers and how that promise would have to be kept, adding the points: "Take from us and give to the enemy the hundred and thirty, forty, or fifty thousand colored persons now serving us as soldiers, seamen, and laborers, and we cannot longer maintain the contest. . . . It is not a question of sentiment or taste, but one of physical force, which may be measured and estimated, as horse-power and steam-power are measured and estimated. And, by measurement, it is more than we can lose and live. Nor can we, by discarding it, get a white force in place of it. There is a witness in every white man's bosom that he would rather go to the war having the negro to help him than to help the enemy against him."

In addition Lincoln had a final point: "Allow me to remind you that no one, having control of the rebel armies, or, in fact, having any influence whatever in the rebellion, has offered, or intimated, a willingness to a restoration of the Union, in any event, or on any condition whatever." Having dwelt on this in several phases Lincoln's final sentence carried implications that could have several constructions. "If Jefferson Davis wishes for himself, or for the benefit of his friends at the North, to know what I would do if he were to offer peace and reunion, saying nothing about slavery, let him try me."

In the writing of this letter Lincoln probably meant it to be one of his devastating propaganda shots, his latest addition to the letters to Greeley, Conkling, Hodges, letters that had gone far and had for the time convinced many readers that they were receiving from the President's published letter practically the same direct explanations he would have made had they met him personally in the White House. Yet other and more immediate matters pressed for his decision, so that he could not finish or revise the letter. Or he held it back in a belief that in the gloom and confusions of the hour no letter could be framed that would help. Only military victories would help.

The letter from Robinson had been handed to Lincoln by Judge Joseph T. Mills and ex-Governor A. W. Randall of Wisconsin. In their interview at the Soldiers' Home Lincoln unburdened himself.

"Mr. President," said Randall, "why can't you seek seclusion, and play hermit for a fortnight?"

"Ah, two or three weeks would do me no good. I cannot fly from my thoughts—my solicitude for this great country follows me wherever I go. I do not think it is personal vanity or ambition, though I am not free from these infirmities, but I cannot but feel that the weal or the woe of this great nation will be decided in November. There is no program offered by any wing of the Democratic party but that must result in the permanent destruction of the Union."

"But, Mr. President, General McClellan is in favor of crushing out this rebellion by force. He will be the Chicago candidate."

"Sir, the slightest knowledge of arithmetic will prove to any man that the rebel armies cannot be destroyed by Democratic strategy. It would sacrifice all the white men of the North to do it. There are now in the service of the United States nearly 150,000 able-bodied colored men, most of them under arms. The Democratic strategy demands that these forces be conciliated by restoring them to slavery. The black men who now assist Union prisoners to escape are to be converted into our enemies, in the vain hope of gaining the good-will of their masters. We shall have to fight two nations instead of one. . . . There have been men base enough to propose to me to return to slavery the black warriors of Port Huron and Olustee, and thus win the respect of the masters they fought. Should I do so, I should deserve to be damned in time and eternity. Come what will, I will keep my faith with friend and foe. My enemies pretend I am now carrying on this war for the sole purpose of abolition. So long as I am President, it shall be carried on for the sole purpose of restoring the Union. But no human power can subdue this rebellion without the use of the emancipation policy, and every other policy calculated to weaken the moral and physical forces of the rebellion. . . . Let my enemies prove to the country that the destruction of slavery is not necessary to a restoration of the Union. I will abide the issue."

And what hopes, what envisionings, what dawns real or false, were moving behind one remark to Randall? "Freedom has given us 150,000 men, raised on Southern soil. It will give us more yet. Just so much it has subtracted from the enemy, and, instead of alienating the South, there are now evidences of a fraternal feeling growing up between our men and the rank and file of the rebel soldiers." It would seem that he welcomed "fraternal feeling" between Union and Confederate troops. Yet it was also his regret that his proclamations failed to bring death to the enemy. "Breath alone kills no rebels." And he was telegraphing Grant, "Chew and choke as much as possible," and he considered it axiomatic that the war would end when enough rebels had been killed. None the less he mentioned to Randall evidences of "a fraternal feeling growing up between our men and the rank and file of the rebel soldiers." This gave him a glow. He seemed to welcome news of fraternal feeling rather than hate, as though should the Union be saved, that fraternal feeling could be built on.

Judge Mills in writing this interview for a Wisconsin country paper either reported Lincoln's words with a rare accuracy or he requested Lincoln to make sure it was correctly notated, for Nicolay and Hay considered it perfect as a transcript. The Badger State visitors saw Lincoln enter the room with shoulders inclined forward, gait rapid "and shuffling, ample understandings with large slippers, and Briarian arms, a face radiant with intelligence and humor." Judge Mills saw the President as "not a mere joker but a man of deep convictions . . . the great guiding intellect of the age . . . of transparent honesty, republican simplicity, gushing sympathy for those who offered their lives for their country, utter forgetfulness of self . . . Heaven's instrument to conduct his people." This peculiarly significant interview *Harper's Weekly* of New York reprinted from the *Grant County Herald* of Wisconsin, whereupon scores of newspapers in America and the London *Spectator* and other journals in England gave it to their readers.

And Mr. Raymond, editor of the only Administration daily newspaper in New York, steadfast opponent of Greeley, chairman of the Republican National Executive Committee, what would be the "prompt and bold step" he told Weed was immediately necessary? "I feel compelled to drop you a line," he began his letter of August 22 to the President. Raymond was hearing but one report. "The tide is setting strongly against us." Washburne in Illinois, Cameron in Pennsylvania, were saying their States at the moment were against the Administration. Only strenuous efforts could carry Indiana,

Governor Morton had written. "This State [New York], according to the best information I can get, would go 50,000 against us to-morrow. And so of the rest." Two special causes were assigned for this feeling against the Administration: want of military success, and "the impression in some minds, the fear and suspicion in others, that we are not to have peace in any event under this Administration until slavery is abandoned." The suspicion seemed widespread that peace with Union was to be had. "It is idle to reason with this belief—still more idle to denounce it. It can only be expelled by some authoritative act, at once bold enough to fix attention and distinctive enough to defy incredulity and challenge respect."

Therefore Raymond would suggest the President appoint a commission to proffer peace to Davis "on the sole condition of acknowledging the supremacy of the Constitution—all other questions to be settled in a convention of the people of all the States." Raymond reasoned that such an offer would require no armistice, no suspension of active war, no sacrifice of consistency. "If the proffer were accepted (which I presume it would not be), the country would never consent to place the practical execution of its details in any but loyal hands, and in those we should be safe. If it should be rejected (as it would be), it would plant seeds of disaffection in the South, dispel all the delusions about peace that prevail in the North, silence the clamors and damaging falsehoods of the opposition . . . and unite the North as nothing since the firing on Fort Sumter has . . . done." Out of the gloom of the hour Raymond could see victory snatched by a peace proffer, ending his proposals in a grave and gentle tone. "I beg you to excuse the earnestness with which I have pressed this matter on your attention. Permit me to add that if done at all I think this should be done at once,—as your own spontaneous act."

Raymond waited in New York. From the President came no reply. In Washington the President was viewing the national situation. He was a candidate for re-election with as yet no opponent. It would be a week or more before the Democrats at Chicago would name a man to run against him. Yet the signs were that he was already beaten by whoever might be named to run against him. In his own later words, "At this period we had no adversary and seemed to have no friends." When his Cabinet members came in for a meeting August 23, he handed each of them a sheet of paper so folded and pasted that what was inside could not be read. He requested each Cabinet member to sign his name across the back of the sheet. Each one wrote not knowing what he was signing. It was a memorandum for possible future use, reading:

Executive Mansion, Washington, August 23, 1864

This morning, as for some days past, it seems exceedingly probable that this administration will not be reëlected. Then it will be my duty to so coöperate with the President-elect as to save the Union between the election and the inauguration; as he will have secured his election on such ground that he cannot possibly save it afterward.

A. Lincoln

"In this peculiar fashion," noted the secretaries Nicolay and Hay, "he pledged himself and the Administration to accept loyally the anticipated verdict of the people against him, and to do their utmost to save the Union in the brief remainder of his term of office. He gave no intimation to any member of the Cabinet of the nature of the paper they had signed."

Two days later Raymond and the National Executive Committee of the Republican party, not having heard from the President that he would publicly proffer peace to the Richmond Government, arrived at the White House. They were, according to Nicolay and Hay, "in obvious depression and panic." Raymond was in a final and confidential session with the President and three Cabinet members when Welles entered. "I went in as usual unannounced," wrote Welles in his diary. . . . "I found Messrs. Seward, Fessenden, and Stanton with Raymond . . . in consultation with the President. The President was making some statement as to a document of his, and said he supposed his style was peculiar and had its earmarks, so that it could not be mistaken. He kept on talking as if there had been no addition to the company, and as if I had been expected and belonged there. But the topic was not pursued by the others when the President ceased. Some inquiry was put to me in regard to intelligence from the fleet at Mobile. . . . Mr. Fessenden rose and, putting his mouth to the ear of the President, began to whisper, and as soon as I could answer the brief inquiries, I left the room. It was easy to perceive that Seward, Stanton, and Raymond were disconcerted by my appearance. Except the whispering by Fessenden I saw nothing particular on his part."

Could Welles have read a letter written that day in the White House by Nicolay to John Hay in Illinois he would have gained more than inklings of what was going on in the room into which he had entered "as usual unannounced." Nicolay wrote as between two cronies: "Hell is to pay. The New York politicians have got a stampede on that is about to swamp everything. Raymond and the National Committee are here to-day. R. thinks a commission to Richmond is about the only salt to save us; while the Tycoon sees and says it would be utter ruination. The matter is now undergoing consultation. Weak-kneed damned fools . . . are in the movement for a new candidate to supplant the Tycoon. Everything is darkness and doubt and discouragement. Our men see giants in the airy and unsubstantial shadows of the opposition, and are about to surrender without a fight. I think that to-day and here is the turning-point in our crisis. If the President can infect R. and his committee with some of his own patience and pluck, we are saved."

And what of the document Welles heard the President say was in his own "peculiar" style, having his personal "earmarks"? Lincoln had written it to meet squarely the proposals of Raymond for a peace proffer to Richmond. Raymond, having the document before him, could judge whether it could be improved on, could visualize its potential effect on the public as a peace proffer. It read:

Executive Mansion, Washington, August 24, 1864

Sir:

You will proceed forthwith and obtain, if possible, a conference for peace with Honorable Jefferson Davis, or any person by him authorized for that purpose. You will address him in entirely respectful terms, at all events, and in any that may be indispensable to secure the conference. At said conference you will propose, on behalf of this government, that upon the restoration of the Union and the national authority, the war shall cease at once, all remaining questions to be left for adjustment by peaceful modes. If this be accepted, hostilities to cease at once. If it be not accepted, you will then request to be informed what terms, if any, embracing the restoration of the Union would be accepted. If any such be presented you in answer, you will forthwith report the same to this government, and await further instructions. If the presentation of any terms embracing the restoration of the Union be declined, you will then request to be informed what terms of peace would be accepted; and, on receiving any answer, report the same to this government, and await further instructions.

The more Raymond looked at it, the more he saw it was off key and in diplomatic lingo inadmissible. Or as Nicolay wrote in his private notebook, the President "and the stronger half of the Cabinet, Seward, Stanton, and Fessenden," showed Raymond that they had thoroughly considered and discussed his proposals of a peace proffer. They gave Raymond their reasons. "He very readily concurred with them in the opinion that to follow his plan of sending a commission to Richmond would be worse than losing the Presidential contest—it would be ignominiously surrendering it in advance. Nevertheless the visit of himself and committee here did great good. They found the President and cabinet much better informed than themselves, and went home encouraged and cheered." And into files to which Greeley and Bennett had no access went the unused, unsent peace proffer which Lincoln had written to show Raymond what it might look like when put in black and white.

Raymond had proposed that a certain state paper be issued by Lincoln. Lincoln wrote such a state paper and let Raymond consider whether it was worth issuance. The Raymond satisfied by this procedure was the same Raymond whose biography of the President published that summer held the statement: "No one can read Mr. Lincoln's State papers without perceiving in them a most remarkable faculty of 'putting things.' . . . His intellect was keen, emphatically logical in its action, and capable of the closest and most subtle analysis; and he used language for the sole purpose of stating, in the clearest and simplest possible form, the precise idea he wished to convey. He had no pride of intellect—not the slightest desire for display—no thought or purpose but that of making everybody understand precisely what he believed and meant to utter." Raymond in that furious and dark summer of fresh maledictions on Lincoln had published in a book his admiration and affection for the President, how Lincoln's practical style in public papers carried "a weight and influence with the mass of the people which no public man of this country had ever before attained." Raymond had put in a book his rich sentiment about some phases of Lincoln. "The atmosphere of humor which seemed to pervade his mind . . . was just as natural to it, and as attractive and softening a portion of it, as the smoky hues of Indian summer are of the charming season to which they belong. . . . He seemed to be incapable of cherishing an envenomed resentment. . . . Easily touched by whatever was painful, the elasticity of his temper and his ready sense of the humorous broke the force of anxieties . . . under which a man of harder, though perhaps a higher, nature would have sunk and failed."

This was the Raymond who now returned to New York and threw amazement into the Republican anti-Lincoln ranks with his positive statements in the *Times* that peace-negotiation stories had no bottom; no commissioners would go from Washington to Richmond seeking an armistice; "the President stands firm against every solicitation to postpone the draft"; and as to rumors of this and that about the Government, "You may rest assured . . . its sole and undivided purpose is to prosecute the war until the rebellion is quelled."

The *New York Herald* Washington correspondent had telegraphed his paper earlier in the month that an armistice might be near at hand, that Fessenden leaned to the idea, that Senator Wilson was taking care of it, that the President seemed to be studying it with favor. Toward the end of the month, however, armistice reports were regarded as "silly," wrote the same correspondent. And perhaps it was the mercurial Bennett himself who in the *Herald*, on the day after Raymond's return from the interview with the President, mocked and gabbed and jibed: "Many of our leading Republicans are now furious against Lincoln. . . . Bryant of the *Evening Post* is very angry with Lincoln because Henderson, the *Post's* publisher, has been arrested for defrauding the government. . . . Raymond is a little shaky and has to make frequent journeys to Washington for instructions." And what did it amount to? "The Republican leaders may have their personal quarrels, or their shoddy quarrels, or their nigger quarrels with Old Abe; but he has the whiphand of them, and they will soon be bobbing back into the Republican fold, like sheep who have gone astray. The most of the fuss some of them kick up now, is simply to force Lincoln to give them their terms."

The Democrats, warned Bennett, had better put no trust in "the Republican soreheads," who would soon be again shouting for Lincoln. "Whatever they say now, we venture to predict that Wade and his tail; and Bryant and his tail; and Wendell Phillips and his tail; and Weed, Barney, Chase and their tails; and Winter Davis, Raymond, Opdyke and Forney who have no tails; will all make tracks for Old Abe's plantation, and soon will be found crowing and blowing, and vowing and writing, and swearing and stumping the state on his side, declaring that he and he alone, is the hope of the nation, the bugaboo of Jeff Davis, the first of Conservatives, the best of Abolitionists, the purest of patriots, the most gullible of mankind, the easiest President to manage, and the person especially predestined and foreordained by Providence to carry on the war, free the niggers, and give all the faithful a fair share of the spoils. The spectacle will be ridiculous; but it is inevitable."

In this same week of August Lincoln had Nicolay send a telegram to Congressman Reuben Eaton Fenton of New York, who arrived on invitation at the Executive Mansion the next day. In a confidential interview Fenton heard the President say, in language as nearly as he could remember: "You are to be nominated by our folks for Governor of your State. Seymour of course will be the Democratic nominee. You will have a hard fight. I am very desirous that you should win the battle. New York should be on our side by honest possession. There is some trouble among our folks over there, which we must try and manage. Or, rather, there is one man who may give us trouble, because of his indifference, if in no other way. He has great influence, and his feelings may be reflected in many of his friends. We must have his counsel and coöperation if possible. This, in one sense, is more important to you than to me, I think, for I should rather expect to get on without New York, but you can't. But in a larger sense than what is merely personal to myself, I am anxious for New York, and we must put our heads together and see if the matter can't be fixed."

As a Republican Congressman of eight years' service and a member in favor with the Seward-Weed-Raymond faction, Fenton understood without names being mentioned that Lincoln meant the old party wheel horse, the Warwick, Thurlow Weed, was "dissatisfied with the disposition of federal patronage in New York City," feeling especially "that Mr. Simeon Draper, Collector of the Port, and Mr. Rufus F. Andrews, Surveyor, were unfriendly to him [Weed], and that he had no voice in those places." Fenton and Nicolay left for New York on the evening train and the next forenoon in Room No. 11, Astor House, Fenton talked with Weed. And the upshot was, according to Fenton, "that Mr. Nicolay returned to Washington with the resignation of Mr. Rufus F. Andrews, and that Mr. Abram Wakeman, zealous friend of Mr. Weed, at once became his successor as Surveyor. From that time forward Mr. Weed was earnest and helpful in the canvass."

Midway of this same gloomy August resistance to the draft had gone so far that State governors were calling on the War Department for troops to enforce the President's proclamation. When Halleck informed Grant that 50,000 troops would be wanted for work at home, Grant replied that the loyal governors ought to organize militia to handle draft uprisings. To draw troops from the field "to keep loyal States in harness" would delay the suppression of rebellion in disloyal States. "My withdrawal now from the James River," wrote Grant, "would insure the defeat of Sherman."

On this matter and other items Lincoln sent John Eaton to interview Grant. The item uppermost with Lincoln however was, in his own words, as Eaton noted them, "The disaffected are trying to get him to run [for the Presidency], but I don't think they can do it. If he is the great General we think he is, he must have some consciousness of it, and know that he cannot be satisfied with himself and secure the credit due for his great generalship if he does not finish his job. I do not believe they can get him to run."

Eaton, with a pass signed by the President which authorized him to "visit Gen. Grant at City Point, Va.," arrived at Grant's headquarters, sat next the General through an enjoyable supper, and in the General's tent watched him open his mail as they talked, Grant pausing at times to take pen and ink and write replies. Grant referred to the battle of the Crater and how he had given special orders for no delay of troops in crossing the big powder-blown chasm. Of a scheme to replace Stanton with Butler as War Secretary, Grant said it had troubled him and Eaton said it had troubled Lincoln too. Stanton had not always co-operated fearlessly, Grant believed, but he was far from wishing Stanton removed. If a change of War Department heads must be made, Grant would recommend his chief of staff, John Rawlins. Of fresh and summary demands by State governors for troops to handle draft uprisings, Grant said he would send the troops, but it involved a change of campaign and moving the army away from the Richmond front.

Grant held strictly to army matters in the talk of the two men that ran past midnight. Eaton was interested, but was trying to find some entering wedge on political affairs. Finally he mentioned to Grant a conversation on a railroad train with army men who knew of Eaton's official contacts, as a Freedmen's Bureau commissioner, with Grant. The army men had asked Eaton if he thought Grant could be induced to run as a citizen's candidate for President. "The question is," said Eaton to Grant, "not whether you wish to run, but whether you could be compelled to run in answer to the demand of the people for a candidate who should save the Union."

The talk till then had been very quiet, but Grant's instant reply amazed Eaton. The General brought his clenched fists down hard on the strap arms of his camp chair, "They can't do it! They can't compel me to do it."

"Have you said this to the President?"

"No, I have not thought it worth while to assure the President of my opinion. I consider it as important to the cause that he should be elected as that the army should be successful in the field."

Eaton, back at Washington, entering Lincoln's office heard the eager question, "Well, what did you find?"

"You were right."

And the President "fairly glowed with satisfaction," noted Eaton, as he heard Lincoln say, "I told you that they could not get him to run until he had closed out the rebellion."

Lincoln then asked what Grant had said about a dispatch Lincoln had sent to him the day before. Eaton said he had left Grant before the dispatch arrived. So Lincoln repeated to Eaton the text of it. Grant could be satisfied completely that the President was backing him on no withdrawal of 50,000 troops to handle draft uprisings. "I have seen your despatch expressing your unwillingness to break your hold where you are," Lincoln repeated to

Eaton. "Neither am I willing. Hold on with a bulldog grip, and chew and choke as much as possible."

Grant resumed his noncommittal attitude toward Lincoln as a candidate for the Presidency. To the country Grant gave no sign that he was for or against Lincoln. To Lincoln himself Grant gave no confidential hint that he hoped Lincoln would still be Commander in Chief after the November elections. In Lincoln's circle ran gossip that the President felt hurt by Grant's aloofness. To the young men such as Nicolay, Hay, Brooks, and Schurz, into whose bosoms Lincoln had on occasion poured confidences he would not for the world have made public, Lincoln gave no word that Grant's course in politics was troubling him. He may have guessed that Grant had a fear of the Washington hotbed of intrigues and the political guile that had been a curse on the Army of the Potomac. The Democratic candidate for the Presidency, it seemed certain, would be McClellan, for whom there was still much affection and some trust in the Army of the Potomac. And A. K. McClure said he had it from Grant that for Grant to speak out in favor of Lincoln would have been "obviously unbecoming" because it would be "a public expression against a general whom I had succeeded." Also McClure may have read more portent than intended in the remark he quoted as from Lincoln, "I have no reason to believe that Grant prefers my election to that of McClellan." Lincoln may have instigated the mission of Congressman Washburne of Illinois in going to Grant and asking him to publish a letter in favor of Lincoln's election. If Washburne then carried back to Lincoln what Grant had to say, Lincoln might have taken a healthy laugh for himself. Grant told Washburne that "for the President to answer all the charges the opposition would bring against him would be like setting a maiden to work to prove her chastity."

Grant's letter for publication dated at City Point, August 16, 1864, took no sides with any Republican or Democratic party faction, was neither pro-Lincoln nor anti. And in its closing paragraph it endorsed by inference the President's emancipation policy, not by a plea that Negroes were human and in justice deserved freedom, but with a prediction that a peace through separation of North and South would send "thousands of Northern men joining the South, because of our disgrace in allowing separation." Keeping free from political alliance or favor, Grant set forth what would await an Administration that listened to Peace with Separation. "To have Peace on any terms, the Southerners would demand the restoration of the slaves already free; they would demand indemnity for losses sustained; they would demand a treaty which would make the North slave hunters for the South; they would demand pay for every slave escaping to the North."

This was Grant's counsel to those, like General Meade in his own army, who demurred at the President having suggested that "abandonment of slavery" would be considered among peace terms. The old Steve Douglas Democrat, Grant, was saying by implication that the slavery issue had progressed to where the complications were inexorable: there was nothing else to do but free the slaves and make a peace that kept the slaves free. Regarding the war and the draft he wished to give the impression that the Confederacy was becoming a hollow shell sucked of its vitality. Grant wrote:

"I state to all citizens who visit me that all we want now to insure an early restoration of the Union is determined unity of sentiment in the North. The Rebels have now in their ranks their last man. The little boys and old men are guarding prisoners and railroad bridges, and forming a good part of their forces, manning forts and positions, and any man lost by them cannot be replaced. They have robbed the cradle and the grave equally to get their present force. Besides what they lose in frequent skirmishes and battles, they are now losing from desertions and other causes at least one regiment per day. With this drain upon them, the end cannot be far distant if we are only true to ourselves. Their only hope now is a divided North, and this might give them reinforcements from Kentucky, Tennessee, Maryland and Missouri, while it would weaken us.

"With the draft quietly enforced, the enemy would be very despondent and make but little resistance. I have no doubt but that they are exceedingly anxious to hold out until after the Presidential election; for they have many hopes upon its result. They hope for a counter revolution; they hope for the election of a Peace candidate; in fact, like Micawber, they hope 'something will turn up.'

"Our Peace friends, if they expect Peace from separation, are much mistaken. It would be but the beginning of war, with thousands of Northern men joining the South, because of our disgrace in allowing separation. To have Peace on any terms, the Southerners would demand the restoration of the slaves already free; they would demand indemnity for losses sustained; they would demand a treaty which would make the North slave hunters for the South; they would demand pay for every slave escaping to the North."

This letter Stanton withheld for later publication, probably after conference with Lincoln, as though written appeals could be of little use in that dark August, and the letter could better be given the public after the army and the navy had produced results to enforce the claims in the letter. In belittling the enemy Grant was "a little hyperbolical in . . . expression," Meade wrote to his wife. "Ten a day would be a liberal estimate of the deserters who have come into our lines for some time past," and in Meade's reckoning there would probably not be as many as 300 rebel deserters a day in all the armies in the field. "He [Grant] is of a very sanguine temperament, and sees everything favorable in a strong light, and makes light of all obstacles. In some respects this is an admirable quality, if it is not carried to extremes." Had Meade consulted Grant on the matter Grant would probably have told him that you couldn't estimate the number of Confederate deserters by the number who came into the Union lines, and that for each deserter coming into Union lines there might be five or ten who were going home for a furtive visit with the womenfolks or else heading for some one of the many bands of bushwhackers and guerrillas that were on the increase.

Grant's letter by itself could at that hour have had small effect among the radicals so widely split and of whom Editor Sam Bowles of the *Springfield Republican* had to write in a letter: "Do you notice that the Anti-Slavery Standard and the Liberator, representatives of the old Abolitionists, are both earnest for Lincoln? Yet a new crop of radicals have sprung up, who are resisting the President and making mischief. Chase is going around, peddling his griefs in private ears, and sowing dissatisfaction about Lincoln. Oh, how little great men can be—the larger the smaller." And how would Bowles have written in a private letter of still other matters too pettily grievous to publish for his newspaper readers? For Chase amid his other doings had opened a correspondence with August Belmont, chairman of the Democratic National Committee, letting Belmont know that if the Democratic party at its Chicago convention would insert a platform plank declaring for the abolition of slavery, he, Chase, would then be willing to run as the Democratic candidate for the Presidency.

And there was fact, detail, information, with no wisdom worth mentioning, in the narrative of Old Man Blair about his "effort at conciliation," as he termed it. "I went on this errand without consulting the President, without giving him directly or indirectly, the slightest intimation of my object, and, of course, without his authority." Nevertheless some New Yorkers had their suspicions that Old Man Blair was not on his own initiative but was doing errands for Lincoln. Blair counted Bryant of the *New York Evening Post* discontented but reliable in behalf of Lincoln, Greeley assuring Blair that "his best efforts would not be wanting to secure the peace of the country and the reëlection of the President," while Bennett of the *Herald* would merely advise, "Tell him [the President] to restore McClellan to the army and he will carry the election by default."

Then Blair had paid a call on McClellan. The Blairs had been adhesive enough to McClellan for such a visit to be justified. Who but Old Man Blair had pleaded with Lincoln not to issue the order removing McClellan from command, on the day Lincoln stretched his long arms and said, "He's got the slows"? So now Blair, one of the ruins still standing, one of the living relics surviving from the Kitchen Cabinet of Andrew Jackson, now Blair opened with stating distinctly to McClellan that he had not come from Mr. Lincoln, that he had no authority or even consent from Mr. Lincoln to make representations or overtures of any sort. McClellan said nothing outwardly, possibly lifting one eyebrow and inwardly, "Yes? Interesting if true." Blair then urged McClellan, with the privilege of age and long friendship, to have nothing to do with the Chicago convention, to refuse to be named for defeat, and on the other hand to make himself an inspiring center and spokesman of the loyal Democrats of the North. By what method? By writing a letter to Lincoln asking to be restored to service in the army, declaring at the same time that he did not seek a restoration to command with any furtive eye on a presidential nomination. "In case the President should refuse this request he would then be responsible for the consequences."

McClellan heard politely, thanked Mr. Blair, said he would give deep consideration to the suggestion, mentioned that he must go to the country to see a sick child, had regrets that he might not talk with Mr. Blair again. Mr. Blair took a train for Washington, repeated to Mr. Lincoln the conversation between himself and General McClellan, and gave his belief that McClellan would probably write a letter to the President asking to be restored to service. And what did Mr. Lincoln reply? Mr. Blair wrote that the President "neither expressed approval nor disapprobation, but his manner was as courteous and kind as General McClellan's had been." That is, Lincoln said nothing outwardly, possibly inwardly, "Yes? Interesting, probably true, and of but slight importance, though the Blair family is curious in undertaking errands where my initiative is suspected no matter how it may be denied." A ruthless autocracy, coldly indifferent to McClellan, held sway at Washington, so believed McClellan if he accepted without question the information sent him in a letter from Allan Pinkerton dated Philadelphia, April 6, 1864: "I arrived here this A.M. from Washington. There is not much to be learned there. The Reign of Terror there is perfect. No one dares to speak—or if they do it is in whispers. From what little I could glean there is no intention of giving you a command which you could accept."

Increasingly, as Welles noted in his diary, Lincoln was "greatly importuned and pressed by cunning intrigues." The summer of '64 had seen plenty of this, more than any previous summer of the war. Beyond the politicians were the people. Lincoln hoped they would see him as "the people's attorney," remarking to one friend, "If the people think I have managed their case for them well enough to trust me to carry it up to the next term, I am sure I shall be glad to take it."

But would the people so think and do? In latter August of '64 all the forecasters, including Lincoln himself, believed he was probably headed for defeat at the end of the nine or ten weeks remaining before election. Yet perhaps the Democrats in their Chicago convention at the end of August would somehow blunder. And perhaps the armies would bring victories to light bonfires of enthusiasm athwart the Northern gloom. Lincoln knew that no words, explanations, persuasions, letters, speeches, could save his cause. Only bayonets triumphant and red-dripping with Confederate defeat could bring anything like magic or potency to anything he might have to say. While decisive events waited he would manage a course as best he could, saying: "The pilots on our western rivers steer from point to point, as they call it—setting the course of the boat no farther than they can see. And that is all I propose to do in the great problems that are set before us."

A summer for sure it had been of steering from point to point, from Sherman's drive toward Atlanta and Grant's lunges at Richmond to the arrival of Early at the gates of Washington and the sinking of the *Alabama* and the capture of Mobile; from the smooth unanimous nomination of Lincoln at Baltimore to the clawing scorn of the Wade-Davis Manifesto; from the peace missions of Greeley at Niagara and Jaquess-Gilmore at Richmond to the secret Republican-party manipulations hoping to replace

Lincoln at the head of the ticket; from draft legislation authorizing conscripts to buy substitutes to the attempt to detach 50,000 men from Grant's army to enforce the draft in Northern cities, oath-bound secret societies threatening to take over the Government at Washington and one committee of Republican-party leaders begging the President not to make his call for a draft of a half-million men until after the November election. He had given reply: "What is the Presidency worth to me if I have no country?" If, in his view, the opposition could have their way against him, there would be not one country but many.

"If this country gets ultimately through," then wrote Franz Lieber, scholar and liberal, "safe and hale, no matter with how many scars, a great civil war with a presidential election in the very midst of it (while the enemy has to stand no such calamity), I shall set it down as the most wonderful miracle in the whole history of events."

Midsummer, Lincoln had told a *Boston Journal* man: "I have faith in the people. They will not consent to disunion. The danger is, in their being misled. Let them know the truth and the country is safe." He looked haggard and careworn to the correspondent, who said, "You are wearing yourself out with work."

"I can't work less. But it isn't that. Work never troubled me. Things look badly, and I can't avoid anxiety. Personally, I care nothing about a reëlection, but if our divisions defeat us, I fear for the country."

The correspondent suggested that right must eventually triumph, that for himself he had never despaired of the result. Lincoln: "Neither have I, but I may never live to see it. I feel a presentiment that I shall not outlast the rebellion. When it is over, my work will be done."

The welcome Lincoln gave to William Bross of Chicago one August day was "cordial but rather melancholy," according to Bross. A brother of Bross had fallen at the head of his regiment in fighting before Petersburg and Bross was on his way to recover the body. Bross, deep-chested, heavily full-bearded with bristling hairs, flashing-eyed, one of the owners and editors of the *Chicago Tribune*, was the Union-party candidate for lieutenant governor of Illinois. Lincoln asked Bross anxiously for news from the West. Gloom hung over the West and the entire country, Bross believed. Lincoln agreed that neither of them could shut their eyes to the condition. The Wilderness losses, the Crater blunder, were a weight on the mind. To a question from Lincoln, Bross answered that the people expected a more vigorous prosecution of the war; more troops and appliances would be forthcoming from the people, if called for. And Bross felt assured that Lincoln spoke his "inmost sentiments" in a brief and graphic commentary which Lincoln plainly wished Bross to carry back to the Union men of Illinois: "I will tell you what the people want. They want and must have, *success.* But whether that come or not, I shall stay *right here* and do my duty. Here I shall be. And they may come and hang me on that tree [pointing out of the window], but, God helping me, I shall never desert my post."

In the progress of the war Lincoln had constantly drawn closer to the churches in personal contacts and in a spirit of piety and an acquaintance with the speech of piety. From officers and memberships of church bodies had come a loyal and tenacious support of the Union cause of such proportions that Lincoln as their political Chief Magistrate identified himself with their good works and sacrifices for the Union, employed their phrases in a way to convince many that a somber trust of some form of religion underlay and interfused his personality. He replied to one delegation in May of '64: "It may fairly be said that the Methodist Episcopal Church, not less devoted than the best, is by its greater numbers the most important of all. It is no fault in others that the Methodist Church sends more soldiers to the field, more nurses to the hospital, and more prayers to heaven than any. God bless the Methodist Church. Bless all the churches, and blessed be God, who, in this our great trial, giveth us the churches." And replying to a Baptist delegation later in the same day: "I have had great cause of gratitude for the support so unanimously given by all Christian denominations of the country. I have had occasion so frequently to respond to something like this assemblage, that I have said all I had to say. This particular body is, in all respects, as respectable as any that have been presented to me."

Late in the summer of '64 came a committee of colored people from Baltimore, their spokesman in an elaborate address presenting Lincoln with a richly wrought Bible. The occasion seemed fitting for "a lengthy response," he assured them. "I would make one if prepared; but I am not. I would promise to respond in writing had not experience taught me that business will not always allow me to do so." He could only now say as so often before, "It has always been a sentiment with me that all mankind should be free." And the Bible? "In regard to this great book, I have but to say, it is the best gift God has given to man. All the good Saviour gave to the world was communicated through this book. But for it we could not know right from wrong. All things most desirable for man's welfare, here and hereafter, are to be found portrayed in it. To you I return my most sincere thanks for the very elegant copy of the great Book of God which you present."

While the merciless governmental dragnet of the draft of '64 was preparing, in a letter to the Quaker Eliza P. Gurney, Lincoln dwelt on the searchings of conscience that might divide a man in time of war. "Your people, the Friends, have had, and are having, a very great trial. On principle and faith opposed to both war and oppression, they can only practically oppose oppression by war. In this hard dilemma some have chosen one horn, and some the other. For those appealing to me on conscientious grounds, I have done, and shall do, the best I could and can, in my own conscience, under my oath to the law. That you believe this I doubt not; and, believing it, I shall still receive for our country and myself your earnest prayers to our Father in heaven." The letter was intimately somber and openly affectionate, saluting Mrs. Gurney as "My esteemed Friend," and saying: "I have not forgotten—probably never shall forget—the very impressive occasion when yourself and friends visited me on a Sabbath forenoon two years ago. Nor has your kind letter, written nearly a year later, ever been forgotten."

Then came Lincoln's freshly worded meditation arriving at the same results as in a similar one many months before, a memorandum that John Hay found on his desk and copied. The President wrote for Mrs. Gurney his contemplations of God as a Power beyond man yet intimately associated with the works of man. "In all it has been your purpose to strengthen my reliance on God. I am much indebted to the good Christian people of the country for their constant prayers and consolations; and to no one of them more than to yourself. The purposes of the Almighty are perfect, and must prevail, though we erring mortals may fail to accurately perceive them in advance. We hoped for a happy termination of this terrible war long before this; but God knows best, and has ruled otherwise. We shall yet acknowledge his wisdom, and our own error therein. Meanwhile we must work earnestly in the best lights he gives us, trusting that so working still conduces to the great end he ordains. Surely he intends some great good to follow this mighty convulsion, which no mortal could make, and no mortal could stay."

CHAPTER 55

THE FIERCE FALL CAMPAIGN OF '64

BEFORE boarding a train in Washington for the journey to Chicago to report the Democratic National Convention, Noah Brooks heard Lincoln express a wish that Brooks write him two letters on the tone and temper of the convention and the delegates. "Write just what you would talk, but wouldn't print." And in the ears of the young newspaperman lingered the forecast: "They must nominate a Peace Democrat on a war platform, or a War Democrat on a peace platform; and I personally can't say that I care much which they do."

In the same Wigwam in Chicago where Lincoln had been nominated for the Presidency in June of '60, the Democratic National Convention met August 29, a boiling kettle of partisans that included Peace Democrats, War Democrats, Whigs, Know-Nothings, Conservatives, States' Rights extremists who endorsed the doctrine of secession, millionaires in broadcloth, run-down politicians in paper collars, men who had braved the wrath of violent communities and suffered for the rights of free speech and a free press, and a remnant of Confederate loyalists who necessarily could not be open in their efforts. The delegates were called to order by August Belmont, a German-born Jew, head of the American branch of the Rothschild international banking house, president of the American Jockey Club, chairman of the Democratic National Committee, saying: "We are here not as war democrats nor as peace democrats, but as citizens of the great Republic, which we will strive to bring back to its former greatness and prosperity, without one single star taken from the brilliant constellation that once encircled its beautiful brow. [Cheers.] . . . Under the blessings of the Almighty, the sacred cause of the Union, the constitution and the laws, must prevail against fanaticism and treason." Belmont dwelt on "four years of misrule, by a sectional, fanatical and corrupt party" having brought the country to "the very verge of ruin." He introduced as temporary chairman former Governor William Bigler of Pennsylvania, who said "the first indispensable step" toward rescuing the country "is the overthrow, by the ballot, of the present administration." In a discussion of credentials which followed, Governor Wickliffe of Kentucky read letters from Delegates John W. Leathers and J. R. Buchanan explaining their absence by saying they were in jail and the victims of a military despotism which refused them opportunity to establish their innocence.

On taking the gavel as permanent chairman, Governor Horatio Seymour of New York said the present Administration could not now save the

Union if it would, but "If the administration cannot save this Union, we can. [Loud applause.] Mr. Lincoln values many things above the Union; we put it first of all. He thinks a proclamation worth more than peace; we think the blood of our people more precious than the edicts of the President. [Cheers.]" The platform then adopted declared for the Union, the Constitution, civil liberty, and "care, protection, and regard" for the soldiers of the country.

Against a heavy and persistent opposition Vallandigham in the Resolutions Committee carried through a straight-out peace plank. The war was a failure and should come to an end by no more fighting, said this plank, a distillation of the views Vallandigham had always stressed. It read: "This convention does explicitly declare, as the sense of the American people, that after four years of failure to restore the Union by the experiment of war, during which, under the pretense of a military necessity, or war power higher than the Constitution, the Constitution itself has been disregarded in every part, and public liberty and private right alike trodden down and the material prosperity of the country essentially impaired,—justice, humanity, liberty and the public welfare demand that immediate efforts be made for a cessation of hostilities, with a view to an ultimate convention of the States, or other peaceable means, to the end that at the earliest practicable moment peace may be restored on the basis of the Federal Union of the States."

This plank would have been written somewhat differently by some of the Democrats. The agreement seemed to be that a War Democrat would be nominated for the Presidency in exchange for the Peace Democrats being permitted to record a pledge that the War Democrat nominee would be opposed to war. Such was the dilemma and its straddle, in a platform of few paragraphs saying scarcely more than that the war and the Administration were failures, and both should be ended. The definite measures of immediate action on taking power, directly pledged in the platform, were: (1) that the armies would be ordered to cease hostilities and go home; (2) that the Southern States would then be asked to join a convention to restore the Union; (3) that free speech and a free press would be allowed and no matter what opposition might be raised against the Government there would be no arbitrary arrests, while habeas corpus and trial by jury would return like the sweet perennial blooms of spring. Whether the army commanders on being told to stop fighting and go home would agreeably bow low and yield to orders was one question. Whether Jeff Davis and his associate Confederates would wait till the mythical areas of hell froze over before they would join in a convention to restore the Union was another question. Out of an agglomeration of practical politicians who wanted again to feel their hands running the governmental machine, and sincere haters of war who wanted nothing so much as an end to war, only a platform of negatives could have been expected, with a high note on hate.

Delegate Stambaugh of Ohio believed "they might search hell over and they could not find a worse candidate than Abraham Lincoln." Delegate Alexander, a circuit-court judge from Kentucky, made public, according to the *Chicago Times*, his favorite anecdote "of a Kentucky gentleman who thought that as Mr. Lincoln was so fond of the negro, he should have one of the slain ones skinned and made into a pair of moccasins for his daily wear." The Honorable W. W. O'Brien, a Peoria delegate, according to the *Chicago Times* was certain that the convention's candidate for President would on the next fourth of March "apply his boot to 'Old Abe's posterior' and kick him out of the Presidential chair." Editor C. Chauncey Burr of the Old Guard declared the party must cry loud for peace in order to overthrow the Lincoln despotism. The people had submitted to "the infamous orders of the gorilla tyrant that usurped the Presidential chair," according to Burr as reported in the *Chicago Times*, "because they were a law-and-order people." Besides stealing Southern slave property Mr. Lincoln was a horse thief and a looter who approved the larceny of household silver and women's jewelry in Southern homes, in the view of Mr. Burr, who would have it, "Mr. Lincoln has stolen a good many thousand negroes, but for every negro thus stolen, he has stolen ten thousand spoons."

Burr, with Vallandigham, was a peace man. Vallandigham had come to the convention with a following. On the streets he was cheered. As a delegate he was a presence. Echoes of his jail term and exile, echoes of the New York draft and race riots, open resistance to the Government, were heard. Free speech held sway in the convention and newspapers free as the *Chicago Times* reported it in full. Moreover, John J. Van Alen of New York early intimated that he and others would not accept the nomination of McClellan for President, nor any candidate "with the smell of war on his garments." Congressman Long of Ohio told the convention that McClellan in his arrest of the members of the legislature of Maryland in '62 had gone even further than Lincoln in the perpetration of tyrannical measures, and that almost any other man than McClellan would satisfy the Northwest as a candidate. These anti-McClellan peace men were given a free hand in writing a peace plank.

On the final showdown McClellan had 202½ votes as against little more than one-tenth of that number for one T. H. Seymour of Connecticut. Vallandigham amid cheers moved that the nomination of McClellan for President be made unanimous, which was done with further cheers. Senator George H. Pendleton of Ohio, on his record entirely satisfactory to the peace men, was named for Vice-President. And the convention, ominously, did not as usual adjourn sine die. On motion of Wickliffe of Kentucky it had been resolved to "remain as organized" subject to call of the national executive committee. Delegates from the West, said Wickliffe, believed things might happen, "circumstances may occur between this and the fourth of March next" making it proper for the convention to meet again.

With a platform crying out loud for peace while keeping silence on the pivotal issue of slavery that had fomented the war, with a candidate who was a professional man of war expected to end the war without more war, the delegates, the politicians of a party organization which previous to Lincoln's election had for thirty years controlled the United States Government went home fairly well satisfied. Was not victory in the air? In that week did not everyone know that the leading prophets and weathervanes of the Republican party were conceding defeat, were saying the outlook was gloom and shipwreck ahead? Would not Governor Seymour of New York, as chairman of the committee to notify George B. McClellan of his nomination for President, be sure to mention this gloom in his letter of notification to General McClellan? And would General McClellan forget to hint about it in his response?

Then fate stepped in. Like a moving hour hand on a clock of doom came news flung world-wide, news setting crowds of Northern loyalists to dancing with mirth and howling with glee, news centering about one little dispatch wired to Washington by Sherman September 3: "Atlanta is ours and fairly won." In the War Department telegraph office Lincoln read a flimsy saying: "So Atlanta is ours and fairly won. . . . Since May 5th we have been in one constant battle or skirmish, and need rest."

The dull ache of defeat and failure that had stirred in many hearts took a change. Even the stern-faced and imperturbable General George H. Thomas, on first hearing of it from Sherman, galloped his horse, "snapped his fingers, whistled, and almost danced." In all news sheets the first item, the one story overwhelming all others, was around that precious little communication: "Atlanta is ours and fairly won." A strategic crossroads, supply depot, and transportation center of a pivotal Cotton State in the Deep South was gone. Vicksburg, New Orleans, and the Mississippi River gone, Kentucky, Tennessee, and Nashville gone, Mobile gone. Lee and his army penned between Grant and Richmond for how long? As Union men of the North looked at the picture it had more hope. Because Atlanta was "ours and fairly won," the picture had changed. Bells rang again, guns boomed in salute. Grant wired Sherman he was ordering "every battery bearing on the enemy" to release shot and shell.

The President on this September 3 jubilated in four different expressions. One requested thanksgiving to be offered in all places of worship the next Sunday. Another ordered salutes of gunfire at the arsenals of thirteen various ports and navy yards in celebration of Farragut's naval and military victories. Another ordered thanks and rejoicing over Farragut's clinching the capture of Mobile Harbor by the reduction of the last forts guarding it. Another read: "The national thanks are tendered by the President to Major-General William T. Sherman, and the gallant officers and soldiers of his command before Atlanta, for the distinguished ability, courage, and perseverance displayed in the campaign in Georgia, which, under divine favor, has resulted in the capture of Atlanta. The marches, battles, sieges, and other military operations that have signalized the campaign must render it famous in the annals of war, and have entitled those who have participated therein to the applause and thanks of the nation."

A Congregational minister and army chaplain, the Reverend J. P. Thompson, entering Lincoln's office with Charles A. Dana on September 6, saw the

President alone at a table covered with documents he was studying, at his elbow a basket of fine peaches. Thompson spoke of the pleasure with which the proclamation for a Thanksgiving on the next Sunday would be regarded.

LINCOLN. I would be glad to give you such a proclamation every Sunday for a few weeks to come.

THOMPSON. The victory at Atlanta has wiped out one-half of the Chicago platform, and if General Grant will give us Petersburg, that will wipe

Harper's Weekly in mid-September presumes what the President might be saying

out the other, and we shall simply go through the form of reëlecting you, Mr. President, by acclamation.

Dana interposed that he believed the revival of Union feeling was due quite as much to the platform itself as to the victory.

"I guess," said Lincoln, "it is more due to the victory. At any rate that will better bear *repetition*."

McClellan's acceptance of his Chicago nomination had not yet been signified, and Thompson thought the General seemed "about as slow in getting up on the platform as he was in taking Richmond."

And Thompson noted "a marvelous brightening of eye" as Lincoln said, "I think he must be *intrenching*."

New York rumor had it, the chaplain suggested, that the General would decline the nomination on that platform.

LINCOLN. Well, he doesn't know yet whether he will accept or decline. Somebody must do it for him. For of all the men I have had to do with in my life, indecision is the most strongly marked in General McClellan—if that can be said to be strong which is the essence of weakness.

This, noted Thompson, was said with "head leaning forward, as if he would thrust his face into yours; but trenchant as was the sarcasm, there was no maliciousness in his tone, no trace of personal rivalry or animosity," being "the utterance of a deliberate judgment."

On Dana's giving the news that the cavalry marauder John Morgan was dead, Lincoln exclaimed to Dana, "Is that so?" and turning toward Thompson as though to recognize a profession having to do with last things: "I wouldn't crow over anybody's death, but I can assure you that I take this as resignedly as I could take any dispensation of Providence. This Morgan was a nigger-driver. You Northern men don't know anything about such low, mean, cowardly creatures. Southern slaveholders despise them. But such a wretch has been used to carry on their rebellion."

Thompson was startled at the tone of the President. It carried passion.

A messenger now brought word that a lady at the door wished to know his decision in a certain case. Then slow words from the President: "Tell her that I shall do nothing about it."

"Need I say just that to her? She is terribly distressed. Can't I say, sir, that you are still considering it?"

"Well, if you choose. But I shall not interfere." Then turning to a pile of papers on the table: "Here is the case of a man condemned by a court-martial for bounty-jumping, desertion, and inducing others to desert. It is a very clear case; and as the officers say that pardons relax all discipline, I suppose I must not interfere." He had been studying all night to find some flaw in the evidence on which he might annul the sentence, and between justice and compassion, as Thompson saw it, was "almost unmanned" by the report of a woman weeping at the door.

The conversation shifting to the political campaign, Thompson told of meeting an Irishman at Resaca, Georgia, who said: "It wasn't myself that made Mr. Lincoln President. But these rascals down here said he shouldn't be President, and I'm bound to fight till he is. And sure I think the jointilman that begun the job is the one to go through with it."

"I am glad," laughed Lincoln, "to know that any Irishman is going to vote for me, and especially for such discriminating reasons."

If re-elected he could carry on his policies and so desired to do, Lincoln made clear, and when Thompson mentioned "the unanimity of the religious sentiment" of the country for him, Lincoln remarked that he relied very much on the religious element for the support of his Administration. Thompson named several prominent ministers working for his re-election, among them Dr. Bacon of New Haven. Whereupon Lincoln told of reading a book on slavery by Dr. Bacon. "It had much to do in shaping my thinking on the subject of slavery. He is quite a man."

On Thompson's drifting into a distinction in Mosaic law between "domiciliary imprisonment" and chattel slavery, Lincoln said it would relieve the question of Hebrew servitude, though "I have sometimes thought that Moses didn't quite understand the Lord along there."

Thompson on leaving the White House felt that he had shaken a cordial hand, looked into "gentle, loving, and magnetic eyes," nor could he begin to tell of "the brilliancy of repartee, the readiness of wit, the affability of manners, the frankness of soul," that had surprised him.

A few days later the country read of Governor Seymour notifying McClellan that he was nominated for President, and McClellan having the honor to acknowledge the notification. Both were more even in tone than the proceedings at Chicago. McClellan's letter carried his dignity and his evasions. He threw no slightest gleam of light on what he would do about slavery except let it alone. "The Union is the one condition of peace—we ask no more." He glided from point to point as though "a spirit of conciliation and compromise" would correct and adjust the fiercely cardinal doctrine of faith in the South that each State was sovereign and had the right to secede at will. McClellan's awareness that many a brave soldier still was a loyal comrade stood forth in a paragraph which came as a slap in the face to the peace cohorts of Chicago. It had to be read slowly and carefully to make sure what he was saying. Then it dawned that he was saying the Chicago convention which had nominated him meant the opposite of what it had to say about peace. The real sentiment of the convention was "unexpressed," according to McClellan, and therefore he would assume it was for him to express it.

As gently as McClellan could put it to those favoring immediate peace on any terms—and they were an influential fraction of his party—he seemed to be saying with a finality, hesitant yet final, that if the States out of the Union refused to come back on his invitation if he were President, then he would fight them. He hoped for peace "without the effusion of another drop of blood" but possibly there might have to be more fighting if the Union were to be saved. The General wrote: "Let me add, what I doubt not was, although unexpressed, the sentiment of the Convention, as it is of the people they represent, that when any one State is willing to return to the Union, it should be received at once, with a full guarantee of all its constitutional rights. If a frank, earnest and persistent effort to obtain those objects should fail, the responsibility for ulterior consequences will fall upon those who remain in arms against the Union. But the Union must be preserved at all hazards. I could not look in the face my gallant comrades of the army and navy who have survived so many bloody battles, and tell them that their labors and the sacrifices of so many of our slain and wounded brethren had been in vain, that we had abandoned that Union for which we have so often periled our lives. A vast majority of our people, whether in the army and navy or at home, would, as I would, hail with unbounded joy the permanent restoration of peace, on the basis of the Union under the Constitution, without the effusion of another drop of blood. But no peace can be permanent without Union."

Having thus deftly and gently thrown out the main plank and the most-labored point of the Chicago platform, McClellan closed his letter to the notification committee with reliance on the Ruler of the universe and his acceptance of the nomination in a belief "that the views here expressed are those of the Convention and the people you represent."

Vallandigham for the Peace Democrats a few days later scoffed at McClellan's repudiation. "The Chicago platform enunciated its policy and principles by authority and was binding upon every Democrat, and by them the Democratic Administration must and should be governed." Mainly on this basic clash of convictions did Lincoln base his frequently registered view that if the opposition to him won in November it would be on such terms that if the Union were to be saved it would have to be in the interval between the November election and March 4 of '65.

Now in this month of September Phil Sheridan was heard from. Lincoln on the twelfth was but echoing the readiness of Grant and Sheridan to take a chance when he telegraphed Grant: "Sheridan and Early are facing each other at a dead-lock. Could we not pick up a regiment here and there, to the number of say ten thousand men, and quietly but suddenly concentrate them at Sheridan's camp and enable him to make a strike? This is but a suggestion." Grant didn't need this suggestion from Lincoln, but it did him good to know the President would take a chance. Three days later Grant rode to Sheridan's headquarters. He ended their conference with the order "Go in!"

Since August 7, when he took command of the Army of the Shenandoah, Sheridan had not won the results predicted for Grant's thirty-three-year-old tryout against the veteran Early, whose men had in July marched into sight of the Washington Capitol dome. The press already complained that Sheridan was not heard from. Halleck had been telegraphing Grant that if Sheridan was not strong enough to break Early's hold on railroads hauling coal to Washington, Sheridan should be reinforced, for fuel supplies in Washington and Baltimore were running low.

Yet Sheridan had not been idle in moving his army from Frederick, Maryland, by way of Slabtown and Buckystown on down to Cedar Creek and into camp at Charlestown, where five years before Old John Brown was hanged after prophesying that many more lives than his would be spent before slavery vanished. "I think I can manage this affair," Sheridan said in one telegram to Halleck. "I have thought it best to be very prudent every-

Above and below, campaign cartoons of the National Union party on the dilemmas and predicaments of the Democratic candidates

thing considered." And to Grant: "Mosby has annoyed me and captured a few wagons. We hung one and shot six of his men yesterday. I have burned all wheat and hay, and brought off all stock, sheep, cattle, horses, &c., south of Winchester."

For the first time in the war the Shenandoah Valley saw a destroyer with a system. Whatever would nourish man or provide fodder for beast was to be taken or burned or spoiled. When Grant's order should be met, then a crow would have to carry its own rations flying over the valley. At Harrisonburg from Gibbs Hill residents counted twenty barns in the same hour lighting the dark night of the valley as the flames roared upward and later sunk sputtering.

Four days' fighting at Winchester and Fisher's Hill followed Grant's order "Go in!" and Sheridan's telegram to Grant the night of September 19 hummed on the wires and had first place in all news sheets of the country: "I attacked the forces of General Early . . . and after a most stubborn and sanguinary engagement, which lasted from early in the morning until five o'clock in the evening, completely defeated him, and driving him through Winchester, captured about 2,500 prisoners, 5 pieces of artillery, 9 army flags, and most of their wounded." To his army the next day Sheridan gave a telegram signed "A. Lincoln" reading: "Have just heard of your great victory. God bless you all, officers and men. Strongly inclined to come up and see you." Two days later, on September 22, Sheridan telegraphed Grant: "I achieved a most signal victory over the army of General Early at Fisher's Hill today . . . only darkness has saved the whole of Early's army from total destruction. My attack could not be made until four o'clock in the evening, which left but little daylight to operate in. . . . The victory was very complete."

There was a note here that the North had not heard before from the Shenandoah Valley. The tone ran as though the war was on and would yet be over. "We have just sent them whirling through Winchester and we are after them tomorrow," was a Sheridan sentence picked from one of his telegrams to Grant and passed along on street and farm in the North. The combined losses in the two battles had been: Union 749 killed, 4,440 wounded, 357 missing; Confederate 250 killed, 1,777 wounded, 2,813 captured. Valor enough there had been on both sides, with the result that a Confederate army of proved fiber had been routed. As a performance it gave no comfort to those chiming with the *Chicago Times* saying that Lincoln could not win the war with armies enrolled from "conscripts, foreign hirelings, and niggers." A *Harper's Weekly* writer had noticed a man at a news bulletin board reading one of Sheridan's dispatches to Grant and commenting, "A few more such victories and Abe Lincoln will be elected in November." They were what Lincoln had wanted. No campaign speeches could equal them. The least he could do was appoint Sheridan a brigadier general in the regular army and place him in permanent command of the Middle Division, which he did.

Down the Shenandoah Valley went the destroyer, 6,000 head of cattle

A savage campaign cartoon, caricaturing both Lincoln and Davis in a prize fight, with an international gallery and 500 horses being taken by one cavalry body, not less than 3,000 sheep killed and issued to his army. One telegram to Grant served notice that Sheridan had "destroyed over two thousand barns filled with wheat, hay and farming implements," over seventy mills "filled with wheat and flour." In Rockingham County, where Abraham and Bathsheba Lincoln, the grandfather and grandmother of President Lincoln, had farmed and heard rumors of better farming farther west, a committee appointed by the county court later estimated $25,000,000 worth of property had been destroyed by Sheridan's troops, itemizing 50,000 bushels of corn, 100,000 bushels of wheat, 450 barns, 1 furnace, 3 factories, 30 dwelling houses, 31 mills, besides livestock. Grant's order had aimed at desolating the Shenandoah Valley this year and the next. "Carry off stock of all descriptions, and negroes, so as to prevent further planting. If the war is to last another year we want the Shenandoah Valley to remain a barren waste." From the Blue Ridge to North Mountain, Sheridan wrote to Grant to show the order was being strictly followed, the country had been "made untenable for a rebel army." Now indeed the crows could eat—if they brought their own rations.

To the stride of the war came political responses. In a Washington dispatch to the *St. Louis Democrat* Whitelaw Reid voiced those who had sought to replace Lincoln with another candidate. "The general apathy and discontent and the apparent certainty of Mr. Lincoln's defeat" had all changed. Greeley announced that the *Tribune* would "henceforth fly the banner of Abraham Lincoln for President." Chase spoke likewise and prepared to go on the stump with speeches alongside Ben Wade and Henry Winter Davis. "Sherman and Farragut have knocked the bottom out of the Chicago nominations," said Seward in a Washington speech just before the Sheridan victories. Gloomy August became a September edged with a few splinters of dawn.

The 1856 Republican-party candidate was nevertheless in mid-September still heading a third-party ticket. Frémont was still in the running. And what could be done about Frémont? Senator Zach Chandler and many others asked. And Chandler, afraid of nothing alive, abashed at no rules or formalities, went and saw Frémont and then went and saw Lincoln, besides Wade, Winter Davis, and others. Of what precisely was said Chandler made no record. If there was a deal, a cold piece of political horse-trading, Chandler, the shrewdest real-estate buyer and dry-goods merchant in Detroit, did not put it on paper. But two things happened that dovetailed as nicely as anybody could ask. On September 22 was published a letter of Frémont dropping his third party and coming out for Lincoln. And on the next day Lincoln asked Blair to leave the Cabinet and Blair so did. Whether Lincoln made a deal for Frémont's return to the fold on condition of Blair's being ushered out of the Cabinet was anybody's guess. That Lincoln gathered strength and cohesion for the National Union party was the general comment.

"Precisely why Mr. Lincoln thought this action called for at this moment, rather than at any other time in the last four months, we are not told," wrote Greeley in the *New York Tribune*. Bennett in his *Herald* insisted that Blair was the victim of a bargain between Lincoln and Chase, Wade, and Davis, and that Fox, Welles, and Seward would next feel the ax of dismissal. Chandler, the gossips buzzed, told Stanton he had taken a good drunk for himself on the strength of the Blair dismissal, Stanton saying he would like to have joined had he "known when and where."

For the single result of drawing the Frémont third party behind him Lincoln might have agreed to drop Blair from the Cabinet. But there was a large array of other interests and individuals that were glad to see Blair go. They would also have liked to add Seward. But the President would not give them Seward's head on a platter. He let them have Blair's. A muddle of human relations stood forth. The Blairs had at first been the outstanding friends of Frémont, so intimate that Monty Blair in '61 had unbosomed himself to Frémont in letters that later, when they became bitter enemies, Frémont had given to the press. The letters had passages of confidence wherein Blair wrote: "The main difficulty is with Lincoln himself. He is of the Whig school, and that brings him . . . to the feeble policy of the Whigs. It costs me a great deal of labor to get anything done, because of the inclination of mind on the part of the President." The abolitionists Sumner, Wade, Winter Davis, and their group blamed Blair only next to Seward as a counselor hostile to them at the President's Cabinet table. In public speeches and private advices Blair had sometimes spoken as if he might be taken for an Administration mouthpiece, though he had not consulted the President on what he was saying. Between Blair and Stanton the enmity was open. Yet these things did not mean that Blair was disloyal to Lincoln. Blair had never connived and plotted in a web of personal ambition after the manner of Chase. It did not come hard nor easy, it came as a necessary piece of work for Lincoln to write his letter dated September 23, 1864, addressed to Blair:

"My dear Sir: You have generously said to me more than once that whenever your resignation could be a relief to me it was at my disposal. The time has come. You very well know that this proceeds from no dissatisfaction of mine with you personally or officially. Your uniform kindness has been unsurpassed by that of any friend; and while it is true that the war does not so greatly add to the difficulties of your department as to those of some others, it is yet much to say, as I most truly can, that in the three years and a half during which you have administered the general post-office, I remember no single complaint against you in connection therewith."

The Cabinet met on this September 23, discussed newspaper rumors of peace, adjourned early. Bates and Welles walked out of the Executive Mansion together and were in conversation when Blair joined them remarking, "I suppose you are both aware that my head is decapitated,—that I am no longer a member of the Cabinet." Welles said he must beg pardon, he was not sure he heard aright, and would Mr. Blair repeat what he had just said? On hearing it again Welles asked what it meant and how long he had had the subject submitted or suggested to him. Blair said never until today; that he came in this morning from Silver Spring and found this letter from the President for him. Taking it from his pocket, he read it to Welles. Welles thought, and so wrote in his diary, it was "couched in friendly terms." The remark of Blair that he was willing to leave the Cabinet when the President thought best Welles remembered having heard both Blair and Bates make, though for himself Welles considered it unnecessary to make any such remark, because the President's wishes and purposes, whether right or wrong, should and must rule.

Welles asked Blair what had led up to it. There must be a reason. Blair said he had no doubt he was "a peace-offering to Frémont and his friends." They wanted an offering and he was "the victim whose sacrifice would propitiate them." The President the day before had quoted to Blair from Frémont's letter of withdrawal as a candidate for the Presidency, said Blair to Welles, how Frémont in this letter stated "the Administration was a failure, politically, militarily, and financially," and how Frémont regarded the entire Cabinet as misfits except perhaps the Navy head and the Attorney General.

As Blair and Welles walked toward the western gate of the White House grounds Welles said Frémont could not have been "the moving cause" with the President. "Oh," said Blair, "there is no doubt Seward was accessory to this, instigated and stimulated by Weed." Welles thought about that and then said to himself, "I am not certain that Chase has not been more influential than Seward in this matter."

They parted and Blair went to his office, wrote his resignation as Postmaster General and then began a letter with the word "Dearest." Writing to his wife, then visiting her mother in Portsmouth, New Hampshire, Blair told her that when the Baltimore convention had passed a resolution requesting the President to reorganize his Cabinet, "I told him not to stand on any ceremony with me but to be frank and tell me whenever he thought it advisable for him that I should quit. This morning he wrote me saying that time had come, and accordingly my resignation has now been written and will be delivered when I go to the other end of the Avenue. He made no explanation and I asked none. I suppose, however, that he thinks it will help to appease the Frémonters and Radicals, if I am dropped, and I think myself it will give them a temporary triumph. . . . The President has, I think, given himself, and me too, an unnecessary mortification in this matter; but then I am not the best judge and I am sure he acts from the best motives."

Welles in his office had just finished writing in his diary what Blair had told him two or three hours before. Then Blair dropped in to say he had handed his resignation to the President. Though the President's letter that morning had surprised him, Blair thought it right and it would "eventuate well." Blair said the President did not intimate that Seward had advised the call for his resignation, though Blair still believed Seward had so done. "The President," wrote Welles in the diary, "tells him [Blair] that Washburne recommended it. Strange if the President is influenced by so untruthful, unreliable, and mean a man as Washburne. But Washburne thinks it will help the President among the Germans. The President thinks it is necessary to conciliate Weed (he might have said Chase also). . . . Such are Blair's conclusions and . . . my own. Yet I cannot but think there must be something ulterior, for it is unlike the President to dismiss an acknowledged and true friend. . . . My impression is that the President does not intend to part with Blair, and I shall be disappointed if he is not recalled, perhaps to some other position in the Cabinet, perhaps to act in an important capacity for

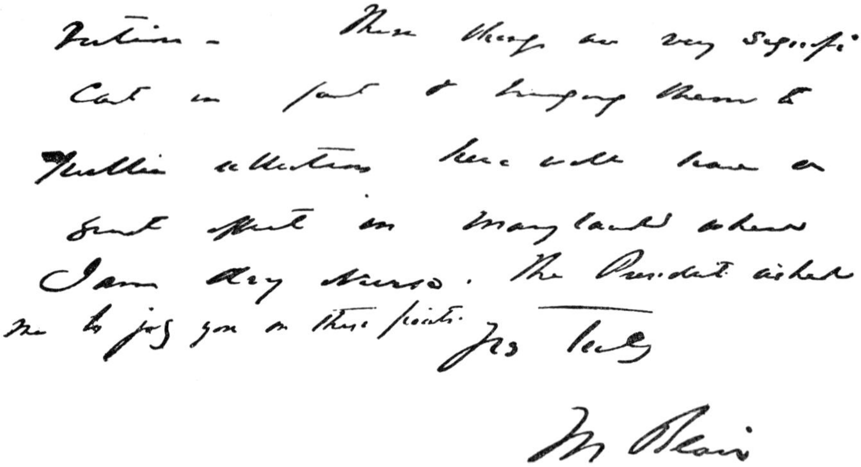
[illegible] — These things are very signifi-
cant in fact & bringing them to
public attention here will have a
great effect in Maryland where
I am dry nurse. The President asked
me to jog you on these points. Yrs truly

M Blair

Reproduction of part of a note of Montgomery Blair to William Douglas Wallach, editor of the *Washington Star*, asking the editor to "blow a little on the progress of the Emancipation cause" in the Border States, writing: "These things are very significant in fact & bringing them to public attention here will have a great effect in Maryland where I am dry nurse." Then, apparently as an afterthought, but worth putting in, Blair writes, "The President asked me to jog you on these points." Original from Crosby Noyes Boyd.

the restoration of the Union." And later Welles had it from the President that Mr. Chase had many friends who felt wounded that he should have left the Cabinet alone. "If Montgomery Blair left the Cabinet, Chase and his friends would be satisfied, and this he (the President) thought would reconcile all parties, and rid the Administration of irritating bickerings."

The secretaries Nicolay and Hay would not stress any one factor as bringing the President to oust his Postmaster General. Throughout the summer hate against Blair had piled up from many quarters. Appeals for Blair to go began increasing. "The President's mail was filled with such appeals." Senator Wilson of Massachusetts wrote September 5: "Blair everyone hates. Tens of thousands of men will be lost to you or will give a reluctant vote on account of the Blairs." And the President had waited until he felt "it was his duty no longer to retain in his Cabinet a member who, whatever his personal merits, had lost the confidence of the great body of

Republicans." Blair under the attacks piling in on him became more jealous and suspicious, "wearied the President by insisting upon it that all the leading Republicans were Lincoln's enemies," held Seward to be flirting with the Copperheads, insisted that Seward and Stanton were double-crossing the Administration.

Lincoln grew tired of these denunciations, lost the fine edge of his patience, once saying to Blair in the hearing of John Hay, "It is much better not to be led from the region of reason into that of hot blood by imputing to public men motives which they do not avow."

The dismissal of Blair when it finally came, it would seem, was related to many particulars. The willingness of Frémont to be again a Republican provided Blair was told to walk the plank, whether the offer was carried directly to Lincoln by Chandler or someone else, was convenient and timely for Lincoln's purpose. "The union of the Republican party has become a paramount necessity," ran Frémont's letter withdrawing his candidacy in favor of "the Republican candidate pledged to the reëstablishment of the Union without slavery . . . however hesitating his policy may be." In doing his part toward preventing the Democratic candidate from entering the White House Frémont believed he was "consistent" to his principles. "In respect to Mr. Lincoln I continue to hold exactly the sentiments contained in my letter of acceptance. I consider that his administration has been politically, militarily, and financially a failure, and that its necessary continuance is a cause of regret for the country."

When friends of influence with the Administration had asked Frémont if he would accept a high command again if the President offered him one, he said he had tried often enough and would again be put in a wrong light if he went into the army. Frémont could have said too that fate was playing hard with him in his 44,000-acre Mariposa estate in California, once valued at $10,000,000, that debts on it had reached a total of $1,250,000 with interest charges of $13,000 monthly, that negotiations with the Rothschilds and with Paris bankers had failed to bring favorable loans, that one fee of $200,000 had been charged him by David Dudley Field for attorney's services, that Field, George Opdyke, and Morris Ketchum had while Frémont was engaged in politics and war manipulated his vast estate "always to their own benefit," that by frauds not strictly illegal and by mismanagement and bad turns of luck he was slowly being eased out of possession of an almost fabulous fortune in land and gold. His brownstone mansion on West Nineteenth Street, between Fifth and Sixth avenues, New York, and his luxurious Pocaho summer home two miles north of Tarrytown, with a hundred acres of lawn and woodland, his own horses which he rode with friends and the Kentucky thoroughbreds of his daughter, his gardens and the big gray-stone house that commanded a beautiful view of Tappan Zee, these were all to go in pawn and then fail to meet the demands. Frémont could in September of '64 have set forth many explanatory details on why he was less eager than in '61 for a military command under appointment from President Lincoln.

"Frémont recedes—honest patriot that he is," wrote Gurowski in his diary September 13, and on September 21: "In a few days Postmaster Blair will be thrown overboard by Lincoln. A victory by the radicals. . . . Lincoln begins to be a man." And on September 24: "Blair out of the Cabinet. A victory over Blair and Seward almost equal to that won by Sheridan. Lincoln behaved splendidly *à la* Macchiavelli . . . in a masterly, cool, unconcerned, statesmanlike manner. No *porphyrogenus* could have behaved more sovereign like. The victory was won exclusively by Senator Chandler. He fought single-handed and won the country's gratitude."

On the heels of the Blair dismissal some newspapers made much of a remark dropped by Simon Cameron, that in the event of a re-election the President would call around him fresh and earnest men. Hay referred to this. Lincoln said: "They need not be especially savage about a change. There are now only 3 left of the original Cabinet with the Government."

A letter of Old Man Blair published in the press gave with good political effect his version of his summer negotiations with McClellan. Lincoln agreed with John Hay that its calm and discreet tone was in contrast with the indiscretions of the son Monty. Lincoln was reminded of a man he had heard of who sat in a barroom among strangers and overheard them telling of his father being tricked in a trade. And when the man said they were liars about his father and they asked what he meant: "Why the old man ain't so easy tricked. You can fool the boys but ye can't the old man."

An Ohio lawyer who was president of the Exchange Bank of Columbus and also president of the Columbus & Xenia Railroad Company, Governor of the State of Ohio the first two years of the war, permanent chairman of the Baltimore convention of the Union party, and a cordial friend of the Blair family, was in Lincoln's mind to fill the vacant Cabinet office. Except for Justice David Davis writing to Lincoln in June, suggesting this man for chairman of the Baltimore convention, and that in case of Cabinet modification "you could not get a wiser counselor," there had been no pressure, no names mentioned to Lincoln that had come to the ears of the secretaries Nicolay and Hay. A telegram from the President went September 24 to William Dennison, its two sentences reading: "Mr. Blair has resigned and I appoint you Postmaster-General. Come on immediately." John Hay wrote in his diary of that day:

> This morning I asked the President if the report of the resignation of Blair were true. He said it was.
>
> "Has Dennison been appointed to succeed him?"
>
> "I have telegraphed to him today—have as yet received no answer."
>
> "What is Mr. Blair going to do?"
>
> "He is going up to Maryland to make speeches. If he will devote himself to the success of the national cause without exhibiting bad temper towards his opponents, he can set the Blair family up again."
>
> "Winter Davis is taking the stump also. I doubt if his advocacy of you will be hearty enough to be effective."
>
> "If he and the rest can succeed in carrying the State for emancipation, I shall be very willing to lose the electoral vote."

The '64 National Union party candidate for President, Abraham Lincoln. Photograph by Brady

The '64 Democratic-party candidate for President, George Brinton McClellan

The '64 National Union party candidate for Vice-President, Andrew Johnson

The '64 Democratic-party candidate for Vice-President, George Hunt Pendleton

From the Meserve collection

The Astor House, New York City

From an engraving in the Barrett collection

August Belmont

William Henry Aspinwall

From the Meserve collection

To Nicolay in New York Hay wrote that day of taking to the President a dispatch from Nicolay, and, "he told me to tell you you had better loaf around the city a while longer. You need some rest . . . & may as well take it in N. Y. . . . Besides you can't imagine how nasty the house is at present. You would get the 'painter's cholic' [sic] in 24 hours if you came home now. Politicians still unhealthily haunt us. Loose women flavor the anteroom. Much turmoil & trouble. . . . Write to me some morning while you are waiting for your cocktail & tell me how's things. Give my love to the fair you are so lucky as to know."

But Nicolay in New York had little rest. On an errand for the President he was on that day hunting for the adroit manipulator Thurlow Weed, telegraphing the President that T.W. had gone to Canada, writing a letter to Hay with the same message. Hay showed the letter to the President, who said: "I think I know where Mr. W. has gone. I think he has gone to Vermont, not Canada. I will tell you what he is trying to do. I have not as yet told anybody." Then Lincoln told of Governor Smith of Vermont, "a little dark . . . sort of man," and a cousin, "though you wouldn't think it," of General Baldy Smith, who "is large, blond, florid." And the Vermont Governor had come to Lincoln with a story, giving General Baldy Smith as his authority. As West Point cadets and later in Washington McClellan and Baldy Smith were intimates. When McClellan sought promotion for Smith from the President, he got it. McClellan was free and confidential with Baldy Smith about plans and prospects, till one day on the Peninsula Fernando Wood and another politician visited McClellan and stayed in camp a few days. Smith mentioned to McClellan that he seemed cool and reserved for some reason. McClellan told Smith that his recent political visitors had urged him to stand as an opposition candidate for President, that in line with their proposition he had written them a letter, not yet sent, "giving his idea of the proper way of conducting the war, so as to conciliate and impress the people of the South with the idea that our armies were intended merely to execute the laws and protect their property," and pledging himself to conduct the war in that style.

On Baldy Smith saying the letter "looks like treason" and would be the ruin of McClellan, his generals, and his army, the commander of the Army of the Potomac before Baldy Smith's eyes destroyed the letter and thanked Baldy for frank counsel. They were friends again until after the battle of Antietam; McClellan again seemed to be avoiding certain old intimates and free talk with them. Seeing a light in McClellan's tent one night, Baldy stepped in to report on duty for the day, saw several other persons there, gave his report, was about to leave when the General asked him to stay. After the others had gone McClellan told Baldy his visitors had renewed their proposition about his running for the Presidency, and this time he had agreed and had written them a letter pledging himself, a letter which he read to Baldy Smith, who immediately thereafter applied to be transferred from that army, Franklin, Burnside, and other major generals asking for transfer about the same time. Thus Lincoln gave Hay the story he had heard from Governor Smith of Vermont.

"Now that letter must be in the possession of Fernando Wood, and it will not be impossible to get it. Mr. Weed has, I think, gone to Vermont to see the Smiths about it." And Lincoln sketched briefly for Hay his reasons for relieving McClellan from command and referred to his dismissal of McClellan's associate Major Key "for his silly, treasonable talk because I feared it was staff talk & I wanted an example." He referred to a letter of General Buell that Hay knew about which furnished "another evidence in support of that theory." He would remind Hay of "the story you have heard Neill tell about Seymour's first visit to McClellan," also tallying with Baldy Smith's story of the strange personal ambitions of McClellan and the sordid political guests permitted so many hours in McClellan's camp.

Whatever political letter McClellan had written from his camp headquarters, if any, on the persuasions of his camp visitors Seymour and Wood, was being sought by Weed on the suggestion of Nicolay, the President's secretary. Nicolay, returning from New York to the White House, said Weed was "on the track of the letter and hoped to get it." In the course of time it would seem that Weed was not to get it. And it might have been that such a letter never was written and therefore was not to be gotten. In the meantime for campaign purposes both Republicans and Democrats made use of the long letter which McClellan had handed to Lincoln at Harrison's Landing more than two years before. The Democrats published it in their leaflets. They offered it as a modest self-portrayal of a Christian gentleman, a soldier, and a statesman who would have conducted the war with decency and courtesy. The Republicans picked at it in editorials and squibs, the more radical editors saying its frank ego and its covert insolence should have brought the President's instant removal from the army of a general stepping so completely out of the military field into politics.

On one point regarding the Harrison's Landing letter the Republicans and Democrats seemed to agree: that on July 7, 1862, when he dated that letter, and for some time before, McClellan had the definite notion in his head that he might make a good President and had carefully studied what he would announce as his policies if he were President or a candidate for the Presidency. Whether or not Fernando Wood had seduced McClellan into politics, as Baldy Smith believed, it was now in McClellan's favor that Wood announced in view of McClellan's repudiation of the Chicago platform he, Wood, could not support McClellan for President.

"The conspiracy against Mr. Lincoln," wrote Weed to Seward September 20, had embraced more leading men than Weed had supposed possible, had collapsed, and had held its last conclave at the house of David Dudley Field "early last week." Among the thirty or more present Weed named individuals in effect much less conspiratorial toward Lincoln than

Weed himself. That Seward might at times have been misled by the trends and assumptions of Weed was evident in this letter. The points where sincere self-deception ended and convenient pretense began could be not easily marked in a Weed letter. September 20 he wrote of those he termed conspirators, "Knowing that I was not satisfied with the President, they came to me for coöperation; but my objection to Mr. Lincoln is that he has done too much for those who now seek to drive him from the field." Weed wrote this as though it covered the fact that he too in the weeks of gloom preceding military victories had been saying much the same thing as the "conspirators" he refused to join.

State elections in Vermont and Maine in mid-September showed Unionists gaining in Vermont and a little better than holding their own in Maine. The straws in the wind favored Lincoln. The solidarity of Unionist ranks

DON'T SWAP HORSES.

JOHN BULL. "Why don't you ride the other Horse a bit? He's the best Animal."
BROTHER JONATHAN. "Well, that may be; but the fact is, OLD ABE is just where I can put my finger on him: and as for the other—though they say he's some when out in the scrub yonder—I never know where to find him."

A campaign horseplay cartoon in *Harper's Weekly*

that had come in September was partly if not mainly the result of Lincoln's cool and patient management, his keeping his head and letting the plans to replace him develop till suddenly they were wrecked by events, his acceptance of Frémont's withdrawal timed to Blair's dismissal with Blair's loyalty to the Union ticket unquestioned, his moderate course permitting such foes as Greeley and Weed to work together, his disposal of fresh patronage to Weed, his refusal to be led into a break beyond repair with

Chase, his summoning into the Cabinet as Postmaster General an Ohioan of more practical resources than Chase.

When this September swing into party unity had been accomplished Lincoln was in "a more gleeful humor," according to Lamon, who found him alone one evening and met the greeting, "I am glad you have come in. Lamon, do you know that 'we have met the enemy, and they are *ourn*'? I think the cabal of obstructionists 'am busted'! . . . I now am inspired with the hope that our disturbed country further requires the valuable services of your humble servant. 'Jordan has been a hard road to travel,' but I feel now that, notwithstanding the enemies I have made and the faults I have committed, I'll be *dumped* on the right side of that stream."

Of the few "obstructionists" still unyielding was Wendell Phillips, writing as late as September 27 to Elizabeth Cady Stanton: "I would cut off both hands before doing anything to aid Abraham Lincoln's election. I wholly distrust his fitness to settle this thing, and indeed his purpose. Lincoln wishes the end; won't consent to the means. I still reject Lincoln's quarter loaf. Justice is still more to me than Union." Yet even Phillips in the passing of days was to see himself so alone in his stubborn course, and so overly zealous to be "absolutely right" that he too would join those who believed Lincoln's quarter-loaf better than nothing and that it might become a half-loaf. His most scathing denunciation of Lincoln perhaps had been in connection with a speech by Blair condemning race amalgamation. Phillips assumed that this and other anti-Negro expressions in Blair's speech came by consent of Lincoln. "If it were possible to defeat God, in that speech of Blair is the poison," said Phillips to a Framingham, Massachusetts, audience. In the light of history and every page he ever read, he was "an amalgamationist, to the utmost extent," seeing no hope for the future "but in that sublime mingling of races, which is God's own method of civilizing and elevating the world." Blair in his denial of Negro rights had sunk the war from "the august level of a revolution" to "the deadly miasma of politics."

Yet the Niagara of events at hand would sweep aside the Lincolns and the Blairs who might try to check it, said Phillips. "At the same time, remember this: the man who, sitting as President, and speaking by the voice of his agent, appeals to prejudice, to loathsome ignorance, to all the worst enemies of the country, is not to be trusted as a leader." Thus Phillips had spoken in Massachusetts, meeting, the reporters noted, "Applause" and again "Prolonged applause." And now the Blair he had excoriated was out of the Cabinet, by Lincoln's request, in some tacit agreement with Frémont. And Phillips was writing Elizabeth Cady Stanton that he would "cut off both hands" before he would do anything to aid Lincoln's election. This was September. October was to see him on the stump for Lincoln, along with Frederick Douglass and William Lloyd Garrison.

October was to see Thad Stevens commending "the firm grasp of the pilot at the helm," who had risen above "Border State seductions and Republican cowardice" and thereby "elevated himself to the full height of his moral stature." Though he was beset with unheard-of difficulties at first, Mr. Lincoln's "kind nature inclined him to favor those who were more favorable to our erring brethren. . . . But all this is in process of correction. Above all, the President has declared there shall be no compromise with traitors. Submission, the integrity of the Union, and the abandonment of slavery are his only terms. Let us forget that he ever erred, and support him with redoubled energy." Before the Union League Club of Lancaster Stevens struck at "vipers" who would restore slavery. "I doubt if there can be found in the hottest corner of pandemonium cinders black enough . . . to make hearts for such wretches."

At the customary procedure of collecting a campaign fund from party men drawing government pay, Welles protested. Happening into the President's office one day, he did not take a good look at the President's other caller who was pouring a line of low-modulated conversation into the President's ear. On the President loosening up to say, "Here he is; it is as good a time as any to bring up the question," Welles saw the visitor was Henry J. Raymond and that Lincoln preferred to have the two of them iron out their difficulties before him. Raymond told Welles that the navy-yard commandant had forbidden the collection of campaign levies at the navy yard, this resulting in "great dissatisfaction to our party friends, for these assessments had always been made under preceding administrations." Welles said he doubted collections had been made "in such an offensive and public manner," that he "was aware parties did strange things in New York" but the stationing of collectors at navy-yard gates to solicit a share of the wages of employees was "inexcusable and indefensible." Raymond admitted the course was "not politic" but repeated that former Administrations had practiced it. Welles again questioned that former Administrations had. Raymond held to it that the collections would have to be made, though "it doubtless might be done in a more quiet manner." They parted with Lincoln having said nothing to put him on either side.

Collections for the campaign went on, among government employees and elsewhere. Leonard Swett wrote to his wife that he and Congressman Washburne had managed to get a campaign fund of $100,000, assuring her: "Don't think it is for improper purposes. It is not. . . . Innumerable expenses have to be incurred."

Seasoned politicians not averse to any legitimate and paying horse trades brought to the White House a notion that at first seemed a merry waggery. John Hay noted in his diary September 23: "Senator Harlan thinks that Bennett's support [with the *New York Herald*] is so important, especially considered as to its bearing on the soldier vote, that it would pay to offer him a foreign mission for it, & so told me. Forney has also had a man talking to the canny Scot who asked plumply, 'Will I be a welcome visitor at the White House if I support Mr. Lincoln?' What a horrible question for a man to be able to ask. I think he is too pitchy to touch. So thinks the Presd't apparently." Six weeks passed, however, and for reasons satisfactory to himself, and undoubtedly to others, Lincoln, it seemed, verbally committed himself as definitely as anyone could ask to a promise that he would appoint James Gordon Bennett to be the United States Envoy Extraordinary and Minister Plenipotentiary to France. An associate, confidant, and go-between of Bennett's, W. O. Bartlett, wrote to Bennett the following letter:

New York, Nov. 4, 1864

My Dear Sir:

I am from Washington, fresh from the bosom of Father Abraham. I had a full conversation with him, alone, on Tuesday evening, at the White House, in regard to yourself, among other subjects.

I said to him: "There are but few days now before the election. If Mr. Bennett is not *certainly* to have the offer of the French Mission, I want to know it *now*. It is important to me."

We discussed the course which the *Herald* had pursued, at length, and I will tell you, verbally, at your convenience, what he said; but he concluded with the remark that in regard to the understanding between him and me, about Mr. Bennett, he had been a "*shut pan*, to every body"; and that he *expected to do that thing* (appoint you to France) *as much as he expected to live*. He repeated: "*I expect to do it as certainly as I do to be re-elected myself*."

I wanted to see you; but I am obliged to do some work in Pennsylvania, about the election, and cannot till my return.

Truly yours,

James Gordon Bennett, Esq. W. O. Bartlett

Thus ran the report of a responsible and careful go-between acting for a stern executive who, in such an instance, would resent any slovenly transcript of the language used by the President. It carried Lincoln's vocalism. Regarding the Paris Mission the President had said and done nothing to give anyone else hope of landing it; he had been a "shut pan, to every body"; this was Kentucky household and farm speech of basic simplicity and clarity. The inference was that Bennett and his *Herald* were of moment for the election a week away. And far more in the labors to follow a re-election would it count for Lincoln to have the goodwill and some degree of co-operation from the most influential and humanly interesting newspaper in the Western Hemisphere. The press chronicled of November 5, the day after Bartlett wrote to Bennett of being "fresh from the bosom of Father Abraham," that General McClellan "paid a lengthened visit to Mr. James Gordon Bennett" at the latter's country home, which might mean anything. If Bennett was extracting promises from both presidential candidates that he could have the Paris Mission, it would be like him and in tone with his sinister mirth.

Though Hay seemed unaware of what the President, through Bartlett, had promised Bennett, the diary entry of Hay on November 7, 1864, indicated that Mrs. Bennett had probably learned of that promise, that she was keen to go to the American Legation at Paris, and that McClellan had again guessed wrong. The entry read: "Bartlett writes to President that Mrs. J. G. B. has become an earnest Lincolnite. Poor M^cs^ visiting those people and compromising himself to them has been of no avail and must be terribly humiliating to a man so well bred as McC. is."

And did Lincoln early in the campaign just as definitely promise to another go-between that he would appoint Horace Greeley Postmaster General? One George G. Hoskins of Wyoming County, New York, an ally of Congressman Reuben E. Fenton, at a later time Speaker of the New York State Assembly, so alleged. Just after the Chicago convention, according to Hoskins, he had interviewed Lincoln at the White House, had heard Lincoln say that Benjamin Franklin was the first Postmaster General of the country and Greeley as a later Franklin would be a worthy successor, and this would have been told Greeley had he accepted an invitation to visit the White House. Hoskins was not sure he understood the President. Was he at liberty to tell Greeley of this promise? "Certainly. This is what I intended to tell him if he had come himself. I shall not fail, if God spares my life, to keep this solemn promise."

Hoskins on reaching New York that evening reported the words to Greeley, who with fishy eye and in natural falsetto asked, "Hoskins, do you believe that lie?" Hoskins said he believed Lincoln would keep the promise. "I don't," retorted Greeley, Hoskins saying as he took leave, "I will stake my life upon it." Hoskins believed that the editorial next day in which the *Tribune* announced that it would "henceforth fly the Lincoln banner," and the consistent and friendly support of Lincoln from then on through the campaign, were in part the result of Greeley's being offered place as Postmaster General. Hoskins's story had a discrepancy in saying that his interview with Lincoln took place while Lincoln shaved himself, which Lincoln never did. Had Hoskins said that a barber shaved Lincoln during their interview it would have been more credible. Yet Hoskins could reply that his discrepancy was slight and nothing would have been more like Lincoln, everything considered, in that first week of September of '64 than such an offer to Greeley. The words, according to Hoskins, were that Greeley would be appointed Postmaster General, "if I am re-elected and reinaugurated."

Greeley's incessant criticisms and misrepresentations, according to Chauncey Depew, "annoyed Mr. Lincoln probably more than anything which happened during his administration." Lincoln talked one day to a friend of Depew about Greeley's methods "and the false light in which they put him before the country." Then came the earnest suggestion to Lincoln: "Why don't you publish the facts in a card? They will be printed in every newspaper in the United States. The people will then understand exactly your position, and your vindication will be complete." Lincoln's reply, as Depew noted it from his friend: "Yes, all the newspapers will publish my letter, and so will Greeley. The next day he will take a line and comment upon it, and he will keep it up, in that way, until, at the end of three weeks, I will be convicted out of my own mouth of all the things which he charges against me. No man, whether he be private citizen or President of the United States, can successfully carry on a controversy with a great newspaper, and escape destruction, unless he owns a newspaper equally great, with a circulation in the same neighborhood."

The campaign strode on with McClellan's personality in high contrast with that of Lincoln. And marshaled solidly behind McClellan were power-

The voice of the Law telling McClellan and Pendleton they must get off the Capitol grounds with their grind-organ act—circulated by the National Union Committee

ful forces, the banking and transportation interests linked with August Belmont, Dean Richmond, Aspinwall, the industrialist churchman seen preeminently in Cyrus H. McCormick of Chicago, an array of respectably wealthy and intellectual or aristocratic types embodied in Horatio Seymour of New York and Robert C. Winthrop of Boston. Marching along were the two-fisted and riotous elements who formed part of the rank and file of the Democratic party, joined by those to whom the race issue was uppermost, fearful the Emancipation Proclamation might bring political and social equality. The recoil over McClellan's repudiation of the peace platform came in some of the most vocal sections of the party. The *Metropolitan Record* and the *Daily News* in New York announced that they could not go along with McClellan. The *Crisis* at Columbus, Ohio, held that "fraudulent sale is not binding in law" and the "sell-out" in Chicago was treachery. With Vallandigham these organs continued their attacks on Lincoln, pouted disapproval of McClellan, and seemed to be saying they hoped McClellan could be elected, after which they could force him into respect for the Chicago demand for peace through "cessation of hostilities." This too seemed to be the position of McClellan's running mate, Senator George H. Pendleton, who had been among the foremost at Washington in urging peace and conciliation at any price. Republican cartoons had horses at both ends of the Democratic wagon, McClellan driving east and Pendleton west. The dissatisfied Democrats, however, were a minority. The heavy guns were with McClellan, newspapers, orators, campaign managers with a chest of funds, the traditions of an old and powerful party, and McClellan himself on horseback, the warrior, hero, and myth.

Besides appeal to blood and passion were arguments addressed to the reason. In behalf of the Democratic cause Robert C. Winthrop quoted, "We should so be patriots as not to forget that we are gentlemen," privately deplored "the insolent tone" prevailing in Boston "towards all who cannot find it in their conscience to support Lincoln," and inquired as to martial law, arrests without examination or trial, men silenced by force for speaking their minds freely under a supposed free Government. "Who can help being alarmed for the future?" And Winthrop spoke of a trend that Lincoln was only too familiar with, in saying, "The Republican party have so thriven and fattened on this rebellion, and it has brought them such an overflowing harvest of power, patronage, offices, contracts and spoils, and they have become so enamoured of the vast and overshadowing influence which belongs to an existing administration at such an hour, that they are in danger of forgetting that their country is bleeding and dying on their hands."

Seymour raked over "the frauds and failures of the administration," seemed to have fewer specific cases than would warrant his tone, yet managed questions that someone should have been asking. "When the Government is spending such an enormous amount of money, and the liability to peculation is so great, the Administration that will say to contractors, as has been openly said in circulars: 'You have had a good contract, out of which you have made money, and we expect you to use a part of that money to assist to replace us in power,' renders itself a partner in fraud and corruption. The contractor will say to this Government: 'You shall not make a peace that shall put an end to all my profits.' "

Of course, other politicians and attorneys-at-law were aware that Seymour did not like to name names, because contractors shifted from party to party and the Democratic ranks likewise were not lacking swindlers. Seymour would have, as in England, the humblest home a castle of refuge, whereas "in our country the meanest and most unworthy underling of power is licensed to break within the sacred precincts of our homes." Yet

A cartoon caricaturing Lincoln and each Cabinet member–widely circulated by the Democratic-party organization. From the Lincoln Library of the University of Chicago.

his own rank-and-file party men had wrecked, burned, and looted more homes and private domiciles during the New York draft riots than the Lincoln Administration in any other hundred Northern cities. So delicate and combustible was the subject that neither party cared to go into details about those New York riots, the Democrats because their record was so lawless and shameful, the Republicans because they were still conducting the draft over the country. Thick pamphlets, virtually small books, were widely circulated by the Union party, titled *War Powers of the President*, reprinting an extended study by Solicitor William Whiting of the State Department, who cited for the President, Congress, and their military and naval establishments about all the legal authority they might want for anything they had done or might want to do "in relation to rebellion, treason and slavery."

In a tone of genial tolerance masking a lofty patronization, Robert C. Winthrop in a speech at New London, Connecticut, thrust at the vulgarity and incapacity of his old Congressional Whig-party colleague, Abraham Lincoln. "You know already, I am sure, all that you care to know about President Lincoln. Yet, perhaps, I can recall a little passage in his public life which may at least amuse you. His only term of Congressional service was during the period when I had the honor to preside over the House of which he was a member. He helped me to the Speaker's chair by his own vote, and I really wish I could find it in my conscience to return the compliment at this moment. [Laughter.]" Then Winthrop of the ancient and honorable line of Winthrops of Boston read from Lincoln's 1848 speech in Congress ridiculing General Cass. "By the way, Mr. Speaker, did you know that I am a military hero? Yes, sir; in the days of the Black Hawk war, I fought, bled, and came away. . . . If General Cass went in advance of me in picking huckleberries, I guess I surpassed him in charges upon the wild onions." From this Winthrop proceeded to the point that the Lincoln who by his own admission was a military failure in the Black Hawk War should have blessed his country by never attempting to control and direct armies in the present crisis.

Then Mr. Winthrop, a Henry Clay Whig who had been in Congress ten years, who had once held the Senate seat vacated by the death of Daniel Webster, who was a distinguished scholar and deeply instructed by the history of the past, soberly spoke his prophecy: "If Mr. Lincoln is re-elected, the people of the South will fight for thirty years."

The campaign would decide whether ever again there should be a President over the whole United States of America, Winthrop believed, and to restore the old Union and bring peace "almost any other party would be more able than the Republican party, and almost any other President would be more likely than Abraham Lincoln, to accomplish that consummation which every Christian patriot . . . must have at heart." Had the President frankly recognized the antagonisms and hates he had created, and had he six months ago with self-denial and magnanimity told the country he would not again be a candidate and would favor the selection of a new

President, "Ah. my friends," said Winthrop, "ah, my friends, what a glorious example of patriotic self-denial . . . this would have been!" On the contrary, "President Lincoln . . . has quite forgotten that *one-term* principle to which he and I were committed as members of the old Whig party. We see him clinging eagerly and desperately to patronage and place. We see him demanding to be renominated, demanding to be re-elected, and claiming it almost as a test of patriotism and loyalty that we should all with one accord support him for four years more. . . . You may swap Secretaries of War, as you did Cameron for Stanton [Laughter.]; you may swap Secretaries of the Treasury, as you did Chase for Fessenden; you may swap Postmaster-Generals as you have just done, Blair for Dennison [Continued laughter.]; you may change your candidates for the Vice-Presidency, 'handy-dandy,' and leave Mr. Hannibal Hamlin to shoulder his musket in a Bangor militia company. [Laughter.] Thus far you may go, but no further. You must not touch me. [Laughter.] You must not change Presidents. Patriotism requires that Abraham Lincoln should be exempt from all casualties. And so we are all to be drummed into voting for him under a threat of the pains and penalties of treason."

In the course of his speech Mr. Winthrop emphasized the need for "a wise, conciliatory, healing policy" toward the South instead of the "peculiar" method of the Administration. He would offer some "plain, common-sense views which President Lincoln himself seems to have expressed" regarding the need for change. Winthrop quoted from a letter of the Reverend Dr. Moncure Conway dated July 20 and published in the *Boston Commonwealth.* Conway, with antislavery associates of Massachusetts, had interviewed the President on the matter of appointing Frémont as the Provisional Governor of North Carolina. And the careful and scrupulous Conway recorded the President as saying:

"Gentlemen, it is generally the case that a man who begins a work is not the best man to carry it on to a successful termination. I believe it was so in the case of Moses, wasn't it? He got the children of Israel out of Egypt, but the Lord selected somebody else to bring them to their journey's end. A pioneer has hard work to do, and generally gets so battered and spattered that people prefer another, even though they may accept the principle."

Conway's own comment followed: "Under him [Lincoln] the war was begun; he had to deal with the disaffected; is it not possible that he has become so *battered and spattered* as to make it well for him to give up the leadership to some Joshua?"

Mr. Winthrop read this to his New London audience. The reporters noted "Loud laughter and cheering." A moment later they heard "Laughter and cheers" when Mr. Winthrop said, "Some of us are not a little afraid that the same fatality which attended the ancient Moses, is about to find a fresh illustration in the case of our modern Abraham."

Mr. Winthrop then argued that the Southern States had seceded because of the election of Abraham Lincoln as President and they would stay seceded and never return to the Union if Abraham Lincoln should now be re-elected. Mr. Winthrop's New London speech was joined to letters of General McClellan in a pamphlet which the Democrats gave wide circulation. On its back cover was a list of groceries and dry goods showing they cost the average man and woman two to ten times as much as before the war.

The printing press worked overtime. The electorate saw literature hauled by the ton. Pamphlets, leaflets, brochures, cards, tracts, envelopes colored with party emblems, in quantity lots came into the hands of voters. The Republicans seemed to outdo the Democrats in the amount of educational material, but no voter went hungry who wanted reading matter that lambasted Lincoln and sang the praises of McClellan. Each side had pamphlets titled *What Lincoln's Administration Has Done*, but no voter could believe both. McClellan's military record was torn to shreds in the Union-party literature; Lincoln's conduct of the war was macerated as unspeakably cruel and atrocious in the Democratic tracts. That McClellan had arrested enough members of the Maryland Legislature to stop them from seceding their State from the Union was fairly well proved in one Union pamphlet. That Lincoln and Seward had egged him on and led him into it was not emphasized in that particular piece of literature. In Campaign Document No. 11 the Democrats took up *Miscegenation Indorsed by the Republican Party*, quoted the Negro leader Frederick Douglass as saying that "the President of the United States received a black man at the White House just as you have seen one gentleman receive another," quoted various radicals and extremists on the race question, and ended with claiming that Republicans favored intermarriage between the two races and the more of it the better. A list of horrors, including the debauchery of young women and the jailing of boys in foul and dismal cells for two years, filled a fearsome Democratic brochure titled *Mr. Lincoln's Arbitrary Arrests.*

That those whom the Lincoln Administration had arrested arbitrarily had been themselves somewhat arbitrary in conduct was the thesis of a Unionist pamphlet giving the report of Judge Advocate General Joseph Holt on the Order of American Knights, alias the Sons of Liberty, which Holt termed "a western conspiracy in aid of the Southern rebellion." The works of their "temples" and "lodges," oaths and rituals, storing of guns and ammunition, propaganda, kidnappings and assaults, were recited as a sober presentation of evidence. Under date of London, September 30, 1864, a political ghost walked in the flesh again in a pamphlet titled *Letter of Honorable R. J. Walker in Favor of the Reëlection of Abraham Lincoln.* Walker took old Steve Douglas men by the flank in writing: "In voting against Mr. Lincoln in 1860, I did so to save the Union from peril. In voting for him now, it is to suppress the rebellion and maintain the Union." News of the re-election of Mr. Lincoln would send Confederate stocks down to rise no more. American securities, Federal bonds and State bonds, railroad and other issues, "will all be immensely appreciated," forecast Walker. He predicted too that an established Southern Confederacy would trouble the North with its wishes for conquest of Cuba and Puerto Rico, its aims to extend slavery to Central America. "The temple of Janus will never be closed on our continent, and war will be our normal condition."

One Union-party leaflet spoke for the army. The Mayor of Atlanta having written a bitter protest at one order, Sherman replied that he was seeking peace not only in Atlanta but in all America. "The South began the war by seizing forts, arsenals, mints, custom-houses, &c., long before Mr. Lincoln was installed. . . . You might as well appeal against the thunder-storm as against the terrible hardships of war. They are inevitable, and the only way the people of Atlanta can hope once more to live in peace and quiet at home is to stop this war. . . . We don't want your negroes, or your horses, or your houses, or your land, or anything you have; but we do want and will have a just obedience to the laws of the United States. That we will have, and if it involves the destruction of your improvements, we cannot help it. You have heretofore read public sentiment in your newspapers, that live by falsehood and excitement, and the quicker you seek for truth in other quarters the better for you. . . . I want peace, and believe it only can be reached through Union and war. . . . When that peace does come, you may call on me for anything. Then I will share with you the last cracker, and watch with you to shield your homes and families against danger from every quarter. Now, you must go, and take with you the old and feeble; feed and nurse them, and build for them in more quiet places proper habitations to shield them against the weather until the mad passions of men cool down, and allow the Union and peace once more to settle on your old homes in Atlanta."

This letter was the beginning of Sherman's coming to be regarded in the North as a fighting prophet. The same leaflet had Grant's letter saying "a determined unity of sentiment" in the North would win the war hands down. Speeches of Major General Joe Hooker in Brooklyn and New York were included, with "Great applause" indicated at his saying: "There are no Copperheads in the army. The troops will fight well, and they will vote well."

Leaflet No. 61 of the Loyal Publication Society in New York gave Sherman's reply to Hood's charge of "studied and ungenerous cruelty." Sherman told Hood why he was ordering the old people and children removed from Atlanta. "You yourself burned dwelling-houses along your parapet, and I have seen to-day fifty houses that you have rendered uninhabitable because they stood in the path of your forts and men." Sherman gave cases where Hood and other Confederate commanders were cruel not because they enjoyed it but because necessity dictated. "In the name of common-sense, I ask you not to appeal to a just God in such a sacrilegious manner. . . . Talk thus to the marines, but not to me. . . . If we must be enemies, let us be men, and fight it out . . . and not deal in such hypocritical appeals to God and humanity. God will judge us in due time, and he will pronounce whether it be more humane to fight with a town full of women and the families of a brave people at our back, or to remove them in time to places of safety among their own friends."

Included in this leaflet was an anecdote from General Schenck in an Ohio speech. The Chicago peace platform with a war candidate reminded Schenck of an old lady selling apples at the courthouse door in Cincinnati. On a customer asking, "Are they sweet or sour?" she would lead on into finding out what might be wanted by the assurance, "Why, sir, they are rather acid; a sort of low tart, inclined to be very sweet."

A speech of Carl Schurz at Philadelphia, September 16, was an extraordinary effort in persuasion. The Union Congressional Committee circulated it among all groups, with emphasis on the Germans. Schurz had grown restless in command of a corps of instruction at Nashville and had taken to the stump after a conference with Lincoln. Undoubtedly they had one of their long talks again. And undoubtedly Lincoln wrote parts of Schurz's speech or Schurz, with his remarkably acute literal memory, incorporated something of the flair and wording of Lincoln's conversation into a speech. "The mouth of the Mississippi in the hands of a foreign power? Let it be so and half our independence is gone. . . . The people of the United States have bought the mouth of the Mississippi, once with their money, and twice with their blood. To give it away would be merely to produce the necessity of buying it a fourth time. Can the South yield it? No. Can the North do without it? No. And then?"

Schurz at Philadelphia asked how if hostilities ceased they could compel Jeff Davis to meet them at a convention to restore the Union, as the Chicago platform proposed. "Will you tacitly acquiesce in the establishment of the Southern Confederacy? Or will you resume the war? What then in the name of common-sense will you do? Here we look upon a jumble of contradictions so glaring that our heads begin to reel, and we wonder how it could happen to the whole wisdom of a great party in solemn convention assembled to hatch out so bottomless an absurdity."

Was Schurz, fresh from a long White House conference, voicing the moving involvements of the conscience of Lincoln, in addressing the Democrats? "I tell you in the face of your protestations and those of your candidate, if you permit yourself once to be infatuated with the idea that you can coax and buy the rebels back into the Union by concession, and whatever they may ask of you, you will do it, for it is only the first step that costs—and surely, Jefferson Davis will not spare you, for his foot is too familiar with the necks of his old Northern friends. [Great applause.] The old silly cry, 'Do not irritate the South! do not irritate it by the blockade! do not irritate it by the armed negroes!' [Laughter.] will again have its old sway; your desires and delusive hopes will give birth to the most obsequious schemes, and soon you will be in a state of mind of which it will be difficult to say where folly ends and treason begins."

Schurz quoted from an official dispatch of Lord Lyons to his Government. "Several of the leaders of the Democratic party sought interviews with me." They wanted "foreign mediation between North and South." But they were afraid "of its coming too soon." They held it should "be deferred until the control of the Executive Government should be in the hands of the Conservative party."

The enlightened opinion of the liberal masses of Europe was with the Lincoln cause, said Schurz, making special reference to his mother country. "You have heard of the people of Germany pouring their gold lavishly into the treasury of the United States. [Applause.] You have heard of a loan of a thousand millions having been offered, and being now in progress of negotiation."

A comparison between the Chicago Democrats and Lincoln's predecessor in the White House followed. "Although Buchanan is dead and buried, those who indulged in the soothing delusion that such a man could leave no progeny, find themselves mistaken. Behold, a whole brood of young Buchanans has risen up and met in convention in Chicago. [Continued laughter.] The laurels of their father do not let them sleep. I see again the cunning twinkle of the eye, I see the white necktie again [Great laughter.]; they try to adjust it like a halter around the throat of the Republic, to throttle her to death. [Continued cheers.] Truly the sons are greater than the sire. For what he did, we may say he did as a weak old man, whose life had been spent in a constant exercise of his knee-joints; and who, when the rebellion first raised its Gorgon-head, had neither the firmness of a patriot nor the courage of a traitor. But what they do, they do after thousands have stained battlefields of their country with precious blood, after the people have poured out money like water to save the Republic, when the hero of Vicksburg is thundering at the gates of Richmond, when our flag waves over Atlanta, and Victory is the cry! [Long-continued cheering.]"

Schurz turned to discuss McClellan's middle way. "He ignored the platform and took the nomination, wrote a skillfully worded political letter showing that the art, How not to say it, can be brought to as high a degree of perfection as the art, How not to do it. [Laughter and cheers.]" At the suggestion of Vallandigham for Secretary of War and Fernando Wood as Secretary of the Treasury, there were, the reporter noted, "peals" of laughter.

The vote for the platform at Chicago was far more unanimous than the vote for the candidate, in which connection Schurz would speak from experience: "There is no American who does not know that a President's policy is not made by him alone, but by those who have made him."

In closing Schurz let the American Eagle scream. In fifty years the country would have 100,000,000 people, in another century 500,000,000, and the purpose of the North was a free Republic "so strong that its pleasure will be consulted before any power on earth will undertake to disturb the peace of the world." The rebellion had lifted the nation from its childhood. "She did not know before how strong she was."

Again on October 7 Schurz delivered an address, this time in Brooklyn, New York, a discourse historical, allusive, extended, evidence enough that he was a first-rate scholar in politics and a second-rate major general whose instinct was for the public rostrum. "The Emancipation Proclamation is the true sister of the Declaration of Independence," said Schurz. And he was one of the few campaign orators who laid stress on the friendship for Lincoln of the laboring many in England. He asked if they remembered "the touching address of the workingmen of Manchester" to the President of the United States in '62. "While the instincts of despotism everywhere conspired against us, while the aristocracy of Great Britain covered us with their sneering contempt, while the laboring men in England began to suffer by the stopping of the cotton supply, and the nobility and the princes of industry told them that their misery was our fault, the great heart of the poor man rose in its magnificence, and the English laborer stretched his hard hand across the Atlantic to grasp that of our President, and he said: 'Although want and misery may knock at my doors, mind it not. I may suffer, but be you firm! Let the slave be free. All hail, American people! we are your brothers!' "

Schurz however was not one more ordinary campaign freedom-shrieker. He had been a hunted man in the 1848 revolution in Germany. He had whiffed the smoke of conflict against rulers who held liberty to be no phantom but a reality that could be shot down and stuffed as a trophy and set up like a slave's bloody head on a pike. The same voice of experience was in a Union-party pamphlet wherein Professor Edouard Laboulaye spoke for French liberals. "The world is a solidarity, and the cause of America is the cause of liberty." So long as a society of 30,000,000 people across the Atlantic lived "under a government of their choice, with laws made by themselves," Europe could hope. "But should liberty become eclipsed in the New World, it would become night in Europe," and power would go to "the whole school which believes only in violence and in success." Therefore Laboulaye and his associates were "praying God that the name which shall stand first on the ballot [of November] shall be that of honest and upright Abraham Lincoln." From the English liberal leader John Bright in a letter to Greeley came the wish that Lincoln be re-elected because it would over Europe "and indeed throughout the world" deepen men's faith in republican institutions. His own countrymen hoped "with an intense anxiety" for another Lincoln term. "It is not because they believe Mr. Lincoln to be wiser or better than all other men on your continent, but they think they have observed in his career a grand simplicity of purpose . . . regarding his Presidential path with the calm judgment which belongs rather to history than to the present time."

In mid-September, being invited to a Union mass meeting in Buffalo, Lincoln began writing a draft of a letter to be read at the meeting. But he was in no mood for it. He seemed to have detected that what he had written lacked the flash of his letter to Conkling the previous year, which had carried highly effective persuasion. Also he seemed to have decided this was not the expedient moment. He would let events march on, laid aside what he had written, courteously notified the Buffalo Unionists that to address them would be a breach of precedent, that if he once began to write such campaign letters it would be difficult to discriminate between meetings having equal claims.

Three speeches of Lincoln to Ohio regiments, "three months' men" going home, gave his attempt to tell in a few simple words what the shooting and crying, the war, was about. "A free government where every man has a right to be equal with every other man" was endangered. The main question, he told the sunburned young men in blue before him, was "whether your children and my children shall enjoy the privileges we have enjoyed." In the practical workings of the system there might be inequalities. "But if we should wait, before collecting a tax, to adjust the taxes upon each man in exact proportion with every other man, we should never collect any tax at all. There may be mistakes made sometimes; and things may be done wrong, while the officers of the government do all they can to prevent mistakes." In no Administration could there be perfect equality of action and uniform satisfaction for everybody. "I beg of you not to allow your minds or your hearts to be diverted from the support of all necessary measures . . . by any miserable picayune arguments addressed to your pockets, or inflammatory appeals made to your passions and your prejudices." In spite of the acts of any man or set of men their free government was worth every effort. "Nowhere in the world is presented a government of so much liberty and equality. To the humblest and poorest amongst us are held out the highest privileges and positions. The present moment finds me at the White House, yet there is as good a chance for your children as there was for my father's." Under their free government was "an open field and a fair chance for your industry, enterprise, and intelligence."

The President begged the Ohio troops to remember this. And he would be vividly specific. "I happen, temporarily, to occupy this White House. I am a living witness that any one of your children may look to come here as my father's child has."

The issues of the hour were not easy for the editor of the *Corydon* (Ohio) *Democrat*. He arranged them three-in-one, up, down and across, the first column Secessionist, the second Abolitionist, the third, reading across and taking it all in, was Democratic. Being a Democrat himself, he assumed that the Abolitionist column represented the Republicans. As an exercise in ideas and emotions it was ingenious. (See page 267.)

In Tennessee the revolution snarled and whanged, reaching the White House in more than slight echoes. At a convention called for loyal men to meet in Nashville and frame a program to get the State back into the Union, the radicals and the soldiers had it their way. When a conservative Democrat moved that the convention be governed by the Constitution of the United States and that of Tennessee, and when later he presented his ultimatum that his group must have a chance to vote as they saw proper, he was howled down in such jeers and cries that he and his followers left the convention. After endorsing the Lincoln-Johnson ticket and demanding emancipation of slaves in Tennessee, the convention arranged an oath to be taken by those who would vote in November. Each was required to swear solemnly, so help me God, "that I am an active friend of the government of the United States; that I sincerely rejoice in the triumph of its armies and navies . . . that I will cordially oppose all armistices or negotiations for peace with rebels in arms . . . and that I will heartily aid and assist the loyal people."

These were not easy words for Tennessee McClellan Democrats, with the right hand on the Bible, to repeat. A committee of them carrying an elaborate document of protest arrived at the White House and John Lellyet of Nashville read the recital of their wrongs to Lincoln. Lellyet finished. Lincoln was brusque. "May I inquire how long it took you and the New York politicians to concoct that paper?" Lellyet replied that none but Tennesseans had had a hand in it. Lincoln: "I expect to let the friends of George B. McClellan manage their side of this contest in their own way, and I will manage my side of it in my way." Adding that he might make some further answer in writing, Lincoln closed the discussion. He was abrupt. They saw he was abrupt and had no doubt nothing more should be said. So they filed out.

The secretaries Nicolay and Hay believed this one occasion when the President might not have valued his self-control. They wrote, "It is not impossible that, in a moment of irritation at the presentation of a petition which was in itself an insinuation that he was making a selfish and corrupt use of his power, the President may have treated Mr. Lellyet with scant courtesy; but he took the protest, nevertheless."

A few days later he wrote the McClellan electors of Tennessee, "I have nothing to do with the matter," the President being charged with no duty to conduct elections in any State; nor did he see any reason for military interference. In an independent movement "of at least a portion of the loyal people of Tennessee," he could not perceive in their plan "any menace of violence or coercion toward any one." They objected to the plan. "Leaving it alone will be your perfect security against it. Do as you please on your own account, peacefully and loyally, and Governor Johnson will not molest you, but will protect you against violence so far as in his power." And a faint humor of understatement crept in. "I presume that the conducting of a presidential election in Tennessee in strict accordance with the old code of the State is not now a possibility." He reminded them that the Executive Department also would not decide whether votes in Tennessee after being cast were entitled to be counted. "Except it be to give protection against violence, I decline to interfere in any way with any presidential election." On thus hearing from the President, and considering it an off year for them in Tennessee, the McClellan electors drew out of the race.

Mingled flamboyance and romance of democracy as it moved in Andrew Johnson came to the fore one October night as he rose to address the torchlighted faces of a crowd that included practically the entire Negro population of Nashville. They knew beforehand a high hour was to be theirs. And the Military Governor's voice rang out that the hour had come when the last vestige of slavery must be removed. Therefore, "without reference to the President or any other person," he had a proclamation to make: "Standing here upon the steps of the Capitol, with the past history of the State to witness, the present condition to guide, and its future to encourage me, I, Andrew Johnson, do hereby proclaim freedom, full, broad and unconditional, to every man in Tennessee." A roar of rejoicing and a wild clamor of gladness broke from Negro throats, drums and trumpets added jubilation, and banners waved over circling torches. After this punctuation Johnson's voice rang again. "This damnable aristocracy should be pulled down. No longer should the wives and daughters of the colored men of Tennessee be dragged into a concubinage compared to which polygamy was a virtue." If the law shielded them, he asked, "Will you endeavor to be true to yourself, and shun . . . the path of lewdness, crime and vice?" The shouts burst in a mass: "We will! We will!"

Clearly the black faces and the mystic hopes moved the Governor. He spoke hope that as in the days of old a Moses might arise "to lead you safely to your Promised Land of freedom and happiness."

"You are our Moses!" came the shouts. And in a surge of wild mass cheering, "We want no Moses but you!" His response: "Humble and unworthy as I am, if no better shall be found, I will indeed be your Moses, and lead you through the Red Sea of war and bondage to a fairer future of liberty and peace."

Packed with emotion and drama, the incident as published and interpreted in the North seemed a foretokening of the war entering another phase, tentative and experimental, touched with the hazards of the race question being dominant in any reconstruction of the Union. Radicals who had found Lincoln a poor instrument for their measures began saying, "Johnson is our man, one of us." They counted it in Johnson's favor that ex-Governor Wise of Virginia should be saying Johnson was "as dirty as cart-wheel grease."

Singing "Blow ye the trumpet, blow," in opening, the John Brown song midway, and "From all that dwell below the skies" in closing, 144 delegates of the National Convention of Colored Men met in Syracuse, New York, four October days. They spoke for the free Negroes of eighteen States, including seven Slave States. In speeches, committee reports, and a Declaration of Rights and Wrongs they voiced the demands, prayers, and fears of the organized free Negro. The Reverend Henry Highland Garnet of Washington, D.C., called the convention to order; John Mercer Langston of Oberlin, Ohio, was elected temporary chairman and Frederick Douglass president, with fifteen vice-presidents and five secretaries. The officially published proceedings noted, "The President introduced Miss Edmonia Highgate, an accomplished young lady of Syracuse. Miss Highgate urged the convention to trust in God and press on, and abate not one jot or tittle until the glorious day of jubilee shall come." Behind him on the platform, said Douglass, were younger men who "had come up in this time of whirlwind and storm." The convention would deal with the state of feeling in the country toward the colored men, Douglass added, and "answer the question, as we pass to and from this hall, by the men on the streets of Syracuse, 'Where are the damned niggers going?' " In what was to be done "we shall give offence to none but the mean and sordid haters of our race."

An Ohio speaker was certain "the effort we are making to secure rights for the colored men is also one to secure recognition of the rights for the white men of the country," for both "are slaves to the oligarchy which inaugurated the present rebellion." Garnet as an officer of the African Civilization Society said he believed in a "Negro nationality" and described a New York draft-and-race riot mob hanging a man to a tree. "Then a demon in human form, taking a sharp knife, cut out pieces of the quivering flesh, and offered it to the greedy, blood-thirsty mob, saying, 'Who wants some nigger meat?' and then the reply, 'I!' 'I!' as if they were scrambling for pieces of gold." Garnet referred to the nationality of those in the mob, and said he could not tell how it was that men crossing the ocean only should change as much as they. He had traveled from Belfast to Cork, and from Dublin to the Giant's Causeway, meeting kindness and always kindness. He had stood in public side by side with that hater of oppression Daniel O'Connell—and at the name of O'Connell the free Negro delegates broke into cheers and applause. Why the change? asked Garnet. Why should crossing the ocean give the Irish people a hate for the Negro? Garnet would answer it was "the debasing influence of unprincipled American politicians."

Saluting a battle flag stained with the blood of free Louisiana Negroes, Dr. P. B. Randolph of New York said, "We are here to ring the bells at the door of the world," proclaiming to nations, white men, slaves, kings, and the universe, "*We are coming up* . . . and going up to *stay*." John S. Rock of Boston held there was no middle ground between the two political parties. "The one headed by Lincoln is for Freedom and the Republic; and the other, by McClellan, is for Despotism and Slavery." The two systems represented could not exist on the same soil. One would have to annihilate the other. As between the Romans and Carthaginians "there always existed either a war, preparations for war, or a deceitful peace."

The convention proceeded to organize the National Equal Rights League, saying in its declaration, "As a branch of the human family, we have for long ages been deeply and cruelly wronged by people whose might constituted their right," and petitioning Congress to remove "invidious distinctions, based upon color, as to pay, labor, and promotion" among Negro troops. Thanks were accorded the President and Congress for opening the way to colored mail-carriers, for abolishing slavery in the District of Columbia, for recognition of the Negro republics Liberia and Hayti, for a retaliatory military order invoked because of "barbarous treatment of the colored soldiers of the Union army by the rebels." Further and special thanks were accorded Senator Sumner and General Butler.

They protested the official journal of the anti-American Anti-Slavery Society in its policy of denial of the ballot to colored men, and that William Lloyd Garrison's weekly paper, the *Liberator*, "apologizes for excluding the

DEMOCRATIC
CATECHISM
Of Negro Equality.
JULY 4th, 1863.

Who said that all men are created equal? Thomas Jefferson, the Father of Democracy.

Who gave the negroes the right of suffrage in New York? The Democratic party.

Who presided over the Convention which gave this privilege to negroes? Martin Van Buren, a Democrat.

Who married a negro woman, and by her had mulatto children? Richard M. Johnson, a good Democrat.

Who elected Richard M. Johnson Vice President of the United States? The Democratic party.

If President Van Buren had died, and Richard M. Johnson had become President, who would have become the Democratic mistress of the White House? This same negro woman.

Who made the negro a citizen of the State of Maine? The Democratic party.

Who enacted a similar law in Massachusetts? The Democratic party.

Who gave the negro a right to vote in New Hampshire? The Democratic party.

Who permitted every colored person owning $250 in New York to become a voter? A General Assembly, purely Democratic.

Who repealed the laws of Ohio which required negroes to give bonds and security before settling in that State? The Democratic party.

Who made mulattoes legal voters in Ohio? The Supreme Court of which Reuben Wood was Chief Justice.

What became of Reuben Wood? The Democratic Party elected him Governor three times, and he is still a leader of the Democratic party.

Who helped to give free negroes the right to vote in Tennessee, under her Constitution of 1796? General Jackson.

Was General Jackson a good Democrat? He generally passed as such.

Who with the above facts, and many others staring them in the face, are continually whining about "negro suffrage" and negro equality? The Democratic party.

All these things were done by Democrats, and yet they deny being in favor of negro equality, and charge it upon the Republicans—just like the thief who cries "stop thief" the loudest.

N. B.—Send your Democrat friend one of these Valuable Documents

This circular aims to give any Democrat a certificate of consistency and respectability in joining the National Union party. From the Barrett collection.

colored men of Louisiana from the ballot-box." In this "they injure us more vitally than all the ribald jests of the whole proslavery press." Yet this was a slight anxiety compared to what might await them. While they were still demanding their right to freedom with the ballot, it was possible that freedom *without* the ballot might vanish. "There is still room for painful doubt and apprehension." The Republican party still put Union above the abolition of slavery. "However antislavery in sentiment the President may be, and however disposed he may be to continue the war till slavery is abolished, it is plain that in this he would not be sustained by his party." A single reverse in arms might throw the issue into the hands of the South. There freedom hung on a slender thread. It did not help, read their address, that the Administration spokesman Seward in a recent speech had said that on the insurgents laying down their arms the war would cease and all war measures, "including those which affect slavery," would cease also.

The main text of their adopted "Address to the People of the United States" presented their claims to the ballot. "We are asked, even by some abolitionists, why we cannot be satisfied, for the present at least, with personal freedom; the right to testify in courts of law; the right to own, buy, and sell real estate; the right to sue and be sued. We answer, Because in a republican country, where general suffrage is the rule, personal liberty and the other foregoing rights become mere privileges, held at the option of others. What gives to the newly arrived emigrants, fresh from lands governed by kingcraft and priestcraft, special consequence in the eyes of the American people? Not their virtue, for they are often depraved; not their knowledge, for they are often ignorant; not their wealth, for they are often very poor; why, then, are they courted by the leaders of all parties? The answer is, that our institutions clothe them with the elective franchise, and they have a voice in making the laws of the country. Give the colored men of this country the elective franchise, and you will see no violent mobs driving the black laborers from the wharves of large cities, and from the toil elsewhere by which he honestly gains his bread. You will see no influential priest, like the late Archbishop Hughes, addressing mobocrats and murderers as 'gentlemen'; and no influential politician like Governor Seymour addressing rowdies of New York as his 'friends.' " The right to vote was "the keystone of the arch of human liberty," and "If you still ask why we want to vote, we answer, Because we don't want to be mobbed from our work, or insulted with impunity at every corner. We are men, and want to be as free in our native country as other men."

The rebellion in the South suppressed, then what? "A sullen hatred towards the National Government, transmitted from father to son as 'sacred' animosity? . . . We may conquer Southern armies by the sword; but it is another thing to conquer Southern hate." For a counterpoise they would have the ballot and, "if need be, arms," in the hands of 4,000,000 Negroes in the South.

Thus the free Negroes in convention assembled made clear where they stood in the political campaign of 1864. Every point which they brought to the fore was a living human issue that had taken on new intensity with every month of the war, that had dominated the discussions in Congress, that had come and was yet to come to the desk of the President in written proposals and to his ears in the pronouncements of men holding themselves crusaders and evangels. "The freedmen are wards of the nation," he once remarked to Stanton, who replied, "Yes, wards in chancery." In law this meant they were cases in separate courts of equity with no remedy in common law. In boxing it meant "with head held under opponent's arm being pommeled."

And William Lloyd Garrison, the early and unquenchable veteran of abolitionist agitation, where was he in the campaign? In the campaign biography of Lincoln by William Thayer, he was quoted: "We are making progress in the right direction every day, and every hour of the day. I believe that under this administration we have advanced a quarter of a century in a single year." And what was his argument that so grieved the free Negroes assembled at Syracuse? It was his defense of Lincoln's reconstruction policy in Louisiana and a forecast of what would happen if the freed blacks were given the ballot. He had written: "Chattels personal may be instantly translated from the auction-block into freemen, but when were they ever taken at the same time to the ballot-box, and invested with all political rights and immunities? According to the laws of development and progress it is not practicable. . . . Besides, I doubt whether he [the President] has the Constitutional right to decide this matter. Ever since the Government was organized, the right of suffrage has been determined by each State in the Union for itself, so that there is no uniformity in regard to it. . . . In honestly seeking to preserve the Union, it is not for President Lincoln to seek, by a special edict applied to a particular State or locality, to do violence to a universal rule, accepted and acted upon from the beginning till now by the States in their individual sovereignty. . . . Nor, if the freed blacks were admitted to the polls by Presidential fiat do I see any permanent advantage likely to be secured by it; for, submitted to as a necessity at the outset, as soon as the State was organized and left to manage its own affairs, the white population with their superior intelligence, wealth, and power, would unquestionably alter the franchise in accordance with their prejudices, and exclude those thus summarily brought to the polls. Coercion would gain nothing."

Around the very issues set forth by the Negro equal-rights league, Missouri was in turmoil between the conservative "Claybanks" and the radicals, the anti-Lincoln Germans. Lincoln sent Nicolay with messages to the moderate Unionists that their childish quarrels ought to end. Nicolay reported to his chief that "with the exception of a very few impracticables, the Union men will cast their votes for you," and that "in practice nearly everybody is right and united, while in profession everybody is wrong or at cross-purposes." The *Corydon* (Ohio) *Democrat* summarized:

Hurrah for	The Old Union
Secession	Is a curse
We fight for	The Constitution
The Confederacy	Is a league with hell
We love	Free speech
The rebellion	Is treason
We glory in	A free press
Separation	Will not be tolerated
We fight not for	The negroes' freedom
Reconstruction	Must be obtained
We must succeed	At every hazard
The Union	We love
We love not	The negro
We never said	Let the Union slide
We want	The Union as it was
Foreign intervention	Is played out
We cherish	The old flag
The stars and bars	Is a flaunting lie
We venerate	The habeas corpus
Southern chivalry	Is hateful
Death to	Jeff Davis
Abe Lincoln	Isn't the Government
Down with	Mob law
Law and order	Shall triumph

A leaflet carried the "Black Republican Prayer" and addressed "Abraham Lincoln, who art in the White House at Washington." It proceeded: "Thy Presidency has come, thy will must be done. We implore thy Royal Highness to gag the Democrats and their press that they may not speak evil of thee. Centralize thy power, that we may become a strong government, that the people will kneel before thy Royal Highness, and worship thee. And O, we humbly pray that thou wilt carry on the war with vigor, lay waste the Southern States, murder the inhabitants, confiscate their property, ravish their women, and burn their cities and towns. And O, Father Abraham, when the cry of the widow and the orphan ascendeth to heaven, and the wrath of the Great Jehovah descendeth upon us for our wickedness, and cruelty, and our grand armies are defeated, do thou open thy balmy bosom and hide us from that vile rebel Jeff Davis and his army; for thou art to rule with power and with glory, forever and ever. Amen." Then was printed a "Benediction" which read: "May the blessings of Emancipation extend throughout our unhappy land, and the illustrious, sweet-scented Sambo nestle in the bosom of every Abolition woman, that she may be quickened by the pure blood of the majestic African, and the spirit of amalgamation shine forth in all its splendor and glory, that we may become a regenerated nation of half-breeds and mongrels, and the distinction of color be forever consigned to oblivion, and that we may live in bonds of fraternal love, union and equality with the Almighty Nigger, henceforward, now and forever. Amen."

One 48-page pamphlet, its author anonymous, was published by J. F.

Feeks in New York, titled *The Lincoln Catechism: A Guide to the Presidential Election of 1864: wherein the Eccentricities and Beauties of Despotism are Fully Set Forth.* It put questions and then gave the answers. "What is the Constitution? A compact with hell, now obsolete. By whom hath the Constitution been made obsolete? By Abraham Africanus the First. To what end? That his days may be long in office. What is a President? A general agent for negroes. Have the people any rights? None but such as the President gives. What is the meaning of the government? The President. What is the meaning of an oath? To swear not to do anything you promise. Is amalgamation now practiced to a greater extent than formerly? It is. Is it prosperous in Washington? It is, so much so that more than five thousand of the fruits of amalgamation have been born in that city since the election of Mr. Lincoln. Is it spreading elsewhere? Yes, wherever the officers of our army go in the South, it is doing well. How is it in New Orleans? Well—but there are a great many squint-eyed yellow babies there, supposed to have been occasioned by fright at the presence of Ben Butler. Was Mr. Lincoln ever distinguished as a military officer? He was, in the Black Hawk war. What high military position did he hold in that war? He was a cook. Was he ever in any battle? No, he prudently skedaddled and went home at the end of the first engagement. Who is Mrs. Lincoln? The wife of the government. Who is Mr. Lincoln? A successful contractor to supply the government with mules. Who is Master Bob Lincoln? A lucky boy, yet in his teens, who has been so happy as to obtain shares in Government contracts by which he has realized $300,000. Is it disloyal to refer to the size of Old Abe's feet? It is. Is it disloyal to speak of white men as a superior race? It is, very. Is it disloyal to allude to the rate at which the Republicans are plundering the Treasury and the people? It is. Is it disloyal to allude to the difference between an old fashioned Democratic gold dollar and the Republican green paper dollars? It is. Have the loyal leagues a prayer? They have: Father Abraham, who art in Washington, of glorious memory since the date of thy proclamation to free negroes. Thy kingdom come, and overthrow the republic; thy will be done and the laws perish. Give us this day our daily supply of greenbacks. Forgive us our plunders, but destroy the Copperheads. Lead us into fat pastures; but deliver us from the eye of detectives; and make us the equal of the negro; for such shall be our kingdom, and the glory of thy administration."

The Union party circulated in reply *The Copperhead Catechism: for the Instruction of Such Politicians as Are of Tender Years*, which was "authorized and with admonitions by Fernando the Gothamite, High Priest." Here too were questions duly followed by answers. "What is the chief aim of a Copperhead in this life? To abuse the President, vilify the Administration, and glorify himself. What are the articles of thy belief? I believe in One Country, One Constitution, One Destiny; And in George B. McClellan, who was born of respectable parents; Suffered under Edwin M. Stanton; Was refused reinforcements and descended into the swamps of the Chickahominy; He was driven therefrom by fire and by sword, and upon the seventh day of battle ascended Malvern Hill, from whence he withdrew to Harrison's Landing, where he rested many days; He returned to the Potomac, fought the battle of Antietam, and was then removed from his high command, and entered into Oblivion; From this he shall one day arise and be elevated to the Presidential chair, there to dispense his favors unto all who follow him. I also believe in the unalienable doctrine of State Rights, And I finally believe in a Peace which is beyond everybody's understanding.

This gives the tone of the fierce, primitive passions let loose in the fall campaign of '64; *Harper's Weekly* sets forth Columbia with Union shield and sword defending herself against Copperheads—the National Union party circulated reprints of it

Have any precepts been laid down for thy guidance? Yes, two. What are they? Thou shalt hate the Nigger with all thy heart, and with all thy soul, and with all thy mind, and with all thy strength. This is the first and great commandment. And the second is like unto it: Thou shalt hate an Abolitionist like the devil."

In campaign literature the Republicans surpassed, in torchlight parades the Democrats. Kerosene was a help. Along Broadway, New York, up State Street in Chicago, in every large Northern city, moved the ranks of voters, each with a McClellan torch, each an attestation he was against the rule in sway at Washington, in squads and platoons of flaring testimonials marching between crowded sidewalks, taken by themselves as living shouting omens of the end of Lincoln and all his works. In Chicago when the sidewalks called "Hurrah for Lincoln!" the parade hooted "And a rope to hang him!" It was an American custom that year. The lighted boxes called trans-

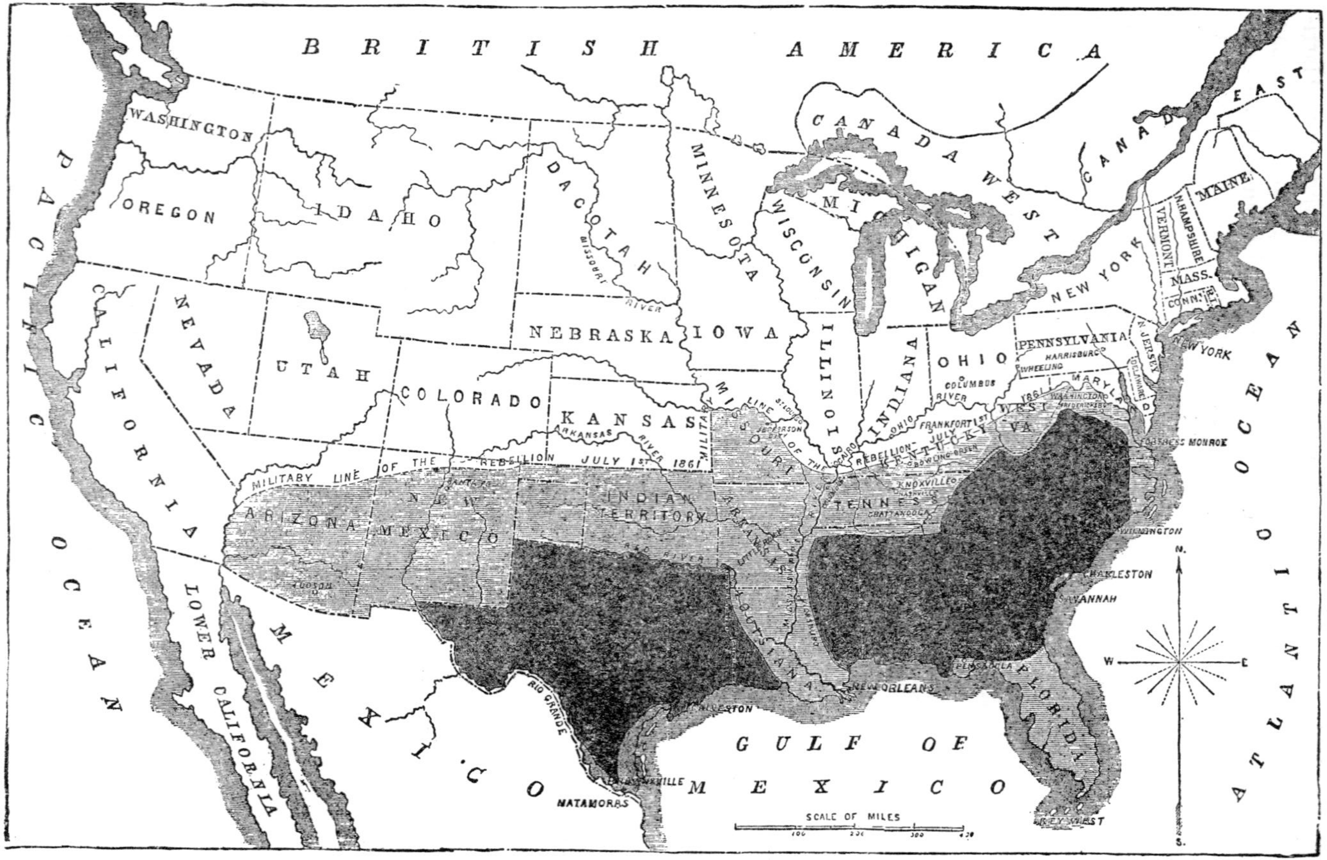

The National Union party circulates this map of the United States, shaded portions showing territory occupied by Federal forces, the black area still to be overcome. Original in the author's collection.

parencies carried little sentences for the sidewalks to read and ponder. Much could be said around any one of them. The *New York World*, the *Chicago Times*, the *Detroit Free Press*, from day to day filled entire pages with speeches around the stubby little propositions in these lighted boxes of the torchlight processions. "Old Abe Removed McClellan. We'll Now Remove Old Abe." "To Whom It May Concern—for President, George B. McClellan." "Time to Swap Horses, November 8th." "We Demand the Habeas Corpus." "Fort Lafayette, to Let." "The Constitution As It Is, the Union As It Was." "No Emancipation; No Miscegenation; No Confiscation; No Subjugation." "No More Vulgar Jokes."

Newspaper squibs traveled from New York and Philadelphia to the tall-grass sections of the Midwest, where the *Bureau County Patriot* would reprint: "Prentice thinks that a lock of the President's hair clipped from the spot where he scratched his head when he was writing his Emancipation Proclamation, might perhaps bring almost a fortune at one of our sanitary fairs."

Passion spun the plot and called it good. At Quincy, Illinois, in the City Park overlooking the Mississippi River to where the waters washed the border of the Slave State of Missouri, a Republican mass meeting of 10,000 people heard General Richard Oglesby, Union candidate for Governor, not yet recovered from wounds received in battle. They heard young Clark E. Carr of Galesburg and young Colonel Robert G. Ingersoll of Peoria. While Carr spoke there were hurrahs for Jeff Davis. At a call "Three cheers for Jeff Davis!" a small group lustily joined in three cheers. They met no violence. In the close of freethinker Ingersoll's speech, however, they heard him pay his personal regards:

"God bless the soldiers of the army of the United States, wherever they may be—whether they be fighting on the hillside, the open plain, or in the dark valley, whether weary and footsore on the long march, whether parched with thirst they are dying on the field or are ministered to by loving hands in the hospital, whether they be tossed upon the uncertain waves of the great deep, whether they be writing letters to their friends by the dim light of the camp-fire, or reading letters from home, God bless the soldiers of the army of the United States, God bless their friends, and God damn their enemies!"

Never before came such rolling thunders of applause and cheers, thought Carr. He noticed the Reverend Dr. Horatio Foote, a distinguished and scholarly clergyman, seated on the platform, pounding the boards with his cane. Someone asked, "Doctor, is not that blasphemous?" The doctor, pounding on with his cane: "Inspiration, gentlemen, inspiration." Then came billows of joined voices, for everybody by now knew "The Battle Cry of Freedom," one of many songs by the Chicago music teacher and publisher George F. Root. It had an elation of gathered forces, was not an effective solo, but required a chorus. It was a rallying song:

The Union for ever, hurrah, boys, hurrah!
Down with the traitor; up with the Stars!
While we rally round the Flag, boys,
Rally once again,
Shouting the battle cry of Freedom!

Not far away, over at Lewiston on the Spoon River, a Union-party county convention and mass meeting was not so helter-skelter as the *Chicago Times* correspondent reported. The report, however, had campaign savor and American speech. "The Convention was called to order by the election of one S. A. Gee, a one-horse country pettifogger who left the Democratic party and sold himself to the Union League of Canton for a mess of abolition porridge in the shape of the office of Police Magistrate. The candidate for School Commissioner is a 'war democrat' abolitionist and says that Lincoln has the power and ought to suspend the Constitution of the United States. . . . The meeting at the grove was a brilliant affair. One Bob Ingersoll of Peoria said he was not in favor of the Union as it was. After Bob was through, a mass of legal stupidity, by the name of Burrough, arose, told the crowd it was time for him to go home, and he started. The crowd was a perfect disgrace to a civilized community. No way could you turn your eyes but what you could see men reeling and stumbling from the effects of whiskey; while curses, oaths, and indecent and brutish yells, intermingled with hurrahs for Lincoln, filled the air. Several fights occurred, in one of which poor, miserable Bill Phelps, Provost Marshal of Fulton County, was rather roughly handled. It was intended not to allow people to hurrah for Vallandigham: however cheer after cheer went up for the noble, brave and true Ohio patriot, right in the very teeth of the abolitionists. The crowd was not more than half as large as that at the recent Democratic meeting here. There is to be speaking tonight at which some of the smaller guns will make asses of themselves, and thus will end the 'great mass meeting' of shoddy contractors, Assistant Provost Marshals, precinct statesmen, and corner grocery orators."

Along the Spoon River and over the old Eighth Circuit the barbs of Unionist satire in the *Weekly Illinois State Journal* were read. "Dear Brother Vallandiggers, our great long-eared and one hoss Anti-Wah apostle from the land of the Buckeyes, has eloquently expressed it in his quotation from Spokeshave: Blessed are the Peacemakers, the Anti-Wah men, when there be Wahs and Rumors of Wahs, for they shall drink pure Corn lager fresh from the fountains of Bull Run, ah. Afore the foundation of the Southern Conthieveracy, Benedict Arnold and that good old traitor Aaron Burr, was threatened with suspension of the writ of habeas corpus. I find that our Dear Uncle Jeff Davis and his Anti-Wah men down South, for the sake of peace have skedaddled occasionally, and let themselves get whipped a number of times, and from the very first have sung the beautiful Hymn of Peace and still their cry is: 'Down with the Stars and Stripes, dissolve the American Union, and give us a One-Horse Republic, whose chief cornerstone is Slavery.' What is worse, Uncle Jeff Davis & Co. are in a tight place.

in a bad row of stumps, and expect soon to be badly whipped by a mighty army sent against them by a man called Honest Abe, and led by some mighty Wah men, who will make them skedaddle unto the Mountains of Hepzidam, where the Lion of Secession and Nullification roareth, and where the whangdoodle of Disunion and Slavery mourneth for its first born, ah. This being the case I will now let my remarks come to a close, kerflummix, so that we can pass some resolutions of Peace and Anti-Wah. Brother Doughface, please pass around your Coonskin Hat and make a wee bit of a collection, but don't take anything but Confederate scrip."

Breezy campaign humor. From the Barrett collection.

One orator of excess was reported in *Leslie's Weekly* as having closed his appeal to a barbecue audience: "My fellow citizens, were I an angel from heaven, with wings dipped in sunbeams, I would fly from the cold North to the sunny South, from the wild shores of Maine to the golden regions of California, proclaiming Democracy! Democracy! Democracy!" The *New Orleans Era* described a speaker at a Free State meeting as having either inherited or by constant exercise developed a powerful pair of lungs. "On this occasion, when he got fairly warmed up by, whatever it was, he spoke so loud it was quite impossible to hear him."

On October 11 the stump speakers and the tub-thumpers paused slightly, the torchlights and the transparencies halted a moment, and there was less fury in the pamphlets blown loose as wild geese across the autumn sky. The electorate went to the polls that day in Pennsylvania, Ohio, and Indiana. At eight o'clock in the evening the President with Hay walked over to the War Department. The usual entry door was locked and Stanton upstairs with the key. In a moonlight that fell on scurrying leaves of autumn paced a sentry, buttoned and shivering. He saw it was the President and took them around by the Navy Department and into the War Office by a side door.

The first flurry of telegrams showed gains in Indiana and Ohio, a lead of 2,500 in Philadelphia, with Democrats of prominence giving up the State.

Awaiting more dispatches, the President took from his pocket a book and read several chapters of the doings and ideas of the Copperhead martyr Petroleum V. Nasby. "They were immensely amusing," noted Hay. "Stanton and Dana enjoyed them scarcely less than the President, who read on, *con amore*, until 9 o'clock." A few flyers from the soldier camps near Washington showed Ohio troops voting about ten to one for Union, Pennsyl-

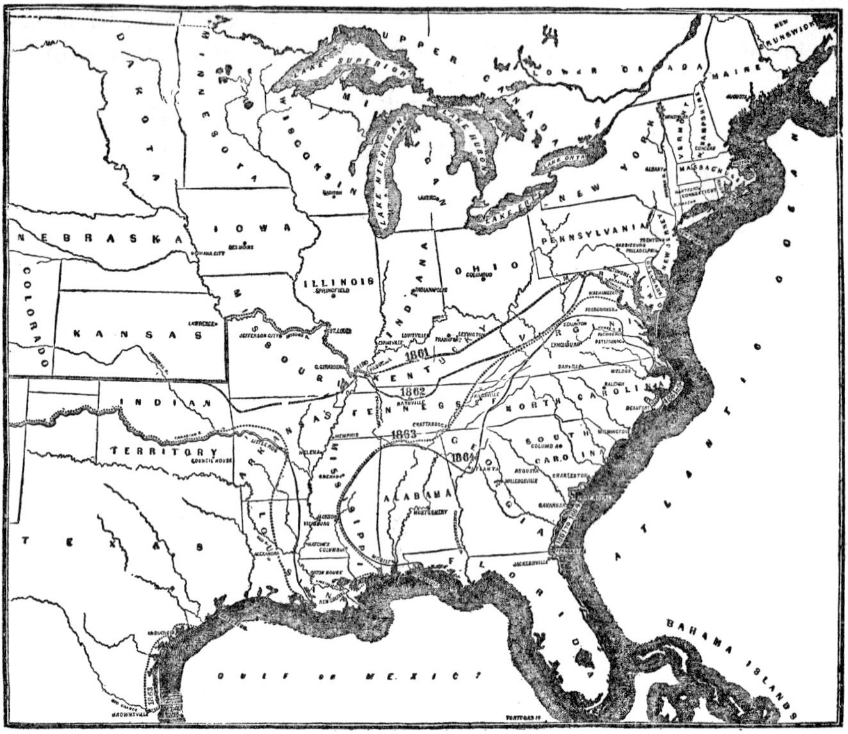

Another map issued by the National Union party, with lines indicating how Federal forces pushed farther south each year. Original in the author's collection.

vania less than three to one. Carver Hospital, which Stanton and Lincoln passed every weekday on their way to the country, gave about one out of three for Union, Lincoln saying, "That's hard on us, Stanton—they know us better than the others." The President's personal guard, Company K, 150th Pennsylvania Volunteers, voted 63 to 11 for Union.

The telegraph keys clicked. Governor Morton and the entire Republican ticket in Indiana were elected by 20,000 majority, with a gain of 4 Congressmen. Pennsylvania's Congressmen, equally divided between two parties, changed to 15 Republicans against 9 Democrats. The Union ticket carried Ohio by 54,000 and the 14 Democrats and 5 Republicans of '62 shifted now to 17 Republicans and 2 Democrats in Congress. The defamatory Peace

Anna Elizabeth Dickinson

Walt Whitman

John Murray Forbes

Matthew B. Brady

Francis Bicknell Carpenter

Ralph Waldo Emerson

From the Meserve collection

Reading from top to bottom: *First row:* Garrett Davis, John Adam Kasson, John Brooks Henderson, William Sprague. *Second row:* James Alexander McDougall, Willard Saulsbury, Horace Maynard, Samuel Jordan Kirkwood, Thomas E. Bramlette. *Third row:* William Gannaway Brownlow, Austin Blair, James Samuel Wadsworth, Henry Laurens Dawes

From the Meserve collection

Democrat "Sunset" Cox lost his seat to Samuel Shellabarger. Not least was the news from Maryland and her adoption of a new State constitution abolishing slavery. The majority was slim, the soldier vote giving emancipation its day. It was of less importance that, as Hay wrote, "W[inter] Davis' clique was badly scooped out in the mayoralty election at Baltimore."

The returns were slow coming in. A little after midnight Lincoln wired Simon Cameron at Philadelphia: "Am leaving office to go home. How does it stand now?" And the next day when Grant telegraphed for news of Pennsylvania, Lincoln replied: "Pennsylvania very close and still in doubt on home vote."

In this week Lincoln estimated Illinois as with the opposition. "Imminent danger of our losing this State," Washburne had written him from Galena. "Everything is at sixes and sevens; and no head or tail to anything." Lincoln laid the letter aside with one penciled comment: "Stampeded." Ten days later saw Washburne crowing. "Logan is carrying all before him in Egypt." Seward brought a letter unfolding a plot of the Democrats on election day "to abstain from voting." Lincoln returned the letter with the indorsement, "More likely to abstain from stopping when once they get at it." He seemed amused at the idea of Democrats not voting, as though the last thing a Democrat would "abstain" from would be the fun of his say at the ballot box.

The President had been "extremely anxious," even "despondent," about what might happen, wrote Hay, who believed that now Indiana was rescued from "sedition & civil war." A Copperhead Governor in Indiana, Hay had no doubt, would have afforded "a grand central rallying point" for the secret orders and a dissatisfied electorate.

Lincoln during his life had seen himself so often a loser when victory seemed just ahead that he had a habit of underconfidence. On October 13 he penciled in the war telegraph office on a telegraph blank his estimate of how many votes he would get as against McClellan in the Electoral College. He gave to McClellan in this realistic calculation the electoral votes of New York, Pennsylvania, New Jersey, Delaware, Maryland, Missouri, Kentucky, Illinois. To himself he gave the New England States, Michigan, Wisconsin, Minnesota, Iowa, Oregon, California, Kansas, Indiana, Ohio, West Virginia. The total figured 117 for Lincoln, and 114 for McClellan. Out of 231 votes he could see himself probable winner by a bare majority of 3 votes. Major Eckert took the memorandum and added the 3 electoral votes of Nevada, which Lincoln had forgotten. Otherwise Bates considered it a feat of political skill and memory that Lincoln carried in his head the exact number of electoral votes accorded each of the States.

Now on October 12 Roger Brooke Taney died. Now the President was required to name a new man to hold the august seat of Chief Justice of the United States Supreme Court. Now the austere and provocative Taney was gathered to his fathers. And spheres of influence formed and sought to have Lincoln name Montgomery Blair, Bates, Fessenden, Salmon P. Chase, or some other one for the place of head interpreter of the Constitution. And Lincoln was to hear them and to wait and to consider carefully and hold his patience till the momentous election day of November 8. "It is," wrote Hay to Nicolay in Missouri, "a matter of the greatest personal importance that Mr Lincoln has ever decided."

Funeral services over Taney had not yet been held when Lincoln's old associate Browning called on Secretary Fessenden and transacted matters in behalf of cotton-trading permits for his client, William Butler of Springfield, Illinois. Then Browning sounded Fessenden on whether he would permit his friends to mention him to the President for Chief Justice, heard Fessenden's refusal, and went away to take part in various moves to "procure," as he termed it, the high seat for the right man, once proposing Stanton's name to the President.

To the War, Treasury, and State departments in the morning, to his room in the afternoon, went Mr. Browning, ex-United States Senator Browning, holder of the seat vacated by Steve Douglas until Illinois had gone Democratic again, the one old-time Illinois lawyer associated with Lincoln who most often was seen at the White House. "At the Departments in the forenoon, and at work at my room in the afternoon" ran the most frequent item of his diary, though the next most frequent seemed to be "At night went to the President's." And unless the President was over at the War Department Browning was let in. The President liked his company, though it seemed that along in the fall of '64 the President came to look at Browning as one of the most peculiarly befuddled individuals that had come out of the war, and he became less free in outpourings of mind and spirit to Browning. When Smith had retired as Secretary of the Interior, Browning had hoped that the President would agree with Mrs. Lincoln that he should have the place. When Browning brought to the President the matter of the vacant Chief Justiceship, he was not without faint hope he might be the man. Known as a familiar of the President, for him doors swung open when he sent his card in at the departments. He rode with the President and navy heads to the navy yards to witness the throwing of rockets and signals from 6- and 12-pound guns. "Went in President's carriage and returned at 10 O'clock last night." He worked in his office till night "then went and saw the President about fees in the Phillips cases, about Adml Wilke's case, and about appointment of Eben Moore to Montano"

Browning refused the request of Seward and the President that he take the appointment of Commissioner for claim adjustments of the Hudson Bay and Puget Sound Agricultural companies. "I find the duties will be very arduous, and the compensation $5000 inadequate." When the hay contractors Covert & Farlin had been arrested and put on trial before a court-martial charged with fraud, the hay contractors hired the two lawyers in Washington nearest to the President in confidence and the longest in acquaintance, Orville H. Browning and Leonard Swett. To the War Department, to the Quartermaster General, to the Judge Advocate went Browning, sometimes in company with Swett, with the result that the hay contractors got "an extension of 30 days to enable them to fill their contracts—They discharged from arrest and proceedings in Court Martial suspended," according to Browning's diary.

Wearing a serenity somewhat blank and colorless, almost empty of humor, precise in the forms and manners, scrupulous and overly vain about his scruples, busy as a proverbial busy bee, Browning went here and there, saw everybody who was anybody, made the entries in his diary, two lines, ten lines, without elation or melancholy, earnest and careful. When a band of serenaders came to his Quincy home on the night of McClellan's nomination for President, Browning was earnest and scrupulous enough to tell them he was not a Democrat, yet sufficiently careful to repeat that McClellan was "a great general" and would have his support if elected President. In like manner he would support Frémont or any other administration. The name of Browning's intimate personal friend and political benefactor, then a candidate for re-election, escaped his mention. He may have wished that Lincoln might be President another four years, but the wish did not reach his tongue. It was likewise when Browning spoke before a crowd jubilating over the capture of Atlanta. Then too, as he wrote in his diary, "I carefully avoided subjects of a merely partizan character, and made no allusion to the Presidential candidates." On Friday, September 16, 1864, his entire diary entry read: "Honorable C. B. Lawrence dined with me today. Has urged me earnestly to declare myself in favor of the re election of Mr. Lincoln"

And the days ran on through the campaign and Browning was to wait perhaps for inquiries and solicitations from Lincoln and hearing none, was to hold back from any word that he would vote for Lincoln. His calls on the President seemed to increase and nearly always the favor he asked was granted him. "At night went to the Presidents and got order for release of Capt Saml Black." "At Presidents and got order for Judge Advocate Burnett to examine & report on cases . . . and of Captain Black" Where other advocates would have met delay in the case of Captain Black, Browning could go straight to the Executive Mansion and get immediate action. Nothing less than "an interview of three hours" with the President was accorded him one evening "in regard to Capt Blacks case." Or again one Sunday: "At night went to the Presidents, and got an order for the release of Ludwell Y. Browning, a rebel prisoner at Camp Douglas." Or again, meeting the President by appointment at the Arsenal: "Talked with President on behalf of E L Baker of Springfield [Illinois] about contract of E S Fowler & Co; also about discharge of son of Dr. Alf Baker, a boy of 16 who had been decoyed into enlisting—President promised to discharge him"

On behalf of Dixon & Zane, Browning took the President to see General Ramsay "about the Absterdam projectile." His clients had engaged an attorney with connections. "At night went to see the President about getting contract for Dickson [sic] & Zane for manufacture of Absterdam's projectiles." The errands of Browning, always legitimate, sometimes missions of mercy, were on occasion lucrative. "Went with Dr. Fowler and Goodell of Illinois to Commissary department on their business and got it arranged for which they are to pay me $5000" within two weeks. To both Browning and Lincoln the Jonas family could be thankful, the diary saying one day: "Went to the President and got Chas H Jonas, a rebel prisoner at Johnson's Island, paroled for three weeks to visit his father, who is dying," and a week later: "At night I went to the Presidents and got his promise to appoint Mrs Jonas Post Mistress at Quincy in place of her dec^{d} husband."

When the War Department questioned methods of J. W. Parrish & Company of St. Louis in ice contracts, Browning alone shortly adjusted the matter. In the case of the Parrish pork contract Swett worked with Browning, though it required several visits of the two of them at various offices to arrange for "proper" future deliveries of pork. On the President's request Browning left with him overnight a paper requiring the President's signature, which would authorize William Butler to bring out cotton from the South and sell it North. On the Banks Red River expedition Butler had lost his cotton and the money invested, but was going to try again. Permits for such trading were scarce. Lincoln again accommodated an old friend. "Finished Mr Butlers business," noted Browning, "by getting permit to bring out cotton signed by Secy of Treasury and the President."

Only once in his diary did Browning record an open rebuff from the President. Browning possibly omitted some points of circumstance in his entry, which read: "At night went to see the President on behalf of Mrs Fitz, a loyal widow of Mississippi owning a cotton plantation there, and from whom the U S Army had taken all her slaves amounting to 47, and 10,000 bushels of corn—She is now a refugee in St Louis, reduced to indigence She asks no compensation for her slaves, but wishes the government to give her a sufficient number of negroes out of those accumulated upon its hands to work her farm the ensuing season, and enable her to raise a crop of cotton, she to pay them out of the proceeds the same wages which the government pays those it employs. I made the proposition to the President thinking it reasonable and just, and worthy at least of being considered.

"He became very much excited, and did not discuss the proposition at all, but said with great vehemence he had rather take a rope and hang himself than to do it. That there were a great many poor women who had never had any property at all who were suffering as much as Mrs Fitz—that her condition was a necessary consequence of the rebellion, and that the government could not make good the losses occasioned by rebels. I reminded him that she was loyal, and that her property had been taken from her by her own government, and was now being used by it, and I thought it a case eminently proper for some sort of remuneration, and her demand reasonable, and certainly entitled to respectful consideration. He replied that she had lost no property—that her slaves were free when they were taken, and that she was entitled to no compensation.

"I called his attention to the fact that a portion of her slaves, at least, had been taken in 1862, before his proclamation, and put upon our gun boats, when he replied in a very excited manner that he had rather throw up, than to do what was asked, and would not do anything about it. I left him in no very good humor."

In the case of the young Frenchman named Shiff, Browning found the President more agreeable. A surgeon in the Confederate Army, captured at the Wilderness and brought to Old Capitol Prison in Washington, Shiff had signed an oath of allegiance to the United States Government and won release to join his mother in Paris. Now his mother was afraid that if the Confederates learned that her son had sworn loyalty to the Union, they would confiscate large property interests of hers in the South and stop collection of debts due her family. Therefore Browning petitioned leave for his client "to withdraw the oath" of allegiance to the Union.

"The President was very amiable, and seemed inclined to grant the request, but said he would consult Secy Seward, and see what his views were," noted Browning. "He sent for Seward. We waited a half hour, and he [Seward] did not come. The President then asked me to go over and see him." Seward on hearing an argument that Shiff as a surgeon was a noncombatant became "excited, boisterous and profane," saying that Shiff was one of the "d m d rebel belligerents" who could be thankful he was allowed to go away to Paris with his head on his shoulders. To Browning the next day the President said Seward had been over to see him, and had urged objections to granting the request, "that he did not see that any injury could result from it, but as Seward objected he believed he would do nothing" This closed the incident. But all the numerous past incidents of trust, affection, and benefits bestowed on him did not bring out Browning in favor of Lincoln for President. He said nothing for nor against a second term for Lincoln. To that extent Browning helped the McClellan ticket and cause.

Unionist serenaders from Baltimore arrived at the White House in late October, and facing them, Lincoln made reference to a Seward remark "construed by some into a threat that if I shall be beaten at the election I will, between then and the end of my constitutional term, do what I may be able to ruin the government." Seward's speech some six weeks earlier had dwelt on the paralyzing effects that would follow a Democratic victory with the Chicago peace platform. Seward had inquired as to who could then "vouch for the safety of the country," meaning to imply that McClellan would be helpless to control armed and disorderly peace factions of his party. Democratic newspapers set up a clamor, repeated in many ways their charge that the Lincoln Administration aimed to keep its power whatever the verdict at the polls in November. Lincoln told the Maryland serenaders that in contrast "others regard the fact that the Chicago Convention adjourned, not *sine die*, but to meet again, if called to do so by a particular individual, as the intimation of a purpose that if their nominee shall be elected he will at once seize control of the government." He hoped the people would suffer no uneasiness on either point, delivering himself of the most momentous words he spoke during the campaign:

"I am struggling to maintain the government, not to overthrow it. I am struggling, especially, to prevent others from overthrowing it. I therefore say that if I shall live I shall remain President until the 4th of next March; and that whoever shall be constitutionally elected therefor, in November, shall be duly installed as President on the 4th of March; and that, in the interval, I shall do my utmost that whoever is to hold the helm for the next voyage shall start with the best possible chance to save the ship.

"This is due to the people both on principle and under the Constitution. Their will, constitutionally expressed, is the ultimate law for all. If they should deliberately resolve to have immediate peace, even at the loss of their country and their liberty, I know not the power or the right to resist them. It is their own business, and they must do as they please with their own. I believe, however, they are still resolved to preserve their country and their liberty; and in this, in office or out of it, I am resolved to stand by them.

"I may add that in this purpose—to save the country and its liberties—no classes of people seem so nearly unanimous as the soldiers in the field and the sailors afloat. Do they not have the hardest of it? Who should quail when they do not? God bless the soldiers and seamen, with all their brave commanders."

This was reassurance to political independents such as Edward Everett, now trying to swing to Lincoln the votes that had come to him in 1860 on the Bell-Everett ticket of the Constitutional party. A call signed by eminent and influential Democrats of the past endorsed the Lincoln-Johnson ticket. The call asked what kind of a Democratic party it was that excluded John A. Dix, Alexander T. Stewart, Theodore Roosevelt, Sr., R. B. Roosevelt, Peter Cooper, John A. Logan, John M. Palmer, and many others who till now had had no political home except the Democratic party. "If these men are not Democrats, who are?"

"Should the soldier in the field have the right to vote in elections?" Two Union-party pamphlets called the roll on the various States. *Harper's Weekly* summarized the points. In New York the Union men passed a soldier-vote bill by 65 Yeas to 59 Copperhead Nays; Governor Seymour vetoed the bill, but the Unionists went over his head and against prolonged Copperhead opposition procured a soldier-vote amendment to the State constitution. In New Hampshire the law passed the legislature by 175 to 105. In Rhode Island, Connecticut, Maine, Michigan, Ohio, and other States the only opposition was from McClellan-for-President men. In New Jersey 31 Copperhead Nays against 19 Union Yeas defeated the soldier vote, and likewise in Delaware. In Michigan the soldiers in the field were accorded the ballot over the opposition of "the *Detroit Free Press* and the entire Copperhead press." In California, Iowa, Minnesota, and Missouri it was Union men against Copperheads that won the soldier's right to vote. In Indiana a Copperhead legislature naturally refused it. In the adjacent State of Ohio in the October election, out of 55,000 soldier votes a majority of 48,000 were for the Union-party candidates. Edward W. Harrington, Copperhead candidate for governor in New Hampshire, was quoted as hoping "every Union soldier would come home in a box." An Ohio State senator was quoted: "No Government ever survived the vote of its armies."

Twenty-nine regiments and two batteries of Hoosiers were in Sherman's army. In the hope that some of them might be sent home to vote in the October election Governor Morton telegraphed the President, "While we do not urge that any troops be withdrawn from where they are needed, we suggest a mere request to the commanding General upon the matter." So Lincoln took his pen and worked on a message dated September 19 that would convince the flaring and blunt-spoken Sherman of a genuine emergency. By a special messenger who had traveled the tortuous route from

POLITICAL DIALOGUES.

Soldiers on their Right to Vote, and the Men they should support.

SOLDIERS' PEACE ARGUMENT:

MOBILE,
HATTERAS,
PORT ROYAL,
FORT DONELSON,
SHILOH, VICKSBURG,
DRAINSVILLE, CORINTH,
GAINESVILLE, FORT HENRY
CEDER MOUNTAIN, BELMONT,
ROANOKE ISLAND, SHARPSBURG,
ISLAND NO. 10, CEDAR MOUNTAIN,
PORT HUDSON, PEA RIDGE, OPEQUAN,
WINCHESTER, ANTIETAM, GETTYSBURG,
WILLIAMSBURGH, VICKSBURG, MILL SPRING,
SOUTH MOUNTAIN, FORT PULASKI, ATLANTA,
MURFREESBORO', NEW ORLEANS, COAL HARBOR,
CHICKAMAUGA, SPOTSYLVANIA, REAMS' STATION,
CHATTANOOGA, LOOK-OUT MOUNTAIN, FISHER'S HILL
MALVERN HILL

Headlines and pyramidal type arrangement from the top and the bottom of a circular of the National Union party. From the Barrett collection.

the White House to Sherman's headquarters, Sherman was handed a letter from the President, tore it open and read: "The State election of Indiana occurs on the 11th of October, and the loss of it, to the friends of the government, would go far toward losing the whole Union cause. The bad effect upon the November election, and especially the giving the State government to those who will oppose the war in every possible way, are too much to risk, if it can possibly be avoided. The draft proceeds, notwithstanding its strong tendency to lose us the State. Indiana is the only important State, voting in October, whose soldiers cannot vote in the field. Anything you can safely do to let her soldiers, or any part of them, go home and vote at the State election will be greatly in point. They need not remain for the Presidential election, but may return to you at once. This is in no sense an order, but is merely intended to impress you with the importance, to the army itself, of your doing all you safely can, yourself being the judge of what you can safely do."

Sherman read it carefully, of course, and considered what he might do for anxious men in the North who so thoroughly understood his own viewpoint. Then began moves of the Confederate forces near him, of enough menace to his long thin line of communications northward so that he would have been taking risks unjust to his army had he let Hoosiers go home to vote. From posts in Tennessee and Kentucky a few Indiana regiments went to their home townships and precincts to ballot, most of them in disapproval of the Democratic Copperhead majority of the 1863 legislature which refused to let them vote in the field. A formidable political faction it was which had the State legislature formally declare that "while the President persists in his abolition policy Indiana will never voluntarily contribute another man or another dollar to be used for such wicked, inhuman and unholy principles."

The draft meanwhile proceeded. The relentless dragnet moved. Grant and Sherman wanted the men. On the draft being postponed a few days in early September for technical reasons, Seward in a speech, published in newspapers, declared the draft would never be enforced, Halleck writing Sherman . . . "these infernal old humbugs cannot tell the truth when it is to their interest to do so." Sherman telegraphed Stanton that if Lincoln modified the draft or "to the extent of one man" wavered in its execution, he was gone forever. "Even the army would vote against him." Stanton sent Sherman's telegram over the Northwest as notice to politicians that conscription must be enforced. Nevertheless able politicians of tried years came to Lincoln predicting that the draft would bring defeat in November. "Leading Republicans all over the country," noted Nicolay and Hay, "fearing the effect of the draft upon the elections, begged the President to withdraw the call or suspend operations under it." Cameron advised against it in Pennsylvania. Chase telegraphed from Ohio urging a three weeks' suspension. To an Ohio committee earnestly requesting suspension until after the November elections, Lincoln quietly answered, "What is the Presidency worth to me if I have no country?"

Twice came Governor Morton of Indiana, whose soldiers could not vote in the field, applying for the return of all Indiana soldiers possible on election day. And at Lincoln's refusal to go over the heads of his generals and order the soldiers home to vote, it was suggested that if Indiana went Democratic she could give no more help to the Government. Lincoln met this point: "It is better that we should both be beaten than that the forces in front of the enemy should be weakened and perhaps defeated on account of the absence of these men." Morton suggested that no Indiana troops be kept in hospitals outside his State and that all troops unfit for service be sent home. On these points Lincoln got action. And Stanton had Lincoln's approval in ordering home from Sherman's army for campaigning in Indiana six prominent Hoosier officers, along with Major Generals Logan and Frank Blair to stump Indiana and near-by States. In fact, Logan at a later time wrote to Sherman that "when I left on leave after the Atlanta campaign, to canvass for Mr. Lincoln, I did it at the special and private request of the President. This I kept to myself and never made it public." Logan was criticized as speechmaking when he should be fighting. Not even to Sherman, however, would he at the time reveal that the President had put him up to it.

Black Jack Logan had been a power among the Democrats in the days before the war. And a brother-in-law of Mrs. Logan, on the news of his coming home to campaign, bet a span of mules against $500 in greenbacks that Black Jack would be for McClellan when he took the platform to speak. At his first speech some of the crowd, according to newspapers, were moved to tears by his appeal for the Union and Lincoln. When it was over they went to a barn and got him the span of mules his speech had won. Through part of the campaign he was hauled by these mules from town to town, a crowd sometimes unhitching the mules and themselves taking hold of the tongue and the whiffletrees and pulling Logan's buggy.

Sherman, like Grant, was reserved in the national political fray. Each had in his army a proportion of able soldiers who favored McClellan and hated "race equality." Sherman wrote his brother as though certain comfortable stay-at-homes of the North had little right to be balloting. "No man should vote now unless he has a musket on his shoulder." And was Sherman himself on an odd spot? "I am not a voter . . . not a citizen of any State unless it be Louisiana." Howsoever, "if government must be inflicted I suppose Lincoln is the best choice." This was in a private letter. And when the mercurial strumpets of the *New York Herald* wrote a lie peddled industriously by the pro-McClellan press, Sherman from "Headquarters, in the Field" wrote October 11 to John C. Hamilton, Esq., a reply short and to the point, which the pro-Lincoln press published:

"My Dear Sir,—There is not one word of truth in the paragraph you sent me cut from the New York Herald of September 20. I never thought, said, or wrote that McClellan would get 'ninety-nine out of every hundred' votes in the army. I am as ignorant of the political bias of the men of this army as you are at a distance of a thousand miles, and I would as soon think of tampering with a soldier's religion as with his preference for men. I have not and shall not attempt to influence a vote in the coming struggle. I believe Mr. Lincoln has done the best he could. With respect, etc."

Besides nailing a lie, this carried the positive stride of the North. With the Administration it said Yes to more war immediately as the only way to end future wars between States of the Union. Against it the Democrats had mainly negatives: avoiding war, avoiding abolition, avoiding issues beyond evasion. The chairman of the board of directors of the Illinois Central Railroad, William H. Osborn, in October in New York discussed evasion of issues in the campaign. It was a private chat in the office of Abram S. Hewitt, a gun-barrel-iron maker. To Hewitt and a son of Peter Cooper, Osborn told why he believed them mistaken in their guess that McClellan would win in November. Having seen both Lincoln and McClellan at close range in his position earlier as president of the Illinois Central, Osborn gave his blunt opinion: "No, Lincoln will beat McClellan, for he has the courage of his convictions and *does things*, but McClellan, while able and great in preparation, lacks confidence in himself at critical times. Even if elected he would be a failure in the responsible position of President. He could, and did, build the best and strongest bridges on our road, but I always noticed that at the finish he hesitated to give the order to send over the first train."

The draft marched on. But not in the one large city most hostile to Lincoln, not where draft and race riots the year before had for three days overthrown the Government, not in New York City. There under conditions some wit had discovered the draft was not put into motion. *Harper's Weekly* put it briefly: "The War Department has credited New York City with 18,448 men enlisted in the navy from April 15, 1861, to February 24, 1864. There was a surplus over the last draft of 1,137. This surplus, together with the naval enlistments and 1,616 recruits enlisted under the last call, amounts to 22,010. The quota of the city is 23,124, leaving a balance in favor of the Government of 1,114 men. There will therefore be no draft in this city." In other words, if a boy from Ohio or Iowa became a gunner or seaman on a warship, the enlistment was credited to the quota of New York City if that was where he signed the papers. The device was raw, but it fended off disorder in a community peculiar to itself.

In preparation for soldier voting in November the New York secretary of state, Chauncey Depew, went to Washington for required data as to where New York troops were located, scattered over the South in all the armies. Stanton in a flurry of temper said that such information given to politicians would reach the newspapers and help the Confederates. He sent Depew away sore. Meeting Congressman Washburne, Depew said he would have to publish a card in the New York newspapers that the soldier vote could not be taken because of a decision of Secretary Stanton, which would result in the Electoral College vote of New York being lost to Lincoln. According to Depew, Washburne answered: "You don't know Lincoln. He is as good a politician as he is a President, and if there was no other way to get those votes he would go round with a carpetbag and collect them himself." So Washburne went straight to Lincoln, had an immediate interview, and in fifteen minutes an orderly let Depew into Stanton's office. What Depew had asked of Stanton a half-dozen times before was now granted with even temper and courtesy. Depew left Washington on an evening train with a list giving the location of every organization of New York troops.

One State received special attention from Lincoln. "He said he was anxious about Pennsylvania," noted Hay just after the October 11 elections, "because of her enormous weight and influence, which, cast definitely into

A soldier's ballot. From the Barrett collection.

the scale, w^{d} close the campaign, & leave the people free to look again with their whole hearts to the cause of the country." More than a third of the soldiers voted for McClellan. "Serious evils" had attended the draft in Pennsylvania, noted the *Appleton's Cyclopaedia* observer. "The large sums offered in some places in the competition for men have demoralized many of the people, and the most atrocious frauds connected with the system have become common. The men of some of the poorer counties have been nearly exhausted by their volunteers being credited to richer counties which paid higher bounties. Of the number of men to whom bounties have been paid, it is believed that not one-fourth have been actually placed in the ranks of the army, and even those who have joined it have probably not, on an average, received for their own use one-half of the bounty paid *for* them." One decision of the State supreme court had held the draft law unconstitutional. Then a changed court had reversed the decision.

Now was at hand the confusion, favoritism, and corruption which Lincoln, Stanton, Fry, and Schenck had tried to correct with a conscription act that would end the buying of substitutes. When a Pennsylvania boy in a poor county enlisted as a substitute, taking the bounty paid him by a man in a rich county, the boy was credited as from the rich county. And the poor county to maintain its quota had to dig up someone else for the army. For these and other reasons the political sentiment in Pennsylvania was delicately balanced. To Lincoln it was darkly doubtful.

Just after the October elections he sent for Alexander K. McClure, as he had several times before in connection with Pennsylvania matters, as he did in the previous spring when Dana heard Seward say to Lincoln, "My advice is to send for Aleck McClure." Now Lincoln and McClure discussed the October political weather in the Keystone State, Lincoln winding up with a request that McClure give his personal services at the party State headquarters continuously till the November election. Cameron was running the headquarters, McClure reminded Lincoln, and might take it as "obtrusive" if McClure stepped in. "Of course, I understand that. But if Cameron

a refuge from ANARCHY.

Annexed is the *Pennsylvania Electoral Ticket*, pledged to *Abraham Lincoln* and *Andrew Johnson*. Let us **VOTE FOR IT**; let us **WORK FOR IT.** The election takes place on Tuesday, November 8. Every consideration of enlightened self-interest, every sentiment of honor, every feeling of humanity, and every dictate of patriotism, demands that we maintain the present efficient and patriotic NATIONAL ADMINISTRATION. Let us show ourselves worthy of our fathers who made the UNION, and worthy of our brothers and sons who have DIED to defend it. We inherited its blessings, let us transmit them unimpaired to our children.

By order of the National Union City Executive Committee.

ROBERT T. GILL, WM. R. LEEDS, } *Secretaries.*

WILLIAM ELLIOT, *President.*

☞Polls open at 8 o'clock, A. M., and close at 8 o'clock, P. M.

Closing part of a circular issued in Philadelphia. From the Barrett collection.

shall invite you can you give your time fully?" "Gladly." And McClure went away and soon had a nice letter from Cameron inviting him to come on to the Philadelphia headquarters, which McClure did. Thus in the final weeks of the campaign Lincoln had the leaders of two factions watching and helping each other. McClure found Cameron "mortified" over the October showing of Pennsylvania in comparison with Ohio and Indiana, and believed Cameron was giving every possible effort toward winning in November. "I never was at headquarters except for confidential conference with Cameron himself," wrote McClure. "And, as requested by Lincoln, I wrote him fully every night my impressions of the progress we were making."

A week passed and Lincoln sent Postmaster General Dennison to talk things over and McClure had to tell Dennison the State still looked doubtful, that if in another week it looked no better he would go to Washington and personally report to Lincoln. Another week and no material advantage had been gained that McClure could see; he thus advised Lincoln from day to day. "And I telegraphed Lincoln that I would see him at ten o'clock that night. I found him waiting, and he exhibited great solicitude as to Pennsylvania . . . if he lost New York and with it Pennsylvania on the home vote, the moral effect of his triumph would be broken and his power to prosecute the war and make peace would be greatly impaired. His face was shadowed with sorrow when I told him that I saw no reasonable prospect of carrying Pennsylvania on the home vote."

On the whole situation having been presented, Lincoln inquired what was to be done. McClure said it was "simple and easy." Grant was idle in front of Petersburg, Sheridan had won all possible victories in the Shenandoah Valley. "And if 5,000 Pennsylvania soldiers could be furloughed home from each army the election could be carried without a doubt." Lincoln brightened and McClure went on, "Of course, you can trust Grant to make the suggestion to him to furlough 5,000 Pennsylvania troops for two weeks?" Lincoln made no answer. McClure felt disconcerted but went on, "Surely, Mr. President, you can trust Grant with a confidential suggestion to furlough Pennsylvania troops?" Lincoln still having nothing to say, McClure pressed, "It can't be possible that Grant is not your friend." Lincoln hesitated, and McClure was sure he caught the slow answer, "Well, McClure, I have no reason to believe that Grant prefers my election to that of McClellan."

To McClure this was appalling. He reminded Lincoln that when he, McClure, in that very room had voiced an almost universal demand for Grant's dismissal that Lincoln alone had stood by Grant and had replied, "I can't spare this man—he fights!" To this warm reminder Lincoln said nothing or, as McClure had it, "as usual answered intemperance of speech by silence." McClure then suggested that General Meade was commander of the Army of the Potomac. "Send an order to him from yourself to furlough 5,000 Pennsylvania soldiers home for two weeks, and send that order with some trusted friend of the War Department, with the suggestion to Meade that your agent be permitted to bring the order back with him." Lincoln's slow response to this was, "I reckon that can be done," and to McClure's query, "What about Sheridan?" a brightening face like a noonday sun emerging from a dark cloud, "Oh, Phil Sheridan, he's all right."

McClure's transcript of this conversation with Lincoln, Nicolay would say, was fantastic if not false. Others who knew McClure as well and perhaps better would say McClure could not be far wrong as to essentials. The upshot of this conversation with Lincoln McClure recorded: "Before I left his room that night he had made his arrangements to send messengers to Meade and Sheridan. The order was sent to Meade, and he permitted it to be returned to the President, but Sheridan needed no order. The 10,000 Pennsylvania soldiers were furloughed during the week."

"There was a constant succession of telegrams from all parts of the country," wrote Dana of the War Office, "requesting that leave of absence be extended to this or that officer, in order that his district at home might have the benefit of his vote and political influence. Furloughs were asked for private soldiers whose presence in close districts was deemed of especial importance, and there was a widespread demand that men on detached service and convalescents in hospitals be sent home. All the power and influence of the War Department, then something enormous from the vast expenditure and extensive relations of the war, was employed to secure the re-election of Mr. Lincoln. The political struggle was most intense, and the interest taken in it, both in the White House and in the War Department, was almost painful."

Of the President as a vote-getter Horace White of the *Chicago Tribune* would repeat and emphasize these points as essential: "Mr. Lincoln never gave his assent, so far as my knowledge goes, to any plan or project for getting votes that would not have borne the full light of day. At the same time, he had no objection to the getting of votes by the pledge of offices, nor was he too particular what kind of men got the offices. His preference was always for good men; but he could not resist pressure where persons were concerned, even though his conscience told him that he was doing wrong."

Governor Seymour appointed some fifty civilians to oversee the soldier voting, commissioning each one "to be present as an Inspector on the part of the Democratic party of the State of New York," leaving the Republican State Committee to choose and pay its own inspectors. Two of these Seymour inspectors were found to have in their possession bundles of voting papers to which the names of soldiers and officers had been signed, according to one Inspector Ferry, who testified before a military commission in Baltimore that he and his associate Inspector Edward J. Donohue had written the names. Their trial in the last week of October was open to the public. The *New York World's* cries of tyranny in its editorial columns were oddly refuted in its own news-column reports and those of its rivals, which covered the testimony in considerable detail. The military commission found Donohue and Ferry guilty of forgery and impersonation of a United States officer, and sentenced them to imprisonment for life.

Lincoln considered reports and supplemental reports of the case, the opinion of Major General Lew Wallace and Judge Advocate Joseph Holt that the facts were of grave import, "conspiracy fully exhibited," the disclosure complete of "a carefully matured plan for defrauding the soldiers of the State of New York now in the field of their votes at the approaching Presidential election." Lincoln signed his approval of life sentences in prison for Donohue and Ferry. Commissioners from Governor Seymour came to Lincoln with claims that only the State of New York had the right to try the prisoners, admitted that "irregularities" may have been committed, but no crime. Furthermore, the commissioners from Seymour wished added information as to why others of Seymour's inspectors had been thrown into close confinement in Carroll Prison, given coarse food, straw sacks to sleep on; no newspapermen let in to see them, no friend allowed to see them until Seymour's commissioners talked through the bars with them. One of the commissioners, Amasa J. Parker, said after their interview with the President that he received them "very cordially, heard what they had to say, told them he would examine into the matter of the arrests and see that no injustice was done; but he did not promise anything, and while the interview was very pleasant it was not entirely satisfactory to the Commissioners." They went to Albany and so told Governor Seymour.

Seymour could not with ease take this from Lincoln. He had his State judge advocate general prepare a ram's-horn blast. The *New York World* printed it in full. Suppose all the charges were true, he inquired, what had a Federal military commission to do with them? The prime movers were "abolition journals" and "conspirators at Washington," who used "government spies and pimps" in the interest of "military despotism." Page after page of hoarse vituperation hardly intended as argument, as though in the gravity of the case convenient allegations would be accepted as fact. "A shameless court" had been the "tool" of an "abolition cabal" which ruled from Washington. The leading witness "has always been an abolitionist" and was "manifestly a sanctimonious villain." The convicted Donohue "admitted that he had signed to certain voting papers a fictitious name as a certifying officer." But what of it? Was not Donohue the victim of an "insensate" prosecutor whose case rested on "Mr. Lincoln's stool-pigeons"?

The three-line newspaper item saying that President Lincoln while paying the soldiers in greenbacks was himself drawing his salary in gold had in October grown to more lines that went the rounds of the opposition press as follows: "Jeff. Davis's salary is nominally twenty-five thousand a year, but by the depreciation of the Confederate money is equal to about fifteen hundred dollars, and on this practically he has to live. Abraham Lincoln's salary is legally twenty-five thousand dollars a year. But his legal-tender money, having depreciated to less than half its nominal value, he refuses to take, and demands and receives his pay in gold or gold certificates, while the soldiers of his army have to take their pay in greenbacks. Isn't this patriotic and honest in Old Abe, and ought not he to be re-elected to another four years' hard money for himself, and of largely depreciated money for the people?" In reply to this fabrication a letter of F. E. Spinner, United States Treasurer, whose signed name in facsimile adorned greenbacks, published in Administration journals, held "this story perhaps as true as other slanders that have been heaped upon the head of Mr. Lincoln." Mr. Spinner had "great doubts as to the propriety of answering this foul falsehood," but he would make a statement in official form:

"The salary of the President is, in accordance with law, paid in warrant drafts on the Treasury of the United States for the amount, less the income tax, which have been sent him regularly monthly. Instead of drawing his money on these drafts, he has been in the habit of leaving it for a long time without interest. In one case all his salary so remained for eleven months. On several occasions I solicited the President to draw what was due him, urging that he was losing largely in interest on the amount due him. He asked me, 'Who gains my loss?' On my answering, 'The United States,' he replied, 'Then as it goes for the good of the country, let it remain. The Treasury needs it more than I do.'

"Having at length satisfied the President that it was necessary to the closing of my annual accounts that the drafts on the Treasury that he held should be presented and paid, he indorsed and handed them to me. I drew the amount in United States notes, and placed it to his credit as a temporary loan at five per cent, per annum, payable, principal and interest, in greenbacks. Since then his salary has been from time to time mostly invested in the stocks of the United States, purchased at current rates by his friends for him. The interest of these stocks is payable in coin. When this interest became due, I tried to induce him to draw it. Failing in doing so, the amount due him was sent by Honorable John C. Underwood, Judge of the United States Court for the District of Virginia. The result of his interview with the President is best told in the letter of Judge Underwood to me, which is herewith enclosed to you.

"I have caused an investigation to be made of the transactions of the President with the receipt of his salary, and the investment of the sums in United States stocks, and enclose you herewith the letter of Le Roy Tuttle, Esq., the Assistant Cashier, from which it appears that Mr. Lincoln, from his forbearance in collecting his dues, has lost at least four thousand dollars, and which he has virtually given to the people of the United States."

Along the Canadian border and the shore lines of the Great Lakes, from the British end of the suspension bridge at Niagara Falls to the high walls holding the Confederate prisoners at Camp Douglas on Cottage Grove Avenue, Chicago, there were in the summer and fall of '64 plots, adventures, explosions, robberies, espionage, propaganda. From the dwindling hoard of Confederate gold, Jacob Thompson of Mississippi, formerly Secretary of the Interior under President Buchanan, passed money to Sons of Liberty for armed revolts to be started in various States. "Lincoln had the power and would certainly use it to reëlect himself," wrote Thompson later in a report to Judah P. Benjamin at Richmond, "and there was no hope but in force. The belief was entertained and freely expressed, that by a bold, vigorous and concerted movement . . . Illinois, Indiana, and Ohio could be seized and held." To Mason and Slidell, Thompson sent the news: "In order to arouse the people, political meetings, called 'peace meetings,' have been held and inflammatory addresses delivered, and wherever orators have expressed themselves for peace with restoration of the Union and, if that cannot be, then peace on any terms, the cheers and clamor of the masses have known no bounds." Plans were laid in detail for a general uprising on an appointed day, seizure of arsenals at Indianapolis, Springfield, Chicago, and

Columbus, release of Confederate prisoners at four camps, arming of prisoners, overthrow of the State governments in Ohio, Indiana, Illinois, Missouri, formation of a Northwestern Confederacy. Then they would dictate peace.

The uprising collapsed. A few stolen ships on the Great Lakes were lost before they could be used. A bank robbery by Confederate soldiers who suddenly threw off their disguises in St. Albans, Vermont, killed one innocent bystander, and on livery-stable mounts made their way to Canada, resulted in proceedings before one Judge Coursol, who let the raiders off with $87,000 of cash belonging to Vermont depositors. On General Dix's instructing military commanders to cross the Canadian border in pursuit of robbers and murderers, the Confederate Government at Richmond hoped the United States would soon be at war with Great Britain. Lincoln joined with General Dix in resentment over robbery and murder committed by Confederate raiders who went unpunished in Canada, but he also gently insisted that no department commander should be allowed to embroil the United States in a war with a British Dominion. General Dix defended what he termed "the right of hot pursuit" but the President required him to revoke his instructions about crossing the Canadian border.

After conferences with London the Canadian Government sought the St. Albans bank-robbers and killers, and arrested them, while the Canadian Parliament reproved Judge Coursol, who had released them, and suspended the Judge from office. The leader of the St. Albans raiders, it was brought out in a trial at Montreal, was no common, ordinary bank robber at all but Lieutenant Bennett H. Young, a commissioned officer of the army of the Confederate States of America. From Clement C. Clay, an associate of Jacob Thompson, Lieutenant Young had received $400 with which to finance the St. Albans raid. "The attack on St. Albans," said the court, Mr. Justice Smith, in turning the prisoners loose, "must therefore be regarded as a hostile expedition, undertaken and carried out under the authority of the so-called Confederate States by one of the officers of their army." Higher up were Canadian authorities who rated Mr. Justice Smith a pettifogger and worse. They had Lieutenant Young and his raiders arrested again for a trial they hoped would be more in accord with Anglo-Saxon customs. Furthermore, the Canadian Government eventually refunded the United States $58,000 in gold as payment for the $87,000 of gold and greenbacks found on the raiders when arrested but which disappeared after their release by Judge Coursol. Also the chief of police of Montreal was forced to resign for having been so blundering or corrupt as to let the robbers out of his custody with the $87,000 they did not have on them when again arrested.

John Yates Beall commanded twenty Confederate soldiers disguised as passengers on an unarmed merchant vessel, the *Philo Parsons*, plying between Detroit and Sandusky. Beall suddenly ordered revolvers out and took possession of the steamer and what money was in the office. Meeting another unarmed steamer, the *Island Queen*, they took what they wanted aboard of her. Then they put the passengers ashore, lashed her to the *Philo Parsons*, took her out in Lake Erie and scuttled her. The plan now was to capture a Lake Erie war steamer, the *Michigan*, and use her to release Confederate prisoners on Johnson's Island in Sandusky Bay. But the plan didn't work out, seventeen of Beall's men saying it was too rash. Beall and his crew scattered over Canada, to be heard from later.

Assistant Secretary of War Dana brought Lincoln and Stanton into a hurried conference after church one Sunday. The Union spy who had wormed his way into the confidence of the Richmond Government and its agents in Canada was again in Washington with a dispatch and again in the War Department the seal was broken and the paper read. "It showed unequivocally," wrote Dana, "that the Confederate agents were making use of that country [Canada] as a starting point for warlike raids to be directed against frontier towns in Vermont." Stanton thought this dispatch should be kept for evidence to be used in dealing with the British Government. But Stanton sent Dana to the President to arrange for a discussion of what to do. Lincoln was going to church to hear Dr. Gurley preach. He would meet Stanton and Dana after church. They met in Stanton's office and Stanton gave his reasons for retaining the dispatch. Lincoln turned to Stanton's assistant. "Well, Dana?" And Dana said it would be too bad to stop such a channel of information and that it would be stopped if they kept the paper now in their possession.

"Oh," said the President, as Dana quoted him, "I think you can manage that. Capture the messenger, take the dispatch from him by force, put him in prison, and then let him escape. If he has made Benjamin and Clay believe his lies so far, he won't have any difficulty in telling them new ones that will answer for this case."

And this foxy piece of espionage suggested by the President was followed out. Carrying the dispatch and riding toward Washington on a south road where troops of General Augur, commanding the District of Columbia, were ready and waiting, the spy was arrested and searched, the dispatch seized, the spy held in prison. Then Lincoln's suggestion "Let him escape" was followed. The spy conveniently escaped. And the spy met Lincoln's challenge that if he had so far made the Confederate high officials believe his lies he would find no difficulty in telling them new ones to fit this case. According to Dana, he shot himself in one arm, showed Dana the wound, and Dana thought it was a nice specimen of a wound, an impressive exhibit for the young man leaving for Canada to show Thompson and Clay, saying, "They caught me and I got shot breaking away." Dana rated the youth one of the best actors he had ever seen and a brave, resourceful secret-service operative who rendered valuable aid to the Government. Lincoln seemed a little suspicious, as though any spy until long tested would bear plenty of watching.

The Confederate operations from Canada annoyed the North. But they were more noisy than effective. Jacob Thompson, who was Jeff Davis's personal choice for the work of embroiling the Northwestern States in an uprising, lacked the required touch. Thompson moved at cost and found the result was a rubber dagger limp on the hide of a rhinoceros. The messages between him and Richmond were carried by the young Union spy who stayed long enough in Washington on each trip for the communication to be copied and a properly sealed new envelope fabricated. Dana, Stanton, and Lincoln studied these messages and moved toward checkmate. That these activities of the Richmond Government flared on the Canadian border in the fourth year of the war was ascribed in part to a Confederate belief in the necessity of defeating Lincoln and in part to a desperate hope that a war which it seemed could not be won against Grant and Sherman might be saved through internal convulsions in the Northern States. The secret service of Thompson, he reported to Richmond, required "expenditures on all accounts" of about $300,000. His operations gave an illusion of results attained until the fall of Atlanta and the smashes of Sheridan in the Shenandoah Valley changed the Northern mood of the-war-is-a-failure.

Reading at Meade's headquarters the Richmond journals to be sent on to the War Department and the Executive Mansion, Colonel Theodore Lyman wrote in mid-October, "At no time during the war have the Rebel papers talked so desperately; they speak of the next month settling the questions, and of arming the negroes." Until now the Confederates had not wanted guns in the hands of the black men. Their man power having run low, they now seriously considered giving freedom to Negroes who would fight for their former masters. Lyman noted that while the Army of the Potomac was not putting on any showy combats, "They perfectly hate what we are doing now, going a couple of miles and fortifying, then going two more and fortifying again; then making a sudden rush, taking a position and a lot of cannon, and again fortifying *that.* All these moves being a part of what we may call a throttling plan. Their struggles, though often apparently successful, do them thus far no good. They flank us on the Weldon railroad, and brush off 2000 prisoners: no use! we hold the road. They flank us again at the Pegram house and capture 1000 more: no use; we hold the Pegram position and add it to former acquisitions."

One of the old and established New England Lymans, an officer of the old Army of the Potomac not yet become a thoroughly co-ordinated body responsive to Grant, Lyman analyzed himself: "How shall I vote? I don't know that I shall be given the chance; but, if I am, I shall vote for the blue-blooded Abraham. It was with a feeling of depression that I heard the first rumors that the Dems had carried Pennsylvania, Ohio, and Indiana; and when the truth came out, I felt glad. This proves to me that I look on the Mac party with misgivings." Nevertheless without grumbling he would confess, "I can't be enthusiastic about such a government as Lincoln's, when I see, under my nose, the petty tyranny and persecution they practice against subordinate officers." Then he named "a petty, scheming, political officer" who sent letters to newspapers and telegrams to Stanton about the enthusiasm for Lincoln in the army, and was looked on with favor, while another officer of proven valor as one of Sedgwick's staff, being a McClellan man who talked openly for McClellan, was "without any warning mustered out of the service."

Stanton could use an iron hand. Lyman was correct. Stanton had cleaned out some of McClellan's political palaverers who were third-rate fighters, and then in his bureaucratic and indiscriminate purging had unjustly dismissed McClellan men of fine records as soldiers. Lyman's resentment about it ran to an extreme, however, and was allied to the vague uneasiness of Meade and his circle about Grant, Lincoln, "the abandonment of slavery," and the war. It was a matter of temperaments not adjusted to each other, along with shadows inherited from the early Army of the Potomac. Meade in an October letter wrote his wife: "I note all you say of politics, but in the army we take but little interest except earnestly to wish the election was over, as we see, until it is, nothing else will be thought of and no proper thought given to the war. It is generally believed here that McClellan has very little chance. I think he is very unfortunate in his friends and backers. I see the *Chronicle* announces me as a supporter of Mr. Lincoln and is pleased to class me among the ill-treated generals who have been driven into the opposition. Well, the one has as much authority for his assertion as the other."

In more than one case officious army politicians refused a pass, previously promised, to a soldier wearing a McClellan campaign badge. Friends of one such soldier brought his case before Lincoln, who investigated, sent for the soldier, and then handed him a pass in the President's own handwriting along with a handshake and "God bless you, my boy. Show them that. It'll take you home." Another instance was more flagrant. A lifelong Democrat and a McClellan man serving as adjutant general to the commander of the defenses of Baltimore, E. W. Andrews, went to a Democratic mass meeting in September to accommodate some old friends who invited him. "As I could not well refuse, I agreed to go for a few minutes only," ran Andrews's story. "To my surprise and annoyance, I was called on by the audience for a speech, and the calls were so persistent that I was placed in a most embarrassing position. Forced to say something, I contented myself with brief expression of my high regard for McClellan as a soldier, and a statement of my intention to vote for him. I made no reference to Mr. Lincoln and soon left the hall."

Stanton the next day ordered that Andrews be mustered out of the service, no reason assigned, no questions asked Andrews. Word came to Andrews that Stanton, on hearing of Andrews standing before an audience and saying he would vote for McClellan, raged and spoke threats of what he would do to Andrews. Having always been an unwavering Union man, having a brother and three sons in the army with clean records, Andrews went to Washington and interested a Republican member of Congress, who went to Lincoln and asked whether Stanton had done this thing with his order, knowledge, or consent. The President's answer, as the Congressman carried it to Andrews, was immediate: "I know nothing about it. Of course Stanton does a thousand things in his official character which I can know nothing about, and which it is not necessary that I should know anything about." Lincoln heard from the Congressman that Andrews was a man of parts, had been admitted to the bar in Connecticut and practiced law, later becoming a Congregational minister holding the pastorate of the Broadway Tabernacle Congregational Church, appointed by President Fillmore a member of the West Point Board of Visitors, again entering

UNCONDITIONAL

UNION TICKET.

For President,

ABRAHAM LINCOLN,

OF ILLINOIS.

For Vice-President,

ANDREW JOHNSON,

OF TENNESSEE.

Specimen soldier's ballot

law practice in the State of New York and leaving it in '62 to raise a regiment of infantry with himself captain of one company. Andrews's speech at the Baltimore meeting had been short and was that of a friend of McClellan and not one of the Lincoln-haters. Having heard the case the President gave his opinion:

"Well, that's no reason. Andrews has as good a right to hold on to his Democracy, if he chooses, as Stanton had to throw his overboard. If I should muster out all my generals who avow themselves Democrats there would be a sad thinning out of commanding officers in the army. No! when the military duties of a soldier are fully and faithfully performed, he can manage his politics in his own way; we've no more to do with them than with his religion. Tell this officer he can return to his post, and if there is no other or better reason for the order of Stanton than the one he suspects, it shall do him no harm; the commission he holds will remain as good as new. Supporting General McClellan for the Presidency is no violation of army regulations, and as a question of taste of choosing between him and me, well, I'm the longest, but he's better looking."

Again Sheridan, his men, his horses, were heard from. Below the northern end of Massanutton Mountain, Virginia, over which it was supposed no troops could cross, his men encamped at Cedar Creek. Sheridan left his army, arrived at Washington October 17 for a few hours of conference with Stanton and Halleck. Leaving Washington the afternoon of October 17, he arrived at Martinsburg, an easy journey, and stayed there overnight. On October 18 he could easily have rejoined his army, but he paused at Winchester and stayed overnight. Why Sheridan traveled so slowly on these two days and what transactions or pleasure might have delayed him became nobody's business in the light of what happened on the nineteenth.

A few nights before, Early's officers on the headland of Massanutton Mountain had looked down through field glasses on Sheridan's sleeping army, its campfires and pickets. Now on the morning of October 19, clear, cold, and still, before daybreak in the light of a waning moon, Early and his forces marched over trails near the river, skirting the base of the mountain. The moon waned and faded and dawn arrived and a slow fog began sliding into the valley.

While Sheridan slept at Winchester fourteen miles away, Early surprised and smashed the first lines of the left flank of the Union army at Cedar Creek, tore through the second lines, and in an irresistible sweep of fighting sent Sheridan's forces reeling and routed up the valley, up toward where Sheridan slept, their hurried retreat covered by the 6th Corps under General Horatio Wright.

The five-o'clock fog held through six, seven, and eight o'clock. In that fog the broken Union columns were saying they had lost a battle. In that same fog the Confederates were saying at last they had won—and they lingered. They might in those hours have clinched a victory. Why some of them rested on their arms and waited, why others looted the Union camps and stores, became afterward a matter of dispute. In the fog destiny was kind to Sheridan while he slept at Winchester twenty miles away.

At six o'clock an officer knocked on Sheridan's door. "I hear artillery firing at Cedar Creek."

"Is it a continuous firing?"

"No, it is irregular and fitful."

"It's all right. Grover has gone out this morning to make a reconnoissance. He is merely feeling the enemy."

General Sheridan tried to go to sleep. But it was not his morning for sleep. He got into his clothes. The officer came to the door again. "The firing is still going on, sir."

"Does it sound like a battle?"

"No."

"It probably is Grover banging away at the enemy to find what he is up to."

Then suddenly Sheridan ordered breakfast in a hurry and the horses saddled. On his powerful black Rienzi he began riding toward the gunfire. Rienzi knew he wanted speed and gave it, Rienzi who had been given him by a 2d Michigan Cavalry colonel and had taken wounds and seen fighting from the Shenandoah Valley to near the gates of Richmond when Jeb Stuart was killed.

Here were soldiers at the roadside, lighting fires, cooking coffee. "Turn about, boys. We're going to sleep in our old camp tonight. We'll lick them yet!"

Farther along on the pike as he pulled in the reins on the now sweating Rienzi were lines of stragglers. "Men, by God, we'll whip them yet! We'll sleep in our old camp tonight!"

These were men who had come to believe in him as a commander. He had taken care of them in rations and supplies, and when he had ordered fighting it had always turned out right. "Fighting Phil! Hurrah!" They swung their hats. He doffed his. An officer galloped up crying out bad news in the uproar. And Sheridan in a soft voice, leaning over the foaming neck of his black horse: "Damn you, don't yell at me!"

When the hour cried for it Sheridan had the genius of a daredevil who could make other men in the mass want to be daredevils. At ten o'clock that night of October 19 Sheridan telegraphed Grant: "My army at Cedar Creek was attacked this morning before daylight, and my left was turned and driven in confusion; in fact, most of the line was driven in confusion with the loss of twenty pieces of artillery. I hastened from Winchester, where I was on my return from Washington, and found the armies between Middletown and Newtown, having been driven back about four miles. I here took the affair in hand, and quickly united the corps, formed a compact line of battle, just in time to repulse an attack of the enemy, which was handsomely done at about 1 P.M. At 3 P.M., after some changes of the cavalry from the left to the right flank, I attacked, with great vigor, driving and routing the enemy, capturing, according to the last report, forty-three pieces of artillery, and very many prisoners. . . . Affairs at times looked badly, but by the gallantry of our brave officers and men disaster has been converted into a splendid victory."

General Early, whose daring and adroit operations three months before had brought him in sight of the Capitol dome at Washington with the hope of capturing an Executive Mansion and carrying away its most hated occupant, wrote later his view of what had happened: "This was the case of a glorious victory given up by my own troops after they had won it, and it is to be accounted for on the ground of the partial demoralization caused by the plunder of the enemy's camps, and from the fact that the men undertook to judge for themselves when it was proper to retire."

Grant telegraphed Stanton October 20 that each of the armies before Richmond had fired a salute of one hundred guns in honor of Sheridan's victory. "Turning what bade fair to be a disaster into a glorious victory, stamps Sheridan what I have always thought him, one of the ablest of generals."

Lincoln telegraphed Sheridan October 22: "With great pleasure I tender to you and your brave army the thanks of the nation, and my own personal admiration and gratitude, for the month's operations in the Shenandoah Valley; and especially for the splendid work of October 19, 1864."

When on October 20 a dispatch telling of Sheridan's victory was brought in by a messenger saying, "An important telegram, Mr. President," he was in conversation with a nurse about special-diet kitchens for the soldiers and the relation of better food to the health of soldiers. The nurse, Mrs. Annie Wittenmyer, went so far as to say that better food would have the effect of reducing the number of furloughs requested by soldiers. The President talked as though he understood her, though she believed she caught "a far away look in his eyes." He picked up the telegram, read it to himself, then read it to her, with a smile. "This is good news indeed. This Sheridan is a little Irishman but he is a big fighter."

"The nation rings with praises of Phil Sheridan," said a Chicago newspaper, a New York journal saying, "His exploit is recited in prose and chanted in verse." Twenty days before the November elections Sheridan gave the North one of the most dramatic victories of the war, following a methodical devastation of the Shenandoah Valley, with the result soon to come that his own army and the shattered forces of Early would be transferred to operations before Richmond. From innumerable platforms of the North were recited the verses of "Sheridan's Ride" by Thomas Buchanan Read. As a campaign tract it was fetching. The emotional elocutionist James E. Murdoch in the last week of October declaimed it to an excited audience in Cincinnati:

The first that the general saw were the groups
Of stragglers, and then the retreating troops.
What was done? what to do? A glance told him both,
Then striking his spurs, with a terrible oath,
He dashed down the line, mid a storm of huzzas,
And the wave of retreat checked its course there, because
The sight of the master compelled it to pause.
With foam and with dust, the black charger was gray;
By the flash of his eye, and the red nostrils' play,
He seemed to the whole great army to say,
"I have brought you Sheridan all the way
From Winchester, down to save the day!" . . .

Hurrah! hurrah for Sheridan!
Hurrah! hurrah for horse and man!

As he heard this piece many and many a time Sheridan said he believed that what people liked best in the poem was the horse. National Union party campaign managers were thankful for Rienzi, the fast black one, with such legs and sound wind. Sheridan and that horse were imprinted on the minds of many who had heard and read of the war being a failure. Herman Melville, the profoundly imaginative genius who had created Moby-Dick, was seized by the event and wrote that October of Sheridan at Cedar Creek:

Shoe the steed with silver
That bore him to the fray,
When he heard the guns at dawning—
Miles away;
When he heard them calling, calling—
Mount! nor stay. . . .

House the horse in ermine—
For the foam-flake blew
White through the red October;
He thundered into view;
They cheered him in the looming,
Horseman and horse they knew.
The turn of the tide began,
The rally of bugles ran,
He swung his hat in the van;
The electric hoof-spark flew. . . .

Shroud the horse in sable—
For the mounds they heap!
There is firing in the Valley,
And yet no strife they keep;
It is the parting volley,
It is the pathos deep.
There is glory for the brave
Who lead, and nobly save,
But no knowledge in the grave
Where the nameless followers sleep.

The poets had spoken. And what were the gold speculators saying? From day to day in their gamblings they bet it would go down, down. From 254 before Sherman took Atlanta gold had fallen to 191 after Sheridan's ride to Cedar Creek.

Soon now, on November 8, the American electorate would choose between Lincoln and the Baltimore platform and McClellan and the Chicago platform as revised by McClellan. That day of ballots would fix a momentous decision in the life of the American people.

CHAPTER 56

LINCOLN'S LAUGHTER—AND HIS RELIGION

For unspeakable mysteries in the Scriptures are often delivered in a vulgar and illustrative way; and being written unto man, are delivered, not as they truly are, but as they may be understood.
—SIR THOMAS BROWNE, *Religio Medici*

BUSTS of Dan Rice, the burnt-cork blackface minstrel, and of Abraham Lincoln, the storytelling President, stood side by side as a duo facing throngs of the Sanitary Fair in Chicago in early '64. The one label for the two busts, said *Leslie's Weekly*, read THE TWO AMERICAN HUMORISTS.

In estimates of Lincoln as a person, a reality, a political tradition among masses of people who were to vote for or against him in November, the matter of his laughter was considered. He was the first humorist, real or bogus, to occupy the White House. No other President of the United States had come to be identified, for good or bad, with a relish for the comic. To what extent was this flair for the funny, this sense that scrambled nonsense with serious common sense, to operate for or against him? Had he gone too far in so often being openly, and some said flagrantly, ready for participation in the witty, the grotesque, the foolish, the flippant, lighter-minded phases of life during a war drenched with grief and draped with sorrow?

This side of him was momentous in one respect at least. It had brought him to folk masses as a reality, a living man who moved and thought and spoke, however rightly or wrongly. It raised the question whether his gift of laughter was a proper national belonging. Did he truly have something of the cartooned figure of Uncle Sam, benign, sagacious, practical, simple, at times not quite beyond taking a real laugh for himself and the country? Whatever the elements of this trait, it rested on American material, connected with an immense variety of American circumstances and incidents, and had become inevitably associated with Lincoln's name and personality.

The English novelist Anthony Trollope on an American tour was interested to hear Emerson in a lecture: "Your American eagle is very well. Protect it here and abroad. But beware of the American peacock!" Trollope would have been further interested that Captain John Potts of the Washington military patrols heard Lincoln speak of a garrulous politician who reminded him of a peacock farm in Kentucky. "That's a fine bird," was suggested. Lincoln: "Yes, he's a very pretty bird, and if he would only keep his mouth shut, people would never know what a blamed old fool he is."

In the very state papers of the President were exaggerations, thinly shaded jests, outright jokes, detected by the *Saturday Review* of London. "The Northerners have never loved the war for itself, and have never gone into it heart and soul, as soldiers or lovers of martial deeds. They accept it resolutely enough as a means of saving the Union, but they do not glory in it as we have gloried in the battles of the Peninsula or in the Crimean war. Hence their readiness to make jokes. We never treated lightly our Indian mutiny, nor did our forefathers ever laugh at the great colonial revolt; but then we have not Yankee esprit, nor the recklessness which is its root. One advantage which the Americans now have in national joking is the possession of a President who is not only the First Magistrate, but the Chief Joker, of the land. Collections of American jests are advertised as containing 'Mr. Lincoln's latest jokes,' and some of his stories are certainly good. Some of them are in his 'earlier manner,' when as yet coercion was not considered essential to the dignity of the North. The basis of nearly all American wit was irreverence, speaking lightly of serious events, treating alligators, lightning, big rivers, trackless mountains, as mere material for jest. This was natural enough, in the English view, for the lank, lean-faced pioneers had faced all these things, had given out their dry-daring jokes with smileless lips amid swamp fever, starvation, and death itself."

Besides, continued this English study, the Americans of the North had a startling readiness to treat with jesting familiarity even the most sacred themes. Religious subjects provoked the irreverence of professional jokers. Orators, writers, talkers, were jocose about grave matters that Americans themselves sincerely respect. This came from the Puritan element which dominated the North with their factual religion. "They spoke of Jehovah and Christ, of Heaven and Hell, of Death and the Judgment, as they would of serious familiar facts of daily life—as they spoke of their long barn, or their fifteen-acre field, or their new clearing. The Devil was as real as the Red Indian, was spoken of as a real living enemy to be met and overcome. Puritanism in its day, in our own country, was much the same thing. The American irreverence that translates the Bible into newspaper jokes is therefore descended, on one side, from the fearless Puritan handling of religious names, thoughts, and facts; but, on the other side, it is derived from the audacious, wild-cat Yankee evoked by New World facts.

"Men who have had to encounter the hardships and perils of backwoods life, must, above all things, have courage; and the courage that habitually faces danger, discomfort, rough life, gouging, bowie knives, and free fights, soon becomes recklessness. Take your Puritan far from the 'means of grace,' as prayer meetings are called; give him, instead of imaginary wrestlings with Satan, some tough fights with grizzly bears; show him chances of cheating Red Indians, of larruping niggers, of striking a trade with a Yankee less keen than himself; and you have, as the result, an odd mongrel—one-third Fifth Monarchy, one-third Red Indian, one-third Joe Miller with the Bible twang; grave, lantern-jawed, and lean, like the aborigines; with the Old English love of humour, but humour dried, cut into slips and preserved—English beef 'jerked,' with a peculiar flavour of its own.

"When Bishop Simpson of Pennsylvania said that 'God could not do without America' we had the essence of the Yankee Puritan. It came out in another shape when the *New York Herald*, wishing to monopolize the telegraph wires that it might have the first announcement of the Prince of Wales landing at Halifax, instructed its reporter to engage them three hours in advance, and 'send on the Book of Job.' The Puritan familiarity without intention of irreverence we have in the camp story of the Colonel (reprinted in all American papers), who, hearing from his Baptist chaplain that there had been ten conversions in a rival regiment, exclaimed, 'Do you say so? Sergeant Jones! detail fifteen men of my regiment for immediate baptism.' There is another story—invented of course—indicating a recklessness in profanity that it is difficult to characterize. A chaplain, dressed unclerically, knelt by the side of a dying soldier, and abruptly asked, 'My man, do you know who died for you?' The Yankee soldier opened his eyes and replied, 'Wal now, stranger, I guess this is not the time for asking conundrums.' Such a jest it is very hard for Englishmen to understand."

No comment was offered on the epitaph in a Baton Rouge cemetery: "Here lies the body of David Jones. His last words were, 'I die a Christian and a Democrat,'" though the *Saturday Review* demurred to the American war joke about the man who claimed exemption from the draft because he was "a Negro, a minister, over age, a British subject, and an habitual drunkard."

The American President happened to join comic and mystic elements. Renan's observation held: "Human affairs are always an approximation lacking gravity and precision." The bronze figure of a woman symbolizing Liberty atop the Capitol building, seen for miles around Washington, was cast by slaves. Negro chattels of the sculptor Clark Mills did the foundry work on this statue of Freedom, before they were accorded their own personal freedom under the act of Congress abolishing slavery in the District of Columbia. One human affair was this lacking gravity and precision.

English interpretations of American humor, their comments on the birth of an American language, were signs of a distinctive American national culture emerging. "Yankee Doodle" and the Declaration of Independence were in speech tone out of old England; "Jim along Josey" and some of Lincoln's letters and speeches were fresh from young America.

An American audience was prepared for Lincoln's humor, was seen in creative bursts of it. At a second-rate production of *Hamlet* in Nashville the crowded house was divided between Union and Confederate sympathizers, the latter perhaps predominating. The gravedigger scene was on, and the actor overmouthing the soliloquy on Yorick's skull, a soldier away to the rear cracked out so the whole audience could hear, "Say, pard, what is it, Yank or Reb?" The house went into an uproar. From their seats in the back of the theatre Generals Sherman and Grant quietly rose with their staff men and took a quiet leave without being recognized.

The joking habit of the President was considered a vulnerable point by the political opposition. They laid on his doorstep jokes he hadn't fathered. The *Metropolitan Record* of New York, as an instance, protested a "telegraphic joke" not spoken by Lincoln:

> The ever-flowing humor and inexhaustible fund of jokes possessed by the sixteenth chief magistrate of the United States renders what was an indispensable adjunct to the court of olden times entirely unnecessary at the White House, for the principal occupant of the Presidential mansion is a sort of dual character, and so saves the Nation the expense of supporting a jester.
>
> But we are forgetting the telegraphic joke; and as our readers may be somewhat impatient to see it, here it is as it comes over the wires:
>
> The rebel pickets informed ours that they had a new general on their side who treats the army with great severity. On inquiring his name, they replied—General Starvation.
>
> What do our readers think of that? If that is not in every way worthy of the last successor of Washington, we are no judge of a Presidential hit.
>
> Is there no publisher sufficiently enterprising to collect all the witticisms, all the puns, and all the anecdotes of the Executive, and give them to the world in an imperishable form? It strikes us that Barnum is just the man to undertake the task.

Before Lincoln's renomination at Baltimore the *New York Herald* did its best to attach infamy to Lincoln as a jester, "a joke incarnated, his election a very sorry joke, and the idea that such a man as he should be the President of such a country as this a very ridiculous joke." This editorial continued: "That was a fine joke when he removed General Frémont, on the very eve of victory, and allowed Price's army to escape. That was another fine joke when he held back McDowell, and permitted the Peninsula army to be cut to pieces. That was still another brave joke when he removed McClellan, after the triumph of Antietam, and so brought about the massacre at Fredericksburg and the subsequent invasion of the North. The people do not appreciate these stupendous military jokes, however. Perhaps the loss of life and property takes away some of the fun. Nevertheless, we are assured that somebody laughs at them—down below."

The sarcastic *Old Guard* quoted Lincoln to a Provost Marshal: "If you hear any man say that I know better how to tell stories than how to conduct the affairs of the nation, he is disloyal—arrest him."

The *Detroit Free Press* in reprinting the *New York Herald* attack indulged in its right of free speech: "Bennett is getting decidedly disloyal, and should be waited on with an oath of allegiance or something else to prevent his weakening the love, respect and veneration felt by the people for 'honest Old Abe.'" That the *Springfield Republican* during the '64 campaign swung into complete and unreserved support of Lincoln, with eloquent tributes, did not get reprint in the *Detroit Free Press,* which enjoyed giving its readers such items as the *Springfield Republican* advising

Lincoln, "It would add materially to the dignity of his position if he would leave off his jokes altogether till he retires from the Presidency."

Of Lincoln cartoons before and during the campaign, one comment held they were "more often terrible than ridiculous"; he looked too powerful to be merely grotesque, too formidable to be just silly, too solemn and gaunt for a devotee of the ribald and lewd. Both the lithographic and the literary cartoons often missed. Crayon sharpshooters usually found enough sheer fun handling "Old Abe" so that it ran over into their pictures. In one little mock biography, originally intended to wrap up Lincoln as entirely ridiculous, the writer had too good a time; a genius of nonsense let himself go:

"Mr. Lincoln stands six feet twelve in his socks, which he changes once every ten days. His anatomy is composed mostly of bones, and when walking he resembles the offspring of a happy marriage between a derrick and a windmill. When speaking he reminds one of the old signal-telegraph that used to stand on Staten Island. His head is shaped something like a rutabago, and his complexion is that of a Saratoga trunk. His hands and feet are plenty large enough, and in society he has the air of having too many of them. The glove-makers have not yet had time to construct gloves that will fit him. In his habits he is by no means foppish, though he brushes his hair sometimes, and is said to wash. He swears fluently. A strict temperance man himself, he does not object to another man's being pretty drunk, especially when he is about to make a bargain with him. He is fond of fried liver and onions, and is a member of the church. He can hardly be called handsome, though he is certainly much better looking since he had the small-pox." An Ellsworth Zouave, M. A. McClellan, later told his fellow Kansans Victor Murdock and William Allen White that he had seen Lincoln deliver his Cooper Union speech. "When he sat in his chair before being introduced I knew there was something unusual about the way he was sitting. I couldn't figure out what it was till finally I noticed that he had his legs crossed—and both feet flat on the floor!"

Congressman Julian wrote his impression of Lincoln seeming gay while the Army of the Potomac was wading in blood one day in '62: "He looked thin and haggard, but seemed cheerful. Although our forces were then engaged in a terrific conflict with the enemy near Richmond and everybody was anxious as to the result, he was quite as placid as usual, and could not resist his 'ruling passion' for anecdotes." Congressman James M. Ashley of Ohio on this occasion went farther than Julian. He challenged the President:

> I went up to see him about McClellan—got there early in the morning. He hadn't got into his room. When he came in he expressed some surprise, talking to himself, as I supposed. He hesitated a moment, and said:
>
> "Well, General, what are you doing here so early?"
>
> "I came here to see you."
>
> "What can I do for you?"
>
> "Nothing, sir." I shut my mouth as tight as I could.

"You have come up to see about McClellan?"

"Yes, sir."

"Well," said he, "that reminds me of a story."

I was determined to have a solid talk with him. So I said, rising to my feet: "Mr. President, I beg your pardon, but I didn't come this morning to hear a story."

He looked at me, and said, with such a sad face: "Ashley, I have great confidence in you, and great respect for you, and I know how sincere you are. But if I couldn't tell these stories, I would die Now, you sit down!" . . .

That was the peculiar character of the man.

In a little card circulated by the opposition was the announcement that he had returned to law practice in Springfield, Illinois:

A. LINCOLN

ATTORNEY AND COUNSELLOR AT LAW

SPRINGFIELD, ILL.

———o———

To Whom It May Concern

My old customers and others are no doubt aware of the terrible time I have had in Crossing The Stream, and will be glad to know that I will be back on the same side from which I started on or before the 4th of March next, when I will be ready to Swap Horses, Dispense Law, Make Jokes, Split Rails, and perform other matters in a small way.

This was gratuitous rhetoric from an enemy engaged in full exercise of free speech. Not so with the cartoon in the usually rather generous *Harper's Weekly* of January 3, 1863. There against a wall stood Lincoln and Stanton, worried and guilty-looking, with the angry woman Columbia, symbolizing the nation, flinging an accusing finger at them, crying: "Where are my 15,000 sons—murdered at Fredericksburg?" Below were the lines of Lincoln: "This reminds me of a little joke," and Columbia: "Go tell your joke at Springfield!!"

An Illinois cavalry colonel, John F. Farnsworth, quoted Lincoln on his storytelling: "Some of the stories are not as nice as they might be, but I tell you the truth when I say that a funny story, if it has the element of genuine wit, has the same effect on me that I suppose a good square drink of whiskey has on an old toper; it puts new life into me. The fact is I have always believed that a good laugh was good for both the mental and the physical digestion." Lamon said he used stories as a laugh cure for a drooping friend or for his own melancholy, yet also to clinch an argument, to lay bare a fallacy, to disarm an antagonist, but most often the stories were "labor-saving contrivances."

Often however his storytelling ran back to a humor of blood, to a talent which was part of his temperament, to an instinct for democracy snatching at false dignity resting on externals, on looks only. "I am glad to take the hand of the man, who, with the help of Almighty God will put down this rebellion," said an earnest citizen in line at a reception. The answer flashed, "You are more than half right, sir." To one asking whether the town of Lincoln, Illinois, was named after him, Lincoln said with gravity: "Well, it was named after I was." A New Yorker found it strange that the President of the United States and the President of the Confederate States were born in the same State. Lincoln laughed. "Oh, I don't know about that. Those Kentucky people will tell you that they raise 'most anything in their State, and I reckon they're mighty near right." On a mortar vessel docked at the Washington navy yard the gunners manned a piece expertly for the inspecting President, and the master's mate reported, "I have the right elevation and can land a shell on the dome of the Capitol, sir, if you wish." The President, smiling: "No, leave it where it is. That is the best place for it." Handing over an appointment to be assessor in the Wall Street district of New York (as Carpenter heard it), Lincoln said: "Gilbert, from what I can learn, I judge that you are going upon good 'missionary' ground. Preach God and Liberty to the 'bulls' and 'bears,' and get all the money you can for the government!"

No other President unless possibly Andrew Jackson had made it a custom to meet so many people, of all classes, as part of his scheme to be in close touch with what the masses as well as leaders were saying and wanting. The owner of a yoke of oxen came asking to get the tax off his personal property. Lincoln knew the man, recalled the oxen, and "Are those the oxen I see standing at the corner whenever I go to the Treasury? I never saw them move. Maybe they're not movable property. Perhaps we can get them put down as real estate." Usually to those who entered with their cases, causes, requests, he was pleasant or severe or immediately practical. Scores of men saw him often and said they never heard a story from him, nor a funny saying, they receiving plain consideration of business immediately at hand.

A flowing ease of behavior, relieving another man's embarrassment, was there when an Ohio man named Brand interviewed the President. A regiment arrived outside the White House and set up a loud clamor for a speech. Lincoln asked Brand to go with him out on the portico, meantime carrying on their talk. When they reached the portico, the regiment lifted a rousing cheer, and an aide stepped up to Brand and told him it would be necessary for him to drop back a few steps. Lincoln without a flicker of hesitation relieved all concerned. "You see, Mr. Brand, they might not know who was the President." Thus it was later told in Ohio, having particular interest for an Ohio namesake of Mr. Brand named Brand Whitlock.

Perhaps one-sixth of the stories credited to him were old acquaintances, Lincoln told Noah Brooks. The other five-sixths came from other and better storytellers than himself. "I remember a good story when I hear it, but I never invented anything original. I am only a retail dealer." His seeking to know what brand of whisky Grant drank, so that he might send a few barrels to his other generals, was not original. More definitely so was his mocking wail over the loss of one brigadier and twenty horses: "I can make more brigadiers, but those horses cost $125 apiece." Some versions had mules instead of horses. The remarks about the brigadiers varied. Nicolay noted, as in the hearse-horse story from the painter Conant, how Lincoln wove in odd interpolations, in a way made the story his own.

In the telegraph office one evening Lincoln confessed to David Homer Bates that his storytelling was a habit. He couldn't break himself of it. "It had been formed in his younger days," wrote Bates, "and later he found it difficult to refrain from clinching an argument or emphasizing a good point by means of a story." His case, Lincoln told Bates, was like that of an old colored man on a plantation, who let his work slide to preach to the other slaves. His master rebuked him, but the old man had the spirit of the gospel in him, kept on preaching, even when he knew the lash might be waiting for him. At last one day he was ordered to report at the Big House. There the master scolded, told him he would get hard punishment the very next time he was caught preaching. Tears came to his eyes:

"But, marsa, I jest cain't help it; I allus has to draw infrunces from de Bible textes when dey comes into my haid. Doesn't you, marsa?"

"Well, uncle, I suspect I do something of that kind myself at times, but there is one text I never could understand, and if you can draw the right inference from it, I will cancel my order and let you preach to your heart's content."

"What is de tex, marsa?"

" 'The ass snuffeth up the east wind.' Now, uncle, what inference do you draw from such a text?"

"Well, marsa, I's neber heerd dat tex' befo', but I 'spect de infrunce is she gotter snuff a long time befo' she git fat."

Some yarns and anecdotes attributed to Lincoln were definitely inventions, made up for various reasons or none at all. They were spurious, lacking his known personal touch and flavor. Others were dubious. He might have told them. More likely he didn't: he was a convenient peg on which to hang them: they took on added interest with foreword that Lincoln had told them, or they might damage him politically if they were dirty and alleged to have come out of his mouth. His own admitted and acknowledged anecdotes and stories might number a hundred, noted Nicolay. On the flyleaf of a replete book of *Anecdotes of Abraham Lincoln* later edited by A. K. McClure, Isaac N. Arnold wrote that in his judgment about half were probably stories that Lincoln had actually told. His own, along with those he had from others which he "retailed," might be trifling puns or spontaneous and indefinable flashes. They might be sheer rollicking fun or darkly implicative beyond their humor, having the stuff of homespun fables and parables. The materials were out of near-by and modern sources, Nicolay noting Lincoln's point that he "did not care to quarry among the ancients for his figures."

His treasures of memory being "inexhaustible," wrote the prime story-teller and raconteur John W. Forney, he never failed for illustrations. "He liked the short farce better than the five-act tragedy. He would shout with laughter over a French, German or Negro anecdote, and he was always ready to match the best with a better. More than once, when I bore a message to him from the Senate, he detained me with some amusing sketch of Western life. He seemed to have read the character and to know the peculiarities of every leading man in Congress and the country, and would play off many an innocent joke on them." Around much of this, wrote Forney, was "a sort of sacred confidence which could not be violated without offence to many good men." To repeat some of the more hilarious outpourings of Lincoln, considered Forney, "would give unnecessary pain."

The Indiana banker Hugh McCulloch, standing high as a counselor of the Treasury Department, called with friends on Lincoln just after the first battle of Bull Run. "The President received us kindly," wrote McCulloch, "and tried to amuse us with anecdotes. I was surprised that he should relate anecdotes when the Government of which he was the head seemed to be in imminent peril." The banker left the White House feeling his previous judgments of Lincoln were mistaken, fearing Lincoln would fail as a President. When later McCulloch as an officer of the Treasury Department saw the President more freely and often, he changed his mind: "story telling was to Mr. Lincoln a safety-valve . . . relief from oppressing cares." Nevertheless the graces were lacking, to McCulloch, whose appraisal ran, "In appearance Mr. Lincoln was unprepossessing, in manners ungraceful, in taste unrefined, or at least peculiar." In this, McCulloch felt the deficiencies were Lincoln's and not McCulloch's. In other directions the admiration of McCulloch ran high: "in sagacity, Mr. Lincoln had no superior"; with reference to "bravery of a higher and rarer kind" Mr. Lincoln was "one of the bravest of men." Was McCulloch of a type? Lacking even a slight comic element in himself, did he see Lincoln as lacking to the extent that Lincoln lived and exulted in the comic? Having sagacity of a sort himself, was it easier for McCulloch to see and praise Lincoln's sagacity?

On an eight-day trip on a revenue cutter up the Potomac and around Fortress Monroe, a small cabin spaced off by four partitions quartered officers and guests. "We never lost sight of each other," said General Egbert L. Viele, in charge. "We were constantly engaged in conversation and discussion about war matters, much of the time being occupied in listening to Mr. Lincoln's wonderful fund of reminiscences and anecdotes. If I had been a stenographer it seems to me that I could have filled a large volume made up of these remarkable stories. Of course I could not remember all of them. I remember many of them. Some of them it would be hardly right to print."

Isaac N. Arnold, whose humor, like that of Nicolay, seldom rose to the surface, quoted "What has made this joyous merry man so sad? What great sorrow lies at his heart?" The mingling of these extremes in Lincoln affected his loyal friend. "Mirthfulness and melancholy, hilarity and sadness, were strangely combined in him. His mirth was sometimes exuberant. It sparkled in jest, story and anecdote, while at the next moment, his peculiarly sad, pathetic, melancholy eyes would seem to wander far away, and one realized that he was a man 'familiar with sorrow and acquainted with grief.'" In '61 there was an immense secret hostility to him at home, Arnold emphasized, while abroad the *Times* of London voiced a ruling-class belief in exulting: "The great republic is no more. The bubble is burst." In this chaos Arnold saw a prairie humor and sagacity bringing order. As to "coarse and indecent anecdotes," Arnold interceded: "The charge, so far as it indicates any taste for indecency, is untrue. His love for the humorous was so strong, that if a story had this quality, and was racy or pointed, he did not always refrain from narrating it because the incidents were coarse. But it was always clear to the listener that the story was told for its wit and not for its vulgarity. 'To the pure all things are pure,' and Lincoln was a man of purity of thought as well as of life."

Carpenter throughout his stay of six months in the White House, as a witness of Lincoln's "intercourse with nearly all classes of men," could not "recollect to have heard him [Mr. Lincoln] relate a circumstance to any of them, which would have been out of place uttered in a ladies' drawing-room." Isaac N. Arnold endorsed this as tallying with his own observation of Lincoln over a twenty-year period. "Scores of stories of this character have been falsely attributed to Mr. Lincoln," believed Arnold. He quoted Dr. Stone, the family physician: "Lincoln is the purest-hearted man with whom I ever came in contact." Undoubtedly these three close friends and associates spoke truly of what they saw and heard. They were neither the crony familiars nor the bores and nuisances to whom Lincoln told his stories or fables questioned as "not in good taste." It was accident that they didn't happen in when he was in the mood or amid circumstances that called out stories and lines like those deleted from the "expurgated" editions of Shakespeare's plays.

Lincoln's transition from mood to mood impressed Andrew D. White, educator and a member of the New York State senate. White saw Lincoln in the White House "dressed in a rather dusty suit of black," resembling "some rural tourist who had blundered into the place." Lincoln entered the room and approached White's group. He seemed, to White, "less at home there than any other person present" as he "looked about for an instant as if in doubt where he should go." Others had seen and written of the same thing. And White's impression recorded itself: "As he came toward us in a sort of awkward, perfunctory way his face seemed to me one of the saddest I had ever seen, and when he had reached us he held out his hand to the first stranger, then to the second and so on all with the air of a melancholy automaton. But suddenly someone in the company said something which amused him and instantly there came in his face a most marvelous transformation. I have never seen anything like it in any other human being. His features were lighted, his eyes radiant, he responded to sundry remarks humorously, then dryly, and thenceforward was cordial and hearty.

Taking my hand in his he shook it in the most friendly way, with a kindly word, and so passed cheerily on to the others till the ceremony was finished." It interested White to hear later from Robert Lincoln that "when any attempt was made to photograph his father or to paint his portrait, he relapsed into his melancholy mood."

George Bancroft, historian and educator, saw nothing seriously impressive, met the hilarious and humdrum and thought it could be done better. In a letter of February 24, 1864, to his wife Bancroft wrote: "Last night I went to the President's reception. He took me by the one of his hands, and trying to recall my name, he waved the other a foot and a half above his head, and cried out, greatly to the amusement of the bystanders: 'Hold on—I know you; you are—History, History of the United States—Mr.—Mr. Bancroft, Mr. George Bancroft' and seemed disposed to give me a hearty welcome, expressing a hearty wish to see me Sunday apart from the crowd. S—— wanted Abe's autograph in a copy of his Gettysburg speech; finding him so good-natured, I asked for it; and he very readily promised it."

Among callers one evening in '64 Carpenter saw disappointment on their faces. The President didn't measure up. "One rough-looking sovereign from Cape Cod, or Nantucket, had listened attentively, but taken no part in the conversation. Turning away at length, with an expression of deep disgust, he muttered: 'A set of consummate fools! Nominate a man for the Presidency who has never smelt salt water!' "

Isaac N. Arnold once waited with friends for the President to finish his session with a congressional delegation. From the President's room, noted Carpenter, came presently, through the walls and transoms, "an unmistakable voice . . . in a burst of mirth," Arnold remarking as the sound died away, "That laugh has been the President's life-preserver!" Of this Carpenter too noted: "Mr. Lincoln's 'laugh' stood by itself. The 'neigh' of a wild horse on his native prairie is not more undisguised and hearty." One evening the President, Mrs. Lincoln, and the secretaries had gone to the opera, and Carpenter worked late and the house was quiet. But this quiet did not last. "Towards twelve o'clock I heard some persons enter the sleeping apartment occupied by Mr. Nicolay and Major Hay, which was directly opposite the room where I was sitting; and shortly afterward the hearty laugh of Mr. Lincoln broke the stillness, proceeding from the same quarter. Throwing aside my work, I went across the hall to see what had occasioned this outbreak of merriment. The Secretaries had come in and Hay had retired; Mr. Nicolay sat by the table with his boots off, and the President was leaning over the 'footboard' of the bed, laughing and talking with the hilarity of a schoolboy. It seemed that Hay, or 'John,' as the President called him, had met with a singular adventure, which was the subject of the amusement. Glancing through the half-open door, Mr. Lincoln caught sight of me, and the story had to be repeated for my benefit. The incident was trifling in itself, but the President's enjoyment of it was very exhilarating. I never saw him in so frolicsome a mood as on this occasion."

By mid-1863 several large editions of Lincoln joke books had been printed and sold. *Old Abe's Jokes—Fresh from Abraham's Bosom* ran the title of one whose cover alleged it contained "authentic jokes and squibs" of the President. *Old Abe's Joker, or Wit at the White House* ran the title of another. The preface of the latter said it had been calculated that "any efficient circus-clown will save more lives in the course of the year than four physicians." The typesetters on the job had grown so fat they were eating only *four* meals a day. "The joke, you see, produces the exhilarating laugh,

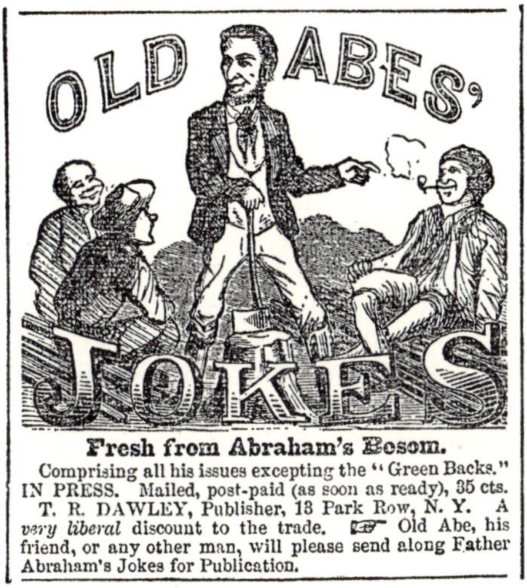

Advertisement in *Harper's Weekly*

which shakes up the midriff, clears off the lungs, carries off the morbid humors, and does other obliging things." The preface implied that though the President was a man of humor, he hadn't originated the contents of the books. "We have christened this child 'Old Abe's Joker,' for what could be more natural than to associate with 'quips and cranks and wanton wiles,' the name of one who so greatly enjoys and successfully perpetrates the fine, old full-flavored joke. 'Wit at the White House' is in full blow, now, so our little book may be considered quite in season. When traveling, reflect that you took good care to put 'Old Abe's Joker' up along with your toothbrush and other necessaries." There were pages of puns and tomfoolery, much from Joe Miller, and assorted jests, some of them folklore. "An old lady living on Long Island is so fat that the neighbors use her shadow for griddle greasing. To keep her from flipping out of bed, her husband rolls her in ashes." "A man in Mississippi is so lean that he makes no shadow at all. A rattlesnake struck at his legs six times in vain, and then retired in disgust." Old Abe once asked the vote of a blacksmith, who said, "Mr. Lincoln, I admire your head, but damn your heart!" "Mr. Blacksmith," returned Abe, "I admire your candor, but damn your manners!"

One page had a bad-tempered old fellow calling to a noisy boy, "What are you hollering for when I'm going by?" The boy: "What are you going by for when I'm hollering?" This was not credited to Lincoln, though it did happen that one day Lincoln came into the telegraph office, found Major Eckert counting greenbacks, and Lincoln said it seemed the Major never came to the office any more except when he had money to count. Eckert said it was just a coincidence, but it reminded him of Mansfield, Ohio, where a certain tailor was very stylish in dress and airy in manner. A groceryman, seeing the tailor passing one day, puffed himself up and gave a long blow, the tailor snorting, "I'll learn you not to blow when I'm passing," the groceryman answering, "And I'll learn you not to pass when I'm blowing." Lincoln found this very good—like the man in an open buggy caught at night on a country road in a pouring shower of rain. He was hurrying to shelter, passing a farmhouse where a man somewhat drunk put his head out of a window and yelled, "Hullo! hullo!" The traveler stopped his buggy in the rain and asked what was wanted.

"Nothing of you," came the voice at the window.

"Well, what in the damnation do you yell hullo for when people are passing?"

"Well, what in the damnation are you passing for when people are yelling hullo?"

The joke books created a figure in the White House more trifling and nonsensical than Lincoln's most dignified critics or humorless friends ever pictured him. Yet the same joke books also credited him occasionally with some of the keenest wit and philosophy of the time, in creations of anonymous newspaper writers widely reprinted. One of these pieces assumed that the President had been West in 1862, which he hadn't, and on the hurricane deck of a gunboat was questioning a Socratic old Negro. "He rather interested me, I made some inquiries, and found that he had really been with the 9th Illinois Infantry at Donelson." Then came a dialogue that thousands of soldiers read aloud in camp to hilarious little audiences:

"Were you in the fight?"

"Had a little taste of it, sa."

"Stood your ground, did you?"

"No, sa, I runs."

"Run at the first fire, did you?"

"Yes, sa, and would ha' run soona, had I knowed it war comin'."

"Why, that wasn't very creditable to your courage."

"Dat isn't my line, sa—cookin's my profeshun."

"Well, but have you no regard for your reputation?"

"Reputation's nuffin to me by de side ob life."

"Do you consider your life worth more than other people's?"

"It's worth more to me, sa."

"Then you must value it very highly?"

"Yes, sa, I does, more dan all dis wuld, more dan a million ob dollars, sa, for what would dat be wuth to a man wid de bref out ob him? Self-preserbation am de fust law wid me."

"But why should you act upon a different rule from other men?"

"Different men set different values on their lives; mine is not in de market."

"But if you lost it you would have the satisfaction of knowing that you died for your country."

"Dat no satisfaction when feelin's gone."

"Then patriotism and honor are nothing to you?"

"Nuffin whatever, sa—I regard them as among the vanities."

"If our soldiers were like you, traitors might have broken up the government without resistance."

"Yes, sa, dar would hab been no help for it. I wouldn't put my life in de scale 'g'inst any goberment dat eber existed, for no goberment could replace de loss to me."

"Do you think any of your company would have missed you if you had been killed?"

"Maybe no, sa—a dead white man ain't much to dese sogers, let alone a dead nigga—but I'd a missed myself, and dat was de p'int wid me."

Likewise the story titled "Uncle Abe and the Copperhead" may or may not have been told by Lincoln, but it was published as a mild rebuke given by the President to a politician who came to the White House with denunciation of the Administration. A Dutch farmer elected justice of the peace faced the first couple that came to him.

"Vell, you want to be marrit, do you?"

"Yes," answered the man.

"Vell, do you lovish dis voman as goot as any voman you have ever seen?"

"Yes."

Then to the woman:

"Vell, do you love this man so better as any man you have ever seen?"

She hesitated and he repeated:

"Vell, vell, do you like him so vell as to be his vife?"

"Yes, yes," she answered.

"Vell, dat ish all any reasonable man can expect; so you are marrit. I pronounce you man and vife."

The man drew out his pocketbook and asked the justice what was to pay.

"Nothing at all, nothing at all, you are welcome to it if it will do you any goot."

The joke books made free with any religious austerity Lincoln might have assumed. "It is said of Old Abe," chattered *Old Abe's Joker*, "that he once attended a church where a minister made an estimate that out of the whole human race not more than one in a thousand would be saved. On the announcement of this, Abraham took his hat and walked out saying as he went, 'Gentlemen, if any of you want my chance you are welcome to it.

It is not worth staying for.' " The President was credited with telling of a fresh young lawyer at a town meeting losing in an argument with a farmer and snorting, "Sir, do you know that I have been at two universities, and at two colleges in each university?" "Well, sir," said the farmer, "what of that? I had a calf that sucked two cows, and the observation I made was, the more he sucked the greater calf he grew." Likewise a tanyard in Virginia where the owner, to attract customers, bored an auger hole in a door-post and stuck a calf's tail into it, with the bushy end flaunting out. And a man of grave face came and stood looking through his spectacles at this sign. As he gazed and gazed without moving, the tanyard man stepped out and said good morning. But the stranger never moved, murmured good morning, but kept his eyes on the sign. "You want to buy leather?" asked the tanyard man. "No." "Do you wish to sell hides?" "No." "Are you a farmer?" "No." "Are you a merchant?" "No." "Are you a lawyer?" "No." "Are you a doctor?" "No." "Who are you, then?" "I'm a philosopher. I've been standing here for an hour, trying to see if I could ascertain how that calf got through the auger-hole. I can't make it out to save my life." This might have been told by Lincoln; it was told on the old Eighth Circuit.

Lincoln heard from Alexander Stephens when they were in Congress, and may have retailed, the incident of an undersized lawyer in an acrimonious stump debate with the massive Robert Toombs. Toombs called out, "Why, I could button your ears back and swallow you whole." The little fellow retorted, "And if you did, you would have more brains in your stomach than you ever had in your head."

Amid specimens of humor published as current in the White House was one of a bashful farm boy in Maine calling on a farmer's daughter. Finding it hard to keep the conversation going, he suddenly asked her if she knew anybody that wanted to buy a shirt. "I don't," said she. "Have you got one to sell?" "Oh, no, I only asked to make talk." Also there was a lawyer in Hartford, Connecticut, cross-examining a woman who swore that her son had worked on a farm ever since he was born. The lawyer had her repeat this and then asked, "What did he do the first year?" The reply: "He *milked*." Also there was a teacher examining a wild boy on punctuation. He knew a comma but the next mark he didn't know, answering, "Now y've got me where the hair's short." She rebuked his slang, asked again about the mark; he didn't know, and the teacher said it was a period. The bad boy looked more closely at the mark, burst out, "Ha! ha! now I've got you where the hair's short, that ain't nothin' only a fly-dirt"—and for this he was dismissed. Also there was the man who married a second wife and was saying, "I intend to enlarge my dairy." "You mean *our* dairy, dear," said the wife. "No," he returned, "*my* dairy," whereupon she seized a poker and with each blow on his back called out, "*Our* dairy," while he called, "*My* dairy," finally retreating under the bed. When later he slowly thrust his head out, like a turtle, she asked what he was looking for. "*Our* breeches, my dear."

Hundreds of newspapers reprinted, as though Lincoln told it, the anecdote from *Old Abe's Joker*, of Old Jake Tullwater who lived in Pennsylvania, got a fever, became delirious, imagined the Last Day had come, and he was to judge the world. He called up his friends and acquaintances, millers like himself, and spoke the questions and answers:

"Shon Schmidt, come up here! Vot bees you in dis lower world?"

"Well, Lort, I bees a miller."

"Well, Shon, did you ever take too much toll?"

"Oh, yes, Lort, when the water was low, and the stones were dull, I did take too much toll."

"Well, Shon, you must go to the left among the goats." And having put among the goats all of the millers he knew, he came to himself.

"Shake Tullwater, come up here! Well, Shake, vat bees you in dis lower world?"

"Well, Lort, I bees a miller."

"And, Shake, didn't you ever take too much toll?"

"Oh, yes, Lort, when the water was low and the stones was dull, I did take too much toll."

"Well, Shake—well, Shake"—scratching his head—"well, Shake, what did you do mit dat toll?"

"Well, Lort, I gives it to de poor."

"Ah! Shake—gave it to the poor, did you? Well, Shake, you can go to the right amongst the sheep—but it is a tam'd tight squeeze."

Was this funny? Should an intelligent person respond to this with laughter or at least a smile? Some said No. It was merely silly. Yet rural America had such stories. On farms and in villages the freeholders and citizens couldn't help telling them. The compilers of *Old Abe's Joker* considered it funny and put it in the book. Also the compilers of *Old Abe's Jokes—Fresh from Abraham's Bosom* considered it funny and put it in their book with a prefatory note: "President Lincoln says the prospect of his election for a second term reminds him of Old Jake Tullwater who lived in Illinois." Readers of the book thought it funny and read it aloud to others. It was not a priceless gem of a humorous narrative but it was "plumb ridiculous" to many that Old Jake Tullwater in a deathbed delirium should let himself into heaven by "a tam'd tight squeeze," while Lincoln saw his second-term chances about even with those of Old Jake Tullwater for entry into heaven.

The President laughed heartily, it was alleged in print, telling of a German colonel on Frémont's staff in West Virginia doing some quick thinking in an emergency, bringing up howitzers strapped to the backs of mules, turning the rear ends of the mules on the advancing enemy and repelling the attack with volleys of grape and canister. Part of the fun was in the sudden cry, "Pring up de shackasses, pring up de shackasses, for Cot's sake, hurry up de shackasses im-me-di-ate-ly!"

In several of the more widely repeated and reprinted stories, men and boys supposed to be half-wits proved not so dumb as they looked. A careless fellow with a rusty gun managed to shoot more prairie chickens than anybody else in his Illinois neighborhood. Another hunter, with improved fowling-pieces and fancy bird dogs, asked Jake, "How is it you never come home without a lot of birds?" Jake grinned, half-closed his eyes. "I jes go ahead and git 'em." After several questions and a promise that the secret wouldn't be revealed, Jake put his mouth close to the ear of the fancy sportsman and whispered, "All you got to do is jes hide in a fence corner an' make a noise like a turnip—that'll bring the chickens every time." Another yarn had a smart city man send his big wolfhound into underbrush to eat up some timber wolves. The dog-owner, togged up fancy, rode his horse up to a farmhouse a long way off and asked the farmer leaning at the gate whether he had seen a dog and wolves. "Yep." "How were they going?" "Pretty fast." "What was their position when you saw them?" "Well," and the farmer was very deliberate and easy, "the dog was a leetle bit ahead."

Another "fresh from Abraham's bosom," with the preface "President Lincoln tells the following story," was about a Colonel W., once a member of the legislature and county judge, pompous, enjoying big words. His ox, Big Brindle, often broke down neighbors' fences, spoiled the corn, and was otherwise annoying. "One morning after breakfast in the presence of Mr. Lincoln, who had stayed with him overnight, and was on his way to town, he called his overseer and said to him, 'Mr. Allen, I desire you to impound Big Brindle, in order that I may hear no animadversions on his eternal depredations.' Allen bowed and walked off, sorely puzzled to know what the Colonel meant. So after Col. W. left for town, he went to his wife and asked her what Col. W. meant by asking him to impound the ox. 'Why, he meant to tell you to put him in the pen.' " And Allen, with much running, yelling, and sweating, at last got Big Brindle into a pen. The next day, before company at dinner, Col. W. asked Allen if he had impounded the ox. "Yes, I did, sir, but old Brindle transcended the impannel of the impound, scatterlophisticated all over the equanimity of the forest." The company roared, the Colonel's face got red as he asked, "What do you mean by that, sir?" "Why, I mean, Colonel," said Allen, "that old Brindle, being prognosticated with an idea of the Cholera, ripped and tared, snorted and pawed dirt, jumped the fence, tuck to the woods, and wouldn't be impounded nohow!" The company roared again, the Colonel joined in and Allen left, saying, "I reckon the Colonel won't ask me to impound any more oxen."

A short biography and kindly comment in *Honest Abe's Jokes* gave the impression of an intensely alive man in the White House, serious though quizzical, close to the plow, with kinship for the common man and "the folks." Possibly this impression reached as far and as deep as any made by the President's addresses or letters in winning affection for him, in blunting the edges of war hatred. The *Spectator* of London was quoted in the joke book: "Although Mr. Lincoln may not always have risen fully to the level of a great emergency, he has seldom failed to display a noble impartiality, a great firmness of purpose, and a sagacious if somewhat utilitarian judgement; we believe a juster man never held the reins of government." Opening pages of this joke book stressed Lincoln's upbringing as a Christian, how he had been drilled in the Ten Commandments, learning to repeat favorite ones of his mother: (III) Thou shalt not take the name of the Lord thy God in vain; (IV) Remember the Sabbath Day to keep it holy; (V) Honor thy father and thy mother, that thy days may be long upon the land which the Lord thy God giveth thee; (IX) Thou shalt not bear false witness against thy neighbor. "In this way many Sabbaths of Abraham's boyhood were spent, so that he became familiar with the Bible. For a boy of his age, he was excelled by few in his acquaintance with the Scriptures."

A current quip was adapted as personal to the President. "I feel patriotic," said an old rowdy. "What do you mean by feeling patriotic?" inquired the President, standing by. "Why, I feel as if I wanted to kill somebody or steal something." With the preface "Abe tells the following story" was a brief dialogue between a captain and a private, both drunk. "Private Smith, I'll give you t'l (hic) four o'clock to gissober in." "Cap'n, as you're (hic) —— sight drunkerniam, I'll give you t'l five o'clock to gissober in."

Old Abe was credited with asking a Union soldier in jail what he was in for. The answer: "For taking something." Lincoln: "What do you mean?" And the explanation: "One morning I did not feel very well, and went to see the surgeon. He was busy writing and when I went in he looked at me saying, 'You do look bad; you had better take something.' He went on with his writing, and left me standing behind him. I looked around, and saw nothing I could take except his watch, and I took that. That's what I'm in here for." Under the heading "Old Abe's Story of New Jersey"—politically more anti-Unionist than any other of the Northern States—was the tale of a shipwrecked sailor drifting toward land, where friendly hands flung him a rope. He took hold of the rope, asking, "What country is this?" and hearing "New Jersey" let go the rope and moaned, "I guess I'll float a little farther!" More like something based on an actual event, and touched up by various humorists as it traveled, was one with the prefatory note, "The President often tells the following, which may be considered rich":

> Company K of the first Iowa Cavalry, stationed in Tennessee, received into their camp a middle-aged but vigorous contraband. Innumerable questions were being propounded to him, when a corporal advanced observing, "See here, Dixie, before you can enter the service of the United States you must be sworn."
>
> "Yes, massa, I do dat," he replied; when the corporal continued:
>
> "Well, then take hold of the Bible," holding out a letter envelope, upon which was delineated the Goddess of Liberty, standing on a Suffolk pig, wearing the emblem of our country. The negro grasped the envelope cautiously with his thumb and finger, when the corporal proceeded to administer the oath by saying:
>
> "You do solemnly swear that you will support the Constitution of the United States, and see that there are no grounds floating upon the coffee at all times."
>
> "Yes, massa, I do dat," he replied. "I allers settle him in de coffee pot."
>
> Here he let go the envelope to gesticulate by a downward thrust of his forefinger the direction that would be given to the coffee grounds for the future.
>
> "Never mind how you do it," shouted the corporal, "but hold on to the Bible."

"Lordy, massa, I forgot," said the negro, as he darted forward and grasped the envelope with a firmer clutch, when the corporal continued:

"And you do solemnly swear that you will support the Constitution of all loyal States, and not spit upon the plates when cleaning them, or wipe them with your shirt-sleeves."

Here a frown lowered upon the brow of the negro, his eyes expanded to their largest dimensions, while his lips protruded with a rounded form as he exclaimed:

"Lordy, massa, I never do dat. I allers washes him nice. Ole missus mighty 'ticler 'bout dat."

"Never mind ole missus," shouted the corporal, as he resumed: "and do you solemnly swear that you will put milk into the coffee every morning, and see that the ham and eggs are not cooked too much or too little."

"Yes, I do dat, I'se a good cook."

"And lastly," continued the corporal, "you do solemnly swear that when this war is over you'll make tracks for Africa mighty fast."

"Yes, massa, I do dat. I allers wanted to go to Cheecargo."

Here the regimental drum beat up for dress parade, when Tom Benton—that being his name—was declared duly sworn in and commissioned as chief-cook in Company K of the first Iowa Cavalry.

A man visiting a hospital in Washington noticed a soldier in one bed "laughing and talking about the President." The visitor was educated, drew fine distinctions, and said to the soldier, "You must be very slightly wounded." "Yes," said the soldier. "Very slightly—I have lost only one leg." Vouched for as "a good story and true" was the incident of a private writing: "Dear President—I have been in the service eighteen months, and I have never received a cent. I desire a furlough, for fifteen days, in order to return home and remove my family to the poor house." The President granted the furlough. On one page were printed words as from Lincoln's mouth which sounded like a man of authority going his own way, yet speaking more peremptorily than was the custom with Lincoln, particularly if he knew he was to be quoted. The words came as a reply to a Senator who protested against keeping Chase in the Cabinet when it was well known that Chase was opposed to Lincoln. "Now, see here," the President was quoted, "when I was elected I resolved to hire my four presidential rivals, pay them their wages, and be their boss. These were Seward, Chase, Cameron and Bates; but I got rid of Cameron after he had played himself out. As to discharging Chase or Seward, don't talk of it. I pay them their wages and am their boss, wouldn't let either of them out on the loose for the fee simple of the Almaden patent." The President's views on the liquor question were set forth in *Honest Abe's Jokes* in a sober report of an earnest conference at the White House:

The twenty-first anniversary of the "Sons of Temperance" was appropriately celebrated in Washington. The "Sons" on reaching the White House, were invited to enter the East room, which was nearly filled by the ladies and gentlemen participating in the ceremonies. President Lincoln, on entering, was enthusiastically applauded, and, in the course of his response to the address presented to him, said that when he was a young man, long ago, before the Sons of Temperance, as an organization had an existence, he in an humble way made Temperance speeches, and he thought he might say to this day he had never by his example belied what he then said. As to the suggestions for the purpose of the abandonment of the cause of temperance, he could not now respond to them. To prevent intemperance in the army is even a great part of the rules and articles of war. It is a part of the law of the land, and was so he presumed long ago, to dismiss officers for drunkenness. He was not sure that, consistently with the public service, more can be done than has been done! All, therefore, that he could promise, was to have a copy of the address submitted to the principal departments, and have them consider whether it contains any suggestions which will improve the cause of temperance, and repress drunkenness in the army any better than it is already done. He thought the reasonable men of the world had long since agreed that intemperance was one of the greatest, if not the very greatest, of all the evils among mankind. That was not a matter of dispute. All men agreed that intemperance was a great curse, but differed about the cure. The suggestion that it existed to a great extent was true; whether it was a cause of defeat he knew not; but he did know that there was a good deal of it on the other side. Therefore they had no right to beat us on that ground. (Laughter.) The remarks of the President were listened to with great interest and repeatedly interrupted by applause.

Immediately in *Honest Abe's Jokes* followed a fabricated anecdote of a young man examined for the Zouaves by a pompous major who inquired, "How old are you, and what are your qualifications?"

"Twenty-two, and a strong stomach."

"What is the first duty to be learned by a soldier?"

"How to draw his rations."

"If you were commanding skirmishers, and saw cavalry advancing in the front and infantry in the rear, which would you meet?"

"Neither; I would mass myself for a bold movement, and shove out side-ways."

"If you were captured, what line of conduct would you pursue?"

"I would treat my captors with the utmost civility."

"What are the duties of Home Guards?"

"Their duty is to see that they have no duties."

"What will you take?"

"—— Bourbon, straight!"

Of one interview with the President, Hay wrote in his diary for September 29, 1863: "Today came to the Executive Mansion an assembly of cold-water men & cold-water women to make a temperance speech at the Tycoon & receive a response. They filed into the East Room looking blue & thin in the keen autumnal air; Cooper, my coachman, who was about half tight, gazing on them with an air of complacent contempt and mild wonder. Three blue-skinned damsels did Love, Purity, & Fidelity in Red, White & Blue gowns. A few invalid soldiers stumped along in the dismal procession. They made a long speech at the Tycoon in which they called Intemperance the cause of our defeats. He could not see it, as the rebels drink more & worse whisky than we do."

The cause of the war in its later phases was given in a folk tale of Lincoln and Jeff Davis meeting on neutral ground and deciding to settle the war by

GOOD FOR THE MIDDIES!

Midshipmite.—"LOOK HERE, UNCLE ABE, WE'VE LEFT SCHOOL, NOW, AND WANT TO GO RIGHT STRAIGHT INTO BUSINESS!"

Vanity Fair cartoons a playful and fatherly President welcoming into the United States naval service the brand-new graduates from the Annapolis naval academy

dividing the territory and stopping the fighting. "Lincoln took the Northern States, and Davis the Gulf and seaboard Southern States. Lincoln took Texas and Missouri, and Davis Kentucky and Tennessee; so that all were parcelled off except Arkansas. Lincoln didn't want it—Jeff wouldn't have it—neither would consent to take it. And on that they split; and the war has been going on ever since."

The book of *Old Abe's Jokes*, with like published material, wove a legend. However true the legend might be in proportion and detail, it was a creation peculiar to its age. As much, perhaps, as his speeches and letters, the joke book played its part toward the end Lincoln wished—that people would say of the White House as the chess-player said of the automaton, "There is a man in there!" Myriad newspaper references to him as a story-teller, mouth-to-mouth repetitions of his sayings, were making a portrait of him for his own generation. He might be baffling, anomalous, vacillating, vague, or Machiavellian in his policies of state—but for a large mass of people the impression formed of a plain, neighborly, somewhat droll man, nobody's fool, at home to common folks and even simpletons or charlatans who might step into the White House for a look at him.

A farmer came saying he wanted to hear him tell a story. "Where you from?" "State of New York." Lincoln: "That's a good enough place to come from without a story." A Boston man wished information. "You never swear, Mr. President, do you?" And Lincoln laughed, not loud but deep, the Bostonian noted. "Oh, I don't have to. You know I have Stanton in my Cabinet."

A heavy-headed philosopher came with a theory of public-opinion currents being like surface water and undertows that flowed in and out of the Mediterranean, the Black Sea, and the Atlantic Ocean. Lincoln, half wearily: "Well, that don't remind me of any story I ever heard of." An old friend kept begging for a foreign mission, where the climate was notoriously unhealthful, but was satisfied and reconciled with Lincoln's refusal: "Strangers die there soon, and I have already given the position to a gentleman I can spare better than you." Others besides Thomas Wentworth Higginson in 1862 went so far as to say in letters, "The President really says very good things."

To some who visited the White House Lincoln had a schoolmaster look. Hawthorne and others noted it. The country was taking sentences of his everyday talk, phrases of his letters and speeches, finding maxims and a rough eloquence. "As likely to capture the man in the moon as any part of Lee's army." "A short and feeble existence, as an animal with a thorn in its vitals." "A jury too frequently has at least one member more ready to hang the panel than the traitor." "Every foul bird comes abroad and every dirty reptile rises up."

At a navy-yard experiment with signal rockets, one soared up with a bright flare, and then fizzled out halfway up. Lincoln: "Small potatoes and few in a hill." Thus Hay wrote it in the diary. In the White House Lincoln philosophized no less than in earlier days, in the same manner as when, after hearing many theories and noisy wranglings in a big law case, he had walked out on the Rock Island bridge, coming on a boy with a fishing-pole whose legs dangled idly from the ties above the water. "I suppose you know all about this river," he ventured. The boy, brightly: "I guess I do. It was here when I was born, and it's been here ever since." And Lincoln smiled. "I'm mighty glad I walked out here where there is not so much opinion and a little more fact." He sought realities by the same procedure as when in an Illinois court two farmers disputed over who owned a mule in the hands of the sheriff. One farmer testified the mule was a family pet fed on milk. So judge, lawyers, witnesses, claimants, went with the farmer, who carried a pan of milk to the mule. And the mule drank of the milk. "Try it on the other mules," laughed Lincoln. And each of five other mules on the public square eagerly lapped up the milk—in the finish Lincoln's client winning the disputed mule.

Grown-up men and women, even nations, at times were like the little girl Lincoln told Gustave Koerner about. She asked her mother if she could run out and play. The mother refused, and the girl begged harder, kept teasing till the mother gave her a whipping. When that was over the girl said, "Now, ma, I can surely run out and play."

A newly elected Congressman came in, Lincoln knowing him to have a sense of humor, for the gay greeting was: "Come in here and tell me what you know. It won't take long." Meeting a Congressman elected for the second time by the same large majority, he said, "Your district is a good deal like a jug—the handle is all on one side." Two Pennsylvania Congressmen bringing in five six-foot-high soldiers from their State, Lincoln sized them up in a long glance. "Are they all from your State?" and taking a quick survey of the Congressmen, "Why, it seems to me that your State always sends its little men to Congress." A major general from General Scott's staff had his arguments tangled by Lincoln's questions and defended himself. "That is the opinion of General Scott and you know, Mr. President, he is a very able military man." Lincoln: "If he is as able a military man as he is *un*able as a politician, I give up."

Alexander K. McClure, the Pennsylvania editor, wrote of a range or gamut of moods. "I have known Mr. Lincoln many times to silence a controversy by a humorous story with pointed application. I have often known him within the space of a few minutes to be transformed from the saddest face I have ever looked upon to one of the brightest and most mirthful. In the gravest consultations of the Cabinet where he was usually a listener rather than a speaker, he would often end dispute by telling a story and none misunderstood it. Often when he was pressed to give expression of particular subjects, and his always abundant caution was baffled, he many times ended the interview by a story that needed no elaboration." He didn't know beforehand when the mood of humor would come. It bubbled up, unexpected, and often unsettled the most carefully studied arguments. "I have many times been with him when he gave no sign of humor, and those who saw him under such conditions would naturally suppose that he was incapable of a humorous expression. At other times he would effervesce."

A presidential trip on a special train was under discussion, and it was suggested that one railroad president would take pleasure in supplying the transportation. Lincoln agreed, but said that if he believed what some people were saying of that railroad president the case might be different. He told of a son of President Tyler, a Democrat, going to a Whig railroad superintendent and receiving word that the railroad was not running special trains for the accommodation of Presidents just then. "What!" said the young man. "Did you not furnish a special train for the funeral of President Harrison?" "Yes," said the superintendent calmly, "and if you will only bring your father here in that shape you shall have the best train on the road." At a White House breakfast with Brooks, Lincoln mentioned a captain of volunteers convicted of misuse of government funds. To the captain it was a minor affair and he didn't care much about his defense, but when he was charged with the crime of treason, disloyalty to the Government, he broke into hot excitement and put up a fierce defense; the captain smiled at being called embezzler but the name of traitor stung him. Lincoln was reminded of a hen thief convicted in Illinois, one juryman saying afterward: "Why, when I was young, and my back was strong, and the country was new, I didn't mind taking off a sheep now and then. But stealing hens! Oh, Jerusalem!"

Standing at the fireplace of a parlor in the Soldiers' Home one evening Lincoln had explained for a sedate New England judge that if he liked a thing he read, it stuck with him after one reading. He told from the Orpheus C. Kerr papers, of a dying sailor who asked hospital attendants to bring in his grandmother that he might say farewell. Thereupon a messenger is sent to the Navy Department to implore Secretary Welles to put on petticoats and impersonate the grandmother for this occasion Welles declines with regret, giving the excuse that he is busy examining a model of Noah's Ark, with a view to its introduction in the United States Navy. Having told this, Lincoln turned to Noah Brooks and said, "I hope Mr. Welles will never hear that I told this story on him." Brooks: "It will not be your fault, Mr. President, if he does not hear of it, for I have heard you tell it at least a dozen times." Lincoln: "Well, I can't resist telling a good story." The company gone, Lincoln made a semiapology to Brooks: "I was only using you as an old friend. I was afraid Judge P. would go and tell that I had been repeating that."

A District of Columbia official called with a party of politicians to ask appointment of a man opposed by the Senators of his own State. Lincoln suggested they ought to get the Senators on their side. They said local complications made it impossible. Lincoln retorted that nothing was impossible in politics, that the peculiarities of one Senator referred to were well known, and by the use of a little tact and diplomacy he might be brought around to clinch the appointment. The matter was delicate, devious, so far as the Senator was concerned, and Lincoln brought up an incident from real life to make clear his point. A distinguished Tennessee lawyer, James Quarles, presented his evidence in a case and rested. The defense then produced a witness who swore Quarles completely out of court; the verdict was for the defense. Later a friend came to Quarles and said, "Why didn't you get that fellow to swar on your side?" "I didn't know anything about him." "I might have told you about him, for he would swar for you jest as hard as he would for the other side. That's his business. Judge, that feller takes in swarin' for his business."

To illustrate a shifting political policy, Lincoln told of a farm boy whose father instructed him in plowing a new furrow. "Steer for that yoke of oxen standing at the further end of the field." The father went away. The boy followed instructions. But the oxen began moving. The boy followed them around the field, furrowed a circle instead of a line! A footloose and conniving clergyman once came under discussion. Lincoln held the judgment pronounced on the man too hard. "He reminds me of a man in Illinois arrested for passing a counterfeit bill." The man's lawyer, hearing of evidence to be used, asked him before going to court, "Did you take the bill to the cashier of the bank and ask him if it was good?" "I did." "What was the reply of the cashier?" "He said it was a pretty tolerable, respectable sort of a bill." So Lincoln's opinion ran that the man under discussion was "a pretty tolerable, respectable sort of a clergyman."

An ex-governor made a plea for a lieutenant, an orphan from Missouri, convicted of corruptly receiving $40 while an officer on duty. The lieutenant cut in on the ex-governor's reading of a document. "Stop there! Why, Mr. Lincoln, beg pardon, Mr. President, it wa'n't but thirty dollars." The ex-governor put in, "Yes, Mr. President, it was only thirty dollars, as we can prove." Lincoln kept a straight face and gravely told of a man in Indiana wrangling with a neighbor, one charging that the other's daughter had three illegitimate children. "Now," said the man whose family was thus slandered, "that's a lie and I can prove it, for she has only two." Lincoln went on: "This case is no better. Whether the amount was thirty dollars or thirty thousand dollars, the culpability is the same." And reading the papers in the case, he said he would leave it where it was left by the officers who tried it.

The ex-governor brought up another case, that of a woman named Betsy Ann Dougherty. "She did my washing for a long time. Her husband went off and joined the rebel army, and I wish you would give her a protection paper." Lamon was listening, looking on, noted the President masked his humor and with inimitable gravity inquired, "Is Betsy Ann a good washerwoman?" She was indeed, said the ex-governor. "Is your Betsy Ann an obliging woman?" She was certainly very kind, the ex-governor responded soberly. "Could she do other things than wash?" the President asked without batting an eyelash. Oh, yes, she was very kind—very. "Where is Betsy Ann?" It came out she was in New York, wanted to come back to Missouri, but was afraid of banishment. "Is anybody meddling with her?" "No; but she is afraid to come back unless you give her a protection paper." Thereupon, noted Lamon, Lincoln turned to his desk and wrote on a card, which he signed: "Let Betsy Ann Dougherty alone as long as she behaves herself." Handing over the card, he said it should be given to Betsy Ann. "But, Mr. President, couldn't you write a few words to the officers that would insure her protection?" "No, officers have no time now to read letters. Tell Betsy Ann to put a string to this card and hang it around her neck. When the officers see this, they will keep their hands off your Betsy Ann."

Lamon gave this as an instance of Lincoln using "mirth-provoking trifles" out of the day's routine for relaxation. When the ex-governor, accompanied by a committee from Missouri, had left with his card for Betsy Ann, Lincoln had a laugh about it, and then, said Lamon, "relapsed into his accustomed melancholy, contemplative mood, as if looking for something else—looking for the end." He sat in thought for a time at the desk and turned to Lamon. "This case of our old friend, the governor, and his Betsy Ann, is a fair sample of the trifles I am constantly asked to give my attention to. I wish I had no more serious questions to deal with. If there were more Betsy Anns and fewer fellows like her husband, we should be better off. She seems to have laundered the governor to his full satisfaction, but I am sorry she didn't keep her husband washed cleaner."

An Englishman in service as an admiral of Chile's navy came to the White House to get permission to buy and export two vessels for the use of that country in troubles with Spain. While Seward glanced over the Chilean state paper making so unusual a request, Lincoln said: "Admiral, I must tell you a little story. When a young man I was anxious to read a book which belonged to a neighbor. 'Could you lend me this book?' I asked. 'Certainly,' he replied, 'you can come here and read it whenever you like.' As the book was rather a bulky one I thought this was rather an odd way of lending it to me, but I let that pass. A short time afterward he came to me. 'Lincoln,' he asked, 'can you lend me your bellows?' 'Certainly,' I replied, 'here they are: you can come here and blow away as much as you like.' And that is exactly the case now, Admiral. You can come here and blow away as much as you like, but we cannot let you take the ships away."

During the Trent Affair Lincoln urged, "The less risk we run the better," and mentioned a recent battle where amid furious fire of shot and shell an officer drew his revolver and ordered a running soldier: "Go to the front with your regiment or I'll shoot you." The private yelled, "Shoot and be damned—what's one bullet to a whole hatful?!" Once when the interference of foreign nations with American affairs was under discussion, the President was quoted in a reminiscence of early Indiana days when he had called at a farmhouse overrun with children managed by a redheaded mother who kept a whip and made everyone come to time at her orders. "There's trouble here, and lots of it," she blurted, "but I kin manage my own affairs without the help of outsiders. This is jest a family row, but I'll teach these brats their places ef I have to lick the hide off every one of them. I don't do much talkin', but I run this house, an' I don't want no one sneakin' round tryin' to find out how I do it, either." Lincoln ended: "That's the case with us. We must let the other nations know that we propose to settle our family row in our own way."

Assistant Attorney General Titian J. Coffey explained to Lincoln that a sudden activity had developed among United States Marshals to control a $100,000 fund appropriated by Congress to be spent under the President's direction in defending United States officers in suits for false arrests and illegal seizures. Until the special fund was created these Marshals had called on the Attorney General for defense; now they were after the cash. Coffey was submitting to the President for his approval some rules under which payments of this money should be made. "Yes," mused Lincoln, "they will now all be after the money and be content with nothing else. They are like a man in Illinois, whose cabin was burned down, and according to the kindly custom of early days in the West, his neighbors all contributed something to start him again. In his case they had been so liberal that he soon found himself better off than before the fire, and he got proud. One day, a neighbor brought him a bag of oats, but the fellow refused it with scorn. 'No,' said he, 'I'm not taking oats now. I take nothing but money.' "

A committee of clergymen from three denominations urged a change in the system of appointing regimental chaplains, saying many of the chaplains were notoriously bad. Lincoln replied that the Government had little to do with the matter, as the chaplains were mostly chosen by the regiments at that time. The committee pressed their points, Lincoln heard them through, and said that without disrespect he would tell a story. "Once, in Springfield, I was going off on a short journey, and reached the depot a little ahead of time. Leaning against the fence just outside the depot was a little darkey boy, whom I knew, named 'Dick,' busily digging with his toe in a mud-puddle. As I came up, I said, 'Dick, what are you about?'

" 'Making a "*church,*" ' said he.

" 'A church?' said I; 'what do you mean?'

" 'Why, yes,' said Dick, pointing with his toe, 'don't you see? there is the shape of it; there's the "steps" and "front-door"—here the "pews," where the folks set—and there's the "pulpit." '

" 'Yes, I see,' said I, 'but why don't you make a "minister"?'

" 'Laws,' answered 'Dick,' with a grin, 'I hain't got *mud* enough!' "

At a mention of some persons' not capitalizing the name of the Deity, the President was reminded of a Confederate soldier's letter saying the Yankees would be licked in the next battle "if goddlemity spares our lives."

Recruiting in Kentucky for the 5th United States Colored Cavalry, Colonel James Sanks Brisbin met various troubles. As an abolitionist orator in Ohio Brisbin had known Senator Ben Wade, and he went to Washington for help. He and Wade called at the White House. "Mr. Lincoln assailed us with a perfect avalanche of jokes," according to Brisbin, who rated the President as "undoubtedly the champion joker of the United States." The clock hand was past eleven, the Senate was to meet at twelve noon, and Wade chafed at the delay. "Sit down, Mr. Wade, I am going to tell you a story," smiled the President. Wade rejoined that it was almost time for the Senate to convene. "Well, well, if the Senate meets without you, why, let it meet," smiled Lincoln again, and turning to Brisbin, asked about the people of Kentucky. Were they loyal? And the conversation, as published in the *Philadelphia Times* and other newspapers, and credited to Brisbin:

"Sometimes the Kentucky people are loyal and sometimes not. When they think the Union is going to win they get loyal until Lee gains a battle on the Potomac, and then when it looks better for the Confederacy, they become disloyal again."

"That reminds me of the high- and the low-combed cock," said Abe, "and as it is a capital story I must tell it to you."

"Now, Mr. Lincoln," said Wade, "I must be going, as it is nearly 12 and I have barely time to reach the Senate before it assembles. I have a little business with you, and–"

"Sit down, sit down, man," cried Lincoln; "the Senate can assemble, I say, without you being there, and I must tell you this story; besides I won't be five minutes, and you can surely give me that much of your time." Uncle Abe then related the following story, as nearly as I recollect it in my own words:

"When I was a youngster out in Kentucky there was a chap who had a high-combed cock that could lick all the roosters in the country. One day an emigrant came in to settle who said he had a low-combed cock he reckoned could thrash anything in them parts, the high-combed cock included. The interest became intense, and the chickens were examined by all the boys. Both looked well, and seemed to be genuine game-cocks. A meeting was arranged to come off between the cocks, and the whole neighborhood was excited over it. Squire C—— was a noted man and very sharp. The Squire was always right, but no one could ever find out exactly what his beliefs were, his reserved opinions being the correct ones. The Squire was consulted about the roosters, as he was about everything else, and putting his spectacles on his nose, he examined both roosters carefully. He said the high-combed cock had 'pints' about him which indicated he would win, but the low-combed cock was much the heaviest rooster of the two, and by sheer weight might beat his antagonist. The young fellows who wanted to bet questioned the Squire closely, but they could not get any nearer to his opinion of the real merits of the chickens. The day came for the battle, and with it a great crowd. The Squire presided, for in those days more than now, racing, fighting and betting were the height of a Kentuckian's glory. Close attention was given to the Squire's position on the fight, as he was both oracle and judge.

" 'I propose,' said the Squire, 'this yere shell be a fare fite, and tharfore we will give three cheers for both roosters.' It was done with a will, and the fight began. At every turn in the battle the Squire would cry out: 'Hurrah for the high-combed cock! Hurrah for the low-combed cock!' Once he made a bet on the high-combed cock, but immediately hedged by betting on the low-combed cock. At last, after a bloody contest, the low-combed cock got the worst of it, and turned tail and ran. 'Hurrah! hurrah! hurrah for the high-combed cock! Gentlemen, I knew that rooster would win in the end, but it is always unfair to express an opinion in a contest like this in advance of the rale issoo. Now, gentlemen, you have had all the fun, but you see that high-combed cock was bound to win. Why, look at his comb! Any man can see with half an eye he is a real game chicken, while that other one is only a dunghill fowl!'

"Now," cried Uncle Abe, "that is the way it is with those fellows out in Kentucky. They want to be on both sides of this fight and hurrah for the high- or the low-combed cock as policy dictates. If we win, they will be good Union men, but if Jeff Davis were to win, they would be the best Rebels in the world. General," he said, seriously, "I think we have got the high-combed cock in this fight. We must see to it that our rooster wins, and then in the end we will be all right."

I sat and looked in astonishment at the great man before me. I had come to Washington to explain to him my embarrassments in Kentucky on account of the anomalous position of the State and the varying temper of the people. Kentucky was then a State in the Union, with a representation in our Congress, but she had sent no less than thirty-four thousand men to the Rebel army, and had also a representation in the Rebel Congress at Richmond. I had expected to have some difficulty in making my embarrassments understood, but here was a man who knew everything, and by a simple story had not only explained my situation, but had pointed out what I would do.

Brigadier General John Gross Barnard, chief engineer to the Army of the Potomac in the Peninsula campaign, told of McClellan's plan early in the war to surround Washington with fortifications. At the review by Lincoln and his Cabinet of troops and forts, the President asked General McClellan why such heavy embankments and gun emplacements had been located to the north of the capital city. According to Barnard, McClellan's reply ran: "Why, Mr. President, according to military science it is our duty to guard against every possible or supposable contingency that may arise. For example, if under any circumstances, however fortuitous, the enemy, by any chance or freak, should in a last resort get in behind Washington in his efforts to capture the city, why, there is the fort to defend it." The precaution, said the President, was doubtless a wise one, and the clear explanation of the General reminded him of a question discussed once at a lyceum in Springfield when he was studying law. "The question," Lincoln rambled on, "was, 'Why does man have breasts?' and after long debate the question was submitted to the presiding judge who wisely decided 'that if under any circumstances, however fortuitous, or by any chance or freak, no matter what the nature or by what cause, a man should have a baby, there would be the breasts to nurse it.' "

One fable Nicolay heard in use by Lincoln, its central character the hard-worked backwoods housewife in her messed-up log cabin, many ragtag children running around, the pioneer struggler making "the best of things." A wandering Methodist preacher tried to sell her a Bible. She was polite to begin with, but she didn't like the way he pushed some questions. Shouldn't every home have a Bible? Did they have a Bible in this home? Her sharp answer came that of course they owned a Bible. If so, where was it? the man asked. She began a hunt, finding no Bible. She called the children and they joined in the hunt for the missing Bible. At last one of them dug up from some corner and held up in triumph a few torn and ragged pages of Holy Writ. The man tried to argue this was no Bible, and how could they pretend it was? The woman stuck to her claims. Of course they had a Bible in the house. "But I had no idea we were so nearly out!"

The glib representations of one military report, concealing disgrace and defeat involved, reminded Lincoln of the young fellow who shouted at the plowing farmer, "I want your daughter!" The farmer went on plowing, merely shouting over his shoulder, "Take her," whereupon the youth stood scratching his head: "Too easy, too durned easy!"

The seizure early in the war of all copies of dispatches in the major telegraph offices of the country uncovered names, individuals, disloyalties, to an extent shocking, even appalling. Lincoln thought of an Illinois farmer who for years had prized and loved a soaring elm tree that spread its majestic branches near his house. Chasing a squirrel one day, the farmer saw the little animal scurry up the giant elm's trunk and suddenly disappear in a hole. Looking farther, the farmer found the great tree to be hollow, the whole inside rotten, a tree ready to fall at the next heavy storm wind. Lincoln quoted the farmer as moaning to his wife, "My God! I wish I had never seen that squirrel!" And pointing to the piles of telltale copies of dispatches: "And I wish we had never seen what we have seen today."

An overly officious general made wholesale arrests of citizens in one of the Border States, recalling to Lincoln the judge in flush times in Alabama. The hushed quiet of the courtroom was broken by the slam and clatter of a falling stovepipe. In a collapse of nerves, and not knowing what had happened, the judge cried out, "Sheriff, arrest every one of them!" and to the court clerk, "Enter a fine against every one in the room, women and children alone excepted."

An old man came from Tennessee and asked a pardon for his son condemned by court-martial to be shot at sunrise. Lincoln promised he would attend to the matter. The old man cried out that tomorrow wouldn't do—the shooting was at sunrise. Lincoln drawled a story to the old man, of a regiment where the colonel had made his troops promise that he would do all the swearing and they would lay off. But a mule-driver, stuck in mud to the hubs, one day let out a volcano of profanity just as the colonel came along and heard the tumultuous oaths, and asked what about it. "Colonel," said the teamster, "I did vow to let you do all the swearing of the regiment, but the cold fact is, that the swearing *had* to be done thar and then or not at all—and you weren't thar." With that Lincoln handed the old man a signed pardon and said, "I may not be there, so you take this and do the swearing him off."

A caller asked a pardon for a young Confederate surgeon who for fairly good and humane reasons had passed through the Union Army lines, was captured and sentenced to prison for the duration of the war. Lincoln said he couldn't offend the Secretary of War by interfering. The caller said the very reason he had come was because the President was known to be more patient and humane. Lincoln admitted there was a difference between him and Stanton, and was reminded of a Maine man who had a bull terrier that could whip any other dog in the neighborhood. Its owner was asked how it came his dog could outfight all others, and said it wasn't peculiar. "Your dog and other dogs get half through a fight before they are ready; my dog is always mad."

Whatever incident was related to the President, it never failed to remind him of something similar, noted Carpenter. In a night walk over to the War Department, Carpenter told of a "contraband" who had fallen into the hands of some good pious people and they were teaching him to read and pray. Going off by himself one day, he was overheard commencing a prayer by explaining and identifying himself to God Almighty as "Jim Williams—a berry good nigga to wash windows—'spec's you know me now?" This, laughed the President, was a "direct way of putting the case," and went on: "The story that suggests to me, has no resemblance to it save in the 'washing windows' part. A lady in Philadelphia had a pet poodle dog, which mysteriously disappeared. Rewards were offered for him, and a great ado made without effect. Some weeks passed, and all hope of the favorite's return had been given up, when a servant brought him in one day, in the filthiest condition imaginable. The lady was overjoyed to see her pet again, but horrified at his appearance. 'Where *did* you find him?' she exclaimed. 'Oh,' replied the man, very unconcernedly, 'a negro down the street had him tied to the end of a pole, *swabbing* windows.'"

A Midwest friend remarked that Lincoln looked about the same as he did out in Illinois, reminding Lincoln of a farmer who put an old horse out to pasture to "recuperate," the farmer declaring after some months that the horse was looking the same as ever: "He neither recupes nor decupes."

Out of conscription routine came the story of a recruit unable to name his father, explaining, "Captain, sir, I guess I'm just a camp-meetin' baby." When this at a later time was repeated to John Hay he chuckled. Hay had heard Lincoln tell "that one." More long-spun was one Lincoln told Lamon, in connection with the current turmoil between North and South. A man chased around a tree by a bull gained on the bull and got it by the tail. The bull pawed, snorted, broke into a run, the man after it still holding to the tail and bawling, "Darn you, who commenced this fuss?"

New Orleans Unionists at the White House asked the President if he had heard the prize Delta conundrum, "Why are greenbacks like the Jews?" He crossed his legs, smiled, gave it up, and they roared the answer, "Because—because they are the issues of Father Abraham, waiting for a redeemer." His sides shook. "I owe you one, and here it is. You remind me of a cow in Illinois," but here Stanton came in, and Lincoln walked out with Stanton and with a messenger who later told the New Orleans visitors that Stanton had wanted to know from Lincoln who was "that lean cur at General Butler's heels" who for three days had insisted on telling Stanton how the Department of the Gulf should be managed. "He is not a cur," laughed Lincoln. "You are too severe, Mr. Secretary. He is only a burr. Someone flung him at Butler, in sport, and the fellow has the facility of sticking."

Joseph W. Fifer of Bloomington, Illinois, believed a story that he heard Richard Oglesby swear was true. It was "about a clergyman who appeared to think he was specially anointed of the Lord; kind of a pompous fellow," and as Fifer told it:

> He came to the White House with some impossible request or recommendation and he had a lot of papers with him that told how well anointed he was. The President had to refuse the request, or whatever it was, and the rector lost his temper. In those days St. John's church, across from the White House, was called "exclusive," and when the clergyman flounced out of the President's study Lincoln called after him, "Here, here, doctor, you've forgotten your papers!"
>
> "Never mind my papers," shouted the visitor, and kept going.
>
> "Better take 'em, doctor," said Lincoln. "You may need 'em to get into St. John's church next Sunday!"

Was there humor, grim in its breath of brevity, in one verbal Lincoln message carried back to Illinois? Governor Yates gave it to the 10th Illinois Cavalry, according to the *Chicago Tribune* of February 4, 1864. It came from "My friend Bill Greene of Menard County," said the Governor. Greene in closing an interview with the President, had asked, "Mr. Lincoln, what shall I say to the people of Illinois?" "Say to them," replied the President, "that I have Jeff Davis by the throat." And from the 10th Illinois Cavalry applause and cheers roared.

Of the agility of one spy who had come through the enemy lines with valuable information Lincoln said to Seward: "Did you ever try to put your finger on a flea to find he wasn't there? That's the way with my man. He got these plans and immediately wasn't there." Thus one of the secret service told it.

A California member of the Republican National Committee, Cornelius Cole, with a colleague Thomas Shannon, paid an official visit on a matter of business so tangled that it reminded Lincoln of a young Universalist preacher who came to Springfield. Three ministers of orthodox churches agreed "to take turns and preach this young fellow down." It fell to the Methodist to preach the first sermon. "He commenced by telling his large congregation how happily they were all situated in Springfield. Launching into his sermon the Methodist shouted, 'And now comes a preacher preaching a doctrine that all men shall be saved. But, my brethren, let us hope for better things.' " This one Seward too had heard, repeating it as a sample of Lincoln humor.

Another caller told about a friend of his, early in the war, ordered out of New Orleans as a Unionist. He had asked a committee of Confederates to see the writ by which he was expelled, and the committee told him their government had made up their minds to do nothing illegal, were issuing no illegal writs, and he would have to get out of his own free will. Lincoln was reminded of a St. Louis hotel-keeper who claimed a record no one had ever died in his hotel. "Whenever a guest was dying in his house, he carried him out to die in the street."

A general was being outmaneuvered in West Virginia. At the high danger point Lincoln said the general reminded him of a man out West who put his boy inside a barrel to hold up the head while the father pounded down the hoops. When the job was done the father saw he hadn't figured on how to get the boy out again. "Some people can succeed better in getting themselves and others corked up than in getting uncorked."

Once when results were slow from armies in the field the President, according to Alexander K. McClure, had regretful comment: "Some of my generals are so slow that molasses in the coldest days of winter is a race horse compared to them. They're brave enough, but somehow or other, they get fastened in a fence corner, and can't figure their way out." Of a Union and a Confederate army maneuvering as if they might soon be fighting, though not reaching the combat stage, Welles noted the President's remark they were like "two dogs that get less eager to fight the nearer they come to each other." Another general constantly telegraphed Washington, afraid to move without advice from the War Department. Lincoln was reminded of what a Tammany man told him about John Morrissey's absolute control in New York of organization members. When two members met one time and one said he was going to be married, the other looked anxious. "Ain't you glad I'm to get married?" "Of course, but," as he put his mouth close to the ear of the other, "have you asked Morrissey yet?" And the President added, "This general of whom we are speaking, wouldn't dare order the guard out without asking Morrissey." Fears were telegraphed by Burnside's command, lost down in Tennessee and not heard of for some time. Lincoln was reminded of Sally Ward on an Illinois farm with fourteen children. Sometimes one of them got hurt and let out a loud cry somewhere in the cornfield or the timber. Then Sally Ward would sing out, "Thank Heaven there's one of my children that ain't dead yet."

Illustrative, in a backwoods way, was the anecdote from Lincoln when delegations early in the war urged the sending of fleets to Southern ports with the strategic aim of drawing off the Confederate Army from Washington. Lincoln was reminded of a girl in Illinois troubled with a "singing" in the head. Various remedies had failed her when "a common-sense sort of man came along" who inquired, examined, said the cure was very simple. "What is it?" "Make a plaster of *psalm-tunes* and apply to her feet and draw the 'singing' *down*."

An aloof quality, not alien to humor or even fantasy, was there in Lincoln meeting a Confederate blockade-runner who, for reasons known to the President, had been let out of Old Capitol Prison. Lincoln heard the released man speak thanks, and responded, "I am happy to know I am able to serve an enemy." To an elegantly dressed Maryland woman asking release for her brother, an officer of the United States Navy who had resigned and had been put under arrest, the President said he recognized the powerful influences used in behalf of her brother, "but the fact is there are some of us here who have taken an oath to support this old Government." Once a petitioner, of doubtful loyalty, handed the President a letter signed by an influential Marylander. While the President read it another man in line spoke up saying the signer of the letter had been dead several months. The petitioner turned pale, sank into a chair in a half-faint. Lincoln: "Never mind, sir, never mind. I would rather get a letter from a dead man than from a live man any day." An Englishman who spoke the goodwill of his country's people for the Union cause quoted the President: "We have a good deal of salt water between us. When you feel kindly toward us we cannot, unfortunately, be always aware of it. But it works both ways, when you in England are cross with us, we don't feel it quite so badly." One visitor had heard the President suffered for want of advice. "Yes," said Lincoln, "I am suffering for it. I remember a clock-peddler in McLean County, Illinois, who told the people that they were actually suffering for clocks." This aloof quality was there high-lighted in the diary entry of Hay on July 1, 1864: "This evening I referred to Wilkeson's blackguardly statements in today's *Tribune* & asked if I might not prepare a true statement of facts to counteract the effects of these falsehoods. He [the President] answered, 'Let 'em wriggle.'" It was a day earlier in the war that Nicolay found, on an envelope holding a raving, vituperative letter, the memo of his chief: "Send him a copy of my debates."

Sarcasm edged some of the fables. A man came to a farm to have a look at a rare specimen of a big hog. The farmer insisted on charging 25 cents for the look. The stranger paid the two bits, started walking away, and the farmer called, "Don't you want to see the hog?" "No, I've seen as big a hog as I care to see for today." Or again when politicians already well taken care of came asking for more jobs in a certain department, conditions in that department put Lincoln in mind of two fellows calling on the daughters of a widow who kept a lot of hounds, three or four of them spread around the fireplace, two or three more in the corners of the room as the boys arrived to see the daughters. Another hound was trying to edge in at the door when the old woman gave him a kick, saying: "Get out of here. There's too many dogs in here now." A New Jersey Congressman brought in two heavy constituents to whom he had made a promise he would show them the one and only Old Abe in person. "Mr. President, this is Mr. X and Mr. Y, and they are among the weightiest men in southern New Jersey." They left and Lincoln had to "wonder that end of the State didn't tip up when they got off it."

Signing a brigadier general's commission for Napoleon Jackson Tecumseh Dana, Lincoln pronounced the name; it would "certainly frighten the enemy." He was told of an author he considered "tedious" that of this profound historian "it may be doubted whether any man of our generation has plunged more deeply in the sacred fount of learning." "Yes, or come up dryer," said Lincoln. The same thrusting style he had used in Congress in 1848 when satirizing General Cass was in a note to Frank P. Blair, July 30, 1863: "I would like to know who is the great man Alexander, that talks so oracularly about 'if the President keeps his word' and Banks not having 'capacity to run an omnibus on Broadway'? How has this Alexander's immense light been obscured hitherto?"

Wishing to check a newspaper Biblical reference to the Frémont Cleveland convention, Lincoln asked for a copy of the Bible. A polite offer to go get a Bible came from Albert Johnson, Stanton's secretary, described by David Homer Bates as "a very obsequious, dapper little man." Johnson soon brought in and laid before the President a Bible. Lincoln looked up the reference he wanted. Johnson meantime had left the room. Then, according to Bates, who said he was there and saw and heard it, Lincoln arose with a smile, saying: "I am always interested in the movements of Johnson. Now let me show you how he did that." Then as a performance in pantomime and mimicry, Lincoln took the Bible in his hands, presented it in a very obsequious style to Major Eckert and said, "That is the way Johnson did that." This, noted Bates, created a laugh among those looking on. An odd little functionary, a curious and incessant yes-man to Stanton, Lincoln impersonated in a funny little errand with a Bible.

Another impersonation was given for Governor Yates of Illinois, Secretary Seward, and Judge Steele of the land division of the Indian Bureau. The business of the group having been transacted, Lincoln introduced H. P. H. Bromwell of Illinois to Seward and began telling of an 1856 political rally at Grandview, Illinois, "when we had fun." He rehearsed flighty and curious lines spoken by Judge J. P. Cooper of Clark County and the replies by one Dr. A. Goodell of Kansas. The Doctor in the course of his vituperation said, "The new Republican party is composed of the essence of the putrescence of purulent matter and it has agitated and shaken this great fabric from center to circumference." Judge Cooper's reply in part: "Fellow citizens, I am going home and when I get there I am going to take down my dictionary and if I find one word in it I have just listened to, I'll burn the thing in the cook-stove so none of it can escape." In his mimicry Lincoln included such particulars, according to Bromwell, as Judge Cooper screaming, "I'll take anything in the world from you, but for God's sake don't give me any of your pills," Dr. Goodell shouting back, "I've got no pill that would help your case—I don't treat delirium." Flourishing a cane and limping, short and stout with a lame hip, Lincoln went back and forth, "doing" Judge Cooper. Laying the cane on a table, he then "took off" Dr. Goodell. The room, as Bromwell remembered it, roared with laughter.

Congressman J. B. Grinnell of Iowa once reminded Lincoln "that you with some of the rest of us were out last night." Lincoln rejoined, "Yes," he was in the theatre audience the previous evening, "and they said my coarse laugh was very audible. But what did you think, Grinnell, was the best thing there last night? I will tell you what convulsed me." Then, as Grinnell told it: "Mr. Lincoln rose from his chair and stepped out from behind the table, struck an attitude and raised his hand as if in holy horror: 'Lord, how this world is given to lying.' " This bit of pantomime and speech over, he continued, "We had some good war news yesterday and I was glad to unbend and laugh. The acting was good, and true to the case, according to my experiences, for each fellow tells his story and smirches his rival."

Those who believed Lincoln entirely a tenderhearted man, his humor and laughter merely for relief from the heavy cares of office, were mistaken, in the view of Colonel Donn Piatt, recruiting Negro troops in Maryland. Piatt believed Lincoln may have shed tears when his friend Baker was killed at Ball's Bluff but Piatt wouldn't believe the report that after the Chancellorsville slaughter Lincoln threw himself on a sofa in Stanton's office and burst into tears. With General Schenck, Piatt had called on Lincoln, heard the President say he "ate his rations and slept well," and Piatt believed Lincoln's looks sustained the assertion. "What man of keen, delicate sensibility could find relief from cares of any sort in jests so coarse that they cannot be put to record?" Piatt asked. "This habit ran through his life from the time he was a day-laborer. While a railsplitter in his early manhood he was noted for his jokes and stories. Had he then the necessity for relief? As a member of the bar he was accustomed to amuse his associates in the same way. Did the reason for relief apply in that case? As a member of Congress he was a habitué of the cloakroom, holding a circle of amused members, listening to the recital of his funny stories. Were the cares of legislation so heavy that this was necessary? It is all nonsense. The habit of life that had come to be second nature clung to him."

And Piatt emphasized his opinions that President Lincoln had no worry, had strong confidence in himself, a deep reliance on the rule of right, exercised power without the loss of nerve-force, "ate with appetite, and slept the sleep of the just." Lincoln's tough hide, or lack of fine sensibilities, in Piatt's view was traced tersely by the Wendell Phillips expression that Lincoln was "the white trash of the South spawned on Illinois."

Thus educated men troubled themselves with attempts to reduce to simple points the shifting lights and glooms of the Lincoln personality. They would deny the wriggling in one human frame of Hamlet and Falstaff.

Piatt's temperament ran to the same color as Chase, whom he counted one of the heroic figures of the war. Neither would tell such reminiscences, half-ridiculing themselves, as Lincoln did in the White House, once recalling an old hard-boiled Democrat stepping up to him at Decatur, just after the State Republican convention had nominated him for President. "So you're Abe Lincoln?" "Yes, that is my name." "They say you're a self-made man." "Well, yes, in a way what there is of me is self-made." "Well," said the old man with a long survey, "all I've got to say is that it was a damned bad job."

Young Horace White of the *Chicago Tribune* saw Lincoln through the debates with Douglas and on through years in the White House—and White wrote with feeling and color of how Lincoln's sense of humor was fatefully intermeshed with the man's everyday behavior and democratic habits. "I have seen him a hundred times," noted White, "his lantern jaws and large mouth and solid nose firmly set, his sunken eyes looking at nothing yet not unexpressive, his wrinkled and retreating forehead cut off by a mass of tousled hair, with a shade of melancholy drawn like a veil over his whole face. Nothing more unlike this can be imagined than the same Lincoln when taking part in a conversation, or addressing an audience, or telling a story. The dull listless features dropped like a mask. The melancholy shadow disappeared in a twinkling. The eye began to sparkle, the mouth to smile, the whole countenance was wreathed in animation, so that a stranger would have said, 'Why, this man, so angular and somber a moment ago, is really handsome.' "

A sense of humor made him wary of "ornament" in his speeches, thought White. "Although gifted with the power of humor to an extraordinary degree, he seldom employed it in his later years except in private circles. Thus it came about that this growing master of logic, this profound and earnest debater of the most serious questions of the day, was the most popular of tavern loungers, and could draw more people together and hold them longer by mere drollery and *cameraderie* [sic] than any other man I ever knew."

Directly from this the hard-boiled newsman White moved to an associated phase. "Mr. Lincoln's nature was one of almost child-like sweetness. He did not 'put you at your ease' when you came into his presence. You felt at your ease without being put there. He never assumed superiority over anybody in the ordinary intercourse of life. . . . His democracy was of the unconscious kind—he did not know anything different from it. Coupled with this was a habit of unselfishness and kindly temper most engaging to all who knew him. At the same time he knew when he was imposed upon, and it was unsafe for anybody to presume upon his good nature or to take him for a flat."

White was just out of college, "callow and self-confident" when first thrown with Lincoln. "I was often with him when he had no other companion. He always paid marked deference to my opinions, and if we differed he would argue the point with me as earnestly as though I had been the opposing counsel in a lawsuit. And this he would do with anybody, young or old, ignorant or learned. I never heard him express contempt for any man's honest errors, although he would sometimes make a droll remark or tell a funny story about them. Deference to other people's opinions was habitual with him. There was no calculation, no politics in it. It was part and parcel of his sense of equal rights." This peculiar sincerity he wore "as he wore his clothes, except that it fitted him much better than his garments usually did."

In some respects Lincoln simply gave no thought to his cultural advance, or rather he maintained an indifference to some forms of conventional polish. Welles recorded Lincoln's reference to one politician as "a mighty onhandy man." Galusha Grow told of his taking a Pennsylvania infantry company to see the President, who stepped out of the White House, looked around, put his hand behind him. "When I get this handkerchief out of this coat-tail pocket I intend to shake hands with you boys!" Casual mention by a White House visitor of an old mutual friend brought the reminiscence: "I have known him now for almost thirty years; my first board bill in Springfield began on the 15th of April, 1837, and he came along about strawberry time." Four picked New York soldiers who were plumbers stacked arms in the White House kitchen, began a repair job, and the Commander in Chief of the Army and Navy entered, half-sat and half-leaned on a table, holding one knee in his hands, and chuckled. "Boys, I certainly am glad to see you; I hope you can fix that thing right off, for if you can't the cook can't use the range and I don't suppose I'll get any grub to-day."

One Eastern critic of Lincoln could not accommodate himself to Lincoln's saying of some move "It has petered out," and of someone's plan "It won't jibe," and when Lincoln was asked if the war and the Union cause were not a great care, his reply: "Yes, it is a heavy hog to hold." These phrases were to Lincoln durable and worn devices. Common in the

Midwest was the neighborhood butchering when the hog carcass, stripped of its hair by scalding, with a gambrel bar slit through its hocks, was swung clear of the ground. In this moving and hoisting of a wet and slippery animal, weighing perhaps two hundred pounds, it took a good man to "hold the hog." And Lincoln being asked whether the war and the Union cause weighed him down, reverted to a familiar and belaboring experience. "Yes, it is a heavy hog to hold."

To the army and to the President there was fun in the German picket who heard the password "Potomac" from another German as "Bottomic" and gave it to another as "Buttermilk." An officer that night trying to return through the lines was challenged, gave the word "Potomac" and was told, "Nicht right; you don't pass mit me dis vay." "But I gave you the right word, and I will pass." "No, you stan'," said the picket, putting his bayonet at the breast of the officer, who now asked, "What is the word then?" "Buttermilk." "All right—Buttermilk—let me pass." "Das is right; now you pass mit youself all about your pizziness."

One story James M. Scovel said Lincoln told to illustrate the petty jealousies and bickerings among Congressmen and army generals. Lincoln was reminded of two Illinois men, one Farmer Jones, a churchman gifted in prayer, the other Fiddler Simpkins, welcome at every country merry-making. At one Wednesday evening prayer meeting Brother Jones made a wonderful prayer which touched the hearts of all. And Brother Simpkins felt called on to rise and say, "Brethring and sistring, I know that I can't make half as good a prayer as Brother Jones, but by the grace of God I *can* fiddle the shirt off of him."

In an afternoon call on Lincoln, Dr. Robert Boal of Lacon, Illinois, said he noticed the dignity of high authority about the President, but on a second call in the evening, "he had thrown off his reserve somewhat, and would walk up and down the room with his hands to his sides and laugh at the joke he was telling or at one that was told to him. I remember one." It was about Tom Corwin going down to Alexandria that day and coming back to Lincoln with a report about an old man he met who knew George Washington. And this old man told Tom Corwin that George Washington was addicted to the vices and infirmities of man, and gave cases. This so relieved Corwin that he "just shouted for joy."

Of General Schenck's methods in Maryland, forcibly enlisting Negroes without asking consent of master or slave, Hay heard "the Tycoon" observe: "The fact is Schenck is wider across the head in the region of the ears, & loves fight for its own sake, better than I do." Hay noted too that Seward spoke one morning in November of '63 of a dispatch revealing that General Banks had been on the point of firing upon the Mexican border town of Matamoras, opposite the town of Brownsville on American soil.

"He was about to fire on them, then?" said the Prest.

"Yes," said Seward. "Our consul at Matamoras asked for protection and he brought his guns to bear on the castle for that purpose. I wrote to him at once that that would be war. That if our consul wanted protection he must come to Brownsville for it. Firing upon the town would involve us in a war with the Lord knows who."

"Or rather," said the Tycoon, "the Lord knows who not."

While the President sat with his Cabinet one morning an outsider managed to get a card put into the President's hands: Mr. E. A. Becker, D.N.T.A., Chicago, Illinois. Lincoln asked the doorman if he knew what the D.N.T.A. meant, and he didn't. Lincoln threw the pasteboard to Seward, to Chase, and passed it on to the rest of the scholars; not one could tell what title or office was designated by D.N.T.A. Becker was called in and Lincoln insisted he must first of all tell the high men of the United States Government what D.N.T.A. stood for. Becker beamed as he said, "Deputy North Town Assessor." And the Cabinet meeting proceeded after Lincoln had granted a pardon to Becker's brother-in-law on evidence that the convicted man had deserted his regiment for the one reason that he had been refused a furlough to go home while his wife bore a child.

For the Unionist Governor Pierpont of Virginia Lincoln repeated Orpheus C. Kerr's yarn of a man eagerly seeking an interview with Secretary Welles, being told over and again that Secretary Welles was "busy." Finally he was let in. "And, my son, what do you think I saw? There sat the Secretary of the Navy, in profound contemplation, studying the last and most improved model of Noah's ark." Of this Pierpont noted Lincoln as saying: "Nothing . . . since I came to Washington has afforded me so much amusement. You must not say anything about this, as coming from me. If Mr. Welles should hear that I was laughing at his expense he might think hard of it."

With a lighted face he told Pierpont in early '63, "If an intelligent angel from heaven would drop down in one corner of this room and sit there for two weeks hearing all that is said to me, I think he would come to the conclusion that this war was being prosecuted for the purpose of obtaining cotton from the South for the Northern cotton mills."

A California man informing Lincoln of an old Springfield storyteller he had met on the West Coast, Lincoln was reminded that the former Illinois man, a dry wit, had been Secretary of State once and a meek, cadaverous stranger entered the office one day requesting a permit for a room in the Capitol to deliver lectures. "May I ask what is to be the subject of your lectures?" "Certainly. The course I wish to deliver is on the Second Coming of Our Lord." "It is of no use. If you will take my advice, you will not waste your time in this city. It is my private opinion that if the Lord has been in Springfield once He will never come the second time."

"Can this man Lincoln *ever* be serious?" wrote Richard Henry Dana in a letter. For the President would tell, in the midst of tremendous efforts to draft a new army, of the boy under fire whose commanding officer called, "You are crying like a baby," getting the answer, "I knows it, Ginral. I wish I was a baby, and a gal-baby, too, and then I wouldn't have been

The campaign of '64 carte-de-visite cartoons of presidential candidates

From the Barrett collection

Lincoln with Nicolay and Hay

Frederick William Seward

Sara Jane Clarke Lippincott
(Grace Greenwood)

Adam Gurowski

La Fayette Curry Baker

From the Meserve collection

conscripted." In the middle of the night he left his room in the White House and routed out Colonel Schuyler Hamilton to tell a yarn that had got the best of him. As they laughed Lincoln noticed he had nothing on but his red flannel undershirt, and it didn't reach below his waist. He started back to bed saying, "Colonel, either I have grown too long or the shirt has grown too short, I know not which!" *Leslie's Weekly* of July 11, 1863, ran the note: "Mr. Lincoln said the other day that almost every officer, whether entitled to a staff or not, had four aides—promenade, lemonade, serenade, and gasconade." The *New York Evening Post* printed a paragraph:

> It is told by a general correspondent who is probably "reliable" that Mr. Lincoln was walking down Pennsylvania Avenue the other day, relating a "little story" to Secretary Seward, when the latter called his attention to a new sign bearing the name of T. R. Strong. "Ha," says Old Abe, his countenance lighting up with a peculiar smile. "T. R. Strong but coffee are stronger." Seward smiled but made no reply. We don't see how he could reply after so atrocious a thing as that.

It was a punning era; newspapers and periodicals were peppered with puns; Lincoln responded to the air of the time that set people punning, just as he had rollicking laughter with army men over the huckleberry cavalry officer in Arkansas who got his men mounted with two orders, first, "Prepare to git on your creeters," and second, "Git." He appreciated the way Dick Oglesby said he had found Kentucky soil "the yallerest kind of yaller." The *Bureau County Patriot* in Illinois and hundreds of newspapers reprinted in May of 1863 a distorted incident under the heading of "Old Abe's Valentine" as follows:

> It is stated that President Lincoln, on last Valentine's Day, received a valentine in the shape of a picture of the American Eagle, busily engaged in picking up and swallowing gold coin, while at that portion of the bird most remote from the head was a pile of "Greenbacks," into which the yellow coin seemed to have been mysteriously transmuted. The President, who takes all things philosophically, acknowledged the palpable hit with good-natured cheerfulness, and went with his valentine to the Secretary of the Treasury, in order that the latter might enjoy the joke with him. Mr. Chase, however, did not seem disposed to take the matter in the same spirit the President did; but appeared much out of humor at the hieroglyphical attack on the Finances; he declared his belief that the joke had been got up by some of the subordinates in the Treasury Department, and said he would give a hundred dollars to know who was the perpetrator of it. The President remarked that the offer sounded liberal, but he could make up his judgment better upon that point, if Mr. Chase would tell him "from which pile he proposed to pay?" At this point the Secretary only became still more angry, till the President remarked, "O, never mind! never mind, Mr. Chase! We can soon remedy all this when the war is over. All we have to do is turn the bird end for end, and get him to eating 'greenbacks,' and all will come out right!"

In the telegraph office Lincoln and David Homer Bates discussed Thomas Hood's poem "The Spoiled Child," rehearsed with the operators the scenes: First, the nurse places baby in an armchair before the fire and covers it with a shawl to shield it from the heat; next the fussy aunt comes into the room, and, being nearsighted, fails to observe the sleeping baby and flops into an easy chair when, of course, there is a scream; then the nurse enters and rescues the baby from the heavy weight of the aunt and holds it in her arms edgewise so that when the father of the now *spoiled child* comes in the baby is mashed so flat that the father can't see it. Lincoln, said Bates, produced a counterpart of the Hood story. A man enters a theatre just as the curtain goes up. So interested is the man in looking at what is happening on the stage that he puts his tall silk hat, open side up, on the seat next to him, without noticing a very stout woman who is nearsighted, like the aunt of the spoiled child in the Hood poem, and does not see the hat. She sits down. There is a crunching noise. The owner of the flattened hat reaches out for it as the stout woman rises. He looks at his hat, looks at her: "Madam, I could have told you my hat wouldn't fit you before you tried it on."

Dozens of stories like the foregoing were repeated and in the repetitions came to be told as though Lincoln were an actor, a participant in what happened, that he in a theatre had bowed politely and remarked, "Madam, I could have told you my hat wouldn't fit you before you tried it on." Or Lincoln was the man to whom a fellow came to borrow a boiled shirt, or he personally knew Simpkins who could fiddle the shirt off Deacon Jones, and so on. Noah Brooks, as an instance, after telling one Lincoln story, made the correction, "I am not certain now whether Mr. Lincoln told this story out of his own experience or second-hand." Many who freely recited "Lincoln stories" could have likewise corrected themselves.

Those who might try to analyze humor, and explain the burst of laughter at the climax of a comic anecdote, could focus on a story Bates heard of Lincoln telling, about a man going into an asylum and meeting a little old fellow who demanded a salute. "I am Julius Caesar." The salute was given, the man went on his errand, returned soon, and again the little fellow demanded a salute. "I am Napoleon Bonaparte." "Yes, Napoleon, but a while ago you told me you were Julius Caesar." "Yes, but that was by another mother!" Likewise the anecdote of the man who asked a friend to loan him a clean boiled shirt, getting the answer, "I have only two shirts, the one I have just taken off, and the one I have just put on—which will you have?" Into the ear of Monty Blair Lincoln sent an incident of many details concerning human fright as a cure for boils, of how a certain colonel had ordered his men forward into action while he got off his horse on account of boils that pained him when he sat in saddle. When in a few minutes his troops surged backward in retreat under hot fire the colonel sprang into the saddle, forgot his boils, rode furiously to the rear and got off his horse to find the boils cured—by fright. Similar nonsense pertaining to serious human conduct underlay such press items as *Leslie's Weekly* of November 29, 1862:

Senators Chandler and Hale called lately on the President to thank him for having removed General McClellan. Mr. Lincoln replied by telling his visitors a story, the moral of which was so pointed that they have not yet repeated it, whereby "Abe's last and greatest joke" has not yet been published.

Long before the war Lincoln had heard Illinois variations, in other settings, of the story of the woman picking up chips for a wood fire when suddenly through a timber road came a company of soldiers quietly marching toward the enemy. An officer tiptoed up to the woman, put his arm around her, kissed her—and stepped back to be out of the way of a slap in the face that might be coming. As the woman straightened, sized him up for a nice enough fellow, she said slowly, "Yeou'll find me right here every mornin' a-pickin' up chips." And there was the man asking a new hired boy what he meant by saying he was not Irish though born in Ireland. "Och your honor, if that's all, small blame to that. Suppose your cat were to have kittens in the oven, would they be loaves of bread, do you think?"

Ingenious and entertaining Negro speech and dialect, accredited to Lincoln by his good friends of *Harper's Monthly*, ran through a story going to show black folk acute and logical reasoners. In a Negro debating society in Kentucky the question was: If one hen lays ten eggs, and another hen sits on them and hatches out those eggs, which of the two hens is the mother of the chickens? This had been threshed out, up and down, from many sides, and the chairman, or umpire, was about ready to give his decision on the arguments. Then a battered old-timer rose from a barrel in a far corner and in a tremulous and cracked voice intoned the serious query: "But, Mis'er President, sposin' dem eggs what dat dar ole hen lay, the obdentical eggs what dat dar udder hen she hatch out, be duck eggs? Den dis nigger is like fer to know, if the char please, who am de mudder ob de chickens?" This at first seemed a poser to the umpire, but after a moment's hesitation he replied: "Dat wenerable pusson, my 'tickler fren Mis'r Jeemes, will please for to resume his barrel, as de duck eggs am not in the question for dis ebening." He then concluded in the following words: "De pedigree ob de fowl specie am ginerally monstrous oncertain, and the tickler birds what the s'iety been 'cussin' on dis kashun am periently more onsartiner nur de generality of de hen genus. Mebbe dis 'ere chicken got ten fadders; den, agin, mebbe, he ain't got but one; but dat he had two mudders am, in the pinion ob dis char, sartin sure."

On the day after Fredericksburg Isaac N. Arnold entered Lincoln's office to find the President reading the works of Artemus Ward. The staggering defeat, the rivers of blood gone, the topic of informed men everywhere, was not touched by the President. He asked Arnold to sit down and he would read Artemus Ward's description of a visit to the Shakers, a sect who had a communal form of life, believed in plain clothing for all occasions and fantastic moaning and holy rolling at their religious services.

Ward wrote that one spring he got "swampt in the exterior of New York State, one dark and stormy night, when the winds Blue pityusly, and I was forced to tie up with the Shakers." He knocked at a door. "A solum female, looking sumwhat like a last year's beanpole stuck into a long meal bag, axed me was I athurst and did I hunger? to which I urbanely ansered 'a few.' " That Lincoln should wish to read this sort of nonsense while the ambulances were yet hauling thousands of wounded from the frozen mud flats of the Rappahannock River, was amazing to Congressman Arnold. As he said afterward he was "shocked." He inquired, "Mr. President, is it possible that with the whole land bowed in sorrow and covered with a pall in the presence of yesterday's fearful reverse, you can indulge in such levity?" Then, as Arnold said it happened, as he saw and heard, the President threw down the Artemus Ward book, tears streamed down his cheeks, his physical frame quivered as he burst forth, "Mr. Arnold, if I could not get momentary respite from the crushing burden I am constantly carrying, my heart would break!" And with that pent-up cry let out, it came over Arnold that the laughter of Lincoln at times was a mask.

Possibly only a crony from the old Eighth Circuit could have called out the peculiar humor that Leonard Swett met one gloomy day of the summer of '64. Grant was pounding toward Richmond, the ambulances groaned with their heavy loads, hospitals filled beyond capacity. Men should be rushed to the front. This and much else Swett poured out to Lincoln, with a flood of suggestions on what should be done and immediately. "The President was sitting by an open window," noted Swett. "And as I paused, a bird lit upon a branch just outside and was twittering and singing joyously. Mr. Lincoln, imitating the bird, said: '*Tweet, tweet, tweet;* isn't he singing sweetly?' I felt as if my legs had been cut from under me. I rose, took my hat, and said, 'I see the country is safer than I thought.' As I moved toward the door, Mr. Lincoln called out in his hearty, familiar way, 'Here, Swett, come back and sit down.' Then he went on: 'It is impossible for a man in my position not to have thought of all those things. Weeks ago every man capable of bearing arms was ordered to the front, and everything you suggested has been done.' "

Without doubt there were persons justifiably annoyed at "the White House joker," their opinion resting on fabricated or distorted Lincoln jokes. As though old neighbors, comedians and punsters, could step into the White House any time and tickle the ribs and fraternize with the President, an item went the rounds of newspapers, usually about as printed in the *Chicago Journal* July 28, 1864:

> Setchell, the comedian, says he was present at the White House the other day when the following was perpetrated: An old farmer from the West, who knew President Lincoln in days bygone, called to pay his respects at the presidential mansion. Slapping the chief magistrate upon the back, he exclaimed, "Well, old hoss, how are you?" Old Abe being thoroughly democratic in his ideas, and withal relishing a joke, responded, "So I'm an old hoss, am I? What kind of a hoss, pray?" "Why, an old draft hoss, to be sure," was the rejoinder. Good, even for Setchell.

This caught the eye and won the favor of thousands who couldn't find time that same week to read the involved denunciations of Lincoln in the Wade-Davis Manifesto.

Far and wide through newspaper reprints went an eyewitness account of Lincoln's pertinence, bordering on horseplay, during a spiritualist séance in the White House. Curiously enough there was little or no hostile comment on this procedure. Any ordinarily acrimonious editorial writer with a satirical touch and an air for trifles could have done much with it. It was one of a series of odd incidents that built up a portrait of an American in the White House who could be keen, possibly wise, amid the ludicrous, the shallow, the bottomless. A *Boston Gazette* writer described the evening. His recital would have been rather dull reading except for the interspersals of comment from the President. The account printed in scores of newspapers, reaching a large section of the literate population of the country, read as follows, usually with the heading "Spiritualism at the White House":

Washington, April 23, 1863

A few evenings since, Abraham Lincoln, President of the United States, was induced to give a spiritual soirée in the crimson room at the White House, to test the wonderful alleged supernatural powers of Mr. Charles E. Shockle. It was my good fortune, as a friend of the medium, to be present, the party consisting of the President, Mrs. Lincoln, Mr. Welles, Mr. Stanton, Mr. L—— of New York, and Mr. F—— of Philadelphia. We took our seats in the circle about eight o'clock, but the President was called away shortly after the manifestations commenced, and the spirits, which had apparently assembled to convince him of their power, gave visible tokens of their displeasure at the President's absence, by pinching Mr. Stanton's ears and twitching Mr. Welles's beard. He soon returned, but it was some time before harmony was restored, for the mishaps to the secretaries caused such bursts of laughter that the influence was very unpropitious. For some half-hour the demonstrations were of a physical character—tables were moved, and the picture of Henry Clay, which hangs on the wall, was swayed more than a foot, and two candelabras, presented by the Dey of Algiers to President Adams, were twice raised nearly to the ceiling.

It was nearly nine o'clock before Shockle was fully under spiritual influence, and so powerful were the subsequent manifestations, that twice during the evening restoratives were applied, for he was much weakened; and though I took no notes, I shall endeavor to give you as faithful an account as possible of what took place.

Loud rappings, about nine o'clock, were heard directly beneath the President's feet, and Mr. Shockle stated that an Indian desired to communicate.

"Well, sir," said the President, "I should be happy to hear what his Indian Majesty has to say. We have recently had a visitation from our red brethren, and it was the only delegation, black, white, or blue, which did not volunteer some advice about the conduct of the war."

The medium then called for pencil and paper, and they were laid upon the table in sight of all. A handkerchief was then taken from Mr. Stanton, and the materials were carefully concealed from sight. In less space of time than it has required for me to write this, knocks were heard and the paper was uncovered. To the surprise of all present it read as follows:

"Haste makes waste, but delays cause vexations. Give vitality by energy. Use every means to subdue. Proclamations are useless; make a bold front and fight the enemy;

leave traitors at home to the care of loyal men. Less note of preparation, less parade and policy talk, and more action. HENRY KNOX."

"That is not Indian talk, Mr. Shockle," said the President. "Who is Henry Knox?"

I suggested to the medium to ask who General Knox was, and before the words were from my lips the medium spoke in a strange voice: "The first Secretary of War."

"Oh! yes, General Knox," said the President; who turning to the Secretary, said: "Stanton, that message is for you; it is from your predecessor."

Mr. Stanton made no reply.

"I should like to ask General Knox," said the President, "if it is within the scope of his ability, to tell us when this rebellion will be put down."

In the same manner as before, this message was received:

"Washington, Lafayette, Franklin, Wilberforce, Napoleon, and myself have held frequent consultations on this point. There is something which our spiritual eyes cannot detect which appears well formed. Evil has come at times by removal of men from high positions, and there are those in retirement whose abilities should be made useful to hasten the end. Napoleon says, concentrate your forces upon one point; Lafayette thinks that the rebellion will die of exhaustion; Franklin sees the end approaching, as the South must give up for want of mechanical ability to compete against Northern mechanics. Wilberforce sees hope only in a negro army.—KNOX."

"Well," exclaimed the President, "opinions differ among the saints as well as among the sinners. They don't seem to understand running the machines among the celestials much better than we do. Their talk and advice sound very much like the talk of my cabinet—don't you think so, Mr. Welles?"

"Well, I don't know—I will think the matter over, and see what conclusion to arrive at."

Heavy raps were heard, and the alphabet was called for, when "That's what's the matter," was spelt out.

There was a shout of laughter, and Mr. Welles stroked his beard.

"That means, Mr. Welles," said the President, "that you are apt to be long-winded, and think the nearest way home is the longest way round. Short cuts in war times. I wish the spirits could tell us how to catch the *Alabama*."

The lights, which had been partially lowered, almost instantaneously became so dim that I could not see sufficiently to distinguish the features of anyone in the room, and on the large mirror over the mantelpiece there appeared the most beautiful though supernatural picture ever beheld. It represented a sea view, the *Alabama* with all steam up flying from the pursuit of another large steamer. Two merchantmen in the distance were seen, partially destroyed by fire. The picture changed, and the *Alabama* was seen at anchor under the shadow of an English fort—from which an English flag was waving. The *Alabama* was floating idly, not a soul on board, and no signs of life visible about her. The picture vanished, and in letters of purple appeared: "The English people demand this of England's aristocracy."

"So England is to seize the *Alabama* finally?" said the President. "It may be possible; but, Mr. Welles, don't let one gunboat or monitor less be built."

The spirits called for the alphabet, and again "That's what's the matter," was spelt out.

"I see, I see," said the President. "Mother England thinks that what's sauce for the goose may be sauce for the gander. It may be tit, tat, toe, hereafter. But it is not very complimentary to our navy, anyhow."

"We've done our best, Mr. President," said Mr. Welles. "I'm maturing a plan which, when perfected, I think, if it works well, will be a perfect trap for the *Alabama*."

"Well, Mr. Shockle," remarked the President, "I have seen strange things and heard rather odd remarks; but nothing which convinces me, except the pictures, that there is any thing very heavenly about this. I should like, if possible, to hear what Judge Douglas says about this war."

"I'll try to get his spirit," said Mr. Shockle; "but it sometimes happens, as it did to-night in the case of the Indian, that though first impressed by one spirit, I yield to another more powerful. If perfect silence is maintained, I will see if we cannot induce General Knox to send for Mr. Douglas."

Three raps were given, signifying assent to the proposition. Perfect silence was maintained, and after an interval of perhaps three minutes Mr. Shockle rose quickly from his chair and stood up behind it, resting his left arm on the back, his right thrust into his bosom. In a voice such as no one could mistake who had ever heard Mr. Douglas, he spoke. I shall not pretend to quote the language. It was eloquent and choice. He urged the President to throw aside all advisers who hesitate about the policy to be pursued, and to listen to the wishes of the people, who would sustain him at all points if his aim was, as he believed it was, to restore the Union. He said there were Burrs and Blennerhassetts living, but that they would wither before the popular approval which would follow one or two victories, such as he thought must take place ere long. The turning-point in this war will be the proper use of these victories. If wicked men in the first hours of success think it time to devote their attention to party, the war will be prolonged; but if victory is followed up by energetic action, all will be well.

"I believe that," said the President, "whether it comes from spirit or human."

Mr. Shockle was much prostrated after this, and at Mrs. Lincoln's request it was thought best to adjourn the séance, which, if resumed, I shall give you an account of.

Yours as ever,

MELTON.

What were Lincoln's motives in this little affair? He had permitted a metropolitan news-writer to be present, had thrown no air of privacy around the séance, and seemed entirely willing to have a story of it go out to the country. First of all perhaps there was his own curiosity about the psychic-phenomena manipulators, who had become rather numerous and were preying on many good people over the country. The war had intensified speculation over departed spirits and communication with "the spirit world." From the *New York Herald* down to small-town papers there was advertising of many pretenders, Russell of the London *Times* having noted with accuracy: "It is strange to see in journals which profess to represent the civilization and intelligence of the most enlightened and highly educated people on the face of the earth, advertisements of sorcerers, wizards, and fortune-tellers by the score, 'wonderful clairvoyants,' the 'seventh child of a seventh child,' 'mesmeristic necromancers,' and the like, who can tell your thoughts as soon as you enter the room, and secure the affections you prize, give lucky numbers in lotteries, and make everybody's fortunes but their own."

A spiritualist medium passing by the name of Colchester pretended to be the illegitimate son of an English duke, had many other pretenses, and through the White House seamstress Mrs. Keckley met Mrs. Lincoln and induced her to let him give a séance at the Soldiers' Home. There in a darkened room he pretended to produce messages from her dead son Willie in a script scratched on the wainscoting and in tappings on the walls and furniture. To another of these exhibitions by Colchester Mrs. Lincoln invited Noah Brooks. He declined, but spent a dollar to attend "a Colchester sitting" in the Washington home of a spiritualist believer. In a room with lights out, with silence broken by the thumping of a drum, the twanging of a banjo, and the ringing of bells, Brooks suspected that Colchester had by some hocus-pocus freed his hands from his neighbors' and was himself creating the supposed sounds of the mystic spirits in the air. Loosening his own hands from his neighbors', Brooks reached in the direction of the drumbeat sound and found himself holding hands not mystic at all, but solid and fleshy. Shouting to a friend, "Strike a light!" Brooks held on to the solid hands he was holding, took on his forehead a bloody cut from the metal drum-edge swung by someone. Lighted gas jets the next instant showed Colchester glowering at the drum and the bells in his hands. The séance ended. Colchester slipped out amid confusion. A day or two after, wrote Brooks: "I was astonished by a note from Mrs. Lincoln requesting me to come to the White House without a moment's delay, on a matter of the most distressing importance. On my arrival, the lady, somewhat discomposed, showed me a note from 'Colchester,' in which he requested that she should procure for him from the War Department a pass to New York, and intimated that in case she refused he might have some unpleasant things to say to her."

Mrs. Lincoln arranged for Colchester to come to the White House the next day. Brooks was introduced. Colchester muttered that he had been insulted. "You know," said Brooks, "that I know you are a swindler and a humbug. Get out of this house and out of this city at once. If you are in Washington tomorrow afternoon at this time, you will be in the Old Capitol prison." With what result? "The little scamp . . . sneaked out of the house," wrote Brooks, "and I never saw or heard of him afterward."

Joined to whatever of fun, frolic, wit, or macabre humor of psychic phenomena Lincoln might have thought he could get from an evening session with a spiritualist, there may have been the mixed motive of publicity, with much pleasantry, discrediting it so that Mrs. Lincoln would give less time and worry to the numerous tribe of mediums.

Though white paper was costly in '64 and its newspaper size diminishing, the *Charleston Mercury* went on reprinting occasional Lincoln wit from Northern newspapers. One incident it told of went far. A minister in line with a delegation meeting the President "hoped the Lord is on our side." The President: "I don't agree with you." There was amazement. The President continued: "I am not at all concerned about that, for we know that the Lord is always on the side of the right. But it is my constant anxiety and prayer that I and this nation should be on the Lord's side."

Also widely published was an incident of the summer of '64 when

Bishop Simpson spoke in the Methodist church at the corner of Four-and-a-half and F Streets in Washington on "The Providence of God as Seen in Our War." Lincoln was ushered to a pew in front of Secretary Stanton. The sermon over, the Bishop was escorted to the President's pew. Soldiers seeking a Lincoln handshake blocked the pew entrances. But finally the President and the Bishop had their little conference, the President voicing satisfaction over the way in which the Bishop in his sermon had traced the course of events leading to the war, inventions and discoveries that had made for the progress of the country. With a gleam of humor the President added: "But, Bishop, you did not 'strike ile.'" This, noted John Eaton, was "widely reported in the press, for the discovery of the great oil fields was new then. It certainly illustrated Lincoln's shrewd appreciation of current events." Others added it was interesting to see a President on a Sabbath day play on words and pun with a bishop.

Bennett of the *New York Herald* hired writers with gifts of satire and persiflage. They took facts and ran away with them. The fun got mixed with malice and readers could not always be sure where history ended and horseplay began. "War in the Cabinet" was headlined in October of '63 and disagreements over the next presidential nomination were forecast in the *Herald*. "Mr. Lincoln is very hard to move when he sets his foot down and he sheds political bullets as the monitors shed cannon balls when he is in battle trim, with his hatches fastened down and his fighting flag hung out. Ordinarily Honest Old Abe does not display much energy and spirit. So long as he is left in peace to read Artemus Ward's book and crack his own little jokes, he is happy. But when an emergency comes, Old Abe is ready to meet it. We should not be at all surprised to learn that at this moment Lincoln has a masked battery ready to open upon Chase and blow him to atoms whenever he is ready. Chase has too much confidence in himself. He thinks he can easily vanquish Lincoln when really Lincoln wears a coat of mail under his ordinary habit and carries a big bowie knife up his sleeve."

In the same week the *Herald* played fast and loose with facts, invented untruth, and then dealt satirically with it, as follows: "President Lincoln has decided to send one of his sons to the University of Heidelberg and Mrs. Lincoln herself will carry the youth to Europe. We are informed that Mrs. Lincoln is on her way to Heidelberg to place the President's first born on the matriculate list of that University, a preference not over-complimentary to Harvard or other Yankee seats of learning. The result of this experiment may determine whether chopping German metaphysics or rail splitting be more conducive to future success in American life." A month later "military apathy" was laid at the door of "the utter brainlessness of the administration in Washington." Southern recovery of force was just ahead, for which "Thank the Washington imbeciles."

"Lincoln is called the American Aesop," said the *Herald*, November 21, 1863, a week later taking the liberty of putting a comic speech and a long anecdote in the President's mouth, throwing quotation marks around it, and so presenting it that any careless reader, or one not fairly well informed, might easily believe the President had actually said what was put in his mouth. The advantage was with the *Herald.* Its mimicry of Lincoln's style in storytelling was near enough perfect for the laugh to be one in which Lincoln himself might have joined. In a speech to the Cabinet and the foreign diplomatic body Lincoln was represented as telling "his best story," rambling on and on:

"In my position it is not wise to talk foolishly and I would therefore not talk at all. . . . As for the 'war for succession,' about which the *Herald* and Mr. Phillips appear crazy, I will say some few words. Men oftenest betray and defeat themselves by overanxiety to secure their object just as the widow Zollicoffer's negro did down in Bourbon County when he had been eating her cranberry jam. (Laughter.) The widow while making her jam, was called away to a neighbor who was about to increase the population. 'Sam, you rascal, you will be eating my jam while I am away.' Sam protested he would die first but the whites of his eyes rolled and hung towards the bubbling crimson. 'See here, Sam,' said the widow taking up a piece of chalk. 'I'll chalk your lips and then I'll know if you have eaten any when I come back.' So saying she passed her forefinger heavily over the thick lips of her darkey, *holding the chalk in the palm of her hand and not letting it touch him.* Well, when she came back, Sam's lips were chalked a quarter of an inch thick and she needed no further evidence against him.

"Now it is much the same about the Presidency. (Loud laughter.) A good friend of mine declared he would not take it at any price, but his lips were heavily chalked when he came back from Ohio. (Great merriment with Mr. Chase joining in heartily.) So were General Frémont's out in Missouri when he issued his 'emancipation order.' And General Butler's were not only chalked but had the jam on and had it thick. Senator Seward once chalked very badly but gave it up as of no use when he quarrelled with the machine proprietor of his own State. (Loud laughter.) Mingled jam and chalk might be seen on the lips of General Banks; while the same compound formed quite a paste around the orifice through which his good friend Governor Seymour supplied the wants of nature. (Roars of laughter.) I have never seen any chalk on the lips of Secretary Stanton nor General Halleck but with these exceptions there was scarcely a man connected with the army who did not chalk his lips. (Continued mirth, the foreign diplomatic corps joining in heartily.)"

Later in this evening, the *Herald* artist in persiflage rambled on: "The President, who had been sitting curled up in an arm chair with his legs loosely crossed one over the other, now began to rise, slowly untwisting the kinks of his back and towering up like one of the genii released from a jar or jug in which he had been bottled up for centuries under the seal of Solomon. 'Aisy!' exclaimed Mr. Luke Clark with unaffected dismay. 'It's dashing your brains out against the ceiling you'll be or tangling your shoulders in the top notches of the chandelier.' At length Mr. Lincoln reached his full height and said that he did not quite catch the drift." Still later the

President was saying to Miles O'Reilly, the poet, "Tell us if you can, what the people say of us, what they say of Chase, of Seward. You needn't be afraid, Miles, we are not of a thin-skinned family and we know before asking that you have an awkward knack of telling the truth."

Farther along in this same evening, according to the *Herald's* mimic and word caricaturist: "Mr. Lincoln begged Count Mercier not to utter the titanic, unspeakable word (that embalmed sublimity of English wrath) which Colonel Cambronne at the head of the last square of the Imperial Guard at Waterloo, hurled against the English general who asked him to surrender. . . . As to dancing, Mr. Lincoln said he never danced. As to his being a candidate for reëlection, it reminded him of what old Jesse Dubois said to the preacher at Springfield when he asked from the State House for a lecture on the subject: The Second Coming of Our Saviour. 'If our Saviour,' retorted old Jesse, 'had ever come to Springfield and was lucky enough to get away with his life, he would be too smart to come again.' This is very much my case about succession. . . . As I see you are all buttoning up to go away, I will not detain you, more especially as Louis Burgdorf has been making secret signs to me for the last half hour that Mrs. Lincoln and the child will have cold turkey for their Thanksgiving dinner if I don't cross over to the other side of the building shortly."

Thus free speech in a democracy had its innings. The *Herald* writer was permeated with Lincolnisms of manner and vocabulary. That he counted on his readers being likewise somewhat permeated in latter '63 was an evidence of the extent to which the Lincoln personality had reached out across the country and made its impress as alive and breathing.

To run down all the suspicions, insinuations, inveracities, innuendoes, uttered against a man in his place, said Lincoln, "would be a perpetual flea hunt." This was published in England. Gradually, by 1864, a constantly enlarging British audience had studied the ways of Lincoln, had come to see glimpses of an ancient Anglo-Saxon, more Anglican and more Saxon than many an h-dropping reader of the *Times* of London. The press now and then ascribed wit to Lincoln not heard of in America. In a mixed company, hearing one say matrimony was Hell and another say it was Heaven, Lincoln judged, "We had better take a middle course and call it Purgatory." They had him opening sentences with, "Did you, by God," and "I trow, sir." They gave him "an uncle who kept a mill down west" not "out West." They took the blunt American version of the incident of a disgruntled office-seeker saying, "Why, I elected you," with Lincoln's reply, "And a nice mess you got me into," making it over into this: "A visitor soliciting a government post, urged his claim for the appointment on the ground that it was solely through the applicant's exertions Mr. Lincoln was elected President. 'Oh, indeed,' said Abe. 'I now look upon the man, who of all men, has crowned my existence with a crown of thorns—no post for you in my gift, I assure you: I wish you good morning.'" They had Mrs. Lincoln alluding to "his well-known love of tobacco." They credited him with telling a lieutenant who complained that the Irish gave his company the most uneasiness, "Sir, our enemies, the rebels, make the same complaint." They had the ex-slave woman Sojourner Truth a man, the President welcoming *him*, "Lies are pictured as being as black as Erebus; but thou, *Truth*, art black also."

Nothing short of goodwill and fine kindliness was in the British ascription to Lincoln personally of some prime American folklore, having him mention a baby he had seen in Massachusetts, "only six months old, sitting in its mother's lap, viewing its own cradle, to see if it could not invent a better, or, at least, suggest an improvement." A Federal ram having been built with the fatal flaw that it lacked space for stowing requisite fuel, Lincoln asked the constructor "if he intended the vessel to be driven by the force of circumstances." As a youth, said English prints, Lincoln in New York City had his watch stolen and "the young joker" inserted the following in the *New York Herald:* "Stolen, a watch worth $100. If the thief will return it, he shall be informed gratis, where he may steal one worth two of it, and no questions asked."

The foremost funnymen of the age, the leading American comics, however, understood the ways of Lincoln. At least they shaded their foolery and colored their jests as if in the White House was one of their own, a fellow of the craft of clowning who nevertheless carried merit and a dignity. Artemus Ward, Petroleum Vesuvius Nasby, Orpheus C. Kerr, Miles O'Reilly, the young burblers of the satirical weekly *Vanity Fair*, all wrote with a gay though covert affection for the President. Of course, it came to them that the President was one of their faithful readers, seemed to believe they were important voices of democracy in a living Republic, but they also knew it was a lonesome and more often thankless job held by their "O. Abe," as Ward abbreviated.

The President reveled in the Ward items sprinkled in city and country papers, the toast of the waxworks showman "to the phair sex" at a county fair: "May you allers be as fare as the son, as bright as the moon, and as butiful as an army with Union flags—also plenty of good close to ware. Tu yure sex we are indetted for our bornin. Yure 1st muther was a lady and all her dawters is ditto. Hopin that no waive of truble may ever ride akross yur peaceful brests, I konklude these remarks with the following centyment: *Woman—She is a good egg.*" The swagger of Yankee Doodle with corncobs twisted in his hair, growing up to find he was no longer so young as he had been, was in Ward's paragraph:

"At the time Chris. orrove on these shores (I alood to Chris. Columbus) the savajis was virtuous and happy. They were innocent of secession, rum, draw poker, and sinfulness gin'rally. They didn't discuss the slavery question as a custom. They had no congress, faro banks, delirium tremens, or Associated Press. Their habits were consequently good. Late suppers, dyspepsy, gas companies, war politicians, thieves and other metropolitan refinements, were unknown among them. No savije in good standing would take postage stamps—you couldn't have bought a coonskin with a barrel of 'em."

More than buffoonery was in Ward's opinion in latter 1862: "Onless there's different management right off, the American eagle will have to disguise hisself as a shanghai rooster, and make tracks for Canady." Forty thousand copies had been sold of *Artemus Ward: His Book* published in May, 1862. The author, Charles Farrar Browne, was only twenty-eight years old, born in Waterford, Maine, his father a justice of the peace, his mother of Puritan stock, the son writing, "I think we came from Jerusalem, for my mother's name was Levi, and we had a Moses and a Nathan in the family, but my poor brother's name was Cyrus so, perhaps, that makes us Persians." He learned typesetting on the *Skowhegan Clarion;* in Boston worked on the *Carpet-Bag* edited by B. P. Shillaber, creator of Mrs. Partington, who travestied correct diction by exclamations to her boy Ike: "I am almost tempered to take corrosive measures, and punish you within an inch of your skin. Such a fragrant outrage I never saw in one so young. Boys that show such a moral turpentine never come to an end." Drifting west as a tramp printer, Browne finally took a $12-a-week job as reporter on the *Cleveland Plain-Dealer.* The lean, long-nosed, heavy-and-drooping mustached Maine boy found minstrel shows using his jokes, newspapers far and wide reprinting his letters.

On the staff of *Vanity Fair* in New York Browne worked up lectures on "Babes in the Woods" and "Sixty Minutes in Africa," advertising that his lectures were not merely endorsed by O. Abe at Washington but also by James Buchanan, Wheatland, Pa., Wendell Phillips, Boston, C. L. Vallandigham, Canada, William Lloyd Garrison, Mass., Mr. Czar of Russia, Russia, Mr. Lucy Stone, New England, The Bedouin Arabs, Ireland, Mr. Smith, Wisconsin, Young Albert Wales and Wife, England. Amos Pilkins certified that his wife, "afflicted with the pipsy-wipsy in the head for nearly eight years," recovered on hearing one Ward lecture, Pilkins adding, "Send me another five dollar bill and I'll write another certificate twice as long as this." For the opening lecture in Clinton Hall, New York, placards were scattered over the city reading "Artemus Ward Will Speak a Piece." Midway in his lecture he paused to say, "Owing to a slight indisposition we will now have an intermission of fifteen minutes" and after the audience had puzzled a moment, he rubbed his hands, "but, ah—during the intermission I will go on with my lecture." An Englishman came from the Artemus Ward lecture and wrote of it:

> When he first comes on to the platform, with his long, hollow-cheeked face, and his bright, sad, interrogative eyes, we should expect from him almost anything rather than cause for laughter. He might be a philanthropist or preacher, eager to enlist the rest of the world in some crusade. He never smiles, but looks, on the contrary, pleading and entreating, as if he were above all things solicitous to get his thoughts really disentangled. When he hits on a deep thought, and says, for instance, with a sort of hesitating, perplexed candor, as though he were getting a little beyond his own depth and his audience's too,—"Time passed. You may have noticed that it usually does, that that is a sort of way Time has about it, it generally passes on," a joke of no absolute merit takes a very great humour from his hesitating anxious way of appearing to show

the analysis of his own embarrassed thoughts to the people he is addressing. He drifts about in search of words and phrases, often conveying a sense of difficulty and of conscious error, and then correcting himself by the use of a phrase still more ludicrous. and on what he seems to have been landed by an imperious necessity. Thus, when he says that he used to sing, but not well, he stumbles in the most natural way, and is a prey to melancholy that he can't hit on the proper phrase; "as a songer," he said, "I was not successful"; and then, in a depressed and self-correcting way, conscious he had gone wrong, "As a singster I was a failure. I am always saddest when I sing—and so are those who hear me." The art with which he gives the impression that he is floundering along is beyond praise. So, again, when he finds the seventeen young Mormon widows weeping, and asks them, "Why is this thus?" he falls a victim to embarrassment and goes on helplessly, "What is the cause of this thusness?" The humour of all this is the humour of letting your thoughts drift idly with the most absurd association that crosses them, and never rescuing yourself by any insurrection of common sense.

The Englishman thus analyzing would have understood much better than Congressman Isaac N. Arnold of Illinois precisely why Lincoln wanted to read aloud from Artemus Ward when the Union cause was embarrassed, perplexed, and floundering after the Fredericksburg defeat and disgrace. After the tension Lincoln wanted to "let thoughts drift idly." For him there was hilarity in Ward's signing a letter, "Yours for the Perpetration of the Union, and the bringin of the Goddess of Liberty out of her present bad fix." And while Lincoln wrestled with his brigadiers and major generals, there was comfort in reading of Ward as member of a military company. "We air progressin pretty well with our drill. As all air commandin offisers, there aint no jelusy; and as we air all exceedin smart, it ain't worth while to try to outstrip each other." Or the cry of a woman at a war meeting in Baldwinsville, "We want you able-bodied men to stop speechifying, which don't amount to the wiggle of a sick cat's tail, and go to fi'tin; otherwise you can stay at home and take keer of the children, while we wimin will go to the wars!" The Ward sketch "In Washington," published in 1862, had an impudence requisite to democracy yet also a blither penetration not so often joined to impudence. The mock interview with Lincoln read:

I called on Abe. He received me kindly. I handed him my umbreller, and told him I'd have a check for it if he pleased. "That," sed he, "puts me in mind of a little story. There was a man out in our parts who was so mean that he took his wife's coffin out of the back winder for fear he would rub the paint off the doorway. Wall, about this time there was a man in a adjacent town who had a green cotton umbreller."

"Did it fit him well? Was it custom made? Was he measured for it?"

"Measured for what?" said Abe.

"The umbreller?"

"Wall, as I was sayin," continnerd the President, treatin the interruption with apparent contempt, "this man sed he'd known that there umbreller ever since it was a parasol. Ha, ha, ha!"

"Yes," sed I, larfin in a respectful manner, "but what has this man with the umbreller to do with the man who took his wife's coffin out of the back winder?"

"To be sure," said Abe—"what was it? I must have got two stories mixed together, which puts me in mind of another lit——"

"Never mind, Your Excellency. I called to congratulate you on your career, which has been a honest and a good one—unscared and unmoved by Secesh in front of you and Abbolish at the back of you—each one of which is a little wuss than the other if possible!

"Tell E. Stanton that his boldness, honesty, and vigger merits all prase, but to keep his under-garmints on. E. Stanton has appeerently only one weakness, which it is, he can't allus keep his under-garmints from flyin up over his hed. I mean that he occasionally dances in a peck-measure, and he don't look graceful at it."

I took my departer. "Good bye, old sweetness!" sed Abe, shakin me cordgully by the hand.

"Adoo, my Prahayrie flower!" I replied, and made my exit. "Twenty-five thousand dollars a year and found," I soliloquised, as I walked down the street, "is putty good wages for a man with a modist appytite, but I reckon that it is wuth it to run the White House."

Life was ridiculous, its forms and appearances deceptive and ludicrous, and any pomp and power would drop into collapse and shuffle with a limping dignity if looked at long enough—such stark gargoyles of thought were implied by the horselaugh philosophers praised by Lincoln. The fields of politics and war saw swindlers, pretenders, hypocrites, demagogues, charlatans, bootlickers, snivelers, shifters, incompetents. They and their works implied constantly that democracy, the experiment of popular government, could never be anything else than a series of approximations, imperfections incessantly present or arriving. Democracy would be achieved only through humanity, its operations conducted by and through the members of the human family. And what was humanity, or as Lincoln termed it, "the family of man"? A species of biped creatures on the surface of the earth with which these horselaugh philosophers were concerned. Behind the exterior of mirth, under the jokery, seemed so often to be the quizzical thrusting: "What is man? Why does he behave as he does? Is it absurd that I, who am a man, should cut up and play such capers as you see me in?"

While Artemus Ward tried to lay out comic patterns of humanity in general, David R. Locke dealt more immediately with the human race in America and its current issues. His letters dated at "Confederate X Roads which is in the State of Kentucky," had their signer, the Reverend Petroleum Vesuvius Nasby, set up as pastor of a church and a seeker of office. Lincoln kept a pamphlet of these Nasby letters in a desk drawer. Locke was a year older than Ward, and like Ward had been a tramp printer, learning to set type on the *Cortland* (New York) *Democrat,* serving on the *Pittsburgh Chronicle,* having a hand in running newspapers in Plymouth, Mansfield, Bucyrus and Bellefontaine, Ohio. In April, 1862, in a Findlay, Ohio, newspaper he ran the first of the Nasby letters, dating it at Wingert's Corners, a village in Crawford County where the citizens almost to a man were secessionists.

Fifteen Negroes had arrived at the place, "yisterday another arrove," and P. V. Nasby, alarmed, prepared resolutions: "Wareas, we vew with alarm the ackshun uv the President uv the U. S., in recommendin the immejit emansipashun uv the slaves uv our misgided Suthern brethrin, and his evident intenshun uv kolonizin on em in the North, and the heft on em in Wingert's Corners; and Wareas, Eny man hevin the intellect uv a brass-mounted jackass kin easily see that the 2 races want never intendid to live together; and Wareas, Bein in the magority, we kin do as we please and ez the nigger haint no vote he kant help hisself; therefore be it Resolved, That the crude, undeodorized Afrikin is a disgustin obgik. Resolved, That this Convenshun, when it hez its feet washed, smells sweeter nor the Afrikin in his normal condishun, and is there4 his sooperior. Resolved, That the niggers be druv out of Wingert's Corners, and that sich property ez they hev accumulatid be confiscatid, and the proseeds applide to the follerin purposes, to wit: Payment uv the bills uv the last Dimekratik Central Committee, Payment uv the disinterested patriots ez got up this meetin, The balence to remane in my hands. Resolved, That the Ablishnists who oppose these resolushens all want to marry a nigger. Resolved, That Dr. Petts, in rentin a part uv his bildin to niggers, hez struck a blow at the very foundashens uv sosiety. Fellow whites, arowz! The enemy is onto us! Our harths is in danger! When we hev a nigger for judge—niggers for teachers—niggers in pulpits—when niggers rool and controle sosiety, then will yoo remember this warnin!"

The combined hilarity and political values of the foregoing so pleased Lincoln that he carried a clipping of it in his vest pocket and read it aloud. In time he memorized the whole of it, and Noah Brooks told of an evening at the Soldiers' Home when visitors came and talk fell on the slaves released into freedom, of a sort, in the Border States. Lincoln stood before the fireplace and recited the Wingert's Corners piece, dwelling on the latter part of it as especially good:

"Arouse to wunst! Rally agin Conway! Rally agin Sweet! Rally agin Hegler's family! Rally agin the porter at the Reed House! Rally agin the cook at the Crook House! Rally agin the nigger widder in Vance's Addishun! Rally agin Missis Umstid! Rally agin Missis Umstid's children by her first husband! Rally agin Missis Umstid's children by her sekkund husband! Rally agin all the rest uv Missis Umstid's children! Rally agin the nigger that cum yisterday! Rally agin the saddle-culurd girl that yoost 2 be hear! Ameriky for white men!"

Lincoln at intervals used to quote these mock rallying cries, said Brooks, long after other men had read and forgotten them.

P. V. Nasby outdid Artemus Ward in the matter of interviewing the President. Of the many imaginary interviews with Lincoln his was easily the boldest, the most cunningly conceived and contrived. A piece of satirical journalistic writing born out of the issues and personalities of the time, it was rated a masterpiece. Home folks of the North and their boys in the field read it aloud to each other, and knew the weapon of ridicule for its worth. This Nasby paper read:

Church uv St. ———————, November the 1st, 1863.

I felt it my dooty to visit Washinton. The misarable condishon the Dimocrisy find themselves into sinse the elecshun, makes it nessary that suthin be did, and therefore I determind to see wat cood be effectid by a persnel intevew with the Presdent.

Interdoosin myself, I opened upon him delikitly, thus:

"Linkin," sez I, "ez a Dimocrat, a free-born Dimocrat, who is prepared to die with neetnis and dispatch, and on short notis, fer the inalienable rite uv free speech—knoin also that you er a goriller, a feendish ape, a thirster after blud, I speek."

"Speek on," says he.

"I am a Ohio Dimocrat," sez I, "who has repoodiatid Valandigum."

"Before or sinse the elecshun did yoo repoodiate him?" sez he.

"Sinse," retorted I.

"I thot so," sed he. "I would hev dun it too, hed I bin you," continuered he, with a goriller-like grin.

"We air now in favor uv a wiggeorus prosecushen uv the war, and we want you to so alter yoor polisy that we kin act with you, corjelly," sez I.

"Say on," sez he.

"I will. We don't want yoo to change yoor polisy, materially. We air modrit. Anxshus to support yoo, we ask yoo to adopt the follerin' trifling changis:

"Restoar to us our habis corpusses, as good ez new.

"Arrest no moar men, wimmin and children, fer opinyun's saik.

"Repele the ojus confisticashen bill, wich irrytaits the Suthern mind and fires the Suthern hart.

"Do away with drafts and conskripshens.

"Revoak the Emansipashen proclamashen, and give bonds that you'll never ishoo a nother.

"Do away with tresury noats and sich, and pay nuthin but gold.

"Protect our dawters frum nigger eqwality.

"Disarm yoor nigger soljers, and send back the niggers to their owners to conciliate them.

"Offer to assoom the war indetednis uv the South, and plej the Government to remoonerate our Suthrin brethrin fer the losses they hev sustaned in this onnatral war.

"Call a convenshen uv Suthern men and sech gileless Northern men ez F. Peerce, J. Bookanon, Fernandough Wood and myself, to agree upon the terms of reunion."

"Is that all?" sez the goriller.

"No," sez I, promptly. "Ez a garantee uv good faith to us, we shel insist that the best haff uv the orifises be given to Dimocrats who repoodiate Valandigum. Do this, Linkin, and yoo throw lard ile on the trubbled waters. Do this and yoo rally to yoor support thowsends uv noble Dimocrats who went out uv offis with Bookanon, and hev bin gittin ther whisky on tick ever sinse. We hev maid sakrifises. We hev repoodiated Valandigum—we care not ef he rots in Canady—we are willin to jine the war party, reservin to ourselvs the poor privilidg uv dictatin how and on what prinsipples it shel be carried on. Linkin! Goriller! Ape! I hev dun."

The President replide that he wood give the matter serious considerashen. He wood menshen the idee uv resinin to Seward, Chais and Blair, and wood address a serculer to the Postmasters et settry, an see how menny uv em wood be willin' to resine to accommodait Dimocrats. He hed no doubt sevral wood do it to wunst.

"Is ther any littel thing I kin do fer yoo?"

"Nothin pertikler. I wood eccept a small Post orifis, if sitooatid within ezy range uv a distilry. My politikle daze is well-nigh over. Let me but see the old party wunst moar in the assendency—let these old eyes onct moar behold the Constooshn ez it is, the Union ez it wuz, and the Nigger ware he ought 2 be, and I will rap the mantel uv privit life arownd me, and go in2 delirum tremens happy. I hev no ambishen. I am in the sear and yaller leef. These whitnin lox, them sunken cheak, warn me that age and whisky hev dun ther perfeck work, and that 1 shell soon go hents. Linkin, scorn not my wurds, I hev sed. Adoo."

So sayin I wavd my hand impressively and walked away.

PETROLEUM V. NASBY,
Paster uv sed Church, in charge.

Sometimes before reading aloud from the pamphlet of Nasby papers taken from his desk drawer, Lincoln made such remarks as one to Sumner, "For the genius to write these things, I would gladly give up my office," or as he told two Senators, a Congressman, and several officials and private citizens one evening, "I am going to write Petroleum to come down here, and I intend to tell him if he will communicate his talent to me, I will swap places with him." It was, for one thing, an affinity of temperaments. The style of Nasby, his use of coarse dialect, violence to good grammar and diction, with pointed caricature and barbs aimed to puncture the puffed-up, these were the characteristics of the anonymous letters Lincoln twenty years earlier had sent to a Springfield newspaper, resulting in the Shields challenge of Lincoln to a duel. These javelins of horselaugh journalism Lincoln welcomed. They fought for his cause. It was not strange he got out of bed and paraded around the White House past midnight to find someone else awake to share his reading of Nasby.

Nasby and Ward were two of a kind, but Orpheus C. Kerr (Office Seeker) was something else. He didn't go in for twisted misspelling; he wrote of farcical American affairs in an utterly dignified and chaste English. "A comic military authority," his publishers termed him. In the 749 pages of his two volumes that had been published by 1863 was a series of satirical thrusts at McClellan as a military hero, along with persistent clever references of praise and affection for Lincoln. On June 17, 1863, when a report reached the War Department of a big scare, stragglers and baggage trains of one unit of the Army of the Potomac throwing terror into each other and fleeing on parallel roads toward Harrisburg, Welles noted in his diary:

"The President was in excellent humor. He said this flight would be a capital joke for Orpheus C. Kerr to get hold of. He could give scope to his imagination over the terror of broken squads of panic-stricken teamsters, frightened at each other and alarming all Pennsylvania. Meigs, with great simplicity, inquired who this person (Orpheus C. Kerr) was. 'Why,' said the President, 'have you not read those papers? They are in two volumes; any one who has not read them must be a heathen.' He said he had enjoyed them greatly, except when they attempted to play their wit on him, which did not strike him as very successful, but rather disgusted him. 'Now the hits that are given to you, Mr. Welles, or to Chase, I can enjoy, but I dare say they may have disgusted you while I was laughing at them. So *vice versa* as regards myself.' He then spoke of a poem by this Orpheus C. Kerr which mythologically described McClellan as a monkey fighting a serpent representing the Rebellion, but the joke was the monkey continually called for 'more tail,' 'more tail,' which Jupiter gave him, etc., etc."

Like the other two leading comics, Robert H. Newell, creator of Orpheus C. Kerr, was under thirty. He was of Scotch-Welsh stock, a New York City boy; his father was the inventor of a bank lock and key that permitted new combinations every day, and of a sewing machine that had won gold medals at the London and Vienna World expositions. While young Newell served as assistant editor of the *New York Sunday Mercury,* he wrote letters dated at Washington or in the field with the Army of the Potomac. He opened one with "not wishing to expire prematurely of inanity." On the face of them his sketches were an escape from inanity. Of the national capital he alleged: "The most interesting natural curiosity here, next to Secretary Welles' beard, is the office of the Secretary of the Interior. Covered with spider-webs, and clothed in the dust of ages, sit the Secretary and his clerks, like so many respectable mummies in a neglected pyramid." His dog Bologna met with other dogs in conflict over bones, leading to the surmise: "Dogs, my boy, and men, are very much alike in their hostile meetings, neither seeming to know just exactly which is truly their *magnum bonum.*" He set forth unvarnished philosophizings: "This is a dull day, my boy; and when there is no longer any sunshine to make steel bayonets and brass buttons glimmer to the eye, war is stript of half its pomp, and the American mind takes a plain, practical view of the strife. Truth to tell, this secession is a very shabby, unromantic thing to fight about. There is really no poetry at all about it, my boy, and when one would rhyme about it, the mantle of poesy refuses to fall upon him, although a bogus sort of Hood may possibly keep him in countenance."

Orpheus C. Kerr gave out ornate prophecies in October of '62. "The North, my boy, has not yet begun to fight; and as the stolid centuries roll on, and the hoary years move one by one into the sunless solitude of Eternity, it becomes daily more evident that the North's actual putting forth of all its strength is merely always a question of time. The giant is only just rousing from his slumbers, and nothing but his legs and feet appear to be thoroughly awake yet." Visiting a museum in Washington, he noticed "a fine young chap just in front of me who has recently been appointed to the staff of the Commander-in-Chief in consequence of his great experience in the coal business." He would quote a Copperhead newspaper: "I'm the best advertising medium in the country, and have reptile contemporaries." He twitted the New York newspapers: "It takes so long to get the news of the war from New York, that our citizens grow languid in the intervals."

Kerr sprinkled his letters with fool verses, referred often to his Gothic steed, Pegasus, and to horses in general. "The horse, my boy, is the swarthy Arab's bosom friend, the red Indian's solitary companion, and the circus proprietor's salvation." The public wanted more about his Pegasus, so he wrote: "The splendid architectural animal has just enough slant from his backbone to his hips to make a capital desk, my boy; and then his tail is so handy to wipe pens on. In a moment of thirst he swallowed a bottle of ink, and some fears were entertained for his life; but a gross of steel pens and a ream of blotting paper, immediately administered, caused him to come out all write. In a gothic sense, my boy, the charger continues to produce architectural illusions. He was standing on a hillside the other day, with his rear elevation toward the spectators, his head up and ears touching at the top, when a chap, who has been made pious by frequent conversation with the contrabands, noticed him afar off, and says he to a soldier, 'What church is that I behold in the distance, my fellow-worm of the dust?' The military veteran looked, and says he, 'It does look like a church; but it's only a animated haystack belonging to the cavalry.' " When a "leftenant" was asked how he would get important Confederate prisoners out of Fort Warren, the reply was: "I'd sue out a writ of Habeas Jackass, and get the *New York Herald* to advise the Government not to let them out." As January of '63 arrived: "The New Year again dawns blithely upon our distracted country as accurately predicted by the New York Tribune Almanac; and having given much deep thought to the matter, I am impressed with the conviction that the first of January is indeed the first of the year."

While this humorist steadily upheld Lincoln and the Union cause, and directed ridicule at the South and the Copperheads, he also kept on with sarcasm and irony aimed at the pretenses and pomps of war, at showy military heroes, at loud-mouthed statesmen. His serious view, not written in a public letter, held that so long as the world is inhabited by mankind there will always be more or less war, yet it tends, "when waged as the heartless pastime of kings, or the sinister tool of national ambition, to unduly exalt manual over moral force, and make mere tawdrily colored, plundering, wantonly destroying, murderous machines of men." Mankind's readiness for war lay in "the dazzling glare, heroic glow, romantically associated with march and battle, in the common mind." Briefly: "One nation under bellicose excitement, is much like another, the world over; one war is much like another, whatever the cause. The plain, often ludicrously incongruous, realities of all that dazzling glare of steel and gold, heroic glow of patriotic ferocity, and miraculous splendor of strategical and personal achievement, through traditional imagination, have long made all peoples ready military sacrifices."

That was his private opinion. Publicly for his large audience he wrote in March of '63: "To the youthful soul this war is a vast phantasmagoria of mighty giants struggling together in the clouds. There was a time when I, too, was able to see it to that extent; but time, and some experience, have reduced my giants in the clouds to brigadiers in the mud; and from seeing our national banner in the character of a rainbow dipped in stars, I have come to regard it as an ambitious attempt to represent sunrise in muslin." He quoted a garrulous, patriarchal statesman: "My friends, this war is like a great struggle between two hostile armies; it will continue until it has ceased, and it will cease when it is no longer continued. Peace is the end of

War, as war is the end of Peace; therefore, if we had no war, peace would be without end, and if we had no peace, war would be endless."

In another Washington letter: "We took a hack to the White House, my boy, and on arriving there were delighted to find that the rooms were already filling with statemen, miss-statemen, mrs-statemen, and officers, who had so much lace and epaulettes about them that they looked like walking brass-founderies with the front door open." He asked whether a large ornamental pair of brass tongs, figured in blue enamel, near the fireplace was a gift of the Japanese Legation. "Thunder," said a general, "that's no tongs. It's the young man which is Captain Villiam Brown." In deep cogitation the general ventured to say, "Strategy, my boy, is a profound science, and don't cost more than two millions a day, while the money lasts."

Kerr mocked at the McClellan addresses to the army in imitation of Napoleon. "Fellow-Soldats: Should any of you happen to be killed in the coming battle, let me implore you to *Die without a groan.* It sounds better in history, as well as in the weekly palladiums of freedom. How well it reads, that 'Private Muggins received a shot in the neck and *died without a groan.*' Soldats! bullets have been known to pass clean through the thickest trees, and so I may be shot myself. Should such a calamity befall our distracted country, I shall *die without a groan,* even though I am a grown person. Therefore, fear nothing. The eyes of the whole civilized world are upon you, and History and Domestic Romance expect to write that you *died without a groan.*" Kerr had one soldier punished for saying he would rather "groan without a die." He burlesqued McClellan's careful instructions for the return of slaves to their owners, with the order: "If any nigger comes within the lines of the United States Army to give information, whatsomever, of the movements of the enemy, the aforesaid shall have his head knocked off, and be returned to his lawful owner, according to the groceries and provisions of the Fugitive Slave Ack."

In the month that Lincoln finally removed McClellan, Kerr argued that as the army had marched fifteen miles in six weeks, they were going up steep hills and Lincoln had a choice of removing either the Blue Ridge or McClellan. To have removed the Blue Ridge would have been "construed into proof that the Honest Abe had yielded to the fiendish clamor of the crazy Abolitionists." Also it would occasion heartburnings among the Democrats. "Hence our Honest Abe has concluded to leave the Blue Ridge where it is, and remove the idolized General."

With the publication of the Lincoln-McClellan correspondence, Kerr parodied a note of Lincoln to the General on the matter of withdrawing troops from the defense of Washington. "If the capital is weakened, it follows very clearly, that it will not be strengthened. My plan is directly the reverse of your plan, so that your plan is immediately opposite to my plan. How can your plan, by differing from my plan, save Washington according to my plan, which is not your plan?"

In August of '62, when Lincoln's plans lagged in execution, Kerr wrote:

"Notwithstanding the fact that President Lincoln is an honest man, the genius of Slumber has opened a large wholesale establishment here, and the tendency to repose is general." At a White House reception "the President wore his coat and whiskers, and bowed to all salutations like a graceful door-hinge." A Connecticut inventor came to the White House with a design for an immense ship with colossal clamps for reaching out and clutching enemy vessels "athwartships." The inventor admitted to begin with that the design needed only one thing to make it perfect. He finished a long statement of its workings. "The President's gothic features lighted up beautifully at the words of the great inventor, but in a moment they assumed an expression of doubt." The President asked what if the privateer fired while being seized by the colossal clamps. "My dear sir," says the inventor, "I told you I had only one thing to discover before I could make the machine perfect and that's it."

One midnight of July, '62, as Kerr made it up, a man arrived at the White House front, having made a bet with another fellow that "he couldn't by any possible means, speak to the President without hearing a small anecdote." He thundered at the White House door till "the Honest Abe stuck his night-capped head out of the window" and asked, "Is that you, Mr. Seward?" "No, sir, I'm a messenger from the army. Another great strategic movement has taken place, and our whole army have been taken prisoners by the Southern Confederacy." "Hem!" says the Honest Abe, shaking a mosquito from his nightcap, "this strategy reminds me of a little story." And there came a long yarn of a man out in Iowa who played one game of checkers after another, losing each time but saying each time he had yet "one cute move" to make, and when at last they asked him what was this famous move he had left up his sleeve, he got up from the table saying pleasantly, "Why, it's to move off for a little change."

Kerr knew it was a trifling story when he wrote it for print, but his theory was that the national scene of the hour looked a little silly. Likewise in October of '62, when he opened a letter: "Our Honest Abe may lack these brilliant qualities which in the great legislator may constitute either the live-oak sceptre of true patriotism or the dexter finger of refined roguery, as the genius of the age pivots on honesty or diplomacy; but his nature has all the sterling characteristics of the heartiest manhood about it, and there is a smiling sun in his composition which never sets. That he is in his anecdotage, is a fact 'which nobody can deny; or if they do, they lie!' Yet even his anecdotes have that simple sunlight in them which is, perhaps, a greater boon to the high place of a nation in the dark hour, than the most weird and perpetual haze of crafty wisdom could be."

With this utterly serious preface the letter drifted into telling of a New York chap perforating the White House to find "Honest Abe sitting with his boots on the window sill, carving a pine toothpick from a vagrant chip." The stranger asked why the army wasn't doing more. "Hem!" says the Honest Abe, combing his locks with his right hand, and placing a small bit of the chip in the right corner of his Etruscan mouth: "Perhaps I cannot better answer your question, neighbor, than by relating a small tale." Then came a long-spun yarn of an Iowa farmer invaded by a squatter sovereign from Missouri. They quarreled, picked out a bare spot where the grass never grew, and there they rassled and chawed each other, without victory on either side, the Missouri man going home under agreement to come back the next spring and finish the fight. When the Iowa farmer was asked why the show was put off till next spring he spoke of "the cantankerous spot where we fit" and said: "I'm just waiting till that thar spot has a trifle of grass on it."

Having heard this narrative, "the dignified, conventional chap hurried from the White House scratching his head; and I really believe, my boy—I really believe that his sensitive soul detected an analogy not gushingly flattering to national strategy and the President of the United States for 1865. Soon after I met him at Willard's, and says I: 'Well, my sagacious Mirabeau, what is your final opinion of our Honest Abe?' He merely paused long enough to swear at a button which happened to burst from the neck-band of his shirt just then, and says he: 'The Honest Abe is a well-meaning Executive, enough. He's a well-meaning Executive,' says the dignified chap, with an air of slightly irritated good nature; 'but I wish he'd do something to save his country, instead of telling small tales all the time.'" Having ended the foolery Kerr added: "Our President is an honest man, my boy, and the glass in his spectacles isn't exactly made of the paper they print [war] telegrams on."

The most extended and overstressed imitation of the Lincoln manner in storytelling, connected directly with current political events, was in a Kerr letter dated Washington, November 7, 1862:

The late election in New York has electrified everybody except our Honest Abe, who still goes about smiling, like a long and amiable sexton, and continues to save our distracted country after the manner of an honest man. On Tuesday night, a high moral Democratic chap, of much watch-seal, who had just received a dispatch all about the election, went to see the Honest Abe, for the express purpose of telling him that the Democratic party had been born again, and was on the point of protesting against everything whatsoever, except the Constitution of our forefathers. He found the Honest Abe cracking some walnuts before the fire, and says he:

"The celebrated Democratic organization, of which I am Assistant Engineer, has carried the State of New York in a manner impossible to express, and will now proceed to demand of you a vigorous prosecution of that unnatural strife in which are involved our lives, our liberties, and the pursuit of happiness. We admire to see your harmless honesty," said the chap, blandly, "and we believe you to be a fresh egg; but we protest against the arbitrary arrest of men which is patriots, only conservatively Democratic; and we insist upon a vigorous prosecution of Constitutional hostilities against our misguided brothers who are now offering irregular opposition to the Government."

The Honest Abe cracked a walnut, and says he: "You say, neighbor, that the organization still insists upon a vigorous prosecution of the war?"

The Democratic chap sliced a toothpick from the arm of the chair with his knife, and says he: "That is the present platform on which we are *E Pluribus unum*."

"Well," says the Honest Abe, "I believe that you mean well; but I am reminded of a little story.

"When I was practising law out in Illinois," says the Honest Abe, twisting the bow of his black necktie around from under his left ear, "there was an old cock, with two sons, living near me in a tumble-down old shanty. He lived there until half his roof blew off one windy night, and then he concluded to move to a new house, where the chimney didn't take up all the upper story. On the day when he moved, he'd got most of all his traps changed to the other residence, and had sent one of his sons to see that they were all got safely indoors, when suddenly a shower commenced to come up. The old man and his other offspring, who had stayed to hurry him, were taking up a carpet from the floor at the time the first dose of thunder cracked, and the offspring says he, 'Hurry up, old crazy-bones, or we'll be ketched in the freshet before you get up this here rich fabric.' The stern parent heeded the admonition, and went ripping away the carpet around the edges of the room, until he came near where the offspring was standing, and there it stuck. He pulled, but it wouldn't come, and he says, says he: ''Pears to me that dod-rotted tack must be a tenpenny nail—it holds on so.' You see, the old screw was very blind without his specs," says the Honest Abe, buttoning his vest askew, "and he couldn't see just where the tack was. Another peal of thunder at this moment made the irascible offspring still madder, and he says, says he: 'You misabul old cripple, if you don't hurry up we'll be ketched, I tell you!' As he made this dutiful remark he went stamping to the window, and at the same moment the cantankerous tack came out, and the aged parent went over on his back with the carpet up to his chin. He got up and dusted, and says he: 'Well, now, that *is* cur'ous—how suddent it went.' Then he proceeded to rip away again, until it came near the window, and there it stuck once more. The wild offspring saw him tugging again, and it made him so wrathy that he says, says he: 'Why in thunder didn't you take the nails out first, you crooked old sinner, you? It's enought to make me weep afresh for the old woman, to see how you—' But he didn't finish his observation; for as he walked toward where the hammer lay, the tack came out, and the old 'un went to bed again under the carpet. Up sprang the sad parent, spitting rags, and he says, says he: 'Well, now, how cur'ous—to think it should come so suddent!' Still on he went, until the carpet was all up from around the edges; but when he tried to draw it away on his shoulder, it was fast somewheres yet. R-r-*rwn*-bum-boom! went the thunder; and says the unfuriated offspring, says he: 'Well, I never did see such a blundering old dad as you be. We'll be ketched in the rain sure as grasshoppers; and all because you didn't take my advice about the hammer in the first place.' The poor old 'un tugged, and pulled, and panted, and says he: 'Well, now, it *is* cur'ous, I swun to massey. There can't be no tacks way out in the middle of the floor here, can they?' To make sure, the old blind-pate was going down on his knees to take a mouse-eye view, when all of a sudden he gave a start, and he says, says he: 'Why, 'pears to me, Sammy, *you're standing on the carpet yourself!*' And so he was—so he was," says the Honest Abe, smiling into the fire, "and that was why the carpet had stuck fast in so many places.

"Now," says the Honest Abe, poking the Democratic chap in the ribs with his knuckles; "if your organization wants me to move vigorously in this war, tell them not to be standing on my carpet all the time. Otherwise, I must still keep tacking about."

The Democratic chap had been slowly rising from his chair as this small moral tale drew toward its exciting conclusion, and at the last word he fled the apartment with quivering watch-seal.

Another imitation of the Lincoln manner was long-spun and had to do with a henpecked husband whose wife was on a sickbed, and a clergyman inquiring, "How do we find ourselves now, my dear madam? Are we about to die this pleasant morning?" She answered feebly, but later her husband beamed on the parson that she would get well. "I know it. Why, didn't you hear yourself? *She's begun to call me names!*" The letter having this yarn, dated January 4, 1863, led off with a solemn deep-toned psalm of praise to Lincoln. The unreserved devotion of Robert H. Newell, alias Orpheus C. Kerr, to the President of the United States recorded itself without a flicker of fun or pun. At the beginning of the darkest period of gloom that enveloped the nation's Executive came a eulogy more lavish perhaps than any ever flung at him in the length of his career till that time. It read:

"The more I see of our Honest Abe,—the more closely I analyze the occasional acts by which he individualizes himself as a unit distinct from the decimals of his cabinet,—the deeper grows my faith in his sterling wisdom. Standing a head and shoulders above the other men in power, he is the object at which the capricious lightnings of the storm first strike; and were he a man of wax, instead of the grand old rock he is, there would be nothing left of him but a shapeless and inert mass of pliable material by this time. There are deep traces of the storm upon his countenance, but they are the sculpture of the tempest on a natural block of granite, graduating the features of young simplicity into the sterner lineaments of the mature sublime, and shaping one of those strong and earnest faces that God sets, as indelible seals, upon the ages marked for immortality. Abused and misrepresented by his political foes, alternately cajoled and reproached by his other foes,—his political friends,—he still pursues the honest tenor of the obvious Right, and smiles at calumny. His good-nature is a lamp that never goes out, but burns, with a steady light, in the temple of his mortality through all the dark hours of his time:

> " 'As some tall cliff that rears its awful form
> Swells from the vale and midway leaves the storm;
> Though round its base the rolling clouds are spread,
> Eternal sunshine settles on its head.' "

Nowhere else in the extensive writings of Kerr was any similar surge of personal feeling, nor any like salutation to a past or present public character. Of compliments he was spare. Once Kerr went so far as to give McClellan's opinion of Kerr. "I asked the General the other day what kind of a flower he thought would spring above my head when I rested in a soldier's sepulchre? and he said, 'A cabbage!' my boy—he said 'A cabbage!' " Lincoln saw in Orpheus C. Kerr not merely an advocate who reached a large audience, but a kindred spirit to the politician who asked an Illinois gathering whether they saw any cabbages sprouting from his face. Hours of easy reading for two years prepared Lincoln's reply to General Meigs's query who this person Orpheus C. Kerr might be. "Why, have you not read those papers? They are in two volumes; any one who has not read them is a heathen."

The Orpheus C. Kerr papers were uneven and sporadic in production as compared with those of Nasby and Ward, this possibly resulting from his adventures in search of a wife. He married in September of '61 the actress-poet Adah Isaacs Menken, who had divorced Alexander Isaacs Menken, a wealthy Cincinnati dry-goods merchant, her first husband, and John C. Heenan, a famous prize fighter, her second husband. Her dazzling stage success in Baltimore a few weeks after their marriage brought her a gift of diamonds worth $1,500; she announced herself a secessionist, was arrested and released on parole, while her husband went merrily along writing Union propaganda. He sailed with her in July of '63 to San Francisco, where she met and won the general plaudits of a group including Mark Twain, Bret Harte, Artemus Ward, Joaquin Miller, and others. Orpheus C. Kerr in April of '64 sailed with her from San Francisco down to the Isthmus. There she embarked for London, where her poetry and acting met higher praise than ever before—and her husband in New York never saw her again.

While his beautiful and insatiably ambitious wife pursued her career, Kerr followed his bent toward nothing in particular. He would have been heartbroken except for the balance wheel that once enabled him to write, "Our President, my boy, has a tale for every emergency, as a rat-trap has an emergency for every tail."

Thus the three most eminent American literary artists in the field of the comic favored Lincoln in their clowning, and generated goodwill and affection for him. They had helped Lincoln and the Union cause sustain themselves through bitter years without sinking. Ward, Nasby, Kerr, were a trio. Or rather that trio with Lincoln added made a quartet. Their laughter in the American scene could not be dismissed as lacking historic play.

Except for the satirists and airy jugglers of persiflage on the *New York Herald*, and an ironic inkslinger, at his best not lacking majesty, on the *New York World*, there were scarcely any wielders of effective humor in the opposition to Lincoln. Those making attempts at wit or sarcasm often failed of their target or overshot or met a recoil. One signing himself "Major Jack Downing" tried in behalf of the Peace Democrats to write funny and spell scrawny like Ward and Nasby; he awakened little enthusiasm and less laughter. His preface to the collected *Letters of Jack Downing* published in 1864 had a proclamation signed "A. Linkin" announcing that "every person purchasing a copy of the Major's Letters shall be exempt from the draft," and so on. He portrayed himself interviewing Lincoln at the White House and telling the President, "Our Constitution is a Dimmycratic machine, and it's got to be run as a Dimmycratic machine, or it *won't run at all!*" " 'Wal,' ses Linkin, 'things do look kinder dark. I don't know whar we will come out, but I guess I'll issoo a proclamashin for the ministers to pray for us.' " This reminded Major Downing of a wicked old sinner of a farmer telling a pious elder who suggested prayer for an ailing cornfield, "I'll be darned if I don't beleave that this corn needs *manure* a tarnel sight more than it does prayin' for." Thereupon Major Downing advised, "Ses I, 'Now, Linkin, I think this country needs statesmanship a good deal more than prayin' for.' Linkin didn't seem to like that observashin of mine much, for he turned the subjick, an he ain't axed me what it was best to do with the niggers sence." This had Downing's flavor at its best. He was mainly prolix, dubious, dig-

There once was a Copperhead vile, who attempted to damage a file,
So he tried it in truth, but soon broke every tooth
On that rusty and crusty Old File.

From a campaign pamphlet of cartoons, fables, verses, circulated by the National Union party. Original in the Henry Horner collection.

nified, and signaled when to laugh instead of luring and ambushing the reader.

With one great living folk figure Lincoln seemed to have little or no acquaintance. Of the many who spoke with Lincoln none seemed to have heard him speak of Stephen Collins Foster, whose songs had already gone deep into millions of Americans. That Lincoln had heard Foster songs at blackface minstrel shows he favored, there was no doubt. Their impress on him was not such, however, that he mentioned them. They did not linger with him. Lincoln was at home with the great humorists of his country; in his own sphere and way he more than duplicated their performances. And though he had a musical ear and in his prose paragraphs lurked poems of cadence and color, he had no habit of vocal singing. No one, it seems, ever heard him even trying to hum a tune. He had song favorites, but nothing of Stephen C. Foster was among them. Had he heard "Doo-Dah" or "Oh, Susannah," they would have struck him. The originals of these two songs were parodied and used in both the 1860 and the 1864 political campaigns. Their fun was sheer American stuff. They possessed Lincoln so little, however, that he seems never to have named them as worth the country's time. The homely somberness of the melancholy Foster songs matched Lincoln's own streaking, but they too seemed to have made no impress. This was so possibly because the field of vocal song in itself was one not touching Lincoln's life deeply. The best exhibit of Foster at writing a Unionist song of popularity was the tune of "We Are Coming, Father Abraam [or "Abra-

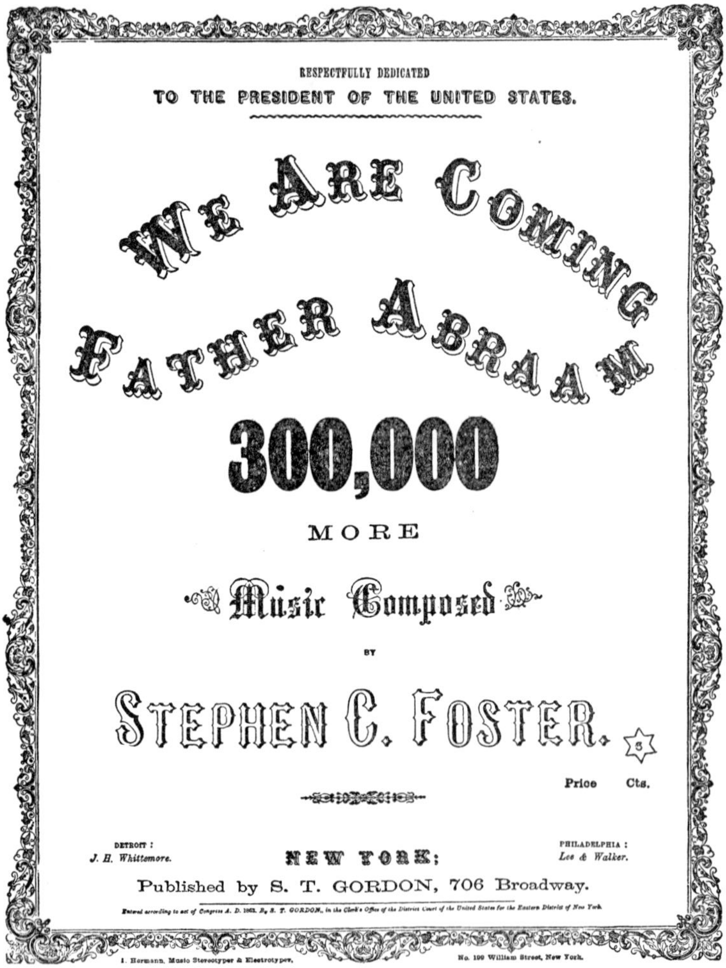

ham"]." When Foster at thirty-eight died, a familiar of strong drink and wrecked women, a great folk artist, meagerly paid for his songs, the date was January 13, 1864, the place New York City, and when in a few days he was laid in a grave a brass band played "Old Folks at Home" and "Come Where

My Love Lies Dreaming." Many journals made comment in the tone of *Leslie's Weekly:* "If singers who have profited by his compositions entertain a proper regard for his memory, they will doubtless manifest it by the construction of a fitting monument." Foster had already become a far-lengthening shadow, but Lincoln's crowded days knew him not.

Two Quakeresses in a railway coach were overheard in a conversation:

"I think Jefferson will succeed."

"Why does thee think so?"

"Because Jefferson is a praying man."

"And so is Abraham a praying man."

"Yes, but the Lord will think Abraham is joking."

This in newspapers had the added information that Lincoln said it was the best story about himself he had "ever read in the papers." Lincoln let this story spread. He loved it. Nevertheless his most deliberate public appearances and utterances encouraged no one to take him for a trifler. The stump-speech letter of September, 1863, read to a Springfield, Illinois, rally of Unionist men, approached hilarity, had its smacks of elation and humor, but closed: "Let us be sober." The series of photographs by Brady, Gardner, and others without exception portrayed a man sober, solemn, grim.

Under the heading "A Good Story," the *Salem* (Illinois) *Advertiser,* distinctly anti-Lincoln in policy, printed November 19, 1863, one of several other versions of the anecdote of the two Quakeresses. An earnest and pious minister of the Gospel, returning North from service that had brought him in touch with the Southern people, said to a brother minister: "I tell you God will always bless those who really and truly pray to him for what they need. And President Davis, sneer at him as you will, is a pious man. In all his official documents, he acknowledges his dependence on God, and in secret he prays to him, and that is the reason God has so wonderfully prospered their cause." The more practical Northern minister interposed: "*But suppose both sides pray?* Mr. Lincoln too is a man of strong religious convictions, and doubtless often prays for success. Don't you believe his prayers are as likely to be heard as Jeff Davis's?" "Yes—oh, yes, I suppose so, if he really does pray, only, God would be sure to think he was joking."

Was there here the seed of an idea Lincoln might project in an address to his own nation, to go world-wide to other nations? The idea of a dilemma faced by any two nations, peoples, or armies wherein "both read the same Bible and pray to the same God; and each invokes his aid against the other"?

Having swung far into laughter, did Lincoln at times need another swing back, into the borders of melancholy? Was it some such need that urged him to ask Lamon on the Antietam battlefield to sing "the little *sad* song"? Or again, as Nicolay noted when in Parlor No. 6 at Willard's in February of '61, "Miss Williams sang, and Mr. Lincoln enjoyed her music in moments of rest, and asked for 'something sad' "—was this the same need?

In as prominent and widely circulated a national journal as *Leslie's Weekly,* in its issue of October 3, 1863, ran an item: "We learn from a San

Francisco paper that President Lincoln was once a Catholic. According to this authority he was received, with his family, into the Catholic Church, in the year 1852, at La Salle, Ill. Rev. Father Raho, now pastor of a congregation at Los Angeles, California, administered to him the sacrament of baptism." Similar items appeared sporadically in various newspapers, marking the rise of pamphlets and books which argued, on the basis of fabrications and fantasies, that Lincoln was a Roman Catholic.

As early as March of '61 the London *Times* man, William Howard Russell, had published an account of a dinner in New York City where "an innocent question of mine, 'What church does Mr. Lincoln belong to?' created surprise. No one knew for certain—the subject had never given them any concern."

Continuously Lincoln gave his wide-flung public no definite impression that he belonged to any particular church or that he endorsed any special faith or doctrine. That he was a man of piety and of deep religious belief was conveyed to large numbers of people by unmistakable expressions in his speeches and messages. A much smaller public was aware of the information, occasionally published, though with meager details, that the President had a pew and regularly attended services of the New York Avenue Presbyterian church in Washington. His attendance there naturally brought persons who wanted to see the President of the United States. On such occasions as he attended the weekly prayer meeting of the church, it was said by members of the church, he "usually sat alone in the pastor's room from which he could hear the service without being seen, thus avoiding the interruptions of the many people who gathered to consult him at its close." A check signed by Lincoln under date of January 25, 1863, drawn on the bank of Riggs & Co., read: "Pay to Rev. Dr. Gurley (for church) or bearer Twenty-five Dollars."

The President and his wife usually drove to the church but sometimes walked, accompanied by a guard, arriving punctually and never delaying Dr. Gurley's opening of the services, wrote the guard Crook. A stone tablet they passed on the first floor read "The Second Presbyterian Congregation Church of the City of Washington," listing the names of eight Trustees, with the Masonic item: "This Corner Stone Was Laid the 29th Day of July Anno Domini 1820 by the Worshipful Grand Master of the District of Columbia—A.M. 5820." Ascending to the second floor, the President and his wife would walk down the center aisle, and on the right take the eighth pew from the pulpit. During this proceeding, wrote Crook, "out of respect for the great office he occupied, those in the church when the President arrived would rise from their seats and remain standing." The same formality was omitted at the close of the services, when Mr. and Mrs. Lincoln "would slowly walk along surrounded by others, exchanging a few words, shaking hands with those they knew."

The piety of the House and Senate chaplains, and the curious reference of one of them to the President's habits, were the topic of a Noah Brooks news letter April 9, 1864. Chaplain Channing of the House "gave the Lord a graphic description of the statue of Liberty on the Capitol dome in his prayer one morning," wrote Brooks. The House chaplain however had not offended any of his audience as had the Senate chaplain, Senator Saulsbury of Delaware offering this for passage:

> *Resolved,* That the Chaplain of the Senate be respectfully requested hereafter to pray to and supplicate Almighty God in our behalf, and not to lecture Him, inform Him what to do, or state to Him, under pretense of prayer, his (the said Chaplain's) opinion in reference to His duty as the Almighty; and that the said Chaplain be further requested, as aforesaid, not, under the form of prayer, to lecture the Senate in relation to questions before the body.

Senator Howard of Michigan objected to reception of the resolution as unworthy of the Senate. It was laid over. Saulsbury gave his word he would offer it every day of the session. Brooks wrote: "It must be said, however, that the worthy Chaplain of the Senate, Rev. Byron Sunderland, is given to sensation and lecture in his prayers. He once alluded to Uncle Abe's having been at the theater the night before by praying that we might not imitate Nero while Rome was burning, by gazing with open-mouthed wonder upon the mimic representations of the painted stage, and so on."

Of visitors and associates somewhat acquainted with Lincoln's ways of speech not more than three or four, it would seem, heard him using profane language. "By jings" was the most frequent approach to it. Perhaps only two competent witnesses had him using the word "damn." One instance was touched with humor. David Homer Bates of the War telegraph office took note of Lincoln September 21, 1863, receiving a telegram indicating that General Burnside's army was on its way to Jonesboro, Tennessee. This meant that Burnside was marching away from Rosecrans instead of toward him, as ordered. When Burnside's telegram was shown him, Lincoln said, "Damn Jonesboro!" and again telegraphed his slow, well-meaning friend Burnside to go to the help of Rosecrans.

A diary entry of Hay on May 3, 1861, read:

> This morning in the President's mail I came across some warlike documents. One from Fernandy Wood offering his services in a military capacity which was very cool but not so arctic as the cheekiness of Govr. Harris of Penn. who demanded an immediate explanation of the seizing of the *Hillman* at Cairo (which the Tycoon glanced at & quietly observed, "He be d——d.")

The good, upright, usually well-tempered Fessenden, it was told over Washington, in a rage over some unjust distribution of patronage turned loose a flow of "intemperate language" on Lincoln one morning. Lincoln took it. He kept cool. The fury of his Maine friend spent itself. Lincoln inquired gently, "You are an Episcopalian, aren't you, Senator?" "Yes, sir. I belong to that church." "I thought so. You Episcopalians all swear alike. Seward is an Episcopalian. But Stanton is a Presbyterian. You ought to hear him swear." Then Lincoln went on into telling about different kinds of swearing, how there are several varieties of profanity, and some who are proficient convey nice distinctions between punishments in this life and damnations in the world beyond. It was after this philosophical discussion of blasphemy that Lincoln and Fessenden settled down to an even-toned conversation about patronage.

The press in October of '63 reported a call paid Lincoln by members of the Baltimore (Old School) Presbyterian Synod. Lincoln's pastor, the Reverend Dr. Phineas D. Gurley, introduced the Moderator, the Reverend Dr. Septimus Tustin, who said the synod wished as a body to pay their respects, and that each member "belonged to the Kingdom of God, and each was loyal to the Government." The President's reply had overtones not to be gathered in one reading. It was an avowal of religious faith, an implied wish that all religious organizations and their memberships could be unified for the war, and a direct wish that he himself could be a more devout man than he was. Plainly it was no perfunctory address. The Associated Press report of it read:

> I can only say in this case, as in so many others, that I am profoundly grateful for the respect, given in every variety of form in which it can be given, from the religious bodies of the country. I saw, upon taking my position here, that I was going to have an Administration, if an Administration at all, of extraordinary difficulty. It was, without exception, a time of the greatest difficulty that this country ever saw. I was early brought to a living reflection that nothing in my power whatever, in others to rely upon, would succeed without the direct assistance of the Almighty—but all must fail.
>
> I have often wished that I was a more devout man than I am. Nevertheless, amid the greatest difficulties of my Administration, when I could not see any other resort, I would place my whole reliance in God, knowing that all would go well, and that He would decide for the right.
>
> I thank you, gentlemen, in the name of the religious bodies which you represent, and in the name of the Common Father, for this expression of your respect. I cannot say more.

The President seemed to be deeply moved, according to the *Cincinnati Gazette,* when he said, "I have often wished that I was a more devout man than I am," to which sentence "he gave a very tremulous utterance." Dr. Gurley came forward: "Mr. President, these are members of this Synod, and if you have time they would like to take you by the hand." The President: "Certainly, I shall be most happy to shake hands with all of them." The members of the synod then came forward, personally paid their respects to the President "and retired heartfully gratified with the interview."

To Methodist and Baptist delegations of ministers the President had spoken with rich praise of their support of the war and the need for reliance on God. His speech one May day in '62 began: "I welcome here the representatives of the Evangelical Lutherans of the United States. I accept with gratitude their assurances of the sympathy and support of that enlightened, influential, and loyal class of my fellow-citizens in an important crisis which involves, in my judgment, not only the civil and religious liberties of our own dear land, but in a large degree the civil and religious liberties of mankind in many countries and through many ages." He had re-

The actress-poet Adah Isaacs Menken and her husband Robert Henry Newell (Orpheus C. Kerr)

From the Meserve collection

David Ross Locke (Petroleum Vesuvius Nasby)

From the Barrett collection

Charles Farrar Browne (Artemus Ward)

From the Meserve collection

Lincoln, February 9, '64. A Brady photograph of exceptionally sharp definition of line

The Washington Monument in later days. In '64 it was built only to 200 feet.

From a stereograph in the Barrett collection

Lyman Trumbull

Owen Lovejoy

From the author's collection

luctantly accepted the issue of battle forced by internal enemies. "You all may recollect that in taking up the sword thus forced into our hands, this government appealed to the prayers of the pious and the good, and declared that it placed its whole dependence on the favor of God." That he had a creed of some religious faith, which he might be able to amplify in extenso if required, he would have them know by his closing statement to them: "I now humbly and reverently in your presence, reiterate the acknowledgment of that dependence, not doubting that, if it shall please the Divine Being who determines the destinies of nations, this shall remain a united people, and that they will, humbly seeing that Divine guidance, make their prolonged national existence a source of new benefits to themselves and their successors, and to all classes and conditions of mankind."

Bishop Ames as chairman and the Reverend Dr. Joseph Cummings as secretary headed a large Methodist delegation that came to the White House in May of '64 to present an address. One member had called the day before, notified Nicolay that on the next day a delegation from the General Conference of ministers assembled in Philadelphia, "representing the largest, most loyal, and influential church of the country," would hope to see the President. Nicolay brought the President, who took the prepared address of the delegation and said he would think about his reply for the next day. The Methodist Church was taking as strong a stand as Lincoln could ask in support of the Government and the war. When their delegates were ushered in the next day and Secretary Seward had introduced them to the President, Dr. Cummings noted, "In his reply the President playfully remarked, much to the surprise of those members of the committee who knew nothing of the arrangement, that he had seen the address before, and had prepared his reply." He read to them his reply, on which he had deliberated:

> Gentlemen. In response to your address, allow me to attest the accuracy of its historical statements; indorse the sentiments it expresses; and thank you, in the nations [sic] name for the sure promise it gives.
>
> Nobly sustained as the government has been by all the churches, I would utter nothing which might, in the least, appear invidious against any. Yet, without this, it may fairly be said that the Methodist Episcopal Church, not less devoted than the best, is, by its greater numbers, the most important of all. It is no fault in others that the Methodist Church sends more soldiers to the field, more nurses to the hospital, and more prayers to Heaven than any. God bless the Methodist Church—bless all the churches—and blessed be God, Who, in this our great trial, giveth us the churches.
>
> May 18, 1864. A. Lincoln.

After handshaking, the delegates took leave amid a general smile over one saying, "Mr. President, we all hope the country will rest in Abraham's bosom for the next four years." While a few waited for a copy to be made of the President's address, noted Dr. Cummings, "There was a general conversation relative to public matters and on the state of the Methodist Church in the South; and it was amusing to see how Mr. Lincoln evaded a direct answer to Bishop Ames's request for an opinion relative to our rights to the Methodist churches in the South."

In proclamations, in recommendations of thanksgiving or of fasting and prayer, in numerous references to God, Providence, the Almighty, the Common Father, sometimes having their meaning colored by special events or conditions, Lincoln had given the impression to a multitude that he might have a creed. At a later time a clergyman sought to formulate such a creed from Lincoln's own words, changing the text merely to the extent of trans-

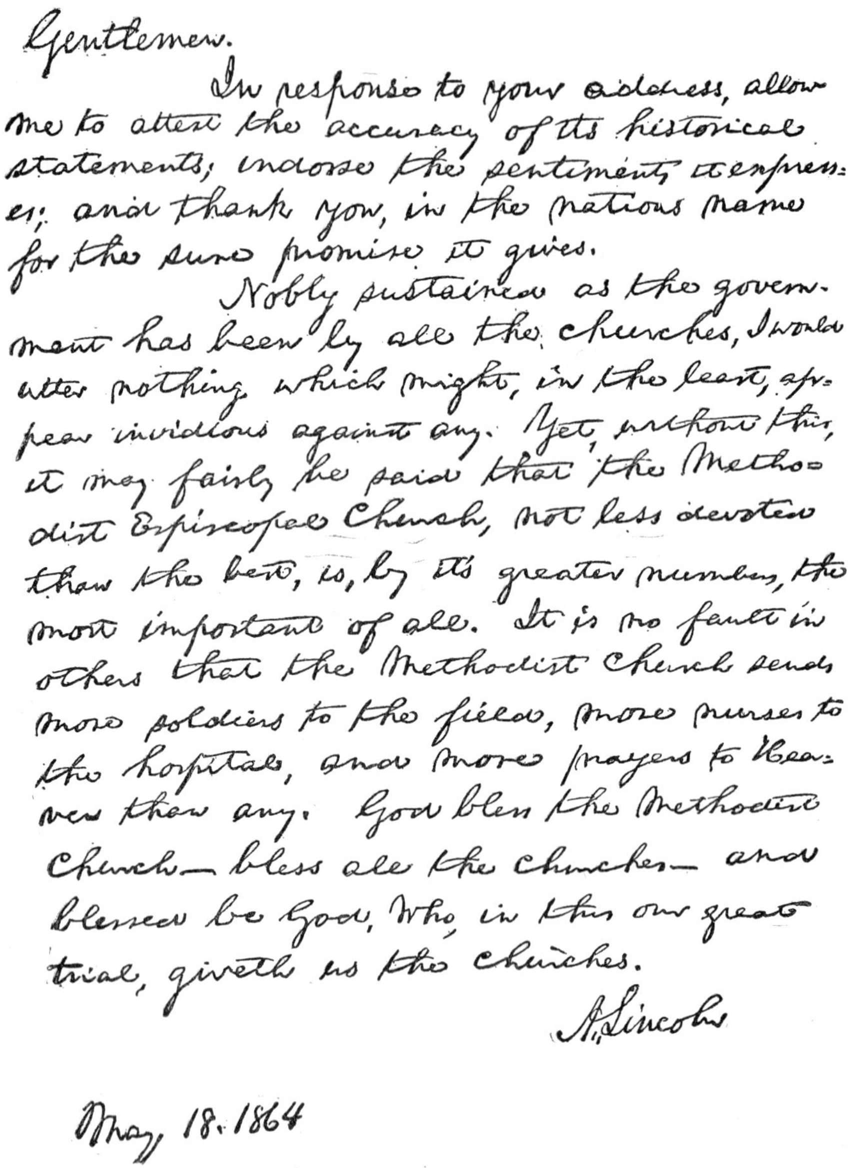
Gentlemen.

In response to your address, allow me to attest the accuracy of its historical statements; indorse the sentiments it expresses; and thank you, in the nations name for the sure promise it gives.

Nobly sustained as the government has been by all the churches, I would utter nothing which might, in the least, appear invidious against any. Yet, without this, it may fairly be said that the Methodist Episcopal Church, not less devoted than the best, is, by it's greater numbers, the most important of all. It is no fault in others that the Methodist Church sends more soldiers to the field, more nurses to the hospitals, and more prayers to Heaven than any. God bless the Methodist Church—bless all the churches—and blessed be God, Who, in this our great trial, giveth us the churches.

A. Lincoln

May 18. 1864

posing pronouns from plural to singular, making other slight modifications, and prefixing the words "I believe." Further additions to such a creed, possibly carrying it to such a length of form that it is rather a liturgical expression of faith, a partial arrangement of the declarations of the Chief Magistrate and the public man Abraham Lincoln, would give this result:

I believe it is fit and becoming in all people, at all times, to acknowledge and revere the supreme government of God; to bow in humble submission to his chastisements; to confess and deplore their sins and transgressions, in the full conviction that the fear of the Lord is the beginning of wisdom; and to pray with all fervency and contrition for the pardon of their past offenses, and for a blessing upon their present and prospective action.

I believe, in our beloved country now afflicted with faction and civil war, it is peculiarly fit for us to recognize the hand of God in this terrible visitation.

I believe that the united prayer of the nation may ascend to the Throne of Grace.

I believe it has pleased Almighty God to vouchsafe victories to the land and naval forces engaged in suppressing an internal rebellion, wherefore they should especially acknowledge and render thanks to our Heavenly Father for these inestimable blessings.

I believe it is the duty of nations as well as of men to own their dependence upon the overruling power of God; to confess their sins and transgressions in humble sorrow, yet with assured hope that genuine repentance will lead to mercy and pardon; and to recognize the sublime truth, announced in the Holy Scriptures and proved by all history, that those nations only are blessed whose God is the Lord.

I believe we may justly fear that the awful calamity of civil war which now desolates the land may be but punishment inflicted upon us for our presumptuous sins, to the needful end of our national reformation as a whole people.

I believe we have been the recipients of the choicest bounties of Heaven, preserved these many years in peace and prosperity, grown in numbers, wealth, and power as no other nation has ever grown; but we have forgotten God, the gracious hand which preserved us in peace.

I believe that intoxicated with unbroken success, we have become too self-sufficient to feel the necessity of redeeming and preserving grace, too proud to pray to the God that made us.

I believe it behooves us to humble ourselves before the offended Power, to confess our national sins, and to pray for clemency and forgiveness.

I believe in national humiliation, fasting, and prayer, in keeping a day holy to the Lord, devoted to the humble discharge of the religious duties proper to such a solemn occasion.

I believe in hopes authorized by the Divine Teachings, that the united cry of the nation will be heard on High.

I believe in Him whose will, not ours, should be done.

I believe the people of the United States, in the forms approved by their own consciences, should render the homage due to the Divine Majesty for the wonderful things He has done in the nation's behalf, and invoke the influence of His Holy Spirit to subdue anger.

I believe in bounties so extraordinary they cannot fail to penetrate and soften the heart habitually insensible to the ever watchful providence of Almighty God.

I believe no human counsel hath devised, nor hath any mortal hand worked out, these great things we have received; they are the gracious gifts of the Most High God, who, while dealing with us in anger for our sins, hath nevertheless remembered mercy.

I believe in the interposition of the Almighty Hand to heal the wounds of the nation, and to restore it, as soon as may be consistent with the Divine purposes, to the full enjoyment of peace, harmony, tranquillity, and union.

I believe in penitential and pious sentiments, in devotional designs and purposes, in homages and confessions, in supplications to the Almighty, solemnly, earnestly, reverently.

I believe in blessings and comfort from the Father of Mercies to the sick, the wounded, the prisoners, and to the orphans and widows.

I believe it pleases Almighty God to prolong our national life, defending us with His guardian care.

I believe in His eternal truth and justice.

I believe the will of God prevails; without Him all human reliance is vain; without the assistance of that Divine Being I cannot succeed; with that assistance I cannot fail.

I believe I am a humble instrument in the hands of our Heavenly Father; I desire that all my works and acts may be according to His will; and that it may be so, I give thanks to the Almighty and seek His aid.

I believe in praise to Almighty God, the beneficent Creator and Ruler of the Universe.

One public document carrying Lincoln's signature went far and wide to persuade many that the President was a practicing Christian to the extent of being a stern observer of the Seventh Day, a strict adherent to the Sabbath kept with propriety. This was the notable paper headed "General Order Respecting the Observance of the Sabbath Day in the Army and Navy." It read:

Executive Mansion,
Washington, November 15, 1862

The President, commander-in-chief of the army and navy, desires and enjoins the orderly observance of the Sabbath by the officers and men in the military and naval service. The importance for man and beast of the prescribed weekly rest, the sacred rights of Christian soldiers and sailors, a becoming deference to the best sentiment of a Christian people, and a due regard for the Divine will, demand that Sunday labor in the army and navy be reduced to the measure of strict necessity.

The discipline and character of the national forces should not suffer, nor the cause they defend be imperiled, by the profanation of the day or name of the Most High. "At this time of public distress"—adopting the words of Washington in 1776—"men may find enough to do in the service of God and their country without abandoning themselves to vice and immorality." The first general order issued by the Father of his Country after the Declaration of Independence indicates the spirit in which our institutions were founded and should ever be defended: "The general hopes and trusts that every officer and man will endeavor to live and act as becomes a Christian soldier, defending the dearest rights and liberties of his country."

Abraham Lincoln

Official: E. D. Townsend
Assistant Adjutant-General

The text and tone of this order indicate definitely it was composed by someone else than Lincoln. An assistant adjutant general, T. M. Vincent, was to clarify in his statement: "I myself took the famous Sunday-Observance order, in Mr. Stanton's handwriting, to Lincoln, who approved it without suggesting a change, and it was issued as coming from him. It gained great credit for the supposed author." Stanton, according to his secretary, Albert E. H. Johnson, kept at his desk a facsimile stamp with which he attached Lincoln's signature to orders and other communications. General Vincent and others of Stanton's immediate assistants spoke as though their chief often wrote pieces of high merit for which Lincoln got the public credit, and in their view the Sunday Observance order was an outstanding instance.

To what degree the hand of Seward, an Episcopalian versed in forms and rituals, participated in the texts of the executive proclamations, no one could say. They were issued over the President's signature and by the Secretary of State, who countersigned them. In some paragraphs a reader familiar with Lincoln's style would say this or that was undeniably his. In sentences and phrases here and there, the devotee and churchman, the ritualist accustomed to forms, was present in a manner to indicate that Seward probably wrote them. Possibly their sharing in these texts varied, as it did in the documents showing on their early drafts what Lincoln wrote and what Seward wrote, as in the first inaugural address, where Seward lent a softening influence, or in the note to Great Britain, where Lincoln took the edge off Seward's warlike tone. That Lincoln omitted to put a reliance on God in the Emancipation Proclamation until reminded by Chase was evidence that Chase was more than Lincoln sensitive to the need for a note of piety in such a document. That Lincoln's first draft of the Gettysburg Address omitted mention of the Deity might indicate that Seward suggested it on the late evening visit of Lincoln; or Lincoln may have inserted the words "under God" on his own initiative. A distinct trend toward a deeper religious note, a piety more assured of itself because more definitely derived from inner and private growths of Lincoln himself, this could be seen as the President from year to year fitted himself more deeply and awarely into the mantle and authorities of Chief Magistrate.

To others beside Alexander H. Stephens, Lincoln had a "mystic" zeal for the Union cause. In one sense Lincoln saw himself as a crusader and a holiness preacher for an indissoluble unity of one common country. To the sacred devotions of his own cause he would join any others of capacity for sacred devotions.

The extent of the loyalty of the churches, as compared, for instance, to that of the newspapers, drew him in response to the churchmen and to church heads. He could not be impervious to the Reformed Presbyterian Church ("Scotch Covenanters"), through a committee in dark months of 1863, "by every consideration drawn from the Word of God" enjoining him "not to be moved from the path of duty on which you have so auspiciously entered, either by the threats or blandishments of the enemies of human progress." Likewise the New School Presbyterians in 1862 through their General Assembly sending word: "Since the day of your inauguration, the thousands of our membership have followed you with unceasing prayer, besieging the throne of Heaven in your behalf. . . . When we look at the history of your Administration hitherto, and at the wonderful way in which this people have been led under your guidance, we glorify God in you." Their delegation in 1863 presenting loyalist resolutions, with approval of the President's antislavery policy, was headed by John A. Foote. a brother of the Admiral. In his reply the President said it had been his happiness "to receive testimonies of a similar nature from, I believe, all denominations of Christians." This to him was gratifying. "From the beginning I saw that the issues of our great struggle depended on the divine interposition and favor. . . . As a pilot I have used my best exertions to keep afloat our Ship of State, and shall be glad to resign my trust at the appointed time to another pilot more skilful and successful than I may prove. In every case and at all hazards the government must be perpetuated. Relying, as I do, upon the Almighty Power, and encouraged as I am by these resolutions which you have just read, with the support which I receive from Christian men, I shall not hesitate to use all the means at my control to secure the termination of this rebellion, and will hope for success."

The German Reformed Synod, the Lutheran General Synod, the Moravian Synod, had passed resolutions of varied texts declaring themselves in favor of the war, terming it the duty of every Christian to support it by his means, efforts, influence, and prayers. State conferences of the Congregational churches adopted resolutions in key with the Massachusetts body of 1864 declaring the surest and shortest way to peace was not "to relax our grasp upon the enemy" but to present a united and loyal front "and an unconquerable determination to prosecute the war till the power of the Government meets no longer armed resistance." In the autumn of 1864 the Congregational churches of New York, New Jersey, and Pennsylvania placed themselves squarely in favor of Lincoln's re-election through the declarations of their General Association: "Make the decision of the people on the 8th of November final and fatal to the hopes of traitors in arms and conspirators in political councils." They used Lincoln's Niagara Conference phrase in favoring "that policy which looks to the abandonment of slavery as the condition of permanent union and peace." The armies and the Government "in the field and at the polls, we will sustain with our votes."

The Roman Catholic Church was less demonstrative and vocal than the Protestants. But it was a Roman Catholic, General William S. Rosecrans, who had resisted the pressure of Greeley to place him at the head of the Union ticket instead of Lincoln. And General Rosecrans' brother, a Catholic bishop at Cincinnati, had continuously approved of Lincoln's progressive antislavery policy. Archbishop John Hughes of New York, despite his tardiness of action during his illness while the New York antidraft riots raged, had kept in close touch with Secretary Seward and rendered important loyalist service. In the ranks and among the shoulder-straps of the Union armies Catholics of several nationalities, and particularly the Irish, had records for gallant and distinguished service.

As a Chief Magistrate having a common bond with all of these faiths and churches that moved toward a national unity beyond any future breaking, Lincoln's piety was manifest. A blood fellowship of death and suffering moved him. When he thanked one group of religionists "in the name of the Common Father," and gave his tremulous utterance, "I have often wished that I was a more devout man than I am," he had cogent reasons besides intuitions that he deemed valid.

To Joshua Speed's mother the President sent a photograph of himself inscribed: "For Mrs. Lucy G. Speed, from whose pious hand I accepted the present of an Oxford Bible twenty years ago."

By two of their leading points of religious teaching, the Quakers were in a hard way, caught between the two doctrines: hatred of slavery and nonparticipation in war. They acted according to individual conscience, followed various paths, as told by the address of the 1864 Yearly Meeting of the Society of Friends: "Many of our young men, overcome by the spirit of war, have rushed into the conflict where some of them found an early death; some have purchased their release from the draft by the payment of money; others have remained steadfast to their faith in the hour of trial, thereby subjecting themselves to the penalty for desertion." With the Quakers, however, and with members of other religious societies whose teachings forbade participation in war, the Government dealt with a more gentle hand, "exercised a leniency," Congress legislating to accommodate them, the Executive favoring these acts with no reservations.

Answering a kindly letter from Rhode Island Quakers, Lincoln acknowledged that he expected no reputation as a peace man while up to his armpits in war blood. "Engaged as I am, in a great war, I fear it will be difficult for the world to understand how fully I appreciate the principles of peace inculcated in this letter and everywhere by the Society of Friends." That such true and perfect lovers of peace as the Quakers could send him from their Iowa organization, through Senator Harlan, an address voicing accord with him, was deeply moving. As though here were people whose basic thought and feeling required no particular appeals or corrections, as though his conscience at its roots ran with theirs, in phrases shaded with a faint glad music, he wrote the Iowa Quakers: "It is most cheering and encouraging for me to know that in the efforts which I have made, and am making, for the restoration of a righteous peace to our country, I am upheld and sustained by the good wishes and prayers of God's people. No one is more deeply than myself aware that without his favor our highest wisdom is but as foolishness, and that our most strenuous efforts would avail nothing in the shadow of his displeasure. It seems to me that if there be one subject upon which all good men may unitedly agree, it is in imploring the gracious favor of the God of Nations upon the struggle our people are making for the preservation of their precious birthright of civil and religious liberty."

A current of mysticism in Lincoln seemed to run parallel with a strain of rationalism. Beyond the natural and seen was there an operating force of the supernatural and the inscrutable? In the little sheet of paper on which he wrote in latter '62 a private memorandum, copied by Hay, never given to the public by Lincoln, penned in a frame of mind "absolutely detached from earthly considerations," so believed Hay, he seemed to work in a mid-ground between the seen and the unseen. "In the present civil war it is quite possible that God's purpose is something different from the purpose of either party; and yet the human instrumentalities, working just as they do, are of the best adaptation to effect his purpose. I am almost ready to say that this is probably true; that God wills this contest, and wills that it shall not end yet."

On certain occasions when the air was charged with high emotion connected with some immediate event, Lincoln gave his accord to those who spoke sympathy with him, and voiced faith in a guiding Supreme Power. On the morning of the funeral of Willie Lincoln, Mrs. Rebecca Pomeroy of Chelsea, Massachusetts, saw the boy's father as a man under heavy affliction. She was a widow who had recently buried her husband and as a volunteer nurse had come to Washington for service in military hospitals. During the sickness of Willie and Tad Lincoln she entered on duty as a White House nurse in special charge of the two boys. As a Baptist Church member and a devout Christian woman she assured Lincoln that many Christians were praying for him. Tears stood in his eyes, said Mrs. Pomeroy, as he replied: "I am glad to hear that. I want them to pray for me. I need their prayers." As they were going out to the burial, he thanked her gently for further expressions of sympathy, and said, "I will try to go to God with my sorrows." To her kindly question a few days later whether he could not trust God, his answer was: "I think I can, and I will try. I wish I had that childlike faith you speak of, and I trust He will give it to me." To this he added a memory tenderly spoken of: "I had a good Christian mother, and her prayers have followed me thus far through life."

From several accounts it seemed that Lincoln never was curt, patronizing, offhand, nor in any way even slightly resistant to any expression of religious faith or any offer of spiritual consolation made to him with sincerity. As he had told the Presbyterian Synod callers, "I have often wished that I was a more devout man than I am," so he probably told the White House children's nurse, "I wish I had that childlike faith you speak of."

Mrs. Pomeroy was the only White House resident who spoke of having heard the President on one occasion in his room praying aloud earnestly and reverently. General Daniel E. Sickles told of Lincoln saying to him that when so many were panic-stricken just before the battle of Gettysburg, "oppressed by the gravity of our affairs, I went to my room one day, and I locked the door, and got down on my knees before Almighty God, and prayed to Him mightily for victory." Were these accounts of Lincoln as a praying man strictly accurate? It is rather likely they were not. Lincoln was a praying man, but not in the conventional and demonstrative sense these two conveyed. Nicolay and Hay, Stoddard, Carpenter, Chaplain Neill, the guard Crook, these White House residents with far better opportunities for observation, left no record of having seen nor reliably heard from the President or anyone else of his having thus invoked the Lord. They saw him as having piety and spiritual resources, but more subdued about it than Mrs.

Pomeroy or General Sickles represented. Such accounts coming to the man most closely associated with Lincoln before he became President, William H. Herndon, he advised one seeker after light on Lincoln's intricate inner faith, "You had to *guess* at the man after years of acquaintance and then you must look long and keenly before you guessed, or you would make an ass of yourself."

Carpenter published an account of one interview with Lincoln, giving it as though it were credible coming from the Reverend Francis Vinton, rector of Trinity Church, New York. Willie Lincoln having died on a Thursday, the father in grief on the following Thursday "shut himself away from all society," and again on the second Thursday "would see no one," wrote Carpenter. About this time the Reverend Dr. Vinton, as an acquaintance of Mrs. Lincoln and her sister Mrs. Edwards and on their invitation, came to the White House, and in the course of conversation admonished the President that he was unfitting himself for his high post by giving way to his grief. Heathen, not Christians, mourned the departed as *lost.* The account then proceeded:

"Your son," said Dr. Vinton, "is *alive,* in Paradise. Do you remember that passage in the Gospels: 'God is not the God of the *dead* but of the living, for *all* live unto him'?"

The President had listened as one in a stupor, until his ear caught the words, "Your son is alive." Starting from the sofa, he exclaimed, "Alive! *alive!* Surely you mock me."

"No, sir, believe me," replied Dr. Vinton; "it is a most comforting doctrine of the church, founded upon the words of Christ himself."

Mr. Lincoln looked at him a moment, and then, stepping forward, he threw his arm around the clergyman's neck, and laying his head upon his breast, sobbed aloud. "*Alive? alive?*" he repeated.

"My dear sir," said Dr. Vinton, greatly moved, as he twined his own arm around the weeping father, "believe this, for it is God's most precious truth. Seek not your son among the dead; he is not there; he lives to-day in Paradise! Think of the full import of the words I have quoted. The Sadducees, when they questioned Jesus, had no other conception than that Abraham, Isaac, and Jacob were dead and buried. Mark the reply: 'Now that the dead *are* raised, even Moses showed at the bush when he called the Lord the God of Abraham, the God of Isaac, and the God of Jacob. For he is not the God of the dead, but of the living, *for all live unto him!*' Did not the aged patriarch mourn his sons as dead?—'Joseph is not, and Simeon is not, and ye will take Benjamin also.' But Joseph and Simeon were both living, though he believed it not. Indeed, Joseph being taken from him, was the eventual means of the preservation of the whole family. And so God has called your son into his upper kingdom—a kingdom and an existence as real, more real, than your own. It may be that he too, like Joseph, has gone, in God's good providence, to be the salvation of *his* father's household. It is a part of the Lord's plan for the ultimate happiness of you and yours. Doubt it not. I have a sermon," continued Dr. Vinton, "upon this subject, which I think might interest you."

Mr. Lincoln begged him to send it at an early day—thanking him repeatedly for his cheering and hopeful words. The sermon was sent, and read over and over by the President, who caused a copy to be made for his own private use before it was returned. Through a member of the family, I have been informed that Mr. Lincoln's views in relation to spiritual things seemed changed from that hour. Certain it is, that thenceforth he ceased the observance of the day of the week upon which his son died, and gradually resumed his accustomed cheerfulness.

The account was unique in the one respect that it was the first time Lincoln was portrayed as throwing his arm around someone's neck, laying his head on another man's breast, and sobbing aloud. This was the extreme limit of emotional displays accorded Lincoln by observers during the war. An eminent clergyman, widely versed in the materials bearing on Lincoln's religious life, at a later time weighed the Vinton incident as one that could not be wholly false nor conceivably wholly true. "That Lincoln talked with Dr. Vinton concerning his recent sorrow, and was comforted by his assurance of immortality is not improbable, nor that he accepted Dr. Vinton's sermon and had it copied; but the scene as finally described has every appearance of being much colored."

As a user of words having to do with the involved relations of God and man, Lincoln was graphic and precise, according to an interview reported by the Iowa Congressman, chairman of the House Judiciary Committee, James F. Wilson. In June of '62, when Jeb Stuart had taken his gray horsemen in a circle around McClellan's army and cut the communications, Lincoln had remarked there was no news: "Not one word. . . . I don't know that we have an army." One member of the delegation with which Wilson called urged a more resolute policy on slavery. "Slavery must be stricken down wherever it exists," this radical emphasized. "If we do not do right I believe God will let us go our own way to our ruin. But if we do right, I believe He will lead us safely out of this wilderness, crown our arms with victory, and restore our now dissevered Union."

Wilson kept an eye on the President, saw that this trend of speech affected him deeply, and expected "from the play of his features and the sparkle of his eyes" there would be a response. The listless Lincoln slowly arose to full height, "his right arm outstretched towards the gentleman who had just ceased speaking, his face aglow like the face of a prophet," saying to his admonisher, "My faith is greater than yours," agreeing fully with what had been said of the role of God and Providence. Then he proceeded: "But I also believe He will compel us to do right in order that He may do these things, not so much because we desire them as that they accord with His plans of dealing with this nation, in the midst of which He means to establish justice. I think He means that we shall do more than we have yet done in furtherance of His plans, and He will open the way for our doing it. I have felt His hand upon me in great trials and submitted to His guidance, and I trust that as He shall further open the way I will be ready to walk therein, relying on His help and trusting in His goodness and wisdom."

The transcript by Wilson ran remarkably close to the reasoning of the private memorandum Hay found on Lincoln's desk. It was near the core of Lincoln's philosophy of the faiths of men as related to the acts of God in the conduct of the war. "The manner of this delivery was most impressive," recorded Wilson, adding that Lincoln, with his dejection gone, resumed his seat and in a reassured tone continued. His faith told him the present dark hour would be followed by a bright morning. "Sometimes it seems necessary that we should be confronted with perils which threaten us with disaster in order that we may not get puffed up and forget Him who has much work for us yet to do."

A young Tennessean, Opie Read, was to write later of a friend George McCormack saying that in the course of a talk with Lincoln he asked, "What is your conception of God?"

"The same as my conception of nature."

"And what is that?"

"That it is impossible for either to be personal."

On McCormack's observation, "Man is humiliated only when he feels his weakness has been spied upon; he has no self-shame," Lincoln rejoined: "I don't agree with you. A rat gnaws alone; and so does a moral weakness within us, even though we know that it is securely hidden. I have seen a dog alone, suddenly become ashamed and sneak off."

"But the dog must have known that you saw him."

"No, when I was hidden from his view. Now, I don't know what the soul is, but whatever it is, I know that it can humble itself."

A hotel-keeper from Quincy, Illinois, an old client of Lincoln, called at the White House. Between them there might be frank speech. For this was George P. Floyd, who had been honest enough to overpay Lincoln's fee, Lincoln in return being honest enough to return nearly half the fee, finishing their 1856 transaction with writing Floyd: "You must think I am a high-priced man. . . . I send you a receipt for fifteen dollars, and return to you a ten-dollar bill." In the course of their talk these years since Lincoln had taken that long look up and down the Mississippi from the tall bluffs of Quincy, Lincoln said, according to Floyd: "I have not suffered *by* the South. I have suffered *with* the South. Their pain has been my pain. Their loss has been my loss. What they have gained I have gained." To Floyd, Lincoln could say such a thing. To Donn Piatt or Thad Stevens or many others he could not begin to mention it. Harriet Beecher Stowe would have understood it and been wrenched by it; her brother Henry Ward Beecher might have suspected it to be a piece of easy dramatics for political effect.

What Lincoln had of mystic faith and inner outlook was of hidden and slowly incessant growth. "I am very sure," he said once in cheerful mood to Noah Brooks, "that if I do not go away from here a wiser man, I shall go away a better man, for having learned here what a very poor sort of a man I am." Reticent, shy of discoursing much of his own mental exercises, thus Brooks saw him in this mood refer to "a process of crystallization," a result of the interplay of the outside world and his own personality. "Referring to what he called a change of heart, he said he did not remember any precise time when he passed through any special change of purpose, or of heart; but he would say, that his own election to office, and the crisis immediately following, influentially determined him in what he called 'a process of crystallization,' then going on in his mind."

Many who came away from seeing Lincoln carried a dominant and lasting impression of him as a sober and sad man, his lapses into wit or humor fading most often into the austere or the abstracted. John W. Widney of Piqua, Ohio, a sergeant wounded at the Wilderness, starting a furlough home for complete recovery before return to duty, saw Lincoln on the White House walk from the War Office, "dressed in black, with frock coat, stovepipe hat, walking slowly, shoulders bent forward, hands folded behind his back." He reminded Sergeant Widney of a Piqua man, "old Mr. Orputt, an old time shoemaker, who lived in Park Avenue, an old time member of the Greene Street Church, who always came to church in the same style clothes and wore a stovepipe hat." Lincoln asked the Sergeant, "What State and regiment?" Widney answered, and Lincoln, with a "God bless you and I hope you will get home safe," passed into the White House while Widney stood gazing and feeling a "burden of sorrow" on the shoulders under the stovepipe hat. Widney was a churchman who favored his Bible and said that no other words fitted the moment for him like those of (to use his words) an old prophet: "O Jerusalem, Jerusalem, how often would I have gathered thee beneath my wings, as a hen gathers her chicks, but ye would not."

This was akin to Gustave Koerner's feeling in March of '61 about the "neglected and unkempt" White House figure. "There is something about the man, about the face, which is unfathomable." Or of Henry Laurens Dawes saying in the same month: "There is something in his face which I cannot understand. He is great. We can safely trust the Union to him."

CHAPTER 57

THE MAN HAD BECOME THE ISSUE

THE man Lincoln, his person and mind, had come to be the pivotal issue of the 1864 campaign. Some would vote for him with no particular faith, rating him low as statesman and leader, nevertheless preferring him to the only other candidate. Others would vote for him in a loyalty that had seldom or never swerved since he became President; they had arrived at an abiding faith in him. A character and personality had become a reality inwoven with their own hearts and passions. In the chaos of the times he was to these folk a beacon light that shone, that wavered, that in moments almost flickered out into a black despair, yet returned to shine without wavering.

In various angles this generation of citizens saw him as a public man, a politician and statesman first of all, living in terrific high lights of scrutiny and interpretation, of representations ranging from the utterly true to the unutterably false; he was a home man, a husband and father with the routine of family life in a house seldom untroubled with visitors and intruders; he was a churchman to more than the extent of being a pew-renter and a regular attendant at divine services—a theatregoer—a participant in public functions, secret interviews and closed conferences; he was a magistrate of solemn proclamations, a high commander issuing specific orders, a writer of private memoranda for his own eye only, as well as a correspondent whose missives might be marked "Confidential"; a lonely walker and meditator, he had a personality intricate and mysterious even to himself.

On one of Sheridan's forays, crossing the Pamunkey River near the White House, a pack mule fell off a bridge thirty feet to water, turned a full somersault, struck an abutment, went under, came up, swam ashore and rejoined the troop column. Lincoln in the course of the war felt the Union cause occasionally had that mule's luck.

"The great West is with you," Ralph Emerson of Rockford, Illinois, assured him.

"Yes—but I am sometimes reminded of Old Mother Partington on the sea beach. A big storm came up and the waves began to rise till the water came in under her cabin door. She got a broom and went to sweeping it out. But the water rose higher and higher, to her knees, to her waist, at last to her chin. But she kept on sweeping and exclaiming, 'I'll keep on sweeping as long as the broom lasts, and we will see whether the storm or the broom will last the longest.' " At the final words, according to Emerson, Lincoln's jaws came together, his face grim rather than funny.

Out in Illinois, Dick Oglesby, recovered from bullet wounds, was running for governor on the Union ticket and saying that in 1858 at Urbana in a walk together with Lincoln—he distinctly recalled it—Lincoln told him, "Remember, Dick, to keep close to the people—they are always right and will mislead no one."

Would the dream of democracy go down? Was fate to write that popular government and its most hopeful experiment should "perish from the earth"? This hazard troubled Lincoln. He phrased it briefly in the Gettysburg speech. It connected with his melancholy, though Nathaniel Hawthorne could not see this masked behind the politician who so deftly and genially greeted the present of a fancy buggy whip from a Massachusetts delegation. The profound Hawthorne did not become aware that his own somber contemplations of humanity had a parallel in Lincoln's darker and more intricate moods. For both Lincoln and Hawthorne it was a loss. Hawthorne went away to nurse his grief over the awful war game played out by men before his eyes with a shame and a depth of ignorance that overwhelmed him. From this grief Hawthorne died in 1864, mostly of heartbreak, mostly from looking too close and too long at the riddle Lincoln had formulated in the Gettysburg speech. Hawthorne phrased it: "The Present, the Immediate, the Actual, has proved too potent for me. It takes away not only my scanty faculty, but even my desire for imaginative composition, and leaves me sadly content to scatter a thousand peaceful fantasies upon the hurricane that is sweeping us all along with it, possibly, into a limbo where our nation and its polity may be as literally the fragments of a shattered dream as my unwritten romance."

There were sensitive human spirits spun so finely that the war news, war imaginings, war chaos and its seeming lack of meaning, slowly wore away their life threads. Did this happen to Hawthorne? Into America reached a discussion begun by an English bishop who held that nations can go completely insane, the same as individuals, and a national or civil war rests on a form of community madness, a malady scientists should be encouraged to study. Slow ghosts of war pulled Hawthorne down? "Mr. Hawthorne cannot walk ten minutes now without wishing to sit down," wrote his wife to his publisher. "He is indeed *very* weak. I hardly know what takes away his strength. It almost deprives me of my wits to see him growing weaker with no aid. He seems quite bilious, and has a restlessness that is infinite." Her points would go for many of the more sensitive over the country, even in the army. They grew weaker hardly knowing what took away their strength. They had "a restlessness that is infinite." The mockery of it touched young Henry Adams at the war's beginning when he wrote that only a man "cool as death" could take hold and win results.

While her husband was away two years before, Mrs. Hawthorne had written him of "a paragraph in the paper about your being at Washington, and that the President received you with especial graciousness." She wrote as she might have talked over the morning coffee. "The President has had a delicious palaver with a deputation of black folk, talking to them as to babies. I suspect the President is a jewel. I like him very well." She loved her husband, did Sophia Peabody Hawthorne, and wrote as a lover. "If it were not such a bore, I could wish thou mightest be President through this crisis, and show the world what can be done by using two eyes, and turning each thing upside down and inside out, before judging and acting. I should not wonder if thy great presence in Washington might affect the moral air and work good. If you like the President, then give him my love and blessing."

Her next reference was probably to Lincoln's proclamation revoking General Hunter's emancipation decree, joined with Lincoln's plea for gradual compensated emancipation, urging, "I do not argue—I beseech you to make arguments for yourselves." Of this she wrote quaintly, with the air of one who can read words and go behind them and fathom personality. "The President's immortal special message fills me with unbounded satisfaction. It is so almost superhumanly wise, moderate, fitting that I am ready to believe an angel came straight from heaven to him with it. He must be honest and true, or an angel would not come to him. Mary Mann says she thinks the message feeble, and not to the point. But I think a man shows strength when he can be moderate at such a moment as this. Thou hadst better give my regards to the President. I meant to write to him; but that mood has passed. I wish to express my obligations for the wisdom of his message."

So she meant to write Lincoln, but the mood passed. The lights of such spirits as hers, however, did reach Lincoln. Messages came from those joined to him by like purposes. Or if the purpose were clouded and often overshadowed, they had come to trust in him. Precious affection came his way. Motives beyond price were unbosomed to him. He was in the wakeful day thoughts and restless dreams by night of some who were sure he must be honest and true or angels would not come to him with messages. What had these humble and steadfast friends and lovers done to Abraham Lincoln? Giving him riches of the heart he had never known, how had they lighted and changed and deepened him, perhaps saddened him? Did he have hours when he hardly knew what took his strength away, and in "a restlessness that is infinite" black ghosts tried to pull him down? He did. The somber dream that democracy might perish from the earth wore him pitilessly.

Only shallow dreams and shabby motives, however, could be seen by various incessant critics as animating Lincoln. To them he was one more accident of politics, tending his onions. The *New York Herald* surpassed in a rippling and not entirely malicious humor with which it currently interpreted the President. To picture the President's anxiety to be President again through re-election, the *Herald* in an editorial in late November of '63 drew on the ancient authoritative writings of the Jews known as rabbins:

"A dispute once arose between the original Abraham, the ancestor of so many speculators, and Nimrod the mighty hunter. Nimrod did not conduct the dispute on the most approved principles of fair play and Abraham received the worst of it. Thereupon the Father of his People by some occult means sent a plague against the mighty hunter. Now this plague was a gnat. It buzzed in Nimrod's ears, in his eyes and nose, in his mouth, and stung him again and again. Nimrod could not in any way get rid of it. Life became a misery. At last a glass case was made to enclose the hunter's head and he had peace. But not for long. The gnat got inside. Indeed he bored through into Nimrod's brain. Surgery was out of the question. Servants resorted to a course of hammers. All hours of day and night they pounded the hunter's head with hammers so Nimrod could not hear the noise of the gnat. Just now Mr. Lincoln is in the position of the hunter. There is a gnat in his brain. The army of the South, the Mexican muddle, the English rams, the wants of the country, are like so many tilt-hammers against his head for he hears only the hum of the gnat. The gnat is his idea of the next presidency."

How did Lincoln register to such satire? Perhaps as when Lamon asked him if he had read a vitriolic speech of Wendell Phillips saying: "Mr. Lincoln is a politician. Politicians are like the bones of a horse's fore-shoulder—not a straight one in it." Lincoln had not read this nor certain other emanations in July of '64. His view was calm. "Time will show whether I am right or they are right, and I am content to abide its decision."

Events moved him to change his policies. Some were baffled by his transitions. Congressman John B. Alley suddenly found the President differed with him on a matter where they had been agreed. "Mr. President, you have changed your mind entirely within a short time." "Yes, I have. And I don't think much of a man who is not wiser today than he was yesterday."

Could T. C. Durant of New York have an interview with the President? The President wired Durant: "As I do with others, so I will try to see you when you come." Should punishment be accorded a man on trial for violating confidence and making public a letter of the President? The President wrote that he agreed with General Schofield's suggestion to drop the proceedings. "While I admit that there is an apparent impropriety in the publication of the letter mentioned, without my consent or yours, it is still a case where no evil could result, and which I am entirely willing to overlook."

From Bardstown, Kentucky, a few miles from Lincoln's birth cabin, came two stories that as published may have reached Lincoln. If so, he might have said again, "Time will show." One was given in the "Editor's Drawer" of *Harper's Monthly* in July of 1864. "The accomplished and beautiful wife of a volunteer officer," ran a foreword, "tells the following":

> When she was at the Louisville Hotel, while our army was gathering strength to spring upon Bragg at Bardstown, a little boy, whose parents were noted for their secession sympathies, was dangling by the neck over the baluster a toy, known in the nursery vocabulary as a "limber-jack," exclaiming between his little teeth, "There now, old Abe, I told you I would hang you!" giving, as he spake, the string a vindictive jerk. This lady, who was standing by, said, "Johnnie, I'll report you as a rebel, and have you put in the military prison." He quickly drew up his extempore gallows, put the cord into his pocket, and running up to her, said, "Oh, please, don't tell! It's not Mr. Lincoln, it's a limber-jack; I was only playing hanging Yankees!"

The other story from Bardstown was about a small boy whose heart was stirred by the flags and drums of the marching files of Union troops he saw moving through the streets of the town. They made the war and what he had heard about it more real to him. The next day he saw a rainbow arching across the sky and ran to his mother with a cry, "Mother, God is a Union man!" The mother asked him whatever could he mean. He pointed her to the sky. "Look! see the flag! it's red, white and blue! I tell you God is a Union man!"

Seven biographies published in 1864 presented Lincoln favorably for various audiences of readers. Several small paper-covered books issued by

On the 50-cent greenbacks and on the $10 bill (above) a steel engraving representing Lincoln's face became familiar to all who looked at it

the opposition were chiefly humorous and satirical. Immense editions were sold of an issue of the monthly *Beadle Dime Library* by O. J. Victor and another "popular life" by the Reverend William M. Thayer of Boston. Each emphasized the opportunity before any American poor boy who wished "to climb the heights." Greatness was not thrust upon Lincoln—"he achieved it," wrote Victor. "Through long days of labor, and nights devoid of ease, he forced his way from obscurity to renown." Thayer's book of 1863, *The Pioneer Boy*, caught the affections of such a wide array of readers that he rewrote it in 1864. Titled *The Character and Public Services of Abraham Lincoln*, it began to repeat the success of Parson Weems's *Life of Washington*. Thayer portrayed "the model President, the champion of Freedom, and the Emancipator." Industry, honesty, perseverance, and cheerful devotion to duty had been seen in *The Pioneer Boy*, and now, wrote Thayer, on his elevation to the Presidency "have sustained him in that high office." As a campaign document, said the *Chicago Journal* in July: "This is said to be the best. We have heard of several copperheads being converted by reading it." Less emotional and melodramatic was another biography by Benjamin F. Barrett of Cincinnati.

Most solid and impressive of biographies was the one of 495 pages by the *New York Times* editor Henry J. Raymond, the title page reading "*History of the Administration of President Lincoln: Including His Speeches, Letters,*

Addresses, Proclamations and Messages, with a Preliminary Sketch of His Life." Raymond had talked with Lincoln about the main drift of the book. As editor of the most steadily consistent Administration organ in New York City and as a political collaborator with Lincoln, Raymond probably had Lincoln's approval that it should be an arrangement chiefly of the papers and speeches setting forth, according to Raymond's preface, "the motives which have prompted the successive acts of his Administration." In this preface Raymond made clear that "in any exact or important sense" a history of the Administration would require "access to sources of information which cannot, from the nature of the case, be open to the public for many years to come." Available for the first time was a book four-fifths document, with Lincoln's changing points of view as he himself had given them on his major decisions, and policies as they developed. In one sense it was four-fifths autobiographical, Lincoln's story in his own words, an advocate's statement with explanations and running text interspersed by Raymond. "It forms no part of the object of this work to deal in eulogy of President Lincoln and his Administration," noted Raymond in a few pages at the close. "Its purpose will have been attained if it places his acts and words in such a form, that those who read them may judge for themselves." In taking up his gigantic task Mr. Lincoln "had no overweening estimate of his own sagacity," wrote Raymond. "He was quite sensible of his lack of that practical knowledge of men and affairs which experience of both alone can give." But he had faith in the people and in republican government, "and in that intuitive sagacity of a great community which always transcends the most cunning devices of individual men, and, in a great and perilous crisis, more nearly resembles inspiration than the mere deductions of the human intellect."

Therefore, wrote Raymond, "at the very outset of his Administration, President Lincoln cast himself, without reserve and without fear, upon this reliance." He was reproached for not assuming "to lead and control" public sentiment, for his content at being "the exponent and the executor" of the public will. "Possibly an opposite course might have succeeded, but possibly, also, it might have ended in disastrous and fatal failure." Then came a paragraph welling up with unmistakable feeling from the heart of Raymond, dwelling on "a reputation, with the great body of the people, for unsullied integrity," maintained through terrible trials. "He had command of an army greater than that of any living monarch; he wielded authority less restricted than that conferred by any other constitutional government; he disbursed sums of money equal to the exchequer of any nation in the world; yet no man, of any party, believes him in any instance to have aimed at his own aggrandizement, to have been actuated by personal ambition, or to have consulted any other interest than the welfare of his country, and the perpetuity of its Republican form of government." Enormous grants of power were "lavishly and eagerly" conferred upon Mr. Lincoln, "because it was known and felt everywhere that he would not abuse them." Party factions had not marked him, and weapons of party spirit had "recoiled harmlessly from the shield of his unspotted character."

Union journals were unanimous in praise of the Raymond biography. "An admirable summary of the official career of Mr. Lincoln," said *Harper's Weekly*, "a most convenient political handbook of the times." The cavaliers who called Oliver Cromwell merely a "man with a wart on his nose" had the same propriety as those terming Lincoln merely "a joker," commented *Harper's*. The *New York World* had left-handed bouquets for Raymond for his "lucid clearness of expression, a plausible air of candor, dextrous evasion of difficulties." The reader could glide through it "without much emotion indeed, but always without fatigue." A skillful advocate was required for writing "a book which shall shuffle as Mr. Lincoln has shuffled . . . if the cause of Mr. Lincoln shall appear weak in the hands of so shifty and versatile, and, truth compels us to say so, so really able an advocate, it must be intrinsically weak indeed."

The book held internal evidence "of having been written with Mr. Lincoln's privity and consent," continued the *World*, surmising it contained "some materials and documents which only he could have furnished." Raymond had a "footing of confidential intimacy" with Seward and other high officials, which when taken with other indications, showed this book now fresh from the press to be a campaign document and plainly "the joint manifesto of the writer and the administration."

The *Chicago Times* deduced from "the New York press of all parties" that Raymond as historian was "cheerfully supplied with material by the President." Mr. Lincoln's contradictions of "snow and charcoal" could not be reconciled, and Mr. Raymond, the editor of the *New York Times*, reminded the *Chicago Times* of Phoenix's verse:

> There was a man whose name was Ames.
> His aims were aims of mystery.
> His story, I think, by G–d,
> Would make a famous history.

Lincoln's political career, the *Chicago Times* told its readers, was that of a thimblerigger, "evasive," "pettifogging," "absurd," "a muddy pool," and no charm or candor on Raymond's part could "clothe it with a semblance of decency or dignity." It was, to quote Shakespeare, the tale of

> a hungry, lean-fac'd villain,
> A mere anatomy, a mountebank,
> A threadbare juggler, and a fortune-teller,
> A needy, hollow-ey'd, sharp-looking wretch;
> A living-dead man.

Harper's Weekly rose to inquire in its issue of September 24, 1864, how men who vociferated that they were "conservatives" could use such language as was applied to "the Constitutional President of the United States." Not since Washington was bespattered with invective had there been so disgusting a "partisan ribaldry." *Harper's* collected a list of "terms applied by the friends of General M'Clellan to the President":

Filthy Story-Teller,	Ignoramus Abe,
Despot,	Old Scoundrel,
Big Secessionist,	Perjurer,
Liar,	Robber,
Thief,	Swindler,
Braggart,	Tyrant,
Buffoon,	Fiend,
Usurper,	Butcher,
Monster,	Land-Pirate,

A Long, Lean, Lank, Lantern-Jawed, High-Cheeked-Boned Spavined, Rail-Splitting Stallion

Leslie's Weekly quoted Jack Falstaff, "I would I knew where a commodity of good names could be bought," and enumerated "sweet scented compliments" paid by the opposition press to the President of the United States, namely: ape, gorilla, fool, filthy storyteller, despot, liar, thief, braggart, buffoon, usurper, monster, tortoise, ignoramus, old scoundrel, perjurer, robber, swindler, tyrant, fiend, butcher, land pirate.

Document No. 18 of the Democratic party, titled "Republican Opinions about Lincoln," printed in full the Wade-Davis Manifesto of the previous summer, quoted liberally from the Pomeroy Secret Circular, set forth with no defamatory adjective lacking Frémont's letter of acceptance to his third party. The long editorial in *Brownson's Quarterly Review* of April, 1864, was included, setting up Lincoln, the Executive, as an almost incomparable ignoramus and dull clown. "His soul seems made of leather, and incapable of any grand or noble emotion. He never adopts a clean policy. When he hits upon a policy, substantially good in itself, he contrives to belittle it, besmear it, or, in some other way, to render it mean, contemptible and useless." Yet with this thumping denunciation was carried the little hedging disclaimer: "He is a good sort of man, with much natural shrewdness and respectable native abilities; but he is misplaced in the Presidential chair." Likewise the extended official commentary which opened the pamphlet had its mingled judgment, "This excellent man, though honest as the sun, and perhaps the best story-teller in the world, is not the statesman to pluck this country from the grovelling mire." The pamphlet closed with a *New York Tribune* editorial protesting that "nine-tenths of the arbitrary arrests thus far, had better not been made," with much else in the Greeley style, with no excuses, nothing in extenuation of the Lincoln Administration.

Perhaps bluff old Sam Medary editing the *Crisis* in Columbus, Ohio, was as consistent, unvarying, and incorruptible a journalistic critic as the Lincoln Administration had. He had been mobbed and raided, seen his printing plant wrecked, undergone personal suffering. Yet he was sticking to his guns, in his September 14 issue in '64 saying, "We shall continue to oppose the war, whether carried on on Lincoln's or McClellan's plan." Medary declared that in 1864, as in 1861, there were those who would not give way to "the money-plunderers of Wall Street." Thus far Medary had not struck directly at Lincoln's personal integrity, but now without giving particulars, the *Crisis* said: "A reward should be set upon the head of the fellow who first gave Old Abe the prefix of 'Honest.' It has been his only popular capital for three years, and, like the bogus insurance companies, nobody is liable to find it."

The effect of this savage verbal warfare? In October of '64 *Harper's Weekly* dealt with that question. "The personal character of the President is the rock upon which the Opposition is wrecked. It dashes against him and his administration, hissing and venomous, but falls back again baffled. From the day when covert rebellion lay in wait to assassinate him in Baltimore, through all the mad hate of the rebel press to the last malignant sneer of Copperhead Conservatism and foreign jealousy, the popular confidence in the unswerving fidelity and purity of purpose of the President has smiled the storm to scorn." The complaint of despotism was shrilled against the Administration, was thundered and volleyed. With no cessation came assorted varieties of the assertion that "we are all the cowering, shivering subjects of the bloody Emperor Abraham, who brings us all to our knees by pointing to one of the innumerable bastiles which shadow the land." This *Harper's* read as an appeal to indifferent voters who like to see any administration overthrown, to the timid who wish peace at any price, to party spirit which "plays the dangerous game of seeking political power by tampering with national existence." Was such an attack having effect? "Nothing balks such an attack as personal qualities which no calumny can reach."

What could be done, asked *Harper's,* with those Democratic leaders who charged that the President to serve his own political ends was prolonging the war by not sending enough men to his generals, when those same Democratic leaders were opposing the draft? "When you ask them how the President can send men to the Generals if men are not raised, they reply that it is no wonder he can not raise them for such a wicked war." These frantic efforts would be vain. "The profound confidence of the great mass of the people in the President is unshaken. It is simply impossible to make them believe . . . that he is a monstrous despot or a political gambler."

The President had chaos for daily fare, said *Harper's,* in October quoting the *Richmond Dispatch,* infuriated by Early's repulse at the gates of Washington: "The Yankees are the most mercenary of God's creatures. If the ministry of our Saviour had been among them instead of the Jews, instead of lasting three years it would not have lasted three days. Some Yankee Judas would have sold Him in less than half that time. . . . The best road to peace lies through the blood of the Yankees. The more we kill, the nearer we approach to peace." Would the American people be interested in surrendering their Government to such armed enemies? *Harper's* asked the Yankees.

From the *Charleston Mercury* this mid-October of '64 came sorry words. There was mention of Central America; the matter had already been considered of where Southern men might go if they lost the war and became fugitives. "Any man will fight rather than be kicked out of his own house, or be hanged, or starved in the wastes and wilds of Central America. And these are Lincoln's alternatives." Alleging that McClellan meetings in the

North were broken up "by volleys of stones from soldiers, posted for the purpose," it saw this as Lincoln's work. "In a word, Lincoln has the upper hand because he has the armed hand . . . Lincoln and his gallows, Lincoln and the death of millions, the long train of exiles." Cryptic words this mid-October of '64 from the Rhett newspaper, laying its hope on a McClellan victory at the Northern polls in November: "Perhaps the Ruler of events, intending to create and save the Southern Confederacy, so wills. If McClellan were elected, there are doubtless many, very many, persons in the South who would believe the restoration of the Union to be possible." It was cryptic as well as vague, possibly masking hope of some end to the war short of conquest and surrender.

The *Atlantic Monthly* for November, 1864, in a nine-page article of calm pitch and even tenor identified the Union cause in the one person and name of Abraham Lincoln. "The war was made . . . because of Mr. Lincoln's election to the Presidency. The North was to be punished for having had the audacity to elect him even when the Democracy were divided. . . . He, a mere man of the people, should never become *President of the United States!* The most good-natured of men, it is known that his success made him an object of aversion to the Southern leaders. They did their worst to prevent his becoming President of the Republic, and in that way they wronged and insulted the people far more than they wronged and insulted the man whom the people had elected . . . and the people are bound, by way of vindicating their dignity and establishing their power, to make Mr. Lincoln President of the *United* States." The majesty of the law could best be asserted "by placing President Lincoln a second time at the head of the Republic, the revolt of the slaveholders being directed against him personally as well as against that principle of which he was the legally elected representative." And the President's slavery policy? "Many of us thought that the President issued his Emancipation Proclamation at least a year too late; but we must now see that the time selected for its promulgation was as skilfully chosen as its aim was laudable." What would stand as "the noblest fact in President Lincoln's history"? The *Atlantic* would reply "that by the same action he announced freedom to four millions of bondmen, and secured his country against even the possibility of foreign mediation, foreign intervention, and foreign war."

Harper's Weekly, *Harper's Monthly*, the *Atlantic Monthly*, *Leslie's Weekly*, *Godey's Lady's Book*, with by far the larger part of the more formidable and solid periodicals, either in quiet and reserved tones or with direct and sonorous declarations, favored Lincoln and the National Union ticket during the campaign.

The American Republic was being reborn, amid storm and convulsion, for a new life and a fresh career, said the *Springfield Republican*, Sam Bowles writing: "Every man, loose from the bondage of political ambition, and loose from the greed of power and the love of slavery, thinks well of Abraham Lincoln, and casts in his lot with him. Thousands of Democrats, converted to freedom by the war, have, from the moment of their conversion, become his friends. His way of saving the country is recognized as the only way. A conquered peace is the only peace deemed possible."

At recurrent intervals rose in the public prints verses out of a deep reverence, having a phase of hero worship. In their backgrounds these verses would half acknowledge from the author, "I can't write poetry but this welled up in my heart and is my free offering." One little sheaf, dated at Philadelphia, Grand Central Fair, June 16, 1864, was typical, reading:

TO PRESIDENT LINCOLN

Proudest of all earth's thrones
  Is his who rules by a free people's choice;
Who, 'midst fierce party strife and battle groans,
Hears, ever rising in harmonious tones,
  A grateful people's voice.

Steadfast in thee we trust,
  Tried as no man was ever tried before;
God made thee merciful—God keep thee just.
Be true!—and triumph over all thou must.
  God bless thee evermore!

It came to no national reputation, had no influence worth mentioning, nor was it quoted for its valued opinions, but in August of '64 the *Chicago Journal* and other newspapers chronicled the rise in Reading, Pennsylvania, of a newspaper styling itself the *Father Abraham.* That was its name, platform, creed, and code. Its life was not long. Copies became scarce. But it had stood up and testified.

Reporting the 1864 campaign for his readers in the London *Daily News,* the journalist Edwin Lawrence Godkin was sure Lincoln "had been gaining ground steadily with all the moderates though losing it with the radicals." It was in Godkin's mind that the English publicist Mr. Beresford Hope, "in one of those extraordinary outbursts of rage which he called 'lectures' on the American war, likened him [Lincoln] to the most sensual and unscrupulous of Eastern tyrants." In which connection Godkin must record: "I have never heard of his [Lincoln's] uttering or writing one word to show that these shameless attacks ever aroused in him a single angry impulse. How many men of high breeding and culture are there who would pass through a similar ordeal with as much credit?" Godkin would recall the first feeling of a portion of the public about Mr. Lincoln "when he made his appearance on the Presidential stage." It was a feeling of "mixed mortification and disappointment." The horror felt by "nobility, gentry and clergy" in England at the cut of his clothes, the length of his legs, his beard, his manner of receiving company, "called forth a corresponding amount of sympathy here" in America. On every side his want of education was lamented. "In looking round, as the manner of an Anglo-Saxon public is in times of trouble, for a victim, Lincoln was selected as . . . the best mark for popular indignation. During the autumn of 1862 he reached the lowest point in the estimation of all classes."

In the period of deepest national gloom, Godkin saw Lincoln as having "a courage, a constancy, and firmness which astonished his enemies and reassured his friends." The more furiously factions raged, the more completely he kept himself free from their control. "He had refused to issue a decree of emancipation when half the people of the North thought the South could be subjugated in thirty days; he issued it when Lee had only just retired from the gates of the capital. Most people thought him crazy, but it proved that he had made a decided hit. It did not emancipate all the slaves, but it emancipated a great many, and it committed the North decidedly to an anti-slavery policy, without laying the author open to the charge of violating the Constitution." These statements represented the beliefs of the liberal Godkin, with the emphasis placed where he considered the British public needed it.

The speeches, state papers, even telegrams of Lincoln came under the eye of a London *Spectator* writer. "Not one is to be found," he wrote, "that is not stamped deep with the impression of a mind at once singularly representative and singularly personal." He could see other great men of history as organs, spokesmen, transmitters for a class, a nation, or a national mind, "convincing without being personal, without being winning." With Mr. Lincoln it was quite otherwise, "nothing of the *mere* public man about him." With little borrowing and few exterior derivations Mr. Lincoln had slowly and awkwardly, but pertinaciously, built up every conviction for himself by the sheer force of his own intellectual strength and moral veracity. Mr. Lincoln's mind? "A political transparency, in which the nation could see an individual character of great power working out the problems set before them all, working them out slowly indeed, but upon a method in which they all felt the most perfect confidence, working them, too, with a sincerity that was unmixed with the faintest pretension, and showing evidences of a long and patient rather than passionate grappling of his powerful intellect with the difficulties of each question presented to him, evidences which must have touched as well as convinced the great people who followed so anxiously the slow tentative progress of his thought."

Mr. Lincoln's political patience was joined to a political understanding "more lucid than the national understanding" for an ethical reason: he can never tolerate the tyranny of mere words, and always presses through the words to the reality behind them. "There are no State papers in history more remarkable for their refutation of mere *cries* than Mr. Lincoln's." This English writer ascribed to Lincoln as a national statesman the same method that Sangamon County lawyers had long ago reckoned as difficult to overcome: to assume his adversary's position and use his weapon for him "till its use led to absurd and inadmissible results." In the style of this overseas friend were signs he was the same writer who had wrestled with Lincoln's message to Congress in December of '61, finding then a mystical dreaminess in Lincoln: "The thoughts of the man are too big for his mouth."

What of Lincoln's mind in its impress on those near him in daily joined and responsible labors? Charles A. Dana, from his frequent contacts and observations as Assistant Secretary of War, was to write, "Even in his freest moments one always felt the presence of a will and an intellectual power which maintained the ascendancy of the President." Among his Cabinet members, as Dana saw the matter, "It was always plain that he was the master and they the subordinates. They constantly had to yield to his will," and "If he ever yielded to theirs, it was because they convinced him that the course they advised was judicious and appropriate."

John Hay from his years of service near Lincoln saw him as having a sort of natural pride, certainly something the opposite of humility, in the way he often handled other men, associates, colaborers, men in degrees of eminence for strength of mind and will. "It is absurd to call him a modest man," wrote Hay to William H. Herndon. "No great man was ever modest. It was his intellectual arrogance and unconscious assumption of superiority that men like Chase and Sumner could never forgive." The people understood Lincoln well, believed Hay, but there was "a patent-leather, kid-glove set who know no more of him than an owl does of a comet blazing into his blinking eyes." Their estimates of Lincoln were in many cases "disgraceful exhibitions of ignorance and prejudice." They lacked the "Lincoln republicanism incarnate—with all its faults and virtues," with its rudeness and foibles. "Their effeminate natures," wrote Hay to Herndon, "shrink instinctively from the contact of a great reality like Lincoln's character."

More gently and at a later time Hay again wrote: "The evidence of all the men admitted to his intimacy is that he maintained, without the least effort or assumption, a singular dignity and reserve in the midst of his easiest conversation. . . . While men of the highest culture and position recognized his intellectual primacy there was no man so humble as to feel abashed before him." Hay quoted Frederick Douglass, the Negro leader: "I felt as though I was in the presence of a big brother and that there was safety in his atmosphere."

On the point of Lincoln's intellectual arrogance, as Hay termed it, John Eaton of Toledo, Ohio, was to write of Cabinet complications, of how he sat one day in the summer of '64 watching Lincoln sign papers. Chase had just resigned from the Cabinet, yet Lincoln had just signed an appointment of a Chase man to an important position. "So great was the opposition to Mr. Lincoln's re-election at this time," wrote Eaton, "that I not unnaturally felt that a good deal of care ought to be exercised in guarding from his enemies positions of any degree of influence." And Eaton recalled to memory his old Ohio feelings about Chase, spoke of them to Lincoln. His account of their conversation:

> Mr. Lincoln listened with pleasure to all I could say in Mr. Chase's favor. From my college days he had been for me something of an ideal. He was a native of the same State, graduated from the same college, and as Governor of Ohio had won the admiration of every one by his masterly conduct in bringing that State out of bankruptcy. As a resident of Toledo and superintendent of schools there, I had become

much interested in his career, and had employed a niece of his, I remember, in one of the schools under my superintendence. Mr. Lincoln was very earnest in commending what he had done, but at the same time he was compelled reluctantly to admit that his idiosyncrasies as a cabinet officer would have tended to defeat the main aims of the Administration. This I was quite prepared to realize, having experienced complications in my own work which were in part derived from Mr. Chase's Negro policy.

In my enthusiasm for another member of Mr. Lincoln's Cabinet, I exclaimed, "Mr. President, you meet with no such difficulties from your Premier!" I had originally looked upon the failure to nominate Mr. Seward for the Presidency as a great defeat of Republican principles, and had expected everything of him as the head of Mr. Lincoln's cabinet.

My amazement, therefore, could hardly be expressed when the President, who was leaning back in his arm-chair, his great length stretched out at ease, his head thrown back, suddenly raised himself and swung the large effective head forward until his chin rested on his bosom, exclaiming, "Seward knows that I am his master!" He then went on to tell me how he had pushed the prompt surrender of Mason and Slidell as an act of justice toward England, realizing that in the light of international law the Trent affair might justly have given ground for reprisal. Seward would have temporized, and so risked a most unwelcome complication with England.

A notation by Donn Piatt was extreme in viewpoint, inadequate in statement, too easy and offhand in its judgments, yet it conveyed much the same sense as Eaton's report of his interview with Lincoln wherein Lincoln spoke of himself as "master." Unobtruding and even unassuming as Lincoln was, wrote Piatt, "he was not modest in his assertion," and he as quietly directed Seward in foreign policy as he "controlled" Chase and Stanton. The word "control" thus used by Piatt would not strictly apply. Chase and Stanton got beyond Lincoln's control often. Essential fact mingled with too high a dramatization of it in Piatt writing of Seward, Chase, Stanton, "These men, great as they were, felt their inferiority to their master, and while all three were eaten into and weakened by anxiety, he ate and slept and jested as if his shoulders did not carry, Atlas-like, the fate of an empire." Likewise Piatt's facility led him to write, "The sense of superiority possessed President Lincoln at all times." This, for accuracy, might omit the "all."

Letters written by Lincoln in December of '63 to General Banks indicated that Lincoln had a deliberate theory as to use of the word "master." A man invested by due process with certain authority was master if he maintained that authority. To the extent that his authority was cut down by others he was not master. In the reorganization of Louisiana, Lincoln wrote Banks, "I have all the while intended you to be master." Others had set up claims against Banks. Specific language was required as to Banks's authority. Therefore, repeated Lincoln, "I now tell you that in every dispute with whomsoever, you are master." The status of Banks must not possibly be misconstrued by any who refused to co-operate with him. So Lincoln rephrased it a third time in this letter: "In all cases, you are master while you remain in command of the department." Six days later, on a chance that the first letter might have miscarried, Lincoln sent Banks a copy of the first letter, once more and finally declaring, "I intend you to be master in every controversy made with you."

Again in the matter of Arkansas reconstruction Lincoln stressed the word "master," writing in a letter February 17, 1864, to William M. Fishback: "I have sent two letters to General Steele, and three or four despatches to you and others, saying that he, General Steele, must be master. . . . Some single mind must be master, else there will be no agreement in anything, and General Steele, commanding the military and being on the ground, is the best man to be that master."

Lamon and Piatt accepted with full credence an account by the economist and financier Amasa Walker of an interview he and Chase had with Lincoln about a proposed greenback issue which Chase feared was unconstitutional. The case seemed one where Lincoln would override so portentous a barrier as the United States Constitution in order to master events threatening to overwhelm both the Constitution and the Government of which it was the instrument. Piatt wrote:

> Mr. Chase made a long and elaborate constitutional argument against the proposed measure. "Chase," said Mr. Lincoln, after the Secretary had concluded, "down in Illinois I was held to be a pretty good lawyer, and I believe I could answer every point you have made, but I don't feel called upon to do it. This thing reminds me of a story I read in a newspaper the other day. It was of an Italian captain, who ran his vessel on a rock and knocked a hole in her bottom. He set his men to pumping and he went to prayers before a figure of the Virgin in the bow of the ship. The leak gained on them. It looked at last as if the vessel would go down with all on board. The captain, at length, in a fit of rage at not having his prayers answered, seized the figure of the Virgin and threw it overboard. Suddenly the leak stopped, the water was pumped out, and the vessel got safely into port. When docked for repairs, the statue of the Virgin Mary was found stuck head-foremost in the hole."
>
> "I don't see, Mr. President, the precise application of your story," said Mr. Chase.
>
> "Why, Chase, I don't intend precisely to throw the Virgin Mary overboard, and by that I mean the Constitution, but I will stick it in the hole if I can. These rebels are violating the Constitution to destroy the Union. I will violate the Constitution, if necessary, to save the Union, and I suspect, Chase, that our Constitution is going to have a rough time of it before we get done with this row. Now, what I want to know is whether, Constitution aside, this project of issuing interest-bearing notes is a good one."
>
> "I must say," responded Mr. Chase, "that with the exception you make, it is not only a good one, but the only way open to us to raise money. If you say so, I will do my best to put it into immediate and practical operation, and you will never hear from me any opposition on this subject."
>
> The people eagerly accepted the loan which the capitalists were prompt to depreciate and dishonor.
>
> No one can measure correctly the masterly management of this statesman, who does not accept and appreciate the difficulties that beset his way. The intense selfishness of the class that owed its all to the Government he was struggling to sustain, bade fair to be more fatal to us than all the armed legions of the South, fierce and successful as they were. While our soldiers in the field and the laborer left at home accepted the greenback at par, hungry, unpatriotic capital higgled over its marble counters, discounting the currency that was the life-blood of our Government.

The principle or viewpoint that actuated Lincoln here concerning law and forms of law had expression in decisive and unmistakable language in a letter delivered to General Grant. It was addressed: Major General U. S. Grant, Governor Johnson, and all having military, naval, and civil authority under the United States, within the State of Tennessee. It read:

Executive Mansion, Washington, October 21, 1862

Maj. Gen. U. S. Grant:

The bearer of this, Thomas R. Smith, a citizen of Tennessee, goes to that State seeking to have such of the people thereof as desire to avoid the unsatisfactory prospect before them, and to have peace again upon the old terms, under the Constitution of the United States, to manifest such desire by elections of members to the Congress of the United States particularly, and perhaps a Legislature, State Officers, and a U. S. senator friendly to their object.

I shall be glad for you and each of you to aid him, and all others acting for this object, as much as possible. In all available ways give the people a show to express their wishes at these elections.

Follow law, and forms of law, as far as convenient, but at all events get the expression of the largest number of the people possible. All see how such action will connect with and affect the proclamation of September 22. Of course the men elected should be gentlemen of character, willing to swear support to the Constitution as of old, and known to be above reasonable suspicion of duplicity.

Yours very respectfully,
A. Lincoln

This letter became public property and was seized on by the opposition. Here they believed his guard was down and they could hit him. "Follow law, and forms of law, as far as convenient," says the President. They quoted. Then they deduced. What further evidence could be asked? Had not the usurper here admitted his usurpation? What was the law or the Constitution to him? "That is exactly what all tyrants and despots have done in every age," screamed the *Detroit Free Press.* "They all follow the law and its forms when convenient. This is, and has been, the governmental policy ever since 'A. Lincoln' has been at the head of affairs."

Labor strikes in the navy shipyards in December of '63 had come to the President for review and decision. Precisely what was his action did not appear in the record. General Gillmore had studied the matter and proposed some sort of concessions. The terms of those concessions, the demands or grievances of the strikers, the ironing out of the differences, seemed to escape both official record and press publication. In a note marked "Private" for the Secretary of War, December 21, 1863, the President said: "Sending a note to the Secretary of the Navy, as I promised, he called over and said that the strikes in the ship-yards had thrown the completion of vessels back so much that he thought General Gillmore's proposition entirely proper."

The incident probably concerned one of a series of adjustments of labor unrest at the Government navy yard. Hours and wages of navy-yard workers, "shall conform," said the Federal laws of 1861 and 1862, "as nearly as is consistent with public interest, with those of private establishments in the immediate vicinity of the respective yards." Navy-yard commandants were authorized to fix hours and wages "subject to the approval and revision of the Secretary of the Navy." In his annual report covering 1864, the Secretary was to observe that this rule had not worked to the satisfaction of either the men employed or the Government. The method was "an unceasing source of disturbance and discontent." Workmen's committees had found it "difficult to obtain reliable data." The private establishments either refused information or gave only part of what was wanted. This brought confusion and resentment. Another factor was the reduction, in effect, of wages through currency inflation and through the rising cost of life necessaries such as food, clothing, and house rents. Then, ran Welles's summary, "The impression that there is some unfairness is engendered, complaints and strikes follow or are threatened, vigilant officers who are faithful to the government become obnoxious, and discontent prevails." Welles recommended repeal of the Federal acts governing the situation.

Lincoln's decision, which seemed to lean toward "General Gillmore's proposition," whatever that was, had the effect at least of keeping the strikes so quiet that they made no flare or noise adding to the national turmoil. Had the Administration thrown itself against the strikers, there would have been liberal quotation by the *New York World* and the *Chicago Times* of Lincoln's earlier words at New Haven, Connecticut, when he placed himself definitely on the side of the shoe-factory strikers of Lynn, Massachusetts. "Be it understood that I do not pretend to know all about the matter [of the Lynn shoe strike]," he said, but he would speculate about some of its phases. "At the outset I am glad to see that a system of labor prevails in New England under which laborers can strike when they want to, where they are not obliged to work under all circumstances, and are not tied down and obliged to labor whether you pay them or not! I like the system that lets a man quit when he wants to, and wish it might prevail everywhere."

The relation of wage labor to employer was in this hour at no such crisis as that of Negro slave and owner. On the latter issue, slowly and cautiously Lincoln had been more and more outspoken in public about his inner feelings. His scorn for the peculiar array of respectable elements opposing emancipation, his view of any act of emancipation requiring a long slow process to gain its ends, stood forth in a little private notation made during the debates with Douglas, and not made public. Too high- and wide-ranging in its irony, it would not have done for him as President to give out such a psalm of scorn as reposed among his private papers, reading:

"I have not allowed myself to forget that the abolition of the slave trade by Great Britain was agitated a hundred years before it was a final success; that the measure had its open fire-eating opponents; its stealthy 'don't care' opponents; its dollar and cent opponents; its inferior race opponents; its negro-equality opponents and its religious and good-order opponents; that all these opponents got offices and their adversaries got none. But I also remember that though they blazed like tallow candles for a century, at last they flickered in the socket, died out, stank in the dark for a brief season, and were remembered no more even by the smell." This had an odd final sentence, considering it was written five years before he signed the Emancipation Proclamation, which had erected him in a world folklore to the figure of a Liberator. It read: "I am proud in my passing speck of time to contribute an humble mite to that glorious consummation which my own poor eyes may not last to see."

Colonel McKaye of the commission investigating freedmen's conditions told Lincoln personally of the incident with which the commission's report closed. The venerable "praise man" among the South Carolina blacks corrected a dispute as to who and what "Massa Linkum" was. "Brederin, you don't nosen' what you'se talkin' 'bout. Now, you just listen to me. Massa Linkum, he eberywhar. He know eberyting," and with a solemn upward look, "*He walk de earth lak de Lawd!*"

Hearing this moved Lincoln. He got up from his chair. And, as McKaye told Carpenter, Lincoln "walked in silence two or three times" across the room. As he took his chair again he said, "It is a momentous thing to be the instrument, under Providence, of the liberation of a race."

Until the Union Army arrived, Colonel McKaye had explained, the Negroes had an idea that only God, the Almighty, had power greater than their masters. Seeing their masters flee and scatter before the Union Army, the Negroes saw this army as directed by a power greater than their masters. This power they called "Massa Linkum." And in this was no humor for Lincoln. He "did not smile," noticed McKaye.

One late October evening in 1864 a torchlight procession of some hundreds of Negroes marched to the White House lawn, carrying banners and transparencies, a brass band blaring irregularly, loud and repeated cheers bringing the President. He looked from the portico out on jubilant black faces, heard in the half-lighted darkness their moving hoarse voices, and began, "I have to guess, my friends, the object of this call which has taken me quite by surprise this evening." Then according to Noah Brooks's news report, a spokesman shouted, "The emancipator of Maryland, sah!" The newly adopted constitution of that State was in their favor. The President proceeded: "It is no secret that I have wished, and still do wish, mankind everywhere to be free. [Great cheering and cries of "God bless Abraham Lincoln."] And in the State of Maryland how great an advance has been made in this direction. It is difficult to realize that in that State, where human slavery has existed for ages, ever since a period long before any here were born—by the action of her own citizens the soil is made forever free. [Loud and long cheering.] I have no feeling of triumph over those who were opposed to this measure and who voted against it, but I do believe that it will result in good to the white race as well as to those who have been made free by this act of emancipation. And I hope that the time will soon come when all will see that the perpetuation of freedom for all in Maryland is best for the interests of all, though some may thereby be made to suffer temporary pecuniary loss. And I hope that you colored people, who have been emancipated, will use this great boon which has been given you to improve yourselves, both morally and intellectually. And now, good-night." Whereupon, wrote Brooks, there was more cheering, and after some boggling about the order of march, the dark torchlighters gathered themselves up, and hurrahing, disappeared in the darkness.

Of all the gifts and testimonials received in the White House none gave the President "more sincere pleasure," according to Carpenter, than the Bible from the colored people of Baltimore. They had scraped together

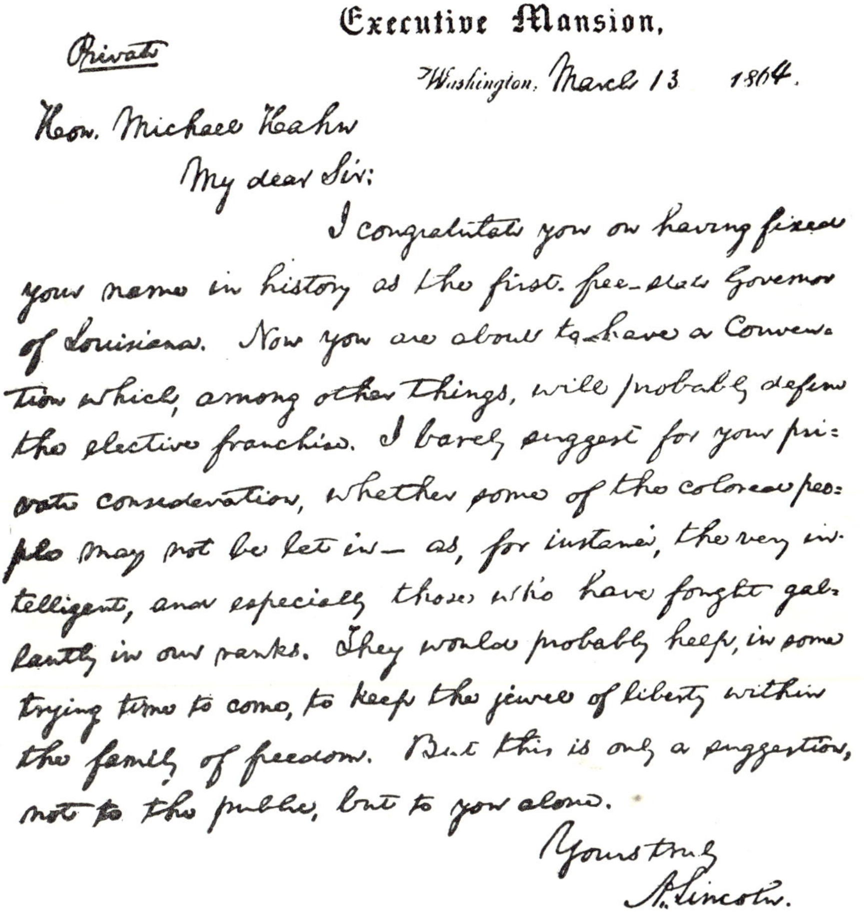

Executive Mansion,

Private

Washington, March 13 1864.

Hon. Michael Hahn

My dear Sir:

I congratulate you on having fixed your name in history as the first-free-state Governor of Louisiana. Now you are about to have a Convention which, among other things, will probably define the elective franchise. I barely suggest for your private consideration, whether some of the colored people may not be let in—as, for instance, the very intelligent, and especially those who have fought gallantly in our ranks. They would probably help, in some trying time to come, to keep the jewel of liberty within the family of freedom. But this is only a suggestion, not to the public, but to you alone.

Yours truly

A. Lincoln.

The President's most significant committal in writing on civil rights for the freed Negroes. Original from Roger Barrett.

$580.75 to pay for this volume, of pulpit size, bound in violet-tinted velvet, corners banded of solid gold, with platings of gold one-fourth of an inch thick. On the left-hand cover was a design representing the President in a cotton field knocking the shackles off the wrists of a slave, who held one hand aloft to bless his benefactor. The plate of the right hand cover bore the inscription:

> To ABRAHAM LINCOLN, President of the United States, the friend of Universal Freedom. From the loyal colored people of Baltimore, as a token of respect and gratitude. Baltimore, July 4th, 1864.

A slave-born woman of Philadelphia, Caroline Johnson, in active duty as a hospital nurse during the war, arrived at the Executive Mansion, with her minister. The President was to see her at one o'clock. She was to present him with a stem table ornamented with an ingenious and handsome collection of wax fruits, which she had prepared with reverence and affection for the President. She had arranged her table in the center of the room, had made her bows on meeting Mr. and Mrs. Lincoln, heard her minister deliver a little speech of presentation, at the end of which she heard him saying, "Perhaps Mrs. Johnson would like to say a few words?" In her own words afterward: "I looked down to the floor, and felt that I had not a word to say, but after a moment or two, the fire began to burn, [laying her hand on her breast,] and it burned and it burned till it went all over me. I think it was the Spirit, and I looked up to him." Then these words came from her:

"Mr. President, I believe God has hewn you out of a rock, for this great and mighty purpose. Many have been led away by bribes of gold, of silver, of presents; but you have stood firm, because God was with you, and if you are faithful to the end, He will be with you."

Furthermore, as Mrs. Johnson's account ran in the *Anti-Slavery Standard*, "With his eyes full of tears, he walked round and examined the present, pronounced it beautiful, thanked me kindly, but said, 'You must not give me the praise—it belongs to God.' "

When the tall, gaunt, slave-born black woman Sojourner Truth, eighty years old, arrived at the Executive Mansion, it was for her the end of a journey from Battle Creek, Michigan, a long and halting journey made, as she said, "with the unalterable purpose of seeing the Emancipator of my race before my death." Part of her travel funds came from sales of photographs of herself. Out of this arose a story that she gave the President a photograph, saying, "I am selling the shadow to sustain the substance but this one is for you without money and without price." He took it, thanked her, and to her suggestion that she would like his photograph replied he had none at that particular time. Her query came then, "But, Mr. President, isn't that your photograph on the back of the new ten dollar bills?" Whereupon the President handed her a ten-dollar bill. The first half of this little yarn was probably true. The second half did not quite run true to Sojourner Truth, prophetess, orator, educator, humble instrument. She had dignity, a sense of occasions, and probably would not have marred what was for her a great event near the close of her life. Her own account more likely had the facts.

Eight o'clock in the morning she entered the President's reception room, saw a dozen persons waiting, among them two colored women. She saw the President meet one colored woman "with much attention," speaking to her

The President's seal, and the right hand of Lincoln molded from life by Leonard Wells Volk

Originals in the Barrett collection

Robert John Walker

Oliver Perry Morton

William Darrah Kelley

John Bassett Alley

Lincoln in '64. Three photographs in a sitting for Brady

Thurlow Weed

WITH EACH OF THESE OTHER MEN THE PRESIDENT HAD CONFIDENCES AND SECRETS

From the Meserve collection

with "kindness and tenderness." This petitioner was sick and liable to be turned out of her house as lacking rent money. "He said," noted Sojourner Truth, "he had given so much he could give no more, but told her where to go and get the money," requesting Sojourner's companion to go along and help. To the President seated at his desk Sojourner's companion now said, "This is Sojourner Truth, who has come all the way from Michigan to see you." The President arose, gave Sojourner his hand, bowed. "I am pleased to see you." Then Sojourner released the speech poem which poured from her heart in singing syllables:

"Mr. President, when you first took your seat I feared you would be torn to pieces, for I likened you unto Daniel, who was thrown into the lions' den; and if the lions did not tear you to pieces, I knew that it would be God that had saved you; and I said if He spared me I would see you before the four years expired, and He has done so, and now I am here to see you for myself."

The President congratulated her on having been spared. Her response: "I appreciate you, for you are the best President who has ever taken the seat." His rejoinder held that other Presidents and emphatically Washington "were all just as good" and would have done just as he did in his Emancipation Proclamation. "If the people over the river"—pointing across the Potomac—"had behaved themselves, I could not have done what I have; but they did not, and I was compelled to do these things." Sojourner: "I thank God that you were the instrument selected by Him and the people to do it." The Bible from the colored people of Baltimore was shown her by the President. She gazed, admired, spoke. "This is beautiful indeed; the colored people have given this to the Head of the Government, and that Government once sanctioned laws that would not permit its people to learn enough to enable them to read this Book. And for what? Let them answer who can." He took the little book she brought out, and as Sojourner phrased it, "The same hand that signed the death-warrant of slavery wrote as follows":

For Aunty Sojourner Truth,
Oct. 29, 1864. A. Lincoln

On her leaving he took her hand, said he would be pleased to have her call again, and she went away to say: "I felt that I was in the presence of a friend, and I now thank God from the bottom of my heart that I always have advocated his cause, and have done it openly and boldly. I shall feel more in duty bound to do so in time to come. May God assist me."

Wide circulation was given an item from the *Washington Chronicle* of January 2, 1864: "Years ago had a colored man presented himself at the White House at the President's levee, seeking an introduction to the Chief Magistrate of the nation, he would have been, in all probability, roughly handled for his impertinence. Yesterday four colored men, of genteel exterior, and with the manners of gentlemen, joined in the throng that crowded the Executive Mansion, and were presented to the President of the United States."

That Lincoln had signed a check payable to a "one-legged colored man" was not known to the public. And how and why he endorsed notes for other Negroes was not a matter of publicity and news. To the ears of Nicolay it came, however, that a cashier of one of the Washington banks, meeting an old friend of Lincoln on the street one morning, had to say: "That President of yours is the oddest man alive. Why, he endorses notes for niggers!"

An escaped Negro slave woman working as a cook in the Harewood Hospital had been arrested and was held in jail by Marshal Lamon under the Fugitive Slave Law for her return to her Virginia master and owner under a warrant from District of Columbia commissioners. General William E. Doster of the District military authority found that a paper of "military protection" from a general at the front had been given the woman, where-

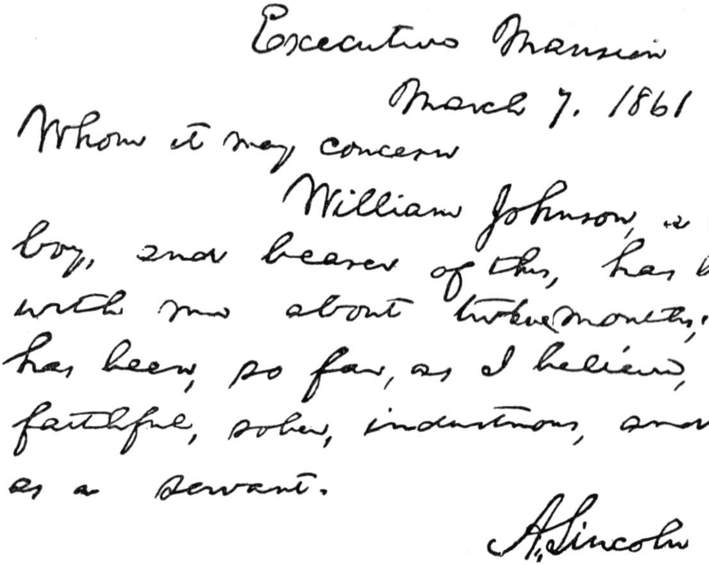
Executive Mansion
March 7. 1861
Whom it may concern
William Johnson, a colored boy, and bearer of this, has been with me about twelve months; and has been, so far, as I believe, honest faithful, sober, industrious, and handy as a servant.
A. Lincoln

Lincoln writes a note of recommendation for a dismissed colored boy of honest and faithful service. Noah Brooks noted that in the early years of the Administration, when the President was sensitive and hesitant about revealing himself on the race issue, there were no Negro employees at the Executive Mansion. After the emancipation policy had made progress several persons of the colored race entered White House service. This recommendation addressed to "Whom it may concern" reads: "William Johnson, a colored boy, and bearer of this, has been with me about twelve months; and has been, so far, as I believe, honest[,] faithful, sober, industrious, and handy as a servant." Original in the Barrett collection.

fore he asked Lamon for her release. Lamon pointed to his warrant and refused. Doster took a company of infantry to the jail and threatened to break down the door. Senator McDougall made a speech and cited court decisions favoring the release. General Doster offered to refer the matter to the military government. Lamon refused this and offered to submit the matter to the Supreme Court, which General Doster refused. Finally they agreed to go to Lincoln and let him decide. He heard both sides, said he must decline to interfere, but, speaking to General Doster, "I guess if you want to take the woman, Lamon can't prevent it." Whereupon Jailer Lamon gave up the woman and General Doster took her to Harewood Hospital, where she resumed her duties as cook.

Against a leg of the President's desk, noted Carpenter, usually leaned a map, service-worn, shaded to show by degrees of blackness the proportions of slave and free populations in the Southern States. Carpenter took it for use in his painting. Lincoln, strolling in one afternoon, noticed it. "Ah! *you* have appropriated my map, have you? I have been looking all around for it." Putting on spectacles, taking the map to a window, sitting on a trunk, he studied it. Then he pointed to where on the map a Union cavalry raider was last heard from in Virginia. "It is just as I thought it was. He is close upon —— County, where the slaves are thickest. Now we ought to get a 'heap' of them, when he returns."

On a letter in April of '64 to Mrs. Horace Mann, widow of the famous educator who had been a fellow member with Lincoln in the 1848 Congress, opinion differed. Some held it one more piece of political palaver, others the outpouring of a reverent humanitarian. Its two sentences read:

> The petition of persons under eighteen, praying that I would free all slave children, and the heading of which petition it appears you wrote, was handed me a few days since by Senator Sumner. Please tell these little people I am very glad their young hearts are so full of just and generous sympathy, and that, while I have not the power to grant all they ask, I trust they will remember that God has, and that, as it seems, he wills to do it.

Had James T. Brady–Irish, brilliant, influential, a New York lawyer for months a steadfast Unionist, then wavering–written a letter to United States Senator Morton Smith Wilkinson of Minnesota, the details might be more accurate as to a conversation he and Lincoln had. As Senator Wilkinson told it the gist of what Lincoln and Brady said and did was probably there. Lincoln early in the war sent for Brady and dumfounded him with the information that his duty was to see that a brigade of Irish troops was raised and officered in New York City. Brady protested that he wasn't military, wouldn't know a major from a colonel, Lincoln replying: "You know plenty of Irishmen who do know all about such matters, and, as to the appointment of officers, did you ever know an Irishman who would decline an office or refuse a pair of epaulets, or do anything but fight gallantly after he had them?" The upshot of the conference was that Brady went back to New York, saw the brigade raised with no difficulty, and as 3,000 Irishmen in blue, with muskets, flags, and drums, marched down Broadway headed for battle fronts, they were a pro-Unionist argument. When later the Irish were accused of being the bulwarks of the draft riots in New York City, James T. Brady entered the public prints with citations of Irishmen in the Union ranks. "Mr. Lincoln's object was fully realized," noted Senator Wilkinson. "I have given the above fact exactly as it was related to me by Mr. Brady at the time."

Recurrent gossip and published items held that Lincoln himself did not write some of his more impressive papers and speeches. Wilkes in his popular and ably edited weekly *Spirit of the Times* intimated that Seward wrote the Gettysburg speech. A *New York Evening Post* correspondent wrote in April of '64 that such statements had attracted the attention of Mr. Lincoln, who, the correspondent heard, pronounced them "entirely erroneous." Every public document of his, since he became President, was his own composition except the address to English clergymen, which Seward wrote. This, of course, did not cover the matter adequately. Undoubtedly the versatile and facile, overly facile, hand of Seward was to be seen in some of the proclamations and more formal documents. Hay wrote occasional letters so frigidly correct that it was patent Lincoln could not have written them. Seward's help on the first inaugural address had been concrete and worthy. It was more than balanced by the concrete and worthy help Lincoln had given Seward in certain state papers. The two of them probably had a good time together in the humorous masterpiece concocted for the King of Siam. Lincoln's own indubitable personal style had by now penetrated to so wide a public that gossip and published items about his need for help in his paragraphs made little headway. The President lacked polish, but had substance, ran the inference from a letter of Sumner to his British ally, Richard Cobden. Sumner enclosed Lincoln's letter to the Union mass meeting in Springfield, Illinois, in September of '63. "You will read the President's letter," wrote Sumner. "It is like him, unique and characteristic; but he states the case very well."

The word "but" thus used by Sumner would not have the approval of Harriet Beecher Stowe. She wrote for the campaign readers of '64 that, true enough, politicians were somewhat "shocked" at Lincoln's state papers at first and saying, "Why not let *us* make them a little more conventional, and file them to a classical pattern?" She could see Lincoln replying to this, "No, I shall write them myself. *The people will understand them.*" Mrs. Stowe had more confidence in the President's choice of words than did John Hay, whose diary entry for October 9, 1864, closed:

> The President is fighting today to get time to write a letter to the Baltimore meeting but is crowded as usual by visitors.
>
> P.S. Wrote the letter. I changed the word "posted" to "informed."

At noon one day in the autumn of '64 Robert Dale Owen with three other callers had a short visit with the President. One was a young woman who later wrote to E. S. Nadal, author and diplomat, of Lincoln's ways and manners. Nadal sketched the young woman as brilliant, handsome, transparent, impulsive, courageous, "such a character as only appears in times of great public agitation, when people's minds are full of exciting ideas." Her letter to Nadal read in part:

"The President gave us a cordial welcome, and seemed annoyed when we told him that the servant had refused to admit us. He was cordial to us, extremely so, and, on hearing that I was an abolitionist and had once manumitted a few slaves, he addressed the most of his conversation to me and, as I was young, wild, and chatty, he seemed amused and perhaps pleased at my audacity. He asked me what I thought the best way to destroy slavery. I quickly replied, 'It is always well to do right, without delay and on the instant.' He smiled ironically, saying that that could not be right, to do things without reason or order, to which I replied: 'Mr. William Lloyd Garrison, the greatest man that had ever lived (again he smiled) has informed me that there could be no delay or tarrying in doing right or in rendering justice.' The President said, as he patted me on the shoulder, 'What a little enthusiast you are! I am neither a red nor a black Republican.' 'I am both,' was my reply. 'So I perceive,' was his rejoinder. He seemed both amused and startled at my intensity, and when taking leave of us, he again patted me on the shoulder and said: 'I like your enthusiasm and earnestness. I hope we shall meet again.' . . . I might have told you in confidence that during the interview Mr. Lincoln sat with his foot and leg lifted on a rather high table."

Nadal's own comment on one feature of the interview was that "the charitable" would attribute the peculiarity of manners mentioned in the last sentence to "his origin and bringing up." Nadal would sum up: "I don't believe that. It seems to me that it was a personal deficiency of his own." Nadal saw a personal deficiency, took it as habitual, not interested that only in this instance and possibly one or two others across many years, had Lincoln kept his feet, or a foot and a leg, on the table in the presence of women. Nadal easily made himself believe that Lincoln enjoyed showing his boots and feet on an elevation for a woman visitor. A problematic factor of physical weariness and mental strain did not occur to Nadal. The casual extenuating circumstance did not cross Nadal's mind that the personal deficiency was not in evidence every day. Nor the consideration that Lincoln at times grew weary of excessively polite persons. They had surface manners and costly apparel overlaying swine motives. Lincoln in certain moods met them with bad grammar and worse manners. In one known instance he brought out one of his smuttiest stories to get rid of elegant bores who were trying to fetch off something for nothing and had little grace about it.

Carl Schurz's private letters held opinions about Lincoln that he could not fully and conveniently have given in his orations to the immense metropolitan audiences that heard him in the autumn of 1864. To Theodor Petrasch, a newly arrived emigrant, once a schooldays chum of Schurz in Germany, went a letter in Schurz's exquisitely executed German script, dated Bethlehem, Pennsylvania, October 12, 1864. "I wish to enlighten you on two other points. You are underrating the President. I grant that he lacks higher education and his manners are not in accord with European conceptions of the dignity of a chief magistrate. He is a well-developed child of nature and is not skilled in polite phrases and poses. But he is a man of profound feeling, correct and firm principles and incorruptible honesty. His motives are unquestionable, and he possesses to a remarkable degree the characteristic, God-given trait of this people, sound common sense. Should you read his official documents and his political letters, you would find this verified to a surprising extent.

"I know him from observation as well as anyone, and better than the majority. I am familiar with his motives. I have seen him heroically wage many a terrible struggle and work his way through many a desperate situation with strength born of loyalty to conviction. I have criticized him often and severely, and later I found that he was right. I also know his failings; they are those of a good man. That he has committed great errors in the endless embarrassments of his position cannot be denied, but it can be explained. Possibly other persons, if in his position, would not have committed the same errors, but they would have committed others. Moreover, Lincoln's personality has a special importance in this crisis. Free from the aspirations of genius, he will never be dangerous to a liberal government. He personifies the people, and that is the secret of his popularity. His Administration is the most representative that the history of the world has ever seen.

"I will make a prophecy that may now sound peculiar. In fifty years, perhaps much sooner, Lincoln's name will be inscribed close to Washington's on this American Republic's roll of honor. And there it will remain for all time. The children of those who persecute him now, will bless him."

Lincoln's own views of his education were so plainly and humanly interesting that when the Reverend John P. Gulliver wrote a full-length newspaper column account of his interview with Lincoln in 1859, even so hostile an organ as the *Detroit Free Press* in 1864 published it. "As to education, the newspapers are correct—I never went to school more than six months in my life," Lincoln was quoted. Euclid, the clergyman suggested, "well studied, would free the world of half its calamities . . . if they could only get the people to read it. It would be a means of grace."

"I think so," laughed Lincoln. "I vote for Euclid."

His life in the White House, his decisions, speeches, and messages issued from there, went out over the country for interpretations, for thanks, curses, doubts. Those interpretations would be told of in the November 8 ballot boxes. As election day drew nearer in the fall months, telegrams from all parts of the country poured in a constant succession into the War Office. They asked leaves of absence for this or that officer, "in order that his district at home might have the benefit of his vote and political influence," wrote Charles Dana. The political struggle was intense, and, further noted Dana, the interest taken in it, "both in the White House and in the War Department, was almost painful." Furloughs were asked for private soldiers in close districts; their personal influence at home would count. Widespread demands came that men on detached service and convalescents in hospitals be sent home. "All the power and influence of the War Department, then something enormous from the vast expenditure and extensive relations of the war, was employed to secure the re-election of Mr. Lincoln."

In, through, and around the city of Washington moved the signs of human storm. Into the White House and over its heavy carpets and past the tall mirrors came the spick-and-span, the dustily ragged and worn, out of the storm, and back into it. Before Lincoln's eyes the drama surged in lines and waves, and his mood varied from telling a man, "The only thing to do is to keep pegging away," and once murmuring half-dreamily to a Michigan woman: "I'm a tired man. Sometimes I think I'm the tiredest man on earth."

One June day in '64 the President, Cabinet members, many government officials, and a long procession of citizens followed a brass band playing dirges, hundreds of girls and young women in white dresses, and a sorrowful line of eighteen hearses. The eighteen dead were young women who had worked at cartridge-making in the United States Arsenal. "The disaster was due to culpable carelessness of the pyrotechnist of the Arsenal," wrote Noah Brooks for the *Sacramento Union*. His material lying drying in the sun took fire and spread. "Some sensational stories about rebel emissaries being instrumental are in circulation, but no sensible man believes such reports. Suffice it to know that gross carelessness, practiced for years, hurried to a premature grave this band of young, lovely and estimable women."

The city, its suburbs, the Capitol, the front of the White House, the saloons, dives, and cheap theatres, Pennsylvania Avenue and all the main streets, in latter '64 swarmed with soldiers, "more than ever before," wrote Walt Whitman in his journal. Blue pants and coats were everywhere. From the northward, from hospitals and neighboring camps they poured in. "The clump of crutches is heard up the stairs of the paymasters' offices, groups often waiting long and wearily in the cold. Furloughed men, singly, in small squads, make their way to the Baltimore depot. Patrol detachments move around, examining passes, arresting all soldiers without them. They do not question the one-legged, or men badly disabled or maimed, but all others are stopt." Of a large brick mansion on the banks of the Rappahannock, used as a hospital during a battle, Whitman had noted, "Out doors, at the foot of a tree, within ten yards of the front of the house, I notice a heap of amputated feet, legs, arms, hands, &tc., a full load for a one-horse cart."

Dr. John Shaw Billings told in later days of his first assignment as a young physician to a field hospital. Piled roundabout a ramshackle building he saw amputated limbs, bloody bandages, flies covering varieties of filth. Inside he found things even worse—no medical supplies, no attempts at sanitation, so he thought. Taking himself very seriously, young Dr. Billings spoke to the hospital chief about the crying need for improvements—and heard an explosion of wrath: "I tell you I never wanted to come here anyway! And now when I can't get supplies I requisition for, now when I can't get help I call for, a young whippersnapper like you comes along and tells me I don't know my job. I tell you, young man, I'd rather be in *Hell*—with a broken *back*—trying to eat *soup*—out of a *bottle*—with a *fork*—than be in this damned hole!"

The bloody battles of the Army of the Potomac that year had turned the city of Washington into one immense hospital. In the single battle of Spotsylvania Court House the casualties added up to 13,416. On railroad flatcars, in boxcars with floor and roof piled close with bodies, the wounded arrived to be unloaded at wharves and platforms, there to wait patiently or with cursing and crying until ambulances carried them to hospitals. The inadequate and cruder equipment of the earlier war years had grown into a vast establishment, much of it still temporary and improvised. Churches, private homes, and government buildings were commandeered. Board barracks and white army tents met the eyes of the President on almost any walk or ride he took around the city. Many hospital tents were located away from the woodland undergrowths, in clearings near the road. Driving from the White House to the Soldiers' Home, the President could look from his carriage through tent openings into the cots and bunks of sick and wounded. One of the best-managed hospitals, Armory Square, had personal attention from Lincoln. He had called Dr. D. Willard Bliss from the field to help in perfecting a general hospital system over the city, and for a long time twice a week held consultations with Dr. Bliss. Once, according to Bliss, he had asked why no one had planted flower seeds on the Armory Square grounds. Bliss said he would if he had the seeds, whereupon the President ordered the Department of Agriculture to send seeds, and each of the long barracks of the hospital soon bloomed with nodding petal and green vine.

"The President conceals an enormous tenacity under his mild gawky western manner," wrote Whitman in a letter of '64. "That he has conserved the government so far is a miracle itself." The tenacity to which Whitman referred was needed after the Wilderness battles, when the wounded so crowded Washington that proper care was impossible. "Mother," wrote Whitman, "it is most too much for a fellow, and I sometimes wish I was out of it." "Many of the amputations have to be done over again. . . . Many of the poor afflicted young men are crazy. Every ward has some in it that are wandering. They have suffered too much, and it is perhaps a privilege that they are out of their senses."

Of a day late in October of '64 Whitman wrote of seeing squads of Union Army deserters, over 300 of them, marching between armed guards along Pennsylvania Avenue, a motley collection, "all sorts of rigs, all sorts of hats and caps, many fine-looking young fellows, some shame-faced, some sickly, most of them dirty, shirts very dirty and long worn, &c. . . . a huddling mass, not in ranks. I saw some of the spectators laughing, but I felt like anything else but laughing. These deserters are far more numerous than would be thought. Almost every day I see squads of them, sometimes two or three at a time. . . . (I hear that desertions from the army now in the field have often averaged 10,000 a month. One of the commonest sights in Washington is a squad of deserters.)"

Less easy to think about were the firing-squad shootings, the hamstringings and the hangings, done in retaliations real and fancied between guerrillas and roving cavalry detachments, Confederate and Union. Reciting atrocities he heard from eyewitnesses, Whitman wrote they gave but an inkling of the war, "the passionate, boiling volcanoes of human revenge for comrades, brothers slain—with the light of burning farms, and heaps of smutting, smouldering black embers—and in the human heart everywhere black, worse embers."

The time beat of the war went on, bluecoat streams pouring south and south, miles of men and boots, leather, hardtack, tents, steel, lead, powder, guns. And as miles of wagon supplies, mountains of hardtack, were used up, more and more poured south. And moving north, flung back out of the muddy and bloody recoils, came stragglers, deserters, bounty-jumpers, the furloughed, the sick and wounded—while beyond the battle fronts toward the south, living skeletons in prison offered prayers that the time beat of the war would end, that the sad music of rifle volleys and cannonading guns would close over in some sweet silence.

Dim echoes and direct shocks of every phase of the war lived and rang and refused to die down in the rooms of the White House, where, according to William H. Crook, assigned to guard duty, "As he went upstairs and entered his own room, Lincoln's last act was to turn to the guard on duty in the corridor and wish him good-night. Then he would enter his room, and close the door, and I—if it were my turn to stand guard—would settle down for eight hours of duty. My chair stood in the corridor, within easy reach of the door opening into the President's room. I could see every inch of the whole length of the corridor, so lighted that no shadows could even partly conceal any one who might try to slip through it."

Outside on the lawn near the front portico stood in moonlight or rain the statue of Thomas Jefferson, a remembered President, jealous of the rights of States and liberally quoted in the South, yet also a believer in some form of *equal* human rights, wherefore he was liberally quoted in the North. Jefferson, a name, a paradox, maker of documents and poems lingering on; Jefferson, red-haired, a violin-player, a composer of slogans and tumults—he too had lived in the Executive Mansion.

Near the Executive Mansion's portals too were three iron mortars with lifted mouths. They had stood there so long in years of peace that birds felt invitations to come inside and make their homes. Rent-free and gay, the birds flew out and in these iron rooms. In June of '62 John James Piatt wrote verses of how:

> Deep in the awful chambers
> Of the gigantic Death,
> The wrens their nests have builded
> And dwelt with loving breath.

In the silence of the night was despair—and hope. Though torn with intestinal violence, the Government of the United States was still a vast going concern, having immense transactions in land, money, shipbuilding, immigrants thronging United States consulates in Europe with anxiety to go to "the free country" overseas, the first tentative projections of the Union Pacific Railway under way, an around-the-earth international telegraph system being wrought toward reality, mails being carried, pensions paid to widows and orphans, river and harbor works in process—the question running over the world: Would the Union Government be able to hammer out an indissoluble unity of its States? And alongside this world of red war and this other world of constructive realities in which Lincoln had to immerse himself daily, there was the formal realm of conventions, of "society," of ordained contacts necessary to the role of being President.

The airy and bubblesome lightness of part of this other realm was set forth by a young lady writing for *Godey's Lady's Book* in '64, of how she was pressed and rushed onward toward Mr. and Mrs. Lincoln at a White House reception, so excited that she was comforted to hear the rustling and sweeping of her skirts behind her; in the jam and the whirl those garments, ran her dizzy impression, might have been lost. "I moved onward. A voice uttered my name. A gracious hand clasped mine, a kind voice said a few words of greeting. To this moment I believe it to have been my gown that made the courtesy, not myself. I, who had intended to have looked, not only at the lion but the lioness, saw nothing but a pair of polished boots and the hem of a silk robe. I retreated to meet mamma who, paying her respects in passing, was smiling in dignified composure. On the soft seats we sank down, and before us passed the groups who had preceded us and those that following us had just left the President. Waxen-faced girls in white, the débutantes, with excited, shy faces; haughtily confident beauties in every tint of flounce and flower; brides in their wedding finery; and such astonishing old ladies! What blazing jewels! What rustling silks! A dress-maker would die of it 'in aromatic pain.' Such dignified old generals! Here a Spanish attaché, olive-tinted, with long black mustache; there a squat yellow figure grinning hideously; a bronze face in scarlet and gold next a smooth-faced lieutenant in new uniform; a young lady with red arms, from the country, beside a warrior so fierce he can only be a volunteer. They dawdle here, and gossip, and look out for notabilities, and criticize a little, and talk a little scandal, and groups form. Gentlemen saunter about gallant and pleasant, or with severe criticism drawl out, 'You never do see a pretty face nowadays!' Possibly it is in the hope of some day seeing one that they stare so. One more crush through the crowded hall, and then the lovely gowns and their fond wearers step into their carriages, and the levee is over."

White House visitors usually had an unobstructed range over the East Room and one or two of the adjoining parlors. "Accordingly," wrote Noah Brooks in a news letter of latter '64, "relic-hunters (let us hope they are no worse) have acquired the practice of cutting out and carrying off bits of rich carpet, damask hangings, and even large pieces of rings, cords, tassels, gilt scroll-work and the covering of damask sofas. A few weeks ago an officer was caught, in company with two ladies who had his penknife and were cutting a square of brocade from one of the East Room chairs, while he stood guard. The *ladies* were let off and the officer was sent to the Old Capitol. Yesterday a man in the garb of a private soldier was caught while skinning off a damask cover of a sofa. He was sent to the guard-house. Well might an astonished Dutchman say, 'Mine Gott, vat a peoples!' "

Orderly persons there were, however. They emphasized keeping the Sabbath day holy. "Our virtuous city government," wrote Brooks of latter

1864, "has passed an ordinance prohibiting the crying of newspapers on Sunday; so last Sunday was signalized by the advent of a lot of dumb newsboys—a monstrosity in the newspaper line. Meanwhile the street cars fracture the Sabbath, but in a noiseless manner, the bells being taken off on that day out of regard for the feelings of Sabbatarians."

The night of the weekly reception—more often termed a levee—"was always a trying one to the President," wrote Carpenter. As persons in line gave him expressions of sympathy he usually turned them off playfully. Occasionally his offhand comment ran that the tug at his hand was much easier to bear than that upon his heartstrings daily for all manners of favors beyond his power to grant. Having been an onlooker at his first levee in the White House Carpenter stepped up for his handshake, meeting the query, "Well, Carpenter, you have seen one day's run—what is your opinion of it?"

In this realm of chatter one White House visitor, a young Englishman known as Lord Hartington, or the Marquis of Hartington, M.P., was a topic in early '64. His speeches in England on American affairs had revealed a "perversion" which required "correcting, publicly," said an open letter of Richard Cobden. "He signalized his visit by insulting all faithful American citizens," commented *Harper's Weekly*, "by wearing a rebel badge in the drawing-rooms of Mr. August Belmont, for which he was not reproved by his host, but was called to account by a young Union officer." He had dined with General Lee at Fredericksburg. And when, self-important and ebullient, he came to a White House reception, was introduced to the President and tried to carry on a running conversation, he was interrupted several times by the President addressing him as "Mister Partington." The raillery probably missed him. Chances were against his having read any lines of the Mrs. Partington who had a gift for malaprops, for sayings that mocked at vulgarity unaware of itself, Mrs. Partington who scolded her boy for a "fragrant outrage," and predicted a bad end for one of such "moral turpentine."

The formalities wore Lincoln unless he more or less mocked at them. A California man found him at his office dressed for a state dinner, his large hands at the ends of his long conspicuous arms encased in white gloves. He raised and flourished them, recalled an Illinois man who could never see him in this "predicament" without being reminded of "canvassed hams."

A crowd on the White House lawn one Saturday afternoon in the summer of '64 was enjoying the weekly concert of the Marine Band. Lincoln stepped out on the portico to look over the crowd and enjoy the music with them. But they saw him first. There were handclappings, calls for a speech. He bowed his thanks, excused himself, stepped back into the circular parlor, slowly stretched himself on a sofa, murmured to Carpenter, "I wish they would let me sit out there quietly and enjoy the music."

Carpenter thought it proper at this moment to say he believed no President since the days of Washington had secured the hearts of the people and carried them with him as Lincoln had done. "To this he replied," noted Carpenter, "that, in such a crisis as the country was then passing through, it was natural that the people should look more earnestly to their leaders than at other periods. He thought their regard for any man in his position who should sincerely have done his best to save the government from destruction, would have been equally as marked and expressive; to which I did not by any means assent."

The President ate a noon lunch, usually with no company, at irregular hours, depending on the day's business. "Almost daily, at this hour," noted Carpenter of his six months' stay, "I met a servant carrying a simple meal upon a tray up-stairs." There the food might be eaten soon or perhaps two hours later.

George E. Baker, private secretary to Seward, described how Lincoln had changed his practice from year to year in the matter of signing the many public documents brought to him by Baker. During the first few months of his Administration he read each paper carefully through, remarking, "I never sign a document I have not first read." At a later period he asked the messenger, "Won't you read these papers to me?" Still later he requested merely "a synopsis of the contents." And in the fourth year his expression most often was, "Show me where you want my name." Seward's secretary mentioned this development as though Lincoln might have been more expeditious to begin with. This was not entirely so. The first year had been given to training Seward in several respects. And as the two had fraternized and policies in degree clarified, their mutual understanding was such that Lincoln could now usually say with perfect safety, "Show me where you want my name," whereas during the first year he would have been near ruin more than once had not his habit been to say, "I never sign a document I have not first read."

Letters written by Lincoln during the two years of 1863 and 1864 doubled in number those of the two previous years. The occasions on which he had answers and was ready to give them seemed to have doubled. In 1861 he wrote 216 letters, in 1862 he wrote 211, in 1863 he wrote 543, in 1864 he wrote 536. For reasons connected with events and with his own outlook, the times and moments in which he believed it worth while to speak on paper doubled.

At eleven o'clock one night Carpenter, who was trusted and had the run of the house, found Lincoln seated alone signing military commissions. Carpenter sat down beside him. He dipped his steel pen into a heavy hexagonal glass inkstand, some five inches in diameter and not easy to knock over. He went on signing, presently remarking, "I do not, as you see, pretend to read over these documents. I see that Stanton has signed them, so I conclude they are all right." He paused and read part of one, So-and-So "is hereby appointed adjutant-general, with the rank of captain" and so on, "E. M. Stanton, Secretary of War." And putting his own signature in the opposite corner, "There, that fixes *him* out." He chatted and wrote, finished the lot, rose, stretched, "Well, I have got that job *husked out*, now I guess I will go over to the War Department before I go to bed, and see if there is any news."

The duel to the death to have been fought with James Shields on a Mississippi River sandbar, which never came off, was "an affair of honor" which seemed to have been mentioned to Lincoln only once in the White House. Vague and often inaccurate references to it were made occasionally in hostile newspapers. As a topic Lincoln strictly forbade it, according to an army officer who related an incident to Carpenter. Once during a pleasant hour of entertainment with Mr. and Mrs. Lincoln the officer turned. "Is it true, Mr. President, as I have heard, that you once went out to fight a 'duel' for the sake of the lady by your side?" With a flushed face came Lincoln's advice, "I do not deny it, but if you desire my friendship, you will never mention the circumstance again!"

What had become of the Shields who was to kill him unless he killed Shields? A mine superintendent in Mexico when the war began, Shields had come to Washington, Lincoln had signed his commission as brigadier general in August of '61, and in Shenandoah Valley service Shields had seen much fierce action and taken a bad wound, resigning from the army in 1863 and moving to California. Was he the same overly elegant dandy that Lincoln had satirized in the published sketches that brought on the challenge to a duel? No, Shields had changed. Perhaps Lincoln had reports of him like the one Private W. F. Goodhue of the 3rd Wisconsin wrote home to his folks: "I send you a picture of brave old Shields. . . . I saw him on our retreat from Harrisonburg. . . . How different he looked in comparison to other generals I had seen, no staff of well-dressed officers stood around him, he wore *not* the yellow sash and epaulettes denoting his rank, there he stood leaning on a cannon, very plainly dressed, a soldier a few rods off holding his horse. . . . The old Mexican Hero and rebel-thrasher."

Not only the fashion world read with interest in the press of Mrs. Lincoln at the New Year's Day reception wearing "a delicately shaded purple silk, trimmed with black velvet, with a rare lace neck-tie, a pearl brooch at the throat, a drooping white feather in her hair"; of her paying a complimentary visit to General Scott at West Point and receiving a salute of fifteen guns; of her going to Harvard College in June to attend the graduation of her son Robert; of her buying a set of earrings and a pin for $3,000 and a shawl for $5,000 on successive shopping trips to New York City; of her sister Martha Todd White of Selma, Alabama, receiving a pass signed by the President giving her passage, with baggage, through the Union Army lines, resulting in rumors and accusations that she had been accorded special privileges and had smuggled contraband goods, including, *Leslie's Weekly* alleged mistakenly, "a rebel uniform, the buttons of which were of gold, worth $40,000."

Of the son Robert the father saw little. When Robert at a later time was requested for information that might help toward a biography of his father he wrote to the inquirer, J. G. Holland: "My father's life was of a kind which gave me but little opportunity to learn the details of his early career. During my childhood and early youth he was almost constantly away from me, attending courts or making political speeches. In 1859 when he was beginning to devote himself more to practice in his own neighborhood, and when I would have had both the inclination and the

Harper's Weekly presents Mrs. Lincoln to its readers and the country

means to gratify my desire to become better acquainted with the history of his early struggles, I went to New Hampshire to school & afterwards to Harvard College & he became President. Thenceforth any great intimacy between us became impossible. I scarcely ever had ten minutes' quiet talk with him . . . on account of his constant devotion to business." This was of a color with Robert Todd Lincoln also saying at a later time to a friend: "I returned from college in 1864 and one day I saw my father for a few minutes. He said, 'Son, what are you going to do now?' I said, 'As long as you object to my joining the army, I am going back to Harvard, to study law.' 'If you do,' said my father, 'you should learn more than I ever did but you will never have so good a time.' That is the only advice I had from my father as to my career." There was surmise at this time as to Robert's future, several newspapers carrying an item similar to one in the *Chicago Journal* of July 15, 1864: "It is rumored that Mr. Robert Todd Lincoln, the President's son, on graduation from Harvard College, will immediately enter the army as a private."

In contrast was the father's fond intimacy with Tad, who could pile chairs and settees of a living-room into a barricade. Behind this Tad hid till his father came into the room, when he would pitch the whole works tumbling toward his laughing elder. Uniforms and military titles were wheedled from the War Department for Tad. He drove his team of goats into a room where his mother was receiving ladies in crisp crinoline. On official Executive Mansion stationery Tad wrote telegrams and sent them in such style as:

> EXECUTIVE MANSION, WASHINGTON, OCT. 4TH. GUS GUMPERT 1226 CHESTNUT STREET PHILADELPHIA GUS I WANT TO KNOW ABOUT THAT BOX YOU WAS TO SEND ME PLEASE LET ME KNOW RIGHT AWAY IF YOU PLEASE AND OBLIDGE COL TAD LINCOLN.

He addressed a telegram to Thomas W. Sweney, No. 1231 Chestnut Street, Philadelphia, regarding a "double Sett of harness" with the information, "I bought it at the Same place that you purchased my wagon at." He went to his father for a written one-sentence communication, "Will Mr. Dickson please pump the water out of a certain well which Tad will show?" From this Mr. Dickson might gather that whatever the water was doing in the well, it served none of Tad's purposes and should be removed. The system of signal bells, connected by cords throughout the White House, suddenly was disrupted and completely useless, investigation showing Tad up to mischief—and soon forgiven. Going to Stanton's office and getting himself commissioned a lieutenant, Tad went to an ordnance officer and ordered a lot of muskets sent to the White House. The painter Carpenter sat in Nicolay's room that night about ten o'clock when Robert Lincoln came in with a flushed face to say, "I have just had a great row with the President of the United States!" explaining that Tad had discharged the regular White House guard, had mustered into service all the gardeners and servants, given them guns, drilled them, and put them on duty. "I found it out an hour ago," Robert went on, "and thinking it a great shame, as the men had been hard at work all day, I went to father with it; but instead of punishing 'Tad,' as I think he ought, he evidently looks upon it as a good joke, and won't do anything about it!"

Tad went to bed, fell asleep, his guards were quietly dismissed, and the Executive Mansion for one night had no guards, and the next day was more normal.

The boy enjoyed strutting along with Captain Bennett inspecting the cavalry on White House guard duty. The Captain one morning saw the men getting lax and bawled them out. "The condition of the quarters is

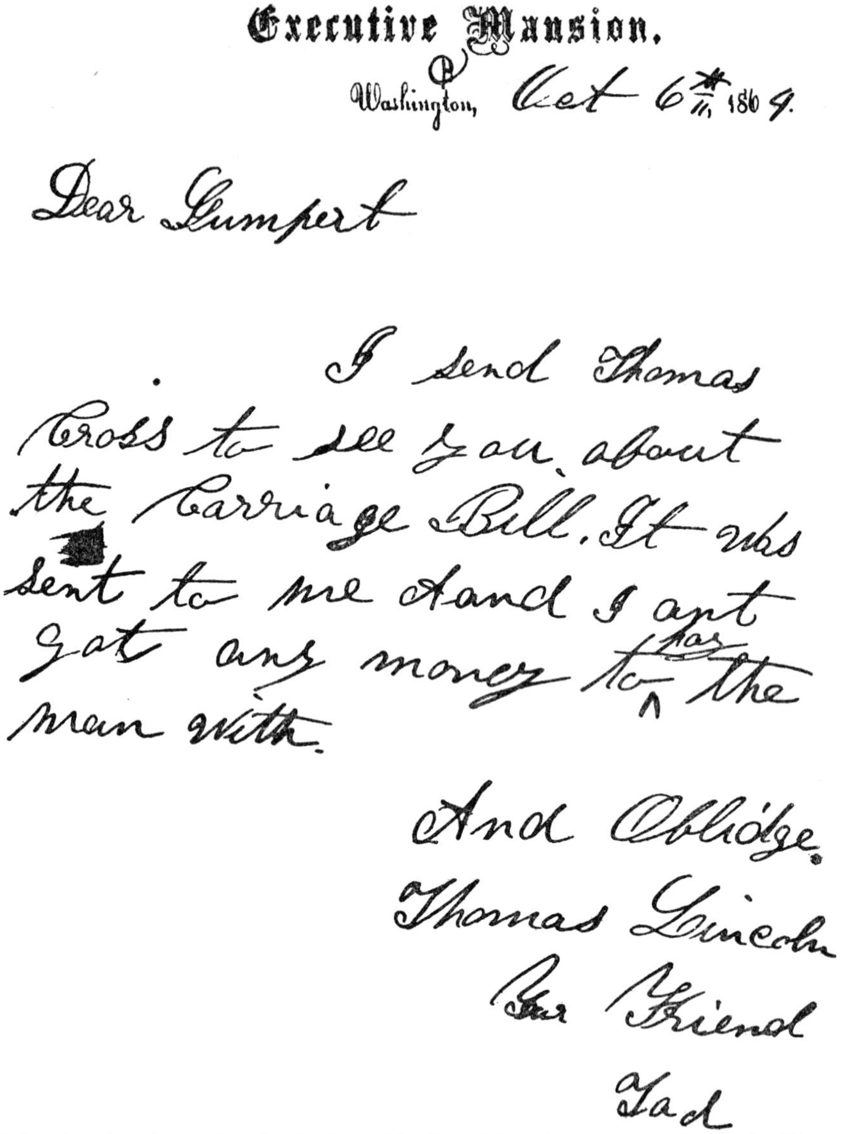
Executive Mansion,
Washington, Oct 6th 1864.

Dear Gumpert

I send Thomas Cross to see you about the Carriage Bill. It was sent to me And I ant got any money to pay the man with.

And Oblidge.
Thomas Lincoln
Your Friend
Tad

Tad writes in a large free hand about his financial embarrassment. From the Barrett collection.

disgraceful," his voice rasped. "Instead of being kept as they should be kept, they look like —" and while he hesitated Tad shrilled "hell!" For the rest of that day discipline was not so good. Nor again one cold night when the corporal of the guard every half-hour blew a police whistle signaling sentinels to walk their horses fast and change places. This lessened monotony and helped warm men and horses. Tad that night went to the corporal of the guard, asked to see the whistle, took it, and ran for the White House. From a second-story window he leaned out and blew it. The men and horses shifted places. Again the whistle and again the shod horses sounding on the cobblestones. For a half-hour Tad kept this up till he had had his fun and then came out and handed back the whistle to the corporal of the guard, along with a bowl of Roman punch from the reception room, where the diplomatic corps was having a party. Thus Robert W. McBride of the guard detail, and others, told of it.

Stereoscopic photographers called in by Carpenter, to make pictures that would help him toward sharper reality in his painting of the President, stored their chemicals in a room that Tad considered his private hangout. In this room with the help of servants Tad had arranged a miniature theatre with curtains, stage, orchestra pit. One or two photographic plates had been made of the President when one of the camera crew came in to say that Tad had locked the room, carried away the key, and now what? In the midst of this, wrote Carpenter, Tad burst in, in a passion, laying the blame on Carpenter. The father, in the chair where he had been posed by the photographers, said mildly, "Tad, go and unlock the door." Tad went off muttering. Carpenter followed, coaxing, Tad refusing. Returning, Carpenter found the President in the same chair. "Has not the boy opened that door?" Carpenter said he could do nothing with him. "Mr. Lincoln's lips," wrote Carpenter, "came together firmly, and then, suddenly rising, he strode across the passage with the air of one bent on punishment. . . . Directly he returned with the key to the theatre, which he unlocked himself. 'There,' said he, 'go ahead, it is all right now.' He then went back to his office, and resumed his seat. 'Tad,' he said, half apologetically, 'is a peculiar child. He was violently excited when I went to him. I said, "Tad, do you know you are making your father a great deal of trouble?" He burst into tears, instantly giving me up the key.' "

With something like affection for an own son Lincoln followed the career of Admiral John A. Dahlgren's boy Ulric, not yet of voting age when Lincoln commissioned him a colonel. In a cavalry raid Ulric Dahlgren's horsemen captured important dispatches from Jefferson Davis to General Lee just after Gettysburg, Ulric losing a leg. Tall, slight, pale-faced, in February of '64 he said gaily to Lincoln, "I am waiting for my new leg and then we shall see whether I can ride again." And with 400 men he did ride, in a wild attack on the outworks of Richmond, confused reports reaching Lincoln, who telegraphed General Butler, "Please send me at once all you know or can learn of his fate." From a Confederate deserter Butler gleaned that "a one-legged Colonel and about a hundred men were taken prisoners." The President and Secretary Stanton, on receiving this news, called upon Admiral Dahlgren, according to press dispatches, "to convey the glad tidings and congratulate him upon the safety of his gallant son." But later news over the wires said, "Colonel Dahlgren is dead." Then followed a controversy, involving the laws of civilized warfare between the Washington and Richmond governments over papers alleged to have been found on the dead person of the boy.

Carpenter's six months' stay in the White House was drawing to a close. His painting titled "The First Reading of the Emancipation Proclamation by President Lincoln to His Cabinet" was nearly finished. He and Lincoln had passed many pleasant hours. Thirty-four years old, slender and delicate, with bushy black hair, devout in religion and strict in manners, Carpenter had a loyalty to the President and a belief that his painting would be a help to the Lincoln cause. "I must go in and take one more look at the picture before you leave us," said Lincoln one July day. And going to the East Room and sitting in front of it for a while, he said there was little to find fault with. "The portraiture is the main thing, and that seems to me absolutely perfect." He suggested that Solicitor Whiting's book *War Powers of the President* looked like an old sheepskin volume of the *United States Statutes* and should have the face of its binding changed. Carpenter thanked him, said the change would be made, asked if there was anything else. "No," replied Lincoln, and then, according to Carpenter, he added, "It is as good as it can be made." Carpenter was touched, spoke of his enthusiasm and devotion in the work, the unvarying kindness the President had always shown him. Lincoln listened, kept gazing on the picture, and when Carpenter was through voicing appreciation and thanks, turned to say, "Carpenter, I believe I am about as glad over the success of this work as you are." With those words and a good-by handshake they parted.

Before this final session of Lincoln and Carpenter, on July 22, the President and the Cabinet adjourned from their regular meeting and in a body viewed the painting of themselves in the state dining-room. Lincoln gave his "unschooled" opinion, as he termed it, and Carpenter wrote that it was all he could ask. By permission of the President the painting was placed in the East Room, thrown open to the public for two days. The porters estimated visitors each day at several thousands. Later the canvas was taken down, rolled up, and moved away, eventually bringing a price of $25,000 from a patriotic purchaser.

Nearsighted Horace Greeley in a June visit had comment "not particularly gratifying" to Carpenter on his picture. The steel engravings in his own book *The American Conflict* Greeley believed much superior. Carpenter pointed to a newspaper in the foreground "symbolizing the agency of the 'Press' in bringing about *Emancipation*," worked out from a copy of the *New York Tribune*. Greeley's face relaxed. "I would not object to your putting in my letter to the President on that subject." Carpenter then had the idea he might get Greeley and Lincoln together for an interview so they could clear up misunderstandings. Leaving Greeley with the picture, he went upstairs to see if Lincoln would come down and meet a guest who inclined to stay downstairs. Lincoln looked up quickly, seemed slightly startled at the editor of the powerful *New York Tribune* being in the

White House, recovered himself, spoke blandly, "Please say to Mr. Greeley that I shall be *very* happy to see him, *at his leisure.*"

On two occasions, it seemed, Lincoln had requested Greeley to call. Once in '64, in connection with Greeley's proposed Niagara peace conference, Greeley had refused. And once in '62 Greeley had accepted, and the report of their conversation had Lincoln saying: "You complain of me. What have I done, or omitted to do, which has provoked the hostility of the *Tribune?*" Greeley: "You should issue a proclamation abolishing slavery." Lincoln: "Suppose I do that. There are now twenty thousand muskets on the shoulders of Kentuckians, who are bravely fighting our battles. Every one of them will be thrown down or carried over to the rebels." Greeley: "Let them do it. The cause of the Union will be stronger if Kentucky should secede with the rest than it is now." Lincoln: "Oh, I can't think that."

This seemed about the sum total of personal conversation reported between the President and the foremost "liberal" journalist of America. On occasion it seemed that Greeley was motivated by suspicions of Lincoln controlled by Seward—radical antislavery leaders were incessant on this point—so Greeley included Lincoln in his ancient and bitter feud with Seward. Now in '64, after Greeley had for a year made every possible attempt to replace Lincoln in the White House with Rosecrans or someone else, Greeley strolled into the Executive Mansion to see and talk with almost anyone except the Executive the mansion was built for. There was a tried patience in the way Lincoln spoke of Greeley, as though life has bitter flavors to which one can become accustomed. Slight was the change, if any, in Greeley since in 1860 he had said of Lincoln, "He has got a lot of people out here in Illinois who seem to see something in him that the rest of us have not seen yet."

Into the White House came gifts and tokens from near and far. Miss Addie Brockway of Newburyport, Massachusetts, sent a pair of wool socks she had knitted. At the top in yarn colors was the Stars and Stripes and on the foot bottoms the secession flag—Miss Brockway wished that her President might always have the banner of rebellion under his feet. From California friends arrived a three-inch-long gold box filled with golden crystals, the President's initials wrought in an oval of quartz on the lid. From the noted Californian hunter Seth Kinman came a chair made of elk horns. A wedding cake from the newly wedded Prince of Wales was transmitted by the bridegroom to his chamberlain and via the British Minister of Foreign Affairs on to Lord Lyons at Washington, who delivered it to Secretary Seward, who passed it on to the White House, where Mrs. Lincoln carved it on April 1 and found it somewhat dry. William O. Snider sent through Governor Curtin a cane for the President, with an accompanying letter, whereof Lincoln wrote to Curtin of the sender, "For my life I cannot make out his name; and therefore I cut it from his letter and pasted it on, as you see." So Snider received a letter of thanks with his name in his own handwriting pasted at the heading of it.

For the benefit of the New York Sanitary Fair an American eagle was portrayed on heavy cardboard with human hair scissored from the heads of Abraham Lincoln and his Cabinet members—excepting Secretary Welles, who had none to spare—and two score of Senators not bald. On silver mountings of two highly ornamented Colt revolvers went the inscription "From the President of the United States to Kubrisli Pasha, Governor of Adrianople" in token of the Pasha's having publicly executed death sentence on three brigands who had murdered an American missionary in Adrianople. To Hawaiian missionaries on the Marquesas Islands who had saved an American sailor being manhandled by natives, the President sent two gold watches, two guns, two silver medals, and a consignment of clothing. At the top of two sheets of elaborate penmanship ran the salutation "Abraham Lincoln, President of the United States of America to the Regent Captains of the Republic of San Marino." The message opened, "Great and Good Friends" and proceeded, "I thank the Council of San Marino for the honor of citizenship they have conferred upon me." Their dominion small, their State was "nevertheless one of the most honored in history." Their kindly feelings toward a representative government in America undergoing trial from "the dangers of domestic faction" were deeply appreciated. "Wishing that your interesting State may endure and flourish forever and that you may live long and enjoy the confidence and secure the gratitude of your fellow citizens, I pray God to have you in his holy keeping." Below his subscription "Your Good Friend" was the signature "Abraham Lincoln" in full and the authentication by the Secretary of State, William H. Seward.

Months after the battle of Fredericksburg came word of the Massachusetts soldier who had carried over his heart a pocket Bible in which a rifle ball became imbedded. The President sent the boy another Bible, with a personal inscription.

Cases of assorted wines and liquors piled higher in the White House cellar, the clerk Stoddard writing that possibly kindly souls had an idea of stimulating the President's war efforts. Stoddard noted loads of champagne, green seal and other seals; red wines of several kinds; white wine from the Rhine; wines from Spain and Portugal and the islands; whisky distilled from rye, from wheat, from potatoes; choice brandy, Jamaica rum, and Santa Cruz rum. Arrivals of these were acknowledged with thanks and the information that the wines and liquors were distributed among hospitals.

One press item in early '64 ran, "It is utterly impossible for the President to answer the great number of applications made for his autographs, to be sold at sanitary and other fairs, his time being wholly engrossed with public business." The British Minister Lord Lyons requested an autograph for a woman of title and received a written message: "Mr. Lyons has informed me that Lady Villiers has expressed a wish for my autograph. I beg that her ladyship will accept the assurance of my sincere gratification at the opportunity of subscribing myself—A. Lincoln." Possibly this routine matter devolved on John Hay; either he or Lincoln could have composed it—it sounded like Hay.

Lady Villiers was not to be met as abruptly as William C. Baker, Esq., whose note from the President read, "You request an autograph and here it is." The tone of a secretary making a routine acknowledgment was in a note to Charles L. Flint, Esq.: "Allow me to thank you cordially for the copy of your work on 'Insects Injurious to Vegetation' which you have had the kindness to send me and believe me—Yours very sincerely."

Humility was quite lacking in a woman member of Henry Ward Beecher's church who had "views" on the military, political, and moral aspects of the war. She journeyed from Brooklyn to Washington expressly to tell the President how the whole Government should be managed. She took her husband along. The two waited while their card was sent in to the President. Word came the President was engaged on important business and could not be seen. The woman sent back word, according to press accounts, that her business was of "the greatest consequence" and must not be postponed a single day. Unwilling to send away an influential member of Beecher's church who might have some reasonable personal favor to request, Lincoln excused himself from a conference and went to listen to her. She began with a wide outline of her plan for combined military, political, and moral strategy for the suppression of the rebellion. She would require probably another hour to complete her statement of what she evidently regarded as a masterly and comprehensive grasp of the American problem and its solution.

Lincoln slowly rose from his chair, stood at full height. And the woman paused in her rush of words. In a tone abrupt and impatient the President said, "Madam, all this has been thought of a hundred times before," and without another word hurried from the room.

Three members of the Freedmen's Inquiry Commission, extremists on emancipation and Negro troops, in frequent conferences pressed Lincoln toward measures beyond his announced policies. They were getting "super-serviceable," as William A. Croffut put it, and Lincoln cautioned them one day: "See here! If I don't look out you'll run away from me."

Along Pennsylvania Avenue, around the War Department and the Treasury Building, and in the White House neighborhood, the newsboys cried their papers. In the *Morning Chronicle*, owned and edited by John W. Forney, Lincoln could read that his Administration was doing well, in the morning *National Intelligencer*, an old-time Whig party organ, that "cordial support to the nomination of General McClellan" was desirable for the country's good. Of the dignified *Chronicle* one writer held it "spread large pieces of bread with small pieces of butter, tucking in moderate ideas under very large quilts." Seven-o'clock morning trains brought the *Baltimore Sun*, *Clipper*, and *American*. Two hours later came the *Philadelphia Inquirer* and the *Philadelphia Press*. The latter was also a loyal Administration paper, owned by Forney. The *Philadelphia Inquirer* Brooks rated "a lively sheet, but utterly unreliable and possessing not one particle of reputation for truthfulness." In the afternoon arrived the *New York Herald*,

Tribune, Times, World. Of these Brooks had deliberate judgments, which he may have discussed with Lincoln, writing: "The *Tribune* has the most accurate Washington news, and the *Times* the least accurate. The *Herald* is sensational and distorted in its Washington telegraph correspondence, and the *World*, though quite accurate in the main, shows all of its proclivities in its Washington news, sent, strange as it may seem, by a clever gentleman loyal to the administration." The afternoon *Washington Star* came out at two o'clock and four, though between noon and evening it might put out six extras. It favored sensational stories, kept sufficiently loyal to be on speaking terms at the War and Navy departments, and was edited by W. Douglas Wallach, a Virginian, brother of the Mayor of Washington. The *Star* had no particular leanings in policy, though it voiced opposition to McClellan, mildly. Of the other afternoon paper, the *Republican*, Brooks indicated it was "Republican in name only," had no special politics, was thoroughly loyal, liberal, and gossipy, but not very reliable.

In October of '63 Brooks wrote of the *Washington Republican* having contrived to secure for itself the reputation of being "the organ of the President," wherefore "misplaced importance was sometimes attached to some of its few editorials." S. P. Hanscomb, formerly of the *New York Tribune*, was its editor, and Brooks dwelt on his exaggerated stature. "The solution is that Hanscomb, a pushing and persevering man, has managed to so ingratiate himself with the President that he has almost exclusive access to the office of the Executive, and there obtains from our good-natured Chief Magistrate such scanty items of news as he is willing to give out for publication, and so the enterprising editor gets up his daily column of 'official intelligence,' much to the annoyance and jealousy of the New York and other Washington correspondents whose dependence is upon the current news of the day, which must be gained before a single hour has blown upon its freshness. As for the *Republican* having any authority to reflect or indicate the views of any member of the administration upon any subject whatever, it is the most complete invention of those who circulate such a foolish yarn. Lincoln believes in letting the newspapers publish all that will not benefit the enemy; he disapproves of many of the arbitrary edicts of the press of Secretary Stanton; and he is more free to converse upon matters pertaining to his Department than any of his Cabinet, though the rack of torture could not extort from him what he chooses to conceal; but he abhors the thought of an 'organ.'"

Carpenter saw the President do very little newspaper-reading. Many ambitious editors believed they were helping run the Government when they sent their marked copies to the White House. They might have been disappointed to hear Carpenter say the marked copies were "usually appropriated by the servants." He could recall "but a single instance of newspaper reading on the part of the President" during six months in the White House. The Washington dailies were usually laid on a convenient table. Lincoln seemed to scan the telegraphic news and let the editorials and oddities go. Nicolay and Hay were his main dependence as to what editors in general were doing for and against the Administration. In the office of the secretaries Carpenter noticed were the *Philadelphia Press* and *North American;* the *Baltimore American* and *Sun;* the *New York Tribune, Evening Post, Independent, Times, Herald,* and *World;* the *Albany Evening Journal;* the *Boston Advertiser, Journal,* and *Transcript;* the *Chicago Tribune* and *Journal* (the latter valued chiefly for the letters of its war correspondent, B. F. Taylor); the *St. Louis Republican* and *Democrat;* and the *Cincinnati Gazette* and *Commercial.*

Few were the difficulties of news-writers who knew Lincoln personally. They found him courteous, ready and willing to grant interviews, noncommittal in his replies to many questions, but anxious to go as far as his responsibilities would permit in helping them to current information. With editors and publishers such as Bennett, Greeley, Storey, he had embarrassments and stormy weather, though in these he so moved that they could not become quarrels or enmities beyond healing. He gently interceded with his generals in the field when they sometimes gave correspondents rough handling, but it was counsel and suggestion to the generals, not orders. He had no complaint over the treatment he personally received at the hands of William Howard ("Bull Run") Russell of the London *Times,* but he joined himself with those who decided it was best to exile Russell back to good old England because of Russell's overly lurid account of the Union Army panic at Manassas.

The press was seen as an institution of mixed benefits and evil results, a few editors having printed their opinion placing "newspapers and politicians" first in blame for the war. Lincoln undoubtedly agreed with whatever Artemus Ward had in mind in pointing to the aboriginal Red Men of America having "no Congress, faro banks, delirium tremens, or Associated Press."

When the State governors after a conclave in Altoona, Pennsylvania, were to hold a session with the President in December of 1862, young William A. Croffut of the *New York Tribune* asked if he could properly be present. "Certainly," was Lincoln's cheery response, according to Croffut. "You can, as far as I am concerned." Croffut felt a little out of place, as the governors were seating themselves; so as not to seem there in disguise or under false pretenses, Croffut took out his notebook, brandished pencils, and tried to look as if he was not a governor but was frankly and openly a scribe. Lincoln requested all to be seated, spoke a welcome, mentioned the Antietam victory, said he would be glad to advise with officials present. Curtin began a response, alluded to their grave errand. Governor Yates of Illinois arose and cut in to ask, looking directly at Croffut, if all present were State executives. Croffut said, "I am an exception," started to go, was pulled back by his friend Governor Buckingham of Connecticut. Buckingham said he had invited Croffut and could not conceive the session as secret. Lincoln added his information that Croffut had applied to him, was there by his consent, adding further: "We shall not say or do anything today that is secret, in any sense, and our only chance is to take the American people frankly into our confidence. However, it is for you gentlemen to say." This last Croffut felt was given "with a whimsical smile of acquiescence." But Croffut thought he saw disapproving faces, and made for the door—later getting a full account of what was done at this "executive session."

Lincoln knew by face and name perhaps every one of the news-writers and men of printer's ink assembled at a dinner they gave to Schuyler Colfax, Speaker of the House, and editor of the *South Bend* (Indiana) *Register.* One of them had written inaccurately early in '64 that Speaker Colfax favored Lincoln for a second presidential term, Colfax issuing for publication a denial that he was committed to any candidate. A few of them had been kindly and had shaded stories to favor Lincoln. Others had written doubts and misrepresentations. They were journeymen pencil-pushers, sometimes wearing out a line of lead pencils in the writing by hand of thousands of words in a single day when news broke heavy. Noah Brooks listed these as present at the complimentary dinner, the first five being special guests with Colfax: Henry Bowen Anthony, Senator from Rhode Island and former editor of the *Providence Journal;* James Brooks, member from New York and editor of the *Express;* John D. Baldwin, Representative from Massachusetts and editor of the *Worcester Spy;* Edward McPherson, clerk of the House and formerly editor of the *Harrisburg Telegraph;* Samuel Wilkeson of the *New York Times;* L. A. Gobright of the Associated Press; E. Kingman of the *New York Sun;* John R. Young of the *Philadelphia Press;* W. D. Wallach of the *Washington Star;* J. D. Defrees, Superintendent of Public Printing; D. W. Bartlett, of the *New York Evening Post;* Whitelaw Reid of the *Cincinnati Gazette;* B. P. Poore of the *Boston Journal;* J. A. Whiteley of the *New York Herald;* J. M. Ashley of the *New York Herald;* Frank Henry of the *New York Times;* Adam S. Hill of the *New York Tribune;* G. W. Adams of the *New York World;* U. H. Painter and W. B. Shaw of the *Philadelphia Inquirer;* J. B. McCullagh of the *Cincinnati Commercial;* Noah Brooks of the *Sacramento Union;* J. N. Platt of the *New York Times;* J. R. Macartney and G. C. Bower, Jr., of the *Washington Chronicle.*

Some of the "long-headed reporters," especially on New York and Philadelphia newspapers, had turned honest pennies, according to Noah Brooks, "by availing themselves of their knowledge of events not made public, telegraphing their Wall St. agents how to buy or sell." Treasury Department decisions, rulings in the Internal Revenue Bureau, the New Almaden decision of the Supreme Court, were cases where "a great deal of money was made by the knowing ones." Some reporters were spies for brokers, sending code wire messages to Wall Street. "There is every appearance of rain" might mean to "hedge" on the market. Or "The wheat crop in the west is reported to be improving" might mean Grant had won a forward movement which would affect the price of gold when the rest of the country knew about it. "It is sad," wrote Brooks. "We cannot expect to prosper while the war interest is looked upon by so many in the same light as the wheat or cotton or stock-raising interests of the country."

One jolly and bumptious news-writer printed a joke which he ascribed to the President, "a very witty and dirty and insolent pun," according to Stoddard. The President's face flushed and darkened when his eyes lighted on "the brand-new pattern of foul humor given him." He sent for the newsman, who was ushered in smiling and came out with no smile at all on his face, as Stoddard read it.

George Alfred Townsend, who had covered the McClellan and Pope campaigns for the *New York Herald* and in 1864 was permitted by the *New York World* to sign his letters and telegrams from the Army of the Potomac, told of a newspaper proprietor going to Lincoln. He had been out electioneering for the President. And what happened? "In my absence you have had my editor arrested. I won't stand it, sir. I have fought better administrations than yours." The President said he didn't know much about it: "I suppose your boys have been too enterprising. The fact is, I don't interfere with the press much, but I suppose I am responsible." The newspaper-owner insisted either his editor be released or he himself be sent to Old Capitol Prison. The President "laughed the other man into good humor," wrote Townsend, quoting Lincoln: "In fact, I am under restraint here, and am glad of any pretext to release a journalist."

"An acquaintance of mine, a printer," further wrote Townsend, "once went to Mr. Lincoln to plead for a man's life. He had never seen the man he pleaded for, and had no acquaintance with the man's family. Mr. Lincoln was touched by his disinterestedness, and said to him: 'If I were anything but the President, I would be constantly working as you have done.'" And in a commonplace way Lincoln issued a pardon. "He would," noted Townsend, "do a great deed in dishabille as promptly as in full dress. He never aimed to be brilliant."

To the White House often had come the master photographer Matthew B. Brady. Since February of 1860, at the time of the Cooper Union speech, Brady had in the autumn of 1864 photographed Lincoln more than thirty times. From his profitable portrait gallery on Broadway and Tenth, New York, Brady had come to the war with his camera. Out in the camps, on the march, and on battlefields Brady and his assistants made both single and stereoscopic wet-plate exposures and were achieving a camera record comprising thousands of convincing likenesses of scenes and people. It was said Brady urged Lincoln to have him co-operate with the Government and make as complete as possible a camera chronicle of the war for the War Department archives, and that Lincoln had refused to support the plan. As next best, Lincoln wrote and signed a heavy card with the large scrawl "Pass Brady," which took Brady nearly anywhere he cared to go.

Collections of cartes de visite, photographs of fine clarity and definition of line, mounted on small cards usually 2¼ by 3½ inches in size, were in many thousands of homes. Brady and Gardner photographs of Lincoln were often on show there. Frequently the illustrated weeklies,

Harper's and *Leslie's*, and occasionally the daily newspapers, published large drawings from photographs, so that Lincoln's face and figure had become familiar to the literate population, to those who read, and of course to some who enjoyed pictures though they read not.

Montgomery Blair told Carpenter that one of the early pictures of Lincoln, "a hideous painting," had given an unfavorable impression of the President's looks. Carpenter replied: "My friend, Brady the photographer, insisted that his photograph of Mr. Lincoln, taken the morning of the day he made his Cooper Union speech . . . was the means of his election. That it helped largely to this end I do not doubt. The effect of such influences, though silent, is powerful."

A Connecticut painter's portrait of Lincoln, done for Secretary Welles, hung temporarily on the wall of Lincoln's office. Welles, turning toward it one afternoon, said it was a successful likeness. From Lincoln came a hesitant "Yes," noted Carpenter, and a story of a Western man who had himself painted secretly and gave his wife the picture for a birthday present. "Horridly like," she pronounced it. "And that," said Lincoln, "seems to me a just criticism of *this!*"

In the Executive Mansion for the first two years no colored persons were employed. "But," wrote Brooks, "the President has succeeded in getting about him a corps of attachés of Hibernian descent." Some of them had manners and style Brooks didn't like. He wrote of the Irish coachman: "One morning the President happened to meet him at the door and asked him to go out and get the morning paper. The Jehu departed, but like the unfilial party of whom we read in Scripture, he said, 'I go' but went not. And the anxious President went out himself and invested five cents in a *Morning Chronicle*. It afterwards transpired that the coachman did not consider it his business to run errands. This coming to the President's ears he ordered up the carriage the next morning at six o'clock and sent a member of his household in the equipage to the Avenue where he bought a paper and rode back, with the mortified coachee on the box."

On Capitol Hill shone the great white dome surmounted by the woman in bronze tokening liberty. From the Capitol grounds to the White House ran the straight and wide Pennsylvania Avenue. Halfway stood Willard's Hotel. There an idler could drop in and hear anything. Often in subdued corners was talk of Colonel La Fayette C. Baker, chief of the Detective Bureau, a czar of various underworlds. He had 1,000 men, 2,000, operating under his orders, their webs and tentacles flung out among the just and the unjust. "You do not know Baker? The head of the secret service?" inquired Stoddard, who held that any man in Washington long enough, "with anything dubious about him," was known to Baker. "He sometimes comes to the White House, and he is a very useful officer, one of the long fingers of the Executive branch." None of Lincoln's closer associates recorded that he had any intimacy with Baker, whose bureau was under Stanton. Baker's grandfather, named Remember Baker, was a Revolutionary

War captain under Ethan Allen, and his father, named Green Mountain Boy Baker, was a Michigan farmer whose boy went East, then West, to become one of the most active members of the Vigilante Committee that overrode the openly lawless of San Francisco.

Early in the war La Fayette Baker had gone afoot, so he said, to Richmond, and returned with a detailed story of being arrested, jailed, and having several interviews with Jefferson Davis during his three-week trip. It became definitely known of him that he could tell a story to his own advantage, that he could be careless with facts. He was often clever—or again merely glib and loose. Stanton believed him useful in tracing conspiracies and thwarting Confederate spies. His work was naturally such that he made enemies and roused ill will. In February of '64 he came to Welles asking a pass to Fort Lafayette, saying his purpose was to get a confession from a convicted Navy Department employee. Welles wrote that from what he had heard and seen Colonel Baker was "wholly unreliable, regardless of character and the rights of persons, incapable of discrimination, and zealous to do something sensational." Senator Hale with lowered voice informed Welles that Baker "tells some things about your Chief Clerk that are very suspicious." Welles replied that Baker had "little regard for truth, believed everything bad, suspected everybody," and that he, Welles, would be answerable for the honesty of his Chief Clerk; "having heard Baker's scandal and suspicion, I requested him [Senator Hale] to bring me a fact, or find one if he could from his lying detective."

Register of the Treasury Lucius E. Chittenden pictured Baker as "cruel and rapacious"; his detectives put on the rolls "without recommendation, investigation, or any inquiry." Usually the suspect arrested was handcuffed, and brought to Baker's office, then in the basement of the Treasury building, not far underneath Chittenden's own desk and a lounging corner to which Lincoln came occasionally for rest and seclusion. There the suspect was "subjected to a brow-beating examination, in which Baker was said to rival in impudence some heads of the criminal bar," this examination being repeated as often as he, Baker, chose. "Men were kept in his rooms for weeks, without warrant, affidavit, or other semblance of authority. If the accused took any measures for his own protection, he was hurried to the Old Capitol Prison, where he was beyond the reach of the civil authorities."

These methods naturally were in the trail of war, particularly civil war. More grave was Chittenden's notation: "Corruption spread like a contagious disease, wherever the operations of these detectives extended. . . . Honest manufacturers and dealers, who paid their taxes, were pursued without mercy for the most technical breaches of the law, and were quickly driven out of business. The dishonest rapidly accumulated wealth, which they could well afford to share with their protectors." Turning to a concrete and detailed instance, Chittenden wrote of catching Colonel Baker in the act of forgery and "Perfectly unabashed, without a blush, the fellow smiled as he looked me in the face and said, 'That game didn't work, did it?' " This was the secret-service head who once said he had 2,000 men working their ramifications inside and outside Washington, reporting to him their findings, and he at the central controls.

Baker had a way of talking and writing as though he were a confidant and a trusted operative of the President, as though the President often sent for Baker, and unbosomed himself of some difficulty on which Baker then went out and got action. "I was sent for by Mr. Lincoln," Baker would say. Or he would write, "I was summoned to report in person to Mr. Lincoln," or, "I was summoned to the White House." And though he sought to convey an impression that he was often consulted on weighty matters, there was no record of the President writing any communication to Baker or to anyone else about Baker. In the hundreds of cases handled by Baker there was no occasion for Lincoln at any time to say in writing directly or indirectly whether Baker's work was meritorious or whether Baker himself was worthy of trust. Probably the President did, as Baker alleged in writing, personally ask for an investigation of reports of brutal treatment of slaves in lower Maryland. And it was probably true that Baker laid before Lincoln the case of 110 slaves belonging to a Maryland planter who had been convicted of aiding the enemy and sentenced to two years in Fort Delaware. "I did not like to assume the responsibility of their liberation," said the chief of the Detective Bureau to the President, quoting the President as replying, "Baker, let them alone, and they will free themselves!"

Undoubtedly Baker sent to the President a report on lower Maryland, weak in particulars, but heavy with a general indictment of Maryland planters that might excuse any methods of raid or seizure that Baker employed against them. The colored people, wrote the detective chief, were "daily subjected to a more ferocious despotism, and more flagrant and shameless outrages, than were ever before tolerated by any Government. . . . Depredators in Washington, D.C., break into the houses of colored citizens, thrust loaded pistols into the faces of terrified women and screaming children."

Lincoln possibly studied the motive behind one paragraph regarding armed bands from Maryland pursuing slaves into the District of Columbia. Baker wrote: "Not less than forty slaves (human beings), by these lawless encounters, were killed; and I have information, that no less than three dead bodies of slaves, thus cruelly slaughtered, are now lying in the woods almost within sight of your own house." Thus in a matter of wholesale murder Baker preferred to be meagerly circumstantial, leaving the information vague, but setting up general charges. Baker, it seemed, wished Lincoln would picture to himself the bodies of three murdered Negro slaves "lying in the woods almost within sight of your own house," seemingly unaware that Lincoln's mental picture would have been helped by the added information that the bodies of the murdered Negroes were lying in woods north toward Rock Creek, northwest toward the Bladensburg Turnpike, or in some other direction and locality. This was like Baker. He could be vague and blatant toward his own end. Where he went on his searches and seizures he was the Law and the Power unless those he dealt with could go higher up.

In one case, according to Baker, he had arrested the son of an influential Pennsylvania politician for fraud in a government contract, and the father had reached the President, who sent for the detective chief. Baker asked and got permission from the President to hold the prisoner twelve more hours. During those twelve hours Baker got from the prisoner a confession and a return of money of which the Government had been defrauded, and according to Baker, this was "but a solitary instance, among many others of a similar kind." He made his reports to Stanton, verbally. Stanton rated him an able sleuth. Baker portrayed himself as not having tasted intoxicating liquors in twenty years, nor having on any occasion indulged in profanity. He warned the keepers of cheap saloons on "two sides of an entire square occupied by the lowest places of intoxication" that they must close the next day at four o'clock, then bided his time, having given them many previous notices about their closing hour. "At the expiration of the appointed time, with my employees, all armed with axes, I proceeded to the dens of Bacchus, and commenced the work of destruction. Soon the long lines of liquor shops were leveled to the ground, and only broken and empty barrels, crushed decanters, and rubbish remained." In Baker's phrasing there were at the time in Washington "not less than three thousand, seven hundred such fountains of ruin in active operation." In this matter he seemed to have had no interview with the President.

But in the field of gambling Baker noted that the President sent for him and opened the meeting, "Well, Baker, what is the trouble between you and the gamblers?" Baker finished his explanations with the remark, "I cannot fight the gamblers and the Government both," the President assuring him, "You won't have to fight *me*." After which Baker went forth and cleaned out the gamblers of Washington, to hear him tell it, or in Baker's words, "The result was, the business was effectually spoiled in Washington."

A trade in bawdy photographs and smutty literature, carried on by "human vampires," a "fiendish business of ruining the morals and bodies of men," was uncovered by Baker. With the approval of the Post Office Department he searched mailbags and found large quantities of these "vile goods" on their way to the army, purchase-price value estimated at $22,000. Of the outcome Baker wrote: "It was decided to make a bonfire of this sensual trash. Our pure-minded President intimated that he would like to see the conflagration. It was kindled in front of the White House, and he enjoyed the sight, with the zest of a noble nature, to which vice was a loathing." Of this curious incident, which would have been spectacular as a scene, Baker seemed to be the only recorder. And the White House bonfire of bawdy photographs may have existed in no other mind but that of the fertile detective chief who so often overdramatized his role. As though it actually happened, he told of the capture of a woman spy at Fairfax Court-House who had wormed herself into the confidence of Union

Army staff officers boarding in the same house. The Confederate Government had issued to her a commission as a spy, according to Baker. "This document, in its original form, was found through the confidence reposed by Miss F. [the supposed spy] in a female subordinate in my bureau. Miss F. opened her heart to the young adventurer and also her bed, in which between the mattress and its nether companion, was concealed the prized and useful paper. It was found there when the fair spy was arrested by my order.

"The work of the detective," ran Baker's definition, "is simply deception reduced to a science or profession." He took pride in his disguises, glibly recounted how he could swiftly change from a loafer in slouch hat to an honest farmer, a Jew peddler, or a mumbling drunk, and the disguise would pass. To hear him tell it he had repeatedly sprung at a man about to fire on him, disarmed the man and arrested him; or he could handcuff a desperado with a left hand while keeping him covered with a pistol in the right hand. But for treachery and corruption in other departments of the Government Baker with his bureau alone would have ended bounty-jumping, so his narrative implied. He pictured himself the heroic foe of "traitors, Copperheads, scoundrels, and rebels," not to mention Confederate spies, fraudulent contractors, draft-evaders, forgers of draft papers, saloon-keepers, gamblers, dealers in bawdy pictures. His habitual boasting won Lincoln's habitual mistrust of the secret-service head.

Blue Room, East Room, Red Room, Green Room, long and stately with lofty ceilings, with gas chandeliers spreading like huge jungle flowers of glass further decked with glittering balloons of whitened glass—these on the downstairs floor of the White House overlooked much small talk and idle chatter. Under them passed many polite persons, some wearing masks over hidden intentions, some with little or no purpose in life worth trying to mask. To an occasional farmer the deep carpets stretched from wall to wall gave his feet an illusion of walking on air. The gilt scrollwork across doorways, Japanese screens, fireplaces, spoke across the rooms to niched palms, fern table arrangements, little bronze statues, and lambrequins. In satin-covered ebony chairs, in gold and blue furniture, the visitors could sit and gaze at special porcelain importations from foreign Ministers, at wide mantels, rosewood bureaus, mirrors now in vertical lengths and then in horizontal, paintings of age and dignity that hid large expanses of wall-paper. In the President's private dining-room were cabinets holding the china, glass, and silver pieces used for state dinners. These were bought and installed under the Lincoln Administration, and included dishes of porcelain with purple and gold decorations, an eagle with full wingspread mounted on a shield having below it the scroll "E Pluribus Unum."

Seven o'clock strictly was the hour for state dinners, according to the Department of State. On request it furnished the White House with elaborate details on the requirements of tradition and accepted form. Advice ran that one must never say "Sir" to a titled foreigner. Gentlemen should wear "coat, black dress, or ditto blue with bright buttons." A frock coat was in bad taste. "At evening calls of diplomats it is well for the President to go down." Thus on the downstairs floor of the White House. Upstairs in the western end of the building lived the Lincoln family and servants. The offices were upstairs in the east end. At times the stairways leading up were blocked with callers and curiosity-seekers bent on real or imaginary errands.

From this little labyrinth of traditions the tale went forth and became published as fact that Senator Sumner strolled in to find the President polishing his own boots.

SUMNER. Why, Mr. President, do you black your own boots?

THE PRESIDENT. Whose boots did you think I blacked?

Congressman Alley's version ran that Salmon Portland Chase found Lincoln rubbing his leather footwear with a brush. Remarks were exchanged.

"Mr. Lincoln, gentlemen don't black their own boots."

"Whose boots do they black?"

Here in this labyrinth was need for concentration. Once near midnight came the Canadian ornithologist A. M. Ross, whose services had been solicited by Senator Sumner, bringing the President letters that had been found addressed to or written by Confederate conspirators on the Canadian border. The President welcomed Ross, who spoke regrets at arriving so late at night. "I then laid before the President the 'rebel mail.' He carefully examined the address of each letter, making occasional remarks. At length he found one addressed to Franklin Pierce, ex-President of the United States, then residing in New Hampshire; and another to ex-Attorney-General Caleb Cushing, a resident of Massachusetts. He appeared much surprised, and remarked with a sigh, but without the slightest tone of asperity, 'I will have these letters enclosed in official envelopes and sent to these parties.' When he had finished examining the addresses, he tied up all those addressed to private individuals, saying, 'I won't bother with them; but these look like official letters; I guess I'll go through them now.' He then opened them and read their contents slowly and carefully." Ross studied Lincoln's face. "A marked change had taken place since my first interview with him. He looked much older, bore traces of months of painful anxiety and trouble. Wrinkles about eyes and forehead were deeper, the lips firmer."

On Lincoln's finishing his reading of the letters, Ross said he would go. The President said it was now three o'clock in the morning, led Ross to a bedroom, told Ross to take a good sleep. At eleven o'clock—before Ross had breakfast in the morning—Lincoln told Ross that he had studied over the intercepted letters till daylight, that they seemed to coincide with news received by Secretary Stanton, with whom he was to have a conference that morning on Canadian-border plots.

After breakfast Ross entered Lincoln's room to find him writing busily, "at the same time repeating in a low voice the words of a poem which I remembered reading many years before." He passed the sheet of written verses to Ross. "Have you ever read them?" Ross said he had, many years ago, and that he should be pleased to have a copy in Lincoln's handwriting when Lincoln had time and inclination for such work. "Well, you may keep the copy, if you wish." The matter was almost as though after a night of little sleep it rested Lincoln to copy these verses now become ancient to him.

The parallels of telegraphic instantaneous communication and certain operations of the human mind and eye became the subject for a little discourse from Lincoln one day in the telegraph office. He had been reading aloud from a printed page and was led on into talk, as David Homer Bates noted it, of numerous and sometimes radically different impressions communicated from eye to brain and then back to the vocal organs by means of the most delicate nerves. His contemplation ran that the eye may rest at the same instant not only upon a single letter of the alphabet, but upon a series of letters forming a given word, and upon a moving procession of words in a sentence, and not only that, but the resultant record of all these numerous and different impressions is translated by the brain into thought and sent back, telegraphed as it were, to the organs of speech, each organ selecting its own particular message, the whole sentence then being spoken aloud even while the eye is still resting upon the printed page. Lincoln was then pondering the same intricacies of certain mental operations he had discussed in his lecture on "Discoveries and Inventions" in Springfield a few years before.

Going over a series of pardon papers one morning with Judge Advocate General Holt, Lincoln added the date to one document, and "Does your mind, Judge Holt, associate events with dates? Every time this morning that I have had occasion to write the day of the month, the thought has come up, 'This was General Harrison's birthday.' "

In the White House he had arranged a mirror and a couch and repeated the experiment performed in his home in Springfield in 1860 when his eye saw distinctly two images of himself, one more pale than the other. "I tried to produce the same effect *here*," Carpenter quoted him . . . "without success." At first when he had casually seen this double image of himself in the mirror he had been disturbed about it, almost superstitious. Later, as it seemed to Carpenter, he was inclined to believe it was a natural phenomenon of refraction and optics that could be accounted for on scientific principles.

The President of the Sanitary Commission, the Reverend Dr. Henry Whitney Bellows, was ushered into Lincoln's office to find the President signing a pile of documents. He had nodded to Dr. Bellows, and then gone on scanning papers, dipping his pen and writing his signature, well aware that Dr. Bellows had come again on a matter pressed with powerful backing: the appointment of Dr. William Alexander Hammond to be Surgeon General of the United States Army. While the President went on with his routine duty Dr. Bellows spoke. For ten or fifteen minutes he argued in favor of the appointment of Hammond. As Dr. Bellows himself told it, he had nearly run out of breath, and Lincoln's pen was still traveling along signing away at the documents, when Lincoln spoke as he was writing:

Lincoln. Photograph by Brady, February 9, '64

The President's wife in ceremonial costume

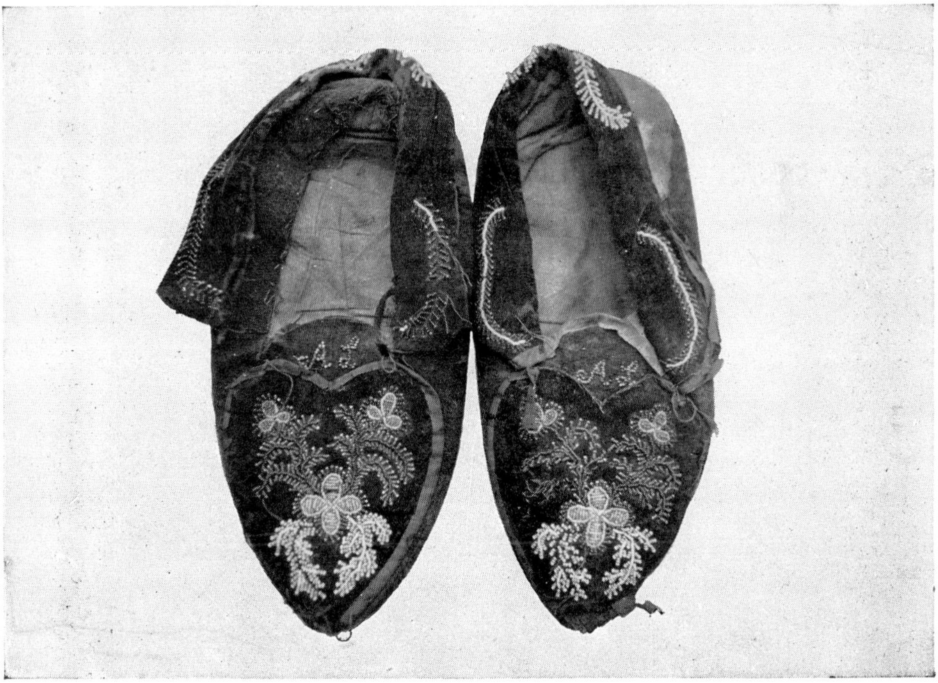

Beaded, initialed moccasin slippers worn by Lincoln

Originals in the Barrett collection

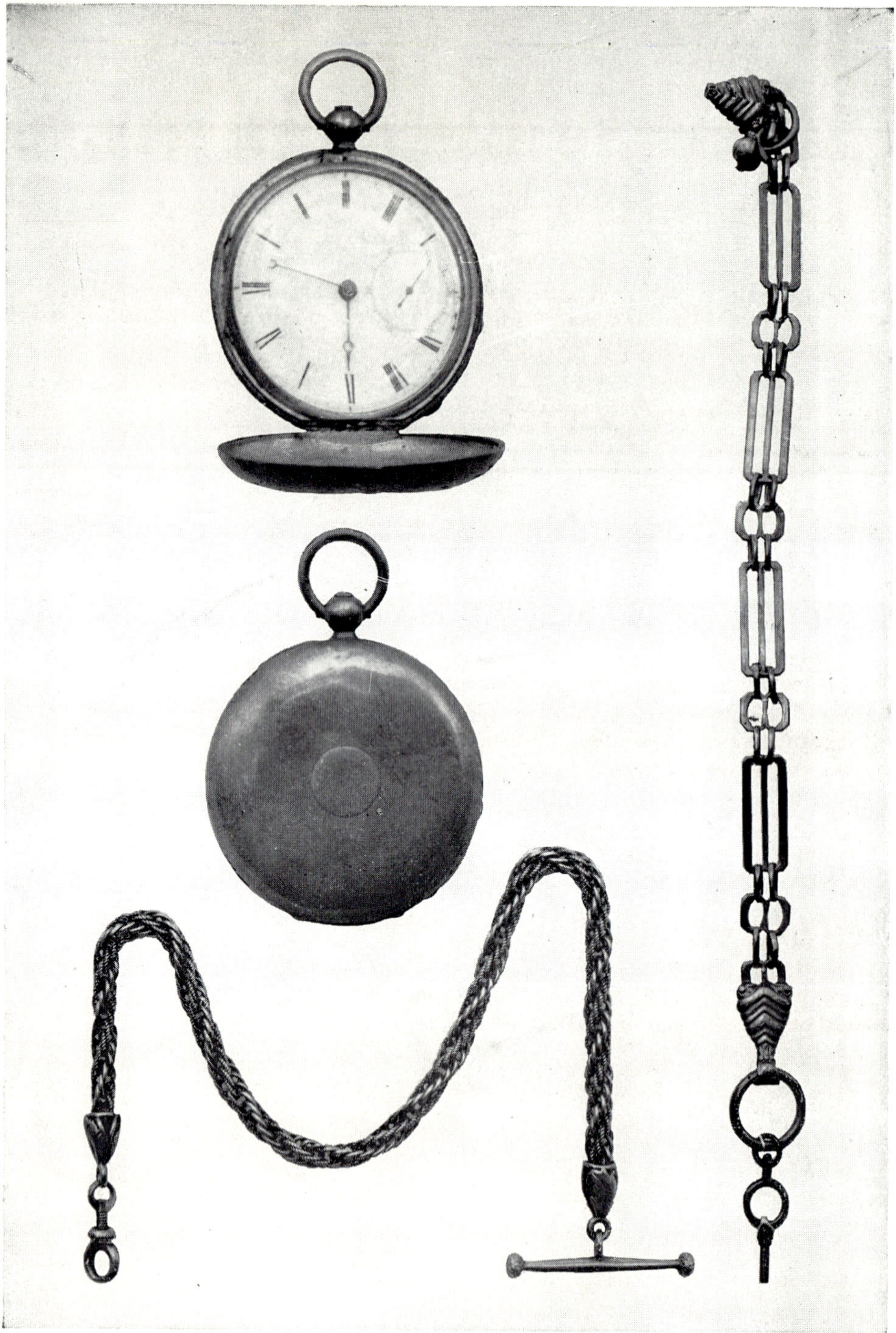

Lincoln's watch used by him during three war years, a silver Waltham case No. E279, William Ellery movement, key winder No. 67613, presented in '64 to Dennis Hanks with the chain at the right; looped below, the gold chain presented to Lincoln by a California delegation

Originals in the Barrett collection

"Shouldn't wonder if Hammond was at this moment 'Surgeon-General,' and had been for some time."

"You don't mean to say, Mr. President, that the appointment has been made?"

"I may say to you"—for the first time looking up—"that it *has;* only you needn't *tell* of it just yet."

A dusty and worn dispatch-bearer with secret papers of importance handed them to the President seated alone in his office. And young Major Gerrard Whitehead of the Philadelphia City Troop took a seat where the President motioned him and watched the President fall into a deep study, lost entirely in the revelations of the dispatches.

"The one window of the room was open," ran Whitehead's account. "Across the sultry sky came up heavy thunder clouds. The storm broke and rain began to pour into the room. The officer did not think of moving while the Commander-in-Chief of the Army was so engrossed. So he sat and watched the rain form a pool on the floor and slowly trickle across it, almost to the feet of the President, absorbed and unconscious. At last Mr. Lincoln made his decision, seemed to rouse from his deep reflections and becoming conscious of the young despatch bearer, told him to return in an hour, when the answering despatch would be ready for him."

On other and different occasions Lincoln kept a weather eye on his caller, as when in April of '64 press items told of "the lunatic who harangued the President, claiming to have been elected President in 1856." And again when an incoherent individual styling himself "Major General of the Anti-Renters," babbled that he had been imprisoned in "Castle Thunder" in Richmond, raved over vast schemes to end the war, and was led away and adjudged insane. Or again the moment reported by Lieutenant George C. Ashmun of the 7th Indiana Troop of cavalry escorting the President's carriage to the Soldiers' Home one evening when suddenly a saber scabbard clattered against a wheel spoke "causing Mr. Lincoln's face to appear at the carriage window with a questioning look."

That the President's earlier suspicions of Count Adam Gurowski were partly justified was seen in August of '64 when that neurotic growler was locked up in a police station and after a hearing before a magistrate was fined $5. Witnesses testified that Gurowski had "attempted to discipline" the Washington Fire Department. Yelling that they were moving too slow toward the conflagration, "he drew a pistol on the firemen to make them run faster." In the same week Gurowski wrote in his diary of a national fast day named by the President, "Well, the people may fast to propitiate Divine Providence, but what kind of atonement shall Lincoln and his associates practice that God may forgive them?"

In December of '63 the Pennsylvania infantry guards on White House duty were reinforced by the Union Light Guard, officially known as the 7th Independent Company of Ohio Volunteer Cavalry. Governor David Tod of Ohio had organized the company with picked men for the special service of bodyguard and mounted escort for the President, performing errands of trust in and about Washington. The company barracks were on Fifteenth Street immediately south of the Treasury building, with stables on the north side of East Street. One evening Robert W. McBride, serving as corporal of the guard, picketed his horse in the rear of the White House and was standing in the driveway of the front portico. As he stood there he saw the President come out alone and walk to the edge of the portico where the steps began. There under a lighted gas jet the President stood, alone. His hands behind him, he stood there in a reverie. A few feet away, across the driveway, Corporal McBride had drawn his saber and stood at attention. As a corporal it was his duty to stand at attention and salute any officer, and particularly the Commander in Chief of the armies of the United States.

"Just how long he stood there I do not know," said McBride. "I know he stood there so long I became very tired." It was to McBride as though, were some marksman hidden anywhere, the President wished to make himself a perfect target by standing alone in the full light of the gas jet. But after a time, possibly several minutes, he came down the steps, and hardly seeming to notice the corporal, nevertheless gravely lifted his hat as a return salute and walked toward the War Department, alone. In about a half-hour he came back, alone.

Having noticed these things, Corporal McBride was not surprised later to hear of a plan to kidnap the President "by seizing him on a dark night while in the shadows of the park, lifting him over the brick wall that bordered the south side of the pathway, and hurrying him across the Treasury Park to a vacant house belonging to a rebel sympathizer where he could be kept concealed in the cellar until taken across the Potomac in a boat." The plan, McBride believed, "was practicable, and I have never understood why it was abandoned."

Stanton's anxiety over the President's safety continued. He gave one standing order. Although the President might come at midnight alone, as happened often, he should never be permitted to return alone, but must be escorted by a file of four soldiers and a noncommissioned officer. "I was on duty every other night," wrote Henry W. Knight, in charge of the guard at the War Department. "When Mr. Lincoln was ready to return we would take up a position near him, and accompany him safely to the White House. I presume I performed this duty fifty times. One night about one o'clock when it was raining very hard, he started back. As he saw us at the door, 'Don't come out in this storm with me tonight, boys, I have my umbrella and can get home safely without you.'" "But," replied Knight, "Mr. President, we have positive orders from Mr. Stanton not to allow you to return alone; and you know we dare not disobey his orders." "No, I suppose not; for if Stanton should learn that you had let me return alone, he would have you court-martialed and shot inside of twenty-four hours."

During the autumn of '64 the cavalry guard at the Soldiers' Home was cautioned repeatedly to be "extremely vigilant," and according to its lieu tenant, George C. Ashmun, "the whole company was kept under arms with horses saddled," ready for any night disturbance. The President was leaving the house late at night, taking solitary walks. Of one Lincoln ramble alone under the stars Ashmun noted: "One beautiful Indian Summer night, about 12 o'clock, as I was returning across the grounds from a visit to one of our pickets who had fired at something, I saw a man walking leisurely and alone across the path I was taking. As I came nearer I saw it was Mr. Lincoln. At an earlier hour I would have kept from speaking, but, prompted

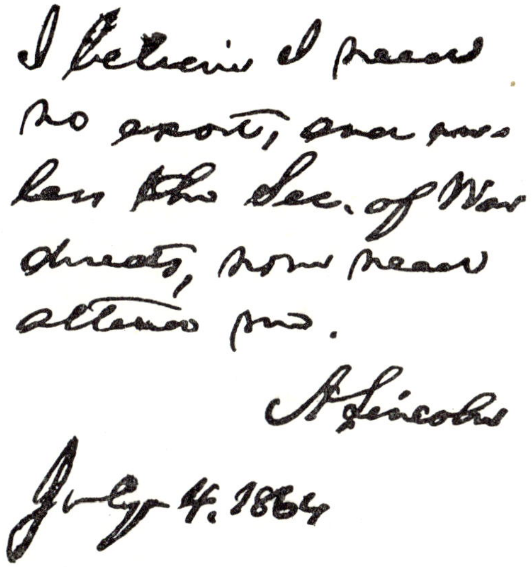

On an officer's provisional order for an escort Lincoln writes: "I believe I need no escort, and unless the Sec. of War directs, none need attend me." Original in the Barrett collection.

by anxiety, I said, 'Mr. President, isn't it rather risky to be out here at this hour?' He answered, 'Oh, I guess not—I couldn't rest and thought I'd take a walk.' He was quite a distance outside the line of infantry guards about the house where the family was staying. He turned back after I spoke to him, and I passed on to where the escort was camped."

Four police officers in November of '64 were detailed by the chief of police of the District of Columbia, to serve as special guards for the President. They were John F. Parker, Alfonso Dunn, Alexander Smith, and Thomas Pendel. On Pendel's later being appointed doorkeeper, that vacancy was filled by William H. Crook. In the usual routine, according to Crook, two of these police officers were on duty from eight in the morning to four in the afternoon, guarding the approach to the President's office or whatever room he might be in, and supposedly accompanying him on any walks he might take. At four in the afternoon another man went on duty till midnight, or later if the President had gone outside the White House and not returned. At midnight the second night guard went on duty and stayed till relieved at eight in the morning. "We were all armed with revolvers," noted Crook. "The night guards were expected to protect the President on his expeditions to and from the War Department, or while he was at any place of amusement, and to patrol the corridor outside his room while he slept." From this description of the duties of the guards, it seemed that on the night when Corporal McBride saw the President come out alone and walk to and from the War Office alone, the President had either eluded the guard on duty, or instructed the guard to let him go alone—or else the guard was off duty from sickness or from neglect of duty.

Surmise still went on as to the extent or reality of the alleged plot to kill Lincoln on his expected visit to Baltimore in February of '61. A former Baltimorean named Byrne, a gambler by profession, being arrested and put on trial in Richmond on the charge of keeping a gambling house, was released on the representations of Wigfall of Texas. Several constructions could be placed on a *Providence Journal* item which seemed to assume that Wigfall was a responsible witness. The gist of the item was that "Wigfall testified to Byrne's loyalty to the rebel cause, and gave in evidence that Byrne was captain of the gang who were to kill Mr. Lincoln, and upon this evidence, it appears, he was let go."

In March and April of '64 the *New York Tribune* gave the country several news letters from a Washington correspondent who named one Colonel Margrave as having submitted to the Confederate War Department plans to kidnap President Lincoln and carry him to Richmond, "or if it should be found impossible to escape with him to the rebel lines, to assassinate him." One hundred and fifty picked men were to go secretly north, take quarters in Washington, Georgetown, Baltimore, and Alexandria. On a day when notified by their leader they were to join up in Washington, where, it was claimed, "the President could be easily seized at a quiet hour, at the White House, or in going to or returning from church, or on some other favorable occasion, and thrust into a carriage and driven off." Twenty-five or thirty armed men on horseback, waiting outside the city, would escort the carriage to Indian Point on the Potomac, about twenty-five miles south of Washington, where a waiting boat would cross the river and land the captive a few miles south of Occoquan. From there they would work their way through the woods by night to the Confederate Army lines. To stop pursuit, every bridge between Washington and Indian Point was to be mined, and after captive and captors had crossed, blown up. Huge trees were to be sawed ready for quick toppling across the roads, to embarrass pursuers. "The Secretary of War [at Richmond] thought this scheme might succeed," wrote the *New York Tribune* correspondent. "But he doubted whether such a proceeding would be of a military character and justifiable under the laws of war. He promised, however, to consult the President and Mrs. Benjamin; but what conclusion was arrived at I am unable with certainty to say."

The correspondent further had been in Richmond, so he wrote, and had talked with a Confederate War Department clerk there named Wellford, "familiar with all the secrets of the Department." To his question whether Colonel Margrave's plan to kidnap Lincoln had been adopted, Wellford answered, "You will see Old Abe here in the spring as sure as God." Also, wrote the correspondent, he had come into possession of a letter addressed to Wellford by a North Carolina captain signing the name of Cullum, writing that "the *ruse de guerre* to capture 'Honest Abe' " interested him, that his wounded arm was nearly well, that "I would willingly sell my soul to the devil for the honor of playing a conspicuous part in the destruction of the *great hydra*." The letter quoted a member of the Confederate Congress as saying "the affair would probably be managed by individual enterprise rather than by the Government." Regarding Colonel Margrave, the correspondent would say on good authority he was a native of South Carolina whose real name was Rhett, that he had been wounded at Shiloh, that he was "one of the most cool and reckless villains in the Confederacy—one who can smile and murder while he smiles."

The story was inconclusive, did not quite stand up, yet was taken in some circles friendly to Lincoln as having some basis—"Where there is so much smoke there must be some fire." The *New York World* said: "This ridiculous canard was telegraphed all over the country, and has found its way into nearly every journal in the land. It is absurd on its face. Mr. Lincoln is of much more service to the rebels where he is than if they had him in Richmond. If by any lucky accident the rebels could bag the whole administration, including Lincoln, Welles, Stanton and Chase, we believe the North would experience a sense of relief, as there would then be an excellent prospect of a speedy ending of the war." A reply to this viewpoint came from the *Tribune* correspondent in a news letter: "The same copperhead journals that pretend to doubt my revelations of schemes to kidnap or assassinate President Lincoln, have never questioned with a single line the statements with which the Southern papers recently teemed, of plots on the part of Yankee spies and Union men in Richmond to assassinate Jeff. Davis. They can readily believe that Union men are capable of murdering the rebel President, but they cannot believe that rebels would be guilty of murdering the Union President."

The Margrave scheme to kidnap the Union President was not the only one he had heard of, wrote the *Tribune* correspondent. A group of "wealthy citizens" in Richmond had started a fund toward the undertaking; circulars inviting subscriptions had been mailed to trustworthy Confederates elsewhere, "and an immense sum of money was subscribed," Maury & Company, Richmond bankers, underwriting $10,000, Sumner & Arents, Richmond auctioneers, $5,000. "One man in Charleston, South Carolina, whose name I have forgotten, subscribed $20,000." Allegations of the correspondent were many, his evidence scant. On one point he was insistent. "Whether these schemes have been abandoned, or whether the kidnappers are only awaiting a favorable opportunity to execute them, remains to be seen; but certain it is that too much caution cannot be observed by the President, or the military commanders stationed at the Capital."

According to a legend accepted by Georgia Confederates who were Unionist at heart, one kidnapping plot did reach a point where Lincoln went with two Confederate operatives into a carriage waiting at the White House, Lincoln riding away with them, Lincoln trading hats with the one who mounted the driver's seat, each side outwitting the other and parting good friends. In the course of the incident Lincoln was reminded of the man who set out to play ghost in a Western village. "He had tolerable success, until he happened to run across a crabbed old fellow who had a good deal of money out at interest. The ghost says, 'Squire Brown, you've got too much money. What'll you do with it when you die?' Squire Brown gripped his hickory, and says, 'You talk lots too natural for a ghost,' and with that he lit in and frailed the fellow out."

The kidnapping Georgians were won to Lincoln as he was won to them. "Down our way," said one of the Georgians, "they say you're a Yankee, but if that's so, the woods is full of Yankees in Georgia, all born and raised right there." And again, "I can only say this, Mr. President, that if the plain people of the South knew you as well as we know you, the war wouldn't last much longer." Whereupon Lincoln spoke of the blood cost of a war of brothers and of his hope for Union and peace. Joel Chandler Harris, a Georgian, wove the tale intricately and persuasively as though it came to him from participants in a fine piece of folly. Harris believed that in the year 1863, the time of the adventure, Lincoln hoped for a reunited nation whose wounds were to be healed, that Lincoln was pleased to circumvent a plot for his kidnapping which had been instigated by a Union secret-service man seeking personal advancement. It was precisely the sort of an affair which, if it happened anything like the way Harris told it, would during the war have been kept confidential by all concerned. Harris's preparation for his portrayal of Lincoln in this story was indicated in a letter of his to E. A. Townsend: "I have most of my ideas of Abraham Lincoln from a long talk I once had with Alexander H. Stephens. . . . Mr. Stephens was a fine talker, and he drew Lincoln's portrait for me much as [Sir Walter] Scott draws some of his characters. . . . It was Lincoln who said to Mr. Stephens, 'Put a man in my place and every weakness he has will grow a beard.' "

Of an odd affair about mid-August of '64, nothing should be said of it, ran Lincoln's advice to John W. Nichols, a guard from the summer of 1862. Nichols, on duty at the large gate entrance to the Soldiers' Home grounds, one night about eleven o'clock heard a rifle shot in the direction of the city and soon after heard the hoofbeats of a horse coming nearer and nearer. In two or three minutes a horse came dashing up. On it Nichols saw the President, bareheaded, and Nichols helped to quiet a favorite saddle horse. The President was now saying: "He came pretty near getting away with me, didn't he? He got the bit in his teeth before I could draw rein." To Nichols's query about his hat the President answered that somebody had fired a gun off down at the foot of the hill, and that his horse had become scared and had jerked his hat off.

Nichols led the horse to the executive cottage, held it while the President dismounted and went into the house, then saw the horse to the stables. Nichols with a corporal began a search for the hat. At a point where the sound of the shot had come from, a driveway intersection with the main road, they found the President's hat, the familiar plain silk stovepipe. "Upon examination," proceeded Nichols's story, "we discovered a *bullet-hole* through the crown. We searched the locality thoroughly, but without avail. Next day I gave Mr. Lincoln his hat, and called his attention to the bullet-hole. He made some humorous remark, to the effect that it was made by some foolish marksman and was not intended for him; but added that he wished nothing said about the matter. We all felt confident it was an attempt to kill the President, and after that he never rode alone."

This made twice that Lincoln lost his hat while riding, having joked with Lamon about the previous occasion. Lamon's continuous warnings went unheeded. In latter '64 Lamon in exasperation sent in a letter of resignation. Lincoln would not accept it. In this Lamon wrote: "To-night, as you have done on several previous occasions, you went unattended to the theatre. When I say unattended, I mean you went alone with Charles Sumner and a foreign minister, neither of whom could defend himself against assault from any able-bodied woman in this city. And you know, or ought to know, that your life is sought after and will be taken unless you and your friends are cautious."

To the theatre Lincoln continued to go. Though warned that he was making himself too easy a target, he went on playgoing. He was aware too of the murmurings of clergymen who disapproved of his moral support of the playhouse. His political opposition seized on it. "The fact comes to be reported," said the *Detroit Free Press* of February 4, 1864, "that President Lincoln spends almost every other evening of the week at some of our city theaters. A good play is not a bad thing, of course, but it is very poor business for the President of the United States to be constantly appearing before the public as a sight-seer, when our poor country is convulsed to its foundation by intestine war." The friendly *Chicago Journal* on August 25, 1864, told of street corners in Washington blazoned with large posters reading: "Ford's Theatre: His Excellency, the President of the United States: Friday Evening," the account proceeding: "The impression was a little queer, thus putting His Excellency where the original Christy ought to be, but approaching the bill you discover a line in very young type that clears up the mystery: 'Has Accepted an Invitation to be Present.' "

One Hay diary entry read: "Spent the evening at the theatre with President, Mrs. L., Mrs. Hunter, Cameron and Nicolay. J. Wilkes Booth in the 'Marble Heart.' Rather tame than otherwise."

Alone often, yet again with varied companions, Tad or Mrs. Lincoln, or Hay, Brooks, Sumner, and others, the President went to the drama, visiting Grover's Theatre perhaps a hundred times since coming to Washington. When there was opera at Grover's, Mrs. Lincoln invariably attended with the President. "Do you know, Mr. Grover, I really enjoy a minstrel show?" was Lincoln's suggestion once, and when Grover at the White House later named the next list of attractions he mentioned that Hooley's Minstrels would follow after the regular season had closed. "So you remembered that," laughed Lincoln. "Well, that was thoughtful of you." Grover's boy picked up an acquaintance with Tad, five years older, helped furnish Tad's miniature theatre upstairs in the White House, fished out goldfish from the Executive Mansion fountains, and one day the two of them tricked up as two little red devils, in costumes stolen from the Grover Theatre wardrobe, marched up Pennsylvania Avenue having fun with the sidewalk public.

Once in '64 Tad quietly slipped away from his father, seated in a box at Grover's. The next the father saw of Tad his boy walked out on the stage with a chorus singing "The Battle Cry of Freedom," Tad half lost in a Union Army blue uniform blouse. The play titled *The Seven Sisters* was billed as a "spectacular extravaganza" depicting "the birth of Cupid" and showing the pranks of "the seven daughters of Satan" who had escaped from the lower regions. The star John McDonough recognized Tad, walked over and placed a large silk flag in his hands. And the boy waved it before the cheering audience as the chorus sang, "We are coming, Father Abraham, three hundred thousand more."

Sitting alone in a box one evening, Lincoln sent word for Grover to join him a while. A half-hour passed and Stanton entered unannounced. Lincoln introduced Grover to Stanton, and according to Grover: "I was about to withdraw, when Mr. Lincoln asked me impressively to remain. Inferring that my presence might be useful to him, I sat slightly behind them and in the center, leaving the President in front nearest the stage, and the Secretary beside him and slightly to his left. Mr. Stanton immediately began a conversation in a low tone of voice, the nature of which I made it my business not to hear. Mr. Lincoln responded in a short sentence and let his eyes drift away to the stage. Mr. Stanton resumed in a longer statement. Mr. Lincoln turned quietly, nodded two or three times gently, and again his eyes sought the stage. This was repeated, Mr. Stanton's speeches, always low, as both were in sight of the audience, growing in length, and Mr. Lincoln listening, nodding in an affable manner that said neither yes nor no, and then turning to the stage. This continued for some minutes until Mr. Lincoln's nods grew more infrequent, till finally he would do the nodding while his face was turned away, and he was apparently occupied with the performance. Then Mr. Stanton twice deliberately reached out, grasped Mr. Lincoln by the lapel of his coat, slowly pulled him round face to face, and continued the conversation. Mr. Lincoln responded to this brusque act with all the smiling geniality that one might bestow on a similar act from a favorite child, but soon again turned his eyes to the stage. I had pushed myself a little to the rear, to indicate that I was not listening, and in fact, I don't think I heard a word from first to last. I imagined that Mr. Stanton might be pursuing a subject that Mr. Lincoln had come away from the White House to avoid, and that Mr. Lincoln was not so much interested in the play, as desirous that Mr. Stanton should think he was. Finally impressed with the futility of his efforts, Mr. Stanton arose, said goodnight, and withdrew. Mr. Lincoln vouchsafed no explanation to me, but appeared to get much satisfaction out of the play."

The eminent actors Lester Wallack and Edward Loomis Davenport played in *Macbeth* one evening, Lincoln in a box with Tad. Malcolm had pronounced the lines, "Let us seek out some desolate shade and there Weep our sad bosoms empty." Macduff gave response: "Each new morn New widows howl, new orphans cry, new sorrows Strike heaven on the face." One commentator wrote that after these lines Mr. Lincoln leaned back in his chair out of the lights into the shadows, "and for a long time wore a sad, sober face, as if suddenly his thoughts had wandered from the playroom far away to where his great armies were contesting."

Between acts at Grover's Theatre groups of seats emptied and bars of near-by saloons lined with patrons. Out of doorways staggered drunken men, sometimes cursing the Emancipation Proclamation and its maker. "Scenes of violence with pistol and knife were of frequent occurrence," wrote Grover of "the immediate neighborhood of my theatre." The provost guard arrested loose talkers. For some months just after the Emancipation Proclamation was issued "much feeling was shown in Washington against that measure by many officers of the army," noted Grover, and, "with the prevailing sentiment against emancipation, threats of violence against its author were not uncommon." Grover understood that his theatre was not the safest place in Washington for the President to go so often. And his own guess was that the President might not have gone so often had he realized what was the talk in the near-by saloons; he believed "that Mr. Lincoln was in ignorance of the prevailing temper."

To Grover's one night came Mr. and Mrs. Lincoln with Speaker Colfax, and no guard or other company. Grover met them at the curb, conducted them from their carriage through a private passage to their box. After the play he took them by the same passage to the street, where they found a crowd of more than a hundred jeering and laughing around the President's carriage. Grover opened the carriage door, handed his guests in, and then studied a scene both comic and sad.

Up on the box of the carriage holding the reins of two spirited horses sat a one-armed boy. That the President of the United States should have his horses and carriage in charge of a boy was curious, and that the boy should have only one arm to drive with, this was funny. They did not know that the boy had been a drummer in the army and had his arm shot off in battle and had then been given a place in the White House service. The crowd did see, however, that the one-armed boy was not the regular coachman. The drunken young man jabbering with a fuddled Irish dialect, clumsy from strong liquor, trying to climb up the wheel and onto the box, this was the regular coachman. Three hours before he had been invited for a few drinks, had left his horses in charge of the one-armed drummer boy and was now trying to climb up where he could drive.

Off the wheel the crowd saw him fall to the cobblestones of the street. Would he now get up? The crowd pressed forward to see. Yes, he slowly got to his feet. Now what? "He staggered slightly," wrote Grover, "and then with a supreme effort, clambered over the wheel, landed on the box, seized the reins from the hand of the drummer-boy, and turning to take his seat—fell sprawling his full length on the sidewalk. The jeering shout which followed had a threatening tone. Any overt act, the throwing of a stone, might have resulted in catastrophe."

Then Grover stooped over swiftly, took the reins from the hands of the stupefied coachman on the sidewalk, sprang to the box, started the span of horses, stopped to ask the President where to drive, took Speaker Colfax home first, then delivered the White House carriage and its occupants to their home.

On the White House portico Lincoln took one of Grover's hands, Mrs. Lincoln the other, Lincoln saying, according to Grover: "Mr. Grover, you have done me a very great service tonight, and one that I shall never forget. I have this to say to you; if at any time you want anything and it is in my power to grant it, you have only to ask and it shall be done." And Mrs. Lincoln: "Remember, Mr. Grover, what Mr. Lincoln says he means." What Leonard Grover had done came to be talked of. He himself wrote with a modest accuracy: "Some people went so far as to say that I had saved Mr. Lincoln's life. I knew that I had extricated him from a very annoying situation." What became of the drunken coachman, whether he continued to forget himself with drink, Grover did not record. The one-armed drummer-boy too was lost in the confusion of chronicles.

On a Bay Line boat from New York to Boston in August of '64 Grover met Postmaster General Blair. They became intimate enough for Blair to say: "Mr. Lincoln will give a great deal of consideration to anything you tell him. I have heard him mention a service you rendered him. You ought to see him and impress upon him the possible danger of defeat if he continues to retain Mr. Stanton." Grover said he couldn't take such a liberty with the President. Blair argued as though Grover's word might swing the election. "I am afraid my head began to grow," wrote Grover afterward, "for at last I assured him that if opportunity offered, I would place my opinion before the President." When a few weeks later Grover was outlining next season's plays for Lincoln, and when Lincoln asked him, as Blair had predicted, what he had heard in his travels about the coming election, Grover managed to say there was an opinion among many that Stanton in the Cabinet was a handicap. "Mr. Grover," came the President's voice slowly and decisively, "many people tell me that. I feel that Mr. Stanton is not generally popular. And if they'll find me a man who will do his work, I'll dismiss him." Grover noted a ringing accent on the word "work."

Grover, accurate of speech and persuasive as an observer, wrote of Lincoln coming to his theatre on the evening of the second day of the Baltimore convention. "There is a convention, as I suppose you know, Mr. Grover, and I thought I would get away for a little rest, lest they make me promise too much." Thus Grover heard him as he was placed in a box —alone—where a theatre audience could see him. He was not hiding from anyone who might want to ask about something. Yet hardly anyone would think of seeking him, on this particular night, at a theatre. Perhaps he had decided suddenly that a theatre box in public view would be a fair hiding-place. He took a program from Grover and looked at it. "Let's see what you are giving us tonight." The play began. Nine o'clock came. Grover brought him a telegram sent over from the White House. Grover noted: "It is safe to say that in ordinary conversation, of twenty remarks made by Mr. Lincoln nineteen of them were accompanied by a genial smile. 'Well,' said he, with the characteristic smile, 'they have nominated me again.'" Grover spoke congratulations and predicted re-election. "I think it looks that way, but I am a little bit curious to know what man they are going to harness up with me. Still I reckon I'll stay a little while longer and look at the play."

Of this particular visit to the theatre Grover wrote an abiding impression: "The solitary presence of Mr. Lincoln on that occasion, when the one thought of the entire nation was upon him, when the White House was invaded and surrounded by an army of partizans, office-holders and office-seekers, argues that he sought the theater as a sanctum of repose, his tired soul and body seeking a little rest, a little relaxation."

For the art of the theatre Lincoln had more than an amateur's interest. Congressman William D. Kelley took note of how the actor John McDonough, a partisan Democrat who regarded Lincoln as "a mere buffoon," came to change his mind about it. McDonough was to play Mrs. Pluto in *The Seven Sisters*, and the evening before opening Kelley coaxed him into going to the White House. Kelley also took along a Methodist minister, the Reverend Benjamin R. Miller, chaplain of the 119th Pennsylvania Volunteers. Lincoln knew offhand what corps the chaplain was from, asked about officers and the condition of the troops, then, turning to the actor: "I am very glad to meet you, Mr. McDonough, and am grateful to Kelley for bringing you in, for I want you to tell me something about Shakespeare's plays as they are constructed for the stage." McDonough was willing to give anything he might have in this field. Lincoln walked to a shelf, took down a well-thumbed volume of *The Plays of Shakespeare*, resumed his seat, arranged his glasses, read from *Henry VI* a long passage, and queried, "Mr. McDonough, can you tell me why those lines are omitted from the acting play?" They discussed this, with no definite conclusion, Lincoln later asking for the view of both the actor and the minister on the stage edition of *Richard III*. "It opens with a passage from *Henry VI*, and the finest soliloquy in the play, if we may judge from the many quotations it furnishes, and the frequency with which it is heard in amateur exhibitions, was never seen by Shakespeare, but it was written, was it not, Mr. McDonough, after his death, by Colley Cibber?" This was discussed, with no fresh light on it. The evening closed with Lincoln quoting a few verses from "Why Should the Spirit of Mortal Be Proud?" and remarking, as

Kelley noted it: "You have given me the benefit of a long holiday. I have not enjoyed such a season of literary recreation since I entered the White House."

Another Shakespearean evening Lincoln shared with Carpenter, who painted the sitting President on Wednesday, March 2, 1864. Samuel Sinclair, a New York friend Carpenter had invited, joined in the conversation, which shifted from the latest war news to the English dramatist, Lincoln saying, "It matters not to me whether Shakespeare be well or ill acted; with him the thought suffices." Lincoln had recently seen for the first time a performance of the play of *Hamlet.* It was put on at Grover's Theatre, with Edwin Booth in the leading role. It was a play that had "at all times a peculiar charm for Mr. Lincoln's mind," noted Carpenter, and the mention of it on this evening "waked up a train of thought" Carpenter was not prepared for.

"There is one passage of the play of 'Hamlet,' " the painter noted Lincoln saying, "which is very apt to be slurred over by the actor, or omitted altogether, which seems to me the choicest part of the play. It is the soliloquy of the king, after the murder. It always struck me as one of the finest touches of nature in the world."

Then the one man in the world in that hour charged by his enemies with having bloodier hands, more foul with mass murder, than any other man that ever lived, recited from *Hamlet* his favorite passage. Ambition, power, justice, bribery, repentance, the most darkly woven themes of personal human life, ran through it. He took up the words, throwing himself into the spirit of it:

O! my offence is rank, it smells to heaven;
It hath the primal eldest curse upon 't;
A brother's murder! Pray can I not,
Though inclination be as sharp as will:
My stronger guilt defeats my strong intent;
And, like a man to double business bound,
I stand in pause where I shall first begin,
And both neglect. What if this cursed hand
Were thicker than itself with brother's blood,
Is there not rain enough in the sweet heavens
To wash it white as snow? Whereto serves mercy
But to confront the visage of offence?
And what's in prayer but this two-fold force,
To be forestalled, ere we come to fall,
Or pardon'd, being down? Then, I'll look up;
My fault is past. But O! what form of prayer
Can serve my turn? "Forgive me my foul murder?"
That cannot be; since I am still possess'd
Of those effects for which I did the murder,
My crown, mine own ambition, and my queen.
May one be pardon'd and retain the offence?
In the corrupted currents of this world,

Offence's gilded hand may shove by justice,
And oft 'tis seen the wicked prize itself
Buys out the law; but 'tis not so above;
There is no shuffling, there the action lies
In his true nature, and we ourselves compell'd,
Even to the teeth and forehead of our faults
To give in evidence. What then? what rests?
Try what repentance can: what can it not?
Yet what can it, when one can not repent?
O wretched state! O bosom black as death!
O limed soul, that struggling to be free
Art more engaged! Help, angels! make assay;
Bow, stubborn knees; and heart with strings of steel
Be soft as sinews of the new-born babe.
All may be well.

The entire passage moved from him smoothly, as though his memory had long held it. As a performance with feeling and shadings, Carpenter rated it "unsurpassed by anything I ever witnessed upon the stage." Sinclair repeatedly said afterward to Carpenter that he had never heard the passage "rendered with more effect by the most famous of modern actors." This reading over, Lincoln thoughtful a few moments, went on: "The opening of the play of 'King Richard the Third' seems to me often entirely misapprehended. It is quite common for an actor to come upon the stage, and, in a sophomoric style, to begin with a flourish:

"'Now is the winter of our discontent
Made glorious summer by this sun of York;
And all the clouds that lour'd upon our house
In the deep bosom of the ocean buried.'

Now," said he, "this is all wrong. Richard, you remember, had been, and was then, plotting the destruction of his brothers, to make room for himself. Outwardly, the most loyal to the newly crowned king, secretly he could scarcely contain his impatience at the obstacles still in the way of his own elevation. He appears upon the stage, just after the crowning of Edward, burning with repressed hate and jealousy. The prologue is the utterance of the most intense bitterness and satire."

With a natural ease Lincoln then stepped into the character of Richard and gave the famous soliloquy with a power that to Carpenter "made it seem like a new creation." Carpenter laid down palette and brushes, gave a burst of handclapping applause, saying "half in earnest," so he noted, "that I was not sure but that he had made a mistake in the choice of a profession, considerably, as may be imagined, to his amusement."

So they had a good time of it, in a quiet corner of the White House, the three of them, the painter, his friend, and a lonely national chieftain. It was long since he had heard Jack Kelso deliver Shakespeare on the green banks of the flowing Sangamon.

To Carpenter he once read aloud his letter to the Owen Lovejoy Monument Association, as though the lines might have reading value with his intoning: "Let him have the marble monument along with the well-assured and more enduring one in the hearts of those who love liberty unselfishly for all men."

The months had passed into years, however, without circumstance bringing together Lincoln and a poet who lived plainly close to poverty and ranged the streets of Washington a neglected figure, though Emerson, Thoreau, and others rated him a high voice of democracy. Once walking quietly along F Street Walt Whitman was seized by a policeman and at the station charged with being in disguise and wearing a mask. The lieutenant on duty released the poet. "You looked so queer," explained the flatfoot who had made the arrest. "Your long white hair and whiskers, sir, and your eyes set well back, and your pink face looking as if it was painted." "Well, well, never mind," said the poet. "We all of us wear masks."

William Dean Howells—whose 1860 biography of Lincoln had brought royalties of $160, who was to write stories and novels—had called at the White House to see his friends Nicolay and Hay. Also Howells would have liked to thank the President personally for having appointed him to a $750-a-year consulate at Venice, Italy. "As I left my friends," wrote Howells, "I met the President in the corridor, and he looked at the space I was part of with his ineffably melancholy eyes. I faltered a moment in my longing to address him, and then decided that every one who forbore to so speak needlessly to him, or to shake his hand, did him a kindness. He walked up to the water-cooler that stood in the corner and drew himself a full goblet from it, which he poured down his throat with a backward tilt of the head, and then went wearily within doors." From Donn Piatt, Howells later heard that Lincoln this day wanted a greeting from him. Howells's biography had been carefully read by Lincoln and its few misstatements corrected in Lincoln's handwriting. But Howells thought Piatt mistaken about Lincoln wanting to meet him. The war roared on. Neither Whitman nor Howells got his handshake from Lincoln.

Bayard Taylor, author of travel volumes, novels, magazine articles, his hurriedly written books timed for and aimed at immediate public interest and large sales, was not so hesitant as Howells about bringing himself before Lincoln. Taylor believed his record as chargé d'affaires in the Russian Legation at St. Petersburg, after Minister Simon Cameron departed and before Minister Cassius M. Clay arrived, justified him in seeking the higher post. "Seward can testify, from my despatches, that I am fully capable of conducting the Legation," Taylor wrote to his publisher George P. Putnam. From St. Petersburg by correspondence he had already won Vice-President Hamlin, the historian Bancroft, and Cameron into consent to bring his matter favorably before the President, wrote Taylor, though as to William Cullen Bryant, "I beg that you will speak to him in my behalf," believing "a simultaneous use of all to the interest which I may be able to obtain, in addition to Cameron's testimony, may be sufficient to move the President." Taylor it was whose official dispatch had reported the words of Prince Gorchakov, Foreign Affairs head, that Russia would join no intervention by European powers. "Russia alone has stood by you from the first, and will continue to stand by you. . . . We desire above all things the maintenance of the American Union, as one indivisible nation." Seward it was who notified Taylor that President Lincoln had expressed gratification at Taylor's act in securing so important an expression from a Great Power.

Politics, however, decreed that Lincoln must appoint Clay to the Russian post, but Cameron wrote to Taylor that it was altogether likely that the President would even matters by appointing him to a special mission to Persia. A few weeks passed. Taylor suddenly appeared at the White House in Washington. Lincoln was surprised. He said he had believed Bayard Taylor to be in Persia. Taylor's view was that Secretary Seward alone knew why instructions and funds had not been sent to him two months before at St. Petersburg. Taylor went away from the White House and soon ended his foreign service. He wrote a sonnet titled "A Statesman" with reference to Seward as "Chief Eunuch," how "he did not deceive us all," was "mean to the friend, caressing to the foe."

Seward's explanation of why he had to treat Bayard Taylor shabbily might have been as simple and inexorable as the motives that Lincoln laid before Senator Sumner and Congressman John B. Alley. Those two Bay State partisans urged the President to appoint a Massachusetts man to be a secretary of legation. They came several times, Lincoln always saying No with emphasis, that he should give the appointment to a man having strong support in another State, although, wrote Alley, "Mr. Lincoln acknowledged that he did not think him fit for the position." On hearing this, Sumner and Alley were, as Alley noted, "naturally indignant." They wished to know if one of acknowledged fitness was to be rejected because he was a Massachusetts man, and one whom the President was willing to say was not fit should be appointed.

"Yes," said the President, "that is just the reason," lightly adding, "I suppose you two Massachusetts gentlemen think that your State could furnish suitable men for every diplomatic and consular station the Government has to fill." The two Massachusetts men agreed. They thought so, and seriously. Then, as Alley put it, "Mr. Lincoln appeased our displeasure by saying he thought so too," that he considered Massachusetts the banner State of the Union and admired her institutions and people so much that he had sent his boy Bob to Harvard for an education. He said he could do nothing further in the way of appointments for Massachusetts because he could not afford to and she did not need it. Massachusetts being intelligent and patriotic, her people would do right and support his Administration, even if he offended scores of her most esteemed public men. "But not so with this other State. It is a close State. I can mention half a dozen of her public men, Republicans, who have influence enough, combined, if I should seriously offend them, to carry the State over to the other side. For this reason I cannot afford to disregard the wishes of these men." This reasoning, along with the compliments, as Alley had it, "restored our good humor, and we went away satisfied."

In vital matters Lincoln was tough and unbending, Alley inclined to believe. But in small and unimportant matters "Mr. Lincoln was so yielding that many thought his excessive amiability was born of weakness." His incessant storytelling too "made him an enigma to many people," and the distinguished men of the country in daily intercourse with him who "thought but little of his capacity as a statesman" were not few but many, as Alley saw it. "Very few of the members of the Senate and of the House were in favor of his renomination for the Presidency in 1864." In result, then, whatever of genuine enthusiasm or deep faith there might be among the people of the country for their President in the autumn of '64 came from elsewhere than among the large majority of House and Senate members. Not through them as transmitters had the personality of Lincoln reached the country.

One weakness had Lincoln, in Alley's view and that of all but a few Senators and Congressmen: he was "more or less oblivious to the faults of dear friends." Alley cited "an exceedingly obnoxious nomination for a United States Judgeship," the nominee a very old friend of the President. The Senators in large majority were against the man and his record. The President was determined to have him confirmed. One Senator telling Alley that the Senate would never vote to make this man a Federal judge, Alley replied: "You do not know Mr. Lincoln. He greatly desires the confirmation and it will be done." The Senator: "Never, never." Yet it was done. The Senate confirmed the nomination and Sumner was the only Senator to speak in opposition to it.

Alley in this referred to the case of Mark Delahay of Kansas, to whom Lincoln had written on March 16, 1860, that on Delahay's being elected a delegate to the Chicago convention, "I will furnish one hundred dollars to bear the expenses of the trip," and on Delahay's failing to be elected delegate, Lincoln writing on April 14, "Come along to the convention, and I will do as I said about expenses." In a letter to Lyman Trumbull, March 16, 1860, Lincoln had urged support of "our friend Delahay" for United States Senator from Kansas. In April of '61 Lincoln appointed Delahay to be surveyor general for Kansas and Nebraska—at a time when decisions as to land titles and records were momentous across a vast area just opening up to homesteaders and exploiters. It was easily one of the worst appointments Lincoln ever made. When in October of '63 Delahay resigned and Lincoln named him to be United States District Judge for Kansas, the letters and speeches against Delahay had to do mainly with his being "so ignorant as a lawyer that no one would employ him," and with his itch for unearned money and his heavy drinking. Yet Lincoln over a powerful opposition drove through the nomination. And the friend to whom Lincoln had shown so unfailing a loyalty began a course of conduct on the Federal bench that resulted eventually in Delahay's being impeached on charges of incompetency, corruption, drunkenness on and off the bench, Delahay resigning while the impeachment committee was taking testimony.

Thus ran in brief essentials the tale of the only man of whom it was ever known that Lincoln promised him money for personal political promotion. On the surface it might seem that Lincoln miscalculated his man, an instance where Lincoln's judgment as a shrewd reader of men failed. Delahay didn't deliver one Kansas delegate for Lincoln at the Chicago convention, losing election as delegate himself. Delahay's influence at the convention as a "hustler" for Lincoln amounted to little or nothing. Whether Lincoln paid him the promised money or whether in Delahay's visit to Springfield after Lincoln's election there was an understanding that the matter would be taken care of by an appointment was not evidenced in any known letters or papers. Whether Delahay performed political service worth naming in support of Lincoln in the stormy Kansas area did not appear; he was in bad odor, stood forth not merely lacking distinction but rather as a drag and a hindrance to the Lincoln cause in Kansas.

What was Lincoln's guiding motive in the case of Mark Delahay? Nearly always he seemed to have a keen eye for scalawags and pretenders. Often he liked to humor them. Seldom did they fool him. As John Hay had once commented as to his insight when a certain overdressed fraud appeared before Lincoln, "He looked through the man to the buttons on the back of his coat." How would that apply in the case of Delahay? How could Lincoln move him up from a high land-office place to a seat on the Federal bench? Where were Lincoln's scruples about justice and the austere requirements of the judiciary? Was the old association of Jim Lane and others with Delahay operating, and did the favors to Delahay count materially for Lincoln's cause in Kansas because of Delahay's connection with others? Whatever the underlying facts, they were probably more essential than any that came to light, this because the Delahay case was not typical in Lincoln's political methods. It stood by itself. Lincoln would early have gone to ruin in politics had there been the lack of scruples or insight which stood forth from the surface in the judicial appointment he presented to a drab rascal.

Shortly after inauguration and more than once since then, Lincoln had told a Congressman or a Senator who asked an office for a constituent that he had no means of knowing whether it would be a good appointment, and therefore, "If you will sit down at the table and write out what you have told me about this man, and recommend his appointment, and sign your name to it, I will appoint him, and if your man proves unworthy I will hold you responsible."

Senator Wilkinson of Minnesota heard presentations to Lincoln by Senators Sumner, Wade, and others, hotly urging removal of a prominent department official. "The President listened attentively, with his head down," noted Wilkinson. "At the conclusion he looked up with a sorrowful expression of face and said, 'Well, gentlemen, it does seem to me that whenever

I have a particular friend in office, everybody is down on him.' This ended the matter, and the official was not removed."

At another time Wilkinson with Senator Wade and Congressman Covode called with an agent of the Bureau of Indian Affairs. The red men had been on the warpath in Minnesota and Dakota and this Indian agent gave elaborate assurances of what he would do if the President appointed him a brigadier general with full powers. He would put down outbreaks, restore quiet on the frontier in six weeks, save the lives of hundreds of settlers besides millions of dollars to the Government. He was rambling further on about how thoroughly he understood Indians and how to handle them, when Lincoln's patience gave out and he interrupted: "Sir, since the war began I have received a great deal of advice from all classes of men, and in the army great promises have been made, and my experience and observation have been that those who promise the most do the least." This ended the interview, noted Wilkinson. "Mr. Lincoln was a keen judge of character. He saw through this fellow at once, and that his object was to make money out of the scheme."

Among odd political fish with whom Lincoln dealt was one he named in a note to Stanton in November of 1863: "I personally wish Jacob Freese, of New Jersey, to be appointed colonel for a colored regiment, and this regardless of whether he can tell the exact shade of Julius Caesar's hair." Nothing seemed to come of this. Freese the next year while editing a newspaper in New Jersey wrote to Secretary Chase proposing that he be made collector of revenue in that State. This could be done through Chase removing the man holding the office, who was "a warm Lincoln supporter." Once in office as collector, Freese explained, he could make certain that all Treasury officials would be Chase-for-President workers at the proper time. Furthermore, the office would furnish an excuse for Freese visiting all parts of the State and building a Chase-for-President movement. This didn't seem to interest Chase, possibly because Freese's newspaper never had any real Chase-for-President editorials or news items. In September of '64 Lincoln wrote the New Jersey Senator John C. Ten Eyck: "Doctor J. R. Freese, now editor of a Union Journal in New Jersey, resided for a time in Illinois where and when I made his acquaintance, and since when I have enjoyed much of his friendship. He is somewhat wounded with me now, that I do not recognize him as he thinks I ought. I wish to appoint him a provost-marshal in your State. May I have your approval?" Thus in the moving stream of politics Lincoln accommodated himself to changing events regardless of the exact shade of Julius Caesar's hair.

Well enough Lincoln knew that two men he had just appointed to nice offices had talked mean about him. And Lamon then asking why he should put them in office, he answered that Lamon couldn't *think* one of them to be half as mean as he *knew* him to be. "But I can't run this thing on the theory that every officeholder must think I am the greatest man in the nation."

Several delegations had called and presented their claims, each for his own man to get a forthcoming appointment. And Lincoln one day refused to receive as a caller an old and dear personal friend, because the friend was one of the candidates for the appointment. Carpenter heard his regrets: "If I was less *thin-skinned* about such things, I should get along much better." Another time he had to refuse a sutlership to a soldier who had served three years with an honorable record, because of Stanton saying the place should go to a soldier who had lost an arm or a leg.

"I have thousands of applications like this every day," ran the President's

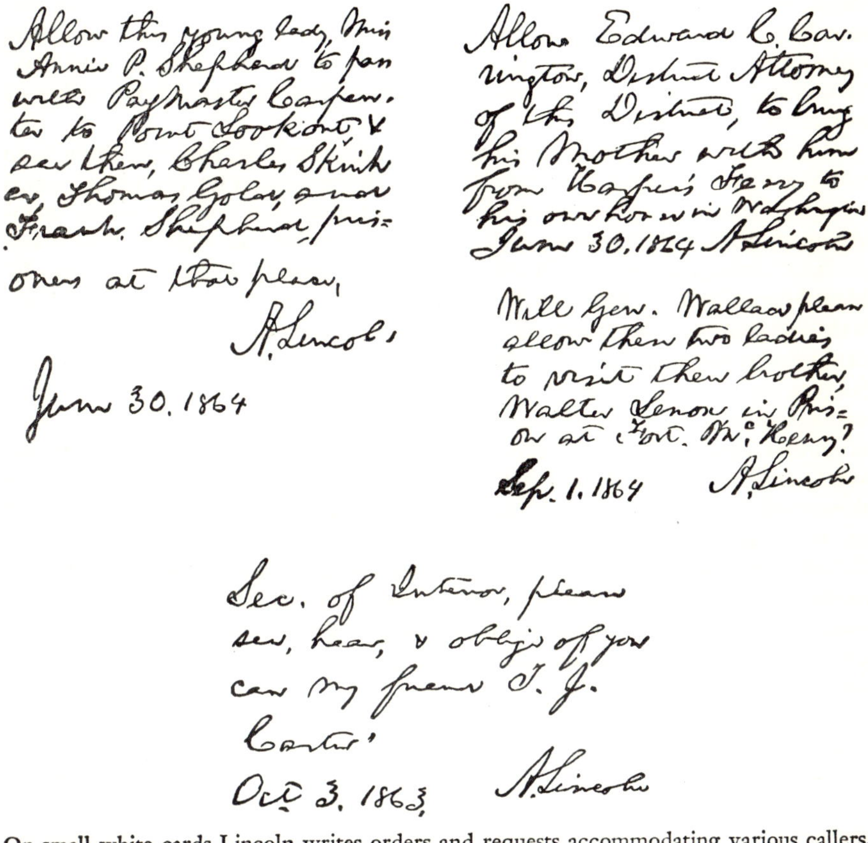

Allow this young lady, Miss Annie P. Shepherd to pass with Paymaster Carpenter to Point Lookout, & see there, Charles Skinker, Thomas Gold, and Frank Shepherd, prisoners at that place,
A. Lincoln
June 30. 1864

Allow Edward C. Carrington, District Attorney of this District, to bring his Mother with him from Harper's Ferry to his own home in Washington
June 30, 1864 A. Lincoln

Will Gen. Wallace please allow these two ladies to visit their brother, Walter Lenon in Prison at Fort McHenry?
Sep. 1. 1864 A. Lincoln

Sec. of Interior, please see, hear, & oblige if you can my friend T. J. Carter.
Oct. 3. 1863. A. Lincoln

On small white cards Lincoln writes orders and requests accommodating various callers. Upper right left: "Allow the young lady, Miss Annie P. Shepherd to pass with Paymaster Carpenter to Point Lookout, & see there, Charles Skinker, Thomas Gold, and Frank Shepherd, prisoners at that place." Upper right: "Allow Edward C. Carrington, District Attorney of the District, to bring his Mother with him from Harper's Ferry to his own home in Washington." Lower right: "Will Gen. Wallace please allow these two ladies to visit their brother, Walter Lenon in Prison at Fort McHenry?" Bottom: "Sec. of Interior, please see, hear, & oblige if you can my friend T. J. Carter." Originals in the Barrett collection.

refusal, "but we cannot satisfy all for this reason, that these positions are like office-seekers—there are too many pigs for the tits."

Whitney noted his repeated refusals to a man who wanted appointment as an inspector of army horses, and the final outburst, "I hain't got anything to give you!" To an officer wishing a staff appointment the President read from the book of laws and regulations which authorized him to make such appointments only on request of the general commanding a brigade, division, or corps. "I have no more power to appoint you, in the absence of such request, than I would have to marry a woman to any man she might desire for a husband without his consent." From far out in Oregon a woman whose husband's health had failed wished a post-office appointment, writing that long ago when she lived in Illinois he used to stop at their house and once when she had sewed a button on his coat he laughingly thanked her—"I will not forget you when I am President." This was added to the file of ingenious recollections.

In one State two party factions were each pushing for their own man to fill a high position. They pleaded and threatened. The President passed by both factions, made an appointment neither faction could criticize, naming an able army officer who in distinguished service had valiantly lost a leg.

Not having landed the Hackensack, New Jersey, post office, Curtis H. Hall wrote about the customs department, reminding Lincoln that his, Hall's, wife's stepfather, was a son of D. E. Ruckel. Lincoln endorsed this letter, "I do not remember Curtis H. Hall, the writer of the within, but Daniel E. Ruckel, mentioned, was a dear friend of mine; and any favor done a member of his family would be appreciated by me." How could the President possibly find time to follow through, on these many appeals that reached his heart, and where he would have liked to make sure the decent and just thing was done? Mrs. Lotty Hough may or may not have "got a place" of some sort as a result of A. Lincoln signing a note of recommendation October 3, 1864: "I have but slight personal acquaintance with the bearer of this Mrs. Lotty Hough; but I have known something of her by reputation for several years and never heard aught against her. She is now struggling to support herself and her little boy, and I hope she may be afforded fair opportunities to success."

The phrase "lame duck" entered American political lingo through a chance remark of Lincoln. A Western Senator on introducing his successor to Lincoln put in his request for the place for himself of Commissioner of Indian Affairs, then held by George W. Dole. Lincoln cut him short, it was said, and later explained: "I hate to have old friends like the Senator go away. And another thing I usually find out is that a Senator or Representative out of business is a sort of *lame duck*. He has to be provided for."

A Methodist minister, claiming relation to the inventor of ironclad gunboats, wished to be a hospital chaplain. The President could do nothing and said so curtly. The place-seeker had heard that such appointments were made by the President. "I will just tell you how that is," the President made clear; "when there are vacancies I appoint, not without."

The clergyman then handed the President a printed war sermon he had lately preached and bowed himself out. The President tossed the sermon out of sight. Carpenter picked it up and read it. He believed the President might have been interested in one incident in the sermon. Two Irish soldiers fighting, one had the other down. A clergyman onlooker rebuking them both, the one underneath called out, "Plase your *riverince,* I am willing to give up this minute, solely out of respect for your *riverince.*" Likewise, the moral was adduced, the South should be made to say "in regard to the Constitution."

A little New Orleans real-estate owner, a Unionist, since military rule in Louisiana could not collect his rents which had hitherto been his livelihood. He spoke with a French accent, haltingly, not used to politics. "Your case, my friend," said Lincoln to this petitioner, "may be a hard one, but it might have been worse. If, with your musket, you had taken your chance with our boys before Richmond, you might have found your bed before now. But the point is, what would you have me do for you? I have much to do, and the courts have been opened to relieve me in this regard."

The small landlord, embarrassed: "I am not in the habit of appearing before big men." Lincoln: "And for that matter, you have no need to change your habit, for you are not before very big men now," then playfully, "I can't go into the collection business." The little man moved off as though Yes, sure enough, the President was not running a rent-collection office.

When Stanton arrested and Halleck ordered court-martial of General Milroy in connection with Shenandoah Valley blunders, Milroy's defense involved an order from General Schenck, who declined summons to appear before the trial board. Piatt rode to the White House with General Schenck's protest. From the White House Piatt went to the War Department, met the President coming out, gave his message. They walked toward the White House. "Let me see the protest," said Lincoln.

"General Schenck ordered me, Mr. President, to read it to you."

"Well, I can read," said Lincoln sharply. Piatt handed over the paper. Lincoln read as he strode along. At the White House entrance the carriage and horse guards waited to take him to the Soldiers' Home.

On the portico steps Lincoln sat down to study Schenck's protest. "A strange picture he presented," wrote Piatt. "His long, slender legs were drawn up until his knees were level with his chin, his long arms held the paper, which he studied regardless of the crowd before him. He read on to the end." Then looking up:

"Piatt, don't you think that you and Schenck are squealing, like pigs, before you're hurt?"

"No, Mr. President."

"Why, I am the Court of Appeal, and do you think I am going to have an injustice done Schenck?"

"Before the appeal can be heard, a soldier's reputation will be blasted by a packed court."

"Come now," an ugly look shading Lincoln's face, "you and I are lawyers, and know the meaning of the word 'packed.' I don't want to hear it from your lips again. What's the matter with the court?"

"It is illegally organized by General Halleck."

"Halleck's act is mine."

"I beg your pardon, Mr. President, the Rules and Regulations direct that in cases of this sort you shall select the court; you cannot delegate that to a subordinate any more than you can the pardoning power."

"That is a point," Lincoln said, slowly rising. "Do you know, Colonel, that I have been so busy with this war I have never read the Regulations. Give me that book, and I'll study them to-night."

"I beg your pardon, Mr. President," Piatt suggested as he handed over the book, "but in the meantime my general will be put under arrest for disobedience, and the mischief will be done."

"That's so. Here, give me a pencil." And tearing off a corner of the paper General Schenck had sent, he wrote, according to Piatt, an order suspending the Milroy court-martial until further orders.

The coachmen, the horses, the horsemen, moved off with the President to the Soldiers' Home. Of the next morning Piatt wrote, "I clanked into the court-room with my order, and had the grim satisfaction of seeing the owls in epaulettes file out, never to be called again."

Of Lincoln as wrathful and ready with a strong hand Donn Piatt gave an incident of which he said, "I never saw him angry but once, and I had no wish to see a second exhibition of his wrath." Piatt as a colonel on the headquarters staff of General Schenck at Baltimore had been counseling with Henry Winter Davis and others. He directed officers raising a Negro brigade in Maryland "to recruit slaves only." In the absence of General Schenck, Piatt issued an order to this effect. Before General Schenck had taken leave Piatt had asked him for authority to issue such an order, but Schenck said it must come from the War Department. Recruiting aimed to bring in slaves began. And soon a delegation of eminent Maryland Unionists protested to Piatt, got scant comfort, and went to President Lincoln. The War Department ordered Piatt to Washington. Piatt went. At the War Department he was told he would find Stanton at the White House.

Piatt soon found himself in the President's office, facing Lincoln alone. "I do not care to recall the words of Mr. Lincoln," wrote Piatt. "I wrote them out that night, for I was threatened a shameful dismissal from the service, and I intended appealing to the public. They were exceedingly severe, for the President was in a rage. I was not allowed a word in my own defence, and was only permitted to say that I would countermand my order as well as I could. I was saved cashiering through the interference of Stanton and Chase, and the further fact that a row over such a transaction at that time would have been extremely awkward."

Of what he had done Piatt wrote, "My one act made Maryland a free State." Piatt saw a touch of the heroic in an unauthorized paper he gave out. He wrote about it as though it never entered his mind that Lincoln had his own plans for liberating the slave Negroes of Maryland. "The President never forgave me."

And when Schenck had resigned from command at Baltimore to take a seat in Congress, Maryland and Delaware Unionists, immediate emancipationists, requested Lincoln to appoint Piatt a brigadier in charge at Baltimore. Lincoln heard them patiently, according to Piatt, and then refused: "Schenck and Piatt are good fellows, and if there were any rotten apples in the barrel they'd be sure to hook 'em out. But they run their machine on too high a level for me. They never could understand that I was boss." And from Stanton, Piatt later had word that when the War Department more than once sent to the President a list of officers worthy of promotion, "Lincoln would quietly draw his pen through my name."

A major walked in one day and handed Lincoln "important dispatches" from General Sherman. At least Sherman had told him they were important. The major was C. J. Stolbrand from the West, a Swedish-blooded citizen who had volunteered at Lincoln's first call in '61 and served continuously, at times in field emergencies acting as colonel or brigadier general. No promotions coming, he was leaving the service. Sherman didn't want to lose his Major Stolbrand, asked him to go home by way of Washington and hand some "important dispatches" to the President. Lincoln opened the sealed papers from Sherman, read them, and put out his hand. "How do you do, General?" Stolbrand corrected, "I am no general; I am only a major." Laughed Lincoln: "You are mistaken. You are a general." And in a few hours, with his commission signed by Lincoln, he was on his way back to Sherman's army.

Old Jim Conner of Miami County, Indiana, arrived home from a long trip to tell what had happened between him and Lincoln and Stanton. His four sons and some neighbor boys were with the Army of the Potomac and he had gone with his Congressman to ask Stanton for a pass to see the boys and to give them knickknacks from the home women. Stanton said No, and soon Old Jim Conner and the Congressman were seeing Lincoln, Conner crying, "My God! I'll never go back home to face those women." The President thought it over, and then: "Conner, I can't overrule Stanton, but I need a special commissioner to go among the rank and file of the army to find out what the soldiers of this country think of the government of the United States in its greatest crisis. Conner, will you be a special commissioner?"

A German clothier and merchant tailor of Baltimore, under arrest in '64 for contraband trade with the Confederacy, had his case appealed to the President by a delegation of a dozen or so of his friends and employees. Their spokesman showed himself not unaccustomed to public speaking, referred to himself as "an humble tobacconist," declared they were all good Union men, had voted for Mr. Lincoln and intended to do so again, had a right to be heard, were sure their friend and employer was innocent, and in fact he had given several hundred dollars toward carrying on the war for the Union. When the oratory had diminished and finally completely died down, the President, according to press reports, spoke:

"Gentlemen, this Government is a big machine, even in times of peace; it is no small thing to keep it in good running order—but now, when added to the usual duties of my position, I have on my hands this great rebellion, *which is to be put down*, I have no time to waste. I have been visited already more than once by parties from Baltimore, urging my interference in this case. You protest that this man is innocent; then let him await his trial, when he can easily prove it."

"But," said the speaker, in behalf of his friend, "but we vote for you."

"Can't help it; it is not so essential that I have votes, as that the rebellion be crushed. To what purpose is it that you vote for me; that you pay a small sum of money to soldiers, as a cover up, while you supply the rebels with goods or arms? I tell you, gentlemen, it will not do. Already has the War Department declared to me that it could not and would not stand by me in this work of subduing the rebels, if every time they catch a rascal, I let him loose. Gentlemen, I ain't going to do it."

"Well, but, your excellency, I am a fighting man. I once paid three hundred dollars for knocking a man down."

The President drew himself back, and with much good nature said:

"Let me beg you not to try that on me."

Then the speaker, in behalf of the accused, took another turn.

"Mr. President, even your enemies say you have much goodness of heart. Will you not parole this man, accepting bonds, which we will procure to any amount?"

The President could not be moved. When appeals were made to his sympathy, he said, with great decision:

"I will not listen."

"But, Mr. President, you *can* do this thing."

"Certainly I *can*, and I can end this war and let the rebels have their own way; but I am not going to do it." And the delegation, including a humble tobacconist orator, went away.

Secretary Welles had removed a Navy Department agent named Isaac Henderson on charges of mishandling government money. Word came to Welles that the United States District Attorney in New York had remarked it was "not worth while to prosecute, that the same thing was done by others." Welles told this to Lincoln, who brought out letters exchanged between him and William Cullen Bryant. Henderson was, according to Bryant, an innocent victim of the principal witness against him, a man named Savage, also arrested and under bonds. To the President it seemed to count that the character of Savage before his arrest was as good as Henderson's before he was arrested. Of Henderson the President said he knew nothing until Welles had brought to his notice the removal of Henderson. Was Welles satisfied the man was guilty? He was. Then, said the President, "Go ahead, let him be removed." Welles added that it was a clear case and should be prosecuted.

So it seemed a major point with Lincoln that the two main figures had each borne good characters before their arrest. If the witness Savage had been shady in other affairs that would have been something else. As between Secretary Welles and Editor Bryant, Lincoln in this case took Welles. Nor was this an easy course. Isaac Henderson, slated to go to trial on the decision of Welles and Lincoln, was the publisher of the *New York Evening Post*, founded long ago by Alexander Hamilton and now edited by William Cullen Bryant. Wrote Welles in his diary July 15, 1864: "The *Evening Post* manifests a belligerent spirit, and evidently intends to make war upon the Navy Department because I will not connive at the malfeasance of its publisher. In a cautious and timid manner they have supported the policy of the Navy Department hitherto, though fearful of being taunted for so doing. Because their publisher was Navy Agent they have done this gently. But they now, since Henderson's arrest and trial, assail the monitors and the monitor system, which they have hitherto supported, and insidiously and unfairly misrepresent them and the Department.

"I am surprised at the want of judgment manifested in hastening to make this assault. It would have been more politic, certainly, to have delayed, for the motive which leads them to make this abrupt turn cannot be misunderstood. They know it is painful for me to prosecute one of their firm, that it pains me to believe him guilty, but that when the facts are presented, they should know me well enough to be aware that I would not cover or conceal the rascality even to oblige them. I claim no merit, but I deserve no censure for this plain and straightforward discharge of my duty."

Into the diary of Welles went many entries about Isaac Henderson, "standing high in the community as a man of piety and purity," nevertheless "getting rich at public expense." Henderson's Congressman, friend, and fellow churchman, Odell, "has looked into the subject, and says he has committed great frauds." A letter from Bryant spoke fear that Seward and Weed, to implicate Henderson, had framed a conspiracy in which Welles was "supposed to be an instrument in their hands, and so is the President." To Attorney General Bates, Welles transmitted a report of his own department attorney "inculpating" District Attorney Delafield Smith of New York in the management of the prosecution of the Navy Department against Henderson for embezzlement, suggesting "that it be laid before the President for such action as he may order." As to Smith, there was a hitch, Welles noted. "He is a pet of Seward, who sometimes closes his eyes to the obliquities of his friends." Furthermore, "It will not surprise me if Seward, Weed, and Smith make friends with Henderson and the *Evening Post* concern, with whom they have hitherto quarrelled, and try to screen or exculpate Henderson." Months passed without action in court. Welles consulted with the President about special counsel to prosecute Henderson. They agreed as to attorneys and the President approved of Welles's course.

Many months were to pass with no trial of Henderson. In one of those months Thurlow Weed's defense, in a libel suit brought against him by Mayor Opdyke of New York City, called as witness one H. D. Stover, a government contractor giving "strange testimony," as Welles phrased it. The same Stover was a material witness to be called to testify against Isaac Henderson. And in another of the months that Henderson evaded trial, Stover was by court-martial found guilty of fraud on three charges, fined $5,000, and sentenced to one year "in such prison as the Secretary of the Navy may select." Welles considered Stover "a dishonest man" who would use his "money, obtained by fraudulent means from the government," for many legal delays. The Secretary of the Navy therefore deliberated and came to a conclusion. He would send Stover to Fort Lafayette instead of a penitentiary. Where was Stover? He had left Philadelphia for New York. "I have," wrote Welles, "therefore written to Admiral Paulding to arrest and send him to Fort L.[afayette]. The President concurs."

The Smith brothers, Benjamin G. and Franklin W., of Boston, Massachusetts, held for many months the center of a web of intrigue and political trading where Welles and Lincoln had to yield to necessities. In its beginning both the Secretary of the Navy and the President plainly believed these contractors in navy supplies deserving of close scrutiny. Also in agreement with this view in June of '64, when Welles ordered the Smith brothers court-martialed, were the Navy Department attorneys and technicians, including Gustavus Vasa Fox, Assistant Secretary of the Navy. It was Fox who had picked the chief detective for the case, H. S. Olcott. He was the man-hunter type, Welles seeing him as "a cormorant, searching papers, utterly reckless."

Welles didn't like Olcott and told Fox what kind of a detective was needed for the job, "a firm but mild man," with some slight understanding of the civil and constitutional rights of suspects. But Fox couldn't think of any detective who was firm but mild. Fox was about ready to use any aggressive or even unscrupulous man-hunter to bring to justice men tampering with the quality of articles delivered to the navy. "Fox," wrote Welles, "is violent against these men, who, he believes, are hypocrites and rascals. While I may not differ with him in that respect, they have rights in common with us all that must be respected and not rudely violated." The desperation of Fox in handling rich, respectable pretenders to patriotism and religion, who were defrauding the Government, seemed to have reached the point where he would use an instrument having no respect for their civil and constitutional rights. When the court-martial gave the Smith brothers light fines and prison sentences, Fox wished Welles to return the papers "for revision," giving heavier punishment, preferably five years in prison and a fine of $100,000. Welles in this case was keeping his head better than Fox. A more severe sentence, he wrote, would "endanger a reaction."

Fox was not meeting, as Welles and Lincoln were, the recoil from Boston and Massachusetts. Congressman Rice of Massachusetts called on Welles and read a midnight telegram from Mrs. Smith, "in great distress." Congressman Rice was saying the Smith families were ruined forever, whether innocent or guilty, and that he believed the Smiths innocent. Counsel for the

Smiths sent word they were going to prosecute the court-martial for false imprisonment. They notified Navy Department counsel they intended to hold Secretary Welles accountable and to have him arrested when he came to New York.

Now came word to Welles that the chief detective termed himself an investigator and a commissioner because the word "detective" lacked true dignity. Welles sketched him: "He is a harsh, rough instrument, and I shall be glad when he shall have done service with me. Yet in saying this I admit from what I have seen he has some good qualities as a detective. I have seen nothing to doubt his honesty; he is industrious and indefatigable, but vain, reckless, regardless of private rights, and all his qualities have been exercised in the case of the Smiths, who are shrewd, piously honest, self-righteous, and wary as well as sharp. It will not surprise me if they prove an overmatch for him and the lawyers."

The bluster and arrogance of the detective put such a face on the case that the court-martial verdict was set aside and a new trial ordered. Two able lawyers from Boston, serving the Smith brothers, talked to Welles two hours on a Saturday and a half-hour on a Tuesday, asking a four-week postponement of the trial and hoping it would take place in Boston.

The President on this Tuesday sent for Welles. Arriving at the White House, Welles found there in discussion with the President the same two lawyers who had left his office two hours before. With the President "they had gone over the whole subject that they had previously discussed with me. The President heard them kindly and then said he could not act without consulting me. I remarked that I had given the subject a hearing and examination, and supposed it was disposed of. The President said he could not interfere, but should be glad if it could be arranged so as to give them time and also a trial at Boston."

Nearly a month later the President sent to Welles a bundle of papers. Welles opened them. And what did he see? "A petition," he wrote, "drawn up with great ability and skill, signed by most of the Massachusetts delegation in Congress and a large number of the prominent merchants in Boston, asking special favors in behalf of Smith Brothers, who are under arrest for fraudulent deliveries under contract, requesting that the trial may be held in Boston and that it may be withdrawn from the military and transferred to the civil tribunals. Senator Sumner and Representative Rice wrote special letters to favor the Smiths. The whole scheme had been well studied and laboriously got up, and a special delegation have come on to press the subject upon the President."

About this latest turn of the case Welles talked with Lincoln that day, after Lincoln had heard the Boston delegation. "He urged me to relieve him from the annoying and tremendous pressure that had been brought to bear upon him in this case by religious or sectarian and municipal influence." Welles wrote as though both he and Lincoln understood that a disagreeable transaction was called for on their part. The Smith brothers were to be favored with a new trial in a city of their choice, their home town, by a civil court. The favor was to be given them because of the large and respectable political strength they could raise behind their cause.

"I went briefly over the main points," wrote Welles; "told him the whole subject ought to be referred to and left with the Navy Department in this stage of the proceedings, that I desired him to relieve himself of all care and trouble by throwing the whole responsibility and odium, if there was odium, on the Navy Department, that we could not pursue a different course in this case from the others,—it could not be made an exception. He then asked why not let the trial take place in Boston and thus concede something. I told him this might be done, but it seemed to me inexpedient; but he was so solicitous—political and party considerations had been artfully introduced, against which little could be urged, when Solicitor Whiting and others urged that three Congressional districts would be sacrificed if I persisted—that the point was waived and the President greatly relieved."

That Welles did not quite understand the mixed motives of Lincoln, the hazardous political considerations involved, was evident in the tone of his final comment on this particular interview: "The President evinced shrewdness in influencing, or directing me, but was sadly imposed upon by the cunning Bostonians." Welles in this assumed that Lincoln let himself be imposed on while not aware he was being imposed on. Lincoln knew well what he let himself in for that day. Lincoln probably surmised that day the case of the oily and tainted Smith brothers would be heard of for many months to come. This was August of '64, the blackest month of the year and the war.

Also as executive and magistrate Lincoln gave a little study in August of '64 to one Mr. Bailor, who sought through Welles an interview with the President. On Welles's mentioning Bailor, Lincoln seemed surprised. Since Bailor claimed to be on an errand requiring uttermost secrecy to begin with, it was natural Lincoln should be slightly surprised at State Department matters getting over into the Navy Department. Bailor claimed nothing less than that he was a commissioner duly authorized by the State of Georgia to negotiate for peace. His credentials? They had vanished. And his dispatches from his own sovereign State of Georgia? They too had vanished. And how? Bailor told Welles, told Seward, and was hoping to tell Lincoln. He had given them into the hands of Consul Allen at Bermuda. From Allen they were stolen "when going from Hamilton to St. George's, at a house where he [Allen] stopped with a lady who had come with him that distance." Consul Allen had hurried to St. George's, where the packet was about to sail, penned a brief line, and gave his story to a Connecticut man known to Welles. This Connecticut man, believing the story, had brought it to Welles.

Meantime Bailor himself had arrived from Bermuda, dined with the Secretary of State, and wished now an interview with the President. Would the President see Bailor? Welles asked. The President said Bailor "had been here and got in with Seward, who had become sick of him." For himself the President believed Bailor a "shyster." Welles introduced his Connecticut man, whose certification of Bailor did not remove the previous impression from the President's mind. Bailor was still a "shyster" to the White House—and so remained.

Congressman Odell of New York asked release of an Englishman jailed under charges of having swindled soldiers out of their pay. Brigadier General W. E. Doster handed Lincoln the papers in the case. He looked them over, handed them back to Doster, and told Odell he must refuse to interfere.

In a voice of high rage a crippled private soldier was cursing out the Government from the President down. Everybody in hearing could get what he was saying near the War Office, just as Lincoln happened along and asked what was the matter. "I want my money. I've been discharged here and can't get my pay." Lincoln told the private he used to practice law and maybe could help. Lincoln sat down at the foot of the tree, ran over the papers handed him, wrote a notation on the back of one and told the private to take them to Chief Clerk Potts of the War Department. Lincoln walked on, and A. W. Swann of Albuquerque, New Mexico, who had been looking on from near by, asked the private if he knew who he had been talking with. "Some ugly old fellow who pretends to be a lawyer," was the guess. Then Swann went with the private, saw him get the money due him, saw him stand sort of puzzled as to whether he ought to be glad or sorry he had cursed the President to his face.

H. P. H. Bromwell and other downstate Illinoisans had finished an interview with Lincoln when a doorman spoke. "Mr. President, that soldier is out here waiting to see you again." To the doorman the President said: "Tell him I can't see him any more about that matter. I've seen him as many times as I can," and according to Bromwell, explaining himself to the others: "I wish that man would let me alone. I've seen him again and again. I've done everything for him that I can do, and he knows it just as well as I do; and I've told him over and over and he ought to let me alone, but he won't stop following me up. He knows I can't do anything more for him. I declare, if he won't let me alone, I'll tell him what I did to a fellow the other day, that I'll undo what I have done for him."

An army quartermaster serving a five-year penitentiary term for gambling with government money had his case presented to Lincoln by the extraordinarily keen and able congressman Henry Laurens Dawes. The prison doctor and an eminent outside physician signed a petition for the man's pardon, with statements that his health was bad and he would die soon unless let out.

"Do you believe that statement?" Lincoln asked Dawes, who said he certainly did or he would not have brought it to the President. "Please say so," said Lincoln, "here on the back of it, under these doctors." Dawes signed, adding in writing, "And because I believe it to be true I join in this petition."

As Dawes signed Lincoln remarked, "We can't permit that man to die in prison after that statement," and immediately under it all wrote, "Let this man be discharged. A. L." Dawes took the paper to Stanton, who smiled about it and assured Dawes he was going over to the White House pretty soon.

Dawes heard from two Michigan Congressmen that the pardon was being held up, that Stanton had refused to execute the order for it, that the President had given them an account of Stanton's refusal. "He told me," said the President, "that it was a sham, and that Dawes had got me to pardon the biggest rascal in the army, and that I had made gambling with public funds perfectly safe. I couldn't get him to let the man off. The truth is, I have been doing so much of this thing lately that I have lost all influence with this administration, and have got to stop!"

Dawes hurried to the White House. Lincoln told Dawes much the same as the two Michigan Congressmen. What then of the order for a pardon, which Stanton had returned? Dawes offered to pay the expense of a messenger to go to the Albany prison and make certain of the truth or falsity of the statement as to the convict's health. Lincoln replied: "I think, if you believe it, I will. At any rate, I will take the risk on the side of mercy." So the pardon went out. The man was released. And Dawes himself let it be known that when he went back home, after adjournment of Congress, he was startled to meet on the street his "dying" quartermaster. The shattered convict had returned to robust health, fit as a fiddle. Stanton had the laugh on Dawes and Lincoln. And Lincoln was on record as having done a favor sincerely requested by a Congressman of able service.

A Pennsylvania election commissioner appointed by Governor Curtin to supervise soldier voting in the field in November of '64 was jailed by Stanton as "a damned rebel," was paroled, not discharged, by Lincoln, and performed his duties under the continued protest of Stanton that he was "a damned rebel." It was at the suggestion of Governor Curtin that A. K. McClure sought Jere McKibben of Philadelphia to represent the Democratic party in the count of the Pennsylvania troop votes, McKibben instantly responding, "Why, Stanton would put me in Old Capitol Prison before I was there [in Washington] a day. He hates our family for no other reason I know of than that my father was one of his best friends in Pittsburg when he needed a friend." McClure said surely Stanton would not dare jail a commissioner named by Governor Curtin. McClure added his personal pledge to protect McKibben. With the other commissioners McKibben left Philadelphia for Washington.

In less than two days McClure had a telegram from McKibben: "Stanton has me in Old Capitol Prison; come at once."

Hurrying to Washington, McClure interviewed Lincoln, finding (so ran McClure's statement) that Lincoln knew of Stanton's old grudge against the McKibbens, that Lincoln had met it when Jere's brothers, who were officers in the army, would have failed of promotion but for Lincoln's interposition. Over this latest spitework of Stanton, Lincoln seemed greatly distressed, according to McClure, saying it was a "stupid blunder," and he would release McKibben at once on his parole.

McClure urged that the commissioner should have a complete and honorable discharge. Lincoln gave his view: "It seems hardly fair to discharge McKibben unconditionally without permitting Stanton to give his explanation. You know, McClure, McKibben is safe, parole or no parole, so go and get him out of prison." McClure persisted. Lincoln agreed to the extent that he would arrange a meeting with Stanton for the next morning. With that understanding McClure left for the Old Capitol Prison, with the President's order, and saw the doors open for the release of the Democratic election commissioner appointed by Governor Curtin to supervise troop voting in the field.

McClure sat in the President's room the next morning as Stanton came in, pale with anger as he exploded, "Well, McClure, what damned rebel are you here to get out of trouble this morning?"

"Your arrest of McKibben was a cowardly act; you knew McKibben was guiltless of any offense, and you did it to gratify a brutal hatred." McClure went farther in his outburst that closed with a demand for honorable and unconditional discharge of the parole of McKibben.

Stanton walked the floor, nervous, excited, sneering: "I decline to discharge McKibben from his parole. You can make formal application for it if you choose, and I will consider and decide it."

McClure put in that he didn't know what McKibben would do. "But if I were Jere McKibben, as sure as there is a God I would crop your ears before I left Washington."

Stanton had no more words. He swung and walked out of the room. Lincoln sat without a word through the scene. Now he spoke. "Well, McClure, you didn't get on very far with Stanton, did you? but he'll come out all right; let the matter rest."

To a formal request for the discharge of McKibben's parole Stanton sent his decision in his own handwriting, that the application, having been duly considered, "could not be granted consistently with the interests of the public service." And there the matter rested a long time.

Perhaps no one in the American scene had studied more anxiously and deeply the two men Lincoln and Stanton, in moments of high decision, than Grant. What was Grant's judgment of the two? They stood foremost in the executive end of the Government, these two. How would Grant contrast them? He was to write:

"They were the very opposite of each other in almost every particular, except that each possessed great ability. Mr. Lincoln gained influence over men by making them feel that it was a pleasure to serve him. He preferred yielding his own wish to gratify others, rather than to insist upon having his own way. It distressed him to disappoint others. In matters of public duty, however, he had what he wished, but in the least offensive way. Mr. Stanton never questioned his own authority to command, unless resisted. He cared nothing for the feeling of others. In fact it seemed to be pleasanter to him to disappoint than to gratify. He felt no hesitation in assuming the functions of the executive, or in acting without advising with him. If his act was not sustained, he would change it—if he saw the matter would be followed up until he did so."

These two executive officials were generally supposed to form the complement of each other, noted Grant. "The Secretary was required to prevent the President's being imposed upon. The President was required in the more responsible place of seeing that injustice was not done to others." Possibly a majority of the people held this view, believed Grant, writing that in his estimation, it was "not a correct view," for "Mr. Lincoln did not require a guardian to aid him in the fulfilment of a public trust." Out of numerous delicate and hazardous situations Grant arrived further at this deadly parallel: "Mr. Lincoln was not timid, and he was willing to trust his generals in making and executing their plans. The Secretary was very timid, and it was impossible for him to avoid interfering with the armies covering the capital when it was sought to defend it by an offensive movement against the army guarding the Confederate capital. He could see our weakness, but he could not see that the enemy was in danger. The enemy would not have been in danger if Mr. Stanton had been in the field. These characteristics of the two officials were clearly shown shortly after Early came so near getting into the capital."

Should Stanton have been acquainted with the very few members of Congress who were thoroughly and continuously loyal to Lincoln? Should he at least have accorded them ordinary courtesy if he could not grant their requests? Such questions rose in connection with one statement by the sober and scrupulous Congressman Isaac N. Arnold. That Stanton was neurotic, of curiously balanced mentality, with nerves often on edge during his heavy duties, entered into consideration. Also that Stanton was arbitrary and willful to the extent that General Grant refused to send important telegrams which had to pass through Stanton's department because in Grant's experience his telegrams too often had their purposes changed in transmittal. If Stanton had no hesitations about tampering with messages of the high commander ranking second only to the President, what might be his attitude or assumption with regard to the President? When every extenuating circumstance was considered in connection with Arnold's statement, it became rather evident that Stanton could be ungenerous and crotchety and, for a War Department head, too easily ruffled. Not many officials of high place could have gone so far as to let loose scoldings and harsh reproaches on a young man who had lost a hand in battle. Arnold's little story, with his carefulness and his peculiar sobriety, with his quiet understatement, read:

> In the early spring of 1862, a young lad, who had lost his right hand at the battle of Belmont, came to Washington to obtain an appointment as assistant quartermaster. He arrived on Saturday, and calling at my house found that I was out of the city. With the confidence of youth, he did not wait my return, but, having very strong recommendations, went to the Secretary of War, and was greatly disappointed when Mr. Stanton refused to appoint him. In the evening he came to me in great distress,

and stated his case. I told him I would go with him on Monday to the War Office, but that his case was injured by his having been once rejected.

On Monday we called on Mr. Stanton, who was receiving and dispatching a multitude of suitors. I noticed that the Secretary was in an ill humor; however, we took our turn, and I stated the case. Turning to the young soldier, Stanton said: "Were not you here Saturday, and did I not refuse to appoint you? And now here you are again on Monday, troubling me again. I cannot and will not have my time wasted in this way."

I said: "Mr. Stanton, I am responsible for this second application." But he would not listen to me, and continued to scold at the young soldier. I thought him rude and uncivil, but seeing his irritability, retired as soon as possible, saying to the young soldier: "We will stop at the White House, and see what the President has to say to this."

We found Mr. Lincoln alone in his office, and I had scarcely stated the case, when he took a card and wrote on it: "Let — be appointed Assistant Quartermaster, etc A. Lincoln." He had not then become familiar with one-armed and one-legged soldiers and he seemed touched by the empty sleeve of the fine-looking young man. Putting the card in my pocket, I went to the Capitol. In the course of the day, Stanton came on the floor of the House, and as he seemed in good humor, I went to him and said: "Mr. Stanton, you seemed very harsh and rude to my friend and constituent this morning. It seems to me that those who lose their right hands in the service of the country should at least be entitled to kindness and courtesy from the Secretary of War."

"Well, well," he replied, "I was vexed and annoyed this morning. Take your young friend to the President. He always does anything you ask him, and he will, I doubt not, appoint him."

"Mr. Stanton," I replied, "if the President grants my requests, I take care never to ask anything but what I am sure is right; but in this instance you do the President no more than justice. He has already directed the appointment, and I beg you will not interpose any obstacle or delay, as you sometimes do."

Taking the card, Mr. Stanton said: "I will send you the commission as soon as I get to the War Department." An hour later a messenger brought the commission.

Where Stanton in this particular instance considered himself "vexed and annoyed," Arnold in the same instance held him "rude and uncivil," or as he said to Stanton, "You seemed very harsh and rude." Then as though his morning mood of vexation and annoyance had passed, and as though the matter rested on a more just and relevant basis, Stanton would dismiss it offhand: "Take your young friend [a Union soldier of honorable battle service with a hand gone] to the President. He always does anything you ask him." Why should Stanton refer to "your young friend" as though he might be an ordinary office-seeker, some manner of nuisance or culprit? And again why should Stanton leave an inference that there was something wrong about the President's doing "anything" that Congressman Arnold asked? And why more especially when Lincoln's trust in Arnold was to have the result that in 1864 Arnold was the only member of the Congress who gave a complete and unequivocal support of the President for renomination and a second term? Was this some form of obtusity in Stanton, or was it a phase of the "timidity" which Grant read in him that made him distrustful of the acts, plans, and decisions of others than himself? An ego, queer to some, weird to others, underlay much of what he did.

An Iowa private on sick furlough had sent a surgeon's reports to the War Department, and according to his Congressman's presentations to Lincoln, these reports had miscarried and on the private's return to the army he found himself on the rolls as a deserter. Stanton refused to correct the soldier's status in the records, saying, "Every man of them when caught or in hiding or asking for relief, has some plausible excuse." The Congressman James F. Wilson said he would take it to the President. Stanton: "Go to the President, if you please. I will not consider the case, nor will I execute such an order."

The President when seen wished to know if Congressman Wilson was sure the facts in the papers were correctly stated. Wilson said he had personal knowledge of the facts, and gave the President his sources. The President had him make a signed endorsement to that effect on the papers. As the President was then about to add his signed recommendation, the Congressman said the President should also be informed that Stanton had said he would never execute such an order. The President seemed interested, signed the requested order, and returning the paper: "Your persistence in this case is right. There is the order and I guess it will be obeyed."

The thankful Congressman was about to go, paused for one more point. What if Stanton declined to execute the order? "Report the fact to me, but I guess he will obey that order. I know it is a small thing, as some would look at it, as it only relates to a private soldier, and we have hundreds of thousands of them. But the way to have good soldiers is to treat them rightly. At all events that is my order in this case. Let me know what comes of it."

Stanton, according to Congressman Wilson, was vexed as he read the order, feelingly repeated that he would not obey it. Wilson reported completely his interview with Lincoln. Stanton was unmoved. Wilson picked up his papers, said he would go again to the President. At the outer door of the building a messenger overtook him. He returned to find Stanton in a better mood. Endorsing the order, Stanton said: "It seems to me that the President would rather have a fuss with anybody than miss a chance to do a kindness to a private soldier. But I suppose this case is all right. At all events I like your dogged persistence in it." At the White House Wilson told how it ended, the President saying: "I'm glad you stuck to it. I meant it should so end, if I had to give it my personal attention. A private soldier has as much right to justice as a major-general."

Joshua Speed told of being with Lincoln when two women asked for releases, one of her husband, the other of her son, serving time for resistance of the draft in western Pennsylvania. The older woman couldn't afford a lawyer, "So I thought I would just come and ask you to let me have my boy." The President, turning to the young woman: "And it's your husband you want?" "Yes." He sent for the papers. Charles A. Dana brought them.

Lincoln counted the names of the prisoners. "There are twenty-seven of these men. Is there any difference in the degree of their guilt?"

"No. It is a bad case and a merciful finding."

"Well," said the President, looking out of the window and half soliloquizing, "these poor fellows have, I think, suffered enough. They have been in prison fifteen months. I have been thinking so for some time, and have said so to Stanton, and he always threatened to resign if they are released. But he has said so about other matters, and never did. So now, while I have the paper in my hand, I will turn out the flock."

He wrote a wholesale discharge, turned to the women. "Now, ladies, you can go. Your son, madam, and your husband, madam, is free."

Lincoln's recommendation joined others that Stanton should appoint J. J. S. Hassler, a drillmaster, to be a regular-army officer. Stanton refused. Adjutant General Townsend said it could be fixed. "Let it be understood by the President that Hassler will step across the street and enlist as a private in the regular army, at the same time resigning his commission as an officer of volunteers. He can then at once be promoted." This worked. Stanton was a little gruff about it, but it went through.

An earnest Republican of proved deeds asked that his son be appointed an army paymaster. How old was the son?

"He is twenty—well, nearly twenty-one."

"Nearly twenty-one! I wouldn't appoint the angel Gabriel a paymaster if he wasn't twenty-one!"

With one arm over a fence railing and one foot on a stone coping, near the gateway toward the War Department, the President leaned and heard for some minutes the difficulties of a plain-looking man whose face he searched as the man talked. He had no interruptions. The man finished. The President asked, "Have you a blank card?" The man ran his hands around in his pockets. No, he had no blank card. A well-dressed bystander came forward. "Here is one, Mr. President." More bystanders had by now collected. Carpenter called it a good scene and sketched it: "Taking a card and a pencil, Mr. Lincoln sat down upon the low stone coping, presenting almost the appearance of sitting upon the pavement itself, and wrote an order upon the card to the proper official to 'examine this man's case.' While he was writing this, I observed several persons passing down the promenade smiling, at what I presumed they thought the undignified appearance of the head of the nation, who, however, seemed utterly unconscious, either of any impropriety in the action, or of attracting any attention. Rising to his feet he handed the man the card, with a word of direction."

At the War Department repeated promises had been made of back pay for a brigadier general of able service whose appointment lacked confirmation of the Senate. No Senator was opposing confirmation. It was just one of those cases arising occasionally where the Senate adjourned without attending to a required formality. The Committee on Claims in the House had certified the claim as correct but Congress had adjourned before action on the report. And to a caller who made these presentations, with documents, to Lincoln, his first remark was, "Mr. G—, when you entered you said you had not called to ask for an office for yourself or any of your friends, but you have presented a matter here that I am afraid I shall find more difficulty in disposing of than I should have found in an application for an office." At all other places justice had been refused, said the caller, having pointed to a good war record of the brigadier general. Lincoln took up the documents, read them once, glanced through them a second time, and then, deliberately: "I do not see how the Government of the United States can afford *not* to pay its officers for rendering it their services, and this case is evidently one of meritorious services that should be paid for. Now, sir, where shall I send you to have it done?" The caller would prefer the Paymaster General to the War Department and its delays.

Tying up the roll of papers, Lincoln endorsed it: "Let the facts be ascertained as to the length of service of the within named J. B. S— and let him be paid for the time he was in service, without formality." With good humor he commented that many cases of this sort came to him, where he must decide the procedure. "I am sitting here from day to day, just like a Justice of the Peace, hearing and determining this class of cases."

This same caller, whose press account of his interviews with Lincoln was signed with the initials W.I.G., received at his Washington hotel a young lieutenant who in service with Frémont in Missouri had been wounded in the shoulder. During months in hospital "piece after piece of bone found exit through the large ragged, open wound." Then he had gone on to West Virginia, rejoined Frémont, who got for him a commission as lieutenant of artillery from the Governor of West Virginia. After months of broken health and on leave of absence he came to Washington and could not arrange to draw his back pay. The War Department ruled that commissions issued by the Governor of West Virginia to officers in the Frémont command could not be recognized. He had no acquaintances in Washington, and haggard, worn, slouching in a threadbare and faded uniform, he seemed to get nowhere in telling his story and showing his papers of commission and opening for those who would look his little parcel of forty pieces of bone that had oozed out of his shoulder wound in hospital.

The advice given him was that he should go to the President's reception room, wait till the usher had announced the reception was over, and then step in and see the President. He did this. Secretary Seward was ahead of him, but the President delayed going to a Cabinet meeting set for that hour. This cadaverous young man of so white a face, his clothes hanging so loose, what was his errand? He was given a chair. He talked for half an hour about himself and army conditions, under Lincoln's questioning. The forty pieces of bone were laid out on the desk and examined. On his original commission the President wrote an endorsement. When this was presented next morning to the officer having power to act, the officer looked disturbed, finally said, "This seems peremptory in its terms," and issued an order for the back pay due. After a furlough the young lieutenant returned to service and within a year stepped into the President's office to pay his respects, to say he was thankful for a commission as captain, and to show Lincoln that he was now plump, erect, and hoping he looked every inch a soldier, even though forty pieces of bone were lacking from one shoulder.

Past Senators and generals one afternoon went a young man into the President's office, having with fear and trembling sent in a card saying he was a wounded soldier. The President was reading a letter as he entered, raised his head a little, and over his spectacles looked the youth in the eye, then scanned his head as though searching for the wound. The soldier explained that he had returned to Washington to find that because of the severity of his wound he had been honorably discharged, and "Is there not some way I can serve my country more?"

"Well, my boy, you are serving your country by being wounded. However, I am glad you want to serve your country more."

The President took off his spectacles, laid them on a long table piled with books and maps, stood up and walked slowly around to the boy, who now no longer had any fear or trembling but was saying to himself he felt as though he had met his best friend. On his shoulder rested the warm, bony hand of the President. "And you would like to go back to the front. But you are too badly wounded for that. Wait a little. Go back home and get well and strong. We are thinking of organizing an Invalid Corps to displace able men now on guard duty, and when we are ready for wounded recruits, send in your name, and you shall do more duty for your country!" He asked young George Edward Hall then where and when he was wounded, and on hearing the story commented, "Oh, yes, these bad bulls that ran, but the last was not so mad-bad as the first." He asked about officers, management, and discipline in the army—while Senators and generals waited outside. Then warmly and with a lighted face: "My dear boy, don't forget to send in your name for the Invalid Corps. God bless you, goodbye!" And the boy later enlisted again, was appointed a lieutenant and assigned to guard duty not far from the White House.

After months in Libby Prison at Richmond, young Will Upham of the 2nd Wisconsin made his way to Lincoln's office, talked long under sympathetic questioning of the President, told of battles and prison fare, and went away carrying an appointment as a West Point cadet.

What were these soldier boys of his talking about in the camps and on the march? Always that question dwelt with Lincoln. In each army, corps, brigade, regiment, battalion, company, were the same major subjects in interest while the minor topics and cares and joys always varied. In letters home the boys wrote of matters on which they could not directly inform the President. From many of the best marchers and fighters, young in years but seasoned with wisdom and devices, Lincoln in his familiar talks with them got at what was going on in their heads and hearts. How did their confessions run? What would they tell and what hold back? No two of them as witnesses were precisely alike, but on the big, main trends they were often amazingly in agreement.

William Fletcher Goodhue of Company C, 3rd Wisconsin Veteran Volunteer Infantry, might serve as an instance. He had enlisted May 4 of '61, fought under McClellan, Burnside, and Hooker in Virginia, and on October 1 of '64 was in Atlanta with Sherman. He was a type of the volunteer citizen soldier, enlisted for duration of the war, writing home with patience and humor about bloody combats, hardships of camp fare and marching, about his sore feet, about one week of dysentery when "you might as well cut out the seat of your pants." Goodhue wrote to his "Dear Parents" the full particulars of what most interested him and his immediate associates, the camp talk. He delivered himself of just the sort of vital and significant gossip that Lincoln sought with his endless questioning of rank-and-file soldiers at the White House, in hospitals and camps. Many a private, corporal, sergeant, poured into Lincoln's ears a tale of active service in much the same tone as Goodhue in October of '64 writing to his Wisconsin home folks:

"Politics is the all absorbing element nowadays. A great many, I fear, think light of it and do not consider that there *is* something deeper and more to their interest than the hollow name Politics. There are just McClellan men enough in camp to raise a stink and with some few exceptions they are nearly all Recruits. They, these (McClellan Recruits) came out last spring from under the Draft, consequently they oppose the Government who called them out. They have no pride for the Regt they serve in, they grumble at the officers, are discontented and would like to go home. Let anyone apply an insulting remark to their Regt. in presence of an old member and there will be a fight in short notice, let a recruit hear it & he would join in and add to it. Yet what I have written would not apply to all the Recruits by any means, there are many of them who are as good Union men and soldiers as you will find.

"The old Army of the Cumberland to show their Jealousy of the 20th Corps have raised the story that the 20th Corps is unanimous for McClellan. They think because we have served under him *we still wish to serve longer*. Election day the 20th Corps will show them votes for Lincoln that can match their votes as well as we can match them in the field. I never in my life saw such a conceited set of men as the Cumberland Army. They think the Vicksburg Army and the Potomac Army have done all the *playing* during this war, and they, the Army of the Cumberland, have done all the work, when to tell the truth either the Vicksburg or the Potomac Army have seen fighting that will make a 'Cumberland' man stare. . . .

"We got 200 substitutes from Wis. a few days ago. They all got from $1,000 to $2,000 bounty. The copperheads call the army Lincoln's hirelings. To the men who enter the army nowadays it applied first rate, but it is a slur on the volunteers. It makes me feel more repugnant to a soldier's life to see such men in the ranks with us and fighting under the name of Wiscon. Vet. Vols. Yet to conquer we must submit to it; why do we have such men in the army, the reason is, the infernal copperheads keep what patriotism there is in the north dormant; they discourage volunteering, then drafts must be made, they counsel the people to resist the draft, try to degrade the army by calling us 'hirelings.' Consequently able bodied men get substitutes, so that they may not be degraded by entering the army. . . .

"Maj Stone, Paymaster U.S.A. is here. He is paying the 150th New York. He pays us next. There is considerable stir among the vets of the Regt. We were never mustered out of service, nor have we received our Discharge papers, consequently the Paymaster will not pay the veteran bounty as we have nothing to show that we are veterans. He says he will pay us up to the 1st of July 1864, the expiration of our first enlistment. I don't let myself think that I am going out of the service yet the facts of the case is this: if we are *not* mustered out of the service for our original three years, we are not legally mustered in as veterans, as the order from the Sectry. of War, is: 'That men on reenlisting shall be mustered, by reason of reenlistment as vet. vol. and so stated on their Discharge papers.' Col Hawley and the Corps Generals will do all in their power to keep us even if we are *not legally* in the service. It is too late to mend the matter now, if we are not legally mustered in they cannot make us take the oath to serve longer. We will all go to the Dry Tortugas first."

This manner of fighting man had Lincoln's affection and loyalty in a deep way. On these who knew his language and were ready for ordeals and sacrifice—on these he must rest for justification and authority. Their bayonets carried his Government. The unwilling drafted men, the substitutes and bounty men, the citizens who evaded service or taxes for the sake of comfort and were pleased to do so—what light or hope could they hold for the causes of which he was the spokesman?

At one crowded White House reception in '64, when so many people pressed into the room that handshaking had to be dispensed with, Lincoln stood bowing acknowledgments. Then his eyes fell on a soldier, pale, crippled, moving through with a plainly dressed mother. Before they could get to the door Lincoln made his way to them, took each by the hand, told them he was interested that they had come, and he could not let them go without his welcome.

A young naval lieutenant reported the talk of a Confederate prisoner: "Our boys say General Sherman never makes but one speech. When ready for a movement, he says: 'Now boys, let's get ready to go'; and they get ready on both sides." Lincoln rejoined that this "mother-wit" put him in mind of Rappahannock pickets after Chancellorsville. On a frosty morning one butternut called across the river, "Where's Old Joe?" meaning the defeated Hooker. The ready bluebelly reply was "Gone to Stonewall Jackson's funeral." The Union boy added, "What's the reason you 'Johnnies' never have any decent clothes?" The retort flashed: "We-uns don't put on our best to kill hogs in."

The fine audacity of the rank and file shone in one incident reported by Stanton. Noah Brooks noted that Lincoln repeated it fondly. Stanton with a major general, aboard a tugboat up the Broad River in North

Carolina, reached the Union outposts, to hear a picket yell, "Who have you got aboard that tug?" The severe and dignified response: "The Secretary of War and Major-General Foster." In a flash the picket roared back, "We've got major-generals enough up here—*why don't you bring us up some hard-tack?*"

Among regimental pets were a half-grown bear with a Minnesota unit that had smelt powder in a dozen engagements; several badgers and one coon with Wisconsin regiments; two gamecocks with the 49th Illinois; a large black-and-white dog named Jack that had marched with the 102d Pennsylvania, seen twenty battles—Jack had taken a wound at Malvern Hill, and twice captured, was held prisoner once six hours, another time six months. The regiment loved Jack as "a brave soldier dog." His reputation was surpassed only by that of a majestic eagle of the 8th Wisconsin Volunteers named Old Abe. Weighing ten and a half pounds, measuring six and a half feet from one wing tip to the other, his snow-white head and neck topping a brown plumage shaded with gold, Old Abe with his regiment took the oath in October of '61, and had been carried with his regiment through active service in seven States. At State expense an eagle perch was made of hardwood, a shield in the shape of a heart, inscribed with the regimental insignia. One man's sole duty on march was to carry this bird, held by a twenty-foot hemp cord. In battle Old Abe, held at three-foot cord length, was assigned to ride to the left of the color-bearer. Verses had been written in tribute to this eagle. Newspaper battle accounts told of his delight when smoke enveloped the regiment, his greeting the roar of action with fierce, wild screams. Twice, said the *Viroqua* (Wisconsin) *Times*, "Old Abe has been hit by secession bullets; one shot carried away a third part of his tail-feathers. He is a universal favorite. Thousands flock to see him, and he is fast becoming famous."

As the fall campaign approached Lincoln said to young Henry E. Wing, the *New York Tribune* cub who scouted among many regiments and reported to the President on the rank-and-file feeling in the armies, "I would rather be defeated with the soldier vote behind me than to be elected without it."

The number of soldiers who felt that they had met Lincoln personally, now in latter '64 ran into thousands. At many a review he had dismounted from his horse, walked along the company lines, shaken hands with soldiers in the front rank and reached through to the rear file and spoken such words as, "Glad to see you looking so well, boys, glad to meet you all." He might look tired when saying it, but many a trooper held a memory of being looked squarely in the eye as he heard, "I am always glad to meet one of our soldiers."

Henry Watson of the 16th Maine Infantry Volunteers would never forget the President among their tents and along their company streets. A whittling soldier was drawing a jackknife toward him, and Lincoln, seeing it: "Boy, my father taught me never to stand astride of a rail when splitting it or to draw a knife toward me. Always whittle like this." And he showed how while troops stood by at attention. The President handed back stick and knife to the seated soldier, who sprang to his feet with a salute, and: "The Commander-in-Chief is right. He is always right and damn the man that says he ain't." The President, with a slight twinkle of eye, before moving on: "Boys, if we are right we will win, if we are wrong we will lose. Your country appreciates your patriotism and let us hope the result of this war will be a just reward to us all."

To the Blue Room one day came young William M. Wires of Lynn, Massachusetts, from a signal corps at Red Hill in Georgetown with a message for the President. A reception was on and young Wires said to himself he would deliver his message personally to the President and have a handshake for once. He stood in line, moved up, reached the President, put out his hand. Just then a pompous officer in full regalia jumped in ahead of him. The President raised his arm showing an open palm of his hand and, to the officer: "This young man has got something very important to say to me, so wait a moment, please." Young Wires delivered the message, heard the President's "I thank you" as they shook hands. Wires said he was sure thankful for the privilege and wrote home to his girl: "I shall always remember the manly way that Lincoln assumed in this case. His face was one of the pleasantest I have looked on, his voice was soft and his figure was very attractive."

Blankets, pup tents, sutlers, graybacks, jiggers, blanket rolls, bivouacs, hardtack, letters from home—of these the President knew from talk with hundreds of soldiers. Of the manners and reputation of officers as they reached the rank and file, of everyday grumbling to be expected and the note of complaint that is a warning signal, these he knew too.

The flimsy excuses that some brought him, hoping for a furlough, the good and valid reasons that others had—these too he knew. Out of the hospitals from fevers and amputations they came, some of them to the White House, some of them pale, wistful, shaken, palsied, dumb, blind—a wide range of men from the realms of trial and pain and bewilderment came Lincoln's way. And he knew there were wrecks beyond coming his way. Thousands read in the *Atlantic Monthly* of a George Dedlow in one of the ten thousand hospital beds of Nashville, then in the Stump Hospital, South Street, Philadelphia, filled with men who had lost one arm or leg, or one of each, Dedlow saying, "I saw men who had lost both legs, and one who had parted with both arms, but none, like myself, stripped of every limb." Wounds, gangrene, amputations, had left Dedlow just a head and a torso. Later at an army hospital for nervous disorders Dedlow saw "one man who walked sideways, another who could not smell, another dumb from an explosion," one whose shoulder blades stood out like wings and had earned him the nickname of "Angel," another hysterical from pain and carrying a sponge and a bottle of water for constantly wetting a burning hand, occasionally pouring water in his boots to relieve his burning feet. At both of these hospitals Dedlow saw care, cleanliness, intelligence, skill, and science giving its best toward making men again of men unmade in the terrorizing routines of war.

Nearing Carver Hospital and its front gate one evening at twilight, Lincoln in his carriage saw what seemed to be a young man groping his way across the road as though blind. Hearing the carriage and its escorting cavalry, the young man turned and walked straight in the direction of the carriage and horses. "Mr. Lincoln quickly observed this," said Henry W. Knight commanding the cavalry guard, "and shouted to the coachman to rein in his horses, which he did. I shall never forget the expression of Mr. Lincoln's face on this occasion. Standing beside the carriage was the young man, in the uniform of a private soldier. He had been shot through the left side of the upper part of the face, and the ball, passing from one side to the other, had put out both his eyes. He could not have been over sixteen or seventeen years of age, and, aside from his blindness, he had a very beautiful face. Mr. Lincoln extended his hand to him, and while he held it asked of the boy in a voice trembling with emotion, his name, regiment, and where he lived. The young man answered these questions, and stated that he lived in Michigan. Then Mr. Lincoln made himself known to the blind soldier, and with a look that was a benediction in itself spoke to him a few words of sympathy and bade him good-bye."

The incident seemed closed. The newspapers, hearing nothing of it, printed nothing. Knight however happened to visit a chum at Carver Hospital and while there casually asked about the boy soldier who had lost his eyes. They told him that on the day after the President's carriage horses came near trampling down the blind youth, a commission had arrived from the President naming him a first lieutenant in the Regular Army of the United States along with an order that he should be retired on full pay.

Widows and mothers who had lost husbands and sons in the war numbered more than 150,000 in February of 1864, according to claims filed in the Pension Office. Not often was the President troubled by claimants in connection with the dead. But those with petitions in behalf of the living came every hour of the day. And many of the living were young. The war was being fought by the young. Not yet voters, all of them under twenty-one years of age, were some 30 per cent of the troops in the United States armies. Another 30 per cent were twenty-one to twenty-four. Still another 30 per cent were from twenty-five to thirty, leaving only 10 per cent over thirty. The heavy work, the toils and sacrifices, to decide the fate of the Union were in the hands of the young, in the arms, legs, and human spirit of the young.

Of a seventeen-year-old boy Lincoln wrote that General Meade could keep him in service or let him go, but the soldier was pardoned "on account of his tender age." And again to Meade, "I am unwilling for any boy under eighteen to be shot, and his father affirms that he is yet under sixteen." Of another whose release from prison was ordered he asked: "What possible injury can this lad work upon the cause of the great Union? I say let him go." Recommending further consideration in the cases of several young lieutenants, cashiered by court-martial for misconduct in battle, the President wrote he was "very unwilling for these young men to be ruined for so slight causes."

A fourteen-year-old who had run away from his Kansas home and enlisted began crying as he read a note Lincoln wrote for him to carry to Stanton. The boy had expected he would be shot at sunrise. But instead he read words to this effect: "Hadn't we better spank this drummer boy and send him back home to Leavenworth?" Lincoln sent the lad to a hotel and arranged for his ticket home.

"The boy is not going to be *shot*," Congressman Kellogg of New York cried at a refusal from Stanton, near midnight, the execution set for sunrise. Kellogg went to the White House, broke down the refusals of the guards, reached the room where the President lay in bed, and cried: "This man must not be shot. I can't help what he may have done. Why, he is an old neighbor of mine; I can't allow him to be shot!" Lincoln stayed in bed, listened quietly to the pleas of a man he had known many years, then slowly: "Well, I don't believe *shooting* will do him any good. Give me that pen."

On the White House portico one morning shortly after the battle of the Wilderness in May of '64 a brother and sister waited from seven o'clock till nine, when the President arrived from the Soldiers' Home. And they shook hands with him. But that was all. They were too bashful to ask him for what they wanted. Their brother Joseph H. Johnston of New Paltz, New York, had his left thigh shattered while going over a rail fence in a charge, and on the amputating table the surgeons said he could live only a few hours.

In the fury and the hurry he had been left under an oak tree, the army had moved off, he had kept warm by piling leaves over himself, the blood from his wound soaking leaves that gradually formed a heavy garment. And by some chance came a young girl day by day with a pail of milk that she fed from a dipper to the wounded, a mysterious doer of good, deaf and dumb, never speaking when spoken to. Ten days Johnston subsisted on milk, lay under an oak in a garment of leaves. Johnston's brother had seen his name in a casualty list, brought him to Washington, saw him washed and given two days' rest.

Then the brother and sister went to the White House—and couldn't summon enough courage to ask the President for a furlough. But the brother did go again the next morning, heard the President's, "Young man, what do you wish?" and later, "Go tell your brother he shall have a furlough." Out of the White House on a run down Pennsylvania Avenue he went to find his brother on a hospital cot holding a furlough paper that had already been brought by a cavalryman. At the railroad station a car had been set aside for the wounded man. A carpenter had hooked rubber rings to the top of the car to hold the four arms of the stretcher, so as to moderate the jolting. The President arrived as the car was ready to leave at five o'clock, shook hands with Private Joseph H. Johnston, saying, "Young man, you have done all for your country you can do, good-bye."

And Joseph's brother said: "My brother got home and lived nineteen days, long enough to see all his friends. When he had seen them all he said he was ready to die." And for kindly consideration they were ever thankful to the President and to the deaf-and-dumb girl who came day by day for ten days with milk for wounded men scattered among wilderness trees and underbrush.

With all its complaining and its tone of gloom there was a graphic touch in a misspelled, ungrammatical letter that came to Lincoln's hands from "a poor farmer boy." This boy's list of miseries would go for thousands of others. His gloom and exaggeration of his fate, his unwillingness to march on into more sufferings, his hope that the war might, for him, come to an end, was in the hearts of many. His letter, having many fancies of penmanship:

Written to the President of the United States
Camp near Culpeper
Feby the 20th 64

Presadent Sir, Mr. A. Lincoln.

I this evning I sit down to write to you (a Soldier Friend!). Mr. L, I am a private in Comp. H. 150th Regt. Pa. Vol. I enlisted in the year 1862, September the 1st and sworn into United States Survice on the 4th day September. I was a Stought and heartey Farmer Boy then. My first Sickness was braught on by lying on the ground allthough it was warm wether and on the 28th of Oct. 62 I was taken to Carver Hospital with the Typhoid Fever and where I had a hard Strugle betwene life and deth, and since then I havent ben fit fore a Soldier; and in January I left Carver Hospital fore my Regt I had hered that I was gowing to leave fore Vergina and I wanted to go with them allthough I was not fit, and I went with them to Bell plain Landing whare we landed on a very fine day and marched about 2 miles where we Encamped we made tents or Shelters from the gum blankets ore Ponshows, and we laid down on the Cold ground which frose that night hard and it rained till near Midnight and then it comenced to snow and it snowed all that day, and I was agane put in the Regt. Hospital and about a Week or two after I was Detailed fore Teamster in the Ordanence Department. I was sick there about two weekes and then I was in purty good health such as it was I was Teamster about 6 months that was till after the Gs.Burg Battel when we came to Raphanack River there I was taken with the Cronick Diareah and then with Typhoid Fever I was sent to Fairfax Simunary where onder the good care of Dr. Huselton I was brought around so I could walk I was then sent from there to Chestnut Hill Hospital whare I receved very good atension from Dr. Budd and on the 18th of January 1864 I left Chestnut Hill Hosp fore my Regt. I arived at Convalescent Camp January the 22d 64 here I aught to have ben Examend but was not although I made an aplication fore it they told me that none ware Examind there at that time they told us that we would be examind at Jenareal Mead Head Quar. but we was not now I am in my Regement agane and not fit fore duty at all as the Typhoid Fever has as I think and the Doctors say Disabled me for life. I am Entirely lame in my left Side the Medical Directors at Convalesants Camp told me to appley to my Capt and to the Comander of the Regt. fore my Discharge well this Evning the Captain Came back from his forlow and came to see me and he wanted to know how I was geting along I told him how it was and Showed him my Sertificates of Dibility but he said he dident no what to due about it he sead he couldent do Enything fore me that he new of he said that the Doctors would be likely to keepe me till the Army Moved and then they would send me of to the Hospital at Washington agane.

Now Mr. L. I am but a poor farmer Boy. I have lost my health in this Nobel Cause of ours in trying to put down this Rebelion the Tradors of the South they that tore down that Nobel flag of General Washington the Flag that our fore Fathers gave to us. Mr. Lincoln I am as I told you a poor farmer son my Mother is a widow she was willing to let me come to help to crush this Rebelion but alas that young man of 20 years that was then in full Bloom is now but a faided flower of the North nothing but a Skeliton that onst wore those Rosey cheeks of helth. I have 8 Brothers and Sisters all younger then myself the next oldest to me has broken his leg So he is a cripel for life so I am all my Mothers Suport if I was at home where I could get the Comforts of life I think I would get back my health at least so I could Earn my living and be a grate Comfort to my Mother where heare I am only Expence to the Goverment and doeing my Country no good.

My kind Friend of Friends you have the power to help me a grate deal you have the power to due it if I am not mistaken which I hope not my Friend will you please see to my case I am in Misery heare last night I had the Eare ache most all night and I have a bad sore throat. will you my dear Friend see to my case fore me you can due it a grate deal fore me; help me fore my poor widow Mother sake healp me out of my misery as I am in misery as long till I can lay in Some beter place than on the cold damp ground healp me before it is to late and I will bless you as long as there is breath in me. I would willingly help my fellow comrads put down this rebelion but my health wont permit me to due so.

I must close my letter by Sending my blessings of which I ask of god upon you and may god Bless you the Remandier of your life is the prayer of your soldier friend —— —— – –.

Mr Lincoln

if you wish to write to my Captain ore Cornel Address Cornel Wister 150 Reg P.V. Captaine (James) Reisinger of Comp H 150 Regt. Pa Vols

if you will write to me and tel me if you can due anything fore me, address —— —— ——

Comp. H 150 Reg pa Vol
in care of Capt Reisinger
Washington D. C.

please help me if you can your obedent Survent —— —— ——

I hope Mr. Presadent that you will foregive me fore my forewardness to you and in Asking of you such a faveret

I speak not ill of my Comanders they say that they can not due me enything at all Sir I have Certificates sined and sworne to in my posesion by Reliabel Doctors and if you wish to see them I will send them to you.

I am sory to put you to in eny way in trouble of eny kind, but I did not no ho to turn to fore Redress and some of my friends told me to write to the *Presadent* that there I would get my right.

I have a grate Confidence in our Good Presadent hoe has dun a grate deal fore us poor Soldiers

Mr Lincoln

there are a few more of such men ore boys as myself hear are not fit to be a Solder than I am.

The letter arrived at the White House, went through the "regular channels," ended at the headquarters of the writer's regiment, 150th Pennsylvania Volunteers, one of the Bucktail Brigade. Its Lieutenant Colonel, Thomas Chamberlin, noted that nearly every company had "at least one disillusioned youth who found soldiering anything but the picnic he had painted it." From his comrades the grumbler and whiner usually won ridicule, and from his officers scant sympathy. Of such letters as that above "President Lincoln no doubt received many," wrote Chamberlin, adding the information, "The 'faded flower of the North' in a few weeks outgrew his complicated ailments, bore his musket manfully, and was counted among the seriously wounded in the fierce encounter of the Wilderness."

Of different streaking was another veteran of the Wilderness. *Harper's Weekly* published some of his diary entries to show how cool and impassive a soldier might be while death took a harvest all around him. Of days that saw the bloodiest warfare known to the century this veteran wrote:

May 8.–Marched all night down through Spottsylvania.–Went into the fight at 10 o'clock, made two charges on the rebs, got drove back–loss very heavy.–Rested.–Ordered out in front: only 200 men left.–Stand picket all night.

May 9.–Pleasant morning.–Started early, marched out, formed a line of battle.–Laid down. Laid all day in the hot sun, with our straps on.–Attacked the rebs a little before night, drove them back, then laid down and slept.

May 10.–Pleasant morning.–The battle commenced anew at noon, lasted till 9 o'clock, when we passed to the front to support the skirmishers.–Staid there until dark; drew back, lay down for the night.

May 19.–Cloudy.–All quiet on the line.–Our boys changed papers with the rebs this morning.–Wrote a letter home.–Relieved from picket at 9 o'clock: laid behind breast-works all night.

May 23.–Cloudy and cool.–All quiet this morning.–We are in Bowling Green, beginning to move forward.–Marched nine miles, forded the North Anna River at 2 o'clock.–The rebs attacked us at 6 o'clock.–Fought an hour and a half; whipped them.

May 28.–Pleasant morning.–Started at sunrise, marched 10 miles, crossed the Pamunky River, and formed a line of battle: threw up breast-works.

June 3.–Rainy morning.–The battle opened at six o'clock.–Continual roar of musketry and artillery until evening: rained all the time.–I was on the skirmish line from 9 till 5: balls and shells fell thick all around me.

June 6.–Cloudy, but warm. Stopped at 6 o'clock near Cold Harbor.–Cooked our breakfast, washed. got a letter from home: ordered to pack up and go on picket at evening.–Got a good night's sleep.

June 7.–Cool and cloudy.–The boys go in swimming in the mill-pond.–Went out on picket at 8 o'clock: relieved at sundown.–Marched five miles and bivouacked for the night.

Out of the Cold Harbor slaughter emerged Carter E. Prince of the 4th Maine Volunteers, his life saved by a small pocket edition of the New Testament. A bullet hit his suspender buckle and carried it through the Testament that lay in the pocket of his blouse. Pushed by the bullet, the buckle penetrated the back cover and through all the chapters between Revelation and St. Mark and came to rest at Mark 12:36, where is recorded the saying of the Lord: "Sit thou on my right hand, till I make thine enemies thy footstool."

With such incidents and with men who could speak at first hand of them Lincoln became familiar.

To Lincoln's desk, to the tents of his generals in active field service, came the appeals of valorous fighters found guilty of drunkenness, of looting, of being absent without leave, of many varieties of insolence or disobedience. Lincoln's view joined that of General Tecumseh Sherman regarding some of his 8th Missouri lawbreakers: "Their conduct for courage under my own eye was such that I would have pardoned them for anything short of high treason." Sherman held, "This may not be good morality, but is war," and recalled the case of a high officer guilty of shameful behavior in repeated drunken sprees, and President Jackson's dismissal of the complaint: "Any man who fought as he did may get drunk as often as he pleases."

Press accounts told of an army surgeon court-martialed and his attorney bringing the papers to Lincoln, who read the indictment of "drunkenness," commenting, "That's bad, very bad," and further along as to "insulting a lady": "That's bad, too. An officer shouldn't insult a lady, by any means. I'm afraid I can't reinstate this man."

On the attorney's request Lincoln read further the specifications regarding an attempt to kiss a lady, scratched his head, looked up to the attorney. "Really, I don't know about this. There are exceptions to every rule but as a general thing it's very hard to insult a lady by kissing her. But it seems the doctor only attempted to kiss her—perhaps the insult consisted in his not fully succeeding. I don't know as I ought to interfere in behalf of a man who attempts to kiss a lady and doesn't do it."

The attorney urged that a third party had made the complaint, with no evidence that the lady herself felt insulted. "That's a fact," said the President. "We can easily dispose of the kissing part. But I must look into the drunkenness a little. I can't overlook that. I'll have to get good evidence that it was strictly a New Year's offence, and is not a common occurrence with the doctor." The case was taken under advisement.

A Pittsburgh boy came with his story of having enlisted at seventeen, of fighting and marching, of fever that had wasted him. Lincoln believed his story, wrote the Secretary of War to see this "very young" soldier. If the Secretary gave the soldier a furlough or any other favor and was criticized, he could point to the President writing that in this case "I shall be satisfied with whatever you do." Benjamin Shultz of Newark, New Jersey, a member of the English New Jersey regiment, tried several ways in latter '63 to get a furlough and failed. Then his mother wrote to Lincoln that she was a widow, that two of Ben's brothers were in the army, that Ben himself had taken a hand in nearly every battle fought by the Army of the Potomac. Now she wanted to see him once more, put her arms around him, and then let him go back to the war. This furlough Lincoln ordered without a moment's delay.

In April of '64 came a letter from a Quaker girl in Washington County, Pennsylvania. She had hesitated "to inform you of my troubles." Now in order to make her case clear "it is necessary to give you a brief history connected with myself and would be husband." They had been engaged for some years. In August of '62 he enlisted for three years. In October of '63 he was furloughed to go home and vote. "It was our design to marry while he was at home and under those determinations we very foolishly indulged too freely in matrimonial affairs and at last our union was defeated by my Father. In consequence of him [the father] he [her lover] was forced to return to the army a single man. The result of our indulgences are going to bring upon us both an unlawful family providing you do not take mercy upon us and grant him a leave of absence in order to ratify past events. I am Honored Sir one that circumstances must apologize for the boldness to ask of you this favor under these aggravating circumstances. I hope and pray that you will not cast me aside in scorn and dismay. Remember that I have a father and mother and a wide circle of friends and if we cannot remedy past events I only pray that Death may come to me at an early period of time. Allow him if it is thy will to remove me to Philadelphia, Pa. to reside during his stay in the army. Dear Sir I can only ask and it lies in your power to grant my request. May God soften your heart if need be. May you view this subject as a serious one connected with me."

Then she named the father of her unborn child, a private in the 140th Pennsylvania Volunteers with the Army of the Potomac. Word had come from him that army orders forbade soldiers writing furlough-begging letters to those higher up. Therefore she wrote to the President.

On the back of her letter Lincoln wrote to the Secretary of War the endorsement, "Send him to her by all means." April 14, 1864, was the official dating of this furlough granted for the sake of the legitimacy of the birth of a child to come.

David R. Locke, on the second of the only two calls he paid Lincoln in Washington, asked a pardon for an Ohio deserter who had enlisted and kissed good-by to a girl he was engaged to marry. She would be true to her hero who had marched away to war. So he believed as he marched away. Then rumors came to him. A rival whom she had rejected, a rival whom he hated, was keeping company with her. She was pretty. She liked company. What was happening? While he was at the battle fronts perhaps the hated rival would win her. He applied for a furlough. It was refused him. Reckless and half-crazy, he deserted, went home, found the rumors partly true, but he had come in time. He married the girl. Then came his arrest, trial, and sentence to be shot. "I stated the circumstances, giving the young fellow a good character," wrote the creator of Petroleum V. Nasby, "and the President at once signed a pardon."

With the pardon went Lincoln's comment to Locke: "I want to punish the young man—probably in less than a year he will wish I had withheld the pardon. We can't tell, though. I suppose when I was a young man I should have done the same fool thing."

Locke in this connection and out of other affairs gave his opinion: "No man on earth hated blood as Lincoln did, and he seized eagerly upon any excuse to pardon a man when the charge could possibly justify it. The generals always wanted an execution carried out before it could possibly be brought before the President."

Governor Morton brought up the matter of three young drafted Quakers. Two had paid their $300 each for exemption. The third, Allen Jay, was ordered to report to Lafayette, Indiana, for training—or pay his $300. He sent word, "If I believed that war is right I would prefer to go myself than to hire someone else to be shot in my place." A military officer came to Jay's farm, took his pick of horses, cattle, hogs, and was writing bills for their public sale when he was called to dinner. The Jay family insisted the officer should eat with them. He did, saying: "If you would get mad and order me out of the house, I could do this work much easier, but here you are, feeding me and my horse while I am arranging to take your property from you. I tell you it's hard work!" The drafted young Quaker, Allen Jay, said there were no "unkind feelings" toward him, as the officer posted the sale bills on trees, fences, and walls in the neighborhood. On the day set for the sale, however, the officer came saying it was postponed, and "You can go on using your horses." At a later time, wrote Allen Jay, "I learned that Governor Morton, in Washington at about that time, spoke to President Lincoln about it and he ordered the sale to be stopped."

Three captured North Carolina Confederate soldiers were Quakers, conscripted into service and at heart Union men, according to an application for their release, which Lincoln endorsed: "This paper is presented to me by Friends John W. Tatum of Delaware, and Joseph Tatum of New Jersey, who are satisfied that the statement is correct. Let the men within named be discharged on affirming according to the oath of December 8, 1863, and that they will remain North."

A deserter wrote from Canada that religion had won him to repentance, and at a certain hour he would be seen on the White House grounds, ready for military service again. Identified by clothes he said he would be wearing, he was arrested and detained. The President wrote on his letter that he should be returned to his regiment without penalty, except that when his term of enlistment service expired he should serve in prison the number of days he was absent by desertion.

From Hannah Armstrong back in Sangamon County came word. She who had fed young Abe Lincoln, given him a roof, and mended his clothes, was asking the President to let her son Duff leave the army. This was the same Duff or William Armstrong that Lincoln had helped clear of a murder charge. Was the case now such a one that Lincoln as a personal favor to an old woman would obey her wish? It was. Duff himself explained it:

"When the war broke out the four brothers of us enlisted in the army. Jim was wounded at Belmont. Pleasant died. I served on. Mother took a notion she wanted me. People laughed at her when she said she would write to the President, but she said, 'Please goodness, I am a-going to try it.' She got Squire Garber of Petersburg to write to 'Uncle Abe,' and in a few days mother got a telegram signed 'A. Lincoln,' telling her I had been honorably discharged. I was at Elmira, New York, helping pick up deserters, and a discharge was the last thing I dreamed of."

Lighted with an old boyhood sentiment, Lincoln wrote to a Missouri commandant: "N. W. Watkins, of Jackson, Mo., (who is half-brother to Henry Clay) writes me that a colonel of ours has driven him from his home in Jackson. Will you please look into the case and restore the old man to his home if the public interest will admit?"

After the Amnesty Proclamation of the President in December of '63 questions arose continuously around the point of whether this or that man had violated his oath of allegiance to the Union Government. Into War Department files went a series of endorsements in Lincoln's handwriting, authorizing officers to discharge prisoners suspected of Confederate sympathies. Where the officers had mainly suspicion with merely slight proof, Lincoln's word usually was to let the man go. Often it was evident from Lincoln's written endorsement that he had first read the documents in the case and then personally interviewed the man. Where no crime or overt act was involved and a man was accused of holding wrong beliefs, though not having been noisy enough with his spoken beliefs to affect recruiting, Lincoln's humor came into play.

Some he let out of prison as though he might have said privately to each one that his feet should be trained to more careful walking. On one War Department paper he indicated with delicacy a guiding rule: "On principle I dislike an oath which requires a man to swear he has not done wrong. It rejects the Christian principle of forgiveness on terms of repentance. I think it is enough if the man does no wrong hereafter."

The load of blame the President himself carried moved him at times. The *New York Tribune* Washington correspondent, Wilkeson, called one morning with his sister-in-law, Elizabeth Cady Stanton, radical on slavery and woman suffrage. Carpenter knew that the President stood for a little lecture from her on how he should do better. Later on this day Carpenter brought in some New York friends, one of them warmly endorsing the Amnesty Proclamation and its spirit of reconciliation toward the Confederates. "This approval appeared to touch Mr. Lincoln deeply," noted Carpenter, seeing on the President's face a look he could never forget. Lincoln meditated: "When a man is sincerely *penitent* for his misdeeds, and gives satisfactory evidence of the same, he can safely be pardoned, and there is no exception to the rule."

From Camp Morton at Indianapolis a prisoner in June of '64 wrote a personal appeal: "Mr. President, I never was, am not, and never can be, a secessionist. I have been of a highly nervous temperament, with weak lungs, and easily excited. I was shamefully deceived by a supposed friend, who made me believe that I would be killed unless I fled from my home and native State to seek safety in the South." Lincoln read this and much more and endorsed: "This man being so well vouched, and talking so much better than any other I have heard, let him take the oath of December 8, and be discharged."

Lawyers and politicians, whose names did not appear in the proceedings, wrought their designs, perpetrated their frauds, and did not hesitate at perjury, to win favors for clients, friends, constituents. When other authorities had refused release or immunity it was known there was yet left a Chief Magistrate with a general reputation as softhearted. In order to have a record of who was sponsoring a release or parole, Lincoln named them in many of the orders issued. On an order directing that William T. Dazey, on taking the oath, be bailed to his brother, Michael, Lincoln wrote on the brother's letter, "Senator Browning personally knows, and vouches for the writer of this letter." In this case Browning had spoken in person to the President in behalf of Dazey's brother. Thus far nothing in writing put any responsibility on Browning. So for convenience and if necessary future reference as to Dazey's behavior, Lincoln entered the name of Browning as a voucher.

An eighteen-year-old boy, Henry N. Warfield, with other Confederate prisoners, escaped from Camp Douglas, Chicago, in December of '62 and made his way to the home of a Unionist brother-in-law, Dr. L. W. Brown, near Jacksonville, Illinois. The boy followed his brother-in-law's advice, gave himself up to Union authorities, and took the oath of allegiance. Nearly a year later, when Governor Yates, Senator Trumbull, two Congressmen, and other officials petitioned Lincoln for the boy's release from prison, Lincoln wrote an order: "Let Henry N. Warfield, named within, be paroled and delivered to the custody,—bailed, so to speak,—to his brother-in-law, Dr. L. W. Brown, who and whose brothers are very near friends of mine in Illinois."

Charged with disloyalty, Thomas Thoroughman of St. Joseph, Missouri, had been held in jail for some time when formidable appeals for his release were made to the President. On the face of a large envelope holding the papers of the case, Lincoln wrote an order closing the matter: "Will the Secretary of War please direct that Mr. Thoroughman may be disposed of at the discretion of Abram Jonas and Henry Asbury of Quincy, Illinois, both of whom I know to be loyal and sensible men?"

Senator Sumner asked Lincoln's attention to a letter written by one Samuel Breck, a fellow townsman of George C. Alden, Company K, 7th Massachusetts regiment. Alden was under death sentence for sleeping on picket duty. Breck attested that Alden was known to be subject to fits of sleeping sickness against which he was powerless to struggle. Below Sumner's recommendation of delay Lincoln wrote his judgment for the record: "I know nothing of this case—know not where Mr. Alden is—whether any proceedings are on foot against him. I should not knowingly let him be punished, if shown he has the infirmity stated in the affidavit, though the infirmity may be sufficient reason for dismissing him from the service."

In the chronicle of Confederate spies saved from death by Lincoln was Lieutenant Samuel B. Davis of Delaware, son of a Presbyterian minister, twenty-four years of age, tall, slender, handsome, dauntless, distant in kin to Jefferson Davis, who sent him on a secret mission to Ohio. His hair dyed, traveling on a British passport with a false name, he was recognized by two Union soldiers who got on at Newark, Ohio, as an officer on duty when they were Confederate prisoners. In the main room of the Newark jail young Davis was seen to remove his coat, rip open the linings, take out dispatches and drawings penciled on white silk. These he burned at a stove around which the other prisoners were gathered.

On trial, Davis pleaded "not guilty of being a spy" but "guilty of being a bearer of dispatches." The Judge Advocate argued that he had been found within the Union lines in disguise and under a false name at places where he could have obtained valuable information, whether he did or not. Lieutenant Davis proposed to show by testimony of Confederate President Davis and Secretary of State Judah P. Benjamin that he was sent as a bearer of dispatches. The court-martial refused a continuance of the trial for the purpose of getting such testimony. Young Davis made a speech. He faced, as he spoke, several haggard and battered Union veterans, some with empty sleeves. They were cold as he began. When he finished his very short speech they were not so cold.

The day was set for his hanging on Johnson's Island near Sandusky, Ohio. Among those who went to Lincoln asking suspension of sentence were William T. McClintick, president of the Cincinnati & Marietta Railroad, and Senator Saulsbury of Delaware, one of the most violent of Senate critics of Lincoln. Saulsbury wrote to Lincoln: "You know I am neither your personal nor political friend, but Senator Douglas once told me you were a kind-hearted man. Read the inclosed speech of this young officer condemned as a spy. There is nothing like it in history save Robert Emmet's. I ask you to act in this matter as the President of the United States should act."

How could Saulsbury, reputed the hardest drinker in the Senate, sometimes attending public sessions drunk, have guessed that such a note would hit where Lincoln was weakest? Lincoln undoubtedly read more than once the little gem of a note from Saulsbury with its wonderfully sober dignity. Then he must have read more than once the little speech of Lieutenant Samuel B. Davis facing haggard and battered Union veterans, some with empty sleeves, at Newark, Ohio: "I fear nothing on this earth. I do not fear to die. I am young and I would like to live, but I deem him unworthy who should ask pity of his foemen. Some of you have wounds and scars. I can show them, too. You are serving your country as best you may. I have done the same. I can look to God with a clear conscience, and whenever the Chief Magistrate of this nation shall say 'Go,' whether upon the scaffold or by the bullets of your soldiery, I will show you how to die."

The day set for the hanging drew near. Lieutenant Davis wrote to Major Lewis H. Bond: "The court of which you are the judge-advocate having sentenced me to be hung, at least grant the request of one whose days are numbered. I desire that, if possible, one or more members of the court will come and witness my execution. Take this as the request of one who is about to be launched into eternity. Come and see it done, and you shall at least have the satisfaction of knowing that you hung a brave man. Be kind enough to answer this hasty note. It is not written through disrespect, but for the reason I have already assigned." Judge Advocate Bond wrote that he would be there with regret and sadness, that "by your manly conduct and heroic bearing under the most trying circumstances, you have won the respect and excited the admiration of your foemen."

The evening before the hanging date the scaffold lumber had been tested, likewise the rope, and the headquarters commandant at Johnson's Island had gone to bed expecting the first thing in the morning to witness the neck of young Davis broken in due process of law. The commandant had gone to sleep when there was a knocking at the door, a pounding that woke him from his sleep. It was a messenger with an order from President Lincoln directing that the execution be suspended and the prisoner sent to Fort Warren. And when much later men tried to get Davis to tell of his mission to Ohio in '64 his quiet answer was, "That is a secret that will die with me."

Young Davis had traveled from Richmond, Virginia, to Baltimore, then to Columbus, Ohio, and up to Detroit and across to Windsor, Canada, where it was known he had connected with Jacob Thompson and other instigators of border plots and violence aimed at entangling the United States in a war with Great Britain. The grounds in international law for a death sentence were clear. But Lincoln held international law not always applicable to a civil war where hope was nursed of reconciliations to come.

A smoking revolver in his hand, a dead Union officer at his feet, Dr. David M. Wright, a leading and reputable citizen of Norfolk, Virginia, was arrested, tried by a military commission, sentenced to be hanged. Two able attorneys managed his case and spoke for him. The verdict was murder. Judge Advocate General Holt, on Lincoln's request, sent a transcript of the trial to the President, with his personal opinion that the deed was "undefended assassination." Petitioners surpassing in number those of any other pardon appeal during the war, it seemed, protested to Lincoln. From the North and the South, and from Canada, they protested with letters, telegrams, personal calls. "Do not let execution be done until my further order," Lincoln telegraphed the commandant at Fortress Monroe.

A crying issue stood out. Up one of the main streets of Norfolk July 11, 1863, had marched a company of Negro troops. At their head was Anson L. Sanborn, a second lieutenant of the 1st United States Colored Troops. From the sidewalks came taunts and hoots. Among the most feverish of the jeering Confederate sympathizers was Dr. David M. Wright, a man of exceptional works and good character, widely known. He was suddenly in a clash with Lieutenant Sanborn, drew a revolver, shot the twenty-year-old officer dead.

Southern friends of the Doctor petitioned President Davis to make efforts. War Secretary Seddon at Richmond endorsed one petition with sympathy over the "natural indignation of Dr. Wright at the shameful spectacle [of Negro troops], and his prompt vindication of his honor." To a Raleigh citizen Jefferson Davis wrote, "I would gladly do anything in my power to rescue him from an enemy regardless alike of the laws and customs of civilized people."

The daughter of Dr. Wright was permitted an extended visit alone with him in his prison cell. He walked out of the prison—in her clothes—beginning his escape. A Union officer in the street noticed his walk. It was not the kind of a walk that went with woman's dress; it was "a masculine stride." He stopped Dr. Wright and took him back to his cell.

It was now October 7 and Lincoln had delayed execution nearly three months. On that day he wrote that no proper question remained open except as to the alleged insanity of the accused. On that point he had caused a very full examination to be made, including all evidence from counsel of the accused, by an expert of high reputation in that professional department. This was Dr. John P. Gray, a noted alienist, who had a long interview with Lincoln on September 10 before going to Norfolk. The findings were that Wright was not insane prior to the killing, "that he has not been insane since, and is not insane now." Therefore the President was directing that the sentence of death be carried into execution.

The date of October 16 was fixed for the hanging. On pleas of one of Wright's attorneys Lincoln ordered postponement of the execution to October 23, adding, "This is intended for his preparation and is final."

On October 17 the Fortress Monroe commandant telegraphed Lincoln that Dr. Wright's wife desired to visit Washington to intercede with the President for her husband's life. Would Lincoln put himself to the test of denying an agonized woman's prayers for mercy? He replied: "It would be useless for Mrs. Dr. Wright to come here. The subject is a very painful one, but the case is settled."

On the day before October 23, according to David Homer Bates of the War Telegraph Office, his office associate Richard O'Brien, "was approached by a man who said that if he would anticipate a telegram which was hourly expected from President Lincoln granting a reprieve, he would be paid $20,000 in gold, and would be given free passage to England on a blockade runner. O'Brien indignantly refused the bribe."

October 23 dawned. Hope had not died in some quarters that in the last hour a telegram from Lincoln might arrive. Hours passed. No Executive Mansion telegram came. At 11:20 in the morning word was put on the wires: "Dr. Wright was executed this morning."

Thus a skilled physician who in his twenty-five years of practice had saved many human lives was given the penalty accorded to murderers. On the scaffold his last words came from tremulous lips: "Gentlemen, the act which I committed was done without the slightest malice."

For some of his own spies, secret-service operatives, and professional man-hunters, Lincoln had little respect and sometimes contempt, as shown in the case of the Reverend Henry M. Luckett. After a lifetime of Midwest Methodist preaching Luckett in the shocks of war finance had lost his investments and with broken health and shattered nerves was visiting a niece in Memphis, a city held by Federals under General Hurlbut. Haunted by his losses, in fear of becoming a pauper and dying a public charge, Luckett turned into a monomaniac on that point. Government detectives,

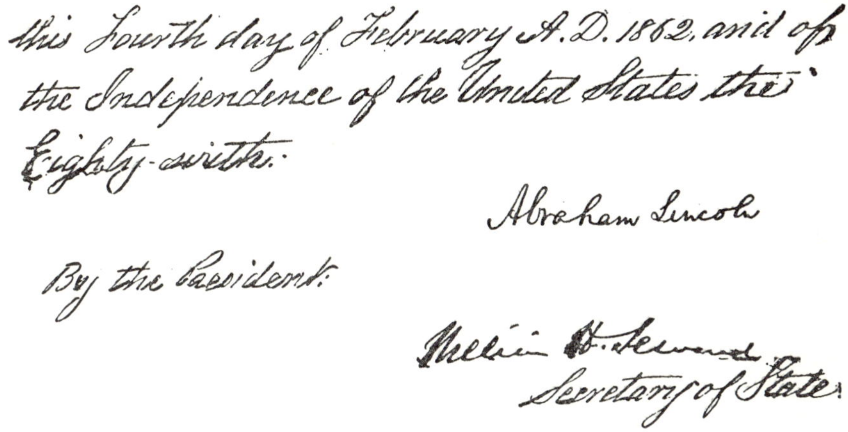
this Fourth day of February A.D. 1862, and of the Independence of the United States the Eighty-sixth.

Abraham Lincoln

By the President:

William H. Seward
Secretary of State.

Not always a pardoner, Lincoln signs the death warrant of the first slave-trader convicted and hanged by the Federal Government. From the Barrett collection.

finding him Southern-born and voicing sympathy with the sufferings of the Southern people, wormed their way into his confidence. They would put up the money for quinine and percussion caps to be carried by Luckett and others into the Confederate lines in the false bottom of a wagon. When they had led the weak and harassed old man into believing he might have a profit that would save him from the poorhouse, when his consent to it had him committed to a grave crime, they arrested him, put the irons on, and a quick trial saw him sentenced to be shot.

Democratic Congressman Voorhees of Indiana went to the Republican Senator Henry S. Lane of Indiana. Would Lane go to the White House with him and intercede for Luckett? "If the man," said Lane, "has been supplying the rebels with ammunition and quinine, I would not interfere if he were my own brother." Then Lane went home, at dinner talked it over with Mrs. Lane, then sought out Voorhees and decided to join him in a White House call. Also joined were Democratic Senator Hendricks of Indiana, Colonel William R. Morrison, soldier and Republican Congressman of Illinois, and a Mr. and Mrs. Bullitt of Kentucky who had first interested Congressman Voorhees. Mrs. Bullitt was a daughter of Luckett, was shaken with distress over her father in forty-eight hours having to face a firing squad. Voorhees quieted her with assurances that Lincoln was a plain, kind man and she could talk to him without dread or awe.

They filed into the President's room. He slowly turned in his chair, inclined his head and spoke. "I saw at a glance," noted Voorhees, "that Mr. Lincoln had that sad, preoccupied and faraway look during which it was difficult at times to engage his attention to passing events." Senator Lane in swift words made known the case. "Mr. Lincoln looked at him in a patient, tired sort of way." In an awkward pause no one spoke. Then Mrs. Bullitt's voice from a chair near the President, "Mr. Lincoln," and "he turned to her with a grave, benignant expression, and as he listened his eyes lost that distant look." Suddenly as she was pleading brightly and rapidly for her father, Lincoln interrupted:

"Lane, what did you say this man's name was?"

"Luckett."

"Not Henry M. Luckett?"

"Yes," interposed Mrs. Bullitt. "My father's name is Henry M. Luckett."

"Why, he preached in Springfield years ago, didn't he?"

"Yes, my father used to preach in Springfield."

"Well, this is wonderful!" Lincoln rambled along. "I knew this man well. I have heard him preach. He was a tall, angular man like I am, and I have been mistaken for him on the streets. Did you say that he was to be shot tomorrow? No, no! There will be no shooting nor hanging in this case. Henry M. Luckett! There must be something wrong with him, or he wouldn't be in such a scrape as this. I don't know what more I can do for him, but you can rest assured, my child," turning to Mrs. Bullitt, "that your father's life is safe."

He touched a bell, dictated a dispatch to General Hurlbut at Memphis to suspend execution and await further orders. They were thanking him, taking their leave, with him repeating as though not to them but to himself, "Henry M. Luckett! No, no! There is no shooting or hanging in this case."

The order to Major General Hurlbut at Memphis read: "I understand you have under sentence of death a tall old man by the name of Henry M. Luckett. I personally knew him, and did not think him a bad man. Please do not let him be executed, unless upon further order from me, and in the meantime send me a transcript of the record."

"Pass the bearer through the lines . . . unmolested and her baggage undisturbed" ran the words of a pass Lincoln wrote for a Southern woman, sedate and respectable-looking, sixty years old, who seemed harmless enough. Bearing this presidential pass, she went to Syracuse, to New York City, and elsewhere buying supplies much wanted in the South. Stanton and Allan Forman, a secret-service operative, managed to have her a prisoner and, her baggage opened, enough contraband material found to show that she was criminally planning to give aid and comfort to the enemy. She was passed through the lines with instructions not to return during the war. Lincoln remarked at a later time that he was pleased on some accounts that it had happened, for it gave him an excuse ever after, when urged to grant a similar pass, to cite this instance.

S. S. Bradford in a pass signed by the President was authorized to go by any route to his home in Culpeper County, "there to remain so long as he does not misbehave." Photographer Brady later came into possession of this pass and enjoyed showing it for its Lincolnian flavor.

A young Virginia woman whose family had long been familiars of the Blairs was brought to Lincoln by Old Man Blair. He had warned her beforehand: she was impulsive and must now be careful and not by any word betray her Confederate sympathies. She wished a pass to visit her brother, a Confederate soldier and a prisoner in the Union lines. Her eyes flashed. She was a vivid presence. The President bent toward her, searched her face, and, "You are, of course, loyal?"

She hesitated a moment, met his gaze frankly, then, "Yes, loyal to the heart's core—to Virginia!" He kept his eyes on her face a moment longer, went to a desk, wrote a line or two and handed her a folded paper. She bowed herself out with Mr. Blair, who was saying: "Didn't I warn you to be very careful? You have only yourself to blame." She unfolded the paper and read words to this effect signed by the President: "Pass Miss —— ——; she is an honest girl and can be trusted."

In the case of another Confederate loyalist Lincoln moved as a shadow and alone. This was revealed long afterward by a young woman of Richmond. In the spring of '61, when war was to be let loose and no one more aware of it beforehand than Abraham Lincoln, her father had an evening visitor. Her father was too well known as a friend of the Confederacy, said the evening visitor. It was possible and even probable that the next day her father, if he stayed in Washington, might be forcibly detained for questioning, and his movements embarrassed, a stay in jail not unlikely—so said the evening visitor. She and her father and mother journeyed that night to Richmond. So she told it. The evening visitor was Abraham Lincoln. He mentioned a favor her father had done for some friend of his. He added that he well knew her father too worthy a character to stay in Washington and be involved as he surely would be. The hates of war had raged on, but in this particular home in Richmond they had a silent affection and regard for Lincoln. Long afterward the young woman told the incident plausibly and with detailed circumstances.

With the North squeezing the South toward its last loaf of bread and final bullet, Lincoln looked to the day when it would be an advantage to have a political record free from vengeance, with no avowals of punishment and retribution to come. Welles meditated in his diary in the summer of '64 on how "greater severity might well be exercised, and yet it would tend to barbarism." Nevertheless Welles could not banish his feeling that the President was going too easy and that sterner measures were wanted. "No traitor has been hung," wrote Welles. "I doubt if there will be, but an example should be made of some of the leaders, for present and for future good. They may, if taken, be imprisoned, or driven into exile, but neither would be lasting. Parties would form for their relief, and ultimately succeed in restoring the worst of them to their homes and the privileges they originally enjoyed."

This was the mild-mannered little bewigged Secretary of the Navy speaking. What would he have? Deaths and more deaths. So long as the high men of the Confederacy lived anywhere on earth, they would threaten the peace and amity of the Union. Therefore hang them or shoot them. "Death," wrote Welles in that summer of '64, "is the proper penalty and atonement." But as to this becoming a policy he had his misgivings from what he had noticed near the President. "I apprehend there will be very gentle measures in closing up the Rebellion."

A story became current which probably didn't happen precisely as told, but did have an actual similar incident as a basis. To a Senator's question as to what he intended to do when the war was over, Lincoln quickly made answer, "Reconstruct the machinery of this government."

And the Senator responded: "You are certainly crazy. You talk as if treason was not henceforth to be made odious, but that the traitors, cut-throats and authors of this war should not only go unpunished, but receive encouragement to repeat their treason with impunity! They should be hanged higher than Haman, sir! Yes, higher than any malefactors the world has ever known!"

The President stood cool, taking it all, pausing a moment. "Now, Senator, suppose that when this hanging arrangement has been agreed upon, you accept the post of Chief Executioner. If you will take the office, I will make you a brigadier-general and Public Hangman for the United States. That would just about suit you, wouldn't it?"

"I am a gentleman, sir. And I thought you knew me better than to believe me capable of such dirty work. You are jesting, Mr. President."

"You speak of being a gentleman. Yet you forget that in this free country all men are equal, the vagrant and the gentleman standing on the same ground when it comes to rights and duties, particularly in time of war. Therefore, being a gentleman, as you claim, and a law-abiding citizen, I trust, you are not exempt from doing even the dirty work at which your high spirit revolts."

The Senator took his hat, vanished, was not seen at the White House for a long time, being too far down the hallway to hear the President's chuckle. "He won't bother me again."

Lincoln's refusals and consents in the case of Colonel Frank Wolford of the 1st Kentucky Cavalry had his opposition harassed. During the Kentucky uproar against the Emancipation Proclamation Colonel Wolford in an elaborate ceremony received from the citizens of Lexington a costly sword, sash, pistols, and spurs in token of his service in fighting against Confederate forces. To the amazement of his audience Wolford in his acceptance leaped forth into violent denunciations of "the Lincoln government," charged it with violation of solemn pledges as to the purposes of the war, with breaking the rules of civilized warfare in the "indiscriminate, wide-spread ruin which he is sowing broadcast throughout the South." According to the *National Unionist*, Wolford elaborated two ideas: "Old Abe was a rascal, and ought to be hung, and McClellan was a great Democrat and ought to be elected President." In every public assembly, Wolford closed, were "pimps and informers" who reported to the "fountains of power and patronage." Such "ilk" could inform Mr. Lincoln that his army minions regarded him as "a tyrant and a usurper."

Praise showered on Wolford then from the conservative Unionists of Kentucky who favored McClellan. General Stephen Gano Burbridge, a lawyer, merchant, and farmer who had early in the war raised a regiment of Kentuckians, with loyal service had won advancement to brigadier general, was in charge of martial law if and when applied in Kentucky. General Burbridge consulted with Dr. Robert J. Breckinridge and other Lincoln men. Then he arrested Wolford.

Immediately the case came before Lincoln through Congressman Robert Mallory and Senator Powell of Kentucky. "We called on Mr. Lincoln, and I can assure you that we were in no very pleasant mood," ran Mallory's account as given at a public meeting in Frankfort, Kentucky. "We gained admittance to his presence, and told him we had come to learn the cause of the arrest. Mr. Lincoln replied, 'Well, I don't know exactly what he was arrested for, but I reckon he was arrested for making speeches calculated to prevent men from enlisting in the army.' "

Mallory insisted that Wolford actually was raising a regiment at the time of arrest, and quoted Lincoln's reply, "Well, I don't know, but I have understood that in his position of loyalty, he had ifs and buts."

A sharp dispute then arose between Mallory and Lincoln as to who was loyal to the Constitution, Mallory quoting Lincoln: "I don't want to argue with you, Mallory; you will beat me in the argument; but I have established my rule in this matter, and intend to stand by it."

"What is your rule?"

"To arrest anybody who says or does anything calculated to prevent any person from enlisting in the army or discouraging enlistment, either white or black."

Mallory's account then proceeded: "I told him I was afraid I should violate this rule, as I expected to go home and enter into the campaign against him. If he expected to arrest all who did this he had as well detain us while we were there and save the trouble of arrest and transportation. He said he reckoned not, and that if we were arrested by any of the small fry to appeal to him and he would have us released. So I feel safe! I then asked him why he did not re-arrest Vallandigham; that he had returned in defiance of his order, and was making speeches vastly more bitter against him than anything Wolford had ever said. His reply was that 'he had not been officially notified of these facts; but whenever he learned certainly that Vallandigham was making such speeches he would arrest him at once.' Powell, who had been sitting by all this while, and had grown about as mad as a man can well get, replied, 'No, sir, you won't; you are afraid to arrest him again, and you know full well that if you undertake it 200,000 freemen from the State of Ohio, and as many more from other States, will rush to his rescue. You dare not make the experiment.' Lincoln responded, 'That's the way you all talk, and now if I release Wolford, you will say that I did it because I was afraid to hold him.' Lincoln then wanted to tell us an anecdote, but I checked him, and told him with feelings of contempt that that was no fit occasion to indulge in anecdote, and the interview ended. And I understand that he, in a subsequent interview with Wolford, said he would like to tell him a joke, but that I had told him this was no time for them, and that he must charge me with having deprived him of a good one."

After this much-ado-about-Wolford and depriving Mallory and Powell of a good anecdote, Lincoln decided not to deprive Wolford of his freedom and issued an order for his release from jail. The *Old Guard* and other hostile journals, however, were printing in October of '64, as campaign material, a note of Lincoln to Wolford, with a blank parole, "which as you choose, you can sign and be discharged." The blank parole read: "I hereby pledge my honor that I will neither do nor say anything which will directly or indirectly tend to hinder, delay or embarrass the employment and use of colored persons as soldiers, seamen, or otherwise, in the suppression of the existing rebellion, so long as the United States government chooses to employ and use them." The endorsement by the President read: "Colonel Frank Wolford is discharged from his parole, given me July 7, 1864, and allowed to go at large upon the condition of the parole by him signed on the other side of this paper." Linked with this was Colonel Wolford's reply to the President July 30, 1864, that frankly "I cannot bargain for my liberty and the exercise of my rights as a freeman on any such terms." By no word or act had he encouraged the enemy, wrote Wolford, and "I may say, without presumption, that I have done more to enlist white men in the army of the Union than any other man in the State of Kentucky. I have done nothing to hinder the enlistment of negroes, because I do not associate with them, and have no influence over them." Then came his accusation, delivered, wrote Wolford, with the bluntness of a soldier. "You, Mr. President . . . have caused me to be arrested and held in confinement contrary to law, not for the good of our common country, but to increase the chances of your election to the Presidency. . . . Much as I love liberty, I will fester in a prison, or die on a gibbet, before I will agree to any terms that do not abandon all charges against me."

The publication of this Lincoln-Wolford correspondence in October of '64 would of course have had more political effect if Wolford had not months before been released on order of the President.

John M. Bullock, son of a Presbyterian minister in Baltimore, came to say: "Mr. President, parole my brother, Lieutenant Walter R. Bullock, from Johnson's Island, where he is sick and wounded. Release him so that he may come home to die."

"Will your brother take the oath?"

"No, sir, he will not. He will have to die if that is the only alternative."

"I cannot parole him. I should like to do so but it is impossible unless he will take the oath."

Bullock pleaded. His brother would soon die. They wanted him to die at home. Only one man in the country had absolute power in such a case to do what he wished no matter what people said or thought—the President. And according to Bullock's account, Lincoln sat with elbows on knees, face in hands, gazing into a log fire, suddenly straightening—"I'll do it, I'll do it," then writing on a visiting card a parole order. The man paroled had been a captain in the terroristic and marauding Morgan cavalry. Also he was a nephew of the former Vice-President of the United States, now a Confederate brigadier, distant kinsman of Mrs. Lincoln, John C. Breckinridge. There was plenty for Lincoln to consider while gazing into a log fire.

"Not always stern" was Lincoln, found Cassius M. Clay. Three of Clay's good friends who happened to be Kentucky Democrats were locked in Ohio prison cells for disloyal utterances. "I asked their pardon," noted Clay, "saying I was sure they would keep their mouths shut and be loyal to the government thereafter. Without a word Lincoln wrote their pardon."

The army service records of the four sons of a Tennessee Union Democrat, Thomas A. R. Nelson, were reviewed by Lincoln when their father applied for the release of a son held in a Northern prison. Two of his sons, the father stated, were serving with Union armies. Another son had from choice gone into the Confederate Army, served twelve months, and been discharged. A fourth son, the father represented, had been practically forced into Confederate service, though he had always favored the Union side. In behalf of this fourth son, who had now spent several months in prison, the father asked a discharge. Lincoln endorsed the application: "Hon. Mr. Nelson, of Tennessee, is a man of mark, and one whom I would like to have obliged." The boy took the oath of Union allegiance and was released.

Another captured Confederate soldier whose Unionist father besought Lincoln to spring the prison doors for his son was Charles O. Roby of Fairfax County, Virginia. The son, according to the father's affidavit, was a conscript who had tried to escape Confederate service. "My impulse," wrote Lincoln on the affidavit, "would be to say, 'Let Charles O. Roby take the oath and be discharged,' yet I do not so say, not knowing what valid objection there may be at the War Department." The bringer of the affidavit was a former New York Congressman, afterward resident in Virginia, continued Lincoln's endorsement. "He is vouched to me as a respectable and worthy gentleman. I submit the case to the Secretary of War." Not long after, on taking the oath, young Roby was released on order of Stanton.

In such an instance the President once dropped a few kind words about the enemy. They were human beings—were they not? One could not be completely remorseless, even in war. The line must be drawn somewhere. His remarks to this effect were overheard by an elderly woman in the reception room. She flashed forth a question of how he could speak kindly of his enemies when he should rather destroy them. "What, madam?"

slowly as he gazed into her face, "do I not destroy them when I make them my friends?" This type of anecdote gained circulation, in both England and America, giving the tone of his policies looking toward reconciliation.

A Philadelphia merchant of wealth and good reputation, a Republican-party man, at the War Department had his request denied when asking a permit to take home his son Paul, wounded in Union Army fighting. The gray-haired father went with a Congressman to Lincoln, who said it wasn't customary but he would make an exception. Handing the old man the wanted permit, he asked if there was anything else he could do. The thankful merchant said there was nothing, turned to go, reached the door, heard Lincoln calling him, and the two men met halfway. In one hand the President held a paper. The other hand he placed on the old man's shoulder, and handing him the paper: "Here is a release for your other son James who was captured in a battle with the Federal troops and is now a wounded prisoner in Washington. Take your boys home with you. May they prove a blessing to you in your declining years." Thus a father with two sons of service in opposing armies traveled homeward hearing his two boys talk about how came their wounds.

One woman asked release of her husband, a Confederate soldier captured in field action. She was not prepared for her interview with the President. He asked whether her husband hadn't gone out to destroy the Union. She so admitted. And while in prison wouldn't he be safe from harming the Union? This too she admitted, had no point to urge against it, and went away puzzled and lacking a pardon.

Mrs. Thomas Theophilus Brown, her baby in her arms, came to the President September 7, 1863, saying she had been to the War Department and elsewhere, having now only fear and anxiety over her husband and his brother who had been taken prisoners at Gettysburg. Their home was in Alexandria, Virginia. Though they had fought with the Confederate Army, they were not spies. Yet they had been held for weeks in Old Capitol Prison and it was whispered would be shot as spies. Lincoln gave her all the time she wished to tell her story. She was crying when she finished. Her baby, however, was smiling and making eyes at Lincoln. It was confusing. Lincoln added to the confusion. He lifted the baby up in his arms and held her to his cheeks. The baby burbled, "Papa." Lincoln laughed, put the baby back in the mother's arms, walked to and fro a few times, then wrote a paper for Mrs. Brown to take to Stanton. At the door he said, "Mrs. Brown, you are a brave little woman." The paper she carried read in part: "This lady says . . . they were conscripted into the rebel army, and were never for the rebel cause, and are now willing to do anything reasonable to be at liberty. This may be true, and if true they should be liberated. Please take hold of the case, and do what may seem proper in it."

Official action for this woman was rapid. Having taken the oath of Union allegiance, three days later at the prison gates the two brothers walked out free men. And Mrs. Thomas Theophilus Brown kissed her ragged, shaggy husband, trembling with fever and nerves, his feet torn and

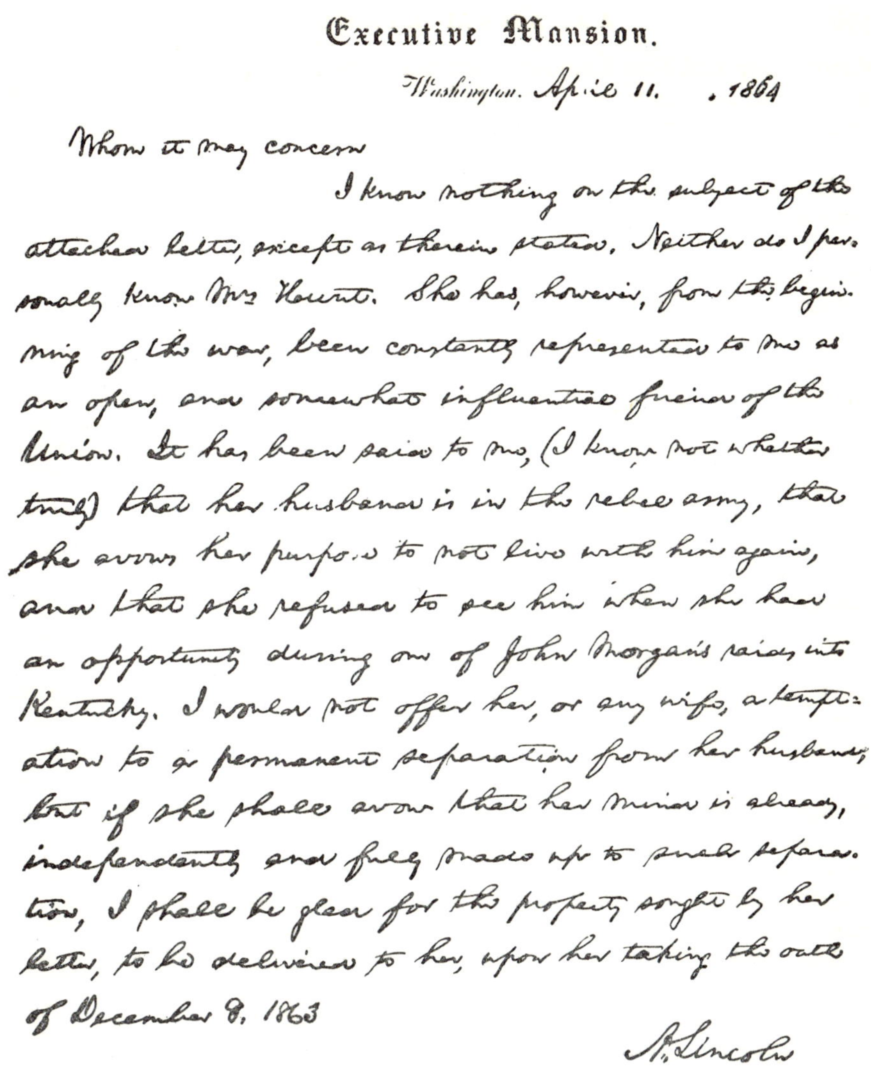

Executive Mansion.

Washington. April 11. , 1864

Whom it may concern

I know nothing on the subject of the attached letter, except as therein stated. Neither do I personally know Mrs Hunt. She has, however, from the beginning of the war, been constantly represented to me as an open, and somewhat influential friend of the Union. It has been said to me, (I know not whether truly) that her husband is in the rebel army, that she avows her purpose to not live with him again, and that she refused to see him when she had an opportunity during one of John Morgan's raids into Kentucky. I would not offer her, or any wife, a temptation to a permanent separation from her husband; but if she shall avow that her mind is already, independently and fully made up to such separation, I shall be glad for the property sought by her letter, to be delivered to her, upon her taking the oath of December 8. 1863

A. Lincoln

Lincoln umpires between wife and husband, making clear that the woman, if a Unionist, is entitled to property sought by her, though he hopes a property offer is not going to tempt her to separate from a husband she may love even though he is a "rebel." The delicately shaded statement, addressed to "Whom it may concern" reads: "I know nothing on the subject of the attached letter, except as therein stated. Neither do I personally know Mrs. Hunt. She has, however, from the beginning of the war, been constantly represented to me as an open, and somewhat influential friend of the Union. It has been said to me, (I know not whether truly) that her husband is in the rebel army, that she avows her purpose to not live with him again, and that she refused to see him when she had an opportunity during one of John Morgan's raids into Kentucky. I would not offer her, or any wife, a temptation to a permanent separation from her husband; but if she shall avow that her mind is already, independently and fully made up to such separation, I shall be glad for the property sought by her letter, to be delivered to her, upon her taking the oath of December 8, 1863." Original in the Barrett collection.

scarred. She took him home to Alexandria and nursed him back to health, waiting till he was strong again before she dared to tell him of the man farther up the river, in the White House, who understood her language and heard their baby call him "Papa."

In some areas both sides were requiring oaths of allegiance. To Lincoln came such stories as that of the captured General Jeff Thompson at Pilot Knob, Missouri, who told the Union post commander there that "these fellows in south-east Missouri" had seemed reliable and friendly enough to the Confederate cause two years before. But now, "hang me if they didn't have to stop and think which oath of allegiance they took last!"

Attorney General Bates, a Virginia-born Missourian with many kinfolk in Virginia, asked Lincoln for the parole of a Confederate soldier taken prisoner just across the Potomac. The boy was not in good health. His father was "at heart a Union man," Bates would put it. "I want you to give me a prisoner," he said to Lincoln. It was the Christmas season. And the Kentucky-born Illinoisan, Lincoln, said he had a parallel case of a young fool who had run away from home to join the rebels, was now in prison, with a broken-hearted father giving pledges he would see that the boy stayed home if set free. "Bates, if you and I unite our influence with this administration I believe we can manage it together and make two loyal fathers happy." Which was done.

They were both "pigeon-hearted," Lincoln said of Bates and himself. Bates spoke of Mr. Lincoln "very near being a perfect man" and lacking but one thing. The painter Carpenter queried, Would that one thing be official dignity? Not that, believed Bates. "His deficiency is in the element of *will*. I have sometimes told him, for instance, that he was unfit to be intrusted with the pardoning power. Why, if a man comes to him with a touching story, his judgment is almost certain to be affected by it. Should the applicant be a *woman*, a wife, a mother, or a sister,–in nine cases out of ten, her tears, if nothing else, are sure to prevail."

Senator Wilkinson of Minnesota entered the President's office one morning in the summer of '63, saw Lincoln put a hand on a large pile of papers and heard him say they were the entire proceedings of a military court with trial, testimony, death sentence, for a boy. "I have read just three pages," said the President, "and I have found this: 'The boy said when first arrested that he was going home to see his mother.' I don't think I can allow a boy to be shot who tried to go home to see his mother. I guess I don't want to read any more of this." Perhaps the boy had thought up an excuse, but until other circumstances overshadowed his excuse it would stand good.

Following his interview with "an intelligent woman in deep distress, as Lincoln described her, he sent two telegrams in one day to General Meade. The first telegram ordered execution suspended of "a man by the name of King." Later it haunted the President that Meade would think it peculiar the President could not give the full name in so grave a matter. The second telegram read: "An intelligent woman in deep distress, called this morning, saying her husband, a lieutenant in the Army of the Potomac,

"The Proclamation of Emancipation," painted by Carpenter during six months' residence in the White House; Lincoln represented as holding the pivotal document of the war

Published by the Lincoln Art Publishing Co.; from the Lincoln Library of the University of Chicago

Reading from top to bottom: *First row:* James Birdseye McPherson, John Sedgwick, Horace Porter. *Second row:* Edwin McMasters Stanton, Winfield Scott Hancock, James Barnet Fry, Lorenzo Thomas. *Third row:* George Henry Thomas, Robert Cumming Schenck, Samuel Peter Heintzelman

From the Meserve collection

was to be shot next Monday for desertion, and putting a letter in my hand, upon which I relied for particulars, she left without mentioning a name or other particular by which to identify the case. On opening the letter I found it equally vague, having nothing to identify by, except her own signature, which seems to be 'Mrs. Anna S. King.' I could not again find her. If you have a case which you shall think is probably the one intended, please apply my dispatch of this morning to it."

Under date of March 18, 1864, Lincoln sent Stanton a letter one paragraph long. Six more paragraphs about equally long, in the original draft of the letter, Lincoln omitted and withheld from Stanton. Here and there the omitted paragraphs had a human quality of natural mercy rather alien, and necessarily so, to the War Department. Also they had a tone of complete kindliness toward the South, as though a spirit of reconciliation would be required for a work of reconstruction to be done if and when the North finished its tragical task of subduing the Southern military forces. Lincoln may have omitted some of these expressions because with certain possible political changes they could be maliciously used against him. Or he may have had several other more pertinent reasons. Or he may have withheld them from Stanton's eye merely on an intuition that another time would be better for any training of Stanton toward a less harsh attitude. The first paragraph, the only one sent to the Secretary of War, read:

"My dear Sir: I am so pressed in regard to prisoners of war in our custody, whose homes are within our lines, and who wish to not be exchanged, but to take the oath and be discharged, that I hope you will pardon me for again calling up the subject. My impression is that we will not ever force the exchange of any of this class; that, taking the oath and being discharged, none of them will again go to the rebellion; but the rebellion again coming to them, a considerable percentage of them, probably not a majority, would rejoin it; that, by a cautious discrimination, the number so discharged would not be large enough to do any considerable mischief in any event, will relieve distress in at least some meritorious cases, and would give me some relief from an intolerable pressure. I shall be glad, therefore, to have your cheerful assent to the discharge of those whose names I may send, which I will only do with circumspection."

Then followed in Lincoln's first draft the six paragraphs which he did not send to Stanton. They constituted a miniature self-portrait of Abraham Lincoln in March of '64, executed in shadows, with torch flares and drooping silhouettes on a dim horizon background. They read:

"In using the strong hand, as now compelled to do, the government has a difficult duty to perform. At the very best it will by turns do both too little and too much. It can properly have no motive of revenge, no purpose to punish merely for punishment's sake. While we must by all available means prevent the overthrow of the government, we should avoid planting and cultivating too many thorns in the bosom of society. These general remarks apply to several classes of cases, on each of which I wish to say a word.

"First. The dismissal of officers when neither incompetency, nor intentional wrong, nor real injury to the service, is imputed. In such cases it is both cruel and impolitic to crush the man and make him and his friends permanent enemies to the administration if not to the government itself. I think of two instances: one wherein a surgeon, for the benefit of patients in his charge, needed some lumber, and could only get it by making a false certificate wherein the lumber was denominated 'butter and eggs,' and he was dismissed for the false certificate; the other a surgeon by the name of Owen, who served from the beginning of the war till recently with two servants, and without objection, when upon discovery that the servants were his own sons he was dismissed.

"Another class consists of those who are known or strongly suspected to be in sympathy with the rebellion. An instance of this is the family of Southern, who killed a recruiting officer last autumn in Maryland. He fled, and his family are driven from their home without a shelter or crumb, except when got by burdening our friends more than our enemies. Southern had no justification to kill the officer, and yet he would not have been killed if he had proceeded in the temper and manner agreed upon by yourself and Governor Bradford; but this is past. What is to be done with the family? Why can they not occupy the old home and excite much less opposition to the government than the manifestation of their distress is now doing? If the house is really needed for the public service, or if it has been regularly confiscated and the title transferred, the case is different.

"Again, the cases of persons, mostly women, wishing to pass our lines one way or the other. We have in some cases been apparently, if not really, inconsistent upon this subject—that is, we have forced some to go who wished to stay, and forced others to stay who wished to go. Suppose we allow all females with ungrown children of either sex to go South, if they desire, upon absolute prohibition against returning during the war; and all to come North upon the same condition of not returning during the war, and the additional condition of taking the oath.

"I wish to mention two special cases, both of which you well remember. The first is that of Yocum. He was unquestionably guilty. No one asking for his pardon pretends the contrary. What he did, however, was perfectly lawful only a short while before, and the change making it unlawful had not, even then, been fully accepted in the public mind. It is doubtful whether Yocum did not suppose it was really lawful to return a slave to a loyal owner, though it is certain he did the thing secretly, in the belief that his superiors would not allow it if known to them. But the great point with me is that the severe punishment of five years at hard labor in the penitentiary is not at all necessary to prevent the repetition of the crime by himself or by others. If the offense was one of frequent recurrence, the case would be different; but the case of Yocum is the single instance which has come to my knowledge. I think that for all public purposes, and for all proper purposes, he has suffered enough.

"The case of Smithson is troublesome. His wife and children are quartered mostly on our friends, and exciting a great deal of sympathy, which will soon tell against us. What think you of sending him and his family South, holding the sentence over him to be reënforced if he return during the war?"

The strong hand, compelled by turns to do "both too little and too much," involved itself in affairs where justice was mocked by men "cultivating too many thorns in the bosom of society." A pitiless logic at times led men from bad to worse, with no going back. In more than one case Stanton and other Cabinet members very strictly were on the side of right and abstract justice with Lincoln ordering another course for the sake of political considerations not to be laughed off lightly in a Republic at war with itself. Some anecdotes were interpreted "as meaning that Lincoln could not control Stanton," wrote James B. Fry, Provost Marshal General. "The inference is erroneous. Lincoln, so far as I could discover, was in every respect the actual head of the administration, and whenever he chose to do so he controlled Stanton as well as the other Cabinet ministers." Fry cited one high instance. Some of its details were odd, even whimsical.

The infantry company detailed to guard Lincoln was part of a Pennsylvania regiment of which Henry S. Huidekoper of Meadville was lieutenant colonel. Huidekoper was short of stature, Dutch in ancestry. Lincoln gave him short-boy jokes, asked the ancient conundrum, "What is the difference between an Amster-dam Dutchman and any other dam Dutchman?" Huidekoper came from four years at Harvard, where he had met Robert Todd Lincoln. Huidekoper had a brother Herman, just past twenty, commanding a colored regiment being drilled to go to the front. Lincoln took an added interest when Henry Huidekoper came back from Gettysburg minus one arm, seeking lighter duty until he could return to his regiment. According to Huidekoper, the President wrote to the Adjutant General October 23, 1863, "Please grant such request as Colonel Huidekoper may make." Colonel Hardee and others at the War Department, wrote Huidekoper, agreed no such carte-blanche order had ever before come from the President to the War Department.

In August of '64 Colonel Huidekoper was at home in Meadville when, by his account, he met an old schoolmate named Wilson, who had served in the Confederate Army and finished a term as prisoner at Rock Island, Illinois. And Wilson was saying that the majority of his associates in the military prison "were tired of fighting the United States, and so were averse to their exchange and return to the South." It occurred to Judge Pettis of Meadville "that these men might be used by the Government to advantage against the Indians." Huidekoper agreed. Pettis went to Washington and saw Lincoln. Lincoln asked Pettis if Huidekoper favored the scheme, and on hearing that Huidekoper did approve, said he would like to talk with

Huidekoper about it. Pettis telegraphed Huidekoper to come on to Washington. The two of them drove out to the Soldiers' Home.

Lincoln came from dinner, stretched on a sofa, and started a general conversation. A servant brought in a card. Lincoln directed her to say he was engaged for the evening. She came back with word that the caller must see the President. A third time she returned to say the man would stay outside and await the convenience of the President. Lincoln, abruptly: "Tell the man I will not see him." The wheels were heard rumbling down the roadway and Lincoln laughed. "That is a most persistent man. As an officer he was dismissed from the army, and now wishes me to reinstate him, so as to relieve him from the imputation of 'conduct unbecoming an officer and a gentleman.' " The man was related to a former political antagonist of his, Lincoln added, mentioning names. He would like to befriend him but army discipline required otherwise. After a half-hour of general talk Lincoln turned to Huidekoper. "Pettis has been talking to me about making use of the rebel prisoners at Rock Island, and I wish you would call at the White House at nine tomorrow morning, that I may talk the matter over with you." That was all.

Huidekoper the next morning urged that it took one year to make a good soldier out of a recruit, that the cost to the Government in pay, rations, and clothing during training was not a small sum, that if a brigade of seasoned, efficient Federal troops could be relieved from watching the Indians, it was worth trying to so relieve them "with reconstructed rebel soldiers," ready for the field almost at once. How many such Confederate prisoners would enlist and stay at Indian fighting? Huidekoper had confidence in his old schoolmate Wilson's statement that a majority would, though "of course it would be better if the men could be stationed where desertion would endanger their scalps."

"The President then left me," noted Huidekoper, "and went into a private office, where it took him some time to draft an order. On his return he read to me what he had written, and seeing that he had brought me into the business, which I had not wished or intended, I suggested some changes in the wording of the paper, particularly in the clause that referred to the bounty-money the men were to receive. The President made, without hesitation, the alterations I suggested, and I then accepted the responsibility of the novel scheme the details of which were left, almost entirely, to Judge Pettis." Thus written, Lincoln's order read:

"It is represented to me that there are at Rock Island, Illinois, as rebel prisoners of war, many persons of Northern and foreign birth who are unwilling to be exchanged and sent South, but who wish to take the oath of allegiance and enter the military service of the Union. Colonel Huidekoper, on behalf of the people of some parts of Pennsylvania, wishes to pay the bounties the government would have to pay to proper persons of this class, have them enter the service of the United States, and be credited to the localities furnishing the bounty money. He will therefore proceed to Rock Island, ascertain the names of such persons (not including any who have attractions Southward), and telegraph them to the Provost-Marshal-General here, whereupon direction will be given to discharge the persons named upon their taking the oath of allegiance; and then upon the official evidence being furnished that they shall have been duly received and mustered into the service of the United States, their number will be credited as may be directed by Colonel Huidekoper."

According to Huidekoper, the President then said: "Now we will take this to the Secretary of War's office, and I wish you to notice how they treat me in there. They do not think I know anything in their line of business, or should ever give them any direction concerning it." The two of them went to the desk of Provost Marshal General Fry. "General Fry remonstrated vigorously," noted Huidekoper, "telling the President that Mr. Stanton had considered the question some time before and had decided against the measure, and that he [the President] must withdraw the order. As we left the room, Mr. Lincoln remarked upon the want of deference shown him, evincing some amusement at the opposition."

Nicolay and Hay believed the President "did not understand the full scope and effect of the order." General Fry believed, and wrote his belief as to what might be under cover in the scheme, in a later statement: "After compulsory military service was resorted to, States and districts tried to fill their quotas, and save their own citizens from being drafted into the army, by voting bounties to buy men wherever they could be found. The agent appointed by a county in one of the Middle States, and supplied with bounty money, learned that some Confederate prisoners of war at Chicago were about to be released and enlisted in our army for service against the Indians in the North-west. The thrifty thought occurred to the agent to pay these prisoners a bounty for what they were going to do without any pay at all, and in return for this payment have them credited as soldiers furnished by his county. Being an acquaintance of Lincoln, the agent obtained from him an order to have the men credited as desired. But the Secretary of War refused to have the credits allowed. Indignant and disappointed, the agent returned to the President, who reiterated the order."

Twenty days later the President wrote an endorsement, according to Huidekoper, on his original order. It was short, polite and positive in tone, reading: "The bearer will present the list of names contemplated within. The provost-marshal-general will please take the proper steps to have them examined, mustered in and discharged from prison, so as to be properly credited; all according to the within."

This order Lincoln himself carried to Stanton's office. A scene took place, not noisy though tense. General Fry was there and reported, as he had previously done to the Secretary alone, that the captured Confederate soldiers imprisoned at Rock Island already belonged to the United States, being prisoners of war; that they could not be used against the Confederates; that they had no relation whatever to the county in Pennsylvania to which it was proposed they should be credited; that all that was necessary toward enlisting them in the Federal Army for Indian service was the Government's release of them as prisoners of war; that to give them bounty and credit them to a Pennsylvania county which owed some of its men for service against the Confederates would waste money and deprive the army operating against a powerful enemy of that number of men, and so forth. Of what followed this recital of points against Lincoln's order Fry wrote:

> Stanton said:
>
> "Now, Mr. President, those are the facts, and you must see that your order cannot be executed."
>
> Lincoln sat upon a sofa with his legs crossed, and did not say a word until the Secretary's last remark. Then he said in a somewhat positive tone: "Mr. Secretary, I reckon you'll have to execute the order."
>
> Stanton replied with asperity:
>
> "Mr. President, I cannot do it. The order is an improper one, and I cannot execute it."
>
> Lincoln fixed his eye upon Stanton, and in a firm voice, and with an accent that clearly showed his determination, he said:
>
> "*Mr. Secretary, it will have to be done.*"
>
> Stanton then realized that he was overmatched. He had made a square issue with the President and been defeated, notwithstanding the fact that he was in the right. Upon an intimation from him I withdrew and did not witness his surrender. A few minutes after I reached my office I received instructions from the Secretary to carry out the President's order. Stanton never mentioned the subject to me afterward, nor did I ever ascertain the special, and no doubt sufficient, reasons which the President had for his action in the case.

Nicolay and Hay were sure that Lincoln in this wished neither "to humiliate the Secretary of War or compel him to violate his convictions of duty." Somewhere in the time between Fry's leaving the room and Stanton's signing the order "Lincoln had doubtless explained to Stanton, with that irresistible frankness and kindness with which he carried all his points of controversy, the reasons for his insistence."

Huidekoper was pleased that when Captain Rathburn was sent by Stanton to watch the mustering in at Rock Island of Confederate prisoners for Indian service, each received his $100 bounty, and the Captain said he had changed his mind about the undertaking being unwise. "The 1,800 soldiers enlisted were formed into two regiments," Huidekoper wrote, "which did excellent service. Not a man ever deserted, and all proved loyal in their new allegiance. From other prisons, other men were subsequently enlisted, making in all 5,738 reconstructed rebels who served under the old flag."

Lincoln, however, two days after his stubborn conference with Stanton, wrote a letter to Grant saying Stanton was "wholly free of any part in this blunder," and giving the impression that some sort of necessary politics had dictated his course. The letter of September 22, 1864, to Grant read:

"I send this as an explanation to you, and to do justice to the Secretary of War. I was induced, upon pressing application, to authorize the agents of one of the districts of Pennsylvania to recruit in one of the prison depots in Illinois; and the thing went so far before it came to the knowledge of the Secretary that, in my judgment, it could not be abandoned without greater evil than would follow its going through. I did not know at the time that you had protested against that class of thing being done; and I now say that while this particular job must be completed, no other of the sort will be authorized, without an understanding with you, if at all. The Secretary of War is wholly free of any part in this blunder."

On occasion Lincoln issued a request with a written proviso that the War Department might, for reasons unknown to the President, refuse it. Governor Curtin and prominent Pennsylvanians recommended in writing that Colonel Payton, a recruiting officer at Philadelphia, be allowed an extension of thirty days to fill a quota. Lincoln endorsed it: "Allow Colonel Payton the additional time required, unless there be reason to the contrary." Under this Stanton wrote, "There is good and valid reason for not extending the time, and the Secretary of War refuses to do it." Thus John P. Usher, Secretary of the Interior, gave the incident to show one kind of veto power Lincoln gave Stanton.

Once Thad Stevens asked a pardon for a young constituent of his who had so far forgotten himself, in spite of the hullabaloo about it, as to go to sleep on picket duty. Lincoln handed Stevens a telegraph blank, Stevens wrote a reprieve, signed "A. Lincoln" to the dispatch, and sent a messenger on the run to a telegraph office. This happened soon after an informal agreement between Lincoln and Stanton that the President would consult the War Secretary on reprieves in capital cases.

"I see, Mr. President," huffed Stanton on his early entry into Lincoln's room office, "you have signed another reprieve contrary to your agreement not to do so without first consulting the War Department."

"No. I have signed no reprieve. I have kept my word."

"But I just saw one going over the wires. And your name is signed to it."

"But I did not write it."

"Did not write it! Who did write it?"

"Your friend, Thad Stevens."

Stanton took his hat and left without another word. The trick was not repeated. Not often was Lincoln's sense of justice and enjoyment of humor so well satisfied.

Quite dispassionately calm and loyally Unionist was the 1864 issue of *Appleton's Annual Cyclopaedia.* Under the head of "Habeas Corpus" it indicated that military commissions, supposedly dealing out justice, inevitably had a proportion of petty tyrants. During a real or imaginary crisis of political circumstances, it was held, "The true end of military commissions, if they are allowed for any purpose, is to inquire and develop, not to judge or convict. It always, however, unfortunately happens, that the same state of political or party agitation which brings the commission into existence, creates a sort of demand that it shall deal finally and vindictively with some who come under its notice. . . . It is not to be understood that persons tried are always convicted; on the contrary, many are allowed to escape.

The difficulty is that in many cases it is impossible to penetrate the curtain which conceals from the observer the power behind the court."

The President had suspended, then later modified, the privilege of the writ of habeas corpus, the War Department following with "an order prohibiting, under pain of dismissal from the army, officers from giving information concerning the sentence of civilians by military commissions before the execution of the sentence." That the *Annual Cyclopaedia* annalist believed a subtle procedure with reference to the President was under way stood forth in the statement: "Upon the representation of the facts, a number sentenced to the penitentiary had been pardoned by the President, and this order [of the War Department] was calculated to get the prisoners fully incarcerated before their friends could be able to ascertain the necessity of appealing to the Executive."

In a crowded room near the President's office a Congressman noticed one morning an old man crouched in a corner, sobbing. The Congressman hurried on in to see the President. The next morning he saw the old man there again, sobbing as the day before. He talked with the old man and then took him in to tell to the President his story, which was short. His son with Butler's army had been convicted of a crime and sentenced by court-martial to be shot. The President read the old man a telegram from General Butler protesting against executive interference with army court-martials. The old man was dazed a moment, then shook with a desperate grief, Lincoln watching a minute, and "By jings, Butler or no Butler, here goes," wrote a few words. He showed them to the old man, a presidential signed order that the son was "not to be shot until further orders from me."

The old man was still in grief. "I thought it was to be a pardon. But you say 'not to be shot till further orders,' and you may order him shot next week."

Lincoln smiled. "Well, my old friend, I see you are not very well acquainted with me. If your son never looks on death till further orders come from me to shoot him, he will live to be a great deal older than Methuselah."

A private in the 72d Pennsylvania Volunteers, Isaac P. Baird, was in the regimental guardhouse on August 12, 1862, when Lincoln wrote to Stanton that the mother of Baird "tells me that she is a widow; that her two sons and only support joined the army, where one of them still is." Furthermore, young Isaac "could not take the benefit of returning under the proclamation on that subject." If the War Department ascertained this information to be correct, "let him be discharged from arrest and go on duty. I think, too, he should have his pay for duty actually performed. Loss of pay falls so hard upon poor families."

Did this spring the guardhouse doors for young Baird? It seemed not. Or if it did the lad went wrong again. And his mother was at the White House beseeching the President. For he wrote to Stanton this note: "A poor widow, by the name of Baird, has a son in the army, that for some offense has been sentenced to serve a long time without pay, or at most with very little pay. I do not like this punishment of withholding pay—it falls so very hard upon poor families. After he had been serving in this way for several months, at the tearful appeal of the poor mother, I made a direction that he be allowed to enlist for a new term, on the same conditions as others. She now comes, and says she cannot get it acted upon. Please do it." Thereupon young Baird was transferred to another regiment, permitted to re-enlist, and his mother heard from him on army paydays.

A young woman in neat and plain dress was heard with respect and frank speech. "My poor girl, you have come with no governor, or senator, or member of Congress, to plead your cause. You seem honest and truthful, and *you don't wear hoops;* and I'll be whipped but I'll pardon your brother!"

In shadows and ironic twilights justice was often measured out as a thing none should ask for with a straight face of honest expectations. So often those dealing it out in their daily decisions knew it was in quality adulterated and shoddy while in politics expedient and necessary. An ancient rule of abstract justice held that pirates should be hanged. Nevertheless Lincoln pardoned a pirate named Alfred Rubery, captured in San Francisco in March of '63 and held in jail for months till released on order of the President. Two reasons were given the public. The pirate was a British subject. And John Bright had written to the President asking the pardon as a favor. "In consideration of Mr. Bright's eminent services, the President at once acceded to his request," said *Leslie's Weekly*, January 2, 1864. "Mr. Bright has some strange friends." The comment was too easy. Lincoln saw little to be gained in that hour by hanging a British subject. And he believed John Bright was entitled to one pardon and no questions asked.

More intricate was the case of Louis A. Welton, sentenced to prison. Senator Morgan and Thurlow Weed, of New York, also Henry J. Raymond of the *New York Times*, were asking Lincoln to pardon him. Lincoln plainly believed the man to be a liar and a scoundrel taking profits out of trading with the enemy. Yet Lincoln pardoned Louis A. Welton. It was the last week in August of '64, the dark and desperate month. The three men asking Welton's pardon were not to be thrust away with abrupt refusals. Lincoln wrote a statement giving his belief that Louis A. Welton was a falsifier and a species of traitor intent on money-making from treason, and his further belief that Welton ought not to be pardoned. However if Messrs. Morgan, Weed, and Raymond would on the same sheet with his statement of the case write their requests for Welton's pardon it would be done in deference to their wishes. Two of the three petitioners did so. Welton was saved from prison. Lincoln held in his possession a paper which the opposition would have seized on as luridly scandalous had it been made public. Lincoln's statement in his handwriting on this paper read:

Executive Mansion,
Washington, August 31, 1864

Mr. Louis A. Welton came from the rebel lines into ours with a written contract to furnish large supplies to the rebels, was arrested with the contract in his possession.

and has been sentenced to imprisonment for it. He, and his friends complain of this, on no substantial evidence whatever, but simply because his word, only given after his arrest, that he only took the contract as a means of escaping from the rebel lines, was not accepted as a full defense—He perceives that if this had been true he would have destroyed the contract so soon as it had served his purpose in getting him across the lines; but not having done this and being caught with the paper on him, he tells this other absurd story that he kept the paper in the belief that our government would join him in taking the profit of fulfilling the contract. This is my understanding of the case; and I can not conceive of a case of a man found in possession of a contract to furnish rebel supplies, who can not escape, if this be held a sufficient ground of escape—It is simply for the accused to escape by telling a very absurd and improbable story. Now, if Senator Morgan, and Mr. Weed, and Mr. Raymond, will not argue with me that I *ought* to discharge this man, but will, in writing on this sheet, simply request me to do it, I will do it solely in deference to their wishes.

A. Lincoln

Then appearing on the same sheet of paper were the endorsements:

We respectfully request the President to pardon the within named Louis A Welton, now at Fort Delaware.

Thurlow Weed.

I have read Mr. Weltons statement and if it is true, (and I know no reason for distrusting it,) his pardon would be an act of *justice*. I concur in Mr. Weed's request.

H. J. Raymond.

Abraham Samuels was another trader caught passing through the Union lines on a questionable errand. His application to the President for release from prison recited that his real purpose was to escape from the South. The President wrote on the application: "It is confessed in this case that Samuels, when arrested, had on his person a paper *prima facie* showing that he was going North to obtain medical supplies for the rebels. Will the officer in command at Fort Monroe please give him an opportunity of trying to prove that this was not his real object, and report the evidence, with his opinion on it, to me?" When later, after considerable testimony had been taken by military officials, the original application turned up, Lincoln signed his name after the six words "Let the prisoner Samuels be discharged."

A former Collector of the Port of New York, a Democrat, caught short of funds belonging to the public, was under sentence to hard labor in prison because of his breach of trust. A delegation of ladies and gentlemen from New York friendly to the former collector used their influence in his behalf in Washington. None other than Cassius Marcellus Clay of Kentucky in a major general's uniform headed a committee and in the President's office spoke for mercy. "The President heard me with great patience and silence," wrote Clay. Clay finished his speech. The President rose, and slowly and sternly: "If I pardon this man, and *my* Collector takes away the public money, what shall I do?" This closed the interview.

Congressman Alexander H. Rice of Boston brought Lincoln a petition signed by many prominent citizens of that city. They asked pardon for a boy convicted of opening United States mail and taking money out of it before it was delivered to his employer. The boy had come to the big city

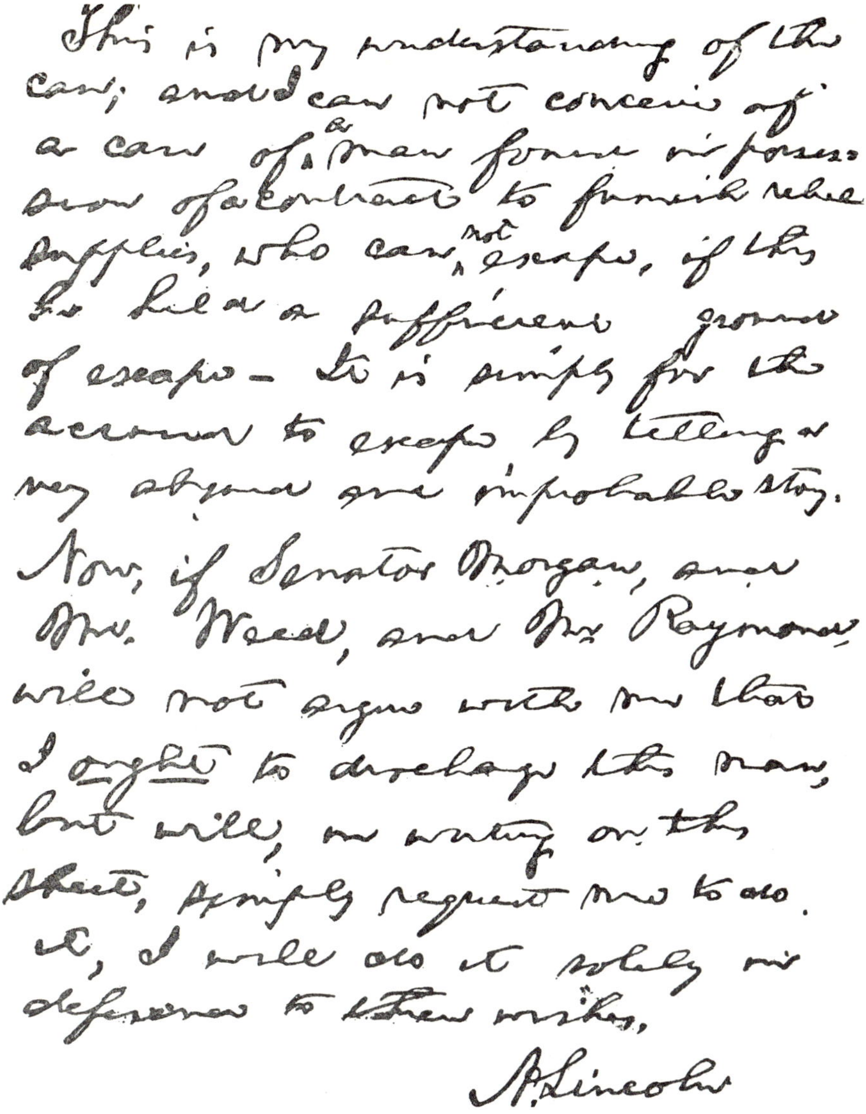
This is my understanding of the
case; and I can not conceive of
a case of a man found in posses-
sion of a contract to furnish rebel
supplies, who can not escape, if this
be held a sufficient ground
of escape— It is simply for the
accused to escape by telling a
very absurd and improbable story.
Now, if Senator Morgan, and
Mr. Weed, and Mr Raymond,
will not argue with me that
I ought to discharge this man,
but will, in writing on this
sheet, simply request me to do
it, I will do it solely in
deference to their wishes.
A. Lincoln

Reproduction of part of Lincoln's memorandum that he believes Louis A. Welton guilty of crime but he will let Welton go free if Welton's friends will "not argue" but "simply request" the prisoner's discharge from Fort Delaware. Inside a folded sheet Thurlow Weed and Henry J. Raymond signed their names and thereby opened the cell door for a convict Lincoln believed guilty of contracting to furnish supplies to the enemy for a money profit. Highly contrasted signatures of Weed and Raymond are presented on the following page. Original in the Barrett collection.

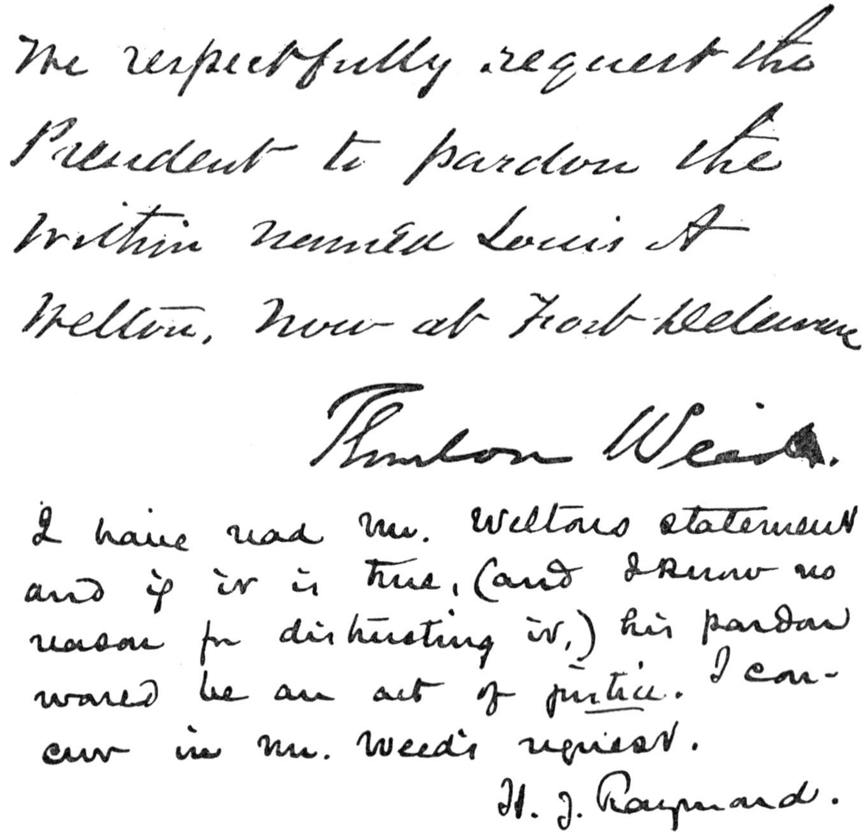
We respectfully request the President to pardon the within named Louis A Welton, now at Fort Delaware

Thurlow Weed.

I have read Mr. Welton's statement and if it is true, (and I know no reason for distrusting it,) his pardon would be an act of justice. I concur in Mr. Weed's request.

H. J. Raymond.

from his father's farm, wanted money to enjoy the glitter and dazzlement of the city, and while carrying his employer's mail to and from the post office had fallen into the habit of stealing money out of the envelopes trusted to him. Now that the boy was convicted and serving a penitentiary term, those who had put him there felt the disgrace had been enough and they were willing he should be out. The father of the boy, jurors who had convicted the boy, along with several respectable Boston citizens, came with Congressman Rice to interview Lincoln. Rice introduced the father, then handed the petition to Lincoln. "Mr. Lincoln put on his spectacles," noted Rice, "threw himself back in his chair and stretched his long legs to their utmost extent, and thus read the document." Having finished reading, Lincoln asked Rice if he had met a man on the stairs going down as he came up. Mr. Rice had.

"Well," began the President, as Rice noted it, "he was the last man in this room before you came and his errand was to get a man pardoned out of the penitentiary, and now you come to get a boy out of jail. I am bothered to death about these pardon cases; but I am a little encouraged by your visit. They are after me on the *men*, but appear to be roping you in on the *boys*. What shall we do? The trouble appears to come from the courts. Let's abolish the courts, and I think that will end the difficulty. And it seems as if the courts ought to be abolished, anyway; for they appear to pick out the very best men in the community and send them to the penitentiary, and now they are after the same kind of boys. According to that man's testimony who was just in here, there are few men so upright as his client; and I don't know much about boys in Massachusetts, but according to this petition there are not many such boys as this one outside the Sunday schools in other parts of the country." Then the boy got his pardon.

For William Tuckerman, convicted of robbing the mails between New York and Boston, went a pardon from the President. Sentenced to twenty years, he had served eight, his conduct, said press items, "such as to gain the sympathy of all connected with the prison."

Charges of irregularities in the award of liquor contracts having been brought against Surgeon General William A. Hammond, and a court-martial having dismissed him from the army in August of '64, Lincoln withheld any participation in the case. "The proceedings, findings, and sentence of the court-martial were approved," wrote Hammond, "without, as I have every reason to believe, the President having read a single page of the record." Hammond's counsel wrote asking whether the President would consider a review of the address of the Judge Advocate. To this the President gave no answer. Then Mrs. Hammond called at the White House and asked for an interview with the President "in order that she might ask him to listen to evidence which had not been brought before the court." And according to Hammond, the President sent out her card with his signed endorsement: "Under the circumstances, I should prefer not seeing Mrs. Hammond."

The case was not clear as daylight. Lincoln's hands-off attitude may have meant he had heard enough of the case to believe that the court-martial findings were probably true and correct. Or it may have implied that, much as he would have liked to take a day or two for the study of the extended evidence in the case, he had no such day or two to spare. It was August of '64.

Congressman Orlando Kellogg of New York brought in the affair of a helter-skelter lad who before the war served six months in the regular army, deserted, came home, told his father nothing about it, sobered up and settled down. Later the boy volunteered at the beginning of the war, helped raise a regiment, was elected one of its officers, and in a charge across a bridge during one battle saw his colonel at his side killed and took wounds himself. Then an old-timer of the regular army recognized him, and let him know he would be exposed as a deserter. He managed to get furloughed home, told his father he would "die first" rather than be arrested as a deserter.

This in short was the story Kellogg told. Lincoln wasn't interested until the charge across the bridge.

"Do you say the young man was wounded?"

"Yes, badly."

"Then," musingly, "then he has shed his blood for his country." And with a brightening, "Kellogg, isn't there something in Scripture about the 'shedding of blood' being the 'remission of sins'?"

"Guess you're about right there."

"It is a good point, and there is no going behind it." The President took a pen, wrote a pardon without condition or reservation.

Pardon appeals where an executive Yes or No must decide whether a soldier face the firing squad—these troubled from several approaches. When Lincoln was a boy the opposition to General Jackson for President circulated a picture of six soldiers standing ready to fall into six coffins as a firing squad prepared to end their lives; they were deserters Jackson in the War of 1812 had ordered shot. From a cold practical viewpoint it was good politics to have a reputation as a pardoner, softhearted rather than hardhearted, even though it affected army behavior.

Mothers and sisters wept as the President one day signed a reprieve. "Well, I have made one family happy, but I don't know about the discipline of the army!"

Lincoln heard of his archantagonist Jefferson Davis likewise tangled as between political human impulses and army discipline. Longstreet's adjutant general in latter '64 reported to Lee that General Pickett was holding some one hundred men in the guardhouse charged with desertion, Pickett explaining that "every man sentenced to be shot for desertion in this division for the past two months had been reprieved." Lee had inclinations toward mercy, had often shown them, but now he wrote to the Richmond War Department that desertion was on the increase notwithstanding his efforts to stop it, advising, "A rigid execution of the law is [best] in the end. The great want in our army is firm discipline." Davis replied sharply to Lee that deserters arrested should be tried, "and if the sentences are reviewed and remitted that is not a proper subject for the criticism of a military commander." Both Davis and Lincoln often had good political reasons for their use of the pardoning power, though Davis to his complaining commanders was the more peremptory about it.

In the seven days between December 26, 1863, and January 3, 1864, six soldiers received pardons or stays of death sentences from the President. "Do not execute him till further order" or "Suspend execution of sentence and forward record of trial for examination" was the repeated essential of the telegrams dated at the Executive Mansion. The most sweeping order of this class ever sent out by the President was on December 10, 1863, to Major General Butler at Fortress Monroe, Virginia: "Please suspend execution in any and all sentences of death in your department until further order." To the army of no other general than Ben Butler did it seem that Lincoln issued so inclusive an order regarding stays of execution. The involved horrors of civil war stood forth.

The Confederate Major General George E. Pickett had court-martialed and hanged twenty-two North Carolinians taken prisoner, one designing, lying Union general reported. "Their supposed offence," wrote Butler, "was that they, being enrolled in the Confederate army, had enlisted in the Union army." One of Butler's generals notified General Pickett that President Lincoln had ordered that "for every soldier of the United States killed in violation of the laws of war, a rebel soldier shall be executed." Pickett responded that he was holding as prisoners some 450 officers and men of the United States Army, "and for every man you hang I will hang ten of the U. S. Army. . . . Very respectfully, your obedient servant."

Butler seemed to be the one major general who openly and directly blamed his military losses on the President's lack of severity. One of Butler's brigadiers had conducted a brilliant march and troop management, according to Butler, "but success was snatched from him, because of the escape, from his guard at Williamsburg, the night before the expedition started, of a prisoner who had been ordered to be executed for the wilful murder of an officer, and who had been reprieved by the President." Butler gave his answer why the war was lasting so long: "Pusillanimity and want of executive force of the government."

As a strictly political general Butler had his guesses about Lincoln's purposes. One Lincoln telegram to Butler in April of '64 read: "I am pressed to get from Libby, by special exchange, Jacob C. Hagenbuck [sic], first lieutenant, Company H, Sixty-seventh Pennsylvania Volunteers. Please do it if you can without detriment or embarrassment." This was a very special request. Not once in a year did Lincoln single out for exchange one particular man among the thousands languishing in Southern prisons. Butler undoubtedly asked himself why Jacob Hagenbuch should be given such a pleasant distinction; possibly he guessed that some political interest in Pennsylvania was being allied to Lincoln's purposes. No one, however, neither Lincoln, Butler, nor Hagenbuch, was going to be involved in anything questionable. This was covered in Lincoln's direction that it must be done "without detriment or embarrassment" to Butler. Whatever Butler decided was "without detriment or embarrassment" would be good enough for Lincoln and Hagenbuch —and the hoped-for Union political victory in Pennsylvania in 1864.

Butler noted that on his White House call, when returning from his dismissal at New Orleans, he spoke to the President of "clemency in not having deserters speedily and universally punished by death." With a sorrowful face Lincoln demurred, "But I can't do that, General." On Butler suggesting he could throw the responsibility on the General in Chief, Lincoln still more sorrowfully insisted, "The responsibility would be mine, all the same."

Donn Piatt wrote of how he sat with Brigadier General Daniel Tyler of Connecticut in an antechamber of the War Department after adjournment of the Buell court of inquiry, of which they were both members. Lincoln, just leaving a conference with Stanton, saw the two of them. "Well, gentlemen . . . have you any matter worth reporting, after such a protracted investigation?"

"I think so, Mr. President." Then General Tyler laid reverses in Kentucky and Tennessee to the one condition that Bragg, the Confederate commander, had shot his deserters, but "if we attempt to shoot a deserter, you pardon him and our army is without discipline." Speaking toward the President's now perplexed face Tyler went on: "Why do you interfere? Congress has taken from you all responsibility."

The President, swiftly and impatiently: "Yes, Congress has taken the responsibility and left the women to howl about me." So he strode away.

To Piatt, General Tyler remarked that the President didn't need to see those women and to endanger an army by such a course was feeble. Piatt however saw other motives in the President, "far more policy of course than kind feeling." Piatt saw the President as "not lost in his high admiration for brigadiers and major-generals," having "a positive dislike for their methods and the despotism on which an army is based," aware that he was "dependent on volunteers for soldiers, and to force on such the stern discipline of the regular army was to render the service unpopular." Finally, in Piatt's view, "it pleased the President to be the source of mercy, as well as the fountain of honor, in this direction."

Many opponents and critics of Lincoln believed that realistic political and military purposes moved him entirely in his pardons. The popular belief in Lincoln's mercy was "erroneous," Donn Piatt would say. "His good-natured manner misled the common mind." Piatt doubted whether Lincoln "had at all a kind, forgiving nature." Piatt pointed to history and successful leaders of men as "round, oily, elastic" on the outside, giving way in trifles, while "angular, hard," on the inner purposes. In his guess at this phase of Lincoln, Piatt was half-correct at least. Lincoln had disciplined himself to hide his deeper purposes under the spoken immediate ones. He could be smooth toward rough ends when he considered it necessary.

"I heard Secretary Seward say," wrote Piatt . . . "that President Lincoln 'had a cunning that was genius.' " Coming from Seward that was some manner of tribute. Piatt's appraisals at times were drawn from poor hearsay. Once he contrasted how "on the very field [Gettysburg] that he [Lincoln] shamed with a ribald song he left a record of eloquence." Piatt accepted the story that Lincoln had asked Lamon to sing a questionable song amid dying soldiers, Piatt not knowing the battle had been finished on that field three weeks before Lincoln came to it, not knowing that Lincoln sang neither sacred nor ribald songs, not knowing that Lincoln asked Lamon for "a sad little song." Also it slipped Piatt's memory that all published accounts gave the battlefield as Antietam and not Gettysburg.

Many common soldiers believed it not a bad thing to have high over the military authorities a Chief Magistrate to whom their friends and relatives could appeal from a court-martial judgment. In Charles G. Halpine's ditty was a kernel of feeling that lurked in many soldier hearts:

Long life to you, Misther Lincoln!
May you die both late an' aisy;
An' whin you lie wid the top of aich toe
Turned up to the roots of a daisy,

May this be your epitaph, nately writ—
"Though thraitors abused him vilely,
He was honest, an' kindly, he loved a joke,
An' he pardoned Miles O'Reilly!"

And for the same act while I've breath in me lungs
Or a heart in me body beatin'
It's "long life to you, Misther Lincoln!"
That meself will keep repeatin':—
If you ain't the handsomest man in the world
You've done handsome by me, an' highly;
And your name to poshterity will go down
Arm in arm wid Miles O'Reilly!

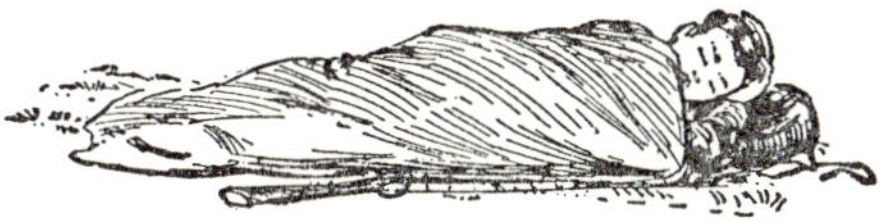

Possibly in some one case, as a legend had it, Lincoln did get out of bed and rush over to the war telegraph office to make sure a death set for morning was put off. On dozens of dispatches ordering execution postponed were little notes by Lincoln or his secretaries to the chief dispatcher: "Major Eckert, please send the above despatch," or "Will you please hurry off the above? To-morrow is the day of execution." Or again a telegram might be repeated or would have the inquiry follow trailing it, "Did you receive my dispatch suspending sentence of ——?"

Motives underlying fear or courage wove through evidence connected with pardon appeals. Cowards of one day were brave the next—and vice versa. Horace Porter of Grant's staff probably gave Lincoln the story of two soldiers in a desperate charge up a hill to capture a battery. One of them halfway up turned to the other. "Why, you're pale as a sheet; you look like a ghost; I believe you're afraid." And the other: "Yes, I am, and if you were half as much afraid as I am you'd have run long ago." Troops refreshed by rest and a good meal stood their ground under fire that would have sent them scampering had they been tired and hungry, observed Porter. He had seen them go into action cool and steady under the screeching of shot and shell as though it was "the music on which they had been brought up." After two days' fighting their nerves gradually lost tension, they were less gay and buoyant, "dangers they would have laughed at the first day often sent them panic-stricken to the rear on the third." And in camp after a three days' fight nerves were sensitive. "Men would start at the slightest sound, and dodge at the flight of a bird or a pebble tossed at them. One of the chief amusements on such occasions used to be to throw stones and chips past one another's heads to see the active dodging that would follow."

Raw recruits at Chickamauga had rushed into dangers from which veterans would shrink, yelling and springing over the Confederate earthworks to the amazement of enemy veterans, the watching General Granger saying of these men of his: "Just look at them; they don't know any better; they think that's the way it ought to be done. I'll bet they'll never do it again." Out of witnessing such bloody action Porter wrote that recklessness often masqueraded as courage and was rather audacity. "Courage born of passion or excitement should always be looked upon with suspicion." The new-coined American word "skedaddle" reached England, where a verse-writer ascribed to Lincoln the lines:

None but cow-hearted men, Europeans to wit,
Run away like a herd of scared cattle;
True Yankees, when licked, may skedaddle a bit,
But ne'er run like base cowards in battle.

With camp discipline and mild sentences ordered by military commissions the President seldom interfered, though always having grave hesitations over the death penalty

When the quota was fixed of drafted men required from the Third Ward of Washington, where President Lincoln resided, he directed one N. D. Larner of that ward to procure a substitute for him. The arrangements being completed, a few days later the *New York Herald* gave these details: "This morning John S. Staples, President Lincoln's representative recruit, was arrayed in the uniform of the United States army, and accompanied by Provost Marshal General Fry, N. D. Larner of the Third Ward, and his (Staples's) father, was taken to the Executive Mansion, where he was received by President Lincoln. General Fry introduced him by saying, 'Mr. President, this is the man who is to represent you in the army for the next year.' Mr. Lincoln shook hands with Staples, remarked that he was a good-looking, stout and healthy-appearing man, and believed he would do his duty. He asked Staples if he had been mustered in, and he replied that he had. Mr. Larner then presented the President with a framed official notice of the fact that he had put in a representative recruit, and the President again shook hands with Staples, expressed the hope that he would be one of the fortunate ones, and the visiting party then retired." Staples, who was then twenty, received $500 from Lincoln, and was enrolled in Company H, 2nd District of Columbia regiment, of which his father was chaplain. Thus far in the passing months Staples had rendered steady and faithful service.

It may have come to Lincoln's knowledge that one Nels H. Peterson, away out in the little prairie town of Knoxville, Illinois, five miles from Galesburg, had enlisted in Company C of the 43d Illinois Volunteers. And there were so many other Petersons in the regiment, and these other Petersons were getting mixed so often in the roll calls and pay rolls, that he changed his name to Nels H. Lincoln. Since then Nels had gone on through the battles of Shiloh, Antietam, Winchester, Fisher's Hill, Cedar Creek, after marching, skirmishing, or outpost duty, answering roll call to his name of Lincoln. At Shiloh Private Nels H. Lincoln had seen his captain, Olof S. Edvall, killed, and of the 100 Swedes and 3 Germans in Company C who went into action 17 killed and wounded.

The President once said he could understand the man "overcome by a physical fear greater than his will." Neither privates nor generals came in for blame in Lincoln's direct replies to Congressman H. C. Deming of Connecticut, who asked when the war might have ended if commanders had managed better. There were three such high points, the President believed, "At Malvern Hill, when McClellan failed to command an immediate advance upon Richmond; at Chancellorsville, when Hooker failed to reinforce Sedgwick, after hearing his cannon upon the extreme right; and at Gettysburg, when Meade failed to attack Lee in his retreat at the bend of the Potomac." Congressman Deming at this moment expected denunciation or complaint or censure. Instead Lincoln further clarified: "I do not know that I could have given any different orders had I been with them myself. I have not fully made up my mind how I should behave when minié-balls were whistling, and those great oblong shells shrieking in my ear. I might run away."

An anxious old woman came in company with Congressman Charles Denison of Pennsylvania. She was the mother of John Russell, a private soldier under sentence to be shot in forty-eight hours. Lincoln heard them, sent for the papers in the case, and issued a peremptory order. Not only did this order revoke the court-martial sentence that young Russell was to be shot in forty-eight hours. It also restored Russell to his regiment. It seemed that in a recent bloody battle Russell's captain had run away and after the battle found half of his command were lost. Russell had been among the last to give way to the enemy. Meeting his captain, he walked toward him, rifle in hand, and burst out, "Captain, you're a damned coward and ought to be shot for cowardice." The captain pulled his revolver and Russell was getting ready to aim his rifle at the captain when others came between them. The captain then had Russell arrested, preferred charges of insubordination, got a court-martial to give the lad a death sentence. Lincoln refused on the basis of the evidence to accept the court-martial findings. He seemed to think it a packed and subservient body. According to James Scovel, in this case he went a step farther than customary, saying to Scovel, "And I did more—I dismissed the cowardly captain from the army."

A private in Meade's army was arrested as a deserter, tried, and given the death sentence, the court-martial refusing to accept his story that he had been in the thick of fighting and got separated from his command. Lincoln suspended sentence. The case was not clear. Later came complete evidence that the man had fought bravely. His delay in retreating had separated him from his command. *Leslie's Weekly*, January 16, 1864, for its national audience, summarized the record, with an unfair reflection on General Meade.

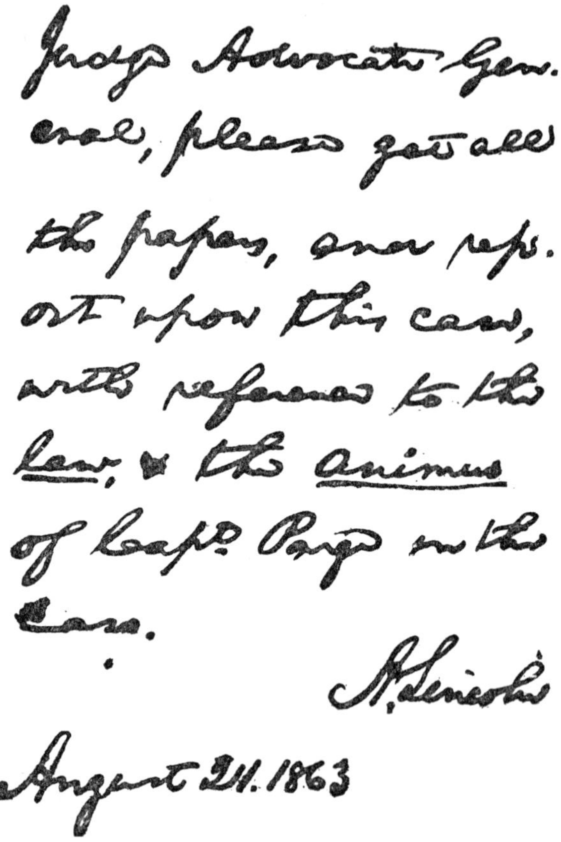
Judge Advocate Gen-
eral, please get all
the papers, and rep-
ort upon this case,
with reference to the
law, & the animus
of Capt. Page in the
case.
A. Lincoln
August 24. 1863

The President presses inquiry "with reference to the *law,* & the *animus*" of an officer toward a man of the rank and file. Original in the Barrett collection.

"The *Washington Republican* gives the particulars of a case where a young soldier was ordered to be shot for desertion when he ought to have been promoted for gallantry. The President was just in time to prevent the poor man's execution. General Meade is very active in shooting his own men, and it would appear, rather carelessly."

In another case later Lincoln wrote to Meade on the day a man was to be shot. Lincoln wished Meade to know that he had examined the record. "And it shows too strong a case for a pardon or commutation, unless there is something in the poor man's favor outside of the record, which you on the ground may know, but I do not." Lincoln in this went the limit in putting the final decision in Meade's hands. "My note to you only means that if you know of any such thing rendering a suspension of execution proper, on your own judgment, you are at liberty to suspend it. Otherwise I do not interfere." A somewhat like note went the same week to General Dix at New York. Lincoln telegraphed suspension of execution April 20. He telegraphed withdrawal of the suspension April 21, "leaving the case entirely" with General Dix. "The man's friends are pressing me, but I refer them to you, intending to take no further action myself."

In the summer of '64 the eminent scientist Joseph Henry sent a friend two papers "as an evidence that Mr. Lincoln desired to do what is proper in the case you and Professor Horsford presented to him." Lincoln's memorandum read:

> Professor Henry. A few days ago a friend of yours called and urged me to pardon Private McCarthy, & upon my refusal, went away dissatisfied, and I thought a little out of temper. After he was gone I telegraphed Gen. Meade that if he and McCarthy's Colonel would consent, I would send him back to his regiment, and the within is Gen. Meade's answer.
>
> Yours truly
>
> A. Lincoln
>
> June 10, 1864

General Meade's telegram enclosed read:

> Mr. President Your dispatch of yesterday in relation to private James McCarthey of Co "K" 140th New York is received. On inquiry I find that Private McCarthey was a Drafted Man who deserted in two (2) or three (3) days after he joined the Regt & was apprehended by our Pickets attempting to pass our Lines towards the enemy when arrested. He attempted to bribe the Pickets to allow him to pass. I cannot recommend any mitigation of the sentence in his case.

Lincoln seemed to fear he might absorb the military viewpoint, as though his first thought must be the civil population whence came the armies. If he lost touch with the civilian mind and approach, then what? The sound of musketry fire blew from Virginia camps into the White House one afternoon as Lincoln sat with John Eaton of Toledo. He stepped to an open window and looked to the Virginia shore. "When he turned again, the tears were running down his cheeks," wrote the responsible John Eaton, who heard him say, "This is the day when they shoot deserters." It was "they" who were shooting, not "we." It was as though to some mindless, heartless, inhuman, pitiless abstract force, a mechanism without remorse or memory, had been committed the lives of boys who were dying for doing they knew not what—"they" not "we" were having this "day when they shoot deserters."

Nevertheless it was not so easy as that. By his pardons he had lowered the army morale. "Some of our officers feel that," he said to Eaton. "Our" officers had that feeling. After all it was "our" army and he too was part of "they" who were shooting deserters. Still and all, he told Eaton, "I am wondering whether I have used the pardoning power as much as I ought." To Eaton and to others he spoke this recurring misery of a dilemma that would be with him so long as the war lasted. He might resolve to help "our" officers, but days came when he was heard to say as he signed papers, "I think the boy can do us more good above the ground than under."

"Death warrants . . . how he dreaded and detested them," wrote Lamon, who said that volumes could be filled with the ever varying names and

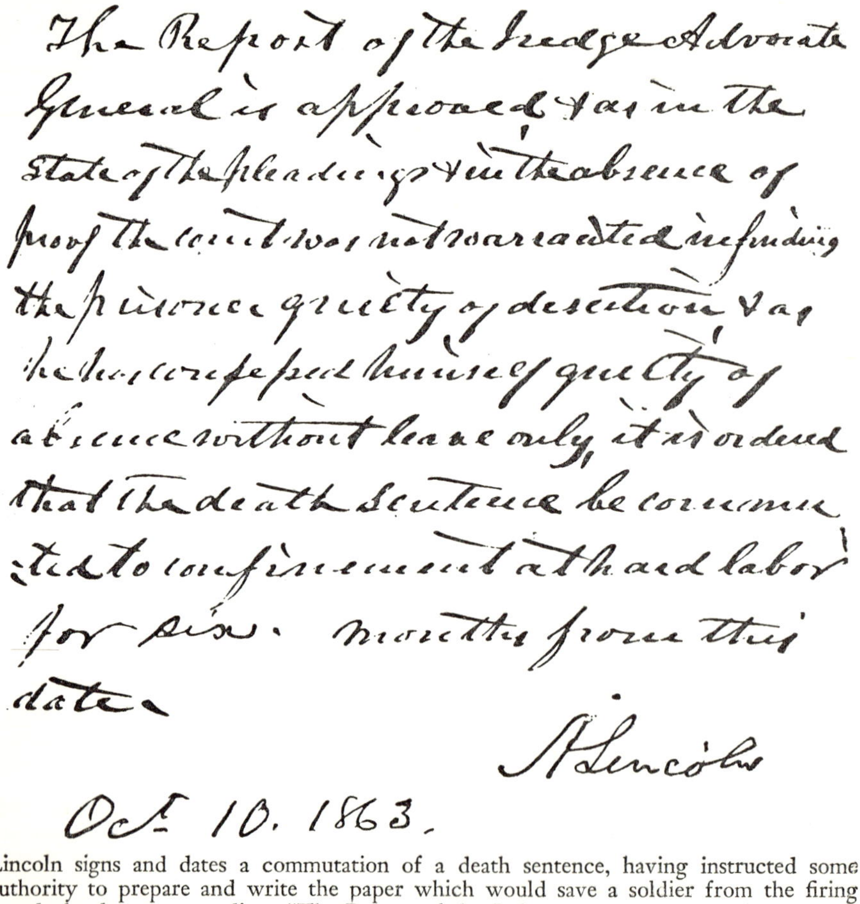

The Report of the Judge Advocate General is approved & as in the state of the pleadings & in the absence of proof the court was not warranted in finding the prisoner guilty of desertion, & as he has confessed himself guilty of absence without leave only, it is ordered that the death sentence be commuted to confinement at hard labor for six months from this date.

A. Lincoln

Oct. 10. 1863.

Lincoln signs and dates a commutation of a death sentence, having instructed some authority to prepare and write the paper which would save a soldier from the firing squad, the document reading: "The Report of the Judge Advocate General is approved & as in the state of the pleadings & and in the absence of proof the court was not warranted in finding the prisoner guilty of desertion, & as he has confessed himself guilty of absence without leave only, it is ordered that the death sentence be commuted to confinement at hard labor for six months from this date." Original in Barrett collection.

anecdotes of disgraced soldiers, prisoners of war, civilian spies, whose papers came to Lincoln's desk for an irrevocable Yes or No. Whether boys unknown to him were facing a firing squad over in Virginia where the shots could be heard at a White House window, or whether friends and familiars of old days met death with perfect valor on the battlefield, he took it too hard, thought Lamon, burdened himself "with an unreasonable sense of personal responsibility." He was in "one of the saddest moods in which I ever saw him," wrote Lamon of the day when news came that the third and last of the Black boys of Danville had fallen in battle. Their mother, the widow of a learned Presbyterian minister, had married Dr. Fithian of Danville, Illinois. Lincoln had often visited their home, seen the boys in and out of the doorways. Two of them fell wounded within five minutes of each other and only thirty yards apart in a charge at Pea Ridge, their father across months nursing them back to life and sending them back to the army. Then the eldest son at Prairie Grove had fallen so badly hit he would live on a mangled man if he lived at all. Lamon took to Lincoln a letter from Dr. Fithian telling of his boys and afraid they would not live. "Mr. Lincoln read it, and broke into tears," wrote Lamon, who heard the outcry: "My God, my God! It is too bad! They worked hard to earn money to educate themselves, and this is the end! I loved them as if they were my own." Not long after he telegraphed Major General Curtis at St. Louis: "If my friend Dr. William Fithian, of Danville, Illinois, should call on you, please give him such facilities as you consistently can about recovering the remains of a step-son, and matters connected therewith."

The news of General W. H. L. Wallace killed at Shiloh "Mr. Lincoln felt bitterly and deeply," wrote Lamon. "He knew his character as a man and his inestimable value as a soldier." Two women relatives of General Lew Wallace sought news at the White House, and getting it, spoke glibly their gladness it was "not our Wallace." Lincoln's rebuke took the form of mournfully meditating aloud, "It was somebody's Wallace, wasn't it?"

He might also then have been thinking of the dead General Wallace's wife, the daughter of a lawyer with whom he had often tried cases. She had a premonition before the battle of Shiloh was fought. At midnight in a wild storm she started a six-hundred-mile journey that brought her, after many excuses and expedients, to the battlefield. There she saw her husband borne to the rear with a shell-torn head. He died in her arms a few days later, saying to her and to soldier kinsmen standing by, "We shall meet again in heaven." Lincoln knew "it was somebody's Wallace."

To what extent did the President's frequent pardons interfere with army discipline? Chauncey M. Depew of New York was to answer that question later by quoting from a conversation he said he had with General William Tecumseh Sherman. "How did you carry out the sentences of your court-martials and escape Lincoln's pardons?" he asked. Sherman answered, "I shot them first!" Whatever the irregular or illegal device used by Sherman in this respect, it was probably also used by Grant, Thomas, Sheridan, and every other commander who won campaigns and battles without such incessant croakings about executive interference as were heard from Butler, who won no campaigns or battles worth mentioning. Able commanders who won effective results, the records indicated, heard no rebukes from the President because of any summary methods they considered necessary for discipline or the winning of objectives.

Once came a telegram that a deserter was to be shot the next day without the facts having been submitted to him. Lincoln replied that he had gone over the facts, found the case "really a very bad one," and nevertheless had already commuted the death sentence to imprisonment at hard labor. "I did this, not on any merit in the case, but because I am trying to evade the butchering business lately."

Well enough was it known in the army that being saved from a firing squad by a President's pardon did not win a life of ease and a bed of roses. More often it meant iron bars, prison fare, close confinement, hard labor, the ball and chain. Far and wide went the press item in 1864: "President Lincoln directed that the sentences of all deserters who had been condemned to death by court-martial, and that had not been otherwise acted upon by him, be mitigated to imprisonment during the war at the Dry Tortugas, Florida, where they would be sent under guard." In a tropical climate, cut off by the sea, with war-torn States and the Atlantic Ocean between them and the Northern home States, some of the deserters, thieves, cowards, "leg cases," mutineers, malingerers, bounty-jumpers, doing the lockstep in the Dry Tortugas Islands wrote back to old comrades that it was a hard life.

The highly wrought emotions, the wild imaginings and hysteria, so often accompanying the event of a pardon gave rise to exaggerations, inventions, false stresses in the telling. Some were dubious, others spurious on the face of them. One of the latter ran in several versions. A woman in tears pleaded that her only son had left the army for a one-day visit with her, returning to the army the next day, being then arrested and ordered to be shot as a deserter. The hour for the execution was near. Lincoln seized her by the hand, ran with her to the War Office, where the woman could not remember regiment nor location of her son. Stanton begged Lincoln to drop the matter. Lincoln rose to full height, declaiming: "I will not be balked in this. Send this message to every headquarters, every fort, and every camp in the United States: 'Let no military execution take place until further orders from me.'" This fabricated incident was told and published widely. Yet the official records and personal testimonies of no one army or its officers gave a basis to the story. The nearest approach to it was the President's order to General Butler to suspend all military executions until further orders in that one department.

The incident was published of a general sending the President warrants for the execution of twenty-four deserters by firing squads. The President refused to sign the papers. The general traveled to Washington and told the President he must make an example of these men, saying: "The army itself is in danger. Mercy to the few is cruelty to the many." The President:

"Mr. General, there are already too many weeping widows in the United States. For God's sake, don't ask me to add to the number, for I won't do it!"

With court-martial records piled on the desk before him Lincoln one day ended a pleasant talk abruptly: "Get out of the way, Swett. Tomorrow is Butcher Day, and I must go through these papers and see if I can not find some excuse to let these poor fellows off."

Two New Yorkers brought a formidable petition for pardon of a seaman acting as mate of a vessel; he had struck one of his men a blow that resulted in death. Though now convicted of manslaughter, his previous reputation was excellent. "Well, gentlemen," said Lincoln, "leave your papers, and I will have the Attorney-General, Judge Bates, look them over and we will see what can be done. Both of us being pigeon-hearted fellows, the chances are that if there is any ground whatever for interference, the scoundrel will get off!"

A Kentucky Unionist friend of Lincoln brought the case of a young Kentuckian who had enlisted with a Confederate force, become disgusted, returned home to find himself arrested later by Union authorities and condemned to be shot as a spy. Thus in brief the story. Lincoln heard it through, and then, "Oh yes, I understand some one has been crying to your good wife and worked on her feelings and you have come here to work on mine." Which was a correct guess. But the friend persisted with more details, fully convinced Lincoln of his own sincerity but only half convinced him of the innocence of the supposed Confederate deserter.

Lincoln deliberated, began writing, and spoke his hesitations as he wrote: "If a man had more than one life, I think a little hanging would not hurt this one, but after he is once dead we cannot bring him back, no matter how sorry we may be, so he shall be pardoned."

From Joseph Holt, Judge Advocate General of the army earlier in the war, came an account of a batch of death-penalty documents he laid before the President. Having heard Holt explain the first case, Lincoln took the papers with "I will keep this a few days until I have more time to read the testimony." In the second case, "I must put this by until I can settle in my mind whether this soldier can better serve the country dead than living." In the third, "The general commanding the brigade is to be here in a few days; I will talk the matter over with him." Finally came a flagrant case of a soldier in the heat of battle, affecting others by his cowardice, throwing down his gun and hiding behind a tree stump. The court-martial found he had neither father nor mother living, nor wife nor child; he was a thief, stealing from comrades on duty, by all standards unfit to wear the uniform. "Here is a case," said Judge Holt to the President, "exactly within your requirements; he does not deny his guilt; he will serve his country better dead than living . . . no relations to mourn for him . . . not fit to be in the ranks of patriots."

The President ran his long fingers through his hair: "Well, after all, Judge, I think I must put this with my leg cases."

Judge Holt frowned. Was Lincoln getting humorous about a matter of life and death? "What do you mean by leg cases, sir?"

"Why, why, do you see those papers crowded into those pigeon-holes? They are the cases that you call by that long title 'cowardice in the face of the enemy,' but I call them, for short, my 'leg cases.' But I put it to you, and I leave it for you to decide for yourself: if Almighty God gives a man a cowardly pair of legs how can he help their running away with him?"

This was Lincoln's later application of points made in a speech in Springfield, Illinois, years earlier. Then he referred to refugees from justice affected in their heels with a "running itch," the malady operating as the cork leg in the comic song did on its owner, "which when he had once got started on it, the more he tried to stop it, the more it would run away." To this was coupled the anecdote of an Irish soldier who explained his running away in battle, "Captain, I have as brave a heart as Julius Caesar ever had, but somehow or other, whenever danger approaches, my cowardly legs will run away with it."

Candor could go no farther than Lincoln's endorsement on some papers filed with him. On one, said Holt, he wrote: "I wish to grant a pardon in this case, and I will be obliged to the Judge-Advocate of the Army if he will inform me as to the *way* in which it is to be done."

In a single year the army court-martials were handling 30,000 cases of offenders against military law. Many capital cases eventually drifted to Lincoln's desk. Of one hot summer afternoon John Hay wrote in his diary that the President spent six hours on court-martial transcripts, catching at any fact that would justify saving a life. To Holt's plea once that it was better to enforce the law rigidly, he responded, "Yes, your reasons are very good, but I don't think I can do it." In one case he doubted "it would make any man better to shoot him," urging that if the Government kept him alive it could at least get some work out of him. One endorsement read, "Let him fight instead of shooting him." Of one who had escaped to Mexico and was beyond Federal authority: "We will condemn him as they sell hogs in Indiana, 'as they run.'" One recourse was to make sure whether some decisive State governor might not incline to mercy. "What do you remember," he wired Governor Morton of Indiana, "about the case of John O. Brown, convicted of mutinous conduct and sentenced to death? What do you desire about it?"

The Reverend Dr. R. K. Rodgers of Princeton, New Jersey, sent his card up to the President's office and was admitted without waiting. He entered with his wife, their baby in her arms. Lincoln: "You are a minister, I believe. What can I do for you, my friend?"

"A young man from my congregation in the army has so far forgotten his duty to his country and his God as to desert his colors, and is sentenced to die. I have come to ask you to spare him."

"Then you don't want him hurt, do you?"

"Oh, no, I didn't mean that. He deserves punishment, but I beg for him time to prepare to meet his God."

"Do you say he has father, wife, and child?"

"Yes."

"Where do you say he is?"

With this required data, Lincoln spoke in an undertone to a secretary who took notes, and turned to the Reverend Dr. Rodgers, "You have your request. Tell his friends I have reprieved him."

"God bless you, Mr. President."

The young Indiana Democratic Congressman Daniel W. Voorhees, to be known in time as "The Tall Sycamore of the Wabash," saw Lincoln occasionally, had favors from Lincoln, though in the *Congressional Globe*, as reported, his speeches gave few favors to the Lincoln Administration. But something in the vivid style of the Tall Sycamore may have interested Lincoln so that he spoke with exceptional candor, Voorhees saying later that he heard from Lincoln the confession: "No one need ever expect me to sanction the shooting of a man for running away in battle. I won't do it. A man can't help being a coward any more than he could help being a humpback, if he were born with one. Voorhees, were you ever scared?"

Yes, Voorhees had had some little experience that way.

"So have I," laughed Lincoln in a high tenor. "And I know just what it means. And in any contest or controversy which arises between the head and the heels, I never knew the heels to get anything but the best of it. No, sir, they needn't send any leg cases to me at all. I'll never order a man shot for any such offense."

It was on another White House call, according to Voorhees, that Lincoln, with a pathetic look of anxious pain, made the little inquiry, "Voorhees, doesn't it seem strange that I should be here—I, a man who couldn't cut a chicken's head off—with blood running all around me?"

Assistant Secretary of War Charles A. Dana wrote from continuous and close observation of Lincoln, "A thing it seemed as if he could not do was to sign a death warrant." Dana instanced General Augur, commanding the forces in and around Washington, coming to his office with information of a spy caught cold, tried by court-martial, convicted on evidence beyond reasonable doubt, sentenced to death.

"Here is the warrant for his execution," said General Augur, "fixed for tomorrow morning at six o'clock. The President is away. If he were here, the man certainly wouldn't be executed. He isn't here. I think it very essential to the service and the safety of everything that an example should be made of this spy. The punishment which every nation assigns to them should be inflicted on at least one of these wretches. Do you know whether the President will be back before morning?"

"I understand that he won't be back until tomorrow morning."

"Well, as the President is not here, will you sign the warrant?"

"Go to Mr. Stanton. He is the authority."

"I have been to him, and he said I should come to you."

Dana signed the death order. He agreed with General Augur that the spy should face a firing squad at six the next morning.

At eleven o'clock of the next morning Dana met General Augur and asked how things were.

"The President," said General Augur, "got home at two o'clock this morning and he stopped it all."

To a woman asking promotion of her husband to be brigadier general Lincoln said earnestly, "He is too young," her response being prompt:

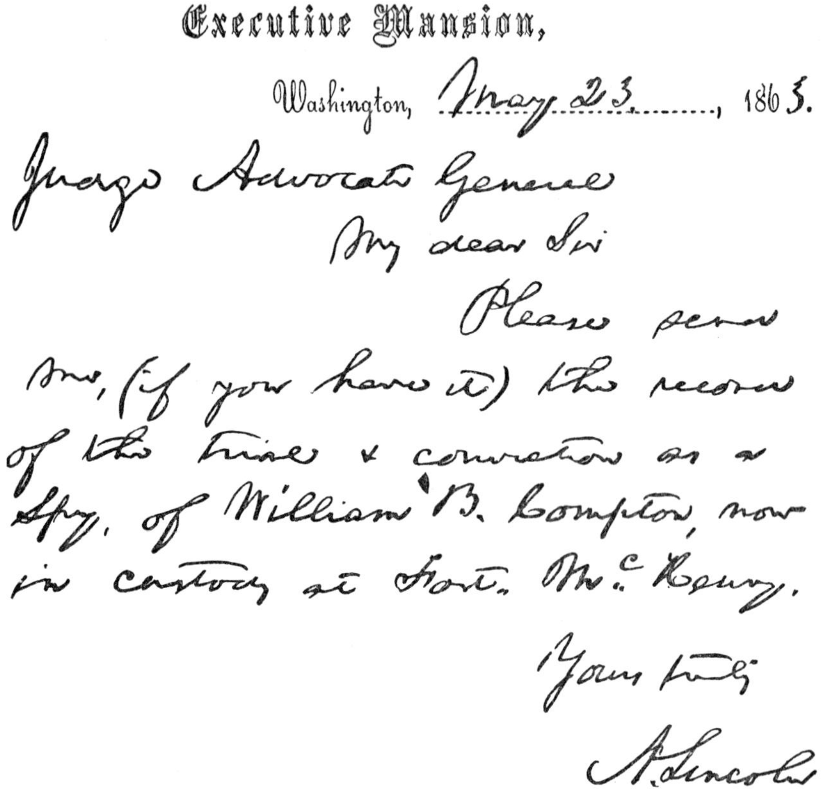
Executive Mansion,

Washington, May 23, 1863.

Judge Advocate General

My dear Sir

Please send me, (if you have it) the record of the trial & conviction as a Spy, of William B. Compton, now in custody at Fort. McHenry.

Yours truly

A. Lincoln

The President asks for the evidence on which William B. Compton was convicted as a spy. Original from the author's collection.

"Not too young to be killed in the service and leave me a widow." What could he say to that? She wrote that "the bonhomie of a courtier" was in his reply, "Well, you would have no trouble in finding promotion then." This, she suspected, was for Mr. Lincoln "quite a flirtatious remark."

While they chatted pleasantly a doorkeeper handed in a card, whispered as the President put on his eyeglasses. Then came a long sigh near to a groan. The mirth of a moment before vanished. "This poor woman's son is to be shot tomorrow." The officer's wife felt her strength leaving her but managed to offer as comfort her opinion that such things were inevitable in time of war.

"Yes, that's so," said Lincoln slowly, his hand pressing his forehead, as he reverted to boyhood Kentucky lingo. "But there's so many on 'em, so many on 'em."

Crook, the White House guard, took note of a woman intercepting Tad in a corridor, telling Tad her boys and girls were cold and starving because their father was shut up in prison and couldn't work for them. Tad ran to his father with the story. The father sat at a desk with papers, an absent look on his face, said he would look into the case as soon as he had time. Tad clung to his father's knees and begged till his father listened. And Tad ran back and told the woman her husband would be set free. The woman blessed him and cried, and Tad cried, and Crook said his own eyes didn't behave well.

A rough rider of the Confederate Mosby's raiders awaited the firing squad while his wife came to Lincoln with her story. The President, knowing how fierce Mosby's men were in the field, asked her what kind of a husband her man was. Did he get drunk? Did he beat her and the children?

"No, no," said the wife. "He is a good man, a good husband. He loves me. He loves the children. And we can't live without him. The only trouble is that he is a fool about politics. I live in the North, born there, and if I can get him home he will do no more fighting for the South."

"Well," said Lincoln as he thumbed through the papers, "I will pardon your husband and turn him over to you for safe keeping."

Here the woman broke into tears, into a sobbing beyond control.

"My dear woman, if I had known how badly it was going to make you feel, I never would have pardoned him."

"You don't understand me," she cried between sobs, in a fresh flow of tears.

"Yes, yes, I do. And if you don't go away at once I shall be crying with you."

A woman knelt to give thanks for the release of her husband. "Don't kneel to me but thank God and go" was the President's dismissal of her.

John W. Forney brought to the White House a woman who set forth reasons why a private soldier sentenced to death for desertion should be pardoned. The shooting was set for the next morning. Forney went back to his work as clerk of the Senate, had a busy and exciting day, had forgotten about the woman he introduced to the President, when at ten o'clock at night she came rushing in, and according to Forney these were her very words: "The Cabinet adjourned and I sat waiting for the President to come out and tell me the fate of my poor soldier, whose case I had placed in his hands after you left. But I waited in vain—there was no Mr. Lincoln. So I thought I would go up to the door of his Cabinet Chamber and knock. I did so. There was no answer. I opened the door and passed in. And there was the worn President asleep, with his head on the table resting on his arms, and by his side my boy's pardon signed. I quietly waked him, blessed him for his good deed, and came here to tell you the glorious news."

There were tender scenes with no overplaying of them. A woman with tears filling her eyes tried to speak gratitude for a "suspension of execution" granted her husband. "Good-by, Mr. Lincoln. I shall probably never see you again till we meet in heaven." She had taken one of his hands. He took her right hand in both of his. They walked to the door as he spoke softly: "I am afraid with all my troubles I shall never get to the resting-place you speak of. But if I do, I am sure I shall find you. That you wish me to get there is, I believe, the best wish you could make for me. Good-by."

"If he has no friend I'll be his friend," was Lincoln's remark as he penned a reprieve for one unbespoken. Once he sat up in his nightshirt, just awakened from sleep, heard the story of a nineteen-year-old boy having fallen asleep on picket duty, wrote a reprieve in bed, then worried that the order might go wrong, dressed himself and went over to the War Department to make sure the order was understood. This was one story and a likely one. Another ran that in fear a similar pardon order might go astray he sent telegrams to four different authorities. Of one of these pardons saving the life of a sleeping picket, he remarked to a Congressman as he read an order he had written: "I could not think of going into eternity with the blood of that poor young man on my skirts. It is not to be wondered at that a boy, raised on the farm, probably in the habit of going to bed at dark, should, when required to watch, fall asleep; and I cannot consent to shooting him for such an act."

The most dramatic pardon episode that wove itself around Lincoln during the war concerned the President and Private William Scott, Company K, 3rd Vermont Volunteers. "He," read the court-martial findings, "being a regularly posted sentinel did go to sleep upon his post; this at the hour between 3 and 4 A.M. on the 31st day of August, 1861, while on picket guard near Camp Lyon, District of Columbia. And the Court, two-thirds of the members concurring therein, does sentence him . . . to be shot to death . . . on Monday, the ninth of September, 1861, at such hour and place as the brigade commander may designate."

Then, according to later newspaper accounts, and according to stories passed from mouth to ear, and according to a dramatic poem by Francis de Haes Janvier, and descriptions in magazine articles and narratives published in books, and most vividly and extendedly of all in pages written by Lucius E. Chittenden, Register of the Treasury, Lincoln and Scott shared in exciting roles.

At the White House Lincoln heard a delegation of Green Mountain boys, farm hands and backwoodsmen, testify that Scott had taken a comrade's place on picket duty the night before he was found asleep, that Scott was as brave a man as ever lived and they would guarantee that if he were given his freedom he would show valor on the coming battlefields. They went away.

Hours passed. Lincoln in the sweep of affairs suddenly remembered the case of Scott, doomed in a few short hours to go down from firing-squad bullets. He ordered his carriage, looked at his watch, saw he might be too late, told the driver to lose no time, that it was a matter of life and death.

In a cloud of dust from furious driving, the horses foaming with sweat, the President arrived at the tent where Scott was under guard, went inside. "My boy," he said to Scott, "stand up here and look me in the face." And Scott looked him square in the eye. "My boy, you are not going to be shot tomorrow. I am going to trust you and send you back to your regiment." He put his hands on the boy's shoulders. "There is only one man in the world who can pay my bill, and his name is William Scott. If from this day William Scott does his duty, so that, if I was there when he comes to die, he can look me in the face as he does now, and say, I have kept my promise, and I have done my duty as a soldier, then my debt will be paid. Will you make that promise and try to keep it?" And the answer, as Scott told his comrades, was: "I said I would make the promise, and, with God's help, I would keep it. I wanted to tell him how hard I would try to do all he wanted, but the words would not come, so I had to let it all go unsaid. May God forget me if I ever forget his kind words or my promise."

Then the months passed and on April 15, 1862, at Lee's Mill on the Peninsula, the 3rd Vermont Volunteers charged across a stream nearly shoulder-high with water, dashed themselves at earthworks and rifle pits of the enemy, met a bloody repulse, leaving half their number dead and wounded in a river and woods. In the lead and with all the valor anyone could ask was William Scott.

"He was shot all to pieces," said one of his comrades. "We carried him back and laid him on the grass to die, his blood pouring from many wounds." In a hospital tent they gathered around to hear his failing and whispering voice say: "You all know what you can tell them at home. I tried to do the right thing."

And a light came on his face with his last words: "If any of you ever have the chance, I wish you would tell President Lincoln that I have never forgotten the kind words he said to me at Chain Bridge, that I have tried to be a good soldier and true to the flag, that I should have paid my whole debt to him if I had lived. I think of his kind face and thank him again." And before closing his eyes and crossing his hands on his breast he murmured as a completely happy man, "Good-by, boys, good-by."

Thus the legend. Thus one of the strangest tales of the war, part fact and part myth, and more fact than myth. And the entire fact story of what did happen was nearly as interesting, if not as spectacular, as the half-myth story told and retold, written and published, read silently or declaimed aloud for tense wartime audiences.

Scott was one of three sentinels posted at a hut guarding the Chain Bridge across the Potomac, a key entry to Washington. Only one man was required to stay awake, according to War Department records, but all were expected to be ready for giving an alarm in case of an attack or an attempt to run the bridge. Watches were four hours each. Scott had eight hours for sleep, if he needed it, before going on duty. Between three and four in the morning, the captain of the guard, making his rounds, found all three of the farm-boy soldiers asleep. They all agreed, including Scott, that they should have been awake. Scott was arrested, held three days, tried, sentenced to be shot. General McClellan approved the findings and sentence, set the execution date for September 9.

Scott's record had been good. The Vermont farm boys inclined to think that while sleeping might be wrong, it wasn't a crime. Where they came from "you worked in the daytime while it was light and when night came you took your sleep in the dark: didn't God mean the night for sleep?" They were just learning this war business, raw recruits of only a few weeks' service.

Excitement ran high along the company streets. A petition for pardon, addressed to Brigadier General William F. (Baldy) Smith, was signed not only by privates but by most of the officers of Scott's regiment. They held a meeting, organized a committee of privates, with one or two officers, who went to see L. E. Chittenden, Register of the Treasury, himself a Vermonter. He took them to Lincoln's office.

Lincoln hailed the little parade from Vermont with some such humor as: "What is this? An expedition to kidnap somebody, or to get another brigadier appointed, or for a furlough to go home to vote? I cannot do it, gentlemen. Brigadiers are thicker than drum-majors and I couldn't get a furlough for myself if I asked it from the War Department." They pleaded their cause, evidently moved him. He queried, "Do your Green Mountain boys fight as well as they talk?" He probably said, as Chittenden quoted him: "I do not think an honest, brave soldier, conscious of no crime but sleeping when he was weary, ought to be shot or hung. The country has better uses for him," and addressing an officer, "Captain, your boy shall not be shot—that is, not tomorrow, nor until I know more about this case," and speaking to Chittenden's point that they were burdening him: "Scott's life is as valuable to him as that of any person in the land. You remember the remark of the Scotchman about the head of a nobleman who was decapitated. 'It was a small matter of a head, but it was valuable to him, poor fellow, for it was the only one he had.' "

The regimental chaplain, seven captains, and many privates had their names by now on four sheets of a petition to Brigadier General Smith for a pardon. General Smith endorsed it, sent it Sunday, September 8, 1861, by a major to General McClellan's headquarters six miles away in Washington, the major stopping in at the White House to show it to the President. It was probably earlier on this Sunday that the President called on McClellan, as under this date of September 8 McClellan wrote to his wife: "Mr. Lincoln came this morning to ask me to pardon a man that I had ordered to be shot, suggesting that I could give as a reason in the order that it was by request of the 'Lady President.' " This might mean that Mrs. Lincoln had interested herself in the case, or that Lincoln preferred that the appeal should seem to come from her, or at any rate that the White House rather than thrusting its interference on Little Mac was requesting a favor. The favor requested was in process of being granted. The major from General Smith's headquarters, before leaving Washington that Sunday, told newspapermen

Cartes de visite of the photographed soldier—Lincoln sought them, met them, read them

Cartes de visite of wartime women North and South—hundreds of them month by month during the war called on Lincoln with requests, prayers, suggestions, patriotic offerings that William Scott was not to be shot the next day. The press published it as an item of news the next morning.

Also that same Monday morning the 3rd Vermont Volunteers regiment was drawn up to hear the reading of General Order No. 8, issued by General McClellan. It began with reciting Scott's trial and sentence, the appeals of brigade, regiment, and company officers, together with privates, that Scott's life be spared. "And," it continued, "the President of the United States had expressed a wish that, as this is the first condemnation to death in the army for this crime, mercy may be extended to the criminal. This fact, viewed in connection with the inexperience of the condemned as a soldier, his previous good conduct and general good character, and the urgent entreaties made in his behalf, have determined the Major General to grant the pardon so earnestly prayed for." Then came a warning that pardons might not always be given to boys who slept on sentinel duty, as it was an offense to which "all nations affix the penalty of death." Then came the order releasing Scott from guardhouse confinement and putting him back on duty with his regiment.

The press immediately treated the incident as though the President's "expressed wish" for a pardon was equivalent to his actually issuing one. The *New York Tribune* dispatch of September 9 said, "The pardon was read to the regiment, which heartily expressed their appreciation of Executive clemency." The *National Republican* editorially said, September 10, "The President has very properly saved the life of the offender, but we hope he will save no more." The *Sunday Morning Chronicle* of September 15 said: "The President . . . interfered and granted a pardon. It is a lesson to the volunteers, and a high tribute to the great goodness of heart of our excellent President."

William Scott seven months later among the fresh growths and blooms of Virginia springtime at Lee's Mill took the burning messages of six bullets into his body. His life was spent. All he could give Lincoln or his country or his God was now given.

William Scott? Yes, wasn't that the fellow who slept on sentinel duty and was pardoned by the President? soldiers and newspapermen asked. And though Scott had died, according to the regimental surgeon, in a coma, lacking speech, imagination played on what he might have said and what would have been good theatre for him to say.

"His comrades caught him up," wrote the *New York Commercial* correspondent in an account published April 21, 1862, "and as his life blood ebbed away, he raised to heaven amid the din of war, the cries of the dying, and the shouts of the enemy, a prayer for the President, and as he died he remarked to his comrade that he had shown he was no coward and not afraid to die." Two miles to the rear under a cherry tree singing with white blossoms, amid holly and vines, the comrades stood with uncovered heads at the burial. "The chaplain narrated the circumstances. He prayed for the President, and paid the most glowing tribute to his noble heart that we ever heard. The tears started to their eyes as the clods of earth were thrown upon him in his narrow grave, where he lay shrouded in his coat and blanket."

A government department employee named Francis de Haes Janvier, who had written "The Stars and Stripes" set to music and sung at the Lincoln inauguration in 1861, now took his pen in hand and achieved a long narrative rhymed piece titled "The Sleeping Sentinel." It was, some readers declared, drenched with feeling. In the United States Senate chamber on the evening of January 19, 1863, James Edward Murdoch, lecturer on Shakespeare, teacher of elocution, author of a book on how to cultivate the voice, was introduced to an audience by Vice-President Hamlin and read Janvier's poem "The Sleeping Sentinel." The *National Republican* writer held its author "need write nothing more to establish his fame beyond cavil as one of the first poets of the day." He summarized the poem: "All our readers will recollect the story of the Vermont soldier who was condemned to die for sleeping at his post. He was pardoned by President Lincoln, and afterwards died on the battlefield, calling his comrades around him to see how a brave soldier could die for his country." Those who "thronged the Senate Chamber on the occasion" included "many of the élite and a very large representation of the beauty and fashion of Washington." Also Lincoln had a seat and heard himself declaimed as a shining dispenser of mercy. "The President and Mrs. Lincoln were there." They had heard Murdoch give Janvier's poem in a private recital at the White House. And how did the reader perform in the Senate chamber? "Mr. Murdoch enchained his auditors in almost breathless interest, except the frequent applause which it was impossible to restrain." And from Washington Murdoch went to Philadelphia and with "thrilling effect" read "The Sleeping Sentinel" before 3,000 people in the American Academy of Music. From Philadelphia he went elsewhere reading stanzas having these lines:

> Then suddenly was heard the noise of steeds and wheels approach,—
> And, rolling through a cloud of dust, appeared a stately coach.
> On, past the guards, and through the field, its rapid course was bent,
> Till, halting, 'mid the lines was seen the nation's President!
>
> He came to save that stricken soul, now waking from despair . . .
> The woes of thirty millions filled his burdened heart with grief;
> Embattled hosts, on land and sea, acknowledged him their chief;
> And yet, amid the din of war, he heard the plaintive cry
> Of that poor soldier, as he lay in prison, doomed to die!

In May of 1864 T. B. Peterson & Co. of Philadelphia announced in *Godey's Lady's Book* publication of a book *The Sleeping Sentinel*, which they believed was "already so widely known that perhaps few of our readers are ignorant of its title." Lovers of poetry would find it "patriotic and pathetic," readings of it having "taken the heart of our great public by storm." When often declaimed to large audiences, "few listened to the end with dry eyes."

As the story of Lincoln and William Scott spread far, it was overcolored in several points. One fact was that Scott had died without naming Lincoln, his mother, his comrades, or anybody. A second fact was that Lincoln had not gone to Scott either on a walk or on horseback or in a carriage or a cab. Yet the myth went out and was taken as a living testament of honor, trust, patriotism, and the supreme sacrifice, deeply moving to many who had sons, brothers, dear ones, in the army. Ralph Waldo Emerson, among others, felt the myth overdone. Emerson believed Lincoln had a habit of riding furiously out to pardon this and that culprit, and wrote in his journal, March, 1863: "President Lincoln should remember that humanity in a ruler does not consist in running hither and thither in a cab to stop the execution of a deserter, but, as Napoleon said, 'justice is the humanity of kings.' "

The very death sentence of Scott, in the first place, probably was meant by Generals McClellan and Baldy Smith as a dress rehearsal to throw fear into all the troops around Washington for the sake of better discipline. McClellan won a peculiar affection with the rank and file of the Army of the Potomac and had no reputation for severity. He probably knew beforehand that Baldy Smith would send in a major with a petition for pardon. Baldy Smith was a Vermonter and had once been colonel of Scott's regiment. The indications were that they planned for some days to have a lot of serious thinking among all enlisted men about the gravity of sleeping on picket duty. Lincoln's course really consisted of adding his wish and signature to an already formidable, almost overwhelming, petition for pardon. But when fate decreed the dramatic and heroic death of Scott, the story took a new turn. And newspapermen, poets, writers, dramatic readers, and publishers carried a highly colored story to an immense audience.

Early in 1862 the *Philadelphia Press* and other newspapers gave their readers the story of a 9th Indiana Volunteers deserter. He stands blindfolded before five regiments drawn up to see him shot. A firing squad of twelve men stand ready to shoot. Behind the one lone doomed man is a long black box—his coffin. He shudders as though he might topple over; this day for the shooting has been fixed, put off, fixed again and once more put off; his nerves are shattered. The voice of an officer rings out, "Take aim!" A brigade of five regiments waits for the next order of "Fire!" That order does not come. On a sweat-streaked, foaming horse a dusty rider gallops in. His hand in the air waves a paper. He hands the officer a reprieve. The pardoned man wavers off his feet, his legs crumple, he falls back on the coffin. They run to him. Is he dead? No, but he might as well be. "Reason had taken its flight. He became a hopeless maniac. He was discharged from the army and sent home to his friends." And the plan had never been to shoot him. The intention was to throw "a healthy scare" into the army, "to solemnly impress upon the whole assemblage of soldiers the necessity of a strict observance of duty and obedience, under the penalty of an ignominious death."

On several bounty-jumpers Lincoln let the firing squads do their work. He refused mercy to bounty-jumpers—or again he intervened. The eccentric versatility of Robert Lane appealed to him. Lane enlisted first in Loomis's battery, left the service on a physical-disability discharge, stayed in Detroit, bobbed up in Nashville with a sutler, clowned with a circus, performed as a sword-swallower, rode a horse in a Kentucky cavalry regiment, was next heard of as a sergeant in one Indiana infantry company, leaving that one for another. While held in an Indiana penitentiary Robert Lane was by court-martial ordered to be shot. Lincoln for reasons known to himself commuted the sentence of this flagrant bounty-jumper and scalawag to one year's hard labor with chain and ball. Possibly he saw genius and wit allied to madness in the case of Robert Lane.

Chaplain Edward D. Neill of a Minnesota regiment told of a convalescent soldier at Elmira Hospital, New York, who drugged and robbed a fellow soldier. When the overdrugged victim died, a court-martial sentenced the convalescent to be hanged. Friends claimed insanity. Among reports sent to Lincoln was one by an asylum superintendent. Lincoln withheld a decision. Weeks passed. The assistant adjutant general at the War Department, General James A. Hardie, asked Chaplain Neill to see the President. Neill did.

The President pointed toward the pigeonholes at the top of his desk, saying: "There they are. Tell him they are still in soak." More weeks passed. General Hardie told Chaplain Neill: "The soldier ought to be hung or pardoned. Will you again see the President?" Neill did. The President asked if Neill had read the report of the asylum superintendent. Neill had. The President rose, found the report, aware exactly of where he was keeping it, and read to Neill the last sentence of the report: "Although I cannot pronounce the person insane, he certainly is peculiar." Wherewith Lincoln observed, "Now if these last words had not been written I should have had no hesitation in disposing of this case."

A soldier home on sick furlough failed to report to his regiment as required. A court-martial found him guilty of desertion. His brother, in company with Congressman S. F. Miller of New York, called on the President, requested a pardon, said the soldier while at home went partially insane, had recovered and was on his way to his regiment when condemned as a deserter. The President at once ordered an examination by a board of physicians as to the soldier's mental condition. Congressman Miller said this course seemed proper and he was satisfied. On leaving the President's room the Congressman was interested that the soldier's brother remarked, "The trouble with your President is, that he is so afraid of doing something wrong."

A boy in a New York regiment had twice deserted, had poisoned a prison guard who died, and was under death sentence. His mother heard refusals from Stanton. Going to Lincoln, she heard only refusals. She then went and found a friend who reached Senator Harris of New York with her side of the case. Harris got the President out of bed near midnight of a

Wednesday. On Thursday morning the boy was to be shot, pleaded Harris, but the boy was insane, irresponsible, and to shoot him would be murder; pardon was not asked, but a reprieve until a medical examination could be made.

Lincoln agreed with the Senator, ordered a telegram sent to Elmira, New York, delaying execution. Early the next morning the President sent another telegram by a different line, and before the hour of execution had arrived he had sent no less than four different reprieves, by different lines, to different persons, so haunted was he by a thing he might have set right had he in the first instance believed the mother's story.

A washerwoman of Troy, New York, had better luck. Her boy, a physical stalwart, though mentally an imbecile, had been lured into the army by swindlers who took his bounty money from him. She wanted her boy back home, though she couldn't even say which New York regiment he was in. She hung around the White House hoping to see the President, couldn't manage to slip into one of the weekly public receptions to petitioners. As Lincoln walked one afternoon to the War Department she spied him and "in no time at all" had a card ordering a search for her boy and his release to her.

A drunken Negro of low grade, having with an ax killed a man in a Washington suburb, awaited hanging. The question arose whether Marshal Lamon as jail-keeper should run the hanging, or local authorities. Chaplain Neill at the White House heard Lincoln say, "There is a dispute as to the hanging of a black man, and I have determined to settle the controversy by not having him hung." Holding the President's commutation of sentence from death to life imprisonment, Marshal Lamon reached the scaffold as the local authorities were fastening the rope around the condemned man's neck. "It took some time for the city authorities," noted Neill, "and a longer time for the dull-headed negro, to comprehend that there was to be no hanging, and that the paper carried by the Marshal was a commutation signed by President Lincoln."

Two white murderers escaped the noose by the same procedure. *Leslie's Weekly* of April 6, 1864, duly chronicled: "The President has commuted the sentence of two men, Hendricks and Pollard, condemned to be hung April 1, to imprisonment for life. Marshal Lamon had previously declined to hang them, assuming the ground that it was not his duty to do so, the recent act of Congress having deprived him of the custody of the jail and placed that institution under the charge of a warden, independent of his [Lamon's] control."

Pardon was sought for a teamster sentenced to the penitentiary for stealing from government property two pairs of pantaloons and a pair of shoes. One witness, it was shown to Lincoln, had testified that he sold the defendant the shoes in question. "Yes, so much for the shoes, but nothing about the pantaloons. The jury had the whole facts before them and I am sorry for his wife and children, sir, but the man must be punished."

A newspaperman and an Ohio colonel, after an interview on Great Lakes commerce, requested Lincoln to hear an old man waiting outside whose boy was to be shot. They waited. Nicolay came in with the old man's card, leaned over Lincoln's chair and whispered. Lincoln spoke, harassed yet decisive: "Tell him I will not see him. I cannot. Don't ask me again. Tell him I have read the papers in the case, all of them, fully, word for word. The boy deserted three times, the last time when on guard at Washington, and he cannot be pardoned. I will not interfere. He must be shot."

To the Fort Warren commandant one day went an order suspending death sentence of a deserter, Charles Carpenter, and the next day a telegram: "The order I sent yesterday . . . is hereby withdrawn and you are to act as if it never existed." To Christiana A. Sack at Baltimore went the telegram: "I cannot postpone the execution of a convicted spy on a mere telegraphic despatch signed with a name I never heard before." To an Ohio man queries were telegraphed: "Can there be a worse case than to desert, and with letters persuading others to desert? I cannot interpose without a better showing than you make. When did he desert? When did he write the letters?"

From a Border State of strife and atrocities came the case of a guerrilla, a lawless raider belonging to no command on either side. Lincoln went through the evidence carefully and completely. He favored the death penalty as a lesson for that region. To the signers of a long petition for pardon, to various influential citizens, he gave no comfort. The hour for the execution came near. A large delegation, eminent names among them, called at the White House. And according to William O. Stoddard, the White House mail clerk, Lincoln told the callers he could take no action without reviewing the papers in the case. He instructed Stoddard to look for the papers. Stoddard looked and hunted, brought word he couldn't find them. Lincoln suggested to the delegation that they should go to the War Department. They did so. They returned to say the War Department believed the papers had been sent to the White House at the President's own request. Further search was made at the White House. The papers couldn't be found. The delegation went away, puzzled, sorrowful. Soon after a telegram was handed the President. Thereupon he remarked, according to Stoddard:

"What did you say? A telegram from ——? You don't tell me! Has that man been actually hung? It's a pity about his papers! It seems to me—well, yes, I remember now. I know where— Well, if I did, I guess I wouldn't; not now! But if they're ever called for again, and they won't be, they ought to be where they can be found. Certainly, certainly. But it's just as well that one murderer escaped being pardoned by Abraham Lincoln. Narrow escape, too! The merest piece of luck in all the world!"

One pardon case after another was laid before the President by Judge Holt one Tuesday morning, noted Carpenter. The clock struck twelve. Lincoln heard it. He drew back from the table, stretched his arms. "I guess we will go no farther with these cases to-day. I am a little tired, and the Cabinet will be coming in soon." After a slight pause came his afterthought: "I believe I have not yet had my breakfast,—this business has been so absorbing that it has crowded everything else out of my mind."

Next morning was taken up with the same kind of cases. Carpenter noticed a score of political applicants impatiently pacing the floors of the hall and the waiting-room. At one o'clock a throng was let in. They took most of the afternoon. Carpenter saw an elderly woman, plainly but comfortably dressed, give the President her story. Her son was in a Baltimore prison. While serving in the Confederate Army he had heard of his sister at home lying dead and his mother dying. He had made his way through Confederate and Union lines, had heard the welcome news that no one was dead, then had fallen sick himself. The mother kept him hid in her house till he was well again. On his way back to his regiment he was captured. Now he was anxious to take the oath of allegiance to the Union. The mother said she was sure hereafter he would "have nothing to do with the Rebels."

Lincoln sat quietly through this story, "his face in half shadow," noted Carpenter. The woman had finished. With some impatience then came Lincoln's assessment of her words. "Your word, what do I know about your word?" He finally took the application, wrote something upon the back of it, and returned it to her: "Now, I want you to understand that I have done this just to get rid of you!" "Oh," said she, "Mr. President, I have always heard that you were such a kind-hearted man, and now I know it is true." And so, with satisfaction glowing on her face, she went away.

A woman with two men came next. The woman asked release of her husband, a prisoner of war. Might he be permitted to take the oath and go free? Furthermore, one of the men interposed, it might interest the President to know that he was an acquaintance of Mrs. Lincoln. This left no slightest impression on the President. He inquired of the woman, who appeared upper-class, what position her husband had held in the enemy service. "Oh, he was a captain."

"*A captain!* indeed!—rather too big a fish to set free simply upon his taking the oath. If he was an officer, it is proof positive that he has been a zealous rebel; I cannot release him."

Again now one of the men made it known he was an acquaintance of Mrs. Lincoln. The President pulled a bell rope. An usher was at hand. "Cornelius, take this man's name to Mrs. Lincoln, and ask her what she knows of him." The usher returned soon to say "the Madam" knew nothing of the man whatever. The man said it was very strange. "Well, it is just as I suspected," said the President. The three callers tried to start all over again with fresh pleas. But they heard only: "It is of no use; I cannot release him."

One guerrilla failing of mercy at Lincoln's hands was a Missouri leader named Nichols. Judge Holt gave Carpenter details about Nichols. "He was in the habit of filling the ears of Unionists who fell into his hands with gunpowder, setting fire to it, and blowing their heads to pieces. When captured, a number of human *ears* were found on his person."

Political interests of influence intervened in behalf of a notorious spy named Burroughs, wrote Carpenter, who was in the room one Tuesday morning where Judge Holt presented the cases to Lincoln for review. As Holt opened the record he informed the President that Burroughs, under sentence of death, had tried to escape from prison and was shot dead by a guard. Lincoln: "I ought to be obliged to him for taking his own fate into his hands; he has saved *me* a great deal of trouble."

A woman begged the President, "as a husband and father," to get a trial for her husband in prison. The President was sorry this could not be done. Such cases, he told her, were like sacks of grain at a country grist-mill, "waiting their turn to be ground," and it would be unfair for the "miller" to show "partiality." The woman left. Seeing her the next day, Lincoln asked if anything "new" had happened.

"No," said the woman, "but I have been thinking, sir, about what you said concerning the 'grists,' and I am afraid *mine* will get 'mouldy' and 'spoil' before its turn comes around. So I have come to ask, Mr. President, that it may be taken to some other 'mill' to be ground." This was much in the President's own style; he at once wrote for the woman an unconditional discharge for her husband.

On November 2, 1864, the Reverend George Harmon Blackslee, pastor of the Court Street Methodist Episcopal Church of Binghamton, New York, entered the room where Lincoln was receiving petitioners at two o'clock in the afternoon. Blackslee came from a month of special religious services among troops in the field and in hospitals. While waiting for an autograph which the President gave him, writing their two names and the date, Blackslee noticed other callers. In a little black notebook that evening Blackslee wrote of what he saw. Four young men with anxious faces asked the President's help in some matter that Blackslee could not quite understand. Lincoln told them in a kindly tone, "I can do nothing for you." They pressed the matter, urged their papers should be read. Again in a kindly tone: "I should not remember if I did. The papers can be put into their proper places and go through their proper channels." They turned away.

A woman presented a paper. He read it, replied: "This will not do. I can do nothing for your husband."

"Why not?"

"Because he is not loyal."

"But he intends to be. He wants to take the oath of allegiance."

"That is the way with all who get into prison. I can do nothing for you."

"But you would if you knew my circumstances."

"No, I would not. I am under no obligation to provide for the wives of disloyal husbands. Hasn't your husband the consumption?"

"No."

"Well, it is the only case. Nearly all have the consumption."

Another woman presented her similar case with a like result. She was followed by a man whose card read "E. W. Breckinridge." Lincoln queried, "What is your name?" the caller replying, "Breckinridge, rather a suspicious name, but I am loyal. I have long desired to see you and take you by the hand. I am glad to see you bearing your labors so well. You have the prayers of the people."

An Illinois major shot and killed the colonel of his regiment. The major's wife came to the President pleading that he must read the evidence in the case and commute the death sentence of her husband. Clutching a handkerchief tightly in a hand that shook against her bosom, she moaned that her husband had been insulted as "coward" and "dog" and had warned the colonel not to repeat such words as between two soldiers. But the colonel had repeated the insults. Lincoln sent the woman away saying he would look into the case. She came again at his appointment. She stood before his desk. He was about to tell her that he had commuted the death sentence to two years in prison. Before he could tell her, the woman swayed and slid to the floor in a dead faint. Lincoln helped lift her up, saw her taken from the room, then paced back and forth, Senator Henderson of Missouri hearing him say: "Poor woman! I don't believe she would have lived if her husband had been shot. What a heap of trouble this war has made!"

The Reverend Phineas D. Gurley told of one of his church members whose son in Confederate service was captured, court-martialed, sentenced to death. The President on an appeal from Dr. Gurley commuted the death sentence to a prison term. Later Dr. Gurley, in belief that the mother of the youth would lose her mind unless he was pardoned, signed an appeal for pardon. This paper the father presented to Lincoln, who broke out in wrath: "I saved the life of your son after he had been condemned to death, to be shot. Now you come here so soon, when you know I am overwhelmed with care and anxiety, asking for his pardon. You should have been content with what I have done. Go—and if you annoy me any more, I shall feel it my duty to consider whether I ought not to recall what I have already done." A few days later, however, Lincoln sent for the father and amazed him by handing him the wanted pardon. To Dr. Gurley, Lincoln said later, "I dismissed him roughly; afterward I felt ashamed of myself for having lost my temper."

Into the hands of Josiah Gilbert Holland, special writer for and one-fourth owner of the *Springfield Republican*, came a letter written by an extraordinary woman who had six interviews with President Lincoln on six successive days. Her account of these six days achieved a vivid word portrait of a man writhing, elusive, tormented, lighted with awkward humors, using words sometimes to mask his thought. To her it was that Lincoln said, "I shall never be glad any more," as a climax of much that had gone before. Her account was put in print by Holland, who identified her merely to the extent of saying she was "a lady of great intelligence and the keenest powers of observation," and, "the widow of one who had died while serving the soldiers of the State of which he was the Governor."

In archives of the State of Wisconsin she was known as Mrs. Louis Powell Harvey, wife of the Governor of Wisconsin elected in 1861. Her husband was drowned while moving supplies for soldiers wounded in the battle of Shiloh. His last letter to her, dated at Pittsburg Landing, April 17, 1862, had only three sentences: "Yesterday was the day of my life. Thank God for the impulse that brought me here. I am well, and have done more good by coming than I can well tell you." That letter and the death of her husband moved Mrs. Harvey. She asked Governor Edward Salomon of Wisconsin for permission to visit hospitals in the Western military depot as an agent of the State. At St. Louis and southward along the Mississippi River she visited many general hospitals, besides post hospitals of Wisconsin troops. She saw Northern boys wasting away in the heat of semitropical summers, noxious and contagious diseases bringing the mortality too high, taking many who might under different climatic and sanitary conditions have lived. She met surgeons appalled at conditions they had to work with, and some hospital attendants who shrank from care of the sick and removal of the dead. Near Vicksburg late in the spring of '63 she herself went down, and believed she would not have recovered had she not gone North. She came to President Lincoln with specific proposals that lay deep in her and for which she was a skilled advocate. She was keen-eyed and highly sensitized, could tell her story, and her account of her interviews was reporting of a kind not common among those who dealt with Lincoln.

She entered alone to find the President alone in "an office-like room, with no elegance around him, and no elegance in him." In a suit of black, poorly fitted, he sat "in a folded-up sort of way, in his arm-chair." Around him were unpretending sofas and chairs, covered with green worsted. Head bent, chin resting on breast, he held her letter, made a feint at rising, looked from under his eyebrows. "Mrs. Harvey?" He took her hand, "hoped she was well," gave no smile of welcome. Her business would interfere with his policy and plans. She read his face, deep-lined, almost stern.

He motioned her to a chair. As he read her letter she went on searching his face. He finished her letter, looked up, ran his fingers through his slightly silvered dark-brown hair. "Madam, this matter of northern hospitals has been talked of a great deal, and I thought it was settled; but it seems this is not the case. What have you got to say about it?"

"Simply this," she replied, "that many soldiers, sick in our western army on the Mississippi, must have northern air, or die. There are thousands of graves along the Mississippi and Yazoo, for which the government is responsible–ignorantly, undoubtedly; but this ignorance must not continue. If you will permit these men to come North, you will have ten men in one year where you have got one now."

Shrugging his shoulders, smiling: "If your reasoning were correct, your argument would be a good one. I don't see how sending one sick man North is going to give us ten well ones."

The lady: "You understand me, I think."

"Yes, yes," said he, "I understand you; but if they go North they will desert, and where is the difference?"

Her reply: "Dead men cannot fight, and they may not desert."

"A fine way to decimate the army!" exclaimed the President. "We should never get a man back—not one—not one."

"Pardon me," responded the lady, "but I believe you are mistaken. You do not understand our people. They are as true and as loyal to the government as yourself. The loyalty is among the common soldiers, and they are the chief sufferers."

Almost with contempt Lincoln replied, "This is your opinion!"

In this exhibition of petulance, were there signs the President saw that he was being undermined? "Mrs. Harvey," said he earnestly, "how many men of the Army of the Potomac do you suppose the government was paying at the battle of Antietam? and how many men do you suppose could be got for active service at that time?"

"I know nothing of the Army of the Potomac, except that it has made some noble sacrifices."

"Well, but give a guess," persisted the President.

"Indeed, I cannot," was her answer.

He threw himself awkwardly around in his chair, with one leg over the arm, and spoke slowly: "This war might have been finished at that time, if every man had been in his place who was able to be there; but they were scattered here and there over the North—some on furloughs, and in one way and another gone, so that, out of one hundred and seventy thousand men, whom the government was paying, only eighty-three thousand could be got for action. The consequences, you know, proved nearly disastrous." The President paused.

Her response came: "It was very sad; but the delinquents were certainly not in northern hospitals, for we have had none; so your argument is not against them."

The President appreciated this logic: "Well, well; you go and call on the Secretary of War and see what he says." He then took her letter, and wrote on the back: "Admit Mrs. Harvey at once. Listen to what she says. She is a lady of intelligence, and talks sense. A. Lincoln."

"May I return to you, Mr. Lincoln?" she inquired.

"Certainly," said he, gently. Then Mrs. Harvey found her way to Mr. Stanton's office, and was listened to and treated with great respectfulness and kindness, but he had to be guided by the medical authorities.

She bade the Secretary of War good morning, and returned to the President. No one was waiting. At the invitation of the messenger she passed directly into the President's room. Mr. Lincoln motioned her to a chair, inquired what the Secretary of War had said to her. She gave him a full account of the interview, and added, "I have nowhere to go but to you." He replied: "Mr. Stanton knows there is an acting Surgeon-general here, and that Hammond will not return these two months. I will see the Secretary of War myself, to-night; and you may come again in the morning." He then dismissed her, she noted, "in the kindest manner and with the kindest words."

Had he from this moment determined to grant the woman her request? In these interviews he seemed to be arguing against and opposing his own decisions.

In the morning, she returned. The President said good morning, pointed to a chair, seemed annoyed at something, and waited for her to speak. She waited for him.

"Well?" said he, after a minute of delay.

"Well?" replied his visitor.

He looked up under his eyebrows, a little startled, and inquired, "Have you nothing to say?"

"Nothing," she replied, "until I hear your decision. Have you decided? You know you bade me come this morning."

"No, I have not decided; and I believe this idea of northern hospitals is a great humbug, and I am tired of hearing about it."

The woman pitied him in his weak and irritable mood. "I regret to add a feather's weight to your already overwhelming care and responsibility. I would rather have stayed at home."

With a feeble smile, he responded, "I wish you had."

She was earnest, and replied: "Nothing would have given me greater pleasure, sir; but a keen sense of duty to this government, justice and mercy to its most loyal supporters, and regard for your honor and position, made me come. The people cannot understand why their husbands, fathers and sons are left to die, when, with proper care and attention, they ought to live, and yet do good service for their country. Mr. Lincoln, I do believe you will yet be grateful for my coming. I do not come to plead for the lives of criminals, nor for the lives of deserters; but I plead for the lives of those who were the first to hasten to the support of this government, who helped to place you where you are—for men who have done all they could; and now, when flesh and nerve and muscle are gone, who still pray for your life, and the life of the republic. They scarcely ask for that for which I plead. They expect to sacrifice their lives for their country. I know that, if they could come North, they could live, and be well, strong men again—at least many of them. I say I know, because I was sick among them last spring, surrounded by every comfort, with the best of care, and determined to get well. I grew weaker and weaker, day by day, until, not being under military law, my friends brought me North. I recovered entirely by breathing northern air."

While she was so earnestly speaking, Mr. Lincoln's expression of face changed often, but he did not take his eyes from her. He seemed distressed at being convinced she was speaking the truth. His face contracted almost painfully. "You assume to know more than I do."

The tears almost came in the woman's eyes. "Pardon me, Mr. Lincoln, I intend no disrespect; but it is because of this knowledge, and because I do know what you do not know, that I come to you. If you had known what I know, and had not already ordered what I ask, I should know that an appeal to you would be in vain; but I believe in you. I believe the people have not trusted you in vain. The question only is—do you believe me, or not? If you believe in me, you will give us hospitals; if not—well."

"You assume to know more than surgeons do," said Lincoln, sharply.

"Oh no," she replied: "I could not perform an amputation nearly so well as some of them do! But this is true: I do not come here for your favor. I am no aspirant for military favor or promotion. While it would be the pride of my life to command your respect and confidence, still, even this I can waive to gain my object—waive for the time. You will do me justice, some time. Now the medical authorities know as well as you and I do, that you are opposed to establishing northern hospitals; and they report to please you. They desire your favor. I come to you from no casual tour of inspection, having passed rapidly through the general hospitals, with a cigar in my mouth and a ratan in my hand, talking to the surgeon in charge of the price of cotton, and abusing our generals in the army for not knowing and performing their duty better, and finally coming into the open air with a long-drawn breath as though I had just escaped suffocation, and complacently saying to the surgeon: 'A very fine hospital you have here, sir. The boys seem to be doing very well. A little more attention to ventilation is desirable, perhaps.' It is not thus that I have visited hospitals. For eight long months—from early morning until late at night, sometimes—I have visited the regimental and general hospitals on the Mississippi, from Quincy to Vicksburg; and I come to you from the cots of men who have died, and who might have lived if you had permitted it. This is hard to say, but it is true."

While she was speaking the last sentences, Lincoln's brow set with hard furrows; a look of pain gathered on his whole face. Then he sharply asked her how many men her State had sent to the field.

She replied, "About fifty thousand."

"That means," he responded, "that she has about twenty thousand now." With an unpleasant voice and manner he continued, "You need not look so sober; they are not all dead." The veins filled in his face painfully; one across his forehead was fearfully large and blue. Then, with an impatient movement of his whole frame: "I have a good mind to dismiss them all from the service, and have no more trouble with them."

Mrs. Harvey was astonished. She knew he was not in earnest. They sat looking at one another in silence. He had become very pale.

At last she broke the silence. "They have been faithful to the government; they have been faithful to you; they will still be loyal to the government, do what you will with them. But, if you will grant my petition, you will be glad as long as you live. The prayers of grateful hearts will give you strength in the hour of trial, and strong and willing arms will return to fight your battles."

The President bowed his head and, with a look of sadness she thought impossible for language to describe, said, "*I shall never be glad any more.*"

All severity had passed away from his face, and he seemed looking inward and backward, unconscious that he was not alone. Great burdens he had borne, terrible anxieties that had poisoned his life at the fountain, peaceful scenes he had forever left behind—did these sweep across his memory? And then the added thought that perhaps his mistaken judgment had done injustice to the men who had fought the nation's battles?

The woman said, "Oh! do not say so, Mr. Lincoln, for who will have so much reason to rejoice as yourself, when the government shall be restored—as it will be?"

"I know—I know," he said, pressing a hand on either side, "but the springs of life are wearing away, and I shall not last."

She asked him if he felt that his great cares were injuring his health. "No," he replied; "not directly, perhaps." She asked him if he slept well. He never was "a good sleeper," he replied, and of course slept now less than ever before.

The woman, feeling that she had occupied too much of his time, rose to take her leave. "Have you decided upon your answer to me?"

"No," he replied, "come to-morrow morning:—stop, it is cabinet-meeting to-morrow. Yes, come at twelve o'clock; there is not much for the cabinet to do to-morrow." Then he bade her a cordial good morning.

The next morning, Mrs. Harvey found that her interview had prostrated her; but at twelve o'clock she was at the White House. The President sent her word that the Cabinet would adjourn soon, and that she must wait. For three long hours she waited, receiving occasional messages to the effect that the Cabinet would soon adjourn, and he would then see her.

She was in distress, expecting defeat. She walked the room, and gazed at the maps, and at last she heard the sound of feet. The Cabinet had adjourned.

The President did not send for her, but came shuffling into the room, rubbing his hands, and saying, "My dear madam, I am sorry I have kept you waiting so long, but we have this moment adjourned."

"My waiting is no matter," she replied, "but you must be very tired, and we will not talk to-night."

Bidding her to a seat, she having risen as he entered, he sat down at her side, and quietly remarked, "I only wish to say to you that an order which is equivalent to the granting of a hospital in your State, has been issued from the War Department, nearly twenty-four hours."

The woman could make no reply, except through the tears that sprang at once. Lincoln looked on, and enjoyed it.

When at last she could command her voice, she said: "God bless you!" Then, as doubts came as to the order, she said earnestly, "Do you mean, really and truly, that we are going to have a hospital now?"

With a look full of benevolence and tenderness—such a look, the woman wrote, "as rarely illuminates any face"—he said, "I do most certainly hope so." Then he told her to come on the following morning, and he would give her a copy of the order.

But she was too much affected to talk; and noticing this, he changed the subject, asking her to look at a map which hung in the room, representing the great battlegrounds of Europe. "It is a very fine map," said he; "see—here is Waterloo, here are all the battle-fields about the Crimea." Then suddenly, turning to her: "I'm afraid you will not like it so well, when I tell you who executed it." She replied: "It is a great work, whoever executed it. Who was it, Mr. President?" "McClellan," he answered, and added: "He certainly did do this well. He did it while he was at West Point."

The next morning, sick with the excitement through which she had passed, Mrs. Harvey was at the White House again. She found more than fifty persons waiting for an audience; so she sent in her name, and said she would call again. The messenger said he thought the President would see her, and she had better be seated. Soon afterward, he informed her that the President would see her. As she passed in, she heard the words from one of the waiting throng: "She has been here six days; and, what is more, she is going to win."

As she entered, Mr. Lincoln smiled pleasantly, drew a chair to his side, and said, "Come here, and sit down." As she did so, he handed her a copy of the coveted order. She thanked him, and apologized for not being more promptly at the house; she had been sick all night.

"Did joy make you sick?" he inquired. "I suppose," he added, "you would have been mad if I had said 'no.'"

She replied, "No, Mr. Lincoln, I should have been neither angry nor sick."

"What would you have done?"

"I should have been here at nine o'clock this morning."

"Well," said he, laughing, "I think I have acted wisely then."

Then he turned suddenly and looked into her face as he said, "Don't you ever get angry?" She replied that she never did when she had an important object to attain. There was more conversation on the naming of the hospital. The woman rose, and said, "You will not wish to see me again."

"I did not say that, and I shall not say it," said the President.

"You have been very kind to me, and I am very grateful for it."

He looked up at her from under his eyebrows, in his peculiar way, and said, "You almost think I am handsome, don't you?" His face was full of benevolence, and his countenance lighted by a cordial smile; and it was not strange that Mrs. Harvey exclaimed, "You are perfectly lovely to me *now,* Mr. Lincoln." The President colored a little, and laughed a good deal, at the impulsive response, and reached out his hand to bid her farewell.

She took it reverently, bowed her head upon it, and, bowing, prayed: "God bless you, Abraham Lincoln!" Then she turned, heard his good-by, and was gone.

Thus ran one transcript, more scrupulously complete and accurate, without a doubt, than perhaps half the accounts of what Lincoln said and did within eyesight and earshot of those who gave the accounts. For others as well as for her, his greeting with the handshake was "I hope you are well," but none of the others had written that one of his greetings was in the words "I hope you are well"—an item not important but interesting, like his occasionally writing the word "whomsoever." Her return from the Secretary of War to say "I have nowhere to go but to you" struck him with its unbeatable simplicity. Her waiting for him to speak was proper. Her "Well?" to his "Well?" could not have been better. To his startled "Have you nothing to say?" came her "Nothing until I hear your decision," the perfect essence of truth. His saying "No, I have not decided" was probably correct, though he was completely incorrect and was either in "a weak and irritable mood," as the woman believed, or had his own designs in ungraciously blurting to her, "I believe this idea of northern hospitals is a great humbug, and I am tired of hearing about it." To her abrupt point that she would "rather have stayed at home" than add "a feather's weight" to his overwhelming care, his "I wish you had" was probably with design, as again his later "You assume to know more than I do."

She was stung deep into responses and explanations that probably swept away his final defenses against her project. Out of her moving words, so joined to human suffering anywhere, she sent him into meditations, into grief beyond speech from which issued the one low cry—"I shall never be glad any more." She asked if he slept well. Few were so kind as to ask that genuinely. And where to the smart and ebullient Donn Piatt he had replied, "I enjoy my rations and sleep well," to this keenly sensitive woman he answered he "never was a good sleeper" and now slept "less than ever."

And during this fourth interview in which he told her that he wished she had stayed home and that he believed her project "a great humbug," everything she asked for had already been granted, an order issued, as he told her the next day, "issued from the War Department, nearly twenty-four hours." Then in their fifth and sixth interviews he had been luminous with humor, shining with a benevolent wit, sharing with her the gladness that came through her tears, refuting his own cry that he would never be glad again—though possibly he had meant that any gladness which might come to him again would be interlined with suffering and tears. Nevertheless some old Kentucky and Indiana boyhood gladness, naïve and bubbling, was there in his query "You almost think I am handsome, don't you?" Then with her God-bless-you she was gone. He was not to see her again. He had a sectional and civil war on his hands.

Mrs. Harvey went away to be a witness of the building of the Harvey Hospital at Madison, Wisconsin, named for her husband, another general hospital at Prairie du Chien, and still another in Milwaukee—three hospitals resulting from her six interviews with her President.

A woman who wrote in *Putnam's Magazine* an article signed M. Wentworth gave a record of what her keen sympathetic eyes and ears met during a stay of hours in Lincoln's office while petitioners came and went.

The President made it a custom, she wrote, to hear petitions at certain hours of the day from all who chose to present them. They were required merely to have the written or spoken introduction of some member of Congress. Miss Wentworth had pleaded for a fifteen-year-old brother of hers who had run away and joined the army. The President granted a discharge of the boy, asked her if he could do anything more for her. Yes, she would like to be present at a series of these public interviews and write notes of them for publication. The President was willing.

She stayed in the background, though within hearing, many hours, a recording witness of a human procession somber, drab, comic, heroic, moving. "All day long the President had received petitioners, and still they came. He could hear the murmur of voices in the outer room, as they were anxious to be admitted, yet, he *must* rest for a few moments."

"Tad, my dear son, go to your mother, you must be tired here."

"No, no, Papa; I don't want to go now—I want to stay and see the people." And Tad forced his hands down deep into his pockets, threw himself on the floor under a writing desk near his father, and, settling his head on a cushion, continued, "Ain't you tired of folks, Pa?"

The little bell which the President sounded, a signal for the doors to be opened, remained unrung. He sat with his hands clasped together and his head drooping forward.

His little son moved softly from the room, returning in a few moments with a sad-faced woman holding a baby. The President motioned her to a chair. She had come from a town in the Far West, she modestly stated, to plead for the life of her husband, who was sentenced to die in six weeks for desertion.

"He ran away from his regiment, then?"

"No, sir; but they think he did."

The President frowned, shook his head rapidly from side to side.

"Of course, madam, *you* think that he did not."

"Oh, sir! Oh!—" And she began to cry aloud, the baby joining.

The President seemed much annoyed but, turning to her, kindly said: "If you can prove to me that your husband did not run away from nor desert his regiment, I will have him pardoned. Will you go on with your story, and stop your crying?"

"How kind you are, sir!"

A faint smile played upon the President's face, as he answered, "Please go on with your story."

She told him she was dangerously sick, and her husband, hearing it from a comrade, went home, about three miles from the camp. The next day he was seized as a deserter, and dragged away. As soon as she could walk a little, she had gone to the officers to plead for him, but they would not listen to her. She was sick after that long walk, and as soon as she could get up again she had started for Washington.

"It was a long and tiresome journey," he said sympathetically.

"Yes, sir; but, someway, I felt, if I could only see you, and tell you, that you would believe my story. I have no letters to speak for me, only this one," moving her hand toward her pocket.

The President shook his head. He was twisting a piece of paper over and over through his fingers. Lifting his eyes suddenly to her face. he asked:

"Who is that letter from?"

"It is from a kind minister; I asked him to write it. He said you did not know him, and would in all probability not read the letter; yet, if it would be any comfort to me, he would write it."

"Let me see it."

As he bent forward to take the letter, the infant seized his hand. The President patted the little hands and face, and then leaned toward the light to read.

Anxiously the woman watched him. His countenance gave no sign. He folded the letter carefully; slowly he handed it back to her.

"I am satisfied with it. I believe your story. I shall pardon your husband."

The baby looked up steadily at him; the woman arose.

"Oh, Mr. President, how can I thank you!"

"Take this note to the War Department, and they will give you a paper of release for your husband from the charge of desertion. It will make your journey home more comfortable. Good night."

"God bless you!" she answered, and was gone.

The President, noted Miss Wentworth, struck the little bell, and a tall usher opened wide the door, until the room was filled. Some of these petitioners were insolent beyond human endurance; some were silly to excess; some were ludicrous in their pompousness, displaying piles of letters of introduction, which the President would not look at. They would, however, persist in their endeavors to make him look at *such* letters from *such* persons.

The President soon became exasperated, as he listened to one and another. In vain he shook his head and stamped his feet, and brought his hands violently down upon the table, telling them that he *would* not and *could* not listen to such petitions. They, with an assurance never to be imagined, would still go on.

Men with defiant faces, men whining and pleading, and forward women, grasped his arms to arrest his attention. His patience with such rudeness was wonderful. If he expressed contempt for affectations, he also did not forget to respect modesty and real sorrow when he met it.

Again the little bell was rung, and again the room was filled. Those who had just gone out muttered their dislike for the man who listened from early morning until late at night to people of every grade.

Often the President impressed Miss Wentworth as grave to sadness. Her eyes saw him for hours in succession express no anger, no mirth. Petition after petition presented in rapid succession the same story of sorrow—of fathers, brothers, and husbands in prison, each pleading for theirs to be the first released in the exchange of prisoners. Some had dear ones dying in camp, beyond the lines; they were begging to go to them. Hundreds had made the same request.

"Oh, let us go to them—only let us go!"

There were bands of poor, oppressed sewing women stating their wrongs —peace commissioners, and Southern refugees.

Toward the close of the day the President was alone for a few moments. The door opened a little, softly, as though begging an invitation to open wide. A merry face and broad shoulders were visible; and, to the President's cheerful "Come in," the whole man entered.

"Nothing to do, eh?" said the President, lifting his eyebrows, and assuming for an instant the most mirth-provoking attitude.

"That's it—just it, Mr. President, your honor! Ushers and watchers have only to stare at each other. I thought I'd show my better bringing up"; and he apologized for laughing and laughed for apologizing, and the President helped him.

"So you thought you'd show your better bringing up—show off by coming up here to disturb me! Maybe you're afraid I rest too much—get too much sleep, eh?"

"Oh, no, Mr. President!" and the speaker shook his white head, adding: "You will be so funny! Only I thought I'd just step up and tell you that there is just one solitary lady wanting to speak to you, and you know—"

"No, I don't know."

"And you see—"

"No, I don't see."

"Beg pardon! but I meant to say, that I could not very well let her go away without telling you."

"Where is she?"

"Outside, in a carriage. There is an old black woman with her, who keeps telling her that Massa Linkum will sure for sartin' let her come up!"

"Yes, yes—of course: I must not refuse any person," and the President laughed again in a weary fashion. "Fetch her up," he added, fatigue sweeping over his face.

The little man soon returned, saying:

"She won't be fetched. This is her name"—handing a card. "When I told her you said she could come right up, she turned pale, and trembled like a leaf, and said, 'Please ask the President if I may come in the morning, and I will be deeply grateful to him.' The black woman said she was 'jes' done ober trablin' in dem ingines. She'd be right pert in de mornin', and tell Pres'ent Linkum all 'bout it.' "

"I'm disengaged now," answered the President, with a frown, "but tomorrow—what do I know of tomorrow? Tell her to come right up. No—tell her to come tomorrow morning at precisely eleven o'clock."

"Deeply grateful!" laughed the President, when the door closed. "I hope there will be no more women here tonight," he added, wearily.

But there *were* women. Each set of petitioners were women, from first to last.

Many times the President started to go to his private room; but sad faces pressing up the stairway stopped him as he was crossing the hall, and he went back again.

"Do, kind President, grant my request!"

The woman's voice was very plaintive, and large tears were falling, but she made no *sound* of crying.

"No, no, I cannot! I cannot, good woman—I cannot! I might grant such requests a thousand a day. I can't turn the Government inside out and upside over. I can't please everybody. I must do my duty—stern duty as I see it. Nobody wants their friends drafted—nobody wants them taken as deserters. He should not have been absent so long; he should not have taken upon himself the appearance of a deserter. How do *I* know—how does anybody know—how does the War Department know—that he did not intend to stay upon the boat where the soldiers found him? How does anybody know that he didn't *think* about his furlough being ended? Didn't think! That was his business to *think*. I am sorry. Everybody ought to be sorry for those who do wrong. When he knew the laws, why did he break them? When he knew the penalty, why did he bring it upon himself? You plead for him, and tell me how upright he is. That's all very well. It is easy for us to overestimate the goodness of those we love. You are his neighbor. It is very kind in you to come so far and plead so strongly; but—I can't—I can't do anything for you!"

"Please, President Lincoln!"

"No, no! No, no! I can't—I won't—I won't!" and he sprang to his feet, but in an instant resumed his former position in his chair, and leaned forward to snap the little bell.

"Oh! oh!"

It was a sound of intense grief, disappointment, and surprise. Miss Wentworth heard them as all mingled together. Coming up so from the heart as this peculiar sound did, it arrested the hand upon the bell, lifted the eyes that were growing cold and stern to the pleading face of the woman before him. She had left her chair, and stood so near that her clothes brushed against him. Heavy were the lines upon her face—lines of care and sorrow; earnest were the tear-dimmed eyes.

"Do, kind sir, consider my case a moment more—oh, President Lincoln! Remember, you were poor once—and—and—"

"Had no friends, do you mean?" He interrupted, almost scornfully.

"No—oh, no!—had a *few* friends—tried and true friends, who would never forsake you. Only one of them I know—ONE, who is alike a friend to you and to me. For his sake—for our dear Lord's sake—grant my petition!"

A striking solemnity was in her whole attitude. The President turned very pale, his eyes misty, sad, and then sadder, as he repeated, slowly and reverently:

"For our dear Lord's sake!"

"Here are three hundred dollars; it was made up by his neighbors.

Couldn't you save him from an ignominious death, which he does not deserve?—no, he does not deserve!"

"Take back your money!" cried the President, throwing away from him her extended hand. "Take it back! I do not want it!"

Only an instant his hand and voice were raised, and then he resumed, kindly:

"I shall not have your money, good woman; the War Department will not have it. Take it back where it came from; and you shall take back his release. Your petition shall be wholly granted."

"Oh, President Lincoln! I believe you are a Christian. I thank God for it. I will pray for you every day with my whole heart."

"I have need of your prayers; I have need of all the prayers that can be offered for me."

"Oh, Mr. Lincoln, that is the Christian spirit—that is faith in Jesus! Oh, let me hear you say that you believe in Him!"

"I do," was the solemn answer. "I believe in my Saviour."

And when she arose to depart, the President also arose and opened the door for her, and led her through the outer room and across the hall to the head of the staircase, and shook hands, said good-by, and went back again to receive more and still more petitioners.

It was past three o'clock; the Executive Mansion was silent and dark, with only the shaded light beside the President, as he sat with folded hands and mournful eyes, alone.

"Mr. President, your Honor," said a languid woman in a languid voice, opening and closing her pale-blue eyes; "Mr. President, your Honor," she repeated, with a slight emphasis; and then, as though it were the last effort she could ever make, succeeded in saying again, "Mr. President, your Honor."

He regarded her with an amused air, and said, "My name is Mr. Lincoln—Abraham Lincoln. I suppose you call me 'Old Abe' when you're at home."

She dropped her head and raised her handkerchief to her face, heaving the folds of it with a deep-drawn sigh, as in one small eye one small tear stood irresolute, and she murmured, "How you mistake me, honored sir!"

She paused a moment to recover from her emotion, and another woman, less delicate, pushed her way up, and, with a stout voice and an important manner, began to tell her qualifications and show her certificates, and wished to have a place given her in the Treasury Department.

"I'd have a different order of things there, Mr. President. I could do the work of two, and do it well. It's a bad thing," she went on, "to have so many young girls there; it's a crying shame—it's a disgrace. You ought to turn them all out, and put in their places persons of my age."

Before the President could answer, a very tall man stumbled over the feet of two or three, and, as he picked himself up and his scattered papers, he exclaimed eagerly:

"Look at these, Mr. President—read all these letters; they will tell you that I am qualified for a high position," and he stumbled again, in his hurry to get up to the President.

"I need not look at your letters; you speak for yourself, sir. It was a waste of time for you to get these letters."

"Won't you read them, Mr. President, your Honor?"

"No, sir. We have enough paymasters, that are known to us—enough, sir—enough; we have more of *them* than we have money for, and out of charity to taxpayers, I ought to dismiss about fifty of them."

"It is an important thing to have a man you can trust, Mr. President—one who is perfectly honest. It is an easy matter for money to get lost, if in the hands of easy, careless people."

"Yes, it certainly is; and, judging from the manner in which these precious letters of yours have been flying about, I should say Government property would be very, *very* safe with you."

"But there is excuse for me now, sir. Time is very short with me."

"Time is short with all of us—or at least we ought to consider it so. No, sir; I can give you no appointment."

The man began to tell the President that he would never regret it; he would see how faithful he would be, and he would be satisfied that he was better fitted for paymaster general than the one who held the position now.

"Oh, you wish to be paymaster general! Well, well! you wish me to turn out the man I *do* know, and put *you* in his place, whom I don't know! You may go, sir."

The President frowned, and waved his hand toward him.

"And you," he said, turning to the woman with a stout voice, "you can't have an appointment. I am very sorry so many young girls are in the Treasury Building; but that is something over which I have no control."

"And *you*, madam," turning to the languid woman, "you have not yet stated your petition."

Another sigh, and then, as though reinforced by sudden vitality, she produced a parcel of letters, saying:

"Read these, sir; they can tell you who I am. I am too timid."

"That's nothing to me," he answered sharply.

"Just read them, sir."

"I can't; I have no time."

"They are from head people at the South."

"I have no doubt of it."

"They plead for me. I have no confidence in myself."

The President was getting very much annoyed, and shook his head from side to side, as he always did when he was out of patience.

"If you can tell me, madam, what you wish, I will listen; if not, I will go on with the others."

"Read this one," she said, picking it out very carefully.

"No, I cannot." Then, suddenly looking up with an odd smile, he asked, "Have you one from Jeff Davis?"

She did not see the expression of the President's face, and she replied, in a faint voice, with her eyes cast down, "I have not, but I can get one."

"Oh, don't put yourself to that trouble; I can know as much from you as from him. I'll take your word for it that you *can* get one." And the President's sleeves shook a little. "Please go on and tell me your story."

"Well—it is—it is—of great account to me. It's about—about my poor cow—which your cruel soldiers killed, and—and—I want the Government to restore the loss—to buy me a new cow."

"I am sorry for your poor cow; but we cannot buy you a new cow. I've had several cow petitions. I expect next to have some person bewailing the loss of a cat. I have plenty of spare time, of course—have nothing to do, and ought by all means to see that every loss is made good."

"I'd like to go home," the woman said.

"I am perfectly willing that you should, madam."

"But how can I go, with my petition refused?"

"I cannot grant it," frowned the President.

"I supposed you were a kind-hearted man," persisted the *timid* woman.

"I'll not listen to you!" he said, loudly, calling forward some others.

"You are just about as much of a gentleman as I expected to find you," added the woman as she flounced out of the room.

(These were the scenes one by one which Miss Wentworth saw and heard. She rendered Lincoln, the listener to petitions, more completely perhaps than any other onlooker and hearer. Impressionable, sensitive, seeming to miss no valid point, she sat with her notebook and witnessed further the comings and goings.)

A Catholic priest entered, with two women. He looked at the writer with a face which plainly said he would rather she would not be there. She moved from the desk toward the door. The President waved his hand, saying, "Come back; I do not wish you to go."

The priest, turning to the President, said:

"I should like a private interview."

"I do nothing privately," was the calm answer. "All I do is public," and he gave the signal for more petitioners, upon whom the priest looked with unconcealed anger, and to the President said, pompously:

"Then we are to have no hearing?"

"Certainly, you shall be heard. I will listen to you now."

"That will not do. I wish to see you alone."

"I can only tell you, as I did before, that I do nothing privately," answered the President, coldly.

The priest angrily rose and left the room, followed by the two women. The President went on with his work, unruffled. He was quite used to all sorts of addresses, manners, and degrees of respect.

The last of these petitioners was a young girl of singular beauty.

"I cannot let you go down there," said the President, dwelling sadly upon his words. "*How* can I?" he asked, looking up at the sweet face, so earnest and truthful, and the deep, spiritual eyes trembling with heavy tears. "I cannot let you go, and I cannot refuse you. What *shall* I do?"

"Let me go there," she pleaded. "I am not afraid. God will take care of me."

"I don't know—I don't know," he said. "Your faith is beautiful—but I don't know," he added, in a low, sad tone. Then, looking up sorrowfully, he continued, "There is not a woman down there."

"I know it," she answered, thoughtfully.

"Are you not afraid—not the least afraid?"

"No, sir; I am not afraid. I have trusted our heavenly Father many times before, and He has never forsaken me."

"And He never will!" exclaimed the President, springing to his feet. "No, my child, He never will." And, drawing a chair close to the fire, he went on: "Come, sit here, until you are quite warm. I will write you a pass. You shall go to your father."

Then, as though he felt pained at seeming inquisitiveness, he stopped suddenly when just upon the verge of asking something; but the interest he felt in the petitioner prevailed, and he asked if she were fully prepared for her journey.

"Yes, sir; I have plenty of money. If money could make the heart glad, I have enough; but I have no mother, and my father is perhaps dying. I cannot stay to get warm—I can *never* get warm. Good-by, President—kind, good President Lincoln! I shall never see you again in this world; so shake hands with both of mine."

A moment more and she had gone.

The President leaned forward, touched the bell, and the room was again filled.

"You take up too much time," said a woman, pushing, and stepping in front of another. "I will talk with the President *now*, and then you can finish what you have to say. Mr. President, your Honor, my husband lost a limb in the last battle, and I want the War Department to settle a pension upon him without delay. I believe in 'first come, first served'; and I want my son to have a position in Washington, if it is no higher than clerk in the Treasury Building. Only two petitions I ask of you. I am in a hurry, for every day I spend in Washington costs me five dollars. I have been here eight days, and, because of the insolence of your ushers, I could not get up to speak to you before. Couldn't you teach them how to treat a lady? It's a great disgrace to an establishment to have saucy servants." Then, in a higher key, she went on: "Only a pension for my husband, and a position for my son. He is just like me—he will repay you for all you can do for him. I have brought him up never to be under obligations to any person."

She paused to take a good long breath, and the President interrupted her with:

"I can do nothing for you, madam."

"Not give my husband a pension?"

"No; the War Department will attend to that."

"Not give my son a position?"

"No, madam."

Her face told her anger; but the President bowed her and her indignation from the room. Once she turned in her exit, saying, "I am proud and sensitive, or I would give you a piece of my mind."

A singular specimen of humanity next came forward, entering the room alone.

"Mr. President, your Honor, will you give me a position in one of your hospitals, as nurse? I am a doctor—a clairvoyant."

"Indeed!"

"Yes, I am ahead of many others, and just now, with these *natural* eyes of mine"—lifting her hands toward two particolored, stony-looking orbs —"with these eyes I can see right into your heart, and liver and lungs; and what do you think I might see with my spirit eyes?"

"I don't know, I am sure."

"No, sir: of course you don't know. It isn't *given* to you to know. Your lungs and heart are all right, but your liver is in a sad condition. I can give you a prescription that will make you a well man, and make you live to a good old age. I want to get into a hospital, for it is an extensive field for my talents, which will expand as I exercise them. I have been sick for years and years; I can sympathize with sick ones. I raised myself up from a bed of suffering to perform my mission. Have you a place for me, do you think?"

"Well, no; I think not," answered the President. "You know rather too much for a hospital."

"Mr. President, your Honor, I have come from the State of New York," said a man with wonderful physical development. "Mr. President, your Honor," he continued, with a flourish of his cane, "I have brought a complaint against Governor Seymour. He takes no interest in these exciting times. He takes no notice of petitions presented to him. He makes no effort to bring things to a focus."

"A focus!" exclaimed the President. "I am glad he is so sensible; for it would take forty lifetimes to do that. Allow me to say, sir, that I do not wish any complaints against your Governor. Go home, sir—go home, and do not molest me." And the President went on with the other petitioners, who were scarcely dismissed before the room was again filled.

The clairvoyant came in a second time on tiptoe, and her voice was soft as a peacock's. Her light-blue eye was fixed on vacancy as she approached the President, saying:

"Kind sir, I believe that you will change your mind about interesting yourself in getting me a position, when I tell you that I have had a vision. I have seen and talked with those who occupied this mansion before they took their departure from this gross world to that region of perfect loveliness—that region to which I lift my eyes—to which my soul goes every night only to return each day to my mission here—my mission, to heal the sick. A few manipulations with these hands"—displaying monstrous specimens—"a few manipulations will cure disease. I can cast out evil spirits. I can lift up the weak and drooping. And, in my vision, the great doctor who has control of my gifts told me to come to you again. I do not expect the world to praise me, for I am not of the world. I find my comfort with those beings with whom I commune." Here her *blue* eye, more susceptible than the gray one, shed a solitary tear.

The President: "Well, don't tell me anything more. I am only a poor, weak mortal. I can't stand it—I can't, indeed."

"Oh, I don't propose to rub *you*," she answered, solemnly. "I want a position in one of the hospitals."

"Well, I tell you confidentially," he replied, dropping his voice and moving his head sideways with his oddest of odd smiles, "I tell you, good woman, those fellows at the hospitals are a rough set; it would take forty such kind and considerate persons as you are to rub faith into one of them; and, of course, if they had no faith, you could do them no good."

"That's true, sir; it all depends upon their faith. Without it, I could not help them."

"Then do not waste your time in an unsuccessful attempt."

"I am sensitive," she continued, sorrowfully. "I am very sensitive; perhaps I could not survive the hospitals. I believe I will go home." And the blue eye and the gray eye looked at the President kindly, as she extended her prodigious hand.

A clergyman pleaded for permission to cross the lines—to go down among the prison pens.

"You shall go," answered the President, extending his hand to him. "It is a perilous work," he added, looking up at the calm intellectual face, and feeling the influence of those sympathetic eyes. "I can't exchange these poor prisoners half fast enough. I have great faith in those laboring for them; but what can a few do? Lee can help them—may you send this letter to him? Of course you may, Miss W——. What have you written? Very well —just to the point! If Lee can't get food for the prisoners, he can let them go."

"He says he has wept tears of blood over this terrible Rebellion; but he could not fight against the State in which he was born."

"That's all bosh!—fight against his State! If a man is born in a bad State, the best thing for him to do is to get out of it as quickly as possible."

A young girl who had much trouble to get an audience at last succeeded. She begged to go to her brother, who was reported very sick. She told the President that Senator —— said he could not introduce her, but he would get somebody else, for there was a feud between the President and himself.

"A feud!" laughed the President. "Well, we are a little out on politics, and that little 'outness' has detained you. Perhaps it is for the best—who knows?"

The room was quite full. A soldier, wan and lame, pleaded for eight weeks' furlough to go home and get strong. The young girl uttered a cry of surprise.

"My brother!—my dear brother!"

The President gave him a furlough of three months.

The petitioners came and went until far into the night. Their pleadings were the same heard thousands of times before. To each one the petition was new and all-absorbing; to the President, only the echoes of the vast army already gone.

Often persons pushed themselves into the Executive Chamber only to irritate the President. Many of these were women who sympathized with the Confederacy, and their elegant courtesy of manner was really amazing. Such a one had kept her chair during the going and coming of five or six relays of visitors, watching each as they presented their claims, following them with her eyes to the door, and then staring at the others. The President, annoyed at her presence, said, rather sternly, "Have you a petition to present?"

She lifted her eyes in a peculiar manner, with an arrogant expression, but she only said, "Yes, sir."

The President said, "It is time you told me what you have to say; you have been here a good while."

"Yes, sir," she replied, brightly; and, confident that he had not gained this time, folded her hands with an air of perfect satisfaction.

"Will you give me your errand, or shall I go on with the others?"

"Yes, sir." And she coolly stroked her muff.

The President jerked himself in his chair, and went on with the rest. These had all gone, and still she sat there.

"Shall I talk to you *now*, or do you intend to stay all day?" he exclaimed in a voice which would frighten any ordinary person.

"Yes, sir." And the brazen woman actually smiled at him. He snapped the bell, and the room was filled. Her presence was almost insupportable. It was almost night. Silent contempt and expression of anger were alike unavailing. For more than an hour the President had ignored her presence, but at last said:

"Will you, madam, prepare to give me your errand, or leave me alone."

"Yes, sir," was the unblushing answer.

The President groaned, shook his head from side to side, stamped his feet, and, bringing his hand down heavily upon the table, cried, "I will call some person who will escort you from the building."

He moved toward the door.

"Yes, sir," said the amiable lady. And, agile as a cat, she sprang in front of him, and passed out of the room.

"President Lincoln, I have a very gifted daughter," said a silly-looking woman. "She is an authoress, and has been ever since she was seven years old."

"Ah, indeed!"

"Yes, sir; and the publishers have a game of keeping her writings until we forget all about them, and then publish them without giving her any remuneration; and she always marks the price upon the first page. I have a piece with me now—it is a story—a story in one hundred and twelve chapters. Will you read it, and give me your opinion? Please write me a note," she added, quickly. Giving the President not an instant to reply, she went on, "If you write me a note, it will have weight with the publishers, and—"

"If the manuscript," interrupted the President, "has merit, there is no need of any note. If it has no merit, all the notes in the world would do it no good."

"Oh, it *has* merit!" replied the woman, assuming an indignant air. "It *has* merit! My daughter is a genius; but I thought it would be better to have a note from you. Everybody has recommendations nowadays. Just read a little," she added, coaxingly. "It is very fascinating," she went on earnestly. "Won't you read it?"

"I can't; I don't like novels."

"Novels! Sir, it is not a novel; it is a story. I would not allow *my* daughter to write a *novel*. I am a Christian. This is a little girlish, thrilling story. It displays a knowledge of history *far* beyond her years." And she went on with a good deal more of the same sort.

A young man desired a clerkship. He was sure he would be made for the world if he had a position in Washington.

"You are mistaken, young man," the President answered. "You are mistaken. What you ask for would ruin you. No, no; go home, and do anything there that comes to you, rather than be deluded by such false ideas. Washington is no place for a young man to come to from a good home."

"I am very steady," answered the young man, modestly.

"That may be; but this is no place for you. Temptations abound here. Believe me to be your friend, young man. Take my advice, and go home."

Seeming much disappointed, he gracefully bowed to the President as he moved backward from the room. The President, pleased with his manner, said as the petitioner's hand touched the door:

"You will thank me, three years from now; yet, I know I seem unkind to you—very unkind."

"It does seem splendid to have a position in Washington," was the earnest answer.

"Three years added to your present good sense will reveal to you the quicksands from which you will be saved by going *now* directly to your home. Will you do it?"

"Yes, sir."

The President spoke to Miss Wentworth of sudden death.

"I believe you are ready to die at any time," she said.

"No, I am not ready," answered the President, mournfully. "Each day, as I look over its events and incidents, as I think of those I have made happy, of those I have made miserable, I see that I might have been truer to my neighbor, truer to my God."

There was some confusion among the next set of petitioners; for one singular-looking individual found much trouble in getting a seat to his liking, and, being rather tall and rather awkward, and very stiff, had much difficulty in assuming a position.

"How are you, my good fellow?" asked the President, shaking the stranger's hand warmly, adding, with a hearty laugh, "It's just the weather for rheumatism."

"Ah, sir," answered the stranger, with a mysterious air, his zigzag mouth zigzagging at a rapid rate. "Oh, sir," he repeated, in almost a whisper, and with his finger lifted, probably to inspire awe, "I have come on a serious errand—an errand which involves the whole nation." And then, rolling his dull eyes, he continued, in the same mysterious manner, "I want you to listen to me, and do exactly as I say, for I have had a vision—"

"Of angels?" interrupted the President.

"Well, I can't say as to them being exactly angels, but they *be* disembodied spirits—Washington, and some of the Presidents. Washington sent a message to you."

"Ah?"

"Yes, he did. But first, before I tell you, I must sound you, to see how deep your faith is. If you have no faith in Washington, why, I can't give you any."

"I *have* faith in him, of course," said the President.

"Then you will believe just what I tell you?"

"That's a *different* thing. You are very honest, no doubt, yet you may be mistaken. I do not believe any messages come from another world, only as our own souls tell us. If there is anything for me to know, my soul will find it out. Perhaps I will not listen to my soul; then I must suffer for it. Perhaps you will not listen to your soul; then you will suffer."

A brief conversation with Miss Wentworth turned to Mrs. Lincoln's fear that some of the Southern women might have hidden weapons to take his life, and it was her earnest request that women should not be admitted, except in company of gentlemen known to the executive departments.

The President answered, with much animation, that he did not feel afraid, and then he added, solemnly: "I do not consider that I have ever accomplished anything without God; and if it is His will that I must die by the hand of an assassin, I must be resigned. I must do my duty as I see it, and leave the rest with God. I go to amusements very much against my inclinations. I go simply because I must have change. I laugh because I must not weep; that's all—that's all."

Had the people and events of those tornado years shaped Lincoln more and more into a man paradoxically harder than ever, yet also more delicate and tenuous in human judgments and affairs? Was there more often a phantom touch in what he did? Did certain men and women who studied him either close up or from far away feel that a strange shade and a ghost, having often a healing power, moving toward wider and surer human solidarity, lived and spoke in the White House? For such as there were of these, who knew an intimacy with Lincoln even when he was at his loneliest, who were ready to uphold him when they had no inkling of where his next decision might bring the country—for these one writer tried in *Harper's*

Weekly of September 24, 1864, to voice a faith and offer a parable bearing on the election to come November next. This was George William Curtis, not signing his singing paragraphs but giving his initials.

He could see a ship torn and worn with a long voyage, met by head winds and baffling currents as she slowly drew near her port. "A feeling of disappointment and despondency takes possession of the passengers and the crew, and each one attributes to the officer of the ship the inevitable and necessary delays and discouragements. Instead of looking forward to the near and certain land they turn their eyes resolutely backward, and persuade themselves that all the troubles in the past are to be gone over anew, and that the momentary delay from which they are suffering could have been avoided had a different course been pursued in some previous part of the voyage."

Then the long-wished-for land heaves into view. "Certainty takes the place of disappointed hopes, and they feel with mortification and regret how unjust they have been to the officer whose every hour and thought has been devoted to their welfare, and who has at length brought them with safety, and with a prosperous voyage, to the end of their journey. Long after every other incident of the voyage has faded from their minds they remember and long to recall the unreasonable and unjust accusations that a moment of impatience caused them to utter toward one to whom their safe return was in so large measure due."

In just such a situation, wrote G.W.C., "do we find ourselves at the present time." He could see that the voyage was nearly over. "We can almost feel the land-breeze . . . we see the land birds fluttering around us; our charts and observations all give us assurance that we are near the end of our journey; but because we can not see the land and put our feet upon it, we are disposed to be anxious and captious, and to lay blame on our faithful and vigilant leader. Let us be more manly and more just. Let us remember how upright and courageous our President has been in the dark and anxious days we have passed through. How manfully and persistently he has met disaster and defeat, always hopeful and always calm in the midst of the greatest dangers and trials."

The record of Mr. Lincoln was written. So deep was the record cut, its main text and asseverations could not be changed or blotted or eroded. "It is not of so great importance to Mr. Lincoln's future fame that he should or should not be elected for another term. . . . In a few short months we may be at the end of our great troubles, and, let us hope, free forever from the anxieties that now beset us. But when that time comes, when history and tradition repeat beside every fireside in the land the trials and the dangers and the heroism of each most faithful and noble veteran, then it will be said, 'And he, too, never faltered; he marched with us side by side; he believed in us when so many desponded; he risked all to support and sustain and reinforce us. We and he worked together with one heart to remove the dark stain of Slavery from our national honor; and if we deserve any credit for what we have done in restoring our land to unity and peace and justice, he with us shall ever receive a common share.' "

Beyond parties or partisan success were other motives to which G.W.C. would appeal in this popular pictorial weekly magazine going to nearly all the towns and camps of the country. The humblest soldier and the most distinguished general would be sustained by each Union loyalist saying, "Walk as nearly in his steps as you can." Like the tenacious President, "Be slow to come to a decision, and slower to change from it; dare to be unpopular in the performance of imperative duty; set an example of calm confidence and religious trust in the hour of gloom and despondency; and you, like him, shall have it written on your tombstone and on the hearts of your fellow-countrymen, 'He, too, was worthy to be an American citizen.' "

Possibly in the roar and press of duties Lincoln missed seeing this rugged psalm of praise to a living President—just before the November election of 1864. Possibly he read it twice and pondered a few moments over it and felt himself strangely moved over such wreaths of high affection and dark adoration being hung on his name. How would the same words look after the November decision of the American electorate? Even his strongest enemies, wrote G.W.C., had "no ardent wish" to replace in the White House "so manly and modest a character, so faithful to every duty, so forgiving and so generous, with a sagacity so eminent, and exercised with so much intelligence and such an absence of guile."

Though no loyal heart could envision Mr. Lincoln replaced "by some other, any other, man," there was the consideration that his influence could not end with his discontinuance of power. "There is a fame which no station or absence of station can add to or diminish. His work, like that of the most obscure soldier who lies buried under the sod of Gettysburg or Antietam, has been done, and faithfully done, and no act of others can destroy or weaken or increase its honor. Faithful and consecrated to the service of his country, his memory, though it were nameless as that of any private in our armies or any nurse in our hospitals, will, like theirs, be sweet in the heart of every true American so long as the humblest hamlet remains to keep up the tradition of a good citizen."

A San Francisco woman wrote for a home newspaper of how she quoted for Lincoln a line from Starr King's burial speech for Ned Baker—"Hither in future ages they shall bring . . . the sacred ashes of the advocate and soldier of liberty"—and of how in evening mist among the Soldiers' Home trees Lincoln kindled to the picture of a grand procession in solemn hush winding its way through street crowds of San Francisco on up the heights to the open grave on Lone Mountain. "It seemed to rise before them out of the quiet sea, a vast mausoleum from the hand of God, wherein to lay the dead."

There amid grasses where sea wind and land wind met they had laid for his long sleep the old and treasured friend whose death at Ball's Bluff had meant tears and grief to Lincoln. Now, thought the woman, this weary though lighted and strange man, Lincoln, seemed almost to be dreaming of rest for himself sometime, perhaps in envy of the rest that had come to the bright and daring Ned Baker. He gave a eulogy of his old friend "in a few deep-toned words."

CHAPTER 58

ELECTION DAY, NOVEMBER 8, 1864

ON the evening of November 8, 1864, John Hay wrote in his diary: "I have nothing to say till the day after tomorrow. God save the Republic!"

The White House was "still and almost deserted" on the day of the national election. "Everybody in Washington, not at home voting, seems ashamed of it and stays away from the President," noted Hay. The President took the day, believed his secretary, as "one of the most solemn" in his life, seeming to have "a keen and surprised regret that he should be an object in so many quarters of so bitter and vindictive an opposition." He commented, "It is a little singular that I, who am not a vindictive man, should have always been before the people in canvasses marked for their bitterness: always but once; when I came to Congress it was a quiet time. But always besides that the contests in which I have been prominent have been marked with great rancor."

The sky hung gray. Rain fell. "About noon I called on President Lincoln," wrote Noah Brooks, "and to my surprise found him entirely alone, as if by common consent everybody had avoided the White House." At the Cabinet meeting earlier in the day only two members came. Stanton was in bed with chills and fever. Seward, Usher, Dennison, had traveled home to vote. Fessenden closeted himself with New York financiers over new loans. So only Welles and Bates had come to the short Cabinet session.

Lincoln had no ease over what was happening at the polls, saying to Brooks: "I am just enough of a politician to know that there was not much doubt about the result of the Baltimore convention; but about this thing I am very far from being certain. I wish I were certain." Brooks wrote that he spent nearly the whole afternoon with the President, "who apparently found it difficult to put his mind on any of the routine work of his office, and entreated me to stay with him." He told Brooks of Tad's turkey, Jack, of how Tad called him to the window to watch the Pennsylvania troops on the river front of the White House, "voting for Lincoln and Johnson." The father asked what business the turkey had stalking around the polls. "Does he vote?" "No," flashed the boy; "he is not of age."

At noon came a telegram to the President from General Butler saying New York on election day was "the quietest city ever seen." Butler with

Grant's consent had detached four regiments, about 3,000 troops, from the Army of the Potomac, had moved these troops to New York and stationed them on ferryboats, with wire communication to Butler's headquarters in the city. Any sign of the mob disorders of July, 1863, would be reported and a regiment with artillery landed at the ferry slip nearest the danger point. This ready and waiting military force was well hidden from the people of the city. On the crowded streets, among lines of voters at the polls, no soldiers were in sight. Everybody knew however they were not far away, by order of the President, as Butler announced, prepared for any interference with a fair election. Published reports and common rumor credited the Federal Government with an army of from 12,000 to 15,000 at hand.

In the "multitudinous gabble" of the New York street crowds, noted the observer for *Leslie's Weekly*, "it was clear that 'little Mac' was the undoubted favorite." On the sixty lines of wire connecting Butler with all sections of the city came the repeated message through the day: "All quiet." The only special matter reported to Butler was "that Mr. August Belmont lost his vote, which was challenged on the ground that he had made a bet on the result of the election, and under that challenge he declined to vote." The press announced the wagers offered by the sportsman-banker, chairman of the Democratic National Committee, as "$10,000 that if Lincoln is elected the war will last his term, and that the Union will be broken up," also "$10,000 that if McClellan is elected the Union will be restored before his term expires, and that there will be peace on that basis."

A few telegrams came to the White House in the afternoon, with no real news. At seven o'clock in the evening Lincoln with Hay stepped out of the White House into a night of rain and stormy dark weather. They splashed across the grounds to the War Department telegraph office. At a side door stood a wet and steaming sentinel huddled in a rubber coat. As Lincoln entered the second-floor telegraph office a dispatch was put in his hands from Forney at Philadelphia claiming 10,000 majority there. "Forney," said Lincoln, "is a little excitable." From a Republican worker in Baltimore came a telegram, "15,000 in the city, 5,000 in the State. All Hail, Free Maryland!" Boston telegrams now gave majorities around 4,000 for two Unionist Congressmen. Lincoln in surprise asked if this was not a clerical error for 400, but other messages soon repeated the 4,000. The re-elected Congressman Alexander H. Rice, later quoted a constituent, without irreverence, "The Almighty must have stuffed the ballot-boxes."

Shakiness and doubt early in the evening gave way to lighter moods. Eckert came through the door of the telegraph office and shook rain off his cloak, his trousers showing mud, too much mud. They bantered him. He admitted having too much fun chuckling over another fellow's fall when he went down himself. Which reminded Lincoln: "For such an awkward fellow, I am pretty sure-footed. It used to take a pretty dextrous man to throw me." He told of an 1858 rainy night when he walked home after hearing returns that elected Douglas. On a hog-backed and slippery path, "my foot slipped from under me, knocking the other one out of the way, but I recovered myself & lit square, and I said to myself, 'It's a slip and not a fall.' "

To Mrs. Lincoln he sent over early reports, saying, "She is more anxious than I."

In Stanton's office a little later Lincoln talked with Gustavus Vasa Fox and delivered himself more freely than usual about critics and opponents. Fox was lit up over returns showing disaster for "two fellows . . . specially malignant to us"—meaning the Navy Department—"Hale and Winter Davis." Retribution had come upon them both.

"You have more of that feeling of personal resentment than I," said Lincoln, as Hay noted it. "Perhaps I may have too little of it, but I never thought it paid. A man has not time to spend half his life in quarrels. If any man ceases to attack me, I never remember the past against him. It has seemed to me recently that Winter Davis was growing more sensible to his own true interests and has ceased wasting his time by attacking me. I hope for his own good he has. He has been very malicious against me but has only injured himself by it. His conduct has been very strange to me. I came here, his friend, wishing to continue so. I had heard nothing but good of him; he was the cousin of my intimate friend Judge Davis. But he had scarcely been elected when I began to learn of his attacking me on all possible occasions. It is very much the same with Hickman. I was much disappointed that he failed to be my friend. But my greatest disappointment of all has been with Grimes. Before I came here, I certainly expected to rely upon Grimes more than any other one man in the Senate. I like him very much. He is a great strong fellow. He is a valuable friend, a dangerous enemy. He carries too many guns not to be respected in any point of view. But he got wrong against me, I do not clearly know how, and has always been cool and almost hostile to me. I am glad he has always been the friend of the Navy and generally of the Administration."

The wires worked badly on account of the rain-and-wind storm. In a long lull about ten o'clock, wrote Brooks, "The President amused the little company in the War Office with entertaining reminiscences and anecdotes naturally suggested by the political intelligence that dropped in from time to time." A New York dispatch claiming that State by 10,000 the President doubted, and said that a Greeley telegram predicting the State by 4,000 was more reasonable. In and out of the door moved Eckert, handing telegrams to Stanton, who read them, the President then studying them and commenting. "Presently there came a lull in the returns," wrote Charles A. Dana of the evening, "and Mr. Lincoln called me to a place by his side." And of what happened immediately Dana recorded:

"Dana," said he, "have you ever read any of the writings of Petroleum V. Nasby?"

"No, sir," I said: "I have only looked at some of them, and they seemed to be quite funny."

"Well," said he, "let me read you a specimen"; and, pulling out a thin yellow-covered pamphlet from his breast pocket, he began to read aloud. Mr. Stanton viewed these proceedings with great impatience, as I could see, but Mr. Lincoln paid no attention to that. He would read a page or a story, pause to consider a new election telegram, and then open the book again and go ahead with a new passage. Finally, Mr. Chase [sic] came in, and presently somebody else, and then the reading was interrupted.

Mr. Stanton went to the door and beckoned me into the next room. I shall never forget the fire of his indignation at what seemed to him to be mere nonsense. The idea that when the safety of the republic was thus at issue, when the control of an empire was to be determined by a few figures brought in by the telegraph, the leader, the man most deeply concerned, not merely for himself but for his country, could turn aside to read such balderdash and to laugh at such frivolous jests was, to his mind, repugnant, even damnable. He could not understand, apparently, that it was by the relief which these jests afforded to the strain of mind under which Lincoln had so long been living, and to the natural gloom of a melancholy and desponding temperament—this was Mr. Lincoln's prevailing characteristic—that the safety and sanity of his intelligence were maintained and preserved.

As the evening wore on the wires worked badly from Illinois and from States west of the Mississippi. The returns in, however, were more than satisfying to Lincoln. They were running close to the tabulation he had made weeks before of his own estimates. Toward midnight, noted Brooks, "It was certain that Lincoln had been reëlected, and the few gentlemen left in the office congratulated him very warmly on the result. Lincoln took the matter very calmly, showing not the least elation or excitement, but said that he would admit that he was glad to be relieved of all suspense, grateful that the verdict of the people was likely to be so full, clear, and unmistakable that there could be no dispute." At a midnight supper, noted Hay, "The President went awkwardly and hospitably to work shovelling out the fried oysters." It was two o'clock in the morning when he started to leave the War Office, at the door meeting serenaders with a brass band, music, and cheers, calling for a speech. The rain, the storm, was over.

He had been informed, the President told them, that this compliment was "paid me by loyal citizens of Pennsylvania, friendly to me." He would not pretend to say that they embraced "all the patriotism and loyalty of the country," but he believed and trusted, without personal interest, that the welfare of the country needed such support and endorsement as they gave the Administration and himself. "I earnestly believe that the consequences of this day's work, if it be as you assume, and as now seems probable, will be to the lasting advantage, if not to the very salvation, of the country. I cannot at this hour say what has been the result of the election. But, whatever it may be, I have no desire to modify this opinion: that all who have labored to-day in behalf of the Union have wrought for the best interests of the country and the world; not only for the present, but for all future ages.

"I am thankful to God for this approval of the people; but, while deeply grateful for this mark of their confidence in me, if I know my heart, my gratitude is free from any taint of personal triumph. I do not impugn the motives of any one opposed to me. It is no pleasure to me to triumph over any one, but I give thanks to the Almighty for this evidence of the people's resolution to stand by free government and the rights of humanity."

The serenaders then crossed Lafayette Square to the home of Secretary Seward, who spoke from a second-story window. Not in a long time had he been feeling so good. The humor, the play of fancy and imagination, that Lincoln had come to love in his Secretary of State shone this evening in an opening fable, in a spirit of goodwill and fellowship welcoming the Southern States back into the old Union in a warmth of affection for everything human. Seward began:

> Fellow Citizens—You remember that once Paul, in his own country, took an appeal to Caesar, and went from Judea across the Mediterranean to follow out his appeal to Caesar. After being shipwrecked, and after having encountered all manner of dangers at Malta and elsewhere—dangers by sea and land—he at last reached the coast of Italy, landing at the Hot Springs, near Naples. From there he proceeded up towards Rome, and when he got within about eighteen miles of Rome he came to a place called Appii Forum, or the Place of Three Taverns; and it is recorded in Scripture that the brethren, when he got within the suburbs of the city, came out to meet him. Thereupon Paul thanked God and took courage. So I think that, having been tossed about on this tempest of secession and revolution for three and a half years, I have at last got to Appii Forum—[Laughter.]—the Place of the Three Taverns. Although there is not a hotel on this street—[Laughter.]—at all events I am sure the brethren have come out to meet me—[Laughter.]—and thereupon I do now here to-night, with all my heart, and in all reverence and humility, thank God. [Cries of "Amen."] Amen. We all of us thank Him, and I hope you will all take courage for the rest of the way, which I think will be a short journey. [Cheers.]

Seward mentioned the many Tories in the country during the War of the Revolution. As a boy he heard his father and mother talk about those numerous Tories. As a boy he hoped to meet a Tory and have a good look at one. "What surprised me above all things was, that at the expiration of thirty years there was not a Tory to be found in the whole United States. [Laughter.]" Seward spoke his judgment "that we will all come together again; that when the Stars and Stripes wave over Richmond the rebellion will go down; and that within one, two, three and four years after that, you will have to look mighty sharp to find a man who was ever a secessionist or an aider of rebellion. [Cheers.]" He was certain that with slavery removed "the only element of discord among the American people will have ceased to work its mischievous fruits." He saw "our proud career among the nations" advancing. And a touch of austerity moved the Secretary of State:

"I know that it will not be the fault of the Administration if we do not have an era of peace and harmony. The election has placed our President beyond the pale of human envy or human harm, as he is above the pale of human ambition. Henceforth all men will come to see him, as you and I have seen him, a true, loyal, patient, patriotic and benevolent man. ["That's so," and cheers.] Having no longer any motive to malign or injure him, detraction will cease, and Abraham Lincoln will take his place with Washington and Franklin, and Jefferson and Adams and Jackson, among the benefactors of the country and of the human race."

The serenaders cried "Go on!" Seward said he had spoken more than intended. "I wish you would go around and see the Secretary of the Treasury and the Secretary of War, and keep them in good humor," he went on in a vein no other Cabinet member could have taken, "for if the Secretary of the Treasury fails us in funds we may come to grief, and if the Secretary of War does not get better within a few days than he is now, I shall begin to be concerned for what is to happen to us all. And while you are about it, you could not do anything better than to call and see my excellent friend and compatriot, Gideon Welles [Laughter.] and tell him that if it is possible for him to close up Wilmington I shall have a great deal less trouble in my foreign relations."

The crowd formed into a procession, with a brass band leading, in high humor marched to Secretary Welles's home, yelled their cheers for Welles and the navy. The solemn little owlish Secretary of the Navy made his speech short, scholarly, formal: "National freedom and national union, those immortal and inseparable conditions of national welfare, have been worthily represented in the wise and just statesman towards whom the hearts and hopes of the people have again turned, and upon whom they have, by a majority so overwhelming as to be almost an acclamation, conferred a new measure of responsibility and a new lease of power. Fellow citizens, Abraham Lincoln, as in the past he has been, so in the future he will be, worthy of the trust." The serenaders moved to Secretary Fessenden's home, found him away, marched to Stanton's house, learned that he was sick in bed and could not respond.

A day of great fate was over. The returns were in. There was no going behind the returns. Complete tabulations were yet to come, a mere formality, a tally sheet of the figures by which the victors won.

A day of rain and wind—and great fate—was over. No shooting, no bloodshed, no casualty lists, no newspaper columns of hundreds of names of dead and wounded. At thousands of polling places some 4,000,000 men marked the pieces of paper called ballots. A nation made a decision.

Chaos, hate, suspicion, mistrust, vengeance, dark doubts, were in the air. But the marking, handling, counting, of the ballots went on in quiet and good order, fraud or violence showing only in minor incidents. The miscounts and repeaters were only ordinary. Free speech and license to print were so operating that either side would have flared forth about any flagrant departure from the customary election methods.

The American electorate, designated in the Constitution's first three words, "We, the people," spoke on whether a colossal, heavy, weary war should go on under the same leadership as it had begun, on whether the same guiding mind and personality should keep the central control and power. To this the electorate, "We, the people," by a majority said Yes. In Washington this was accepted. In New York, New England, the Midwest, on the Great Plains, in the intermountain region, on the West Coast, this was accepted. Lincoln, his Administration, its army and navy, were to go ahead. The people so signaled. On a day of rain and wind that wrecked telegraph systems—a day of great fate—the people said Yes to Lincoln.

On the day after, the President said to Noah Brooks, "Being only mortal, after all, I should have been a little mortified if I had been beaten in this canvass before the people; but the sting would have been more than compensated by the thought that the people had notified me that my official responsibilities were soon to be lifted off my back." On the same day he dictated to Brooks a dispatch to be sent to Dr. A. G. Henry in Washington Territory: "With returns and States of which we are confident, the re-election of the President is considered certain, while it is not certain that McClellan has carried any State, though the chances are that he has carried New Jersey and Kentucky." Brooks finished the writing and passed it to Lincoln for signing, but Lincoln declined to "blow his own horn," as he put it. "You sign the message, and I will send it."

Brooks thought Lincoln might remember that in all these cares as President he was daily remembered, as no man before had ever been remembered, by those "who prayed, not to be heard of men." Lincoln caught at the homely phrase. "Yes, I like that phrase, 'not to be heard of men,' and guess it is generally true, as you say; at least, I have been told so, and I have been a good deal helped by just that thought."

In his news letter dated at Washington, D.C., November 11, 1864, published December 10 in the *Sacramento Union*, Brooks wrote: "I ought to say for the encouragement of loyal, Christian hearts, who daily remember their care-worn Chief Magistrate, 'and all others in authority,' that no man within the length and breadth of this Christian land feels more deeply than he the need of divine support, guidance and wisdom in these great straits than does Abraham Lincoln."

Brooks then directly quoted Lincoln as saying on the day following the election: "I should be the veriest shallow and self-conceited blockhead upon the footstool if, in my discharge of the duties which are put upon me in this place, I should hope to get along without the wisdom which comes from God and not from men."

The election returns held comfort. But when analyzed they admonished humility. True enough, the victory was overwhelming as seen in the Electoral College vote: all States except Kentucky, Delaware, and New Jersey went to Lincoln. But it was not so sweeping a triumph in the total of popular ballots. They gave Lincoln a majority of slightly more than 400,000. The votes cast for Lincoln from coast to coast, 2,203,831, represented 55.09 per cent of all that were cast (*Appleton's Annual Cyclopaedia*, 1864). McClellan had 44.91 per cent of the total: between New York and San Francisco were 1,797,019 male voters opposed to Lincoln, his Administration and his policies. In New York City McClellan carried by 78,746 against Lincoln's 36,673; in the Empire State Lincoln won with 50.47 per cent of the vote as against McClellan's 49.53 per cent. It was formidable that 212 of the Electoral College votes should go to Lincoln, with McClellan getting only 21.

But a study of three States with the largest electoral votes, New York, Pennsylvania, and Ohio, showed Lincoln receiving 930,269 to 843,862 for McClellan, a difference of only 86,407 votes, but giving Lincoln 80 in the Electoral College. Had these three key States by their narrow margin gone for McClellan and been joined by two or three other States, McClellan would have been elected.

The very uncertainties of politics that Lincoln so often mentioned were in the offing on November 8. The very sober and humble Lincoln of November 8 was undoubtedly prepared in his mind for the action he would take if the election went against him.

Humility was counseled even in the one little bulletin off the news presses: "The official majority of votes cast for General McClellan in Mr. Lincoln's own county of Sangamon, Illinois, is 376." Also a study of Illinois returns showed that every county bounding Sangamon had gone for McClellan and against Lincoln. The old district that had once sent Lincoln to Congress, however, elected the Union candidate Shelby M. Cullom, by a majority of 1,785, thus retiring Lincoln's old-time law partner, John T. Stuart. Seymour, the devious New York Governor, had gone down before the Unionist Reuben E. Fenton. There were other satisfactions, such as Samuel S. ("Sunset") Cox in Ohio retired in favor of Samuel Shellabarger, whose majority of 3,169 was heavy with soldier votes.

And in the one spot in the returns where Lincoln's heart would have been sore had not the ballots thundered and roared high for him—the soldier vote—there he won home big, the forecast being fulfilled that they would vote as they shot.

The oddity was chronicled: "Abraham Lincoln is the first President, from the Northern States, who has been twice elected." A wag wrote: "Dear Old Abe—Yesterday I worked hard for you all day and wore out my boots. Please send a new pair by mail." Horatio L. Wait of Chicago, shaking hands at the White House, wished Lincoln had been "elected for life instead of four years." Lincoln laughed. "Oh, no, that would be too much of a good thing."

Telegrams and messages of congratulation flooded into the Executive Mansion. Grant wired from City Point, "The victory is worth more to the country than a battle won." General Frank P. Blair wrote to Hay from Georgia, where he headed an army corps under Sherman, "The vote in this army today is almost unanimous for Lincoln. Give Uncle Abe my compliments."

And high-lighted in the background of Lincoln's victory was the fact that hundreds of thousands of soldiers whose ballots would have been given to the President had no chance to vote, either because of required marching and fighting, or because their home-State legislatures had refused them the right of voting in the field. And in the foul rooms of Libby Prison at Richmond the votes were 276 for Lincoln, 95 for McClellan.

On the night of November 10 a procession with banners, lanterns, transparencies, and the hue and cry of a festive occasion marched to the White

House. The marchers and the throng in their wake surged around the main entrance and filled the grounds. As far as the eye could reach from that front portico were the acres of human faces, cheers, songs, band music, roar of cannon. The Republican clubs of the District of Columbia were putting on a serenade for the President. Inside the White House Tad ran from window to window arranging an illumination with lanterns of his own, having fun over the big panes of glass shivering as cannon went off in the near-by driveway. Also inside the White House the President was writing a speech. Publication of it would go far and be taken as his solemn appraisal of the issues at hand, his outline of the ideas and feeling he would like to see moving the nation. He wrote the speech "hastily," according to Hay, and stepped out of a window opening on the north portico.

The crowd went into an uproar. It was many minutes before the deafening racket let down enough for the jostling serenaders to hear what their hero of the evening might have to say. He made ready for reading his script to the people. Hay stood alongside with a candle to light the written page. "Not very graceful," he smiled to Hay, "but I am growing old enough not to care much for the manner of doing things." Yet there was accomplished style and woven substance and content in the hurriedly written address given to the far-swept throng spotted and dusky amid its banners and lanterns. Seldom did so gay a crowd hear so grave and deliberate a counseling.

In a rather strict sense he was giving his latest redefinition of what he meant by his phrase at Gettysburg, "government of the people, by the people, for the people." It was his interpretation of the Tuesday preceding, with lights and shadows thrust toward many more Tuesdays to come in the life of the Republic. "It has long been a grave question," he began, from the candlelit page, under the night stars, before floating thousands of witnessing faces, "whether any Government, not too strong for the liberties of its people, can be strong enough to maintain its existence in great emergencies. On this point the present rebellion brought our republic to a severe test, and a presidential election occurring in regular course during the rebellion, added not a little to the strain. If the loyal people united were put to the utmost of their strength by the rebellion, must they not fail when divided and partially paralyzed by a political war among themselves? But the election was a necessity. We cannot have free government without elections; and if the rebellion could force us to forego or postpone a national election, it might fairly claim to have already conquered and ruined us."

He voiced his philosophy of applied democracy. "The strife of the election is but human nature practically applied to the facts of the case. What has occurred in this case must ever recur in similar cases. Human nature will not change. In any future great national trial, compared with the men of this, we shall have as weak and as strong, as silly and as wise, as bad and as good." The incidents of this one could be studied for wisdom to be learned from them, "and none of them as wrongs to be revenged."

The election, with its "incidental and undesirable strife," had done good,

Long Abraham Lincoln a Little Longer.

Harper's Weekly rejoices after the November 1864 election returns too. "It has demonstrated that a people's government can sustain a national election in the midst of a great civil war. Until now, it has not been known to the world that this was a possibility. It shows, also, how sound and how strong we still are. It shows that, even among candidates of the same party, he who is most devoted to the Union and most opposed to treason can receive most of the people's votes. It shows, also, to the extent yet known, that we have more men now than we had when the war began. Gold is good in its place, but living, brave, patriotic men are better than gold."

The election over, the rebellion continued. He voiced the human spirit he would prefer to have breathing across the future. "May not all having a common interest reunite in a common effort to save our common country? For my own part, I have striven and shall strive to avoid placing any obstacle in the way. So long as I have been here I have not willingly planted a thorn in any man's bosom. While I am deeply sensible to the high compliment of a reëlection, and duly grateful, as I trust, to almighty God for having directed my countrymen to a right conclusion, as I think, for their own good, it adds nothing to my satisfaction that any other man may be disappointed or pained by the result. May I ask those who have not differed with me to join with me in this same spirit toward those who have? And now let me close by asking three hearty cheers for our brave soldiers and seamen, and their gallant and skilful commanders." Applause and cheers had punctuated the speech. At the final call the crowd raised three cheers that ran into extras for the re-elected President. Then slowly the faces, lights, and voices dwindled. The White House lawn took on its accustomed night shadows of trees, fences, buildings. The meditative bronze statue of Thomas Jefferson before the front portico stood as a vague silhouette.

The outlook Lincoln now voiced was toward conciliation—no retaliation, no reprisals, no thorns knowingly into the bosoms of others. General Butler sending suggestions for punishment of flagrant offenders in New York, the President rejected them. "We must not sully victory with harshness."

Henry J. Raymond, having nearly lost his election to Congress, wanted stern dealing with a treacherous Custom House clique. "To-day I got a letter from Raymond," wrote Hay this week, "breathing fire and vengeance against the Custom House which came near destroying him in his district. I read it to the President. He answered that it was the spirit of such letters as that that created the faction and malignity of which Raymond complained. It seems utterly impossible for the President to conceive of the possibility of any good resulting from a rigorous and exemplary course of punishing political dereliction. His favorite expression is, 'I am in favor of short statutes of limitations in politics.' " A delegation from Maryland counted it his rare discretion that resulted in Maryland becoming a Free State. He spoke deep appreciation of their courtesy; those who differed from and opposed "us" would yet see that defeat was better for their own good than if they had been successful.

The gloomy month of August, with Lincoln about hopeless of election, was recalled. Six days before the Chicago convention nominated McClellan he wrote a memorandum, folded it oddly, signed it himself, had all his Cabinet members sign it without knowing what they were signing, a curious proceeding. Now on November 11 he brought out this paper. Cabinet members for the first time read what they had signed. Hay wrote:

"At the meeting of the Cabinet today, the President took out a paper from his desk, and said, 'Gentlemen, do you remember last summer I asked you all to sign your names to the back of a paper of which I did not show you the inside? This is it. Now, Mr. Hay, see if you can get this open without tearing it?' He had pasted it up in so singular style that it required some cutting to get it open. He then read as follows:—

" 'Executive Mansion
" 'Washington, Aug. 23, 1864

" 'This morning, as for some days past, it seems exceedingly probable that this Administration will not be reelected. Then it will be my duty to so cooperate with the President elect, as to save the Union between the election and the inauguration; as he will have secured his election on such ground that he cannot possibly save it afterwards.

" 'A. Lincoln'

"This was indorsed: William H. Seward, W. P. Fessenden, Edwin M. Stanton, Gideon Welles, Edw[d] Bates, M. Blair, J. P. Usher. August 23, 1864.

"The President said, 'You will remember that this was written at a time . . . when as yet we had no adversary, and seemed to have no friends. I then solemnly resolved on the course of action indicated above. I resolved, in case of the election of General McClellan, being certain that he would be the candidate, that I would see him and talk matters over with him. I would say, "General, the election has demonstrated that you are stronger, have more influence with the American people than I. Now let us together, you with your influence, and I with all the executive power of the Government, try to save the country. You raise as many troops as you possibly can for this final trial, and I will devote all my energies to assisting and finishing the war." '

"Seward said, 'And the General would answer you "Yes, Yes"; and the next day when you saw him again, and pressed these views upon him, he would say, "Yes, Yes"; and so on forever, and would have done nothing at all.'

" 'At least,' added Lincoln, 'I should have done my duty and have stood clear before my own conscience.' "

On election day McClellan resigned as a major general in the regular army. To fill this vacancy Lincoln signed a commission for General Philip H. Sheridan. McClellan began on his plans for a trip to Europe, which would keep him away from the American scene and its war for many months.

Four days after the election the *Charleston Mercury* published the news of it. Then in two days more came an editorial titled "The Days." What were the days saying? The days counted. "The people of these Confederate

States," the editorial began, "constitute a portion of the world, and God is its governor." Did this assume that some recent action or event had read them out of the world as forgotten of God? It proceeded, "Of the family of Christian nations, they are under His special protection." This pretended that they had been recognized by other Christian nations, which had not happened; they had been accorded by Great Britain and France the rights of belligerents. "Standing on the moral principles of the Bible, they are fighting a war of self-defence, against the fanatics of a higher law and the soldiers of dominion. They are breasting a cruel sea of suffering and of blood." This had more the tone of the original Robert Barnwell Rhett. Then came words strangely akin to those heard from Lincoln in his November 10 serenade address. "Human reason is incompetent to 'reconcile the ways of God to man,' and, therefore, humility, submission and trust are the height of wisdom. But we know well enough that we are sinful and faulty. There are, doubtless, good acts to accomplish. Penitential resignation, hopeful, prayerful patriotism, and the correction of sins, public and private, become us as a people on this day of solemn thought and appointed intercession."

Not yet had their dauntless city, so white-walled and lovely by the sea, so proud over her own State flag and her declared sovereign rights as a State, so rooted in her three hundred years of traditions still as green as her own flowering magnolias—not yet had their city been taken. Not yet had Lincoln's November 10 speech of humility, resignation, penitence, and forgiveness reached the *Charleston Mercury*. On November 22, however, it printed that speech, in full, completely accurate, with no garbling. The news item preceding the speech read: "The Abolition Clubs of Washington went to Lincoln's White House on Thursday evening, and, after firing off a cannon, proceeded to hurrah, etc., until the Gorilla came out and made the following speech."

Confederate newspapers in the main interpreted for their readers the election of Lincoln as an advantage to their cause. A soldier in Lee's army, said the *Richmond Sentinel*, November 12, had written that the news of Lincoln's re-election "gives general satisfaction here." The newspaper commented: "There is no such terror, it seems, in the name of Abraham Lincoln as to run men crazy. Four years of cruel war have taught us to hold him as our implacable and barbarous enemy; but four years of successful resistance tells us that we are not to fear him. We are not to dread him now, when with a people weary and divided, he pursues the failing war with weakening exertions. Had Lincoln been substituted by his competitor McClellan, an accomplished soldier, there would have been more cause for solicitude. But Abraham Lincoln we know to be a different grade of man, the hero of an indecent jest, but not of a battlefield. He has a ruler's ambition but not a ruler's skill. His election gives 'general satisfaction' to our people." The size of the vote cast against Lincoln indicated that "the means he employs excite a disgust and abhorrence in the minds of vast multitudes of his people, which their political defeat is not calculated to remove or abate."

The editorial gave a prophecy: "Those against the war before Lincoln's re-election will be but confirmed in their opposition. If the vote cast against him is any indication of the strength of the anti-war sentiment. then, indeed, while his war will be against a united enemy, his rule will be over a divided house."

A *Richmond Sentinel* commentary held Lincoln not so low as others of his Government. A score board of odiums and execrations read: "There are some names more odious among us even than that of Abraham Lincoln. We know Seward as a snake, a cunning plotter of mischief and contriver of

Leslie's Weekly caricatures two antagonists

frauds wherever his faith is pledged. We know Sumner as a mouthing thunderer of great words, but of weak spine and trembling knees. We know Butler as a beast. Compared with these detestable qualities Mr. Lincoln's joking propensities appear, if puerile, yet harmless. If they excite our contempt, they yet appeal to our good nature. In the midst of our resentments we are 'reminded of a little joke.' But as the head of a great war, Mr. Lincoln has sanctioned the infamies of his officers, and thus made them his own. The world execrates Butler, but Lincoln voluntarily partakes of his shame. We will fight him, therefore, as we would Butler, while we rejoice to know that he is far less formidable than the soldier whom he has beaten in the Presidential contest."

Since the November 8 returns there were men who breathed easier, as though on a boat that had negotiated a dangerous river curve and its rapids, as though on a wagon that had traversed a mountain pass at a high divide with the going downgrade from then on, as though a patient had passed a crisis of a fever, as though some sweet certitude had taken the place of a sour and bitter doubt. Longfellow wrote in his journal on November 10: "Lincoln reelected beyond a doubt. We breathe freer. The country will be saved." Ralph Waldo Emerson wrote to a friend: "I give you joy of the election. Seldom in history was so much staked on a popular vote. I suppose never in history." Motley at Vienna wrote his daughter, "I am, as it were, struck dumb . . . realisation of my highest hopes leaves me with no power of expression except to repeat over and over again, 'O Grosser Gott im Staube danke ich dir.' [Oh, great God, from the dust I thank thee.]" Charles Francis Adams at London wrote to a son that the moral effect of the election must be prodigious. "In the face of intrigues of every kind carried on for months between traitors both without and within the lines, in the face of the serious difficulties attending the maintenance of a terrible struggle, a large majority of the people, spread over the whole country, with geographical or sectional lines to mark a difference, have expressed their deliberate sense of the necessity of perseverance in the policy once commenced. This is an extraordinary escape from what at one time looked like a portentous hazard."

Henry, the son of Charles Francis, was more eloquent than his father. "The result is so decisive as to answer all our wishes and hopes," he wrote his brother. "Systems of government are secondary matters, if you've only got your people behind them. I never yet have felt so proud as now of the great qualities of our race, or so confident of the capacity of men to develop their faculties in the mass. I believe that a new era of the movement of the world will date from that day, which will drag nations up another step, and carry us out of a quantity of old fogs. Europe has a long way to go to catch us up." The brother Charles Francis Adams, Jr., in the Army of the Potomac wrote to his father that the last election had given him "a new and almost unbounded faith in the faculty of a free and *intelligent* people to manage their own affairs." In the immediate future he could see evils from the crude methods of raising men and money. "Currency juggles and draft juggles are only swindles," he wrote. "These things need to be brought before the people and the Cabinet should do it, for the President, we know, is not equal to it. What a superb thing it would be to have some man at the head of affairs who could now lead this people!"

Harper's Weekly held that "the true men of all the old parties" stood together for the Government, that Mr. Lincoln was not elected because he was a Republican, nor General McClellan defeated because he was a Democrat. "The election is the expression of the overpowering determination of the people that there shall be no parties during a war for the life of the nation." More vivid was the private letter of George William Curtis to Charles Eliot Norton the day after election. Curtis had been in suspense over the thought that there might be enough misunderstanding and mutiny on the Ship of State to throw the Captain overboard. Now Curtis wrote: "Let us thank God and the people for this crowning mercy. I did not know how my mind and heart were strained until I felt myself sinking in the great waters of this triumph. We knew it ought to be; we knew that, bad as we have been, we did not deserve to be put out like a mean candle in its own refuse; but it is never day until the dawn. . . . Fernando Wood and James Brooks are defeated—God be praised!"

A cartoon in *Harper's Weekly*, titled "Long ABRAHAM LINCOLN a Little Longer," stretched Lincoln's length of form till he soared to an impossible height. In *Leslie's Weekly* a cartoon had Jeff Davis in bed, from his pillow gazing on a doubled-up ghost between him and the footboard and the lines: "Is that you, still there, LONG ABE?" "Yes! and I'm going to be FOUR YEARS LONGER!"

Charles Sumner in Faneuil Hall greeted the election returns as a "great joy" betokening that "the hour of deliverance" had arrived for the slaves. Sumner's jubilance was evangelical, embraced the world and its cosmos: "Let the glad tidings go forth to all the people of the United States, at length made wholly free; to foreign countries; to the whole family of man; to posterity; to the martyred band who have fallen in battle for their country; to the angels above—ay, and to the devils below."

Some newspapers treated the election rather as though it had not happened, as though the more things are different, the more they are the same. They pointed to the large vote given McClellan and said it must be respected. But they were no help on whether the President should now respect the McClellan or the Vallandigham divisions of the vote for McClellan. The peace wing wanted peace right away, the terms to be made after the peace. The other wing wanted the Union saved—with slavery saved. And now their mouthpieces were saying the almost 2,000,000 voters for McClellan couldn't be wrong and must be respected. The *New York World* had about used up its malice in the campaign and now sulked in a sullen daze, reached in a befuddled way for new scares to throw into the country. "The greatest danger which now threatens the country" was nothing less than that before Mr. Lincoln's four years of power were over "he will have made a peace recognizing the independence of the South—a disunion peace." This was to be the scare. To this the *World* tried to join a hope. After Lincoln should wreck the Union, by a shameful peace recognizing the South, then the McClellan cohorts would step in and—they would save the Union. "Now as ever, the Democratic party will, in the language of its noble standard-bearer, who has well deserved the highest honors of the nation, stand steadfast, firm, immovable, and faithful to 'the Union at all hazards.' "

What bubble of pretense was this? Union editors asked. The *Lansing* (Michigan) *State Republican* saw the *World* "taken all at once with a violent fit of patriotism," inquired why the leading McClellan organ had no rebukes for peace-at-any-price Pendleton, McClellan's running mate, or for Vallandigham, Cox, the Wood brothers, and other frank sympathizers with the Confederacy. "The explanation of such patriotism doubtless is that it pays better than treason." The pro-McClellan *Ann Arbor* (Michigan) *Journal*, on the other hand, freely confessed: "If McClellan must go down, we are glad that the Woods, Cox and Vallandigham have gone down with him. He may rise again but they have gone down to rise no more." Of such press opinions on the election there was a wide variety. At bottom they generally gave the impression the Democratic party must be kept alive for incessant opposition to the Republican party, and toward this end any tried and venerable devices of politics were justifiable.

Mr. Lincoln was now President "under very different circumstances," endorsed by "the Union sentiment of the country," no longer forced "to choose his counsellors from among men who were either fools or fanatics," said the *New York Herald*. He was far more free and independent, and "If he fails in realizing what he has been a second time chosen for, it will be from a weakness in his character, and not from the lack of a generous and unselfish support on the part of the people." A man of even less ability than Mr. Lincoln ought to be able to give the country what it expected, said the *Herald*, leading up to statements closely studied and much discussed: "The military situation is divested of all cause for anxiety. Within a given time it is mathematically certain that the resisting power of the rebellion must give way."

Overseas that political fraction known as liberals had relief and joy over Lincoln's re-election. The *Revue des deux mondes* in France, pleased with the orderly progress of the election "in the midst of the freest competition of parties," took pride that a war and its vast convulsive play had not "deranged the mechanism of the noble and glorious Constitution of the Union." Few events in contemporary history would leave so deep a trace as the re-election of Mr. Lincoln in the United States, said the *Journal des débats*. "It is the first time that a people in possession of universal suffrage has been called to pronounce directly and finally for or against the continuation of a painful war." Never in any other land, it seemed, had a people in the waste and anguish of war voted Yes or No, freely and without hindrance, whether a war should go on. "None of the nations of the old world has yet been submitted to such a test, no government has yet been reduced to try it. In electing Mr. Lincoln by a sweeping majority, the American people has given to the world a not unexpected, but very remarkable proof of intelligence and patriotism. It has shown, first, that the federative form did not prevent the national sentiment from developing quite rapidly in the United States and from throwing out roots deep enough to carry it through the roughest experiences. It has proved moreover, that it can choose with discernment the executors of its will, and it has not permitted itself to be deceived by appearances."

From one extreme revolutionary organization came salutations to Lincoln in a fraternal tone. This was the Central Council of the International Working Men's Association, its banner a red flag, its pivotal proposal the international overthrow of the capitalist system by the united workers of the world. Their leading philosopher and tactician, corresponding secretary for Germany, Karl Marx, author of *Das Kapital*, drafted a letter to the American people, addressed to Abraham Lincoln, the President of the United States. "Sir: We congratulate the American people upon your re-election by a large majority. If resistance to the Slave Power was the watchword of your first election, the triumphal war-cry of your re-election is Death to Slavery. From the commencement of the titanic American strife the workingmen of Europe felt distinctively that the Star-spangled Banner carried the destiny of their class." A territorial question had been the immediate cause of the war, and was not the war "to decide whether the virgin soil of immense tracts should be wedded to the labor of the immigrant or be prostituted by the tramp of the slave-driver?" An oligarchy of 300,000 slaveholders had dared for the first time in the annals of the world to inscribe "Slavery" on a banner of armed revolt. This in the very places "where hardly a century ago the idea of one great Democratic Republic had first sprung up, whence the first declaration of the Rights of Man was issued, and the first impulse given to the European Revolution." There a counter-revolution (the Confederate secession) with systematic thoroughness gloried in rescinding what it called "the ideas entertained at the time of the formation of the old Constitution," maintained "slavery to be a beneficial institution," and indeed, the only solution of the great problem of the "relation of capital to labor." Cynically it proclaimed "property in man" as a cornerstone of its edifice.

Then, continued the address, "the working classes of Europe understood at once, even before the fanatic partisanship of the upper classes, for the Confederate gentry had given its dismal warning that the slaveholders' rebellion was to sound the tocsin for a general holy war of property against labor, and that for the men of labor, with their hopes for the future, even their past conquests were at stake in that tremendous conflict on the other side of the Atlantic. Everywhere they bore therefore patiently the hardships imposed upon them by the cotton crisis, opposed enthusiastically the pro-slavery intervention—importunities of their betters—and from most parts of Europe contributed their quota of blood to the good of the cause." As further bearing on this point Marx in November of '64 wrote to Joseph Weydemeyer, then in the United States, regarding their General Council: "Its English members are mostly chiefs of the local trades unions, hence the real labor kings of London, the same people who gave Garibaldi such a rousing welcome, and who by their monster meeting in St. James' Hall

[Bright in the chair] prevented Palmerston from declaring war against the United States when he was on the point of doing it."

Two short paragraphs closed this first letter from organized workingmen of Europe to American kin. One sketched the sardonic interwoven economic relationships of the Negro and the white-skinned laborer. The other paid a gesture to Lincoln's historic significance. The signers at London of the document were George Odger, president of the council, corresponding secretaries for France, Germany, Italy, Poland, Switzerland, and fifty-one others representing practically all the lands and corners of continental Europe and the British Isles. The close of their address read:

> While the workingmen, the true political power of the North, allowed slavery to defile their own republic, while before the Negro, mastered and sold without his concurrence, they boasted it the highest prerogative of the white-skinned laborer to sell himself and choose his own master, they were unable to attain the true freedom of labor, or to support their European brethren in their struggle for emancipation; but this barrier to progress has been swept off by the red sea of civil war.
>
> The workingmen of Europe feel sure that, as the American War of Independence initiated a new era of ascendency for the middle class, so the American Antislavery War will do for the working classes. They consider it an earnest sign of the epoch to come that it fell to the lot of Abraham Lincoln, the single-minded son of the working class, to lead his country through the matchless struggle for the rescue of the enchained race and the reconstruction of a social world.

The letter was delivered by a committee to Minister Adams at London. After some weeks Adams replied. Their address had been duly transmitted to the President of the United States, and "So far as the sentiments expressed by it are personal, they are accepted by him with a sincere and anxious desire that he may be able to prove himself not unworthy of the confidence which has been recently extended to him by his fellow-citizens, and by so many friends of humanity and progress throughout the world." Then came the State Department's velvet-worded warning that it did not approve of revolutionary propaganda and doctrines of force. "The Government of the United States of America has a clear consciousness that its policy neither is, nor could be, reactionary; but at the same time it adheres to the course which it adopted at the beginning of abstaining everywhere from propagandism and unlawful intervention. It strives to do equal justice to all states and to all men, and it relies upon the beneficent results of that effort for support at home, and for respect and good will throughout the world."

On the election news reaching England, the comic weekly *Punch* at once gave its readers a cartoon captioned "The Federal Phoenix," with Lincoln's face lifted in what was meant for malignant arrogance above the ashes of fagots labeled United States Constitution, Credit, Free Press, State Rights, Habeas Corpus, Commerce. The assignment was not an easy one for the cartoonist. Possibly he liked Lincoln a little, for the face and head in the caricature had a touch of majesty and a Yankee Doodle readiness for combat if trod on. Nor in the same month did *Punch's* parody of Lincoln

The cartoonist Sir John Tenniel in *Punch* of London aims to show the re-elected Lincoln an American dictator more ruthless and cruel than before

speaking to his people quite come off. It was too facile and more like a stereotyped British imitation of American manners than an effective take-off on Lincoln. It read: "Well, we've done it, gentlemen. Bully for us. Cowhided the Copperheads considerable. Non nobis, of course, but still I reckon we have had a hand in the glory some. . . . Now I am sovereign of the sovereign people of this great and united Republic for four years next ensuing the date hereof, as I used to say when I was a lawyer. (You are! Bully for you!) Yes, gentlemen, but you must do something more than bully for me, you must fight for me, if you please, and whether you please or not. As the old joke says, there's no compulsion, only you must. . . . Rebellion is a wicked thing, gentlemen, an awful wicked thing, and the mere nomenclating thereof would make my hair stand on end if it could be more stand-on-ender than it is."

An impartial observer could see no reason for alarm at the re-election of Mr. Lincoln, said the London *Times*. "Nay, it may probably be that we are safer in the hands of Mr. Lincoln than we should be in the hands of any one else. As regards Foreign States, ourselves in particular, we may reasonably believe that he has sown his wild oats; he has gone through the course of defying and insulting England, which is the traditional way of obtaining the Irish vote, and we may not unreasonably hope that he is unlikely to repeat the experiment." The London *Herald* held that Mr. Lincoln was the candidate of his party not owing to "any belief in his personal merit, but to accidental circumstances." To what then did he owe his re-election? "To the strength of his party and to his own lawless abuse of executive power, not to the belief of the people that no better man could have been chosen." Mr. Lincoln had not himself "connived at peculation," the London *Herald* would like to believe, even though he had shielded Ministers who had robbed the public. "Mr. Lincoln's predecessors were gentlemen; men of some experience either in military, diplomatic or political life, men at least of average intelligence, and of unquestioned personal integrity. . . . Mr. Lincoln is a vulgar, brutal boor, wholly ignorant of political science, of military affairs, of everything else which a statesman should know."

With evident reference to the case of Simon Cameron, the *Herald* said that "in the only case in which scandal was too bad to be hushed up at home, Mr. Lincoln appointed the guilty party to a first-class embassy." The *Herald* went on to confess frankly its rejoicing over the defeat of General McClellan, as a prelude to the defeat of the North. "We rejoice that the cause of oppression, robbery and injustice is entrusted to the hands of a vacillating, helpless imbecile, rather than to those of an able, resolute and efficient soldier." Much more in the same vein ran through the London *Herald*, while the London *Standard* said the same things, merely using different words. "Against Lincoln the South must fight to the death; the dishonor of asking terms from such a creature would be intolerable. For the North the renewal of Mr. Lincoln's term is the inauguration of a reign of terror. It may be that at the last moment the Northern people will take heart of grace, and resolve to fight for their liberties. If so, the Federal Government will have a double war on its hands." Mr. Lincoln's sole idea of government, it seemed to the *Standard*, was to repress opposition with violence. "Of statesmanship, it is needless to say, he is profoundly ignorant; of finance he knows still less; and when the final crash comes, for which Mr. Chase and Mr. Fessenden have been so long preparing, in all probability the one man in America whom it will take by surprise is the President of the United States. . . . Never were issues so momentous placed in so feeble a hand; never was so great a place in history filled by a figure so mean."

These opinions of London newspapers reached old Sam Medary, the stout-hearted Peace Democrat of Columbus, Ohio. He published them in his weekly, the *Crisis*, as of importance to his Buckeye and Hoosier readers, for their counsel and enlightenment on what kind of a man their Sucker neighbor, Lincoln, might be, in case they couldn't figure out what Lincoln was up to.

What Lincoln's re-election actually did to feeling and opinion in Britain was not easy to measure and estimate, even for a keen observer on the spot in London. "Anything that produces a great effect in our favor on this side," wrote Henry Adams to his brother, "usually produces a sort of general silence as the first proof of its force. So this election has been met on this side by a species of blindness. People remark the fact with wonder and anger, but they have only just such a vague idea of what are to be its consequences, as shuts their mouths without changing their opinions."

The December number of *Littell's Living Age* gave its influential American clientele a reprint of an article in the *Economist* of London. "Nothing is so dangerous as to read a sermon to another nation," it said truly enough. And again pertinently enough: "It always seems like forgetting our own sins to attend to other people's. It often misses the mark, because, though the broad result is true, some local detail is missed. But, nevertheless, thought and philosophy are truthless unless they enable us to interpret events and derive teachings from what we see."

So far, so good. And then what? "It is a lesson of events that America should be obliged to elect such a man as Mr. Lincoln in admitted default of a better to such a place as his at such a moment as this. The President is, for practical purposes, omnipotent at this crisis; Congress is unheard of and unthought of. It is not even contended that Mr. Lincoln is a man of eminent ability. It is only said that he is a man of common honesty, and it seems this is so rare a virtue at Washington that at their utmost need no other man can be picked out to possess it and true ability also. Even supposing the American people could manage one of the vastest executive administrations without great ability, that ability would still be of the first necessity. For ages a certain greatness in speaking has belonged to the rulers of great States, and the Old World expects it even if the New World can dispense with it. Mr. Lincoln has been honest, but he has been vulgar; and there is no greater external misfortune than for a great nation to be exclusively represented at a crisis by a person whose words are mean even when his actions are important."

This priggish patronization was the cue for the undaunted Richard Cobden to say in a November speech at Rochdale, "There is a real danger in the ignorance of what, for want of a better term, I may call the ruling classes of this country—their total ignorance of everything relating to America." If he were a rich man, said Cobden, he would endow a chair of American history at Oxford and at Cambridge. Bring any undergraduate of those universities to a map of the United States and ask him to put his finger on Chicago. "And I will undertake to say that he does not go within one thousand miles of it. Yet Chicago is a place of one-hundred-fifty thousand inhabitants, from which one to two millions of people in our own country are annually fed."

One middle-class organ of liberal opinion in England printed a remarkable commentary on Lincoln's re-election. It had overstresses and errors, but in depth and accuracy of gauging it equaled any single editorial appraisal published in America in latter '64. This was in the *Spectator* of London, November 26, and undoubtedly from the pen of the same writer in that periodical who had several times before executed keen little profiles of Lincoln, once saying of his "mystic dreaminess" about the American Union in relation to world democracy, "The thoughts of the man are too big for his mouth." Events of several European uprisings and outbursts of the people were mentioned and compared to the re-election of Lincoln and the civil and sectional war to which the recent balloting gave approval. In this American war alone had the struggle in modern history between the two great political ideas of mankind, aristocracy and democracy, "the rule of the many for the benefit of the few, and the rule of the many or the few for the benefit of all," been brought into direct and visible collision, stripped of false or misleading appearances. "The reticent, statesmanlike, selfish aristocracy, the slow, loud-tongued, unselfish democracy, each left to itself, each guided by its own highest average and no more, has been fighting out foot to foot and face to face, as the Athens and Sparta of the New World, the ancient political battle of mankind."

Now the North had pronounced by a majority that "through hardship and defeat and financial difficulty, though its land be covered with hospitals and its cities filled with bankrupts, though every family weep for its sons and the course of material civilization be thrown back centuries, it is ready to fight manfully on rather than freedom should be proved a chimera not essential to a grand national life. . . . Had the North shrunk, or even faltered, had she refused the necessary sacrifices or accepted the evil compromise, the cause of liberty would have received a heavy, perhaps a deadly wound." Aristocracies the world over would have said: "Look at the nobleness of your chosen demos! It cares, like kings, only for aggrandizement and wealth." The middle class would have chimed in, "Look! your demos, whatever its merits, is weak, cannot guard national life, cannot keep a nation secure, cannot guarantee that consols shall always be paid." And the hostile and the timid, "the few who mean to rule for themselves and the many who care only that rule should always be strong"? They would have moved toward a logical termination, the legalization of slavery, and in further forms. "The slaveholding interest is the outwork of aristocracy throughout the world, as the American demos is the defence of the masses in every land. The re-election of Mr. Lincoln does not of course ensure the success of the Christian political idea, but it does guarantee that before it yields it will have faced the Pagan one to the death. . . . The re-election of Mr. Lincoln means for all, for the Lancashire operative as much as the slave, for the serf of Mecklenburg-Schwerin as much as the freeman of Maine, that the conflict . . . shall be steadily fought out to the end. We may and shall hear much more in Europe of the crimes of democracy, though all the masses have committed in all ages do not equal those of the single line of Hapsburg, but we shall be free at least of the taunt that liberty means weakness, that self-government threatens national life, that a free people must be a people incapable of energetic and persistent war."

McClellan had spoken out for the war, for the Union, for the Monroe Doctrine, for all that his antagonist could promise, *except* the final extinction of the cause of the whole calamity. New England, the West, the great States of New York and Pennsylvania, had declared that Mr. Lincoln, "this shrewd peasant with his noble purpose and his deadly tenacity, expresses their resolve; that despite endless charges of oppression and occasional realities of failure, despite uncouthness and occasional want of tact, he is the fitting mouth-piece of the nation in its struggle for life or death." Hatred of slavery had penetrated at last, from principle or from political conviction, into the very heart of the people. "The change to all who understood American feeling, who knew how deeply contempt for the coloured races had penetrated the American mind, seems absolutely marvelous. It is like the adoption of a new faith, the growth of a new *system* of thought in a nation, and must produce in the end effects far beyond the mere freedom of the black."

Why this deep change? It was not beyond explanation. First, the *Spectator* would lay claim: "This journal alone in England has pointed out steadily, not as an argument, but as the one necessary datum for argument, that the American Republic is not in times of excitement governed by its talking class." Who then held the ultimate sovereign power? "The quiet, dour, half-cultivated freeholders of whom no one ever hears. . . . These men have sent their sons to the war, have watched its progress as men only watch affairs which do involve their sons, have suffered new ideas to filter drop by drop into their minds and harden there to crystalline clearness and immobility, and they have been ennobled by the suffering which they have undergone. It is they who have filled the voting-boxes, who in New York have carried the State in the teeth of the vast vote of the great city, who in Pennsylvania have overborne the fears of the border counties, the selfish indifference of the old German settlers, and who have carried New England, the six poor frugal 'Yankee' States, which produce nothing except schools, and men. . . . Secure of their support, Mr. Lincoln can afford to disregard the clamour of city mobs and the apprehensions of the mercantile class, and it will be a curious problem to watch the effect of re-election upon him and his policy."

What had brought on Lincoln his strangely added solemn tone since his re-election? Was it in part because of new powers and fresh assurances given him? Was a more exquisite justice and a more tantalizing expediency than ever before now required of him? Had Tuesday, November the eighth, and its result intensified the entanglements to be faced in the work of reconstruction?

The *Spectator* writer from his long-distance view listed the mighty factors of advantage that lay with Lincoln. "He is securely President until March, 1869," having with him all who hoped for office, all who regard compromise as henceforth hopeless, and all who thirst for speedy peace. "He may pursue his policy unchecked, carry on the war without hurrying armies for political purposes, increase the area of freedom with that slow tenacious persistence which he has all along displayed. Having time and the assurance of public support he will undoubtedly be more lenient in his action, more disposed to regard hostility from within as something to be despised, to treat it as an English Secretary of State treats an impertinent deputation." His new platform bound him to reconstruct the Union without slavery, "to re-admit State after State to all its privileges as soon as it has submitted and enfranchised its working class." Victory now needed only persistence. "And persistence is the one quality Mr. Lincoln is certain not to lack. Slowly as the armies penetrate South, at a pace more like that of colonizers than of soldiers, State after State will be made to choose between a purposeless resistance and the instant attainment of all the rights of freemen."

And the President of the United States would have probably agreed quickly and heartily to nothing in the *Spectator* commentary so much as the line: "What further development time may bring to his mind time alone can show."

McClellan on the high seas was to journey to other lands, a private citizen never again to lead or mislead an army, honored by many who joined with *Leslie's* in the admonition, "Let not political rancor blind his fellow-citizens to his merit and services as a soldier, and his integrity and worth as a gentleman and a Christian." Vallandigham had gone back to law practice in Dayton, Ohio, never again to enter Congress.

In Middletown, Connecticut, torchlight paraders passing the house of a clergyman read a transparency: "The Angel of the Lord Called unto Abraham out of Heaven the Second Time. Genesis 22:15."

Near daybreak and dawn of the morning after election day, in the White House, were covered in Hay's diary: "W.H.L. [Ward Hill Lamon] came to my room to talk over the Chief Justiceship; he goes in for Stanton & thinks, as I am inclined to think, that the President cannot afford to place an enemy in a position so momentous for good or evil.

"He took a glass of whiskey and then, refusing my offer of a bed, went out &, rolling himself up in his cloak, lay down at the President's door; passing the night in that attitude of touching and dumb fidelity, with a small arsenal of pistols & bowie knives around him. In the morning he went away leaving my blankets at my door, before I or the President were awake."

CHAPTER 59

LINCOLN NAMES A CHIEF JUSTICE

BEN WADE, in '64 when it seemed for a time that Lincoln would not be re-elected, told Clark E. Carr of Galesburg, Illinois, "When Judge Taney got sick after Lincoln's election [in November, 1861] I was scared for fear he would die before the inauguration and give Buchanan a chance to appoint his successor, and I prayed to God to spare his life until Buchanan should go out of office. Damned if I did not overdo it. He's going to live out Lincoln's term." The Nicolay and Hay version quoted Wade: "No man ever prayed as I did that Taney might outlive James Buchanan's term, and now I am afraid I have overdone it." This profane wit epitomized a fury and an anxiety that played around the point of who should be named Chief Justice to fill the high seat vacated by the death of Roger B. Taney in October of '64.

From his circuit bench in Baltimore Taney had challenged the legality of several of Lincoln's acts, had declared that the President overrode the Constitution in the denial of a writ of habeas corpus in behalf of a man at Fort McHenry under detention as a recruiting agent of the Confederate Army. The Dred Scott decision of Taney was still considered, in anti-slavery circles, a prejudiced and vile interpretation of the Constitution. When Lincoln in October of '62 appointed three new Justices, legalists were more than anxious about possible havoc from the Supreme Court. Richard Henry Dana, as an attorney of reputation and a citizen loyal to the Union, then wrote to an associate: "Contemplate, my dear sir, the possibility of a Supreme Court deciding that this blockade is illegal! What a position it would put us in before the world whose commerce we have been illegally prohibiting, whom we have unlawfully subjected to a cotton famine and domestic dangers and distress for two years! . . . Such an event is legally possible. . . . There was danger of such a result, when the blockade was new, and before the three new judges were appointed. The bare contemplation of such a possibility makes us pause in our boastful assertion that our written Constitution is clearly the best adapted to all exigencies, the last, best gift to man."

Before Lincoln's three appointees, Davis, Swayne, and Miller, took their seats in latter '62, six Justices, all of them Democrats, three from slave-holding States, composed the Supreme Court. Beside the five Associate Justices Wayne, Catron, Nelson, Grier, and Clifford, there was the pro-Southern Chief Justice Taney, his Dred Scott decision vehemently challenged, his quiet but definite accusations pointed straight at President Lincoln as a usurper of ancient and sacred Anglo-Saxon civil rights. The

Administration had long hoped for the death of "the venerable Chief Justice," said the *Chicago Times* in January of '64, adding, "There is one bulwark of our liberties which the impious hands of Mr. Lincoln and his crazy administration have not been able to strike down . . . the Supreme Court of the United States."

And now what? Now Lincoln and his allegedly "impious" and "crazy" Administration had been given a fresh lease of power. Now what was to happen to the Supreme Court? Who would be named as Chief Justice?

In the press, in political circles, across teacups and over whisky toddies in Washington, there was guess and gossip. The eminent New York attorney William M. Evarts, was he in favor with the President? And Justice Swayne, was it not known his legal abilities were highly regarded by the President? And Justice David Davis, had he not been Lincoln's foremost political manager of influence in the 1860 campaign? Of these there was mention. Little was heard publicly of Attorney General Bates, who mentioned in his diary that his appointment as Chief Justice would be a fitting close to his career. Orville H. Browning noted in a diary entry, October 18, "The President . . . told me that Atto Genl Bates had personally solicited the Chief Justiceship of him." Nor was anything heard publicly of Fessenden for the vacant seat, though Browning on the day after Taney died recorded that he went to Fessenden and asked whether he would take the place "if his friends, without his participation, would procure him to be appointed Chief Justice." Fessenden said any such efforts in his behalf would be in vain; he could not consent. Three days later, on a Sunday evening, Browning called at Stanton's house, finding the Secretary of War had gone to City Point. But Mrs. Stanton was at home. "She expressed to me a great desire," wrote Browning, "to have her husband appointed Chief Justice . . . wished me to see the President upon the subject. I fear Mr Chase's appointment, and am anxious to prevent it. Mr Stanton is an able lawyer, learned in his profession . . . a just man—honest and upright . . . I, therefore, think would be an appointment most fit to be made. I will see the President upon the subject tomorrow."

The mother of Stanton may have told Browning that her son had received from Robert Cooper Grier, an Associate Justice of the United States Supreme Court, a letter dated on the day of the death of Taney, saying in reference to the chief-justiceship, "I think, that the President owes it to you that you should retire in this honorable position." Then again the mother of Stanton may not have known of this letter.

And the astute Browning—astute though neither wise nor subtle—wrote of the next day: "Called on the President and urged on him the appointment of Mr Stanton as chief Justice. He said nothing in reply to what I urged except to admit Mr Stantons ability, and fine qualifications. I think he was pleased with what I said and I have some hope that he will adopt my suggestion."

Another to suggest Stanton for Chief Justice was Bishop Matthew Simpson of the Methodist Church. Lincoln's reply, according to one Stanton biographer, was, "If you will find me another Secretary of War like him, I will gladly appoint him." Another Stanton biographer listed Governor Oliver P. Morton and Governor John A. Andrew as favoring Stanton, and quoted Lincoln's reply to Bishop Simpson: "If Mr. Stanton can find a man he himself will trust as Secretary of War, I'll do it." The second reply sounded more like Lincoln. He knew Stanton would trust no one but Stanton as War Department head. The involved relationship between Lincoln, Stanton, and Bishop Simpson was sketched by General Clinton B. Fisk, a close friend of the bishop: "After Mr. Stanton came into the Cabinet, the bishop's relations with the President became more intimate. The bishop was used by Mr. Lincoln to modify the War Secretary's views, and to gain points which he wished to reach. . . . The bishop was of the same mind as the President [on a more lenient treatment of Border State Confederate sympathizers], and was sent to Stanton to bring him over to the President's way of thinking."

Attorney General Bates wrote in his diary of November 22 that Isaac Newton, a Pennsylvania Quaker serving as Commissioner of Agriculture, who often came to Bates with political news, had called that morning. "He had had a free conversation with the President, who if not overborne by others would gladly make me Ch[ief] J[ustice]—That Chase was turning every stone, to get it, and several others were urged, from different quarters. And (!) that the leading *Friends* would urge me." Then Bates, aware that he had little chance, wrote with grace and finality in his diary: "I am happy in the feeling that the failure to get the place, will be no painful disappointment for my mind is made up to private life and a bare competency. If I get it, it is a mere gratuitous addition, to be held only for a little while, and as a crowning and retiring honor."

Formidable pressure arose for Montgomery Blair. James Gordon Bennett and Thurlow Weed, an odd team of editors, went to Washington and held a conference with Blair on how to stop Chase, whom everyone considered in the lead. Seward was agreed with Weed, it seemed, as so often before. More exceptional was the point of Welles being joined with Seward in opposition to Chase. Old Man Blair, hardly a week after Taney's death, wrote to the President, starting the letter, "I beg you to indulge me with a little conference on paper about a thing which as involving a good deal of egotism, I am ashamed to talk about face to face." He recited the Union loyalty record of the Blairs, his son's "unswerving support of your administration," the "unfaltering attachment to you personally," all of which "fits him to be your representative man at the head of that Bench." The father had hesitations about mentioning the fine qualities of his son, and assured the President he could do nothing better to remove the ostracism which had descended upon Montgomery as a result of his removal from the Cabinet. The father urged the matter with earnestness. Nevertheless, "You will not infer that I set up any claim. You have done enough for the Blairs to entitle you to their gratitude & of their posterity."

Welles recorded his interview with the President on November 26. The

Chase movement was going strong but would not win, believed Welles that day. "I have not much idea that the President will appoint him, nor is it advisable he should," wrote Welles. Having dispatched his routine business, Welles brought up the matter of the next Chief Justice. "The President said there was a great pressure and a good many talked of." After Congress commenced its session in December he would take up the subject. "There is," said the President, "a tremendous pressure just now for Evarts of New York, who, I suppose, is a good lawyer?" This was put inquiringly. Welles estimated that Evarts stood foremost at the New York bar. Welles went on into a little lecture on what kind of a man a Chief Justice should be—judicial, upright, of strict integrity, not too pliant, a statesman and a politician, no partisan. And the man who had these points, Welles went on, was Montgomery Blair. "The President at different points expressed his concurrence in my views, and spoke kindly and complimentarily of Mr. Blair, but did not in any way commit himself, nor did I expect or suppose he would."

After leaving the White House Welles talked with Monty Blair, suggested he would like to see Blair heading the War Department, Blair saying this would be agreeable but Seward wanted a tool there and would be against him. Yet Blair was a little puzzled by an assurance from Seward a week before that Seward favored him for Chief Justice. "I told him," noted Welles, "that he [Seward] could hardly be sincere in this, for Evarts would not consent to be a candidate nor think of it if Seward was not for him. Blair seemed a little shocked with this view of facts, and remarked that if Seward was not for him he was an infernal hypocrite." This was possibly another occasion when Welles's diary surmises went astray, the indications being that Seward had seen that only a united opposition would avail against the Chase movement and therefore Seward was joined with Weed and Bennett in taking Blair as the best hope for blocking Chase.

Many were the embarrassments across November while the President heard a series of delegations and individual callers and gave them no committals. Welles recorded a visit from Postmaster General Dennison, who seemed a little dazed over having called on the President to recommend Justice Swayne, "and the President then remarked that that seemed a settled question in which all were agreed." Dennison acted "embarrassed," judged Welles, "for he feels particularly friendly to Blair." The Secretary of the Navy and the Postmaster General were agreed in thinking it impossible that Chase should receive the appointment, "that it is one which the President cannot properly make." Dennison was sure that if Chase were appointed he would "exhibit his resentments against the President," that Chase never forgot nor forgave those who had once thwarted him. In the same week, however, Stanton was writing to Chase, "My belief is that you will be offered the appointment."

Chase himself hoped for the appointment. He would like to be Chief Justice only a little less than to be President. In his diary entry of July 6 the summer before it was plain that he would have enjoyed seeing a new party formed by his own Republican faction joined to Democrats "cut loose from slavery." If enough Democrats would accommodate to that extent, "I would cheerfully go for any man they might nominate," wrote Chase. He saw Senator Pomeroy and himself in the same boat. "He can not support Lincoln, but won't desert his principles. I'm much of the same sentiments." To various factional friends Chase wrote of lack of harmony, of the mistaken policies of Lincoln, of the follies of Mr. Lincoln's chosen advisers. Summering in the mountains of New England, he hoped for a party revolt. The *Springfield Republican* editor, Samuel Bowles, wrote September 4 in a letter: "Chase is going around, peddling his griefs in private ears and sowing dissatisfaction about Lincoln."

With the fall of Atlanta and the brightening Union outlook Chase changed his tune. "I have seen the President twice," he wrote in his diary of a mid-September visit to Washington. . . . "Both times third persons were present, and there was nothing like private conversation. His manner was cordial and so were his words; and I hear of nothing but good-will from him. But he is not at all demonstrative, either in speech or manner. I feel that I do not know him, and I found no action on what he says or does. . . . I have been told that the President said he and I could not get along together in the Cabinet. Doubtless there was a difference of temperament, and on some points, of judgment. I may have been too earnest and eager, while I thought him not earnest enough and too slow. On some occasions, indeed, I found that it was so." Thus on and on went Chase mirroring himself in his diary as a man of almost entire justice having many perfections. "Mr. Lincoln sympathized more with those who assailed and disparaged than with those who maintained the views held by me." There would have been no difficulty "could he have understood my sentiments just as they were." At home in Ohio during the fall campaign Chase brought himself to make an open declaration favoring Lincoln as against McClellan for President. On election day he voted the Union ticket and wired the President Ohio and Indiana results were "all right."

A delegation from the Union League Club of Philadelphia came to the White House, spoke for Chase, and read a signed memorial of reasons why. The President, "in a deliberate manner," according to press accounts, replied, "Will you do me the favor to leave that paper with me? I want it in order that, if I appoint Mr. Chase, I may show the friends of the other persons for whom the office is solicited by how powerful an influence and by what strong personal recommendations the claims of Mr. Chase were supported." The Union Leaguers from Philadelphia were pleased and satisfied at this. Then they noticed the President had not finished what he meant to say. He had merely paused. Now he went on. "And I want the paper also in order that, if I should appoint any other person, I may show his friends how powerful an influence and what strong personal recommendations I was obliged to disregard in appointing him." So the Philadelphians walked out knowing no more than when they came.

Senator Henry Wilson of Massachusetts, as Nicolay later gathered from a conversation with him, one day met Montgomery Blair near the War Department. Wilson heard Blair asking him to put in a good word with the President, and was startled at the confident tone of Blair's statement that Chase would certainly not be nominated. Wilson went at once to the President, repeated to the President arguments already made in favor of Chase, saying the President could well afford to overlook the harsh and indecorous things Chase had said during the summer.

"Oh! as to that," replied Lincoln, according to Wilson, "I care nothing. Of Mr. Chase's ability and of his soundness on the general issues of the war there is, of course, no question. I have only one doubt about his appointment. He is a man of unbounded ambition, and has been working all his life to become President. That he can never be; and I fear that if I make him chief-justice he will simply become more restless and uneasy and neglect the place in his strife and intrigue to make himself President. If I were sure that he would go on the bench and give up his aspirations and do nothing but make himself a great judge, I would not hesitate a moment."

Richard Henry Dana and Judge E. R. Hoar called together at the White House and with perfect courtesy told Lincoln they had their impression of what sort of a man ought to be named Chief Justice; if however, as rumor had it, Lincoln had determined to appoint Chase they would not proceed to suggest men in their opinion admirably fitted. Lincoln's reply as Judge Hoar afterward wrote it: "Mr. Chase is a very able man. He is a very ambitious man and I think on the subject of the presidency a little insane. He has not always behaved very well lately and people say to me, 'Now is the time to *crush him out.*' Well, I'm not in favor of crushing anybody out! If there is anything that a man can do and do it well, I say let him do it. Give him a chance."

With several Iowans Congressman Josiah Bushnell Grinnell urged the President to appoint Chase. The President was courteous and noncommittal. Later alone with Grinnell, Lincoln asked whether appointment as Chief Justice ought not to banish political ambition, adding that outsiders were of good hope "but I must do the right thing in this critical hour."

Another who saw Lincoln at the instigation of Chase was former Congressman Albert Gallatin Riddle of Ohio. "Mr. Chase desired that I should interview the President on this grave matter," wrote Riddle. "I undertook it reluctantly, but his wish was law." The White House conversation covered vital points. Riddle gave his record of it:

MR. LINCOLN. Do you expect that Chase will relinquish his desire to become President?

MR. RIDDLE. Mr. Chase's ambition springs from a consciousness of great ability to serve. It is said that a man once bitten of the Presidency dies of it.

MR. LINCOLN. I should deplore seeing a man trying to swap the Chief-Justiceship for the Presidency.

MR. RIDDLE. Mr. President, you are fully aware that Mr. Chase is a man of the most elevated character, and that personal dignity in him rises to grandeur. A traffic such as you suggest would be impossible. There is a consideration which I beg to suggest. The weighty matters involved in this war have been thoroughly discussed by Congress and the President. They are undergoing the arbitrament of battle. They will next inevitably be submitted to the Supreme Court for the last and final human decision. Do you know a man in the world to whom you would sooner submit them?

MR. LINCOLN. Would you have me pack the Supreme Court, Mr. Riddle?

MR. RIDDLE. Would you appoint a man with no preconceived notions of law? There is not a man at our bar whom you or I would call a lawyer, who has not convictions on these questions.

MR. LINCOLN. This is a matter for reflection.

Mr. Riddle then departed. He had come reluctant and he went away likewise.

Another statement by Riddle of what was said in this interview was partly the same in content. But the feeling was deeper and the tone of language more blunt. This other statement ran:

> After hearing what I had to say, Mr. Lincoln asked, "Will this content Mr. Chase?"
>
> "It is said that those bitten of the Presidency die of it," I replied. His smile showed he would not take that answer. I added: "Mr. Chase is conscious of ability to serve the country as President. We should expect the greatest from him."
>
> "He would not disappoint you, were it in his reach. But I should be sorry to see a Chief-Justice anxious to swap for it."
>
> I said then what I had already said to Mr. Chase: that I would rather be the Chief-Justice than the President. I urged that the purity and elevation of Mr. Chase's character guaranteed the dignity of the station from all compromise; that momentous questions must arise, involving recent exercises of power, without precedents to guide the court; that the honor of the Government would be safe in the hands of Mr. Chase.
>
> "Would you pack the Supreme Court?" he asked, a little sharply.
>
> "Would you have a Judge with no preconceived notions of law?" was my response.
>
> "True, true," was his laughing reply; "how could I find anyone, fit for the place, who has not some definite notions on all questions likely to arise?"

Chase personally seemed to have high hopes at first. Later he was not so sure what the President would do. To Senator John Sherman he wrote November 12 that he would be on his way to Washington if it were not for "a sort of indelicacy" that could be twisted to mean he was seeking an office. From his Cincinnati home he was writing: "I think it due to myself as well as to the President to await his decision here; though, if appointed, I hope the appointment will be considered as made from the country at large rather than from Ohio alone. . . . Please write me, if you can, when the President will act."

Days passed into weeks. From the President came no word. The President was delaying. The deliberation of the President seemed ominous to Chase. He wrote Senator Sherman on December 2 that he was starting for Washington, that after a dedication speech for a Methodist college at Pittsburgh "a number of leading men of the denomination assured me of the profound wishes of themselves . . . for my appointment." The church sentiment for him seemed to be almost "universal," wrote Chase. "So that I cannot doubt that the President's adherence to his declared intention is more important to our cause and to his administration than it is to me personally. Not to be appointed after such declarations and expressions would, no doubt, be a mortification; but it would not, I think, be any serious injury to me."

On Chase's suggestion Senator Sherman called on the President and spoke for Chase. "We had a brief conversation," noted Sherman. "He asked me pointedly whether if Chase was appointed he would be satisfied, or whether he would immediately become a candidate for President." Sherman then gave his opinion that an appointment as Chief Justice ought to and would satisfy Chase's ambition.

Chase's right-hand man in the Treasury Department, Hugh McCulloch, Comptroller of the Currency, an intimate and trusted friend, was called in one day by Lincoln, who seemed to McCulloch "under the apprehension that he [Chase] might be somewhat rigorous in his judgment of some of the executive acts, and especially those of the Secretary of War, if suit should be brought involving questions that could only be settled by the Supreme Court." To McCulloch the President spoke his fears that Chase as Chief Justice might render decisions that the Government had been too high-handed in certain actions. "Why, Mr. President," McCulloch said, "you have no reason for fears on that score. Mr. Chase is in the same box with you and Mr. Stanton. He favored and advised, as he has himself informed me, the dispersion by force of the Maryland Legislature, and if anything more illegal than that has been done, I have not heard of it." This was about all. "The President," noted McCulloch, "did not say that reminded him of a story, but he laughed heartily, and the interview was ended."

Behind the scenes and away from public view it seemed that Lincoln had only one distinct doubt about appointing Chase. This doubt he spoke to one after another of those who came to the front for Chase. So haunting was this doubt that an intention began shaping. Why not send for Chase and say frankly to him that the way was open to him to become the greatest Chief Justice the Supreme Court had ever had if he would dismiss at once and forever the subject of the Presidency from his mind? But when Lincoln broached this to Senator Sumner, noted Nicolay and Hay, "he saw in a moment's conversation how liable to misapprehension such action would be . . . the construction which Mr. Chase would inevitably place upon such a proposition coming from his twice successful rival."

When one day Nicolay brought a letter from Chase, Lincoln asked, "What is it about?"

"Simply a kind and friendly letter."

Lincoln, without reading it and with a shrewd smile: "File it with his other recommendations."

Likewise behind the scenes were at least two men to whom Lincoln had come near a complete assurance that he would name Chase for Chief

Justice. As far back as the spring of '64 he had spoken to Sumner of his favoring Chase for Chief Justice when that seat should become vacant. To the philosopher Franz Lieber, Sumner wrote immediately after Taney's death: "Last spring, after a long conversation, Mr. Lincoln promised me to tender the chief-justiceship to Chase. He has referred to that promise since his break with Chase, and declared his willingness to nominate him." Sumner had this in mind in writing to Chase just after Taney's death: "I have written to the President without delay, and urged anew the considerations to which he yielded last spring, in favor of your nomination as Chief-Justice. Of course, you will accept. Yes! accept, and complete our great reformation by purifying the Constitution, and upholding those measures by which the republic will be saved. God bless you!" Chase wrote swiftly to Sumner, voicing his gratitude, adding that he had heard nothing definite of authority from Washington, that what he did hear led him to think the President was of the same mind as in the last spring, that while it was not correct for a man to say what he would do in regard to an appointment not offered him, "it is certainly not wrong to say to you that I should accept."

To the President, Sumner had already written his plea, "A chief-justice is needed whose position on the slavery question is already fixed and will not need argument of counsel to convert him." What was Lincoln's response to this continuous pressure from Sumner? Did he go so far as to offer Sumner the seat vacated by Taney's death? If so the fact would be based on only one witness, a former New York Congressman, a European traveler and art collector, Caleb Lyon, friend and admirer of Sumner. "Soon after Chief Justice Taney's death," wrote Lyon, "he [Sumner] showed me a card from the President, upon which was written, 'Honorable Charles Sumner: The vacant chief justiceship is placed at your disposal. A. Lincoln.' He [Sumner] then said, 'There was a time when this office would have been the realized dream of my youth; but now it must not, cannot be. The breach between Mr. Chase and the President is growing wider and wider, and this will close it. No personal sacrifice is too great, nor can anything tempt me to desert my post. The Republican party must remain intact until its mission is fulfilled.' " To this Lyon added the point that Sumner scrupulously restrained himself from letting any word get to Chase that Sumner himself could have had the appointment. Sumner's secretary noted that on November 20, to a friend who had written that he wished Sumner could be named as the new Chief Justice, the Senator wrote that he was not a candidate for the office, had never been, that he felt "the grandeur of the judicial office," but he was out of the question for it and still convinced that Chase should have it. "The President, in my opinion, errs by his delay."

To another man, Fessenden, Lincoln had spoken with some assurance in favor of Chase. Eight days after Taney died Fessenden wrote to Chase: "I think there can be no doubt about your appointment to the chief-justiceship. The President said to me of his own motion, 'I have not forgotten our conversation,' but as things were going well, he thought it best not to make any appointment or say any thing about it until the election was over. Your friends need give themselves no anxiety, whatever may be said by the papers. I believe all is right." A month later Fessenden was writing Chase he had no doubt Chase would be Chief Justice. "I have neither seen nor heard any thing to indicate a change of intention." Stanton at the same time was writing Chase: "In regard to the chief-justiceship, I learn from outside sources that Swayne is the most active and Blair the most confident of the candidates. My belief is that you will be offered the appointment."

To still another man Lincoln seemed to have given a flat prediction that no one else but Chase would be named. Noah Brooks broached the subject and noted: "Mr. Lincoln had been, for him, very gay and cheery; but as soon as Chase and the chief-justiceship were mentioned, his visage lengthened, and with great seriousness he pointed to a pile of telegrams and letters on his table and said: 'I have been all day, and yesterday and the day before, besieged by messages from my friends all over the country, as if there were a determination to put up the bars between Governor Chase and myself.' Then after a pause, 'But I shall nominate him for chief justice nevertheless.' " And, continued Brooks, "It was therefore with amusement that I learned from one of Chase's most ardent friends, about an hour later, that 'Lincoln was not great enough to nominate Chase as chief justice'; and with inward satisfaction I bore in silence much contumely and reproach from Chase's fast friends."

From active enemies of Chase in Ohio came spoken and written protests against his appointment. From Treasury Department officials, from the Blair and other groups, came many descriptions of Chase as too partisan, too ignorant of men, too much of a grumbler and a marplot. "The President received them not too affably," noted Nicolay and Hay: he heard with respect any points of merit against Chase but when they tried to remind him of how and when Chase had sought to undermine him, "he sternly checked them." The secretaries believed it was altogether probable that Lincoln intended from the first to appoint Chase but was resolved to say nothing about it until he was ready to act. To Nicolay he said, using boyhood Kentucky lingo, "I shall be very 'shut pan' about this matter."

To the young Illinois Congressman Shelby M. Cullom came the report that when Chase letters with mean insinuations about Lincoln were offered for the President's reading, he commented, "If Mr. Chase has said some hard things about me, I in turn have said some hard things about him, which, I guess, squares the account." Likewise on a similar occasion, "I know meaner things about Mr. Chase than any of these men can tell me."

The first week of December had come. Congress had assembled.

On December 6, at whatever risk and not unaware there were risks, guided by joined motives of statecraft and political balances, the President named Chase for Chief Justice.

"He communicated his intention to no one," noted his secretaries. He wrote out the nomination with his own hand in a script exceptionally large and signed it not as ordinarily, "A. Lincoln," but with the more rarely used name of "Abraham Lincoln."

Addressed to the Senate of the United States it read: "I nominate Salmon P. Chase, of Ohio, to be Chief Justice of the Supreme Court of the United States, *vice* Roger B. Taney deceased." Without reference to a committee and with no discussion the Senate at once unanimously confirmed the appointment.

At the doorway of his home in Washington when he arrived that night Chase met his brilliant, handsome, and ambitious daughter, Kate Chase Sprague. She saluted her father by his new title of Chief Justice. And they were very happy together about it. Thus the version that Nicolay and Hay, and others, gave of how the news of the appointment first came to Chase. A friend of Chase, however, one Robert Bruce Warden, later a biographer of Chase, had another version. He said he had it from Senator Charles Sumner shortly after Chase's death.

"I called on Mr. Sumner," ran Warden's account. . . . "It was evidently hard for the great man from Massachusetts to say much of Chase. For five words about our hero [Chase], he gave me twenty-five about himself. But, after all, I learned some new things about Chase, and among them an anecdote, which, I have learned, Mr. Sumner related to at least one person other than myself. Mr. Sumner was the first to tell Mr. Chase of his confirmation as Chief Justice. As he came out of the room in which that information had been imparted, he met Mrs. Sprague, who, shaking her right fore-finger at him, said: 'And you, too, Mr. Sumner? You, too, in this business of shelving papa? But never mind! I will defeat you all!' "

Shortly after hearing this anecdote from Sumner, Warden heard it from Justice Swayne of the Supreme Court as Swayne heard it from Sumner. So it would seem that whatever may have happened to Chase himself regarding his ambition to be President, his daughter was unchanged. She would plan and plot to the last in the hope of seeing her father—and herself—in the White House.

For the hour, Chase was less dissatisfied with himself and the country and its prospects than at any time since he had been Secretary of the Treasury. He took pen and paper. He wrote to the President: "Before I sleep I must thank you for this mark of your confidence, and especially for the manner in which the nomination was made. I will never forget either, and trust you will never regret either. Be assured that I prize your confidence and good-will more than nomination to office."

Congressman John B. Alley, so he wrote, had entered the President's library the morning of that day to hear a greeting, "I have just sent Mr. Chase word that he is to be appointed Chief Justice, and you are the first man I have told of it." Alley said that, considering what Chase had been saying about the Administration, "Mr. President, this is an exhibition of magnanimity and patriotism that could hardly be expected of anyone." Alley remembered and Lincoln had not forgotten that Alley with Senator Sumner had called one day to plead for Chase and had heard Lincoln urge the defects of Chase so that, as Alley phrased it, "We were both discouraged and made up our minds that the President did not mean to appoint Mr. Chase." Now Lincoln was replying, "Although I may have appeared to you and to Mr. Sumner to have been opposed to Chase's appointment, there never has been a moment since the breath left old Taney's body that I did not conceive it to be the best thing to do to appoint Mr. Chase to that high office; and to have done otherwise I should have been recreant to my convictions of duty to the Republican party and to the country." Alley repeated that the action was magnanimous and patriotic. Lincoln: "As to his talk about me, I do not mind that. Chase is, on the whole, a pretty good fellow and a very able man. His only trouble is that he has 'the White House fever' a little too bad, but I hope this may cure him and that he will be satisfied."

At the Cabinet meeting that day Lincoln gave his high advisers not a word about naming Chase. "I am sorry he should have withheld the fact, which we all knew in less than one hour," wrote Welles. . . . "Dennison informs me that he went to the theatre with the President last evening and parted with him after 11 o'clock, and not a word was said to him on the subject. I hope the selection may prove a good one. I would not have advised it. . . . Chase has mental power and resources, but he is politically ambitious and restless, prone to, but not very skillful in, intrigue and subtle management. . . . He will be likely to use the public for political advancement." Eight days later, December 15, Welles wrote that the "malcontents," meaning the antislavery radicals, were "not in better mood" than before the election. "Chase's appointment gives satisfaction to Senator Sumner and a few others; but there is general disappointment. Public sentiment had settled down under the conviction that he [Chase] could not have the position. Sumner helped to secure it for him. The President told Chandler of New Hampshire, who remonstrated against such selections, that he would rather have swallowed his buckhorn chair than to have nominated Chase." This last sentence of Welles's diary had a remark perfectly like Lincoln. Yet would Lincoln have made so decisive a remark in connection with Chase for Chief Justice? No one else mentioned hearing him say anything at all like it. It may have been more likely that Welles in his fluent diary entry applied to the chief-justiceship a remark of Lincoln to Zach Chandler in connection with Chase's summer resignation from the Cabinet, when it was in character for Lincoln to say, "I would rather swallow this buckhorn chair than not to accept this fourth resignation of Chase."

More of portent was Welles's paragraph in his diary of the same day. "Sumner declares to me that Chase will retire from the field of politics and not be a candidate for the Presidency. I questioned it, but S. said with emphasis it was so. He had assured the President that Chase would retire from party politics. I have no doubt Sumner believes it . . . as if he had assurance. My own convictions are that, if he lives, Chase will be a candidate and his restless and ambitious mind is already at work. It is his nature."

As events moved they were to prove the guess of Welles correct. In the phrasing of Nicolay and Hay: "After all, the fears of the President in regard to the Chief-Justice were better founded than his hopes. Mr. Chase took his place on the bench with a conscientious desire to do his whole duty in his great office . . . but he could not discharge the political affairs of the country from his mind. He still considered himself called upon to counteract the mischievous tendencies of the President towards conciliation and hasty reconstruction. His slighting references to him [the President] in his [Chase's] letters and diaries continued from the hour he took his place on the bench." Nicolay and Hay took it as unfair when the Supreme Court should come to pass on the legal status of greenbacks "that the father of the National currency should ever disown his own offspring."

Congressman George S. Boutwell wrote of his calling to say to the President he was glad Chase had been named. He heard the President's response that there were three reasons why Chase should be appointed and one why he should not be. "In the first place he occupies a larger space in the public mind, with reference to the office, than any other person. Then we want a man who will sustain the Legal Tender Act and the Proclamation of Emancipation. We cannot ask a candidate what he would do; and if we did and he should answer, we should only despise him for it. But he wants to be President and if he doesn't give that up it will be a great injury to him and a great injury to me. He can never be President."

The *New York World* was baffled. Having lost the election, the hour was such that it could not resume its tone of eight months before when it maintained that Chase and Lincoln in seeking presidential nominations were giving favors to "shoddy bank men" who sought only to "line their own pockets," this leading to a question and answer: "What can be said in favor of men like Chase and Lincoln, who can thus only study their own selfish interests in this extremity of their country's peril? Such men have just intellect and heart enough to match coppers on the corpse of their mother!"

To the *Cincinnati Gazette* Whitelaw Reid wrote a long account of the "pressure" on the President to appoint Chase. From this account the *Crisis* said it was evident the contest for the chief-justiceship was carried on "in the same manner as a canvass for any other fat position," with "log-rolling, lying, trickery," on both sides. The President had, since the appointment, spoken very frankly of his reasons for it, the *Cincinnati Gazette* related, quoting the President as saying: "I could not fail to recognize Mr. Chase's fitness for the place, or the popular desire that he should be elevated to it. I wanted a man certain to sustain the emancipation and financial policy of the Administration. I could not ask a man beforehand how he would decide such questions if he was appointed. The man who would answer an interrogatory of the kind would be unfit for the place. But I *knew* where Mr. Chase stood, and felt sure that all these great questions would, in his hands, be safe."

Opposition partisans and critics agreed with the *Crisis:* "Mr. Chase was certainly a party to the emancipation proclamation, and he is the author of the financial policy of the Administration. Does President Lincoln understand that Chase, as Chief Justice, will sit in judgment on his own schemes?

Is the man who originated the financial policy of the Administration, whose reputation is intimately connected with the greenback bubble, to assume the judicial robes and decide upon the legality or unconstitutionality of his own policy? It seems that the President *does* so understand, and that he boldly avows this understanding to be the cogent reason for the appointment he has made. Who can measure the depth of degradation to which the administrators of the government of Washington, Jefferson, and Jackson, have fallen, when such infamous corruption as this, is conceived, avowed and executed by the highest officer in the land?"

Such Administration opponents did not refresh the memories of their readers on the point that the dead Roger B. Taney had been Secretary of the Treasury under President Andrew Jackson, who named Taney Chief Justice with tacit understandings but no pledges of what would be Taney's course on the bench regarding Jackson's policies.

The *Crisis* of course was the voice of partisan politics keeping to the high-pitched tone of the recent campaign. Its main point could be laughed off with Lincoln's acknowledgment to Riddle, "True, true, how could I find anyone, fit for the place, who has not some definite notions on all questions likely to arise?" Yet this would not cover the other point, on which Lincoln had shown plenty of anxiety. Chase was not definitely an able jurist. He might become one. By forgetting he was a politician he might grace his high place. But if he again spent his time seeking the Presidency, he would fall short of the great jurist Lincoln hoped to see robed as chief on the Supreme Court bench.

Yet it seemed furthermore that Lincoln was meeting stern political necessity in naming Chase. A war was being fought by the Union Government for the sake of certain issues or questions. What greater folly could be thought of than to put on the Supreme Court bench a Chief Justice who might be hesitant or evasive or shifting? This lay in the mind of Lincoln and of many who approved the naming of Chase. As Lincoln was quoted, "These great questions would, in his [Chase's] hands, be safe." This was one end Lincoln tried to serve. The other was strictly political. As Nicolay and Hay observed, "The name of Mr. Chase had been especially pressed upon the President by the public men who represented the most advanced antislavery sentiment of the North." Lincoln for his own political reasons was giving them what they wanted. He was hoping for more harmony toward his own plans for reconstruction in the South.

As the author of the National Bank Act, as an acquaintance of August Belmont who proposed in the summer of '64 the conditions under which he would join the Democratic party, as a man of "a certain solid weight of character," Chase was not offensive to a large section of conservatives. The appointment, once made, met with little opposition, and, noted Nicolay and Hay, was "received with the greatest satisfaction throughout the Union." The face of Chase on the $1 greenbacks had become more familiar in the eyes of the people than that of any other man in America. His explanation was natural to him. "I had put the President's head on the higher priced notes, and my own, as was becoming, on the smaller ones." Continuously Chase measured up to the estimate of General Egbert Viele, from observation on a Treasury Department steamer trip down the Potomac: "Had he been more cordial he would have been less dignified, and had he been more dignified he would have been less cordial."

Nicolay and Hay in their review of the event faintly and gently implied what was more explicitly stated by Noah Brooks, who held it "unfortunate that some of the new Chief Justice's overzealous and indiscreet friends gleefully claimed that President Lincoln was coerced into making that appointment, and scornfully insisted that it was a popular choice forced upon the President by men who controlled confirmations in the Senate." To Brooks it was lamentable "that when Lincoln willingly paid a noble honor to one who had been his competitor for the presidential nomination, he could not have at least the poor satisfaction of knowing that the purity of his motives and the fixity of his intention were appreciated by those who made Chase and Chase's ambitions the excuse for conspiring against the good name of Lincoln." As a matter of history, wrote Brooks, "it should be recorded that Lincoln never intended to appoint any other man than Chase to the chief-justiceship, and never for one moment had he entertained the name of any other person. It was a peculiar trait of Lincoln that, in order to preclude all possibility of doubt in his own mind concerning the expediency of any contemplated act, he would state to those with whom he came in contact many doubts and objections not his own, but those of others, for the express purpose of being confirmed and fixed in his own judgment. . . . As a matter of truth, it may be said that when Sumner and others importuned President Lincoln to nominate Chase to the chief-justiceship, and he replied in a doubtful manner, he had really made up his mind to nominate Chase."

Were the lines being more sharply drawn for a more continuous challenge by Congress of the executive power? It seemed so when in latter November Attorney General Bates resigned because of age and long service and to fill the vacant office the President sent to the Senate the appointment of James Speed of Kentucky. This brother of Joshua Speed, Lincoln's old bosom friend, had been a Union loyalist from the first, was credited among the foremost who had been outspoken, raised troops, and otherwise served in practical ways to keep Kentucky in the Union. As an able attorney his record was unspotted.

The Senate Judiciary Committee held up the President's nomination several days, according to Noah Brooks, not because they hesitated at confirming Speed, but, as one of that committee said, "to convey a mild insinuation to the President that they did not know who James Speed of Kentucky was."

On the point of ability the retiring Attorney General had favored his first assistant, Titian J. Coffey of Pennsylvania, to succeed him, it seemed. And according to Coffey, Lincoln had sent for him and asked for help, saying: "My Cabinet has *shrunk up* North, and I must find a Southern man. I suppose if the twelve Apostles were to be chosen nowadays, the shrieks of locality would have to be heeded. I have invited Judge Holt to become Attorney-General, but he seems unwilling to undertake the Supreme Court work. I want you to see him, remove his objection if you can, and bring me his answer."

Coffey shortly returned from this errand. He had seen Judge Holt, explained that he had charge of the government cases in the Supreme Court and that they were in such shape that Holt need not appear unless he chose to do so. Holt had decided to decline Lincoln's invitation. The President, on hearing this from Coffey, said: "Then I will offer it to James Speed of Louisville, a man I know well, though not so well as I know his brother Joshua. That, however, is not strange, for I slept with Joshua for four years, and I suppose I ought to know him well. But James is an honest man and a gentleman, and if he comes here you will find he is one of those well-poised men, not too common here, who are not spoiled by a big office."

The Senate Judiciary Committee's delay in confirming Lincoln's latest Cabinet appointee brought embarrassment. Five times the somber and dignified old Supreme Court room was filled to its limits with people who came to see Chase sworn in as Chief Justice. Five times these crowds filed out from the august chamber in disappointment. The prescribed forms required that the Attorney General of the United States should put his seal on the letters patent of a Justice of the Supreme Court. And as the matter stood there was no such Attorney General. One had resigned. Another was not yet confirmed. The Senate Judiciary Committee was having fun, of its own grim kind, with the Chief Executive of the United States, resulting in what was unpleasant sport for their friend the newly appointed Chief Justice.

On December 15 the crowd was there for the sixth time, the solemn old room overflowing with dignitaries, personages, ladies in crinoline, Congressmen, foreign Ministers, bureau officials. So great was the rush that into the section reserved for the bar, for lawyers licensed to Supreme Court practice, went a human crush, mostly women. There sat famous lawyers, Tom Ewing, Reverdy Johnson, Seward, Ben Wade, many others. Senator Sprague and Kate Chase Sprague were there, Kate never looking more handsome and impudent. To the rear of the Supreme Bench, on the right, leaning against a marble pillar in a fine and studied pose, in view of all, was a classical-featured one; all knew he was feeling good that day. It was Charles Sumner.

An usher called in a loud and official tone, "The Honorable Justices of the Supreme Court of the United States." Through a side entrance came the gowned justices, headed by Justice Swayne, the senior member, arm in arm with Salmon Portland Chase. The Justices took their seats, bowing left and right. The bar, standing, bowed in return. The new Chief Justice came toward his chair, received a paper from Justice Swayne, and in a clear but tremulous voice read: "I, Salmon P. Chase, do solemnly swear that I will, as Chief Justice of the Supreme Court of the United States, administer equal and exact justice to the poor and to the rich, in accordance with the Constitution and the laws of the United States, to the best of my ability." Then, laying down the paper, he lifted his right hand, looked upward to the noble dome of the old room, and with deep feeling, "So help me God."

Over the room was a breathless hush. The Chief Justice took his seat. The clerk, in a trembling voice, read aloud the letters patent of the Chief Justice. Routine business began. The crowd had witnessed a ceremony of historic importance. They began moving out. Noah Brooks came face to face with Senator Ben Wade. He was surprised. The tough old Buckeye had tears in his eyes and was saying with grim feeling, "Lord, now lettest thou thy servant depart in peace, for mine eyes have seen thy salvation."

At the White House Lincoln had received the Electoral College members from Maryland. They spoke their satisfaction over the Chase appointment. Of the President's reply Brooks noted his saying "he trusted the appointment would be for the best." The country, he added, needed some assurances on two points of great national importance; and there was an assurance that could be better given by the character and well-known opinions of the appointee than by any verbal pledges. By the appointment of Mr. Chase all holders of United States securities in America and Europe felt assured that the financial policy of the Government would be upheld by its highest judicial tribunal. In sustaining that policy, Judge Chase would be only sustaining himself, for he was the author of it. "The other point to which Lincoln referred," continued Brooks, "was that relating to the constitutionality of the emancipation policy of the Government. He said that other distinguished gentlemen had been named as competent to undertake the great trust now borne by Judge Chase; but these did not bear the same relation to those important issues that Chase did, although they were doubtless equally sound." To this report of what Lincoln stated so explicitly to friends of Chase, Noah Brooks added his speculative thought: "When we reflect that the financial policy of the Government, so far as it was involved in the legal-tender law, was subsequently disapproved by the distinguished author of it [Chief Justice Chase], we may well wonder what Lincoln would have thought."

Strictly confidential, for the private eye of an old friend and crony, one of the Associate Justices of the Supreme Court wrote briefly his dominant impression of the naming of the Court's newest member. This was Lincoln's earlier appointee, the old Eighth Circuit friend, David Davis. Four days after Chase was sworn in he wrote to General William W. Orme of Bloomington, Illinois: "The appointment of Chief Justice did not take me, from what I heard, much by surprise. It is not the part of a good or deep philosophy to make yourself unhappy about what is inevitable. . . . This nation are really a people of office seekers."

And in the Buckeye State some who had politically long known Salmon P. Chase were unkind enough to recall a saying they had heard from him—"Be satisfied with skim milk when you can't get cream."

The daughters of the dead Roger B. Taney were before long to go to work as ordinary clerks in the Treasury Department of the national capital where their father had been the supreme interpreter of the basic legal instrument of the nation. He had lived plainly, wanted little money, was beyond the reach of money influence, and his small investments had melted away with the fears and changes of war. His Dred Scott decision, however, stayed as a shadow.

Trumbull of Illinois reported a bill to place a bust of Taney in the Supreme Court room. Trumbull was the only Republican to speak for it. Sumner, Wilson, Hale, Wade, lashed out as though a crime were proposed instead of a humble emblem. Senator Reverdy Johnson of Maryland, long a friend of Taney, in turn lashed out, lost his control, never had hurled more bitter phrases at Northern colleagues. Recess suspended debate. The bill lay over.

Nine years later Chase was to die. Then a resolution was to come before the Senate to place side by side in the Supreme Court room busts of both Taney and Chase, the resolution passing unanimously and without debate. On that day, however, there would have been debate had not Sumner lain sick, had not Sumner been in bed with the malady that in two months would send him to join the Great Majority where Chase and Taney had gone.

CHAPTER 60

THE BITTER YEAR OF '64 COMES TO A CLOSE

THE days passed and Grant's point telegraphed to Lincoln held true. The November election counted for more than a great battle won. It answered many questions.

On November 28, 1864, "the minimum standard of height for recruits" was fixed in a War Department order "at five feet instead of five feet three as heretofore."

Would the war go on? Yes, more brutally than before. Would conscription go on? Yes, and with less outspoken opposition. Those claiming free speech and a free press? They would be less noisy and foul, though not giving up old habits. Some were a little stunned and helpless. And the propertied institution of slavery, sanctioned by the Constitution? Sooner or later it would go—the question still waited answer as to how it would have its legal status swept away. And the Union of States? The old map, the same rivers, mountain ranges, coast lines, would hold—out of further turmoil, agony, and high cost it would go on. These were dominant impressions as the war moved into a new phase.

The American future, as Motley at Vienna saw it, would be "more really prosperous" than ever in the past. "The volcano above which we have been

The United States Supreme Court in '64, shortly after Lincoln's appointment of a new Chief Justice. Left to right: *Seated*, *David Davis, *Noah Haynes Swayne, Robert Cooper Grier, James Moore Wayne, *Salmon Portland Chase, Samuel Nelson, Nathan Clifford, *Samuel Freeman Miller, *Stephen Johnson Field—those starred appointed by Lincoln. *Standing*, D. W. Middleton, clerk

From the Meserve collection

William Tecumseh Sherman

From the author's collection

Sherman's army enters Atlanta

From a stereograph in the Barrett collection

living in a fool's paradise of forty years, dancing and singing and imagining ourselves going ahead, will have done its worst, and spent itself, I trust, forever."

To guide a course beyond that volcano was Lincoln's task. Huge labors were yet called for. He would dig deeper in himself for faith to match those who had renewed trust in him. He could be glad the world-traveled English geologist Charles Lyell, a Union loyalist, was writing of human strata in America: "Whatever it may be for the rich, I certainly think that for the millions it is the happiest country in the world."

An opposition was regaining its tongue, biding its time, hoping again sometime to ride into power, keeping its organization intact. The *New York World* was to continue its thrusts. "If Mr. Lincoln trod in crooked ways to secure his re-election, the easiest way for him to extricate himself now is by a frank adherence to the Constitution."

The London *Times*, having in '62 said that Mr. Lincoln had "played his last card," was out of favor as a prophet since the November election had given Mr. Lincoln more and higher cards. The primitive fury, the low passions sought to be raised, by this pretended recorder of events and personages, this whited sepulcher of journals, had failed to come. Picturing a dull, vindictive instigator of Negro uprisings, the *Times* had said, "When blood begins to flow and shrieks come piercing through the darkness, Mr. Lincoln will wait until the rising flames tell that all is consummated, and then he will rub his hands and think that revenge is sweet." This repeated forecast was now hardly worth offering a public jaded by it. Performing armies and an upsurge of American voters had repudiated as false and malicious the London *Times* estimate of Lincoln: "Here is a would-be conqueror and a would-be extirpator who is not quite safe in his seat of government . . . who by his pompous proclamations . . . is more like a Chinaman beating his two swords together to frighten the enemy."

Of the London *Times* as not at all the voice of the English people, Goldwin Smith, Canadian-born, professor of modern history at Oxford University, England, wrote in the December, 1864, *Atlantic Monthly*. The first owner of the *Times*, who had built it into power, was a man with many faults, yet "a man of the people" at war with the aristocracy to the end. "His heir, the present proprietor, born in the purple . . . a wealthy landed gentleman," sitting in Parliament for a constituency of landlords, hoped for a peerage. "It is accusing him of no crime to suppose, that, so far as he controls the 'Times,' it takes the bias of his class," its voice "not that of the English people, but of a rich conservative squire."

And the editor, employed by the owner, was much talked of in England as a toady of the aristocracy: "The lords of the Money Power, the thrones and dominions of Usury." These potentates, ran Professor Smith's version, which he intended as an open letter to all Americans, "happen . . . to be unfriendly to your cause. . . . Caressed by peers and millionaires, the editor of the 'Times' could hardly fail to express the feelings of peers and millionaires towards a Republic in distress." The *Times* editor, one could think, had overacted his part. "No English gentleman would deliberately sanction the torrent of calumny and insult which the 'Times' has poured on this nation. There are penalties for common offenders . . . none for those who scatter firebrands among nations."

Now however a change was to come. The *Times* "must veer with victory," must eat its words as the Union armies marched where the *Times* had said they couldn't go. If the *Times* in the process did not lose authority its readers would be "not only prejudiced, but idiotic." Thus an eminent Canadian scholar publicly apologized to America for a newspaper that garbled and adulterated its news, poisoned the facts, omitted essentials of information, and fed its readers falsehood and prejudice.

Other English newspapers, some having more readers than the *Times*, had spoken goodwill for America, wrote Professor Smith. "I will not deny that it [the *Times*] is a great power of evil," he continued, yet until it had the English people as a support it would not succeed "in producing a fatal estrangement between two kindred nations." Then in justice to his own country Professor Smith must point out that the worst things said about America in England "have been but the echo of things said here" in America. He referred to slanders published and believed in England which originated in American circles. "I have [in America] seen your President accused of wishing to provoke riots in New York that he might have a pretence for exercising military power. I have seen him accused of sending to the front, to be thinned, a regiment which was likely to vote against him. I have seen him accused of decoying his political opponents into forging soldiers' votes in order to discredit them. What could the 'Times' itself say more?"

In the peasantry of England was no understanding of America nor of anything else except perhaps "the struggle for daily bread, of which they have barely enough for themselves and their children." For some of them America might open a door of hope. "Hands now folded helplessly in English poorhouses may joyfully reap the harvests of Iowa and Wisconsin." In the English cities, however, you would find the workingmen with "eyes almost as keen and hearts almost as anxious as your own" on "the great issue between Free Labor and Slavery." In Exeter Hall in London, in the Free-Trade Hall at Manchester, Professor Smith had seen immense throngs give ringing cheers for the cause of Free Labor in America. Of the textile workers, their industry paralyzed by the cotton shortage, the sympathy was an offering to the Northern cause as costly as it was sincere. "Your slave-owning aristocracy had made up their minds that chivalry was confined to aristocracies, and that over the vulgar souls of the common people Cotton must be King. The working-man of Manchester, though he lives not like a Southern gentleman by the sweat of another's brow, but like a plebeian by the sweat of his own, has shown that chivalry is not confined to aristocracies."

The mass in England saw itself one with the mass in America. Lincoln, if his eyes happened to scan the *Atlantic* article, took as a good sign this from the professor of modern history at Oxford University: "If the victory in this struggle has been won, it has been won, not by a man, but by the nation; and that it has been won not by a man, but by the nation, is your glory and the pledge of your salvation. We have called for a Cromwell, and he has not come; he has not come, partly because Cromwells are scarce, partly, perhaps, because the personal Cromwell belonged to a different age, and the Cromwell of this age is an intelligent, resolute, and united people."

The November election added prestige to American Ministers abroad. Consul Bigelow at Paris wrote on November 22 of Lincoln's election as "more important and more significant than is realized even in America." This was the first President ever re-elected from a Free State. "His predecessors from Northern States have all either forfeited the support of the South by their unwillingness to regard slavery as an institution of Divine appointment, or they have forfeited the confidence of the North by acquiescence in that brutal dogma. Lincoln's election shows that the cause of free labor has, to use a mechanical phrase, 'passed the centre.'"

Like others who on further thinking about the fact and looking at it saw it loom larger, Bigelow two weeks later, in a letter to Seward, went farther: "The result of the late election . . . was more worthy of a National thanksgiving than any event, humanly speaking, which has occurred since the Revolution."

After that election the *Richmond Enquirer* spoke more frankly about offers to Britain and France, a fond dream now abandoned. "If we [of the Confederacy] are successful, there immediately arises on this continent a balance of power, or political equilibrium similar to that of Europe, which would check the progress and power of the United States, restore commerce to its normal condition, oppose to the navy of that country [the United States] the navy of these [Confederate] States and of Mexico, which, uniting with a Canadian navy, would at all times effectually keep the Yankees within the bounds of propriety, and from disturbing the peace of the world."

This was the scheme and vision offered at London, Paris, Madrid, Mexico City. But "these governments are indifferent to our cause . . . all has been in vain." Of no use had it been for Confederate diplomats to tell France that when the United States won the war France would lose her hold on Mexico, or to tell Spain she would lose Cuba, or to tell Britain the United States would take over the Western Hemisphere for its own and would when it pleased visit cotton famines on English industry. The declarations of Lincoln and Seward on these matters were as satisfying to Napoleon III and Palmerston as any exchanged between those two smooth international poker-players among themselves. "France fears that England may prove false and unite with the United States and sweep the French navy from the seas, while we have no navy to bring to her assistance," said the *Richmond Enquirer*. "England fears that France has designs on California and the East India commerce. Thus these two great powers, with no faith or trust in each other's pledges, neutralize each other's influence, and for dread of treachery permit us to fight the fight out, notwithstanding their own interests are involved in our cause as directly as they would be in open war with the Yankees."

What was this new candor of a Confederate Government mouthpiece which Lincoln and Seward now scanned daily? Why now lay all the cards on the table? Why now the revelation of what had been spoken behind doors closed in the chancelleries of Europe? Had the November election been a culminating event? First came a tentative admission in this *Richmond Enquirer* editorial: "The fate of war may go against these [Confederate] States—such an end is possible; and if it does, every Confederate citizen would demand from the United States . . . armies for new crusades, armies for Mexico, armies for Canada, armies for Cuba. The continent of North America, from the Straits to the Isthmus, would become the United States of America, and the Isles of the Sea swallowed up in the mighty confederation." This was the picture offered Lincoln. What would he do about it? "This grand object," continued the editorial, "might even now be obtained if reason and common sense could find a resting place in Washington." In the re-elected Lincoln of wider authority they had a frail hope of finding what they termed "reason and common sense." The editorial closed:

> The recognition—the recognition of the independence of these Confederate States by the enemy, with a treaty offensive and defensive, providing for an army and navy proportionate with the population of the two countries; with a customs union of free trade and uninterrupted travel between the States of both confederations, with the free navigation of the Mississippi, would give to both peoples all the practical advantages of the old Union, without the evils that have produced the present war. The foreign policy of both nations should, then, be the Monroe doctrine applied to the whole continent of North America and adjacent islands, Canada and Mexico, Cuba and the Sandwich Islands, Central America and the Russian Possessions, all from Behring's Straits to Darien's Isthmus should be made American in interest and republican in form of government, and each and all united by treaties similar to that proposed for the United States and the Confederate States. Instead of wasting the lives of the citizens, and consuming the resources of the two countries in a war of mutual ruin, such an alliance would open a future of progressive power and influence which would eventually make the confederacies of North America the dominant power of the world.

This had the same color as presentations in the *New York Herald* and other newspapers. They offered an alluring dream to be wrought by the United States and the Confederate States as allies. The slavery issue as a factor went unmentioned, as though it would not again harass and embarrass. Notable however was a note of hoped-for reconciliation, faint though definite, in the opening lines of the *Richmond Enquirer* editorial: "The Monroe doctrine, the *New York Herald* thinks, will yet prove the means of consolidating both countries, uniting in one cause the armies now battling against each other, and reviving the love for the Union in the hearts of Confederates."

The hour for such good-neighbor approaches to negotiation had passed. A similar appeal, made openly, earlier in the war, before the deepening anti-slavery opinion developed, would have had influence in favor of the South

The repeated and varied statements of Lincoln on peace and the causes of the war had deepened a vast sentiment favoring one undivided country. This living and active sentiment Governor Joseph E. Brown dealt with in his annual message to the Georgia Legislature in '64: "The statement of Lincoln, that we offer no terms of adjustment, is made an artful pretext that it is impossible to say when the war will terminate, but that negotiation, not the sword, will finally terminate it." Therefore the idea should be kept before the Northern people that "we are ready to negotiate when they are." Brown directly suggested that the attitude of negotiation was not seen often enough in President Davis. "After each victory," Brown advised, "our government should make a distinct offer of peace" on terms of Southern independence. "Should the course of any State be doubted, let the armed force be withdrawn, and the ballot-box decide. If this is refused even a dozen times, renew it, and keep it before the North and the world that our ability to defend ourselves for many years has been proved."

In these words lurked the definite feeling that the statements of Lincoln to the North and to the world had continuously outmatched those of Davis. Earlier in the war Brown's advice would have been more practical "after each victory." In all of '64, however, there had been no Southern hours of elation and triumph such as after First Bull Run in '61 and Second Bull Run in '62, nor such hours of shame for the North as after Fredericksburg in late '62 and Chancellorsville in early '63. And now overwhelmingly momentous in fate for the South had been the November election of '64 and its antislavery mandate written into the Baltimore platform.

Four prominent Georgians in free conversations with Sherman in September spoke to him their belief that further resistance was impossible. They suggested the possibility of State action being started by Governor Brown to take Georgia out of the Confederacy. Through these Georgians Sherman sent messages to Governor Brown. Sherman proposed that the Governor issue a proclamation withdrawing Georgia State troops from the Confederate Army, in which case Sherman would drop his policy of devastation, keep to the highroads, and pay for the corn and meat which he needed and must seize. Also in September Sherman telegraphed Halleck that Governor Brown was letting his State militia go home to gather the corn and sorghum crops. This telegram was shown to Lincoln. He read Sherman's peculiar sentence, "I have reason to believe that he [Governor Brown] and Stephens want to visit me and have sent them a hearty invitation." Lincoln at once wired Sherman: "I feel great interest in the subjects of your despatch mentioning corn and sorghum, and the contemplated visit to you."

Sherman then sent word to Lincoln of his attempted dealings begun with the Governor of Georgia, saying it was delicate work, "but it would be a magnificent stroke of policy if we could, without surrendering principle or a foot of ground, arouse the latent enmity of Georgia against Davis." The weeks had passed, however, and Sherman, with the help of prominent Georgians who saw only ruin ahead, was unable to interest Governor Brown, who had said to his legislature of the war, "Negotiation, not the sword, will finally terminate it."

To Grant came word of steps Lincoln was taking in Georgia in September. "Please advise the President," Grant wired Stanton, "not to attempt to doctor up a State government for Georgia by the appointment of citizens in any capacity whatever. Leave Sherman to treat all questions in his own way, the President reserving his power to approve or disapprove of his actions." In this Lincoln learned Grant's opinion of some sort of "doctoring" Lincoln had tried his hand at.

"Our people are excited," read a telegram November 25 from Governor Curtin at Harrisburg, "by a rumor that three States have offered to return to their allegiance. Is it true?" Lincoln's instant and positive reply: "I have no knowledge, information, or belief, that three States, or any State, offer to resume allegiance."

More than a hint of desperation on the part of the sinking Confederacy could be read in the projects set on foot by Jacob Thompson from Canada with funds of some $300,000 supplied by the Confederate Government. Secretary of State Benjamin had information of Thompson's design, though later it became doubtful that President Davis definitely linked himself to it. Thompson wrote to Benjamin that a Mr. Minor Major (not Mr. Major Minor), his accredited agent to burn steamboats on the Mississippi, was given "two thousand dollars in Federal currency and soon afterward several boats were burned at St. Louis, involving an immense loss of property to the enemy." Thompson also wrote Benjamin of money advanced to a Mr. Churchill of Cincinnati "for the purpose of incendiarism in that city." Then came what Thompson perhaps considered his masterpiece.

In the metropolis where Lincoln had been voted down in '60 and '64, where a mayor had tried to secede the city from the Union, the torch of arson came into service on the evening of November 25, 1864. With phosphorus and turpentine as starters, eleven New York hotels began blazing at about the same time. The flames were caught in time and put out by quick-witted hotel workers. At Barnum's Museum, at Niblo's Garden where an audience of 3,000 was seeing a play, at the Winter Garden Theatre where Edwin Booth was playing *Julius Caesar* for a Shakespeare Monument Fund benefit, the terrorizing cry of "Fire! fire!" was raised. Cool heads slowed down the near-panics while fires were snuffed out. In this episode the same Federal secret-service operative who had carried dispatches between the Richmond Government and the Confederate commissioners in Canada brought Stanton, Dana, and Lincoln at Washington information that enabled them to have men trailing the arson bugs in New York. One of the guilty was hanged, others sent to prison.

"The bane and curse of carrying out anything in this country," wrote Thompson from Canada to Benjamin in Richmond, "is the surveillance under which we act. Detectives, or those ready to give information, stand at every street corner. Two or three cannot exchange information without a reporter." It may have been that Thompson expected a job at Chicago to be his masterpiece. There at Camp Douglas, holding 8,000 Confederate prisoners, on the night of election day, November 8, the plot was that Sons of Liberty should throw in their forces, outnumber the little garrison, attack it, release and arm the prisoners, "cut the telegraph wires, burn the railroad depots, seize the banks and stores containing arms and ammunition, take possession of the city and commence a campaign for the release of other prisoners of war in Illinois and Indiana." The commandant at Camp Douglas, however, early got word of the plot, and two nights before the break was to come he arrested an English soldier, four Confederates, two Sons of Liberty. Later he arrested seven more Sons of Liberty. A military commission dealt out prison sentences to several and decreed death for one.

Was the South in heartbreak and despair now using tactics it would not have considered when the war opened?

Midyear of '64, Lawrence M. Keitt—who had in 1860 cried to Mrs. Clay and President Buchanan, "Hurrah! South Carolina has seceded! Thank God!"—had gone down with a fatal wound at the head of his regiment in the gory Cold Harbor fighting. Now in December of '64 Roger A. Pryor—who had fomented the firing on Fort Sumter and in April of '61 cried from a balcony in Charleston, South Carolina, "Strike a blow! strike a blow!"—had been taken prisoner near Grant's picket lines. And the daring, elusive cavalry raider John H. Morgan, who had taken his men and horses farther into Northern territory than any other Confederate troop body, who had spoiled millions of dollars' worth of barns, crops, and other property, who had made away with thousands of picked horses and mules—John Morgan had been encircled by Federal soldiers, penned in a Tennessee farmhouse, and while running for escape across a cabbage patch shot through the heart. Parson Brownlow wrote a brutal obituary with one line worth citing: "There should be a salute fired in front of every horse-stable in the land, in honor of his death, and all fine horses and mules should be notified that they may now repose in quiet at night and graze in peace in the daytime."

Charleston, birth city of secession, against land and sea forces held her own. "Fanatics" of the North would yet be worn out "by heroic fighting, heroic praying, and heroic suffering" in the South, counseled the *Mercury*. "We have done too much not to do more. We have fought too well not to fight better." Suffering had come to Charleston, seared by a fire loss of $7,000,000, raked by shells, bombs, the awe of single incidents such as the killing of Miss Pickens, daughter of ex-Governor Pickens. One May morning she was married to Lieutenant de Rochelle, ran the *Mercury* account. "The wedding party had assembled at the house of General Bonham, when a shell from the Union forces penetrated the house and wounded the bride so that she died soon afterward. The marriage ceremony was completed as she lay dying on the floor."

Over at Camden Mrs. Chesnut was haunted by her memory of little Joe Davis, son of the Confederate President, killed by falling from a high porch to a brick pavement, and she in the drawing-room of the executive mansion at midnight hearing the tramp of Mr. Davis's step as he walked up and down the room above, not another sound, the whole house silent as death, and the next day thousands of children at little Joe's grave, each with a green bough or a bunch of flowers to throw on a pile of crosses and evergreens. Now at home in Camden to Mrs. Chesnut it seemed a bad dream. Yet she could recall it happened, the funeral procession winding among tall white monuments, above a hillside over the tumbling James River among rocks and islands, "the dominant figure, that poor, old, gray-haired man, standing bareheaded, straight as an arrow, clear against the sky by the open grave of his son . . . the bereft mother . . . in her heavy black wrappings, and her tall figure drooped . . . those two dark, sorrow-stricken figures stand; they are before me now!" In high places and low sorrow, sorrow, drove sometimes in a streak of macabre gaiety, as one day in '64 when Mrs. Chesnut wrote:

> February 24th.—Friends came to make taffy and stayed the livelong day. They played cards. One man, a soldier, had only two teeth left in front and they lapped across each other. On account of the condition of his mouth, he had maintained a dignified sobriety of aspect, though he told some funny stories. Finally a story was too much for him, and he grinned from ear to ear. Maggie gazed, and then called out as the negro fiddlers call out dancing figures, "Forward two and cross over!" Fancy our faces. The hero of the two teeth, relapsing into a decorous arrangement of mouth, said: "Cavalry are the eyes of an army; they bring the news; the artillery are the boys to make a noise; but the infantry do the fighting, and a general or so gets all the glory."

The fighting men of South Carolina had all gone to the front, wrote Mrs. Chesnut. "Only old men and little boys are at home now." She read a column list of South Carolina dead and wounded in clashes with Grant's men, shuddering at news of Grant receiving 25,000 fresh troops in one relay. "Old Lincoln says in his quaint backwoods way, 'Keep a-peggin.' Now we can only peg out." A harsh play on words. The peg legs were too many. Her imagination was alive. The facts would not fly away.

Over a bank of violets, lilacs, roses, with orange blossoms and magnolia near her window, the soft south wind blew in with its bloom smells. Yet comfort and any letdown of sorrow refused to blow in with healing. "It is impossible to sleep here," wrote Mrs. Chesnut, "because it is so solemn and still. The moonlight shines in my window sad and white." She was as grave and vivid now as when in April of '61 and the first guns booming to bring down the parapets of Fort Sumter, she had leaped from her bed and knelt in prayer over what was to come.

In her Richmond stay she had gone shopping, "and paid $30.00 for a pair of gloves; $50.00 for a pair of slippers; $24.00 for six spools of thread; $32.00 for five miserable, shabby little pocket handkerchiefs." Money—it was getting ridiculous, Confederate money; as it sank in value from month to month pathos and pity touched deeper the Confederate cause. The barrel of flour rising in price from $200 to $500 in six months, dropping in late summer to $300, reaching $700 in early winter, this got into everyday profane talk.

Ten dollars for one head of cabbage, $5 for a quart of potatoes, another paper $5 for a stick of firewood—the Richmond diarist J. B. Jones saw this affected human dignity. The clothes of all being shabby, it was not unstylish to be shabby, he noticed. "The wonder is that we are not naked, after wearing the same garments three or four years."

September 21 this year of '64 Jones wrote of class lines drawn ever sharper, of speculators and hoarders making money and living fat, of the wealthy cajoling or buying arrangements for themselves and their sons to keep out of the thinning armies. "Many of the privates in our armies are fast becoming what is termed machine soldiers, and will ere long cease to fight well—having nothing to fight for. Alas, the chivalry have fallen! The lagging land proprietors and slaveowners (as the Yankees shrewdly predicted) want to be captains etc. or speculators. The poor will not long fight for their oppressors, the money-changers, extortioners, etc., whose bribes keep them out of the service." This could mean much about the morale of the South. Jones was by nature no croaker, though he now wrote of "faint-hearted croakers anxious for peace and reconstruction." Off south and west from Richmond often could be heard the growling of the cannon of Lee and Grant. And—"What for?" Jones wrote of every tree on Governor Wise's farm cut down by Grant's endless gunfire. The naïve Jones asked: "What harm have the poor trees done the enemy? I love trees, anywhere."

Now in the close of '64 it was taken in the North and in Europe as full of portent that President Davis recommended to his Congress that slaves be drafted for the Confederate armies. This plan would throw 400,000 able-bodied and armed black men against the Northern armies. Slavery would not be abolished, but the enlisted Negroes would be given freedom. To Europe went an emissary from Davis, one Duncan F. Kenner, hoping to win foreign recognition of the Confederacy by this concession to world opinion. On this partial emancipation, however, planters and slaveholders of influence squarely opposed Davis. Factions in the Confederate Congress with polite contempt offered other plans to fill the thinning armies.

A movement to impeach Davis gained headway. Vice-President Stephens, the Rhett following in South Carolina, Governor Brown of Georgia, Governor Vance of North Carolina, moved slowly and guardedly, backed by a considerable public opinion in the South which held President Davis too arbitrary, too lacking in a spirit of co-operation, empty of the genius of leadership required for the terrible and immediate problems. A congressional committee sent a member to General Robert E. Lee to ask him if he would take charge of the sinking and chaotic affairs of the Confederacy—as sole dictator. Lee couldn't see that he was the man for such a post, and the old order was resumed.

If the North had its Vallandigham of Ohio, the South had its Henry S. Foote of Mississippi, an editor and lawyer, one-time United States Senator, who had opposed secession but was nevertheless elected to the Confederate Congress. There he took a lonesome route, incessantly criticizing the administration, and across '63 and '64 speaking openly in favor of the peace proposals of President Lincoln. Foote was to resign in disgust over the failure of the Richmond Government to meet proposals from Lincoln, and after a short jail term, like Vallandigham be turned loose into enemy territory. But unlike Vallandigham, Foote stayed in the enemy territory, traveled to Europe, and returned to begin law practice in Washington.

Lincoln in latter November, writing his message to Congress, heard of this growing war weariness at the South. To his desk came such items as one from the *Mobile Register* in August: "In General Lee's tent meat is eaten but twice a week, the General not allowing it oftener because he believes the indulgence in meat to be criminal, in the present straitened condition of the country. His ordinary dinner consists of a heart of cabbage, boiled in salt water, and a pound of corn bread." Southward in Georgia were good rations for Lee and his army—grain and meat lacking transport. The railroads of the South, with no replacements during the war, were rusting and shattered. Forges, mills, machine shops, what few the South had, were almost out of commission. The blockade was letting few new materials in. The extortions of salt speculators had forced the Richmond Government to take over saltworks and issue rations. Meat, sugar, drugs, medicines, wool, coffee, of these in many homes they learned how to do with little, to do without entirely, or to use substitutes. On every doorsill of the South were shadows and imprints of a war going on, with none of the flare and gaiety that marked its beginning.

Unfailing and undying devotion to the cause there was, perhaps most notable among women. A proposal that all Southern women cut off their hair for sale in Europe, to bring $40,000,000 for the cause, would have been carried out if practical. In plenty of instances they denied themselves meat, coffee, wines, blankets, sending these to the army and to hospitals. One invalid denied herself good food with "I think it is a sin to eat anything that can be used for rations." When by order of Sherman the population of Atlanta was ordered away, "a beautiful girl," according to one witness, "was seen to step from among her companions, and kneeling to kiss passionately the soil she was about to forsake."

As with each year of the war the South had dwindled in man power, in money and economic resources, in commerce and industry, in the comforts or necessities of life, the North had gained in each of these points. In steel, oil, railroads, munitions, textiles, and other industries, scores of large fortunes were already made, many others on their way. The fast and luxurious living in most of the large cities still contrasted with sacrifices on the march, in camp, and on the battlefields. From Great Britain, especially Ireland, and from Germany and the Scandinavian countries, fresh populations poured in. *Leslie's* said in July of '64 that Irish newspapers spoke of the emigration to America as being near to a panic. "From the small port of Sligo alone, 3,000 persons have sailed in five weeks for the United States." With Sherman's army was one regiment of Norwegians from Wisconsin who in service through several campaigns had lost more than half their men from death in battle, from wounds and sickness.

Westward across the plains and to the West Coast poured an endless migration, some of it to escape the draft. From March 1 to August 10 of '64, nine thousand three hundred teams and wagons passed Fort Kearney, Nebraska. One fast traveler on the road from St. Joseph, Missouri, to Fort Kearney passed four hundred wagons in one day. At the Council Bluffs ferry in April and May a line of teams three miles long waited their turn day after day to cross a ferry whose capacity was 200 in its operation day and night. By the middle of June it was estimated 75,000 men, 30,000 horses and mules, 75,000 cattle, made the crossing. With each year farmers of the Midwest and Northwest bought more planters, reapers, threshers; their help counted for putting in crops and harvesting them; otherwise the North could not have readily spared so many men for Grant and Sherman. Several foreign travelers from Europe commented in surprise at reaching the seaboard cities of a North at war with few signs of war and such throngs of spenders and pleasure-hunters as in no European cities.

America had these lights and contradictions in 1864. Any historian of them in their vast and moving variety needed a gift for showing chaos in the present scene and a weave of paradox leading to the future. A mystic dream of a majestic Republic holding to human freedom and equal opportunity ran parallel to motives of hard cash and pay dirt. These were to shape a future already begun, swaying indistinctly in many a sentence of Lincoln.

Such were backgrounds in late '64 for the dramatic military performances of Sherman and Thomas and their armies in the Central and Deep South. For the first time during the war, observers in America and Europe hung breathless and wondering over the audacity and fate of a general and an army who vanished. To his wife the head of this adventure wrote that he would come out of it reputed a great general or just plain crazy. Sherman had not seen the newborn baby who had arrived to them in June. The baby would die while he was gone, while millions were wondering where he was, and he would accept this as war.

"If you can whip Lee," Sherman wrote to Grant as between family men, in September, "and I can march to the Atlantic, I think Uncle Abe will give us a twenty days' leave of absence to see the young folks." This he was writing in Georgia, where he had taken Atlanta. Near by was Hood's army, which Jefferson Davis was saying had every advantage of being on home ground, so that it would yet cut Sherman's communications and destroy Sherman. To Grant, Sherman offered his plan. He would divide his army, give Thomas 60,000 with which to take care of Hood's 41,000, and then himself start on a thousand-mile march which was to end by joining Grant in Virginia, pausing at Savannah-by-the-Sea. "I can make the march and make Georgia howl!" Hood was maneuvering to draw Sherman out of Georgia, Sherman saying, "If Hood *will* only go North, I will furnish him with rations for the trip." Long ago everyone in authority knew Sherman's theory was to punish and destroy in the South till its people were sick of war and willing and anxious for peace. "War is cruelty and you cannot refine it.' Down where he was he would not consider defensive warfare. "Instead of guessing what Hood means to do he would have to guess at my plans. The difference in war is full twenty-five per cent." Thousands of people abroad and in the South would reason, wrote Sherman, "If the North can march an army right through the South it is proof positive that the North can prevail in this contest. . . . Mr. Lincoln's election, which is assured, coupled with the conclusion thus reached, makes a logical whole."

What Sherman was proposing sounded as peculiar and as touched with fantasy as Grant's plan a year and a half back for taking Vicksburg. Grant had every faith in Sherman. And by instinct Grant favored this latest hope of Sherman. Grant at this point did what Lincoln so often did. He raised objections almost as though to reassure both himself and Sherman that they were headed right and not moving too fast. He mentioned to Sherman his doubt whether Sherman could get along without a seacoast base prepared for him. He added his doubt about leaving Thomas with too few men to make sure of beating Hood. Sherman replied he was sure he could strike into Georgia without a seacoast base and was also sure that Thomas, his old classmate at West Point, whom he knew well as a slow but safe fighter, would take care of Hood.

On October 11 Grant had not yet told Sherman he could go, and good luck to him. In fact on October 11 Grant sent to Lincoln by wire a statement of reasons for disapproving of Sherman's plan. Then the next day Grant changed front, wired Sherman, "On reflection, I think better of your proposition. It would be better to go south than to be forced to come north." He would have Sherman "clean the country of railroad tracks and supplies . . . move every wagon, horse, mule, and hoof of stock," arming the Negroes and giving them "such organization as you can."

Meantime came word to Grant from Lincoln. He agreed with Grant's reasons for not yet letting Sherman head south to the sea. A telegram from Stanton read: "The President feels much solicitude in respect to General Sherman's proposed movement and hopes that it will be maturely considered. The objections stated in your telegram of last night impressed him with much force, and a misstep by General Sherman might be fatal to his army."

Halleck, it was known, though personally friendly to Sherman, had a plan of his own, different from Sherman's, which he sent to both Sherman and Grant, and which did not favor an immediate start. Undoubtedly Halleck had given the President his views. That was usual. More unusual was it that Grant's chief of staff, John Rawlins, was in bitter gloom about what Sherman proposed, and as Grant learned later, "finding that he could not move me, he appealed to the authorities at Washington to stop it." Colonel Horace Porter, also of Grant's staff, had returned in October from a trip to Sherman, had been completely persuaded by Sherman. A long and heated argument that used up the evening went on at Grant's headquarters one night, Grant enjoying it till he went to bed, but about one o'clock in the morning poking his head out of the tent and crying: "Oh, do go to bed, all of you. You are keeping the whole camp awake."

Not until long afterward did Grant know how deeply Rawlins took this matter and the extent of Rawlins's personal disloyalty. Starting west with orders for Rosecrans in Missouri, Rawlins stopped a day in Washington, and according to Grant's secretary, Adam Badeau: "Here he saw the President and the Secretary of War, and expressed so forcibly his apprehensions as to the result of allowing Sherman to move south and leave Thomas to contend with Hood, that he actually induced the government to send a despatch to Grant, desiring him to reconsider his decision." Then Grant again exchanged telegrams with Sherman about destroying Hood before marching across Georgia. Both their minds seemed to be playing around the idea that Hood wanted to decoy Sherman's army out of Georgia northward. And the strategy of both Grant and Sherman more often ran to finding the one thing the enemy didn't want you to do and then doing that very thing. Grant agreed with Sherman. "I say then, go on, as you propose."

Grant now wired Lincoln: "Sherman's proposition is the best that can be adopted. . . . Such an army as Sherman has, and with such a commander, is hard to corner or capture." This seemed to be the day of an acid test for Lincoln on the matter of whether he would get behind his two best proven generals. Within three hours after Grant's telegram arrived, Stanton telegraphed Sherman complete approval. "Whatever results, you have the confidence and support of the Government." Halleck added that "the authorities are willing," serving Sherman notice that at Savannah a fleet would be waiting for him with supplies.

It seemed as though Grant trusted Sherman completely, except for a day or two of wavering on the point of Sherman's faith that Thomas could take care of Hood. In the end Grant decided he would accept Sherman's judgment of what Thomas could do. And Lincoln, with his natural caution enforced by the bitter opposition of Grant's chief of staff, Rawlins, and by Halleck's placid routine disapproval, had nevertheless thrown himself into complete trust of Grant and Sherman. This trio of Lincoln, Grant, and Sherman now worked in a co-operation as smooth as that which had long existed between Lee and Davis. Grant's later recollection ran that the President's apprehensions, induced by his advisers, went so far as to move him "to ask me to suspend Sherman's march for a day or two until I could think the matter over . . . out of deference to the President's wish I did send a dispatch to Sherman asking him to wait a day or two, or else the connections between us were already cut so that I could not do so."

Sherman later was surprised "to learn that Rawlins went to Washington from City Point to obtain an order from the President or Secretary of War to compel me, with an army of 65,000 of the best soldiers America had ever produced, to remain idle when an opportunity was offered such as never occurs twice to any man on earth." Sherman felt "uneasiness" that any moment a recall order *might* come from Washington. "Free and glorious I felt when the magic telegraph was cut." Rawlins, wrote Sherman, was "one of the many referred to by Mr. Lincoln who sat in darkness, but after the event saw a great light."

Grant's decision in this was one Sherman had in mind later when he said, "Grant stood by me when I was crazy, and I stood by him when he was drunk, and now we stand by each other." Both of them had practiced and wrought out a technic. Their calculations partook of arithmetic and intuitive cunning learned in hard trials. Sherman had found what he could do in enemy territory. Grant trusted Sherman's faith in his own mobility.

In the advance on Atlanta one backwoods woman spoke to a Union officer of Sherman's capacity to have his army disappear and reappear. "You-uns don't fight we-uns fair. When Johnston crossed the High Tower he made a line and wanted you all to come square at him at Atlanta; but instead of that you-uns went away off to Dallas, and we had to leave and make a line for you there. But there again you all wouldn't fight fair, for when our line was made afront of yours, Captain Hooker, with his big regiment, came round and pitched into we-uns' eend. No Gineral can fight such unfair ways as that." This ran counter to Jefferson Davis's prediction that Atlanta would be to Sherman what Moscow was to Napoleon. As a forecaster Davis was losing reputation. Atlanta was burned, not as much as Moscow, but Sherman ordered the torch put to it. Grant found one ingredient lacking. "Mr. Davis has not made it quite plain who is to furnish the snow for this Moscow retreat."

Sherman had not intended to burn as much of Atlanta as did burn. His chief engineer under orders wrecked all railroads in and about Atlanta, heated the rails red-hot and twisted them around trees. Then smokestacks were pulled down, furnace arches broken, steam machinery smashed, holes punched in all boilers, all devices of industrial production sabotaged out of possible use. Battering crews knocked down walls and then put the torch to wrecks of what had been passenger depots, freight sheds, roundhouses, machine shops, mills, factories, a tannery, a laboratory, an oil refinery, theatres, and all hotels but one. Before this work had begun, firebugs had set in flame a score of buildings, General Slocum offering a reward of $500 for the detection of any soldier involved. Public dwellings and churches were spared, and it was not in Sherman's plans to burn the business sections of the city. According to his chief engineer, "lawless persons" without authority had crept through back alleys and laid in ashes stores and shops. Eighteen hundred Atlanta buildings went up in smoke.

Sherman rode into the city with an aide on November 15 near sunset. Roses still bloomed in a few gardens of fine houses and Atlanta was a quiet city, not soothed but calm with a hint of heavy fate. The somber red-haired Man on Horseback was about to say, and did say later, "Pierce the shell of the Confederacy and it's all hollow inside."

The night held little quiet as an engineer corps fired more fallen buildings, as flames spread to a wrecked arsenal and shell explosions rattled the windows of hundreds of homes where no sleepers lay to be awakened. A fire department of soldiers struggled several hours of the night, managing to hold the fire mainly to the downtown and industrial districts, as intended. When Sherman rode out of the city at seven the next morning, a third, perhaps more, of Atlanta lay in ashes.

Toward the east and southward, toward Savannah and the Atlantic Ocean, toward a path that was to twist upward in the Carolinas, Sherman turned his horse. He knew this country. He had crossed many parts of it and lived in it several years of the 1840's. The ways of its people had been under his eye in part when he was superintendent of the Louisiana State Military Academy. No stranger seeing novelties was he now. So the *Macon Telegraph* called him Judas Iscariot, a betrayer, a creature of depravity, a demon "of a thousand fiends."

Toward the east by the Decatur road Sherman paused on a hill and took a last look at smoking Atlanta. On the horizons around him a bright sun slanted down on the shining rifles of 55,000 picked men, veterans of proved capacity for action, for marching, for legwork, for many disease immunities, survivors of hard campaigns. Each man carried forty rounds of cartridges, and in wagons were enough more to make two hundred rounds per man. The sun slanted too on sixty-five cannon, each drawn by four teams of horses. Six-mule wagons, two thousand five hundred of them, hauled supplies and forage. And six hundred ambulances, two horses to each, were prepared for battle service.

Between Sherman and his friend Grant at Richmond lay a thousand miles of cities and towns, lands, swamps, and rivers, alive with a bitterly hostile people hating with a deepening despair. Behind now was smoldering Atlanta and its black smoke and its deathly stillness of ruin. Around him were glistening gun barrels of his 14th Corps, cheery and swinging boys and men, singing and joking about the thousand miles to Richmond. A band struck up the John Brown song. Men sang "Glory, glory, hallelujah!" And to Sherman's ears as he rode along came from more than one soldier something like "Uncle Billy, I guess Grant is waiting for us at Richmond." There at Richmond, as Sherman read their feeling, "there we should end the war, but how and when they seemed to care not, nor did they measure the distance, or count the cost in life, or bother their brains about the great rivers to be crossed, and the food required for man and beast that had to be gathered by the way." Among men and officers Sherman saw a "devil-may-care" feeling that made him feel his full responsibility, "for success would be accepted as a matter of course, whereas, should we fail, this 'march' would be adjudged the wild adventure of a crazy fool."

To his wife Sherman had written less than a month ago that in revolutions men fall and rise, are praised and then insulted. He was in a dark mood then, writing: "Grant, Sheridan and I are now the popular favorites, but neither of us will survive this war. Some other must rise greater than either of us, and he has not yet manifested himself." Of these cheery soldiers singing in sunbright weather on the start from Atlanta he was to write her: "I never saw a more confident army. The soldiers think I know everything and that they can do anything." In late October he had written her he was on a hazardous feat. "And you will not hear from me for months. The War Department will know my whereabouts, and the Rebels, and you will be able to guess."

Heading the Army of the Tennessee, forming the right wing, was the one-armed O. O. Howard with two corps, one commanded by General P. J. Osterhaus, the other by General Frank P. Blair, who was glad he had resigned his seat in Congress and was now so far away from debates in the House. Heading the Army of the Cumberland, forming the left wing, was the cool and tested General H. W. Slocum, with two corps led by General J. C. Davis and General A. S. Williams.

This army had 218 regiments, all but 33 from Western States, 52 from Ohio, 50 from Illinois, 27 from Indiana, 13 from Wisconsin, 10 from Michigan, 15 from Iowa, 3 from Minnesota, 10 from Missouri, 4 from Kentucky. From New York were 16 regiments, from Pennsylvania 10, from New Jersey 3, from Massachusetts and Connecticut 2 each. They would be heard from—sometime. The word of Sherman to Grant, to the War Department and the President, was that communications were cut off from central Georgia and his next message he hoped to send from somewhere on the Atlantic Coast.

In the Eastern regiments was noticeable more antislavery sentiment than among the Western. The emancipation idea had less motivating force among the Iowa, Illinois, Missouri, and Kentucky troops, for instance. Striding over Georgia they were Unionists, not aliens nor invaders; they held they were fighting enemies who sought to take away their Mississippi River, their uninterrupted transcontinental railways, their interstate commerce and peace.

Starting on this November 15, marching in four columns sweeping a path twenty to forty or more miles wide, this army began a systematic campaign of destruction. "The State of Georgia alone," Jefferson Davis had said in a recent speech in Augusta, "produces food enough not only for her own people and the army within but feeds too the Army of Virginia." On this storehouse and granary of the Confederacy worked the destroyers. What the army could not eat or carry away it burned, spoiled, ruined.

What was it other than a human conflagration, a wide-moving cyclone, a plague of locusts, a cloud of giant biped grasshoppers, an Old Testament visitation of the vengeance of Jehovah or the raucous laughter of hell-hounds spawned from the cesspools of demoniac nether regions?

Language and imagery failed to tell the terror that smote this region and ran shuddering through all other yet remaining vitals of the Confederate States of America. War! And the desolation and fallen pride and hunger and deathly quiet lacking majesty because of the smoldering foul smoke and the clean air pungent with the rot and stink of conquest.

Now they had their war, was Sherman's thought, the war they had asked for. Until now the Border States had taken the punishment. Now it had come to the doorsills of the Deep South. Now sometimes you couldn't see the roses and the magnolia trees for the depot and warehouse smoke, for the dust of marching columns and rumbling wagons. Until now hereabouts the war had been fairly polite and far off. Here was a reality with torch crews singing "Thus far the Lord hath led us." Sherman was keeping his promise that he would make Georgia howl, that he would make its people "feel that war and individual ruin are synonymous."

An argument began. It was to last long. Was Sherman a modern impersonation of Attila the Hun, a manner of sadist, a wanton and a monster who took pleasure in seeing an enemy people suffer? Or was he a soldier doing a necessary job, a kindhearted family man who wanted to end the war and saw no other way of ending it than by the tactics he was using? Both sides made out a case. The word in military lingo for the work of Sherman's looters and plunderers was "pillage." When Sherman's men in Georgia drove off the livestock of a farmer without paying the farmer for it—as McClellan's men always did in Virginia and as Lee's men always did (with Confederate money) in Pennsylvania—it was pillage. "In the beginning [of the war]," wrote Sherman, "I, too, had the old West Point notion that pillage was a capital crime, and punished it by shooting, but the Rebels wanted us to detach a division here, a brigade there, to protect their families and property while they were fighting. . . . This was a one-sided game of war, and many of us . . . kind-hearted, fair, just and manly . . . ceased to quarrel with our own men about such minor things, and went in to subdue the enemy, leaving minor depredations to be charged up to the account of the rebels who had forced us into the war, and who deserved all they got and *more*."

His conscience worried Sherman less than his sense of timing. He and Grant would join their armies some day, if their timing was right. Then the war would end. From Richmond to the farthest southwest corner of Texas, "all over the grand theater of war," Sherman wanted "simultaneous action." This lesson had been learned at cost and must be applied. "We saw the beauty of time at Chattanooga and there is no reason why the same harmony of action should not pervade a continent." The man spoke in art lingo and was in some ratings a military artist. He traveled light. The saddlebags which his orderly carried held, as he enumerated the articles, "a change of underclothing, my maps, a flask of whiskey, and a bunch of cigars." He could live as plainly as rank-and-file soldiers; they had seen him sleep in his blanket on cold ground. He watched over details till midnight and past, was out early in the morning, made up lost sleep sometimes with ten- and fifteen-minute naps on the ground during the day. When his troops had orders to do things that at first seemed impossible they said, "Well, *he* can't make a mistake."

A line of bridges on fire toward the rear one day, a private grunted comfortably, "Guess, Charley, Sherman has set the river on fire," Charley answering, "Well, if he has, I reckon it's all right." A stock anecdote had it that two Confederates on outpost duty were overheard trading rumors. "The Yanks can't get any more rations by railroad, for Wheeler has blown up the tunnel at Dalton." "Oh, hell, don't you know Sherman carries along a duplicate tunnel?"

Of the railroad-wrecking, wrote Sherman, "I gave it my personal attention." Bonfires were made of crossties, the iron rails laid on and when red-hot carried to telegraph poles or trees and twisted around to make what were nicknamed "Sherman hairpins." Also they were called "Lincoln gimlets." Or again they were "Jeff Davis neckties." A month of this and 265 miles of railway were unbuilt.

Instead of the fifteen miles a day to which Sherman had accustomed them, the troops on some days saw they were making ten. This gave them extra time to forage, to make trips aside and ahead off the line of march, to

A "Sherman hairpin," "Lincoln gimlet," or "Jeff Davis necktie"

collect corn, molasses, meal, bacon, sweet potatoes, and other foodstuffs. Each brigade commander had authority to detail a forage company, usually about 50 men headed by one or two commissioned officers. Before daylight this party would leave, knowing where to rejoin their command on the march later in the day. On foot five or six miles from the brigade route, they visited every plantation and farm within range. On a farm wagon or a family carriage they loaded bacon, cornmeal, turkeys, ducks, chickens, "everything that could be used as food or forage," to use Sherman's words. They regained the main road, usually in advance of their wagon train, and delivered to the brigade commissary the day's supplies gathered.

"Often would I pass these foraging parties at the roadside," wrote Sherman, "waiting for their wagons to come up, and was amused at their strange collections—mules, horses, even cattle, packed with old saddles and loaded with hams, bacon, bags of corn meal and poultry of every description. Although this foraging was attended with great danger and hard work, there seemed to be a charm about it that attracted the soldiers, and it was a privilege to be detailed on such a party. Daily they returned mounted on all sorts of beasts, which were at once taken from them and appropriated to the general use; but the next day they would start out again on foot, to repeat the experience of the day before." Candidly Sherman admitted, "No doubt, many acts of pillage, robbery and violence, were committed by these parties of foragers, usually called 'bummers.' " Stories came to him of jewelry taken from women, of family silverware dug up from hiding-places, and of plunder of value that never reached the commissary. "But these acts were exceptional and incidental. I never heard of any cases of murder or rape."

Sherman rebuked one day a soldier with a ham on his musket, a jug of molasses under his arm, and a big piece of honey in his hand from which he was eating. The soldier caught Sherman's eye, then in a lowered voice spoke to another trooper, "Forage liberally on the country." This was a quotation from Sherman's general order. Sherman in such cases explained that "foraging must be limited to the regular parties properly detailed." But the unruly and the malicious would get out of hand, and in his official report to the War Department Sherman wrote of this hoodlum element, "A little loose in foraging they 'did some things they ought not to have done.' "

Confederate spokesmen and organs naturally laid blame for all crimes and atrocities on Sherman's "bummers." So loosely was this term applied to any member of his army that the commander in time came to say in fun he was "an old bummer" himself. Yet no careful reading was required of the criticisms voiced by Governor Brown and General Beauregard the previous August to see they meant to say that the Confederate cavalry under General Wheeler had its own bummers. Robert Toombs then was writing to Stephens that Wheeler's band "consumes more than the whole army," was helping "accelerate the evil day," and as to their Confederate commander, Wheeler, "I hope to God he will never get back to Georgia." A letter to Secretary Seddon published in the *Charleston Mercury* went into many particulars of this Confederate unit having plunderers who took carpets, blankets, furniture in private houses, "by force in the presence of the owners."

Kilpatrick's cavalry did more than any other unit to earn a bad name for Sherman's army. They did lay hands on old men and choke them by the throats till the secret hiding-places of coin, silver, or jewelry were divulged. They did put their dirty boots on white bed linen, dance on polished floors to the piano music of howling comrades, smash the piano with gun butts. They did drag feather beds outdoors and scatter the feathers like a small snowstorm. They did scare women, though the incidence of rape was not conclusive in more than one or two cases. They did make free with Negro women and set special value on shapely mulattoes. But they were veteran troopers, hard fighters, afraid of no danger nor hardship—and the army believed Sherman tolerated them, partly because of his own belief that as tough soldiers for loyal active service they were among the best the earth had ever seen, partly because to set up a military police to watch and discipline his own men would delay when delay might be at heavy cost.

Foragers were authorized to appropriate "whatever is needed by the command," forbidden to enter "dwellings of inhabitants or commit any trespass," and particularly and significantly counseled to discriminate "between the rich who are usually hostile, and the poor or industrious, usually neutral or friendly." They were warned against "abusive or threatening language," told to give written certificates of the facts as to what they were seizing, "but no receipts," and they should at all times "endeavor to leave with each family a reasonable portion for their maintenance."

How many hundreds or thousands of stragglers, skulkers, and deserters from the Confederate Army there were at this time in Georgia could not get into official records. In Georgia and all the Southern and Border States at this time were roving bands of bushwhackers and guerrillas, lawless, desperate, living on the country. General Lee, seeing his losses by desertion on the increase in latter '64, suggested to President Davis it might be advisable to serve notice that deserters would have their rights to citizenship and property taken away. Davis the year before had proclaimed amnesty to enlisted men absent without leave who would return. Lee had likewise offered full pardon to some Georgia troops, resulting, said the *Richmond Enquirer* of February 12, 1863, in returns "by dozens, scores, and hundreds," a total of 600 being sent back to their regiments. Governor Vance of North Carolina had the same year given out a long and fierce malediction on "the vile wretch who skulked in the woods, or the still viler coward who aided him, while his bleeding country was calling in vain for his help," telling them they must consider what their brave comrades would do to them when peace and independence were secured. "Ye that shelter, conceal, and feed these miserable depredators, think you that you will be spared? Nay! Never-failing eyes have marked you, every one." Misdeeds near to atrocities had been committed, according to Vance's proclamation. "When the overjoyed wife welcomes once more her brave and honored husband to his home, and tells him how, in the long years of his absence, in the lonely hours of the night, ye who had been his comrades rudely entered her house, robbed her and her children of their bread, and heaped insult and indignities upon her defenseless head, the wrath of that heroic husband will make you regret, in the bitterness of your cowardly terror, that you were ever born. If permitted to live in the State at all, you will be infamous. You will be hustled from the polls, a jury of your countrymen will shun you as a pestilence." This across the State line from Georgia, where Governor Brown had called for a just public opinion to deal with all deserters and stragglers, no matter what their position, wealth, or influence. Disloyal citizens harboring or encouraging deserters, warned Governor Brown, would find him strictly enforcing the law of treason against them, as he was determined to rid the State of all deserters who disgraced her soil.

In more than one case deserters said they had heard that if Lincoln was elected in November the war would be over, that it was common talk that with Lincoln President again the South would quit fighting. Many rumors of the Confederacy being on its last legs encouraged desertion. Union commanders circulated Lincoln's proclamation offering amnesty. Across picket posts, through printed circulars, by means open and secret, the report spread that deserters into the Union lines would meet good treatment. That the earlier Confederate unity was breaking, that cracks and seams had come in their governmental structure, was known to the Georgians, who saw their State legislature joined with those of Mississippi and North Carolina in refusals to take as constitutional the act of their Congress at Richmond in suspending the writ of habeas corpus. And timed with Sherman's march from Atlanta toward the sea ran the rumor that President Jefferson Davis was to be impeached. It was not a harmonious Confederate Georgia over which Sherman was laying devastation. Daily as Sherman's troops swung along on the march came remarks from sidewalks, from roadsides. Most often there was silence. But General Hazen noted that the most typical expression from the Georgians was: "Why don't you go over to South Carolina and serve them this way? They started it."

On the first days out of Atlanta Negroes by hundreds began following "de Linkum sojers," believing "de day of Jubilo" had come for them as they shouted, "Marse Linkum done remember us!" In one rush of the blacks for deliverance, they clung to Sherman's stirrups, pressed their faces against his horse, hailed him as the Angel of the Lord. One of Sherman's staff men wrote of seeing a black woman, holding a mulatto baby, point at Sherman with the cry, "Dar's de man dat rules de world!" At many a crossroads they came singing and cavorting in a faith that now their masters were overcome and the long-promised emancipation was at hand. Sherman however continued his former policy of telling them that in the right and proper hour to come they would have freedom to work for themselves instead of their masters, that they must not now harm their masters. "We don't want that." To Grant's advice that he should acquire Negroes and arm and organize them as best he could, Sherman paid no attention. In a plantation house at the crossing of the Ulcofauhatchee River he explained to an old, gray-haired Negro, "of as fine a head as I ever saw," that "we wanted the slaves to remain where they were, and not to load us down with useless mouths, which would eat up the food for our fighting men; that our success was their assured freedom; that we could receive a few of their young, hearty men as pioneers; but that if they followed us in swarms of old and young, feeble and helpless, it would simply cripple us in our great task." Sherman believed that this old man spread this message far, got it carried from mouth to mouth to an extent that saved the army from taking on a host of refugees that might have spelled famine. Some 25,000 Negroes in all, it was estimated, from time to time joined the army and were fed by it, three-fourths of them perhaps turning back homesick or unwilling or unable to stand the pace.

One raw, cold night Sherman found himself in a double-hewed-log house, saw a box marked "Howell Cobb," learned from Negroes he was in the home of a Confederate brigadier general, one-time United States Senator from Georgia, Secretary of the United States Treasury under President Buchanan. "Of course, we confiscated his property, and found it rich in corn, beans, peanuts, and sorghum-molasses." Sherman sent word to a staff general "to spare nothing," and that night on the Cobb plantation "huge bonfires consumed the fence-rails, kept our soldiers warm, and the teamsters and men, as well as the slaves, carried off an immense quantity of corn and provisions of all sorts."

Arriving the next day at the State capital, Milledgeville, they found Governor Joseph Brown, the State officials, and the members of the legislature gone, the Governor's mansion stripped of carpets, curtains, furniture, food, these latter shipped away on railroad tracks soon wrecked by the Union troops. Here Federal troops used stacks of Confederate paper money for a breakfast fire. Here Federal officers held a mock session in the State legislative chamber, repealed the Ordinance of Secession, voted the State back into the Union, made sarcastic speeches, and appointed a committee officially to kick the buttocks of Governor Brown and President Jefferson Davis. Here were late newspapers from over the South, one having an appeal from General Beauregard to the people of Georgia to arise, obstruct, be confident, be resolute, and "Sherman's army will soon starve in your midst." Also a proclamation from Senator B. H. Hill, cosigned at Richmond by Secretary of War Seddon, that with firm and prompt action, "You have now the best opportunity ever presented to destroy the enemy." And while Sherman in Milledgeville read these and other items, thousands of bales of cotton got the torch, many cotton gins and presses were wrecked, and as Sherman reported, "I burned the railroad buildings and the arsenals; the state-house and Governor's Mansion I left unharmed." That Governor Brown had transported the cabbages from his cellar and left the State archives for the invaders was taken by Sherman as a sign of a hurried departure, if nothing more.

The marching army moved on, no pauses, no days of rest, feeding on the fat of the land with a more savory bill of fare than any army during the war thus far. "It was gravy every day." Juicy steaks, pork chops, fried chicken, ham and eggs, yams rolled in Indian meal, sorghum syrup—at moments the war was a picnic and a frolic. Not so of course when the route shifted from east southward toward Savannah, when ground under the feet of one column heaved in explosion and several men were torn by shells and torpedoes, whereupon Sherman ordered Confederate prisoners to be marched ahead. They accommodated and dug up a line of buried torpedoes.

Sherman's army feinted toward the cities of Augusta and Macon, made no real move at them, slipped smoothly past them. No time now for the taking of cities. At Macon he would have been delayed by General Howell Cobb's State reserves. Governor Brown had called into service all white males from sixteen to sixty-five, except ministers, telegraphers, and railroad employees. From the Georgia members of Congress at Richmond came a message that the President and Secretary of War would do everything possible to help Georgia, and meantime "let every man fly to arms"; remove Negroes, horses, cattle; burn what could not be removed, burn bridges, block the roads, assail the invaders in front, flank, and rear. By a policy of destruction they would stop the destroyer. To Augusta came General Bragg, the Richmond chief of staff. A call went out for defenders against an insolent foe coming "with his hell-hounds thirsty for plunder," the torch "red in his hands," prepared to "leave beautiful Augusta a smouldering heap of blackened ruins."

Confederate cavalry detached from Hood's army skirmished a little with Sherman's advance but undertook no real clash with the Union horse troops under Kilpatrick. The convicts, on Sherman's approach let loose from the State prison at Milledgeville for military service, were no help to further good order in Georgia that month. Some of them, joined up with other deserters, drifters, bushwhackers, posed as Wheeler's cavalry and raided here and there for loot. "People show little spirit," wired a defending general from Augusta to Richmond. There and at Macon were the only signs of any organized resistance to Sherman, and at these spots Sherman refused to pause. At Macon "every man was in the trenches," said the *Augusta Constitutionalist*, adding that when members of the State legislature passed through the city they were arrested and an attempt made to put them in military service. "But they were exempt by law and refused to serve." The *Macon Confederate* of November 20 said its city could be held against any force Sherman could bring. A rival newspaper, the *Southern Confederacy and Intelligencer*, had an opposite notion and packed up and left.

Sherman's men as seasoned soldiers more often gave misleading than correct information when they were asked what would be the route of the army. Sherman told of halting with his staff at a large plantation where the gray-haired old planter sat on a piazza. Could they have a drink of water? The planter called slaves, who brought a bucket of water and a gourd to drink from. While Sherman and his officers sipped from the gourd the old planter eyed them with curiosity. Hearing one say "General," he turned to Sherman in surprise.

"Are you a general?"

"Yes, sir."

"What is your name?"

"Sherman."

"Sherman; you General Sherman?"

"Yes."

"How many men have you got?"

"A million."

"Now, I'd just like to have you answer me one question more. Where are you going from here?"

"Well, now, that is considerable to request of an entire stranger, and under the circumstances."

"But I promise to keep it a secret."

"Are you sure that you can keep the secret if I impart it to you?"

"Certainly, certainly, I will; on my honor as a gentleman."

"But there is a risk, you know. What if I should tell and my intentions become publicly known?"

"I promise that I will not tell your secret to a single human being. You can trust me implicitly."

"You are quite sure I can trust you?"

"Most certainly I am; with the utmost safety."

"Well, then, I will tell you. I am going where I damn please. Good day."

As the Union army drove deeper south and east across Georgia, a bewilderment allied to panic took hold of the Richmond Government and its ramifications. They were stunned by the audacity of it, shaken by mystification as to whether the army was heading for Savannah or Charleston, or whether in the commander's headlong march there was any logical plan. After the first week or so, Confederate editors seemed to heed a warning that their reports of fact might serve the North. From day to day letters written by Rawlins at Grant's headquarters showed how Sherman's progress could be inferred and gleaned from the Richmond newspapers. Then on November 26 Rawlins wrote: "Richmond papers of yesterday seem studiously to avoid any reference to Sherman, except a dispatch which mentions the fact that his cavalry had been repulsed in its attempt to cross the Oconee River. Their failure to give details of Sherman's movements is construed here to be significant of his success."

Grant at City Point, Virginia, was saying: "Sherman's army is now somewhat in the condition of a ground-mole when he disappears under a lawn. You can here and there trace his track, but you are not quite certain where he will come out till you see his head."

As less and less could be gleaned from Southern newspapers, the Union army marching in Georgia, "the lost army," became a manner of world mystery, for speculation and surmise in the North and in Europe. "If Sherman has really left his army in the air and started off without a base to march from Georgia to South Carolina," said the experts of the *Army and Navy Gazette* in England, "he has done either one of the most brilliant or one of the most foolish things ever performed by a military leader." Sherman would either come out decorated for "the success of sublime audacity" or ridiculed for "the most tremendous disaster that ever befell an armed host," believed the London *Herald*, adding that he might become "the scoff of mankind and the humiliation of the United States" or on the other hand win a tablet of "fame side by side with that of Napoleon and Hannibal." The English were now really getting interested in a spectacular phase of the war. As theatre it had so often led them to yawns. Now the London *Times*, accustomed to patronizing of the American scene, found itself fascinated by a piece of drama. "Since the great Duke of Marlborough turned his back upon the Dutch, and plunged heroically into Germany to fight the famous Battle of Blenheim, military history has recorded no stranger marvel than the mysterious expedition of General Sherman, on an unknown route against an undiscoverable enemy."

People were angry at Sherman's presumption in attempting such a wild project, wrote Henry Adams in early December, from the American Legation to his brother with the Army of the Potomac. "Popular opinion here declares louder than ever that Sherman is lost. . . . The interest felt in his march is enormous, however, and if he arrives as successfully as I expect, at the sea, you may rely upon it that the moral effect of his demonstration on Europe will be greater than that of any other event of the war. It will finish the rebs on this side."

To Grant's tent at City Point came Philadelphians in fear Sherman would be overwhelmed while Grant sat before Richmond doing nothing. Grant lighted several matches, took his time, got his cigar going, then, cool as a cucumber: "Sherman is acting by order and I am waiting on him. Just as soon as I hear he is at some one of the points designated on the seacoast I will take Richmond. Were I to move now without advices from Sherman, Lee would evacuate Richmond, taking his army somewhere South and I would have to follow him to keep him from jumping on Sherman." Cordially Grant wished them to pass along word that "jealousy between me and Sherman is impossible." He offered them cigars. They went away with consolation they had hoped for.

To a serenading party on the night of December 6 the President was brief and intimate in what he had to say. "I believe I shall never be old enough to speak without embarrassment when I have nothing to talk about. I have no good news to tell you, and yet I have no bad news to tell. We have talked about elections until there is nothing more to say about them. The most interesting news we now have is from Sherman. We all know where he went in, but I can't tell where he will come out. I will close now by proposing three cheers for General Sherman and his army."

The serenaders, numbering about 1,000, had first been at the home of ex-Mayor Bowen, where they gave music and cheers for Congressman Reuben E. Fenton, newly elected Governor of New York. Then on to the White House they went, taking the President by surprise. He "didn't know just what he could say to satisfy the crowd and himself," according to Fenton. As they walked from the library to the front portico he asked Fenton to speak first, giving Lincoln maybe "a peg to hang on." But Fenton didn't give him much of a peg. So Lincoln was through speaking almost before he began. He faded from view of the crowd, telling Fenton inside the White House, "I raised a good laugh and it was a good time for me to quit."

General Sherman's brother, the Ohio Senator, came in anxiety over published Southern reports of his brother in retreat and disaster. Could anyone tell him the facts? Lincoln said: "Oh, no, I know the hole he went in at, but I can't tell you what hole he will come out of." Some two weeks after Sherman disappeared A. K. McClure had reached the door of Lincoln's office and was about leaving when he heard, "McClure, wouldn't you like to hear something from Sherman?" McClure turned eagerly and said he certainly would. Lincoln laughed. "Well, I'll be hanged if I wouldn't myself."

Not so funny was an incident that came to Carpenter of Lincoln during a White House reception, shaking hands with a continuous stream of people. And along came an old friend, whose name and face should be perfectly familiar to Lincoln. But Lincoln gave him only the same handshake and abstract greeting as any unknown. The old friend stood still and spoke again to Lincoln, who roused, shook himself out of a mood and a dark-brown study, again took his old friend's hand, and apologized. "Excuse me for not noticing you. I was thinking of a man down South."

From the Richmond newspapers and from reprints in Northern dailies, Grant and the War Department and Lincoln tried to glean information. None could be had from so factless a statement as the *Richmond Whig's*, November 24: "Sherman's march looks more like a retreat than an advance." They could discount some of the proclamations and threats. To sift out the actual facts was not easy. Neither Macon nor Augusta had been captured. Day after day the Richmond dailies repeated this. Also Sherman had not reached any prison camp in Georgia and freed Union prisoners. This too was reiterated. Both statements were correct. But they would not spell out the puzzle of where Sherman was, whether an angry population had risen against him and organized desperate defense, nor whether surprise tactics of some sort had damaged or waylaid him. The most significant thing was that the Richmond papers had no stories of attacks or effective actions against Sherman. Lincoln worried over whether Sherman was safe. "I assured him," wrote Grant to Sherman later, "with the army you had and you in command of it, there was no danger . . . that I would not have intrusted the expedition to any other living commander." Sherman understood Lincoln's feeling. "Judging from the tone of the Southern press, the outside world must have supposed us ruined and lost."

Grant summarized the Southern newspapers as saying Sherman's men were starving, demoralized, "wandering about almost without object, aiming only to reach the sea-coast and get under the protection of our navy." The reprints in the North affected the minds of people, bringing distress to good Unionists who had husbands, sons, and brothers with Sherman, noted Grant. "Mr. Lincoln seeing these accounts, had a letter written asking me if I could give him anything that he could say to the loyal people that would comfort them." Grant answered there was "not the slightest occasion for alarm," that Sherman would get through somewhere and even if worst came to worst he could return North. Afterward Grant heard of Lincoln comforting inquirers with the reply: "Grant says they are safe with such a general, and that if they cannot get out where they want to, they can crawl back by the hole they went in at."

The same point in a less blunt style went into Lincoln's message to Congress on December 6. While writing it he told Noah Brooks that he hoped Sherman would be heard from so that he could enlighten "and possibly congratulate the country." But December came, and what would the President do in his message for those so feverish to have news from Sherman? One night he took a sheet of writing paper from a desk drawer, and putting on a manner of confidence and secrecy, said to Brooks, "I expect you want to know all about Sherman's raid?" Brooks said he sure would, Lincoln saying, "Well, then, I'll read you this paragraph from my message."

Then he read: "The most remarkable feature in the military operations of the year is General Sherman's attempted march of three hundred miles directly through the insurgent region. It tends to show a great increase of our relative strength that our General-in-Chief should feel able to confront, and hold in check every active force of the enemy, and yet to detach a well appointed large army to move on such an expedition. The result not yet being known, conjecture in regard to it is not here indulged."

That was all. Brooks puzzled; here was nothing about the direction of march or the point from which news of Sherman was expected. Laying the sheet of paper down and taking off his spectacles, Lincoln laughed at Brooks's disappointment, and added kindly, "Well, my dear fellow, that's all that Congress will know about it, anyhow."

A curious sentence which could serve several purposes was written into the first draft of the message to Congress. Then later Lincoln ran his pen through this sentence: "We must conclude that he [the General in Chief] feels our cause could, if need be, survive the loss of the whole detached force; while, by the risk, he takes a chance for the great advantages which would follow success." This was dropped. It could be taken to mean that Lincoln was not sharing the "risk" with Grant and Sherman. And the point of superior military resources in the North was treated thoroughly and statistically elsewhere in the message.

In early December Colonel A. H. Markland of Grant's staff was leaving with mail for Sherman's army. He didn't know where he would deliver it, not knowing where he would find Sherman. Grant had told Markland to step in and see whether Lincoln had some message for Sherman. Lincoln was in a conference, but on seeing Markland's card had him shown in at once. He arose from his chair at a table, crossed the room, meeting Markland halfway, and with a handshake: "Well, Colonel, I got word from General Grant that you were going to find Sherman, and that you would take him any message I might have. I know you will find him, because we always get good news from you. Say to General Sherman, for me, whenever and wherever you see him, 'God bless him and God bless his army.' That is as much as I can say, and more than I can write." He held Markland's hand and looked him in the eye all the time he was saying this. Tears gathered in his eyes, his lips trembled, and his voice shook, according to Markland, who noted: "He shook my hand, bade me good-by, and I proceeded toward the door, when he called to me. When I looked back he was standing like a statue where I had left him. 'Now, remember what I say,' and then he repeated the message. I passed out the door and never saw Mr. Lincoln again."

An army for thirty-two days to the outside world "lost sight of," as Sherman phrased it, now had behind it three hundred miles of naked smokestacks, burned culverts, shattered trestleworks, wailing humanity. Of the railroads every rail was twisted beyond use, every tie, bridge, tank, woodshed, and depot building burned. Thirty miles ran the devastation on either side of the line from Atlanta, estimated Sherman. Kilpatrick's 5,000 horsemen had ravaged beyond the reach of foot troops. For the economy of powder they had sabered hogs, knocked horses between the ears with axes, killing more than a hundred horses on one plantation with a fine mansion, and shooting every bloodhound, mastiff, or other dog that looked as though it could track runaway Negroes in swamps and forest. Over many square miles of this area now was left not a chicken, not a pig, nor horse nor cow nor sheep, not a smokehouse ham nor side of bacon, not a standing corn-crib with a forgotten bushel, not a mule to plow land with, not a piece of railroad track, nor cars nor locomotives nor a bunker of coal. "The destruc-

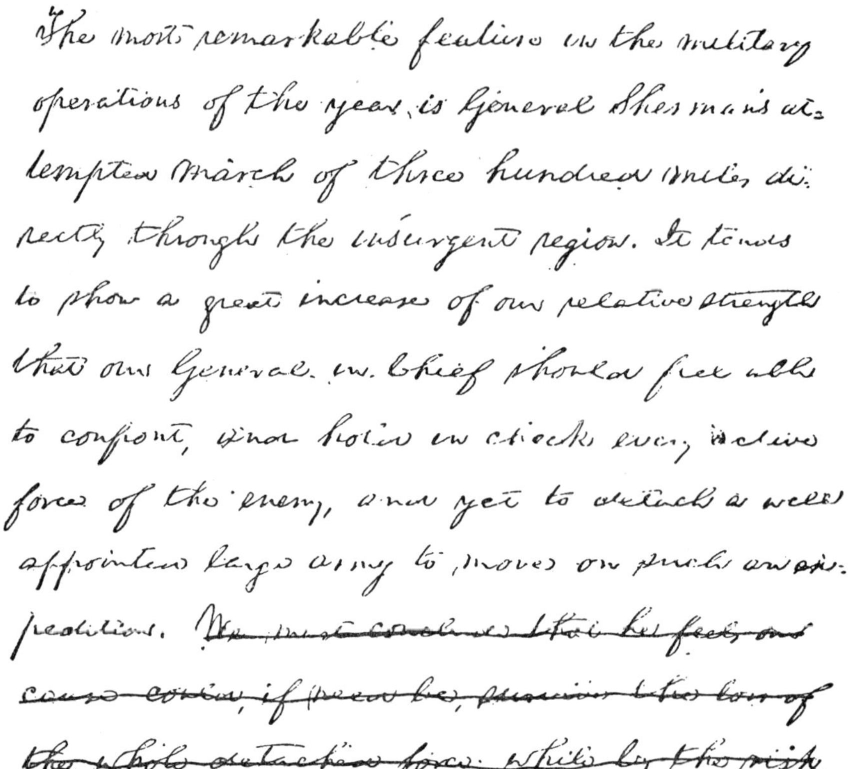

The most remarkable feature in the military operations of the year, is General Sherman's attempted march of three hundred miles directly through the insurgent region. It tends to show a great increase of our relative strength that our General-in-Chief should feel able to confront, and hold in check every active force of the enemy, and yet to detach a well-appointed large army to move on such an expedition. ~~We must conclude that he feels our cause could, if need be, survive the loss of the whole detached force; while, by the risk, he takes a chance for the great advantages which would follow success.~~ The result not yet being known, conjecture in regard to it is not ~~be~~ here indulged.

Lincoln in his '64 message to Congress writes confidently of Sherman's vanished army, drawing his pen through a sentence that mentions "risk." Original in the Barrett collection.

tion could hardly have been worse," wrote one commentator, "if Atlanta had been a volcano in eruption, and the molten lava had flowed in a stream sixty miles wide and five times as long." War as a reality, a pervasive stench of conquest, had come to Georgia.

"We'll give them a bellyful of war," had been a rank-and-file saying. A simoom it was, said a Macon newspaper, another and later observer, seeking metaphors, terming the swath of Sherman's 62,000 men in the fat lands of Georgia like the grind of a glacier, like the rude and laughing Goths who overran Italy, like a Biblical horizon black with locusts who ate and vanished. More than any single military event of the war it captured human imagination as a passage in a terrible epic poem nearing a climax.

On December 10 General Howard's right wing stood ten miles from Savannah. To Washington Howard sent a telegram notifying the Government that the march had won through. By scouts overland to Port Royal, South Carolina, and wire relays this good-news message reached Washington the evening of December 14. The next day Halleck passed on to Lincoln Howard's dispatch: "We have met with perfect success thus far, troops in fine spirit and General Sherman near by."

Over the North flashed this news. Across streets in town, over roads and fields in the country, went the jubilant cry that Sherman had got to Savannah. From Boston to Council Bluffs and points west there were cheers and prayers of thanks.

On December 13 Sherman with staff officers climbed to the top of a rice mill, looked toward the sea for the fleet, looked toward a forest edge where the 15th Corps was ready to move on Fort McAllister. The fort overlooked a river needed for supply transport between Sherman and the fleet—if the fleet had arrived as planned. For hours Sherman and his aides kept their lookout. Hour on hour slipped away and it was getting near sundown when a smokestack took clearer form, at last could be seen, and later a flag wigwagging the words, "Who are you?"

"General Sherman," said the rice-mill flag.

"Is Fort McAlister [sic] taken yet?" asked the ship.

"Not yet, but it will be in a minute."

As though this was a signal, Sherman's old Shiloh division under General William B. Hazen broke from cover, sharpshooters running out to fling themselves flat on the ground and pick off enemy gunners, the whole line soon charging through a hail of shot, shell, and rifle bullets, rushing the defenses, soon dancing on the parapets of Fort McAllister, waving their regimental flags and shooting their happy muskets up at the sky. "It's my old division," cried Sherman. "I knew they'd do it." To General Slocum he wired: "Take a good big drink, a long breath and then yell like the devil. The fort was carried at 4:30 P.M., the assault lasting but fifteen minutes."

By the light of a pale moon this December 13 Sherman rode a fast yawl downstream, boarded the Union ship, the *Dandelion,* and before midnight was writing dispatches to be read five days later by Stanton, Halleck, and

Lincoln—and parts of them passed on to a world starving for news and sure fact.

Over two hundred miles of railroad had been "utterly destroyed," he notified Washington, and now he asked authority to march straight north to Raleigh, North Carolina, giving the intervening country the same operation he had given Georgia, so that Lee must evacuate Richmond. "I regard Savannah as good as gained." The Georgia damage he estimated at $100,000,000, "at least twenty millions of which has inured to our advantage, and the remainder is simple waste and destruction. This may seem a hard species of warfare, but it brings the sad realities of war home to those who have been directly or indirectly instrumental in involving us in its attendant calamities."

Back with his army again, Sherman saw Colonel A. H. Markland with sacks of mail. Men and officers whooped with glee over the first letters from home in many weeks. Sherman's eyes danced when Colonel Markland said he had a message from President Lincoln. "Before leaving Washington, I was directed to take you by the hand wherever I met you and say to you for him, 'God bless you and the army under your command. Since cutting loose from Atlanta, my prayers and those of the nation have been for your success.' " "I thank the President," responded Sherman. "Say my army is all right."

Savannah fell, its garrison of 9,000 under General Hardee moving out and away toward the north on the night of December 20, sensing Sherman's design for their capture. Union troops moved in. Sherman himself arrived on December 22. A Treasury agent suggested a telegram to President Lincoln presenting him with Savannah as a Christmas gift, saying, "The President particularly enjoys such pleasantry." Sherman wrote Lincoln a message:

"I beg to present you as a Christmas gift, the city of Savannah, with one hundred and fifty guns and plenty of ammunition, also about twenty-five thousand bales of cotton." On the day after Christmas Lincoln wrote a letter of thanks to Sherman and sent it South by General John A. Logan, who was to rejoin his old 15th Corps. This letter gave the shadings of Lincoln's anxiety and fear over Sherman's great adventure, with salutations. It read:

My dear General Sherman:

Many, many thanks for your Christmas gift, the capture of Savannah.

When you were about leaving Atlanta for the Atlantic coast, I was anxious, if not fearful; but feeling that you were the better judge, and remembering that "nothing risked, nothing gained," I did not interfere. Now, the undertaking being a success, the honor is all yours; for I believe none of us went further than to acquiesce.

And taking the work of General Thomas into the count, as it should be taken, it is indeed a great success. Not only does it afford the obvious and immediate military advantages; but in showing to the world that your army could be divided, putting the stronger part to an important new service, and yet leaving enough to vanquish the old opposing force of the whole,—Hood's army,—it brings those who sat in darkness to see a great light. But what next?

I suppose it will be safe if I leave General Grant and yourself to decide.

Please make my grateful acknowledgments to your whole army—officers and men.

Yours very truly,

A. Lincoln

There was no doubt that little by little the lingering hesitations that Sherman had about Lincoln were wearing away, and the degree of trust that Lincoln held for him and Grant was deepening. The three were now closer than ever. Later Sherman was to write that the acclaim over the march to the sea pleased him, but "I experienced more satisfaction in giving to his [Lincoln's] overburdened and weary soul one gleam of satisfaction and happiness."

Stanton however refused at this time to join the others in a Merry Christmas mood. To Grant he wrote: "It is a sore disappointment that Hardee was able to get off his 15,000 from Sherman's 60,000. It looks like protracting the war while their armies continue to escape."

In the letter to Sherman, Lincoln referred to "the work of General Thomas," meaning what Thomas had done since he and Sherman parted in northern Georgia. The campaigning was strange and involved, with none of the dramatic simplicity of Sherman's march, General Schofield writing to Sherman that they in Tennessee had the work while he in Georgia had the fun. Schofield on leaving Sherman and trying to connect his force of 29,000 with Thomas at Nashville had to fight a battle with Hood's 41,000 Confederate troops at Franklin. Hood in desperate frontal attacks thrown back with losses of 6,000 as against 2,300 on the Union side, Schofield drew off. Hood followed. Schofield joined Thomas at Nashville. There Hood camped with his army, now reduced to 26,000, intending as he said in a report of December 11 "to force the enemy to take the initiative."

Meantime Washington worried. Stanton on December 2 telegraphed Grant: "The President feels solicitous about the disposition of General Thomas to lay in fortifications for an indefinite period 'until Wilson the commander of the cavalry gets equipments.' This looks like the McClellan and Rosecrans strategy of do nothing and let the rebels raid the country. The President wishes you to consider the matter." On this same December 2 Grant sent two dispatches to Thomas urging him to take the offensive, Thomas replying that in two or three days he would probably be ready. Four days later Grant's sharp-toned order to Thomas ran: "Attack Hood at once and wait no longer for a remnant of your cavalry. There is great danger of delay resulting in a campaign back to the Ohio River." He would obey the order, responded Thomas, adding his belief it would be hazardous with the small force of cavalry at his service. Stanton the next day indulged himself with the telegraphed remark to Grant: "Thomas seems unwilling to attack because it is hazardous, as if all war was anything but hazardous."

Should Thomas have lashed out at Hood with all he had there in early December? Around this question military strategists of either desk or field could argue long. Thomas was naturally slow-moving, preferred walking his horse to a gallop. In the fierce and tumultuous campaign before Atlanta Sherman wrote of one action that it was "the only time during the campaign I can recall seeing General Thomas urge his horse into a gallop." Yet Thomas also, as Sherman saw him, had on occasion a granite-and-glacier certainty of movement. As West Point classmates, as young lieutenants in the same regular-army regiment for ten years, they became "precious" to each other, Sherman feeling that "Never since the world began did such absolute confidence exist between commander and commanded, and among the many mistakes I made I trace some to his earnest and vehement advice." It had been Sherman's decision when his priceless right-hand man, McPherson, was killed near Atlanta, that the command of the Army of the Cumberland should go not to John A. Logan, the one other man considered, but to Thomas. For this Logan, the volunteer, blamed Sherman and those he termed "the West Point clique."

Logan in these days of early December was at Grant's City Point headquarters. He had fought brilliant offensives in the West under Grant and Sherman. He was precisely the kind of a commander who would not have delayed action under the prodding of such telegrams as Grant had been sending Thomas.

On December 8 Grant wired Halleck: "If Thomas has not struck yet, he ought to be ordered to hand over his command to Schofield. There is no better man to repel an attack than Thomas but I fear he is too cautious to ever take the initiative." Even without counsel from Logan, Grant might have had this slant. He believed that Schofield would have moved days ago and that the same Schofield who had savagely lacerated Hood at Franklin was dependable. And time counted. Grant felt that deeply. He was worrying over the possibility of Hood's starting north and reaching the Ohio River, setting ablaze again a low Confederate morale.

To Grant from Halleck came a telegram, in all probability on so grave a matter having had scrutiny or perhaps revision by the President, reading: "If you wish General Thomas relieved, give the order. No one here will interfere. The responsibility, however, will be yours, as no one here, so far as I am informed, wishes General Thomas removed."

Grant tried on this December 8 a further telegram to Thomas: "Why not attack at once? By all means avoid the contingency of a foot-race to see which, you or Hood, can beat to the Ohio." Thomas still delayed. In cavalry Hood outnumbered him four to one; he was getting remounts and hoped to have a force of 6,000. He wired Grant that in troop concentration and transport "I have made every effort possible." Grant, receiving this December 9, wired Halleck that as Thomas had not yet attacked, "Please telegraph orders relieving him at once, and placing Schofield in command."

The order was made out. Before telegraphing it to Nashville Halleck asked Grant if he still wished it to be forwarded. Grant replied, "You will suspend the order until it is seen whether he will do anything."

On Halleck's telegraphing Thomas that Grant was uneasy about the delay Thomas answered that he felt conscious of having done everything in his power to prepare, "and if General Grant should order me to be relieved, I will submit without a murmur. . . . The troops could not have been gotten ready before this. . . . A terrible storm of freezing weather has come on." The rain froze as it fell. A sheet of ice glazed the ground. Men and horses slipped. The weather favored defense. Grant to Thomas: "I have as much confidence in your conducting a battle rightly as I have in any other officer; but it has seemed to me that you have been slow, and I have had no explanation of affairs to convince me otherwise."

Thomas called his corps commanders, told them of the orders to attack Hood. The generals agreed that their commander should not fight till he was ready on the slippery hills around Nashville. No news of an attack reaching Grant, he wired December 11, "Let there be no further delay," Thomas replying, "I will obey the order as promptly as possible. The whole country is covered with a perfect sheet of ice and sleet." He would have attacked "yesterday had it not been for the storm."

Grant on December 13 ordered Logan to go to Nashville and replace Thomas in command. Logan started. Then Grant for the first time since he had become lieutenant general himself started on a trip back West, for Tennessee, to take personal charge there. Grant had reached Washington. Logan was at Louisville, Kentucky, less than a day's travel from Nashville. To both of them came news that Thomas had launched his troops at Hood's army.

Thomas telegraphed, December 15: "I attacked the enemy's left this morning, and drove it from the river below the city very nearly to the Franklin pike, a distance of about eight miles. . . . The troops behaved splendidly, all taking their share in assaulting and carrying the enemy's breast-works." That night the whole army slept on its guns in line of battle and the next day pushed a broken and retreating enemy at all points. "I beheld," later wrote Hood, "for the first and only time a Confederate army abandon the field in confusion." No rout of the war had been so complete. One factor was the cavalry for which Thomas had delayed action. Hood's army as a unit vanished. Parts of it, to the number of 15,000 men, held intact through the generalship of Forrest, who saved them for other Confederate commands. The Confederate losses in killed and wounded at least equaled the Union casualties of 3,000–and 4,462 Confederate prisoners were taken.

Sherman took pride in his friend "Old Tom" and was to write of this battle that it was the only one of the war "which annihilated an army." A famous metaphor was coined: the Rock of Chickamauga became the Sledge of Nashville. Congratulations came from many, including Grant, Sherman, Stanton, Sheridan, Lincoln's of December 16 reading: "Please accept for yourself, officers, and men, the nation's thanks for your good work of yesterday. You made a magnificent beginning; a grand consummation is within your easy reach. Do not let it slip." To a commission naming Thomas for the vacant major-generalship in the regular army Grant and Lincoln joined their signatures.

For Grant the week had been, according to Colonel Horace Porter, "the most anxious period of his entire military career," and before the victory came "he suffered mental torture." To Grant, Thomas was one piece in a big game involving other pieces and Grant was trying to time and co-ordinate them toward destroying the three Confederate armies left. When Thomas won, there would be only two. Porter believed that Grant saw victory right in Thomas's hand and was in grief over Thomas not reaching out and taking it. On top of this Grant was afraid that Hood would do the very thing Grant would do if he were Hood, according to Porter, which would be to march away from Thomas into Kentucky, cutting off Thomas's railroad connections and food communications, and getting to the Ohio River, "the disastrous moral effect of which would be beyond calculation." Furthermore, there were "the authorities at Washington." First had come Stanton's telegram that the President was "solicitous" about Thomas's delay. It sounded more like Lincoln than Stanton: "This looks like the McClellan and Rosecrans strategy of do nothing and let the rebels raid the country. The President wishes you to consider the matter." Then when Grant had suddenly ordered Thomas to be relieved by Schofield, the War Department wired "no one here" wished Thomas removed. So Grant talked with Logan, decided to send Logan on to Nashville, with requisite orders to take charge if Thomas had not moved, telling Logan to "say nothing about it" meanwhile. Then furthermore, according to Porter, Grant foresaw what was going to happen at Nashville and had begun traveling to that battlefield thinking that "his taking command in person would avoid the necessity of relieving Thomas, and be much less offensive to that officer than superseding him by some one else." The extent of Lincoln's hand in the affair did not appear. He seemed to have watched every phase of it keenly, "solicitous" that by no one's mistake should there be more "McClellan and Rosecrans strategy," yet when Grant put it up to him to relieve Thomas he insisted that must be Grant's act. Porter saw the affair in its many changes at Grant's headquarters and summarized it as "mental torture" for the man to whom Sherman could write of "the beauty of time" that the two of them had learned. One of the three remaining Confederate armies having been destroyed, Grant went from Washington to Burlington, New Jersey, and spent a day of rejoicing with his wife and family.

Grant's anxiety to play no favorites, to keep clear of the politics always seething in the army, showed one day in Washington when Sherman's army was "lost" in Georgia. He then gave the President and Secretary of War a list of eight major generals and thirty-three brigadiers whose services the Government "could dispense with to advantage." In the matter of letting out "these useless officers," noted Colonel Porter, Grant was entirely impartial, the list having some of his warm personal friends. The President said: "Why, I find that lots of officers on this list are very close friends of yours. Do you want them all dropped?" General Grant: "That's very true, Mr. President. But my personal friends are not always good generals, and I think it but just to adhere to my recommendations."

Letters and reports on both sides alluded to "the shattered débris" of Hood's army. Lincoln was reminded of a dog that had terrorized a neighborhood, its quarrelsome owner refusing to do anything about it. One day the dog came across a lump of meat and gulped it down unaware that it had a powder charge attached to a slow fuse. "Fragments of the dog were seen flying in every direction. The owner, picking up the remains, said, 'He was a good dog but as a dog his days of usefulness are over.' Hood's army was a good army, and we were all afraid of it, but as an army its usefulness is gone." Chandler of the war telegraph office said that Lincoln told this one in September too when Early's army was scattered by Sheridan.

Piece by piece the Union armies had now carried the Federal flag into an area much more than half the size of the seceded States. The slicing of the Confederacy in two by Sherman's march had now about wrecked Confederate transfers of troops and supplies between eastern and western seceded States. In the war telegraph office one evening Lincoln mused on this and told a story which the operator, Albert B. Chandler, put into writing:

"We had received news of a series of raids into rebel territory. Stoneman had just returned from an expedition into East Tennessee and Southwestern Virginia. Sherman had divided the Confederacy and safely reached Savannah. Grierson and Wilson had each been heard from in Alabama and Mississippi, and no State seemed free from our incursions.

"The President said it put him in mind of a weary traveller in one of the Western States, who, after journeying all day, came at night to a small log cabin. He went in and asked the occupants if he could be accommodated with food and lodging. He was told they could provide him with a place to sleep, but that there was not a 'bite of victuals' in the house.

"The traveller gladly accepted the pallet of straw, and soon fell asleep; but was awakened in a short time by whispers which disclosed that there was a cake baking in the ashes, and the woman and her husband were congratulating themselves on the way in which they had kept their food and deceived the hungry traveller.

"Feeling angry that they should have told him they had nothing to eat when it was not true, and that they were now 'chuckling' over it, he determined to spoil their game. He began to move restlessly, and finally got up and complained of feeling very badly.

"The woman asked him what was the matter.

"He told her he was much distressed in mind and could not sleep, and went on to say that his father when he died had left him a large farm, but that he had no sooner taken possession than mortgages began to appear, and, taking the fire poker, he said: 'My farm was situated like this,' illustrating by drawing the poker through the ashes, so as to entirely surround the ash cake with the lines. 'First one man got so much of it off on this side; then another brought in a mortgage and took off another piece there; then another there, and another there, and there and there,' drawing the poker through the ashes each time to explain locations, 'until,' said he, 'there was nothing of the farm left to me at all, which I presume is the case with your cake.'

"'And I reckon,' said Mr. Lincoln, 'that the prospect is now very good for soon having the Rebellion as completely cut up as that ash cake was.'"

The land areas lost to the Confederacy spelled men lost too. "The need of men was never greater," wrote Lee to Davis in October. The odds against him in troops, "the enemy's numerical superiority," as he phrased it, had brought hazards so that "there is the gravest reason to apprehend the result of every encounter." If the entire arms-bearing population in Virginia and North Carolina, along with Negroes to relieve all labor details, could be gotten into service, "we may be able, with the blessing of God, to keep the enemy in check till the beginning of winter. If we fail to do this, the result may be calamitous." Now after two months Lee's tone to Davis was still graver.

Lee's distressing need for men ran back in part to an order of Grant in April that not another Confederate prisoner of war should be paroled or exchanged until certain conditions were met that Grant probably knew would never be met. Not until August did Grant come out with his real reason for this policy. Cruel it was, he admitted, but necessary. "Every man we hold, when released on parole or otherwise, becomes an active soldier against us at once either directly or indirectly. If we commence a system of exchange which liberates all prisoners taken, we will have to fight on until the whole South is exterminated. If we hold those caught they amount to no more than dead men." At the particular time in late summer when the Confederate Government proposed to exchange prisoners man for man, said Grant, it "would insure Sherman's defeat" and "compromise safety" at Richmond.

Many were the influences brought to bear on Lincoln to reverse or modify this policy of Grant. Arguments based on political power and made in the name of reason, cries and prayers for the sake of humanity, rang in his ears. But Lincoln stood by his general. He let Grant have his way. And at this time there raged over the North a propaganda of horror with proposals of vengeance for the inhuman handling of Union soldiers in Southern prisons. They were starved. And they died of starvation. This was fact. They festered in rags and became living skeletons, chilled and shivering. This, for many, was fact. Atrocities monstrous and almost beyond belief were told of in Northern newspapers and pulpits and on political platforms. These too had some basis of fact. But the South had its answers. And these too held facts. Where in the South were any such parades of pleasure and riots of luxury as could be seen in the metropolitan centers of the North? Measure the South's suffering, estimate its starvation and deprivation, and see how it would compare with that of the North. A shelf of competent testimony would reduce to a verdict of both sides making war as war had always been made, with results of suffering distributed alike among good and bad people, the innocent with the guilty—and meaning brought to the word "agony." The so-called laws of war were being violated, as in former wars, as an incident of humanity in the mass being violated—on both sides. Over this Lincoln troubled his mind and heart and was to refer to it in his second inaugural address.

"Andersonville" in the North meant horror beyond words. A 27-acre piece of marshland in southwestern Georgia, fenced and stockaded for Union prisoners, bare of trees and hiding-places, was Andersonville. Those in the North supposed to inform the kinfolk of a man that he had been sent to Andersonville found it hard to say the name of the place, or they said something else or the tone of voice dropped low. A man going there died a dirty and lingering death; or killed himself by stepping over a line where guards at once put a bullet through him for attempted escape; or lost his mind; or by slim chance issued forth to freedom somehow with a woebegone look and a wild-animal stare in his eyes. When a few of these hunted ones had crept into Sherman's camp one night at Milledgeville, the sight of them had brought mutterings of revenge.

The place named Andersonville won distinction as the one spot on the North American map where war was more hideous to look at than any other spot that could be named. In its close-packed and swarming population was less food and more scurvy and starvation; less soap and more filth, scabs, and lice; less medicine and more gangrene, fever, diarrhea, ulcers, sores, hemorrhages, bleeding gums and swollen lips symptomatic of scurvy, than anywhere else in America.

The bloodiest battle of the war had not taken such a toll of death as Andersonville from June to September, 1864, with its record of 8,589 dying. This reduced the peak population of 32,000 and enlarged the average space of six square feet per man.

Here in September of '64 came Dr. Joseph Jones of the medical department of the Confederate Government, professor of medical chemistry at an Augusta college, to spend three weeks and report with a document of human horror, that the place held "a gigantic mass of human misery." To Vice-President Alexander H. Stephens had come this and like reports. Stephens suggested that Jefferson Davis visit Andersonville, that the Confederate President make a solemn speech to the prisoners and let them loose to go home and tell the North the South was fighting only for independence. Yet President Davis then was listening more closely to General Lee's call of need for his own scurvied and near-starving troops. Davis and Lee knew that desertion was on the increase because good enough men had crossed over into the Union lines to end living like hunted animals.

Where lay the blame? On both sides. So wrote a Confederate prisoner, Henry M. Stanley, later an African explorer, of what he saw at a human "cattle-yard" named Camp Douglas at Chicago. On the way to the latrines Stanley saw "crowds of sick men who had fallen prostrate from weakness, and given themselves wholly to despair, and while they crawled or wallowed in their filth, they cursed or blasphemed as often as they groaned." Every morning came wagons whereon Stanley saw the corpses rolled in their blankets "piled one upon another, as the New Zealand frozen mutton carcasses are carted from the docks!" And why not? The time, the age, wrote Stanley, was "brutally senseless and heedlessly cruel."

Had Lincoln been looking toward a policy of vengeance on the South, had he joined with Thad Stevens and the now powerful group who planned to visit retribution on the ruling class of the South, he could not have wished for a better issue than Andersonville. He could have set in motion such whirlwinds of hate as the war had not yet seen. Two or three pages in his message to Congress reciting high-light horrors would have been playing with dynamite of mass emotion. A grumbling and muttering had begun that the President took no action in this field, assertions, wrote Carpenter, that he showed "a criminal indifference to the sufferings of our prisoners at Libby, Andersonville, and other places." There was the record, said these critics: nowhere in any public address or message of the President could you find any allusion to the Union soldiers murdered by foul treatment in Southern prisons. And this was fact. Purposely Lincoln avoided discussion of it. The issue had not become sharp till this fourth year of the war. For maddening the Northern people into war effort the issue could have been useful earlier in the war. But now it could do no good toward the ends of reconciliation and rebuilding which Lincoln hoped for beyond the war's end. So he was saying nothing. Partly the animus in the matter was political.

"When the reports, in an authentic form, first reached Washington of the sufferings of the Union prisoners," wrote Carpenter, "I know he [the President] was greatly excited and overcome by them." He was told that justice demanded a stern retaliation, that like treatment should be given Confederate prisoners, and according to Carpenter, said to his Congressman M. F. Odell with deep feeling, "I can never, never starve men like that!" and again, "Whatever others may say or do, I never can, and I never will, be accessory to such treatment of human beings."

Stanton in May of '64 had brought the President a proposal that Confederate officers in Union prisons should be given the same rations and treatment as Union soldiers and officers received at Confederate hands. Lincoln, according to the official records, kept silent. No such order was issued. Had Lincoln wished the War Department to publish such an order, or to put such a policy into operation without publication, it would have been done as he wished.

On a visit to General Butler's army the President was taken through hospitals, through wards of wounded Confederate prisoners. And as Butler told it, they were at dinner afterward, Lincoln plainly "weary and depressed." It hurt the General that his guest didn't eat. Was he ill? Pushing away his plate, Lincoln answered, "I am well enough, but would to God this dinner or provisions like it were with our poor prisoners at Andersonville."

The Southern summer heat was bad for men from the North, and the Northern zero winter weather not so good for those from the South. Official statistics ran that twelve of every hundred Confederate prisoners died at the North, while fifteen died of every hundred Union captives in the South. Medical men agreed too that the Southern troops were undernourished because of their own armies' inferior food supply, and therefore less resistant to disease.

Food was a factor. The Union armies were better fed. Nothing in all the letters and communications of Robert E. Lee stood forth more tragically heroic than his calm and but slightly emotional statements to President Davis about the supply wagons going out and coming back with little or nothing. The inference for Davis was that Lee and his men would not cry nor complain, they would go on fighting, though they could fight better on less empty bellies. It was a later time that a loyal Confederate mother was to bring Lee a baby boy for his blessing. He took the little one in his arms, spoke the sacred words, and handed it back to the mother with the words "Teach him he must deny himself."

Want and hunger, however, threatened the life arteries of the Confederacy less than its own internal strife. The November message of President Davis to the Confederate Congress spoke desperately of conspiracies, of traitors and spies inside their own house. Was there one fatal flaw he was barred from discussing? If each State was sovereign, and sufficient to itself in authority, how could the central Confederate Government at Richmond demand or enforce complete loyalty of any State wavering in duty? The Confederacy was built on the basic theory that each State could do as it pleased and the first duty of any citizen was to be loyal to his State. What any State capital announced was more important and authoritative to the people of that State than any proclamations from the Richmond Government. This faith in States' Rights as much as want or military defeat was a gnawing and devitalizing factor in the Confederacy, giving rise to its President being distressed over conspiracies, traitors, and spies within their own house.

The spirit of the dilemma Davis now faced was forecast in Lincoln's first inaugural address: "If a minority in such case will secede rather than acquiesce, they make a precedent which in turn will divide and ruin them; for a minority of their own will secede from them whenever a majority refuses to be controlled by such minority. For instance, why may not any portion of a new confederacy a year or two hence arbitrarily secede again, precisely as portions of the present Union now claim to secede from it? All who cherish disunion sentiments are now being educated to the exact temper of this. Is there such a perfect identity of interests among the States to compose a new Union, as to produce harmony only, and prevent renewed secession?"

Not yet had there been open secession among the Confederate States of America, but the temper and tone in which its Government was challenged indicated that in peacetime, could it achieve a peace, it would be a loose league of sovereign States and not a nation. The *Richmond Whig* had spoken for an element with deep-rooted instincts about States' Rights when it suggested dropping the name of Confederate States and substituting The

Allied Nations or The Allied Republics. "We are sorry to see the word 'national' sometimes used with reference to Confederate affairs. We think it should be henceforth a forbidden word. This Confederacy is not a nation, but a league of nations."

Outside the gates of Richmond sat Grant with 75,000 troops, 20,000 having been sent to take Fort Fisher. And Grant in this December of '64 gave to Colonel Sharpe, his chief of secret information, the cold and brutal facts of the present strategy. Sharpe as an old friend of Colonel Charles Francis Adams, Jr., passed these on to Adams for writing to his father, the United States Minister at London. Sharpe quoted Grant: "Lee's present 55,000 is not at all the old material. It is all that he can rake and scrape—clerks, Government employes, detailed men and all. Of his old fighting stock he has about 22,000 men left. These men *we must kill* before the country can have peace. They are old soldiers and fierce slave-holders. These men have got to be used up." Of his own army, "sadly reduced" from what it was when the spring campaign started, Grant would reply to those saying it had accomplished nothing: "This year in ruining itself in nine pitched battles, it ruined Lee and one week's more fighting would have left him nothing to fight with." And of the present stand: "Lee can keep his army just where it is, but he can't attack, nor can he fight a battle. Victory or defeat would be alike ruinous."

To the White House John Hay returned from a visit in company with naval officers, politicians, and pressmen to Grant's headquarters, gathering no points from Grant as vivid as those written by the younger Adams to his father. The enemy, in Grant's judgment, Hay told Lincoln, could not recover from the blows he hoped to give this winter.

Was it a long time ago now, or only yesterday, that South Carolina had led a procession of sovereign States out of the old Union, like clockwork South Carolina lighting its jubilee bonfires at the signal given by the news of the election of the "Black Republican President" Lincoln? How long now since Ned Baker on the Senate floor, discussing the Crittenden peace resolutions, was saying: "South Carolina and Louisiana are ferocious for disunion, and I am afraid that their young men do want war. There is not excitement enough on the plantation and the farm or in the streets of the towns, but they really want contest, excitement, and bloodshed"—how long? To millions North and South they had seemed the longest slow-dragging years ever known.

Mrs. Chesnut, now in Columbia, South Carolina, wrote when Sherman was two days out from Atlanta moving toward the seacoast, "Fire and the sword are for us here; that is the word." A letter came to her from Mrs. Jefferson Davis saying she was tired of hoping and being disappointed. Her news from Richmond was that some people expected another attack soon, "but I think the avalanche will not slide until the spring." For Mrs. Davis, wrote Mrs. Chesnut, "my heart aches."

Into Mrs. Chesnut's Columbia house came a Connecticut-born woman with Northern relatives who spoke of Sherman opening a way at last so that she could go to Europe or to the North and live in comfort and ease. "I dare say she takes me for a fool," ran the diary entry that day. "I sat there dumb, although she was in my own house. I have heard of a woman so enraged that she struck some one over the head with a shovel. To-day, for the first time in my life, I know how that mad woman felt. I could have given Mrs. S. the benefit of shovel and tongs both."

Now came news of Hood's army broken and scattered, and, wrote Mrs. Chesnut, "maybe I am benumbed." A Miss Rhett was visiting her, "a brilliant woman and very agreeable," who had a saying, "The world, you know, is composed of men, women, and Rhetts." Now, said the diary, "we feel that if we are to lose our negroes, we would as soon see Sherman free them as the Confederate Government; freeing negroes is the last Confederate Government craze. We are a little too slow about it; that is all." Mournful and Biblical was her mood of December 19: "The deep waters are closing over us and we are in this house, like the outsiders at the time of the flood."

In such a December, the fourth December of the war, Lincoln sent his message to the Congress. On the face of it the intention was that it should go to the desks of House and Senate members and possibly have suggestions to them about co-operation between Congress and the Executive. Also on the face of it the intention was to have it read in the South for its information about the present and the immediate future of the war. The tone continuously traveled with high assumption that the United States was a going concern, that the Union of States was fated to become a great World Power, that Northern resources for meeting the Southern insurrection were unlimited, that the door was open for the return of prodigals, that the Emancipation Proclamation still held. Confidence and high expectation ran through it, though it was issued December 6, several days before any news had come from Sherman in Georgia or from Thomas at Nashville.

The President read the message to his Cabinet December 3, his rewriting of his own parts of it "much improved" over a previous version, thought Welles. The briefs of several Cabinet members were kept in the message "pretty much in their own words," noted Welles. One unusual matter came up, indicating the favor in which church leaders were held by Lincoln and an innovation to which, it seemed, he would have consented had the Cabinet agreed. "One paragraph," wrote Welles, "proposing an Amendment to the Constitution recognizing the Deity in that instrument met with no favorable response from any one member of the Cabinet. The President, before reading it, expressed his own doubts in regard to it, but it had been urged by certain religionists."

Foreign affairs were in a "reasonably satisfactory" condition. The African republic of Liberia should be given a gunboat at moderate cost, paying the United States for it in installments. Such a beginning of a navy would "stimulate a generous ambition" in this young Negro nation, while such a show of confidence by the United States in letting her have a gunboat "would win forbearance and favor toward the colony from all civilized nations." An international telegraph system, the Atlantic cable, and co-operation toward "world-encircling communication" were approved. A rebellion "long flagrant" in China "has at last been suppressed," with "the coöperating good offices of this Government and of other western commercial States." Emphasis was laid on "the extension of our commerce" and a "more intimate intercourse" with China, which "seems to be accepting with hearty good-will the conventional laws" toward those ends. Japan in performing treaty stipulations "is inconstant and capricious," though good progress had been effected by the Western Powers "moving with enlightened concert." Money claims of the United States had been allowed by the Japanese or put in course of settlement. One Virginia port, Norfolk, and two Florida ports, Fernandina and Pensacola, were now open, and foreign merchants might consider whether it was not "safer and more profitable" to use those ports than to risk blockade-running.

Thus far the message was chiefly Seward. Lincoln's hand became evident in a paragraph on the slave trade and those who did a business of shipping and selling black folk. "For myself, I have no doubt of the power and duty of the executive, under the law of nations, to exclude enemies of the human race from an asylum in the United States." Where Congress thought authority and regulations lacking he would recommend acts to stop "foreign-slave traders from acquiring domicile and facilities for their criminal occupation in our country." This seemed to be the first use by any President of the United States of the phrase "enemies of the human race."

Canadians could now read that "inimical and desperate persons harbored" in their dominion had made property and life insecure near the American border and unless conditions improved, the United States naval armament on the Great Lakes must be increased, and a passport system put in operation on the Canadian border.

The Treasury Department had taken in nearly $1,000,000,000 in cash and disbursed nearly as much for the army and navy. "Taxation should be still further increased." The public debt was a little under $1,375,000,000, which would go up another $500,000,000 if the war ran another year. This debt, in the form of United States bonds, had become, the President's message set forth, a substantial branch of "national, though private, property." Perhaps both Fessenden and Jay Cooke had helped on the ingenious and appealing sales argument for as many people as possible being holders of Government bonds:

> To favor such general distribution, greater inducements to become owners might, perhaps, with good effect, and without injury, be presented to persons of limited means. With this view, I suggest whether it might not be both competent and expedient for Congress to provide that a limited amount of some future issue of public securities might be held by any bona-fide purchaser exempt from taxation, and from seizure for debt under such restrictions and limitations as might be necessary to guard against abuse of so important a privilege. This would enable every prudent person to set aside a small annuity against a possible day of want.
>
> Privileges like these would render the possession of such securities, to the amount

limited, most desirable to every person of small means who might be able to save enough for the purpose. The great advantage of citizens being creditors as well as debtors, with relation to the public debt, is obvious. Men readily perceive that they cannot be much oppressed by a debt which they owe to themselves.

The paragraph completely and unreservedly endorsing the national banking system probably represented the views of Secretary Fessenden, and with these views Lincoln agreed to the extent that he made few or no changes in what Fessenden wrote. It was the one department of the Government in which Lincoln knew he was farthest from being an expert, and whatever might be the faults of the national banking system, it embodied the work of two Treasury chiefs beyond corruption, Chase and Fessenden, as the most efficient financial establishment for the chaos of the hour. The Cabinet and the President, wrote Fessenden to his family of this time, "know well enough that I am of more, much more consequence to them than they are to me. God knows that I have no private ends to accomplish, and I can, therefore, well afford to be personally independent of everything except my duty." And Fessenden wrote, with probably no slightest change later by the President, this paragraph in the message:

The national banking system is proving to be acceptable to capitalists and to the people. On the twenty-fifth day of November 584 national banks had been organized, a considerable number of which were conversions from State banks. Changes from State systems to the national system are rapidly taking place, and it is hoped that very soon there will be in the United States no banks of issue not authorized by Congress, and no bank-note circulation not secured by the government. That the government and the people will derive great benefit from this change in the banking systems of the country, can hardly be questioned. The national system will create a reliable and permanent influence in support of the national credit, and protect the people against losses in the use of paper money. Whether or not any further legislation is advisable for the suppression of State bank issues, it will be for Congress to determine. It seems quite clear that the treasury cannot be satisfactorily conducted unless the government can exercise a restraining power over the bank-note circulation of the country.

The navy now could show 671 vessels. Across the past year its actual increases over and above all losses by shipwreck and battle was 83 vessels, 167 guns, and 42,427 tons. During the year 324 ships had been captured, making a total of 1,379 since the war commenced. Sales of condemned prize property had brought more than $14,000,000.

For details of military operations, battles and campaigns, the public was referred to the report of the Secretary of War. However since the last annual message, "our arms have steadily advanced," and regions liberated in Missouri, Kentucky, Tennessee and parts of other States which "have again produced reasonably fair crops."

The army and navy could read of "liberal provisions" made by Congress for pensions. During the year ending June 30 last, 16,770 invalid soldiers and 271 invalid seamen had been added to the rolls. Of widows, orphans, and dependent mothers, a total of 22,198 were on the army pension rolls and 248 on the navy rolls.

The war at first glance would seem to have absorbed almost the entire energies of the nation. Wherefore it was of interest that without check or hindrance there had gone on a "steady expansion of population, improvement, and governmental institutions over the new and unoccupied portions of our country." Nevada with rich mountains had come into the Union as a State. The Territories of Idaho and Montana promised to come soon. Rich mineral discoveries were told of in the report of the Secretary of the Interior. Homesteaders had entered more than 4,000,000 acres of public land. Open to settlement were 133,000,000 acres of surveyed land. Though labor and materials costs were high, the project of connecting Atlantic and Pacific oceans by railway had "assurance of success." In the Sierra Nevada and Rocky Mountain regions mining production of precious metals had reached at least $100,000,000 in value. The national resources in materials—and men—"are unexhausted, and, as we believe, inexhaustible."

Of men the North had more than when the war began. Statistical sentences like hammers of doom poured forth on "the most important branch of national resources—that of living men." The President named alphabetically, as though copying from a book, the Northern States holding elections four years ago, gave their total vote, added those of the new States of Kansas and Nevada, showing that the North in spite of war losses had 145,551 more voters at the polls in November of '64 than four years before. To this could be added at least 90,000 votes of soldiers in the field whose State laws did not permit their voting, to which could be further added the new population in the Territories.

The important fact stood out from the cold figures "that we have more men now than we had when the war began; that we are not exhausted nor in process of exhaustion; that we are gaining strength and may, if need be, maintain the contest indefinitely."

Of the word "reconstruction" Lincoln steered clear. Already it had become tinged with suspicion. Important movements had occurred during the year, wrote the President, "to the effect of molding society for durability in the Union." Short of complete success, he admitted, but much in the right direction was it that 12,000 citizens in each of the States of Arkansas and Louisiana "have organized loyal State governments, with free constitutions, and are earnestly struggling to maintain and administer them." Similar movements more extensive, though less definite, in Missouri, Kentucky, and Tennessee "should not be overlooked." And near-by Maryland presented the example of complete success. "Maryland is secure to liberty and union for all the future. The genius of rebellion will no more claim Maryland. Like another foul spirit, being driven out, it may seek to tear her, but it will woo her no more."

Lincoln now dealt with the crowded rumors and flying reports that peace was to be had through negotiation. To this he joined a portrayal of Jefferson Davis, not by name, not by the title of President of the Confederate States of America, spacing off the inexorable issues which now dictated that the war must go on—and on—till one side or the other won. The passage read:

> On careful consideration of all the evidence accessible, it seems to me that no attempt at negotiation with the insurgent leader could result in any good. He would accept nothing short of severance of the Union—precisely what we will not and cannot give. His declarations to this effect are explicit and oft repeated. He does not attempt to deceive us. He affords us no excuse to deceive ourselves. He cannot voluntarily re-accept the Union; we cannot voluntarily yield it.
>
> Between him and us the issue is distinct, simple, and inflexible. It is an issue which can only be tried by war, and decided by victory.
>
> If we yield, we are beaten; if the Southern people fail him, he is beaten. Either way it would be the victory and defeat following war. What is true, however, of him who heads the insurgent cause is not necessarily true of those who follow. Although he cannot re-accept the Union, they can. Some of them, we know, already desire peace and reunion. The number of such may increase. They can at any moment have peace simply by laying down their arms and submitting to the national authority under the Constitution. . . .
>
> After so much the government could not, if it would, maintain war against them. The loyal people would not sustain or allow it. If questions should remain, we would adjust them by the peaceful means of legislation, conference, courts, and votes, operating only in constitutional and lawful channels.

Quickly following this Lincoln pointed to questions "beyond the executive power to adjust." The admission of members into Congress, acts requiring money appropriations, were not for executive decision. Furthermore, the executive power itself would be "greatly diminished by the cessation of actual war." He seemed to leave a quite direct inference here that for himself he would be found, if and when the war closed, using his authority for the help and sustenance of men at the South who might have to consider vindictive enemies in Washington. "Pardons and remissions of forfeitures, however, would still be within executive control. In what spirit and temper this control would be exercised, can be fairly judged of by the past."

Pardon and amnesty had been offered a year ago "to all except certain designated classes." These latter, it was made known then, were "still within contemplation of special clemency." A thousand farces, tragedies, and treacheries of what Thad Stevens called "Lincoln's ten-per-cent plan" were comprised in the President's sentence: "During the year many availed themselves of the general provision, and many more would, only that the signs of bad faith in some led to such precautionary measures as rendered the practical process less easy and certain."

Not Thad Stevens, however, nor the extremist Republican critics of the President, were directly in mind now. Lincoln aimed these carefully written and purposely dry appeals at men of the South. "Special pardons have been granted to individuals of the excepted classes, and no voluntary application has been denied. Thus, practically, the door has been for a full year open to all, except such as were not in condition to make free choice—that is, such as were in custody or under constraint. It is still so open to all; but the time may come—probably will come—when public duty shall demand that it be closed; and that in lieu more rigorous measures than heretofore shall be adopted." Almost cryptic was this. No mention here of the "better angels" of the first inaugural address. Welles on hearing it told Lincoln it sounded too hard, the same Welles who had not long ago written that the President would be too lenient in dealing with the enemy when the war closed. Welles told Lincoln the message should say the Southern people were "not to be considered, not to be treated, as outlaws; that, by returning to their allegiance [to the Union], their persons and property should be respected." The Kentucky-born Lincoln decided against this view of the Connecticut Yankee Welles. Such points could be seized on by those now favoring a punishment policy in the South, and by those Lincoln had in mind the previous April in his mild protest: "It is difficult to say a sensible thing nowadays." Perhaps Welles gave too scant consideration to what Lincoln offered the Southern people. Simply to say now that the door is "still so open to all" was enough perhaps.

More solidarity North and South was Lincoln's aim in his November election interpretations. The calmness and good order of millions of voters spoke for the safety of the Union. Not only those supporting the Union ticket, but a great majority of those opposing it, could be claimed as favoring the Union. One argument was unanswerable. "No candidate for any office whatever, high or low, has ventured to seek votes on the avowal that he was for giving up the Union. . . . The politicians have shown their instinctive knowledge that there is no diversity among the people." In this the election had "vast value."

And slavery? What of this crying, persistent issue? On this the President was brief but more decisive than in any other part of the message. At Gettysburg he had spoken solemnly of government of the people, by the people, for the people. Now he was not unsaying what he had said at Gettysburg, but he was making it clear that if by any chance as President he should be instructed by the people to do a certain thing they would have to find someone else to do it.

The next to the last paragraph of the message declared: "I retract nothing heretofore said as to slavery. I repeat the declaration made a year ago that 'while I remain in my present position, I shall not attempt to retract or modify the Emancipation Proclamation, nor shall I return to slavery any person who is free by the terms of that proclamation, or by any of the acts of Congress.' If the people should, by whatever mode or means, make it an executive duty to reënslave such persons, another, and not I, must be their instrument to perform it."

Dry with a cool Lincolnian finality, touched with a faint preposterous irony, was the closing one-sentence paragraph: "In stating a single condition of peace, I mean simply to say, that the war will cease on the part of the government whenever it shall have ceased on the part of those who began it."

Far and wide went this document. By Union armies it was spread into

Confederate areas where Confederate newspapers had not reprinted it from Northern journals. In Europe it was studied and discussed in state chambers and on the streets. Over the Northern States it was examined for every shading of fear and hope and promise.

In its allusions to friendly Central and South American republics and its "boast" of "inexhaustible resources," J. B. Jones, writing in his diary at Richmond, could read a threat to Great Britain. In references to Mexican affairs he could see Lincoln preparing to menace Napoleon III. The emancipation purposes declared in the message would "prolong" the war. The

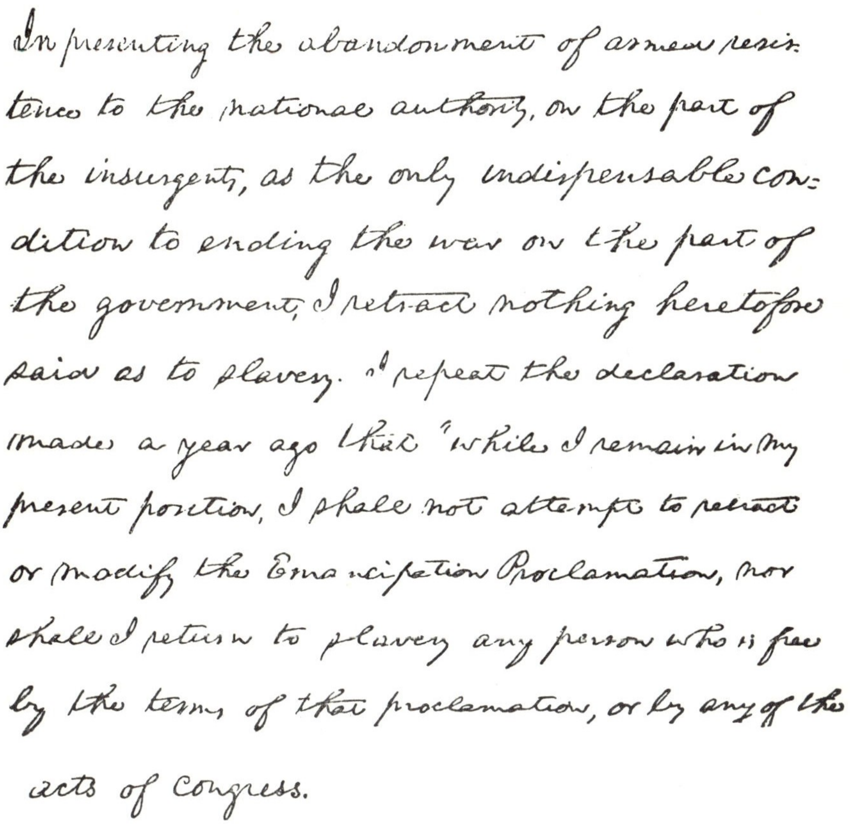

In presenting the abandonment of armed resistance to the national authority, on the part of the insurgents, as the only indispensable condition to ending the war on the part of the government, I retract nothing heretofore said as to slavery. I repeat the declaration made a year ago that "while I remain in my present position, I shall not attempt to retract or modify the Emancipation Proclamation, nor shall I return to slavery any person who is free by the terms of that proclamation, or by any of the acts of Congress.

In the '64 message to Congress the President serves notice that no gains to the Negro from the Emancipation Proclamation shall be lost. Original in the Barrett collection.

amnesty and open-door offers, wrote Jones in his Richmond war-office room, "will certainly cause many of our croakers . . . to submit."

Opposition journals in the North agreed in various ways with the London *Times*, which said: "For ourselves, we never read a public document less calculated to inspire hope," adding the gratuitous and gossipy comment that it was "the most uncomfortable President's address ever read to the American House of Representatives."

La France in Paris agreed that the message portended "maintenance of the destructive policy of which Mr. Lincoln is the representative, perhaps the instrument," being violent and unconciliatory in tone, leaving nothing for the future but more of war, "implacable war, having no parallel for hatred and ferocity, except in the remote ages of barbarism—millions of men slaughtered and thousands of millions of money swallowed up, all to gratify an inflexible pride." *La Presse* in Paris saw no such anger in the American President. "Mr. Lincoln is not a university graduate." That was evident, said *La Presse*. "He does not cultivate the flowers of rhetoric. His elocution comes direct from the backwoods. It has the coarse simplicity of the woodman's ax, but it does its work bravely. It forces its way through thorny obstacles, and opens a path out of apparently inextricable difficulties. . . . We find in its short and condensed chapters the most interesting facts, the most instructive estimates, which say more than the most fluid periods, the most skillfully rounded sounding periphrases; it is as brief, as clear, as precise as a banker's weekly account." *Le Temps* of Paris saw the American President as equivalent to a sovereign, although "It is not a speech from the throne which he addresses to the Congress of his country, but a simple political statement."

To Elizabeth Cady Stanton in New York, December 8, writing a letter to Susan B. Anthony, the President's message was uncomfortable reading. She was later to change her mind about what she wrote this day, but for the hour she traveled in feeling with an element of the Republican party who suspected the President, his words, motives behind his words. "I read Lincoln's message to Congress," wrote Elizabeth to Susan. "What a dry, barren document! The Republican papers make much, however, of the closing paragraphs. He can very safely say that if the people require of him, what he knows they never will, that he will not execute their will. That sounds big, but it is all wind."

In its issue published three days before the President's message went to Congress, *Harper's Weekly* forecast its main drift, saying experience "teaches us that we may trust the President to do the right thing at the right time and in the right way." Nothing finer stood forth from his career than "his passionless but unswerving patriotism." When duty demanded, he did not hesitate "to alienate at times all parties of his immediate adherents . . . secure always of the permanent approval of the people." With no self-seeking, with a sagacious independence in all his actions, "our history does not furnish his master as a statesman."

Of the message itself when published *Harper's* judged it a "calm, simple, concise statement of public affairs," saw eye to eye with the President as to peace prospects, and could understand a Northern opposition, "in common with the rebels," finding the message very "unconciliatory." Its tranquil tone of faith in the people, its dignity toward other Powers, its lofty confidence in peace and union, with much else of justice breathing through it, "make the Message, now familiar to the country, one of the sincerest, most noble, most honorable, and most truly American papers in our political history."

Keen of understanding, Lincoln's anonymous friend in the *Spectator* of London found his later messages as always having a dry, shrewd tenacity. This latest one "is drier, shrewder, and more tenacious than ever." Re-election, while it had not "taught him to write eloquently or to conceal the process of slow thinking so visible between the lines of all his compositions," had made him a little more confident in the success of his own views. Only a year ago he had said, "It is the people who in the end must decide," but this time he was saying that if the people by whatever means made it an executive duty to re-enslave the enfranchised, "another, not I, must be their instrument." Two years more of power, and Mr. Lincoln would probably announce what he already dimly perceives, continued the *Spectator* writer, "that the place of rulers is in the front, that it is his duty to lead, and not merely to follow."

The peace terms offered by Mr. Lincoln were "precisely the terms every monarchy in Europe always offers to rebels." His war policy held to that of the Roman patrician who would "spare the submissive, but war out the proud." His amnesty was free to everybody, "even those specially exempted from amnesty." His proud roll call of national resources, "of which Americans never weary," none the less had great meaning. "Faith is the source of strength, and the wearisome faith in his means which the President exhibits gives him strength to persist to the end." His lumbering but intelligible phrases signified that the Government would offer quarter but not negotiate.

Thus the essence of this commentary of the *Spectator* writer, who reserved to the end his feeling of the awful drama in the American scene, now heightened by this latest document. It held a "steady bovine persistence," a "resolve so iron that it cannot even bend to make phrases." This to spectators was "infinitely impressive," and over the South must create, more than defeat in the field, a sense of hopelessness. Furthermore:

> You may face any man however superior in strength, but the bravest will not stand up to the locomotive. The President does not boast, shows no hate, indulges in no cries of triumph over the "steady advance of our armies," threatens no foreign power, makes no prophecies of speedy success, comforts the people with no assurances of a Utopian future, but as if impelled by a force other than his own will slides quietly but irresistibly along the rails. He is in his groove and moving, and those who are in his path must ride with him, or lie flat, or retreat; must, at all events, recognize that it is they and not he who are to move out of the appointed course. Mr. Hawthorne, who detested Mr. Lincoln for his want of refinement, once doubted audibly whether his detestation was right, for, said he, "I have noticed that the people always in such crises hit on the right man." When the smoke of this struggle ceases to make English eyes smart, they also, we believe, will recognize that the intuition of the man of genius was truer than his taste.

Dry, informative, again casual as a locomotive, came the President's proclamation of December 19 calling for 300,000 more troops. The information

TOPICS OF THE HOUR.

NORTH AND SOUTH.
"*Now, Jeffy, when you think you have had enough of this, say so, and I'll leave off.*"—(*Vide* President's Message.)

UNCLE ABE.—"*Sambo, you are not handsome, any more than myself, but as to sending you back to your old master, I'm not the man to do it—and what's more, I won't.*"—(*Vide* President's Message.)

Leslie's interprets the President's message

ran that on the call for 500,000 men July 18, "credits allowed in accordance with the act of Congress" had reduced the number of men to be obtained to 280,000. The War Department would assign quotas to the States. On February 15 a draft would be made to fill the quotas then unfilled. "In testimony whereof," read the President's document, "I have hereunto set my hand and caused the seal of the United States to be affixed."

Naval operations and the stranglehold of the blockade had now left only one port into which blockade-runners could bring supplies from England.

THE AMERICAN JUGGERNAUT

Punch cartoons war

This port of Wilmington, North Carolina, would be lost if its defending Fort Fisher should fall. General Butler's wily head worked out a plan to run a powder-loaded steamer near the shore under the fort, have a clockwork blow up the boat, and in the ensuing havoc and confusion move in troops to take the fort. "I had no confidence in the success of the scheme, and so expressed myself," wrote Grant later; "but as no serious harm could come of the experiment, and the authorities at Washington seemed desirous to have it tried, I permitted it."

Admiral Porter with a naval squadron, General Butler with troop transports, joined their efforts. After Butler sailed from Fortress Monroe "three days of fine weather were squandered," according to Grant. Then heavy storms delayed action. At last on the night of December 23 the powder steamer was towed in near the fort, the clockwork set, and everybody left. "At two o'clock in the morning," wrote Grant, "the explosion took place—and produced no more effect on the fort, or anything else on land, than the bursting of a boiler anywhere on the Atlantic Ocean." Porter shelled the fort with no damaging results. Butler landed troops, won footings, then drew away, put his troops back on the transports, and told Porter he was through.

Grant telegraphed the President on December 28 that the Wilmington expedition had proved "a gross and culpable failure," that he hoped it would be known who was to blame. Grant, however, on hearing from Admiral Porter that the army had quit when they nearly had Fort Fisher, sent word to Porter to hold on, to stay near Wilmington, that they would soon close that last Confederate port through which came medicine, food, metals, clothing, salt, arms, blankets, from Europe.

General Butler was probably to be the new Secretary of War, said *Leslie's Weekly*, December 3. On that date the rumor sounded less ridiculous than after the Fort Fisher fiasco. The President would soon name another man to replace Stanton, had run persistent reports since the November election. "This subject was brought up by the President in his conversation with the general-in-chief," wrote Grant's aide, Colonel Porter, "and he was considerate enough to say that in case such a change should occur, he would not appoint another secretary without giving the general an opportunity to express his views as to the selection." Grant's reply to Lincoln, as Horace Porter noted it: "I doubt very much whether you could select as efficient a Secretary of War as the present incumbent. He is not only a man of untiring energy and devotion to duty, but even his worst enemies never for a moment doubt his personal integrity and the purity of his motives; and it tends largely to reconcile the people to the heavy taxes they are paying when they feel an absolute certainty that the chief of the department which is giving out contracts for countless millions of dollars is a person of scrupulous honesty." Grant privately continued to believe Stanton "timid" as a warrior, too freely arrogant in the handling of Grant's telegrams when it suited him, but Grant had no one else in mind now who better fitted the needs of the hour.

And Stanton, though in breaking health, regarded himself as an image of war and a hurler of thunderbolts. At the doorway of the war telegraph office one evening he stood, without coming in. At a table sat Lincoln writing. In the doorway Stanton postured volcanic and warlike to look at. The operator Chandler wrote of the tableau: "Mr. Lincoln did not notice him at first. As he looked up from his writing and perceived Stanton standing there, he bowed low and said with much gravity, 'Good-evening, Mars.'"

Robert J. Walker had returned from Europe and was to replace Fessenden in the Treasury, while General Banks would have Welles's portfolio. So ran spoken and published rumors. There was a Cabinet shake-up coming, a housecleaning, a new broom sweeping out old accumulations. This was heard wherever politics was talked. But it was all wind and idle talk. In neither major nor minor offices did Lincoln intend to use a broom. "I have made up my mind to make very few changes in the offices in my gift for my second term," he told one caller. "I think, now, that I shall not move a single man, except for delinquency. To remove a man is very easy, but when

I go to fill his place, there are twenty applicants, and of these I must make nineteen enemies."

One effort at Cabinet change gave life to rumors. An able wheel horse of the antislavery movement, George Luther Stearns, believed that Governor John A. Andrew should sit among the President's confidential advisers. "Mr. Stearns," wrote a kinsman, Frank Preston Stearns, "joined in a desperate effort to obtain a place for Governor Andrew in President Lincoln's Cabinet. He was assisted in this by every loyal son of Massachusetts, as well as by prominent public men in other States, but Lincoln would not listen to it, although Andrew as a judicious manager of public affairs was now considered without a superior in the United States. Mr. Stearns believed that it was owing to the opposition of Seward, who disliked to have anyone near the President who might counteract his own influence."

The President, wrote Welles, was not using his Cabinet, as a Cabinet. He was seeing individual members of it, separately, but not assembling them for joint discussions and judgments. Only three of the members came to the Cabinet meeting of December 20, noted Welles. The course pursued by the President "sustains them in this neglect." Seward was seeing the President every day when there was no Cabinet meeting, and on the days the Cabinet met Seward saw the President at another hour. "As Stanton does not go to the President, the President goes to Stanton. Not unfrequently he [the President] hurries at the close to go to the War Department. Fessenden frets because there are no Cabinet consultations and yet stays away himself."

Nearly four years now Welles had seen something like this going on and could not adjust himself to it. A Cabinet should be a Cabinet, and meet as a joint body helping the President run the country instead of the President's holding private interviews with them each and all, so that no one of them could be exactly sure of what the President was doing or aiming to do. To this view Welles still held in '64, as in '61.

Of Lincoln's Cabinet slate written in Springfield in November of 1860, only two were left. Cameron, Smith, Chase, Blair, one by one had resigned. Of these Cameron's resignation and that of Blair seemed to be the only ones that Lincoln had forced. Smith preferred a life-tenure Federal judgeship. Not till Chase resigned the fourth time, and had formed the habit of expecting to be coaxed back, did he find himself no longer inside looking out. Bates justifiably pleaded advanced age. Seward and Welles still held on, both working hard and most of the time enjoying themselves in their posts, Seward having more authority than he could use, though Lincoln and Welles had more than once checked him from taking authority beyond his title. Welles was a natural-born gossip and it was this that so often lighted his diary with living human action. Oddly enough, he seldom examined his own motives. Welles might have asked himself at least once whether his continuous resentment over the private consultations of Seward with Lincoln was in part due to his cravings of curiosity, to the fact that choice morsels of information were withheld from him.

To Seward the Paris Consul Bigelow more than once sent word, "Burn this Mss when you have read it," Seward once replying that a note was duly "received, read, and burned," as suggested, and "The contents are known only to the President here." This latter concerned the death of Minister William L. Dayton in Paris, December 1, in the hotel apartment of a woman not his wife, the body being immediately removed to Dayton's house. This was done, according to Bigelow, "before the police could interfere, for should they become aware of what had happened they would insist upon holding an inquest upon the premises, which would involve many inconveniences, all of which would be avoided by placing the body within the precincts of the legation." Bigelow recited the insistence of the unfortunate

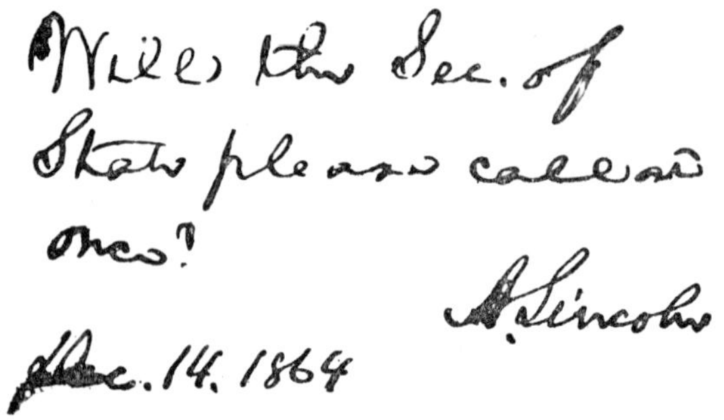
Will the Sec. of State please call at once?
A. Lincoln
Dec. 14. 1864

The President summons Seward. Original in the Barrett collection.

hostess upon riding up to the legation with the body to explain how it happened. They wished to discourage her, but she insisted. "What will Mrs. Dayton think?" she exclaimed. "My reputation is involved. I must go at once." And so she went. According to the doctor's report, wrote Bigelow in a later unofficial account, Dayton "after some pleasantry on entering the apartment, called upon his hostess to give three cheers for Abraham Lincoln, the news of whose re-election had just recently reached Paris. He soon complained of feeling unwell," and died from apoplexy before the doctor's arrival.

Thus a matter kept secret by the Paris Legation in Europe, and by Seward and Lincoln in America, did not reach a press which would have reveled in the details. Other secrets of the diplomatic corps were under discussion by Seward and Lincoln in the private conferences so continuously resented by the gossipy Secretary of the Navy. Also continuously nourished by Lincoln's steady adherence to Seward were the hate and fear of various factions, chiefly the extremist antislavery group, who believed that, as Lincoln once put it to a committee of Senators, whenever he had a good purpose in view Seward "contrived to suck it out" of him.

Lincoln's heart warmed to a notable feature of the work of Grant and Sherman. Personal ambition and petty politics that had so often cursed the armies no longer interfered in the high command. Grant consulted Sherman, leaned on him, asked what next. Sherman replied in kind. A bill in Congress to raise Sherman to Grant's rank of lieutenant general, dividing control of the armies between them, nettled Sherman. He wrote to his brother that he would accept no commission that would tend to create a rivalry with Grant. "I have all the rank I want. I would rather be an engineer of a railroad than President of the United States. I have commanded a hundred thousand men in battle, and on the march, successfully and without confusion, and that is enough for reputation. Now, I want rest and peace, and they are only to be had through war." To Grant, Sherman wrote that he doubted whether the men in Congress fully realized "that you and I are honest in our professions of want of ambition." On the military end Lincoln's load was lighter now by far than it had been. In the political field, however, he saw a work of consolidation ahead, "to the effect of molding society for durability in the Union," desperately complex, calling for every instinct of sagacity he had.

Grant could still use a friend in the White House. He was not yet beyond suspicion in certain influential quarters. The drink habit was on him, ran talk and belief in these quarters and, further ran the tongues of fear and dismay, he might some day try to run the armies while helplessly drunk—and then what? This stale gossip had a renewal in December when the Committee on the Conduct of the War visited City Point to take testimony on the fiasco of the Crater. General Grant spent several hours with the committee, speaking freely and familiarly of various army commanders, "and impressing everyone by his strong common-sense," wrote Congressman George W. Julian.

"While at dinner with us on our steamer," continued Julian, "he drank freely, and its effect became quite manifest. It was a painful surprise to the Committee, and was spoken of with bated breath; for he was the Lieutenant-General of all our forces, and the great movements . . . then in progress, for aught we knew, might possibly be deflected from their purpose by his condition." Not the slightest suspicion had Congressman Julian that the very errands and methods of the committee might have had something to do with Grant's conduct. The more he saw of them, the more he drank—could there be a motive in his so doing? No such course of meditation dawned on Julian. Whether he or others again ran worrying about it to Lincoln and whether Lincoln again groaned, "I can't spare this man—he fights!" Julian did not record.

As the days went by toward the close of the year of '64 the immensity grew of the decision at the November ballot boxes. In returning the National Union party and its leader to the White House, the Ship of State cleared its passage over a fearful bar and sailed on, "all her costly freight of human liberties and human hopes upborne." This in the words of the December *Atlantic Monthly*, holding "that foggy and forlorn Second Tuesday of November the most memorable day of this most memorable year of the war." The outside world was notified that "we have something more than a foul chimney burning itself out over here." The wildfire blaze of the 1861 uprisings was a sudden blowoff and not dependable. Now after four years of "sombre clouds of uncertainty that hung drizzling and oppressive above the whole land," had come a tougher article of iron determination: "This is a war for humanity, and for all time. That . . . the heart of the nation is in it, and that this is no effervescent and fickle heart, the momentous Tuesday stands before the world as the final proof." A motley crew of three elements had been repulsed: (1) reckless politicians; (2) the sheep which those bad shepherds led; (3) respectable conservatives. Now was the false and evil London *Times* lost as a prophet in constantly having taken for granted "that we are a mob, and that a mob is an idiot."

Then came an estimate of Lincoln curiously parallel to that of Professor Goldwin Smith for the same hour. It read: "The nation in its childhood needed a paternal Washington; but now it has arrived at manhood, and it requires, not a great leader, but a magistrate willing himself to be led. Such a man is Mr. Lincoln: an able, faithful, hard-working citizen, overseeing the affairs of all the citizens, accepting the guidance of Providence, and conscientiously yielding himself to be the medium of a people's will, the agent of its destinies. That is all we have any right to expect of him; and if we expect more, we shall be disappointed. He cannot stretch forth his hand and save us, although we have now twice elected him to his high place. Upon ourselves, and upon ourselves alone, under God, success and victory still depend."

To whom had the November election given a mandate—to Congress or to the President? And was it the duty of Congress now to challenge the Executive and begin to cut down powers he had exercised? A test vote on points as to these questions came in mid-December. Henry Winter Davis demanded a vote on his resolution that Congress had "a constitutional right to an authoritative voice" in foreign affairs, and, "it is the constitutional duty of the President to respect that policy . . . in diplomatic negotiations." This raised a rather clear-cut issue. It was so intended by the temperamental orator from Maryland, who had lost his seat in November and was to serve as a "lame duck" until March 4 of the next year.

Without debate or inquiry the House voted on a motion of Representative Farnsworth to lay the Winter Davis resolution on the table. This passed with 69 Yeas, 63 Nays, not voting 50. The moment this result was announced Davis rose to a privileged question, saying he desired to be relieved of further service on the Committee of Foreign Affairs. His speech opened a debate on whether the President was reaching out for more power than entitled to under the Constitution. Supporting Davis were the implacable anti-Administration Democrat Samuel S. Cox of Ohio and the Republican floor leader Thad Stevens, with Blaine of Maine holding that Lincoln and Seward were merely doing what had always been done in foreign affairs. No charge was made that Lincoln and Seward were shaping a wrong policy in Mexico. The fear spoken was that the Executive was overriding the Constitution in not giving Congress its constitutional right to an "authoritative voice" in foreign affairs, thereby failing in "respect" to Congress.

More than one crowned head of Europe was looking anxiously to see whether the House would assert its right as against the Executive, said Winter Davis. "I tell you . . . a shout will go up from one end of despotic Europe to the other when it is known that the House of Representatives has confessed that its resolves are vain breath before the dictation of the President, and that the President is the United States, as Louis Napoleon is France. Insignificant though I be, I am not humble enough to allow my name to be associated with that humiliating abdication." During the course of his speech Davis declared that in his position as chairman of the Committee on Foreign Affairs he stood toward the House as a member of the Cabinet did toward the President, that the vote tabling his resolution "places a great gulf between me and the House." The House however then disagreed with his motion that he be excused from service on the committee.

Thus in mid-December of '64 the respect and adherence of Congress to President Lincoln seemed to hang in a balance of about 69 with him, 63 against him, and 50 undecided, wavering, sick or not interested. Those with him were nearly all his own party men. Those against him were the opposition party, allied with nearly as many of his own party. Those not voting were mostly of his own party. The November election clearly had not been taken by the House of Representatives as a mandate that the President was worth listening to. The November verdict at the polls had not materially changed the complexion of the House. As a year earlier its members had been overwhelmingly against him for another term, did they now estimate him according to Wendell Phillips, "a first-rate second-rate man"?

Not quite. In stature and sagacity the President now stood on a different footing with Congress. The campaign and the election had brought an impression that the President was a politician of keener touch, an Executive of more designing statecraft, than they had given him credit for. Not since Representative Isaac N. Arnold of Chicago early in '64 made the only speech urging the President's renomination and re-election had such fair words and lavish estimates been spoken as Thad Stevens now delivered on the President's message. "It is brief (a great virtue in public documents), it treats of subjects of great importance, not only to the nation but to the whole family of man. I do not think I am extravagant when I say that it is the most important and best message that has been communicated to Congress for the last sixty years."

Both style and content suited Stevens. "The President has never made much pretension to a polished education, yet I nowhere see the least fault found with the composition of his late message. So deeply was he impressed with the greatness of his subject, so free from that vain-glorious and selfish ambition that leads to an inflated and vicious taste, that he expressed his ideas in the purest and simplest English, which, in my judgment, is hardly surpassed by the happiest efforts of Addison. This, however, is of but little importance compared with its principles."

The *New York Express* editor, Representative James Brooks, Democrat, had spoken of the President as lacking tolerance, with no spirit of conciliation or negotiation toward the South. To this Thad Stevens would reply:

"I give the President all honor for his course on this question. Never had a man to decide so important a question under such difficulties. He was obliged to decide it for himself, not only unaided, but in the midst of the most distracting counsels. I am disclosing no secret when I state that his Cabinet has never been a unit." Elsewhere too Stevens saw the President finding not wise suggestions, but timidity, hesitancy, and moral cowardice. The people had stood firm with the President, while "the controlling journals of the party, and able gentlemen whose standing seemed to justify them in tendering their advice, joined in urging the President to pursue the very course which the gentleman from New York now condemns."

The chief anxiety of Brooks, continued Stevens, was to save from destruction "the darling institution of the Democratic party, the institution of human bondage." Compromise on this was sought. "The gentleman condemns the President's determination to insist on the abandonment of slavery." Amid his perplexities, when the President's own leading friends besought him to compromise, he refused to sue for peace. "He took counsel of his own wiser judgment, stood firmly erect, and saved the nation from disgrace. There never was a day since Abraham Lincoln was elected President that he stood so high, or deserved to stand so high in the estimation of the people as at this moment. For purity of heart and firmness of character he would compare well with the best of the conscript fathers."

The guiding fear of Stevens was that the war would end without slavery uprooted. The awful scourge of war would go on, he expected, "until we obey the high behest of the Father of men." The voice of God and humanity called for liberation of a people held in a bondage more cruel and despotic than any of ancient times. "If we still harden our hearts and blood must still flow, may the ghosts of the slaughtered victims sit heavily upon the souls of those who cause it. If it were given to man to look back from a future world and know what posterity will say of them, I fear the gentleman from New York, when he has gone hence and left nothing but his fame behind, would blush at the record which impartial history will make on this subject."

Since the second Tuesday of November, wrote Lydia Maria Child in a letter, "I am a happy woman." As an adorer of Sumner, an admirer of Frémont, an intimate of Wendell Phillips, it counted nothing in particular to her that Lincoln had been named to four more years of power—though she was coming to like him a little and was afraid she might be liking him more if she didn't take care. "There was no enthusiasm for honest old Abe," proceeded her reckoning. "There is no beauty in him, that men should desire him; there is no insinuating, polished manner, to beguile the senses of the people; there is no dazzling military renown; no silver flow of rhetoric; in fact, no glittering prestige of any kind surrounds him; yet the people triumphantly elected him, in spite of all manner of machinations, and notwithstanding the long, long drag upon their patience and their resources which this war has produced. I call this the triumph of free schools; for it was the intelligence and reason of the people that reëlected Abraham Lincoln. He has his faults, and I have sometimes been out of patience with him; but I will say of him that I have constantly gone on liking him better and better. His recent reply to some people who serenaded him charmed me exceedingly. A most beautiful spirit pervaded it."

Such relenting of the heart was not to be seen in Elizabeth Cady Stanton. In a letter of December 29, 1864, she reported a heavy gloom that since the November election had come over the radical opposition to Lincoln. "Phillips has just returned from Washington," wrote Mrs. Stanton to Susan B. Anthony. "He says the radical men feel that they are powerless and checkmated. Winter Davis told him the game was up—'Lincoln with his immense patronage can do what he pleases; the only hope is an appeal to the people.' They turn to such men as Phillips to say what politicians dare not say. Phillips also expresses astonishment, and I share his astonishment, that Cousin Gerrit [Smith] and [William Lloyd] Garrison should defend the proposed apprenticeship system for the emancipated negroes."

John M. Palmer, the Union Democrat of Illinois, waited in a White House anteroom one morning till he was told to enter the President's room. As Palmer told it, he found Lincoln in the hands of the barber, and Lincoln called: "Come in, Palmer, come in. You're home folks. I can shave before you. I couldn't before those others, and I have to do it sometime." They chatted about this and that, Palmer finally speaking in a frank and jovial mood. "Mr. Lincoln, if anybody had told me that in a great crisis like this the people were going out to a little one-horse town and pick out a one-horse lawyer for President I wouldn't have believed it." Lincoln whirled in his chair, his face white with lather, a towel under his chin. Palmer at first thought the President was angry. Sweeping the barber away, Lincoln leaned forward, put a hand on Palmer's knee, and said: "Neither would I. But it was a time when a man with a policy would have been fatal to the country. I have never had a policy. I have simply tried to do what seemed best as each day came."

Palmer's daughter Jessie was to say, "I've heard my father tell that incident many times, putting special stress on Lincoln's saying, 'Come in, Palmer, come in. You're home folks.' "

Gustave Koerner, another of the home folks, wrote of his call on Lincoln in November and Lincoln saying, "I see daylight," as though the strain on him was easing. "More amusing anecdotes than ever before" heard this old Illinois friend from Lincoln, who alluded however "to some of the gloomy and harassing periods he had passed through, and which had almost broken his heart."

The degree of Doctor of Laws, awarded by Knox College, at Galesburg, Illinois, an abolitionist and solidly Republican community, was less a surprise than a like degree conferred by the Trustees of the College of New Jersey. "The assurance conveyed by this high compliment," wrote Lincoln, December 27, "that the course of the government which I represent, has received the approval of a body of gentlemen of such character and intelligence, in this time of public trial is most grateful to me."

Charles Eliot Norton in December was writing to Aubrey de Vere that Mr. Lincoln was constantly gaining in popular respect and confidence. "He is not a man whose qualities are fitted to excite a personal enthusiasm, but they are of a kind to inspire trust." Norton believed that the educated classes in general lacked the sense of history to measure Lincoln or to understand the extent to which his personality had pervaded the masses of people. "He is an admirable ruler for our democratic republic. He has shown many of the highest qualities of statesmanship, and I have little doubt that his course and his character will both be estimated more highly in history than they are, in the main, by his contemporaries."

Contemporaries such as whom? One specimen might be Edward H. Wright, a familiar of General McClellan, writing from Washington December 13, 1864, to the General: "I saw Mr. Lincoln ('that peer of any gentleman in the land,' as Mr. Everett says) last week at the Opera. He has not improved in appearance, seems a little more conscious of his greatness, but deigns still to grin down at his witling subjects. His wife, flanked by Mr. Sumner and 'Bawn' Gerolt, made up what I shall take the liberty, in spite of Mr. Everett, to call a 'peer' less party."

Mr. Wright assumed that General McClellan and he were agreed that Edward Everett in a recent address was mistaken in pronouncing Mr. Lincoln the "peer of any gentleman in the land." In Boston on November 15 at the Revere House, where a dinner was given Captain John Ancrum Winslow and fellow officers of the *Kearsarge*, which had sunk the *Alabama*, Everett had spoken. His response was to the toast "Our President." Long enough had Everett heard certain references to Lincoln in polite society. With the precise and meticulous dignity of the school of classical oratory to which Everett belonged he made himself clear on one point. A newspaper-reading public gathered his meaning as follows: "It may seem hardly worth while to notice the descriptions which represent the President as a person of uncouth appearance and manners. But as Mr. Burke did not think it out of place, in the most magnificent discourse in the English language, to comment on the appearance, manners, and conversation of the exiled French princes, I will take the liberty to say that, on the only social occasion on which I ever had the honor to be in the President's company, namely, the commemoration of Gettysburg, he sat at table at the house of my friend, David Wills, Esq., by the side of several distinguished persons, ladies and gentlemen, foreigners and Americans, among them the French Minister at Washington, since appointed French Ambassador at Madrid, and the Admiral of the French fleet, and that in gentlemanly appearance, manners, and conversation he was the peer of any man at the table."

This public testimony from one of America's foremost and indubitable gentlemen, to the effect that Lincoln too was in the best sense of the word a gentleman, chimed with a letter of the same time. Skeptical at first of any graces Lincoln might have, somewhat shocked at Lincoln's plebeian laughter to begin with, Everett seemed to have slowly grown in a belief that inside of Lincoln moved a motive power of warm goodheartedness, of a love heart that stood hard trials—as with Everett himself. Everett wrote of the President: "He is eminently kind-hearted. I am sure he spoke the truth, the other day, when he said that he had never willingly planted a thorn in any man's bosom. He is one of the most laborious and indefatigable men in the country; and that he has been able to sustain himself under as great a load of care as was ever laid upon the head or the heart of a living man is in no small degree owing to the fact that the vindictive and angry passions form no part of his nature, and that a kindly and playful spirit mingles its sweetness with the austere cup of public duty."

In the realm of manners and style Lincoln in November did a strange little deed and wrote an odd letter which was to go far and reach a vast audience of readers. To Lincoln's desk in September had come a request from Governor Andrew of Massachusetts in behalf of a widow living at 15 Dover Street, Boston. She had sent her five sons into the Union armies and all had been killed in action, according to Andrew's information from his State adjutant general, William Schouler. "This is a case," read Andrew's memorandum for the War Department, which was passed on to Lincoln, "so remarkable that I really wish a letter might be written her by the President of the United States, such as a noble mother of five dead sons so well deserves." Governor Andrew had two years before given this woman $40 to pay her expenses for travel and a hospital visit with one of her wounded sons. In September of '64 the Governor read a report from his adjutant general, including the item: "About ten days ago Mrs. Bixby came to my office and showed me five letters from five company commanders, and each letter informed the poor woman of the death of one of her sons. Her last remaining son was recently killed in the fight on the Weldon Railroad."

On request of the War Department the adjutant general of Massachusetts made an investigation and officially certified that the names, regiments, and dates of death of Mrs. Bixby's five sons were these:

Sergeant Charles N. Bixby, Company D, Twentieth Regiment, mustered in July 28, 1862. Killed at Fredericksburg, May 3, 1863.

Corporal Henry Bixby, Company K, Thirty-second Regiment, mustered in August 5, 1862. Killed at Gettysburg, July 1863.

Private Edward Bixby, recruit for Twenty-second Regiment, Massachusetts Vols. Died of wounds, in hospital at Folly Island, South Carolina. He ran away from home and was mustered in the field.

Private Oliver C. Bixby, Company E, Fifty-eighth Regiment, Massachusetts Vols. Mustered in March 4, 1864. Killed before Petersburg, July 30, 1864.

Private George Way Bixby, Co. B, 56th Reg. Mass. Vols. in March 19th, 1864. Killed before Petersburg July 30, 1864.

The last named, George, enlisted under the assumed name of George Way. The reason why he did not enlist under his proper name was to conceal the fact of his enlistment from his wife.

This document came to Lincoln in mid-October. He could have then written a letter to Mrs. Bixby and made it public for campaign purposes.

Instead, he waited. As on occasion with certain speeches or letters, he probably wrote a first draft of the letter and later changed the phrasing. On November 21 he dated the letter and sent it through the War Department to Adjutant General Schouler of Massachusetts. He addressed it to "Mrs. Bixby, Boston, Massachusetts." Her first name, Lydia, and her address in Boston, were not given. Adjutant General Schouler received the letter in an envelope addressed to himself. He copied the letter. On Thanksgiving Day the General took a holiday dinner and a present of cash money raised among good people of Boston and delivered them at 15 Dover Street to Mrs. Bixby —along with Lincoln's letter to her.

The widow Bixby that day held a sheet of paper in the handwriting of the President of the United States and read it. What she herself thought and felt as she read did not become known. Whether the Adjutant General stayed to see her read it and to hear her comment was not known. What became of the letter delivered to her hands also did not become known. The letter disappeared. Whether Mrs. Bixby was a sensitive woman with a keen ear for delicately organized sentences by a master of language—this too was not recorded by any observers, official or casual. What Lincoln knew and what Andrew well understood, and what the War Department was aware of directly, was that the President of the United States took Mrs. Bixby as a symbol, as a transfigured American mother who deserved enshrinement for loyalty and heroic sacrifice. It was just as well perhaps that no one recorded what Mrs. Bixby may have exclaimed as her eyes fluttered over the written words of the President of the United States. The letter was literary. She was literate, but not literary. Her cue was silence. Her role would best be in shadows and lacking language. Lincoln in the letter was telling her he couldn't find the words to say what he wanted to, and her reply could justly be the same. This was what she read that Thanksgiving Day:

Executive Mansion
Washington, November 21, 1864

Mrs. Bixby, Boston, Massachusetts.
Dear Madam:

I have been shown in the files of the War Department a statement of the Adjutant-General of Massachusetts that you are the mother of five sons who have died gloriously on the field of battle. I feel how weak and fruitless must be any words of mine which should attempt to beguile you from the grief of a loss so overwhelming. But I cannot refrain from tendering to you the consolation that may be found in the thanks of the Republic they died to save. I pray that our heavenly Father may assuage the anguish of your bereavement, and leave you only the cherished memory of the loved and lost, and the solemn pride that must be yours to have laid so costly a sacrifice upon the altar of freedom.

Yours very sincerely and respectfully,
Abraham Lincoln

This was the text as Schouler had copied it and as he gave it to the Boston newspapers. On the day after Thanksgiving the *Transcript* and the *Advertiser* printed it, and a week later the *Army and Navy Journal*, then other journals, so that it had national and world publication in the course of not many weeks. In scores of news sheets ran an item similar to the one in *Leslie's Weekly* of December 24:

"A Boston paper publishes the following facts and correspondence: 'Mrs. Bixby, a lady in the southern portion of this city, whose case has excited much sympathy, had six sons enlisted in the Union army, five of whom have been killed in battle, and the sixth is now at the U. S. Hospital at Readville. Being in indigent circumstances, she has received assistance from some of the churches and Christian women of Boston. Her lonely abode has been made cheerful by the receipt of the following letter from President Lincoln.'"

Later research was to show that of the five Bixby boys Charles did die in action at Fredericksburg, and Oliver met his leaden message of death at Petersburg. Henry was reported killed at Gettysburg, was in reality taken prisoner, exchanged, returned to his mother in good health. George too was taken prisoner, secured his release by enlistment as a Confederate soldier, and was of record as having "deserted to the enemy." Edward Bixby, on the muster rolls as eighteen years of age, became homesick, and his mother swore that he was only sixteen, had enlisted against her will; that he had periods of insanity. The order for his discharge was issued, but the worrying boy had deserted the army and gone to sea as a sailor.

In substance, then, had the actual facts been known, what was the extent of Mrs. Bixby's sacrifice? Whether all five died on the field of battle, or only two, four of her sons had been poured away into the river of war. The two who had deserted were as lost to her as though dead. The one who had returned alive had fought at Gettysburg. If sacrifice could be transmitted into cold figures, she deserved some kind of a token, some award approaching the language Lincoln had employed. From her womb had gone blood to the altars of the Union cause. Lincoln was not deceived. John Andrew had not been fooled. The War Department had not been taken unaware.

Mrs. Lydia Bixby had become an instrument of drama through which Lincoln wrought for the country and the world a psalm of sacrifice. Granted that two and not five of her sons had been piled in graves marked Unidentified, Lincoln could still say, "I feel how weak and fruitless must be any words of mine" and tender her the consolation that might be found in the thanks of the Republic they died to save.

Students of Shakespeare were to come forward and point out that Lincoln as a reader of Shakespeare was probably acquainted with the play of *Coriolanus*. One sentence of the play had hints of the letter to Mrs. Bixby, it would be urged; in the first act Volumnia, mother of Coriolanus, says to his wife, Virgilia: "Had I a dozen sons, each in my love alike, and none less dear than thine and my good Marcius, I had rather had eleven die nobly for their country than one voluptuously surfeit out of action."

As had happened with the Gettysburg speech, there was disagreement about the style and the good taste of the letter to Mrs. Bixby. Tone and content of adverse criticism in the main followed that of an editorial "Cheap

Sympathy" in the *Philadelphia Age,* reprinted December 14 in the *Crisis* of Columbus, Ohio: "Our readers will remember the letter of President Lincoln to Mrs. Bixby, condoling with her on the loss of her five sons in this war. He speaks of the 'solemn pride that must be *hers,* at having laid so costly a sacrifice upon the altar of freedom.' This kind of sympathy is cheap, and easily manufactured; and when one reflects that the man who is ostentatiously shedding his tears over the remains of Mrs. Bixby's five sons, has two sons who are old enough to be laid upon the 'altar,' but whom he keeps at home in luxury, we can easily understand the hypocrisy of all this sympathy for the poor bereaved widow. Why is it, we ask, that Mr. Lincoln's sons should be kept from the dangers of the field, while the sons of the laboring man are to be hurried into the harvest of death at the front? Are the sons of the rail-splitter, porcelain, and these others common clay? Or is it that Mr. Robert Lincoln, the young gentleman whose face is so familiar at watering places and billiard-rooms in the metropolis, has taken his younger brother into the speculation of cultivating cotton on Island Number Ten, through the agency of slave labor, and they can't be spared from their business?"

This style of stench attack, common during the political campaign of the year, had now flared again. The editorial writer probably knew well enough that Tad Lincoln was only eleven years old and still playing with toy pistols and make-believe muskets. Robert Lincoln was twenty-one, and his father was letting a mother of unsound mind have her way that the boy should not go where he might be killed. That Robert was a loafer in cahoots with his younger brother in cotton speculation, cultivating crops with slave labor, was sheer invention. The phrase "cheap sympathy" came naturally from those who had now formed the habit of belittling the President and befouling the President's name. The point could have been made that when the government of a republic reached into a home and by force took away its sons for war, the mother who lost those sons on the field of battle should not be addressed as though she had voluntarily laid her children on an altar of freedom. This point the editorial writer failed to present. He let himself go on the theory of the slogan "Throw mud! and go on throwing mud—some of it is sure to stick."

The response to the Bixby letter, the love of its words and music that arose over the country, lay in the fact that in so many thousands of homes they did love the Union; they did hate slavery; mournfully but willingly, they had sent their boys to take a chance with glorious death on the field of battle. The mystic passion of the American dream of a great Union of States struggling through popular government toward an indefinable goal marked by the word Freedom—this moved Lincoln when he wrote the letter and moved those who read it and clutched it to their bosoms as a token that the war was not all waste and filth and corruption. More darkly than the Gettysburg speech the letter wove its awful implication that human freedom so often was paid for with agony.

As a living human target who daily walked with a lurking and elusive shadow of death, as a Chief Magistrate who had twice had his hat shot off by an unknown would-be assassin, Lincoln was completely entitled to be a spokesman for the boy phantoms who had fought his war and now no longer answered roll call. He saw five vacant chairs in a widow's home, and in writing to her he hoped to reach every home where there were chairs vacant, one, two, or three. Side by side with Governor Andrew's communication to the President about Mrs. Bixby was presented the case of Otis Newhall of Lynn, Massachusetts, and his five vacant chairs at home. George F. Newhall had met the steel of death at Second Bull Run. Edward had begun marching and fighting in October of '61 and had gone on with the Army of the Potomac to the battle of the Wilderness in May of '64, when he was taken prisoner. Henry and Herman Newhall were two sharpshooters who enlisted in October of '61, had stayed on through, and were now with Grant at Petersburg. This left James O. Newhall, who enlisted in January of '62, fought through to Spotsylvania Court House in May of '64, when he received wounds and went to hospital. Now James had recovered, and his father, not wanting all the chairs at home vacant, had proposed Governor Andrew's recommendation to Lincoln that James be discharged "as a graceful recognition of the claim of a patriotic family." To the Newhall family Lincoln gave the discharge asked for, and to Mrs. Bixby a letter the world read.

To those who saw the war as a merely useless human slaughter the letter to Mrs. Bixby was merely "cheap sympathy." To others there was a priceless ring and a precious shine in the "solemn pride that must be yours to have laid so costly a sacrifice upon the altar of freedom." Here was a piece of the American Bible. "The cherished memory of the loved and lost"—these were blood-color syllables of a sacred music.

As the months passed after Lincoln's first inaugural address, his sense of the comic, his occasional role of comedian, stayed with him, while significantly on the other hand he came to know more keenly and fittingly what could be done with the authoritative mantle of President. He learned how better to wear it publicly, to adjust it as the garment of a solemn spokesman. He believed the majesty of the office backed him in telling Congress that "the fiery ordeal" through which they were all passing would be written as history and the players weighed and the balances cast up. At Gettysburg he stood in a ceremonial role. Across many months of '64 his authority hung by such threads that he knew his cue was silence; no statements could be wrung from him. Again in the Bixby letter he performed a rite, managing language as though he might be a ship captain at midnight by lantern light dropping black roses into the immemorial sea for mystic remembrance and consecration.

In quite another key from the Bixby letter was a speech the President made in December, getting it to the public in an unusual way. He sent for Noah Brooks "to hear a story." He had the story partly written on a stiff sheet of white pasteboard, or boxboard, the same supply of paper he used for his message to Congress. With a sheet five or six inches wide on one knee, his legs crossed, sunk comfortably in his armchair, he asked Brooks to wait till he finished. Soon he gave it to Brooks, who saw at the top of the sheet an underscored heading, followed by a paragraph. It read:

The President's last, shortest, and best speech

On Thursday of last week two ladies from Tennessee came before the President asking the release of their husbands held as prisoners of war at Johnson's Island—They were put off till friday, when they came again; and were again put off to Saturday—At each of the interviews one of the ladies urged that her husband was a religious man—On Saturday the President ordered the release of the prisoners, and then said to this lady "You say your husband is a religious man; tell him when you meet him, that I say I am not much of a judge of religion, but that, in my opinion, the religion that sets men to rebel and fight against their government, because, as they think, that government does not sufficiently help *some* men to eat their bread in the sweat of *other* men's faces, is not the sort of religion upon which people can get to heaven!"

A. Lincoln—

"Now!" he remarked to Brooks. "It occurred to me that that was worth printing. What do you think?" And Brooks's account ran: "Having received the answer that he expected, he went on to say that he wanted it copied and printed in the [*Washington*] *Chronicle*, adding, 'Don't wait to send it to California in your correspondence. I've a childish desire to see it in print right away.' "

So Brooks carried off the sheet, copied it, took it to the *Washington Chronicle*, from which newspaper it was widely reprinted over the country. "Lincoln," noted Brooks, "showed a surprising amount of gratification over this trifle and set his signature at the bottom of the page of manuscript, at my suggestion, in order to authenticate it."

The day before Christmas in this December Welles came to the President and asked commutation of sentence for a man condemned to be hanged. "He at once assented," noted Welles. "Is always disposed to mitigate punishment, and to grant favors. Sometimes this is a weakness." Having secured one favor, Welles pressed for another. Miss Laura Jones of Richmond, Welles explained, was engaged to be married to a man in Richmond. This was three years ago. She had then come up to Washington to take care of a sick mother. And having nursed her mother back to health, it seemed she wanted to go back to Richmond and see her betrothed. To get to Richmond she needed a pass through the Union lines. So she had written a letter to her old friend Mrs. Gideon Welles, praying for help in getting a pass. The letter was a touching appeal, noted Welles. "The poor girl . . . says truly the years of her youth are passing away. I knew if the President read the letter, Laura would get the pass."

But without reading the letter the President at once said he would give Miss Laura Jones her pass. Welles now had to make it plain to the President that "her sympathies were with the Secessionists, and it would be better he should read her own statement." But Lincoln wouldn't read her letter to Mrs. Welles. "He . . . said he would let her go; the war had depopulated

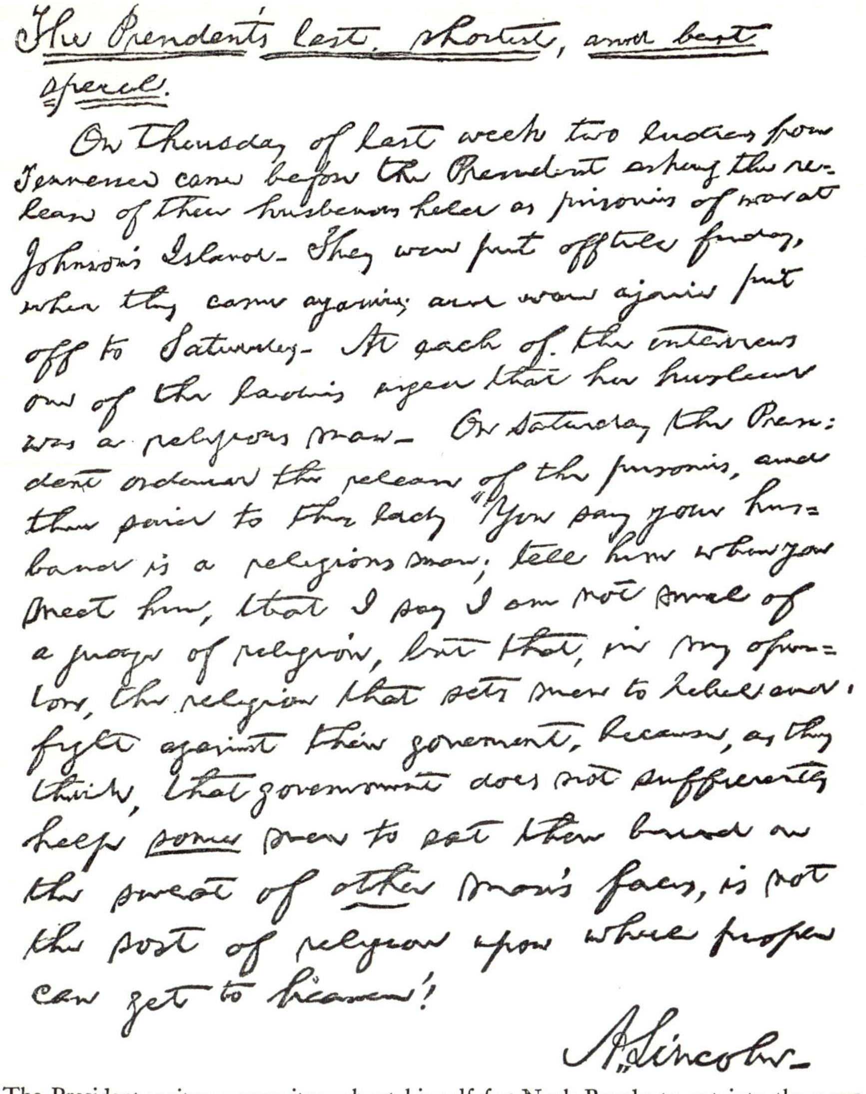

The President's last, shortest, and best speech.

On Thursday of last week two ladies from Tennessee came before the President asking the release of their husbands held as prisoners of war at Johnson's Island. They were put off till Friday, when they came again; and were again put off to Saturday. At each of the interviews one of the ladies urged that her husband was a religious man. On Saturday the President ordered the release of the prisoners, and then said to this lady "You say your husband is a religious man; tell him when you meet him, that I say I am not much of a judge of religion, but that, in my opinion, the religion that sets men to rebel and fight against their government, because, as they think, that government does not sufficiently help *some* men to eat their bread on the sweat of *other* men's faces, is not the sort of religion upon which people can get to heaven!"

A. Lincoln

The President writes a news item about himself for Noah Brooks to get into the newspapers—which Brooks cheerfully does. From the *Scribner's Magazine* article by Brooks.

the country and prevented marriages enough, and if he could do a kindness of this sort he was disposed to, unless I advised otherwise. He wrote a pass and handed me."

This and like incidents that Christmas week, along with Sherman's telegraphed "Christmas present" of the city of Savannah, gave touches of holiday merriment for Lincoln during a war still black with melancholy.

Unionist folk of the North enjoyed Thomas Nast cartoons of the season in *Harper's Weekly*. One titled "Santa Claus in Camp" had the saint of goodwill dressed in the Stars and Stripes giving out presents in a soldier's camp. A double center-page cartoon had two large Christmas wreaths, in one the soldier's family at home, in the other the absent one by his campfire thoughtfully looking at pictures of his loved ones. Lincoln was to term Nast "our best recruiting sergeant," rousing enthusiasm and patriotism "just when those articles were getting scarce."

New Year's Eve came, the fourth for Lincoln in the White House. In the first one McClellan, with a magnificently prepared army, had gone into winter quarters without fighting, the shame of Bull Run not redeemed and the North yet to try its faith in itself. The second New Year's Eve could look back on a year high-lighted by the weary Peninsula campaign, the jubilant capture of Fort Donelson, New Orleans taken, bloody Shiloh, the Second Bull Run shame, McClellan and Lee at Antietam, the preliminary Emancipation Proclamation, the delays of McClellan and his dismissal, the needless red butchery at Fredericksburg. The third New Year's Eve had brought the final Emancipation Proclamation, the rout of Chancellorsville, New York draft and race riots, the turning-point of the war at Gettysburg and Vicksburg, the shouting at narrowly shaded Chickamauga fighting, the cries from men in blue at the top of Lookout Mountain, the speech at Gettysburg, the beginning of the sunset of the Confederacy. Now there was the fourth New Year's Eve looking back on Grant named to head all the Union armies, plunging into the Wilderness and on through Spotsylvania, Cold Harbor, Petersburg, with overwhelming troops and resources battering Lee pitilessly while Early's gray horsemen reached the gates of Washington with their smoke to be seen from White House windows, while Sherman took Atlanta and marched to the sea and took Savannah, while Sheridan scattered Early's army from the Shenandoah and Thomas became the sledge that broke Hood's army into the first Confederate rout of the war, while the navy sunk the *Alabama*, took Mobile, and tightened its throttling grip on all Southern ports—a fateful year that had seen the President of the United States win a party renomination against the almost unanimous disapproval of his party members in the House and Senate, winning a national election in November that looked dark and all lost in August, winning in a fairly conducted contest, amid good order, so that the longer one gazed at the November ballots, the more they seemed to say momentously that the Union would be held together and the underlying cause of the war, the propertied institution of slavery, outlawed forever. Not so bitter as the other three was the taste of this New Year's Eve. Across the horizons of the New Year of 1865, however, were signs of snarling bad weather. The storm was to take new phases. Heavy labors lay ahead, and much human confusion.

The diplomatic corps in sashes and epaulets promenaded over the reception rooms of the White House on New Year's Day, which fell on a Sunday, and members of the Senate and House were there, also the Cabinet—and in larger numbers than ever before the Public was there to shake hands with the President, to have perhaps a greeting and a flash of fun with him. An old American custom was this New Year's levee at the Executive Mansion. And on the first of January, 1865, came a procedure never seen before, never heard of, at this more or less formal social affair. Whether or not it was prearranged for calculated effects, the performance seemed a natural outburst and belonged in the national scene of the hour.

Among the onlookers outside the White House, seemingly innocent bystanders enjoying a show worth while, were groups of Negroes, huddles of blacks and mulattoes watching the whites in fine apparel swarming into the home of the President, gentlemen in high hats carrying gold-headed canes, diplomats and ladies in crinoline lifted from carriages and escorted in silks and ruffles into the Big House. Nearly two hours they hung around gazing at those coming and going, those who had gone through the big doors and come out. Nearly two hours the colored people waited, some of them wearing fine clothes, white linen shirts, others in worn and patched garments, others in curiously slung together pickings from various discards ready for the ragbag.

Suddenly they agreed the time had come for them to go in. Why not? Who would throw them out? Surely not the one man in the house they wanted to see. Soon they were footing it in. And an observer for the New York *Independent* wrote: "For two long hours Mr. Lincoln had been shaking the hands of the 'sovereigns,' and had become excessively weary, and his grasp languid; but here his nerves rallied at the unwonted sight, and he welcomed this motley crowd with a heartiness that made them wild with exceeding joy. They laughed and wept, and wept and laughed—exclaiming, through their blinding tears: 'God bless you!' 'God bless Abraham Lincoln!' 'God bress Marse Linkum!' Those who witnessed this scene will not soon forget it. For a long distance down the Avenue, on my way home, I heard fast young men cursing the President for this act; but all the way the refrain rang in my ears,—'God bless Abraham Lincoln!' "

Had Miss Betsey Canedy of Fall River, Massachusetts, been in line that day and paused for conversation with Lincoln, she could have told him of what she heard while teaching a school of Negro pupils at Norfolk, Virginia. To Negro carpenters at work on the school building one day she showed a plaster bust of Abraham Lincoln. What they said impressed Miss Canedy. She wrote down what some of them said: "He's brought us safe through the Red Sea." "He looks as deep as the sea himself." "He's king of the United States." "He ought to be king of all the world." "We must all pray to the Lord to carry him safe through, for it 'pears like he's got everything hitched to him." "There has been a right smart praying for him, and it mustn't stop now."